Courtly Culture

WITHDRAWN

DD
64
.B8613
1991

Courtly Culture

*Literature and Society in the
High Middle Ages*

Joachim Bumke
Translated by Thomas Dunlap

GOSHEN COLLEGE LIBRARY
GOSHEN, INDIANA

UNIVERSITY OF CALIFORNIA PRESS
Berkeley • *Los Angeles* • *Oxford*

WITHDRAWN

University of California Press
Berkeley and Los Angeles, California

University of California Press
Oxford, England

First published in Germany under the title *Höfische Kultur*:
Literatur und Gesellschaft im hohen Mittelalter. Copyright ©
1986 Deutscher Taschenbuch Verlag GmbH & Co., KG, Munich.

Copyright © 1991 by The Regents of the University of California

Bumke, Joachim.
    [Höfische Kultur. English]
    Courtly culture : literature and society in the high middle ages /
Joachim Bumke ; translated by Thomas Dunlap.
       p.   cm.
    Translation of : Höfische Kultur.
    Includes bibliographical references and index.
    ISBN 0-520-06634-0 (alk. paper)
    1. Germany—Court and courtiers—History. 2. Chivalry. 3. German
literature—Middle High German, 1050–1500—History and criticism.
4. Literature and society—Germany—History. 5. Court epic, German—
History and criticism.   I. Title.
DD64.B8613   1991
943′.02′08621—dc20   90-39790
                                                                        CIP

Printed in the United States of America

1 2 3 4 5 6 7 8 9

The paper used in this publication meets the minimum requirements of
American National Standard for Information Sciences—Permanence of Paper for
Printed Library Materials, ANSI Z39.48-1984 ∞

Contents

Introduction: Fiction and Reality   1

Everyday life and the feast day   1
Courtly society and modern scholarship   5
Literature as a historical source   7
The "Praise of Times Gone By"
(*Laudatio temporis acti*)   14
An overview of the book   16

Chapter I: Noble Society of the High Middle
Ages: Historical Background   21

1. Basic Concepts of the Social Order   22
    The law   22
    Lordship   23
    Estates   26
2. The Hierarchical Structure of
    Society   29
    The king   29
    The princes   31
    The nonprincely nobility   32
    The ministerials   33
    The urban population   36
    The rural population   38
3. The Economy   39
    Economic developments   39

Trade and commerce   41
The economic foundation of
lordship   43
4. The Knight and Knighthood   46
   Ritter-miles-chevalier   46
   Noble knighthood   49
   The formation of the knightly class   50
5. The Court   52
   Itinerant lordship and the formation
   of permanent residences   52
   Court society   55
   The word "*höfisch*" (courtly)   57

Chapter II: The Adoption of French Aristocra-
               tic Culture in Germany   61

1. Society   61
   Economic ties   61
   The state of education   68
   Dynastic connections   75
   The adoption of French social forms   79
2. Language   82
   Language skills   82
   Loan words   85
3. Literature   88
   The chronology and geography of
   the transmission of French literature   88
   Courtly epics   92
   Courtly lyric   96
   The characteristics of the literary
   adaptation   99

Chapter III: Material Culture and Social Style   103

1. Castles and Tents   103
   The construction of castles and
   palaces in the twelfth and thirteenth
   centuries   103
   The architecture of castles and
   palaces   108
   Furnishings   112
   Castles as instruments of lordship   121
   Luxurious tents   126

2. Clothes and Cloth   128
Dress codes   128
The sources for the history of cos-
tume   130
Precious fabrics   132
Sartorial extravagance   134
The courtly ceremony of dress   136
The beginnings of courtly fashion   138
Women's clothes   140
Men's clothes   145
Changes in fashion   150
Criticism from the Church   152
3. Weapons and Horses   155
The history of armament   155
The main weapons of a knight   157
The social significance of weapons   164
The ceremony of knightly single
combat   168
Horses   175
4. Food and Drink   178
Food for the nobility   178
The protocol of the courtly banquet   182
Seating arrangements   183
Service at table   187
Tableware   191
The organization of the meal   193
Courtesy books   196
Literature of feasting and carousing   199

Chapter IV: Courtly Feasts: Protocol and Etiquette   203

1. Court Feasts   203
The court feast at Mainz in 1184   203
Feast and lordship   207
Lodging and food   210
The festive entrance   213
The ceremony of welcome   219
Courtly entertainment   220
Gifts   228
2. Knighting Ceremonies   231
Terminology and ceremony   231
The courtly ceremony of knighting   234

The role of the Church   239
From royal practice to mass promo-
tion   242
3. Tournaments   247
The beginnings of tournaments   247
The mass tournament or melée   251
The buhurt   258
The single joust and the Round Table
tournament   260
The military, social, material, and
political significance of tournaments   264
Prohibitions and criticism of tourna-
ments   271

Chapter V: The Courtly Ideal of Society   275
1. The Chivalrous Knight   276
The traditional image of the ruler   276
The religious concept of knighthood
(*militia Christi*)   290
Courtly virtues   301
Ideal and reality   311
2. The Courtly Lady   325
The new image of women   325
Instruction for women: Upbringing
and education   337
The parameters of women's activi-
ties   346
3. Courtly Love   360
What is courtly love?   360
Love-marriage-adultery   377
Love and society   398

Chapter VI: Criticism of Courtly Life   415

Chapter VII: The Literary Scene of the Courtly
               Age   425
1. Oral Culture and Literacy in Courtly
Society   426
Lay education   426
Oral traditions   436
The development of organized
writing at the secular courts   441

2. Patrons and Sponsors 458
The imperial court as a literary
center 459
The patronage of princes 470
The smaller courts 485
The beginnings of literary life in the
cities 487
3. Author and Audience 488
The social standing of the poet 488
The courtly audience 506
The impact of literature 512
4. The Performance and Spread of
Literature 518
Courtly epic 518
Courtly lyric 545

Notes 573
Glossary 679
Abbreviations 681
Bibliography 687
Index 747

Introduction: Fiction and Reality

EVERYDAY LIFE AND THE FEAST DAY

When scholars in the eighteenth century began to examine the Middle Ages more closely, they emphasized above all the negative sides of medieval life and contrasted them unfavorably with the achievements of their own time. The work of Christoph Meiners, "A Historical Comparison of the Customs, Constitutions, and Laws, of Industry, Commerce, Religion, the Sciences, and the Schools of the Middle Ages with those of our own Century, considering the Advantages and Disadvantages of the Enlightenment" ("Historische Vergleichung der Sitten, und Verfassungen, der Gesetze, und Gewerbe, des Handels, und der Religion, der Wissenschaften, und Lehranstalten des Mittelalters mit denen unseres Jahrhunderts in Rücksicht auf die Vortheile, und Nachtheile der Aufklärung," 1793/4), exemplifies this attitude. This critical view of the Middle Ages did not last. It was not long before the romanticists saw the medieval world in an entirely different light. Discarding historical sources in favor of literary works, they regarded the brave knights and fair ladies of medieval literature, whom they took as reflections of reality, as witnesses of a vanished and more beautiful world, in which man in a spirit of childlike piety had still been at one with himself and with the great order of the universe. This romantic picture of the Middle Ages, later enriched with the nationalistic overtones of emperor-worship, exerted a tremendous influence that has left traces to this day.

Medieval reality was very different. Our sources tell us very little

1

about the lives of the common people, their poverty and troubles, their oppressive bondage. Even for the rich and noble the conditions of daily life were anything but pleasant. Tight, gloomy spaces in the castles, unimaginably primitive hygienic conditions, a lack of light and heating, the absence of expert medical care, an unhealthy diet, rough table manners, degrading sexual behavior towards women: this was the reality. The historical sources illuminate even more harshly the manifestations of public life. Lordship expressed itself all too often as mere oppression and exploitation of the weak. Sale of offices and bribery were common practices. Justice was won by the person who could either pay more or who prevailed in a judicial duel through sheer brute force. Warfare was only in the slightest degree directed towards the exercise of knightly military skills—pillaging and plundering were the customary techniques. Rahewin's account of the wars of Frederick I conveys a vivid picture of this kind of warfare. In 1159 the emperor invaded "Liguria, he burned and devastated the fields, destroyed the vineyards, had the fig trees uprooted and all fruit-bearing trees either cut down or stripped of their bark; he ravaged the entire land."[1] Not that our clerical historiographer described these actions with disgust; he merely recorded what was happening. Prisoners were usually taken only if there was a chance of exchanging them for a high ransom. Those who suffered most from the constant wars and feuds of the magnates were the peasants. In the chronicle of his abbey, the provost Gerhard of Stederburg (d. 1209) recounts the situation in Saxony around 1180, during the final days of Henry the Lion: "We have seen our most valuable possessions plundered, our farms burned, ourselves exposed to plundering, our horses and animals driven off, and our houses abandoned by their inhabitants."[2] In those days even the convents had to be evacuated at the approach of the mercenary bands of the archbishop of Cologne.

Criminal justice was as cruel and brutal as warfare. Otto of St. Blasien tells us of Sicilian noblemen who had conspired against Emperor Henry VI in 1193: "One man, who was found guilty of lèse majesté, was skinned; another, who had aspired to imperial power, was crowned, and the crown was fastened to his temple with iron nails; some were tied to stakes and surrounded with wood: these he killed cruelly by burning them; others were fixed to the ground with stakes driven through their bellies."[3] In those days political murder was nothing out of the ordinary. And it is so contrary to the picture which cultural historians have painted of the Hohenstaufen age that nobody

has bothered to gather and evaluate the many murders that are historically attested. Here are only a few of the most prominent victims: in
1160 Archbishop Arnold of Mainz was murdered, in 1192 Bishop
Albert of Lüttich, in 1202 the imperial chancellor Konrad of Querfurt,
in 1208 King Philip of Swabia, in 1225 Archbishop Engelbert of Cologne, in 1231 Duke Ludwig I of Bavaria. But murder struck down not
only the great magnates. From the *Wormser Hofrecht* [Law of the court
of Worms], promulgated by bishop Burchard in 1024/25, we learn
almost incidentally about "murders" (*homicidia*) "that are committed
almost daily in the bishops' *familia*."[4] It is said that in one year alone
thirty-five serfs of the church of Worms were killed by fellow serfs.
According to the accounts of the historiographers not a few magnates
were poisoned. Even if in some cases these rumors were unfounded,
the fact that such crimes were believed possible throws a revealing light
on the conditions of the age.

The decades during which courtly literature reached its height in
Germany were a particularly terrible period of civil wars and public
disorder. The death of Emperor Henry VI in the year 1197 threw the
land into anarchy. "With the emperor died justice and peace in the
Empire."[5] "At his death the entire world fell into chaos, for many
crimes and wars arose, which then lasted for a long time."[6] "Like hungry wolves"[7] the people are said to have attacked each other in those
days. The situation was exacerbated by the fact that the crops had failed
for several years and prices had risen, which led to catastrophic
famines, especially in the western part of the Empire. In Alsace, "piles
of people who had starved to death were found in the fields and
villages"[8]; in Lüttich "the poor were lying about the streets and
dying."[9] Along the Mosel the old mythical king Dietrich of Bern
appeared as "a ghost of incredible size" (*fantasma mirae magnitudinis*)
and proclaimed that diverse calamities and misfortunes would befall the
entire Roman empire."[10] This prophecy would prove true. In 1198 the
majority of the German princes elected Philip of Swabia king, while an
important minority, led by Adolf of Altena (d. 1217), the archbishop of
Cologne, chose Otto IV. For fifteen years war over the kingship raged
between the Hohenstaufen and the Welfs, devastating large parts of
Germany. Especially hard hit was Thuringia, where the court of Margrave Henry I (d. 1217) was at that time a flourishing center of courtly
literature.

In counterpoint to these negative manifestations of medieval life, the
courtly poets constructed an image of society that lacked everything

that made life difficult and oppressive, and from which all economic and social pressures and all political conflicts were excluded. The only thing people strove for in this world was moral and social self-perfection. Clearly, this extremely unrealistic picture of society was conceived as the opposite of real life, and must be interpreted as such.

But there existed one sphere of reality into which the gloomy aspects of daily life did not intrude, and where noble society did manifest all the glory of its wealth and ceremonial etiquette: the feast at the court. The historical accounts of the great court feasts of the Hohenstaufen period reveal that these festive gatherings were of great importance for the self-image of noble society. Courtly society as a historical phenomenon is best documented on these occasions, and the reason is not only that the sources rarely allow us a glimpse of daily life: it appears that the nobility exhibited only in these exceptional moments a social behavior that was considered particularly courtly.

Since the great court feasts did take place, we must evaluate the descriptions the court poets have given us differently than we do their portrait of daily life. The poetic vision of the festive society gathered at Whitsuntide at the court of King Arthur reflects the modern character of contemporary court life in many details of material culture and courtly etiquette. Even the tendency toward idealized exaggeration, so characteristic of the poetic descriptions, has a basis in reality: those who hosted the great feasts were often driven by the desire to outdo all previous feasts through the most extravagant lavishness. What makes the poetic vision so unreal is not so much the exaggeration as the fact that daily life simply does not appear in courtly literature, thus creating the impression that the feast was the norm of noble life. The old cultural history made the crucial mistake of succumbing to this poetic vision and considering it a true reflection of reality. But every time courtly literature refers even vaguely to the daily life of the nobility outside of the festive setting, we almost always find distinctly uncourtly traits: for example, in the description of the wretched dwelling of the impoverished Count Coralus (Hartmann von Aue, *Erec*, 252 ff.), or the rural "wilderness" (*waste*) to which queen Herzeloyde withdraws after the death of her husband (Wolfram von Eschenbach, *Parzival*, 117.7 ff.); in the description of the economic woes of a country squire, which Gawein held up to his friend Iwein as a warning example (Hartmann von Aue, *Iwein*, 280 ff.); and in the shabby figure of the Knight of Riuwental in Neidhart's songs. These examples, generally overdrawn in the service of satire, reveal clearly just how narrow a slice of reality is presented in courtly literature.

Since the subject of this book is not the reality of medieval life, but the connection between courtly literature and the social culture of the court, the day to day conditions of noble life can largely be ignored. The theme of this essay is the festive society at court, its material culture, its etiquette, its ideas of social perfection, and its literature.

COURTLY SOCIETY AND MODERN SCHOLARSHIP

In the newer works on social history the courtly society of the twelfth and thirteenth centuries rarely appears at all. The reason for this is largely that the Latin sources historians usually work with tell us almost nothing about this society. German historiography in the twelfth century was still largely monastic in character, and this influenced both its view of the world and its value judgments. For the most part the writers were simply not interested in the details of secular society. Other sources supply much more information about the socio-cultural milieu of the nobility. Among them is the "Codex Falkensteinensis" from the end of the twelfth century, in which all the possessions of the Bavarian counts of Neuburg-Falkenstein are recorded. At that time castle Neuburg had "6 silver cups with lids and 5 silver bowls without lids, 3 silver drinking cups with lids and 4 without lids, 2 silver spoons; in addition, 15 coats of mail, 8 iron leggings, 60 lances (i.e. spears), 4 helmets, 6 trumpets, 20 down quilts, 3 gaming boards, 3 chess boards, and ivory game pieces suitable for both the board game and chess."[11] If we compare this to the inventory of objects found at Tyrol castle at the death of Count Otto of Carinthia (d. 1310) (see below p. 192 f.), we get a clear sense of how material culture had developed at the German courts during the thirteenth century. Another source of extraordinary value are the travel expense books of Wolfger of Erla (d. 1218), bishop of Passau, from the years 1203–1204. They are famous in German philology because Walther von der Vogelweide is historically attested in them. But they also reveal the many social contacts the bishop had on his travels, and they give a complete record of the expenses of maintaining his court. Other account books of noble households are not found in Germany before the end of the thirteenth century. The account books of the counts of Tyrol, kept with great accuracy from 1288 on, and the account book from Upper Bavaria from the years 1291–1294, are the earliest examples of this type. These historical sources are undoubtedly important, but if we want to compose a picture of courtly society in action, we depend largely on other sources: literary texts and visual images.

Anyone who wants to find out about the material culture of the high medieval nobility and the social etiquette of the twelfth century must consult the books of the cultural historians of the nineteenth century, especially the great two-volume work of the Prague art historian Alwin Schultz (d. 1909): *Das höfische Leben zur Zeit der Minnesinger* ("Courtly Life in the Age of the Minnesingers"), published in a second edition in 1889. The strengths and weaknesses of the older cultural history stand out clearly in his work. Its lasting value lies in the astonishing range of materials it contains, something that is today beyond the range of a single scholar. Schultz excerpted and evaluated not only the entire German literature of the twelfth and thirteenth centuries, but also a large portion of the contemporary French literature, as well as many Latin sources, some of them quite inaccessible. The flaw that impairs the value of his essay is the same that eventually discredited the older cultural history: an uncritical interpretation of the evidence. Two approaches are especially typical of the methodological deficiencies in his source evaluation. First of all, what the poets described as an unusual and exceptional situation, Schultz presented as a common phenomenon and turned into the social norm. Secondly, the poetic character of most sources was ignored, with the result that the poetic descriptions, which were part of an idealized social image, were naively regarded as reality. This explains why for the modern reader the work of Schultz at times has unintended comical overtones. For example, he says about eating habits: "Calf's brains or stewed plums were spread between two slices of bread and the whole thing was baked in fat" (I, 395); or about women's clothing: "The neckline was closed by a clasp, so that a man could not easily fondle a lady's breasts" (I, 252); or about the peasants: "They spent their leisure hours lying stretched out on the ground being deloused" (I, 439); or about beds: "The beds are either double beds, in which case a knight, who does not want to touch his lady, places a naked sword between himself and her; or the beds are intended for a single person, in which case they are, however, moved together" ("Über Bau und Einrichtung der Hofburgen," p. 27). The cultural history of the nineteenth century did not survive as a great genre of historical writing; it perished from its methodological flaws. It is true that the most comprehensive work of cultural history, the *Handbuch der Kulturgeschichte* edited by Heinz Kindermann, did not appear until the 1930s. But even here, especially in the volume of interest to us—Hans Naumann's *Deutsche Kultur im Zeitalter des Rittertums* (1938) ("German culture in the Age of Chivalry")—we can witness the decay of a once great genre of writing: the focus is no longer on material culture but on the "cultural ideals" that supposedly determined the social life of that age. The influence of Hans Naumann's portrait, so removed from the sources and based on the myth of the Hohenstaufen knighthood, spread far beyond the field of German literature. In some historical handbooks it has shaped the conception of society in the High Middle Ages to this very day. One of the goals of this book is to overturn this image and to reestablish the concept of courtly culture on the firm ground of historical realities.

For some decades now a significant change has been taking place in the study of medieval material culture. Medieval archeology, long left almost entirely to museums, has been developing into an independent science with its own journals and research centers, such as the Institut für mittelalterliche Realienkunde Österreichs in Krems. In Germany, important impulses have been coming from the Zentralinstitut für Kunstgeschichte in Munich and from the Max-Planck-Institut für Geschichte in Göttingen, where the center for the research of imperial palaces (*Pfalzenforschung*) is located. This new field of medieval studies has addressed a broader public primarily through the great medieval exhibits of the last years, especially through some of the superbly documented exhibition catalogs, which offer a wealth of important information for cultural historians.

LITERATURE AS A HISTORICAL SOURCE

The courtly culture of the High Middle Ages has to be reconstructed from a variety of sources:

1. Literary texts in Middle High German make up the largest and most important source. They include highly fictional texts, such as the minnesongs and the courtly epics, as well as didactic poems, political *Spruchdichtung*, rhymed chronicles and similar works which refer to a reality beyond the fictional world of literature. The more fictional a text, the greater the methodological difficulties in using it for concrete historical interpretation.

2. Pictorial evidence forms the second most important source. We have paintings in the form of miniatures and frescoes, sculptures in stone, wood, and metal, and utensils of different materials decorated with pictures. Of particular importance for courtly culture are seals. In interpreting pictures as evidence for social life we face the same methodological problems that we encounter with literary texts. In fact the difficulties are even greater, since the production of visual art was still largely in the hands of members of the Church. The most magnificent pictorial source of the twelfth century comes from the Hohenberg monastery in the Alsace. It is the miniatures in the "Garden of Delight" (*Hortus deliciarum*) of the Abbess Herrad of Landsberg (d. 1196). Unfortunately we possess only a copy, since the original was burned in 1870.

3. Material remains from the High Middle Ages comprise a rich, only partially evaluated source. But few of these remains can be assigned to lay culture, as the majority are ecclesiastical antiquities. Only a handful of art objects and articles of daily life have survived intact: chess pieces, drinking cups and pitchers, mirrors, pouches, belt buckles, candlesticks, wooden boxes, and so on. Much has come down to us only in fragments. Highly valuable evidence are the excavation finds from and the ruins of secular structures—the castles and palaces of the twelfth and thirteenth centuries—none of which have survived the centuries undamaged.

4. Historical sources in Latin play only a minor role in our reconstruction of courtly culture, since the authors of the chronicles and annals largely ignored the social life of the secular nobility. This is true only for Germany, however. In France and England, modern dynastic historiography and the critical writings of John of Salisbury, Peter of Blois, and others supply us with invaluable information about the conditions of life at the courts. This information can also be used to deepen our historical understanding of the cultural situation in Germany.

The courtly poets devoted thousands of verses to the description of weapons, clothes, receptions, meals, and court feasts. It goes so far that the courtly romances seem like poetic handbooks of the culture of the nobility, which is probably how they were in fact understood. The audiences must have taken a keen interest in literary compositions in the French style, and this interest was certainly not limited only to the stories, but extended equally to the descriptions of social life that figure so prominently in this literature. Regardless of how unrealistic King

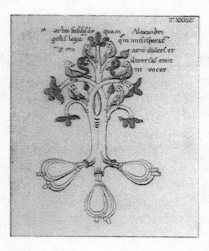

Fig. 1.   Organ-tree. Artificial tree with birds that are made to sing with the help of bellows attached to the roots. From a lost manuscript of the monastery of St. Blasien. Twelfth or thirteenth century.

Arthur's Round Table was, and how fantastic the battles against dragons and giants, in depicting the concrete details of social life the poets were apparently concerned to be accurate and up-to-date. A tendency towards idealization is not incompatible with realism in details. Even when poetic descriptions seem to slide off into sheer fantasy, and we hear of magical devices and marvelous machines, we can glimpse a basis in fact. For example, in the *Straßburger Alexander* we are told of such a machine in the castle of Queen Candacis: "In the middle of the palace a beautiful animal had been set up on her orders. It was made entirely of red gold. This wonderful beast resembled a stag. In the front on its head it had a thousand horns, and on each horn sat a marvelous bird. On top of the animal sat a well-shaped man who was leading two dogs. He had raised a horn to his mouth. Below in the basement lay twenty-four bellows. Each bellows was operated by twelve strong men. Whenever they pumped the bellows the birds in the front of the animal sang, the man blew his horn, and the dogs barked. Also, the wonderful animal would roar like a panther."[12] Organ-trees with singing birds (see fig. 1) were also described in other works, in *Jüngerer Titurel* ("from bellows the air went in so that each bird sang its melody"[13]), and in the *Trojanerkrieg* of Konrad von Würzburg (17562 ff.). As far as we know, such machines did not exist in either Germany or France in the twelfth and thirteenth centuries. But in Byzantium similar devices were already known in the tenth century. Bishop Liutprand of Cremona (d. 972) saw them in the imperial palace on his journey to Byzantium as the emperor's legate in 949: "Before the emperor's seat stood a tree, made of bronze gilded over, whose branches were filled with birds, also made of gilded bronze, which uttered different cries, each according to its varying species. The throne itself was so marvelously fashioned that at times it seemed low, at times higher, and at times very lofty. It was of immense size and was guarded by lions, made either of bronze or of wood covered over with gold, who beat the ground with their tails and gave a dreadful roar with open mouths and quivering tongues."[14] Liutprand indicated that he was familiar with the mechanisms of such machines. The tales of the courtly poets appear in an altogether new light if we can assume the audience knew that machines existed which could be moved artificially and emit sounds.

The question as to the value of literary texts as historical sources cannot be answered theoretically. It is difficult to contend with the view that fundamental methodological problems do not permit us to draw inferences from fictional statements about the reality beyond literature. These methodological doubts have caused the courtly culture of the twelfth and thirteenth centuries to disappear by and large as an object of scholarly attention. Important aspects of social as well as literary history in the High Middle Ages will, however, remain hidden if one rejects out of hand the use of texts based on aesthetic principles. It is therefore preferable to accept the difficulties and limitations that attach to poetic sources, and to try and counterbalance them by making certain that one's conclusions at all times reflect the methodological uncertainties.

The degree of uncertainty varies depending on the object of our inquiry: the difficulties loom largest in the sphere of material culture. Many details are referred to only in literature, and it is impossible to prove that a given object ever existed in real life. As regards the construction of castles and the history of arms, the statements of the poets must be checked against the results of archeological investigation. The information on costume and eating habits must be supplemented by and verified against pictorial evidence. Of course pictures, too, were artistic creations with their own relationship to real life. But when text and picture agree, we can infer in many cases, if not real material objects, at least those things that were considered exemplary in material culture. A masterpiece of courtly description is the appearance of Princess Isolde at the Irish court in Gotffried of Straßburg's *Tristan*. The

Fig. 2.   Seal image of Richardis of Holland. The left hand holds the clasp string. The right hand seems to gather the mantle at the height of the waist. 1258.

poet dwells on the beauty of her appearance, the lovely clothes, the upright gait, the proud look, and the graceful position of her hands: "Where the clasps go, a tiny string of white pearls had been let in, into which the lovely girl had inserted her left thumb. She had brought her right hand farther down, you know, to where one closes the mantle, and held it decorously together in courtly fashion with two fingers."[15] Seals of French and German noble women from the twelfth and thirteenth centuries, which show the hand hooked into the clasp string, attest that this posture expressed a courtly attitude and noble self-consciousness (see fig. 2). This motif was also taken over into sculpture. Like Isolde, Margravine Reglindis in the west choir of the cathedral in Naumburg has one hand hooked into the clasp string, while the other hand holds her mantle together (see fig. 3).

The same methodological difficulties we have mentioned above apply to the ceremony of courtly etiquette, insofar as we are dealing with factual details, as for example tournament practice. Here the evidence of the literary texts can be supplemented with the accounts in historical sources of court feasts, tournaments, and ceremonies of knighthood. The more we focus on the norms of social hehavior, the greater the

Fig. 3. Margrave Hermann of Meißen and his wife Reglindis. Reglindis's right hand is hooked into the clasp string, and her left hand gathers the mantle in such a way that a rich cascade of folds falls down in front. Larger than lifesize statues in the west choir of the cathedral of Naumburg. Thirteenth century.

evidentiary value of literary texts. An example to illustrate this point. Wolfram von Eschenbach described the famine in the besieged castle of Belrapeire: "Famine had reduced them to starvation. They had no cheese, bread or meat. They were not picking their teeth and did not beslabber the wine with greasy lips when drinking."[16] It was a joke that the knights at Belrapeire were following courtly etiquette because they

had nothing to eat and therefore no opportunity to violate table manners, and it could only be fully appreciated by the audience if it was
generally known that one should not pick one's teeth at table, and that
one ought to wipe one's greasy mouth before drinking. We find these
two rules, among many others, in the oldest German courtesy book, the
so-called *Tannhäuser*, which probably dates from the mid-thirteenth
century: "Don't pick your teeth with your knives."[17] "Before you
drink, wipe your mouth, so you won't grease up the drink."[18] From the
funny comments in *Parzival* we can infer that rules for table manners
were already known in Germany as early as 1200, rules otherwise
attested in no other source. Whether such rules were actually adhered to
is another question altogether.

The ideals of courtly society are reflected almost exclusively in literature. The new concept of courtly perfection in knighthood and love can
be drawn directly from an analysis of the literary texts. Yet the con-
troversies over the term and the meaning of "courtly love" reveal that it
is by no means easy to disentangle this ideal from the context of the
fictional texts. Even more difficult are inferences about the nonliterary
world, but we must make such inferences, since the poetic ideals can be
regarded as aspects of a new social ideal only if we can show the social
relevance of the poets' ideas. Only on rare occasions, however, is this
possible. For example, concrete proof that literature actually influenced
the nobility's social self-image can be found in the fact that children
were named after literary characters, and that tournament practice was
refashioned in accord with literary models. But it often remains unclear
to what extent members of courtly society strove to live up to the literary ideals. In this regard a skeptical approach is called for.

While the literary texts thus differ in their evidentiary value in the
various areas of cultural life, they all express the same thing. The reality
to which they can be directly related is not that of material objects or
actual events. Rather, it is the reality of ideas, expectations, and desires,
the reality of social consciousness and cultural norms.

There is yet another dimension to the question regarding the real life
basis of this literature. The courtly poets worked mostly from French
models, and they took over many details in their description of social
life from their French sources, apparently because the noble audience in
Germany was particularly interested in this aspect. We can't always tell
with certainty whether the poet is drawing a portrait of French society,
or whether the German listeners were supposed to recognize details of
the social life depicted as part of their own milieu. In all likelihood both

aspects came into play. For example, when a poet talked about the literary and higher education of a knightly hero, he must have known as well as his audience that princes with a literary education were very rare in Germany, whereas in France the education of a prince in the twelfth century already frequently included training in the higher studies (see p. 426 ff.). In other cases we can show that it is likely that the French objects mentioned by the poets actually existed in Germany or were at least known. A technical innovation on the knight's helmet was the *barbiere*, a metal plate with breathing holes fastened to the front of the helmet to protect the lower half of the face (see p. 158). The earliest evidence comes from France. In Germany it appears for the first time on a seal of Duke Leopold VI of Austria (d. 1230) from the year 1197. Almost at the same time we encounter in Ulrich von Zatzikhoven's *Lanzelet*, written after 1195, the first literary evidence in the form of a French loan word: "Thus the bold Iwein was struck through his *barbiere*, so that the courageous hero began to bleed from his mouth and nose, and the blood ran down his chinguard."[19] This would indicate that the object itself and the name for it were adopted at the same time. Of course neither the Austrian duke's seal nor the passage in *Lanzelet* can prove that at this time German knights wore helmets with a *barbiere*. But we can infer from this that courtly society in Germany knew about the *barbiere*, and that in its eyes it was part of the look that was considered the very model of courtliness.

Why did noble society of the twelfth and thirteenth centuries in Germany take such an avid interest in the poets' descriptions of French innovations in fashion, technical improvements in armament, and the ceremonial forms of courtly etiquette? The answer, it would seem, is that knowledge and mastery of these new social forms became the basis of a heightened self-image that regarded one's own lifestyle as "courtly" (*höfisch*) and dismissed anyone who did not measure up to this standard as "boorish" (*dörperlich*, literally "peasantish"). It is in this sense that the social self-image can be seen as a concrete element of historical reality, and in this sense the literary texts and the pictures for the courtly period are historical sources of exceptional importance.

THE "PRAISE OF TIMES GONE BY" (*LAUDATIO TEMPORIS ACTI*)

Surprisingly enough, the poets presented modern courtly culture not as the achievement of their own age, but projected it back into an idealized past, in comparison with which their own time seemed like a period of decline and decay. This attitude, however, seems strange only at first glance. Already in antiquity the "praise of times gone by" had become a popular way of depicting the present. We must also remember that in the Middle Ages all innovation was seen as the restoration of an older order (*reformatio, restitutio*). The poets occasionally turned this attitude into an effective instrument of social criticism. In *Helmbrecht*, for example, the old steward Helmbrecht draws a touching portrait of the former splendor of noble life and courtly society, with knightly games, dancing, singing, and *Frauendienst* (service to one's lady) (913 ff.), while the young Helmbrecht paints contemporary conditions at the court in gloomy colors: drunkenness, cursing, cruelty, and violence dominate the "new manners" (*niuwen site*) of the nobility (984 ff.). From the rise in such complaints in the thirteenth century scholars have wrongly inferred that the social conditions of the nobility deteriorated rapidly with the decline of the Hohenstaufen dynasty. It was overlooked that already the poets around 1200 had used the literary convention of the "good old days" to contrast their own time unfavorably with the former flowering of courtly life, attributed to the time of King Arthur and the knights of the Round Table. At the end of his description of the festive splendor at Arthur's court, Hartmann von Aue adds this comment: "Truly it grieves me deeply, and I would lament loudly, were it of any use, that today such festive joyousness as was then customary no longer exists."[20] Wirnt von Grafenberg laments the conditions of his time even more bitterly: "The world has changed; its joyousness is in a wretched state. Justice has fled, violence is arising. Loyalty has become brittle, disloyalty and hatred are prevailing. Times have changed completely, and every year it gets worse."[21] In poetry we encounter the complaint about the deteriorating social conditions already in Heinrich von Veldeke: "When proper *minne* was still cultivated, social renown mattered. Now all one can learn day in and day out are bad manners. Anyone who has to witness this and who knows how things used to be, alas, he has good cause to complain. Virtues are trying to change into vices."[22] Similar negative judgments about contemporary times are found in Heinrich von Rugge, Heinrich von Morungen, and Reinmar der Alte. It is especially prominent in Walther von der Vogelweide, with whom the lament about the loss of courtly joy and the changes within noble society became a leitmotif in his songs and *Spruchdichtung*: "Formerly the world was so beautiful, now it is so wretched."[23] The most forceful lamentations come from the moralists and didacticians. Soon after 1200, Thomasin von Zirklaere posed the question: "Why is it that today one does not find as many virtuous people as one used to?"[24] He made the nobility responsible for the moral decay, specifically the lords of the great courts, who no longer surrounded themselves with competent and wise people, but with scoundrels and usurers. Money now ruled the court, and whoever was not rich had no influence (6301 ff.). No longer was there an Erec or a Gawein, "because nowhere in the land was there a King Arthur."[25] Here Thomasin echoed the verdict of the French moralist Guiot de Provins (beginning of the thirteenth century), who held the princes responsible for letting the courts become desolate and no longer hosting great feasts. The knights, barons, and castellans were not to blame, "but the princes are so distraught, so harsh, so uncourtly and mean"[26] that all social life had died off. In former times it would have done the magnates "honor to spend lavishly for a feast, to distribute gifts, and to lead a noble life."[27] But now "the beautiful residences and great palaces that were made to hold court are all abandoned—this I lament."[28] In a different passage Thomasin complained about the decline of lay education: "In the old days every child could read. All noble children were then educated, which is not the case today. At that time the world was in a better state, without hatred and enmity."[29] In reality the trend was exactly the opposite: lay education did not decline but advanced significantly in the thirteenth century. We can also assume that the general social morality of the nobility changed for the better rather than for the worse. The praise of the past was for the courtly poets a way to show the gap between the rough reality of noble life and the new ideal of courtly perfection. The negative description of contemporary life was also an appeal to model oneself after King Arthur and the knights of the Round Table, and to put into practice the courtly virtues which they had already possessed.

AN OVERVIEW OF THE BOOK

It is my intent to present the courtly literature of the High Middle Ages in its relationship to the social and cultural environment that determined the life of the nobility during this period. I want to show to what extent the literary scene of the courtly age was shaped by historical circumstances. The architectural layout of the Hohenstaufen castles and palaces, with the great hall as the center of social life, created the setting that allowed the representative forms of court life to unfold in grand style. Literature also benefited from this development, since it was in the great halls that the poets reached their audience. Without the fundamental change in women's clothing through the invention of the cut in the twelfth century, which made possible the new fashion of close-fitting clothes that accentuated the shape of the body, the new roles of the sexes in courtly entertainment and the culture of courtly love would hardly have flourished as they did. Only the establishment of separate chanceries at the courts of the secular princes at the end of the twelfth century created a written administration on a regular basis, and this guaranteed the poets stable work. These are only a few examples of the link between literary and social culture, a link that has been noted before, but which has never been systematically examined.

This essay is not addressed to specialists. It is in the nature of an introduction, and is meant to be accessible to readers without specialized knowledge.

Without a historical frame the cultural phenomena would make little sense. For that reason chapter one gives a survey of the structure and organization of society in the High Middle Ages. The reader who knows the history and does not need such background can skip this section. The first chapter also contains a historical explanation of the terms "knightly" (*ritterlich*) and "courtly" (*höfisch*) and their meanings for the noble culture of that age.

The courtly culture of the High Middle Ages originated in France. Its reception at the courts of the Gennan princes is the topic of chapter two. The linguistic and literary reception will be placed against the background of social contacts and ties between France and Germany. I will show that the intensification of economic and educational contacts contributed significantly to the spread of French culture.

Courtly culture is historically best attested in its material forms. Chapter three will deal with those spheres of material culture in which the modern character of the nobility's lifestyle manifested itself most clearly: castle-construction, luxurious clothes, knightly arms, and table manners. In each case I will try to bring out the connection between the display of material splendor and the new courtly character of social life.

The ceremonial side of courtly etiquette revealed itself historically nowhere better than at the great imperial diets and court feasts, which were celebrated in magnificent style.

Chapter four examines the social protocol at these great festive occa-

and didacticians. Soon after 1200, Thomasin von Zirklaere posed the question: "Why is it that today one does not find as many virtuous people as one used to?"[24] He made the nobility responsible for the moral decay, specifically the lords of the great courts, who no longer surrounded themselves with competent and wise people, but with scoundrels and usurers. Money now ruled the court, and whoever was not rich had no influence (6301 ff.). No longer was there an Erec or a Gawein, "because nowhere in the land was there a King Arthur."[25] Here Thomasin echoed the verdict of the French moralist Guiot de Provins (beginning of the thirteenth century), who held the princes responsible for letting the courts become desolate and no longer hosting great feasts. The knights, barons, and castellans were not to blame, "but the princes are so distraught, so harsh, so uncourtly and mean"[26] that all social life had died off. In former times it would have done the magnates "honor to spend lavishly for a feast, to distribute gifts, and to lead a noble life."[27] But now "the beautiful residences and great palaces that were made to hold court are all abandoned—this I lament."[28] In a different passage Thomasin complained about the decline of lay education: "In the old days every child could read. All noble children were then educated, which is not the case today. At that time the world was in a better state, without hatred and enmity."[29] In reality the trend was exactly the opposite: lay education did not decline but advanced significantly in the thirteenth century. We can also assume that the general social morality of the nobility changed for the better rather than for the worse. The praise of the past was for the courtly poets a way to show the gap between the rough reality of noble life and the new ideal of courtly perfection. The negative description of contemporary life was also an appeal to model oneself after King Arthur and the knights of the Round Table, and to put into practice the courtly virtues which they had already possessed.

AN OVERVIEW OF THE BOOK

It is my intent to present the courtly literature of the High Middle Ages in its relationship to the social and cultural environment that determined the life of the nobility during this period. I want to show to what extent the literary scene of the courtly age was shaped by historical circumstances. The architectural layout of the Hohenstaufen castles and palaces, with the great hall as the center of social life, created the setting

The conditions in Germany are at the center of this book. It would certainly have been of great value if this work could have taken a comparative approach, including France, Norman England, Sicily, and northern Italy, where at the very same time courtly culture was flourishing. But the groundwork for such a work has simply not been laid. In view of the strong French influence on Germany, however, we must have one eye on developments in France. In chapter five, when we examine the concept of courtly love, French sources figure rather more prominently, since the German sources alone do not convey an adequate picture.

At all times I have tried to check and verify statements from literary texts against historical sources. As a result there are many occasions where evidence from German works of literature and evidence from Latin historical works seem to be uncritically juxtaposed. I am fully aware of the methodological problem in such an approach, but I had to accept it, since it is not possible, within the framework of a comprehensive survey, to examine in detail the historical value of all poetic statements. Furthermore, it is not without some uneasiness that I repeatedly address isolated statements and observations as typical manifestations of their time, without being able to justify this in every case. It is here that the subjective character of the essay is most clear, for it would of course be possible to create a different picture by selecting entirely different passages. Some readers may find these methodological deficiencies so serious that they might question the usefulness of the present study. But in the final analysis every comprehensive essay faces similar problems, especially if it tries to document events and objects with direct reference to the sources.

One of my major concerns is to let the sources speak for themselves, to make the past come alive. All quotations appear in translation in the text and in the original languages in the notes. To allow the reader to verify my arguments, all quotes have references that are listed in the bibliography of sources. I have decided to do without scholarly footnotes. My indebtedness to the scholarly literature is reflected in the bibliography, which is also meant to encourage a broader interest in all aspects of courtly culture. The illustrations play an important role; their visual evidence is meant to complement what is described in the text.

CHAPTER I

Noble Society of the High Middle Ages: Historical Background

If we wish to understand the social basis of courtly literature, we must listen to what historians can tell us about the structure of medieval society. But historians' opinions vary widely, since the social conditions of the twelfth and thirteenth centuries offer a rather confusing picture in which the broad outlines can be discerned only with difficulty. The main reason for this is that the courtly age was a period of profound social change, in the course of which many of the old concepts of social order lost their meaning, and the foundations of a new social and political structure emerged only very slowly. It is this historical transformation with its often contradictory manifestations that we must confront in our effort to describe the social conditions of the courtly age. At the same time we must also take into account changes in scholarly approaches to these phenomena. The traditional concepts of law, state, and constitution in the Middle Ages—associated mainly with the names of Theodor Mayer and Otto Brunner, and nearly universally accepted in German historiography during the last fifty years—have come under attack in recent years. At this time, however, it is not clear whether the old concepts can be replaced by a new integrated view. Given the state of scholarship, it is quite difficult for the nonspecialist to reach a balanced judgment. This must be kept in mind when reading the following sketch, which is no more than a brief outline of the most important phenomena. Of necessity I have had to ignore the regional differences that increasingly shaped the legal and political developments within Germany from the thirteenth century on. Moreover, the following comments are largely focused on German conditions in the twelfth and thirteenth centuries; developments before and after this period are not considered.

1. BASIC CONCEPTS OF THE SOCIAL ORDER

THE LAW

"Nobody is as lofty as the law. For God is truly a righteous judge."[1] The notion that all law had its roots and foundation in God was commonplace in the Middle Ages. In the prologue to the *Sachsenspiegel* we read: "God Himself is justice, and therefore He loves the law."[2] Such statements were the basis of the doctrine of the good old law—described most succinctly by Fritz Kern—according to which the law in the Middle Ages was a "holy law" and had always existed; it was not "made" by mankind but simply "uncovered." No distinction was therefore drawn between subjective and objective, between natural and positive law. Both the law and the sense of justice were rooted in the belief in divine justice. The law lived in the oral traditions, in the memory of wise men who passed it on to succeeding generations. Any legal innovation could be seen as a restitution of the old law. As Eike von Repgow says in the rhymed preface to his *Sachsenspiegel*: "This law I did not think up myself; our venerable ancestors handed it down to us from ancient times."[3] Though it is undeniable that such ideas were ideologically very attractive, it is quite clear that a great discrepancy existed between this concept of the law grounded in religious beliefs and the reality of legal practice. Everybody knew that it was not enough to invoke the old law, that one could only preserve one's right by having it reconfirmed by every new ruler. The twelfth century, in particular, witnessed a new period in legal history, with many codifications that created new laws everywhere: in the form of imperial decrees, public peace (*Landfriede*), princely privileges, ministerial law (*Dienstrecht*), city law, and so on.

As long as there was no official administrative apparatus, public order consisted almost entirely of the courts. The fate of men depended largely on whether and how justice was rendered. To administer the law and to preserve the peace were the noblest duties of a ruler in the Middle Ages. If a ruler was incapable of fulfilling these tasks, or if he suddenly died without having arranged for his succession, anarchy spread over the land. Faced with chaotic conditions after the death of Emperor Henry VI in 1197, Walther von der Vogelweide called upon mankind to follow the example of order in the animal world. Of course there was constant strife among the animals, as among humans, "but in one regard the animals show good sense: they would consider themselves worthless had they not created strong courts; they choose kings, make law, and establish lords and servants."[4] Walther thus considered the establishment of a strong system of justice an essential step in the creation of a functioning state. Middle High German didactic poetry, too, knew that orderly life was impossible without law: "More than anything else the law is the measure, scale, and number of things. Without law nobody can live in peace."[5]

The law manifested itself in the jurisdiction of the king and of the great magnates. Judges are frequently admonished to exercise their office justly, to make no distinction between poor and rich; but at the same time it is very rarely mentioned that not all people stood before the same judge. The Middle Ages knew no equality before the law and no universal common law. Instead, there existed a confusing profusion of different spheres of jurisdiction: territorial law, feudal law, urban law, ministerial law, court law, and so on, which all differed considerably from region to region and from one ruler to the next. Every person lived according to his own law, but even this individual law was not uniform, since any one person could be subject to a variety of jurisdictions.

LORDSHIP

If asked how lordship developed and why there were rulers and subjects, medieval people frequently had only negative answers. The inequality of mankind was explained as the result of the fall from grace, or traced back to Cain's murder of Abel, or—and this theory was most widely accepted—attributed to Noah's curse upon his son Ham: "'Cursed be Canaan and his offspring! They shall be servants and slaves to my other two sons.' Now listen well, my dear friends: in this way noblemen and bondsmen were created."[6] Behind all this was the idea, well known from Roman political theory (Cicero, De officiis I, 21), that all people had originally been equal: "Nature did not assign to us more than to the cattle on the pasture. It gave us all things in common. But then a few people took for themselves that from which many could have lived."[7] Eike von Repgow in the *Sachsenspiegel* expressed most clearly that all lordship is predicated on violence and injustice: "In truth serfdom began with force, imprisonment, and unlawful lordship, and these things were continued from ancient times and turned into unlawful custom, and now some want to consider them law."[8] We don't know how noble society, for which most of the literary texts were created, reacted to such ideas.

Modern constitutional history takes a very different view of the development and nature of lordship. As more and more scholars began to realize that the categories of modern political theory are useless for describing political reality in the Middle Ages, the concept of lordship has gained in importance. Most historians describe the medieval polity as the "rule of the aristocracy." What this means is that for many centuries real power lay in the hands of a relatively small group of families of the highest nobility, which was virtually closed off to people from below. Viewed in this way the continuity of noble rule from the early Germanic period up to the emergence of territorial lordship in the late Middle Ages was the salient feature in the medieval political landscape. Accordingly it would have been of secondary importance that Germany was a kingdom, since kingship differed only in degree and not in kind from aristocratic rule.

Aristocratic rule was lordship over land and people. Using Germanic legal terms, historians distinguish between *Munt* (lordship over people) and *Gewere* (lordship over things). Modern scholarship has been greatly preoccupied with the question whether all the various manifestations of lordship in the Middle Ages—landed lordship, ecclesiastical lordship, territorial lordship, and so on—have one common root. The answer given by Otto Brunner and Walter Schlesinger has decisively shaped the modern notion of medieval constitutional development, and is even today often seen as valid. According to these scholars, the house was the center and starting point of all lordship. It was a sphere of peace, a domain with its own law, in which the lord of the house exercised all authority over people and things. Today this notion, and the entire idea that the continuity of lordship is the fundamental element in medieval constitutional history, has come under criticism especially from legal historians (Karl Kroeschell). In the continuing discussion of these issues, the German terminology of lordship in the Middle High German sources, which has not yet been thoroughly analyzed, could play an important role.

Beyond dispute is the fact that the nature of public authority underwent a fundamental change in the course of the High Middle Ages.
Theodor Mayer summed up the process neatly when he said that the
Personenverbandsstaat (state formed by personal ties) of the early Middle Ages became the *institutionelle Flächenstaat* (institutionalized territorial state) of early modern Europe. What this means is that the power of a ruler in earlier times was based, apart from his own property, on
a network of personal ties of loyalty and dependence, whereas rulers
later managed to extend their control over a solid block of territory by
gathering into their own hands most of the privileges of lordship that
existed there. This process has also been described as the formation of
territorial lordship, or historically as the rise of the territorial states.
There is no clear answer as to what exactly formed the foundation of
territorial lordship. Landed lordship was certainly an important precondition; even more important were apparently the comital rights,
especially high justice. But it is not possible to derive territorial lordship
from a single source of authority. Nor can we consider the extension of
territorial sovereignty simply as the usurpation of older royal prerogatives by the princes, even though the weakening of the kingship in Germany was undoubtedly an important factor in the growing power of the
princes. It is also clear that a number of royal prerogatives were indeed
absorbed into territorial lordship. The great imperial decrees of Emperor Frederick II in favor of the ecclesiastical princes (*Confoederatio
cum principibus ecclesiasticis*, 1220) and the secular princes (*Statutum in
favorem principium*, 1232), legally recognized in perpetuity the princes'
sovereign jurisdiction over the courts, safe passage, minting, tolls, as
well as the building of cities and castles. The regalia became the most
important sources of financial income for the territorial lords, while the
construction of castles and the founding of cities proved very effective
instruments of internal territorial consolidation. The greatest resistance
against the realization of the new form of territorial rule came from
the old noble families, most of whom lost their jurisdictions to the
territorial lords and were integrated into the territorial states. But
almost everywhere the landed nobility managed to acquire a share in
the governance of the land by forming corporate federations. By the
time of an imperial verdict of 1231, King Henry (VII) decided that
no prince or "territorial lord" (*dominus terre*) had the right to pass
new laws without "the consent of the nobles and magnates of the
land."[9] In provisions of this kind lay the beginnings of territorial constitutions.

ESTATES

"God has created three estates: peasants, knights, and clergy."[10] The idea that mankind could be classified into those who work the fields, those who fight, and those who pray, was common from the tenth century on. "The house of God is divided into three and yet considered one. Some pray, some fight, and some work."[11] The appearance of this formula is today generally seen as an indication that by this time the formation of the lower nobility, at least in France, had progressed to the point where it was possible to separate terminologically a noble warrior class from those who were engaged in agricultural work. But we must not forget that Greek philosophy had already known a distinction between agriculture, warfare, and teaching, and that medieval authors were very well acquainted with the classical foundations of this scheme of the estates or orders. In the *Liber lamentationum* (Book of Lamentations) of the notorious misogynist Matheolus (end of the thirteeth century), we read the following: "Moreover, our ancient philosophers already noted three estates. For they assigned to the clergy the responsibility for the doctrine of faith, so that they might guide the others. Next comes the armed knight, who is to guard the common weal. Subservient to them are the peasants and the other laymen, whose work creates the livelihood for the other two estates."[12] However, this hierarchical gradation of the orders was derived more from medieval experience than from a knowledge of classical texts. The ancient idea that the three occupations were in principal of equal worth is found almost at the same time in the German poet Frauenlob: "From the beginning mankind was divided into three groups, as I have read: peasants, knights, and clergy. They all were, each in his order, equal in nobility and birth."[13] Reality, however, was very different: everybody knew that knights and peasants were not "equal in nobility and birth."

Apart from the division into clergy, warrior, and peasants, there were many other possibilities of grouping people according to their "estate." Most divisions were based on the biblical notion—expressed most clearly in the Epistles of St. Paul—that the order of the world rests in God, and that "each [is] in his proper place."[14] Yet this basic idea of the Christian doctrine of the structure of the estates was hardly suitable for describing actual social differentiations. The "estate" in St. Paul denotes merely the place within the large, divinely sanctioned order. "Estates" in this sense were men and women, poor and rich, clergy and laity, sinners and righteous, and so on. Our own phrase "the holy state of matrimony" is reminiscent of this usage. This concept of "estate" must first be related to historical reality. In so doing we must consider that the Middle Ages had no standard term for "estate." Writers used the Latin words *status, ordo, corpus, conditio, gradus,* and in the German texts *name, leben, ê, reht, orde, art,* and *ambet.* The German word *stant* seems to have appeared only in the fourteenth century and was not used until the fifteenth century for the order of estates in the territorial states (*stende des lands*).

Closer to reality was the division of people into "the powerful" and "the poor" (*potentes* and *pauperes*), which could also follow biblical usage. In German one expressed this division as *rîche und arme* or *hêrren und knechte.* The distinction between lord and servant was fundamental to medieval social structure. The hierarchical ladder stood out even more clearly if one distinguished three rungs. The German work *Lucidarius* (end of the twelfth century) gives a division into "free men," "knights," and "serfs."[15] The "knights," who stood between freedom and serfdom, were probably ministerials. Other lists name "princes, knights, and servants (*Knechte*),"[16] or "counts, free men, ministerials (*Dienstmannen*)."[17] One could lengthen the list and vary the terms, but a standard formula did not exist. All enumerations, however, express one thing in common: people were not equal in rank and estate, there were superiors and inferiors. A very original picture of the hierarchy of orders was drawn at the end of the thirteenth century by Berthold von Regensburg in his sermon "On the ten choirs of angels and Christendom." In accordance with the ten choirs of angels, God divided mankind into ten choirs, and among people, as with the angels, the three highest choirs were placed above the other seven. "The first three groups of people are the highest and the most noble, whom God Himself has chosen and to whom the other seven are to be subservient."[18] According to Berthold von Regensburg, the highest choirs included first, the priests (*die pfaffen*), second, the other clergy (*geistlîche liute*), and third, "the secular judges, that is to say the lords and knights who are to protect widows and orphans."[19] This third choir comprised the entire secular nobility: emperors and kings, dukes, free men, counts, "and all secular lords, who are knights and lords, and all to whom our Lord God has entrusted jurisdiction and power on earth."[20] The list of the seven subservient choirs is clearly shaped by the social conditions within the city: 1. "all those who produce cloth or clothing";[21] 2. "all those who work with iron tools";[22] 3. "all those who are engaged in trade";[23] 4. "all those who sell food and drink";[24] 5. "all those who work the field";[25] and 6. "all those who are engaged in medicine."[26] The tenth choir of mankind has, like that of the angels, fallen away from God: "these are the minstrels, fiddlers, drummers, or whatever else they are called, all those who take goods for honor."[27]

To say that feudal society was structured according to estates means that people were not equal before the law. However, the gradations that resulted from the different levels of *wergeld*, as it was laid down in the Germanic tribal laws, or from the varying jurisdictions of the courts, were very different than the estate-formations of the late Middle Ages. When we hear of the "estate of lords" or the "estate of peasants," this kind of terminology obscures the fact that in the early and High Middle Ages there did not exist a structure of estates that comprised all of society. As for the courtly period of the twelfth and thirteenth centuries, one usually refers to the feudal order of the *Sachsenspiegel* to explain the hierarchy of estates. According to its author, Eike von Repgow, there were seven levels in the hierarchy of vassalage (*Heerschildordnung*). The king possessed the highest level, the ecclesiastical princes the second, the secular princes the third, the counts and free lords the fourth, *Schöffenbarfreie* and *Dienstmannen* the fifth and their vassals the sixth; the seventh level, which the *Schwabenspiegel* later assigned to the *Einschildritter* (single-shield knights), was left unnamed in the *Sachsenspiegel*. Quite apart from the fact that this structure had a mostly theoretical meaning, it cannot be regarded as a general hierarchy of estates since it incorporates only one single aspect, that of vassalage; one's place within the law of the land was not affected by vassalage.

The formation of a fixed order of estates was a process that spread from the top down. The first group were the princes, who already by the end of the twelfth century became the estate of the imperial princes (*Reichsfürstenstand*). The subsequent formation of estates was linked very closely with the development of the princely territories into sovereign states. From the end of the thirteenth century on there emerged in a number of German territories an estate of lords (*Herrenstand*) as a corporative federation of the old nobility, usually inclusive of the ministerials. In some territories we also find in the fourteenth century an estate of knights (*Ritterstand*) below the *Herrenstand*. The cities also experienced the formation of estates and were given a place in the territorial diets, where the estates together represented the land vis-à-vis the territorial lord. The formation of an estate of peasants (*Bauernstand*), however, occurred in only a few places. It is only in relation to these territorial constitutions based on territorial estates, which lasted into the nineteenth century, that we can speak of a comprehensive order of estates.

2. THE HIERARCHICAL STRUCTURE OF SOCIETY

THE KING

In political terms Germany in the Middle Ages was an elective monarchy. In theory the king was chosen by the "people" (*populus*), in fact he was elected by the "magnates" of the realm (*principes*). Formal regulations of the election procedure did not exist. The privilege to cast the often decisive first vote in the election was claimed by the archbishops of the Rhineland, especially by the archbishop of Cologne. Eike von Repgow had already written in the *Sachsenspiegel* that a small number of ecclesiastical and secular princes had precedence in the election of the king. In the thirteenth century this group gradually developed into a college of prince electors, which was finally institutionalized as the body of electors in the "Golden Bull" of Emperor Charles IV in 1356. From the very beginning the principle of election in Germany was limited by the royal dynasty's right of blood succession. If a male heir existed the election by the princes was often merely an approval of succession. After the election the king was elevated to the throne and crowned. The prevailing idea around 1200 was that the coronation should take place in Aachen, where the throne of Charlemagne stood, and be performed by the archbishop of Cologne. Later Frankfurt came to be fixed as the site of the election.

The German kingship was a continuation of the Frankish kingship, especially the east-Frankish one. Since the middle of the eleventh century the official title of the German king was "King of the Romans" (*rex Romanorum*); it expressed the connection between the German kingship and the Roman emperorship. "King of the Germans" (*rex Teutonicorum*) was an appelation used almost entirely by foreign writers. The phrase "German kingdom" (*regnum Teutonicum*), however, was occasionally used even by the imperial chancery. Together with the kingdoms of Italy and Burgundy, the German kingdom was part of the "Roman Empire" (*Imperium Romanum*). As emperor the German king called himself *imperator Romanorum* and *augustus*. Ever since the imperial coronation of Otto I in 962, the German monarchs possessed a claim to the Roman emperorship. Many of the problems in the history of the medieval empire have their source in this dual function of the king. To obtain the imperial dignity the king had to be crowned in Rome by the pope. But by the twelfth century Frederick I assumed the imperial title before his coronation in Rome. Later, the notion developed that the newly elected German king was at the same time the "Roman emperor-elect." The last German king to be crowned emperor in Rome by the pope was the Hapsburg monarch Frederick III (d. 1493) in the year 1452.

The king was the highest judge and the highest feudal lord; he called up the feudal army and administered the royal domain. Outward expression of royal power and dignity were the insignia of lordship, especially the imperial insignia that were worn at the coronation and on festive occasions. They included crown, scepter, lance, sword, imperial orb, armlets, festive robes, and imperial relics which the king kept in his treasury. Under the Hohenstaufen emperors the imperial insignia were kept off and on at castle Trifels in the Palatinate; from the fifteenth century on they found a permanent home in Nürnberg, and today they are in the Viennese treasury. The most precious piece is the octagonal imperial crown, richly decorated with images and jewels, and with its characteristic metal arch. The crown itself is thought to be the work of the tenth century; the metal arch dates from the eleventh century. The great importance of the insignia was revealed whenever there were doubts about the legitimacy of the ruler. After the dual election of 1198, the Hohenstaufen Philip of Swabia based the legitimacy of his kingship not least on the fact that he had been crowned with the genuine insignia. In the *Spruchdichtung* of Walther von der Vogelweide this argument looms large: "The crown itself is older than King Philip."[1]

The splendor of the Hohenstaufen emperors under Frederick I (1152–1190) and Henry VI (1190–1197) cannot obscure the fact that the effective basis of royal power in Germany had been seriously compromised. In the thirteenth century the German kingship became the plaything of foreign powers. Already Otto IV (1198–1218) assumed the throne as the candidate of the English king. Frederick II (1215–1250), by birth and language an Italian, was launched by the pope. Another double election in 1257 made German kings of the Prince of Cornwall and the King of Castile. A new chapter in the history of the German kingdom began only with Rudolf of Hapsburg (1273–1291). From that time on the real basis of royal power was the dynastic strength of the princely houses that obtained the throne.

THE PRINCES

In the Middle Ages, the exercise of royal power was hedged about by many restrictions. On all important decisions the magnates of the realm had to give their "advice" (*consilium*). These "magnates" (*magnates, optimates, proceres, principes*) were a not clearly defined group of the leading families of the high nobility, whose members the king gathered around himself at diets and high Church holidays, or who spent longer periods of time at the royal court. In their hands lay the now hereditary public power of the dukes, counts palatine, landgraves, and counts. This group included further the holders of the high ecclesiastical offices: the archbishops and bishops, as well as the abbots and provosts of the imperial monasteries and imperial cathedral chapters. In addition to their own regional power, participation in the exercise of royal and imperial government characterized these princely magnates. As the kingship grew weaker and its center moved increasingly to Italy in the twelfth century, the fortunes of Germany were more and more determined by the magnates of the realm. The fact that they could conduct their own negotiations with foreign powers testifies eloquently to the degree of their independence.

Towards the end of the twelfth century a significant change occurred in the conception and composition of this small group of magnates: from now on the imperial princes (*principes imperii*) formed a separate estate. In 1184 Emperor Frederick I signed an agreement that provided for the elevation of the counts of Hainaut to the rank of imperial princes. That was the first procedure of its kind. The distinction was drawn according to criteria of feudal law: only a lord who held a fief directly from the king belonged to the chosen group. Around 1200, Germany had fifteen to twenty secular imperial princes (*Fahnlehen*, "banner-fiefs") and about eighty ecclesiastical imperial princes (*Zepterlehen*, "sceptre-fiefs"). Later these numbers rose very slightly. As early as the thirteenth century a smaller group crystallized out of the estate of the imperial princes: the seven prince electors, who appeared as the sole electors of the king for the first time at the double election in 1257. Who belonged to this group and how many prince electors there should be was long disputed. Generally those seven princes were named who had already appeared in the *Sachsenspiegel* as the holders of the *Erzämter* (the highest offices in the empire): the three Rhenish archbishops of Cologne, Mainz, and Trier, and as secular princes the count palatine of the Rhine, the margrave of Brandenburg, the duke of Saxony, and the king of Bohemia.

It was of great importance for the subsequent course of medieval German history that the imperial princes became lords of territorial states. In and of itself the concentration of sovereign rights into one hand and the intensive extension of lordship throughout a larger region were not characteristic only of princely rule. All who exercised lordship carried on and strengthened their lands in this way, the king just as much as the nonprincely nobility. Moreover, not all who became sovereign territorial lords were imperial princes. Nevertheless, princely rank and territorial sovereignty were intimately linked. The most important territories that graduallly developed into sovereign states were without exception in the hands of princes. Especially vigorous was the development of the new states in the eastern part of Germany, in the Austrian duchies, in Bavaria, Meißen, Brandenburg, Pomerania, and Mecklenburg. In contrast, only a few extended lordships were able to form in the region of the old duchies of Swabia, Franconia, and Saxony. Particularly in the southwest a great number of small territorial lordships arose, and this gave the political map of Germany in the late Middle Ages such a colorful appearance. Many of these were able to maintain their sovereignty into the nineteenth century.

THE NONPRINCELY NOBILITY

The family histories of the noble houses of the High Middle Ages, including the princely families, can rarely be traced back beyond the eleventh century. The explanation for this seems to lie in the fact that only then did loose family groupings—which, independent of the principle of filial succession, followed the lead of the most prominent members among a wider circle of relatives—gradually develop into clearly distinct noble families with a consciousness of their separateness. This transformation is reflected most clearly in the practice of name-giving. In the older period members of the nobility had only a first name; family names did not yet exist. To designate blood ties one used either those names that frequently reappeared in the family group (e.g. the Ottonians), or the names of a common ancestor (e.g. the Welfs, the Hunfridingers). The noble double names that indicate descent appeared only in the eleventh century. With the exception of the Welfs, who could trace their family history back to Carolingian times, all German noble houses of the High Middle Ages had names of the new type, which were derived from place-names (Hohenstaufen, Wittelsbacher, Hapsburgs). This reveals that the mark of noble descent was now no longer the relationship to other people but the association with a specific place, the ancestral seat and center of the family's power. Almost all new noble names were derived from castle names. Initially it would happen that the various members of a family would call themselves after various castles. Eventually, however, one name came to prevail, and from that time on we get a clear view of the genealogy of the noble houses. Of special importance to the identity of a noble family was the link to its family monastery, where the tomb of the founder-family was frequently located, and where the earliest records of the family history were written. Family traditions and ancestral memories strengthened the self-image of the noble houses. In the twelfth century people began to place pictures and signs onto shields and other parts of a knight's equipment, not only as decoration but as a way of identifying their bearer. This was the beginning of heraldry, though it did take quite some time before the new coats of arms became the unmistakable identity marks of families.

The restructuring of the nobility is linked historically to the intensified exercise of the various forms of lordship and the spread of lordship through entire regions. Monastic advocacy and the building of castles proved to be particularly effective instruments in these efforts. The strengthening of noble lordship developed essentially along the same lines as the efforts of the kings and princes to territorialize their own authority. A few baronial families and some in the ranks of counts were able to make the transition to territorial lordship (e.g. Waldeck, Lippe). The majority of the old nobility, however, could not defend their own positions against the growing might of the princes. The princes succeeded, primarily with the help of the Public Peace (*Landfriede*), in significantly restricting and eventually abolishing altogether the nobility's right to wage private warfare. Step by step the nonprincely nobility thus lost its sovereign rights and became a landed gentry (*landsässig*).

THE MINISTERIALS

A lord's "household" (*familia*) was thought to comprise all those who were subject to a lord and were unfree in their person. Within this large group of "serfs" (*servientes*) and "servants" (*servi*) there existed, however, significant gradations. The chronicle of the Alsatian monastery of Ebersheim distinguished a "three-tiered" family which belonged to the episcopal church of Straßburg. "First, the *familia* of the ministerials, which is also rightly called the knightly *familia*."[2] The chronicler goes on to say: "It is so noble and warlike that it can truly be compared to the free status."[3] Second, "the *familia* of the rent-owing serfs and those obligated to render labor services."[4] Third, "the *familia* of the servants and rent-payers."[5] This part of the Ebersheim Chronicle was written in the first half of the thirteenth century. The ministerials appear here as the upper stratum of the unfree within the lord's *familia*. Modern scholarship agrees with the chronicler's judgment that the unfreedom of the ministerials in the thirteenth century could hardly be distinguished from full freedom, and that the members of this class could already be called "noble" (*nobilis*).

The legal demarcation of the ministerials within the *familia* and the codification of a separate law for them reach back as far as the eleventh century. In view of these developments one can speak of the emergence of a class or estate of ministerials. A uniform ministerial law, however, did not exist; their legal status varied from one lord to the next. In the *Sachsenspiegel* we read: "Now do not be surprised that this book contains so little about the law of the ministerials. It is so varied that nobody can grasp it all. Under each bishop, each abbot and abbess the ministerials have a special law."[6] The law of the Bamberg ministerials, put into writing under Bishop Gunther of Bamberg (d. 1065) in the year 1061/62, was one of the oldest texts of its kind. It decreed that a ministerial could be called upon only for noble services: in war as armored horseman, and at the court as steward, treasurer, marshal, or cupbearer (as a fifth court office the Bamberg law lists the hunting master[7]). Other historical sources attest that some ministerials quite early held genuine fiefs. Scholars have long debated how this highly privileged group of people was recruited. Generally it is assumed that the ministerials for the most part rose from the lower strata of the *familia*. There is, however, plenty of evidence that free noblemen also entered the ranks of the ministerials. A charter of King Conrad III (d. 152) for the monastery of Corvey mentions both of these very different paths into the ministerial class. Permission was granted to free men "to place themselves into the property of the monastery under the ministerial law," and it was also decreed that "the abbot shall have the power to create ministerials from among the lowest ranks of the *lites* and rent-owing serfs."[8]

The most eminent ministerial class was that of the king. Next to the king the bishoprics and the great cathedral chapters early on created their own ministerials. When the secular princes began to organize their court administrations after the royal model in the eleventh and twelfth centuries, they also created court offices and staffed them with ministerials. The Salian emperors of the eleventh century seem to have been the first to use their ministerials consciously as an instrument of politics, by assigning to them important administrative functions and the exercise of sovereign authority. Among the complaints that the princes brought against Emperor Henry IV (d. 1106) was that he "has raised the lowest people without any noble ancestors to the highest honors, taking council with them day and night, and plotting to completely exterminate the high nobility."[9] Disregarding all such opposition, the Hohenstaufen emperors continued and expanded the ministerial policy of the Salians. In the second half of the twelfth century the imperial administration and the military leadership were largely in the hands of the great imperial ministerials, who in some cases rose to prince-like positions. A man like Werner von Bolanden, who as a *ministerialis* was the feudal lord of over a hundred vassals, was certainly an exception, as was the imperial steward Marquart of Annweiler, who as the duke of Romagna became one of the magnates of Italy. But they do embody the kind of hierarchy-breaking opportunities of advancement that the ministerial functions offered their holders in exceptional circumstances.

Like the kings and emperors, the princes, too, used the ministerials as instruments of lordship. As the heads of the central court administration in the emerging territories, as the guardians of their sovereigns' castles, as the princes' representatives in the cities, the ministerials played a crucial role in the expansion and organization of territorial sovereignty. And in the territories, too, their influence and power grew with their functions. Although there were great social differences within the minsterial class, we can say that as early as around 1200, the leading ministerials could hardly be distinguished from the old nobility in regard to their lifestyle. Subsequently the extinction of many families of the old nobility in the thirteenth century led to a steady increase in the percentage of ministerials within the freeholding nobility (*landsässiger Adel*). Legally, however, the *nobiles* and the ministerials remained separated for quite some time. Not until the fourteenth century did the ministerials merge with the remnants of the smaller baronial families to form the lower nobility.

THE URBAN POPULATION

Cities existed in Germany as early as Roman times, but it was only in
the High Middle Ages that they became a decisive factor in social history. During the second half of the eleventh century historical sources
report numerous cases of unrest in the old episcopal cities. The events in
Cologne attracted special attention. In 1074, the burghers occupied the
residence of their overlord, Archbishop Anno II (d. 1075), and forced
him to flee the city. Soon after the archbishop returned with force of
arms and meted out cruel and stern punishment to the inhabitants. Elsewhere the burghers were more successful, as in Cambrai, where in the
year 1076 they "swore a commune (*iuraverunt communiam*) . . . mu-
tually obliging themselves on oath to refuse the bishop reentry to Cambrai unless he recognized the sworn commune."[10] Such "sworn associations" (*coniurationes*) are now seen as the decisive step towards the
creation of a separate urban law. During this same period the cities also
became politically active for the first time. When the princes threatened
to depose Emperor Henry IV in 1073, he found support in Worms: the
burghers expelled their bishop and opened the city to the emperor. He
thanked them with a toll privilege that is among the earliest examples of
imperial policy towards the cities. For the most part the later emperors
also pursued a policy favorable to the cities.

The right of self-government, which the burghers in the old episcopal
seats had to wrest from their overlords in protracted struggles, was
usually granted to the newly founded cities right from the start. During
the first half of the twelfth century there began in Germany a period of
urban foundations that greatly multiplied the number of existing cities
within a short time. One of the earliest examples is the founding of
Freiburg i. Br. by Duke Conrad of Zähringen (d. 1152) in the year
1120. The founding charter has survived. In it the duke promised to
place over his new burghers only a bailiff of their choice, and he granted
them the right to settle their quarrels amongst themselves in accordance
with their own legal customs. Cities were founded in the twelfth century
by kings and the great princes. Many of the new princely foundations
became territorial cities, while the foundations of kings, as well as the
majority of the old episcopal seats, whose inhabitants had won their
freedom from their ecclesiastical lords, later rose to the rank of free
imperial cities.

Characteristic of the legal position of the burgher was the concept of

urban liberty. It meant above all that the burghers were free of all bondage to the soil. The founder of the city gave them their property as a
free, heritable loan without any further obligations to render services or
dues. To this were added the personal liberties, such as freedom of
movement (in contrast to the ties that bound most rural folk to the
land), and the free disposition of their own property and inheritance.
The inhabitants of the old episcopal cities received these rights through
royal charters of liberties: in 1111 a charter went to the citizens of
Worms, in 1114 to the burghers of Speyer. The legal principle "city air
brings freedom" provided that a bondsman who moved into the city
acquired his freedom after a year and a day unless his lord demanded
him back during this time. The principle of the legal equality of all
burghers set urban law fundamentally apart from all other legal systems
of the time, which were structured hierarchically. Yet legal equality did
not mean that the urban population was a society of equals.

In almost all cities a thin upper stratum very soon set itself apart
from the remaining population. These urban nobles often resided in
permanent stone homes, examples of which can still be seen in Regensburg, and gained a controlling influence over city politics and the administration. Nearly everywhere they had social and family ties with the
landed nobility, and in the cities of southern and western Germany they
recruited their members largely from the ministerials to whom the
cities' overlords had assigned important offices (market, mint, tolls,
courts). The descendants of this urban nobility formed the eligible families from whose ranks the members of the city council were elected. The
council governed the city and in turn chose one of their own to be
mayor. Not until the fourteenth century did the guilds rise up against
the rule of the councils. In some cities, such as Straßburg, the guilds
succeeded in displacing the patriciate of the old familes; in others, such
as Augsburg, they gained participation in the council; in a few, such as
Nürnberg, the patricians kept the upper hand.

Not everybody who lived in the city was a citizen. In many cases the
rights of a burgher were tied to the ownership of land within the city.
New immigrants had to pay a burgher fee in order to be admitted to the
burgher oath. Most of the burghers were either merchants, of whom
some managed to rise into the ranks of the patricians eligible for the
council, or artisans, who nearly everywhere organized themselves into
guilds. Those without the citizenship lived in the cities as "inhabitants"
and "dwellers without full civic rights." At the bottom, finally, was a

broad urban class of servants, day laborers, beggars, and poor, who had no share in the liberties of the city.

THE RURAL POPULATION

It is estimated that in the High Middle Ages about ninety percent of the population lived on the land in a state of dependency. Most peasants were personally unfree, being subject to the manorial authority and the manorial law of their lord to whom they owed services and dues in kind. Free peasants did exist in the Middle Ages, especially in the Alpine regions and in Frisia, and their number rose in the course of the twelfth century in the wake of agricultural expansion. When previously desolate land was made arable and settled, no new manors were carved out; instead, the new land was usually given to the peasants as heritable property. By contrast, in the old settlement regions manorial dependency and serfdom persisted for a long time. Yet the concept of bondage is insufficient to describe the condition of the rural population. After all, "free" and "unfree" were relative terms: there was a wide range of personal and property dependencies, and within the manorial *familia* there existed very significant gradations. A steward who supervised a larger economic unit and a poor day laborer were both subject to the manor court, but in terms of social status they had virtually nothing in common.

Very gradually, in a process that stretched over centuries, manorial lordship changed its character. More and more noble lords gave up cultivating their manors themselves and lived only off the income that accrued to them from the ownership of land. The personal services of serfs on the manor, now no longer needed, were commuted to monetary payments. Of course this process showed significant regional variations. On the whole, it resulted in an improvement in the condition of the rural population, especially through the disappearance of the oppressive compulsory labor. We must not, however, accept Neidhart's satirically distorted picture of the rich peasant (first half of the thirteenth century) as a reflection of reality. Nor should we believe that the proud words of the old steward Helmbrecht on the dignity of peasant status sprang from the self-confidence of the rural population: "No matter how eminent a person, his proud nature would be laid low, were it not for peasant labor."[11] The peasants of Neidhart and in the *Helmbrecht* are literary types conceived for the noble court audience. Even if there was some degree of prosperity among the peasants, the mass of the rural population was exposed very harshly to the vicissitudes of life.

3. THE ECONOMY

ECONOMIC DEVELOPMENTS

From the eleventh century on, Europe experienced a vigorous economic expansion which came to an end only with the great crises of the fourteenth century. During this period the population doubled or tripled. Of course the High Middle Ages suffered its share of dreadful crop failures and famines, and the wild fluctuations in grain prices afflicted above all the humbler classes. Nevertheless, on the whole it seems that the living conditions of most people improved during this period. Part of the explanation lies in the fact that the development of a money economy created in all areas a much greater economic flexibility.

The right of coinage was an old royal prerogative. As early as the ninth century, kings granted this right to bishops and monasteries. When secular lords also began to stamp coins in their own domains in the twelfth century, the circulation of money increased dramatically. Frederick II's great privileges of 1220 and 1232 for the ecclesiastical and secular princes recognized their right to mint coins. At this time Germany already had about five hundred mints. The coins most frequently stamped were the silver penny and the half-penny, in many local variations; among them the Cologne Penny was most highly valued. Not infrequently fiscal policy took the form of a continual debasement of the silver content of the coins. Rich silver deposits existed above all in the Harz mountains near Goslar. The attempts of the Salian emperors to expand and strengthen their power base in that region were frustrated by the resistance of the Saxon nobility. In the twelfth century silver mining began near Freiberg in Saxony, near Frisach in Carinthia, in the Lavant valley, in the southern Black Forest, in Silesia, and in Bohemia. Thanks not least to their rich gold and silver deposits, the kings of Bohemia were, at the end of the thirteenth century, the richest princes in Germany.

The increase in money primarily benefited the urban economy. But agriculture also profited: the peasants could now sell their produce at market and acquire in this way the means to pay off in cash the dues and services they owed their lords. A rising demand for foodstuffs,

caused by an expanding population, led to a rise in prices for agricultural produce, and thus to an improvement in the economic situation of
the peasants. In many areas the cultivation of the land was expanded
and intensified; the many rural settlements that were abandoned in later
centuries attest to this. Many new settlements sprang up in the previously thinly populated lower mountain ranges, and especially east of
the Elbe and Saale rivers, in the old Slavic settlement areas. The German
settlers went eastward partly at the invitation of the Slavic princes, and
partly at the initiative of the German territorial lords, who were trying
to expand their power in this way. It was this process that gave the great
east-German territories their historical shape.

The High Middle Ages was also a time of great technical progress. In
agriculture the introduction of the heavy plow had the most profound
consequences. The old scratch-plow could only tear open the soil,
whereas the new heavy plow turned the clods and made possible a
much better use of the land. Where soil conditions permitted, the three-
field rotation was adopted: instead of letting fields lie fallow every other
year, peasants now rotated in a three-year rhythm between summer
crops, winter crops, and fallow. The new method could increase yields
by up to fifty percent. A new harnessing device made the horse the most
important draught animal next to the ox; the emergence of the nailed
horseshoe made the horse a good worker also on rocky terrain. Of great
economic importance was the use of water power. Grain mills had existed for a long time, but it was only in the High Middle Ages that people learned to put the power of the water wheel to other uses: in
brewing, in cloth manufacturing, in metalworking. Trip-hammers and
bellows were now driven by water wheels. The first tanning mills are
attested in the twelfth century, the first saw mills at the beginning of the
thirteenth century. From Persia came the windmill, from China the
crank and the spinning wheel, first attested in 1280 in Speyer. Paper
was another Chinese invention, and its production reached Europe by
way of the Arabs. The first paper mills appeared in thirteenth-century
Italy. The thirteenth century also saw the invention of the counter-
weight clock and eyeglasses. Many of the technical innovations benefited warfare. The modern knightly technique of fighting presupposed
the introduction of the stirrup and the development of a saddle with a
high saddlebow as well as a firm chest strap. The crossbow was adopted
from the Arabs in the eleventh century, while new siege engines with
large catapults of reliable aim spread in the twelfth. Gunpowder was

introduced from Egypt in the thirteenth century, and as early as 1258 rockets were set off in Cologne.

TRADE AND COMMERCE

Of profound significance for the economic development in the High Middle Ages was the flowering of the cities. Twelfth-century Germany had about 250 cities; in the thirteenth century the number rose to over two thousands. Most cities were tiny, with just a few thousand inhabitants. The only metropolis in Germany was Cologne with about thirty thousands inhabitants and an urban space of about forty-four hectares; in 1180 the city began construction of its great wall. Cologne and Regensburg, which could both look back upon a venerable past, were also the major commercial centers. But already in the thirteenth century competing centers arose: Lübeck, founded in 1143 by the counts of Holstein and confirmed in 1158 by Henry the Lion, and Nuremberg, whose development was greatly promoted by the privilege granted to it by Emperor Frederick II in 1219.

The economic activites of the cities were in the hands of merchants and artisans. The concentration of large numbers of people in one place and the economic exchange between city and countryside created brand new markets for the artisans. The city law of Straßburg from the middle of the twelfth century reveals that aside from bakers, shoemakers, smiths, and carpenters, there were a number of trades that worked to satisfy more sophisticated needs: glove makers, furriers, saddlers, armorers, and so on. Characteristic of the development of urban crafts was the growing specialization of artisanal skills. Already in the twelfth century we find trades as specialized as that of the cloth-shearers, dyers, and cup makers. Specialization emerged above all in the flourishing branches of textile manufacturing and metalworking. Fourteenth-century Nuremberg had more than 1200 masters working in fifty different occupations. This trend towards ever more specialization is linked to the peculiar organization of trades in the cities. Quite early the representatives of individual trade branches formed associations that were called "guilds." The oldest such associations were the guild of the fishmongers in Worms (1106/07) and that of the shoemakers in Würzburg (1128). But it took several centuries before all the trades were organized into guilds. The guilds were not exclusively economic associations, but also played an important role in the religious and social life of their members. In time their authoritative character came out more clearly: they controlled prices and wages, set the amount of material to be worked, and determined the techniques of production. Where the guilds did not succeed in gaining participation in city government, as for example in Nuremberg, they fell under the strict supervision of the council.

The dynamic element in the economy of the city was trade, particularly long-distance trade, which experienced a tremendous upsurge in the twelfth century in those cities that were located at the important sites of communication. Given the general insecurity on the routes and the dangers to which the traffic in goods was exposed, especially in foreign countries, long-distance trade always posed a great risk. On the other hand, the profits to be made were immense, vastly exceeding what any artisan or craftsman could hope for. In many cases the great merchant families were able to rise into the ranks of the patriciate that was eligible to serve on the city council.

A very effective way for cities to capture the transit trade was the so-called *Stapelrecht* (staple right): it compelled nonlocal merchants to offer their wares for sale in a city for a given period before they could continue on their way. Sometimes they were prohibited outright from transporting their goods any further; that task now fell into the hands of the local merchants. In Cologne the merchants succeeded in pushing through the *Stapelrecht* against considerable opposition, and the measure played an important role in solidifying the city's economic dominance. In Vienna the *Stapelrecht* was introduced by the new city law of 1221.

From Germany the routes of foreign trade radiated in all directions. Evidence for this is the establishment of German merchants in other countries: in the twelfth century the long-distance merchants from Cologne already owned a permanent home in London, the Guildhall; Novgorod around 1200 had a separate *kontor* ("branch office")—the *Petershof*—for the German Gotland merchants; the *Fondaco dei Tedeschi* in Venice is first attested to in 1228; at the fairs of Champagne the German merchants also had their own houses (see p. 61). The exchange of goods was very varied. Cologne dealt above all in textiles and metal-wares, and it was also the center of the wine trade. Lübeck rose to prominence on the herring-trade. Fabrics were exported across the Baltic Sea, and imports included furs, wax, honey, and amber. From England and Flanders came superior dyed woolstuffs, while the native

German cloth production, primarily coarser wool cloth and linen, also went to Italy and other countries, along with weapons, metals, and glassware. Out of Italy came in return the products of the eastern trade: spices, silk, cotton, ivory, and other luxury items.

The modern merchant of the thirteenth century no longer traveled in person; instead, he supervised his affairs from his *kontor* where he kept his books. The fact that economic activities came to rest on written records was of immense importance for the entire culture of the city. The Italians were the first to use separate accounts for goods and finances, a form of bookkeeping that made it easier to keep track of business. The credit system and mechanisms of cashless transfers developed very quickly; by the thirteenth century most great fortunes were made in financial transactions.

THE ECONOMIC FOUNDATION OF LORDSHIP

The notion that it was among the duties of a good ruler to provide for the economic well-being of his land was common in the High Middle Ages. Sovereign acts concerning economic activity—the founding of cities, the establishment of new markets, regulations regarding transport facilities, mints, or tolls—were frequently justified with reference to the common good. In 1143 the bishop of Passau built a bridge across the river Inn "for the benefit of all."[1] In order "to provide in a useful manner for the well-being of the entire land,"[2] Emperor Frederick I in 1165 confirmed the freedom of navigation on the Rhine. "Out of concern for the common good"[3] Emperor Frederick II granted to Lübeck in 1236 the privilege of an annual fair. To prevent a rise in prices and famine, the Imperial Peace of 1152 decreed the following: "After the feast of the birth of the Virgin Mary, each count shall select seven men of good repute and shall arrange wisely and profitably in each region the price at which grain should be sold in accord with the circumstances of the times."[4] Precautions of this sort to protect the food supply were also taken by many cities in the thirteenth century.

In many cases the measures that served the public welfare also filled the lords' coffers. Especially from twelfth century we have many examples of economic policy that was pursued with the aim of strengthening and organizing a lord's domain. Settlement policy turned out to be as effective an instrument as the foundation of cities and monasteries. Privileges were granted to nonlocal merchants to lure them into the lord's region and thus open the local markets to the international trade. The growing economic strength of the cities soon developed into one of the most important sources of revenue for the territorial lords.

General taxes were unknown in the Middle Ages. The taxes that were levied always fell upon a specific group of people and were based on special legal conditions. The Middle High German word for taxes, *bede* or *bete*, originally meant "request" (*Bitte*), "command," and only later "tax." In the thirteenth century such taxes were regularly demanded from the royal cities. In the territorial states, the notion took hold that general, territory-wide taxes could only be levied in special circumstances: when the lord was in captivity, when his son was knighted, or when his daughter was married.

The economic foundation of royal power were the regalia and the so-called *Tafelgüter*. Regalia were revenue-producing sovereign rights; *Tafelgüter* were the obligatory expenditures for lodging and feeding the king and his court. The following list appears in Frederick I's "Roncaglian Decrees" (1158), with which the emperor was trying to reestablish the sovereignty of the empire over the cities of northern Italy: "Regalia are: public roads, navigable rivers, ports, mooring-dues, dues commonly called tolls, coinage, income from penalties and penances, vacant property, transport services with carts and boats, the exceptional dues for the most blessed military campaign of the royal highness, the right to appoint magistrates for the preservation of justice, offices for the exchange of money, residences in the customary cities, the income from fishponds and salt-works."[5] For a time the Italian policy of the emperor was so successful that, according to the testimony of Rahewin, "about thirty thousand talents flowed into the state treasury every year."[6]

Since the king had no corps of civil servants of his own, he could not exploit many of his sovereign rights. This situation benefited the local rulers, above all the princes, who gradually gained control over most regalia within their domains. Emperor Frederick II's privileges to the princes in 1220 and 1232, in which the emperor renounced these rights, merely gave official approval to what had already happened. How important the regalia were in financial terms in the thirteenth century can be seen from the fact that in Austria, for example, up to fifty percent of the income of the territorial lords came from tolls.

The development of a money economy also had a great impact on the economic situation of the great households. The constantly rising need for money made it imperative to find new sources of revenue. Beginning in the twelfth century, sovereign rights were to a large extent turned into cash income through grants and mortgages, and the trend continued in the thirteenth century. The cities, especially, were in a position to buy economic advantages. Thus in 1226, Lübeck was able to acquire, among other privileges, control over the mint and exemption from tolls for a yearly payment of 750 marks to the king. Treaties were now also couched in terms of privileges, so that one could exact cash payments for them. No enfeoffment or appointment took place any longer without a payment. Entire lordships were sold: in 1179 Emperor Frederick I paid his uncle, Duke Welf IV (d. 1191), a significant sum for a large portion of the old Swabian family lands of the Welfs. War sometimes offered the prospects of great income, if one could force the enemy to make payments, or if prisoners were taken who could be exchanged for a large ransom. At the battle of Bornhöved in 1227, the Danish King Waldemar II (d. 1241) was taken captive by the Count of Schwerin, and had to ransom himself after lengthy negotiations for 25,000 silver marks. Archbishop Gerhard I of Mainz raised 5,000 marks in 1257 to buy his freedom from Duke Albrecht I of Braunschweig (d. 1279). The highest ransom—150,000 marks—was paid in 1194 for the English King Richard the Lionheart (d. 1199). But wars were expensive undertakings even for the victors, since the armies were only in part made up of feudal levies or *ministeriales*. Many vassals preferred to redeem their military service with monetary payments. Most wars were therefore fought with mercenaries. The wealthy kings of England and France, especially, took large bands of professional soldiers into their service. Frederick I used mercenaries for his wars in Italy, and the German imperial princes also recruited them. The burden of their financial obligations not infrequently compelled the princes to take out loans, as guarantees for which they mortgaged various sources of income. The most sought-after lenders were above all the rich Italian commercial houses (see p. 65 f.).

What role money played in big politics as early as around 1200 is revealed by the bribes paid to the German princes after the death of Emperor Henry VI (d. 1197) to influence the election of the new king. While the Hohenstaufen party around Philip of Swabia enriched itself from the rich Sicilian royal treasure brought back to Germany by Henry VI, the election of the Welf Otto IV, a nephew of the English king, was financed primarily with English funds. We hear that Adolf of Altena (d. 1205), archbishop of Cologne, and Duke Henry I of Brabant (d. 1235) received "immense sums of money from the English king"[7] in exchange for their electoral support. The Welf party supposedly bought

GOSHEN COLLEGE LIBRARY
GOSHEN, INDIANA

Archbishop John I of Trier for eight thousand marks (*Braunschwei-gische Reimchronik*, 4882 f.) The archbishop of Cologne allegedly received "nine thousand marks"[8] when he joined Philip of Swabia. For eight thousand marks Landgrave Hermann of Thuringia (d. 1217) switched sides in 1198 to join the Welfs: "He [Otto IV] no doubt gave him eight thousand marks, so that he would swear sincere loyalty in faithful support."[9] In payment for his return to Philip's camp the following year, the landgrave took imperial lands in Thuringia.

At the great court feast in Mainz in 1184 the importance of the gathered princes was measured by the size of their retinue (see p. 204). A century later the princes were judged by the extent of their financial resources. In the "Description of Germany" which has survived as an appendix to the Annals of Colmar, we read the following about the secular prince electors: "One of them is the duke of Saxony, and he has an income of 2,000 marks. One is the count palatine, who is the duke of Bavaria, and he has revenues of 20,000 marks, 5,000 from the palatinate and 15,000 from the duchy. Another is the margrave of Brandenburg, and he has 50,000 marks. Another is the king of Bohemia, and he has 100,000 marks."[10] Though we cannot vouch for these figures, they do convey a good sense of the distribution of economic power in Germany at the end of the thirteenth century.

4. THE KNIGHT AND KNIGHTHOOD

The older scholarship saw the rise of the knightly class as the most important precondition for the emergence of a lay culture and the flowering of courtly literature. Scholarly discussion in recent decades about the foundations and characteristics of knighthood in the High Middle Ages has shown that this notion was mistaken. But no consensus has yet emerged on how we are in fact to understand and interpret the reality of knighthood.

RITTER—MILES—CHEVALIER

There is general agreement that we must approach an understanding of knighthood through its terminology. Historians who work mostly with Latin sources focus on the Latin word *miles*, which in the twelfth century designated the "knight" (*militem facere* = to make someone a knight). *Miles* was an old Roman word, and the history of its meaning and usage up to the High Middle Ages has only been partially clarified.

GOSHEN COLLEGE LIBRARY
GOSHEN, INDIANA

In classical Latin *miles* meant "soldier, warrior," with the emphasis on the fact that the *miles* was a footsoldier in contrast to the horseman, and a common soldier in contrast to the commander. In addition, the word carried the connotation of service: *militare* meant "to serve as a soldier" or generally "to serve." These elements of meaning remained alive throughout the Middle Ages. During the tenth and eleventh centuries *miles* took on two new facets of meaning, both of which became important for the use of the word during the courtly age. On the one hand *miles* could now also describe the noble vassal, the liegeman; it is possible that the vassal's obligation to render military service favored this new usage. On the other hand, it became common not to call all warriors *milites*, but only those who fought as heavily armed horsemen. The differentiation of *milites* (horsemen) and *pedites* (footsoldiers) ran directly counter to the old Roman meaning, without replacing it completely. An explanation for the shift in meaning lies perhaps in the fact that the emergence of a heavy cavalry in the Carolingian period was intimately linked with the development of feudalism and vassalage. The subsequent history of the word *miles* is far less clear, since from then on the various meanings existed side by side, and especially since significant regional variations determined its usage.

Of great importance for the development of the courtly concept of knighthood was the fact that in the twelfth century (in parts of France even earlier) *miles* was used sporadically for members of the high and highest nobility. In addition, *miles* gained a special meaning in relation to the ministerials; it is difficult to decide, however, whether this reflects the rise of the ministerials to quasi-noble status, or whether the word was above all meant to express their bonds of service. Whenever the legal status was in question, the terms noble and ministerial remained separated. The witness lists of charters continued for a long time to distinguish between *nobiles* and *ministeriales*. Only in the course of the thirteenth century—in some regions earlier, in some later—did it become customary to describe the ministerials generally as *milites*.

In developing its high medieval range of meanings, the word *miles* interacted in some way with the French word *chevalier* and the German word *ritter*, but the precise nature of this interaction has been only insufficiently examined. Like *miles*, these two words originated in a low social sphere and underwent the same characteristic social rise. A comparison of usage is rendered difficult by the fact that both *chevalier* and *ritter* are found almost exclusively in poetic texts, while the non-literary usage of these vernacular terms all but eludes us.

Chevalier is derived from the Late Latin *caballarius*, which already in Carolingian times no longer described a "groom" but a "man on horseback." *Caballarii* were frequently unfree men who performed messenger services on horseback. The connection to the horse, which the word *miles* picked up only later, was present from the start in *chevalier*. We encounter the French word for the first time after 1100 in the older *chansons de geste*. Jean Flori's thorough investigations of its usage in the twelfth century have revealed that initially the military meaning was dominant while at the same time an element of servitude almost always characterized the *chevalier*. *Chevaliers* in the French epics could be great noble lords as well as simple soldiers: a legal or social equality of all *chevaliers* is not apparent. In the course of the twelfth century the moral and religious components of the word gradually came to the fore. But not until the verse romances of Chrétien de Troyes, around 1160 to 1180, did the word *chevalier* become the central concept of the new courtly social ideal.

The German word *Ritter* (the forms *rîter* and *ritter* were used synonymously) is attested from the second half of the eleventh century on. Since it is not found in Old High German, we can assume that the word was a neologism that was, very likely from the beginning, influenced by *miles* and possibly also by *chevalier*. This would explain the striking similarities in usage and in the differentiations of meaning. As with *miles*, the main emphasis is on both the military dimension as well as the idea of servitude. As with *chevalier*, the connection with the horse is implied in the word itself. In the texts of the twelfth century, *ritter* generally describes the simple soldier or vassal. But early on the word also developed an honorific sense. This is brought out most clearly in the *Millstäter Genesis* (around 1130), where Potiphar, the Egyptian general[1] and commander-in-chief[2] to whom Joseph was sold in Egypt, is called "knight" (*Ritter*): "They sold him straight away to a knight (*ritter*) Potiphar."[3] In the older Vienna version we read that they sold him "to a Lord (*herren*) by the name of Potiphar."[4] Under the accompanying miniature in the Millstatt manuscript it says "a prince (*fürsten*) Potiphar."[5] The words *ritter*, *herre*, and *fürste* already seem interchangeable here. But it still took more than half a century before the noble concept of knighthood prevailed. A separation from the military meaning is first visible for the adjective *ritterlich* (knightly), which by around 1170 appears in the sense of "stately, beautiful, magnificent." For example, we are told about the clothes of the court ladies: "They wore knightly garments"[6]; and the young ladies at the court of Queen

Candacis were said to be "well shaped and slender and very knightly, beautiful to behold."[7] These passages come from texts that were not composed after French models, which could indicate that it was not the influence of *chevalier* that made the word *ritter* into an attribute of nobility. But it was only with the reception of the epics of Chrétien de Troyes that the courtly concept of knighthood fully developed. After Hartmann von Aue's *Erec*, every prince and every king whose deeds the courtly literature recounted, was "the worthiest man who ever acquired the name of knight."[8]

NOBLE KNIGHTHOOD

The old Roman soldier and service word *miles* became in the Middle Ages an attribute of nobility. The starting point of this transformation was no doubt the military meaning of the word. From the time that *miles* designated the heavily armed cavalryman (thereby moving closer to the cavalry word *eques*), all those who fought in this way could be called *milites*, from the king down to the paid mercenary. When *miles* was used in reference to the common soldier, the emphasis fell on the difference in armament between cavalry and infantry, but when *miles* was applied to noble warriors it almost always took on a moral and ideological flavor. This comes out most clearly in those complementary adjectives that celebrate the noble lord as "a good warrior," "a brave warrior," "a noble warrior." Thus already in eleventh century Latin sources the word *miles*, in conjunction with the adjectives *probus*, *illustris*, *praeclarus*, *egregius*, and so on, could be applied to members of the high nobility. Likewise in the vernacular texts of the twelfth century, the noble *chevalier* was adorned with the qualities *franc*, *gentil*, *noble*, *vaillant*, and so on, and the noble *ritter* with *edele*, *guot*, *wert*, *gemeint*, and the like. In a very similar way the Middle High German word "servant" (*kneht*), which in its original meaning belongs to a very low social sphere, could be used in the phrase *guoter kneht* (good servant) as an honorific warrior name even for great lords: "Charlemagne himself is a good servant."[9]

This usage reveals that noble knighthood was not primarily a social but an ideological phenomenon. Only when one began to justify the use of secular arms on moral grounds did the noble "warrior" became a "knight." The beginnings of that process can be traced back as far as the tenth century, to Cluny, where the idea was formulated that the noble warrior should exercise his arms in the service of the Church and the Christian religion. In the eleventh century this idea found concrete historical expression in the Peace of God movement. In the twelfth century the crusading concept became the dominant element. All those who took the cross went to war as "soldiers of God" (*milites Dei*) and "servants of Christ" (*milites Christi*). In this religious sense the idea of servitude, which was always present in the concept of *miles*, could become a mark of distinction even for the noble lords.

The religious concept of the knight probably also explains the knightly terminology of the noble ceremony of dubbing. When a great lord is called "knight" in the twelfth century, without any adorning adjectives and without any reference to the crusades, the word meant that he had undergone the ceremony of knighthood. Part of the ritual of girding with the sword was the blessing of the sword, which obliged the "new knight" (*novus miles*) to exercise his arms only for good and pious causes (see p. 241). The expression "to make someone a knight" (*militem facere, faire chevalier, ze ritter machen*) was used independent of the social status of the candidate. The title of knight, which one acquired through the ceremony of knighting, was not an indication of rank for the sons of high noble families, but an honorific title.

THE FORMATION OF THE KNIGHTLY CLASS

According to the usage of the sources, a *miles-ritter* in the twelfth century was either a soldier, primarily a cavalryman, a ministerial, or a noble lord who had been knighted.

The older scholarship tried to derive the various manifestations of knighthood from a common bond of class. Historians spoke of a "homogeneous order of knights" which included all those who engaged in knightly warfare, from the king to the lowest ministerial. Originally a professional class, the knightly order was said to have later developed into a class based on birth. This theory, which shows its influence still in some newer scholarship on knighthood, could refer to the fact that in the Middle Ages people were divided into their various professions, with all those who exercised arms being placed into one order of "warriors" (*pugnatores, bellatores, milites*) (see p. 26). Moreover, one could point out that the Middle Ages already knew the terms *ordo militaris* (order of warriors) and *ordo equestris* (order of horsemen), which could be interpreted in the sense of "knightly order." But we must bear in mind that all medieval divisions by occupation were highly theoretical. In real life medieval society was not structured according to occupational groups as long as a social order based on birth had not yet emerged. Instead, from the very beginning the social structure was hierarchical. The "knightly order" (*ordo militaris*) within the occupational scheme must be understood primarily from its clerical usage, where, largely in contrast to the "clerical order" (*ordo ecclesiasticus*), it served to differentiate the secular from the religious life. The term *ordo militaris* or *ordo militum* took on a concrete meaning only in the twelfth century, when it was used, on the one hand, to designate the new military religious orders, and, on the other hand, when it became synonymous with *ordo ministerialis* and served to describe the ministerials.

The formation of the knightly class did not take place in the bright light of an abstract concept of order but against the background of profound social changes that took different courses in France and Germany. In some parts of France a social restructuring began as early as the eleventh century, in the course of which one stratum, whose members are called "knights" (*milites*) in the sources, consolidated into the lower nobility and drew a clear line of distinction against the powerful castelans (*castellani*) above and the rural peasant folk below. A comparable grouping is not evident in Germany. In the German charters, the differentiation within the lower ranks of the nobility between "free noblemen" (*nobiles*) and ministerials was maintained even when the ministerials, or at least the most powerful among them, had long since adopted a noble lifestyle. Only in the course of the thirteenth century— and here, too, there were significant local variations that have scarcely been studied—did the term *ministerialis* disappear from the charters as the chanceries gradually switched to a *miles*-terminology that appears no longer to have emphasized the unfree origin of a person but his noble status.

From the mid-thirteenth century on there is a growing number of examples in the charters where *miles* and *militaris* designate a quality of birth: "of knightly birth" (1244), "of a knightly family" (1252), "of knightly stock" (1254).[10] This terminology reveals that the transformation of the ministerials into the lower nobility and their merging with the remnants of the old baronial nobility had begun. In this way the word "knight" eventually became a term for a class of people at the lower edge of the nobility in Germany as well. Those of knightly birth were defined in contrast to those below, who did not possess noble birth, and to the families of the high nobility above, who now called themselves "Lords" (*Herren*). When a territorial political constitution

based on estates (*landständische Verfassung*) emerged in various territories from the end of the thirteenth century on, we find below the
"order of lords" an "order of knights" that was made up largely by the
descendants of the old ministerial families. This development, however,
was not uniform everywhere. In Austria, for example, where the territorial ministerials had already won significant power in the first half of the
thirteenth century, the "knights" and "squires,"[11] first in evidence as a
separate group in the Territorial Peace of 1281, were not identical with
the territorial ministerials, but had emerged below the "territorial
lords" (*Landsherren*)—as the great ministerials in Austria were
called—from smaller, noble ministerial families. Despite these regional
differences, we can say that in the fourteenth century the term "knight"
became the title that designated the lower nobility.

5. THE COURT

ITINERANT LORDSHIP AND THE FORMATION OF PERMANENT RESIDENCES

In the Middle Ages Germany was a kingdom without a capital. The
king began his reign by riding through the various parts of his realm to
receive the homage of the magnates and to hold court. And thereafter
he and his court were constantly on the road. The king exercised power
by moving about and gathering around himself at stops along the way,
especially at the great Church feasts, the princes, bishops, and local
rulers, who held court with him and gave their advice on all important
matters. Only during the winter months did the ruler usually stay in one
place for a longer period of time. His itinerary was determined partly by
current political developments, and partly by the monarch's preference
for certain places. But above all the king's movement was shaped by the
location of the imperial palaces, the episcopal cities, and those places
that owed *servitium regis*, "royal provisioning." The kings spent a good
deal of time near their own family estates or where larger tracts of imperial lands existed, for example in Goslar in the Harz mountains or in
Altenburg in the Pleißenland. To get a good sense of the nature of this
type of lordship we need only look at the emperor's itinerary during a
randomly chosen year. In May of 1182, Frederick I celebrated Whitsuntide in Mainz, where he had called a general diet that was attended by
many princes. The ceremonial highpoint was the festive crowning of the
emperor and the empress on Whitsunday, followed by a procession in
full imperial array to the monastery of St. Alban. In August, 1182, a

court day was held in Nuremberg, where the bishops of Bamberg, Freising, Münster, and Hildesheim, the margraves of Meißen and of the Lausitz, the counts of Abenberg, and other magnates gathered around the emperor. An even greater number of princes attended the diet in Regensburg a month later, at the feast of St. Michael, where Frederick I reinstated into his office Duke Frederick of Bohemia who had fled to Germany. October, 1182, saw the emperor in Augsburg, accompanied by his sons, King Henry and Duke Frederick of Swabia, as well as several bishops and counts. From there Frederick journeyed to Erfurt, where in November, 1182, in the presence of the counts of Gleichen, Schwerin, Kirchberg, Schwarzburg, Käfernburg, and many other lords, he settled the quarrel between the landgrave of Thuringia and the monastery of Hersfeld. In December, 1182, the archbishops of Magdeburg and Bremen, the duke of Saxony, the margraves of Brandenburg, Meißen, and Lausitz, along with other members of the central and northern German high nobility gathered in Merseburg, where the emperor probably also celebrated Christmas. A court day attended by a number of bishops and counts was held in January of 1183 in Altenburg. In March, Frederick I was again in Nuremberg, where he received the formal submission of the city of Alessandria. From Nuremberg he traveled to Eger, site of a splendid, newly built palace. Frederick celebrated Whitsuntide in June, 1183, in Regensburg in the company of Duke Otto of Bavaria. Then it was on to Constance, host city of the well-attended great diet that began in late June. It was here that the famous "Peace of Constance" was signed with the Lombard League, ending the long struggle for predominance in northern Italy.

It is not easy to get a sense of just how large a royal household was and how its travels and lodging were organized. Our sources rarely mention these things, and we must rely on a few scattered statements that are open to different interpretations. The Saxon Annalist, writing around the middle of the twelfth century, reckoned the daily food requirement at the imperial court at the time of Otto I (d. 973) at "1,000 pigs and sheep, 10 tuns of wine, 10 tuns of beer, 1,000 measures of grain, 8 oxen, also chickens, piglets, fish, eggs, vegetables, and many other things."[1] This seems enough to feed more than one thousand people, and it hardly squares with reality. But newer estimates (by Heusinger and Brühl) assume that the traveling imperial court with its entire train of servants comprised one thousand people and more, a figure that seems very high. Another reason why calculations are so difficult to make is that the size of the imperial retinue was apparently subject to great fluctuations. The investigations of Oehler have shown that there was a constant rotation among the noble members at court and that only a few people spent longer periods of time there. In unsettled times, when a larger number of soldiers accompanied the train, or when military campaigns were planned, the figure must have been substantially higher. And at the great diets and court days, when the princes gathered round the emperor with their large retinues, it is also possible that the numbers went into the thousands. We are told, for example, that Archbishop Albero of Trier (d. 1152) spared no expense or extravagance on these occasions. His biographer Balderic reports that at the diet of Frankfurt in 1149 he had one duke and eight counts in his retinue, "and in addition such a large number of clergy and knights that all who saw it were full of amazement."[2] Albero had come "with 40 houseboats," "not counting the smaller warships, barges, and kitchen boats."[3] The kitchen boats would seem to indicate that the princes themselves organized the provisioning of their retinues. But we don't know whether that was the rule. On a different occasion Archbishop Albero showed up at the royal court "with 500 knights, and he brought along in a seemingly endless wagon train 30 tuns of wine and foodstuffs in immeasurable quantities."[4] Apart from providing for one's own needs, these supplies were also used for political purposes. Our archbishop made a gift of his wine to the magnates gathered at the court, "for he knew very well that in order to prevail and win the hearts of men, more could be done with a store of wine and other food than with an army of many thousand wretches."[5] According to Gislebert of Mons, the famous court day of Mainz in 1184 was attended by a total of 70,000 "knights" (*milites*), "not counting the clerics and the people of different rank."[6] This figure is considered highly exaggerated, but Gislebert was present in Mainz, and he reported the figure, as he emphasizes, "on the basis of a truthful estimate."[7]

The itinerant monarchy was especially pronounced in Germany, but it was not a specifically German phenomenon. The kings of England and France were also constantly on the move with their courts. But in those countries there existed early on a small number of especially favored residences, where the kings would stay for longer periods of time. And in the twelfth century permanent residences began to emerge, as certain sections of the court administration, such as the court and the archives, gradually split off from the royal traveling party and settled down in Paris or London. The same process occurred later in the German territories. Originally the duchies and counties were also ruled on the principle of itinerant lordship, and still around 1200, the princes, like the kings, spent most of their time moving about their lands. Permanent territorial capitals emerged only in the fourteenth century. But the first signs of the emergence of permanent seats are visible in some parts of the empire as early as the mid-twelfth century, and earliest of all in the duchy of Saxony, where Henry the Lion was turning Braunschweig into the center of his realm. He was followed by Henry II (d. 1177), duke of Austria, who built a new residence in Vienna around 1170 and, according to our sources, spent most of his time there. In the thirteenth century we can see the first steps towards permanent seats in Dresden, Gotha, Marburg, Landshut, Munich, and many other places. Everywhere the link between castle and city played an important role in this development, though relations were not always friendly; for while the presence of a court promoted urban development, at the same time it retarded the emergence of an independent urban administration. Thus the Viennese, for example, turned against their overlord Duke Frederick II of Austria (d. 1246) when he was placed under imperial ban in 1236, and they strove to have Vienna declared an imperial city. Such conflicts were particularly violent in the episcopal cities, where in many cases they drove the bishop to set up a new residence outside the metropolis and administer his diocese from there.

The emergence of permanent seats of power was an important step in the creation of territorial states. Only after the court had become stationary could a larger administrative apparatus develop, which in turn was the prerequisite for spreading the authority of the state throughout the land. Permanent residences were also of great significance for literary culture, since a permanent princely court became a great magnet as a social and cultural center. A stationary court gave rise to new forms of princely representation, especially in architecture—the expansion of the lord's living quarters into a palace began at this time—and to new forms of literary patronage. Those who benefited most where the epic poets, who needed the opportunity to work relatively undisturbed on a single piece of literature for several years.

COURT SOCIETY

We know very little about the people who made up society at court. What we find in our historical sources pertains almost exclusively to the imperial court. At the center were always the ruler himself and his family. Although the presence of women and children is mentioned only rarely, we can assume that the empress normally accompanied her husband on his travels through the realm. If the lady lived away from the court for any length of time, as did Beatrice (d. 1184), the wife of Frederick I, who was frequently on her patrimonial lands in Burgundy, we cannot say whether this separation resulted from her desire to avoid the hardship of life on the road, or whether there were other reasons involved. The court included further the numerous court clergy, who were organized into a court chapel and who conducted the daily services. To that end a variety of ecclesiastical equipment was carried along: portable altars, liturgical vestments, missals, and so forth. In addition the court clerics took over a number of functions: the court doctor, the court architect, and the royal tutor were generally chaplains, and diplomatic missions were frequently entrusted to members of the clerical order. The personnel of the court chapel was in part identical with that of the chancery—the notaries and the scribes—in whose hands, under the supervision of the chancellor, lay all the correspondence of the court. It is likely that the mobile imperial chancery also included an archive, but it is very difficult to get any sense of its size. The itinerant court further included the court administration proper, whose most important offices were, by the time of the Hohenstaufen period, heritable within the leading ministerial families: steward, treasurer, marshal, and cupbearer; to which we must add the offices of the kitchen master, the forester, the hunting master, and so on. Each office had its own staff. We can assume that the closest family members of those ministerials who held these court offices also belonged to court society. We must add further all the noble guests who were constantly coming and going to accompany the court or spend time there for shorter or longer periods, as the witness lists of the imperial charters show. Finally there was a much larger number of servants and mounted soldiers who looked after the menial tasks and protected the traveling party.

The society at the princely courts was probably structured fundamentally the same way. Among the few sources that give us any information at all are the travel expense books of Bishop Wolfger of Passau. They don't convey the size and composition of the itinerant court, by they do paint a lively picture of the many and varied people with whom the bishop and his court came into constant contact. Apart from the guests and the various legations and messengers, the court was visited every day by hordes of petitioners and entertainers—the most famous was Walther von der Vogelweide—on whom the bishop bestowed alms and gifts. The account books also record the sums spent on lodging and food for the court. Even more precise information on the organization of a princely court administration and the members of court society can be found in the register of "Offices of the Court of Hainaut" (*Ministeria curie Hanoniensis*), which dates to the beginning of the thirteenth century (see p. 193). From the end of the thirteenth century comes a list with the title: "This is the lord's *familia* in Tyrol" (*Hec est familia domus in Tirol*), which is contained in the account books (*Raitbücher*) of the counts of Tyrol and which names about fifty people who belonged to the administrative personnel and the domestic staff at the count's main castle of Tyrol (see p. 506). The Bavarian court rule (*Hofordnung*) from the year 1294 informs us about the personnel at the court of the Wittelsbach dukes (see p. 506). Based on this varied evidence, we can estimate that a large princely household in the thirteenth century comprised altogether about one hundred to one hundred and fifty people, not counting the guests; however, probably only a quarter at the very most participated in the social life of the princely family.

THE WORD *HÖFISCH* (COURTLY)

When we speak of the "courtly" culture of the High Middle Ages we are following historical usage. "Courtly" was used by contemporaries as the main term for the noble social culture that arose in the twelfth century at the great courts. Apparently the word was itself a fruit of that culture, since it appears only from the middle of the twelfth century on. The oldest examples of *hövesch* or *hubisch* (from the latter variant is derived the modern German *hübsch*) come from the *Kaiserchronik*, where in connection with knightly games and court feasts we already hear of "courtly ladies."[8] In this same work "courtly" is also applied to the sentiment that love called forth in a man: "Whoever experiences the love of a worthy woman will be made well if he is sick, and young if he is old. The ladies will make him very courtly and brave."[9] A decade or two later, around 1170, the abstract term *hövescheit* (courtly character, courtly manner, courtliness) appears in *König Rother*, and it, too, from the beginning described courtly behavior towards the ladies: "And he brought about through his courtliness that the beautiful maiden ran away from her father."[10] In *König Rother* we also find the first usage of the adjective *hovebaere* (courtly) (4316). From this positive vocabulary of courtliness, which quickly became widely accepted and was further enriched by other derivatives of *hof* and *hövesch* (*hovelich, höveschlich, gehovet*), we must separate the verb *höveschen* (to court somebody) and its derivative *höveschaere* (someone who courts another person). The latter were also used in relation to love, but in an entirely negative sense as meaning "to chase after women." In the *Kaiserchronik* we are told of the evil deeds of Emperor Henry IV (d. 1106): "He indulged in an immoral life: he rode a-courting through the land, violating noble women."[11] The words *höveschen* and *höveschaere* soon dropped out of use; apparently they belonged to a now obsolete vocabulary.

It is notable that the oldest examples for this central term of the new culture appear in literary works such as the *Kaiserchronik* and *König Rother*, which were not composed after French models. This goes against the widespread view that *hövesch* and *hövescheit* were created as loan-translations after the pattern of the Old French words *cortois* (courtly) and *corteisie* (courtliness). There is no doubt, however, that from the end of the twelfth century on, the German words had very close contact with the French court terminology. In France *vilain* (peasantish, un-courtly) and *vilenie* (boorish uncourtliness) were used as negative counterparts to *cortois* and *corteisie*; following the same pattern the words *dörperlich* (peasantish) and *dörperheit* (uncourtly manner) were created in Germany. The vowel structure (*dörper* with unshifted *p* as against modern German *dorf*) reveals that these words came into the High German literary language via the lower Rhine, probably from Flanders. Direct borrowing of the French terminology also occurred: the adjective *kurteis* (courtly) and the noun *kurtoisie* (courtliness) appear shortly after 1200 in Wolfram's *Parzival*, Gottfried von Straßburg's *Tristan*, and Wirnt von Grafenberg's *Wigalois*. The French loan word *vilân* (peasant) is found in the *Krone* of Heinrich von dem Türlin (38).

The history of the word *höfisch* and its relation to the Romance vocabulary has yet to be fully studied. We can expect some clarification from Peter F. Ganz, who has pointed out that the German court terminology must also be seen in connection with the Latin terminology. *Curialis* (belonging to the curia) was an old Roman word, but it was used with greater frequency only from the eleventh century on and only very gradually took on the meaning of "courtly." Not until the High Middle Ages was the noun *curialitas* created, which then, along with *urbanitas*, described "wordly refinement," "excellent education," "courtly manner," and with this meaning influenced both French and German court terminology (see pp. 466 ff.) By the twelfth century *curialis* could be used as an ornamental adjective for women. The opposite of *curialitas* was expressed as *simplicitas rusticana* (peasantish simpleness). We also find the opposing pair of *urbanitas* (courtly manner) and *rusticitas* (peasantishness), which Quintilian (first century A.D.) had already used to characterize the refined rhetorician in opposition to the clumsy oaf (*Institutio oratoria* VI.3.17).

In the thirteenth century the German terms *hövesch* and *hövescheit* were at times applied concretely to the institutions of the court: "Whoever wants to show good manners at court should beware of ever doing anything uncourtly at home; for you ought to know that courtly upbringing and courtly manners are the fruits of good habits."[12] When *hövesch* and *hövescheit* expressed the meaning of "what belonged to the court or to courtly society" they could be applied to all ceremonial forms of etiquette and to the whole range of the material objects of noble life, clothes, weapons, and horses: "Listen and hear of the courtliness (*hövescheit*) of the horse she was riding."[13] In most cases, however, the sociological meaning of *hövesch* was second to its ideological content. "Courtly" came to express an entire social ideal, in which outward splendor, physical beauty, noble descent, wealth and renown, were joined with noble sentiment, refined manners, knightly virtues, and piety. It is in this sense of total harmony that we ought to understand the phrase of the "courtly God" that Hartmann von Aue used when Erec killed a cruel giant: "He stabbed him dead upon the earth, just as our courtly God had willed."[14]

In scholarly language *höfisch* is imprecise, a fuzzy word. This is largely due to the fact that literary historians separated the word from the historical surroundings of the court and applied it to an "idea" of courtliness which came to embody the splendor of the Hohenstaufen emperors. Unless we want to avoid using the word altogether, we are well advised to define the various facets of meaning as concretely as possible.

1. *Höfisch* remains a concept of literary history and as such points to the court as the social setting of literary activity. When this literature is called "courtly" literature it means that it was court literature, produced by court poets, who could also be called "courtly" poets, and meant for a court audience or "courtly" audience. In this sense the term "courtly" literature can be used to describe an important tradition within European literature from late antiquity on. This is how Reto R. Bezzola used it in the title of his great five-volume work *Les origines et la formation de la littérature courtoise en occident* ("The Origins and

Development of Courtly Literature in the West"), which covers seven centuries of European court literature from 500–1200. We can trace this tradition of "courtly" literature as far as the eighteenth century, as long as the influence of the court shaped the development of literature. It is more useful, however, to distinguish between the tradition of western court literature and the specific historical phenomenon of the "courtly" literature of the High Middle Ages, which began in Germany in the mid-twelfth century with the reception of "courtly" literature from France, and ended around 1300.

2. Following Middle High German usage, *höfisch* can be applied to various aspects of the new social ideal, that is to the entire sphere of "courtly" culture. At the center was the figure of the "courtly" knight, who dressed in a "courtly" fashion, cultivated "courtly" manners, and exhibited "courtly" sentiment. Here the word "courtly" takes on a pronounced ideological character, which comes out especially when the focus is on "courtly" virtue and on "courtly" love as the central quality of the new social ideal.

3. *Höfisch* also retains a separate meaning as a descriptive term for a literary genre. "Courtly" epic poetry and "courtly" lyric poetry were the major forms of literature promoted at the great courts. While this usage for lyric poetry is straightforward, twelfth century epic poetry is usually subdivided into "pre-courtly," "early courtly," and "high-courtly" texts. But this kind of terminology, which employs the word "courtly" merely to describe a literary style, obscures the fact that even the "pre-courtly" epics such as the *Kaiserchronik* and the *Rolandslied* were court literature and could therefore also be called "courtly." It would make more sense to designate all worldly epics that were intended for a "courtly" audience as "courtly" epic poetry. We could then make an allowance for the fact that Veldeke's *Eneit* initiated a new form of "courtly" epic by calling it, following the French term *roman courtois*, "courtly romance" in the narrower sense. This would have the added advantage that the word "courtly," even as a descriptive word for a literary genre, would remain linked to the court as the central institution.

CHAPTER II

The Adoption of French Aristocratic Culture in Germany

1. SOCIETY

ECONOMIC TIES

The most important trading routes in twelfth-century Europe converged in France. The great fairs of Champagne, held in almost continuous rotation throughout the year in the four cities of Troyes, Provins, Lagny, and Bar-sur-Aube, developed into the flourishing center of the international trade, especially in woolens and textiles. Here the merchants from Italy met with their business partners from France, England, and Flanders. Initially Germans do not seem to have been strongly represented. But soon after 1200 a "German Alley" is attested in Provins[1]; apparently the name stems from the fact that German merchants lodged there, which could mean that their presence was at this time already traditional. Thirteenth-century Troyes had a "German house,"[2] and towards the end of that century a number of German trading cities maintained their own houses in the cities that hosted the fairs: Basel and Freiburg in Bar-sur-Aube, Constance in all four cities. That the German merchants in France traded in linen and other textiles is confirmed by a report that traders from Germany, apparently on their way to Champagne, were robbed of their wares in Lotharingia in the year 1250: they lost primarily furs, and also linen, German gray cloth, and silver (Bourquelot, p. 200). The fairs of Champagne were also used for the international money business. By the beginning of the thirteenth century various German bishops and monasteries conducted financial transactions with the papal curia in Champagne through representatives of Italian banking houses. The archbishop of Cologne made particularly frequent use of these connections.

The Paris tax registers, which begin in the late thirteenth century, reveal not only that the city had several German hotels and wine taverns, but also that more than a hundred Germans maintained a permanent residence there, mostly artisans working as sword-makers, goldsmiths, or in the leather and fur trades (Sprandel, p. 299 f.). According to a guild register from the year 1290, no less than ten percent of the Parisian sword-makers were Germans. By the twelfth century the products of German armorers enjoyed an excellent reputation. In the French literature from that time, especially in the heroic epics, helmets and shields from Bavaria, mail from Mainz, and swords and other weapons from Cologne are frequently mentioned.

Even more clearly attested is Germany's trade with England, which is of special interest to us because Norman England played an important part in the development of modern courtly literature in French. Trade with England was largely in the hands of merchants from Cologne, to whom King Henry II granted permission in 1157 to sell their imported wine in London under favorable conditions (*Hansisches UB* 1, no. 13, p. 8). Another privilege of Henry II from the same time mentions "their London house"[3]: this was the famous *Kauffahrerhof* of the Cologne merchants, the Guildhall, whose name first appears in a privilege of King Richard I from the year 1194, in which he guaranteed the merchants from Cologne free access to all English markets (*Hansisches UB* 1, no. 40, p. 22). During the thirteenth century these rights were repeatedly reconfirmed. We can get a good picture of the intensity of economic ties to England through the Cologne wool merchant Terricus (Dietrich) (d. 1247): he lived and owned property in Stamford, one of the most important cloth centers of England, he traded in cloth and spices and exported wool in his own ships that were anchored in the ports of eastern England (Fryde, p. 4 f.).

The greater portion of the exchange of goods with France and England appears to have been transacted not by Germans but by merchants from Flanders and Brabant, who also played an important role at the fairs of Champagne. Flanders and the region of the Maas was then the center of the European cloth industry. An important trading route led from Ghent via Lüttich or Maastricht to the Rhine, and from there either on land eastwards to the rich ore mines in the Harz mountains, or by boat upstream along the Rhine to southern Germany all the way to the middle Danube. The customs tariff from Constance, confirmed by Emperor Henry IV in 1104, reveals just how large a share the Flemish and Brabantine merchants had of the traffic of goods on the Rhine: the merchants who passed through Constance came partly on the Mosel from Trier, Toul and Metz, partly from the trading cities of the lower Rhine—Deventer, Utrecht and Thiel—but above all they arrived from Huy, Dinant, Namûr, Antwerp, and "the land of Baldwin,"[4] that is, Flanders. By the previous year, 1103, Archbishop Frederick I of Cologne had confirmed to the merchants of Lüttich and Huy their old trading privileges in his city. The same charter tells us that they sold "linen and wool cloth"[5] in Cologne, along with tin, wool, bacon, and lard; some of these goods no doubt came from England. Some of the merchants from the Maas region continued on from Cologne "to Saxony,"[6] whence they returned with copper. The continuity of these trading links is confirmed a century later by the privilege which Archbishop Adolf I of Cologne granted to the merchants of Dinant in the year 1203: it mentions that traders from the Maas region came back "from Goslar"[7] with their copper. Goslar's integration into the international trade is confirmed by a report that in the year 1206 the city was taken and plundered by the troops of Otto IV, who "found there such a great quantity of pepper and spices that these precious goods were divided up into bushels and large heaps."[8] In 1165 Emperor Frederick I guaranteed "the Flemish peaceful coming and going in the land of the emperor."[9] Eight years later Frederick I decreed even more specifically that the Flemish merchants "should have free access up and down the Rhine and on all the other waterways and roads in our realm."[10] The same charter provided for the establishment of "four markets for Flemish merchants"[11] in Aachen and Duisburg; this was apparently a reaction to the quarrel about the rights of Ghent merchants in Cologne which had broken out at that time.

That the merchants from Flanders and the Maas region journeyed up the Rhine to southern Germany and Austria is attested by the market regulations of the city of Enns on the Danube, renewed by Duke Ottokar IV of Styria in 1191. Among the merchants are some "from Maastricht and distant regions,"[12] in all likelihood a reference to merchants from Flanders, who had to pay in Enns on their trip down the Danube market dues of "one-eighth of a mark of silver, one pound of pepper, two shoes and gloves."[13] Merchants from Maastricht, Aachen, and Metz also appear in the Viennese castle toll (before 1221) (Tomaschek, vol. 1, no. 3, p. 5). In 1208 Duke Leopold IV of Austria granted to the Flemish living in Vienna, who seem to have worked primarily as cloth dyers, the same economic privileges that the other inhabitants enjoyed (*UB zur Geschichte der Babenberger* 1, no. 161, pp. 207 ff.).

Among the German trading cities, Cologne held the most important place in international trade. The city had above all flourishing textile and metalworking crafts, whose products were of prime importance for Cologne's long-distance trade. In addition there was the trade in wine, especially to England, and the fur trade, which led the Cologne merchants far eastward. Especially intensive were the connections up the Rhine to southern Germany and Austria. Merchants from Cologne and Aachen appeared in 1191 at the market in Enns, and a year later a charter of Duke Leopold V of Austria spoke of the "quantity of bundled cloths that arrive from Cologne."[14]

Trade along the Danube brought the Cologne merchants into contact and competition with the merchants from Regensburg. Just how dominant a position the Regensburg traders held in the Danube trade is revealed by the fact that the duke of Styria renewed the market regulations of Enns in 1191 "at the urging of the people of Regensburg,"[15] to whom he also transferred the supervision and administration of the market. In 1192 Regensburg had its privileges in Austria confirmed by Duke Leopold V. On this occasion we are also told of the most important trading goods on the Danube. Apart from cloth, they included furs, copper, tin, "bell-bronze,"[16] and herrings. We get an even more detailed glimpse of the traffic of goods on the Danube in the customs tariff of Stein, established around 1200 by Duke Leopold VI of Austria. The merchants from Regensburg, Passau, Swabia, and the "burghers of Aachen"[17] who passed that city with their wares had to pay tolls for metals (tin, copper, lead, iron), swords and arms, grain, legumes, pets and animal products (ham, bacon, eggs, cheese), oil, honey, drinks (mead, wine, beer), spices, furs, and various types of cloth (silk, linen, gray cloth, fustian, buckram, "Passau cloth"), and various items of clothing, among them "shoes, capes, and other precious objects."[18] The Regensburg merchants continued on beyond Vienna to Hungary, Bohemia, and Russia, until the Viennese city law of 1221 forbade the onward movement of all goods. But Regensburg's international trade also flowed to the west and the north. The customs tariff of Constance (1104), which lists Regensburg as the only trading city of southern Germany, shows Regensburg merchants traveling on the Rhine as early as the beginning of the twelfth century. In the twelfth century, cloth from

Regensburg had a good reputation even in France and England. From the middle of that century comes a report that merchants from Lotharingia were offering for sale in London "silk cloth from Constantinople and Regensburg"[19] (in the London *Liber Ordinacionum* the pertinent passage speaks of *gryseyn*, "fur-stuffs" from Regensburg). Around the same time Peter the Venerable (d. 1155), abbot of Cluny, laid down in his revision of the Cluniac Rule "that none should possess purple cloth, or *barracanus* (fustian?), or precious wool cloth made in *Ratisbona*, that is Regensburg, or decorated blankets."[20] The nature and extent of the cloth industry in Regensburg in the twelfth and thirteenth centuries, and especially the question whether the city produced silk at that time, are disputed among economic historians. There is no question, though, that in the twelfth century people as far away as Burgundy associated the name of Regensburg with precious fabrics.

From southern Germany the trading routes went to Italy, and these economic ties to the south must also be considered, since it is not unlikely that the transmission of modern French aristocratic culture occurred also via Italy. In 1162 the merchants of Pisa, and in 1173 those of Venice, were granted by Emperor Frederick I an exemption from duties on their trade within the empire (MGH Const., vol. 1, no. 205 and 274, pp. 282 ff. and 374 ff.). German merchants are attested to in Verona in 1173 (Cipolla, p. 472), and in Genoa in 1190 (Sydow, p. 409). During the thirteenth century such evidence multiplies rapidly. As early as 1225 a German trading house, the *Fondaco dei Tedeschi*, was established in Venice. Of special interest is the merchant Bernhard (Bernardus Teotonicus), of German descent, and around 1200 one of the richest men of Venice. His testament from the year 1213 gives us valuable insights into German-Venetian trading ties. It seems very likely that this Bernhard was identical to the Venetian merchant Bernhard in whose hands lay the collection of the funds that Emperor Frederick I intended to use in 1189 to finance the attack on Constantinople and the continuation of the crusade. A number of princes from southern Germany also took out loans from Bernardus Teotonicus: Duke Otto I of Andechs-Meran in 1209, Duke Leopold VI of Austria in 1214 (Stromer, p. 7 ff.); Margrave Henry of Istria (d. 1228) meanwhile found a lender in Aquileia (Rösch, p. 94 n. 90). The Tyrolian *Raitbücher*, kept since 1288, reveal just how vigorously the economic relations between the southern German princes and the trading cities of Italy developed during the course of the thirteenth century. The counts of Tyrol had at that time very close ties to the Florentine banking and trading house of the Frescobaldi, which received gold from the counts and in return extended credit for their purchases in various northern Italian cities. The count's representatives purchased goods in Venice, Padua, and Verona, especially luxury articles and items from the oriental trade: pepper, almonds, ginger and other spices, rice, figs, sugar, wine, horses and harnesses, saddles, swords, armor, gold and silver vessels, jewelry, furs, and especially precious cloth from dyed wool or silk. We can get a sense of the extent of these imports from a report that a single shipment to Tyrol in 1296 contained 42 bolts of baldekin silk, 10 gilded necklaces studded with precious stones, 10 richly decorated belts, 10 war horses, 141 bolts of multi-colored cloth, various furs, 143 pieces of silk cloth, 6 harnesses and halters for horses, 123 pairs of gilded spurs, 120 swords, and 120 gilded reins (Riedman I, p. 286).

The economic ties and trading routes that I have sketched out are of great importance in tracing the adoption of French aristocratic culture in Germany, since it can be shown that cultural influences traveled along the same roads as the traffic in goods. This may seem surprising at first glance, because trade went from city to city while the aristocratic culture was adopted at the princely courts. The princes, however, took an active interest in the trade in their lands, and in the interest of international trade they would even seek out or use contacts with other rulers. While in Cologne in 1103, the bishop of Lüttich personally spoke for the interests of merchants from his city and from Huy. In a letter of 1157 to Emperor Frederick I, King Henry II of England guaranteed the German merchants "safe trading"[21] in England. On Christmas 1165, the Count of Flanders traveled to Frederick I's diet at Aachen, where he obtained trading privileges for the Flemish merchants; and in 1173, Frederick I established new markets for the Flemish "on the request of our friend the Count Philip of Flanders."[22] Count Philip was personally in Fulda for the occasion and affixed his own seal to the imperial charter. In 1266 King Henry II of England granted the Hamburg merchants trading privileges "at the urging of the noble lord Duke Albrecht of Brunswick."[23]

The personal interest of the princes in the traffic of goods was directed primarily towards the foreign luxury articles that figured so prominently in the material side of courtly culture. From the mid-twelfth century comes a report that Lotharingian merchants arrived in London with luxury goods. On board their ship were gold and silver wares, precious stones, "silk cloth from Constantinople or Regensburg, and linen cloth and chain mail from Mainz."[24] The royal court in London took a special interest in this cargo: the sheriff and the king's chamberlain had the right of preemptive purchase for a period of three tides after the ship had docked. The goods mentioned in the customs tariff of Constance in 1104 were undoubtedly also for the high nobility: slaves, swords, and "hunting falcons."[25] And the shoes and gloves that the Flemish merchants had to pay as market dues in Enns were probably destined for aristocratic buyers as well.

The poets in the employ of the princes also mention repeatedly the economic ties to France and England, and especially the much sought-after products of the Flemish cloth industry. In fact, the trading routes along which the luxury items reached the great courts could even become part of the idealized poetic vision of courtly society: for example, Heinrich von dem Türlein tells us in his *Krone* that as part of the preparations for a great court feast, King Arthur ordered ceremonial arms brought from France (*von Franze*), dyed wool cloth from Ghent (*de Gant*), silk cloth from Greece (*von Kriechen*), and golden tableware from London (*Lunders*). In order to properly decorate his tournament boat, Lord Moriz von Craûn sent "a wagon to Flanders to fetch red-purple cloth."[26] Ruprecht von Würzburg relates the story of a merchant who traveled with "cendale, silk, purple cloth, and precious clothes of various kinds"[27] to the "annual fair in Provins,"[28] that is to the fairs in Champagne. Rudolf von Ems, in *Guter Gerhard*, paints a lively picture of the travels and trading connections of a rich Cologne merchant. In *Servatius*, Heinrich von Veldeke gives a precise description of Maastricht in relation to the geography of trade and commerce: the city is located, so we are told, "on a public road leading from England to Hungary, to Cologne and Tongerns, and also from Saxony to France and by boat—for those who travel this way—to Denmark and Norway: all these roads meet there."[29] While our poet, writing from a provincial local perspective, overstated the importance of Maastricht, there is no question that a significant portion of the flow of German goods to France and England passed through this city. Maastricht was in the twelfth century also the center of a flourishing art industry; emblazoners from Maastricht and Cologne are mentioned in *Parzival* (158.14–15).

The connection between the traffic of goods and the spread of courtly culture becomes especially clear if we trace the paths of linguistic influence. French words that reached Germany in the twelfth and thirteenth centuries apparently used the same routes as did trade, with Flanders and Maastricht playing a particularly prominent role as

mediators. And the trading routes set the basic pattern even for the
geography of artistic and literary activity. New impulses from the West
seem to have reached the Rhine primarily via Brabant, Maastricht, and
Lüttich, or further south on the Mosel route. From there the main
stream flowed southwards up the Rhine, and then eastwards to the area
of the middle Danube. The north, in contrast, was initially untouched
by this or felt the effects only in a few scattered places. In light of the
economic links, the special importance of the cultural ties between the
Rhine-Maas region and Bavaria-Austria, between Cologne and Regensburg, stands out. Along the same roads that brought the Flemish merchants to Vienna traveled one of the most famous artists of the Maas
region, Nicholas of Verdun, or at least his work: an ambo panel of
copper plates with brilliantly radiant champlevé enamel (later reworked
into a retable and therefore also called the "Verdun Altar"), which was
consecrated in the monastery of the Augustinian Canons in Vienna in
1181, as the donor's inscription reveals: "In the year 1181 Wernher, the
sixth provost, joyfully dedicated to you, Virgin Mary, the work created
by Nicholas of Verdun."[30] It was probably also along this same route
that the works of Rupert von Deutz and the German *Annolied* traveled
from the Rhine to Bavaria. The intensity and the literary fruitfulness of
these links between the Rhineland and Bavaria-Austria are also attested
to by the first secular epics in the German language (see p. 534).

THE STATE OF EDUCATION

Even earlier than the merchants, the scholars looked to France. From
there the great Cluniac reform movement had already started in the
tenth century; from there the Peace of God (Treuga Dei) movement
spread in the eleventh century. And it was in France that the idea of the
crusade had its inception: at the Council of Clermont on November 27,
1095, Pope Urban II called upon the French nobility to embark on a
military expedition to the Holy Land.

Around the same time the French schools were acquiring great renown throughout Europe. After the Italian Lanfranc (d. 1089) started
teaching at the Norman monastery of Bec, many students came to hear
him. The cathedral school of Laon became famous through Anselm (d.
1117); Wilhelm of Champeaux (d. 1122), meanwhile, was teaching in
Paris. The cathedral schools of Reims, Orléans, and Chartres also developed during the twelfth century into flourishing centers of higher
studies which attracted, among others, a growing number of German

students. The great prestige that attached to a French education is
reflected in the story in which Bishop Heribert of Eichstätt (d. 1042)
wanted to dismiss a teacher of his cathedral school "because he had
studied at home and not in the Rhine region or in France."[31] The
learned Abbot Williram of Ebersberg (d. 1085), who around 1065 composed a German "Exposition of the Song of Songs" (*Expositio super
Cantica Canticorum*), spoke in the Latin prologue to that work of the
extraordinary fame of the school of Bec under Lanfranc, with "many of
our compatriots flocking there to hear him"[32]; this led Williram to
express the hope that the new learning might bear fruit "also in our
lands."[33] As a young man, the future archbishop of Mainz, Adalbert II
(d. 1141), from the family of the counts of Saarbrücken, was sent by his
uncle, Archbishop Adalbert I of Mainz (d. 1137), first to Reims to study
logic under Alberich, later the archbishop of Bourges (d. 1141), and
afterwards to Paris for further training. The *Vita Adalberti*, composed
soon after Adalbert II's death by an otherwise unknown Anselm,
recounts at great length and with many interesting details the archbishop's student years in France. Just how great was the influence of
a French education can be gathered from the lives of other German
ecclesiastical princes of the twelfth century. Most of the bishops and
archbishops about whose education we know anything studied in
France: Otto of Freising (d. 1158), Konrad of Mainz (d. 1165), Rainald
of Dassel (d. 1167), Hillin of Trier (d. 1169), Henry of Lübeck (d.
1182), Bruno of Cologne (resigned 1193), Ludolf of Magdeburg (d.
1205), and others. Almost all of them belonged to families of the high
nobility, and it is thanks to their high social standing that these details
of their lives were recorded at all. We can assume, however, that there
was also a large number of less prominent people who traveled to
France to study and brought French learning back to Germany. We
happen to know that on his way back to Austria from Paris, Otto of
Freising, a son of the margrave of Austria, put up at the Cistercian
monastery of Morimund with a retinue of "fifteen other specially
chosen clerics who had gone with him."[34] They were probably Germans, and were later "all promoted to various high offices"[35]; the only
one known to us by name is the future Abbot Frederick of Baumgartenburg. Reims was home to a large number of German students by the
first half of the twelfth century, as we learn from an episode in the *Vita
Adalberti*: during games at Christmas time, a German student was
wounded by a rock lodged in a snowball. The incident led to a quarrel,
which threatened to turn into a bloody fight between the *nationes*: "and

so the German cohort went into battle."[36] But young Adalbert restored
the peace with calm and conciliatory words.

Characteristically enough, the German students in France first
appear as a *natio* during such fights. The English historian Roger of
Hoveden reports that the servant of a noble German cleric, the bishop-
elect of Lüttich, was insulted and attacked in a tavern in Paris in the
year 1200. "When word of this spread, a mob of German clerics
gathered. They forced their way into the tavern and beat up the tavern-
keeper."[37] In response the provost of Paris appeared with armed burghers and "attacked the house of the German students"[38]; in the result-
ing fray the bishop-elect of Lüttich and several of his people were killed.
This incident provides evidence that the German students owned their
own house in Paris around 1200, and it has also gone down in the
history of the University of Paris, as it prompted the French King Philip
II Augustus (d. 1223) to place the teachers and students in the city
under his special protection. This same incident may also have been
behind the following entry in the chronicle of the monastery of Lauter-
burg about the Count Dietrich of Sommerschenburg and of Groitzsch
(d. 1207), the brother of Margrave Conrad of Landsberg (d. 1210)
from the house of Wettin: "While he was attending the schools in Paris,
it happened that a quarrel broke out between the burghers and the students. The servants of the count, whom he sent to help the students,
killed someone, whereupon the count despaired of his prospects for
promotion and is said to have renounced his clerical status."[39] That the
Germans enjoyed a reputation for violence comes out in Jacques de
Vitry's (d. 1240) stinging remarks about the Parisian students of various nationalities. The English he characterized as "drunkards" (*pota-
tores*), the French as "arrogant, given to sensual pleasures, and of
womanish appearance" (*superbos, molles et muliebriter compositos*),
the Italians as "rebellious" (*seditiosos*), the Flemish as "excessive and
extravagant" (*superfluos, prodigos*), while "the Germans are said to be
madmen and indecent at their meals."[40] Jacques de Vitry painted the
state of morals among the students in the bleakest colors: "In the very
same house the classrooms were above and a brothel below. In the upper part the teachers instructed, while below the whores engaged in
their foul profession."[41] When we read such comments we must bear in
mind that modern educational activities and life at the higher schools,
with its characteristic looseness among teachers and students, had to
seem very offensive to the representatives of a strict monastic morality.
The judgment of the Augustinian Canon Jacques de Vitry, who later

became the cardinal-bishop of Acre, was echoed by the Cistercian monk Heliand of Froidmont (d. 1237): "The clerics [i.e. students] seek in Paris the liberal arts, in Orléans the [ancient] authors, in Bologna the [legal] writings, in Salerno medicine [i.e. medical knowledge], in Toledo black magic, and nowhere morals. For morals are not even sought last, they are not sought at all. Everywhere they search for knowledge and nowhere for life, without which knowledge is useless and meaningless."[42]

A course of study in another country demanded considerable resources. Complaints about the high cost of living in Paris and the housing shortage there appear in a number of letters written by German students. Listen to a relative of Udalrich, the patriarch of Aquileia (d. 1181), from the family of the counts of Treffen in Carinthia: "For everything in Paris is very expensive, and the number of students is so great that one finds lodging only with the greatest difficulty."[43] In the *Summa dictaminum* of Ludolf of Hildesheim (mid-thirteenth century) we find the model letter of a Paris student[44] asking his father for money, together with the latter's pre-formulated answer. The traveling life of scholars and students found its most important literary expression in the Latin poetry of the *vagantes* (wandering scholars). Scholars no longer accept at face value the portrait that the authors of the songs painted of themselves: they were not a bunch of dissolute students who devoted their life to alcohol, gambling, and the pleasures of sensual love. In fact most of the poets were highly educated, and some of them later filled high offices. This does not exclude the possibility that realistic elements were incorporated into the poetry of the *vagantes*, as for example in the farewell song of a Swabian student who is setting out for Paris: "My studies are calling me to hospitable France"[45]; "Farewell my dear fatherland, my dear Swabia! Greetings to you, beloved France, gathering place of the philosophers"[46]; Once more I hasten to the city of wisdom."[47] The "city of wisdom" is surely Paris, which Caesarius of Heisterbach (d. after 1240) called the "fount of all knowledge."[48]

Germany played only a small part in the educational movement of the twelfth century. But through the educated clerics, who brought back what they had learned in France and Italy, higher studies did gradually gain ground in Germany, and there was a steady rise in the number of those to whom—as Otto of Freising put it in the prologue of his *Gesta Frederici*—"the refinement of subtle reasoning affords greater delight."[49] Otto of Freising was one of the first who knew the entire Aristotelian logic, and he made it known in Germany through a philo-

sophical excursus in his *Weltchronik* (p. 118 ff.). Rainald of Dassel
mentions in a letter the books "which we are bringing back from
France,"[50] and which he loaned to some of his cleric friends. Just how
eagerly the books of the French scholars were sought after in Germany
is revealed by the story of how a theological work with the title "The
Storehouse of the Ant" (*Horreum formice*), attributed to the monk
Liebhart von Prüfening, came to be written. In the prologue the author
praises the "cleverness of the modern teachers" (*modernorum magis-
trorum sollertia*) and the zeal of the students, "who are accustomed to
writing down diligently everything they hear from their teachers, and
who pass these transcriptions on to others."[51] And so when "students
of theology brought back to Germany the *Distinctiones* of the Parisian
teacher Peter [Cantor],[52] a happy circumstance placed the book into his
hands, and he immediately went to work copying it. But, he explains,
since he did not have sufficient time to finish the task, he filled the gaps
with borrowings from other authors. On occasion even secular princes
could have a hand in the transmission of the works of the modern
French theologians, as is shown by an entry in the Vorau manuscript of
the *Commentary on the Psalms* by Gilbert de la Porrée (d. 1154)
(Vorau, Stiftsbibliothek, codex 261, fol. 1ʳ). Provost Bernhard of Vorau
(d. 1202) noted that "the archdeacon Otakar transferred this book to
the Margrave Otakar II and he transferred it to our church."[53] Margrave Otakar II of Styria (d. 1164) had founded the monastery of
Vorau. In the great monastic and diocesan libraries of Bavaria and
Austria—in Freising, Tegernsee, Salzburg, Admont, Klosterneuburg,
and others—the most important teachers of early French Scholasticism
were represented by numerous manuscripts. It is, however, characteristic of the state of learning in Germany that Abelard's theological tracts
reached Germany in great number, whereas his writings on logic remained all but unknown.

In addition to the new ideas of the French scholars, listeners and
readers were also fascinated by their eloquence. In speaking of the
ancient poets of Gaul, Otto of Freising praised "French subtlety and
eloquence."[54] The impression made by the lectures of William of
Champeaux, the head of the cathedral school in Paris, is reflected in the
letter of a student (written around 1100): "When we hear his voice we
think that no man is speaking but an angel from heaven; for the loveli-
ness of his words and the profundity of his thoughts transcends all
human measure."[55] Abbot Wibald of Stablo (d. 1157) lists in one of
his letters the French teachers of his time, "Anselm of Laon, William

of Champeaux, Alberic of Reims, Hugo of St. Victor, and many more, with whose teachings and writings the world is filled,"[56] and places them on a level with Bede and Hrabanus Maurus, the venerable teachers of old. In his chronicle (written around 1210), Otto of St. Blasien mentions among those who "are famous in Paris as outstanding teachers"[57] especially Peter the Lombard and Peter Comestor.

Laymen, at least in Germany, had no access to the new learning. But there were many links between the educational activities at the higher schools and the court culture of the secular nobility. Most of the young clerics who went to France to study came from noble families. The necessary money was in many cases raised by secular relatives, who in some cases even initiated the trip abroad. Margrave Leopold II of Austria (d. 1136) appointed his younger son Otto—the future Bishop Otto of Freising—provost of the monastery of Augustinian canons which he had founded at Klosterneuburg while Otto was still a child. "Then he sent him to Paris to study, supplied with funds from his own [i.e. Leopold's] treasury and from the revenues of the church that he [i.e. Otto] presided over."[58] Secular rulers also promoted the flourishing of schools and the rise of the universities by granting privileges and protection. When King Frederick I stopped off at Bologna in 1155 on his first journey to Italy, he was given a festive reception from the burghers of the city and the members of the university: "Professors and students together came in a festive procession, all eager to call upon the Roman king, the very people who dwell in such large numbers in your city, Bologna, and labor day and night in the various disciplines."[59] The king received them in a "friendly manner" (*placide*, 467) and listened "kindly" (*benigne*, 468) to their complaints about the problems and shortcomings in the city. He then decreed "with consent of the princes" (*principibus consultis*, 494) "that nobody should molest those who wish to pursue their studies either during their stay or when coming and going."[60] He also ordered that the members of the university be exempted from the customary practice of collective legal responsibility. The king admonished the citizens of Bologna "to treat the students in the city honorably"[61] and then departed. This incident is corroborated only poetically, but there is no reason to doubt its authenticity. The ordinance of 1155 was apparently a preliminary step to the general privilege for scholars that Frederick I decreed three years later as part of the legislation passed at Roncaglia. In it he granted "to all scholars traveling about for the sake of studying, and especially to those who teach the divine and holy law, this privilege of our grace, that they themselves as well as their servants may travel to and live safely in those places where higher studies are carried on."[62] A further provision decreed that the students and scholars could be cited before no other court except that of their teachers or of the bishop.

It was not only love of learning that prompted secular lords to promote the higher schools. The key tasks at the royal chancery, diplomatic functions, and the higher administrative offices all required a growing number of educated people, above all lawyers, but also clerics trained in rhetoric and dialectic. Evidence of the interest of secular rulers in the higher training of young clerics is the letter of Emperor Frederick I to Archbishop Eberhard of Salzburg (dated 1155–1164). In it the emperor requested permission for a canon of the church of Salzburg, a relative of the Hohenstaufen house, "to attend [foreign] schools for the sake of higher studies," so that in the future the young man, "equipped with a higher education, will be able to serve more honorably your church and, should we so desire, our court."[63] Some of the German clerics who studied in France later reached important court offices: Rainald of Dassel, for example, who as imperial chancellor exerted a decisive influence on Frederick I's policy towards Italy, or Bishop Henry of Lübeck, who was among the closest advisors of Henry the Lion. Academics and court society were intertwined in many different ways. Worldy values— money and fame—were also important to the representatives of the new learning: "Two things drive men to the study of the law: ambition for offices and a thirst for empty fame,"[64] wrote Peter of Blois in one of his letters around 1180. The most famous teacher of the twelfth century, Peter Abelard, accused himself of having engaged in his profession "out of lust for money and fame."[65] In the extravagance of their lifestyle and the splendor of their courts the highly educated bishops and ecclesiastical princes of the twelfth century outdid most of their secular peers. Abbot Ekbert of Schönau wrote to Rainald of Dassel: "Every day you decorate your mortal flesh with artistically wrought Greek silkcloths and Russian furs, which are preferred in value to gold and silver."[66] We hear this about Archbishop Albero of Montreuil (d. 1152) from his biographer Balderic: "With his magnificent retinue and extravagance he eclipsed all other princes."[67] Archbishop Christian of Mainz (d. 1183) was one of the greatest knightly lords of his time. At the head of his troops he rode into the battle of Tusculum in 1167, "mounted on his horse, with a coat of armor over which he wore a blue tunic, a gilded helmet on his head, and in his hands a three-knotted club."[68] It was said "that the mules in his army caused a greater expense than the entire imperial household."[69]

Ecclesiastical courts played an important role in the spread of aristocratic social culture. Lack of evidence makes it impossible to say with certainty whether they also promoted the reception of French literature. It is noteworthy, however, that the first translations of French epics were done by educated clerics. We do not know where and how Pfaffe Lamprecht (pfaffe = priest) and Pfaffe Konrad acquired their knowledge of French, though it is highly probable that they were among the many Germans who studied in France as early as the twelfth century. There can be no doubt that the upsurge in education in the twelfth century and the rise of the courtly social culture are historically closely connected. In France and England we can see this in the fact that the princely benefactors and patrons, at whose courts the sciences and arts were cultivated, themselves shared in the new education (see p. 426). The situation was different in Germany. Here the princes, who organized their social activities after French models, were generally illiterates and had no personal access to the tradition of Latin learning. One result was that French science was not adopted in Germany with the same intensity as was French literature. It also explains why the Latin court literature of France and England, the works of John of Salisbury, Peter of Blois, Giraldus Cambrensis, Walter Map, Andreas Capellanus, and many others, found no audience in Germany.

DYNASTIC CONNECTIONS

Throughout the Middle Ages, close political and personal ties existed between the high nobility of Germany and that of France. From the North Sea to the Mediterranean, the borders of the Empire embraced large regions of French language and culture, which were important intermediaries between west and east. This applies especially to the northwestern territories: the County of Flanders—the larger portion of which was a fief of the French crown, the smaller an imperial fief—and, bordering it in the east and southeast, the Counties of Namur and Hainaut and the Duchy of Brabant. The culture of these lands, oriented entirely towards France, exerted in the twelfth and thirteenth centuries a strong attraction, which can be shown to have radiated as far as southern Germany. In Swabia, young Gregorius was dreaming of sitting on a horse more splendidly "than the best knight in Hainaut, Brabant and Haspengau."[70] And the Swiss poet Konrad von Landeck wrote as the greatest praise for his lady that "Hainaut, Brabant, Flanders, France and Picardy possess nothing so beautiful."[71]

In the southwest, the entire kingdom of Burgundy as far as the estuary of the Rhone belonged to the Roman Empire. Frederick I once more reasserted the sovereignty of the emperor in those lands, and in 1178 he had himself crowned king of Burgundy in Arles. In the County of Burgundy, the northern portion of the Burgundian Kingdom bordering on the Duchy of Swabia, the emperor had earlier acquired personal rights of lordship through his marriage to Beatrice, daughter and heiress of Count Rainald III of Upper Burgundy (d. 1148).

Marriage connections to France were common in the twelfth century. In many cases it can be reasonably assumed that these dynastic ties were also important in the transmission of French aristocratic culture; in some instances it is certain. Empress Beatrice (d. 1184), described by the Italian historian Acerbus Morena as "with a very beautiful face," demure "in her sweet and lovely speech," "of graceful figure" and "educated,"[72] remained an active patroness of French court literature even after her marriage to Frederick I in 1156. In the prologue of his epic *Ille et Galeron*, the French poet Gautier d'Arras bestowed effusive praise on the empress: he had composed his work "in her honor" (*a s'onor*, 72). From the epilogue of the epic we learn that Count Thibaut V of Blois (d. 1191) also sponsored the poet. We don't know if there were direct literary contacts between the empress and the court at Blois, but a dynastic contact was established soon after. In 1192, Count Palatine Otto of Burgundy (d. 1200), the son of Frederick I and his wife Beatrice, married Marguerite of Blois, the daughter of Count Thibaut V. Marguerite had previously been married to Huon d'Oisy (d. 1190), a French poet of the high nobility who erected a literary monument to her in his politico-satirical "Tournament of the Ladies" (*Tournoiement des dames*). That her second husband, the Hohenstaufen Count Palatine Otto, was also interested in French literature may be inferred from the fact that Otto (along with his father and his father-in-law) is named in the long catalog of donors ("the Count of Burgundy"[73]) which the French poet Guiot de Provins included in his "Bible" (*La Bible*). Count Palatine Otto is probably also identical with the count of Burgundy to whom the trouvère Gontier de Soignies sent one of his songs (No. 10, verse 98 f.).

The Welfs were as closely linked to Norman-French society and literature as were the Hohenstaufen. In 1168 Henry the Lion married Matilda, daughter of King Henry II of England (d. 1189) and his wife Eleanor of Aquitaine (d. 1204). Matilda's importance for the transmission of French literature is revealed by the epilogue to the German *Rolandslied*, where the duke's decision to have the French work translated into German is attributed to her initiative ("the noble Duchess requested it"[74]). After his fall and exile from Germany in 1182, Henry spent several years as the guest of his father-in-law in Normandy, mostly at the royal court at Argentan. This is where Duchess Matilda supposedly came into direct contact with Provençal poetry. Bertran de Born, one of the most famous troubadours of his day, was at Argentan at that time, and according to later reports he courted the duchess. In one of his pieces he sings of the physical beauty of a "Saxon lady" (*la Saissa*, no. 8, verse 5.12), whom medieval commentators were already inclined to identify as Duchess Matilda. Most likely the children of Henry the Lion also received a French education. His second son Otto, the future Emperor Otto IV (d. 1218), grew up entirely in French surroundings. He was very close to his uncle Richard the Lionheart, who became king of England in 1189, and held the title of count of Poitou—the inheritance from his grandmother Eleanor—when he was elected king of Germany in 1198.

Other German princely houses also united with the French through marriage. Matilda of Carinthia (d. circa 1160), daughter of Duke Engelbert of Carinthia (d. 1141) from the house of Sponheim, was given in marriage to Count Thibaut IV of Blois. Agnes of Andechs (d. 1201), daughter of Duke Berthold IV of Andechs-Merans (d. 1204), became the wife of Philip II Augustus in 1196 and thus the queen of France. The Church, however, did not recognize this union, since the French king was still married to Ingeborg of Denmark.

No German family of the high nobility cultivated more intense ties to France than the Zähringen. Duke Conrad of Zähringen (d. 1152), the founder of Freiburg, to whom Emperor Lothair had transferred the exercise of sovereign rights in Burgundy, was married to the daughter of Count Geoffrey of Namur. Conrad's son, Berthold IV (d. 1186), had to content himself with the title "Governor of Burgundy" (*Rector Burgundiae*), since Emperor Frederick had acquired sovereignty over Upper Burgundy through his marriage to Beatrice. Shortly before his death Berthold would marry Countess Ida of Boulogne (d. 1216), a much sought-after match since she was the heiress to the county of Boulogne. His son from his first marriage, Duke Berthold V (d. 1218), the last of the Zähringen, took as his wife Clementia, the daughter of Count

Stephan of Auxonne and a cousin of Empress Beatrice. Even though her mother tongue was French, Duchess Clementia also supported the German poets at her court: the author of the *Wallersteiner Margarete* praises "the noble Duchess Clementia of Zähringen"[75] as his patroness.

Marriage connections with the German-speaking princely houses of the northwestern Rhine region were probably also important for the reception and spread of courtly culture in Germany. Deserving of special attention are the dynastic ties between Bavaria and the Lower Rhine. Count Otto of Scheyern (d. 1183), the first duke of Bavaria from the house of Wittelsbach, was married to Agnes, the daughter of Count Louis I of Laon (d. 1171). The counts of Laon held their county in Haspengau as a fief from the dukes of Brabant. In her homeland Agnes of Laon (or her mother of the same name) was the patroness of Heinrich von Veldeke, and presumably she brought this interest in poetry with her to Bavaria.

It also happened occasionally that German princes sent their sons to France to be educated. The most important piece of evidence from the twelfth century is generally thought to be a letter written by Landgrave Ludwig of Thuringia, probably Ludwig II (d. 1180), to the French King Louis VII (d. 1180). In it, he told the king that he intended "for all my sons to learn to read and write, and the one who proves himself the brightest and most talented shall continue with his studies."[76] The landgrave was informing the king of his decision "to send two of my sons"—apparently he is now talking only of those sons who were being considered for further studies—"to Your Honor at this time, so that with your help and under your protection they might be lodged in Paris."[77] Scholars have inferred from an allusion to the political situation of the time that the letter (whose authenticity is not certain) was written in 1162. The wording shows that the letter is about the intended stay of two of the landgrave's sons in Paris for the purpose of studying. Most likely the young men were being groomed for an ecclesiastical career. The French king was repeatedly contacted by foreign princes who wanted to send their sons to the schools in Paris. Undoubtedly the young men who came with such recommendations established closer contact to the French court. The letter of Ludwig II of Thuringia is supplemented by a document (not precisely dated) from Henry the Lion, also to Louis VII of France. Henry thanked the king because "you have graciously received and until now most graciously maintained"[78] the son of a vassal, whom the duke had sent to the

French court. That the noble families at this time sent their sons off to Paris not only to study theology, but "also to be trained in worldly matters,"[79] is confirmed by Arnold of Lübeck, who says this directly only of the Danish nobility, but emphasizes that in so doing the Danes "imitated the customs of the Germans."[80]

During their sojourns at the French court or on diplomatic missions to France and England, the German noblemen could get to know the style of modern French society. Conversely, it is likely that western diplomats took their culture with them to Germany. An important role was no doubt played by the more than sixty hostages who came to Germany in 1194, when the English King Richard the Lionheart was released from captivity. They spent several years at the imperial court, or in some cases at the court of Duke Leopold V of Austria (d. 1194). All were members of illustrious families. We know that one of them, Hugo of Morville, brought to Germany a work of modern French poetry, a *Lancelot*, and that this work was used by Ulrich von Zatzikhoven as the model for his German *Lanzelet*.

Another setting in which one could encounter French culture was the great court days and the gatherings of princes, which were not infrequently attended by foreign delegations. In 1157 Frederick I held a splendid diet in Besançon, where the entire Burgundian nobility was assembled. Several princes whose mother tongue was French also appeared at the court feast at Mainz in 1184. And in the retinues of the princes came the poets. It is fairly certain that Heinrich von Veldeke was in Mainz in 1184 along with the French poet Guiot de Provins.

THE ADOPTION OF FRENCH SOCIAL FORMS

The beginnings of the influence from France reach back to the middle of the eleventh century, when Emperor Henry III (d. 1056) married one of the great southern French princesses, Agnes of Poitou (d. 1077), the daughter of Duke William V of Aquitaine (d. 1030). It was noted with indignation in conservative German ecclesiastical circles that the fashionable appearance of French lords in the entourage of the empress was applauded and imitated by the German nobility. Our chief witness is Abbot Siegfried of Gorze (d. 1055), who in a letter of 1043 to Abbot Poppo of Stablo (d. 1048) laments the decay of social etiquette. What he specifically had in mind was the emperor's marriage to a French lady:

What now grieves me most and what I cannot keep silent about is that the honor of the realm, which stood in such seemly regard during the time of the earlier emperors in regard to clothes, appearance, armament, and horsemanship, is in our days neglected; the disgraceful fashion of French tastelessness is being introduced, namely the shaving of beards and the highly offensive and to modest eyes insulting shortening and modification of clothes, along with many other novelties, to list all of which would be too tedious.[81]

Of particular concern to the abbot was the fact that those who were adopting the new customs "are finding more favor with the king and some other princes"[82] than those who were resisting them. That some novelties, especially the shaving of the beard, were successful in Germany, is also attested by a story told by Otloh of St. Emmeram (d. after 1070) in the appendix to his work "The Spiritual Race" (*De cursu spirituali*). We hear of a "noble man" (*illustris vir*, col. 242) who suffers the misfortune of having the verdict of an ordeal go against him even though he is innocent. A priest then explains why God is angry with him: "Even though you are a layman and in the custom of the laity should never be clean-shaven, you violated the divine law and shaved your beard like a cleric."[83] The man promises not to shave again, and straightaway the repeat performance of the ordeal ends in his favor, which both proves his innocence and confirms the truth of the pronouncement "that no layman may shave his beard."[84] But this was not the end of the story. The new habit was apparently so seductive that the noble lord soon forgot his promise and started to shave again. He paid a heavy price for his relapse: he fell into the hands of his enemies and was blinded.

Just how shocking the appearance of the young French noblemen with their fashionable *accessoires* and their emphatic worldliness was to the representatives of a traditional monastic ethic, can be seen most clearly in the Norman monk Ordericus Vitalis (d. after 1140). He looked back with sadness upon the "venerable customs of our ancestors"[85] and noted with utter disgust "the new ideas" the noble youths had embraced in the first half of the twelfth century. The young people shaved their foreheads and in the back grew "long curls like women"; they "crimp(ed) their curls with the curling iron"; they sported short beards; they dressed in "very tight-fitting garments" with "long and broad sleeves" and swept the "dusty floor with the excessive trains of their tunics and mantles."[86] Worst of all in the eyes of our ecclesiastical author were the pointy crakows (type of shoe). According to Ordericus, this footwear had been invented by Count Fulk IV of Anjou (d. 1109) to hide a deformity of his feet, and everywhere the count went, he and his shoes found favor with "superficial people crazy for novelties," so that now "nearly everyone, rich and poor alike, wants this type of shoe."[87] Undoubtedly it was partly for these fashionable items that the German nobility of the twelfth century looked to France. But how much was actually imitated and adopted escapes historical proof.

An important clue for the chronology of French cultural influence can be found in princely seals. From the mid-eleventh century on we find in France equestrian seals decorated with the picture of a heavily armed knight on horseback. The first member of the German high nobility to use a French type seal was Count Conrad of Luxembourg in 1083, and shortly thereafter other princely houses in Germany followed suit. In the twelfth century the equestrian type became the standard princely seal.

Another clue is the descriptions of courtly life in contemporary German literature. The poets no doubt responded to the expectations of their audience in presenting French courtly ways as exemplary in every respect. The ladies wore garments and mantles "in the French cut"[88]; they dressed "as French ladies do,"[89] and strove to acquire "the lady-like walk of French women."[90] Men also adorned themselves with clothes and tunics "as is done in France."[91] For the reception of guests, seats were set up and "in the French manner with cushions placed on them."[92] At the festive meal one used "white tablecloths in the French style and Parisian napkins."[93] It was also in keeping with "French custom"[94] that the lady of the court would honor a guest by sitting next to him during the meal. The courtly forms of entertainment included fiddling "in a French melody."[95]

Otto of Freising reports that in 1127 King Lothair of Sipplinburg mounted an unsuccessful siege against the Hohenstaufen city of Nuremberg, and then withdrew to Würzburg. The Hohenstaufen brothers, Duke Frederick II of Swabia (d. 1147) and Conrad, the future King Conrad III (d. 1152), followed him there with their troops. They "moved right up to the walls and put on outside, with the knights of the king, a war game that is now commonly called tournament."[96] The home of the tournament was France. The French nobleman Geoffroi de Preuilly is said to have laid down the rules in the eleventh century. Still in the thirteenth century Matthew of Paris spoke of "French war games that are called 'jousting' or 'tournaments.'"[97] Otto of Freising's report of the Würzburg tournament is revealing in several respects regarding the reception of French aristocratic culture:

1. The date of the occurrence shows that the adoption of French social practices was already well underway in the first half of the twelfth century. In contrast, the literary reception began only a few decades later, around 1150, with the first translations of French epics.

2. It appears that the new practice was adopted along with the word to describe it. Otto's wording that the knightly games were "now" called tournament does leave open the possibility that the French word *tournoiement* did not become known in Germany until after 1127, and it is also possible that the German bishop was not familiar with precise knightly terminology (the exercise put on by the Hohenstaufen outside Würzburg was, strictly speaking, not a 'tournament' but a 'bûhurt', see p. 258). Nevertheless, this is the first evidence of the new word in Germany. Otto wrote the *Gesta Frederici* in 1158; the first book may even have been written in 1146/47. The first poetic examples of the French loan word *turnei* do not appear until around 1170, in Heinrich von Veldeke and Eilhart von Oberg.

3. The vehicle of cultural reception was the high nobility. It is no coincidence that in this regard the secular princes proved more progressive and more modern in practicing French knightly customs. Nor is it a coincidence that the princes who put on this knightly game were the dukes of Swabia, whose territories bordered French-speaking lands.

2. LANGUAGE

LANGUAGE SKILLS

Upon his arrival at the English court, young Tristan immediately caught the attention of King Mark. "Mark looked at Tristan: 'Friend,' he said, 'are you called Tristan?' 'Yes, sire,' said Tristan. 'Dieu vous garde!'—'Dieu vous garde, beau vassal!'—'Merci, gentil roi, noble King of Cornwall,' Tristan said, 'may the Son of God forever bless you and your household.' The retainers thanked him profusely with much 'merci.' They kept saying over and over: 'Tristan, Tristan de Parmenie, comme il est beau, comme il est courtois!'"[1] With this sprinkling of French Gottfried von Straßburg probably wanted to demonstrate to his listeners how refined society expressed itself. Perhaps he could count on the courtly audience in Germany to understand the French greetings and polite phrases. Apparently it was considered elegant in German court society to speak this way.

Linguistic contacts must have played a large role in the adoption of French court culture. Unfortunately our historical sources tell us very little about the language skills of the secular nobility. In the vicinity of the French language border, bilingualism was not uncommon. A command of both languages could at times be a distinct advantage. Thus we are told that Godfrey of Bouillon (d. 1100), one of the leaders of the First Crusade, who as duke of Lower Lotharingia was also a German imperial prince, was well served by his language skills while in the Holy Land: "He also mediated between the French and the German Franks—who enjoyed taunting each other with bitter and hateful jokes—because he had grown up on the border of the two peoples and spoke both languages. In this way he contributed much to their getting along peacefully."[2] From the Belgian monastery of St. Truiden (St. Trond) we hear that language skills were the decisive factor in deciding the election of a new abbot towards the end of the eleventh century. The brothers considered one of the candidates particularly "suited to govern the monastery since he knew both French and German."[3] The further east we go the less likely we are to find a good knowledge of French. But anybody who had studied in France or had spent time at the French court usually also had a command of the French language. It was said that Rainald of Dassel "gave speeches now in Latin, now in French and German."[4] The dynastic connections no doubt also helped to promote language skills. But not every prince who married a French lady could speak her language. When Duke Rudolf III of Austria (d. 1307) came to Paris in 1300 to marry the daughter of the French King Philip III (d. 1289), communication with his bride was very limited as he "could not understand a word she was saying."[5] The retinues of the French ladies who married German princes must have included a certain number of French noblemen, who could spread knowledge of their language at the German courts. Perhaps teachers were even hired to give instruction. In the French epic "Bertha with the Big Feet" (Berte aus grans piés), written by the Flemish poet Adenet le Roi in the second half of the thirteenth century, we read: "At the time of which I am telling you, it was the custom in Germany that the great lords, the counts and barons, constantly kept around them people from France who taught French to their daughters and sons."[6] Whether this statement is true simply cannot be confirmed. If we can believe the German court poets, public reading from French books was a special attraction of the court feast ("much French was read out loud"[7]). They also tell us that a good knowledge of French was to be found above all among the women of the German nobility. It is likely that the noble ladies played a major role in the spread of French taste in Germany.

In many cases people were probably content simply to "color" (*strifeln*) their sentences with a sprinkling of foreign words. According to Thomasin von Zirklaere, it was considered noble "when someone colors his German with French, as is proper. For in this way a German who does not know French will learn many fine words."[8] Tannhäuser parodied this courtly fashion: "I heard there nice *tschantieren* (singing), the nightingale *toubieren* (making music). There I had to *parlieren* (express) how I felt; I felt completely free. I saw there a *riviere* (stream), through the *fores* (forest) ran a brook to the valley across a *planiure* (meadow). I followed her, until I found her, the lovely *creatiure* (creature): the beauty was sitting at the *fontane* (source), lovely in *faitiure* (appearance)."[9]

There were, incidentally, also some French-speaking princes who learned German. Count Baldwin V of Hainaut (d. 1195) sent his son to the court of Emperor Henry VI "that he might learn the German language and the customs of the court."[10] The count had good reason to cultivate relations with the imperial court. But this was not an isolated occurrence. Henry the Lion, in the letter to King Louis VII of France quoted earlier, had this suggestion for the king: "in case you have noble squires whom you want to expose to our land and our language, send them to us."[11]

A particularly problematic question concerns the language skills of those courtly poets who worked from French models. Scholars have advanced contradictory views. The liberties that some German authors took in translating have sometimes been seen as misreadings of the French texts and are interpreted as the result of a deficient knowledge of the French language. This has been the case especially with Wolfram von Eschenbach, who at times turned the French text completely upside down or deliberately and humorously twisted it around. In *Willehalm* he once commented on his knowledge of French: "'to take lodging' in French is 'loschieren': that much I have learned. Of course a peasant from Champagne could speak much better French than I, no matter how well I speak it."[12] These lines were probably not, as has often been thought, a humorous admission of his poor knowledge of French. The statement that the French of a peasant from Champagne (where the best French was spoken) was better than his own can also he interpreted as reflecting considerable self-confidence. Heinrich vor Veldeke, Hartmann von Aue, and Gottfried von Straßburg, who had all received a Latin education, seem to have understood their French models very well. It is a reasonable assumption that their knowledge of Latin came in handy when translating French. The poet of the German *Rolandslied* reveals that he first translated the French *Chanson de Roland* into Latin and then into German (9080 ff.). Whether this was a more common procedure we simply do not know. There were also some courtly poets who knew no French and had their French models translated for them. But such use of interpreters is confirmed only for the late thirteenth century, when the contacts to French literature had already loosened up. Konrad von Würzburg explains in *Partonopier und Meliur*: "I don't understand French."[13] In composing the German version of the French *Partonopeus de Blois* he had the help of two gentlemen from Basle, Heinrich Merschant and Arnold der Fuchs, for whom there is historical evidence. Likewise, Claus Wisse and Philip Colin, two goldsmiths and poets from Straßburg, who in fourteenth century composed the *Nüwen Parzifal* at the request of Ulrich von Rappoltstein, had the French text translated by their fellow citizen Samson Pine (854.27 ff.).

We don't know how the German poets acquired their language skills. Heinrich von Veldeke was at home in Brabant, not far from the French language border. Most of the minnesingers and epic poets who participated in the transmission of French poetry in the twelfth century can be located along the Rhine. But where did Wolfram von Eschenbach, who was born near Nuremberg and whose audience was in Bavaria and Thuringia, learn his French? The early minnesingers learned not only from the northern French trouvères but also from the Provençal troubadours. Can we assume that a knowledge of Provençal was also transmitted across the language border? One of the great connoisseurs of Provençal poetry, Count Rudolf of Feins-Neuenburg, lived in western Switzerland, near the border with Burgundy. The climate for learning the language of the Provençal poets was especially favorable in northern Italy, where the troubadour songs flourished during the second half of the twelfth century. Historical charters attest to the presence in Italy of Friedrich von Hausen and several German poets from his circle.

LOAN WORDS

Just how influential a model French court culture was is documented by the many French words that made their way into German at that time. By the twelfth century three hundred and fifty French loan words are documented, for the thirteenth century seven hundred, and even in the fourteenth century three hundred newly borrowed words are recorded. To this we must add the many parallel word creations (for example *dörperheit* after Old French *vilenie*) and the so-called loan meanings. Under the influence of Old French *fiance* ("assurance," "a knight's word of honor"), Middle High German *sicherheit* became a specialized term in the knightly code of behavior. Even certain linguistic elements that were used in the formation of new words, such as the abstract suffix *-îe* (New High German *-ei*, as in "Schlägerei"), or the suffix *-ieren* for the formation of weak verbs (New High German "buchstabieren"), were adopted.

French linguistic influence began before the first French literature was translated into German. To the oldest layer belong the French words in the religious poetry of the twelfth century, a few of which can be assigned to the sphere of courtly culture: *prîs* "price," *palas* "residence," *turn* "tower," *tanzen* "dance," *firnîs* "make-up." The French words in the *Kaiserchronik* and in *König Rother* must also have been known in Germany by the middle of the twelfth century: *buhurt* "knightly game," *buckel* "shield boss," and the names of precious silk-stuffs (*samît*, *siglât*, *bônît*). The harvest of loan words is surprisingly meagre in Lamprecht's *Alexander*, the first German epic composed after a French model: apart from the already known words *prîs* and *turn* we find only *gemuoset* "inlaid like a mosaic" (716) and *sarrazîn* "saracen" (253), both of which could also have been derived from the Latin. The great stream of loan words began only around 1170, when the reception of French epics intensified. French elements became the primary linguistic characteristic for the great works of around 1200. More than four hundred French words appear in *Parzival* alone, some with great frequency. This vocabulary mirrors precisely those areas in which French culture exerted the greatest influence: courtly dress, knightly arms, living arrangements and eating habits, tournament practice, courtly entertainment, music, the game of love, and so on. Some words had a very fashionable ring to them, others enhanced the expressive capability of the language since the use of French terms could allow a degree of differentiation—in describing, for example, the various gaits of a horse—that was not possible with the German vocabulary alone. Most of the French words used by the poets were never adopted outside of literature, and later disappeared along with the courtly epic.

There must also have existed, however, a French vocabulary not limited to literature but actually used in noble society at court. This is difficult to prove, though, since there are relatively few French words for which we have any clues that point to borrowing and to usage outside of literature. One indication of oral transmission is the adaptation of words for German usage, as for example the change of accent in *palas*, which in Middle High German was accented both on the first syllable (German intonation) and on the second syllable (French intonation). Other indicators are changes of vowel sounds in accordance with German developments (*prîs* became Preis); further changes of loan words with the help of German elements used in word formation (*tanzgeselle, natiurlîch*); the creation of German sound equivalents (*kolze* "leggings" from Old French *chauce*; *schâch* "chess" from Old French *eschac*); finally, the survival of French loan words in German dialects. Nonliterary transmission is also likely for the French castle names that we encounter in western Germany from the end of the twelfth century: in 1190 *Montclair* (near Mettlach) is mentioned; in 1229 *Monreal* (district of Mayen), castle Grenzau (district of Montabaur) appears in 1213 in the French form *Gransioie*, which was apparently supposed to mean "Great Joy" (Jungandreas, p. 562 f.). In some cases scholars believe they can show traces of eastern French dialects in adopted words: the *i* in *ohteiz* "unharmed, sound" (from Old French *ostez*, East French *osteiz*), and the *h* in *schahtel* "castle" (from Old French *chastel*, East French *chahtel*).

If these indications are trustworthy, such words were first adopted along the western language border. Der Marner, a thirteenth-century writer of *Spruchdichtung*, mocked the *höfischen liute* ("courtly people") of the Rhine region who adorned their speech with French words: "They are truly "des gents courtois"; in French breakfast agrees with them."[14] Scholars have discovered three paths along which the words traveled: the first and by far the most important lead via Flanders to Brabant and the Rhine; the second from Metz and Tries down the Mosel; the third through Burgundy to the Upper Rhine. These paths were also the most important trading routes to France.

The northwestern region seems to have played a particularly important role in the transmission of French language and culture. This is confirmed by the fact that along with French words a large number of Low German and Low Dutch words and word formations came into High German. Among them we find such characteristic forms as *wâpen* "weapon" (next to High German *wâfen*) and *dörper* "peasant" (next to High German *dorf*) with their unshifted stops; further *ors* "horse" (next to High German *ros*), possibly also *trecken* "to pull," *tadel* "censure, blame," *baneken* "to romp about," *draben* "to trot," and others. The Low German diminutive suffix *-kîn* with the unshifted *k* (for High German *-chen*), must have held a particular charm for the High German aristocracy. It was used in words such as *blüemekîn* "floweret," *merli-kîn* "little blackbird," *pardrîsekîn* "young partridge," *schapellekîn* "circlet, garland," and so on. Satirical poetry reveals to what extent the use of such forms was seen as the mark of courtly-knightly society. In Neidhart "Flemicizing" (*flämeln*) characterizes the foppishly attired peasant who tried to speak in a courtly way ("he Flemicizes in his speech"[15]). In *Seifrid Helbling*, a "Saxon who was born in Vienna"[16] becomes the target of ridicule. Most effective is the parody of knightly jargon in *Helmbrecht*, where young Helmbrecht, upon his return to his native manor, addresses the staff in Low German: *liebe soete kindekîn* (literally: "dear, sweet little children," 717), which draws this comment from the servant: "According to what I heard him say, he is from Saxony or Brabant. He said: 'liebe soete kindekîn,' I bet he is a Saxon."[17] Even to his parents Helmbrecht spoke only in Flemish: "Ah, what are you saying, my little peasant, and this common women over there? No peasant shall ever touch my horse or my fine body."[18] Unfortunately the translation cannot convey the humor of the original language.

3. LITERATURE

THE CHRONOLOGY AND GEOGRAPHY OF THE TRANSMISSION OF FRENCH LITERATURE

In no other sphere was French influence in the twelfth century more dominant than in vernacular literature. Within the space of a few decades the character of secular literature was completely transformed. The process of imitating and adopting French models created courtly literature with its two main genres, the minnesong and the courtly romance. The vehicle of the literary reception was the same court society that looked to France for guidance in matters of material culture and etiquette.

The first French text translated into German was the epic of Alexander by Alberic of Besançon, which has survived only in fragments. Pfaffe Lamprecht's German version probably dates to about 1150, but where it was composed and who commissioned it is unknown. This was an isolated first attempt, as the main activity began twenty years later. Around 1170 the German *Rolandslied* was written (after the *Chanson de Roland*) and Heinrich von Veldeke was at work on his *Eneit* (after the *Roman d'Eneas*). The *Trierer Floyris* was created (after *Floire et Blancheflor*) at about the same time, as was quite possibly the *Tristrant* of Eilhart von Oberg (after a lost French epic of Tristan). Meanwhile the first courtly minnesongs were composed in Germany after the models of the troubadours and the trouvères. In the half century between 1170 and 1220 the transmission of French literature reached its height. It involved almost exclusively those texts that were new and fashionable in France. In some cases the time lag between the appearance of an original in French and its German adaptation seems to have been less than ten years: a remarkably short time span, considering how long it must have taken in those days for a new work of literature to become internationally known, and how time-consuming the translation of a long epic was. It would appear that the German courts were well informed about the latest works on the French literary scene. The minnesingers, too, sought inspiration primarily from contemporary Romance poets, with whom they may have had direct personal contact.

After 1220 the situation changed drastically. French taste did remain dominant, and the adopted French genres of the minnesong and the courtly romance continued to shape literary work for some time to come. But the direct adoption of French texts ceased as suddenly as it had begun. In the thirteenth century very few French epics were translated into German, and the interest was no longer focused on new works. Characteristic for the literary scene in the thirteenth century are the sources employed by Konrad von Würzburg (d. 1287), who consulted French models for two of his epics. The French works he worked from were at that time nearly a century old: for his *Trojanerkrieg* he used the old *Roman de Troie* by Benoît de Sainte-Maure, which Herbort von Fritzlar had already translated in 1210; and for his *Partonopier und Meliur* he reached back to a famous French adventure romance of the twelfth century, *Partonopeus de Blois*, which was translated into many European languages. The main concern in the thirteenth century was no longer to keep up with the literary activity in France. More and more the focal point for new epics became the great German works of the classic period around 1200, which were continued and which served as models. For this kind of work one could for the most part do without French texts.

French influence radiated from west to east, and appeared first and most strongly along the Rhine. Early epic writing based on French models was centered along the Middle and Lower Rhine. Pfaffe Lamprecht probably hailed from around Trier. Heinrich von Veldeke's home was the Duchy of Brabant. Judging from its language, the *Trierer Floyris* was composed in the border region between the Ripuarian and the Lower Frankish dialects. It is not clear whether Eilhart von Oberg's *Tristrant* also belongs to this group of Rhenish epics. Within a generation the main center of the writing of epics had shifted to the Upper Rhine. This is where Hartmann von Aue and Gottfried von Straßburg worked, along with Ulrich von Zatzikhoven (*Lanzelet*) and Konrad Fleck (*Flore und Blanscheflur*). *Reinhart Fuchs* is another work created in the Alsace. Northern Switzerland, Alsace, and the region of the Upper Rhine remained productive in the thirteenth century. Rudolf von Ems took his name from castle Hohenems south of Bregenz; Konrad von Würzburg wrote his poetry in Straßburg and Basel. The southwest was also the first center of courtly lyric in the French style. Scholars now believe that Friedrich von Hausen's ancestral seat was along the Lower Neckar river. Not far from there lived Bligger von Steinach. Ulrich von Gutenberg and Bernger von Horheim should probably be located along the Upper Rhine. Count Rudolf von Fenis-Neuenburg was at home in Switzerland.

As we move farther east, the traces of French literature become fewer and fewer, and it becomes clear that with increasing distance French influence made itself felt only sporadically and above all at the great princely courts. The appearance of new centers of literary transmission seems to have depended largely on the personal initiative of individual princely patrons. This is most obvious in Thuringia: under Landgrave Ludwig III (d. 1190) there is hardly a trace of any literary activity in the vernacular, whereas the court of Thuringia under his brother and successor Hermann I (d. 1217) developed within a very short time into the most important center for the transmission of French literature. Landgrave Hermann called Veldeke to Thuringia and brought about the conclusion of the *Eneit*. He also obtained the French model that Herbort von Fritzlar used for his *Liet von Troie*, and he introduced Wolfram von Eschenbach to the French source for *Willehalm*. Perhaps some other epics (*Athis und Prophilias*, Otte's *Eraclius*) that were based on French works were also written at the request of the landgrave.

Less clear is the personal influence of the princely patron at the court of the Babenberg dukes of Austria in Vienna, where the courtly minnesong in the French style had its most important center in the last decade of the twelfth century. The crucial initiative must have come from Herzog Leopold V (d. 1194) or his son Frederick I (d. 1198), the patron of Walther von der Vogelweide.

We are even less informed about the situation in Bavaria. Above all, we have no idea where Wolfram von Eschenbach composed his *Parzival* and how he became acquainted with the French source. Wirnt von Grafenberg's *Wigalois* (based on an unknown French work) has been linked to the court of the Bavarian dukes of Andechs-Merran. The Wittelsbach dukes of Bavaria were also active in the thirteenth century in promoting literary works based on French models (*Heiliger Georg* by Reinbot von Durne, possibly also *Jüngerer Titurel*).

Northern Germany participated only marginally in the creation of courtly literature in the French style. There was no Low German court literature based on French sources in the thirteenth century, with the possible exception of the so-called *Locumer Artusepos*, which has survived in so fragmentary a form, however, that we cannot say with certainty what its sources were. Some northern German courts cultivated courtly literature in High German, beginning in Brunswick under Henry the Lion (d. 1195). Perhaps the oldest German Tristan epic, Eilhart von Oberg's *Tristrant*, belongs there.

If we survey the geographic pattern of literary transmission, the same routes of influence emerge that were crucial for language contacts and the traffic of goods between Germany and France. It would appear that the Lower Rhine and the Mosel were critical transshipment points in the adoption of courtly epics. Somewhere between Maastricht and Cleves, Heinrich von Veldeke found his first patron. From there the new literary works made their way both up the Rhine to southern Germany, and further inland to Thuringia. The old trading road between the Rhine region and Bavaria, between Cologne and Regensburg, was apparently the most important line in the geography of twelfth-century literary activity. In some cases we can see how the spread of French literature was linked with the itineraries of poets. Veldeke traveled from the Rhine to Thuringia and there established the new art of French-style epics. Perhaps Pfaffe Lamprecht journeyed from Trier to Bavaria and there composed his *Alexander* for a Bavarian court audience; in any case, the only manuscript containing his work comes from the southeast (the monastery of Vorau).

Manuscripts also traveled. By the twelfth century Veldeke's *Eneit* was repeatedly copied in Bavaria, and conversely the *Rolandslied*, composed in Regensburg, was copied early in regions where Low German was spoken. The travels of princely patrons and their dynastic links were further important factors in the transmission of French literature. When the family of the Thuringian landgraves, on the occasion of the

marriage of Landgrave Ludwig III to Margaret of Cleves, were guests at
the court of Cleves, the first contact was made with Veldeke. It is generally assumed that the contacts of the dukes of Zähringen with Flanders
and Hainaut made it possible to obtain the French sources for Hartmann von Aue. Only in exceptional cases do we know such details. For
the most part it remains a mystery what circumstances and interests
promoted the spread of French literature.

COURTLY EPICS

During the second half of the twelfth century in France, there existed
three types of epics, all derived from different traditions:

1. The heroic epics (*chansons de geste*), based on oral traditions,
dealt with historical material from the Merovingian and Carolingian
periods. The oldest and most famous text was the French *Chanson de
Roland*, probably written down around 1100. The chanson-epics had
their own metrical form: assonant long verses that were combined in
alternating numbers into strophe-like units (*lais*). It is generally believed
that the chansons were presented in a musical performance.

2. A small group of rhymed romances based on ancient material
(*romans antiques*), whose sources were Roman epics in hexameter (Virgil's *Aeneid*; Statius's *Thebaid*) and late antique prose romances (the
Romance of Alexander, the Romance of Troy). Their metrical form—
octosyllabic rhymed couplets—had previously been employed in religious narrative literature.

3. The courtly romances (*romans courtois*) treated largely Celtic
material (*matière de Bretagne*), the stories of King Arthur and the
Knights of the Round Table and of Tristan and Isolde. The works of
Chrétien de Troyes and Thomas of Britanny were translated into almost
all the European languages. Included among the *romans courtois* are
also a few pieces of literature based on oriental-Byzantine sources
(*Floire et Blancheflor*), and love and adventure romances drawn from a
variety of traditions. In metrical form and literary technique, the courtly
romances follow the *romans antiques*.

The *chansons de geste*, the largest group of works in France, aroused
little interest among the German aristocratic audience. The adaptation
of the *Chanson de Roland* by Pfaffe Konrad (around 1170) was among
the first translations, but the German *Rolandslied* did not establish a

new genre. Only Wolfram von Eschenbach, some fifty years later, drew once again on the chanson-epics: his *Willehalm* is a free translation of the *Bataille d'Aliscans* ("The Battle of Aliscans"), the middle work in the great epic cycle about Guillaume d'Orange, the famous slayer of infidels. A little later Der Stricker also used new chanson material for his adaptation of Konrad's *Rolandslied*, as did Ulrich von Türheim for his continuation of *Willehalm*. In addition, the thirteenth century saw the translation of a few works from the Charlemagne cycle (*Morant und Galie*; *Karl und Elegast*), which later passed into the great *Karlmeinet* compilation. But all these remained isolated instances, even though Wolfram's *Willehalm* was, in the late Middle Ages, among the most popular works of narrative. A variety of factors explain the weak impact the chanson-epics had in Germany. To begin with, the metrical-musical form of the *chansons de geste* confronted the translator with a nearly insoluble problem. Furthermore, the national pathos of the French heroic epics was unlikely to meet with an enthusiastic response from the German audience. But above all, the old-fashioned *chansons de geste* lacked precisely what made other French literature so attractive to Germans: the depiction of modern court society with its ideal of knighthood and love. Only much later did the French heroic epics become a powerful force in shaping literary taste in Germany: through the prose romances of the fifteenth and sixteenth centuries, which incorporated material from French chanson-epics on a large scale.

All the epics based on ancient themes—with the exception of the *Thebaid*—were translated into German. But they did not exert their influence as a unified group. Lamprecht's *Alexander*, the first German work based on a French model, seems to have become obsolete very quickly and to have been left behind by literary developments. Only its courtly reworking from around 1170, the so-called *Straßburger Alexander*, had a wider impact. The French *Roman de Troie* of Benoît de Sainte-Maure was first translated by Herbort von Fritzlar (circa 1210?), and again later by Konrad von Würzburg. While Herbort shortened his model by almost half—a unique case among courtly epics—Konrad's *Trojanerkrieg* is a huge work (over fourty thousand verses) which breaks off in the middle of the story. The most important text among the French *romans antiques* was the *Roman d'Eneas*, whose highly developed literary technique prepared the way for the *romans courtois*. Its German adaptation at the hands of Heinrich von Veldeke, begun around 1170 and not completed until 1185, played a crucial role in the development of the courtly epic in Germany. Veldeke was celebrated by the great poets of the next generation as their great common model: "Heinrich von Veldeke, he composed with the highest gift of poetry. He planted the first seeds in the German language."[1]

The period after 1170 also saw the first adaptations of the modern French *roman courtois*. The *Trierer Floyris* and Eilhart's *Tristrant* have survived only in fragments. In both cases their immediate sources are not known. A stroke of extraordinarily good fortune placed the masterpieces of the *romans courtois* into the hands of the greatest German poets of the time. Two of Chrétien de Troyes's epics, *Erec et Enide* and *Yvain*, were translated by Hartmann von Aue (*Erec*, *Iwein*). His *Conte de Graal* ("Story of the Grail") was used by Wolfram von Eschenbach for his *Parzival*. Through Hartmann and Wolfram the type of Arthurian romance created by Chrétien became the standard genre in Germany as well. A fourth epic by Chrétien, his *Cligés*, was apparently translated by Konrad Fleck. This work has not survived; all we have are fragments of a *Cligés* by Ulrich von Türheim, which belong either to a second version or the continuation of Konrad's epic. Only Chrétien's "Romance of Lancelot" (*Le chevalier de la charrete*) did not find a German translator. Quite possibly the Lancelot story with its central theme of adultery was considered too risqué in Germany. In any case, a German *Lanzelet* appeared quite early—that of Ulrich von Zatzikhoven, based on an unknown French source—and it lacks the adultery motif. Thomas of Brittany put the French romance of Tristan and Isolde into its exemplary courtly form. His work has survived only in fragments, but it was a great international success. The German adaptation by Gottfried of Straßburg was left unfinished.

One of the most important French epic poets of the twelfth century was Gautier d'Arras, whose works strangely enough had little influence in Germany. *Ille et Galeron* was not translated at all; his *Eracle* fell into the hands of a mediocre poet by the name of Otte and lost much of its artistic quality in the German adaptation (*Eraclius*).

Most of the anonymous French romances of the twelfth century were also eagerly received by the German public. *Floire et Blancheflor* was translated twice, first in the *Trierer Floyris*, and then at the beginning of the thirteenth century by Konrad Fleck. Unfortunately the German *Athis und Prophilias* (circa 1210?) exists only in fragments: the unknown poet must have been an outstanding figure. The French *Partonopeus de Blois* found a translator only in Konrad von Würzburg. On the other hand, the two romances of Hue de Rotelande, *Ipomédon* and *Protheselaus*, had no impact in Germany, nor did the *Florimont* of

Aimon de Varennes; there are no apparent reasons why this should have been so.

After 1220, French sources were used primarily to continue the unfinished works of Wolfram von Eschenbach and Gottfried von Straßburg. Most of the later Arthurian romances got by without any French models. Der Stricker seems to have been the first poet (circa 1230?) who constructed a new Arthurian romance (*Daniel vom blühenden Tal*) from existing motifs after the pattern of Hartmann's *Iwein*. The same technique was later employed by Berthold von Holle, Der Pleier and others. The extensive production of French romances in the thirteenth century had little influence on Germany. The Arthurian romance *Meraugis de Portlesguez* by Raoul de Houdenc, and the anonymous adventure romance *Blancandin et l'Orgueilleuse d'amour*, both dated to the beginning of the thirteenth century, were the last French romances to be translated. The fact that both German adaptations (*Segremors, Blanschandin*) have survived only in fragments is probably a sign that neither one was widely distributed.

By the end of the thirteenth century there existed over forty German epics based on French sources. In many cases, however, the direct source has not survived, or the German texts exist in so fragmentary a form that a comparative analysis of sources yields no definite results. Even when the German and the French works are available in their entirety, it can be difficult to answer the question of sources. Previously scholars liked to think of secondary sources and lost versions whenever the German adaptations departed from their models. Even today it is occasionally questioned whether Hartmann von Aue and Wolfram von Eschenbach worked at all directly from the epics of Chrétien de Troyes. On the whole, however, scholars now tend to accept the fact that the translators worked with a certain degree of creative freedom.

In France a high form of narrative prose had been created as early as around 1200. Thematically centered in the Arthurian and Grail legends, its characteristic form was the great cycle of romances. In Germany this literature was all but ignored, with one notable exception. It would appear that soon after the creation of the main work of the French prose-cycles, the *Lancelot en prose* (1220–30), a piece of it was translated into German prose. This German *Prosa-Lancelot* of the thirteenth century, whose very existence was proved only by the discovery of the old Amorbach fragments, has raised a number of still unanswered questions. It is, for example, unclear whether the German text is based directly on the French work or whether a Low Dutch version should be placed between them. Scholars are also uncertain just how many pieces of the French cycle were translated by the thirteenth century. What is clear, though, is that this first German prose romance holds an absolutely isolated place in the literary history of the thirteenth century. Only in the fifteenth century did the *Prosa-Lancelot* exert a wider influence in Germany.

COURTLY LYRIC

Courtly lyric was created in southern France. William IX, duke of Aquitaine and count of Poitou (d. 1126), was the first troubadour whose songs have survived. By the first half of the twelfth century Provençal poetry was flourishing at the courts of southern France. After about 1150 the art of the troubadours was taken over by the northern French trouvères. Much later, Provençal poetry reached Italy, where the troubadours sang in their own language.

The second half of the twelfth century was also the time when the influence of romance poetry began in Germany. It is not clear whether the first German minnesingers, Der von Kürenberg and the poet of the so-called Danubian minnesong, who were still composing in the old-fashioned long verse strophe, had already assimilated western innovations. But the reception of romance lyric is clearly visible around 1170 to 1180 in the songs of Heinrich von Veldeke and Friedrich von Hausen. Hausen set the tone for an entire generation of minnesingers: the majority of German poets at this time are assigned to the Hausen-school. Characteristic for the work of this group is a strict thematic and formal adherence to their French models. The great new theme was high minne. The depiction of love, the reflective style, as well as a host of metaphors, images, and analogies were adopted by the German singers. Even more noticeable is the extension of poetic form through the imitation of the French structure of verses and strophes. Upbeat and cadence were subjected to strict rules; assonances were given up in favor of pure rhyme; the poets experimented with complicated rhyming schemes and tried to get by with the smallest possible number of rhyming sounds. Characteristic of this phase of the direct imitation of romance versification are the so-called Middle High German dactyls (*Mich mac der tót von ir mínnen wol schéiden*), which strove to reproduce French decasyllabic or dodecasyllabic verses. Of all the romance strophe types that were tried out in the Hausen school, the tripartite canzone stanza—made up of two identical *Stollen* and a differently constructed *Abgesang*—was most successful in Germany: most German minnesongs are constructed this way.

Sometimes not only individual formal elements were adopted but the entire strophic scheme. Such imitations are called *contrafacta*, and they reveal most directly the indebtednesss of the German poets to the art of the troubadours and trouvères Today there are about twenty *contrafacta* whose authenticity is certain; without exception they belong to the early, romanicizing phase of the minnesong. Graf Rudolf of Fenis-Neuenburg adhered more closely than anyone else to his romance models: more than half of his songs are *contrafacta*. Friedrich von Hausen is well represented with seven *contrafacta* (out of a total of seventeen songs). The *contrafacta* also reveal which poets were taken as models in Germany. Provençal troubadours and northern French trouvères appear in about equal numbers. Among the troubadours we find the famous names of Peire Vidal and Bernart de Ventadorn, but even more frequently two contemporary poets: Folquet de Marseille and Gaucelm Faidit. The trouvères whose strophic scheme was imitated in Germany were all contemporaries of the German minnesinger: Gace Brulé, Blondel de Nesle, Guiot de Provins, Chrétien de Troyes, and Conon de Béthune.

We assume that the German minnesinger also adopted the melodies of the French songs along with the strophic schemes. Whereas hundreds of melodies of minnesongs have survived in France, the courtly lyric in Germany has come down to us almost entirely without notation. Not a single melody exists for the songs of Walther von der Vogelweide. In view of this situation, the melodies of the early *contrafacta* are a precious source. We must keep in mind, though, that the adoption of romance melodies by the German poets is only a hypothesis for which no irrefutable evidence exists. Above all, it has not been proved that the German songs were rhythmized—as we presume the romance songs were—in accord with the medieval theory of the six modes.

Friedrich von Hausen and the poets of his circle must have had direct contact with their contemporary Provençal and French counterparts. Such contact is likely to have continued in the following generation, even though we can no longer prove it through *contrafacta*. Heinrich von Morungen had a thorough knowledge of the art of the troubadours, and the same goes for Walther von der Vogelweide. But around 1200 the emphasis had already shifted away from direct imitation and adoption to the creative reworking of the artistic impulses that came from France. The elaboration of the canzone form into very complicated structures, and the dialogue with the idea of service and high minne no longer required a direct use of romance lyric. In individual cases we have to leave open the question of whether or not the German singers still had access to the musical art of the troubadours and trouvères. That the contacts became much looser in the course of the thirteenth century is also revealed by the fact that the development of the polyphonic secular song had no resonance in Germany.

In addition to the minnesong proper, a few special types of romance lyric were also adopted. As early as Friedrich von Hausen we encounter the courtly crusading song in the style that Conon de Béthune and Guiot de Dijon had given it in France. One of its central characteristics is the connection between the minne theme and the crusading motif, frequently expressed as the poet's perceived conflict between the religious motivations of the crusade and the lady's claim to service.

The courtly dawn song, modeled after the Provençal "alba," appears first in Heinrich von Morungen. The formal characteristic of this genre, the refrain with the word *alba* ("dawn"), was adopted by the German poets only in a few exceptional cases. Instead, the German songs emphasize a unique feature of the "alba": the figure of the watchman, whom we encounter as the friend and protector of the lovers. The German watchman-dawn song was given its typical form by Wolfram von Eschenbach; under his influence the dawn song flourished during the thirteenth century.

The Provençal poem of invective, the "tenzone," had little influence in Germany. But we do find among the works of Albrecht von Johansdorf, Reinmar der Alte, and Walther von der Vogelweide a number of dialogue songs, in which a knight and a lady debate in a humorously pointed way questions of minne, and without the model provided by the "tenzones" these songs would not have been composed.

Distinct from the strophic songs are the Provençal "descorts," which have a different musical setting for each stanza; related to them are the French "lais" and the German *Leiche* ("lay"). Characteristic for this type is a sequence-like structure. The fact that we find the first German lays in the Hausen-school—in Ulrich von Gutenberg and Heinrich von Rugge—in itself makes a French influence highly likely. But we are unable to point to any direct models. The German pieces frequently differ from the romance songs in that they are longer and more complex.

An illuminating light is shed on the social conditions in Germany not only by what the German poets adopted from the troubadours and trouvères, but also by those elements of the art of romance lyric that were ignored in Germany. The pastourelle, very popular in France, was, as a genre, avoided by the German lyricists. But pastourelle-like motifs in Morungen and Johansdorf reveal that the special themes of this genre were known to the minnesingers. Other types of the so-called "genre objectif" ("Chanson de toile," "Chanson de femme," "Chanson de mal mariée," "Rondet," "Virelai"), used in France primarily as dancing songs, were also passed over by the German poets. Absent in Germany, furthermore, are the political song ("sirventes") and the lament ("planh"). For political themes and death lamentations poets in Germany used a different artistic form that was not derived from the romance sphere: the *Spruch*. It is true that the courtly *Spruchdichtung* was also under French influence insofar as the artistic structure of the strophic forms (used by all the *Spruch*-poets after Walther von der Vogelweide) cannot be understood without the model of the strophic structure of romance songs. But in essence the *Spruch* was not a romance form, and its similarity to the Provençal "sirventes" is only superficial. Also without resonance in Germany were the highly developed dialogue songs of the troubadours: the different forms of the "tenzone," the "partimen" and the "cobla."

THE CHARACTERISTICS OF THE LITERARY ADAPTATION

To understand what made French literature so attractive to the princely patrons and the courtly public in Germany, we must appreciate above all the fact that literary adaptation made a revealing selection from the rich palette of French literature by focusing almost exclusively on two genres, the minne-canzones and the "roman courtois." Towards the end of the twelfth century these were the most modern forms of literature in France. Everything else that existed—the "chansons de geste," the short epics of the "lais" and the "fabliaux," the prose romances, the rhymed chronicles, the "pastourelle," the dancing songs, the poems of invective, the secular and sacred plays in the vernacular—radiated into Germany only in a few exceptional cases, or not at all, or only much later. The special qualities of the minnesongs and the courtly romances must explain why the German courts were so strongly interested in these two genres.

The minnesong and the "roman courtois" demand from the poet-translator a high level of artistic creativity and a mastery of lyric form. In emulating the French structural models the poets managed to create

in the space of only one generation a literary public that could reconstruct the ingenious devices of half dactyls and internal rhyme, grasp the
complex structure of the strophes, appreciate rhetorical ornaments, and
follow the demanding artistic creations of the epicists. The self-
reflection of the minnesingers and the psychological motivations in the
adventure and love stories of the romances opened up new dimensions
in the portrayal of human beings, which give this genre its very modern
quality. But above all it was no doubt the details of social life that gave
the minnesongs and the romances their special charm in the eyes of the
German public. No other medium conveyed such an accurate picture of
the material culture, the ceremonial forms of courtly behavior, and the
new ideals and values of French aristocratic society; and apparently this
is what especially interested courtly society in Germany.

   In the past, the relationship between the German adaptations and
their French models was seen largely as a problem of individual artistic
achievement, and the standards of evaluation employed were almost
always clouded by national prejudice. While German scholars took
pains to emphasize the artistic originality of the German works, their
French counterparts tried to dismiss German poetry as mere translation. If the question concerned common approaches to the texts, the
answer was frequently based on a primitive ethnic psychology, according to which the German poets surpassed the formal artistry and elegance of their French models by infusing them with much deeper meaning. Even today it is still difficult to discuss the nature of the literary
indebtedness without biases, as is revealed by the recent debate about
the so-called "adaptation courtoise". The phrase itself sums up the
thesis of Jean Fourquet and his school, who argue that the German
adapters—with the exception of Wolfram von Eschenbach, to whom
they concede a special place—merely used different means of expression and a different descriptive technique, leaving the actual content of
the French texts unchanged. This notion is sometimes so provocatively
overstated that it easily serves to provide fuel for more unscholarly exchanges. The claim that the German poets made only stylistic changes
in their French models is not born out by the facts. But it is certainly
true that the adapters were not primarily concerned with expressing
their own ideas; rather, they were concerned—at least during the first
phase of adoption—with emulating the French formal models as precisely as they could, and were fundamentally interested in conveying to
the German public with the greatest possible authenticity the new social
world of the French texts. The most important result of the debate

about the "adaptation courtoise" is, however, the insight that the process of literary adaptation, beyond individual artistic differences, was also shaped by the divergent social structures in Germany and France. But which concrete historical facts played the most significant role has yet to be clarified. In all likelihood the different educational conditions had a strong influence in shaping the literary manifestations. In France, courtly literature could profit from the rise of higher studies and from the fact that most members of the aristocratic society were literate. The transfer of this French literature to a largely illiterate lay society in Germany had the result that courtly literature took on a different function. Intellectual elements, which appear for example in the playful treatment of love, or in the narrative irony that characterizes Chrétien de Troyes and the best French epic poets, in Germany took a back seat to ideological aspects. Notwithstanding the fact that the texts were also great entertainment, it appears that the German adapters were primarily concerned with the ideal of courtly society. From this perspective we can understand the following differences that set the German adaptations apart from their French models:

1. A tendency toward abstraction, especially in the minnelyric, where the figure of the courtly lady paled in the hands of the German poets more and more into the embodiment of absolute beauty and virtue, whose importance to the courting knights was almost entirely as the representative of courtly ideals.

2. In epic poetry a corresponding loss of suspense and narrative individuality in favor of a heightened exemplariness. This is reflected both in the greater frequency of descriptions of exemplary courtly objects and events, and in the idealization and stereotyping of knightly heroes, whose path to courtly perfection through the motifs of guilt and redemption took on greater ethical importance.

3. The seriousness of the dialogue with the new minne ideal. This appears as early as in the first crusading songs, and later finds expression in Hartmann von Aue's and Walther von der Vogelweide's critique of the courtly ideal of service, and in the great minne-excursus in Wolfram von Eschenbach and Gottfried von Straßburg.

4. The efforts of the German poets to bring together the various aspects of courtly perfection into a unified ideology focused on the notion that the ideal knight had to please both God and the world.

CHAPTER III

Material Culture and Social Style

1. CASTLES AND TENTS

THE CONSTRUCTION OF CASTLES AND PALACES IN THE TWELFTH AND THIRTEENTH CENTURIES

The rise of the noble castle in the High Middle Ages was linked to a development that profoundly transformed the structure of aristocratic society. Beginning in the eleventh century, the families of the high nobility left their ancestral manors and estates and built—often at great expense—castles which served as living quarters. The castles were erected at inaccessible sites, on ridges, or behind moats. This set into motion the process of feudalization and the expansion of lordship that eventually led to the formation of territorial lordship. The personal motives that prompted this move into the wild mountains and forests are unknown. But the construction of castles was of great significance for the self-image of these noble families, as is revealed by the fact that many houses began to call themselves after their castles. From this time on the possession of a castle was an important attribute of the noble lifestyle. "You kings and dukes and all those, to whom the God Almighty has granted power," so we hear in a sermon of Berthold of Regensburg, "one must kneel down before you and rise up before you and one must fear you. You have so much space around you. You ride in splendor and walk in splendor and have high castles and beautiful ladies."[1]

The right to build castles was an ancient royal privilege. As late as the twelfth century we still find scattered cases of royal construction permits. In 1145, for example, King Conrad II allowed the count of Arnsberg "to construct castles in our realm wherever he wishes, on his allodial land or on his fief."[2] Even the *Sachsenspiegel* in the thirteenth century still adhered to a general prohibition of castle construction. Most castles, however, were erected without any special permission. In all likelihood the dukes and margraves derived their right to do so from their authority of office. The territorial lords were later as unable as the kings had been before them to control the building of castles on their lands. It was an exceptional accomplishment in the thirteenth century when the archbishop of Cologne, in his capacity as duke of Westphalia, was able to enforce his sovereignty over all fortifications, a sovereignty that was respected even by the families of the counts.

Few castles existed up to the end of the twelfth century. In the description of the "Conditions in Alsace at the Beginning of the thirteenth century," appended to the *Annals of Colmar*, we read the following: "The nobility in the countryside had small towers it could barely defend against its peers. There were few castles and fortified places."[3] Apart from the king, the castle builders were up to this time almost exclusively princes, dukes, and their families. But even the families of the great counts possessed only a handful of castles: the powerful Swabian counts of Pfullendorf had five castles in the second half of the twelfth century; the counts of Laon (in Brabant) had four, as did the Bavarian counts of Falkenstein. A new phase of castle building set in only in the thirteenth century, when a great number of the smaller noble families and the ministerials began to construct their own castles. The notion that these small knightly castles were the real nurturing ground of courtly poetry and courtly culture is wrong on chronological grounds alone. Most of the castles that today dominate the landscape along the Rhine or in Tyrol date to an even later period.

A castle policy in the grand style was first pursued by Emperor Henry IV (d. 1106), whose attempt to secure the imperial lands around Goslar with a ring of castles was thwarted by the resistance of the Saxon nobility. The emperor began "to look for high and naturally fortified mountains in deserted places and to construct on them such castles as would be a great protection and ornament to the empire if only they could be located at appropriate sites."[4] According to this account Henry IV himself roamed the forests "in search of suitable sites for his castles."[5] At the same time he placed "the speedy and careful implementation of his plan under the supervision of the Lord Benno."[6] Bishop Benno II of

Osnabrück (d. 1088) was famous as "a superb architect and the leading expert of masonry construction."[7]

In the twelfth century it is the Hohenstaufen family which stands out above all the other princes as castle builders, and especially Duke Frederick II of Swabia (d. 1147), who threw a net of fortifications over the entire region of the Upper Rhine, and who used the construction of castles systematically for the consolidation of his territorial lordship: "Continuously moving down the Rhine, he would now erect a castle at a suitable site and subject the surrounding land, and then leave this castle and build a new one."[8] His son, Emperor Frederick I, followed his example. The Hohenstaufen's wealth of castles was enormous, for it is reported that Beatrice, the daughter of King Philip of Swabia, brought with her no less than 350 castles when she married the Emperor Otto IV after the murder of her father in 1208: "He took her as his wife along with her paternal inheritance of many riches and 350 castles."[9] But the Hohenstaufen were not the only ones who engaged in castle building in a grand style. The archbishops of Cologne, the Zähringer dukes in Swabia, the landgraves of Thuringia, and others pursued a similar policy. Most of these royal and princely castles rarely or never served as living quarters for their lords. Their purpose was to secure or expand the lords' sphere of power, and they were usually garrisoned with a castle guard drawn from the ministerial class.

The castle building of this time reached its height in the magnificent imperial palaces newly built or restored by Emperor Frederick I. Castles and palaces cannot be clearly differentiated in the twelfth century. Unlike the older imperial palaces, which were not surrounded by walls, the Hohenstaufen constructions are characteristically well fortified. This had led some to speak of palace-castles (*Pfalzburgen*), distinguished from other castles by their greater spaciousness and a much larger number of buildings (residential wing, royal living quarters, chapel, garrison quarters, and buildings housing the various economic activities). The Hohenstaufen imperial palaces were not merely functional structures, but also expressed an exalted outward manifestation of imperial power linked to the conception of the empire held by Frederick I and his advisors. It is expressed most clearly in the inscriptions preserved in the palaces at Nimwegen and Kaiserwerth (near Düsseldorf). The Nimwegen inscription reads: "In the year 1155 after salvation had been given to the world, the ruler of the world, Frederick, the friend of peace, caused this structure at Nimwegen, which had been neglected and was broken and nearly extinguished, to be artfully and beautifully restored.

Julius had once begun it; unequal was he to the peace-loving renewer Frederick."[10] The reference to Julius Caesar and the peace emperor's claim to universal lordship reflects the desired "renewal of the empire" (*renovatio imperii*), which played such a significant role in the first decades of Frederick I's reign. The two surviving inscriptions from Kaiserwerth date only from the 1180s. Here the building program was tied to the Christian ideal of the just and peace-bringing king (*rex iustus et pacificus*): "In the year of the incarnation of our Lord Jesus Christ 1184, Emperor Frederick exalted the Empire through this ornament. He wanted to strengthen justice, and he desired that peace should prevail everywhere."[11] The second inscription from a great hall (*aula*) emphasizes the severity of imperial justice. These texts are supplemented by Rahewin's account in the *Gesta Frederici* of the emperor's building activities: "Displaying an extraordinary, inborn magnanimity, he [Frederick] restored most magnificently the beautiful palaces originally built by Charlemagne, and the splendidly decorated royal palaces in Nimwegen and near the village of Ingelheim, extremely strong structures that had by now become feeble through neglect and old age."[12] Rahewin also mentions the palaces newly erected by Frederick I in Kaiserslautern and in various Italian cities. How dear these structures were to the emperor is revealed by the letter he wrote to his son Henry VI on November 16th, 1189, while en route to the Holy Land—it was the last sign of life from the emperor that reached Germany—in which he admonished him: "See to it that the water castles of Kaiserwerth and Nimwegen are completed and excellently guarded, for we consider that to be of the greatest advantage."[13] All that is left of the palacial structures in Ingelheim, Nimwegen, Kaiserslautern, Kaiserwerth, and Hagenau are insignificant fragments. To get a sense of the architectural characteristics and the artistic significance of the Hohenstaufen imperial palaces we must examine the more extensive remains at Wimpfen, Eger, Seligenstadt, and especially Gelnhausen. Regardless of their location—Gelnhausen and Hagenau were water castles, Wimpfen and Eger were situated on a mountain ridge—the Hohenstaufen castle-palaces reveal a common architectural concept. Apart from the fortifications—walls and towers—two complexes stand out everywhere: the imperial living quarters and representational structures, and the palace chapel, which usually had the characteristic form of a two-story double chapel. These buildings also displayed the richest architectural decorations: pillars with splendidly ornamented capitals, arcatures, portal frames, free-standing flights of stairs, and especially the magnificent window arcades

Fig. 4.   The imperial palace at Gelnhausen. View of the interior court. On the right is the inner façade of the palas with the window arcades of the great hall. Originally a free-standing flight of stairs led up to the entrance with its artistic portal frame. In the background the gate hall with a chapel on top. Twelfth century.

which give the Hohenstaufen buildings their unmistakable appearance (see fig. 4).

An architectural style identical to that of the imperial palaces and of the same high level of artistic design is found in some castles built by noblemen who belonged to the closest circle of advisers and court officials around Frederick I. Castle Münzenberg in Wetterau, with its two towers and, in the front façade of the residential wing, window arcades that were visible even at a great distance, belonged to Kuno von Hagen, one of the most powerful and influential of the great imperial ministerials. Castle Wildenberg in the Odenwald was erected by Freiherr Rupert von Durne, who appears as a witness in over one hundred charters of Frederick I and Henry VI. The similarity of architectural and decorative forms seems to indicate that the emperor passed on to his followers the architects and stonemasons in his employ. Whether the imperial court also contributed financially to these very expensive enterprises is not known. As it is we know all too little about the financing and the practical execution of the construction work. The information we have about the building activities of Benno II of Osnabrück (d. 1088) and Otto of Bamberg (d. 1139), who, at the request of Emperor Henry

VI, both played major roles in the completion of the cathedral at Speyer, indicates that the construction of large castles and palaces was supervised by the same people who were leaders in the field of church building. Identical decorative elements—such as the capitals and pedestals in the palace chapel at Nuremberg and in the church of St. Jacob in Regensburg—point in the same direction.

THE ARCHITECTURE OF CASTLES AND PALACES

"The name 'castle' is given to a site where a tower stands surrounded by a wall, with both protecting each other."[14] Which architectural elements were considered typical of a castle is revealed by the regulations regarding castle building that appear in the *Sachsenspiegel*. Without the permission of the local judge (*Landrichter*) one could dig only "as deep as one man can shovel out the earth with a spade"; and one was allowed "to build of wood or stone only three stories on top of each other, one story into the ground and two upwards, namely in such a manner that on the first floor the door was no more than knee-high above the ground."[15] In addition, one could "fortify a house with fences, palisades, or walls only to the height that a man sitting on a horse could reach with his hand"; and they should "have no crenelations."[16] Deep ditches, multistory towers with recessed entrances, and high walls, crenelated and fortified, determined the appearance of a castle.

A number of elements made this new type of noble castle, which began to appear in the eleventh century, distinct from the older refuge-castles (*Fluchtburgen*) that were meant for a large number of people: a smaller castle space, improved defenses, and the almost exclusive use of stone as the construction material. In regard to the architectural layout, the main difference is that the tower became the central structure of the castle. The most important impulses for this development seem to have come from Italy, where the noble castle-tower is attested much earlier. Later developments primarily involved an expansion of the fortifications. The walls became higher and thicker; they were strengthened with merlons and towers and protected by moats, outworks, and barbicans. Sometimes the first wall was surrounded by a second one; the space in between was called the outer bailey. Gates were particularly vulnerable, and were protected by drawbridges and portcullises. In some cases several gates were placed in succession, or gate passages and even entire gate castles were constructed. Character-

istic of the development of the German castle in the twelfth and thirteenth centuries is the fact that a building housing the lord's residential
quarters—the *palas*—was usually built in addition to the tower; as a
result the tower acquired a strictly military function and is known in
German as the *Bergfried*. In France and England, on the other hand, the
great residential tower, the "donjon" ("keep"), dominated the appearance of the noble castle. A number of German princes, apparently influenced by the French model, preferred the donjon-type, especially the
dukes of Zähringen (in Breisach, Thun, Burgdorf), the margraves of
Baden (in Besigheim and Reichenberg), the archbishops of Cologne (in
Godesberg), and the counts of Jülich (in Nideggen). The much rarer
fortress type, with a square layout and usually a tower at each corner, is
also traced back to French impulses. In Germany it appears first around
1220 at castle Lahr (Upper Rhine) built by the counts of Geroldseck.
Evidence of French influence in the field of castle building can also be
found in the numerous loan words, especially those for individual elements of fortification: *barbigân* "barbican," *hâmit* "outwork," *tralge*
"iron grate," *erker* "bay." To the oldest layer of French terms belongs
the word "tower" (*turn*). *Palas* is attested from the middle of the
twelfth century on. The entire castle could also be described with a
French word: *chastel*, which appears in German as *schastel* (or
schahtel) and *kastêl* (*kastel* with a short *e* is considered a Latin loan
word). The old German noun for the castle was *hûs*. Other words in use
were *veste* and *burc*. *Burc* was the broader term and could also stand
for a fortified city. But around 1200, the terminological differentiation
of *burc* and *stat* in the sense of "castle" and "city" had not progressed
as far as is usually assumed.

Castle scholarship today is centered on archeology, which has
brought to light an extraordinarily rich range of material, but this material is not always easily accessible to the nonspecialist. Archeologists
classify the many variations of medieval castles into different castle
types, using as criteria either geographic location (high castle, low
castle, peak castle, spur castle, water castle, island castle, etc.), or
architectural layout, which differentiates two main types: the central
layout (ring castle, tower castle, motte, etc.) and the axial layout
(*Abschnittsburg, Schildmauerburg*). Castles can also be classified according to their lords (imperial castles, territorial castles, castles of the
high nobility, ministerial castles).

The most extensive contemporary castle descriptions are found in
courtly poetry. Scholars studying the historical development of castles

have paid little attention to them, because they regard poetic evidence
as unrealistic and therefore of little use. It is certainly true that the poets
were not concerned with furnishing authentic descriptions of normal
castles. They told of castles situated in the magical land of Celtic
legends, whose fantastic splendor surpassed anything in real life. Nevertheless, these descriptions are very informative for the reason alone that
they document a very differentiated German castle terminology that is
attested nowhere else in this period. Moreover, they reveal which
details of castle architecture appealed most to the imagination of the
noble audience. Special attention was paid to those architectural elements that were of importance for this society's outward expression of
status. The amir of Babylon had a gigantic keep erected, built "of such
large stones that one could barely pull up a single one with three
winches."[17] In reality one winch would have been sufficient to hoist up
the stones. Yet the use of giant stone blocks was not a fairy tale motif
for the courtly audience. The *Königschronik* of Cologne reports, under
the year 1217, that the Knights Templar were repairing the old castle of
Districtum (near Caesarea), and that "two towers were being built with
blocks of such size that one stone could hardly be transported in a cart
pulled by two oxen."[18] Castle Brandigan in Hartmann's *Erec* impressed
with the multitude of its towers: "There stood the castle with the towers. Altogether there were thirty of them."[19] If we assume that most
Hohenstaufen castles had only one tower or at most two towers, the
thirty towers of Brandigan seem like sheer fantasy. But Hartmann von
Aue was speaking specifically of wall towers: "The mountain was encir-
cled by a high, thick castle wall. A fortified appearance characterized
the interior of the castle. Towers of mighty blocks rose high above the
merlons."[20] Such magnificent structures were rare in the period around
1200, but they did exist. Coradin of Babylon built on Mount Tabor "a
very strongly fortified castle with seventy-seven towers."[21]

The poets praised the height and thickness of the walls and towers,
the depth of the moats, the number and quality of the fortifications, and
the expansiveness of the entire structure: "There stood a castle, it was
the best structure that existed on earth. The space it enclosed was im-
measurably vast."[22] Even more attention was paid to the splendid decoration: "The towers were decorated on top with bosses of red gold,
each one glimmering far into the land."[23] Today the gray ruins of the
Hohenstaufen castles give no hint of the splendor that once radiated
from them and which the poets captured in their verses: "Then he saw a
castle—ah! with what splendor did it shine!"[24] Gilded roofs, colored

ceramic bricks, encrusted walls, and mosaic floors are historically confirmed for the courtly age only in sacred buildings. The poets speak of these ornamental elements also in castles, and it is quite possible that they are describing something real that has not been documented in any historical sources. Castle Dodone "shone splendidly inside and out. The floor below was made of marble. The wall was of the same material, pieced together in a square pattern like a chessboard with red and white stones."[25] In castle Karidol the palas of the queen radiated in all colors: "The queen had a palas of marble, decorated all over in four colors: red, brown, blue, and yellow. The building was round, and all around were pergolas."[26] The poets' preference for round structures—the embodiment of architectural perfection—and some descriptions of figurative scenes on walls and merlons could have been taken over from classical models. On the other hand, the statements about window decorations reflect the artistic trends of contemporary secular architecture: "Every window was ornamented with two graceful columns."[27] "One palas had round about windows and arches, about five hundred; they were separated by columns of different colors."[28] As decoration for the windows, "leaf and animal shapes had been carved in. Whoever wanted to see masterful artistry cast his glance onto the round columns, on which many magnificent capitals had been cut and chiseled out of stone."[29] Artistically shaped capitals, double columns, and window arcades were among the most striking decorative features of the Hohenstaufen castles. Window panes hardly existed at all at this time. Even in the thirteenth century the great castle windows were usually closed with wooden shutters. But when the poets spoke of glass windows ("along the wall the chamber had many windows, and in front of them glass"[30]) they were probably expressing the kind of luxury their audiences imagined and longed for.

Life in the castles must have been uncomfortable and dreary even for the lord and his family. Conditions behind the castle walls were cramped, cold, dark, drafty, and unhygienic. To relieve themselves the residents used latrines jutting out over the walls and often placed in lofty heights reached only by long passages and stairways. It is not unlikely that sometimes the residents of the castle did not bother to go that far: "Along came a beautiful young lady, like a turtledove, and she quietly stepped outside the palas gate and wanted to relieve herself in front of it."[31] Such motifs, however, are rare in courtly poetry.

More frequently the poets integrated the architecture into their descriptions of social life in the castle. Guests were received in the courtyard of the castle. A particularly splendid impression was created if the side of the palas facing the courtyard had a free-standing flight of stairs, as was the case at Gelnhausen. Ulrich von Liechtenstein relates his reception at castle Felsberg: "The host welcomed me there in a very friendly manner. His wife, the mistress of the house, came down the stairs to meet me, accompanied by many ladies."[32] The trains of the dresses created a nice effect as they fell in beautiful drapes across the stairs. The places most preferred by the ladies were the windows and the balconies: "The windows were crowded with seated ladies."[33] Benches were frequently built right into the window niches or were separately set up and covered with soft cushions: a spot for intimate conversations. An equally popular spot for the ladies was on top of the walls. From there they could observe what was going on in the courtyard or in front of the castle, watch the arrival of strangers or the jousting of the knights. Such scenes were captured in the miniatures of the great minnesinger manuscript in the University Library in Heidelberg. Windows and ramparts were also the refuge for a lady unhappily in love: "She stepped up to a window, as women frequently do who have suffered lover's grief."[34]

A place of private conviviality was the orchard, which was part of every castle. The story *Die Nachtigall* speaks of a garden in which grew not only beatiful flowers but also "many aromatic plants and herbs."[35] Since the air was so good there the lord of the castle had a bower erected in the garden: "It had been built so that the lord could sit there in the summer and take his meals; he thought the food would agree with him more in that place."[36] The orchard was also well suited for secret rendezvous. Isolde was careless enough to set up a bed among the trees in broad daylight and to ask her lover to meet her there (G. v. Straßburg 18143 ff.).

FURNISHINGS

What a castle around 1200 looked like on the inside we can learn from Lambert of Ardres, who in his *History of the Counts of Guines* described in detail the new castle erected in Ardres by Count Arnald of Guines. As was customary in Flanders at that time, the castle was a multistory donjon.

> The first floor stood level to the ground. It housed the cellars and the granary, the great chests, barrels and vats, and other household equipment. On the second floor were the living quarters and the great hall for all the resi-

dents. Here were further the food supplies of the pantlers and cupbearers, and also the great chamber of the lord and his wife, in which they slept, and joined to it the hidden rooms or bedrooms of the chambermaids and pages. In a separated part of the great chamber was a special partition, where a fire was lit early in the morning and at night, and also during illnesses or blood-letting, or to warm the chambermaids and weaned infants. On this floor the kitchen, likewise two stories, was linked with the main house. On the lower level of the kitchen pigs and geese were kept for fattening, along with capons and other fowl, always ready to be slaughtered and eaten. On the second level of the kitchen building only the cooks and kitchen masters worked; here the dishes for the lord and his family were most carefully prepared with all the effort and artistry of the cooks, and were made ready for consump-tion. Here too the food for the members of the court and the service staff was prepared, and the work was planned and carried out day after day. The uppermost floor contained numerous garrets, in which the sons of the lord slept if they wanted to, and the daughters because it was proper. Here also were the watchmen and the servants assigned to the castle guard, who kept continuous watch whenever the lords and ladies went to bed. There were stairs and passageways from one floor to the next, from the main house to the kitchen, from one room to the next, and from the house to the *logium* (pergola), which had that name for a very good reason; derived from *logos*, that is "speech," it was a charming place where people used to sit and talk. There was also a connection between the balcony and the oratory or chapel, which resembled in its architectural decoration and paintings the Temple of Solomon.[37]

This account of Lambert of Ardres is of extraordinary value, since no other historical source of this period reveals in such detail the interior structure of a lord's house. The entire architectural layout revolved around the lord and his family. The central area was, in addition to the great hall, the lord's bedchamber. All other facilities served to feed the lord and his family, protect them, entertain them, and minister to their spiritual well-being.

The castle ruins of the Hohenstaufen period reveal little about the interior furnishings. A few surviving columns and capitals, remnants of door and window frames, and a few random pieces such as the decora-tive stone plates at Gelnhausen (see fig. 5)—works of superb artistic quality—still hint at the splendor of the original decoration and fur-nishings. The greatest care was devoted to the artistic decoration of the capitals. The best preserved are those in the chapels at Nuremberg and Eger, both double chapels with rich architectural ornamentation. Fol-lowing the model of the imperial buildings, ecclesiastical and secular princes also built double chapels in their palaces and castles. In Neuen-burg on the Unstrut, one of the chief castles of the landgraves of Thur-

Fig. 5. Imperial palace at Gelnhausen. Side piece of the fireplace in the great hall. To the left an inlaid stone decorative plate with a wickerwork pattern. Twelfth century.

ingia, and in Klosterneuburg, where the Babenberg dukes of Austria erected a new palace around 1200, much of the old architectural decoration has survived. But as far as the interior furnishings of the living quarters and the other secular buildings are concerned, we are almost totally dependent on the descriptions of the poets.

The social center of the castle was the great hall, usually located on the second floor of the palas and recognizable from the outside by the splendid window arcades. Here the courtly festivities could unfold. "I don't know what would be the purpose of a prince if not from time to time his court were filled with the joyous noise of festivities."[38] The size of the great hall mirrors the heightened desire for representation and display so characteristic of the courtly age. In the imperial castles at Gelnhausen and Eger the halls are more than one thousand square feet in size. The great hall in the house of the landgrave in the Wartburg measured more than twelve hundred square feet. It was probably completed under Landgrave Ludwig IV (d. 1227), and its size and magnificent decoration and furnishings surpassed everything that existed then in Germany. Halls of such size were at that time built only in France

·and England. The great hall in Poitiers, residence of the dukes of Aquitaine, measured twenty-six hundred square feet. The hall in Westminster Castle in London, which King Henry II expanded, covered an incredible five thousand square feet. The largest hall in a German castle (over twenty-six hundred square feet) was built in the middle of the fourteenth century in Nideggen, the main seat of the counts of Jülich. Such huge halls required the kind of pillar construction that Wolfram von Eschenhach described for the castle of Glorjet: "Straight down the middle of the palas many marble pillars had been placed under the vaults."[39] Great halls of fantastic size appear fairly often in literature. The hall in the grail castle Munsalvaesche could seat four hundred knights at tables (W. v. Eschenbach, *Parzival* 229.28 ff.).

The poets especially emphasized the features which most castles, with their cold and gloomy rooms, lacked: light, warmth, and color. The great hall was illuminated by the glow of countless candles when court society assembled there. "One hundred chandeliers"[40] existed in the palas of Munsalvaesche, and in addition "small candles lined its walls."[41]

Rooms were heated, if they could be heated at all, by fireplaces. In the palace at Gelnhausen one can still see the great sidewalls of the fireplace and the richly decorated columns that framed it. The great hall of Munsalvaesche had "three square fireplaces of marble masonry,"[42] which were probably open on all four sides. Wolfram von Eschenbach adds: "Here at Wildenberg none ever saw such great fires."[43] We assume that this was a reference to castle Wildenberg near Amorbach, which belonged to the lords of Durne. The fireplace there is 3.5 meters wide and among the most impressive remains of that castle. Wolfram's verses could have been intended as a compliment to his hosts.

We must picture the great halls as being very colorful. The walls were painted or on festive occasions hung with tapestries. According to the poetic descriptions, the wall hangings were sometimes made of colorful silk damask with interwoven figurative patterns. "There hung a precious tapestry; it was broad and long and interwoven with gold thread. Birds and forest animals in silk were woven into it, with myriad decorations and in many colors. All this I saw. At the upper and lower border one could see knights and ladies beautifully depicted. At the ends and at the borders precious trimmings had been affixed, and ivory hooks that were attached to the mount. If one pulled the tapestry, many small golden bells on it sounded."[44] Literary motifs were very popular as figurative scenes, especially motifs from classical legends. "There gold thread had

Fig. 6.   The Bayeux Tapestry. This detail shows a Norman horseman attacking Saxon warriors at the battle of Hastings. Both Normans and Saxons wear mail armor that reaches down to the knees, pointed helmets with nosebands, and carry large, almond-shaped shields. In the lower edge we can see fallen warriors being stripped of their armor. End of the eleventh century.

been interwoven to depict how lady Helena fled from Greece together with Paris, and in another place how Troy lay in ruin, and further the terrible fate that befell Dido when she had Aeneas as her guest. Moreover, one could see there scenes of the beautiful Lavinia, how Aeneas won her in combat, and the defeat of the Romans. The wall hanging ran around the entire hall and embraced it very suitably."[45] No doubt we would consider such descriptions mere poetic fancy, if we did not possess the Bayeux tapestry, which was made towards the end of the eleventh century, probably at the request of a member of the royal family of England. The tapestry is about seventy meters long—the end is missing—and about half a meter wide. With colored wool stitched onto linen it depicts scenes from Anglo-Norman history, especially the conquest of England by William (d. 1087) and the battle of Hastings in 1066. Pictured are more than six hundred people and a great array of objects: clothes, weapons, horses, boats, and so on (see fig. 6). The tapestry is a major source for the material culture of noble society around 1100. In Germany we have tapestries with secular motifs only from a later period. Outstanding among them are the great Tristan tapestries from the monastery of Wienhausen (near Celle); the oldest piece is dated to about 1300. Considering how delicate the material of these tapestries is, it is not surprising that much has been lost.

This applies even more so to wall paintings, for nowhere has the interior plastering of the great halls survived. According to the testimony of the poets one could see in many castles "beautiful paintings on the walls of the palas.''[46] Preferred themes were, as with the tapestries, literary motifs, along with historical subjects and depictions of modern society, sometimes with reference to the princely patron. We can get a sense of the splendid coloring and festiveness of these paintings as well as the variety of their literary themes from the summer house of castle Runkelstein (near Bozen); the decoration, however, dates only to the period around 1400. In German-speaking regions the oldest surviving wall paintings with scenes from courtly literature are the recently uncovered Iwein frescoes at castle Rodeneck (near Brixen), said to have been created at the beginning of the thirteenth century, and the Iwein images in Schmalkalden (Thuringia), dated to about the middle of the thirteenth century (see p. 527).

As richly decorated as the great hall were the lord's living quarters (*kemenâten* from Latin *caminata* "heatable room"). The countess of Beaumont had her knight led into a chamber for a secret rendezvous, "where the walls were so richly decorated with paintings that it radiated inside like in a church. The ceiling of the room was covered with mosaics, which made it shine like a mirror."[47] In the royal palace of Troy the wounded Hector was taken into a room with silken wall hangings, splendid furniture, and a special artistic decoration: in each corner there stood a human statue on top of a twisted column of precious stone: a knife thrower, a lute player, a woman scattering flowers, and a female fortuneteller, all of which could be made to move mechanically (H. v. Fritzlar 9221 ff.). The ideas for this probably came from classical sources. But it is not unlikely that such luxurious rooms, even with ornamental sculptures, existed during the courtly age. The French poet and bishop Baudri de Bourgueil (d. 1130) composed a long Latin poem (*Adelae comitissae*) of over two thousand verses, addressed to Countess Adele of Blois (d. 1137), the daughter of King William I of England. In it he gives a very exhaustive description of her room in the palace at Blois. The walls were decorated with precious tapestries that had been made under the personal supervision of the countess ("she herself helped by directing the girls who were working on it and showing them with her drawing stick what they should do"[48]). On the first wall were the creation, paradise, and the flood; on the second scenes from the Old Testament; on the third figures from Greek mythology, the siege of Troy, and the history of Rome. The fourth wall hanging was stretched around the alcoves, where the bed of the countess stood. This fourth tapestry was particularly richly ornamented with gold and silver threads, and it depicted the Battle of Hastings and the conquest of England by Adele's father. On the ceiling a sky with all the stars, planets, and zodiac signs had been painted, and on the marble floor one could see a world map with all the rivers, mountains, and cities. The bed of the countess was surrounded by three groups of statues representing Philosophy, the Seven Liberal Arts, and Medicine. Some of the inscriptions on the figures came from Countess Adele herself ("with care and sagacity the ruling countess had composed this inscription for the statue"[49]). The description of Baudri de Bourgueil was not a record of what he had actually seen in Blois. We know the literary models from which some of the descriptive elements were borrowed. But this poetic homage would have made little sense if such a luxurious room had not actually existed.

There is evidence for figurative cycles based on themes from world history, as in Blois, also for Hohenstaufen palaces. Everything we know about the magnificent frescoes painted at Frederick I's request onto the walls of the imperial palace at Hagenau comes from the verses of the court chaplain Gottfried of Viterbo: "In gold paint several wall panels of the room recount all things past and show the future; the family of all kings is depicted there."[50] We can infer from this that the king's chamber in Hagenau was decorated with a cycle of portraits of rulers, comprising probably the entire course of world history ("the family of kings"). This visual program followed a Carolingian tradition. Ermoldus Nigellus (d. after 830) reports in his poem in honor of Emperor Louis the Pious (d. 840) that a similar cycle existed in the great hall of the imperial palace at Ingelheim. In twelve double portraits it depicted the history of the rulers from the Babylonian King Ninus down to Charlemagne, and it included Alexander, Augustus, and Constantine (*In honorem Hludowici christianissimi Caesaris Augusti* 2126 ff.). Nothing of it has survived; the pales in Hagenau has also disappeared.

Petrus de Ebulo tells us of another world-historical pictorial cycle of the twelfth century: Henry VI had six rooms of his imperial palace painted with scenes that traced the entire history of mankind, from the creation of the world and the kings of the Old Testament down to the present. The crusade of his father Frederick I and his death in the Saleph River were the subject of the last room (see p. 649). This pictorial evidence of the twelfth century has so far attracted little interest.

The idea that a ruler would have his palace painted with scenes that established a historical link between himself or his family and the great kings of the past also appears in a contemporary poetic work. In *Pfaffe Amis* we are told that the hero of the story was once commissioned by

·the French king to paint a hall in the royal palace in Paris. To accomplish his task he created a historical cycle that began with David and Solomon, moved on to depict the history of Alexander the Great and the deeds of the Babylonian kings, and in the end—as Amis leads the king to believe—included the patron himself: "Everything that I have painted above deals with you. In this hall I have painted how all your knights together with you enter here and stand around you looking."[51]

The fact that the poets said little about furniture is probably a reflection of reality. Tables and benches were set up specifically for the meals. Chests, which replaced cabinets, are occasionally mentioned, and one can get a sense of what they looked like from the magnificent collection at the convent of Wienhausen in Niedersachsen. Apart from these items, only a single piece of furniture attracted greater attention: the bed, especially the so-called *spanbette* (the sling-bed), which took its name from the ropes that were stretched between the bedposts and formed an elastic frame. Pictorial representations, as for example in the Straßburg manuscript of the *Hortus deliciarum* from the end of the twelfth century, convey a very good idea of its appearance (see fig. 7). Historically such beds are attested as precious gifts. When Frederick I set out for his crusade in 1189, the King of Hungary presented to him, among other things, "a bed with a splendidly decorated pillow and a very precious blanket, and in addition an ivory stool with a cushion which was to be placed in front of the bed."[52] The luxurious beds described by the courtly poets looked no different.

> There in the middle stood a bed, now listen how it was made. It had large, lathe-turned feet, from which ivory carved animals emerged, animals of every kind that the earth brings forth. Between the ivory gold was inlaid, so that its shape radiated from in between. The side boards of the bed were of such wood that even Vulcan himself could not burn it. Stretched across them were four leopard skins, sewn together in the middle. Only rich people can afford this. This is the truth, even though I did not see the bed myself. On the skins lay many soft, large pillows, not lacking covers; they were covered with Greek silk, and on top were a quilt—I believe that even Cassandra never stitched a better one or anyone else of her sex—and a coverlet of fine linen stuffed with precious down.[53]

Since beds were the only comfortable pieces of furniture, they were used for sitting—as a couch—as well as for lying down. In the great hall of Munsalvaesche stood "one hundred beds"[54] on which sat four hundred knights to take their meal, always four to each bed. In most cases the poets speak more of the soft pillows than the bed frame. For that they

Fig. 7. Solomon's bed. A luxurious sling-bed, with the attachments of the ropes visible at the top and foot of the bed. The bed has artistically carved feet and is lavishly covered with pillows and blankets. From the *Hortus deliciarum* of Herrad of Landsberg. End of the twelfth century.

had at their disposal a characteristically courtly pillow terminology that was made up of French and Latin loan words: *küssen* "pillow," *matraz* "cushion," and *kulter* "quilt" were derived from French; *plûmît* "down pillow," *phulwe* "couch," and *tepich* "rug" came from Latin.

Among the most highly prized amenities was a warm bath. Baths were taken simply in a tub of water that was set up in a room or outdoors, as the poets often describe. But it would seem that even smaller castles early on had separate bath chambers. Der Stricker tells the story of how a servant came to a castle and requested to see the lord, whereupon he was sent to the bath room: "Go into the bath chamber, he is inside; the chamber is warm."[55] Assuming that the lord of the castle was taking a bath, the servant undressed and entered stark naked, to the horror of the lord and his family, who were using the bath chamber in the autumn as a living room because the chamber of the castle was not heated until the winter.

On occasion the poets also speak of complicated technical systems, of pipes and pumps that conducted the water throughout the castle. In the great donjon of the amir of Babylon, the water was pumped up to the tower and from there flowed into the various chambers (K. Fleck 4224 ff.). It seems that such installations did in fact exist, if in a simpler form, as we learn from the account of an accident at the Austrian castle of Persenbeug in 1045, which killed the bishop of Würzburg and the abbot of Ebersberg. At the time Emperor Henry III was the guest of Countess Richilde von Ebersberg. When suddenly "a pillar of the wooden construction of the dining hall, in which they were sitting, moved from its place, they fell into the bath chamber [on the ground level] which was just at this moment being filled with water brought in from over the mountain."[56] No doubt water pressure was also used this way in other castles, wherever the geographic location permitted it. But the bathing facilities in the castles were surely not comparable to the much more comfortable and popular bath houses in the cities. Much later, Count Froben Christof von Zimmern (d. 1567) reports in the *Zimmerschen Chronik* that it was largely consideration for the baths that prompted the nobility to abandon its castles and move back into the cities: "Our ancestors once lived on high mountains in their castles and palaces. Back then loyalty and faith still existed among them. But today we are giving up our mountain fortresses and dwell in them no longer; instead we wish to live in the plains, so that we don't have to go far to the baths."[57]

CASTLES AS INSTRUMENTS OF LORDSHIP

Castles were military structures. They offered a means of defense and at the same time consituted a threat to the enemy. Wars in the twelfth and thirteenth centuries were fought almost exclusively around castles and cities, while the open countryside was entirely at the mercy of the attacking troops. Some castles were considered impregnable, but hardly any castle could withstand a serious siege for very long. Even the famous Château Gaillard, built by Richard the Lionheart for the protection of Rouen, was taken by Philip II Augustus in 1204, and the siege lasted at most a month. Frequently the staggered nature of the fortifications created the illusion of military purpose. Particularly questionable was the military usefulness of the *Bergfried*, which appeared from the outside as the fortified center of the castle. In some cases the entrance to this tower was built five to ten meters above the ground and could be reached only with a ladder, and the idea behind this must have been that the tower should still be defended against the enemy who was already inside the castle. But it must have been hardly possible to defend the tower alone when the rest of the castle had been taken. Surrounding the castle with multiple walls also seems to have had little military usefulness. Heinrich von dem Türlin probably judged the situation realistically when he said that a castle was already lost once the enemy had gained a foothold in the *hâmit*, the outwork (*Krone* 11684 ff.). Most Hohenstaufen palace-castles were built in such a way that the palas formed part of the exterior wall. The lavish window arcades on the outer side were, from a military standpoint, superfluous and dangerous. This shows that the architectural design of castles in the High Middle Ages was only in part determined by military considerations. Castles always had in addition a representative—we could also say a symbolic—function. Their mighty walls and towers were visible expressions of the nobility's claim to lordship, of its wealth and power.

The castle was above all the center from which lordship expanded. Next to the control over monasteries—under the legal title of ecclesiastical advocate—and the founding of cities, castle building proved the most effective instrument for the consolidation of territorial lordship, both for the smaller noble families who were trying to establish a compact sovereign territory from their ancestral castles, as well as for the great princes, who engaged systematically in castle building. Since the construction of a new castle almost always went hand in hand with an expansion or intensification of sovereign rights, the claims that radiated from a castle could easily come under the suspicion of being unjust and unlawful tyranny, even if the castle lord was the emperor. This is how Bruno, with a clear anti-imperial bias, reports in *Sachsenkrieg* on the efforts of Henry IV to consolidate territorially the imperial lands in Goslar through a ring of new castles: "But after the garrisons that were quartered in the castles had begun to sally forth in search of booty, to harvest for themselves what they had not sown, to force free men into servile labor, and to make a sport of the daughters and wives of others, then the Saxons finally realized what a threat these castles were."[58] In similar fashion we hear in Strickers tale *Die Gäuhühner* how a noble lord built a citadel at a suitable site and from there subjected all the surrounding land. An evil advisor gave him the fomula:

Expand your power! Show knightly boldness, subject to yourself the people and property in this region, no matter who they belong to, and spare no one. It will soon reach the point when they will consider it their greatest joy to win your goodwill. Then they will gladly be your subjects. The rich fear your power, the poor must serve you. With suitable measures we can easily get the people to serve you day after day without complaining. Whatever we get from them this year through sweet words, they must also deliver next year. They will not dare to resist; thus they will have to pay dues forever. Whoever gives you one chicken this year will deliver next year two or three without protest. Thus your profit and your reputation will grow, and you will be more highly regarded than before. If a peasant wants to resist you, make him your bailiff. Then everything that he will be able to produce will be yours. In this way you shall subject them all, with cunning and force. Thus you will grow old with honors.[59]

This speech is remarkable not only because it lays out in such detail the mechanism of how to expand power, but also because it employs the central concepts of the courtly ethic of a knight to cloak the exercise of unlawful power. It would be difficult to find another text from the thirteenth century that so clearly reflects the awareness that the knightly ideals of the courtly age could be abused for evil purposes.

In the historical sources of the time we hear again and again of acts of violence and abuses of power committed by the lords of castles. To this day cultural historians repeat the mistaken notion that the robber knights were a typical phenomenon of the late Middle Ages and reflected the supposed moral decay of noble society. In truth the robber knights were so prominent in the later Middle Ages because it was only during these centuries that a firm concept of public peace arose, which tried as much as possible to restrict and criminalize all independent military activities of the nobility. Lawlessness had emanated from the castles much earlier. Our historical sources generally mention it only in those cases where acts of violence were punished.

Experiences of this kind could foster the belief that castle building always led to despotic rule, a belief expressed most pointedly in Freidank's *Bescheidenheit*: "Castles are built for one purpose: to strangle the poor."[60] Echoing this sentiment of Freidank (and using the suggestive rhyme *bürge : würge* "castles : to choke"), Hugo von Trimberg complained at the end of the thirteenth century in *Renner* "that Christian people have moved into the wastelands and want to live in the wild forests with wolves and bears, and they construct castles in the wilderness in order to torment the poor."[61]

Castles were also of great importance to economic life. Quite often a manor was attached to the castle, and it secured the food supply for the residents. Frequently new castles were located in sites from where they could control trading roads and shipping routes. If the location was favorable, artisans and merchants settled in the protective shadow of the castle mountain, and not a few cities began this way. In the historical sources we seldom hear of the economic development of a region by castles. The Cologne *Königschronik* speaks once of a castle of the crusaders in Palestine: "The castle, moreover, possesses a good port, well-stocked fisheries, salt mines, forests, pastures, and fertile fields."[62] In general the poets, too, showed little interest in the economic aspects of castle building. But there is one poetic castle description from the end of the thirteenth century—in the religious work *Der Saelden Hort*—that does emphasize the economic side. Castle Magdalun—symbolic for Mary Magdalen—was an idealized structure, but in many details it took account of the needs of economic life. It was situated "on top of a rock where four roads met that were dominated by the mountain."[63] A navigable river flowed around the castle, crossed by a stone-bridge with "vaulted arches."[64] The bridge was protected by strong bridge towers, and over it rolled "many carts and wagons fully loaded."[65] Thanks to "old privileges, dues, and tolls,"[66] the castle took in substantial revenues from this economic traffic. To this was added the income from the forests and fields within the castle's jurisdiction. All people within a radius of ten miles owed dues. At the foot of the castle mountain was a settlement "which derived great benefit from the fact that a strong, navigable river flowed there."[67] The castle was so well fortified that a siege was no great threat. "Everything that a mighty prince and his court need is found there."[68] At the top of the mountain ran a stream abounding in fish, "which allowed one to wash, bake, and grind corn there."[69] The water from several springs was gathered on the mountain into a great pond, which was "so well stocked with fish that one could serve a fish dish every day."[70] The forest and the heath belonging to the castle were unusually rich in animals: there were "squirrels, foxes, rabbits, hares, martens, wild boars,"[71] and also "stags, deer, does, fallow deer,"[72] "hawks, falcons, sparrow hawks,"[73] "partridges and pheasants."[74] Cotton and sheepwool were worked into good cloth. "There also grows the material for women's work: long hemp and soft flax."[75] Honey and wax were supplied by the bees. On one side of the mountain was a crevice, and "there flowed a spring from which salt was boiled."[76] In addition there were meadows, fields, and vineyards that bore rich yields. An especially detailed description is given of the herb garden, where the ladies helped themselves "if they wanted to treat or bathe themselves or their friends,"[77] and "where the apothecary's assistants met frequently to pick herbs, dig for roots, and gather the ingredients for potions."[78] The lovely environs of the castle offered the noble residents many opportunities for recreation: one could take a stroll or organize athletic competitions; "one sees also deer hunting and hawking from the mountain down into the valley."[79] Mining was also done at Magdalun, and the ore was smelted into precious metals. There was a place for washing gold and a tile kiln, and "as a result the houses there were covered only with fired tiles"[80] that shone far into the land. In this description the castle was the center of a harmoniously organized economic system which comprised all important branches of production and trade.

Castles and palaces were particularly important for the use and administration of the forests and game preserves. Political historians have long recognized the great significance of the game preserves for the consolidation of territories. The connection between palace and royal forest emerges especially clearly in Emperor Frederick I's new foundations. The Alsatian palace in Hagenau was at the center of the Sacred Forest; the palace at Kaiserslautern was built inside the royal forest of Lutra; and the palace at Gelnhausen was part of the imperial forest of Büdingen. Apart from the economic exploitation through land clearing and the use of wood, hunting within the forests was of great importance. The enforcement of the lord's hunting privilege had not only an economic motive, but was also an attribute of a noble lifestyle. How important this was is revealed by Rahewin's description of the palace at Kaiserslautern: "In Kaiserslautern he [Frederick I] built a royal palace of red stone and adorned it quite lavishly. On one side he surrounded it with a very strong wall, the other side is enclosed by a lake-like fishpond, which contains for the delectation of the eyes and the palate all delicacies of fish and fowl. An adjoining park offers nourishment to a wealth of stags and deer. The royal splendor of all these things and their abundance, which is greater than one could describe, strikes all who see it with amazement."[81] Such animal parks were also found in France and Sicily. They served not only to satisfy the love of hunting, but were also part of the courtly pomp. All the courtly poets picked up on this motif. A nice example is the hunting lodge Penefrec in Hartmann von Aue's *Erec*. The house stood in the middle of a lake rich in fish. At a radius of two miles the forest was enclosed by a wall, and this walled-in preserve was subdivided again by walls into three sections, one for deer, one for wild boar, and one for smaller animals, foxes and rabbits. "These hunting grounds were richly stocked, so that nobody who loved to hunt could complain that he could not find any game. The lord of the castle had also furnished the hunting lodge with trained dogs."[82] From the ramparts of the castle one could watch the dogs chase the quarry to the lake, where it was killed. Hartmann von Aue described these splendid grounds without any prompting from his French source. He was probably inspired by reality. The palace built by Frederick I in Seligenstadt (on the Main river) also seems to have been a hunting castle. From there one could go hunting in the royal forest of Dreieich, and fish could be caught in the Main.

LUXURIOUS TENTS

Castles were not the only feudal living quarters. When great lords were on the road and could not expect to find lodging with friendly peers every day, they lived in tents. These portable dwellings were used during military campaigns, on pilgrimages, at tournaments, and for the journey to the great assemblies of the princes. In 1184 the count of Hainaut brought his own tents to the court feast at Mainz, and his chancellor Gislebert of Mons acknowledged that he had "more tents and more beautiful tents than the other princes."[83]

Starting with Heinrich von Veldeke's *Eneit*, descriptions of tents are part of courtly epic, and they show that the tents were seen as mobile castles. Aeneas's tent, a gift of Queen Dido, stood visible from afar "as though it were a tower. Twenty pack animals could not transport it."[84] Isenhart's tent was designed "like a palas."[85] The tent that Schionatulander brought as a gift for his lover had "palas, towers, walls all crenelated."[86] In *Wigamur* we hear of a tent "that had twelve beautiful rooms in it."[87] The roof of the tent (the *huot*) and the side walls (the *winde*) were sometimes fashioned from precious oriental silkstuffs and were decorated with the coat of arms of the lord or with figurative scenes.

> The wall of the tent was made of four sections; it was high and broad. One section was of samite, green as grass. Pictures were affixed to it with great artistry. This samite was of better quality than all the silkstuffs of Greece. The second section consisted of rich brown triblât silk, and worked onto it in masterful fashion were scenes of birds and wild animals. The tent could withstand any weather. Of gold was the seam where the samite and triblât

were sewn together. I am telling you the truth: the third side was of red baragân. It shone from afar on the green meadow. Whoever was fortunate enough to enter this tent experienced the greatest joy. Truly, one must say it was an earthly paradise. The fourth side was made of white sea grass.[88]

The description of this tent, a gift from the sea fairy, takes up many more verses.

The terminology also reveals that tents were considered a part of the luxuries of the nobility. Next to the generic terms *zelt*, *gezelt*, only one other German word for tent existed, and it was used for the smaller, canonical tents used by servants and simple warriors: *hütte*. The great luxury tents were usually described with the French words *pavilün*, *poulûn*, first attested in Hartmann's *Erec*. In *Willehalm* we find the words *preimerûn*, *ekub*, *treif*, and *tulant*, which were all borrowed from French (*tulant* is still unexplained).

Luxury pavilions with unbelievably splendid decorations did in fact exist. In 1157 King Henry II of England sent to Emperor Frederick I, together with other gifts, "a huge, magnificent tent. If you inquire about its size: it could be lifted only with machines and tools of every kind and with poles; if you inquire what it was made of: I believe that neither in material nor in workmanship could it ever be surpassed by any structure of its kind."[89] Gunther of Paris supplements Rahewins's account of "this tent worth seeing for its splendid decoration"[90] with additional details: "You ask about the material? It is said to have been of a fabric made of foreign threads. Was it a work of art? They say it carried magnificent pictures."[91] The tent given as a gift to Emperor Frederick I by the queen of Hungary in 1189 attracted just as much attention. Arnold of Lübeck described it: "A very beautiful tent, and on top of it a tent dome of scarlet cloth, and wall hangings equal to the height and length of the roof."[92] This "artistically wrought tent, which three carts could barely move,"[93] is also mentioned in the Cologne *Königschronik*.

The most splendid tents were found in Byzantium and the East. When Henry the Lion visited the emperor in Byzantium in 1171 during his journey to the Holy Land, the Germans saw there "innumerable tents of fine, purple linen, with golden domes, and decorated differently in accordance with the different ranks."[94] They also came upon "a golden tent that glittered from top to bottom with jewels and precious stones."[95] The sultan of Babylon gave Frederick II a particularly beautiful tent as a gift in 1232. It was "a tent fashioned with wondrous artistry, in which the images of the sun and the moon, made to move in artful fashion, ran their course in a determined and correct time and indicated unerringly the hours of the day and night. The value of the tent is said to have exceeded the price of twenty thousand marks."[96] An artificial sky was also part of the luxurious pavilion of King Agrant in *Wilhelm von Österreich*: "Ah, with what splendor the ceiling had been decorated! The story says that the planets Luna, Mercurius, Venus, Sol, Mars, Jupiter, and Saturnus could be seen there in wondrous fashion. At such splendor the heart rejoices greatly. They were affixed in a circular course, and the revolution of the stars was sewn into the sky."[97] How highly Frederick II prized the gift of the sultan is revealed by the fact that the tent was placed into "the royal treasure."[98]

2. CLOTHES AND CLOTH

DRESS CODES

Clothes have always been an attribute of social rank. In the twelfth century, however, they played a special role in shaping the outward appearance of aristocratic society. We find this reflected in an idea propagated by the courtly poets, namely that the exclusivity of noble dress was, or at least should be, guaranteed by laws. In support of this idea the poets invoked the emperor as the highest juridical authority in worldly matters. As early as 1150, the *Kaiserchronik* cites legislation supposedly promulgated by Charlemagne after he had been crowned emperor. It forbade the peasants the wearing of elegant clothes:

> Then he straightaway passed regulations concerning the dress of the peasants. The pope approved them. Now I will tell you what a peasant was allowed to wear according to the law: black or gray, nothing else did the emperor permit. Gores only on the sides, that is appropriate to his social standing, and shoes made only of cowleather and nothing else. Seven ells of cloth for shirt and pants, of rough material. If he wears gores in the back or in front he has violated his social rank.[1]

The gores (*gêren*) on the sides were meant to allow the peasant freedom of movement while working. In front or in back, on the other hand, the extravagant inserts were necessary in the wide frocks worn by noble society. The *Limburger Chronik* (fourteenth century) knew of "skirts with twenty-four or thirty gores."[2] A peasant's frock should have no more than four *gêren*. In Carinthia it was customary that the new duke, before receiving the homage of the lords, appear on the toll field at Klagenfurt dressed in peasant's clothes. On this occasion he was to wear gray pants and a skirt of the same material "with four gores and no more."[3]

The idea that Charlemagne had regulated what the peasants could wear also found its way into Neidhart's songs. In *Winterlied* no. 36, the peasants are warned that their hair will be cut when the emperor shows up. That was meant especially for the peasant Gätzemann, who wore "his long, curly blond hair"[4] like a nobleman. "He and his dancing companions should be told to wear their hair and clothes—following the old traditions—the way it was customary at the time of King Charlemagne."[5] *Seifried Helbling* (around 1300) traced the dress prohibitions for peasants back to ancient Austrian law: "When the law was made for the land, the peasant was permitted only gray, homemade loden, and on feast days good, blue woolcloth; other colors were not permitted to him or his wife. She is now wearing green, brown, and red fabrics from Ghent."[6] Nearly everywhere the discriminatory regulations against the peasants were accompanied by complaints that they were violating them. Heinrich von Melk (end of the twelfth century) expressed outrage that even a woman day-laborer was not content "unless she made her dress so long that the train dragging behind stirred up the dust wherever she went."[7]

These poetic passages could be interpreted to mean that the noble audience at court was interested in protecting its privileges of dress. But actual prohibitions do not seem to have existed before the mid-thirteenth century. In scholarly works on the history of costume we often find the unverifiable claim that King Philip II Augustus of France had published a first code of this kind as early as 1180. The truth is that in 1188, before setting out for the crusade, the French king and Henry II of England drew up a military code, which among other things prohibited the crusaders from wearing costly fabrics and furs during the expedition: "Nobody shall wear colored cloth, gray cloth, squirrel fur, sable, or purple cloth."[8] The first dress code whose exact wording has survived comes from Spain. In the year 1258 King Alfonso X of Castile (d. 1248)—a great friend of the arts and sciences—promulgated an extensive military code. It contained very precise regulations concerning the dress of courtly society, with the aim of restraining the nobility's extravagance while also protecting its right to wear elegant clothes. The most important provisions read:

No nobleman, no knight, nor anyone else shall have more than four sets of new clothes a year. And these clothes shall not be of ermine or nutria, nor of silk or gold or silver fur, they shall have neither long laces nor embroidery, no golden trim, nor sashes, no ornamental hem nor any other decoration. Rather, they shall be made of fur or cloth. One may not wear one suit on top of another. Nobody but the king may wear a purple cape. Everybody shall receive a fur cloak only twice a year, and the cape shall be worn for two years. Nobody except the king or a nobleman may wear light taffeta or silk, except when used for lining. Nobody shall wear costly furs except the king, a nobleman, or a groom, provided he is a nobleman or the son of a nobleman. No nobleman or anybody else may wear a cape of silver fur with precious stones, buttons, long laces, ermine or nutria (except on the trim of the fur coat), and no nobleman shall wear a *tabardo* mantle at court.[9]

The first French dress code dates from the year 1279 and was promulgated by King Philip III (d. 1285). In it, "it is decreed that nobody, no duke, no count, no prelate, no baron, and nobody else, cleric or layman, may own or have made more than four pairs of fur robes a year."[10] Only the most noble could have five robes per year, the smaller lords only two or three; and the burghers were not allowed to have fur unless their total wealth exceeded one thousand pounds. This code must have attracted great attention at that time, and it became known in Germany as well. The annals of Colmar speak of it under the year 1279, but the emphasis is shifted: "The King of France decreed for his entire realm that no peasant, no matter how rich, may wear knight's clothes."[11] The law of Philip III had not mentioned the peasants at all. It seems that in Germany, where laws against the sartorial pomp of the nobility and the rich burghers are known only from later times, one could conceive only of dress prohibitions directed againt the peasantry. The sole German dress code from the thirteenth century is concerned only with peasants, and in this it shows a remarkable similarity to the poetic texts. The Territorial Peace of Bavaria of 1244 decreed in article 71 (*De rusticis*, "Concerning the Peasants"): "Moreover, they shall wear no clothes more elegant than gray and the cheaper kind of blue, and shoes only of cowleather."[12] How effective such prohibitions were is difficult to judge.

THE SOURCES FOR THE HISTORY OF COSTUME

The actual appearance of clothes during the courtly age must be reconstructed from secondary sources, since virtually nothing has remained of the secular dress of the High Middle Ages, except for a few fragments of cloth and some precious items of ceremonial vestments, like the so-called mantle of Charlemagne in Metz or the imperial robes in the treasury in Vienna. Historians of costume therefore rely for this period heavily on pictorial evidence and literary texts. But so far the results of scholarship have not been very satisfying. We know what the individual pieces of clothing looked like, but there are confusing and contradictory notions about the general lines of development. The reason for this is largely because most works on costume examine only part of the existing evidence and reveal an alarming deficiency of critical evaluation. Not many studies on costume can match the high level of scholarship in Germain Demay's book (*Le costume du moyen âge d'après les sceaux*) from the year 1880, in which he examined the French seals of the High Middle Ages for the history of courtly fashion. Among German works only those of Paul Post deserve mention. Above all there is a lack of comparative studies concerning the evidentiary value of pictorial and literary texts.

Courtly literature offers an almost overwhelming wealth of information on the fashionable dress of noble society. We get the impression that the poets possessed specialized knowledge about textile working and tailoring, and that such knowledge was in fact expected of them. It is rare that a poet declines to provide precise information about clothes: "What her skirt looked like? You better ask her chamberlain. God knows, I didn't see it."[13] This deflating of the audience's curiosity was only a rhetorical game, for Hartmann had earlier described the lady's dress in detail.

In describing clothes the poets used a highly differentiated and specialized terminology of textiles and costume, and it appears that the audience wanted and understood it. There were special terms for individual clothes and parts of clothes, such as *kurzebolt* "overgarment," *liste* "hem," *mouwe* "sleeve," *pheit* "shirt," *rîse* "veil," *schürlitz* "undershirt," *stüche* "sleeve," *underzoc* "lining," and so on. We also find a specialized vocabulary for the fashionable working and ornamenting of the fabrics and robes: *bestellen* "to hem," *braemen* "to trim with fur," *durchlegen* "to ornament," *krispen* "to crimp," *lenken* "to pleat," *ricken* "to trim," *rîhen* "to thread," *schraemen* "to chamfer," *schrôten* "to cut to measure," *spengen* "to fit with buckles," *undersnîden* "to put together in a colorful pattern," *verwieren* "to interweave with something," *zerhouwen* "to slit open," and so on. And the poets repeatedly emphasized that the modern cut of the clothes followed French custom: "cut in the French fashion,"[14] "a cut in the French style,"[15] "in the French cut."[16]

To what degree the imitation of French fashion actually shaped the dress of the nobility in Germany is difficult to demonstrate, since the process of adoption in the area of clothes cannot be proven through historical evidence. From the pictorial and literary sources, however, we can deduce that noble fashion in both countries followed essentially the same lines; and the chronological clues that we can gather from the dating of manuscripts, seals, and texts, indicate that France led the development. The extent of French influence in fashion is documented by the numerous loan words. In the older texts of the twelfth century we already find French words for individual items of clothing (*bonît* "cap" (?) in *König Rother, suckenei* "wrap" in *Graf Rudolf, vaele* "mantle" in *Himmelreich*), and several terms for silk borrowed from the French (*samît* and *sigelât* in *König Rother, zendâl* in *Graf Rudolf*). Later many more words for clothes were added: *blîât* "silkcloth" or "silkdress," *garnasch* "outer garment," *jope* "jacket," *kolze* "stocking," *kursît* "fur coat," *schapel* "garland," *schaperûn* "hood," *stival* "boot," *surkôt* "surcoat," *taphart* "wrap," *tassel* "clasp," and so on; and especially words for the fashionable working of the cloth: *ridieren* "to pleat," *fischieren* "to pin," *flottieren* "to serrate," *franzen* "to fold," *furrieren* "to line."

PRECIOUS FABRICS

The precious fabrics used in tailoring clothes attracted just as much attention as the clothes themselves. Most highly prized were Oriental silks. For silk one used the words *side* from Latin *saeta*, and *phellel* from French *paile*. In addition there existed many special terms for silk. For the coronation feast of King Wenzel II of Bohemia in the year 1297, one procured from afar "silkcloth: *zendal* and *baldekîn, samît* and *siglât, phellel* and *blîât*."[17] For his court feast, King Arthur received "brocades of different colors from Greece, purple cloth and *timît, paile, rôsât, siglât, diasper* and *tribelât, blîat,* interwoven with gold, and various other silkcloths, from which clothes were cut to dress the knights and decorate the halls."[18] Whether every one of these words actually meant something must remain unclear. Most were borrowed from French (*baldekîn, blîât, diasper, samît, siglât, zindâl*), some from Latin. Many of these terms for cloth can also be attested in nonpoetic texts.

To indicate the oriental provenance of their silks, the poets often mentioned where they came from. Wolfram von Eschenbach was very creative in inventing fantastic sounding oriental places: he has silk from Ipopotiticôn (*Parzival* 687.9), from Thopedissimonte (*Parzival* 736.15), from Ganfassâsche (*Willehalm* 63.17). In general, though, the writers used places of origin that can be historically verified. Arabia was mentioned most frequently, along with Persia, Syria, Morocco, Libya, and various cities: Alexandria, Baghdad, Ninive, and Almeria in Spain. The importance of Greece in silkweaving and the silk trade was also emphasized by the poets ("one of the best purple fabrics ever woven in Greece"[19]). When Henry the Lion stopped off in Constantinople in 1172 on his pilgrimage to Jerusalem, the Byzantine empress gave him "so many brocades that he could clothe all his knights in silk."[20] On his journey home he received from the Turkish sultan, among other gifts, "a mantle and a surcoat of the finest silk."[21] These pieces were so precious that the duke had a cape and a chasuble made from them. In 1195 Emperor Henry Vl had the Sicilian royal treasure brought to Germany. It included "many very valuable silk cloths,"[22] which probably came from the Sicilian silk manufacture that King Roger II (d. 1154) had set up in Palermo, and which produced primarily for the court. Other silks were brought back by the crusaders as booty. The Cologne *Königschronik* reports for the year 1190 that citizens of Cologne had seized "clothes and mantles and other precious objects"[23] on a crusade in Spain. When Constantinople was taken in 1204, the crusaders found there—as Count Baldwin of Flanders wrote to the archbishop of Cologne—an immense wealth of "gold and silver, silkcloths, precious clothes and gems."[24] The assault on Damietta in 1219 also yielded to the Christians "a great amount of gold and silver, an abundance of silk cloths from the merchants, and vast quantities of costly clothes and worldly ornaments with a variety of household goods."[25]

How highly sought-after precious silks were in noble society is revealed by an episode in Heinrich von Veldeke's *Servatius*. One day, as the wife of Count Giesebrecht was viewing the church treasure at Maastricht, a very un-Christian desire overtook her at the sight of a silk cloth:

> When she viewed the treasure a desire took control of her, on account of the precious and beautiful silk she saw lying there in the treasury. She wanted to have it. It was a great sin that she stole the silk. Secretly she took it with her. It was bad enough that she had such a thought in the first place. When the noble duchess had brought the cloth home, she had it artfully cut and tailored; for it was very costly silk. That is why she had the seams sewn with gold thread. One could not blame her if she had acquired the cloth rightfully."[26]

But when the duchess wore the festive dress to church, the saint punished her harshly for her misdeed.

Fine woolens were also highly esteemed by the court audience, especially the colorful scarlet that came in red, blue, or brown, and *brûnat*, *fritschâl*, *schürbrant*, *stampfart*, and others. Distinctions of quality among woolens depended on where they had been made. The most valuable came from England and Flanders. Among the famous Flemish textile cities, the German poets most frequently mention Ghent, Ypres, and Arras.[27] Even in Austria the beautiful Flemish woolens were very popular: "The clothes of the knights and the squires had to come from the Rhine, from Ypres or Ghent."[28] The wool terminology of the courtly poets mirrored economic reality quite accurately, as we can see from the Viennese cart toll (before 1221), which regulated the size of cloth-loads subject to toll: "Ten pieces of cloth from Ghent are a load. Eight pieces of scarlet are a load. Twelve pieces of cloth from Ypres are a load. Sixteen pieces from Huy are a load. Ten pieces *stampfart* from Arras are a load."[29] And in the account books of the count of Tyrol the precious woolens are also named after Flemish cities: "cloths from Ghent" and "cloths from Ypres."[30]

SARTORIAL EXTRAVAGANCE

Noble society of the twelfth and thirteenth centuries displayed a pomp in clothing that had been unknown before. The most noticeable features of aristocratic dress were the colorfulness of the precious fabrics and the wealth of jewelry and decoration. Gold, pearls, and gems were used to ornament the clothes, sometimes to such excess that "they were dripping from top to bottom with gold."[31] Gold platelets were sewn onto the cloth and the clothes were decorated with ornamental buttons of precious material. Net-like strings of pearls covered the dresses, and special attention was paid to decorating the finely woven braids—used in trimming seams—with pearls and gems. Asked by her brother to prepare clothes for his courtship of Brunhilde, Kriemhild answered: "I have silk of my own. Now get your men to bring us jewels by the shield-ful, and we shall sew your clothes."[32]

While the peasants were told they could wear only gray-blue and black stuff, noble dress radiated in all colors. "Over the body of a knight a colorful robe is fitting,"[33] it is later said in the *Ritterspiegel* of Johannes Rothe (beginning of the fifteenth century). Clerics had been prohibited from wearing colored robes as early as the thirteenth century. A council in Cologne in 1281 decreed: "They may not wear red and green fabrics, decorative sleeves, and laced shoes."[34] The existing large sculptures give hardly a hint of the rich colors of courtly dress. In this respect the colorful miniatures are the richest pictorial source. They agree with the descriptions of the poets. "White, red, yellow, green, black, grey, and blue was her splendid appearance."[35] The dress of the beautiful Amorfina glittered "like a peacock."[36] "Peacock-dresses"[37] were worn by Kriemhild's ladies-in-waiting. The descriptions of clothes often aimed at creating surprising effects of color. Engeltrud wore her mantle of red scarlet such that the lining would shine forth now white, now blue (K. v. Würzburg, *Engelhard* 3098, ff.). Irekel's mantle was "checkered like a chessboard,"[38] made up of small squares of white ermine and black sable. Florie "wore a wide robe made of two kinds of silkcloth, evenly, carefully and splendidly cut. One cloth was green as grass, the other was red, nicely decorated with gold."[39] Apparently the dress was half green and half red. The beginnings of this "mi-parti" fashion can be traced back to the eleventh century. "Gowns cut parti-wise"[40] were also worn by the noble grail maidens at Munsalvaesche: "It was half cloth-of-gold, half silk from Ninive."[41] The color division could run vertical or horizontal, as is shown by the pictorial representations, which, however, appear with growing frequency only from the end of the thirteenth century.

Our historical sources give us little concrete information about the luxurious clothes of the courtly age. Only in exceptional cases did the historians think it appropriate to discuss the splendor of noble dress in any detail. From Caesarius of Heisterbach we learn that shortly before Archbishop Engelbert of Cologne was murdered in 1225, he had exquisite ceremonial vestments made, "of purple cloth and the finest linen, with gold fringes and gold platelets, pearls and gems."[42] The available evidence begins to increase only from the late thirteenth century on. Famous for his sartorial pomp was King Ottokar II of Bohemia (d. 1278), who came to his meeting with King Rudolf of Hapsburg "wearing gilded robes decorated with jewels,"[43] and who also bestowed gifts of sumptuous clothes on his vassals. An obituary notice at his death said: "You nobles of the realm, in the sadness of your hearts mourn your king who dressed you in scarlet and gave you golden ornaments for your clothes, you who were wrapped in the most precious and luxurious garments, from whose purple-colored trim hung glittering fringes."[44] Ottokar of Styria reports on the preparations for the wedding of King Albrecht I (d. 1308) and Elisabeth, the daughter of

Count Meinhard II of Görz-Tyrol, in the year 1298: pack animals laden
with gold and silver were sent to Venice to purchase jewelry, gems, furs,
and precious cloth. Among the latter were "the finest clothes of gold
cloth"[45] from the East. "In addition, colored cloth, ermine and gray
cloth were purchased: many bails were loaded up."[46] "All those,
women and men, who at that time were greatly skilled in threading,
sewing, stitching, or knotting animal shapes onto women's clothes with
pearls and white rubies, were richly rewarded."[47] The account books of
the counts of Tyrol reveal that the festive dresses of the ladies were in
fact studded with thousands of pearls and stones: "To make the dress of
the lady duchess," a larger sum of money was charged on April 16th,
1300, "for 6,000 gilded pearls, 6,000 corals, 3 strands of varicolored
pearls, 5 ounces of white pearls and 6 silken cloths."[48]

THE COURTLY CEREMONY OF DRESS

Clothes were also a sign of lordship, especially the mantle, which constituted an important part of the royal insignia. Several precious examples have been preserved, among them the star-mantle of Emperor Henry
II (d. 1024) in the cathedral of Bamberg. It is nearly three meters in
diameter and made of purple silk, with the orb and the signs of the
zodiac embroidered onto it. A similar star-mantle was described in
Wigalois: "The noble maid had wrapped herself in very courtly fashion
in a wide and long mantle beautifully decorated with gold platelets and
trimmed with ermine as suited her taste. Stitched onto it were the moon
and stars, cut from blue seal fur that was brought from Ireland."[49] The
mantle was also a badge of judicial honor and authority. In the *Sachsenspiegel* we read: "When court is held at the royal ban, neither the lay
assessors nor the judges shall wear hoods or hats or small caps or bonnets, or gloves. They shall wear mantles about their shoulders."[50] If a
lord took a suppliant under his mantle, this gesture had the force of law.
In the *Rolandslied* we hear how the pagan Queen Brechmunde sought
refuge with the great King Baligan after her husband had been defeated
and injured: "Baligan took her under his mantle; he consoled the
queen."[51] In courtly poetry the motive of the protective mantle was
given a specific courtly twist: here it was most often a lady of high rank
who took a man in need of protection or consolation under her mantle.
After the tournament of Kanvoleiz, Queen Herzeloyde placed the fringe
of her mantle around her cousin Kaylet when she came to check on his
wounds (W. v. Eschenbach, *Parzival* 88.9). When Gyburg found Renne-

wart in distress, "she wrapped a part of her mantle around him"[52] to comfort him. A special meaning was attached to this gesture when it was part of a minne scene. "The beautiful queen received the good, noble count with great joy. She pressed him to her breast and kissed him lovingly. She took him under her mantle."[53] "She opened her small mantle and received him under it."[54]

Clothes played a very important role in the courtly ceremonies of greeting and hospitality. Where a noble knight was hospitably received, the presentation of clothes prepared especially for him was part of the protocol of reception. The poets infused this motif with a significance that far exceeded the practical demands of hospitality. When Gahmuret arrived in the royal city of Zazamanc, the clothes for his reception were, as a special honor, quickly embroidered with his coat of arms (W. v. Eschenbach, *Parzival* 22.30 ff.). At great court feasts it was customary to present the guests with farewell gifts of clothes or precious cloth. Wilhelm von Wenden was especially generous to the nobleman of his land, whom he had invited to the court to celebrate his departure: "To all noblemen he sent three kinds of costly cloth: uncut red scarlet and two finely woven silkcloths beautifully interlaced with gold."[55] After his victory over Milan in 1160, Emperor Frederick I dismissed his army and presented to the princes and leaders precious gifts, among them "exquisite garments."[56]

Gifts of clothes also played a role in the courtly ceremony of knighting (see p. 245) and in diplomatic relations. In 1135 the Greek emperor sent to Lothar III, in addition to gold and gems, "purple clothes of different colors, and a great quantity of spices previously unknown in this country."[57] The king of Bohemia received from Byzantium in 1164 "valuable mantles of different types and garments of fabulous workmanship, decorated with gold and gems."[58]

Other ceremonial forms involving clothes are referred to only in literature. No greater joy could come to a knight engaged in minne service than to receive a piece of clothing from the lady for whom he was fighting. At the tournaments Gahmuret attended while married to Herzeloyde, he wore over his hauberk "a white silken shift of the queen's, as it came from her naked body."[59] In this way he used up no less than eighteen shifts, and his wife subsequently wore them again as a sign of her love. Amelie handed over to her friend a brooch with the words: "Now take from me this brooch, my friend and my beloved. It has lain on my naked skin."[60] It was always of prime importance that the love token had touched the lady's body. No piece of women's clothing was used as a token more often than the sleeve. The overlong sleeves, one of the most conspicuous innovations in women's dress, were apparently seen as a particularly powerful erotic symbol. This motif plays an important role in the story of Gawan and little Obilot, who desperately wanted to send her knight a token of her favor. Her father, Prince Lippaut, quickly had a new dress made for her of oriental gold brocade. The detachable right sleeve was simply slipped on by Obilot—"it had touched her right arm"[61] and then taken off and handed over to Gawan, who nailed it to one of his shields and won victory with it. Later he returned the hackedup sleeve to his lady: "At this the maid was overjoyed. Her right arm was white and bare, and she quickly fastened it over."[62] A touch of parody informs the account of Ulrich von Liechtenstein, who dressed up as Lady Venus and rode through the land from tournament to tournament: "I had women's clothes cut for myself. Twelve dresses were made for me and thirty beautiful women's sleeves attached to fine shirts, as was my wish."[63]

For courtly society, splendid clothes expressed self-confidence and a feeling of social elation that was described with the Middle High German word *vreude*. Walther von der Vogelweide saw the decay of courtly *vreude* reflected in the abandoning of courtly dress: "Wheresoever I turn, nobody is cheerful any more. Dancing and singing are overcome by worries. Never before has a Christian seen such a miserable bunch. Just look how the ladies are wearing their headdresses! The proud knights are wearing peasant clothes."[64]

THE BEGINNINGS OF COURTLY FASHION

In looking back to the period at the beginning of the twelfth century, the Norman monk Ordericus Vitalis wrote around 1140 that in those days French youth had changed its looks radically. Young men and women of the nobility let their hair grow in long curls, they wore shoes with very long turned up toes, and dressed altogether in a newfangled fashion. "They considered it beautiful to dress in long-flowing and very tight shirts and robes."[65] Two details of the new fashion were particularly conspicuous: the long trains and the draping sleeves. "They swept the dusty floor with the overlong trains of their shirts and mantles. In everything they do they cover their hands with long, wide sleeves."[66] What Ordericus Vitalis saw as signs of the decay of the good old manners, and for which he blamed the deleterious influence of "womanish effeminacy" ("the frivolous youth embraces womanish effeminacy"[67]), was the beginning of courtly fashion that would shortly conquer all of Europe. In contrast to the sacklike clothes that had been standard since the Carolingian period, courtly fashion brought something completely new. People began to cut clothes to measure, and it was only this tailoring that made possible the characteristic narrowing of the top down to the waist. The cut was a French invention; its aim was to emphasize the human figure, and this gave clothes a new meaning and importance.

As a result of tailoring dress to fit the body's shape, men's and women's clothes were now more distinct than before. As Ordericus Vitalis had already correctly understood, it was the style of women's clothes that came to determine courtly fashion. In any case, the most striking innovations in fashion occur in women's garments. This aspect has not been sufficiently appreciated in the existing works on costume. The prevailing notion that there were no significant differences between women's and men's clothes in the twelfth and thirteenth centuries is based largely on misunderstood literary evidence. In courtly poetry we hear occasionally that women's garments were also worn by men. Tandareis, for example, was supplied by Antonie with her own clothes after his had been taken from him: "The maid gave the knight her mantle and her wrap to wear."[68] A similar thing happened to Wigalois, who had been robbed of his armor and clothes while he was unconscious, and therefore had to meet Countess Beleare stark naked: "Right away she took off her fur coat, it was of beautiful squirrel fur, and had it handed to the knight. He immediately covered himself with it."[69] In *Parzival* we are told that Duke Orilus's wife Jeschute had to wear torn clothes since she was under the suspicion of having committed adultery. But when her innocence was made clear, the duke draped his surcoat (*kursît*) around her (270.11 ff.). Such exchanges of clothing always involved only mantles and loose overgarments, which were cut so generously that they could be worn by both men and women. Even in pictorial representations men and women are sometimes hard to tell apart when they are wrapped in wide mantles.

How the innovations in courtly fashion spread in the twelfth century and came to be widely adopted has not yet been sufficiently studied. Large-scale secular sculptures are especially informative for the developments in France. The famous figures on the west portal of Chartres are an outstanding source, since the master of Chartres has reproduced the details of courtly dress with great accuracy. As for Germany, no attempt has yet been made to document the adoption of

French dress with the help of dated pictorial works and texts. The poets who worked from French models after 1170 were already familiar with the essential characteristics of courtly fashion.

WOMEN'S CLOTHES

In the Old French *Roman d'Eneas* we find a description of the dress that Queen Dido wore when she rode out hunting with Aeneas: "The queen had put on a costly purple-red robe that was wonderfully interwoven with gold thread along the entire body down to the waist and all around the sleeves. She was wearing a costly mantle exquisitely sprinkled with gold. Her hair was decorated with gold thread, and her head was wreathed with a golden braid."[70] In the German adaptation by Heinrich von Veldeke, the description of Dido's dress is five times as long:

> Her shirt was of exquisite cloth, white and artfully sewn. A lot of gold filament was on it. It was laced tightly to her body; she was a shapely woman as beautiful as could be. The fur trim on her shirt was of ermine, white and very costly. The neck-pieces were as red as blood. The sleeves were no wider than was proper. Over the shirt she wore a green silk dress that was perfectly fitted to her body. She would have been very reluctant to do without it. The dress was nicely ornamented and very richly decorated with pearls and braids. It suited her very well, the way she had put it on. To gird herself she used a precious belt fitted with silver and gold as she wanted. Her mantle was of silk, green as grass. The fur lining of white ermine could not have been more exquisite; the sable at the edge was brown and wide."[71]

After Veldeke, descriptions of this kind were standard elements of the style of courtly epic. The poets were concerned primarily with the fashionable style of a woman's dress, which was laced tightly to the body (buttons were at this time used only as decoration since the button hole had not yet been invented). There was a separate vocabulary for lacing up a dress and squeezing in the body: *besten, brîsen, spannen, twengen, fischieren,* and so on. "Her shirt was of silk: she was laced into it."[72] "The lovely woman had laced a shirt very tightly to her body."[73] "Her body had been laced into it with gold laces at the sides."[74] "With her own hands she laced the maid into a shirt."[75] "Her dress had been nicely tailored to her lovely body."[76] "The dress clung closely to her body and was nowhere worn out."[77] If the clothes were cut rather loosely, a belt was used to emphasize the waist. "Her dress was beautifully decorated and nicely belted to her body, as shapely French women are wont to do."[78] Both styles of women's dresses are

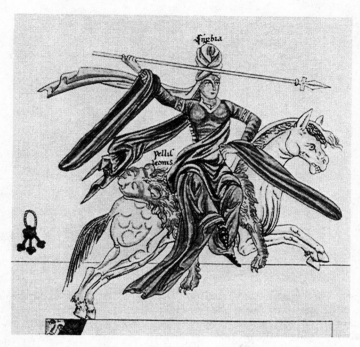

Fig. 8.   Superbia. Fashionable dress with hanging sleeves and train. The upper part down to the waist fits very tightly; the lacing is visible on the right side of her body. From the *Hortus deliciarum* of Herrad of Landsberg. End of the twelfth century.

also well documented in pictorial sources. In the miniatures to the *Hortus deliciarum* of Herrad von Landsberg we can even make out the lacing at the sides (see fig. 8).

A tightly cut top was usually joined to a wide, richly pleated skirt which fell down over the feet. Meliur's dress "clung tightly to her and was taut over her arms and chest. Below it was—for joy!—cut so wide that many folds lay about her feet."[79] This style is best illustrated in the miniatures of the Munich ms. Clm 2599 from the monastery of Aldersbach, in which the Liberal Arts are allegorically depicted as women. Grammatica wears a dress that is laced so tightly on top that the laces stick out like ribs, while below the hips rich casts of folds fall down (see fig. 9). This contrast was brought out most strikingly by Konrad von Würzburg in the later thirteenth century: "The beautiful lady wore a shirt of silk on her body; no more perfectly tailored garment a woman

Fig. 9. Grammatica and Priscianus. Woman's dress with decorative sleeves and train. Above the waist the dress is laced so tightly that the laces stick out like ribs. From a Munich manuscript (Clm 2599) from the monastery of Aldersbach. Beginning of the thirteenth century.

ever wore. It was so delicate, as I have heard, that one could see her skin—it was like a flowering plant—shining through. Her body was laced into the shirt with gold strings on the side. One could see her lovely breasts standing out delicately from under the dress like two apples."[80] Next, Konrad described the precious brooch that held the neckline together, and the broad gem-studded braid across the chest. Then he turned to the lower portion of the dress: "The dress fell to the ground in beautiful folds. The folds were shaped this way and that. Down around the feet one could see them arranged very artistically every which way. They formed strange arches, upwards and downwards. Some fell nicely down, others arched up; some formed hollows like a carved image, others were flat. They ran straight and even, and then intertwined this way and that."[81] The attention then shifted once again back to the top: "The shirt was tailored after an unusual cut and clung so tightly to her splendid body that one could have sworn the lovely lady was entirely naked and bare above the belt."[82] Finally the train was described: "But on account of this the train did not lose any of its beauty; it was clearly visible with its many varied folds."[83] The idea that the naked body could be seen through the delicate material had great appeal with the poets of the time (U. v. d. Türlin 301.16 ff.; Meister Altswert 25.16 ff.).

The shirt was not only an undergarment, but was also worn as a dress, not infrequently with a loose wrap. Only on festive occasions were several pieces of clothing worn on top of each other. In addition to the tight waist and the generous cast of folds of the skirt, the look of courtly women's clothes was shaped by long sleeves and the train. Luxurious sleeves had already been worn in the eleventh century, but only in the twelfth century did the overlong hanging sleeves that reached down to the ground become a trend setting fashion item. Strangely enough they are rarely mentioned in courtly poetry. Women's sleeves appear mostly as love-tokens. Their length was mentioned rather incidentally, as when a lady used her *stûchen* to wipe the sweat of her knight (*Ornit* 476.2), or carried a letter in her sleeve (*Wolfdietrich* A 200.1). The train, called *schwanz*, was also depicted better by the painters than the poets. In dance lyric we hear of trains that had to be gathered up for dancing. When Kriemhild was received by Etzel in Tuln, her train was carried by two princes (*Nibelungenlied* 1350.1 f.). The Franciscan Salimbene of Parma reports that in 1240, the Papal legate Latinus "scared all the women with an order that all women should wear short dresses down to the ground or in excess of that only by one handbreadth. For previously they used to drag along the ground trains that were an arm and a half in length."[84] The legate had this order announced from the pulpits, and threatened to refuse the women absolution if they did not comply with it. "That was more bitter than death to the women," the Franciscan monk continues; "a woman told me in confidence that the train was more important to her than any other piece of clothing she wore."[85]

The courtly dress for women also included a belt and clasps, richly decorated with pearls and gems. Incidentally, the metal belt buckles (*rinken*) are the only part of the secular dress of the nobility of this period of which numerous pieces have survived. Most of them are the products of superior workmanship and confirm the poets' statements about the preciousness of the belts. The breast-clasps (*fürspan, haftel*) were also made of costly materials and were occasionally of exceptional size ("the clasp that was a good handswidth in size was a shining ruby"[86]). As a headdress the young ladies wore flower wreaths or circlets (*schapel*) of precious metal, sometimes decorated like crowns, whereas the whimple became the typical headgear for married women in the thirteenth century. Scarves and veils were also used as headcoverings.

The point of the descriptions of clothes was not merely to list and depict fashionable details. Instead, the poets were concerned to make a connection between the courtly look of women's dress and the new image of the courtly lady. Nearly always the description of clothing was part of an elaborate praise of women, which normally began with an account of physical beauty and which in some cases showed the link between the appearance in society and the splendor of a courtly outfit. Just how closely physical beauty, courtly dress, and noble bearing belonged together is demonstrated, for example, in the appearance of young Isolde at the Irish court, described by Gottfried von Straßburg. Here the posture of one hand hooked into the clasp string while the other gathers up the mantle reveals the full beauty of the garments (see p. 11): "Both things together, posture and dress, have never created a living image more beautiful than this."[87] The lady depicted on a French woman's seal from the year 1247 has one hand hooked into the clasp string while she opens the mantle with the other to show the costly fur lining (see fig. 10). This opening of the mantle was another gesture in which courtly exemplariness and noble bearing expressed themselves. Wolfram von Eschenbach described it at Gyburg's appearance in the great hall of Orange. Gyburg wore a dress and a mantle of oriental silk and had a gem-studded belt around her waist: "Now and then she would open her mantle a little: whoever could see what was underneath it beheld paradise."[88]

Some women of the high nobility were personally engaged in making and ornamenting clothes, and became extremely skilled at it. Of Mahilda, the sister of Bishop Burchard of Worms (d. 1025), we are told: "This lady was herself very creative and most skillful in women's work. She had assistants who were skilled in the various aspects of cloth-working, and she surpassed many other women in the making of sumptuous clothes."[89] The monk Albert of Metz used similar words to praise the cloth-working skills of the Lotharingian Countess Adele (*De diversitate temporum*, p. 702). The Chronicle of Berthold von Zwiefalten reports that Matilda, the daughter of the count of Achalm, "decorated a black chasuble most beautifully with broad gold embroidery."[90] Baudri de Bourgueil tell us that Countess Adele of Blois personally supervised the weaving of her precious tapestries (see p. 117). Queen Candacis, too, had "mastered" the magnificent wall hangings in her palace (*Straßbur-*

Fig. 10.   Seal portrait of Perrenelle de Maubuisson. The left hand is hooked into the clasp string, while the right hand opens the mantle to allow a look "inside" and to reveal the precious fur lining. 1247.

ger Alexander 5969 ff.). In courtly poetry we hear repeatedly of the cloth-working skills of noble ladies. Of Princess Irene of Norway it is said that "she could make in masterful fashion beautiful, noble, artistic, and costly belts."[91] Kriemhild herself cut the clothes for her brother Gunther and his retinue: "Kriemhild the queen summoned from her quarters thirty of her maidens who were especially gifted for such work. They threaded gems onto the snow-white silk from Arabia and the fine silk from Zazamanc, green as clover, and made splendid robes. Kriemhild cut the cloth herself."[92]

MEN'S CLOTHES

We hear much less in courtly literature about the fashionable look of men. What for women is the description of dress, for men is the description of armor and weapons. Rarely is the civilian dress of noble men depicted in as much detail as in Tristan's appearance at the Irish court (G. v. Straßburg 11106 ff.), or when Venus dressed up young Paris (K. v. Würzburg, *Trojanerkrieg* 2896 ff.). Pictorial evidence is therefore all the more important. But most pictures show the ceremonial vestments, insignia of lorship; it is highly unlikely that they followed the trends in fashion.

Texts and pictures reveal that the courtly dress of men was as costly, as colorful, and as richly decorated as that of women. The fashionable cut and style was also the same. Men, too, wore garments that fit snugly on top and, widened through inserts, fell in folds from the waist down. Men's robes, like women's dresses, were laced at the sides: "A young lady laced him into a silk shirt."[93] And men also wore long decorative sleeves: "Thus his elbows lie in two pointy folds: they hang down very low."[94] "One sleeve would supply four men with sufficient cloth for an entire tunic."[95] Like the women, men wore silken and delicately pleated shirts, tops with trim and gold embroidery, mantles lined with rare furs, richly embellished belts, precious brooches, golden circlets, and peacock hats.

But there were also significant differences in dress. A feature unique to men's fashion seems to have been slit garments, which were known as early as the eleventh century: "After this he put on a multicolored fur robe, slit in front and back."[96] Only in the courtly age, however, did slit garments determine the fashion look. At King Mark's court feast the knights wore clothes that were "magnificently slit and cut open."[97] The slits were either underlined with a cloth of different color, or left open to reveal the underlying garment or the naked skin. The effect was particularly striking if the garment treated this way was pants: "He wore slit pants of red scarlet cloth, through which one could see the legs."[98] "The pants of the two [lords] were cut and slit open in courtly fashion. Across the openings was much gold filament, and through it one could see the snow-white linen."[99]

Masculine beauty manifested itself most conspicuously in the legs and what covered them. The "knightly" or "imperial" legs of the courtly knight were often praised by the poets. At the court feast of Tintagel, young Riwalin attracted the attention of the ladies: "'Just look at that young man,' they said, 'what a fortunate man he is. How splendidly he succeeds in everything he does! How handsome he is! How straight his imperial legs are!'"[100] The pants of this period were stocking-like leggings of leather or cloth. Occasionally decorated with gold and pearls, they had to fit very tightly to bring out fully the beauty of the legs. They were "painted onto the legs"[101] in order to fit as though "glued on."[102] "The bold lad was dressed in hose of red scarlet. Goodness, how beauti-

Fig. 11.   Ennius and Flaccus. The lord on the right is wearing a silk mantle that is tightly cut to his body. It has a woven-in floral pattern and a fur lining on the inside. The garment underneath leaves the legs exposed to above the knee. From the Munich Codex Clm 2599. Beginning of the thirteenth century.

ful his legs were!"[103] The uncovering and displaying of the legs was especially offensive to ecclesiastical writers. As early as the middle of the eleventh century, Abbot Siegfried of Gorze had complained about "the very indecent and to modest eyes damnable shortening and disfiguring of the clothes,"[104] which was then very popular among the German nobility. Ordericus Vitalis, however, notes reproachfully that men dressed themselves in "long flowing shirts and robes."[105] This seeming contradiction in their criticism of men's dress is explained if we examine the depiction of the Roman epic poet Ennius in the previously mentioned Munich Codex (Clm 2599) from the monastery of Aldersbach. Ennius is portrayed as a young man wearing a costly upper garment of silk, cut closely to the body and reaching down to the feet. In the front, however, it is cut open to reveal the splendid fur lining and the very short undergarment that exposes the legs to above the knee (see fig. 11). Cicero is also depicted as a courtly lad, with a short upper garment that reaches down no further than the thighs, revealing some of the undergarment; from the knees down the legs are naked; only the feet

Fig. 12. Tullius and Rhetorica. The lord on the right is wearing a very short, tightly cut overgarment, underneath which we can see the undergarment, not much longer; draped over his shoulders is a fur-lined mantle. The hair is artfully curled. From the Munich Codex Clm 2599. Beginning of the thirteenth century.

are covered with nice boots (see fig. 12). Wolfram von Eschenbach tells how young Gahmuret, upon entering Kanvoleiz, displayed his masculine pride by swinging one leg up onto the saddle in front of him. He was not wearing any hose, only "two fashionable boots over naked legs,"[106] and with this outfit he caused quite a stir. Archbishop Albero of Trier (d. 1152) occasionally rode in the same posture, but only—as his biographer assures us—"because an illness forced him to."[107] But since the archbishop usually went about in considerable splendor, it is not surprising that "some thought he did this to attract attention."[108] A distorted caricature of the courtly displaying of legs is given in *Seifried Helbling*: "The robe is so short that one can see his boots. He doesn't think of letting the robe down when he goes out in public. Everyone can see: in the front the garters show, and in the back his private parts which I won't mention by name."[109]

The figurative art of the period knows the motif of the seated or enthroned ruler with his legs crossed. In illustrations to secular texts this was a courtly gesture, as for example in the Munich Tristan manuscript (Cgm 51) from the mid-thirteenth century, where King Mark is shown this way at a reception. In religious art, however, this posture is used only with evil characters, with tyrants like Herod or Pharaoh; apparently it was meant to show their worldly pride.

Men's hairstyles and beards were fertile ground for fashion. From the eleventh century on, secular nobility considered it modern to be cleanshaven, as was the custom in France (see p. 80). At the same time the hair was worn long and curly. This is how Ordericus Vitalis described the appearance of young noblemen in the early twelfth century: "In front their faces are shaved, like thieves; in back they let their hair grow long, like whores."[110] In this context the monk from Saint Evroul also mentioned the implement that was so very important for a man's hairstyle: the curling tongs: "They crimp their hair with a curling iron."[111]

Beard fashions of the courtly age can best be described if we assign them to the different stages in a man's life. The young nobleman was cleanshaven. The middle-aged man sported an elegantly trimmed chin beard, sometimes also a moustache. An elderly man was usually depicted with a full beard. In the Aldersbach Codex all three styles are represented. Ennius is portrayed as a beardless lad with short curly hair. Boethius is a grown man with a nicely curled moustache and a goatee— also treated with the curling iron—that runs over his cheeks to the artificially curled hair on his head. Pythagoras, finally, is depicted as an old man with a full beard artfully braided. Literary sources confirm that the full beard of elderly men was sometimes "plaited into braids and interwoven with gold threads."[112] The middle style had a particularly high representational quality, and it appears on most royal portraits of this time, including the famous Barbarossa head from Cappenberg, which Emperor Frederick I gave to Count Otto of Cappenberg, and which is considered an idealized, stylized bust of the emperor. A connection between the style of beard and the length of the robes is confirmed by pictorial representations of the Three Kings, who are sometimes regarded as representing the three ages of man. In the lavishly illustrated Berlin manuscript of Priest Wernher's *Marienleben* (Ms. germ. oct. 109), which dates to the twelfth century, the young king is depicted beardless, the middle king with a short goatee, and the old king with a long, full beard. Only the young king wears a robe that hardly reaches down to his knees, while the two older kings are dressed in long robes that fall down to the feet (see fig. 13).

Fig. 13.   The Three Wise Men. The first sports a full beard, the second a short chin-beard, the third is clean-shaven and wears a short dress. From the Berlin manuscript of Priester Wernher's *Driu liet von der maget* (Mgo 109). Around 1200.

CHANGES IN FASHION

According to recent works by Joan Evans and Erika Thiel, the development of fashion from the twelfth to the thirteenth centuries was characterized by a reduction of fashionable extravagance, a renunciation of excessive pomp, and a tendency to greater modesty and simplicity. This picture is based largely on the examination of a number of large sculptures, for Germany especially the figures at Bamberg, Straßburg, Magdeburg, and Naumburg. But all these statues are either church decorations or tomb sculptures, and in either case a serious and solemn style without the worldly splendor of clothes must have been considered appropriate. The literary evidence, largely ignored by scholars of costume, reveals a different situation. This evidence is all the more important, since the poets could express the ideas and desires of their noble audience more freely than the sculptors who were commissioned by the Church. It is true that the long sleeves and the wide decorative trims lost some of their popularity in the thirteenth century. But on the whole, the dress of the nobility did not become simpler and less adorned; on the contrary, it became ever more elaborate and refined. There are, incidentally, numerous pictorial sources from the thirteenth century that attest to the luxuriousness of clothes of the time. I refer to the illustrations to secular texts. Created for the most part at the request of lay princes, these illustrations were not subject to the moral restraints of religious art.

The basic styles of courtly dress seem to have continued largely unchanged. Throughout the thirteenth century women wore dresses tailored closely to the body, laced at the sides, and attached to long, elaborately pleated skirts. In addition, as they had done in the twelfth century, people used the more loosely cut robe that was worn with or without a belt. Changes in fashion concerned mostly details, but these did set new accents in the look of the clothes.

Wide surcoats enjoyed a growing popularity with men and women during the thirteenth century. The names for these garments are entirely French: *surkôt, suckenîe, kursît*: a sure sign that this fashion also came from France. The French words appear shortly after 1200 in *Parzival*; *suckenîe* possibly already in *Graf Rudolf* (ab 29; the word cannot be positively deciphered in the manuscript). Pictorial representations seem to be more recent. Judging from the miniatures in the minnesinger manuscripts from Weingarten and Heidelberg (beginning of the fourteenth century), the sleeveless surcoat was one of the most common garments at the end of the courtly age.

Another innovation of the thirteenth century was the clasp-mantle; at least there seems to be no secure pictorial or literary evidence for it from the twelfth century. This type of mantle takes its name from the two clasps (*tasseln*: also a French loan word) that were fastened on the right and left below the collar. A string from one clasp to the other held the mantle together. Literary evidence exists by the beginning of the thirteenth century (*Athis* D 140 ff.). Initially these are all women's mantles, but we must keep in mind that detailed descriptions nearly always concern women's dress. Later the clasp-mantle was also worn by men, as for example by Count Conrad in the west choir at Naumburg. The older type of brooch-mantle also continued in use; it was held together at the chest by a single brooch (*nusche*). The figure of Ecclesia on the south portal of the Cathedral in Straßburg is wearing such a mantle.

The fashionable look of noble women was most dramatically altered by a new headdress: the wimple, consisting of a chin strap and a stiffened headband that was worn like a crown. This innovation, too, seems to have come from France ("The lovely maid was tied in the French manner"[113]). The Old French word for it (*guinple*) was also taken over into German, as *wimpel* (H. v. Aue, *Erec* 8945) and *gimpel*: "She had tied up her chin: the *gimpel* reached to her mouth, very much in the courtly fashion."[114] Usually we find the German word *gebende*, which had been used to describe a woman's headdress as early as the mid-twelfth century (*Kaiserchronik* 11868); it is not clear, though, whether this already referred to the French type. The poets of around 1200 were well acquainted with the *gebende*; in figurative art it appears somewhat later. The *gebende* was considered the mark of a married lady, but it was also worn by unmarried women. The straps around the chin and the cheeks covered most of the face. Kundrie had to take off her wimple before she was recognized at Arthur's court (W. v. Eschenbach, *Parzival* 778.27 ff.). The wimple also interfered with speaking, laughing, eating, and kissing. Kriemhild "pushed her wimple up"[115] in order to greet her second husband, Etzel, with a kiss. It is no surprise that the wimple was considered the symbol of a woman's morals. A lady who loosened her wimple was accused of loose morals (W. v. Eschenbach, *Parzival* 515.1 ff.).

CRITICISM FROM THE CHURCH

The Fathers of the Church had already regarded worldly pomp in dress with suspicion. In a letter to Demetrias, St. Jerome warned: "Beware of the wantonness of those girls who decorate their heads, let their hair fall into their foreheads, polish their skin, use cosmetics, and wear tight sleeves, dresses without folds, and shiny shoes."[116] Vincent of Beauvais (d. 1264) quoted this sentence in his educational tract for princes (*De eruditione filiorum nobilium*, p. 187), and it could also be applied to the fashionable dress of the thirteenth century. In most cases the criticism was aimed at women's clothes and their alleged indecency. Thietmar von Merseburg (d. 1018) combined his praise of the pious Countess Christina with a swipe at certain "modern women," "most of whom gird themselves in an indecent fashion and show openly to all lovers what they have to offer up for sale."[117] This criticism was even more effective if one could claim that the corruption of morals was a foreign import. Empress Theophano (d. 991), the niece of the Byzantine emperor and wife of Emperor Otto II (d. 983), was accused of setting a corrupting example with her Greek ways. In the "Book of Visions" (*Liber visionum*) by the monk Otloh of St. Emmeram (d. after 1070), the empress herself explained why she had to suffer the torments of purgatory: "because I was the first to bring to Germany and France many superfluous and oppulent ornaments for women, which are customary in Greece but were previously unknown in these parts, and because in dressing in excess of what is proper to human nature and appearing in these novel clothes I led other women to the sin of desiring similar things."[118] Around the same time Abbot Siegfried of Gorze also complained that Empress Agnes of Poitou (d. 1077), the wife of Henry III, had brought disgraceful new fashions to Germany from her southern French homeland (see p. 79).

The luxurious display of clothes during the courtly age offered fertile ground for ecclesiastical criticism. The attacks of the clerics are, at the same time, important evidence that fashionable splendor, otherwise referred to almost exclusively in poetic texts and illustrations, did in fact play a large role in the social life of the nobility. In Der Arme Hartmann's *Vom Glauben* ("Discourse on Faith") of the mid-twelfth century, the noble lords were already criticized for their worldly luxuries: "The golden cups, the silver bowls, the gems, the precious ivory, the many artfully woven trims, the elegant jewelry, *pellil* and silk, *cindal* and samite, and also scarlet. The many mantles you own! You have beautiful wall hangings made for yourself, very wide and long tapestries and drapes, full of gold, as your heart desires, and many ornaments besides, which I do not want to list."[119] Heinrich von Melk (end of the twelfth century) especially denounced the young ladies' passion for finery: "They have very beautiful outfits, shirts, and dresses. Their locks are so carefully curled. They like to put on those well-made gloves. One can see the decorative trim shining through the yellow veils. They lace themselves up tightly. The gloves! And the mirrors!"[120]

Very informative are the decrees of Church councils, which reveal that the worldly adornment of dress had penetrated even into convents, many of which were inhabited by daughters of noble families. A synod at Trier in the year 1227 prohibited all monks and nuns from owning "mantles of black or purple *bruneta*, fur coats or other exquisite and precious furs."[121] Moreover, it was decreed "that nuns should have no tight-fitting or stitched-on sleeves, no necklaces, no clasps, no golden or silver rings, no gold fringes, no silk belts, nor any other kind of worldly adornments."[122]

Criticism of dress had no place in courtly epics. It was an exception when the poet of *Reinfried von Braunschweig* (around 1300), as part of an elaborate scolding of women, attacked the indecent tightness of the courtly clothes and the uncovering of the body: "I am very surprised that they run around more than half naked from the waist up. Their clothes are so tight that it strikes me as an abomination; for in the clothes the body entices with shameful readiness."[123] Ecclesiastical criticism of courtly dress reached its height in the works of the preachers and didacticians of the thirteenth century. Hugo von Trimberg criticized above all the fashionable adornment of the nobility's clothes: "Lord Adam had not gusset in his robe. To the day he died he knew nothing of fancy shoes, bonnets, and shirts with figurative scenes."[124] No one was more committed to the battle against sartorial pomp than the eloquent Franciscan preacher Berthold von Regensburg. The fashion elements that aroused his wrath and disgust reveal what was particularly prized by courtly society: "Over here you men with your slit gowns, and over there you women with your dyeing, plucking, sewing."[125] Berthold accused the women of thinking only about their clothes and "whether the sleeves look good or the veil or the wimple."[126] "You ladies, you carry on far too vainly with your robes, your dainty dresses: you sew them in so many styles and so foppishly that you ought to be ashamed in your hearts."[127] The French fashion words also became a target of Berthold's scorn: "When you wear it then with such excessive pride that you *brankieret* and *gampenieret* your body with it."[128] Elsewhere his censure is directed against those "clothes that are too daintily cut or too tightly sewn and tailored the way the women like to do it."[129] The greatest disgust was aroused by the dazzling colors of courtly dress, especially by the ingenious combining of differently colored fabrics:

> You are not content that almighty God has given you the choice among clothes, whether you want them brown or red or blue, white, green, yellow, black. That will not do for you. Instead your great vaingloriousness drives you to cut up the cloth into patches and to place here the red piece into the white and there the yellow into the green, one piece pleated, the other smooth, one motley, the other of two-tone brown, here the lion, there the eagle.[130]

Lion and eagle referred to the costly brocades with embroidered figurative patterns.

The very embodiment of female pride was, for Berthold von Regensburg, the "yellow wimple": "Thus the ladies with the yellow wimple have more trouble than those who modestly wear a white one, since many of them spend half a year fussing with the wimple and the veil."[131] This theme stems from a tradition of court criticism reaching back into the twelfth century. Heinrich von Melk had already railed against peasant women who sewed trains to their dresses, and who wanted to emulate the rich ladies "with their proud gait and with makeup on the cheeks and with yellow wimples."[132] Hugo von Trimberg describes "a maid in a yellow dress with a train"[133] as the bait of sinfulness: "A bare neck and a yellow skirt lure many false suitors. Laces on the dresses and figures on the skirt spoil girls and lads."[134] Yellow was the color of prostitution, worldly pleasure, and pride. In courtly color symbolism yellow was also the color of consummated love. It is not surprising that "the yellow dress and the yellow sleeves"[135] scandalized the preachers. Much later, in the Alsfelder Passion Play of the sixteenth century, Mary Magdalen lists her yellow wimple among the attributes of her sinful worldliness: "Alas for the wreaths of roses! Alas for my train! Alas for the yellow wimple! Alas for my white hands! Alas for my pride!"[136]

3. WEAPONS AND HORSES

THE HISTORY OF ARMAMENT

We are far better informed about the weapons of the High Middle Ages than we are about civilian dress. A separate branch of scholarship, weapons archeology, looks after the extensive material remains. The surviving pieces stem largely from excavations: sword blades, spear heads, spurs, stirrups, all so badly corroded that little remains of the original luster. In addition there are a few precious single pieces that have survived, mostly ceremonial weapons never intended for actual warfare, like the imperial sword in the treasury in Vienna, or grave shields that were suspended over the tombs of noble lords. The complete suits of armor displayed today in castles and museums are all of much more recent date.

To get a more detailed picture of knightly weapons, historians of armament must turn to secondary sources. Extensive pictorial material is available, the most important being seals, which can usually be dated very precisely. Unfortunately the German seals have not yet been studied carefully for their pictorial content. Scholars of weaponry have also made little use of the rich material contained in courtly literature. The poets described knightly arms with the same detailed realism that they lavished upon courtly dress, and the thoroughness of their descriptions shows that in doing so they catered to the interests of their audience. We may suppose that the descriptions of weapons were meant primarily for the male listeners, while the descriptions of clothes appealed to the interests of the ladies. In fact some details of weapons technology are attested only in literature.

The courtly terminology of arms consisted in large part of French words and loan words. The Old German terms for the major weapons, *helm*, *swert*, *sper*, and *schilt*, did remain in use during the courtly age, but changes to these weapons were mostly designated with specialized French terms. For example, the new iron plate on the helmet was called a *barbiere*. The figurative decoration of the helmet was described with two French words, *zimiere* and *kroier*. For the shield buckel one borrowed the French *buckel*. In the courtly period the French loan word *lanze* became the main term for the long thrusting lance of the knight. It replaced *spiez*, which was still used in the *Rolandslied* for all types of lances, but was later found only in heroic epics, mostly with the meaning of "javelin" or "hunting spear." Another borrowed word for the lance was *glavîe*, *glevîn*. The pennant on the lance was also given a French name (*baniere*). For the body armor the poets had at their disposal a great number of different terms: *werc* (*stalwerc*), *geruste*, *gesmide*, *gewant* (*wîcgewant*, *strîtgewant*, *îsengewant*), *wât* (*sarwât*, *wîcgewaete*, *îsengewaete*), *rock* (*stalîn rock*, *îsern rock*), *gar*, *gerehte*, *geserwe*, *wer*, *wâfen* (*gewaefen*). Most frequently used were *brünne* and *halsberc*, which cannot be clearly differentiated. It would seem that the *halsberc* always had an attached mail hood, whereas the *brünne* did not. While *brünne* was especially popular in heroic poetry, the courtly epicists preferred to use *halsberc*, along with the French loan word *harnasch*, which at first designated the knight's entire panoply, but after Wolfram von Eschenbach, specifically the knightly armor. In *Parzival*, *halsberc* is used five times, *brünne* not at all, and the French *harnasch* more than sixty times. The individual sections of the armor of chain mail (*maile* = ring mail) were described almost entirely with French terms. The hood was called *koife* or *hersenier*, its extension that was pulled over the chin and mouth was the *finteile*. The hauberk was also called *panzier* and *hâbergoel*. Sometimes it came with a separate breastplate (*plate*, *bônît*). The armor included further arm guards (*brazel*), kneecaps (*schinnelier*), and greaves (*hurtenier*). The padding worn under the armor was called *senftenier*, the loin belt *lendenier*, the shoulder guard *spaldenier*, and the neck guard *kollier*. All this vocabulary was already known in Germany around 1200 and was part of the modern style of courtly literature. Of the armament of the Trojans we are told in Herbort von Fritzlar: they had *pancir kollir Krocanir testir Armysen vu plate* (4735-37). A single German word appears here (*armisen*) surrounded by French. How greatly the fashionable sound of such words was valued is revealed also by German words that were created with French derivative syllables: for example, *brustenier* "breast guard for the horse" from the German word *brust*; or *mûsenier* "arm guard" from the German word *mûs* "arm muscle."

French weapons terminology was probably transmitted to a large extent through literature. But linguistic borrowing did not occur only via literature, as is revealed by the fact that in Emperor Frederick I's decree on military matters from the year 1158, we find the word *harnasch* used in the sense of "military equipment" ("all his equipment"[1]). Apparently the French word *harnais* was already known in Germany at that time. As in other areas of material culture, we can assume that the words for weapons were adopted along with the objects they described. This is difficult to prove in detail, since the archeological material is not sufficient. Everything indicates, however, that knightly armament in Germany was not different from that in France. Since a number of innovations can be attested earlier in France, there is little doubt that the common elements are the result of the adoption of French types. Only a few details remained unknown in Germany, such as the tail-like ribbons at the back of the helmet, which appear frequently on French seals of the twelfth century, and had either a protective or merely a decorative function. To say that certain weapons were made in France was a mark of high quality: helmets from Poitiers (H. v. Aue, *Erec* 2328), spearheads from Troyes (W. v. Eschenbach, *Parzival* 288.16), gorgets from Chambly (H. v. Aue, *Erec* 2329) and Anjou (*Jüngerer Titurel* 5828.1), breastplates from Soissons (W. v. Eschenbach, *Erec* 261.26). These names were not introduced arbitrarily: they stood for famous armories with an international reputation.

THE MAIN WEAPONS OF A KNIGHT

The knightly armor of the High Middle Ages had a long history reaching back to the heavy cavalry of antiquity. What the armament looked like at the end of the eleventh century is best documented in the many war scenes on the Bayeux Tapestry. Here both the Normans and their Saxon opponents wear knee length mail shirts with half length sleeves and coifs, over which are placed canonical helmets with nose guards. The mounted warriors as well as the foot soldiers carry nearly man-high, strongly curved shields that are either almond shaped or pointy at the bottom. Swords, lances, and battle-axes serve as offensive weapons.

A number of characteristic changes during the course of the twelfth century created out of this weaponry the typical knightly armament of the courtly age.

The hauberk was a mail shirt made of iron rings. Scale armor was rare in Germany. The rings were either stitched onto a leather coat or interlaced and riveted together. The latter type seems to have been the one most widely used. The rivets are occasionally mentioned even in literature: "He struck King Malakin through the riveting of the mail rings."[2] In due course all body parts were surrounded with protective mail. The mail shirt was given long sleeves that reached to the wrist and to which iron mittens were attached. The legs and feet were protected by hose and shoes of chain mail. In addition, the coif was extended in such a way that part of it could be pulled over the mouth and chin and fastened at the side. The fully developed armor, which encased the entire body except for the upper portion of the face, is depicted at the end of the twelfth century on seals and in the miniatures of the *Hortus deliciarum*. The poets tells us what was worn underneath the hauberk. The heavier the armor the more it had to be padded. Of special importance was a thickly padded stand-up collar to protect the neck.

The complete suit of chain mail remained in use throughout the thirteenth century and was continually improved upon. Sometimes the chest received additional protection through a metal plate. Such plates could also be sewn into the tunic, in which case a scale tunic was created; we can see an example of this on the Mauritius figure in the Cathedral of Magdeburg, dated to after 1250. The thirteenth century also witnessed the beginnings of scale armor, which superseded the mail shirt in the late Middle Ages.

The helmet underwent characteristic changes during the courtly period. The canonical Norman helmet with the attached nose guard was still widely used around 1200. Its greatest disadvantage was the lack of adequate protection for the face. This deficiency was remedied by the *barbiere*, a metal plate with breathing holes that was attached to the front of the helmet and covered the lower part of the face. French seals attest this innovation from 1190 on. It appears that it was immediately adopted in Germany. An equestrian seal of Duke Leopold VI of Austria from the year 1197 is considered the first piece of evidence. People in Germany were well acquainted with the new type of helmet, as is shown by a remark in Wolfram's *Willehalm* about the armor of the old Count Heimrich von Narbonne, who rode into battle without the modern face protection, "unprotected by a *finteile*. The lower half of Heimrich's face was uncovered, no *barbiere* surrounded it. His helmet had only a nose guard."[3] There was a special reason why the mighty Count Heimrich was wearing an old-fashioned helmet with a nose guard: Heimrich had a long beard that would not fit into the camail of the coif nor, it seems, under the *barbiere*. Here we see an interesting connection between the style of beards and military technology.

A different change in the shape of the helmet was pointed out in *Athis und Prophilias*: "His helmet was brown, shiny, made of iron, beautifully decorated with metal strips, and in front of the eyes and the face it had an attached *barbiere*; the helmet was canonical in the old style, as used to be customary."[4] Pictorial evidence reveals that the modern helmet with the *barbiere* was usually flat on top. From 1210 on French seals depict flat helmets that reached down to the neck in the back, and whose face guard in front was solidly fused to the helmet leaving open only the slit or window for the eyes. Because of its great weight, this helmet rested no longer on the forehead but on the crown of the head, now furnished, of course, with a suitable insert. This is the earliest style of the *Topfhelm* (pot-helmet). Later extended down to the shoulders and equipped with a movable visor, it remained the typical knightly helmet throughout the later Middle Ages. This innovation, too, seems to have spread very quickly to Germany. It can already be seen on some seals of Leopold VI of Austria from the years 1212–1214, as well as in a miniature of the *Speculum virginum* (see fig. 14). The battle scenes in the manuscripts of the thirteenth century show that the new *Topfhelm* and the helmet with the *barbiere* were initially worn only by a few especially outstanding individuals—by kings and the leaders of armies—whereas the other knights continued, for quite some time, to use the old Norman helmet with nose guard, or a round iron cap with broad brim, which later developed into the chapel-de-fer.

The poets had many terms for the helmet: *helm, helmvaz, stahelvaz, huot, helmhuot, stahelhuot, flinshuot, hûbe*, and more. Poetic descriptions speak of the bright luster of the helmets and of their decoration with gold and gems. Kings wore crown helmets, for which there is also good pictorial evidence. In the course of the thirteenth century it became customary to decorate the helmet with colorful cloths. Ulrich von Liechtenstein was the first to mention such helmet cloths (*Frauendienst* 1405.7 ff.). But the most conspicuous ornaments on the helmet were the figurative crests of wood, leather, linen, or parchment, often colorfully painted, and attached to the top of the helmet (see fig. 15). The oldest

Fig. 14. Battle between the Virtues and the Vices. The allegorical figures are dressed in modern knightly armor: pot-helmets (*Topfhelme*), which cover the entire head; mail coats with attached slippers and gloves; on top of that colorful tabards. On the inside of the shields we can make out the attachments of the hand grips. Single folio from a manuscript of the *Speculum virginum* (Hannover, Kestner-Museum, 3984). Around 1200.

Fig. 15. Turnus and his knights. Helmets with forged-on *barbiere* and different crests: eagle, crown, bird head, griffin-claw, pennant, wing, hand, and wheel. The shield decorations are only in part of heraldic significance. From the Berlin *Eneit* manuscript (Mgf 282). Thirteenth century.

pictorial evidence for a crest is thought to be a seal from the year 1198 belonging to King Richard I of England. The literary evidence reaches back even farther. In Veldeke's *Eneit* a golden flower is mentioned on Eneas's helmet (160.4 f.), and in *Erec* we find an angel on top of a crown used as a crest (2337 f.). The fully developed crest is described by Wolfram von Eschenbach. Gahmuret bore an anchor on his helmet (*Parzival* 36.16), his cousin Kaylet an ostrich (39.16), Orilus a dragon (262.6). In other texts from the beginning of the thirteenth century we encounter helmet decorations in the form of a tree (U. v. Zatzikhoven 4438 f.), a wheel (W. v. Grafenberg 1862 f.), an arrrow (G. v. Straßburg 4941), a ship (W. v. Eschenbach, *Willehalm* 409.20). "One saw there vast numbers of wild animal and birds strutting along atop the solid helmets; trees, too, with twigs and branches, preciously decorated."[5] The crests that have survived all date from later periods. One of the oldest pieces is the lion crest of the Black Prince (d. 1376) above his tomb in Canterbury Cathedral.

The shield usually consisted of leather-covered wood. In the middle and at the edge it had metal mounts (*schiltgespenge*), which were sometimes arranged in ornamental patterns. The large, strongly curved shields depicted on the Bayeux Tapestry are still found around 1200. But on the seals a new type begins to dominate by the second half of the twelfth century: the shields become smaller and flatter, triangular in shape, with a straight upper edge and rounded corners. This new type can be confirmed in France from about 1140 on, in Germany after 1170 (the equestrian seals of Duke Henry II of Austria). A few shields from the courtly age have survived intact. The oldest piece is thought to be the famous Seedorf shield (from the monastery of Seedorf on Lake Lucerne), kept today in the Swiss Landesmuseum in Zurich. It bears the coat of arms of the lords of Brienz—a silver lion on an azure field—and is usually attributed to the founder of the monastery of Seedorf, Arnold of Brienz (d. 1225). Somewhat later in date are the shields in the choir of the Church of St. Elisabeth in Marburg. One of them belonged to Landgrave Conrad of Thuringia (d. 1241) and bears the Thuringian coat of arms: a lion on an azure field with superimposed red and white chevrons. The shield is about eighty centimeters high; nearly seventy-five centimeters broad at the top, it comes to a point at the bottom. It shows traces of paint on the inside—fragments of a minne scene can still be recognized—which is an indication that this shield was in fact used by the landgrave.

The change in the shape of the shield is also echoed in courtly litera-

ture: "His shield was old, heavy, long, and broad; his lances were un-
wieldy and large; half of his body and half of his horse were
unprotected."[6] With such equipment and with the obsolete weapons of
Enite's father—an impoverished count—Erec had to fight a duel. This
passage reveals that the great, heavy shields of former times, as well as
the mail shirt that did not cover the entire body, were already regarded
by the courtly audience in Germany around 1180 or 1190 as evidence
of an antiquated weapons technology. When Erec is later equipped with
new weapons at Arthur's court, his splendidly decorated shields are
especially emphasized. One of them glistened silver, the second was
bright red.

> The third was of gold on the outside and the inside, and on it was a sleeve of
> sable, the finest that existed. Attached to the shield were a buckle and silver
> clasps of suitable size, which covered the entire surface of the shield with
> a beautiful pattern. The sleeve was fastened on top of this. On the inside
> a lady was depicted on the upper part of the shield. The shield strap was
> decorated with a gem-studded braid; but not only the shield strap, the hand
> straps, too, were ornamented in this way.[7]

Here again we find on the inside a painted scene with a minne motif.
The woman's sleeve on the shield indicated a knight engaged in minne
service. Other shield descriptions of this time already depict heraldic
emblems. Eneas, for example, displays a red lion on his shield (H. v.
Veldeke, *Eneit* 162.12). These were the beginnings of heraldry. Figurative decorations on shields are occasionally found before this time, but
not until the second half of the twelfth century did such emblems gradually take on heraldic significance. One of the earliest pieces of evidence is the lion shield of Count Geoffrey Plantagenet of Anjou (d.
1151) on the enamel tomb plate in Le Mans. The oldest German example is probably the eagle on the shield of Duke Henry II of Austria on
his equestrian seal from 1156. Heraldic symbols also appear in the
miniatures of the *Hortus deliciarum* and in the Bern manuscript of the
Carmen in honorem Augusti by Petrus de Ebulo from the end of the
twelfth century. But only in the thirteenth century did the coat of arms
gradually develop into permanent family crests that were regularly displayed on the shield. This development had to do with the social restructuring of the nobility, as well as with the necessity of providing the
knight with an external mark of identification once his face had been
completely covered by the new helmets.

The sword hardly changed its shape since Carolingian times. Swords
dating to the High Middle Ages that have been found in Germany

usually have a short handle, straight quillons (cross-guards), a long blade with a wide groove, and a rounded tip. The seals show that short-er swords with tapering blades and sharp points also existed. In courtly literature we seldom hear of the shape of the swords, while their pre-cious ornamentation is described in great detail: "The pommel and the handle were of gold and enamel."[8] "The hilt was of gold, the sheath of scarlet orphrey."[9] The ceremonial swords preserved from the courtly age attest to the accuracy of such descriptions. The sword of Emperor Frederick II, forged at the beginning of the thirteenth century in Sicily (now housed in the Treasury in Vienna), is decorated on the hilt and the quillons—the pommel was added later—with gold platelets of filigree and cloisonné. The scabbard is encased in a weave of gilded silver wire; in between are gold platelets with inlaid enamel framed by a double row of pearls.

"Beautiful letters were inlaid into the groove of his sword."[10] Such sword inscriptions have actually been preserved. Of particular interest is the ceremonial sword of Konrad von Winterstetten. Excavated in the sixteenth century, it is today in the Historical Museum in Dresden. The double groove bears this inscription: "High-spirited Konrad, noble cupbearer of Winterstetten, herewith remember me, leave no helmet intact!"[11] The imperial minsterial Konrad von Winterstetten (d. 1243) was also active as a patron of German poets (see p. 486). The sugges-tion that the inscription may have been composed by Rudolf von Ems is, however, beyond proof.

The lance developed in the course of the twelfth century into the characteristic offensive weapon of the knight. The battle scenes of the Bayeux Tapestry show that around 1100 the armored horsemen were still using their lances primarily as javelins The new technique of lance warfare, in which the lance was used as a thrusting weapon and couched tightly under the arm, is first attested in figurative scenes on capitals or church portals, some of which may even go back to the eleventh century (see fig. 16). But pictorial representations begin to in-crease only towards the end of the twelfth century. From about 1170 on in Germany, there is also literary evidence for the new technique. The knight's thrusting lance was longer and heavier than the old throwing lance. Shafts of ash wood are frequently mentioned in literature. The vamplate, whose function was to protect and support the hand on the shaft, seems to have become known in Germany only towards the end of the thirteenth century (H. v. Freiberg, *Tristan* 6229). Frequently the shafts were given a colorful coat of paint. The real ornament of the

Fig. 16. Lance fight. The new fighting technique of the knightly joust with the lance couched under the arm. Architrave in the cathedral of Angoulême. Eleventh/twelfth century.

lance, however, was the pennant, the *baniere*, which in the twelfth century was a long, narrow ribbon, and in the thirteenth century took on a long rectangular shape.

THE SOCIAL SIGNIFICANCE OF WEAPONS

We would not do justice to the importance of medieval armament by looking at it solely from a military point of view. The armored knight on horseback seemed at first glance invulnerable, and could strike terror into anyone not equipped in like fashion. But on closer inspection the military worthiness of knightly armament seems rather dubious. And the innovations and improvements in weapons technology during the courtly age exacerbated the problems. The fully developed mail shirt and the new helmets did offer better protection, but at the same time the armor became steadily heavier, making the use of weapons more and more uncomfortable and strenuous. Underneath the modern *Topfhelm* one could see little and hear even less ("therefore he did not hear and see from under the iron armor as well as he would have had he been unarmed"[12]). This made it imperative that the knight have a companion and lookout to warn him of unpleasant surprises. Moreover, the abundant padding under the armor increasingly restricted the knight's mobility. In actual combat the warriors in their chain mail perspired so profusely that even the greatest heroes had to take a break now and then to cool off. On foot one could hardly carry the weighty armor: "I cannot bear my hauberk on foot, it is too heavy."[13] Since the armor could also no longer be put on or taken off by one person alone, knights had to rely on the help of others. That the knight could become the dominant military figure for an entire age can be explained historically only by the fact that for centuries the nobility was able to preserve its monopoly on force. It is also revealing that there were few large-scale battles during the age of the knight. When the knights in the fourteenth century for the first time encountered troops with different equipment and a different fighting technique—the English longbowmen and the Swiss peasants—their military vulnerability was instantly exposed.

The social significance of the weapons went beyond their military function. The poets were less concerned with the fearsome effect of weapons and more with their splendid luster: "Shiny like a mirror was his helmet."[14] "There one could see on them gleaming hauberks white as tin."[15] "In the dark they saw bright shields flashing."[16] It was the whitish shimmering of the metal that inspired the poets with the idea of comparing the knights to angels: "Like an angel the knight stood there in his knightly armor."[17] "He seemed an angel, not a man."[18] The gleam of the gold and gems which, according to the descriptions of the poets, decorated the weapons of the great lords, contributed to this image. Like the luxurious clothes in courtly poetry, the splenidid arms also have a basis in real life. Richly decorated weapons of great value are mentioned by contemporary chroniclers.

In the course of the thirteenth century, the appearance of the armored knight was determined more and more by the nonmilitary, decorative elements of his equipment. Up to around 1200 only two parts were of cloth: the saddle cloth and the pennant, the *baniere*. Things got much more colorful when one began to paint the shields with coats of arms and to decorate the helmets with crests. Two new pieces were also added to the armament: the tabard (*wâpenroc*) and the horse blanket (*kovertiure*). The tabard was a sleeveless tunic, frequently of colored silk, and was worn over the hauberk. English and French seals attest it even before 1150. It must have spread very quickly to Germany: at the battle of Tusculanum in 1167, Archbishop Christian of Mainz wore "a blue tunic" over his armor, along with "a gold-decorated helmet."[19] The first literary example appears in *König Rother* (1110). After Veldeke's *Eneit*, the tabard became a standard element in every description of armor. Scholars of weaponry have suggested that the tabard was intended to protect the chain mail from rain or the knight from the heat of the sun. No doubt of equal importance was its representational function. The same applies to the colorful horse blankets, which appear for the first time in Germany in Hartmann von Aue (*Erec* 737 f.) and in the *Nibelungenlied* (1882.2); the pictorial evidence is later in date. But the covering of the horses also had a military purpose: it served to protect the horses, especially when a blanket of chain mail was placed under the housing (U. v. Zatzikhoven 4414). If, however, the decorative cover touched the ground ("The blanket reached down to the hooves"[20]), it could prove a hindrance in battle.

In portraits of knights from the end of the thirteenth century, the metal of the armor has almost completely disappeared behind the colorful cloths and the decorations. A studied effect was created when the various parts of the armament were matched in color and decorative designs. This was done either by having all cloth of the same color, or by repeating the coat of arms from the shield on the tabard and the housing, later also on the pennant and sometimes even on the crest (see fig. 17). This is how the poets from Veldeke (*Eneit* 200.7 ff.) and Hartmann von Aue (*Erec* 9015 ff.) on described their heroes.

In the High Middle Ages weapons were symbols of rank. In the Territorial Peace (*Constitutio de pace tenenda*) promulgated by Emperor Frederick I in 1152, a general prohibition was decreed against the carrying of weapons by peasants, especially the carrying of swords or lances: "If any peasant bears arms, be it lance or sword, the judge in whose jurisdiction he is found shall take away his weapons or receive for them from the peasant twenty solidi."[21] In the *Kaiserchronik*, which dates to the same time, the regulation against the bearing of arms by peasants is passed off as a law of Charlemagne, and the threatened punishment is much more severe: "On Sundays he [the peasant] shall go to church, carrying his stick in his hand. If a sword is found on him, he shall be bound and led to the church fence. There the peasant shall be held and soundly heaten."[22] What the situation was in real life is difficult to assess. In the twelfth and thirteenth centuries the peasants were occasionally called up for military service, and the later declarations of Territorial Peace did not repeat such a strict prohibition of weapons. The Bavarian Territorial Peace of 1244 permitted the peasants to wear to church "armor and helmets, collar pads and coats of buckram, and Latin knives"[23]; "innkeepers"[24] were additionally allowed to carry a sword. Against this background it would appear that Neidhart's satirically exaggerated peasants, who appear at the village dance with their

Fig. 17.   Walther von Mezze. The cloth components (horse blanket, tabard, and pennant) determine the appearance of the knight in the thirteenth century. Like the shield they carry the heraldic colors. From the Large Heidelberg Song Manuscript (Cpg 848). Fourteenth century.

long swords ("he constantly carries around a sword as long as a hemp-swing"[25]), were modeled at least to some degree after real life. Fundamentally, however, knightly arms were regarded as a mark of noble status.

The sword and the lance also played a significant role as royal insignia. From the Carolingian period on we find imperial portraits showing the ruler seated on a throne flanked by two weapons-bearers with sword and lance. The imperial sword and the imperial lance, the latter considered identical to the Holy Lance found in Antioch in 1098, were among the most venerable symbols of imperial power. The sword was also a sign of judicial authority. On festive occasions the ruler's sword was carried before him as a symbol of his power. The office of the ceremonial weapons-bearer was regarded as a high honor, and was usually assigned to a prince who had just been confirmed in rank or promoted. Thus King Magnus of Denmark (d. 1134) paid homage to Emperor Lothar III at Easter in 1134 at the diet of Halberstadt: "and when the Emperor went in procession to church, Magnus, decorated with the crown of his country, honorably carried the imperial sword before him."[26] Gislebert of Mons reports that at the festive crowning of Emperor Frederick I at the court feast in Mainz at Whitsuntide in 1184, "the most powerful princes claimed for themselves the privilege of carrying the sword at this crowning."[27] The emperor, however, assigned this function to the count of Hainaut, whose promotion into the ranks of the imperial princes had been decided upon at that time. At the crowning of Philip of Swabia in September 1198 in Mainz, Ottokar I of Bohemia (d. 1230) carried the sword before the Hohenstaufen ruler after his own elevation to the kingship. The princes, too, made use of this gesture of lordship. In *Willehalm* the count of Narbonne had his sword carried before him at his festive entrance into the royal court: "And now came Heimrich in his princely power: a baron bore his sword before him, and many noble knights followed him."[28]

THE CEREMONY OF KNIGHTLY SINGLE COMBAT

Courtly literature describes both mass battles and single combat. Pitched battles, however, appear almost exclusively in epics with themes from antiquity, in crusading epics, and in heroic poetry, whereas in the Arthurian romances battle descriptions are rare. In the latter a great deal of space is devoted to accounts of single combat, which often go on for hundreds of verses. The sheer length of these accounts can make reading these texts somewhat tedious especially since they lack any suspense regarding the outcome of the fight. But it would appear that contemporary listeners saw these passages as important and modern, primarily, no doubt, because they portrayed the superior technique of knightly warfare.

Single combat between knights followed a set ritual. It began nearly always as a lance fight, followed in the second phase by a sword fight. The poets frequently emphasized that the beauty and valor of a knight was manifested in his posture. Seated in full armor high on his horse, the lance held upright to indicate his readiness for battle or already

Fig. 18.   Count Wilhelm IV of Jülich. The equestrian seals of the princes and lords depict an idealized image of the knight: the armored horseman in full gallop. 1237.

couched under the arm: this seems to have been regarded as the very embodiment of knightly exemplariness: "No painter could have portrayed him to better effect than as he sat there on his charger."[29] How much this posture expressed the self-confidence of the noble lords can be seen from the fact that the princes of the twelfth and thirteenth centuries used equestrian seals that showed them in this pose (see fig. 18).

In contrast to the older fighting style, the charge with the couched lance was a particularly characteristic element of modern single combat. It was called *hurten* "to charge," and one used mostly French words to describe it: *poinder* "the start," *puneiz* "the attack," *punieren* "to charge with the lance," *sambelieren* "to squeeze with the thighs," *kalopieren* "to gallop," *leisieren* "to ride with a loose rein." Previously, German had had no terms for the different types of gallop. Now one adopted *walap* "gallop" and *rabîne* "full gallop" to express the motions during the charge with the lance. The most difficult part of the charge was the simultaneous control of the horse and the weapons. The knight held the lance in one hand, the shield in the other, and urged the horse on with his legs, using his thighs (*vliegende schenkel*), feet (*enkel*), and spurs: "With pressure from his thighs, with his spurs and his heels he guided the horse at the flanks."[30]

The knightly lance charge was called *stechen* ("tilting"). Sometimes the phrase *stechen unde slahen* ("tilting and striking") was used to describe the lance fight followed by the sword fight. The art of tilting involved striking the opponent with the lance in a particular spot. Two targets were emphasized: "Where the four nails are on the shield, that is where your lance should strike, or where the helmet is laced: these are the two proper targets for the knight and the highest artistry in jousting."[31] These were the two places where a knight was most vulnerable to his opponent's lance. The helmet strap at the neck was only partially covered by the shield; if the lance struck there it could easily penetrate into the *kollier*, the neck guard, or the throat itself: "Where shield and helmet meet and where the throat is surrounded by the *kollier*, that is where my hand struck him, tearing open the *kollier*, so that the strong and brave man slowly sank to the ground."[32] The four nails on the shield were not, as one frequently reads, part of the buckle in the middle, for that is precisely where the shield was strongest; they were rather the externally visible riveting of the hand grip: "Where one could see the attachment of the grips by the nails on the shield, that is where the lance was often aimed with knightly spirit."[33] If the lance struck here the thrust could tear through the shield "to the hand"[34] and disable the opponent.

In many cases, though, the shield withstood the impact of the lance. The result was the famed breaking and splintering of the lances, which had such appeal to the poetic imagination. In the *Kaiserchronik* the phrases *schefte brechen* and *sper verstechen* were already used to describe the joust (14070 f.). Later one also used *sper vertuon*, *schefte zerklieben*, *schefte zerbersten*, *sper verswenden*, *sper enzwei frumen*, and so on. Particularly numerous were expressions describing how the splinters flew about: *die sprundelen hôhe flogen* (H. v. Veldeke, *Eneit* 201.13), *die speltern ûf stuben* (U. v. Zatzikhoven 5294), *die sprîtzen gein den lüften flugen* (W. v. Eschenbach, *Parzival* 37.26). The fame and reputation of a knight were measured by the number of broken lances, which is why a knight keen on performing noble deeds always had to carry along a plentiful supply. As Gahmuret rode into Kanvoleis he ordered his squires to gather his painted lances into bundles: each squire carried a bundle of five lances and a sixth one with a colorful pennant (W. v. Eschenbach, *Parzival* 61.23 ff.). When Ulrich von Liechtenstein, dressed up as Lady Venus, traveled through Friaul and Carinthia in 1227 and fought friendly jousts along the way, he carried along one hundred lances (*Frauendienst* 475.3). One gets the impression that the lances were sometimes made of wood that splintered easily, and that the whole point of jousting was to shatter them. The idea that the breaking of so many lances deforested the woods, and that the knight was a "squanderer of forests,"[35] was often voiced in the thirteenth century. This more than anything reveals that the joust catered to the knights' egos.

Delivered in full gallop and with incredible force, the lance thrust in many cases nonetheless had a relatively modest impact. It could happen that a knight was killed by a lance, but the fatal thrust appears with any frequency only in the older epics. Later the outcome of the clash was usually that one of the knights was unhorsed. This "throwing" of the opponent (*abstechen, ûz dem satele stechen, zuo der erde werfen, entsetzten*) was the climax of the lance fight. It was only decisive, however, if the unseated knight was unfortunate enough to break an arm or a leg in the fall. For the knight still seated it would have been easy to slay the defenseless opponent on the ground, but normally he was not at all interested in doing so. Instead, he would wait until his opponent got up and was ready to continue the fight. In *Erec* we are told why: "He did it so that nobody could claim he had been so dishonorable as to kill him on the ground."[36] Here we see clearly that the knightly duel had a strong ritualistic quality: what was at stake was social reputation, fame or disgrace, more than simply victory itself.

The ensuing battle with the swords was less characteristic of the new weapons technology of the courtly age. Its depiction was also colored more strongly by traditional elements derived partly from classical literature and partly from the oral heroic epics. In the sword fight the opponents ran up and struck each other with their swords until one of them stumbled or sank to his knees. A terrific effect was created by the din of the weapons, which sometimes thundered across the entire battlefield ("palace and towers resounded with their blows as they struck their good helmets with the swords"[37]), and from the sparks that flew from the clashing iron ("the sparks sprang from the helmets"[38]). Not infrequently the sword fight ended in the death of one of the combatants. But a more typical outcome of a duel was that the victorious knight would decline to kill the vanquished opponent. The victor would accept a "surety," a pledge that the loser would place himself into his hands. This courtly "taking of a surety" (*sicherheit nemen*) was also designated by the French word *fianze*: "He gave him *fianze*: in German it is called 'surety.'"[39] To refrain from killing the opponent and instead to accept a pledge was regarded as one manifestation of a courtly attitude.

Fighting with the sword was usually done on foot. Sometimes it was pointed out specifically that the combatants had dismounted (*erbeizen* was the technical term). Hartmann von Aue had some very disparaging words about a sword fight on horseback: "Had they fought with swords seated on their chargers—which they had no intention of doing—it would have been the death of the poor horses. For that reason they were both obliged to refrain from such boorishness and to fight on foot. The poor horses had done them no harm."[40] Wolfram von Eschenbach, however, depicted Parzival's sword fight with Orilus as talking place while they were still mounted, something he specifically emphasized: "This happened on horseback and not on foot."[41] The equestrian seals of the twelfth and thirteenth centuries frequently show the princely knights on horseback with sword raised high above their heads. And pictorial battle scenes from the thirteenth century confirm what the historical sources report, namely that the knights fought with swords while mounted on their chargers. Hartmann von Aue's polemicizing against this practice in the name of courtliness reveals the gap between the poetic fighting scenes and reality.

In some cases the sword fight was followed as a final act by a wrestling match. It would end with one man placing his knee onto the chest of the opponent and forcing him to yield. The wrestling match was a typical motif of the heroic epic and was only occasionally taken up by the courtly poets. The assertion that Erec "had in his childhood in England, so they say, learned to wrestle very well,"[42] was probably meant to portray wrestling as a variant of the courtly duel. Wolfram von Eschenbach even used the decisive wrestling match several times in deviation from his French source.

It is not only these details that have an unreal air about them. The entire construct of the knightly joust was unrealistic in the extreme. What the courtly poets described as the normal knightly trial—the one-on-one confrontation of the noble warrior with a peer armed in like manner—had only a tenuous link to real life. Judicial combat was carried out in the form of a duel, but certainly not as a joust. It could also happen that especially bold knights rode jousts against each other between the lines before battle was joined. When King Ottokar II of Bohemia faced the Hungarians in 1271, "many a joust was ridden on the plain between his troops and theirs, as one still does between the battle lines, driven by a knightly spirit in the desire to be esteemed more highly."[43] It is not unlikely that the chronicler was inspired by poetic images when he composed this description. A more realistic account of such fighting between the battle lines, which was generally a deliberate violation of military discipline, is given by Rahewin in connection with the siege of Milan by Emperor Frederick I in 1158. With great chagrin the emperor had to watch as "some men from his army, driven by the usual thirst for glory and eager to beat the others to it," rushed blindly against the city "in the hope of achieving something memorable."[44] The most prominent among them was the Bavarian Count Ekbert of Pütten und Formbach, who was joined by a large band of armored knights. "They fought first with their lances and then with drawn swords,"[45] and in the turmoil of dust and bodies the German knights were repulsed by the Milanese. Graf Ekbert advanced alone right up to the walls of the city, "as everyone took flight because they could not resist the strength and boldness of this man."[46] But in the end he was struck down by a blow from a lance, "and after he had been stripped of his helm and armor they cut off his head."[47] Such was the reality against which the courtly poets asserted the ideology of the knightly duel.

Nevertheless, there must have been occasions when adherence to the knightly code of behavior was expected even in real life. Ottokar von Steiermark recounts that in the year 1258 the Austrian Marshal Hermann von Landenberg warned the Swabian knights of the uncourtly fighting style of the Hungarian Count Yban von Güssing: "You think this will be like fighting the French. But I have not known Count Yban to be so courtly."[48] The reason being that Count Yban had used light-armed crossbowmen against the armored knights in the army of Duke Albrecht of Austria (d. 1308), who threw the Austrian cavalry into confusion with their bolts and who refused to engage in close combat. A very similar situation had occurred in 1246 at the battle of Laa on the Thaya river, where Duke Frederick II of Austria (d. 1246) employed archers against the Bohemian troops of King Wenzel I (d. 1253). Their arrows penetrated the armored housings of the horse, which drew bitter complaints from the Bohemian knights:

> You lords from Austria, you are all noble fighters. Engage us in knightly fashion and use your swords, and for the sake of all the ladies fight with us in courtly manner. You fire shafts at us that cut through the iron housings and throw us to the ground. That is not the knightly way. Whoever girt you with the sword, may he be cursed; and whoever blessed your shields, may his soul be never saved. He should rather have blessed for you a quiver full of arrows: you would be well served with such a pagan practice.[49]

The appeal fell on deaf ears.

It is revealing that crossbowmen and archers, whose decisive role had already been demonstrated at the Battle of Hastings in 1066, appeared in courtly poetry only where the intent was to portray an unknightly and insidious fighting style. In the adventure of Schastel Marveile, for example, Gawan is unexpectedly showered with arrows from an

ambush and can defend himself only with great difficulty (W. v. Eschenbach, *Parzival* 569.4 ff.). Wherever a band of crossbowmen is mentioned we always find some derogatory adjective attached to them. In
the besieged castle of Belrapeire there were, among other troops, "a
great many vile bowmen."[50] Some scholars believe that the appearance
of the word *arc* ("vile," "worthless") at this point in the manuscript
must be a copyist's error, but they overlook the fact that crossbowmen
with their deadly bolts always seemed base and uncourtly to the poets.
The fulminations against these weapons, whose deadly power the noble
knights had come to know and fear on the crusades, were also supported by the Church. At the Second Lateran Council in 1139 the use of
crossbows against Christians was prohibited on pain of punishment:
"We prohibit furthermore on pain of anathema that the art of the crossbowmen and the archers, deadly as it is and repugnant to God, be used
against Christians and believers."[51]

The reality of warfare was different than the poets depicted it. In his
war against the French, King Peter III of Aragon (d. 1285) had the
watering holes of the horses poisoned: thirty thousand horses are said
to have perished; the remainder died of thirst (O. v. Steiermark 3768
ff.). In the war between England and Flanders, the Flemish, on the
advice of a weaver from Ghent, dug pits and placed sharp stakes at the
bottom that impaled the French knights (ibid. 64298 ff.). At the Battle
of Bouvines in 1214, the Germans in the army of Emperor Otto IV used
a new type of three-edged knife which was considered a particularly
cruel weapon: "The enemies [of the French] used a strange weapon that
had not been seen before. They had long, slender, three-edged knives
with three sharp edges that ran from the tip to the handle. These they
used instead of swords."[52] Ruthlessness and cruelty in battle are also
found in courtly literature if the enemy was not part of courtly society or
if the warfare had a religious motivation. When the pagan King Arofel's
belt broke in battle, Willehalm first chopped off his leg and then his
head (W. v. Eschenbach, *Willehalm* 78.26 ff.). Occasionally such a
rough fighting style was also employed against knightly opponents.
Brought to his knees by a blow from the sword of Prince Pallas, Duke
Turnus from this postition thrust his sword upwards through his opponent's hauberk and into his stomach (H. v. Veldeke, *Eneit* 206.10 ff.).
In his battle against Morolt, Tristan took advantage of the moment
when his opponent was about to mount his horse and hacked off his
right hand. As Morolt then lay before him defenseless, Tristan with his
knightly background did not hesitate to kill him and cut off his head

(G. v. Straßburg 7050 ff.). Tandareis was not content to simply slay his opponent: "In rage he rode over him and trampled him down."[53] To the courtly poets, however, such behavior was unusual.

HORSES

The horse played a very important role within noble society of the Middle Ages. The mobile nature of lordship necessitated that the entire court—including the ladies—was accustomed to a life in the saddle. Coaches and sedan chairs were used fairly rarely. In connection with the new fighting techniques a great culture of the horse developed in the courtly age. It is reflected in many historical sources and found literary expression in a rich vocabulary.

The old German noun for horse was *ros*. From the end of the twelfth century writers liked to use the word in the form *ors* with the *r* inverted. This variant, apparently taken over from Low Frankish, had a very modern Flemish sound to the ears of the noble audiences at the High German courts. Heroic epics preferred the word *marc*, which was avoided by most courtly poets because it seemed old-fashioned. *Ros* and *ors* could be applied to every horse, though in the courtly age they were used primarily for the charger suitable for knightly combat. To distinguish knightly mounts from other horses one had to resort to loan words. *Pferit*, an early borrowing from Latin (*paraveredus*), served mostly to designate the lighter riding horse or a lady's horse. Erec ordered "that his war-*ros* be saddled and Lady Enite's riding-*pfert*."[54] The word pair *ors–pfert* had a Medieval Latin equivalent in *dextrarius-palefridus*. In the military code promulgated by Emperor Frederick I in 1158, we read: if a foreign knight comes into the camp unarmed and "seated on a palfrey,"[55] he should be left alone. But if he arrives "mounted on a charger"[56] and armed with shield and lance he is a legitimate target.

Two other words for horse were borrowed from French: *ravît* for the fast racer, and *runzît* for the less valuable animal that was used mostly as a draft or pack horse. A corresponding terminology is attested in the scientific literature of the thirteenth century. Albertus Magnus distinguished in his work "On Animals" (*De animalibus*) "four types of horses" (*quatuor modi equorum*): first the *dextrarii* or *bellici* ("war-horses"); these were the chargers that "execute jumps and smash into the battle lines biting and kicking" (*dare saltus et irrumpere acies mordendo et calce feriendo*); second, the *palefridi*, used as riding horses;

third, the *curriles equi*, which were especially fast runners; and fourth, the *runcini*, used "as beasts of burden or to pull wagons and carriages."[57] The German terms were of course not always employed in their specialized meaning. *Pfert* could also describe a horse in general and it then overlapped with *ors*. *Runzît* could also designate a good palfrey. But if the poets wanted to draw distinctions they knew precisely which words to use.

Descriptions of horses were part of the modern style of courtly epics. A model was created by Hartmann von Aue: his description of Enite's horse is nearly five hundred verses long (Erec 7286-7766). Praise was heaped onto the figure of the horse, its qualities, and its unusual coloring. Even more space was devoted to the costly riding gear (*gereite*). The saddle was of ivory, decorated with gold and gems and figurative scenes from the story of Aeneas. On top of it lay a silk blanket (*sateltuoch*) interlaced with gold; it reached down nearly to the ground and showed the four elements. The border was ornamented with a broad trim set with jewels. The stirrups (*stegereif*), shaped like dragons, were made of gold. Girth (*darmgürtel*) and stirrup straps (*stîcleder*) were mounted with gold and lined with silk. The saddle cushion (*panel*) displayed the story of Pyramus and Thisbe. A mesh of gold wire covered the horse's croup. The bridle (*zoum*) was a jewel-studded braid. Gems also decorated the headpiece (*schîbe*). And yet this fantastic wealth of luxurious attributes was not without foundation in real life. We know from historical sources that great splendor was lavished on the decoration of horses. Arnold of Lübeck tells us that Henry the Lion, on his journey home from the Holy Land in 1171, received from the Turkish sultan, among other gifts, "thirty very strong horses... with silver bridles and exquisite saddles fashioned from precious cloth and ivory."[58]

The riding gear of the chargers was entirely determined by the new technique of fighting with couched lance. In front and back the saddle was equipped with high saddlebows (*satelbogen*) that ensured the knight a firm seat. If the rear saddlebow broke on impact nothing would keep the knight on his horse. The saddle was secured with two girths (*darmgürtel*), one chest strap (*vürbüege*), and one top strap (*surzengel*, from French *sorcengle*). The chest strap was particularly important, as it prevented the saddle from sliding back at impact. If this strap broke when the lances clashed the knight would land behind his horse. Armor for horses is historically documented from the second half of the twelfth century. Gislebert of Mons recounts under the year 1187 that the count of Hainaut and his knights rode into battle against the

English king "on horses decorated with iron housings."[59] In courtly
epic iron horse blankets appear first around 1200 (îsnîne kovertiure,
U. v. Zatzikhoven 8078). Shoulder blankets and chamfrons (head armor)
are attested somewhat later. The fact that only French words were used
for the armor of horses (kovertiure "housing," gropiere "shoulder
blanket," tehtier "chamfron") undoubtedly indicates the provenance of
these innovations. Another French loan word, gugerel, described the
headdress of a knight's horse: "Of gold was his gugurel, a small tree
with leaves."[60] Later the headdress of the horse usually took the same
form as the crest on the helmet of its rider.

Knightly combat demanded exceptionally strong horses. The notion,
common in hippological literature, that heavy horses were normally
used, cannot be validated for the twelfth and thirteenth centuries. It is
also false to regard the Latin word dextarius as a term for a specific
breed. Only after the adoption of plate armor, which added considerably more weight to the armored knight, was it necessary to use the
super heavy horses that we know from illustrations of the fifteenth
and sixteenth centuries. It has been calculated that late medieval armor
by itself weighed over 250 pounds. There does not seem to be evidence
for the breeding of heavy horses for combat before the end of the fourteenth century. There is also no proof that only stallions were used as
chargers because mares were supposedly too weak. In support of such a
claim, some have pointed to a statement by Wolfram of Eschenbach,
but his comment was probably humorous (or misogynistic). In Willehalm we are told that the pagan King Margot of Pozzident rode into
battle on a mare (jumente) "covered with an iron housing. Spread out
over the iron was a silken blanket, and that was too much for her. Here
in our country the mothers of chargers are not decked out this way: we
ride stallions to the charge."[61]

The best war horses were imported from Spain. In Krone we hear
that King Arthur sends his highest court official, the steward Keie,
to Spain to buy horses: "Lord Keie the seneschal rode to Spain and
brought many horses from there back to England: they were good, fast,
tall, handsome, and strong."[62] Here we see what made Spanish horses
special and what was so highly valued: speed, size, and strength. Spanish
chargers were so well known that the word spanjol became a word for a
horse in German, just like the word kastellân, which indicated the
famed horse breeding in Castile. Historical sources confirm that Spanish horses were brought to Germany. While Emperor Frederick II was
staying in Hagenau in 1235, "envoys from the queen of Spain arrived,

and they presented the emperor with the most beautiful chargers and other splendid gifts."[63] The heavy Scandinavian horses were also well suited for combat. The smaller horses from Hungary were especially popular as riding horses. Palfreys were greatly valued as riding horses because they were so comfortable. Mules, too, were often used for riding. The noblest horse of all was thought to be the Arabian, primarily because of its speed. Historical sources indicate that enormous sums were paid for good horses: in 1298 the Bohemian King Wenzel II came to King Albrecht I "dressed in costly robes and seated on a horse valued at one thousand marks."[64]

4. FOOD AND DRINK

FOOD FOR THE NOBILITY

"Beets and sauerkraut were not brought to the table. Venison and fine fish, well seasoned, were prepared for the lords. An abundance of dishes was there; and along with it the warriors drank the finest wine found on earth."[1] In the High Middle Ages a distinction was always made between noble food (*Herrenspeise*) and peasant food (*Bauernspeise*). "Many a peasant turns old and gray who never tasted almond pudding or figs, fine fish or almonds. Beets and sauerkraut he liked to eat, and sometimes he enjoyed his oat bread every bit as much as the lords enjoyed the meat of game and domestic animals."[2] In *Helmbrecht* the oat bread (*haber*) of the peasants is contrasted to the white rolls (*wîzen semeln*) of the knights, water to wine, grits (*gîselitze*) to boiled chicken (*huon versoten*), and cabbage (*krût*) to fish (471 ff., 1604 ff.). Sometimes the wandering *Spruch* poets had reason to complain that they were not served the same food that the lords ate. Friedrich von Suonenburg was entertained "in an unworthy manner" (*unwirdiclichen*) by an unnamed lord: he was given only "bad wine, the worst food,"[3] and his horse was not fed at all. "His cabbage stew, his dark bread, his cheap wine, let him feed it to the dogs or the pigs!"[4] The rich Cologne merchant Gerhard was well aware that he acted in an un-Christian manner by feasting lavishly while serving inferior food to the poor outside: "I had sour beer and rye bread brought to the door as alms when I saw a beggar outside."[5] Quite different was the behavior displayed in the thirteenth century by the papal legate Martin of Parma whenever he was entertaining high ecclesiastical dignitaries at table. "In front of him on the table he had two large silver bowls, into which the food for the poor

was placed. The cupbearer always brought two plates of every kind of
dish, in the sequence of the meal, and placed them before Brother Rigal-
dus [the archbishop of Rouen]. He kept one plate for himself, from
which he ate, and dumped the other one into the bowls for the poor.
And this he did with every dish and with every new course."[6]

In *Seifried Helbling* we read that Duke Leopold VI of Austria (d.
1230) supposedly published rules governing the food of peasants:
"Their food was determined to be meat, cabbage, and barley porridge.
They were not to have venison. On fast days they ate hemp, lentils, and
beans. Fish and oil they properly left for the lords to eat, that was the
custom."[7] The author—or rather, his fictional speaker—noted with indignation that these regulations were no longer being observed at the
end of the thirteenth century, and that peasants "are now eating the
same as the lords."[8] For him that was an indication that society had
fallen into disorder. As far as we know, there were no such food laws in
the thirteenth century. The first real laws that contained regulations
concerning food were very different in nature: they were aimed at the
excessive lavishness of aristocratic tables. The oldest such document
dates to the year 1279. King Philip III of France decreed "that no duke,
no baron, no count, no prelate, no knight, no cleric, nor anyone else in
the realm, of whatever estate, may serve up for a meal more than three
simple courses."[9] Fruit and cheese, "so long as they were not in the
form of pies or soufflés"[10], should not be counted among the three
courses. A "course" probably means an entire menu composed of
several individual dishes.

As an attribute of rank and lordship, noble food was every bit as
important to aristocratic society of the High Middle Ages as elegant
dress. Strict hunting laws closed the forests, streams, and lakes to practically everybody who did not hold sovereign rights. Along with domestic fowl, venison and fish were therefore among the typical foods of the
nobility. The court had "great stores of noble food: fish, chicken,
venison."[11] In courtly epics we read the names of different types of fish,
especially salmon (*salm*), lamprey (*lamprîde*), and beluga (*hûsen*). Even
the not-so-wealthy ate fish in the High Middle Ages, but mostly
stockfish (dried cod) and salted herring, which were transported far
inland along the trading routes. When it came to wild fowl, medieval
people spurned "neither the crane nor the bustard, neither the heron
nor the capon, neither the partridge nor the pheasant."[12] Even swans
and peacocks were eaten ("roast peacock stood before him"[13]). The
Latin "Lament of the Roasted Swan" (*Olim lacus colueram*) from the

Carmina Burana (no. 130) is still known today in Carl Orff's musical setting. In interpreting these poetic texts, however, we must bear in mind that the only surviving, detailed record of a great thirteenth century noble household, the account books of the Countess of Leicester for the year 1265, mention mostly domestic fowl—chicken, capons, and geese. Partridges, bustards, and pheasants were highly valued game. The great wild birds—herons, cranes, and swans—were apparently dished up very rarely indeed, even at the royal table only on very special occasions. In 1306, King Edward I (d. 1307) celebrated the knighting of his son Edward. At the banquet, "two swans or water birds were served to the king in great splendor, decorated with golden nets and gilded necks."[14] Keeping a proper table required a well-stocked chicken coop. When Parzival arrived at Belrapeire "the coops were empty"[15]: a sure sign of famine in the castle. At great court feasts coops were sometimes set up for the occasion. That was the case in 1184 Mainz, at the great feast hosted by Frederick I: "Two houses were put up there, large and very spacious inside, and throughout equipped with perches. From roof to floor they were so stuffed with cocks or hens that one could not see through them. All this aroused the amazement of many who had believed that so many hens scarcely existed in all the world."[16]

Meat dishes were often served in spicy sauces: "Here are pepper and saffron, ginger and galagan-root, they artfully make food tasty. These spices make the dishes become delicious in smell, taste, and color, thanks to the industriousness of the cook."[17] "In small vessels of gold they received a sauce suitable for each dish, saltsauce, peppersauce, winesauce. All had their fill there, the frugal man and the glutton."[18] In addition to domestic spices one used the costly oriental ones that long-distance trading brought to the courts. Merchants also supplied nuts, almonds, figs, dates, ginger, and raisins, all of which were used for making a variety of desserts. One mark of a noble table was white bread, served either as rolls or in the French variety as a round *gastel*: "Half a bread which is called *gastel*: it is completely round."[19]

A festive meal had to include wine: "If someone hosts a feast, no matter how many courses are served, it is no festive entertainment if good bread and wine are missing."[20] Courtly literature knows the names of many different kinds of wine. Greatly renowned were the heavy wines of southern Europe, especially from Cyprus. Domestic wines were usually fairly sour and were therefore sweetened and spiced. White spiced wine was called *lûtertranc* or *clâret*, a French loan word;

red spiced wine was *sinôpel*, also a French word. In addition one drank mulberry wine (*môraz*), fruit wine (*lît*), and mead (*mete*), whereas beer was considered an uncourtly drink: "No one there was drinking beer: one drank wine and *clarêt*, good *sinôpel* and sweet mead."[21]

The lists of the various dishes and drinks in the feast descriptions could create the impression that the courtly epic poets displayed in their descriptions of culinary customs the same expertise as with courtly dress and knightly armaments. But that was not the case. The order of the menu at the great feasts was reported in a very summary fashion, mostly in the form of a list of typical noble dishes. Contemporary historical sources are equally bare of information about individual dishes. A unique exception is the account of the Italian chronicler Salimbene of Parma about a banquet—though a lenten meal without meat—in the Franciscan monastery of Sens in 1248, to which the French King Louis IX (d. 1270) had invited the leadership of the Franciscan order. Salimbene was also present: "And so we received on that day first cherries, then the whitest bread. Plenty of excellent wine was also served, as befits the glory of the king. . . Afterwards we had young beans cooked in milk, fish and crabs, pâté of eel, rice with almond milk and ground cinnamon, fried eels in an exquisite sauce, cakes and cottage cheese. The usual fruits were also served properly and in abundance. And everything was dished up in befitting manner and eagerly served."[22]

It seems that it was considered bad form in courtly society to speak of the food in excessive detail. Occasionally the poets downright refused to be more specific: "Unversed as I am in culinary arts, I could not name individually the dishes that were brought in with proper ceremony."[23] "Were I to tell you now much about the food and dishes that were served, it would only cause a great din and yet be of no use; I shall therefore refrain."[24] "If someone now asks me when they ate something, let him go to the gluttons and have them tell him about food."[25] Rudolf von Ems put it blunty: "Let a glutton talk about abundant eating."[26]

Ever since antiquity, warnings against gluttony and drunkenness had been part of the maxims of secular morality. The notion that moderation in food and drink was becoming, especially to a person who had everything in abundance, also had a permanent place in the courtly concept of etiquette. "Eat and drink such that the natural needs are satisfied."[27] The didactic poems of the thirteenth century addressed this point at length. "Immoderation in eating and drinking often damages a person in body and soul, in reputation and property."[28] The courtly poets also emphasized repeatedly that noble society strove to exercise proper restraint in food consumption. An exemplary knight behaved as Erec did before the tournament: "He did not indulge in gluttony: he took three bites from a chicken, that was enough for him."[29] In an extreme case even complete abstention could he integrated into the courtly ideal. In the minnegrotto, Tristan and Isolde lived only on love, taking no earthly nourishment (G. v. Straßburg 16811 ff.).

It is difficult to judge the degree to which the courtly style of the meal in Germany was influenced by the social customs of the French nobility, since in this area, unlike with clothes and weapons, there is no detailed information that can he securely dated. It is, however, highly likely that the adoption of French court manners also shaped the protocol of the festive meal. One indication is the fact that many French words were borrowed. These are words for the tableware (*barel* "goblet," *toblier* "bowl"), the meals of the day (*petit mangir* "breakfast," *gramangir* "main meal"), the type of food (*mursel* "delicacy"), and the different dishes, drinks, and spices (*gastel* "cake-bread," *suppierre* "soup," *blamenschir* "almond dish," *clarêt* "white spiced wine," *sinôpel* "red spiced wine," *salse* "spicy sauce," *vînaeger* "wine vinegar," *muscât* "nutmeg," *kubêbe* "raisin," and others).

THE PROTOCOL OF THE COURTLY BANQUET

The festive meal followed elaborate ceremonial rules. In most cases the poets devoted more attention to the courtly arrangements than to the sequence of dishes. To eat "with courtly decorum" (*mit zuht*) was the most important rule of all. The encyclopedic work *De proprietatibus rerum* ("On the Nature of Things") by the English Franciscan Bartholomaeus Angliscu (d. after 1250) lists thirteen points that make a meal splendid and festive. Only three points concerned the food itself: "the great variety of dishes," "the diversity of wines and drinks," and "the deliciousness of everything served."[30] Bartholomaeus adds that one should not set any greasy or common dishes before the guests, "instead, one serves the diners something special, light and delicious, especially at the courts of the great lords."[31] The remaining ten points were devoted to the festive framework of the meal. The "proper timing" of the meal was crucial, as was "suitable space,"[32] with the size, beauty, and safety of the hall being of uppermost concern, "for the nobility are accustomed to celebrating their feasts in spacious, lovely, and secure rooms."[33] The host shall please his guest by "the cheerfulness of his countenance"; "for a meal is worth nothing when the host's face is gloomy."[34] Also of great importance was "the elegant and dignified deportment of the servants," and "the sweetness of the singing and the music," "for noble people do not hold their meals without a harp or organ."[35] "A suitable number of candelabra and wax candles"[36] should also be present. Finally, the host should see to it that the guests are suited for each other, that the meal can be eaten without haste, and that the guests incur no expenses and find their desired comforts after the feast.

SEATING ARRANGEMENTS

In preparation for the meal the hall was decorated. King Arthur "had his entire hall hung with tapestries that glittered splendidly with gold. The floor was covered with costly silk rugs and then sprinkled with many roses."[37] Tables and seats, usually of costly material, were set up especially for the meal. Great care was taken to provide comfortable cushions: "The seats were nicely covered with good quilts of splendid color. The pillows and cushions were of brocade and cendale. No seat was ever more beautifully decorated."[38] The hall for eating should be spacious, so that everything could be splendidly prepared: "Great was the feast, and the seating took up a good deal of space."[39] If the hall was not large enough to entertain all the guests, tables were set up outdoors.

The difficult task of supervising the seating arrangements was usually the responsibility of the steward: "In front of the table stood the steward, who led the lord of the court to his seat. In his hand he held a staff which he used to indicate to the guests where to sit."[40] "There with his staff went the steward of the emperor and made sure that one could eat."[41] There are also pictorial scenes that show how the steward with his staff kept watch over the courtly protocol during the meal (see figs. 19 and 20).

The seating arrangement was strictly hierarchical: "All were seated splendidly but not equally."[42] "In accordance with their rank he seated them on the benches."[43] If several high ranking guests were present, great prudence was required to accommodate all considerations: "Let us praise him who knows how to seat guests festively, below, in the middle, and at the top end of the table."[44] In *König Rother* we hear of a quarrel over rank that turned into a bloody fight, when at the court

Fig. 19. Banquet of Ahasuerus. On the table are three bowls with fish, an assortment of vessels, knives, and bread. Off to the side the steward with his staff. From the *Hortus deliciarum* of Herrad of Landsberg. End of the twelfth century.

In mensa sedet

Fig. 20. Banquet of Archbishop Balduin of Trier. On the table are different dishes and a variety of vessels. Food and drink is served in large bowls and pitchers from high up on horseback. The steward, also on horseback, supervises the serving personnel with a staff. From the Codex Balduini (Koblenz, Landeshauptarchiv, Bestand I C, no. 1). Fourteenth century.

feast of King Constantine both Rother's chamberlain and the chamberlain of Duke Frederick laid claim to the particularly honorable "facing seat" (*daz geginsidile*, 1618), the seat of honor opposite the lord of the court. A historical incident of such a quarrel is reported by Ottokar von Steiermark. In 1298 the German princes journeyed to Nuremberg to pay homage to the new king, Albrecht I (d. 1308). At the banquet, "each prince was separately assigned a seat where he should eat."[45] "Then there arose a great quarrel. The archbishop of Cologne asserted that by ancient custom the archbishop of Cologne was to eat on the right side of the king whenever a court day was held in Germany."[46] The archbishop of Mainz protested and took his seat at the right hand of the king by force, whereupon his colleague from Cologne left the hall in a rage and challenged his rival to settle the matter in a duel.

To preempt disagreements over rank and precedence among the princes, the poets invented the "round table," the *table ronde*, at which the best knights at Arthur's court were seated with equal honor: "The table has nowhere a head or an end, neither corners nor points. Those heroes who by knightly deeds and boldness acquired the distinction and earned in knightly fashion the right to sit there, they are all seated splendidly and equal in high rank."[47]

In real life the tables were very different in shape. They were rectangular and long, with the host seated "at the very head."[48] "The table was low and long. The host sat alone and uncramped at its head."[49] But different seating arrangements were possible. The pictorial scenes of banquets from this period show the lord not at the head of the table but in the middle of one of the long sides, with a decreasing order of rank to his left and right (see fig. 21). It could also happen that the lord sat all alone at a separate table or that only the lady of the court dined with him. It was always a high honor for a guest to be seated next to the host or close by. The pictorial evidence also reveals that one long side of the table was left free during the meal to allow access by the servants. This must have been the arrangement at great banquets, while in the family circle, when the lord took his place at the head of the table, people were probably seated all around.

We possess one unusually detailed report about the seating arrangements at the great banquet given by the French King Louis IX in Saumur in the year 1241 to celebrate the dubbing to knighthood of his brother, Count Alfonse of Poitiers (d. 1271). The account comes from the pen of Jean de Joinville (d. 1317), who was present in person as a sixteen-year-old lad, serving at that time as a page at the royal court.

Fig. 21. Banquet at Munsalvaesche. At the center of the table, with the large hat, sits King Anfortas, to his right Feirefiz and Parzival (the name bands were left empty). Women in precious robes serve at table. The larger female figure with the crown is probably Repanse de Schoie, who hands the Grail to Parzival. From the Munich *Parzival*-manuscript (Cgm 19). Thirteenth century.

> I was there as well and can assure you that it was the most well-ordered court I have ever seen. At the high table, next to the king, sat the comte de Poitiers, whom His Majesty had knighted on Saint John's Day; next to him was the comte de Dreux, another newly made knight; then came the comte de la Marche and next to him the good comte Pierre de Bretagne. In front of the king's table, facing the comte de Dreux, sat my lord the king of Navarre, in tunic and mantle of satin, well set off by a fine leather belt, a brooch, and a cap of gold tissue. I was set to carve his meat.[50]

The king was served by his brother, and three noble lords supervised the royal table. "Behind them stood some thirty of their knights in tunics of silk, to keep guard over their lords. Behind these knights stood a great company of sergeants, in suits of cendale embroidered with the arms of the comte de Poitiers."[51] The banquet was held "in the hall of Saumur, which was said to have been built by the great King Herny of England for his own great feasts. This hall is constructed on the model of a Cistercian cloister; but I do not believe there is any other hall that even approaches it in size."[52] Along the wall where the king was dining, there was still room for a table at which twenty bishops and archbishops were eating. At the opposite wall sat the Queen Mother, Blanche of Castile, who was waited on by two counts,

> and a German lad of eighteen, who was said to be the son of St. Elizabeth of Thuringia. On account of this, so it was said, Queen Blanche kissed the boy on his forehead, as a pure act of devotion, because she thought his own

mother must often have kissed him there. At the other end of the cloister were the kitchens, the wine cellars, the pantries, and the butteries, from which the king and the queen mother were served with meat, wine, and bread. To the right and left of the main hall and in the central court so many knights were dining that it was more than I could do to count them. Many people declared that they had never, on any other festive occasion, seen such a number of surcoats and other garments of cloth of gold and of silk. It was said that no less than three thousand knights were present on that occasion.[53]

Eating at small tables was considered courtly and modern. This practice is documented as early as the eleventh century: "Ruodlieb assigned the seats as he well knew how, where everybody was to sit and which seat was meant for him, and he placed two lords at each table."[54] In the great hall of the Grail castle Munsalvaesche, four knights were seated at each table; altogether the hall had one hundred of them, not counting the royal table (W. v. Eschenbach, *Parzival* 237.1 ff.). That men and women ate separately, either at different tables (Pleier, *Tandareis* 2595 ff.), or even in different rooms (Geoffrey of Monmouth, *Historia regum Britanniae*, p. 456 f.; *Nibelungenlied* 1671.1 ff.), can be attested through the late Middle Ages. The courtly poets, however, preferred to have courtly society dine in a loosely mixed arrangement or in pairs. "A knight and a lady each ate together."[55] "With each prince sat a beautiful lady, lovely, pure, and noble, who ate with him; this elevated their spirits."[56]

SERVICE AT TABLE

The ceremony of the meal required a large number of servants. At the festive entrance of the staff, as Heinrich von dem Türlin described it, there came first "twenty chamberlains, squires of refined manners and great decorum,"[57] who were carrying basins and towels for washing the hands. They were followed by so many servants with candles that the hall was illluminated as bright as day. Then came "thirty fiddlers"[58] together with a band of singers who knew "many fine melodies"[59]: they were to entertain the festive gathering during the meal. A little later the cupbearers entered the hall with wine pitchers, and finally, in a long line, the stewards with the food. The entrance of the stewards and cupbearers is also depicted in a miniature of the Munich Tristan manuscript (Cgm 51) from the mid-thirteenth century (see fig. 22). In addition there were carvers and "food-masters" (*spîsaere*), whose task it

Fig. 22. Banquet of King Mark. The servants kneel to serve the food. On the right the procession of the chamberlains and cup-bearers. From the Munich *Tristan* manuscript (Cgm 51). Thirteenth century.

was to cut the food at table into bite sized morsels, so that no cutlery was needed for eating. At the banquet in Munsalvaesche the four hundred knights were waited on by the same number of pages. Four pages were assigned to each table, "two kneeled down and cut the food; the other two brought the dishes and drinks to table and served the knights."[60] Occasionally girls would serve at table, as is depicted in a miniature in the Munich *Parzival* codex (Cgm 19) (see fig. 21). It was a rare honor if the lady of the court herself served a guest at table as happened to Gahmuret in Zazamanc. The Moorish Queen Belakane "knelt down before him—which was very embarrassing to him—and with her own hand carved him a portion of his food."[61] As an even stronger sign of her favor, the lady would let the lord of her table drink from her cup: "Every time she presented the goblet which her lips had touched, he felt joy once again that he was to drink after her."[62] The new custom of eating in pairs created a connection between the courtly meal and courtly love.

On especially festive occasions the service at table was done by some of the great nobles in attendance. "Very noble chamberlains, the highest in the land, knelt in festive gowns and offered the white towel to the king."[63] It is reported that at the court feast in Mainz in 1184, "the offices of steward, cupbearer, chamberlain, and marshal were attended upon solely by kings, dukes, and margraves."[64] Such service of honor was not always performed voluntarily. When King Albrecht I held court

at Nuremberg in 1298, the prince-electors served him at table. King
Wenzel II of Bohemia (d. 1305), however, tried to avoid the obligation
of waiting on the king as the cupbearer by feigning illness. But when
King Albrecht insisted on his service, the Bohemian monarch turned his
appearance at court into a demonstration of his wealth and power. He
donned the costliest robes, adorned himself with a belt and rings, and
wore the crown on his head as he mounted his horse.

> His head chamberlain carried a golden pitcher and a cup of heavy gold. A
> terrific blare arose from the sound of the trumpets. Flutes and tubas, shawms
> and drummers with huge military drums resounded together. Over the entire
> place, where stood the tables and benches, a noise arose as though every-
> thing was crashing down. Many had to make room and move out of the way
> when the mighty king of Bohemia came riding into the feast in such impe-
> rious manner.[65]

A thousand knights followed the king of Bohemia, who then knelt
down and offered up the wine to King Albrecht, and whom Albrecht
left on his knees until he and the queen had finished their drink. Subsequently the Bohemian monarch handed "the staff and the drinking
vessels"[66] to an assistant and took his seat at the table.

The arrangement of the courtly meal always included music.
"Together with the stewards came trumpeters who blared out before
them. The drums were beaten so strongly that the large hall echoed with
the great sound."[67] From French poetic works of the thirteenth century
we know that every new course was announced with trumpet signals
and the singing of lovely women: "At every course the trumpet sounded. The ladies who were serving there were decorated with golden
robes. Before each course they came in singing."[68] A similar custom
was already described in the *Straßburger Alexander*. When Queen Candacis went to eat, "a thousand squires from her court stood there in a
circle and provided courtly entertainment with all the various string
instruments."[69] Five hundred pages served at table. Five hundred ladies
also appeared: "When the harps sounded the young ladies sang and
danced."[70] Not only the ears, the eyes, too, were entertained with
courtly performances during the banquet: "They ate and drank and
watched a variety of entertainments that were put on before them."[71]

Details about such performances are available only in texts and pictures of a later period. In 1378 Emperor Charles IV (d. 1378) was festively entertained in Paris by the French King Charles V (d. 1380). A
miniature from the *Grandes Chroniques* (Paris, BN f. franç. 2813)
shows how the guests were entertained at table by a lavish play in pan-

Fig. 23. Entertainment for Emperor Charles IV in Paris. On the table are gold-
en drinking boats and other vessels. A great spectacle is performed between
the courses: the conquest of Jerusalem in the year 1099. From a manuscript of
the *Grandes Chroniques* (Paris, Bibliothèque Nationale, f. fr. 2813). Fifteenth
century.

tomime that depicted the conquest of Jerusalem in 1099 and King Richard the Lionheart's journey to the Holy Land (see fig. 23). Whether such performances already existed in the thirteenth century must remain unanswered.

The banquets of the twelfth and thirteenth centuries might seem modest or downright simple in comparison to the culinary refinements and courtly table manners at the Burgundian court in the fifteenth century: huge figures of sugar and marzipan, table fountains and automatic table leaves, an abundance of exotic food, giant pâtés from which dwarfs emerged, the precise coordination of the music with each course, dancers with animal masks, great allegorical plays during the meals, the complicated hierarchy of the service staff, the ceremony of carving and tasting the food, the serving from high up on a horse, and much more. But such a perspective is deceiving. The splendor of Burgundian court culture was only the continuation and intensification of what had begun in the twelfth century, when at the great secular courts—first in France and England—a social style developed that was characterized by a previously unknown material luxury and refinement of etiquette. Through the kind of food it ate and through the courtly ceremony at table, courtly society expressed its claim to a special place above those who did not participate in the noble lifestyle. But even at this time we find ingenious food creations that anticipated later developments. In the French work *Floire et Blancheflor*, "a pâté filled with living birds"[72] was served: when it was broken at table the birds flew out, first smaller ones and then hunting birds who chased them.

TABLEWARE

The wealth of a table was also revealed by the costly tableware of gold and silver: "Drinking vessels and cups of red gold, the bowls nicely wrought of silver."[73] A *kopf* was a goblet-like double cup with a high, round cover; a *napf*, a cup without a cover; a "bowl" was called *vaz*, *schüzzel*, or *toblier* (a French word). Pictorial scenes also show serving pitchers, sauceboats, salt containers, and other utensils. The boat-shaped drinking cups so popular at the time in France and England seem to have been still unknown in Germany. According to the poetic description, vessels were sometimes decorated with figurative scenes with typical motifs from courtly life: a joust (H. v. d. Türlin, *Krone* 8853 ff.) or a minne scene (K. Fleck 3962 ff.), everything fashioned in great splendor. Such costly utensils are also attested historically.

The following was reported about King Ottokar II of Bohemia: "Even
the dishes for his table were of pure gold and silver and most exquisitely wrought. At every course, in unending succession, they were
brought to his table."[74] At the court of Emperor Henry VI, in the year
1196, "the golden and silver vessels for the daily table service, in which
the food and drink was served up, were valued at one thousand
marks."[75] Rahewin recounts that Emperor Frederick I, on the occasion
of a court day in 1159, presented "vessels of silver and gold"[76] as
gifts to the guests. We are told that the court officers of King Richard
the Lionheart once prevailed upon him to cut back his excessive generosity for one year. But the king knew how to circumvent his promise:
from the window of his palace he would throw his costly tableware to
needy knights below: "All the precious vessels that he found on that
occasion he threw down to the needy on the street. Magnificent golden
double cups and many silver bowls his generous arm tossed to the
knights who, poor and in distress, were counting on his help."[77] Wolfram von Eschenbach has described what precautions were sometimes
taken to prevent the precious tableware from being stolen. At the banquet in Munsalvaesche, the golden dishes for the four hundred knights
sharing the meal were wheeled into the hall on "four trolleys"[78] and
then distributed by four knights to the tables. "Each trolley was followed by a clerk whose job it was to return them to the trolley after the
meal was over."[79]

It appears that such lists of precious tableware were in fact kept. The
oldest record of this kind from Germany is contained in the "Codex
Falkensteinensis" from the end of the twelfth century: "In Neuenburg
there are six silver drinking cups with lids and five silver bowls without
lids, three silver goblets with lids and four without lids, one silver knife
(?) and two silver spoons. Altogether there are sixteen silver vessels."[80]
Far longer is the list of tableware that was found in castle Tyrol in 1310
at the death of Duke Otto of Carinthia from the house of Görz-Tyrol:
two drinking cups (*ciphi*) of beryl with gilded feet and gilded lids; five
ciphi of large nuts with silver feet partially gilded; one *ciphus* in the
shape of a bowl of silver; seven *ciphi*, two of them entirely gilded, the
others of shiny silver; one vessel (*stutza*) of nut with a silver foot; one
ciphus of horn with gilded rings; three small silver *ciphi* with lids, ten
large and small cups (*cuppae*) with lids; eleven round, silver *cuppae*
with no lids; two jugs (*flascae*) of silver; two small vessels (*barilia*) of
silver; one *ciphus* of rock crystal with a tall, gilded foot; one *ciphus* of
rock crystal with two gilded rings; six small drinking cups (*ciphuli*);

two great ostrich eggs; one *ciphus* of wood with spiral grain and silver-coated on the inside; two *ciphi* of wood with spiral grain, with two golden lions inlaid on the inside and with silver feet; four silver spoons; nine large and small *ciphi* of wood with spiral grain, all with tall silver feet (Mayr-Adlwang, p. 166).

The protocol of a courtly meal included washing of the hands before and after eating. For this, too, costly vessels were used: water pitchers (*giezvaz*) and hand basins (*beckîn*) of gold and silver, and towels (*twehel*) of pure silk. Matthew of Paris reports that in 1255, Queen Margaret of France presented the English King Henry II with "a splendid washbasin . . . shaped like a peacock."[81]

THE ORGANIZATION OF THE MEAL

Two little-noticed historical sources of the thirteenth century illuminate in greater detail the organization of the lord's table and the ceremony of serving the food. One is the register of the "Offices of the Court of Hainaut" (*Ministeria curie Hanoniensis*), drawn up between 1212 and 1214 by the Hainaut chancellor, Gislebert of Mons, and the Flemish chancellor, William, at the request of Ferdinand of Portugal (d. 1233), who was count of Flanders and Hainaut from 1212 on. It lists all court offices at Hainaut and the people who held them at the time of writing. At the top stood "the chief steward of the entire county of Hainaut,"[82] followed by the "chief chamberlain,"[83] the "chief cupbearer,"[84] and the second-ranking steward. The offices listed thereafter all have to do with the food supply for the court and the service at the comital table, a sure indication that the organization of the meals was of great importance in the social life at court. Listed are Iwan de Frameries, "the buyer and overseer of the kitchen stocks,"[85] as well as several "cooks" (*coqui*). There was further a "female cupbearer" (*pincerna*) by the name of Margareta—a canoness at Mons and the daughter of the chief cupbearer Renier de Mons—"at whose command the wine was brought to the court and served"[86]; it was also her task "to pour with her own hand the wine in front of the lord count and the lady countess."[87] If she was absent her place would be taken by the two helpers who usually assisted her if she performed the service herself. Next were Wacher de Crascol, whose job it was "to store the wine in barrels and pour it into cups or bowls so it could be served at table,"[88] and "two people who carried in the wine and the drinking vessels."[89] Then came the "pantler" (*panitaria*) Sapientia de Hyon, "by whose order the bread from the house of the court baker or from the bread sellers was brought to the court."[90] Pierre de Buselesia held a similar office. Next came Bernerus Malescherie, "the court-baker,"[91] Englebert de Jemappes, "who kept the bread brought to court and the tablecloths,"[92] and Thomas de Crascol, "who set up the tables and placed the tablecloths on them, and who had to carry the bread behind the pantler to serve it and distribute it at court."[93] The register names further a "door-keeper" (*hostarius*), a "porter" (*janitor*), and an under-chamberlain "who had in his care the mantles and hats of all those who paid their respects to the lord count of Hainaut."[94] Another under-chamberlain had the task "of making candles according to the instructions of the chamberlain, and to prepare the candles produced by weight for the chamberlain. He also had to ready the water for the chamberlain, so that the latter could personally offer it to the count and the countess, while the under-chamberlain had to present it to the clerics and knights."[95] Régnier was in charge of the tableware (*scutellarius*). The "potter" (*figulus*) Gautier had "the task of supplying the court with the earthen vessels that were needed in the pantry as well as in the kitchen, and for serving the wine."[96] In addition there was somebody who "had to keep the count's larder at the order of the pantler of Mons."[97] Finally, there were the cleric Martin, "whose office it was to guard the keys to the cellar,"[98] and a man "who had the task of collecting from the estates at Mons the sheep and oats owed to the count."[99] This register from Hainaut reveals that the table service at the great courts at the beginning of the thirteenth century had already reached a level of organization that has usually been assumed only for later centuries. We must bear in mind, however, that the court of the counts of Hainaut at Mons was in its entire culture oriented towards Flanders and France. The same kind of organization cannot be simply assumed for the German courts east of the Rhine.

Of equal interest are the instructions for the maintenance of a household from the pen of the English bishop and theologian Robert Grosseteste of Lincoln (d. 1252). We have a Latin, a French, and an English version of this tract, but their relationship to each other has not been definitely clarified. Apparently the bishop first drew up these instructions in Latin for his own court, and later, in 1240–1242, on the basis of the Latin text composed a detailed version of the "Rules" for the household of Countess Margaret of Lincoln. Under the title "Here begin the rules that Robert Grosseteste, the good bishop of Lincoln, has written for the countess of Lincoln, to guard and govern land and household,"[100] he compiled instructions both for the management of the estates and for the organization of the comital court. The second part, which is of interest to us, deals with the supervision of the court staff, the reception of guests, and the service at the lord's table. Regarding the seating arrangements we are told:

> The [seventeenth] rule teaches you how to seat the people at a meal in your house. Let all noble members of the household and the guests sit together on both sides of the tables, as much as possible, and not four here and three there. You shall always sit in the middle of the high table, so that your presence as lord or lady is visible to all, and so that you can survey on both sides the service and notice the mistakes. See to it that you have every day two overseers at your table, who supervise the meal while you are seated to eat."[101]

Precise instructions were given for the service at table:

> Give the order that your marshall shall supervise in person the assembled group, especially in the hall, and that he keep watch in a friendly manner over the people inside and out, without quarrel or ugly words. At each course he shall direct the servants to go into the kitchen, and he himself shall go in front of your steward up to your seat, until your food has been served to you; then he shall position himself in the middle of the front wall and see to it that your servants proceed everywhere through the hall in good order and without noise until they reach those who have been appointed to serve the food, so that nobody will receive any special treatment during the serving and distributing. And you personally shall keep an eye on the servants until the dishes have been distributed throughout the hall. Then devote yourself to your meal, and see to it that your bowl is refilled and heaped high, especially during the side dishes, so that in courtly fashion you can distribute from your bowl to the right and left at the entire table and wherever else you desire. All shall receive the same food that you have before you.[102]

No other source from this time describes so precisely and so authentically the ceremony of a courtly meal as these "Rules" of Bishop Grosseteste. The instructions further laid down "in what clothes your people shall serve at table,"[103] and how the portions of the meal intended for the poor were to be distributed. The good bishop of Lincoln also made rules concerning the number of courses: "At noontime the court shall be served only two main courses, large and heaping so that more alms are available, and two side dishes, likewise plentiful for the noble assembly. And for the evening meal one lighter course and a side dish and then cheese. If strangers appear for supper, they shall be served with all the things they need most."[104] It is remarkable that advice about the forms of courtly protocol was sought from an ecclesiastical prince. That the "Rules" were put into writing is an exception. But we can assume that a fixed arrangement for the organization of the meals existed at all larger courts.

The poets described the great feasts almost always from the perspective of the host, who had to make sure that everything went according to protocol. How the guests were expected to behave during the meal was touched on only incidentally. We can assume, however, that by around 1200 certain rules had been formulated regarding the behavior at table (see p. 13).

The genre of the courtly courtesy books seems to have been created by the court clerics; the oldest texts are in Latin. The Spaniard Petrus Alfonsi, who won great renown as the personal physician to King Alfonse I of Aragon (d. 1134) and later as court physician to King Henry I (d. 1134) of England, was the first to compile precepts for courtly conduct during a meal in his tract *Disciplina clericalis* at the beginning of the twelfth century. "Do not eat the bread before the first course is placed onto the table, otherwise you will be considered as lacking in self-control. Do not put such a large piece into your mouth that the crumbs fall out left and right, otherwise you will be considered a glutton. Do not swallow what is in your mouth until you have chewed it well, lest you choke. Drink only when your mouth is empty, otherwise you will be regarded as a drunkard. Do not speak while there is something in your mouth."[105] The tract of Petrus Alfonsi exerted a great influence on the Latin as well as the vernacular books of etiquette from the twelfth and thirteenth centuries. Among the later Latin works and for the situation in Germany, the *Phagifacetus* of Reinerus Alemannicus is of special interest, since the author—if the information from several manuscripts is correct—was chancellor or protonotary at the court of the landgrave of Thuringia in the thirteenth century. With a length of 440 hexameters, the *Phagifacetus* is the longest book of etiquette from the Middle Ages. The author arranged his material into different categories depending on the person with whom one shared a table. The largest number of precepts concern the behavior at the table of a noble lord. A meal shared with friends was treated more briefly. The third part compiled rules that one ought to observe in the company of ladies. Here Reinerus seems to presuppose the modern seating arrangement in pairs. One was not to move too close to the lady (381 ff.) and should refrain in her presence from everything crude and unseemly (392 ff.)

The first table manners in the German language appear in the ecclesiastical moralists who were writing for a secular noble audience. The tract on virtues by Wernher von Elmendorf (circa 1170) contains precepts that one should not drink too much (889 f.), should not complain about the food (1927 f.), and should not make any noise while eating (1050 f.). An entire catalog of such rules was compiled by the Italian cleric Thomasin von Zirklaere in his *Der Wâlsche Gast* (circa 1215) (471 ff.), clearly under the influence of Petrus Alfonsi. According to Thomasin's own account, this part of his work went back to a court manual he had written earlier in Provençal. Tannhäuser's *Hofzucht* from the middle of the thirteenth century initiates the line of independent books of etiquette. This new genre flourished in Germany, both in the serious version of the courtly books of etiquette, as well as in the parodistic manuals of manners. In the latter the rules of proper behavior had to be inferred from their opposites, for they describe what went on at table when all courtly manners were ignored. These rude and funny texts reflect no less a serious didactic purpose, but are vastly more entertaining than their sober counterparts.

Some precepts in the courtly manuals seem peculiar. In Tannhäuser's *Hofzucht*, for example, the noble audience is told not to place the gnawed-off bones back into the bowl (49 ff.), not to dip their fingers into the mustard or the sauces (53 ff.), not to blow their noses into the tablecloth (57 ff.), not to blow on a hot drink (85 ff.), not to stretch across the table during the meal (105 ff.), not to scratch their throats with the bare hand (109 ff.), and not to blow their noses into their hands (129 ff.). If we assume that these manuals had a practical purpose and were intended to remedy actual slovenliness, we get a very bleak picture of the real table manners, a picture that is difficult to reconcile with the highly stylized poetic descriptions of courtly meals. Nevertheless, we are dealing with the same reality simply looked at from different perspectives. Most prescriptions of table manners can be explained as rules of hygiene that responded to the actual conditions at table. Courtly society of the High Middle Ages ate with its fingers. The fork was known but used only for precutting. Knives and spoons were used for carving and serving. The pictorial scenes of the time show that usually only a few pieces of cutlery lay on the table, intended for common use. A slice of bread was used as a plate. One had to reach into the communal bowls, and frequently one also had to share a drinking cup with a neighbor (see fig. 24). In view of these conditions, the rule that one should not drink with greasy lips (*Tannhäuser* 93 f.) makes practi-

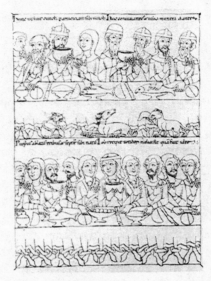

Fig. 24. A banquet. The diners reach into the bowls and pick at the fish with their fingers and take bite-sized pieces. The knives are hardly used. Several diners have to share one drinking cup between them. From a manuscript of Gregory the Great's *Moralia* (Paris, Bibliothèque Nationale, f. lat. 15675). Twelfth century.

cal sense. If one wanted to comply with the proper rules of etiquette and wipe one's mouth, the obvious choice, since there were no individual napkins, was the tablecloth. But that was prohibited by a number of etiquette books. Instead, the *Ulmer Hofzucht* recommended: "Wipe your mouth with your hand!"[106] Other books, however, opposed such a practice, which left the eater in a real predicament. The best solution was to use one's own clothing to wipe the mouth. The situation was similar with blowing the nose: if one could use neither the tablecloth nor one's hand, that left only the sleeve. The admonition not to dip one's fingers into the mustard seems only at first glance a response to crude manners; if there were not enough spoons on the table one really had no other choice. And how was one to get at the food without leaning across the table if the nearest bowl was far away? What to do with the gnawed-off bones if there were no plates? The rule not to scratch oneself during the meal makes sense, since the same hand would then reach back into the communal bowl. In case one felt an itch while eating, Tannhäuser recommends the following: "If that happens, in courtly fashion take your role and use that to scratch: it is better this way than if the hand were to get dirty."[107]

Many rules of etiquette expect a very cultured way of eating. Thomasin von Zirklaere, for example, demands that one must set the cup down before turning to one's table companion (491 ff.), or that one should eat only with the hand that is furthest from one's neighbor (501 ff.). In *Phagifacetus* we read that one must not start eating before the lord of the house does so (112 f.); one should look about pleasantly and not stare incessantly at the food (120 ff.); one should wear fresh clothes to the meal so as not to bring bugs to the table (133 ff.). The books of table manners were based on the belief that by adhering to such rules courtly society would set itself apart from the peasant: "Some take a bite from a piece and throw it back into the bowl, as the peasants do. Courtly people give up such crude manners."[108] In this respect these texts are important evidence for the self-image of courtly society and at the same time for the refinement of social behavior during the courtly age.

LITERATURE OF FEASTING AND CAROUSING

The subject of food and drink also had its humorous side. Kitchen humor has been among the most popular forms of comedy since antiquity. In courtly literature we encounter such themes mostly in deliberate contrast to the courtly ideal of society. Immoderation in food and drink characterizes the behavior of young Parzival, who had grown up without knowledge of courtly manners. In the tent of Duchess Jeschute "he didn't care where the hostess sat. He ate his fill and then drank some heavy draughts."[109] The rudeness of young Rennewart's breach of courtly table etiquette was illustrated in similarly fashion: "He stuffed his cheeks so full with the food that stood before him that not a snowflake could have snowed in."[110] Devotion to the pleasures of the palate could also be used as a critical motif. In *Willehalm* we hear that the French princes abandoned the battlefield because they preferred the comfortable life at court to the hardships of war: "Back there we will have many feasts at which to enjoy ourselves."[111] The poet makes it very clear that he finds such an attitude disgraceful. A different type of kitchen humor appears in the *Nibelungenlied* in the character of the Burgundian court chef Rumolt, who tries to talk the kings out of the dangerous journey to the land of the Huns by conjuring up the delicacies they would get at home; as a special treat he promises "dough fried in oil."[112] It is no coincidence that the only German text from this period in which the individual courses of a meal are described is parodistic in nature. In *Helmbrecht*, at the banquet for the returned son, noble food and peasant food are listed together in comic confusion. The "first course"[113] was "chopped cabbage"[114] with a piece of meat. The second course was made up of "a fatty, ripe cheese."[115] Next came a goose on a spit as well as "a fried and a boiled chicken"[116] and several other dishes "that a peasant had never known before."[117]

In the thirteenth century we find epic and lyric texts that celebrate unabashedly the pleasures of a good meal and liberal indulgence in wine. How these works continued the tradition of Latin drinking literature has not been sufficiently clarified. Stricker's *Weinschlund* and the anonymous *Weinschwelg* begin, by the first half of the thirteenth century, the series of the so-called *Zechreden*, verses in which the virtues of wine are played off against the typical forms of courtly conviviality. "I want to praise wine more than tournaments and dancing. Crown, circlet, and wreath, silk, brocade, and scarlet, all splendor of the world I would not prefer to wine."[118] In Stricker's *Weinschlund*, the boozer justifies his preference for wine by saying that he is not rich enough to participate in courtly life: "I own no hunting dogs, no greyhounds, and no hunting falcons; nor do I have enough horses to ride at tournaments or in knightly battle. I know no women who would give me a friendly reception. I also have no elegant clothes such that I would enjoy showing myself in them in public. Am I supposed to go naked to the dance? I would be the laughingstock of the people."[119]

The real songs of carousing and gluttony appeared in Germany only towards the end of the thirteenth century with the autumn songs of Steinmar and Hadloub. Autumn was the time of the harvest and the delights of the table. With the cry: "I want to indulge now,"[120] the poets embraced the pleasures of autumn while renouncing courtly minne service: "Since she for whom I have so often sung does not want to reward me, behold, I shall praise him who can soothe my sorrows, autumn, who makes the clothes of May fall from the trees. I know well the old story that a tormented lover is a real martyr. Behold, that is what I had been driven to. Well then, I say farewell to that and will give myself to gluttony."[121]

In these songs the poets did not hold back in any way in listing individual dishes. Reveling in the abundance of the food was part of the style of the autumn songs. "Innkeeper, you are to serve us fish, more than ten different types, and also geese, chickens, birds, pigs, sausages, peacocks there shall also be, and along with it wine from Italy. Above all give us plenty and let us fill the bowls. Cups and bowls I will empty to the bottom."[122] With the exception of the sausages (*dermel*), Steinmar mentions only noble food. Later we find ever increasingly the kinds of dishes that do not appear at all in courtly epic. Hadloub's autumn song, *Herbst wil aber sîn lop niuwen*, lists fifteen "courses" (*trahten*): a fatty roast (*veizer brâten*), sausages and ham (*Würste und hammen*), a good plate of selected meats (*guot gesleckte*), entrails (*ingwant bletze*), that is gut and stomach (*terme und magen*), neck pieces (*kragen*), giblets (*kroese*), head and feet (*houbt und vüeze*), brain (*hirn*), legs (*die*), garlic sausages (*klobwürst*), shoulder (*buoc*), and cracklings (*grieben*) (20.5 ff.). The humorous effect of these songs was created not least by this piling up and mixing together of such kitchen terminology. This earthy poetry reached a high point in the fourteenth century in *Neidharts Gefräß*, where no less than forty-two different dishes are named.

In the past the appearance of this literature of gluttony and drunkenness was seen in relationship to social changes. If these texts could not simply be attributed to the bourgeoisie and its supposedly cruder tastes, they were seen as symptoms of the decay of courtly knighthood. This interpretation was thought to be all the more justified, since it could invoke certain statements from the thirteenth century. Special attention was given to *Helmbrecht*, where the old and the new manners of the nobility are contrasted: in the old days the knights were supposedly "courtly and joyous"[123] and their life was devoted to the service of ladies and courtly festiveness, whereas the nobility of the present thought only of gluttony and violence: "This is today life at the court: 'Drink, my lord, drink, drink, drink! Drink it up, I'll drink along!' He who worried more about a lady than good wine was thought a monkey and a fool. Whoever can lie is courtly. Deceit is the custom of the court."[124] The moralists and the preachers of the late thirteenth century confirm that gluttony and drunkenness among the nobility was not merely a literary motif. In Hugo von Trimberg's *Renner*, "Lord Glutton and Lord Gullet"[125] play an important role. Berthold von Regensburg castigated the "immoderation of the mouth,"[126] *überezzen* and *übertrinken* (overeating and overdrinking) as a vice specifically of the German nobility and the rich burghers: "This sin is found nowhere as often as here in Germany, especially among the lords in the castles and among the burghers of the cities."[127] Such attacks were certainly directed against something that was real. But it is wrong to assume that noble society around 1200 lived differently, that in those days the poetic ideals of courtly virtue were actually practiced. Complaints about the gluttony and the carousing of the nobility are already found around 1200. *Der Winsbeke* warns: "My son, gluttony and gambling are the downfall of body and soul."[128] Not the alleged decay of knighthood, but changes in literary life and literary tastes explain why the themes of feasting and carousing began to flourish only toward the end of the thirteenth century.

Courtly Feasts: Protocol and Etiquette

1. COURT FEASTS

THE COURT FEAST AT MAINZ IN 1184

The historical significance of the court feast must be seen in relation to the nature of medieval lordship. On all important issues the king sought the "advice and support" (*consilium et auxilium*) of the magnates of the realm, without whose participation effective governing was impossible. Lacking a permanent residence, the king gathered the princes and lords around himself in different locations, mostly on high Church feasts that were celebrated together. On important political or dynastic occasions, when a great number of princes and foreign delegations were assembled, these court feasts were put on with extraordinary splendor. At no other time did noble society display its material wealth and courtly etiquette more openly. Unfortunately the historical accounts of court feasts have never been compiled and evaluated from the perspective of social history. Only one such event, the famous court feast at Mainz in 1184, has attracted wide attention. In the judgment of the historian Wilhelm von Gislebrecht, this Whitsuntide feast in Mainz was "a high point in the history of the German Empire, indeed a high point of the Middle Ages." Contemporaries already considered this assembly of princes an amazing event such as had never been seen before. No other court feast received such detailed attention from the chroniclers, and this allows us for once to reconstruct with considerable accuracy the external circumstances and the unfolding of the festive program.

"More than seventy imperial princes"[1] were said to have been assembled. The size of their knightly retinue was estimated at tens of thousands. "An incredible multitude of people from different countries and of different tongues was gathered there."[2] In the *Sächsische Welt-chronik* we read: "This was one of the greatest court feasts ever held in Germany. The knights there were estimated at fourty thousand, not counting the other crowds."[3] Gislebert of Mons, who attended the feast in person, gave a number nearly twice as high: seventy thousand knights, "not counting the clerics and the people of other orders."[4] Gislebert also indicated the size of the contingents of the most important imperial princes. The duke of Bohemia is said to have come to Mainz with two thousand knights, the landgrave of Thuringia with one thousand; the same number, we are told, comprised the retinue of Count Palatine Conrad (d. 1195), the brother of Emperor Frederick I. Duke Bernhard of Saxony (d. 1202) was supposedly accompanied by seven hundred knights, Duke Leopold V of Austria (d. 1194) by five hundred. The emperor had made extensive preparations for lodging and feeding this multitude of guests. Many tents had been erected outside the city, along with an entire palace of wood, containing quarters for the imperial court, a large "hall" (*aula*), a spacious church, and "houses for the princes" (*domus principum*) "set up most nobly in a circle."[5] The palace included further buildings housing household activities, among them two large chicken coops which drew the admiration of the guests (see p. 126). As to the food supply, Arnold von Lübeck reports that an abundance of noble foods and drinks "from all countries"[6] had been heaped up there. Apart from the chickens, he mentions especially the stores of wine, "which had been brought from up and down the Rhine."[7] For three days the emperor entertained his guests "most liberally."[8] The expenses for the accommodations were, however, partially defrayed by the princes themselves: "each one, in order to display the splendor of his dignity, bore the cost most ambitiously."[9] The count of Hainaut had brought not only his own tents, but had arrived with his own tableware and a large staff of servants (see p. 210). In all likelihood the other princes had done much the same.

The festivities began on Whitsunday with a ceremonial crowning of the emperor and the empress, followed by a procession of the crowned rulers in which the count of Hainaut carried ahead the imperial sword. In the procession was also young Henry VI decorated with his royal crown; he had been elected king of Germany in 1169. At the subsequent banquet, "prepared most sumptuously with exquisite dishes,"[10] the highest princes served at the imperial table as steward, chamberlain, cupbearer, and marshal. The remainder of the day was spent in games and entertainment. The following day, after the festive mass, the event that most contemporary accounts described as the real reason for the court feast took place: the emperor's two sons, Henry and Frederick, were knighted in a ceremony celebrated "with the greatest splendor and dignity."[11] Henry VI was at that time eighteen years old; his brother Frederick, who held the title of duke of Swabia, was a year and a half younger. The ceremonial girding with the sword was followed by the traditional distribution of gifts by the new knights to the needy ("knights in captivity and crusaders"[12]) and to the entertainers. The princely guests also took part by giving away "horses, costly clothes, gold, and silver."[13] "The princes and other noblemen gave liberally, not only for the honor of their lords—the emperor and his sons—but also to spread the fame of their own names."[14] Afterwards a "war game" (*gyrus*) was held, without weapons, and twenty thousand knights are said to have participated. Emperor Frederick also took part in this exhibition of horsemanship, and "even though in body he was neither bigger nor more handsome than the others, it was proper that he should carry his shield in front of the others."[15] War games on horseback were again held on the third day of the festivities.

The joyous atmosphere was clouded by an incident which some chroniclers say occurred on Whitsunday, others on Monday or Tuesday. The wooden church and several buildings of the palace collapsed in a heavy storm, killing a number of people. While some chroniclers attributed the disaster to an "unfortunate accident,"[16] others wanted to see in it the sign of a "divine judgment,"[17] because "the children of this world were abusing in their lifetime their wisdom, which is foolishness before God."[18] Perhaps as a result of this accident, a tournament which "had been scheduled by the princes"[19] to take place in Ingelheim following the feast in Mainz was canceled.

The days at Mainz were filled not only with courtly festivities. The emperor also took the opportunity "to deal with diverse matters of imperial business."[20] Henry the Lion had come to Mainz from his exile in Normandy, but he could not reach an agreement with Frederick I. Delegates from the count of Flanders were present in Mainz and negotiated with the emperor. The main political event was the treaty with Baldwin V of Hainaut, which stipulated that the county of Namur-Luxembourg be made into an imperial fief and the counts of Hainaut elevated to the ranks of imperial princes.

When contemporaries searched for ways to describe the unprece-

dented splendor of the court feast at Mainz, the biblical Kings Ahasuerus and Solomon came to mind. The magnificence of food and drink
in Mainz was, so wrote Arnold von Lübeck, "equal to that at the banquet of Ahasuerus."[21] The tremendous impression the festivities at
Mainz made can also be measured by the fact that this feast itself became the standard for poetic feast descriptions. When Heinrich von
Veldeke, who was in Mainz in person, sought to describe the wedding
feast of Aeneas and Lavinia—this was the first great depiction of a feast
in German literature—he reminded his listeners of the celebration that
Emperor Frederick I had put on:

> I have never heard of a celebration anywhere that was as large as that of
> Aeneas's wedding, with the exception of the one at Mainz, which I myself
> saw. That feast, when Emperor Frederick knighted his two sons, was indeed
> immensely large, goods worth many thousands of marks were consumed and
> given away. I don't think anyone alive now has ever seen a greater feast.
> What the future may bring I don't know. Truly, I have never heard of a
> knighting ceremony where so many princes and people of all kinds were
> gathered. Enough are still alive who know the truth of it. Emperor Frederick
> won there such renown that one could keep telling wondrous things of it
> until Judgment Day, without lying. More than a hundred years from now
> people will still be speaking and writing about it.[22]

These verses were probably written soon after 1184. The fact that decades later chroniclers were still talking about the splendor of the feast
at Mainz also had something to do with the subsequent history of the
empire. After the mid-1180s the political circumstances in the empire
were hardly ever again so favorable for a peaceful gathering of the
entire high nobility. No such opportunity existed during the reign of
Emperor Henry VI (1190–1197), and during the long period of domestic war following the double election of 1198, the court feasts held by
the rival rulers were attended only by their own supporters. Not until
1235 was there again a gathering that in sheer size was reminiscent of
the Whitsuntide feast of 1184. In that year Emperor Frederick II celebrated, once again in Mainz, his marriage to Isabelle of England. "At
the celebration of the betrothal of Empress Isabelle, the sister of the
king of England, there were present in Mainz and Worms four kings,
eleven dukes, and thirty counts and margraves, not counting the
prelates."[23] But this wedding at Mainz did not capture the imagination
of contemporaries nearly as much as had the knighting of 1184.

Next to the imperial diets, the feasts put on by the princes gained
increasingly in importance. By the 1160s the feasts held at Gunzenle

near Augsburg by Duke Welf VI (d. 1191), the uncle of Emperor Frederick I, attracted wide attention: "Around the same time he invited the magnates of Bavaria and Swabia to the Lechfeld, across from Augsburg, to a place called Gunzenle, and he celebrated there splendidly the feast of Whitsuntide, entertaining in praiseworthy fashion a great throng of people who had gathered from everywhere."[24] A few decades later the Babenberg court in Vienna displayed exceptional festive splendor. The knighting of Duke Leopold VI in 1200 and his marriage to the Byzantine Princess Theodora in 1203 were among the greatest feasts of their time. Throughout the thirteenth century the great princely courts competed with each other in the magnificence of their court feasts. The most resplendent and expensive feasts were celebrated during the second half of the thirteenth century at the court of Prague. These celebrations form the concrete historical background to the literary descriptions, which differ from the historical accounts in that they focus much more closely on the details of social life and the courtly protocol of the feasts.

FEAST AND LORDSHIP

The word for the court feast was *hôchgezît*, *hôchzît* (literally, "high time") (the meaning "wedding"—modern German *Hochzeit*—is a later development), and it expressed the fact that the celebration was elevated above day-to-day life. The German word *Fest* (from Latin *festum*) was used only sporadically in the thirteenth century. One could also describe the court feast as a *hof* and *tac* (court-day). The terms *tagedinc*, *teidunc* (court day [judicial court]) and *lantsprâche* (princes' day) emphasized more the politico-legal character of the assembly. Since the festive meal was usually the high point, a natural word was also *wirtschaft* (feast). Depending on the occasion for the feast, two other words in use were *brûtlouft* (wedding) and *ritterschaft* (tournament).

Most of the feasts described by the poets took place on Whitsuntide, as did the feast in Mainz in 1184. "Whatever we are told of Arthur, the man of the merry month of May, takes place on Whitsuntide or in the blossom time of May. What sweet breezes always waft about him!"[25] More precise dates, such as "the end of April"[26] or "the beginning of May,"[27] are the exception. Whitsuntide was a particularly good time for the great assemblies of princes, since the weather conditions at that time of year made traveling easier and the lodging of guests in tents could be more readily accomplished. The choice of a high Church

holiday as the date for a feast most certainly had something to do with
the fact that the acts of sovereignty exercised on such a day received
the aura of a religious blessing through the accompanying religious
ceremonies.

The occasions for the hosting of great feasts were the same in literature as in real life: weddings, crownings, knighting ceremonies, peace
treaties, and celebrations of the Church holidays. The political business
that was usually transacted on such days is almost never mentioned in
literature. Of prime interest to the poets was always the display of fabulous splendor and the elaborate depiction of refined courtly etiquette.
But the link between the court feast and the nature of feudal lordship is
visible in the poetic works. It could even play a dominant role if the
hero married the lady or heiress of a large principality and assumed the
lordship on the occasion of the wedding. The festive gathering was then
transformed into a politically active council of princes as the bride
negotiated with the magnates of the land and sought their permission
before marrying and handing power over to her new husband. In such
cases the invitation for the feast usually went out in the name of the lady
(Pleier, *Garel* 8702 ff.). Wirnt von Grafenberg gives a detailed description of the procedure in such a transfer of lordship. The entire nobility
of the land was gathered in Korntin for the wedding and coronation
feast. The princess and heiress Larie made her appearance "crowned
like an empress,"[28] and she had the highest princes of her realm carry
before her the sword and lance of her future husband as the insignia of
lordship. Then the marriage to Wigalois was performed through the
exchange of rings. Larie asked the assembled princes whether this was
in accord with their wishes. When they consented, "she ceremoniously
placed the crown on Wigalois's head and with a golden scepter transferred to him the lordship over herself, her people, and her land."[29] The
next day the king and the queen attended mass wearing their crowns.
The liturgy was then followed in the hall by the ceremony of enfeoffment and homage from the princes (9549 ff.).

Frequently the choice of guests by itself would emphasize the nature
of a feast. We do hear of entirely fanciful feasts to which the entire
world had been invited. But more often the invitation went specifically
to the princes of the land (U. v. Zatzikhoven 7762, W. v. Grafenberg
8678 ff.), or, if the host was a prince himself, to the nobility, to "barons
and *Landherren*,"[30] or to "counts, *Freiherren*, and ministerials."[31] If
the guests were politically dependent on the host, the invitation sometimes took on the air of a command, and attendance was then the fulfill-

ment of a feudal obligation. It even happened that the invitation came along with a threat of punishment to those who failed to respond. This motif, however, was used primarily in the portrayal of tyrants, like the Byzantine King Constantine in *König Rother*, who threatened all those who did not answer his invitation to an assembly with death: "So great is my power that if somebody stays away he shall pay for it with his life."[32]

The court feast was one way in which a ruler could bind the nobility of his land more closely to himself. After Prince Wilhelm of Wenden had decided to leave his land secretly as a pilgrim, he took the advice of his wife and once again called together the nobility of his land to a great feast. His conscious aim was to ensure their loyalty to his house during his absence by displaying the splendor of his court and his friendliness and magnanimity: "Let us spare no expense. Let us show our wealth and delight them with gifts and inspire them to feel attached to us."[33] Such motivation is also confirmed historically, as for example in Johann of Victring's description of the court feast hosted by the sons of Count Meinhard II of Görz-Tyrol (d. 1295) in 1299 in St. Veit to consolidate their lordship over the duchy of Carinthia: "At this court feast they consecrated new knights and dressed them honorably, they distributed gifts and displayed the splendor of their wealth. By showing their good-will towards the nobility of the land, they impressed themselves more strongly on this duchy, so that its enemies, if they existed, would be thoroughly red with shame, and their loyal supporters would be more surely devoted to them."[34] For the nobility of the land it was an honor to be summoned to court and have close contact with their ruler. The festivities at court also allowed access to the modern lifestyle patterned after the French model. And beyond the pleasures of a banquet there was the prospect of material profit: a liberal distribution of gifts to the guests was part of the protocol of a feast. All this explains why a ruler who hosted feasts quite frequently enjoyed a special popularity. In *Kud-run* we are told that Uote, the daughter of a Norwegian prince, once complained to her husband, King Sigebant of Ireland, that life at the Irish court was not as festive as at the court of her father (27.2 ff.). Asked what was missing, she explained: "A king as mighty as you should have guests more frequently; he should often ride the buhurt with his people, to his own honor and that of his land."[35] The king took this to heart and, to everyone's delight, held a great feast. The author of *Mai und Beaflor* ends the description of a magnificent feast by lamenting: "Alas, how nice it used to be. Today the princes do little to show

themselves publicly. To be often among people is to them a burden.
Nobody wants to put up any more with the crowds at court. They can
now rule only with force over those to whom they are supposed to bring
joy; these people are forced by the princes into a life of sadness. This is
why courtly joy is entirely dead."[36] Here, too, the hosting of great feasts
is considered part of the courtly exercise of lordship, and is the very
opposite of undesirable tyranny. The second half of the thirteenth century did not witness fewer feasts than before. But apparently these
feasts gradually lost the character of great public spectacles; court society became increasingly a closed society. The French poet Robert de
Blois wrote in the mid-thirteenth century: "Who would believe this of
the princes, unless he had seen it himself or heard of it, that they close
their doors for the meal? So help me God, I cannot keep quiet about it
when the doormen cry out: 'Away with you, my lord wishes to eat!'"[37]

LODGING AND FOOD

As was done in Mainz in 1184, at other feasts, too, buildings were
erected specifically to house the guests. If the assembly was held near a
city, lodging was reserved there. Many times the guests stayed in tents
set up by the host or brought along by the guests themselves. The noblest guests came with a great retinue and sought to impress everyone
else with their wealth. We know that Count Baldwin V of Hainaut
appeared in Mainz in 1184 "with great and splendid furnishings, many
silver vessels and other personal necessities, and servants festively
attired."[38] Of the appearance of Archbishop Albero of Trier (d. 1152) it
was reported: "When he came to the court of the king he was a spectacle for everyone. He alone seemed worthy of admiration. With his
magnificent retinue and outlay he eclipsed all other princes."[39] To the
Frankfurt diet of 1149 the archbishop traveled with forty houseboats
(see p. 54).

The questions of protocol that were raised by the lodging of guests
were best arranged in advance by the marshal of the host and the marshals of the noble visitors (Pleier, *Garel* 19483 ff.). "They sent marshals
ahead to seek lodging for them in the city."[40] In *Reinfried von Braunschweig* we hear that no proper quarters were available in the city at the
great tournament in Linion, because the king of Scotland and the duke
of Berbester had occupied them all (574 ff.). To prevent discontent from
arising, the Danish king saw to it that "small and large tents"[41] were
pitched for the noble guests outside the city. A famous quarrel occurred

during the Third Crusade, when King Richard Lionheart sought lodging in a castle near Emmaus, where the marshal of Duke Leopold V of Austria (d. 1194) had already occupied the best quarters. Enraged about this, the English king ordered "that the banner of the duke, which had been affixed to the inn, be thrown into the gutter."[42] Later the king had to pay for this insult when he was captured in Austria and held at ransom.

In *Gauriel von Muntabel*, the chamberlains and the marshals of Queen Elaete were busy for three days setting up in a meadow the necessary buildings for housing the guests (4015 ff.). On the fourth day pack horses brought everything that was needed for the banquet: "Good pillows and other housewares, drinking vessels and tablecloths of precious material, heavy bowls and cups."[43] A great deal was also spent on gifts for the guests. King Arthur procured "one thousand chargers"[44] and "twelve hundred riding horses"[45] to give away at the Whitsuntide feast. In the description of Heinrich von dem Türlin, war horses were brought from Spain, white mules from Syria, richly decorated weapons from France, dyed cloth from Flanders, various silk cloths from Greece, precious furs from Russia, golden tableware from London, and different kinds of jewelry from Ireland (490 ff.). Jans Enikel reports how for the great feast of King Samson, "one thousand pieces of red and white scarlet were cut,"[46] along with "two thousand bails of linen."[47] In addition, one hundred shoemakers were employed "so that they might present all those who came to the feast with enough shoes."[48] An even closer approximation to reality is the account by Ottokar von Steiermark about the court feast held in 1264 when the son of King Bela IV of Hungary (d. 1270) married the daughter of Margrave Otto III of Brandenburg (d. 1267). The expenses for the feast were born by King Ottokar II of Bohemia, the brother-in-law of Margrave Otto. He had "bridles and riding gear"[49] made of gold and silver. "Scarlet, brunat, baldachin and siglat silk, gray cloth, ermine and fur for more than twenty thousand pounds were purchased for the feast."[50] Messengers carried invitations to the nobility in Bohemia, Silesia, Poland, Saxony, Meißen, and Thuringia. A bridge was specially built across the Danube, wide enough "so ten horsemen could ride across it side by side without danger."[51] A great store of wine was prepared, and for the horses five great piles of feed had been heaped up, "with each pile taller than the church in Solenau."[52] The pastures were covered with fat cows, pigs, and smaller animals that would have sufficed to supply the festive gathering with enough meat for four weeks. Nobody could guess how much bread was used, "until the king's notaries sat down to do the accounts. According to their calculation, the bread that was eaten there, together with what was left over, amounted to one thousand bushels of wheat."[53]

We are particularly well informed about the feast hosted by the sons of Meinhard II of Görz-Tyrol in 1299 in St. Veit. "So splendidly great were their expenses—exceeding all measure—for the various purple cloths and cendales, and for the clothes of different colors bought from the Venetians on credit, that they still have not been repaid. As a result the nobles and the burghers, whom the dukes of Carinthia consider wealthy, have experienced difficulties from the Venetians in their business dealings."[54] In this case the account books of Tyrol allow us to supply hard historical evidence for these statements. Under the heading "For the knighting in St. Veit" (*in sancto Vito ad miliciam*)—the three sons of Meinhard II were knighted at this feast—they list for the year 1299 the expenses for a variety of foreign fabrics. A Florentine trading company supplied wax candles, furs, spices, as well as linen for forty-eight tablecloths and ten towels (Riedmann I, p. 289). How much such a feast could cost is revealed by a comparison with the outlay for the wedding of Duke Henry of Carinthia (d. 1335) with Adelheid of Brunswick in 1315. To finance this celebration, a special wedding tax was levied, and according to the Tyrol account books the money taken in was spent for the following purchases: 2 ermine furs and 3 gold-interlaced oriental cloths for the groom; different kinds of furs, red scarlet, 279 ells of blue cloth, and 285 ells of green cloth for 50 knights; mixed cloth and furs for the notaries; 46 ells of brown cloth and various furs for the chaplains; 128 ells of red and green cloth for the female attendants; furthermore 31 red-dyed gold fabrics, 20 silk cloths for tabards, other various silks and linen cloth, 5 wall hangings, 19 tablecloths, towels, and a silk-covered blanket for the groom. Payment was also entered for 10, 000 gilded pearls, the same number of corals, 9,000 gilded buttons, 10 centners wax, 2 centners pepper, 15 centners rice, 10 centners almonds, 4 centners raisins, 3,000 dates, 17 centners figs, 215 talents sugar, in addition sweets and spices, among them 15 talents saffron, nutmeg, cloves, cinnamon, ginger, raisins, and galagan (Riedmann II, p. 116 f.). The account books also specify the amount of food consumed at the feast: the dried meat of 69 cows and 252 sheep, pork from 58 pigs, 357 pork hocks, 242 lambs and kids, 12 geese, 185 chickens, 8,960 eggs, 2,995 cheeses, 35 bowls of fat, 55,560 breads, and more than 19 tuns of wine (ibid., p. 117).

THE FESTIVE ENTRANCE

Nearly all the descriptions of feasts follow an identical scheme: invitation—preparations—arrival and greeting of the guests—banquet—entertainment and conviviality—gifts for the departing guests. The actual festivities began with the arrival of the guests, which was frequently turned into a great spectacle. To honor a noble guest "the host went out to meet him far in front of the castle gate and greeted him there."[55] The host could also send out a group of festively attired knights and a band of musicians to meet the guests (W. v. Grafenberg 8646 ff.). In special cases the hosts rode out to catch up with the approaching guests several days' journey from the castle (H. v. Aue, *Erec* 10,005 ff.). A magnificent reception was arranged for the English · Princess Isabelle when she came to Germany in 1235 for her marriage to Emperor Frederick II. Upon landing in Antwerp, she was greeted by "a huge multitude of armed noblemen"[56] who had been sent by the emperor to protect her against possible attacks. From everywhere came clerics "with lit candles,"[57] "ringing the bells and singing songs of joy in festive procession."[58] Among them were "masters of every kind with their instruments."[59] They accompanied the future empress for five days all the way to Cologne, where she was solemnly met by ten thousand festively dressed burghers who approached her with flowers and palm branches. "They sat on Spanish horses, which they urged to a fast gait, and shattered lances of wood and cane in tilting against one another."[60] An "ingenious exhibit" (*excogitatum ingenium*) awaited the empress in the city, namely "boats which seemed to be rowing on dry land, pulled by hidden horses covered with silk blankets. In these boats clerics with melodious instruments were playing lovely melodies never heard before, to the great surprise of all who listened."[61] In Germany at that time such boat-shaped floats were known only from literature (*Moriz von Craûn* 627 ff.). We suspect that this unusual parade was arranged on orders from the imperial court. Isabelle took lodging in the palace of the archbishop, and she stayed in Cologne for six weeks. Then a festive procession conducted her up the Rhine to where the emperor received her near Worms.

In such festive processions, instrumental music played an important role. The order of instruments was determined by a fixed protocol: first came the trumpets, whose loud blare attracted attention and created the desired festive noise; in the middle were the drums and fifes; and last, in close proximity to the lord of the procession, came the string instruments, fiddles, *rotten*, and violins. Sometimes the drums and kettle drums were also placed with the trumpets. Ulrich von Liechtenstein describes such a procession, which he put together for himself as he was journeying through Friaul and Carinthia in 1227 dressed up as Lady Venus. At the head of the train rode his marshal and his cook, who arranged for lodging. They were followed by his flag (*banir* 482.5) accompanied by two trumpeters, "whose trumpets blared loudly."[62] Next came three packhorses accompanied by three servants on foot and three squires leading three riding horses with beautiful saddles. Behind them were carried Liechtenstein's shield and helmet. "Then came a flute player who was skilfully beating a drum;"[63] apparently he was playing a one-handed flute. Next were four servants on horseback, each with a bundle of spears, and then two maidens dressed in white. "After them rode two good fiddlers who made me happy, for they played a nice traveling tune."[64] Last came Lord von Liechtenstein himself in his splendid Venus costume. A pictorial depiction of such a musical procession is contained in the Bern manuscript of the *Liber ad honorem augusti* by Petrus de Ebulo. The miniature shows the entrance of King Tancred of Sicily (d. 1194) into Palermo in 1190: in the front of the procession are three trumpeters, further back we see three drummers and two cymbalists (see fig. 25). It is believed that this kind of festive music was taken over from the Arabs.

On their way to the wedding of Prince Mai, the guests joined together to form a large procession. "They arranged everything in an honorable and praiseworthy manner. They ordered their group festively."[65] At the head of the train were pack animals, followed by chargers. Then came squires (*bescheliere* 70.25) with the banners of all the lords in the train. Next came the pages on horseback, and then the nobles, ladies and knights, "festively with courtly manners,"[66] accompanied by an ensemble of string instruments. "How splendid was the festive group. With every lady rode a noble knight, who all along could while away the time with lovely stories. Thus they rode in a beautifully arranged train."[67] There were four hundred ladies in this train and a like number of knights, followed by another five hundred knights in splendid dress and arranged into three groups. Along the way the young knights engaged in war games: "One could see them riding the buhurt next to the ladies."[68] Riding in pairs was considered especially courtly: "To every young lady was assigned a knight who was to render his service to her."[69] It was also very courtly to organize hunts along the way. Many noble guests came to the wedding feast that King Arthur

Fig. 25.   King Tancred's entry into Palermo. The festive procession is headed by archers, who are followed by three dismounted horsemen. Next comes the musical ensemble with trumpeters, cymbalists, and drummers. It is followed by a group of warriors. The king, who rides at the end of the procession, is preceded by the insignia of his lordship. From the Bern manuscript of the *Liber ad honorem Augusti* by Petrus de Ebulo (Burgerbibliothek, 120). End of the twelfth century.

arranged for Erec and Enite, among them ten kings with large retinues who joined together to form a festive train. The young kings, all dressed alike, carried hunting falcons on their fists, the old kings carried hawks. "They had joyous pastime on the three-mile-long journey. The hunting was good: streams and ponds were full of ducks. What a hawk will catch they found there in abundance."[70] There are pictures—if only of somewhat later date—of the adoration of the Magi that depict the entire festive procession of the kings to Bethlehem, complete with great hunts and other courtly entertainment along the way. Best known is the magnificent painting by Benozzo Gozzoli (d. 1497) in the chapel of the Palazzo Medici-Riccardi in Florence.

Special forms of the festive reception existed for the king's entrance into a city. Following classical and oriental models, the Middle Ages developed an elaborate liturgical ceremony for the *adventus* of the ruler, put down in writing in the "Regulations for the Reception of the King" (*Ordines ad regem suscipiendum*). Bearing palm branches and burning candles, the representatives of the city and the clergy, accompanied by the peal of the bells, went out to meet the king and greeted him on the various stations of his journey with songs and acclamations that reflected the elevated sacral nature of the royal dignity. In the coronation city of Aachen it was customary, when receiving the ruler, to carry ahead the imperial sword and to bring along the head reliquary of Charlemagne. The liturgical forms of greeting were expressly reserved for anointed rulers: emperors, kings, and the highest ecclesiastical dignitaries. Thietmar von Merseburg reports that Duke Hermann Billung of Saxony (d. 973) once had the presumption of using the liturgical protocol of the *adventus* for himself: at a court feast in Magdeburg "the archbishop received him and led him by the hand to church while candles were burning and bells ringing."[71] The emperor's indignation at what had occurred was directed not so much against the duke as against the archbishop, whom he ordered as punishment "to send him horses equal in number to the bells he had rung and candles he had lit for the duke."[72]

The reception of the ruler had a special accent if it was simultaneously an act of submission. Otto von St. Blasien recounts how Emperor Henry VI, after quashing the rebellion of the Sicilian nobility with great brutality, marched to Palermo in 1194, destroyed its famous animal park, and forced the city to surrender. After the day of the festive entrance had been determined, "the triumphal procession was prepared with the greatest splendor: the entire city was adorned, and the streets were hung with tapestries and wreaths of different type and costliness; all places within the city and outside were filled with the scent of incense, myrrh, and other aromatic drugs."[73] The burghers then went out in groups to meet the emperor, first the leading citizens, then the oldest, finally the youngest, "with splendidly bridled horses and adorned with clothes of various colors, in a fixed order,"[74] with "some in their manner and artistry offering acclamations on all kinds of musical instruments."[75] When the emperor entered the city, "all shouted out loud laudations"[76] and precious gifts were presented.

The courtly poets made use of the festive entrance into a city also in their descriptions of court feasts. Heinrich von Veldeke gave the first example in Eneas's entrance into Laurente for the celebration of his marriage to Princess Lavinia. Fifty knights in costly dress accompanied Eneas when he entered the city "with a lordly crowd, with flutes and singing, with drumming and fiddling."[77] The city gates were swung open for him, the streets through which he rode were "hung with silk cloths"[78] in his honor. Beautifully attired maidens and women lined his way to the royal palace, where Eneas was festively welcomed by his future father-in-law. In the thirteenth century this type of description was frequently used, most expansively in the addendum to Ulrich von Etzenbach's *Alexander*, at the entrance of the emperor into Tritonia. With a huge retinue Alexander approached the city, "crowned in royal dignity and magnificently dressed."[79] Outside the walls, costly cloths had already been spread out for his reception, and here the emperor was greeted first by the boys of the city with a song of welcome repeated three times. A bit further on the burghers came to meet him and joined in the singing. Crying out "Lord, now we belong to you!"[80] they fell to their knees before him. Following this, and still outside the city walls, the women of the city, festively attired, welcomed him. The emperor politely dismounted from his horse, while "the ladies began softly to sing a song of praise to the exalted Emperor Alexander, the way they sang lovely melodies to the honor of God."[81] Next came the city government with the council and the senate and the eminent burghers, all of whom wore splendid clothes and greeted the emperor with a responsory: "The *legum dominus* [the highest judge of the city] sang first, all others followed him with loud voices."[82] They, too, knelt down and paid homage to the emperor with hands raised high. Alexander bade them to rise and continued on his way. He was now riding under a splendid canopy of gold-interlaced silk, and there was much music in the train: "The roll of drums and the blare of trumpets sounded there in many a way. Moreover, there were many good flute players; four richly dressed fiddlers rode right before the emperor and struck up in proper tempo a very lovely traveling song."[83] At the city gate the noble youths of the city came out to meet him "with all kinds of string instruments."[84] "There were many who sang the psalter and danced to the lyre. Some played the citole, others plucked in lovely fashion the harps and *rotten* that the young people had with them. They were masters of their art."[85] The author emphasizes that only their noble descent made possible such artistry: "These lords of noble families learned this art from nobody who did not possess the nobility for it."[86] The emperor then moved through the city that was decorated with cloths, first to the "oratory" (*bethûs*, 1998), where he said his prayers, and finally to the palace of the governor, the *râthûs* (2064), where the banquet was to be held.

The entrance into the hall was another opportunity for the unfolding of an elaborate ceremony. The entrance of the ladies is not infrequently described as a splendid event. An early example is in *König Rother*, when the Byzantine princess at the feast hosted by her father enters the hall accompanied by one hundred festively gowned maidens (1811 ff.). In the *Nibelungenlied* the entrance of Kriemhild at the victory feast after the Saxon war was carefully orchestrated. One hundred knights, swords in hand, had been chosen by the king to escort the princess and her retinue. They were preceded by chamberlains who made way for the procession. It was a high honor for Siegfried that King Gunther asked his sister Kriemhild to give him a special welcome as the noblest guest present. "The lovely maid said: 'You are welcome Lord Siegfried, good and noble knight.' Siegfried was elated at this greeting, and he bowed devotedly. She took him by the hand. How ardently did he walk beside the lady!"[87]

If the host was of nobler rank than his guests, he might decide to make his festive entrance into the hall only after everyone was assembled. When Duke William of Wenden hosted a farewell feast for the nobility of his land, the duchess appeared first with her ladies, and then the duke in splendid procession with a great retinue and well-arranged music (U. v. Zatzikhoven, *W. v. Wenden* 1545 ff.). Occasionally the lord's procession was even intended as the high point of the entire feast. We are unusually well informed about the festive procession of King Philip of Swabia (d. 1206) and his wife, the Byzantine Princess Irene (d. 1208), on Christmas day of 1199 in Magdeburg. The author of the *Halberstädter Bischofschronik*, who seems to have been present in Magdeburg, has left a detailed account:

> The king celebrated the feast of the birth of Our Lord in Magdeburg with exceptional magnificence. On the holy day he came forth solemnly in royal vestments and decorated with the imperial crown. His wife, the Empress Irene, adorned splendidly with royal ornaments, followed the king most seemly and gracefully. She was accompanied by the venerable Lady Agnes, the abbess of Quedlinburg, by the Lady Judith, the wife of Duke Bernhard of Saxony, and by a bevy of other noble ladies. The bishops present, adorned with their episcopal vestments, walked on both sides of the king and the queen in a reverent and dignified manner. Duke Bernhard of Saxony, who was carrying ahead the royal sword, and the other princes and noble lords, counts, and barons, and the assembled crowd of every estate, burned with

zeal to pay homage to the king and serve him at such a celebration. All those who were there in inconceivably large numbers, were joyous in their hearts and exulted in their souls, they applauded, cheered loudly, and were incessantly active; all found great pleasure in this celebration, which they attended to the end with devoted exultation.[88]

The same event, which seems to have made a great impression on contemporaries, was also celebrated by Walther von der Vogelweide in a *Spruch*. Walther mentions fewer details of the festive protocol; instead he emphasizes the religious consecration of the imperial couple:

> To Magdeburg—on the day Our Lord was born from a maid he had chosen for his mother—King Philip came forth in all his splendor. There walked an emperor's brother and an emperor's son, three names united into one. He bore the Empire's scepter and its crown. He walked majestically and without haste. In measured pace did follow him the well-born queen, rose without thorn, dove without gall. Nowhere was there such measure of courtly decorum![89]

What seems to have made such an impression was apparently not only the public display of imperial majesty, but also the magnificent arrangement of the procession, which bestowed upon this day at Magdeburg a very modern, courtly quality. From the Halberstadt chronicle we learn that the organization of the procession had been in the hands of Conrad von Querfurt, who headed the imperial chancery under Philip of Swabia: "Lord Conrad, the chancellor of the imperial court, arranged everything sagaciously and prudently, and saw to it that everything came off as planned."[90]

THE CEREMONY OF WELCOME

"With gestures and with greetings"[91] the guests were welcomed. The gestures included kneeling, bowing, embracing, and kissing. The greeting was often combined with a religious formula: "Welcome, first to God and then to me."[92] The greeting was a solemn act with legal implications. It was a sign of peace: the welcomed guest was assured of the host's goodwill. If one harbored hostile feelings the greeting would be refused. The close connection between greeting and goodwill was a common theme in minne poetry. For a knight to serve "for a lady's greeting"[93] was not as modest a goal as it might seem at first glance. The lady who extended her greeting to a knight assured him of her good graces, and in the language of the courtly age this could be interpreted already as a partial promise that his desires for love would be granted. Hence the frequent complaints of the minne poets that they did not so much as receive a greeting.

Since greeting also expressed goodwill, it was an act especially befitting of great lords: "Princes ought to be praised for greeting people nicely."[94] Who was greeted and how was determined by a courtly protocol that paid particular attention to differences of rank. When Queen Kriemhild was received in Tulln on the Danube by her second husband, King Etzel, Margrave Rüdiger instructed her precisely about the formalities of the greeting: "Lady, the king desires to receive you here. Kiss only those I tell you to; you cannot possibly greet all of Etzel's vassals the same way."[95] To receive a kiss of welcome from the lady of the court or to be allowed to kiss her was always a high honor. How the kiss of welcome by a lovely young lady could get a bit out of hand is described in Wolfram von Eschenbach's *Parzival*, when Gawan is greeted by Ampflise, the king's sister: "She stood before him most courteously. Said Gawan: 'Lady, your lips so invite kissing, I must have a kiss of welcome.' Her mouth was hot, full, and red, as Gawan pressed his own on hers. What happened there was not the kind of kiss that one gives to a guest."[96] This is precisely why especially young ladies were advised to show restraint. When old Queen Isolde of Ireland appeared before the court together with her daughter, young Isolde, their respective greetings took different forms: "The two ladies were pleasantly engaged with two kinds of welcome: greeting and bowing, with words and in silence. The duties for both were arranged and set. One did the greeting, the other bowed; the mother spoke, the daughter was silent. This is how the two well-bred ladies behaved."[97] The lord of the court would also kiss his guests if he wanted to honor them especially, or he embraced them, took them by the hand and led them to the ladies or to the banquet.

COURTLY ENTERTAINMENT

The splendor of a great feast included a diverse program of entertainment. There was no better way to experience the modern form of courtly conviviality in all its variety. But our historical sources rarely provide us with any details of the entertainment. Among the few exceptions is the account of the Italian chronicler Rolandinus Patavinus about a feast held in 1214 in Treviso, north of Venice. It was "a court feast of pleasure and joy,"[98] to which many noble lords and ladies from Padua and Venice had also been invited. The main event was a great minne play:

> For the play a castle was erected, manned by ladies with their maids, ladies-in-waiting, and female servants, who defended it very cleverly without the help of a man. The castle was fortified all around with defenses of fur and gryce, cendale, purple cloth, samite, *ricellus*, scarlet, baldachin and ermine. What can one say about the crowns with which the ladies protected their heads against the attack of the warriors: they were embellished with gems of every kind, with chrysolites, hyacinths, topazes and emeralds, with *piropis* and pearls. This castle had to be conquered with the following array of missiles and siege machines: apples, dates, nutmeg, rolls, pears, figs, roses, lilies and violets, flasks of balsam, perfume and rose water, ambergris, camphor, cardamon, cinnamon, cloves, *melegetis*, all kinds of fragrant and gorgeous flowers and spices.[99]

What prompted the writing of this report was probably the unpleasant end to the feast: Paduans and Venetians got into a quarrel that turned into a bloody fight. Along the way we also find out that this game of the minne castle included "court arbiters" (*rectores curie*) charged with "supervising the orderliness of the ladies and knights and the entire court or game."[100]

Equally rare is the account of Matthew of Paris about the professional entertainments at the court of Emperor Frederick II. When Count Richard of Cornwall (d. 1271), the brother of Henry III of England, visited the emperor in Sicily in 1241, Frederick received him with great pomp and invited him to participate in the magnificence of his court:

> On orders from the emperor he was presented with and watched with great delight a great variety of unknown games and instruments intended for the enjoyment of the empress. Among the marvelous novelties there was one he especially praised and admired. Two shapely Saracen girls climbed onto four round balls on the smooth floor, such that one placed her feet onto two balls and the other onto the other two balls, and they moved back and forth while clapping their hands. And wherever they wanted to go they moved with the rolling balls, swinging their arms about and turning and twisting their bodies in tune with the music, striking together clashing cymbals and woods with their hands, clowning around and behaving in an unusual manner. Thus they presented a wonderful spectacle to those watching, as did other jugglers.[101]

Frederick II liked to impress his contemporaries with such novelties. A great stir was caused, for example, by an elephant carrying a castle-like structure decorated with banners and manned by trumpeters and other musicians (see fig. 26).

Fig. 26. Emperor Frederick II's elephant. The animal carries a castle-like structure that offers room to an entire ensemble of trumpeters, drummers, and pipers. From a manuscript of the *Chronica majora* by Matthew of Paris (Oxford, Corpus Christi College, 16). Thirteenth century.

Most of what we know about courtly conviviality comes from literary sources. According to the poets, the great court feasts were characterized above all by the abundance and variety of entertainment. "There were games and song, buhurt and festive crowds, piping and dancing, fiddling and singing, organ-playing and stringed music, every kind of amusement."[102] "Whatever anybody wanted, whatever he had his mind set on, he found plenty of it there: buhurts, tournaments, sword-fighting, javelin-throwing, stone-hurling, jumping, fiddling, harping, singing; one could also see there dances by girls and ladies."[103] Much space was also given to military games and knightly exercises, especially in the form of the joust and the buhurt. Archery and crossbow-shooting are rarely mentioned: "Crossbow and bow with bolts and shafts contributed to the entertainment."[104] Athletic competitions were especially popular: javelin throwing (*schefte schiezen*), long-jump (*verre springen*), and stone-hurling (*den stein werfen*) appear most often. There were also races where prizes could be won,[105] hurdle races,[106] target-shooting,[107] running and standing long-jump,[108] wrestling,[109] and ball games.[110] Ball games were activities in which women could also participate. Board games are mentioned more rarely in the descriptions of feasts: "Some were playing *mile* or *wurfzabel* on the board; others were playing chess, others again were throwing dice."[111] A miniature in the Large Heidelberg Song Manuscript shows Margrave Otto IV of Brandenburg (d. 1308) at a game of chess with a lady. In the lower border of the picture is a musical group with two trumpets, a two-handed drum, and a bagpipe: this alta-ensemble was undoubtedly not meant to provide accompaniment for the chess game, but had the function of creating the festive noise that provided the setting for the different kinds of courtly entertainment. A different miniature from the same manuscript depicts the poet Goeli and two lords playing backgammon. The "Codex Falkensteinensis" reveals how popular board games were with the nobility: in his castle Falkenstein, Count Siboto of Falkenstein (d. circa 1200) had "two chess boards and two backgammon boards,"[112] in castle Hartmannsberg "one chess board and one backgammon board,"[113] and in castle Neuburg "three boards each for backgammon and chess, and ivory figures for both games."[114]

Professional entertainers appeared at the court feasts in a variety of roles: as singers and musicians, as acrobats and jesters. "There was plenty of opportunity to see someone lift a huge castle with one hand; and whoever did not wish to see that could watch people flying through the air."[115] "Some were walking on balls and managed to stay on them with their feet. Others tried hard with leaps that had been carefully practiced."[116] The performances of the entertainers are described in considerable detail in *Lippiflorium*, a Latin poem on the life of Freiherr Bernhard II of Lippe (d. 1224):

> When the meal is over, the group of wandering performers start up their acts again. Each one does what he can, and strives to please. One sings and delights the listeners with the loveliness of his voice; another recites songs of the deeds of heroes. This one here skillfully strums the various strings; that one over there makes the lyre sound out sweetly with his artistry. From a thousand holes the flute brings forth sounds of every kind, the beating of the drums creates a frightful din. Another one jumps and does various movements with his limbs, bends forward and back, bent over backwards he moves forward, lets his hands walk instead of his feet, sticks his feet into the air and puts his head down, like a chimera. Someone else makes illusions appear with magic and deceives the eyes with the dexterity of his hands. This one shows off to the people a young dog or a horse, which he commands to act like a person; that one there throws a disk into the air in an arch, catches it on the way down and throws it up again. Such games and more there were on this festive day.[117]

Trained animals are mentioned on numerous occasions. In Charlemagne's camp before Cortes one could see "fierce lions fighting with bears"[118] and "eagles trained to provide shade."[119] Once we hear that "elephants, lions, and bears were shown off for entertainment."[120]

Theatrical performances are never mentioned in the poetic feast descriptions. Philippe de Novare recounts in his *Mémoires* that "the adventures of the Bretagne and the Round Table were performed"[121] at the great feast hosted by Jean d'Ibelin in 1223 to celebrate the knighting of his two oldest sons. This was probably a war game rather than a play. Albertus Magnus distinguished three kinds of play: 1. the "pleasure game,"[122] which "makes the spirit free and vigorous, promotes virtue and the mildness and gentleness of the heart"[123]; he included in this category music, singing, and instrumental music; 2. the "mechanical" or "useful game,"[124] for example the game on horseback, which was useful because it contributed to the defense of the land; and 3. the "detestable and disgraceful game,"[125] meaning by this "the play of actors, who run about naked, expose their genitals, and incite to shameful things,"[126] as well as "the game of dice."[127] In regard to this third category, Albertus was probably thinking more of the tradition of Christian theater critique than of the secular entertainments of his time. Beginning with the Fathers of the early Church, the polemic against the indecency of theatrical performances had a permanent place in Christian lay ethics.

Musical entertainment everywhere played a prominent part. At Daniel's coronation feast, "three hundred skilled and famous Italian fiddlers"[128] made music, along with "sixty superb German musicians on stringed instruments."[129] In addition, "one heard there tambourines and many flutes,"[130] as well as "one hundred harpists, who brought forth lovely sounds,"[131] and "twenty singers."[132] Nearly always on such festive occasions the great variety of instruments is mentioned. Heinrich von dem Türlin tells how "Lady Musica"[133] made her entrance at court with her retinue of fourteen instruments. There were: *fidel* (fiddle), *harpfe* (triangular, plucked instrument), *rotte* (harp-zither), *symphonie* (hurdy-gurdy), *flöite* (flute), *clîe* (flute?), *lîre* (a stringed or plucked instrument), *pusîn* (trumpet), *manichord* (trumpet), *psalterium* (zither), *holre* (elder-flute), *gîge* (violin), *organiston* (a stringed instrument with keyboard), and *tambiur* (drum) (22085 ff.). While no order seems discernible here, the instruments were usually arranged according to their sound and rank. The loud wind and percussion instruments went with knightly war games, while dancing and singing was done to the accompaniment of the lovely stringed instruments, which were either plucked (*rotte*, *harpfe*), or bowed (*fidel*, *gîge*). Among the loud wind instruments, pride of place belonged to the trumpet (*busîne, pusîune*). In composing different ensembles the courtly poets displayed their knowledge of courtly music. Trumpets appear alone or together with kettledrums and drums; woodwinds would also fit in. Sometimes flutes and drums formed a separate group. Woodwinds alone were rare. The miniature of the Chancellor in the Large Heidelberg Song Manuscript shows a flute and a fiddle striking up a tune for dancing. Rarely was a dancing ensemble made of drums and flutes: "There I heard the flutes starting up, here the drums were rolling: to all who wish to sing with us and dance this round, good luck in all you do!"[134]

In *Renner* we read these comments on the different effects of the loud alta-ensembles and the quiet bassa-instruments: "Harps and *rotten* require gentle consideration, decorum and silence. War wants to rage and scream, beat the drum, blow the trumpet and the shawm."[135] It was Albertus Magnus's verdict that the wind instruments did not promote virtue but anger. Petrus of Auvergne (d. circa 1275), a student of Thomas Aquinas, wanted to limit this negative effect to those instruments that were blown with a powerful breath and "produced an immoderately loud tone."[136] There was no room in courtly literature for such derogatory critiques. Quite the contrary, the loud trumpet always signaled courtly splendor and heightened festiveness. But even the court poets put the string instruments, and especially the fiddle, first when it came to the higher art of music: "Behold! I want to praise the fiddle above all other instruments. It is a delight to hear it. The heart wounded by sorrow attains inner peace through the beauty of its clear tones."[137] The ladies, in particular, showed little love for the din of drums and trumpets and much preferred to listen to the soft music of the string instruments: "The ladies would be enchanted neither by drums nor by trumpets. Fiddles, harps, *rotten*, and other lovely tones: that is what they wanted to hear."[138] The enchanting effect of beautiful string music was described on many occasions; most powerfully by Gotffried von Straßburg when young Tristan demonstrated his mastery of the harp at the English court (see p. 514).

With music went dancing, and we find it in every description of a feast: "Good entertainment was had: rounds, leaping, dancing, and lovely turning about."[139] We know exceedingly little about the courtly dances of the twelfth and thirteenth centuries. There are two reasons for this: our poor sources—handbooks on dancing appear only in the fifteenth century—and the fact that the existing evidence, which comes largely from courtly literature, has not been thoroughly evaluated.

What is written in works on cultural history about the difference between peasant dances and court dances, about the forms of the dances
performed with stately steps and those involving energetic leaps, rests in
large part on uncritical and obsolete notions. For the courtly period,
there is evidence for dances of the most diverse type and manner of
performance. Sometimes only the girls danced ("This year one sees the
girls dancing"[140]), sometimes only the men. When Emperor Frederick I
was celebrating Easter in Modena in 1159, "the young princes and the
other knights performed in the center of the imperial court dances after
their custom, with the emperor watching them from the palace."[141]
Frequently knights and ladies danced together: "In the royal palace
there was plenty of joy and entertainment: many a graceful young lady
and many a worthy knight, who was all virtue, danced and leapt with
the ladies and sang many a courtly tune along with the dance."[142] People danced either in pairs (*Ruodlieb* XI.47 ff.) or in a line. The mixed
line was very popular: "Between every two women stood a knight who
held their hands, as is still done when dancing."[143] One miniature of
the Large Heidelberg Song Manuscript shows Lord Heinrich von
Stretelingen in a courtly pair dance with his lady; another miniature
has Lord Hiltbolt von Schwangau dancing between two women.

There were stately dances that were "walked" ("We walk another
small court dance"[144]), and sprightly dances with high leaps ("Let us
jump the round!"[145]), but a consistent differentiation between a walked
dance and an energetic round is not apparent. In the dance of the temple
maids described by Konrad von Würzburg, both movements are used:
"There a splendid dance was performed by them, with steps and leaps,
as one liked."[146] The dances were nearly always accompanied by the
fiddle or the violin, more rarely by the fiddle and the flute. If the dance
had no instrumental accompaniment, all dancers sang together. Alternatively, the precantor, who was also the lead dancer, sang first, with
the others singing only the chorus or repeating what the precantor had
intoned: "A maid, tightly laced, of marvelous beauty, and with a slim
waist, lead by singing a lovely tune; the others all repeated after her."[147]
Neidhart has described how the accompaniment alternated between a
violin and the singing of the lead dancer: "There one could see a lovely
ridewanz. Two men were fiddling. When they stopped—this pleased
the boisterous lads—behold, they competed in leading the song!"[148] "If
the lead dancers stop singing, you are all requested to resume a courtly
dance to the sound of the violin."[149]

More than any other form of courtly entertainment, dancing became

the target of clerical criticism. The Christian polemic against secular
dances was as old as the fulminations against the indecency of the theater: "In the train of filthiness I find dances and rounds."[150] In Jacob of
Vitry we find this thought: "The dance is a circle whose center is the
devil."[151] This sentence comes from St. Augustine, and throughout the
Middle Ages it was repeated in many variations. A sermon from the
fifteenth century, entitled "The harm caused by dancing" (*Was schaden
tantzen bringt*), describes in great detail how the devil used women
during dancing to seduce the men to evil things: "There are above all
three things with which the devil seduces men by using women: looking, talking, and touching. All three occur in dancing. They look at each
other and wink with their eyes, there is indecent talk, gestures, and
songs. The hands and the entire body are touched, which kindles and
increases the fire of unchastity, to which many a virtuous child falls
victim."[152] Dancing men, and more so dancing women, aroused the
special disgust of the clerics "by jumping obscenely and exposing themselves, which incites the lust of the flesh."[153] It was widely believed that
the indecent leaping dances were a modern invention, not like the good
old days, when dancing was done "with dignified movement of the
body and the limbs"[154]: "In modern times the flutes and trumpets
together with their noise have chased away the decent fiddles from the
feasts, and to the accompaniment of this loud din the girls leap about by
wiggling their buttocks rude and indecently like deer."[155]

At almost all the great feasts the palette of entertainments included a
special diversion for the men: if they were so inclined, the lords could
"watch the ladies"[156]: "Whatever one desired to see was offered there:
some went off to look at the ladies, others watched the dance; some
wanted to see the buhurt, others the jousts."[157] Such statements throw
a revealing light on the place of women in courtly society. If admiring
the ladies was not enough, one could seek a courtly conversation:
"Many great princes sat there joyfully and conversed with the
ladies."[158] "Some were talking with the women, others went for a
walk: some were dancing, some were singing, and others were running
a race."[159] *Frauendienst*, service to a lady, also had a place in the conviviality of the feast: "Some were throwing the javelin, some wanted to
drink wine, others wished to be with the ladies and seek to win their
favor."[160]

When men engaged in conversation they usually talked about two
things, minne and adventure: "Some spoke about lover's grief, others
about heroic deeds."[161] "These here talked of money, those others

about the feast; one group was quarreling over which of the ladies was the best."[162] What such men's talk sounded like is described by Heinrich von dem Türlin in *Mantel*. As the festive assembly at King Arthur's Whitsuntide feast was making its way to church, the men were observing the ladies:

> The knights were constantly looking over to the lovely ladies. Great were their compliments and praise. One was asking and another interrupted. This one spoke to his chosen lady, while the other only looked. Yet another said: 'Just look here at those shiny gray eyes and there at the brown eyebrows!' Someone praised the appearance of one lady, someone else that of another, and someone that of a third. There was praise for the neck, for the hands, for the mouth, the whimple, the lovely, beautiful figure, for the golden hair of a lady or a maid, or of both, for her manner, her figure. 'This is the most beautiful lady!' one said. Another nudged him and replied: 'Nonsense! Do you see that one over there? She is the loveliest of all!' 'No, you're mistaken. Do you see the one in the silk dress?' At this point the quarrel ended, for they had arrived at the cathedral where the archbishop was already intoning the introitus for the mass.[163]

Conversely the ladies also entertained themselves by watching the men at their war games and athletic competitions; several miniatures of the Large Heidelberg Song Manuscript have captured such scenes.

According to the descriptions of the poets, the court feasts were also the social setting for courtly literature, for the minnesong and the knightly romance (see p. 521).

GIFTS

The feast came to an end with the distribution of gifts to the guest and a great ceremonial farewell. The greater the value of the gifts, the more clearly they revealed the power and wealth of the host and attested to his courtly virtue of magnanimity. Sometimes the invitation to a feast was coupled with the annoucement that precious gifts could be expected. Thus at Whitsuntide the word went out that "King Arthur intended to break open his treasury and distribute his gold, so that his praise be magnified."[164] At his court feast, William of Wenden bestowed "most liberally upon each lord amazingly costly gifts: gems, silver, gold."[165] In addition, each noble guest received from him "three kinds of magnificent cloth: one uncut red scarlet and two silk-cloths skilfully interwoven with gold thread."[166] Finally, William gave away "chargers and riding horses."[167]

Gifts to the ladies were usually distributed by the lady of the court.

Suitable women's gifts were cloth and precious clothes, and especially jewelry: "One belt, one clasp, and one ring the noble queen gave her."[168] In the historical sources we often hear of very costly and exotic gifts which the great lords exchanged on the occasion of visits or through diplomatic delegations. The distribution of gifts at court feasts is also well documented, and our sources speak of such a display of splendor that the descriptions of the poets cannot be dismissed as unrealistic. At the knighting of Count Baldwin VI of Hainaut (d.1205), celebrated in 1189 at the court of Emperor Frederick I in Speyer, "the count distributed worthy gifts to the knights and clerics of the court and to the servants, namely chargers, palfreys, pack horses, precious clothes, gold and silver."[169] Of Duke Welf VI (d.1191) it was reported that he "bestowed splendid arms and costly vestments upon the knights of his court and their peers, whenever it seemed appropriate to him."[170] After Emperor Frederick I had taken Crema in 1160, he dismissed the German lords who had served in his army, and "distributed with royal magnanimity gold and silver, silver and golden vessels, along with costly clothes, fiefs, and other gifts."[171]

Gifts were graded according to the rank of the recipients. One gave to "every man as was appropriate,"[172] but primarily to "the nobles in accord with their dignity."[173] The noblest guests always received the costliest gifts, while the lesser nobles and the knights had to be content with more modest ones. From the poets we learn that gems were esteemed even more highly than gold and silver. At the wedding of Gahmuret and Herzeloyde, "Arabian gold was distributed to all the poor knights, to the kings and all the princes present Gahmuret gave gems."[174] In the descriptions of feast we hardly ever hear of gifts to the truly poor. Only in works that were more legendary in nature is this motif sometimes found. And then we discover that alms for the poor were reckoned in pennies (*Mai u. Beaflor* 89.15 ff.), whereas the gifts for the wealthy were measured in pounds.

Only one group of needy was never forgotten when gifts were distributed: the minstrels. We know from historical sources that the great feasts usually attracted "a vast number of jesters and jongleurs."[175] According to the poetic descriptions, they came in hundreds and thousands whenever the nobility was celebrating. To the hosts they were always welcome, for as musicians and jesters they contributed to the variety of entertainments. For that reason it was sometimes made known in advance that all minstrels could look forward to generous gifts. Aeneas issued the following announcement prior to his wedding with Lavinia: "All those who choose wealth over honor"—this formula was virtually a definition of the profession of wandering minstrels (see p. 504)—"let them come happily and receive enough to last them and their offspring for the rest of their lives."[176] That these were no empty promises is revealed at the end of the wedding feast in Laurentium: Aeneas

> now looked after the minstrels. He was the first to give presents to the minstrels, as was fitting for a king, because he held the highest position. Whoever received his gifts was truly fortunate, for he was made rich to the day he died, and even his children would profit from them all their lives. The king knew how to give: he was rich enough and had the right attitude. Afterwards the mighty princes bestowed on them costly gifts: precious garments of silk, gold, and fine metal-working, silver and gold vessels, mules and fast horses, uncut cloth of silk and samite, many red bracelets of gold and studded with gems. Sable and ermine the princes distributed, as they could well afford it. Dukes and counts, too, gave liberally to the minstrels, so that all of them departed happily and sang the praises of the king, each one in his own language.[177]

As concerns the type of gifts the minstrels received, it would seem that the poets sometimes piled precious object on precious object. Not infrequently, however, we can detect a gradation. At his own knighting, Wilhelm of Wenden distributed "costly jewels worth many hundred of marks to the nobles, depending on their rank and position; to the minstrels he gave clothes and horses."[178] Horses and clothes[179] were the typical presents for minstrels. King Nabuchodonosor "announced to the minstrels that he intended to wear new clothes at his feast and wanted to give away his old. Thereupon they all flocked there, and all who wanted to have the old garments received them."[180] That the minstrels in most cases had to content themselves with used clothing is also attested to by the *Spruch* poets.

Our Latin historical sources, too, mention gifts for the minstrels. It seemed especially remarkable to the chroniclers when a great lord did not live up to what was expected of him and refused to hand out gifts to the minstrels. Emperor Frederick II acted this way at his wedding to Isabelle of England in 1235, and he is even said to have dissuaded the princes from distributing gifts: "The emperor urges the princes not to waste their gifts on minstrels in the customary manner, since he regards it as the height of folly if someone stupidly bestows his possessions on mimes and jugglers."[181] Whether this report is true cannot be confirmed.

2. KNIGHTING CEREMONIES

The act of knighting was a solemn ritual through which a young noble-man was made a knight. At the center of the ceremony was the girding with the sword, usually in connection with other ceremonial acts. Whoever had gone through the ceremony could call himself a knight, and this was regarded as an honor. Knighting never functioned as an elevation to a particular estate.

The knighting ceremony of the courtly age was historically linked to the old aristocratic tradition of the delivery of arms, which probably went back to a Germanic tradition mentioned as early as Tacitus. In the Carolingian period, a young lord who had reached manhood was custo-marily presented with his weapons in a ceremonial act. Thus in 838 Emperor Louis the Pious "girt" his son Charles the Bald "with the weapons of a grown man, that is, with the sword."[1] This ceremony announced that a young man had come of age and was empowered to act as an independent person. Immediately following the girding with the sword, Emperor Louis the Pious placed the crown on his son's head and transferred to him a portion of the realm. Even in the poetry of the courtly age, the expression "to become a man" (ze man werden) was still synonymous with "to be knighted" (swert leiten) and "to become a knight" (ritter werden). "And so Lord Wigalois became a man,"[2] we are told in connection with his knighting ceremony. The description of the knighting of Flores ends with the comment: "now he is fully a man."[3] Immediately after the ceremony, the new knight would usually engage in his first public act. In 1163, Baldwin V of Hainaut "hastily knighted" his nephew Matthew "to enable him to assume the rulership of the land."[4] In 1170 King Henry II of England "made" his son Henry "a knight, and had him immediately anointed and crowned king, to the amazement and astonishment of all."[5] Philip of Swabia was knighted in 1197, and "after being girt with the weapons he celebrated most splen-didly his wedding feast."[6] The poets, too, regarded the knighting cere-mony as the precondition for a young prince's independence. They de-pict it as occurring at the outset of a campaign, prior to his crowning, and very frequently just before his wedding. When King Arthur reached the age of fifteen, "he became a knight and took a wife."[7] Guter Gerhard's son was not allowed to touch his wife during the wedding night, "because he had not yet in knightly manner reached manhood.

As long as he was a squire his wife was denied him."[8] Prince Mai also thought it his duty to be knighted before marrying, for "my lady shall never feel the warm embrace of a squire."[9] In 1258, Count Meinhard II of Görz-Tyrol married Elizabeth (d. 1273), daughter of Duke Otto II of Bavaria and widow of King Conrad VI, "but he was not allowed to consummate the marriage without having first been girt with the belt of knighthood; after that had been done with great festivity, he entered his lady's chamber."[10]

But the courtly ceremony of knighting was more than the solemn declaration of manhood. We can see this from the fact that in the High Middle Ages the ceremony was not always performed at a fixed date, when a young man legally came of age. The information concerning the age at the time of knighting varies widely. In the poetic sources the spread is more than ten years: Orendel was thirteen when he was knighted (*Orendel* 177); Pippin became a knight only at age twenty-four (*König Rother* 5002). It is historically attested that sometimes two brothers not of the same age were knighted in a joint ceremony. And Count Raimund of Provence was already fifty when Emperor Frederick II "promoted him to the rank of knight" at the urgent request of Raimund's two sons-in-law, the English and French kings, "for they deemed it unworthy that their father-in-law was not a knight."[11]

When and how the old ceremony of the delivery of arms developed into the knighting ceremony is difficult to pinpoint, since our historical sources rarely provide details about ceremonial procedures. An important clue is the change in terminology. It is towards the end of the eleventh century—the oldest examples come from France—that the noble lord who receives the sword is first given the title "knight" (*miles*). From the year 1096 comes the fragmentary "History of Anjou" (*Fragmentum historiae Andagavensis*) from the pen of Count Fulk IV of Anjou (d. 1109), in which the count records that his uncle, Geoffrey Martell, "made me a knight"[12] on Whitsuntide in 1060. Two years later, in 1098, Count Guido of Ponthieu wrote a letter to Bishop Lambert of Arras, informing him of his intention "to decorate [the son of the French king] with knightly arms, to honor him, and to elevate and consecrate him to knighthood."[13] In Germany throughout the twelfth century, the phrase "to gird with the sword" (*gladio accingere*) predominated. The first usage of "to declare a knight"[14] appears in Rahewin's *Gesta Frederici*, composed around 1160. The first German example of "to make a knight" (*militem facere*) seems to be even later: it is found at the end of the twelfth century in the *Annales Aquenses* in reference to the knighting of the emperor's sons, celebrated in Mainz in 1184 (*facti sunt milites*, p. 39).

The abundant historical documentation of the festivities in Mainz allows us to survey the Latin terminology of the knighting ceremony in use in Germany around 1200. The expressions "to take arms"[15] and "to be decorated with arms"[16] stem from the old aristocratic tradition of delivering the weapons to a young man when he reached manhood. Most frequently we encounter "to gird with the sword" or "to gird about with the sword."[17] Rarely was the old word for sword, *ensis*, used instead of *gladium*.[18] Of greatest interest are the phrases that include the words "knightly" and "knighthood" (*militaris*, *militia*): "to gird with the knightly sword,"[19] "to gird with the sword of knighthood."[20] One could also say: "to put on the weapons of knighthood,"[21] "to become bound by the knightly duties,"[22] or simply "to become a knight."[23] The actual word "knight" (*miles*) appears in only a few sources: "to make a knight,"[24] "to declare a knight,"[25] "to be elevated as new knights."[26] All these terms and phrases describe one and the same ceremony.

The German word *swertleite* is documented from about 1160 on. It was used first in *König Rother* (5061), Heinrich von Melk (*Erinnerung an den Tod* 520), and Veldeke's *Eneit* (347.30). Somewhat older is the verbal form *swert leiten* in *Kaiserchronik* (8390 and elsewhere) and in *Trierer Silvester* (584). Whether this word was coined only in the twelfth century must remain unanswered, since prior to 1150 only religious texts, in which such a term would not be used, have survived. In courtly poetry the word is relatively rare; only Gottfried von Straßburg and Rudolf von Ems used *swertleite* and *swert leiten* with any frequency. By the second half of the thirteenth century its usage declined. One of the last instances comes from around 1280 in Konrad von Würzburg's *Partonopier und Meliur* (18732).

The German language also had a variety of expressions to describe the knighting ceremony: "to take arms" (*wâfen nemen*), "to receive arms" (*wâfen enphâhen*), "to take arms" (*wâfen leiten*), "to give the sword" (*swert geben*), "to take the sword" (*swert nemen*), "to receive the sword" (*swert enphâhen*), "to tie on the sword" (*swert umbebinden*), "to gird the sword" (*swert umbegürten*), and so on. The word *ritter* ("knight") appears in connection with the knighting ceremony at about the same time as the first usages of *miles*: "to become a knight"[27] is first used by Heinrich von Veldeke and is subsequently well documented throughout the courtly age; "to become a knight"[28] appears first in Hartmann's *Gregorius* and in the *Nibelungenlied*. Slightly later are "to give knighthood,"[29] "to attain knighthood,"[30] "to consecrate as knight."[31] Quite popular was the expression "to win a knight's name,"[32] first found in *Gregorius* and in the *Nibelungenlied*. Others were "to take the name of knight,"[33] "to aspire to the name of knight,"[34] "to receive the name of knight,"[35] "to attain to the name of knight,"[36] "to take the knightly law,"[37] "to receive the calling of knighthood,"[38] and so on. Wolfram von Eschenbach has the phrase "the calling of the shield" (*schildes ambet*) for the consecration to knighthood: "I shall be a page no longer, I must follow the calling of the shield."[39] In all essential points the German terminology confirms the findings from the Latin sources. The most important fact is that during the second half of the twelfth century the old servile word "knight" was introduced into the vocabulary of the knighting ceremony of the high nobility. It is likely that the new word corresponded to a new phenomenon, meaning that during this time the courtly ritual of the knighting ceremony was developed.

THE COURTLY CEREMONY OF KNIGHTING

There is only one historical source of the twelfth century that describes in considerable detail the procedure of a princely knighting ritual: Jean de Mannoutier's account—written around 1180—of the knighting of Geoffrey Plantagenet of Anjou (d. 1151), celebrated in Rouen in 1127 on the occasion of his betrothal to the daughter of King Henry I of England. On the morning of that day a bath was prepared for the young count, "as custom demands for someone who wants to become a knight."[40] After the bath he was dressed in costly vestments: a linen shirt, an "outer robe spun of gold threads,"[41] and a purple mantle. In addition he put on silk stockings and shoes ornamented with gold. The "companions" (*consodales*) who were to be knighted with him were also clothed in linen and purple cloth. Adorned in this fashion they "showed themselves in public."[42] Horses and weapons were brought and distributed. Count Geoffrey received "a splendidly decorated Spanish horse,"[43] along with a "coat of mail of double-woven links"[44] which could withstand any lance or javelin; the mail hose, too, was made of double rings. Golden spurs were tied to his feet. A shield "with the emblem of the golden lions"[45] was hung around his neck. A gem-studded helmet was placed on his head and he was handed a lance with a shaft of ash wood and an iron head from Poitou. "Finally a sword from the royal treasury was brought to him."[46] Armed in this way the count leapt onto his horse "with amazing agility"[47] without using the stirrups. The entire day was then spent with "war games"[48] and other forms of entertainment in honor of the new knight and to his great delight.

Historians are skeptical about this report since it shows some literary embellishments. Its historical accuracy cannot be verified. But we can at least assume that at the time when the *Historia Gaufredi* was composed such a protocol for the courtly knighting ceremony was in existence. The first detailed acounts in French literature date from the same time when Jean de Marmoutier was writing, and they show the same basic pattern. Of outstanding importance is the *Conte du Graal* by Chrétien de Troyes, composed probably between 1180 and 1190. Here we find two knighting ceremonies which differ in important points of protocol. The first is the knighting of Parzeval at the court of Gornemant de Goort. In the morning Parzeval's host presented him with fresh clothes. Then "the noble lord bent down and tied on his right spur; for the custom was such that he who knights someone must tie on the spurs. There were plenty of pages around, and all those who could join lent a hand in arming Parzeval. The noble lord took the sword, girt him with it, gave him a kiss, and said that with the sword he had now bestowed upon him the highest estate that God has instituted and commanded: it is the estate of knighthood, which must be free of boorishness."[49] In a long speech Gornemant advised the new knight of the duties that the name of knight imposed upon him. "Then the noble lord makes the sign of the cross over him, he lifts high his hand and says: 'Dear brother, God bless you! Go with God!'"[50] More clearly than in Jean de Marmoutier, the emphasis here is on the girding with the sword as the real high point of the ceremony, and hence also on the role of the person who performs it. Both accounts share certain elements: the festive clothing of the new knight, the tying on of the spurs, the arming of the knight, the delivery of the sword (see fig. 27). Absent in Chrétien de Troyes are the ceremonial bath, the presentation of the horse, and the subsequent equestrian games. The *consodales* (companions-in-knighting) are also found only in Jean de Marmoutier. Chrétien, on the other hand, stresses in Gornemant de Goort's speech the connection between the knighting ceremony and the courtly ideal of knighthood.

A different focus and new aspects appear in the knighting ceremony conducted by Gauvain and Queen Yguerne for the pages of the magic castle liberated by Gauvain.

Fig. 27. Roland's knighting ceremony. Emperor Charlemagne girds Roland
with the sword, two other men fasten the spurs to his feet, while a bishop
pronounces the blessing. From a manuscript of the *Chanson d'Aspremont* (London, British Museum, Ms. Landsdowne 782). Thirteenth century.

> The queen had bathing chambers prepared and five hundred tubs of water
> heated. Then she bade all the pages enter to bathe and wash themselves.
> Clothes had been cut for them and they were decorated with them when they
> had left the bath. The clothes were interlaced with gold, the trim was ermine.
> The pages kept a standing vigil in the cathedral until after matins and never
> knelt down. In the morning Lord Gauvain himself tied on the right spur for
> each one, he girt them with the sword and delivered the *colée*. And so he now
> had around himself a proven band of five hundred new knights."[51]

Here we find, apart from the ceremonial bath, two new motifs: the
night vigil in church and the *colée*. It is difficult to determine whether
these are poetic embellishments or a reflection of social practices in
northern France. Around 1200, the monk Helinand of Froidmont (d.
1237) mentions in his tract "On the Good Rule of a Prince" (*De bono
regimine principis*) the solemn night vigil in church as an established
custom: "In certain places it is customary that the knight who is to be

consecrated the next morning spend the entire previous night awake in prayer; he may not lie or sit down."[52] Even more important is the second motif. The older notion that in France the *colée*—a light blow delivered with the hand or the broad of the sword against the neck (hence *colée*)—was already in the twelfth century the central act in the knighting ceremony, was obviously incorrect. Only one historical source attests the *colée* in France during the twelfth century: the "History of the Counts of Guines" (*Historia comitum Ghisnensium*) by Lambert of Ardres, written around 1200 or soon after. Speaking of the knighting of Count Baldwin II of Guines, it recounts that Thomas Becket of Canterbury "recently gird the count with the sword as a sign of knighthood, he tied spurs to the feet of his knight and gave him a blow (*alapa*) on the neck."[53] This event was dated to between 1154 and 1162. The word *alapa* (lit. "a box on the ear") was derived from classical Latin. Lambert's report is so unlike all other accounts in its terminology and concrete details, that Wilhelm Erben doubted the authenticity of the text; recently Johanna Maria van Winter, one of the leading experts on the material, agreed with his verdict. Most historians, however, consider the *Historia comitum Ghisnensium* an authentic source. Perhaps the *colée* was initially an innovation of only regional importance. In any case, it is striking that the two oldest examples come from Flanders. Chrétien de Troyes composed his *Conte du Graal* at the request of the count of Hainaut and probably wrote it at the Flemish court. The small county of Guines borders Flanders directly in the west. In the course of the thirteenth century the *colée* then gradually spread throughout France: this development, however, still requires historical documentation.

There are no twelfth-century German sources comparable to the detailed accounts of Jean de Marmoutier and Chrétien de Troyes. As a result there is a good deal more uncertainty about the protocol of the knighting ceremony in Germany. The contemporary chroniclers of the Mainz court feast in 1184 allow us to grasp the ritual of knighting only in rough outlines. The day began with a mass. The high point of the day was the ceremonial presentation of the arms and the girding with the sword, yet no source mentions who performed the latter act. Afterwards the new knights distributed gifts, and then equestrian games were held. The "Chronicle of Erfurt" states that the sons of Frederick I "were sworn to the knightly oaths,"[54] but it is not clear whether this can be taken as evidence that the emperor's sons were instructed on the ethical duties of knighthood.

For the most part the literary sources also spend more time describing the festive setting than the knighting ceremony itself. In the oldest secular epics we already find knighting ceremonies for the sons of princes and kings (Lamprecht, *Alexander* 357 ff.; *König Rother* 5003 ff.). Interestingly enough the first detailed descriptions date only to the beginning of the thirteenth century, in Wirnt von Grafenberg (1627 ff.), Gottfried von Straßburg (4973 ff.), and Konrad Fleck (7510 ff.). In Heinrich von Veldeke and Hartmann von Aue, who shaped the way German poets depicted courtly society, we find almost nothing at all. It is particularly odd that Wolfram von Eschenbach in his *Parzival* simply ignored the two detailed descriptions contained in his French source, Chrétien's *Conte du Graal*. The explanation for this striking omission must lie in the nature of the ceremony itself.

The literary descriptions of the thirteenth century reveal a fixed procedure: the ceremonial dressing, the girding with the sword, and the subsequent equestrian games are standard elements. The description in Wirnt von Grafenberg, one of the first in Germany, may serve as an example. King Arthur held "a court feast"[55] to celebrate the knighting of young Wigalois. "The queen straightaway sent him six knightly garments; they were of scarlet and of silk."[56] Lord Gawain, the most illustrious member of the Round Table, "presented him with a good riding-horse."[57] The king himself "placed twelve pages at his disposal, along with everything he needed and desired."[58] On Whitsunday[59] the actual celebration began with a mass. "The priests gave him the blessing"[60]; "then the young man girt himself with the sword"[61] Gawain had handed him. "The generous king himself handed him the shield and the lance."[62] Afterwards "many equestrian games started up and a wonderful buhurt with splendid pennants."[63] The only thing unusual is the fact that the new knight girt himself with the sword; in most cases the host of the feast or a close relative performed this act. But Grafenberg's story was apparently no literary invention: Lampert of Hersfeld reports that in 1065 in Worms, young Emperor Henry IV "girt himself with the weapons of war."[64]

What the German poets of the thirteenth century report about the protocol of the knighting ceremony agrees in the essential points with Chrétien's account of the knighting of Parzeval at the court of Gornemant de Goort. But the *colée*, the night vigil in church, and the ceremonial bath had no parallels in Germany at this time. The bath and the vigil appear first in the rhymed chess book of Heinrich von Beringen (first half of the fourteenth century). Whoever desired to become a knight, we read there, "is given the knightly blessing in a temple."[65] "Previous to this a bath has been prepared for him, in which he must wash himself carefully from head to toe."[66] "The night he spends in the temple."[67]

The *colée* appears in Germany as early as the *Orendel*, a poetic work considered to be a twelfth-century *Spielmannsepos*. We hear there of Master Ise's knighting ceremony at the Holy Sepulchre: "How quickly he was girt with the sword! Each of the knights in attendance delivered a firm blow."[68] But the only manuscript of this work dates from the late fifteenth century and therefore has no evidentiary value for twelfth-century conditions. Much the same applies to the description of Lancelot's knighting ceremony in the German *Prosa-Lancelot*: in the evening the young man "was taken to a church, where he spent the entire night awake and in prayer, until the day dawned."[69] The following morning, "all the weapons of those who were to be knighted were brought to the cathedral; the men had to arm themselves in the cathedral, and then the king delivered the blow to the neck."[70] The first part of the *Prosa-Lancelot* is today regarded as a work of the thirteenth century. But the existing version comes from the fifteenth century, and this passage reveals that the original text has been thoroughly reworked.

Only in the fourteenth century is there mounting evidence that the *colée* came into use in Germany as well. One of the earliest pieces of evidence is Suchenwirt's poem *Von hertzog Albrechts ritterschaft*, concerning the Prussian campaign of Duke Albrecht III of Austria (d. 1395) in the year 1377, in which the knighting of the duke is described: "Count Hermann of Cilli unsheathed his sword, he raised it high into the air and said to Duke Albrecht: 'Better a knight than a page!' And he struck the blow of honor."[71] The first pictorial representations of the *colée* in Germany are also dated to around the mid-fourteenth century. The German word *ritterslac* is documented from the second half of the fourteenth century (Suchenwirt IV.421).

THE ROLE OF THE CHURCH

According to the German sources, the knighting ceremony almost always included a church celebration. "In the morning, as day dawned, a bishop began to chant a very beautiful liturgy, and he blessed the sword of young King Tandarnas."[72] The usual procedure we hear about is this: first the blessing of the new knight's sword in church, followed outside the church by the lay part of the ritual, the girding with

the sword. This is how Wirnt von Grafenberg and Gottfried von Straßburg describe it: Young Tristan and his companions "together had
come to the cathedral where they heard a mass read and received the
blessing that was their due."[73] Then the celebrants apparently left the
church. "King Mark took Tristan, his nephew, by the hand and clad
him with sword and spurs. 'Behold, Tristan, my nephew,' he said, 'now
that your sword has been blessed and you have become a knight, be
mindful of the knightly honor.'"[74] We also find that the mass with the
blessing of the sword could take place after the new knight had been
girded with the sword (*Mai und Beaflor* 82.39 ff.), or the ceremonial
girding itself was performed in church: "After mass had been read the
elated young men stepped solemnly before my lord. He blessed their
swords. Then noble knights girt the young warriors with the swords, as
was the custom. After the blessing the young knights hastened from the
cathedral with jubilant cries. Outside they found their horses ready for
them, covered with precious blankets."[75] The expressions "to give the
blessing of the sword"[76] and "to consecrate as knight"[77] were two
alternative ways of describing the knighting ceremony.

Our historical sources rarely mention the mass and the blessing of
the sword (*consecratio ensis*). The reason can only be that the chroniclers usually left out such details. At least we do know that the knighting
ceremony of the emperor's sons at the court feast in Mainz in 1184 took
place on the Monday after Whitsunday following a mass. The blessing
of the sword is attested for the knighting ceremony of Duke Leopold VI
of Austria in 1200: "Duke Leopold of Austria and Styria was honored
in great splendor with the solemn blessing of the sword."[78] The blessing
is also mentioned on the occasion of the knighting of his son Frederick
II, performed in 1232 in the Schotten monastery in Vienna (*Continuatio
Mellicensis*, p. 507). According to the *Continuatio Scotorum* (p. 626)
and the *Continuatio Sancruensis* I (p. 627), Bishop Gebhard of Passau
girt Frederick with the sword. But historical evidence for the blessing of
the sword reaches back to the eleventh century. On Easter in 1065,
Henry IV was girt with the sword in Worms, "Archbishop Eberhard of
Trier pronouncing the blessing."[79] From the twelfth century comes
Otto of Freising's report of the knighting of young King Geza II of
Hungary (d. 1162) on the morning of the battle of Leitha in 1146: "The
next day the king went to a certain wooden church in the plain I have
mentioned. After having received from the bishops the prescribed
priestly blessings, he was girt there with his arms; for up to that time he
had not been knighted as he was still a youth."[80] Otto of Freising's

wording indicates that the blessing of the sword as part of the knighting ceremony was nothing unusual.

The testimony of some twelfth century ecclesiastical writers carries special weight. John of Salisbury, in his *Policraticus*, calls it a "venerable custom that everybody who is decorated with the belt of knighthood enters the church that same day, places the sword onto the altar and vows with a solemn oath obedience to the altar."[81] With direct reference to his day, Peter of Blois wrote that "today the knights receive their swords from the altar, so that they may profess themselves sons of the Church."[82] Even if these statements cannot simply be taken as descriptions of existing customs, they do reveal that the blessing of the sword was a widespread notion in the twelfth century.

The participation of the Church in the knighting ceremony emerges most clearly in the liturgical texts for the blessing of the knightly weapons and their bearer. Such texts are found from the tenth century on, and at the latest from the end of the eleventh century they were written for the specific purpose of the aristocratic knighting ceremony. This is documented most impressively by the "Rite for the arming of a defender of the Church or some other knight,"[83] composed after 1093 in Cambrai, in a French-speaking part of the empire. It lays down the sequence for the blessing of the weapons and the prayers that should be recited. First the banner was blessed, then the lance, then the sword, and finally the shield. The consecration of the sword was followed by the blessing of the knight: "Next the bishops shall girt him with the sword with these words: 'Receive this sword that is given to you with God's blessing, so that you may be strong enough, with the strength of the Holy Spirit, to resist and defeat all your enemies and all the enemies of the Holy Church of God.'"[84] Other texts recite in even greater detail the ethical duties imposed upon the noble warrior by the blessing of the weapons (see p. 300). To what extent such texts were in fact used is impossible to ascertain, but they are an important supplement to our other sources.

The liturgical rites of blessing are important for another reason: they attest to a connection between the knighting ceremony and the royal coronation ritual. Since Carolingian times, the handing over of the consecrated sword and other weapons, along with the vow to uphold the duties of a Christian ruler, had a permanent place in the *ordines* of coronation. Of particular interest in this context is the twelfth-century Burgundian "Ordo for the consecration of the king."[85] It stipulates that on the day of coronation, the king to be crowned should be "fully bathed."[86] Then he is to be festively dressed with a new white garment on top of a linen shirt, over that a purple mantle embroidered with gold, and gold-trimmed shoes and golden spurs. Next "he shall be girt with the precious golden sword."[87] In the subsequent course of the coronation ceremony the archbishop was called upon "to elevate this knight here present to the royal dignity."[88] How this peculiar mix of knighting ceremony and coronation ritual came into being awaits clarification.

FROM ROYAL PRACTICE TO MASS PROMOTION

Historical reports from the Carolingian period concerning the ceremonial delivery of arms and girding with the sword involve almost exclusively members of the Carolingian royal family. It would seem that in the beginning the knighting ceremony was a royal custom, closely linked to the assumption of kingship or the first public act of the young ruler. Developments in post-Carolingian times went along a number of paths. In France, where the centralized royal power receded into the background for several centuries, local rulers soon adopted the royal protocol of knighting for their own use, at first the great royal vassals, then also the smaller nobles who at this time were called *milites* (knights). But we can grasp this development only in rough outlines, since a history of the knighting ceremony in France—which would also have to consider regional differences—has not yet been written. In Germany it would seem that the custom of celebrating a young man's entrance into society with the presentation of weapons remained tied to the royal family much longer. Only in the French-speaking lands of the empire, in Lotharingia and Burgundy, were social practices probably similar to those in France. From Upper Lotharingia comes a charter of the bishop of Toul, dated 1091, which confirms the gift made to the monastery of Cluny by a certain "Wido, of noble family and girt with the knightly arms."[89] Apart from this case, we hear of nonroyal knighting ceremonies in Germany only in the twelfth century, and these reports refer exclusively to members of the most powerful and illustrious princely houses. In 1104 "Margave Leopold of Austria was girt with the sword."[90] In 1110 Count Frederick of Goseck—the counts of Goseck were at this time in possession of the Palatinate of Saxony— "became a young man and girt on the weapons."[91] For the year 1123 it is reported that the Welf Henry the Proud "received the arms."[92] Adalbert, the son of Margrave Leopold III of Austria, was "girt with the sword"[93] in 1125. Otto of Freising reports under the year 1147 that the son of Duke Frederick II of Swabia, the future Emperor Frederick I, at that time "already received the belt of knighthood."[94] The ceremonial knighting of the sons of princes was part of the new style of lordship that was developing at this time in close imitation of the protocol at the royal court. But it would seem that the new custom was slow to spread. Gislebert of Mons tells us that the knighting of Baldwin V of Hainaut— celebrated on Easter of 1168 in Valenciennes "with dignity and joy" (*cum honore et gaudio*)—fulfilled a long-standing wish of his father's, "since for many years it had not happened that a count of Hainaut had seen his son as a knight."[95] In some princely houses the knighting ceremony was performed more frequently: the Hohenstaufen and the Babenbergers—related by marriage—head the list with five and four knightings, respectively; other families never knighted anyone. At no time was the knighting ceremony an obligatory ritual. Inspired by the great feast in Mainz in 1184, a number of princely knighting ceremonies were celebrated with great splendor in the years following. In 1189 the young Count Baldwin VI of Hainaut was made a knight by Henry VI (Gislebert of Mons, p. 237). On Whitsunday in 1192 in Worms, Conrad of Swabia and Ludwig I of Bavaria took the sword in the presence of the emperor (Magnus von Reichersberg, p. 519). The year 1197 witnessed the splendid celebration of the knighting of Philip of Swabia in Augsburg (*Continuatio Admuntensis*, p. 588). In 1200 Duke Leopold VI of Austria took the sword "in great splendor."[96]

The only nonprincely family that celebrated knighting ceremonies as early as the twelfth century were the counts of Hainaut. This comital house, however, was French-speaking, and looked towards Flanders and France for its style of social life. Of interest is an entry in the chronicle written by the monk Berthold of Zwiefalten around 1138. It concerns a son of Count Rudolf of Grüningen, "a youth just recently girt with the knightly arms."[97] Read literally, this would imply that the knighting ceremony was already performed among the comital nobility of southwestern Germany in the first half of the twelfth century. But our interpretation must take into account the uncertainty that attaches to the terminology. The expressions "to gird with the sword" (*gladio succingere*) or "to take arms" (*arma sumere*) did not necessarily refer to the ceremonial act of knighting, but could be used to describe the fact that a young man was now fit to bear arms. Even the term "knightly belt" (*cingulum militiae*), derived from classical Latin, was frequently used metaphorically; "to lay down the knightly belt" (*cingulum militiae deponere*) meant: "to retire," "to renounce the world," or "to enter a monastery."

But we do know for certain that even in Germany by the twelfth century, a significant number of nonprincely noblemen were ceremonially knighted. This was done through a new practice: the mass knighting. We cannot date with any certainty when it became customary to present several "companions-in-knighting" with arms and declare them knights as part of the knighting ceremony of the son of a king or prince. Participation in such a ceremony was regarded as a mark of honor and distinction, quite apart from the material benefits it brought. The oldest historical account of such a mass knighting comes from Poland. The *Chronica Polonorum*—written at the beginning of the twelfth century, most likely by a Frenchman—reports that King Wladislav I of Poland (d. 1102), probably in 1099, "wanted to gird his son [Boleslaw] with the sword," and it adds: "He was not the only one girt that day with the knightly belt. His father, for love of his son and in his honor, also handed the arms to many men of the same age."[98] The first example from Germany concerns the knighting of the Babenberg Adalbert in the year 1125: "Adalbert, the son of Margrave Leopold, was girt with the sword along with one hundred and twenty others."[99] This entry, however, is regarded as a fourteenth-century addition. The first secure report comes only from the end of the twelfth century. Magnus von Eichersberg (d. 1195) tells us that on Whitsuntide of 1192 in Worms, Emperor Henry VI elevated to the knighthood his brother Conrad, and Ludwig of Bavaria, of the house of Wittelsbach; "many counts and a great many noblemen were also girt there with the sword."[100] For the same period we already have literary testimony for this custom. Eilhart von Oberg tells of a mass knighting at which sixty pages received the sword in company with Tristan (521 f.). The *Nibelungenlied*, too, speaks of the taking of the sword by many "noble children,"[101] who were made knights together with Siegfried: "four hundred companions"[102] took part in the ceremony. When the younger works of literature speak of the knighting of a young prince, they almost always mention the participation of numerous noblemen.

By the end of the twelfth century we hear of mass promotions that were not held in conjunction with the knighting of a king's or prince's son. The oldest historical report from Germany refers to the year 1189, when Emperor Frederick I, on his way to the Holy Land, conducted a review of his army. "Elated by the great pleasure he felt at seeing such a huge army, he happily ordered in person that a war game be held, and he promoted sixty young noblemen, who were squires, to the rank of knights and to the exercise of knighthood."[103] Literary examples also appear at the end of the twelfth century. At the double wedding of Gunther and Siegfried in Worms, six hundred young noblemen were girt with the sword "in honor of the kings."[104] Ulrich von Liechtenstein recounts in his *Frauendienst* that in the year 1222 he was among 250 squires who were knighted in Vienna (40.5 ff.) when Duke Leopold VI celebrated the marriage of his daughter Agnes to Duke Albrecht I of Saxony (d. 1261). If we grant Liechtenstein's comic self-portrait the status of a historical source, this would be the first report of the knighting of a ministerial. The house of Liechtenstein was among the leading ministerial families of Styria. Around the same time Rudolf von Ems recounts that Guter Gerhard's son became a ministerial of the archbishop of Cologne before he ceremonially took the sword (R. v. Ems, *Guter Gerhard* 3475 ff.). From the mid-thirteenth century comes the report that Duke Frederick II of Austria, on the fest of St. George in 1245, "gave the sword to 144 noble youths of his land in a splendid ceremony near Vienna."[105] From then on, mass knightings were held with increasing frequency on the occasion of princely weddings, as part of coronation festivities, or during military campaigns, before or after battle. In 1260, before the battle against the Hungarians, King Ottokar II of Bohemia "girt himself and 118 squires with the sword."[106] The future belonged to mass knightings; after the end of the thirteenth century single knighting ceremonies are no longer documented.

The splendidly arranged mass promotions offered the host an opportunity to display the wealth and power of his court. The new knights stood to profit from this, since they were equipped with costly garments and weapons and were sometimes even given rich gifts. At the knighting of Vivianz, every one of the one hundred companions received from Margrave Willehalm a suit of armor (*harnasch*) and two chargers (*kastelân*); in addition, Gyburg cut for each one "three different garments from her own stock."[107] Gifts of clothing to the companions-in-knighting are also mentioned in the historical sources. The annals of Colmar report that in 1298 in Straßburg, Bishop Conrad of Liechtenstein made a number of young men into knights, "all of whom he clothed with at least three garments, namely a costly tunic, a surcoat with fine fur, and a wrap with precious fur."[108] Even more detailed is the account of the knighting of Edward of Carnarvon, the heir to the English throne, celebrated in London on Whitsuntide in the year 1306.

After mass, the king himself, Edward I (d. 1307), girt his son with the sword, while the Earl of Lincoln and the Earl of Hereford, both relatives of the royal house, tied on the spurs. The prince then elevated to knighthood his three hundred companions, who had kept a kneeling vigil during the previous night in the abbey church of Westminster. Each one of them was equipped with weapons (helmet, gorget, lance, sword, spurs) and cloth for the festive garments and the ritual bed. There were materials for a mantle (*cointesia*), a robe with fur trimming (*roba*), a fur frock (*pena*), a cape (*capa*), a cap (*capucium*), a linen shirt and socks, a straw mattress (*matracium*), and a down quilt (*culcitra*); per person that amounted to no less than a hundred meters of cloth (Bullock-Davies, p. XXIII). In preparation for the feast, the king had brought to London eighty bails of colored wool cloth, two thousand ells of linen and four thousand ells of canvas (ibid., p. XVII). A nice effect was created if the companions wore the same outfit as the prince. At the knighting of Wilhelm of Orlens, there were sixty companions "who wore in great splendor the same clothes as Wilhelm. The garments shone with a magnificent radiance. Brocade, silk, baldachin, lined with ermine and nicely set off with sable, that is what the noble man and all his companions wore."[109]

Sometimes the financial expenses involved in a knighting ceremony taxed a noble household to the very limit of its resources. Under the year 1276, the *Magdeburger Schöppenchronik* relates the following about the sons of the duke of Saxony: "Then the young lords of Saxony became knights, and they incurred such expenses that they were imprisoned in Magdeburg on account of the debts they could not pay."[110] Only after they had mortgaged a few cities and castles were they set free. By at the end of the thirteenth century some territorial lords were already demanding the right to levy a special tax not only for the "journey to Rome" (*transire alpes*) and "the wedding of their daughters" (*tradere filiam suam nuptui*), but also for "the knighting of a son."[111]

Complaints that lowborn or unworthy people were attaining knighthood arise as early as the twelfth century. Otto of Freising reports with disgust that it was not unusual in northern Italy to "admit to the belt of knighthood or the higher distinctions young men of inferior station and even artisans who engaged in some vile mechanical art."[112] The German bishop adds that in other countries—no doubt he was thinking of Germany—such people "were excluded like the plague from the more respectable and honorable pursuits."[113] But soon after 1200, a poet in Germany laments: "He who is barely a servant now wants to be a knight. Thus the noble must pay for the wicked. Rarely does anything good come from evil fellows. May God reject those who give the sword to someone who cannot keep up a knightly life, and who from his descent is not born to it. We have lost the old law!"[114] What such lamentation could be referring to is not clear. There are no historical indications that at this time non-nobles were being promoted to knighthood through a knighting ceremony. More likely we should be thinking of the kind of "knightly" career described in *Helmbrecht*: a horse and elegant clothes were all the peasant's son needed to appear a knight and begin his life as a knightly brigand. It seems that only towards the end of the thirteenth century were non-nobles sometimes ceremonially declared knights. The annals of Colmar note under the year 1281: "Many non-nobles became knights in Straßburg."[115] Apparently that was considered something unusual at the time. The complaints about "country yokels"[116] who presumed to play knights probably had a different sociological reason, even though we also hear of the sword blessing in this context: "If one blesses the sword of a rich and renowned peasant, he becomes an unworthy knight."[117] This was probably prompted by the experience that in some rural areas the lines of social distinction were being blurred as better off peasants, who had attained a measure of economic prosperity, were marrying into smaller noble families.

3. TOURNAMENTS

THE BEGINNINGS OF TOURNAMENTS

The origins and development of the knightly tournament are shrouded in obscurity. Martial games on horseback were known in antiquity as well as among the Germanic peoples. What such games were like at the ninth-century Frankish court is described by Nithart, a grandson of Charlemagne (*Historiae*, p. 442 f.). In the tenth century, Widukind of Corvey reports in his "History of the Saxons" that King Henry I (d. 936) proved his skill in war games (p. 78). But these older accounts all lack one element that became characteristic for the later tournament: the clash of compact cavalry formations wielding sharp weapons. Only the new developments in the lance technique created the precondition for the creation in the eleventh century of rules for a new martial sport. This was said to have been the work of the French nobleman Geoffroi de Preuilly. At his death in 1066, it was reported that it was he "who had invented tournaments."[1] The first historically documented tournament was held in 1095 in Flanders, and the new sport claimed its first victim when Count Henry III von Löwen was fatally impaled: his opponent "raised the lance and rode towards him by driving his horse vehemently with his spurs; in this war game he wanted to unhorse him, but he drove the lance into his heart and killed him on the spot."[2] Subsequent reports also come from Flanders and northern France. Galbert of Bruges recounts in his biography of Count Charles of Flanders (d. 1127), written around 1130, that the count fought in France against various princes "for the honor of his land and the training of his knights."[3] By 1130 the first papal prohibition of tournaments had already been promulgated by Innocent II at the Council of Clermont. The heyday of the tournaments in northern France was in the 1170s and 1180s. The best information for this period comes from the "Life of William Marshal" (Histoire de Guillaume le Maréchal), composed by a French-speaking poet soon after William's death in 1219. William Marshal, an English nobleman, was a typical figure of his age. As the younger son of Baron John Fitz Gilbert he was left without feudal property, and so he took his fortunes into his own hands. After being knighted in 1167, he spent many years in France traveling from tournament to tournament and became one of the most famed and feared tournament fighters of his day. In 1170 King Henry II of England entrusted to him the knightly training of his son Henry. Through a later marriage to one of the wealthiest heiresses of England, William Marshal became Earl of Pembroke and a very powerful man; after the death of King John I (d. 1216), he was regent of the realm from 1216–1219. Of the twelve tournaments reported in his "Life," four took place in the Ile de France, four in the County of Blois, and three in Champagne. During this period Flanders and the neighboring provinces, too, witnessed lively tournament activity, as we learn from Gislebert of Mons's Chronicle of Hainaut. Count Baldwin V of Hainaut was knighted in 1168 in Valenciennes, a year after William. Afterwards he participated in a tournament in Maastricht "with a great many knights," for knighthood was at that time flourishing in Hainaut,"[4] and in the following years he visited numerous tournaments in Flanders and Normandy. According to the Histoire de Guillaume le Maréchal, at that time a tournament was held in northern France every two weeks (4974 f.).

"Then the tournament started, as was customary in France."[5] Everybody knew that France was the homeland of the tournament. Radulf of Coggeshall described how the knights galloped at each other with lances couched "in the French manner."[6] Radulf of Diceto and Mat-

thew of Paris spoke of the tournaments as "French fighting."[7] Knights
flocked to France from everywhere, including England, where, except
for a few brief periods under King Stephan I (d. 1154), tournaments
were prohibited by royal decrees in the twelfth century. Only in 1194
did Richard the Lionheart allow tournaments to take place, but he
placed a high tax on participants. Among the reasons that are said to
have prompted the king to permit tournaments in England was the desire "that the French should no longer mock the English knights as
inept and inexperienced."[8] Tournament prohibitions were later renewed in England, and only under Edward I (d. 1307) did the French
knightly sport finally gain acceptance.

The adoption of French tournaments in Germany began quite early.
The oldest piece of evidence is thought by many to be Otto of Freising's
account (written in 1157/58) of the tournament put on by the Hohenstaufen Dukes Conrad and Frederick of Swabia outside Würzburg in
1127 (see p. 82). But since we hear neither of a formal invitation nor a
clash of massed formations, it is doubtful whether this event was anything like a tournament in the French style. Even earlier are some entries
in the chronicle of Zwiefalten, compiled in 1138 by the monk Berthold.
They concern two noble youths from southwest Germany: "Young
Henry of Hapsburg was prone to unseemly gaiety. At one of those ill-
fated war games, a dangerous diversion he frequently indulged in, he
suffered an unfortunate blow and died."[9] "Adalbert, a son of Rudolf [of
Grüningen], a youth just recently girt with arms, was killed not through
the fault of the others but on account of his own carelessness."[10] Here,
too, it is unclear how the events that claimed the lives of these young
men were organized. It is highly unlikely that the French tournaments
were already so firmly established in southwestern Germany in the first
decades of the twelfth century that the monk from Zwiefalten could
speak of them as a well-known practice. Of interest is Berthold's comment about the chronological link between Adalbert's knighting and his
participation in a tournament. From the later period there is a good deal
of historical and literary evidence that young princes and other noblemen rode in their first tournament immediately following their ceremony of knighting.

In the "Life of Archbishop Albero of Trier"—written between 1152
and 1157—we read that in 1148 the armies of the archbishop and of
Count Palatine Hermann von Stahleck (d. 1156) stood facing each
other at the Mosel. For days the knights from Trier waited for the
count's attack, and to while away the time they put on exercises:

What a spectacle you could have seen there! Knights in full armor practicing simulated combat! Wild chargers turning in the smallest space! Knights on horseback clashing with each other, lances splintering with a crash! What shouting of the pursuers and the pursued you would have heard! Skillfully feigned flight you could have seen, the sudden wheeling about of those fleeing and a sudden shift in fortune for those already at their backs! There you could have observed knights now in a tight pack, now suddenly opening up so that by pretended yielding they could meet the enemy with an arched line and enclose him by turning in the flanks! A thousand tricks, a thousand feints one could learn there![11]

Riding in opposing formations and the requisite dividing up of the participating knights into teams were in keeping with French tournament practice. Maneuvers similar to those described by Balderic also appear in the tournament descriptions of courtly literature. Nevertheless, such a war game during a campaign cannot be directly compared to the French tournaments. The latter were separate events to which formal invitations were issued.

It would seem that the French-style tournaments gained ground in Germany only gradually. Because of their poor riding skills, the German knights who joined the Second Crusade in the mid-twelfth century were mocked by the French with the linguistically puzzling taunt: "*Pousse Aleman.*"[12] In fact we know of only one German tournament from the twelfth century that was announced ahead of time, as was customary in France, and in the end it didn't even take place. Following the knighting of Emperor Frederick I's sons at the court feast of Mainz in 1184, a tournament was supposed to be held in Ingelheim, but it was canceled for unknown reasons (see p. 205). The dearth of historical reports is not, however, conclusive proof. What would we know about French tournaments of the twelfth century if we did not have the *Histoire de Guillaume le Maréchal* and Gislebert's Chronicle of Hainaut? Historical sources of this kind didn't exist in Germany at the time.

The *Lauterberg Chronicle*, though written only around 1230, contains a very interesting entry. It reports under the year 1175 that Count Conrad, the son of Margrave Dietrich von der Lausitz (d. 1185), was killed "during a military exercise which is commonly called 'tournament.'"[13] The chronicler then adds: "This pernicious sport had become so entrenched in our region that within one year sixteen knights are said to have been killed by it."[14] If this report is accurate, many more tournaments must have been held in Germany than our historical sources would indicate. It is not clear, though, whether these were tournaments in the French style or war games of some other kind. In most cases we are probably dealing with local events in which only a small number of noblemen participated. Ulrich von Liechtenstein reports in *Frauendienst* that in his youth he took part in twelve tournaments in the course of one summer (47.1 f.). If that is true, it would mean that in Austria around 1230, a tournament was held every other week.

The borrowing of the French word *tornoi* (or *tornoiement*) is attested around 1160 by Otto of Freising (see p. 82). The first occurrences in the vernacular are about a decade earlier. Heinrich von Veldeke seems to have been the first to use *turnei*. It appears only once in his *Eneit*, when Eneas recounts the Greek attack on Troy: "The Greeks found us ready for battle at all times (*bereit zu turneie und zu strîte*), mounted or on foot."[15] This is how the text reads in the younger manuscripts from Heidelberg (H) and Gotha (G); the oldest manuscript, from Berlin (B), instead has: *ze storme und ze strîte* (40.35). This discrepancy makes it uncertain whether the word *turnei* belonged to the original version. What is more, in this instance *turnei* does not have the meaning of "tournament," but is used in connection with *strît* to describe real warfare. The same phrase is found in Eilhart's *Tristrant*: "How much fame he always won in battle (*zu tornei und zu strîte*)."[16] These particular *Tristrant* verses are also found only in younger manuscripts. Apparently the word *turnei* was initially taken over by Veldeke and Eilhart in the meaning of "warfare," a usage that is also documented for the French *tornoi*. The *turnei* as a separate event with its own rules appears first in Hartmann's *Erec*. Following Erec's knighting at the court of King Arthur, "the tournament was set for three weeks from next Monday."[17] *Turnei* was now joined by the verb *turnieren*: "Never did a knight tourney more splendidly."[18] Hartmann's *Erec* also contains the first large tournament description (2404 ff.). From that time on French tournament terminology was firmly established in German literature. The longest tournament description comes from the pen of Ulrich von Liechtenstein, who participated in the great tournament held in Friesach (in Carinthia) in 1224 (*Frauendienst* 177.1-315.8).

THE MASS TOURNAMENT OR MELÉE

Tournaments were mass affairs: the contest took place between opposing ranks and differed but little from ordinary battle. What set a tournament apart from real war was the fact that invitations were issued, rules and conditions were agreed upon, and each team had a safety zone.

The invitation   Invitations to a tournament were usually sent out three to six weeks ahead of time. Most tournaments were set for a Monday. "I fought hard there on three successive Mondays"[19] is another way of saying "I fought in three tournaments." Messengers and letters were dispatched to invite anybody who wanted to come ("In all of France the tournament was announced"[20]), or to challenge a specific opponent (U. v. Zatzikhoven 2628 ff.). Matthew of Paris quotes, under the year 1215, the wording of a letter of invitation from the English barons to William of Albineto: "Therefore we inform you and urge you to attend said tournament with horses and weapons in such a state of preparation that it may be to your honor."[21] What makes this letter even more interesting is the fact that it mentions a prize sponsored by a lady: "Whoever acquits himself best shall receive a bear that a lady is sending to the tournament."[22] Animals seem to have been very popular as tournament prizes. In *Renner*, a young nobleman is scolded "who risks his life for a pig or a bear or a lion."[23] Prizes of a very different nature are also found in literature. Queen Herzeloyde hosted the great tourney of Kanvoleis with the intention of giving her hand in marriage to the winner: she had appointed herself as the prize. When we encounter the same theme in real life—for example at the grail feast of Magdeburg in 1280 (see p. 263), where a prostitute was offered up as the prize—we are dealing with the imitation of literary motifs.

Dividing the teams   Before the contest began, the tourneyers met to set the rules. Normally two teams were formed and the highest-ranking lords were appointed their leaders. Care was taken to make the ranks numerically as equal as possible, which required not a little diplomatic skill since the knightly retinues of the lords could be very different in size. At the tournament of Friesach in 1224, one team was made up of the duke of Austria as the overall leader with 100 knights, the margrave of Vohburg with 12 knights, Albrecht of Tyrol with 40, Hugh of Tufers with 23, Otto of Lengenbach with 22, Reinbrecht of Muoreck with 40, Hadamar of Küenring with 31, Hermann of Kranberg with 20, and Wolfger of Gors with 12 knights. The opposing ranks were led by the margrave of Istria with his 60 knights, and included the duke of Carinthia with 50, Meinhard of Görz with 55, the count of Hiunenburg with 32, the count of Liubenouwe with 25, Hermann of Ortenburg with 8, Hertnit of Orte with 36, and Wölfing of Stubenberg with 34 knights (U. v. Liechtenstein, *Frauendienst* 246.1 ff.). If we add up the figures, each team comes to exactly three hundred knights. In other cases the teams were not so balanced. The *Histoire de Guillaume le Maréchal* mentions one incident where one group was so much weaker that it hardly dared to come out of the gates (3447 ff.).

The poets tell us that hundreds, and sometimes even thousands, of knights attended the tournaments. Here we must bear in mind that they were always describing exceptionally large affairs. Historical figures bear out that the poets' ideas were not sheer fantasy. Count Charles of Flanders is reported to have participated in the tournaments in France with two hundred knights (Galbert of Bruges, p. 564). That was also the size of the retinue of the English crown prince Henry in 1180 at the great tourney of Lagny-sur-Marne, where, according to the *Histoire de Guillaume le Maréchal*, a total of three thousand knights were assembled (4782). The martial exercise put on at Mainz in 1184 following the knighting of the emperor's sons supposedly involved twenty thousand knights (Gislebert of Mons, p. 157).

At the great tournaments, teams were usually divided up in such a way that groups from the same region stayed together. At the tourney of Komarzi, the question "how shall we tourney here?"[24] drew the response: "how else but land against land."[25] Within the regional groupings, however, the feudal ranks remained intact: the great lords formed separate bands with their knights and could operate on their own. From Gislebert of Mons we learn that around 1170 at the tournaments of northern France, the knights of Hainaut usually fought alongside their peers from Vermandois and Flanders against the Frenchmen. When Baldwin V of Hainaut on one occasion joined the French against Count Philip of Flanders, this move had far-reaching political consequences (*Chronicon Hanoniense*, p. 97). Not infrequently tournament opponents were old enemies who had met before on the battlefield. At Kanvoleis, King Kaylet of Spain had to confront the vastly superior forces of King Hardiz of Gascony, who had been harassing him for some time (W. v. Eschenbach, *Parzival* 65. 5 ff.). Enemies also met at the tournament of Komarzi: the son of the French king and the king of Aragon who stood among opposing ranks had just clashed in a military confrontation (R. v. Ems, *Wilhelm v. Orlens* 6121 ff.). In such cases the tourney was a continuation of war by other means. It is not surprising that sometimes the tournament threatened to degenerate into a bloody fight: "And now the tourney turned into a battle, for it claimed lives."[26]

Financial conditions One important question that had to be settled before the tourney could start concerned the financial arrangements.

Two alternative rules were proposed at the tournament of Komarzi: either a defeated knight should lose everything he had,[27] or the stake was everything he could raise,[28] which included a ransom appropriate to his rank. The tourneyers at Komarzi agreed on the first option. In other cases high ransoms were set. At most tournaments the prize was the knight's equipment: "Just as the man appeared on the tourney ground, that was to the prize. In those days one seldom tourneyed under different arrangements."[29]

The safety zone   Each team was assigned a refuge where prisoners could be taken and knights were safe from attack. This zone was called *fride* (zone of peace), *hamît* (barricade), or *litze* (cord, barrier). Except for this, the tourney ground had no boundaries in the early days. As a result, the great tournaments did substantial damage to fields and crops. Only in the thirteenth century did it become customary to mark off the grounds. In literature this is first mentioned in Rudolf von Ems's *Guter Gerhard* (3437 ff.). This was a step in the development that transformed the battle-like tournaments of the early period into the ceremonial pageantry of the late Middle Ages. The safety zones were frequently chosen such that one was located inside a city and the other outside, in which case there was an "inner" and an "outer" team. If the city happened to be the seat of the prince who was hosting the tourney, and if the guests who formed the opposing party were camped out in tents before the city, such an arrangement made perfectly good sense. This may perhaps also explain why especially in the older period martial games were frequently held during sieges.

The "vesper"   Sometimes the tournament proper was preceded on the day before by a preliminary tourney, the *vesperîe*, which, despite its name, was not only held at night. It was a preliminary skirmish without any fixed rules or conditions. In most cases it consisted of a series of jousts, though sometimes the fighting was already done in teams. According to the poets, the most famous fighters liked to hold back and let the others show off their skills first so that later on they might demonstrate even more impressively their superior knightly ability. The *Histoire de Guillaume le Maréchal* reports that Count Philip of Flanders, who fought in more tournaments than most of his peers, owed his success not least to the clever stratagem of joining the fray only when the combatants showed signs of exhaustion (2718 ff.). At times the fighting during the *vesperîe* became so intense that all plans were upset and the real tournament never took place. The most famous literary example of this is the tournament at Kanvoleis, which began at noon on the day before with preliminary skirmishes. Gradually more and more knights in small groups arrived on the tourney ground, and the fighting developed into a full-fledged battle contested with great intensity on both sides. The end result was that by evening most leaders had been captured and the tournament could not be put on the next day: "A tournament had been proclaimed, but it did not take place. A *vesperîe* crippled it. Those who were eager for a fight became so tame that the tournament lapsed."[30]

The fight   The main tourney in the twelfth century was always contested by two massed formations. The leaders of the two teams supervised the positioning of the units and probably also decided when to send them into action. We learn little about tournament tactics from our sources. Apparently each individual lord had more or less independent command of his knightly contingent. The most important consideration was to keep the formation in tight ranks during the charge: "The group that was to begin the tournament charged in formation and stayed close together, which is what one should do against the enemy."[31] The leaders had constantly to impress upon the knights to stay in formation: "Keep together, it's for your own good."[32] "Now squeeze together tightly!"[33] The aim was to smash into the enemy with the full force of a massed formation, in the hope of throwing him back or breaking his ranks. If that was successful, one then tried to ride a "turnabout" (*widerkêre*) by attacking the opponent in the back. It could happen, however, that a formation under attack would initially take to flight only to suddenly wheel about and go on the offensive: "One group gave way and one saw them in headlong flight in tight ranks; but it was not long before those fleeing turned around and were now pushing those who had chased them back across the field."[34]

One passage in *Parizival* mentions tournament rules that are already reminiscent of the tournament orders found in a later period. Parzival's brother Feirefiz boasts that he is skilled in all forms of the joust: "The tournament has five runs, and I have done them all. The first is called *zempuneiz*. The second I know under the name *ze triviers*. The third is *zentmuoten*. Then I have also ridden the good thrust (*ze rehter tjost*) at full charge, neither have I neglected *zer volge*."[35] The meaning of these phrases has occasioned a lively scholarly debate. The three French words seem reasonably clear: *zem puneiz* is the massed charge straight ahead; *ze triviers* is the charge from the side; *ze rehter tjost* probably means the single combat with couched lance. The two German terms are more problematic: *zentmuoten* (manuscript D) or *ze muoten* (other manuscripts) was used in *Willehalm* as the opposite of *zer tjost* (29.15; 361.21 ff.), and may possibly mean the lance fight from standing horses, that is, without a charge, or the simultaneous fight against several opponents. *Zer volge* is, as we learn once again from *Willehalm* (57.11; 88.17), the charge in pursuit. Whether such a systematic differentiation of tournament "runs" already existed at the beginning of the thirteenth century cannot be determined. In any case, the passage reveals that as early as around 1200, the poets, and no doubt the audience as well, were familiar with the details of tournament practice.

The fight would go back and forth until the two formations were so thoroughly intertwined—"group into group, team into team"[36]—that no substantial movement was possible. The tournament now "stood": "The tourney stood still on the spot."[37] "The tournament had now come to a standstill like a wall."[38] Frequently this was the decisive phase. In the general tumult each knight hacked at the opponents with the aim of unseating as many as possible in order to disable or capture them. The attempt to take prisoners was aimed especially at the leaders, since success here promised the greatest material rewards and rendered the opposing team leaderless. There were two techniques of capturing a knight. One could assault the opponent so fiercely with the weapon that he was forced to "pledge surety" so as not to seriously endanger his life; the defeated knight then had to follow the victor into the latter's safety zone without any further resistance. Alternatively, one could drag the opponent off the field by force. This was called "bridling" and it was considered particularly difficult and daring. It entailed taking a hold of the opponent's reins and dragging off the horse along with its rider. Obviously the intended prisoner would fight back, and it required great physical strength to restrain him with one arm. Moreover, one had to deal not only with one opponent at a time: as soon as one of the leaders got into trouble, his knights and squires would surround him to protect him and take him to safety.

The "kippers"   In the tumult of close combat the knights were supported by their squires and servants, the feared "kippers" who were armed with staffs and clubs: "There one could see a great band of kippers with stout clubs delivering blows in the rear."[39] "Each one had good armor, a mail shirt, a chapel-de-fer, and a club well tipped with metal."[40] Though noble lords treated the kippers with contempt, they had an important role, especially during the "bridling" maneuver. Konrad von Würzburg recounts in *Engelhardt* how the leader of one of the teams, the King of Riuzen, was "bridled" by an experienced tourneyer: "He had taken a hold of the noble King of Riuzen's bridle and wanted to pull him under a tree into his safety zone. His servant beat the king on arms and legs with a big club, for the king was decorated with gold as richly as an angel. The knight was also after the horse and armor as ransom."[41] Sometimes kippers were prohibited: "The announcement for the tournament stipulated that no kippers could be brought along."[42] At the tourney of Worms this issue was debated beforehand: "'How do you want it to be,' Rüdiger asked, 'tell me, noble King, whether the tournament shall be without kippers.' 'Yes, on my faith,' the mighty Gunther replied, "to this I pledge my firm promise. If a kipper who is not qualified to take part—be he a squire or a sergeant—touches a knight, his hand shall be cut off.'"[43] The kippers, however, seem to have participated in most tournaments.

At times the tournament could be decided if one entire team was driven back into its safety zone and could not get back out. More frequently nightfall put an end to the fight. Though the usual duration of a tournament was one day, some tourneys extended over several days. Attentive hosts made sure that baths were prepared for the knights in the evening. Afterwards the tourneyers sat around and talked about who had performed the greatest deeds. Much later real tournament juries were appointed to decide who was the victor.

Sharp and blunt weapons   The older scholarship assumed that tournaments were always fought with blunted weapons. That is not so. No evidence indicates that twelfth-century tournaments were contested with weapons different from those used in real warfare. The many reports of fatalities at tournaments leave no room for doubt. The first historical mention of the use of blunt weapons occurs in Roger of Wendover and Matthew of Paris in connection with an English tournament of 1216: "at a game on horseback—called 'joust' or 'tournament'—with lances and cloth armor..."[44] The mention of cloth armor is generally interpreted as an indication that this tournament was not fought with sharp weapons. That weapons were indeed blunted is reported by Matthew of Paris in his account of the Round Table tournament in Walden in 1252, where a knight was killed by a lance "whose tip had not been blunted as it should have been."[45] Blunt weapons are also documented in Germany around 1270/80, in *Jüngerer Titurel*: "Swords that cut no sharp wounds but raised only welts."[46] "They were coronals, not lances with sharp points."[47] The abandoning of sharp weapons reflects the end of the old, dangerous mass tournaments.

THE BUHURT

Entirely different in nature from the melée was the buhurt. The words *buhurt* and *buhurdieren* (from French *behort*, *behorder*) appear in Germany surprisingly early. In the *Kaiserchronik*, around 1150, we hear of games in honor of the god Saturn: "They hurried out onto the field; great was the festive noise from buhurt and jumping, from dancing and singing."[48] In later works the buhurt is also mentioned in connection with other forms of courtly entertainment: "There was a great diversity of courtly pleasures. One could choose how to entertain oneself, whether to ride the buhurt, dance, joust, run, or jump."[49] In *König Rother* we are told that a buhurt was held on the occasion of the knighting of Pippin (5047 f.). The buhurt and the knighting ceremony appear together fairly often, as do the tournament and the knighting ceremony. But while the buhurt was put on immediately following the girding with the sword, the tournament was generally held several weeks later at a different site. Such was the case in Mainz in 1184. After the emperor's sons had been knighted, the knights rode a buhurt carrying only a shield and no other weapons. Following the festivities in Mainz, a tournament had been scheduled to take place in Ingelheim, but, as we have seen, it was canceled (see p. 205).

Like the tournament, the buhurt was ridden in closed formations. For the most part it seems to have been an exhibition, a kind of parade on horseback, with the emphasis on skilled horsemanship. That is the sort of game we must picture whenever we hear of *buhurdieren* as part of courtly entertainment. When Wigalois and his great entourage caught up with Queen Larie, his knights formed a buhurt in her honor: "The knights all began to ride the buhurt with their splendid pennants."[50] This type of buhurt was performed without weapons, which set it clearly apart from the tournament: "It would have become a tournament had they worn their armor."[51] But the buhurt was not always a harmless spectacle. Frequently the knights would ride the buhurt against each other, and things could get pretty rough. At the knighting of Wilhelm of Orlens the knights rode the buhurt in contingents that were grouped according to "nationality," just like the groups at tournaments (R. v. Ems, *Wilhelm v. Orlens* 5805 ff.). In most cases the shield was the only weapon used: "From the stands all the way to the barriers there arose a great shoving and clashing of many shields."[52] In this type of buhurt the aim was to force the opponent aside with the shield or knock him off his horse. "The buhurt got so rough that many a knight along with his horse fell to the ground, where he could find no rest, for the kicks of the horses were so painful that on this day he had no further desire to ride the buhurt for the sake of the ladies; his whole body ached. Not a few broke their shins in the tumult."[53] Knee injuries are mentioned fairly often. Broken arms and legs, and even fatalities occurred at the buhurt held in Antwerp on the occasion of the marriage of Lohengrin and Elsa of Brabant (*Lohengrin* 2428 ff.). Sometimes the buhurt was also fought with lances (*Athis* C 30 ff.), but this seems to have been rather the exception. Swords were never used, and in this regard the difference between buhurt and tournament was always maintained.

The martial games reported by the twelfth-century historical sources from Germany were for the most part some kind of buhurt. During the siege of Cologne by Emperor Henry V in 1114, "knights from both sides exercised as in an exhibition by charging at each other on the open field."[54] Even though the knights here were divided into ranks, this was most likely a buhurt, since the spectacle seems to have been more important than the fight. The same goes for the tournament that the Hohenstaufen dukes put on outside Würzburg in 1127 (see p. 82). The martial games organized in 1147 outside the castle of Count Heinrich of Wolfratshausen were probably also a buhurt: "The Bavarians, and particularly the counts and other nobles, gathered at the castle of the aforesaid count to hold a tournament (*tyrocinium*) which we are now accustomed to calling *nundinae*."[55] The word *tyrocinium* ("first military service or campaign") was used in the Middle Ages for the tournament, as was *nundinae* (classical Latin = "market day"), used especially frequently in ecclesiastical prohibitions of tournaments: "These detestable entertainments (*nundinas*) and celebrations (*ferias*) that are commonly called tournaments."[56]

The kind of martial games that the poets called *buhurt* are well documented for Germany throughout the twelfth century, whereas there are only a few unequivocal references to tournaments. We may infer from this that the buhurt was especially popular in Germany, while the tournament proper had its home in France. An awareness of this basic difference seems still to have been alive in the thirteenth century. When the King of France, at the great tournament in *Partonopier*, attacked the emperor with his lance, the poet comments: "In France it is still the custom and widely known that tournaments are fought with lances and swords. If anyone is eager for a lance fight, he can expose himself there to many dangerous thrusts. In that country the tournament is contested like a real battle, God knows."[57] The equating of the French tournament (*turnei*) with real warfare (*strît*) may also have been the reason why the French loan word *turnei* was used in Germany initially as synonymous with *strît* (see p. 251). The notion that the tournament underwent a general development from a highly dangerous sport to a courtly pageant must be modified as far as Germany is concerned. We must start from the assumption that the brutal game with sharp weapons existed side by side with the parade-like buhurt. Moreover, we have discovered that in Germany the buhurt was the older form of the tournament, and that the battle-like games became known only later. But whereas the buhurt seems to have continued unchanged throughout the courtly age, the tournament proper underwent a profound transformation in the thirteenth century: the dangerous melée became the courtly joust.

THE SINGLE JOUST AND THE ROUND TABLE TOURNAMENT

Unlike the tournament and the buhurt, the joust was a single combat involving only two opponents who charged with couched lances and tried to unhorse each other.

The French loan words *tjoste* and *tjostieren* first appear in Veldeke's *Eneit*: "They charged at each other, as they both desired. They performed a joust in very knightly fashion like two heroes, without artifice. Neither one missed the other, they both thrust so well that their lances shattered and the splinters flew up high."[58] Veldeke, however, was not describing a game but a duel to the death. Not until Hartmann von Aue's *Erec* do we encounter the joust as a form of tournament. On the day before the tournament proper, Erec rode onto the tourney ground ahead of everyone else, without hauberk, armed only with a shield and lances, which he shattered "in a proper joust."[59] When the bands of tourneyers arrived, Erec, now fully armed, was again first. Before the attack of the opposing formations, he used the space between the deploying groups to joust "between the teams"[60] and break twelve lances. Then, finally, the actual tournament began with the charge of the massed ranks. According to this description, the joust, which gave the knight a chance to stand out among the crowd, was held in connection with the tournament, or the vesper, and in the same place, though without being part of the tournament itself.

The distinction between joust and tournament emerges even more clearly in Ulrich von Liechtenstein's account of the tournament of Friesach in 1224. When the Austrian nobility was assembled there, the brothers Ulrich and Dietmar von Liechtenstein decided to use the opportunity for a martial game: "Let us both, together with a retinue of knights, lie in *foreis*, so that anybody who may have the desire, while the assembly of princes lasts, can fight with us in knightly fashion."[61] This is the first recorded use of the expression "to lie in *foreis*." It refers to a special form of the tournament, where a single knight or a group of knights take up a position outside the camp (literally: "in the forest," from Old French *forest*); this was a challenge to others to try their strength with them in single combat. The Liechtenstein brothers were so successful that all the knights gathered in Friesach spent ten days riding jousts. The ecclesiastical princes in attendance were not amused, since they had no opportunity to negotiate the political questions that drew them to Friesach in the first place: "The patriarch of Aquileia said: 'My stay here is getting too expensive.' The bishop of Bamberg [he and the patriarch were brothers of Margrave Henry of Istria (d. 1228), whose quarrel with Duke Bernhard of Carinthia (d. 1256) was to be settled at Friesach] said: 'I would be displeased if we have come for nothing. My brother asked me to come, I mean the noble margrave of Istria, who wants me here.'"[62] To put an end to the knightly game a tournament was finally announced at the suggestion of the duke of Carinthia: "It was proclaimed in the city that the tournament would take place on Monday."[63] Thereupon the jousting stopped instantly, and on the Monday following a one-day tournament was contested in the familiar form of a melée. Here it is clear that the terms *turnieren* (242.5) and *tjostieren* (243.3) described two entirely different affairs.

While there is incontrovertible historical evidence for the buhurt and the tournament proper in the twelfth century, for a very long time the joust is mentioned only in literature. This may be partly due to the fact that especially for the earlier period there are few accounts that supply details about the nature of the martial games. It is, therefore, not impossible that by the twelfth century jousts were already held during the tournament festivities. But only in the thirteenth century did new

forms of knightly games develop, apparently influenced by courtly literature. The best known and most popular type was the Round Table
tournament, whose very name reveals its literary origin. The first recorded examples come from different parts of Europe, but they are
chronologically close together. On Cyprus in 1223, when Jean d'Ibelin
celebrated the knighting of his sons with a great feast, they held a
"buhurt and imitated the adventures of the Bretagne and the Round
Table."[64] In 1232 the English king prohibited a Round Table tournament[65] in his country. In 1235 at Hesdin in Flanders, a Round
Table[66] of the Flemish barons was held. By the end of the thirteenth
century the Round Table games were especially common in England,
which may have something to do with the political interests of the
English kings in promoting the Arthurian cult. The most important
information comes from Matthew of Paris, who in his account of the
great affair of Walden in 1252 also attempted a terminological differentiation of Round Table games and the melée: "In this year the knights
wanted to test their experience and skill in a military exercise, and so
they decided unanimously to try their strength not in the kind of tilting
match commonly called tournament, but rather in the martial game
called Round Table."[67] What exactly differentiated the two kinds of
tournament from each other is not made entirely clear by the historical
sources. Various clues seem to indicate, however, that the Round
Tables, at least in England, were frequently organized in connection
with great court feasts. The presence of ladies is also mentioned on
several occasions, as is the fact that this kind of exercise was less dangerous than the old tournament. If we may generalize from Matthew
of Paris's account, this new type of tournament consisted primarily
of single jousts fought exclusively with blunt weapons. The very detailed descriptions of Round Table tourneys in the French epics of the
thirteenth century, especially in Sone de Nansay, confirm that only single jousts were contested. In Sone de Nansay we hear that a large field
was marked off for jousting, at the edge of which the ladies and judges
took their seats. In the middle of the tourney-grounds stood the pavilion
of the queen of the Round Table. Suspended on it were the shields of a
hundred knights. By touching a shield one challenged its owner to a
single combat. For two days the knights exercised in this way (1153 ff.).
At this affair, as well, blunt weapons seem to have been used.

We have no historical evidence that Round Table tournaments were
held in Germany during the thirteenth century. Not until 1319 did King
John of Bohemia (d. 1346) host a tabula rotunda in Prague. Neverthe-

less, we can assume that this new type was already known in Germany before this time. Our chief witness is Ulrich von Liechtenstein, who recounts in *Frauendienst* that he organized a tournament circuit through Carinthia in 1240 (1400.1 ff.). Dressed like King Arthur, he journeyed through the land and promised admission to the Round Table to any knight who would break three lances with him. Apparently Liechtenstein had already founded a Round Table society with a number of other lords some time before. Of particular interest is the final event of his journey. In Katzelsdorf a great pavilion was pitched: "It was the tent of the Round Table."[68] In front of it they had marked off a fighting area, which the Arthurian knights defended for five days in many jousts. The delimiting of the tourney ground, the gesture by which a challenge was issued, and the restriction to jousts fought only with the lance, are elements that this Arthurian tournament has in common with the Round Table affairs in other countries.

Round table tournaments are next mentioned in German literature only at the beginning of the fourteenth century, in *Reinfried von Braunschweig* ("a knightly Round Table"[69]) and in *Apollonius von Tyrland* by Heinrich von Neustadt: "A tournament was planned and soon held: *foreis* and Round Table."[70] The detailed description of this tournament by Heinrich von Neustadt reveals that various motifs from the Arthurian epics were acted out, among them a ritual challenge with a washbasin and a gong modeled after the adventure of the well in *Iwein*. That such games did take place, in fact as early as the thirteenth century, is shown by a report in the Magdeburg *Schöppenchronik* about the grail feast organized by the citizens of Magdeburg on Whit-suntide of 1280. With "courtly letters"[71] they invited the merchants from Goslar, Hildesheim, Braunschweig, and other cities. In the middle of the festival grounds a grail had been raised (possibly a tent), and next to it the shields of its defenders were hung on a tree. By touching a shield one issued a challenge to a joust. The tournament prize was "a lovely lady, her name was Lady Feie,"[72] apparently a prostitute from Magdeburg. She was won by an old Goslar merchant, who dowered her and married her off honestly, "so that she would no longer lead such a wild life."[73] This Magdeburg grail feast also reveals that by the end of the thirteenth century the burghers of the bigger cities began to emulate the tournament practices of the nobility.

In the course of the thirteenth century the knightly tournament took on an entirely different character. The old mass tournaments, where knights charged each other in closed formations and with sharp weapons, came to an end. Their place was taken by single jousts contested with blunted weapons and subject to an increasingly strict courtly protocol. One of the most magnificent tournaments in the new style was celebrated by Margrave Henry III of Meißen (d. 1288) in 1263 in Nordhausen, "to which place he had called together all the princes of Germany, displaying to them—like Ahasuerus—the pomp and splendor of his lordship."[74] For once we are given details about how such an affair was put on. Outside the city an artificial forest had been erected, in which stood a tree "of marvelous beauty" (*mirae pulchritudinis*), fashioned entirely of gold and silver. "Now if one of the counts and barons, assembled there in such large number, shattered his lance in a joust against someone else, he was given straightaway a silver leaf from the tree as a token of his manliness. If he unhorsed a peer of equal rank with his lance while keeping the saddle himself, he presently earned a golden leaf from that tree."[75] These were the beginnings of a new tournament practice, which exerted an influence on the social style of the court nobility for centuries to come.

THE MILITARY, SOCIAL, MATERIAL, AND POLITICAL SIGNIFICANCE OF THE TOURNAMENTS

A wide range of motivations might prompt a knight to participate in a tournament. "Some took part in the jousting for higher motives; others were solely concerned about profit; many knights were jousting there for no other reason than for the sake of the ladies; some participated to learn something, and others again to win fame."[76] Originally, military reasons were no doubt an important consideration. Since we now know—especially through the work of Jans F. Verbruggen—that feudal warfare of the High Middle Ages did not, as was earlier supposed, revolve primarily around the knight as a single fighter, but was dominated by the charge in massed formations, the military purpose and usefulness of the older tournaments appear in a new light. These tournaments provided training in formation movements and in the technique of the massed charge. However, the enthusiasm with which many noble youths took part in these exercises, in disregard of many prohibitions, reveals that from the very beginning strong personal motivations must also have been present. The rough martial games offered the young knights a chance to distinguish themselves before an audience of their peers, and in this way to win fame and recognition within noble society. The didactic poem *Tirol und Fridebrant* puts it this way: "Tourneying elevates a man's dignity, and for his dignity he is praised by the ladies. Tourneying is a knightly thing."[77]

The courtly character of tournaments was especially evident when women participated. The way this was done was that the knight would tourney for the honor of his lady, as for example in *Moriz von Craûn*, where even the initiative for holding the tournament in the first place came from a lady. After Lord Moriz had already won renown through many knightly deeds in the service of minne, the lady he was courting, the Countness of Beamunt, requested as the final proof of his devotion that he arrange a tournament very close to her home. She justified this wish by saying that she had never before seen a tournament (601). To honor her request, Lord Moriz spared no expense in building and furnishing a float in the shape of a boat. Having announced throughout the land that a tournament would be held, he appeared before Beamunt with this contraption. The description of this tournament shows, however, that the actual circumstances of such an affair did not always suit the story telling needs of the courtly poets, since the clash of massed formations offered few chances to single out an individual knight. The author of *Moriz von Craûn* therefore relegated the course of the actual tournament to the background and emphasized only those details that showed his heroes in action.

An even closer link of the tournament activities to the ladies occurred when they attended as spectators. This is already mentioned in the first half of the twelfth century by Geoffrey of Monmouth in his description of the great Whitsuntide feast that King Arthur celebrated in Carleon. After the banquet, the knights put on a martial exercise outside the city, "while the ladies watched from the top of the ramparts."[78] In German literature this motif also appears surprisingly early, in the *Kaiserchronik* around 1150: "It came to pass one day that the king [Tarquinius] had cause for rejoicing: the Romans were putting on a great martial game. News of this reached the city of Viterbo, and the courtly ladies hastened to the ramparts to watch from above. When the Romans saw the ladies, they strove to charge even better and faster, so that the ladies should say what good knights the Romans were."[79] In Heinrich von dem Türlin's *Krone*, the ladies watching from the palace sent jewelry to the tourneying knights, with the request "that they become their knights and take the blows for the sake of their ladies."[80] Türlin also describes as a special custom of Arthur's court the practice of placing captured knights into the keeping of the ladies (893 ff.). Ladies watching the tourneying knights from the ramparts or windows are depicted in a number of miniatures of the Large Heidelberg Song Manuscript. According to the poets, the tourney grounds were sometimes chosen such "that the ladies could observe from the palace the efforts of the knights."[81] Once King Arthur even had a separate palace erected near the tournament field to allow the queen and the ladies to watch (Pleier, *Tandareis* 11847 ff.). The presence of the ladies was credited with a calming and civilizing influence on the conduct of tournaments: "It was announced that a great many ladies from many countries would come to watch the tournament. For that reason the tourney was arranged in a dignified manner: no beating each other with clubs; the knights should unhorse each other in courtly jousting."[82]

Whether the ladies exerted such influence in real life is difficult to say. As long as tournaments were contested in the old style, that is with no boundaries to the field, it wasn't very much fun for the spectators. The *Histoire de Guillaume le Maréchal* mentions the presence of ladies once, at a tournament held around 1180 near Sens. As William Marshal arrived the day before the tourney, he met the Countess of Joigny with her ladies, who had come to watch. That same evening was filled with courtly entertainment of song and dance, and William himself recited "in a gentle voice"[83] a song that was well received by all. Next came "a professional singer"[84] who performed a composition of his own, a song in praise of William Marshal with the refrain: "Marshal, give me a good horse!"[85] Thereupon William slipped away unseen, mounted his charger, unseated another tourneyer, and returned to present the horse he had won to the young singer before the amazed assembly. His action on this occasion was a noticeable departure from his usual behavior, and we must assume that the presence of ladies accounts for this change. Thirteenth-century historical sources mention fairly often that tournaments were attended by ladies. It would seem that the ladies were attracted above all by the new Round Table tournament, with its literary motifs and courtly setting.

Tournaments gave the knight an opportunity to demonstrate in public that he was motivated not by greed but by a courtly attitude and a desire for fame. Erec turned out to be such a model knight at his first tournament. He unseated his opponents but "paid no heed to their horses,"[86] which caused the other tourneyers to marvel at his selflessness at the sight of the unclaimed chargers: "and so he was highly praised."[87] The poet emphasized "that he took not a single horse, since he had not come there for the sake of material gain; instead, his aim was to become the champion."[88] Erec's exemplary generosity went so far that he even gave away his own horses and weapons whenever he exchanged them during the tournament (2595 f.). In this manner he used up five valuable Spanish chargers and three complete suits of armor without being unhorsed a single time. The beneficiaries of such courtly prodigality were above all the squires, who acted as "criers" (*kroijiraere*) during the tournaments. Later on this developed into the office of herald. From the end of the thirteenth century on they were called "squires of the escutcheons,"[89] since it was one of their duties to announce the coats of arms of the noble participants. These squires were usually in the employ of the tourneying knights and came onto the tournament grounds in their entourage. But there were also professional "announcers" who were among the traveling folk ("the criers who call themselves *Landfahrer*"[90]) and who flocked together wherever a tournament was held. "There were many of the traveling folk. Some 'spoke of the coats of arms,' which is called '*kroijieren*'; these people are allowed to strip the blankets off the horses [that had been brought down]: that is their share of the booty."[91] The *kroijiraere* had to announce their lords when they appeared on the tourney grounds, and had to make room for them. Whenever their cries are quoted verbatim, we find many French words: "*Za, tschavaliers, wikeli wa! Wicha wich! sie kument hie!* (R. v. Ems, *Wilhelm v. Orlens* 6750–51). *Jû, vassel, schevalier za!* (H. v. d. Türlin, *Krone* 871). *Zay, tschâvalier! âvoy diu wîp*" (R. v. Ems, *Guter Gerhard* 3645). Perhap we can infer from this that the tournament language in thirteenth-century Germany was largely French.

By staying close behind their lords during the fight, squires could easily take booty: "It was no mean profit that the squires made, when the knights whom their lords had unhorsed fell to the ground."[92] At the end they were given everything that was left lying on the field: "This delighted the *kroijiraere*, for scattered on the field were silk, jewels, and fine gold."[93] A model of generosity was Moriz von Craûn, who at the end of the tournament gave his entire tournament boat to his squires (1040 ff.). The sails were especially prized, since their costly cloth could be made into clothes: "The first received two ells of it, the second and third were given three ells, the fourth got as much as one needs for a robe."[94] When everything had been distributed, one of the captured knights came up and asked Moriz for a present. As Moriz was just stripping off his armor, he gave him his gorget, and then "he waited to see whether somebody might also want the hose; but there was no one."[95] Such behavior increased one's reputation and added lustre to

one's name. Sometimes the "criers" helped to spread the fame by re-
paying the gifts they had received with public songs of praise for their
benefactor. Of an exemplary tournament knight, it was said: "Seldom
did he miss a tournament; he frequently took part in jousting and in
foreis games. And wherever he had been his praise was sung, for he gave
so liberally to minstrels and free men that they had to proclaim his
praise everywhere with loud voices."[96] The following was reported of
King Richard of England: "All the horses and precious objects he won
he distributed evenly to his squires on the tourney ground, and it was
their task to speak of the splendid shields and helmets. Thus they spread
his praise and his renown. With great zeal they proclaimed him and
cried out loud in unison: 'The virtuous lord of England is a true prince.
Hurta, hurt, well he knows how to win great fame!'"[97] Reality was
surely not like this. But it is not impossible that occasionally some lords
indulged in excessive generosity for the purpose of glorifying their
names.

The life of William Marshal shows that the prospect of material
profit was the driving motivation for some tourneyers. For many years,
William, who had no steady income, lived off the booty he won at
tournaments. Just how lucrative such a "profession" could be for a
skilled tourneyer is revealed by the statement that in the space of ten
months, William and his friend Roger de Gaugi, who was in the same
situation as William, captured 103 knights (*Histoire* 3421). On his
deathbed William was encouraged to repent his sins and to restore all
he had robbed from his fellow man during his life. That, William replied, would be impossible, "for I have captured five hundred knights,
from whom I took their weapons and horses and the entire armor."[98]

In subplots the motif of material gain also appears in courtly literature. With a touch of disdain in his voice, Ulrich von Liechtenstein recounts that Lord Kuon von Friedberg and the Lords Otto and Dietrich
von Buchs at the tournament of Friesach were far more interested in
their opponents' horses than in their own reputation with the ladies:
"One could see them there striving for profit. They didn't care who was
shattering many lances: they strove for profit moreso than for the noble
ladies."[99] In Pleier we encounter three noble brothers who were professional tourneyers: "Their mind and will was focused entirely on tournament profit. If they heard that people were gathering somewhere for a
tournament, they went there solely to enrich themselves. They were
famous fighters. They brought pack horses and each of them had twelve

experienced squires."[100] From the poet's account we can infer that the three brothers and their teams could capture an average of forty to fifty horses at the great tournaments (13199 f.; 13929; 14398 f.). Such people were by no means always regarded with contempt. In *Engelhard* we hear of a strong tourneyer who very nearly succeeded in bridling the leader of one of the teams. Engelhard, however, intervened and took the stranger prisoner. "This experienced knight was a real man of the road, who owned nothing more than what he could win with his shield, as the saying goes."[101] When Engelhard discovered this, he returned the man's horse and weapons and set him free. His action seems to have been motivated by the thought that only rich lords could fight for fame, while the poorer knights had to make a living from it: "Many a noble knight, compelled by want, was only after profit, whereas the great lords strove for fame."[102]

The flip-side of great potential profit was the threat of serious financial loss. Participation at a tournament in a manner suited to one's rank could demand expenses that exceeded the financial means of many a noble family. We hear of the young Count Willekin of Muntaburg: "His sole interest was knighthood, until he had wasted two thirds of his father's property. He was unlucky with material things. He carried on until his father refused to give him any more of what he had. The tournaments are to blame for all this."[103] In a different case a lord suffered total financial ruin, "because he indulged only in tournaments, as he had long been wont to do. Today he sold a manor in order to gain fame, until one day the upright man had sold his entire inheritance."[104] Ulrich von Liechtenstein recounts that on the day after the tournament of Friesach, where 150 knights had lost their horses (306.5 ff.), many had to seek out the money-lenders: "All those who had been taken prisoner had to go to the Jews. One could see them pawning all sorts of valuable possessions. Those who had won profit were glad and in high spirits."[105] From Jean Renart's *Guillaume de Dole* we learn that the great lords occasionally called on the financial help of wealthy burghers to purchase their expensive tournament equipment. Before the great tournament of St. Trond, the hero of the story dispatches "in all haste a letter to Lièges to a wealthy burgher who is well disposed towards him and usually grants him credit. He asks him to have 120 lances painted with his heraldic emblem, along with three shields whose straps should be of silk and gold brocade. And he urges the burgher that each lance should have a pennant."[106] Apparently the expenses of the business friend in Lièges were later repaid with our hero's tournament winnings; in any case, Guillaume had one charger handed over to the burgher from Liéges (2672 f.).

Tournaments also had a political significance. This is quite clear in England: until the later thirteenth century the kings tried to block the independent ambitions of the barons with the help of tournament prohibitions. In France, where no royal prohibition existed—Philip II prohibited his sons from tourneying only because he feared for their lives— the division of the tournament teams into regional contingents reflected the rivalry among the great lords. In Germany most tournaments seem to have been put on by the imperial princes and territorial lords. The tournament in Ingelheim, which was supposed to take place in 1184 following the court feast in Mainz, had also been "arranged on the resolution of the princes."[107] A conflict of interests is visible in Liechtenstein's *Frauendienst*, where it is reported that the spontaneous jousting of the Austrian nobility in Friesach ran counter to the political intentions of the princes, and that the jousts were ended after ten days by a tournament arranged by the duke. The same thing happened again somewhat later, in 1240, at the end of Liechtenstein's "Arthurian journey." When many nobles came to participate at the Round Table jousting in Katzelsdorf, the duke of Austria at first announced that he himself intended to ride a joust against King Arthur (1567.3 ff.). But then the duke prohibited all further jousting (1571.1 ff.); as had been the case in Friesach, a tournament would be held instead. When the two teams had already been drawn up, the duke canceled the tournament altogether without a word of explanation. The assembled nobility was displeased but had to obey: "Then one of them said angrily: 'My lord of Austria ordered us not to tourney. That displeases us sorely.' Young lords, I tell you: we must defer to him and must do it or not, as he desires."[108] Apparently the tournaments were also used by the territorial lords as an instrument of territorial policies, no doubt with the primary aim of binding the nobility of the land more closely to the ruling family. This is especially obvious when tournaments were held as part of great court feasts. In the two cases reported by Ulrich von Liechtenstein, the tournaments of the territorial lords were intended to control those of the nobility and eventually prohibit them. Some scholars believe that the literary dress of Liechtenstein's "Arthurian circuit" conceals concrete political plans: that he intended to forge in this way an alliance of nobles directed against the duke. The text does not support such an interpretation with the desired clarity. But the political constellation in Austria and Styria at the time of Duke Frederick II was such that the noble gatherings could have had such aims.

PROHIBITIONS AND CRITICISM OF TOURNAMENTS

In 1130 in Clermont, Pope Innocent had the Council issue a decree against "those detestable games and celebrations at which the knights are wont to gather by arrangements and where they come together to demonstrate their strength and rashness."[109] This initiated an unbroken series of ecclesiastical prohibitions of tournaments. Violators were threatened with the refusal of a Christian burial or even with excommunication. Only in the fourteenth century, when the old-style tournaments had disappeared, was the universal ban on tournaments lifted. The prohibitions were justified with the argument that the martial games endangered the body and soul of the participants. It was also said that the tournaments kept the knights from fulfilling their crusading vows. Occasionally the clerics succeeded in preventing a tournament, as for example in 1215, when Master Oliver preached against it: "And so he brought about that the tournament which was supposed to take place in the following week was completely canceled. On the tourney grounds he stationed six preachers who successfully proclaimed the word of the cross and made many into crusaders."[110] The frequent reissuing of prohibitions and the many tournaments held in spite of them indicate that the efforts of the Church were not terribly successful. This is all the more important since the ecclesiastical tournament prohibitions represent the most determined attempt by the Church to control the new social lifestyle of the secular nobility. In pursuing this policy the Church willingly risked a serious loss of prestige. The lay nobility had apparently grown so self-confident in the second half of the twelfth century that not even threats of draconian punishment could dissuade them from their courtly lifestyle.

The sermons and didactic works of the thirteenth century reveal even more clearly how clerics perceived and judged the tournament scene. In his sermon "To the Magnates and the Knights,"[111] Jacques de Vitry (d. 1240) applied the catalog of the seven deadly sins to the specific transgressions of the tournament knights. Their first sin is pride (*superbia*), "because these godless and vain men ride in these affairs above all for the praise and glory of mortals."[112] The second sin is jealousy (*invidia*), "since one envies another for being considered more powerful in arms."[113] The third sin is hatred and anger (*odio et ira*), "because one knight beats and manhandles another and frequently inflicts a lethal wound or kills him."[114] The fourth sin is that of indolence or melancholy (*accidia vel tristitia*), because many tourneyers "are very dejected if they cannot withstand the opposing team and flee in disgrace."[115] The fifth sin is greed or pillage (*avaritia vel rapina*), "when one takes another captive and ransoms him, and steals the horse he was after from the person over whom he triumphed in the fight. The tournaments are for them a chance to raise high and excessive monetary demands. Without pity they seize the possessions of their own people, nor [do they refrain from] trampling or laying hands on the crop in the fields; and they sorely injure and vex the poor and the peasants."[116] The sixth sin is gluttony (*gastrimargia*), "because they invite one another to banquets for the sake of worldly pomp, and spend in excessive indulgence not only their own possessions but those of the poor as well."[117] The seventh and final sin is lust (*luxuria*), "because they strive to please shameless women and are accustomed, if they are considered worthy fighters, to wear love-tokens from them."[118] This final point is particularly interesting. It indicates that as early as the beginning of the thirteenth century a connection was perceived between tournament practice and knightly service to a lady. But we cannot exclude the possibility that Jacques de Vitry was influenced here by the courtly poets.

For Berthold of Regensburg, tournaments were a demonstration of the "great pride"[119] to which the nobility, with its love of pomp, was attached. The tourneying knight (*turneiesman*) whose preoccupation with these dangerous games made him forget his pilgrimage to the Holy Land, was to Berthold on the same level as a woman who wore yellow clothes (*gilwerinne*), dressed up (*itelmacherinne*), and applied makeup (*verwerinne*). At one point he lists tourneying among the courtly entertainments and the forms of aristocratic violence: "He who also dances, or attends tournaments, or throws dice, or is indecent, or robs, burns, steals, or perjures himself, or commits whatever sin that sorely displeases our Lord God."[120] Hugo von Trimberg gave one section of his didactic poem the title "Of jousting."[121] "Many a foolish layman lost his life, soul, and possessions through jousting and tourneying: what's the point of this rashness?"[122] In the eyes of this spiritual teacher the tourneying knights were destined for hell: "Many devils are up in the air, they snatch those who show off with horses, clothes, and with expenses for the buhurt and joust and for love of a lady."[123] The real criticism was aimed at the worldly values of the nobility. For the clerics it was a sign of sinful pride when a young man "sits on a strong charger and fixes all his thoughts on how he might please the world."[124]

Didacticians writing for a courtly audience approached the tournament theme differently:

> In the old days tourneying was a knightly affair. Today it is brutish, wild, deadly, boastful. Killer-knives, killer-clubs, sharpened axes in order to kill: that is today's tournament. A lovely lady's eyes turn red and her heart cold when she knows her man to be in such murderous danger. When tourneying was still done to practice the art of knighthood, with magnanimity and courtesy, to win renown, a knight would have been loathe to strangle a brave man for the sake of a horse blanket. But he who does this today and is good at it, considers himself a great fighter.[125]

The old steward in *Helmbrecht* uttered similar sentiments: "The old tournaments are gone, in their stead new ones have been introduced. One used to hear such cries as this: 'Brave knight, be of good spirits!' Today they shout all day long: 'Give chase, knight, chase, chase, stab, stab, strike, strike; maim the one who can still see; chop this one's foot off, let that one pay with his hand; you must hang this one and catch a rich one who will pay us a hundred pounds.'"[126] The belief that the nobility's tournament behavior became more violent and ruthless over time was, historically speaking, wrong. The courtly didacticians of the thirteenth century did not derive their criteria from real life, but from the idealized poetic image of noble life created by courtly literature around 1200. The real development of tournament practice was entirely in line with the demands of the poets: the martial games of the thirteenth century were increasingly absorbed into the ceremony of courtly festivals.

CHAPTER V

The Courtly Ideal of Society

According to the poets, the true meaning of courtly social life with its material splendor and ceremonial etiquette lay in its relationship to the ideal of chivalry, of courtly perfection as it was poetically practiced by the knights of the Round Table at King Arthur's court and by the courtly ladies in the songs of the troubadours and minnesingers. The fact that love was the highest social value in this idealized world reveals just how far removed from reality these poetic visions were. In those days nobody lived like the heroes of the Arthurian romances, whose efforts were directed solely at achieving perfect courtliness in knightly battle and in minne service. The poets described a fairy tale world with none of the political, economic, and social problems and conflicts that confronted noble society in real life. It would not be farfetched to say that courtly literature cast such a spell over contemporary audiences because the poets' stories made it possible to forget, at least for a brief time, the harsh reality.

But this can only have been one side of the picture. The other side is illuminated by the fact that the idealized poetic image had a profound impact and influenced the real social behavior of the noble upper class in many different ways. The courtly knight and the courtly lady became model social figures and remained so for centuries. It is likely that the great interest of the courtly audience in these literary creations was directed not least at the fact that many real details of courtly social life were interwoven into an exalted vision of noble life. Of course one could immediately recognize this vision as something unreal, but it was flattering, and one happily subscribed to it because it was seen to justify and glorify one's own social pretensions and ambitions.

It is not entirely clear to what extent the poets drew upon concepts and ideas already present in the self-image of aristocratic society in formulating their idealized vision. A lively scholarly debate concerning the historical foundations of the courtly ideal of society is currently going on, and no definitive conclusions have yet emerged. Conditions in Germany will undoubtedly be judged differently from those in France or Norman England. In these countries there are indications that from the eleventh century on new forms of social behavior—which were in a very specific sense considered courtly—were gaining acceptance among the nobility. In Germany, on the other hand, it would seem that the courtly ideal of society did not grow gradually but was adopted to a large extent as a literary import from France. The interest of the German high nobility in French social culture was not limited to details of material life and the modern forms of etiquette; it was just as much directed at the transfiguration of the image of society in the ideal of chivalry and love. Within this context secular literature played an important role in the nobility's social self-perception. This is reflected in the respect and esteem which even poets of low birth enjoyed at the courts, and in the readiness of the great princely houses to organize and finance an elaborate literary culture at their courts.

1. THE CHIVALROUS KNIGHT

THE TRADITIONAL IMAGE OF THE RULER

Mirrors of princes   Old and new conceptions of noble perfection were joined in the courtly image of the knight. The modern demands of chivalry were combined with the religious concept of knighthood derived from the Truce of God and the crusading movements, and with elements of a Christianized ruler-image that can be traced back to late antiquity. This traditional ruler-image found expression in a variety of literary forms: in the Latin historiography of the Middle Ages, in coronation rites for emperors and kings, in royal and imperial acclamations and liturgical prayers, in papal and episcopal letters of exhortation to great secular magnates, and in panegyrics. But above all it permeates the so-called mirrors of princes, pedagogical tracts written mostly in response to the practical needs of educating princes, and with the aim of teaching future rulers about their tasks and duties. "Mirrors" of this kind first appear in the ninth century, all intended for members of the Carolingian royal family: "The way of the king" (*Via regia*) by Smaragdus of St. Mihiel, "Of kingship" (*De institutione regia*) by Jonas of Orleans, "The book of the Christian ruler" (*Liber de rectoribus christianis*) by Sedulius Scottus, as well as a variety of writings by Hincmar of Rheims. After a lengthy hiatus and unaware of its Carolingian precursors, the genre of the mirror of princes attained new importance in the twelfth century. At the beginning of this new development stands the *Policraticus* of John of Salisbury, though this work extends beyond its narrower theme of princely education and offers a comprehensive social and political doctrine. The *Policraticus* exerted considerable influence on the mirrors of the late twelfth and thirteenth centuries, which include the following tracts: "On the education of princes" (*De principis instructione*) by Geraldus of Cambrai, "On the good rule of the prince" (*De bono regimine principis*) by Helinand of Froidmont, "The education of kings and princes" (*Eruditio regum et principum*) by Gilbert of Tournai, and "On the education of children of the royal family" (*De eruditione filiorum regalium*) by Vincent of Beauvais. Most of these works come from England, France, Spain, and Italy. Only at the turn of the thirteenth century do the first mirrors appear in Germany with the works of Abbot Engelbert of Admont: "On the governance of princes" (*De regimine principum*), and "The mirror of moral virtues" (*Speculum virtutum moralium*). The author had close contact with the Hapsburg royal court under King Albrecht I (d. 1308).

The mirrors of princes allow us to follow the changes in the image of the ruler from the early Middle Ages to the early modern period. But some elements of the ruler-image persisted virtually unchanged. Among them were the fundamental Christian duties, already formulated by the Church Fathers and throughout the Middle Ages an indispensable part of every tract on princely education. A very powerful expression of these ideas can be found in the seventh-century pseudo-Cyprian work "On the twelve evils of the world" (*De duodecim abusivis saeculi*), especially in the ninth chapter, which deals with the "unjust king" (*rex iniquus*). To the "unjust king" the author opposed the image of the "just king" (*rex iustus*):

> It is the justice of the king not to oppress anyone unjustly by force; to judge people without regard for the reputation of a person; to be a defender of strangers, orphans, and widows; to prevent theft; to punish adultery; not to elevate the unjust; not to support the unchaste and minstrels; to destroy

the godless; not to permit murderers and perjurers to live; to protect the
churches and feed the poor with alms; to entrust the just with the business
of royal government; to have experienced, wise, and prudent advisors; to
pay no heed to the superstitious customs of magicians, soothsayers, and
sorceresses; to suppress rage; to defend the realm bravely and effectively
against enemies, and to trust God in all things.[1]

This text was used or quoted verbatim in many mirrors. It reached its
widest circulation after being incorporated into Gratian's *Decretum*
(twelfth century). During the fifteenth century it was also translated
into German several times. In a very condensed form it sums up the
main themes of the Christian ruler-image. That the king be just in his
rule, punish the godless and promote the worthy, protect widows and
orphans, feed the poor, defend the Church, be brave in war and wise in
council, surround himself with good counselors and place his confidence in God: these expectations comprise the core virtues of a
ruler-image which prevailed for centuries.

   Central to the traditional ruler-image was the notion that justice
(*justitia*) and the keeping of peace (*pax*) were the noblest duties of a
ruler. The ideal of the "just and peace loving king" (*rex iustus et
pacificus*)—which could invoke both Cicero and St. Augustine—also
became the foundation of the courtly ruler-image. Equal in significance to the conceptual linkage of *pax* and *iustitia* was the joining of
iustitia and *pietas*, an association derived from ancient sources
and found in the coronation rites of the High Middle Ages, where the
ruler is promised "the crown of justice and piety" (*Corona iustitiae et
pietatis*, Vogel-Elze, p. 255). *Pietas* in this context also means grace and
mercy; it includes the protection of the Church and the proper relationship to God. In the medieval image of the good ruler, classical and
Christian notions and concepts were fused. This is especially true for
the term "virtue" (*virtus*). On the one hand, used in combination with
clementia (clemency), *iustitia*, and *pietas*, it was part of the Roman-
Augustan tradition: Augustus reports in the *Monumentum Ancyranum*
that these four words were inscribed on the golden shield that the Roman Senate erected in his honor. On the other hand, together with
sapientia (wisdom) it belongs to the "two names of Christ" that Paul
speaks of in 1 Corinthians: "Christ, the power of God and the wisdom
of God."[2]

   Another element of classical emperor glorification became important
for the courtly ruler-image: the "splendor of lordship" (*splendor imperii*), through which the ruler's "virtue" (*virtus*) and his "divine grace"

(*charisma*) were manifested. The ruler's splendor was concretely embodied in the emperor's aura and his crown. A lavish appearance demonstrated the ruler's "majesty" (*maiestas*), his grandeur and "magnificence" (*magnificentia*). In this context the ruler's virtue of "liberality" (*liberalitas, largitas*) assumed special importance, and it found its Christian expression in alms-giving (*largitas elemosiarum*), in loving care for the needy (*caritas*), and in ecclesiastical foundations. Its worldly manifestation was the lavishness of imperial hospitality and gifts. One could also refer to the Bible to prove that the good ruler must not be stingy. In the proverbs of Solomon, the "just king" (*rex iustus*) is contrasted to the "avaricious man" (*vir avarus*) (Liber proverbiorum 29.4).

Model kings   To illustrate the traditional ideal of the ruler, authors invoked the great kings of the past as exemplars. Pride of place among the "model kings" (*exempla regis*) belonged to the venerable royal figures of the Old Testament, Solomon and David. King David in particular, as the prefiguration of Christ (*typus Christi*), became important for the literary and artistic development of the medieval ruler-image. In his dual role as "king and prophet" (*rex et propheta*) he was seen during the Carolingian period as the embodiment of the Christian ruler. Later the idea of his spiritual office became somewhat less important. But as a "just king" (*rex iustus*) and a "humble king" (*rex humilis*), David was celebrated throughout the Middle Ages as an exemplary monarch. The prototype of royal "wisdom" (*sapientia*) was his son Solomon, whom medieval rulers also liked to take as an example because of his wealth and power. Solomon was further given the honorific title "king of peace" (*rex pacificus*). In the "Order for the consecration of the king" (*Ordo ad regem benedicendum*), God was beseeched to let the newly anointed king rule "just as you made Solomon possess his kingdom in peace."[3]

In addition to the kings of the Old Testament, the emperors of antiquity were held up as exemplars for medieval rulers. Apart from Augustus, from whom was derived the title of the medieval emperor, Trajan played an important role among the pagan emperors. He was praised for his justice and affability. In the German *Kaiserchronik* of the twelfth century, we read: "Now let all kings of the world observe as an example how the noble emperor Trajan won the grace of God because he was a just judge."[4] In the courtly age Emperor Alexander came to the fore.

Though he was tainted with the stain of sinful "pride" (*superbia*) for advancing—as the medieval romances of Alexander told—to the gates of paradise, he exerted a strong influence on the courtly ruler-image with his legendary magnanimity and generosity: "Behold Alexander, he gave abundantly, hence his fame spread to all lands."[5]

Among the Christian emperors of antiquity, the highest place belonged to Constantine, whom Eusebius of Caesarea (d. 340) had already fashioned into the ideal Christian ruler in his *Vita Constantini*. Aside from him, Emperor Theodosius was venerated as the paragon of the "humble king" (*rex humilis*) on account of his penitence. Of all the rulers of the past, Charlemagne was the most immediate and vivid. The kings of France and Germany invoked him as their ancestor and the model of their rulership. The poets celebrated him as the ideal embodiment of the Christian monarch: "Charles was a true warrior of God; he forced the pagans to accept Christianity. Charles was brave, Charles was handsome, Charles was steadfast and had real kindness. Charles was praiseworthy, Charles was fearsome. He possessed the highest excellence."[6]

The transfer of royal attributes to the princes   When the mirrors spoke of "princes" (*principes*), they almost always meant members of the royal family, as is revealed by the commissioning of the works and by their dedications. A very important development took place in the twelfth century when the traditional attributes of royal exemplariness were transferred to the secular princes. This process reflects the actual shift in the balance of power in favor of the princes, who took advantage of a weakening kingship, especially in Germany, and laid claim to an increasing number of sovereign rights which had hitherto been regarded as the mark of royal authority. They now used the old royal formula "by the grace of God" (*dei gratia*) in their charters, and had their newly acquired power described in Latin histories. The "History of the Welfs," composed around 1170, emphasized the monarchical position of this great princely house: "As the lords of a domain and strengthened by the possession of a permanent residence, our men began to extend their authority and to acquire in various regions ever more land and prerogatives. In this way they became so rich, surpassing kings in wealth and dignities, that they refused homage even to the Roman emperor."[7] Even more so than Latin historiography, from the middle of the twelfth century vernacular poetry created impressive princely portraits that reflected the new attitude. The first example of

this kind appeared in the *Kaiserchronik* (17097 ff.) and was dedicated
to Duke Henry the Proud (d. 1139). In the glorification of Henry the
Lion in the epilogue to the *Rolandslied*, the laudation of the prince
follows even more closely the typology of the traditional *rex iustus*
image:

> In this day and age we can compare no one more appropriately to King
> David than Duke Henry. God has given him the power to defeat all his
> enemies. He has brought high honor to Christendom; the pagans he con-
> verted. To act thus is his rightful inheritance. Never once has he turned his
> banner in flight; God has always granted him victory. Night never falls on
> his court: I mean the eternal light which never stops shining for him. He
> hates insincerity and loves genuine truth. This prince follows all the com-
> mandments of God, as does everybody in his noble entourage. At his court
> one finds real steadfastness and real decorum. Happiness and joy are there,
> exemplariness and renown. Have you ever heard of anyone blessed with
> more good fortune? To his Creator he devotes himself body and soul, like
> King David.[8]

It was something completely new and unheard of that a prince was
glorified as a second King David and thus placed on the same level as
crowned rulers. Later the courtly poets carried the use of royal attributes to describe their princely patrons even further. Eventually this became part of the image of idealized knighthood: at King Arthur's
Round Table no distinction was made between royal and princely descent. All who were allowed to join were regarded as equal in rank in
terms of their perfect chivalry, and all were bound to uphold an ideal
that had absorbed significant elements of the traditional ruler-image of
the *rex iustus et pacificus*.

Imperial and princely portraits   The standard medieval imperial portrait shows the ruler from a strict frontal perspective seated on his
throne and adorned with the insignia of his power. The basic elements
in this portrait, which gave visual expression to the universality and
loftiness of the imperial majesty, had already been fully developed at the
end of the fourth century under Emperor Theodosius (d. 395), and for a
thousand years they played a part in shaping the concept of kingship,
both in Byzantium and in the West. In the Occident this visual form
experienced its most significant artistic elaboration first in the ninth
century at the Westfrankish court of Charles the Bald, and then under
the last of the Ottonians in the late tenth/early eleventh centuries. The
imperial portraits of Otto III (d. 1002) and Henry II (d. 1024) represent,

Fig. 28.   Emperor Frederick I with his two sons. On either side of the imperial
throne stand Henry VI and Frederick of Swabia. The emperor inclines his head
to his right towards his son Henry. From the Fuldau manuscript of the *Historia
Welforum* (Hessische Landesbibliothek D 11). End of the twelfth century.

in their splendor and costliness as well as their sacral stylization of the
imperial majesty, a high point that was never again attained. But
the solemn picture of the enthroned ruler continued to be used in the
twelfth and thirteenth centuries. The full page portraits of Emperor
Henry in the song manuscripts B (Weingarten-Stuttgart) and C (Heidelberg) attest that this visual tradition was still alive at the end of the
courtly age. For the most part, however, the portrait was less elaborate
during this period, more modest in style and with a more private statement. An example is the image of Emperor Frederick I in the Fuldau
manuscript of the *Historia Welforum* from the end of the twelfth century. As in the older imperial portraits, the enthroned ruler is depicted
in ceremonial garb with crown, scepter, and globe. But on both sides of
the throne stand his sons Henry and Frederick, addressing the emperor
with lively gestures. Frederick has his head turned slightly to the right,
towards his older son Henry, a gesture that breaks the strict frontality
(see fig. 28). The formal portrait has become a family picture. The old
portrait type of the enthroned majesty remained unchanged, however,
on the imperial and royal seals.

Other types of ruler portraits were used less frequently: the coronation picture, in which the coronation of the emperor is depicted as carried out by the hand of God; the devotional picture, which shows the ruler or the ruling couple in a posture of veneration at the feet of Christ; and the dedication picture, in which the emperor presents the model of a church he built to the saint in whose name it was consecrated. The ruler portrait takes on a previously unknown range of variation with the appearance of new visual motifs from the middle of the twelfth century. In the process the emphasis shifts from the symbolism of universal imperial power to a more narrative visual style, which could also depict the emperor in some kind of activity, as we see from the many pictures in the Bern manuscript of the *Liber ad honorem Augusti* by Petrus de Ebulo. The artistic techniques of representation also underwent a change. In addition to painted miniatures we find colored pen and ink drawings. By the twelfth century in Regensburg, a large wall painting was used to portray the ruler. Different kinds of sculpted figurative forms also begin to appear. On the Aachen arm reliquary of Charlemagne (now in Paris) donated by Emperor Frederick I, the emperor, his wife Beatrice, his father, Duke Frederick of Swabia, and his uncle, King Conrad III, are depicted in partial relief on hammered silver. Small stone statues of Frederick I exist in the cloisters of the monastery of St. Zeno in Reichenhall, and—once again in conjunction with Beatrice—on the west portal of the cathedral of Freising. One of the greatest imperial images of the twelfth century is the Barbarossa head of Cappenberg, which Frederick I presented as a gift to Count Otto of Cappenberg (d. 1171). Large stone sculptures begin to appear only around the middle of the thirteenth century in Bamberg, with the figures of Emperor Henry II and his wife Kunigunde, and shortly afterwards in Magdeburg.

From the middle of the twelfth century on, secular princes were also portrayed visually. Older princely pictures are very rare, such as the peculiar image of the Bavarian Duke Henry the Wrangler (d. 995) in the rule book of the monastery of Niedermünster. This Henry was the father of Emperor Henry II and became anti-king after the death of Otto II (d. 983). That might explain why a portrait of him was painted. He is depicted without any royal insignia but with a nimbus, a most unusual motif in secular painting (see fig. 29). The princely portraits of the twelfth century were expressions of the new self-confidence of the great princely families. This is confirmed by the portraits of Henry the Lion, with whom the history of princely pictures in Germany begins.

Fig. 29.   Duke Henry the Wrangler. In his right hand the duke holds a lance as a sign of his lordship, in his left he holds a book. The halo he may have earned as a benefactor of the monastery of Niedermünster. From the rule book from Niedermünster (Bamberg, Staatsbibliothek, Lit. 142). Tenth century.

Henry the Lion commissioned several manuscripts decorated with precious pictures from the monastery of Helmarshausen (near Karlshafen on the Weser river), whose advocate he was. The so-called Gospel Book of Gmund, intended for the Church of Saints Blasius and Aegidius in Brunswick, contains a dedication picture very much in the tradition of the imperial dedication images: the duke, attired in a purple robe, presents the book to St. Blasius, while St. Aegidius next to him greets the Duchess Matilda dressed in the same splendid fashion. The coronation picture in the same manuscript follows the old imperial investiture picture: two hands reach down from the clouds to crown the duke and the duchess, while their noble ancestors stand behind them: on the duke's side his father Henry the Proud and his wife Gertrude as well as her parents, Emperor Lothair III (d. 1137) and Empress Richenza (d. 1141), and on the side of the duchess, her father, King Henry II of England, and his mother Matilda, who had been married to Emperor Henry V (see fig. 30). A third picture of the ducal couple, in the so-called London Psalter, also from Helmarshausen, continued the type of the devotional image: Henry the Lion and Matilda kneel at the feet of the crucified

Fig. 30.   Coronation picture of Henry the Lion. The duke and his wife Matilda are crowned by the hands of God. Behind the duke stand his parents, Henry the Proud and Gertrude, and his maternal grandparents, Emperor Lothar III and Richenza. Behind Matilda is her father, King Henry II of England, and his mother, Empress Matilda. From the Gospel Book of Henry the Lion (Wolfenbüttel, Herzog August Bibliothek, Cod. Guelf. 105 Noviss. 2). Twelfth century.

Christ. In all three instances, the artist used visual types with a long tradition in the history of imperial portraiture.

Not every type of imperial portrait was adopted by the princes. Seals reveal that the image of the enthroned ruler with the insignia of his power remained a prerogative of crowned heads. While the kings of the thirteenth century, including the kings of Bohemia, always used the *majestas* image on their seals, the princes almost never used it. An exception is Landgrave Conrad of Hessen (d. 1241), the son of Hermann I of Thuringia and Grand Master of the Teutonic Order, who in 1232/33 used a seal with the image of the enthroned ruler. How he came to choose this motif is unclear, and even in his capacity as Master of the Order, Conrad used unusual seal images. Apart from this there are only two Mecklenburg throne seals dating to the later thirteenth century. Not until around 1500 was the throne image used again, by the prince-electors of Brandenburg.

The situation was different when it came to coinage. Henry the Lion minted coins depicting an enthroned ruler with a lily scepter and a sword. Similar scenes are occasionally found even on the coinage of

Fig. 31. Seal of Henry VII of Bavaria. The oldest German princely seal. The duke is depicted standing with shield and lance. 1045.

nonprincely persons: a coin of Count Berthold of Ziegenhain (d. 1258) displays the enthroned ruler with sword and five-leafed rose. How these images on coins should be interpreted must remain open for the time being. The analysis of coins in relationship to the history of the medieval ruler-image has barely begun. Perhaps the coin images reflect the awareness that the right of minting coins had originally been the exclusive prerogative of the kings.

The oldest surviving German princely seal is that of Duke Henry VII of Bavaria (d. 1047) from the year 1045 (see fig. 31). It depicts the duke standing (or walking) with lance and shield, a motif that had already been used at the end of the tenth century by Emperor Otto III (d. 1002), and then in the years 1028–1038 by Emperor Conrad II (d. 1039). Such seals with a standing figure were still used in the courtly period by the Askanians in Brandenburg, the Piastes in Silesia, and the Zähringer. Among the oldest princely seals is the half-figure seal of Count Adalbert of Anhalt from the year 1073, which also imitated an imperial model. By the end of the eleventh century the equestrian seal appears as the characteristic type of princely seal. The oldest example comes from the year 1083 (Count Conrad of Luxemburg). It is followed by the equestrian seals of Duke Henry III of Carinthia (1103) (see fig. 32), Margrave Leopold III of Austria (1115), Margrave Conrad of Meißen (1123), Duke Henry the Black of Bavaria (1125), and others. The equestrian seal, which depicts its owner as a heavily armed mounted knight, was typical of the princes and was never used by the emperors. The impulse for it came from France, where the first such seals belonged to Count

Fig. 32.   Seal of Henry III of Carinthia. One of the oldest German equestrian seals. 1103.

Geoffrey II Martell of Anjou (d. 1060), and to the Norman Duke William the Conqueror (d. 1069). In the twelfth and thirteenth centuries the equestrian seal was also used in Germany by members of comital families: Florentin III of Holland (1162), Baldwin V of Hainaut (1164), Dietrich V of Cleves (1191), Adolf III of Holstein (1196), William II of Jülich (1201), and others. But without exception these men belonged to the highest nobility and came largely from the western regions of the empire. Only sporadically was the equestrian seal later—in the second half of the thirteenth century—also carried by minor nobles. These seals always portray a stereotyped and idealized image of the knight, whose details of posture and armament corresponded to the image created by the poets. A distinctly courtly attitude is also displayed by the hunting seals, which portray the unarmed noble lord on horseback with a hunting falcon on his gloved hand. This type, also found on women's seals, was, however, fairly rare.

The rich development of the princely and noble image in the thirteenth century is still an entirely unexplored field. The only study of this material, that of Steinberg and Steinberg ("Die Bildnisse geistlicher und weltlicher Fürsten und Herren"), ends with the year 1200. Given this state of scholarship on the subject, it is not possible to sketch even in broad strokes the subsequent development. But I would like at least to indicate the artistically most important medium, tomb sculpture. Figurative depictions of the deceased on his tomb already existed in earlier times; the graves of bishops and abbots in particular were decorated this way. The figurative royal tomb was also known. Charlemagne was supposedly depicted on his tomb, but nothing of it has survived. The first figurative tomb of a German king is that of the anti-king Rudolph of Rheinfelden (d. 1080) in the cathedral of Merseburg. The cast ledger with a bas-relief of the deceased is of great art historical importance. This royal tomb did not, however, initiate a new tradition; in subsequent years the kings were interred once again in nonfigurative tombs. Only the grave of Rudolf of Hapsburg (d. 1291) in the cathedral of Speyer once again displays the portrait of the deceased. But by this time the figurative noble tomb was in its prime.

Secular tomb sculpture in the thirteenth century was centered in the region of Thuringia and Saxony. The tombs of the nobility could model themselves after the sacred tomb sculpture that was so highly developed in this area around 1200. The tomb of the Magdeburg ministerial Hermann of Plothe (documented 1135–1170) in Altenplathow, with a very old-fashioned portrait of the dead man, is among the oldest examples of the figurative noble grave. Soon after 1200 a different, very modern style prevailed, and with it began the heyday of tomb sculpture in central Germany. Among the most important works is the double tomb of Henry the Lion and his wife, Matilda, in the cathedral of Braunschweig (circa 1230), the tomb of Wiprecht of Groitzsch in the church of St. Lorenz in Pegau (circa 1230), the double tomb of Dedo, the margrave of Wettin, and his wife, Mechthild, in the castle-church of Wechselburg (circa 1230–1240), the knight's tombstone in the cathedral of Merseburg (circa 1250), and the interesting triple tomb of the count of Gleichen and his two wives in the cathedral of Erfurt (circa 1260). Most of these tombs reveal a desire to express an ideal of beauty in the figurative decoration that can be compared directly to the ideas of the courtly poets. Henry the Lion was sixty five years old at his death in 1195, and during the last years of his life he had suffered from various infirmities of old age. But the tombstone in the cathedral of Braunschweig (see fig. 33), erected by his descendants, shows him in almost youthful beauty, with a smooth, unwrinkled face, beardless, with long, flowing, lightly curled hair, and dressed in rich clothes. His right hand gathers up the mantle while holding a model of the church of St. Blasius, which he had built in Braunschweig; in his left hand he holds the sword as the sole attribute of his power. His wife Matilda next to him is wearing a fur-trimmed mantle with a clasp and a rich cascade of folds. Underneath her mantle we can see a dress belted at the waist and with tight-fitting sleeves that reach down to the hands. An even more pronounced courtly accent was given to the magnificent double tomb of the count and min-

Fig. 33.   Tomb sculpture of Henry the Lion and his wife. In his right hand the duke holds a model of the Church of St. Blasius, which he built, and in his left a sword as a symbol of his power. The duchess has her hands folded in prayer. Braunschweig cathedral. Thirteenth century.

nesinger Otto of Botenlouben-Henneberg (d. circa 1245) and his wife, Beatrice, in their monastic foundation of Frauenroth near Kissingen (see fig. 34).

Here we must also mention the twelve larger-than-life donor figures in the west choir of the cathedral of Naumburg. Owing to their exceptional artistic quality, they hold a special place among the sculptural princely portraits of the thirteenth century. All the people represented were members of the princely house of Wettin and their relations by marriage, the Ekkehardinger, the ancestors of the margraves of Meißen who ruled in the thirteenth century, and of Bishop Dietrich of Naumburg (d. 1272), during whose episcopacy these sculptures were in all likelihood created. What connects the Naumburg donor figures with tomb sculpture is that all the people represented are in fact buried in the west choir of the church. This figurative cycle is unusual for another reason: it depicts members of a great noble family in a manner that was usually reserved for saints and emperors.

Fig. 34. Tomb sculpture of Otto of Botenlouben-Henneberg and his wife. The damaged tombstones show the comital couple in courtly dress and courtly posture. The count gathers his mantle with his left hand, the countess has her right hand hooked into the clasp string. Frauenroth, monastery church. Thirteenth century.

THE RELIGIOUS CONCEPT OF KNIGHTHOOD (*MILITIA CHRISTI*)

Aristocratic ethic and the idea of reform   Since the beginning of the Christian church, the concept of *milites Christi* (soldiers of Christ) or *milites Dei* (soldiers of God) had held a permanent place in Christian thinking. Based on St. Paul's words of admonition to Timothy, "labor like a good soldier of Christ Jesus. No one who serves as a soldier for God will let himself be involved in civilian affairs,"[9] the *milites Christi* were initially understood to be the apostles and missionaries, later the martyrs and ascetics, and in the Middle Ages above all the monks who fought the devil with spiritual weapons in service to God. At the same time the term *militia Christi* (the knighthood of Christ) was always sharply opposed to *militia saecularis* (secular knighthood), which from this religious perspective had to seem like a veritable *militia diaboli*, "the devil's soldiery." Against the background of this older terminology, a change of almost revolutionary character occurred at the end of the eleventh century, when *milites Christi* was first used in reference to secular knights and lords who wielded their arms in service to the Church and the Christian faith.

This new, religious terminology of knighthood was the fruit of the Church's many efforts directed at the secular nobility. Of great importance among them was the Peace of God movement, which spread from the end of the tenth century from southeastern France and was aimed at restricting the nobility's feuding. The novel aspect of this initiative was that the maintenance of peace—properly the task of the worldly powers—was taken over by the Church. Individual bishops proclaimed a regional peace, which in its older version consisted in most instances of a special protection for churches and noncombatants (monks, clerics, pilgrims, merchants, peasants, and women). The later version, the so-called *Treuga Dei* (Truce of God), prohibited fighting on certain days— generally from Thursday to Sunday—and during certain times of the year. To enforce these provisions, the Church raised peace militias and made it their religious obligation to fight violators and to protect those threatened by unlawful violence. This service in arms was considered a meritorious act.

From the tenth century as well come the first literary documents of a new lay ethic, created in the reform monasteries and intended as a model for the secular nobility on how to lead a pious life. Of special interest is the vita of Count Gerald of Aurillac from the pen of Abbot Odo of Cluny (d. 942). According to Odo, Count Gerald did not become a saint only after his withdrawal from the world, but already led a saintly life as a worldly ruler. He resisted the temptations of power and luxury and always maintained a "humble disposition."[10] If he resorted to arms it was not to enrich himself but to maintain peace and justice. He would rather suffer hunger than lay hands on the property of others. So as not to shed blood, he fought with his weapons reversed, and when he emerged victorious his thoughts were not of revenge but of mercy and reconciliation. He defended above all the poor and those in need of protection, and bestowed rich gifts on churches and monasteries. Thus Gerald "supported the needy," "fed the orphans," "protected the widows," and "consoled the distressed."[11] These terms appear later again and again whenever we hear of the religious duties of the knights.

Around the middle of the eleventh century, Count Burkhardt of Endôme (d. 1007) was celebrated as the paragon of a pious knight by his biographer, the monk Eudes of Saint-Maur: "He was a loyal defender of the churches, a giver of alms, a consolation to the poor, and a most pious helper of monks, clerics, widows, and virgins serving God in convents."[12] Among texts from Germany we must mention above all the *Ruodlieb*, a mid-eleventh century Latin verse-romance influenced by the ideology of the reform movement. Though descended "from a noble family,"[13] the hero of the work, the *miles* Ruodlieb, remains throughout his life in a position of service. His actions are characterized by a selfless readiness to serve, the renunciation of revenge, and a dedication to peace: "No one is your equal in council, nobody renders justice as righteously and honorably, and no one defends in like manner the widows and orphans when they have suffered injury at the hands of greed."[14] The old royal duties of justice and protection of the oppressed are here transferred to a "knight" (*miles*) who did not exercise any sovereign rights himself.

Towards the end of the eleventh century, Bonizio of Sutri, the most important papal supporter in the literary battle against Henry IV, discussed in great detail the duties of the "knight" (*miles*) in his "Book on the Christian Life." He called upon the knights to render "faithful service to their lords," and admonished them to fight in such a way "that they do not oppose the Christian religion."[15] "Above all, they are obliged to be devoted to their lords, to strive not after booty, to spare not their own lives to protect that of their lords, to fight to the death for the public good, to subdue schismatics and heretics, to defend the poor, widows, and orphans, to violate not their sworn loyalty nor ever perjure their lords."[16] To whom this first "Christian catalog of knightly duties" (Carl Erdmann) was concretely addressed is difficult to say. What stands out is the fact that the idea of service, so strongly emphasized by Bonizo of Sutri, appears here in combination with distinctly royal duties.

The new concept of religiously motivated military service was further elaborated in the twelfth century by ecclesiastical and learned writers. It received a thorough and forceful treatment from John of Salisbury in his *Policraticus*, the sixth book of which is almost entirely devoted to the duties of the *militia* as the "armed hand of the commonwealth."[17] As John of Salisbury saw it, "the duties of real knighthood" consisted above all in "protecting the Church, fighting heresy, honoring the priesthood, eliminating injuries to the poor, pacifying the land, shedding one's blood for one's brothers (as the formula of the oath teaches), and, if necessary, giving up one's life."[18]

Of outstanding importance for the development of the religious concept of knighthood were the liturgical formulae used for blessing swords and other weapons; I have already discussed them in connection with the knighting ceremony (see p. 241). The tenth-century Romano-German Pontifical contains a text with the title "Blessing of the newly-girt sword" (*Benedictio ensis noviter succincti*); it opens with these words: "Hear, O Lord, our prayers, and bless with the right hand of Your Majesty this sword, with which this man, your servant N., wishes to be girt, so that it may be a defense and protection for churches, widows, and orphans, for all servants of God against the fury of the pagans, and that it may strike terror, fear, and dread into the enemy."[19] It is not entirely clear who would have been addressed with these words. In the tenth century, such texts were probably used in the ceremonial delivery of arms to the sons of kings and princes. But in the twelfth century these same texts became part of the knighting ceremony. This is revealed by the fact that the *Benedictio ensis* from the Romano-German Pontifical appears in a late twelfth century manuscript from Klosterneuburg (Stiftsbibliothek no. 622) under the heading: "For making new knights."[20] The words that pledged the knight to defending the Church and protecting widows and orphans were borrowed from the liturgy of the royal coronation. The explanation for an important element in the religious idea of knighthood therefore lies in the fact that religious demands originally imposed on the king became so generalized that they could be applied to all "knights."

Crusading propaganda   The notion of spiritualized warfare found its most impressive exposition in the crusading literature. Of fundamental significance was the great speech delivered by Pope Urban II to a large gathering of ecclesiastics and laymen at the Council of Clermont on November 27, 1095. In it he called upon Christendom to embark on an armed expedition to the Holy Land and to liberate the Eastern Church. While the speech itself has not survived, the various reports about it show that the Pope aimed his exhortation specifically at the French nobility, holding out the promise that as "knights of God" (*milites Dei*) in a just war against enemies of the faith, they could win remission of temporal punishment for their sins and gain eternal reward. It seems that the Pope had harsh words for the customary violence of the nobility in order to paint in brighter contrast the new image of the spiritual knight. The historical accounts differ in their wording but agree in essence: "Let those who have long been robbers now be soldiers of Christ."[21] "Until now you have engaged in unjust wars; again and again you have raised in anger your weapons in mutual murder, solely because of greed and pride."[22] "Turn the weapons which you have bloodied unjustly in killing each other against the enemies of the faith and of Christendom."[23] According to the version of Robert the Monk, Urban II made overpopulation in France responsible for the constant feuding of the nobility, and he promised land in the East to the crusaders:

> Let no property detain you nor any worry about possessions. For the land in which you dwell is closed in on all sides by the sea and the mountains, and it has become crowded on account of your number. It no longer has an abundance of riches and supplies barely enough food to feed its inhabitants. This is the reason why you quarrel and fight, why you start wars and often injure and kill one another. Put an end to the hatred amongst you, cease quarreling, refrain from war, and put to rest all conflicts and dissension. Set out on the journey to the Holy Sepulchre, take that land from that godless race and make it subject to yourselves, the land which God gave the children of Israel to possess, as the Scripture says, "where milk and honey flows."[24]

Balderic of Dol paid particular attention to those passages in Urban II's speech that described the misdeeds of the secular nobility:

> Girt with the belt of knighthood you are haughty in your great pride. You tear your brothers to pieces and cut each other up. It is not the knighthood of Christ that destroys the sheepfold of the Redeemer. The holy Church has reserved warfare for the protection of her children, but you have wickedly perverted it into an evil. To confess the truth, which to proclaim is our duty, you are truly not going the path to eternal life. You oppress orphans, rob widows, commit murder, defile churches, and violate foreign laws. The reward of robbery awaits you for shedding Christian blood. And like vultures smelling the carrion, you cast your eyes to remote parts and seek out war. Truly this is the worst path, for it is altogether turned from God. But if you desire to be mindful of your souls, lay down quickly the belt of such knighthood, bravely join the soldiers of Christ, and hurry to the defense of the Eastern Church.[25]

In Balderic's version, as well, the crusaders were promised worldly possessions: "The goods of the enemies will be yours since you will seize their treasures."[26] It is very interesting that in Balderic's account—written at the beginning of the twelfth century—we also find the idea that female beauty might keep knights from joining the crusade: "Let neither the seductive charms of women nor your own possessions tempt you into not going."[27] This theme would later play an important role in the courtly crusading songs, which appear in France around 1150 and in Germany around 1180.

In contrasting evil, secular robber-knights to the meritorious knighthood of God, writers were fond of using the wordplay *militia–malitia* (knighthood–malice). Bernard of Clairvaux wrote in his crusading exhortation to the east-Franconians and Bavarians in 1146: "Put an end to what was formerly not *militia* but clearly *malitia*, whereby you used to cast down, ruin, and annihilate one another. Now, brave knight and warlike man, there is a knighthood where you can fight without danger, where victory brings fame, and death profit."[28] We encounter this play on words also in the crusading letter of the cardinal legate Henry of Albano to the ecclesiastical and secular princes of Germany from the year 1187 or 1188. Henry condemns with special severity the violence of the nobility: "It was not *militia* but *malitia* when the Christians hitherto were only intent on murdering, robbing, and committing evil deeds, through which they have earned the eternal fire and the torments of eternal Hell. Foreign to them is the blessed knighthood in which victory brings fame, and death even greater reward. To this we are called today by Him who loves our souls."[29]

When the ecclesiastical writers spoke of "knights" (*milites*) and "knighthood" (*militia*), they surely did not always have a clear idea of the socio-hierarchical reality that corresponded to these terms. The crusading exhortation was directed basically at all of Christendom, but specifically at the nobility, both at the great princes and the smaller lords. Only the kings were at first deliberately excluded from the appeal, since the Church wanted to reserve for itself the leadership of this holy undertaking. But as early as the Second Crusade (1147–1149), the decisions of the kings almost always set the tone. No doubt it must have struck the noble lords who followed the call to the crusades as somewhat unusual to be addressed as "soldiers" or "servants" (*miles* could have both meanings). The notion that it could be an honor even for a great lord to be called "servant" if his service was for God and the Christian faith was an important component of the religious concept of knighthood. The Church Fathers had already taught that the concepts of lordship and service, which in reality described sharp social differences, were in an almost paradoxical way identical in relationship to God. From Gregory the Great (d. 604) comes the statement that "serving God is ruling."[30] And St. Augustine in his *City of God* wrote about the princes of God's people: "Those who rule serve those whom they seem to be ruling."[31] How widespread these ideas were during the time of the crusades is revealed by a letter Count Henri of Saint Pol wrote to the Duke of Brabant concerning the conquest of Constantinople in the year 1203. The letter is quoted in the Cologne *Königschronik*: "If anyone desires to serve the Lord—service to whom is ruling—and if he wishes to gain a famous and outstanding name in the world of knighthood, let him take the cross and follow the Lord and come to the tournament of the Lord, to which he has been invited by the Lord Himself."[32] The reformist theologians went still a step further. In their eyes service to the human community—which meant protection for the oppressed and support for the suffering—should also be a duty for those chosen to rule. In its secularized version, this idea of service became an important component of the courtly image of knighthood. *Lippiflorium* tells us of the education of Freiherr Bernhard II zur Lippe (d. 1224), who was initially groomed for an ecclesiastical career but then returned to lay status:

> Dressed with the robes of the laity, he switches over to the exercise of arms. As a servant he carries the yoke of a lord. He wishes joyfully to serve; he does not spurn to endure toil, ready to be obedient and eager not to be indolent. It is not the lack of wealth that compels him to serve, but his inborn virtue, and the praise and goodwill of the people. He serves so that he may be lord; he serves so that he may be elevated by it.[33]

It is difficult to gauge what impact the idea of the *militia Christi* had on the noble lords who were exhorted to join the crusades. The remission of sins granted by the Church to the crusaders (and later to those who made it possible for others to participate), proved to be an especially effective propaganda tool. Though, strictly speaking, the remission covered only the temporal punishment of sins, it seems to have been understood from the beginning as a complete remission of all guilt, and the Church made little attempt to clear up the misunderstanding. In many cases religious motives were probably joined by the hope of material profit. Even though the prospect of winning land and booty always remained a secondary theme in the crusading literature, we can assume that it was precisely this expectation that most attracted the secular participants. The fact that the crusaders came to enjoy a general suspension of interest payments on their debts—first granted by Pope Gregory VIII (d. 1187) in his crusading bull *Quam divina patentia*—was certainly of great practical consequence. What affected the actual conditions of the nobility's life most strongly was probably the special protection that the Church extended to the property of the crusaders. But it is rather doubtful whether the religious propaganda transformed the way of thinking in lay society and created a willingness to change one's way of life as drastically as the idea of spiritual knighthood demanded. In the course of the thirteenth century more and more critical voices were raised. In *Reinfried von Braunschweig*, written at the end of the courtly age, nine reasons are listed why Christian knights journeyed to the Holy Land. "To serve God with a pure heart"[34] was only one of the nine; the remaining eight were all secular motives: one knight went "from a free desire"[35]; the second sought "knightly combat"[36]; the third wanted "to see the world"[37]; the fourth wished "to serve his lady for her love"[38]; the fifth wanted to "suffer pain"[39] for the sake of his true Lord; the sixth was driven by hope of "profit"[40]; the seventh went simply "for pleasure"[41]; the eighth "for the sake of fame."[42]

The military religious orders   In 1118/19 a group of French crusaders led by Hugh of Payens decided to remain in the Holy Land and devote themselves completely to protecting the pilgrims on their way to Jerusalem. They professed a religious way of life and adopted the rule of the Augustinian canons at the Holy Sepulchre. This was the birth of the military religious orders, in which the ideal of Christian knighthood found its most striking realization, even though the political maneuverings that the orders were later involved in revealed but little of the original religious motivation. This fusion of monasticism and knighthood, spiritual and secular warfare, *militia spiritualis* and *militia saecularis*, must have struck contemporaries as a new and initially strange idea, despite the fact that the ground had been prepared somewhat by the *militia Christi* propaganda. Two documents illuminate the peculiar nature of the new orders: the first Rule of the Templars from the years 1128/30, and the "Book to the knights of the Temple in praise of the new knighthood" by Bernard of Clairvaux, written about the same time. By prohibiting all secular pomp, admonishing knights to be obedient, and warning of any association with women, the Rule of the Templars imposed upon the knights of the order the so-called three evangelical vows of poverty, obedience, and chastity: "Knights are not to pay attention to the appearance of women. We believe it is dangerous for any pious man to have excessive regard for the looks of a woman. No brother shall therefore presume to kiss a widow, or a virgin, or his mother, or his sister, or his aunt, or any other woman. The knighthood of God shall avoid the kiss of a woman."[43]

As Bernard of Clairvaux saw it, "the new knighthood" (*nova militia*) of the Templars was distinguished by the fact that it engaged in a physical and a spiritual battle, that it combined the duties of a knight with those of a monk. Both the Rule as well as Bernard emphatically demanded the renunciation of all worldly luxuries. According to the

Rule, the brothers should be content with simple fare, and "on normal days two or three vegetable dishes shall suffice."[44] They are to dress in "clothes of one color,"[45] renounce costly furs, and "wear only sheepskin."[46] It was not permitted "that gold or silver—the marks of wealth—appear on the reins and chest straps of horses or on spurs and stirrups."[47] Knights shall "not hunt birds with hunting birds,"[48] and in general "shall refrain from the hunt in all circumstances."[49] In similar fashion, Bernard of Clairvaux impressed upon the knights of the order "to detest board games and dice, to shrink back from hunting, not to enjoy, as is customary, the sport with hunting birds, to despise mimes, magicians, and inventors of fables, and reject scurrilous songs and performances as so much foolish vanity."[50] Furthermore, Knights Templar shall not wear their hair long, their armor is to be undecorated, and their horses shall not have colorful blankets ornamented with heraldic emblems. "Let them think of battle, but not of pomp, of victory, but not of fame."[51] Such rules reveal that the Church's efforts to spiritualize the military profession took offense not only at how the nobility exercised its rule, at the acts of violence and injustice. Sharp criticism was directed equally at the material luxury of the nobility and its forms of entertainment. At the court feast of Mainz in 1188, where the crusade of Emperor Frederick I was decided upon, Bishop Henry of Straßburg denounced especially the fondness of the secular nobility for actors and theatrical spectacles:

> Oh wondrous thing, oh you excellent knights! Your inborn courage and uprightness has made you famous in the exercise of arms and has distinguished you before the rest of the world. I am amazed, and it is a thing worthy of wonder, that in such a crisis your devotion to God is so disgracefully cool and sluggish, and that you have forgotten your usual bravery, like degenerates and cowards. A minstrel or a theatrical play could easily capture your attention with its allurement, whereas the words of God, which you receive with such a stubborn and deaf mind, find no reception with you."[52]

Ecclesiastical criticism of the courtly social life of the nobility in the name of the *militia Christi* was addressed not only to those who joined the new knightly orders. In his crusading exhortation to Duke Wladislav of Bohemia in 1147, Bernard of Clairvaux demanded that none of the crusaders "wear colored or gray fur or silk clothes."[53] Furthermore, crusaders were prohibited from having gold and silver decorations on the bridles and saddles of their horses. Similar regulations appear in Pope Eugene III's crusading bull *Quantam praedecessores* of December 1145, written apparently under the influence of Bernard of Clairvaux.

They are stated even more bluntly in the new version of the bull in March 1146: "those who serve God with the sword" are called upon "to pay no heed to splendid clothes or the beauty of outward appearance, nor to hunting dogs or falcons or the other things that indicate wantonness."[54] Let them renounce also "colored cloth and fur on their clothes as well as gold and silver on their weapons."[55] Identical prohibitions are found in later crusading bulls, as for example in Pope Gregory VIII's bull *Audita tremendi* from the year 1187. What effect such pronouncements had is difficult to determine. No doubt they were violated often enough. But there is one piece of evidence that the demands of the Church were also accepted as binding by the worldly rulers. When King Philip II Augustus of France and King Henry II of England met at Grisor in January of 1188, they promulgated a military code which adopted the ecclesiastical declarations against worldly luxuries. This remarkable document decreed the following:

> 1. Nobody shall swear an irregular oath. 2. Nobody shall play dice. 3. Nobody shall wear colored cloth, fur, sable, or scarlet. 4. Everyone, ecclesiastics and laymen, shall be content with two courses at a meal. 5. Nobody shall bring a woman along on the pilgrimage, except for washerwomen, who are above suspicion. 6. Nobody shall wear slit or lace-trimmed clothes.[56]

However, decrees of this sort by worldly rulers seem to have been the exception. Nothing comparable is known from Germany, apart from the prohibition of taverns and costly clothes in the military code for the Mongol War of 1241 (MGH Const. 2, no. 335, p. 445). We must also bear in mind that the secular military codes imposed a *temporary* renunciation of certain amenities or privileges on those who took part in a campaign. In contrast, the ecclesiastical exhortations, even when intended for a specific crusade, always raised the demand that the knights make a fundamental and permanent commitment to the idea of spiritual knighthood.

Vernacular sources   Since the ecclesiastical writers who propagated the idea of religious knighthood in the twelfth century wrote their works in Latin—which the lay nobility, at least in Germany, could not read—they undoubtedly reached few of those for whom the new doctrine was intended. At most the crusading sermons were translated, but we know precious little about the content and form of vernacular crusading propaganda. We must assume that the ecclesiastical concept of knighthood exerted a broader influence on lay society only after

it had been picked up by authors who wrote in the vernacular for a
courtly public. It was above all the clerical didacticians who adopted
the ideology of the reform movement and made it accessible to the noble audience. In France or Norman England, the leading figure was
Etienne de Fougères (d. 1178), who was active as a cleric at the court of
King Henry II of England before becoming bishop of Rennes. In his
"Book of Manners," dedicated to the countess of Hereford, he laid out
in detail the moral and religious obligations of a knight while putting
particular emphasis on his ties to the Church. In Germany the most
important voice was that of Thomasin von Zirklaere, who in 1215/16
wrote a lengthy treatise on morality (Der Wälsche Gast) in the German
language. In his discussion of the knightly duties in books VI and VII,
Thomasin, like the crusading preachers before him, started from a
gloomy picture of reality, which made his opposing concept of spiritual
knighthood all the more effective:

> He who kills a poor man does not fight like a true knight; and he who takes
> his possessions has an unknightly disposition. Knights, think of your calling!
> Wherefore have you become knights? God knows, not to sleep. Shall a man
> be a knight because he likes to rest? That is new to me. Do you think you are
> knights because of the good food and wine? If so you are mistaken. Beasts
> like to feed, true enough. You are also not knights because of clothes and
> precious ornaments.[57]

"He who wants to cultivate the calling of knighthood must take more
toil upon himself than eating well."[58]

> If a knight wishes to do what he is obligated to do, let him toil day and night
> with all his might for the churches and the poor. But today there are few
> knights who do that. You should know: whoever does not act thus should
> rather be a peasant, for then he would not be so hateful to God. This you
> must know: whoever exercises his knighthood such that he refuses help and
> council will be deprived of his knightly rank.[59]

But the clerical didacticians were not the only ones who expressed
these sentiments. The idea of spiritual knighthood appears in courtly
literature whenever the crusading theme is touched upon. Middle High
German crusading lyric, like its French counterpart, used the entire
ideological arsenal of ecclesiastical propaganda. The Rolandslied illus-
trates this with a wealth of examples. Courtly lyric, too, was familiar
with the notion that participation in the holy campaign necessitated an
inner transformation and the willingness to devote oneself totally to the
religious cause. "The cross demands a pure disposition and a life free of
sin. Thus one can gain salvation and the highest reward."[60]

The courtly poets had another opportunity to expound the religious aspects of knighthood when describing the ceremony of knighting. The ceremonial girding with the sword was almost always accompanied by words of admonition meant to spell out for the new knight the duties of the knightly calling: "Protect the poor: that is knighthood. Speak on their behalf: that is virtuous; in this way you will be acknowledged before God. It is for this that your sword has been blessed."[61] The knightly virtues in the *Prosa-Lancelot* are fully oriented towards the spiritual dimension: "Knighthood was created especially to protect and defend the holy churches."[62] Hence the knights shall "fight tirelessly to strengthen the faith."[63]

Most courtly poets strove to create a harmonious integration of the religious duties of a knight with the courtly-wordly motifs of knighthood, which found their clearest expression in service to a lady. Margrave Willehalm's address to his troops before the battle against the pagans included these words:

> Let each knight take thought for his honor, as if guided by the blessing that was pronounced when he received the sword; whoever seeks to practice true knighthood must protect widows and orphans from the dangers that threaten them, and this will win him everlasting reward. Yet he may also direct his heart to serve for the rewards of women: that way he will learn the sounds of lances as they burst through shields, how ladies rejoice at the sight, and how a lady comforts her friend's distress. A two-fold reward awaits us: heaven and the favor of noble ladies.[64]

COURTLY VIRTUES

The knightly code of virtues   The phrase "knightly code of virtues" (*ritterliches Tugendsystem*) was coined by Gustav Ehrismann. It is misleading insofar as there never was a systematic courtly doctrine of ethics. Courtly virtues were recited almost exclusively in poetic form. It is true that the poets at times compiled complete catalogs of virtues, but they were hardly interested in systematizing these concepts. Another Ehrismann thesis, that the courtly ethic of knighthood could be traced back for the most part to classical doctrines of ethics, such as those Cicero expounded in his tract "On Duties" (*De officiis*), was also misleading and fraught with problems. It was only at this point of Ehrismann's notion of the knightly code of ethics that the Romanist Ernst Robert Curtius directed his famous critique, which after World War II set off a lively debate within German philology. Looking back at this controversy a generation later, it is difficult to understand how Curtius's attack, laced with unpleasant polemics against German philology, could cause such a stir. We must also note that the entire debate clarified very little and hardly advanced our historical understanding of the courtly concept of knighthood. Not even the very specific question whether a connection existed between the development of the aristocratic social ideal and the arrival of classicism in the twelfth century, found a satisfactory answer. For all intents and purposes, scholarship has to start again where Ehrismann left off in 1916: with a survey and analysis of the concepts and terms of knightly exemplariness in courtly literature.

Sometimes the poets piled up a wealth of virtuous attributes, listing religious, moral, and social concepts without apparent order: "He was a flower of shining perfection, a rock of steadfast virtue, a mirror of magnanimity and courtly deportment, he was pure and humble, of manly kindness, wise, gracious in an understanding way, brave, and with a lofty disposition."[65] Correspondingly broad was the range of teachings that showed the knight the path to courtly perfection. There was, for example, the short thirteenth-century poem "The teacher" (*Der magezoge*), which sought to give the noble youth instructions for proper behavior: "Love God with all your might," "accustom yourself to virtue," "strive for good behavior," "do not speak viciously," "be decent and well-bred," "put up with the hatred of the peasants," "give thanks to him who speaks honestly to you," "let virtue teach you every day," "fear Hell," "follow the teachings of God," "honor your father and your mother," "listen to the advice of the wise," "protect the poor,"[66] and so on. Behind the seemingly arbitrary nature of these lists we can, however, detect fixed organizing principles. The common foundation everywhere is a stock of Christian commandments that must have reached the poets from ecclesiastical sources.

Among the religious virtues of a knight, humility ranked first. Central in the knightly code that Gurnemanz imparted to young Parzival was the advice to "cultivate humility."[67] "Be humble and without deception,"[68] Tristan was admonished at his knighting ceremony. Knightly humility manifested itself in the realization that personal effort amounted to nothing without the blessing of God. "He acted like the wise who thank God for all the honor they attain and see it as a gift from God."[69] The commandment to "love God above all else"[70] was therefore the fundamental injunction also for the courtly knight. Towards his fellow man the knight expressed his humility as pity and mercy: "Let mercy be joined to daring."[71] This meant not only the sparing of defeated enemies, but also protection for those in need of it and pity for the suffering, which Erec demonstrated in exemplary fashion towards the eighty mourning widows in Brandigan: "He took pity on the sorrowful group."[72] The religious instruction for the knights further included the admonition to attend church regularly and to show deference towards clerics.

A great number of praiseworthy attributes was available to describe a knight's exemplary character: *guot, reine, biderbe, vrum, lobesam, tiure, wert, ûz erwelt*. The terms *schame* and *kiusche* designated the purity and decency of one's moral sensibilities. *Güete* stood for inner goodness. The word *triuwe*, too, could have a very broad meaning. In the narrower sense it was a legal term and referred to the loyal adherence to a contract or a vassal's ties to his lord. In the wider sense, *triuwe* meant the honesty and steadfastness of human bonds as such, and the love for God and God's love for humankind ("since God himself is *ein triuwe*"[73]). For the knight, *triuwe* entailed the keeping of moral obligations: "Proper *schame* and noble *triuwe* bestow everlasting fame."[74]

If a writer needed moral concepts that were more clearly defined, he could fall back on the canon of the cardinal virtues in Christian dogma. This applies especially to the terms *mâze* and *staete*, which the poets and didacticians who were addressing a noble audience used with great emphasis. The meaning of *staete* can be explained with the help of the Christian-Latin term *constantia* ("steadfastness"), while *mâze* was related to Christian *temperantia* ("moderation") as well as *medietas*, the proper middle between two extremes: "*Staete* and *mâze* are sisters, they are children of one and the same virtue."[75] *Staete* as firm perseverance was displayed by the knight above all in service to a lady: "Before I would break my knightly *staete* towards good women..."[76] In a broader sense *staete* was the adherence to goodness: "To your goodness I can ascribe constancy without wavering."[77] When it carried this meaning, *staete* could be regarded as the very foundation of the entire moral code: "The other virtues are nothing if *staete* is not among them."[78] *Mâze*, too, was lauded as the "mother of all virtues": "The mother of all virtues suits young people well: *mâze* is her name."[79] No code of knightly ethics was without the injunction to keep moderation in all things and walk the proper middle way. *Mâze* was urged especially upon women: "Noble *mâze* ennobles a person and his reputation. Nothing that the sun ever shone upon is as blessed as the woman who devotes herself and her life to mâze."[80]

Nobility and beauty   A courtly knight was not only pious and virtuous, he was also handsome, rich, fond of splendor, full of desire for fame, and of illustrious descent. The question of how to judge these worldly qualities gave rise to different positions. The concept of *militia Christi* rested on the distinction between worldly knighthood, condemned not only for its violence but also for its courtly pomp, and spiritual knighthood, directed entirely towards God. In courtly poetry this distinction vanished altogether. What the ecclesiastical writers condemned, the poets integrated into the image of perfect knighthood: not, of course, injustice and violence, but the outward display of power, physical beauty, splendid clothes and furnishings, and refined manners. Characteristic of the poetic conception of courtly knighthood was the positive view of aristocratic court culture and the seemingly unproblematic fusion of these worldly values with the notions of virtue derived from the traditional ruler-image.

A theoretical justification for regarding nobility, fame, and wealth as "goods" and placing them among the virtues could be found in Roman moral philosophy. Cicero ranged beauty, nobility, strength, power, renown, and so forth, under the category of "useful things" (*utile*), and divided them into "earthly possessions" (*bona fortunae*) and "bodily goods" (*bona coporis*). One of the most influential ethical works of the twelfth century, the *Moralium dogma philosophorum* (by William of Conches or Walter of Châtillon), picked up on this idea and taught that there was in principle no conflict between "the good" (*honestum*) and "the useful" (*utile*): "Therefore hold most firmly in your mind and do not doubt that everything good is useful, because there is nothing useful that is not good."[81] Through Thomasin von Zirklaere, who was familiar with the *Moralium dogma philosophorum* and used it as a source, the notion of the "useful" (*utile*) was also made accessible to lay society. Thomasin's perspective, however, placed the accents differently: the "goods" in the useful (*utile*) category were to him not unconditionally good but morally ambiguous, simultaneously "evil and good."[82] And what he has to say about them is closer to Christian ethics than to classical philosophy: "Men and women possess five things in their body, and five things not tied to the body. The soul must rule them, otherwise they cause great vices in both old and young. The five things carried in the body are: strength, agility, health (joy of living), beauty, and dexterity. The five goods outside the body are: nobility, power, wealth, renown, and lordship. Whoever cannot control these ten things with his mind should not be called human."[83] Traces of the doctrine of the *bona corporis et fortunae* are also found in other Latin-educated writers. Yet we must not overemphasize the importance of these musings. For most poets the positive depiction of the nobility's social culture was not a philosophical problem. The less one inquired into a theoretical justification, the easier it was to portray the poetic knights and ladies as beautiful, rich, and noble, while simultaneously showering them with all the virtuous attributes. This did not keep the poets from picking up preformulated lines of explanation and justification when they were available.

This also applies to the doctrine of the "nobility of virtue." The idea that a noble lord was in some special way obliged to act virtuously, and that his nobility of birth had to be complemented by a like nobility of character, had played an important role in aristocratic ethics since classical times. In courtly literature, which told of knights who in social rank were the sons of kings and princes, such notions carried special weight. The perfect knight should possess both nobilty of birth and nobility of character:

> In him there was forgotten no virtue that a young knight must have to win high praise. No one was praised as much as he in all the lands. He held both nobility and power; his virtue, too, was great. Yet no matter how vast his worldly goods and how immaculate his descent, which was equal to that of princes, birth and wealth did not honor him nearly as much as renown and high-mindedness.[84]

Occasionally the concept of the nobility of virtue was used to criticize the noble class:

> It is said that no one is noble who does not act nobly. If that is true, many lords must feel ashamed, for they are not without disgrace, indeed they do possess deceitfulness and malice. These three destroy magnanimity, renown, and nobility. Alas, that there was ever a rich man who let disgrace and malice deprive him of his good name! Let him look at those who are poor but high-minded, how they strive for high honor with a courtly disposition. A poor man who takes the proper path of virtue is noble, whereas a rich man who keeps company with disgrace is of the lowest birth.[85]

This kind of criticism, which did not seriously challenge the claim that nobility of birth and nobility of character were identical, was something the nobility was probably happy to submit to. The more one emphasized that nobility of birth had to be complemented by true virtuousness, the easier it was to reverse the argument and deduce inner qualities from outward noble rank. Only rarely was the doctrine of the nobility of virtue given an antifeudal slant and sharpened into the claim that true nobility was not acquired by birth but by a noble character. The ecclesiastical didactician Thomasin von Zirklaere declared: "No one is noble except for the person who professes true goodness with heart and mind."[86] The same idea appears in Hugo von Trimberg: "No one is noble except for the person who is ennobled by character and not property."[87] Freidank put it most bluntly: "He who possesses virtue is noble. Without virtue nobility is worth nothing. Whether serf or free, he who is not of noble descent can acquire nobility through virtue."[88] Courtly society probably regarded such statements as manifestations of an unrealistic ethical rigorism. Everyone knew that the nobility had no reason to fear social competition from the virtuous.

A knight's noble descent was complemented not only by a virtuous disposition, but also by physical beauty. Young Parzival in his peasant dress was "a floral wreath of manly beauty"[89] as he encountered the knights in the forest, who saw in his beauty evidence of his illustrious descent: "'I should think you are of noble stock.' The knights looked him up and down, and indeed he bore the marks of God's own handiwork."[90] From the theologians the poets could learn that human beauty was created by God, and that a person's beauty was a mirror of his inner perfection. Scholastic aesthetics regarded beauty as the visible manifestation of the true and the good: "Hence Beauty is intrinsically the same as goodness."[91] The external beauty of things therefore revealed their inner beauty. "Since then the beauty of visible things is inherent in their forms, correspondingly the invisible beauty can be shown from the visible forms, since visible beauty is an image of invisible beauty."[92] For the poets, this notion of a harmony between inner and outer qualities became one of the most important ways of depicting courtly perfection. If one disregarded the philosophical implications, this doctrine of harmony made it possible to portray the outward splendor of courtly life as the manifestation of a divine purpose.

Beauty was mentioned primarily in relation to women. Elaborate descriptions of male pulchritude are rare. One example appears in Konrad von Fleck:

Flore had nice hair, more blond than brown and slightly curled throughout. His forehead was white and high, free of any blemish, with suitably delicate eyebrows at the proper height, in the color of his hair and just perfect. His eyes were radiant and large, and they looked about in such a lovely way as though they frequently wanted to laugh, which suited him well. His nose was likewise faultless, straight and evenly shaped. Nature had made his cheeks red and white, like milk and blood. The mouth was impeccable, with an even pink color. The regular and straight teeth sparkled with a white lustre. The chin was round, neck and throat lovely, his arms strong and long, his hands straight and white, the fingers flawless and at the tip the fingernails were bright as glass. His chest was nicely rounded, but his waist was slim, his entire figure was straight as a reed. He had splendid legs and nicely shaped calves, not too thick and not too thin, and what are called slenderly arched feet. To leave nothing unsaid: his toes were formed such that he could not have wished for a better shape. Nature had forgotten on him no mark of beauty.[93]

What Konrad says here about the face would also be fitting in a description of female beauty, as would the white hands, the straight figure and the small waist. Gender specific attributes of beauty are only the barrel chest and especially the legs: women's legs remained covered, whereas male fashion was aimed at showing them off (see p. 146).

In addition to beauty, strength was, among the "goods of the body" (*bona corporis*), the most important attribute for the courtly knight. The heroes of the courtly romances are all blessed with tremendous bodily strength, which enables them to gain victory even in the toughest battles: "He was steel in every fight, victorious he laid hands on many a glorious prize."[94] The action in courtly romance is almost always made up of a string of duels in which the hero must prove himself. But these confrontations also showed that brute force alone was not enough to emerge victorious from the diverse adventures. Superior knightly skill frequently enabled the hero to defeat an enemy of greater physical strength. The martial character of the fighting was also muted by the fact that the knights usually fought from noble motives: to protect ladies in distress or to rid the land of monsters. If a warrior was driven solely by the desire for fame, the poets not infrequently considered this an indication that courtly perfection had not yet been attained.

Hövescheit (*courtoisie*)   The distinct nature of the courtly image of knighthood is revealed very clearly in the fusion of moral injunctions with rules of social conduct. A knight should not only possess wisdom, justice, moderation, and courage, he should not only be noble, handsome, and skilled in arms, but should also have a mastery of the refined manners of the court, the rules of decorum and etiquette, the proper forms of behavior, especially towards women. The poets described the courtly concept of etiquette with the terms *zuht* and *vuoge*. "He was handsome and strong, he was upright and good, and he was affable. He had sufficient knowledge, courtly breeding (*zuht*) and decorum (*vuoge*)."[95] Frequently we encounter *zuht* and *vuoge* in combination with the terms that became synonymous with the new social doctrine: *hövescheit*. "He had devoted his time and energy to *vuoge* and *hövescheit*."[96]

The Middle High German word *hövescheit* was probably a loan formation in imitation of Old French *corteisie* or Provençal *cortesia* ("courtoisie"). The Provençal poet Garin le Brun (end of the twelfth century) wrote in his didactic poem: "*Cortesia*—if you want to know—is this: whoever knows how to speak and act well and thereby make himself liked, and who refrains from improprieties."[97] "*Cortesia* manifests itself in clothes and in a beautiful reception. *Cortesia* shows itself in courting (in loving, manuscript N) and in refined speech. *Cortesia* reveals itself in pleasant conviviality."[98] In Germany we encounter *hövescheit* for the first time in *König Rother* (around 1170), in reference to courtly conduct towards ladies: "And with his *hövescheit* he brought about that the lovely maid ran away from her father."[99] In this sense the word spread very quickly. In *Graf Rudolf*, *hövescheit* already comprises the entire field of social conduct, and it stood in opposition to *dörperheit* ("peasantish, uncourtly behavior"), a term applied to all those who did not share the courtly lifestyle. The passage in question concerned the education of Prince Appollinart, which Count Rudolf had entrusted to his nephew:

> For my sake make it your concern to lead him to (*hov*)*ischeit*. Make *dorperichheit* hateful to him. Make him enjoy riding the buhurt and protecting himself with the shield. Moreover, he shall be generous and of a steadfast mind; that is good for his reputation. He shall enjoy seeking out ladies, and shall stand and sit with them in a well-mannered way. In every respect he shall demonstrate good sense, as is proper for him. When he hears brave men speaking of manliness, he shall not be loathe to listen. In doing so he may learn those things that promote his reputation in society.[100]

Sometimes *hövescheit* referred specifically to the artistic forms of courtly conviviality, especially singing and instrumental music. At the court of Queen Candacis, there were "among her entourage one thousand young men who devoted themselves to courtliness with every kind of stringed instrument."[101] Knowledge of foreign languages was also considered a mark of *hövescheit* (G. v. Straßburg 7985 ff.). Occasionally even higher education was introduced into the ideal image of the courtly knight. In the second half of the thirteenth century, the *Spruch* poet Boppe gave a humorous twist to this idealized image:

If a hero were to win the highest prize in five countries, if his body were shaped with perfect beauty, if he were upright, generous, and prudent in speech, if he could write, read, compose poetry, play the fiddle, and also stalk, hunt, parry, hit a target, and in every way handle weapons; if he understood the black books and had mastered the art of grammar, and if his mind were trained in music and for singing all estampies; if he could hurl the throwing rock twelve feet further than all his companions, and if he were able to hunt a wild bear; if all the ladies bestowed on him most graciously their greeting, and if he possessed the treasure of the seven Liberal Arts and could sing and speak it—all that would avail him little if he did not also have money.[102]

A person who met the requirements of *hövescheit* possessed *vreude* and *hôhen muot*. In religious thinking *hôhen muot* meant "pride" ("Wealth causes pride [*hôhen muot*] and arrogance and forgetfulness of God"[103]). In the courtly context it stood for high-mindedness and a knight's feeling of elation in social life. The term *vreude* ("joy") referred also to society. It described not a subjective feeling, but the condition of festive excitement and elevation above the routine of daily life, a heightened self-consciousness as manifested in the bustling noisiness of the court feasts: "There was joyousness and splendor, festive high spirits and great knighthood, and an abundance of all the pleasures of the body."[104] The courtly code of knightly values recited to Tristan at his knighting ceremony closed with these words: "Be always courtly, be always joyful!"[105] Whether or not society lived in the high spirits of *vreude* depended largely on the conduct of the ruler, who imparted *vreude* to his court and his people through his generosity, his friendliness, and his amiable disposition. "To all those to whom he was supposed to bring joy, this lord was throughout his life a sun radiating joyousness. He was to all the embodiment of perfection; he was a model to knighthood, an ornament to his family, a refuge for his land. He lacked no virtue that a lord should have."[106] When Erec in his love for Enite neglected his social obligations, "his court lost all joy and lapsed into disgrace."[107]

Courtly exemplariness was converted into social prestige. The key word for this was *êre*. To ecclesiastical writers worldly renown was thoroughly suspect: "Fame is empty noise."[108] The courtly poets, however, summed up with the term *êre* everything that distinguished a knight in this world. They assigned a central value to worldly fame insofar as they demanded that courtly perfection live up to the commandments of the Christian religion as well as the expectations of society: "When a man's life ends in such a way that God is not cheated out of the soul because of the sin of the body, and who yet retains the world's favor and respect, this is useful toil!"[109] The idea that it should be possible to satisfy both God and the world appears by the middle of the twelfth century. In the *Kaiserchronik*, the Roman Emperor Domitian was held up to all kings as a warning example, so that "they might preserve their souls and also keep their worldly reputation."[110] Like a red thread this idea weaves its way through courtly literature. "Let me teach you a virtue that is useful for your reputation and will also win you God's favor."[111] "A man should possess worldly fame, and yet he should sometimes also show consideration for his soul lest his exuberance lead him too far astray."[112] He who can retain both God and the world is a happy man."[113] Gottfried von Straßburg made the balancing of religious and worldly demands the central aspect of his princely education, and he summed it up in the word *morâliteit*: "*morâliteit* is a sweet science, blissful and pure. Its teachings are in one accord with the world and with God. Through its laws it teaches us how to please God and the world. She is the nurse of all good people, that they may draw nourishment and vigor from her doctrine. For they shall have neither wealth nor honor if they do not also have the code of *morâliteit*."[114] This thought also plays a central role in Walther von der Vogelweide. In his first *Reichsspruch*, the singer appears as a mourner who sits on a rock with his legs crossed, at a loss for an answer to the question "how a man might gain three things at once and not one of them be ruined. Two are the honor and the goods of this life, which often damage each other. The third is God's grace, more precious than the other two. How I'd like to have all three in one casket."[115] Unlike the other poets, however, Walther was doubtful that a harmonious balance could be achieved: "Unfortunately it can never be that in this world wealth and honor come together in one heart along with God's grace."[116] Walther's look at the harsh political reality after the death of Emperor Henry VI was intended to call to mind that the unproblematic balance of religious and worldly values was only a poetic ideal.

The demand that the courtly knight please both God and the world can hardly be seen as the product of serious philosophical reflection. Nevertheless, it makes an important statement of its own, since it manifests the new appreciation of secular culture. In contrast to the traditional Christian teaching based on the idea that a human being had to choose between the temptations of the world and the joys of eternal life, the courtly poets created an ideal which claimed that the demands of both aspects of life could be satisfied. This was clearly meant primarily as a justification of aristocratic court culture in the face of Christian criticism. It is equally clear that a new foundation for lay ethics was laid by the attempt of the poets to integrate the social etiquette and worldly values of the secular nobility into an idealized courtly image that also embraced the traditional ideas of virtue and took seriously the commandments of the Christian religion.

IDEAL AND REALITY

The courtly ideal of knighthood and the social reality of noble life stood in glaring contrast. This discrepancy between the lofty moral claim attached to the title of knight and the experience of real life was seen most clearly by clerics who knew court life and court society from personal experience. Peter of Blois (d. after 1204) was engaged as a princely tutor at the royal court in Sicily, and as court chaplain he belonged to the inner circle around the English King Henry II. In a letter (no. 94) to the archdeacon John, he wrote: "Today the order of knighthood consists of not keeping order. For he who most pollutes his mouth with filthy words, who swears most abominably, who fears God the least, who despises the servants of God, who does not honor the Church, that man is today considered the bravest and most renowned among the knights."[117]

> In former days the knights pledged themselves by the bond of oath to stand up for public order, not to flee in battle, and to give their life for the common good. Even today the knights receive their swords from the altar in order to pledge that they are sons of the Church, and that they have received the sword for the honor of the priests, the protection of the poor, the punishment of the evildoers, and the liberation of the homeland. But this has now turned into the opposite. For as soon as they have been decorated with the belt of knighthood, they rise up against the anointed of the Lord and rage violently in the estate of the crucified. They plunder and despoil the poor servants of Christ, and, what is worse, they oppress mercilessly the wretched and satiate with the pain of others their own forbidden pleasures and unnatural desires.[118]

"Those who should prove their strength in fighting the enemies of the cross of Christ prefer to battle their drunkenness, they indulge in doing nothing, are enfeebled by gluttony, and by spending their degenerate lives in uncleanness they dishonor the name and the duties of knighthood."[119]

If our knights are obliged to go on a campaign, the packhorses are loaded not with weapons but with (wine) skins, not with lances but with cheese, not with swords but with skins, not with spears but with spits. One would think they are going to a banquet, not to war. They carry beautifully gilded shields with them and are more intent on the booty of the enemy than on fighting him; their shields they bring back, so to speak, in a maidenly and untouched condition. They have war scenes and knightly battles painted on their saddles and shields, so that through these imaginary visions they might enjoy the battles they do not dare to engage in or watch in real life.[120]

The one-sidedness of the clerical perspective that emerges here should not lead us to diminish the value of this testimony. Peter of Blois's judgment is confirmed by other contemporary statements, and it was not only the clerics who thought this way. The poets themselves made their listeners aware of the gap between the ideal and the reality of their own day by transferring their poetic vision of knighthood into a distant past, into the time when King Arthur and the knights of the Round Table were alive. On the other hand, one cannot overlook the fact that the courtly ideal of knighthood was also meant as an appeal to live up to it. The poetic descriptions were obviously not intended solely for the literary enjoyment of the noble audience, but wanted also to influence social practices. Whether they succeeded in doing so is difficult to determine. We can indicate, however, those spheres of real life where the idealized demands were used as practical guidelines. That was the case especially in the education of young noblemen.

The education of the nobility   We know little about the education of the nobility. To some extent the reason for this is that the historical evidence has not yet been assembled and analyzed with sufficient thoroughness. It is characteristic for the state of scholarship in this area that the most extensive information for Germany is in Georg Zappert's 1858 essay "Über ein für den Jugendunterricht Kaiser Maximilian's I. abgefaßtes lateinisches Gesprächsbüchlein" ("About a Latin conversation booklet written for the education of young Emperor Maximilian I"). The literary evidence also awaits a critical examination. Both historical and literary sources depict the education of young noblemen as consisting primarily of physical training through athletic exercises and the practicing of horsemanship and knightly fighting techniques. For example, we are told the following about the education of the future Abbot Hugh of Cluny (d. 1109): "His father, wishing for an heir to his temporal possessions, destined his son for worldly knighthood. While the latter was still a youngster, he urged him on to ride with other boys of his age, to wheel the horse about in a circle, to wield the lance, to carry around the shield effortlessly, and—what he abhorred most—to pursue plunder and booty."[121] If the father did not take on the task himself, the knightly education was placed into the hands of an experienced fighter. Emperor Otto III was trained in the use of arms by Count Hoico, Emperor Henry VI probably by Heinrich von Kalden, a member of the family of imperial ministerials von Pappenheim. It was rather unusual for young noblemen to be instructed in worldly skills by an ecclesiastical lord, as we hear of Abbot Notker of St. Gall (d. 975), who "gave a strict education"[122] to the sons of his noble vassals.

There is abundant evidence that young noblemen were sent to other courts to be educated. The *Historia Welforum* says about Duke Welf V (d. 1120): "He maintained his house in the best order, which was why the noblest families of both duchies eagerly entrusted their sons to him to be educated."[123] Next to athletic and military exercises, the acquisition of courtly manners played an important role. Count Baldwin V of Hainaut (d. 1195) sent his son to the German imperial court that he might "learn the German language and the customs of the court."[124] At court the young noblemen served as pages and squires, as Ulrich von Liechtenstein described (*Frauendienst* 26.1 ff.). According to the Bavarian Court Rule of 1294, "eight young lords"[125] were to serve at court at all times; these were "noble children from the land"[126] whose duties included "serving us [the dukes] at table."[127] Young Count Arnald of Guines was sent to be educated at the court of his feudal lords, the counts of Flanders, "to learn the customs of the court and to be thoroughly accustomed to and acquainted with the knightly duties."[128] These two aspects of the knightly education—the teachings of knighthood and the teachings of the court—also determined young Parzival's training at the court of Prince Gurnemanz of Graharz, which was divided into a theoretical and a practical part. Gurnemanz began his instruction with an appeal to *schame*, "purity of mind" (W. v. Eschenbach, *Parzival* 170.15 ff.). Then he turned to the future ruler in Parzival ("you may well be ruler of a people"[129]) and emphasized the Christian virtues of "compassion," "benevolence," "goodness," "humility."[130] Whoever acted thus would be blessed with God's grace (*der gotes gruoz*, 171.4). The largest part of the princely instruction was devoted to rules on the right way to practice generosity. A lord should be neither profligate nor stingy: "Give moderation its due."[131] The injunctions of

lordship were followed by the teachings of the court, which dealt with
the proper conduct within society and sought to prevent *unfuoge*. Here
we find admonitions not to ask too many questions, to give considered
answers, to grant surety to a defeated foe, and to wash after battle
(172.9 ff.). The most elaborate instructions to Parzival concerned social
intercourse with women and "noble love" (*werde minne*, 172.15). This
concluded the theoretical portion. The practical training (173.11 ff.)
was entirely aimed at practicing knightly fighting techniques. Parzival
had to learn to control the gait of the horse, to hold shield and lance
properly, and to unseat his opponent in the joust. The only thing unreal
in this description is the shortened time frame: fourteen days would not
have been enough to transform the Welsh bumpkin Parzival into a
perfect knight.

The training of the intellectual faculties is hardly mentioned in the
courtly-knightly educational program. Parzival apparently remained
illiterate all his life, and in this regard he was no different from most
members of the high nobility in Germany. Only those princes destined
to assume the royal throne were also given a literary and higher education; their teachers were usually members of the court chapel. Otto III,
for example, was taught by Bernard, the future bishop of Hildesheim
(d. 1022); Henry VI's tutors were Konrad of Querfurt, later bishop of
Wurzburg (d. 1202), and Gottfried of Viterbo (d. circa 1200), who dedicated several of his works to the emperor. In this respect other courtly
poets adhered less closely to real life, since they occasionally portrayed
their heroes as having enjoyed a higher education. Wilhelm of Orlens
began his school days at age five. Along with twelve other noble children the young prince was taught reading and writing (R. v. Ems,
Wilhelm v. Orlens 2744 ff.). As was the case in the monastic school,
instruction was in Latin (2745 f.). The emphasis was on grammar and
rhetoric ("speaking and reading books"[132]). Different tutors were
charged with teaching foreign languages to the children (2762 ff.). From
age eight on, Wilhelm learned knightly conduct and courtly manners.
This included the art of horsemanship and the use of weapons, and also
singing, playing chess, and hunting with dogs and birds (2773 ff.). For
his first foreign trip he was not only decked out splendidly; his father,
Duke Jofrit of Brabant, also sent along a complete book of ethics and
manners (3390 ff.). Wilhelm then spent several years at the court of the
king of England, where he waited on the royal table as a page (5246 ff.)
and read out loud from French books to the princesses and ladies-in-
waiting or sang and played with them (3918 ff.). He also found time to

learn how to fight in tournaments (3950 ff.), and was introduced to the rules of minne service (4010 ff.). At fourteen he returned to his country and was knighted. Characteristically enough it was the poets who had received a learned education themselves—Hartmann von Aue, Gottfried von Straßburg, Rudolf von Ems—who bestowed a thorough literary training on their heroes. Perhaps these poetic lords, who could read and write, seemed like foreigners to their German audiences. It was probably known that lay education was much more common among the French nobility than it was in Germany. Tristan, in any case, was described by Gottfried von Straßburg as a French lord, and Wilhelm of Orlens, too, was a member of the French high nobility. There is no indication that the Gennan listeners saw these heroes as an appeal that they should learn to read and write; or if they did, nobody did anything about it.

In twelfth-century France and England, an educated ruler was also expected to have a command of foreign languages. It was said that King Henry II of England "had a knowledge of all the languages that exist between the North Sea and the Jordan."[133] Emperor Frederick II, too, "knew how to speak in many tongues."[134] Count Adolf II of Holstein (d. 1164), who had received a clerical education, "was not only fluent in Latin and German, but knew also the Slavic languages."[135] Archbishop Christian of Mainz (d. 1183) "used the Latin, Romance, French, Greek, Apulian, Lombard, and Flemish languages like his mother-tongue."[136] King Adolf of Nassau (d. 1298) supposedly "knew French, Latin, and German."[137] The courtly poets picked up and elaborated on the idea that knowledge of languages enhanced a knight's reputation. Young Tristan was sent "to foreign lands to learn foreign languages."[138] As Gottfried von Straßburg describes him, not only could he speak Latin, French, and German, he also understood four Celtic and two Scandinavian languages (3688 ff.).

The uneducated German nobility also regarded cultured speech as a mark of a courtly upbringing. We learn this both from historical and poetic sources. Rahewin said about Emperor Frederick I, who had received no formal education: "In his mother tongue he is very articulate."[139] Otto of Freising has handed down an example of the emperor's eloquence. Once, when an embassy of Romans addressed him in arrogant words, he interrupted and spoke to them "in the Italian fashion in lengthy and circuitous periods," whereby he "demonstrated royal dignity in the modesty of his bearing and the charm of his expressions and responded without preparation but not unprepared."[140]

That eloquence was held in high esteem by the secular nobility is revealed by a statement in Berthold's *Zwiefaltener Chronik* about Otto of Streußlingen: "a grandiloquent man, a consummate master of worldly eloquence, whose prudence and council was highly regarded among the princes of the realm."[141] In the ideal knightly image of the poets, the courtly art of speaking also played an important role. The young noblemen had to learn "to speak in a courtly manner."[142] "Seemly words"[143] were seen as a mark of courtly education.

Only from literature do we learn that the training of musical skills was a standard part of the educational curriculum of the secular nobility. Of young Lanzelet we hear: "To play the harp and the fiddle and other string instruments, in this he was very skilled, for that was the custom in that land. At the same time the ladies taught him to sing joyfully."[144] A teacher was especially engaged to instruct Alexander the Great in the musical arts: "The second teacher he had taught him music and how to sing by himself."[145] Of course not every nobleman was educated in this way. But some of them apparently acquired considerable skills. As early as in the *Ruodlieb* we find the motif that the noble layman outdoes the professional musician in playing the harp (XI.37 ff.). At the English court young Tristan gained the king's confidence thanks to his enchanting music (G. v. Straßburg 3545 ff.). In the appendix to Ulrich von Etzenbach's *Alexander*, we even find the claim that only noble lineage enables one to play stringed instruments masterfully (1968 ff.). The singing and harp-playing king, who in the figure of King David played an important role in the medieval concept of the ruler (the David image also explains why in the Middle Ages the harp was considered a symbol of royal lordship), was not merely a literary creation. Emperor Frederick II "could read, write, sing, and compose cantilenas and songs."[146] Even in Germany in the twelfth and thirteenth centuries, many members of princely and comital families wrote and composed minnesongs, though their educational level probably placed them among the illiterates. This is proof that making music and writing poetry existed not only in the poetic world but had a place in real life.

Literature as model   If we seek to discover to what extent the principles of courtly education actually determined the practical behavior of noble lords, we must look first of all at the exercise of knightly arms and at conduct in war. There can be no doubt that many lords held personal bravery and the skillful handling of weapons in high regard and strove to acquire these attributes. The life of the English nobleman William

Marshal shows that a seasoned tourneyer could not only draw a handsome profit from his skills, but that his superiority in knightly combat earned him high respect in noble society. It is also beyond question that the knightly code of honor was sometimes followed in armed confrontations between peers. Though in most cases deceit and cruelty were the salient characteristics of feuds and wars among the nobility, there are also examples that rules of fairness were honored, and that knights were reluctant to attack an unarmed opponent or gang up on someone. There are also instances when vanquished enemies were spared, set free on their word of honor, and when prisoners were treated decently, even if these were probably exceptional cases. The honoring of legal ties and obligations was undoubtedly also regarded as a practical duty by noble society, even if they were not infrequently violated. Honesty and trustworthiness bestowed honor on vassals, ministerials, and feudal lords alike. Many historical sources confirm that the the virtue of generosity was sometimes displayed in impressive fashion during the courtly age, even though in many cases such virtuous behavior probably had a political motive or served to glorify one's name.

The adherence to courtly forms of etiquette does not have such clear historical proof. While the historical accounts of princely assemblies, court feasts, military reviews, diplomatic missions, coronation festivities, and weddings supply abundant illustrations for the development and display of a lavish protocol of state, they rarely ever cast any light on the more private expression of courtesy, as for example towards women. Among the few sources that do provide information about this side of social life is the report of the annalist Saxo about the events in Speyer during the war in 1130 between Emperor Lothair III and his Hohenstaufen enemy, Duke Frederick II of Swabia. The city supported the duke but was forced to open its gates to the emperor: "The wife of Duke Frederick, whom the duke had left behind as encouragement to the inhabitants of the city, and who was sorely afflicted by hunger and privation, was generously enriched by King Lothair with royal gifts and departed with her own troops."[147] Three year later, in 1133, the Bavarian Duke Henry the Proud captured castle Wolfratshausen, which belonged to Count Otto VI of Wolfratshausen (d. 1136). "However, when the wife of the count, who had been among the besieged in the castle, was led before him, the duke received her kindly and with comforting words handed her over to her father, the count palatine."[148] But before we regard such behavior as courtly treatment of noble ladies, we must

bear in mind that in both cases family considerations or political calculation were probably involved. The wife of Frederick II of Swabia
was the Welf Judith, the sister of Duke Henry the Proud, who was the
son-in-law of Lothair III since 1127. And the wife of Otto VI of Wolfratshausen was the daughter of the Bavarian Count Palatine Otto V of
Wittelsbach (d. 1156), who at that time was the only one among the
Bavarian magnates who supported Henry the Proud. Still, courtesy towards women seems to have been an attribute that also had practical
significance. In the spring of 1211, some of the leading German princes
assembled in Naumburg to confer about a rebellion against Otto IV.
Among the reasons given for the planned depositon of the emperor was
his uncourtly behavior: "There they took into consideration the
emperor's rude manners, which they considered little suited for the
imperial court, namely the fact that he did not honor ecclesiastical
dignitaries, that he simply and insultingly calls archbishops 'clerics,'
abbots 'monks,' respectable ladies 'women,' and that he looks down
on all those whom God has commanded to honor."[149] Even if at
Naumburg the archbishops of Mainz and Magdeburg in all likelihood
set the tone of the discussion, it is noteworthy that the secular princes
—the landgrave of Thuringia, the margrave of Meißen, and the king
of Bohemia were among the conspirators—also supported such a justification (provided the account in the Erfurt Chronicle is accurate).
This presupposes that lay society, too, considered respectful treatment
of noble ladies as more than merely a theoretical concept.

It would seem that the norms of courtly behavior changed social
practice only partially and very slowly. That literature served as a guide
and model in this process can be seen from the changes in tournament
practice. The Round Table tournaments, which in the first half of the
thirteenth century displaced the older type of mass tournament, followed in the footsteps of the literary institution at King Arthur's Round
Table. Later we find "Arthurian courts," in which this tradition was
cultivated, in various German cities; there is historical evidence for the
first *curia regis Artus* in Danzig in 1350. In the thirteenth century,
Ulrich von Liechtenstein is the most important witness in Germany for
the effect of literature on the social festivities of the nobility. In 1240
he traveled through Austria in the guise of King Arthur, supported
along the way by noble tournament fans who had assumed literary
names (see p. 263). It is highly doubtful that Liechtenstein's peers
saw him as the fool he makes himself out to be in his ironic self-
portrait in *Frauendienst*. The great interest that his tournament jour-

neys aroused among the local nobility—there is no reason to doubt the factual accuracy of his story on this point—is an indication that festive occasions modeled after literary examples were very popular with the nobility. A basis in fact probably also underlies the knightly journey of the Bohemian nobleman Johann of Michelsberg (d. 1294) to Paris; according to the account of Heinrich von Freiberg, he undertook it in lavish fashion as "the new Parzival" (*der niuwe Parzival*, 178). On Whitsuntide in 1306, the knighting of Edward of Carnarvon, the successor to the English throne, was celebrated in great splendor in London. At the festive banquet King Edward I (d. 1307) made the solemn vow that he would defeat his enemies in Scotland and then journey to the Holy Land. "The son of the king, however, swore that he would never spend two nights under the same roof until, inasmuch as it was within his power, he had reached Scotland in fulfillment of his father's vow."[150] It is very likely that these solemn vows were inspired by literature. In any case, the oath of the prince is reminiscent of the public pledge given by Parceval at his departure from the court of Arthur, "that as long as he should live, he would never sleep two nights in the same inn until he had discovered who was served with the grail."[151]

Further evidence for the influence of courtly literature on the lifestyle of the nobility is that from the thirteenth century on noble families christened their children with names taken from courtly poetry (see p. 514). In addition, in the thirteenth century we find pictorial representations of literary motifs on tapestries, articles of daily life, clothes, and in large-scale paintings (the Iwein-frescoes in Rodeneck and Schmalkalden). The underlying motivation for their appearance was probably the desire on the part of the noble patrons to establish some kind of link between themselves and the literary events and personages portrayed. The French adventure romance *Blancandin et l'Orgueilleuse d'amour* (first half of the thirteenth century) recounts that the young hero of the story, who grew up without any knowledge of knightly weapons, noticed a painting of a knight in the queen's chamber: "In the chamber of the queen a curtain had been suspended; it was completely painted with knights."[152] The sight of this painting aroused in him the desire to become a knight himself: "Blancandin, however, ate little, because in his thoughts he was still with the knights he had seen in their iron armor painted in the room. And he swore by God that he would seek out all the adventures that existed, with jousting and tourneying."[153] In Thomasin von Zirklaere we encounter the notion that painted images had exceptional educational value for all those who could not read, primarily for children but also for illiterate adults: "Painted pictures often please peasants and children. Anyone who cannot understand what an educated man may learn from written texts should be content with pictures. The cleric shall read what is written, while the uneducated man shall look at pictures, since he cannot read."[154] This idea was very common in the Middle Ages. It could refer back all the way to Gregory the Great, who had written: "Pictures should be used in churches for the reason that those who cannot read should at least pick up by looking at the walls what they cannot read in books."[155]

Most difficult of all is the attempt to prove the influence of literature on the moral sense of noble society. All that can be clearly said is that the poets believed they exerted such influence. In the prologue of Wirnt von Grafenberg's *Wigalois* we read: "He who cherishes good poetry and likes to listen to it, let him now courteously keep quiet and pay attention: that is good for him. Poetry purifies the character of many a person, for he will easily find in it that which serves for his improvement."[156] In *Jüngerer Titurel*, too, the model character of poetry is explained:

> He who wants to exercise knighthood in knightly manner, in jest and in earnest, let him never tire of listening when someone reads aloud, speaks, or sings of it. This will give him more skill and courage than wrestling for fun with fools. Sweet courtly manners in speech and gestures, one should aspire to this, so that at court one can engage lords and ladies in courtly fashion. German books were devised with steadfast loyalty to impart virtues. Virtue and manliness one attributes to those great nobles who formerly strove with all their might for honor. Manliness, uprightness, decorum, moderation, and generosity, the refined upbringing of ladies: men and women then had their mind fixed on high honor. I think the same qualities still today bring high renown in the world. In this all noble people are instructed. This book does not teach anything useless. Of those who never listened to German read out aloud to them, one sees more and more coming to ruin.[157]

The ecclesiastical didacticians took a different position than the courtly poets. Thomasin von Zirklaere saw educational value in the courtly romances only when used in educating children: "Young noblemen should hear the stories of Gawein, of Cliges, Erec, Iwein, and from a young age on they should model themselves after Gawein's untarnished exemplariness. Follow noble King Arthur, he places many good teachings before your eyes, and think also of King Charles, the brave hero."[158] Alexander, Tristan, Segremors, and Kalogreant he would also recommend as models to young people (1050 ff.). But since poetry was prone to lying and falsehood ("The poems are frequently very nicely dressed up in lies"[159]), it was of value only for those who could not grasp true wisdom ("Whoever does not understand the deeper meaning shall read poetry"[160]). Yet in principle Thomasin affirmed the didactic value of courtly literature: "Even though poetry presents us with lies, I do not scold it, for it contains images of courtly education and wisdom."[161] "Even if the invented stories are not true, they do show symbolically what every person who aspires to an exemplary life should do."[162] A harsher critic was Hugo von Trimberg, who denounced not only the falseness of secular literature ("These books are full of lies"[163]) but also its poetic ornamentations: "Anyone who strives for unusual verses wants the glue of his artistic sensibilities to stick on the outside to beautiful words while inside there is little that is instructive. In Germany this has acquainted us with Erec, Iwein, Tristan, König Rother, Lord Parzival, and Wigalois, who have found great approval and high fame. Anyone who believes in this is a fool."[164] Hugo of Trimberg even believed that interest in such literature endangered the salvation of the soul: "The way I see it, the teachings of these German books has already cost many a man his life and soul, his possessions and reputation."[165] But this rigid attitude is unlikely to have been popular in lay society. Hugo von Trimberg himself—and this is especially noteworthy about his comment—attests that many nobles took the epic heroes as their models: "For many a man thinks he would be nothing if he did not become like the above-named heroes."[166] It is also significant that Hugo's condemnation was directed only against the courtly epics, whereas he attributed high ethical value to courtly lyric, and this included, remarkably enough, both the minnesong (he mentions Otto von Botenlouben, Heinrich von Morungen, der Schenke von Limburg, Gottfried von Neifen, Walther von der Vogelweide, and others 1184 ff.) as well as *Spruch* poetry (Reinmar von Zweter, Der Marner, Konrad von Würzburg, whose *meisterlîchez tihten* [1214] is praised): "He who esteems the songs of these poets and their noble and beautiful poetry will find virtue, decorum, and fame, wordly courtliness, and the teaching by which his life will become pleasing and offensive to no-one."[167]

Historical preconditions; the role of the court cleric   If it is true that the idealized image of the courtly knight fused traditional concepts of lordship, the religious idea of knighthood of the reform movement,

Christian ethical notions, and the modern code of good manners, educated clerics must have played a decisive role in formulating this ideal,
since only the educated had access to the various traditions. The importance of clerics and court chaplains in the rise of courtly culture was
recognized by Hennig Brinkmann and Reto R. Bezzola; recently
C. Stephen Jaeger has strongly emphasized this point.

The words "courtly" (*curialis*) and "courtliness" (*curialitas*) were
used from the end of the eleventh century to describe a special quality of
social behavior found among bishops and court clerics. Bishop Meinwerk of Paderborn (d. 1036) was "born of a royal family and through
the refinement of his manners was suited to royal service."[168] Cardinal
Guido of Crema (d. 1168) was "a man of illustrious descent, very courtly and honored, and of a pleasing eloquence."[169] Bishop Gardolf of
Halberstadt (d. 1201) possessed "inborn courtesy and extraordinary
magnanimity, and was decorated with the courtliness of his manner and
the utter refinement of his righteousness."[170] But there were also voices
that opposed the idea of praising an ecclesiastical dignitary for his perceived courtly manners. When the history of the abbots of the monastery of St. Bertin says of Abbot Leonius (d. 1145) that he "was educated
in courtly fashion and instructed in courtly manners,"[171] this was,
from the author's perspective, anything but a compliment. The reformist Cardinal Petrus Damiani (d. 1072) had, as early as the eleventh century, spoken of "courtly bishops"[172] who lacked true piety. When the
curialitas of an ecclesiastical lord was mentioned with approval, it manifested itself in high education, amiableness, eloquence, the beauty of
his outward appearance, and above all in his mastery of elegant manners. "Probity of manners" (*probitas morum*), "nobleness of manners"
(*nobilitas morum*), "refinement of manners" (*elegantia morum*), "elegance of manners" (*venustas morum*): these were the phrases used in
the biographies of bishops in the twelfth century to describe a new quality of social behavior. A model of courtly decorum was Bishop Otto of
Maberg (d. 1139), a member of the court chapel under Emperor Henry
IV and famous as a master builder.

> For in all his actions he possessed—and this seemed praiseworthy even to the
> pagans—as a gift from the Holy Spirit, as I firmly believe, an exceptional
> fineness and, I would like to say, such a noble and refined manner, that he
> never allowed himself anything unseemly, tasteless, or dishonorable, be it in
> eating or drinking, in his speech, in his gestures, or clothing. Rather, he
> demonstrated in every outward act an inner attitude distinguished by good-
> ness, learning, and prudent intelligence.[173]

Herbord wrote these comments before 1160.

Even before the middle of the twelfth century the new ideal of *curialitas* was also applied to people of secular rank. Ekkehard of Aura (d. after 1125) said of Count Conrad of Beichlingen (d. 1103) that he had been "one of the great lords, possessed of everything that enhances a person's dignity, that is to say, he was highly distinguished by birth, education, courage, and wealth, amiable and pleasing to all good people on account of his refinement and eloquence."[174] In the *Vita Paulinae*, written around 1150 by the monk Sigeboto, we read that the son of Paulina (d. 1107), the foundress of the monastery, had "shaped his character with courtly teachings and a certain splendid brilliancy to such a degree that among courtiers and men resplendant with worldly fame he committed no boorishness and seemed praiseworthy to all."[175] These words of praise adumbrate essential aspects of the courtly images of knighthood and lordship, upon which the poets later elaborated richly. But the ecclesiastical authors did not bestow courtly attributes without reservations. We learn this from the comments of Gerhoh of Reichersberg (d. 1169) about Duke Frederick II of Swabia (d. 1147), "whom we know as a courtly man, totally devoted to refined living, not to say: to the vanity of the world."[176]

Educated clerics were the authors of the first court manuals. This new genre begins with the *Disciplina clericalis* by the Spanish doctor Petrus Alfonsi, who was active at the beginning of the twelfth century. Here Alfonsi put together a complete courtly educational curriculum. To his son's request: "Dear father, give me the true definition of nobility,"[177] he responds by referring to Aristotle's letter to his student Alexander: "Take a man who is instructed in the seven Liberal Arts, educated in the seven wise precepts, and trained in the seven skills. This I deem perfect nobility."[178] The "seven wise precepts" (*septem industriae*) designated for the most part courtly rules of etiquette: "Don't be a glutton, a drunkard, a voluptuary, a violent person, a liar, don't be greedy or improper in conduct."[179] The "seven skills" (*septem probitates*) referred to knightly training and comprised "riding, swimming, archery, boxing, hunting, chess-playing, and composing poetry.[180] This fusion of knightly athletic skills with courtly manners and a literary education embraces central elements of the courtly ideal of the social person, which was first formulated in this work by Petrus Alfonsi.

As the twelfth century progressed, many Latin works in verse and prose appeared, whose subject matter was proper conduct at court and especially good manners at table. Best known among them are the

Urbanus and the *Facetus*. We still know very little about how these works were transmitted and how the various versions are related. What is clear, however, is that the Latin writings had a decisive influence on the first court manuals in French and German. In Germany the genre begins with a poem entitled *Der heimliche Bote* (dated 1170–1180), preserved only in fragmentary form. The first part contains teachings on minne, for which the unknown author based himself on the *Facetus moribus et vita* ("For the book 'Facetus' tells us sufficiently of good minne"[181]), while the second part addresses the knights with a doctrine of courtly etiquette: "If anyone does what I advise him to, his fame will be green and lasting."[182] A complete court manual in German was put forth by the Italian canonist Thomasin von Zirklaere in the first book of his *Der Wälsche Gast*. Thomasin tells us that this portion of the work was based on a text he had composed earlier "in the Romance language" (in *welhscher zunge*).

As tutors at court the clerics unquestionably exerted a significant influence on the social ideas of the secular nobility. Very widespread during the twelfth century was the idea that a knight could learn refined courtly manners and the art of love from a cleric: "By a cleric the knight was made into a minne servant."[183] This sentence comes from a poetic dispute between two young noble ladies over the question whether a knight or a cleric should be preferred as a courtly lover, a theme that was repeatedly treated in Latin and French poems of the twelfth and thirteenth centuries. Nearly always the decision came out in favor of the clerics, who in the eyes of the ladies (or rather in the eyes of the authors of these poems, who were clerics themselves) were distinguished by their refined manner, their cultivated speech, their affability, and also by their wealth and generosity: "We know that the clerics are friendly, charming, and kind. They possess *curialitas* and honesty. They don't know how to deceive and speak abusively. In love they have experience and diligence. They give beautiful gifts and keep their word."[184] Knights, on the other hand, were in these poems usually portrayed as uncouth, pugnacious, rough, and impoverished. But those ladies who preferred a knight as lover did list some of the positive qualities of knights: their courage, the splendor of their weapons, their willingness to serve; sometimes they were even credited with a higher degree of *elegantia* (*Carmina Burana* 92.16.3). This judgment was expressed most clearly in the famous letter of the thirteenth-century Tegernsee letter collection which ends with the German verses: *Dû bist mîn, ich bin dîn* ("You are mine, I am yours") (MF 3.1). The letter is a lady's response to a warning from her cleric friend and teacher "to beware of knights as though of monsters."[185] She assures him that she will guard against their courtship, but she does not want to deny the knights their merit: "For, as I would like to say, it is they through whom the laws of *curialitas* reign. They are the source and origin of all renown."[186]

2. THE COURTLY LADY

THE NEW IMAGE OF WOMEN

The ideal of beauty   "If I am to speak the truth, there never was, except for the majesty of God, anything as blessed as woman and her kind. This honor God has granted her, that she is to be regarded as the highest good on earth and always praised."[1] No one had ever spoken of women in these tones. In opposition to deeply embedded notions of the inferiority and wickedness of the female sex, the courtly poets created a new picture of beauty and perfection: "Look at her eyes and observe her chin; look at the white neck and note her mouth. She is truly created for love. Never have I known of anything so lovely among the ladies."[2] The poets' praise of beauty was not concerned with personal features of individual women but with an ideal that manifested itself in a fixed stock of attributes. In most instances the poets followed the precepts of rhetoric, which advised a description from top to bottom, from head to feet. The face provided the best opportunity for listing qualities of beauty: curly blond hair, a white forehead, eyebrows straight as though drawn with a brush, beautifully radiant eyes, small ears, a straight nose, the red of the cheeks sweetly mixed with the white of the skin, a red mouth, white teeth, a round chin, a white, translucent throat, a lovely neck. From there the description jumped to the white hands and the small feet; the shape of the body is mentioned only in general phrases. Arms and legs, if they are mentioned at all, are white, round, and smooth, the breasts small, the waist slim. In many cases the praise of physical beauty turned into an elaborate description of the clothes once the poet had reached the neck.

Physical beauty manifested the inner virtue of a woman. The minnesingers celebrated "all her good qualities and her beauty,"[3] "her beauty and her kindness."[4] The harmony of beauty and moral perfection was a central aspect of the courtly image of women. Beauty took a back seat to virtue only when the question was directly raised whether courtly perfection revealed itself more in the outer or in the inner qualities.

Such concerns are found especially with the ecclesiastical didacticians: "Beauty is nothing compared to goodness."[5] "A foolish man sees in a woman only the charm of her body; he does not see what virtue and good sense she possesses inside."[6] "Thus her outer beauty is nothing unless she is also beautiful inside."[7] Even the minnesingers sometimes stated the difference in a remarkably blunt manner: "Let no one ask too much about the beauty of ladies. If they are good, let him be content."[8]

As the embodiment of beauty and moral perfection the courtly lady fulfilled an important social function by transmitting the values she represented to a man:

> Women are definitely the source of all perfection and goodness, women transmit a virtuous disposition, women arouse great joyousness, women lead the wounded heart with gentle concern straight ahead on the lofty path, women break the chains of oppressive cares, women dispense sweet consolation, women call forth courage, women allow victory over the enemy, women are the full measure of goodness, noble women are a man's good fortune.[9]

A woman could fulfill this great task because she kindled in a man the power of high minne through her beauty and perfection: "Who gives the knights heroic courage? Who gives them good qualities? Who lets them attain courtly joy, if not the ladies' power of minne?"[10] "That knights live in knightly fashion, this they get from the ladies."[11]

The courtly image of women was an invention of the poets. The idea that noble lords adoringly looked up to the ladies because they owed them all their knightly abilities and social renown, turned the real relationship between the sexes upside down. In poetic playfulness, and undoubtedly for the enjoyment of their audience, the poets occasionally lifted the veil of literary fiction just enough to reveal that behind it was nothing except poetic imagination. Walter von der Vogelweide was a master at this game. In his song *Lange swîgen des hât ich gedâht*[12] ("I thought of keeping silent for long") he unmasks the unkind lady he has courted as the figment of his own imagination: "She does not want to look at me! She to whom I brought such honor that she is now in high spirits! As though she didn't know that if my song falls silent her fame will also disappear!"[13] The lady's renown exists only in the poet's song, so if he consumes himself in fruitless minne service she will have to "die" with him: "Her life is worth only as much as my life: if I die she is also dead."[14] Hartmann von Aue addressed the same point in his critique of the minnesinger: "You minnesinger, you will always fail. What gives you pain is empty imagination."[15] Neidhart used a different approach to expose the fictitious character of the courtly praise of woman: his knight Riuwental sings about the peasant girls he is court-ing as though they were courtly ladies: "I think no one in the world has found a more perfect girl; except that her little feet are scratched up."[16] Here we see clearly that the praise of women was a tool of poetic technique which could also be used for comic effect.

Women-worship and misogyny   The image of women constructed by the courtly poets seems like a counter-projection to the predominant tradition of Christian misogyny, which was rooted in the fundamental Christian rejection of and contempt for the world and its hostility to the body and the senses. For Christians, a woman was an object of venera-tion only in the state of untouched virginity, graced with the ornaments of chastity and purity. As a sexual being, however, she was accused of succumbing more easily than a man to the sinful desires of the flesh. Proof of this was found in the holy writings of the Bible, especially in the books of instruction of the Old Testament: "All evil is little against the evil of woman. . . . Do not look at the beautiful figure of a woman and do not desire to possess her when looking at her. Great is the anger of woman and her disobedience and transgression. . . . Sin originated with woman."[17] "I found woman more bitter than death: she is a trap for the hunter, her heart is a net and her arms are fetters."[18] "Three things are never satisfied: hell, a woman's desire, and land thirsty for water."[19] On the basis of such biblical passages, St. Jerome (d. 420), one of the Fathers of the Church, could teach: "All evil comes from women."[20] From this perspective one could interpret the story of the fall of man (Genesis 3.4–6): Eve's actions were seen as the manifesta-tion of female nature, of inborn disobedience and weakness towards the temptations of evil. The story of creation was also invoked as evidence for the inferiority of women, for it said there that God had created woman only "as a helper for man" (*ei adjutorem*, Genesis 2.18), which could be taken to mean that she was meant to be subservient and sub-missive. In the Epistles of St. Paul this idea plays a central role: "Wives should be subject to their husbands as to the Lord; for the man is the head of the woman."[21] "Woman shall be silent in the assembly; for they have no license to speak, but should keep their place as the law directs."[22] "A woman should learn in silence and with due submission. I do not permit a woman to be a teacher, nor must women domineer over man."[23] The ousting of women from Church office, from the teaching profession, and from public life in general found its biblical

justification in these sentences. Through the writings of the Church
Fathers ("It is the natural order among humans that women serve
men"[24]) this notion became a permanent part of Christian social doctrine. In the handbook of canon law, the *Decretum* of Gratian (d. circa
1160), it was codified: "Owing to her condition of servitude, woman
shall be subject to man in all things."[25]

Scholastic theology of the thirteenth century combined this outdated
Christian attitude with newly received Aristotelian physics, and this
made it possible to justify the inferiority of woman also on scientific
grounds. According to Thomas Aquinas, a woman was capable of trans-
forming nourishment into blood because of her moister and warmer
composition, but the further transformation of blood into sperm was
something only a man could do. At conception the male sperm was
the active element, the tool, while the mother's blood was passive,
material to be shaped. A man should actually always create male children, since every cause produced something similar to itself. Only if
"adverse circumstances" (*occasiones*) affected conception (if the sperm
or the blood of the womb was defective, or if moist southerly winds
gave rise to children with a higher percentage of water) was a girl
created. A girl was therefore nothing but a "misconceived male" (*mas
occasionatus*). Stated in more general terms: "Woman is an incomplete
man."[26] The incomplete nature of woman revealed itself, according to
Thomas Aquinas, in her diminished physical strength as well as in her
mental and moral inferiority: "Woman has by nature less of virtue and
honor than man."[27] Because of this deficiency a woman was more exposed to the sinful desires of the senses than a man: "In woman there is
not sufficient strength of mind to resist the desires."[28] This is why a
woman needed in every respect the guidance of man. Both in domestic
affairs and in social life, the following principle was to be observed:
"Woman is ruled, man rules."[29] The relationship of the sexes to each
other obliged a man to punish his wife, if necessary, "with words and
blows."[30] With instructions of this kind, Scholastic theology supported
the prevailing legal notions.

No less powerful was the profane tradition of misogynistic literature
based on the Roman classics. Virgil's famous verse was cited: "A fickle
and changeful thing is woman ever."[31] One read in Ovid's "Remedies
against Love" how to train oneself to feel disgust for women: "Whenever
you can, change the good qualities of a girl into bad ones and distort
your judgment a little bit. If she's plump call her bloated; if she's dark
call her black; if she's slim accuse her of being bony."[32] Juvenal's sixth

satire contained a complete arsenal of accusations against a woman's pride, arrogance, quarrelsomeness, deceitfulness, thirst for power, hypocrisy, and especially her untamable sensuality and licentiousness. It also criticized women who laid claim to an education and presumed to talk about literature: "Even more annoying is the woman who, when she has just reclined at table, praises Virgil and defends Dido's suicide, matches and compares poets, placing Virgil in one end of the scale and Homer in the other. Grammaticians leave, rhetoricians are vanquished, the whole crowd falls silent."[33] From such sources learned authors of the Middle Ages drew inspiration for misogynistic poems, excursuses, and tracts in Latin, which met with a good deal of success. This strand of literature would continue unbroken for centuries.

Condemnation and praise of woman was not as far apart as one might think. If one distinguished between good and bad women, one could praise some and denounce others; both praise and blame could be formulated in such a way as though the entire sex were meant. In his "Book of Ten Chapters" (*Liber decem capitulorum*), Bishop Marbod of Rennes (d. 1123) spoke in the chapter "About the whore" (*De meretrice*) of the "evil race, the wicked progeny"[34] of women, and in the next section "About the honorable woman" (*De matrona*) who was "more beautiful than silver and more precious than red gold."[35] From Bishop Marbod's pen also came devotional poems (*Huldigungsgedichte*) for great noble ladies of the time, in which we already hear strains of the courtly veneration of women. Of particular interest is the poem "To the English Queen" (*Ad reginam Anglorum, Carmina varia* no. 24)—the queen in question was Mathilda of Scotland (d. 1137), the wife of Henry I—which celebrated not least the physical beauty of the queen. Mathilda of England was also the recipient of a great prize poem by Hildebert of Lavardin (d. 1133), who also heaped poetic praise on her daughter Mathilda (d. 1167) and Countess Adele of Blois (d. 1137), the sister of Henry I of England. But Hildebert of Lavardin was at the same time the author of the very popular poem "How woman, avarice, and desire for fame are harmful to saintly men."[36] Here women are depicted as the ruin of society as a whole as well as of each individual man. Even more striking is the concurrent glorification and condemnation of women in Andreas Capellanus's Latin tract *De amore* ("On love") from the end of the twelfth century. While Book I, in the conversation of noble society, presents the courtly concept according to which woman "ought to be the cause and origin of everything good,"[37]

Book III is a lengthy compilation of female vices and embraces the entire stock of traditional accusations and suspicions.

Vernacular poetry, too, showed this double-faced character. Tileman Elhen von Wolfhagen (fourteenth century) recounts in his Limburg Chronicle that Lord Reinhart of Westerburg (d. 1353) recited in the presence of Emperor Louis the Bavarian (d. 1347) a song of insult on his lady, which opened with the words: "If I break my neck because of her, who will make up for the damage?"[38] The account in the chronicle then continues: "When the aforementioned Emperor Louis heard the song, he rebuked the Lord of Westerburg for it and said that he wished the lady to receive satisfaction."[39] And so the Lord of Westerburg sang as penance a minnesong in the courtly style of women-worship: "In wretched pain have I been rebuffed by such a lovely lady."[40] It seems the noble minstrel could choose at will between songs of condemnation and songs of praise to suit the wishes of the audience.

In fact, even in courtly poetry the negative sides of the image of women played a greater role than one would suspect at first glance. The new courtly image could blend surprisingly well with those old notions of female inferiority it appeared on the outside to contradict so vehemently. One qualification, however, needs to be mentioned in this context: the misogynistic strains of the Provençal and French poets were frequently muted or entirely eliminated in the process of transmission, with the result that the female image in the courtly poetry of Germany appears on the whole rather more positive. A typical example is the comment by Hartmann von Aue regarding the quick change of mind by Queen Laudine, who decided to marry the man who had killed her husband when the latter was barely in the ground. Chrétien de Troyes remarked at this point "that a woman has more than a thousand moods,"[41] and rebukes Laudine for "a fault" (une falor) she shares with other women: "Almost all act in such a way that they excuse their foolishness, and condemn aloud what they really want."[42] Hartmann von Aue referred directly to this passage: Laudine "just did what women are wont to do. From sheer moodiness they contradict what sometimes seems actually very good to them."[43] But then he rejects this reproach and thus goes directly counter to his literary model: "He does an injustice who says that this is caused by their fickleness. I know better why it is that one often finds them in such an unsteady mood: it is the result of their kindness."[44] Hartmann's argument is not very convincing. But it shows his eagerness to turn a criticism of women into the opposite. The reason is surely not that people in Germany in general had a more positive view of women; it seems that they were simply more interested in the idealized aspects of the female image.

Yet negative elements are not missing in German poetry. In the songs of Kürenberg, the first minnesinger known by name, we find a woman who tried to subject her man to her unbridled desires ("he must leave my land or I shall have him"[45]), and who cursed the beloved who stood at her bed at night without waking her ("may God hate you for it! I was not a wild boar, you know, said the lady"[46]). The latent undertone of mockery in these lines came out into the open if a man felt challenged to break the pride of a strong woman: "Woman and hunting birds can be easily tamed. If you entice them the right way they fly to the man."[47]

The first strophe of female condemnation in courtly minnesong was the work of Friedrich von Hausen (d. 1190), who followed the tone of the Provençal renunciation songs: "Nobody should accuse me of inconstancy if I hate her whom I previously loved. I would be a fool if I considered her stupidity as something good. That will never again happen to me."[48] Hausen found few imitators, and Walther von der Vogelweide's *sumerlaten*-song (72.31)—which threatened the hardhearted lady with blows "from young branches"[49]—also remained an exception. What set the tone in German lyric was the attitude of Reinmar der Alte, who suppressed lamentation over unrequited service because one should say only good things about women: "I could lament to you the greatest distress, except that I cannot speak ill of the ladies."[50] Only when a comic-satiric style prevailed in lyric through Neidhart's peasant songs, Tannhauser's minne parodies, and the autumn songs of Steinmar and Hadloub, do we find with growing frequency derogatory remarks about the whole minne business and about women as the representatives of that culture.

Courtly epic did not know such restraints. The depiction of women in this genre seems frequently more realistic, since the idealization of the courtly lady was more often blended with negative motifs. "Women are simply always women."[51] This profound statement was by no means meant as a compliment: "A woman seldom does what is best."[52] This same notion could be formulated even more sharply: "I have seldom seen a woman—be it maid or wife—who was without taint in soul and body."[53] Where a distinction was drawn between good and bad women, some poets believed that the bad ones were mostly in the majority: "It saddens me that so many are called 'woman.' They all have clear voices. But many are quick to deceive, few are without deceit."[54] "Wise Solomon says that among ten women there is barely one who is pure and truly constant."[55] Not infrequently we hear in courtly epics of Eve and her disastrous role in the "fall of man, and this provided an opportunity for unflattering comments about women in general, their moral weakness, their disobedience, and their lustfulness. Gottfried von Straßburg drew a connection between Eve's actions and the courtly notion of *huote*, the supervision of women: it was pointless to supervise women and prohibit anything, because that would only incite them to transgression. They rebel against every prohibition, "because that is part of their character and nature makes them do it."[56] A woman's greatest task, therefore, was to conquer her nature and become morally "a man": "For if, contrary to her nature, a woman is virtuous, and happily guards her name, her reputation, and herself, she is a woman only in name, but in character a man."[57] "A woman with a man's disposition"[58]: that was the highest praise for a woman that poets and chroniclers could think of. Only in physical strength should a woman not equal a man. Otherwise she would become weird and dangerous, like strong Brunhilde in the Nibelungenlied, who struck the fear of God into the heroes from Worms and was therefore cursed as the "devil's wench": "What now, King Gunther? We are done for! The woman whose love you seek is the devil's own wench."[59] And when on his the wedding night, Siegfried, despite the strength of twelve men that his magic cloak imparted to him, was about to lose the wrestling match against Brunhilde, wounded masculine pride drove him to the utmost exertion: "'Alas,' the hero thought, 'if I now lose my life to a girl, all women can forever afterwards take the upper hand with their men.'"[60]

The moral weakness of women reveals itself clearly when we read of tests of virtue. Emperor Focas invited the noble daughters of his land in order to pick one among them to be his wife. Most ladies were reluctant to accept the invitation: "Among them were very many who would gladly have missed the feast, since they had lost their virginity quite some time ago. Many enjoy their virginity for only a short time. And then there were many who had heard of the game of love and would have liked to have known it all if they had had a good opportunity."[61] When the ladies were assembled at court, Eraclius, who was to select the bride for the emperor, first cast his eyes on one who was still a virgin, but whose sole thought was of enriching herself: "that is evil and is called greed."[62] Then his attention fell on a lady who already had amorous relationships, and who immediately decided to betray her husband: "I will easily make an ape of him, my lord, no matter how smart he is."[63] Thanks to some special talent, Eraclius discovered in every single one "the vice" (*diu untugende*), however deeply it was buried. The depressing finding was that among a thousand noble ladies not a single one was worthy of the emperor. Eraclius dismissed the ladies with the dishonest excuse that he did not wish to honor one at the expense of the others, for all were equally worthy, and "even with the least of them, crown and realm would be in good hands."[64] Here the praise of women has become an empty phrase of courtesy, a lie.

Very popular in courtly epics were tests of chastity with the help of some magical clothes, a mantel or a glove that fit only the woman who was without fault, or a cup from which only she could drink who was completely pure. In France this theme had already been treated repeatedly in the twelfth century in bawdy comedies (*Du mantel mautaillié, Lai du corn*). In Germany the first example is in Ulrich von Zatzikhoven's *Lanzelet*. A magic cloak is presented by a sea-fairy to King Arthur as a gift, and all the ladies at court must try it on. On Queen Ginover, who put it on first, it reached down only to the ankles: though she had not sinned, she was guilty of impure thoughts. The other ladies fared much worse: on one the cloak stuck up in back, on another in front. The misogynistic tenor of this scene was further intensified by the fact that it was a woman, the messenger of the sea-fairy, who interpreted the results of the fittings in line with the traditional catalog of vices: one lady was too desirous of men, another gave in too easily, a third was unfriendly to her husband, a fourth was a gossipmonger, a fifth was simpleminded. In Heinrich von dem Türlin's *Krone*, the Seneschal Keie, feared for his sharp tongue, comments on similar proceedings and with mockery and contempt enjoys to the fullest the unmasking of the women. All these tests had the devastating result that all ladies at Arthur's court, who were usually portrayed as the embodiment of courtly virtue, were tainted and had violated the commandments of chastity.

Not infrequently, courtly epics recount that women were discriminated against, dishonored, tortured, and beaten. These motifs stood in strange contrast to this genre's "official" attitude of venerating women. But it seems as though the poets did not realize this contradiction. In matters of inheritance or the disposal of personal property, the inferior position of women was entirely normal. It would also occasion no surprise if women were treated as objects. Without male assistance they were exposed to the crudest injustices, as Cunneware had to learn. As the sister of Duke Orilus she was among the noblest ladies at Arthur's court, but she was brutally beaten by the Seneschal Keie, the highest court official, when she appeared to have violated a prohibition imposed on her: "For Keie the Seneschal seized Lady Cunneware de Lalant by her curly hair. He wrapped her long, beautiful tresses round his hand and held her tight as with an iron door-hinge. Her back was taking no oath, yet the staff came raining down until its swishing died away: it fell on her through clothes and skin."[65] At the Arthurian court nobody uttered a word of reproach about this abuse, except for the country bumpkin Parzival. Enite was equally helplessly exposed to the advances of Count Oringles after Erec's apparent death had robbed her of male protection. The count was so blinded by Enite's beauty that he wanted to marry her on the spot and threw off all restraints. When Enite refused to sit down to a joyous wedding feast in sight of her deceased husband's body, Oringles became abusive and violent and "beat her with his fist, so that the noble lady bled profusely. He said: 'You will eat now, wretch!'"[66] Criticism from his retainers he brushed off: "Their rebuke angered him. He said agitatedly: 'You lords, you are strange for rebuking me for what I do to my woman. Nobody is entitled to say anything good or bad about what a man does to his wife. She is mine and I am hers; how are you going to keep me from doing with her as I please?' With these words he silenced them all."[67]

Courtly epic offers an abundance of examples for the sheer limitless power of a husband over his wife. That a man would leave his wife in search of adventure, and that his wife would sometimes have to wait years for his return, was relatively harmless. A man could also lock his wife up and have her guarded, he could publicly mock and ridicule her, torture her with accusations. A husband could order his wife not to speak, a prohibition rendered most effective if violation was punishable by death, as happened to young Enite when her honeymoon at Karnant was barely over. Enite also had to endure patiently that her husband made her perform servile tasks and arbitrarily dissolved their marriage bonds. That she not merely put up with all this but actually approved of it demonstrated her virtues as a wife: "Whatever my companion shall do to me, I will bear it for justice's sake. If we wants me as a wife, a servant, or anything else, I am in everything subservient to him."[68] If a husband suspected his wife of infidelity, his punitive authority was unlimited. Duke Orilus tortured Jeschute with privation until she was completely withered and worn out and her dress was in tatters. When it turned out after a year that his suspicion was groundless, Orilus did have to admit that his actions were wrong ("I treated her improperly"[69]), but for his wife he had no word of apology or regret. The poets, too, criticized only the mistake Orilus had made, not his treatment of Jeschute.

Bodily punishment from the husband was also common on other occasions. Kriemhild recounts, not without pride, how Siegfried had exercised his domestic authority over her after she had publicly insulted the Burgundian queen during a quarrel in front of the cathedral: "I have regretted this ever since, said the noble lady. For Siegfried has beaten me soundly for it."[70] To let a woman discourse on the weakness of her own sex was a particularly effective narrative device: "A woman will easily say something she shouldn't. Whoever wanted to punish everything that we women say would have a lot of punishing to do. We women need daily forgiveness for our foolish talk, since what we say is often insulting, but without deceit, dangerous, but without malice: unfortunately we don't know any better."[71]

The ornamental and serving role of women   The ideal of beauty and virtue devised by the poets saw its richest elaboration when the emphasis was on the serving role of women within the festive society at court. At the great court feasts described by the epic poets, it was only the presence of many festively attired women that created the true atmosphere of high spirits, expressed by the word *vreude*. "And at court they experienced in every respect a dream life: many girls and women, the most beautiful from all countries, courted them and made life there very pleasant."[72] At the court feast of King Mark, everyone's attention was focused on Blanscheflur, the beautiful sister of the host (G. v. Straßburg 625 ff.). King Telion in Rome even put on several feasts during the year for the sole purpose of showing off the striking beauty of his daughter Beaflor (*Mai u. Beaflor* 13.12 ff.). The sight of festively adorned ladies was described by Walther von der Vogelweide:

> Whenever a noble, lovely, chaste lady with a beautiful dress and nice whimple enters a large gathering for entertainment, with courtly high spirits and with a retinue, looking about a bit now and then, as the sun outshines the stars, then May can bring us all his splendor: what is so lovely among it as her lovely figure? We leave all flowers be and stare at this magnificent woman.[73]

Courtly ladies had primarily representative functions at festive gatherings. They watched from the ramparts or from windows and bowers as the lords tested their mettle in knightly games; no doubt on such occasions they sent encouraging gifts to the knights. They participated in the courtly dances and games. They engaged in courtly conversation and let the men lead them to table in festive procession. Sometimes they greeted the guests and saw to their well-being. Once, when Kalogreant, a knight of the Round Table, sought lodging in a castle along his way, he got a friendly reception from the lord of the castle and his domestics. "When I entered the castle, I presently saw a young lady approaching, who welcomed me."[74] This young lady matched in every detail the courtly ideal of beauty: "In her I found joined intelligence and youth, great beauty and inner perfection."[75] The courtly maid took off the knight's armor and dressed him in a scarlet robe. Then she lead him into the garden: "She sat down sweetly next to me, and no matter what I said, she listened to it and responded kindly."[76] Sometimes the courtly tasks of a maid included bathing the knight and leading him to his bed.

On special occasions the ladies contributed to the entertainment of court society with artistic performances: "Now it happened often, when her father was in good spirits or when foreign knights were visiting the king at court, that Isolde was summoned to her father in the palace. And then with all her skill in courtly art and with fine decorum she entertained him and many others."[77] The princess commanded an extensive repertoire: "she sang, she wrote poetry, and she read out aloud"[78]; in addition, she delighted her father and the guests by playing on a variety of stringed instruments. King Telion was said to have let his guests choose the skill with which his daughter was to entertain them: "I will look to it that my daughter will read to you everything you want to hear in French. My daughter is very courtly. If you wish to play board games with her, she is very good at it, believe me. She will do anything you want when she keeps you company."[79]

Through their beauty, refined manners, and skills, ladies were to arouse in men the elated feeling of courtly joyousness or encourage them to minne service. How well minne inspiration could be combined with the decorative and serving role of a woman is revealed by the speech of Gyburg to her court ladies after the arrival of the French relieving army. For weeks the women had defended their city single-handedly against a superior force of pagans, and they were still dirty and tired from battle. Now a festive reception was to be arranged in honor of the princes of the army, which meant that the ladies quickly had to switch roles and take their place within the festive society:

Gyburg could now honorably lay aside her armor; she and her court ladies could clean off their armor stains. She said: "Fortune is a circle. For a long time worry oppressed me; this has now partly been lifted off my shoulders. All young ladies here, I urge you to put on your best dresses. Adorn yourselves, fix up your face and hair so that you look lovely, so that a minne-seeking man who offers you his service in return for love does not soon regret it but finds it hard to part from you. Before that there is something else you must do. Adhere to one rule of courtliness and behave as though the enemy caused you no suffering. Do not say much if they ask about your hardships, but respond: 'If you please, don't trouble with our tale. We have no reason to complain, for your comforting arrival has freed us from the enemy's threat. If you grant us your support we need worry no more.' Be obliging. No prince is so mighty that he does not like to hear the words of a maid. Wherever you sit, if a knight takes a seat next to you, behave in such a way towards him that he will recognize your virtuousness. Through a lover a man's boldness grows; the virtue of lady, however, gives a man high spirits."[80]

Rarely was it expressed more clearly to what extent passivity and self-denial were part of the courtly role of a woman. Female beauty and virtue were not values in themselves, but served to please and encourage men. Against the serious background of the pagan war the role of women in festive society strikes one as contrived and rehearsed. Just how brittle the foundation of these social conventions was in the eyes of the *Willehalm* poet is revealed by the fact that Gyburg herself did not follow the instruction she gave to her ladies: while the others feasted, she tearfully recounted to her father-in-law the horrors of war.

INSTRUCTION FOR WOMEN: UPBRINGING AND
EDUCATION

Because female nature was so weak, women had to be instructed and guided more carefully than men. The Church Fathers had already made this discovery, and in many writings they admonished women to remain chaste and warned them of the temptations of the world. The letters that St. Jerome wrote to various ladies of Roman society with advice about the education of their daughters were a prime source for the Christian concept of women's education. How relevant the ideas and instructions of the old Doctors of the Church still were in the courtly age can be seen from the tract "On the education of royal children" (*De eruditione filiorum regalium*) by Vincent of Beauvais, dedicated to King Louis IX of France (d. 1270). In the final chapters, the author compiled all that had to be considered in the education of noble girls. In doing so he could cite almost everything verbatim from the Proverbs of Solomon and from the Patristic writings.

The first commandment was that girls should be strictly guarded to protect their virginity. It was best to keep them at home at all times; on the way to church the mother should accompany the daughter. At home the girls had to be kept busy, otherwise they could get wicked ideas. They should work, pray, and study. Work meant spinning, weaving, and sewing: not fashionable, low-cut dresses, but robes of thick cloth which protected against the cold. Girls should also learn to read and should spend much time with the psalter and the Holy Scriptures. Furthermore, they must be instructed "in good manners and customs" (*in moribus et consuetudinibus bonis*). "Four things especially they should be taught and instructed, namely 1. modesty and chastity, 2. humility, 3. reticence, and 4. maturity of manners and gestures."[81] Modesty and chastity showed themselves by an avoidance of all unnecessary delights of the flesh. Girls should eat and drink only to satisfy their hunger; they should not sleep too much and should not bathe. On this point Vincent quotes from a letter of Jerome to Laeta: "I dislike baths very much in a grown maid, who must blush at herself and who should not see herself naked."[82] The greatest threat to the modesty and chastity of girls arose, according to Vincent, from their passion for worldly finery and from bad company. In their clothing they should avoid everything that might kindle lust; for the dress "is a sign of the soul."[83] They must not wear tight-fitting dresses with trains and slits, no silk or purple, and no precious belts and hair ribbons. Above all they were not to apply makeup or dye their hair: all this was the sinful work of the devil, because it falsified God's creation. Instead of keeping company with loose women and chatterboxes they should choose as their companions widows and maids of proven virtue. Humility, reticence, and decency of manners were displayed in social behavior. A girl should not talk or laugh much, she should dress plainly, possess a dignified walk, and above all should not let her eyes rove about. "Girls should maintain dignity in every gesture, but especially in their glances, for therein is clearly revealed their chastity as well as its opposite, licentiousness."[84] In a separate chapter Vincent of Beauvais compiled everything a girl should know to enter the estate of matrimony. Her parents must tell her that she should seek conjugal intercourse not out of lust but out of obedience and for the sake of procreation. The parents are further to instruct her on how to live with her husband: "To honor her parents-in-law, to love her husband, to rule the domestic staff, to govern the house, and to keep herself above reproach."[85] To show her love for her husband she should obey him, honor and fear him, strive to please him—both to enjoy his love as well as to keep him from loving other women—and bear patiently and lovingly his faults and mistakes. With a disquisition on widowhood and a praise of virginity Vincent of Beauvais closed this part of his work, which conveys an excellent picture of the kind of questions with which the education of noble girls was primarily concerned in the thirteenth century. Most of this reappears in the vernacular literature of the time. In Germany, Thomasin von Zirklaere wrote the most extensive treatment on the upbringing of noble girls in his *Der Wälsche Gast.*

How the upbringing of young girls was organized in practical terms is largely beyond our knowledge. As far as practical skills are concerned, their instruction was most likely in the hands of women. Literary training was normally entrusted to a court chaplain or a domestic tutor hired for that specific purpose. Alternatively one could place the young girl into a religious institution to be educated. In 1223, Ulrich of Dachsberg gifted a piece of property to the Chapter of Canons Regular in Understorf on the condition that his daughter Ottilia "be boarded [there] until she has learned the psalter."[86]

Needlework   Noble girls were supposed to learn how to spin and weave, sew and embroider, and no doubt they spent a good part of their lives engaged in such activities, even if they did not have to live from the work of their hands. The didacticians took it as a bad sign if a lady "hates the distaff, does not weave, spin, or spool," and only wastes her time "making herself nice and lovely and painting herself white and red."[87] Weaving, embroidering, and ornamenting clothes were considered honorable work even for great ladies, while the preliminary steps in the treatment of flax were usually left to the maids. The three hundred noble ladies in *Iwein*, who had fallen into the hands of a giant and had been locked up in a workhouse, had to perform all tasks themselves: "Many of them were busy producing everything one could make from silk and gold thread. Many worked at the loom, and their work was not shameful. Those who had no skill in this sorted the threads and rolled them onto spools; one beat the flax, another broke it, another hackled it; some were spinning, others sewing."[88] Of young Hugdieterich we are told that he managed to gain access to Hildeburg—whose father had imprisoned her in a tower—by disguising himself as a woman of many skills. For an entire year he learned from a master seamstress sewing and spinning, but especially all the art of silk-embroidery, the designing of figurative patterns, and the art of decorat-

ing with ribbons and braids (*Wolfdietrich* B 22.2 ff.). Some women
attained great renown in these skills (see p. 144). The *vita* of Empress
Kunigunde (d. 1033), written around 1200, reports that the empress
"was as experienced in grammar and the other letters as in the skill of
ornamenting ecclesiastical vestments with gold and gems."[89]

Literary and artistic training   It was not unusual that noble girls
learned to read and write; and in connection with this, not a few
women also acquired a basic knowledge of Latin, which enabled them
to read the psalter in Latin. Albert of Stade says that Hildegard of Bingen (d. 1179) "learned nothing more than the psalter, as was customary
for noble girls."[90] The *Landrecht* ("common law") of the *Sachsenspiegel* lists those things that belonged to a "woman's inheritance"
(*rade*): pets, jewelry, and "the psalter and all books which are needed
for mass and in which the ladies are wont to read."[91] The artists of the
thirteenth century portrayed noble ladies with psalter in hand, as for
example the Countesses Gerburg and Gepa in the west choir of the
cathedral of Naumburg. The poets, too, described them this way:
"Every night until daybreak, she reads in her psalter."[92] "She carried
a psalter in her hand."[93] "Kneeling, she read in her psalter."[94] To the
minne poets the constant preoccupation of the ladies with the holy
book was rather an annoying habit: "My heart's love, my queen, . . . do
you wish to become a churchy woman—a "psalter-lady"?[95] The precious psalters that have survived from the courtly age were probably for
the most part produced for women.

Women can be said to have possessed a higher education only by
comparison with lay society as a whole. They were almost entirely excluded from the learned education that was acquired through the study
of the trivium and the quadrivium. It is true that schools did exist in
convents, but in general their academic level does not seem to have been
very high. Apparently the nun's grasp of Latin was frequently so poor
that they had to be preached to in German. This had profound consequences for the emergence of a religious literature in the vernacular:
legends, prayers, and devotional books were translated from the Latin
specifically for a female readership. The abbess of Hohenburg, Harrad
of Landsberg (d. after 1196), who was herself superbly educated, not
only decorated her "Garden of Delights" (*Hortus deliciarum*), a book
intended for the instruction of her nuns, with many pictures, she also
provided the Latin text with over a thousand interlinear glosses, i.e.
with German translations of individual words; apparently she expected

the nuns to have difficulty understanding it. Despite these unfavorable conditions there were always a few highly educated women, not only in the convents but also among the great secular ladies. From the tenth century several members of the Saxon imperial house belong in this group; from the eleventh century the Empresses Gisela of Swabia (d. 1043) and Agnes of Poitou (d. 1077). In the twelfth century we also meet well-educated women at the courts of secular princes. Queen Judith of Bohemia, a daughter of Landgrave Ludwig I of Thuringia (d. 1140), was distinguished not only "by beauty and decorum" (*specie et decore*), but was also "very learned in letters and in the Latin language," which—as the author Vincent of Prague adds—"especially adorns the seemliness of noble ladies."[96] Unfortunately the historical evidence for the education of women in Germany during this period has not yet been gathered. Incidentally, the attitude of Vincent of Prague was not shared by everyone. In a French didactic poem entitled *Urbain le courtois*, a father gives his son this advice: "Don't take a woman because of her beauty, nor one who has "literary education.""[97] Phillipe de Novare, a renowned lawyer, advocated that women should not learn to read and write at all, since they use these skills to violate the commandments of chastity.

A woman should not be taught reading and writing, unless she wishes to become a nun. For many an evil has come from the reading and writing of women. There are men who dare to hand, send, or toss to the ladies letters full of foolishness and requests in the form of songs or poems or stories, things they would not dare to request and say verbally or pass on through messengers.[98]

Even if a woman had no inclination whatsoever toward evil, the devil would nevertheless succeed in bringing her to read and answer the letters. And then "the weakness of the natural constitution of a woman"[99] would give rise to a dangerous correspondence. It seems, however, that there were few who shared Philippe de Novare's ideas on this.

Closely tied to the literary instruction was the development of artistic skills. A courtly lady was expected to be able to play stringed instruments, to sing, and to dance. The game of chess and hunting with birds were also among the courtly arts. What the poets tell us about them is usually completely idealized. But Gottfried von Straßburg's account of the upbringing of young Isolde allows at least a glimpse of those elements of the educational curriculum that were considered exemplary. The princess had initially been instructed by a court chaplain; she had learned French and Latin (*si kunde franzois und latîn*, 7990), and had mastered several stringed instruments. "The talented girl also sang sweetly with a lovely voice."[100] To attain mastery in these areas, her advanced training was entrusted to a skillful wandering teacher (Tristan in disguise). In the literature lessons this new tutor placed the emphasis on applied rhetoric and had the young lady write texts in prose and verse: "She could compose texts and melodies for lovesongs and ornament her works beautifully."[101] In music lessons she practiced above all the modern French song forms and melodic types, which seemed to have been particularly popular with the courtly audience. "She fiddled her dance tunes, songs, and foreign melodies, which could not have been any more foreign, in the French style of Sens and Saint-Denis."[102] "She sang her pastourelle, her rotrouenge and her rondeau, chanson, refloit, and folate as beautifully as could be."[103]

Rules of behavior   An important portion of the education was made up of the rules of etiquette governing the social conduct of a young girl. Thomasin von Zirklaere tells us all the things that had to be kept in mind: "A lady should not jest willfully."[104] "A lady should not look directly at a strange man."[105] "A young lady should talk pleasantly and not too loud."[106] "Propriety prohibits all ladies from crossing their legs when sitting."[107] "When walking a lady should never bring her foot down too heavily or take excessively big steps."[108] "When riding a lady should turn forward towards the head of the horse and not sit entirely crosswise."[109] "When riding a lady should not stick her hand out from under her dress; let her eyes and head be still."[110] "A lady who has regard for propriety should not go out without a mantle. If she is not wearing an overgarment, she should keep her mantle together. It violates good manners if any part of the body can be seen uncovered."[111] "When walking she should look straight ahead and not around too much."[112] "A young lady should speak little if she is not asked; a grown lady should also not speak much, especially while eating."[113] A lady should accept only small gifts from her friend: gloves, mirrors, rings, brooches, circlets, and flowers (1338 ff.). "No decent lady should let herself be touched by any man who does not have the right to."[114]

Even more detailed were the instructions in the *Chastoiement des dames* by Robert de Blois (middle of the thirteenth century), who arranged his etiquette for women into twenty-one points: 1. On the way to church a lady should walk "with measured pace,"[115] neither too slow nor too fast; she should "offer a friendly greeting"[116] to the people she meets and should console the poor with alms or kind words. 2. "Beware and let no man touch your breast, except for the one who has a right to."[117] Only the husband was permitted to do that. "If he wants, let it willingly happen, because you owe him obedience."[118] The brooch had been invented precisely to keep a man from touching a woman where he was not allowed to. 3. Likewise a lady should not allow anyone except her husband to kiss her on the mouth. 4. A lady should guard her eyes and "not look at a man repeatedly."[119] Otherwise he might think "this was done out of love."[120] 5. "If someone asks for your love, take care not to boast about it."[121] To brag of love would be "boorishness."[122] 6. A lady opened herself up to reproach if she exposed too much of her body. "Some openly show their bosom, so that one may see how white their skin is. Another willingly displays her body from the side. Another uncovers her legs too far."[123] A woman who acts thus is called a whore. What a lady is allowed to show are "her white neck, her white throat, her white face, her white hands"[124]: from this one can tell "that she is beautiful under her robes."[125] 7. A lady who is concerned about her name should not accept gifts from a man, for such gifts "cost her honor."[126] Only relatives may present small gifts, "a nice belt or a pretty knife, an alms bag, a buckle or a ring."[127] 8. "Above all I wish to warn you, ladies, not to quarrel."[128] A lady who squabbles and shouts no longer deserves the name "lady." She "lacks good sense and courtesy."[129] 9. A lady should not curse; she should neither drink nor eat too much, for "there is no greater boorishness for a lady than gluttony."[130] "No lady who is drunk can have courtliness, beauty, and intelligence."[131] 10. If a mighty lord greets her, a lady should lift her veil and return the greeting. In fact a lady needs to be veiled only when going to church or riding through the streets. An ugly woman will wear a veil often, a beautiful one won't. 11. "A lady with a pale color or an unpleasant odor"[132] should do something about that. Good wine restores color, and a remedy against bad breath was "to frequently eat anise, fennel, and cumin in the morning."[133] 12. In church a lady had to be especially watchful of her behavior, since so many could observe her. "How one judges you in church, good or bad, is how one will always judge."[134] "One should refrain from laughing and talking too much in church."[135] 13. When the gospel is read one should rise; in the beginning and at the end a lady should "courteously cross herself."[136] 14. When service was over, a lady should let the mass of people leave first. 15. "If you have a good singing voice, sing out freely. Beautiful singing, in the right place at the right time, is a very pleasant thing."[137] But in a social setting one should not sing excessively, for "beautiful song is often boring."[138] A lady should groom her hands. "Cut your fingernails frequently,"[139] for "neatness and cleanliness are worth more than beauty."[140] 17. During a meal a lady should not laugh or talk too much. If she is eating with someone else, let her precut the best pieces for him. She should not put morsels in her mouth that are too big or too hot. "Everytime you drink, wipe off you mouth carefully so that the wine does not get greasy."[141] A lady should not wipe her nose or eyes on the table cloth, and she should not eat too much if she is a guest. 18. "Nobody will love or serve a lady who lies often."[142] 19–21. "Many a lady is so taken aback when she is asked for her love that she does not know what to answer."[143] This was no good, since it created the impression that she was an easy catch. If a man said to a lady: "Mistress, your beauty makes me yearn for you day and night,"[144] and if he described his lover's grief, let her answer: "I love him whom I am supposed to love, to whom I have pledged my loyalty, my love, my heart, and my willingness to serve, in accord with the laws of the holy Church."[145] She could also say that she would forgive his courtship if he never again spoke to her in such a manner. But she should say this in all seriousness and not laughingly.

Some didacticians conceded that it was not easy for a young lady to do justice to all these prohibitions that restricted her social conduct and consigned her to a passive role. If she talked, people said "she talks too much"[146]; if she kept quiet, it was said that "she does not know how to talk to people. This is why a lady sometimes does not know what to do."[147] She should keep the proper measure in everything and impose great restraint on her gestures and talk; "for nice gestures and good talk crown the behavior of a woman."[148]

Ethics   In the education of noble girls, a good deal of time was devoted to the teaching of ethics. A woman should subject her entire life to the norms of ethical conduct and should distinguish herself by "her high morals, her chastity, her good deeds, her uprightness and constancy, her praiseworthiness and courtliness, her good name, her nobility, and her virtue."[149] The ideal of female virtue comprised all the ethical values that were also binding on a courtly knight, but the accents were placed differently. For women, virtuous behavior meant above all keeping their good name untarnished, which was measured almost exclusively by their sexual conduct. Modesty, chastity, and purity headed the list of female virtues, followed by qualities of a rather passive behavior:

gentleness, modesty, mercy, kindness, and humility. At one point Thomasin von Zirklaere contrasted male and female virtues. "Falseness" (*valsch*) was deleterious for everybody, but "a lady should beware even more of falseness than a man."[150] Everybody should be "generous" (*milte*), including women, "though generosity is more fitting for knights than for ladies."[151] "Humility" (*diemüete*) was an ornament to men and women, "but humility suits ladies better."[152] "Courage" (*vrümketi*) was a male virtue. "Uprightness and truthfulness" (*triuwe und wârheit*) were female virtues. A knight should be on his guard against "stinginess" (*arc*); "a lady should be protected from inconstancy, dishonesty, and arrogance, that is a good thing. If she does not possess these virtues, her beauty is worth nothing."[153]

Philippe de Novare began his tract on ethics for women with the injunction that young girls must learn to be obedient, "since our Lord has decreed that woman should always be in submission and dependency."[154] Therefore "they should in their youth obey those who nourish them; and when they are married they are to obey their husband as their lord."[155] This French author also emphasized that some virtues had a different value for women than for men. Generosity was inappropriate for the female sex. Young girls don't need to give gifts, and for married women the situation was this: "If she is generous and her husband is generous, they will be left with nothing. But if her husband is stingy and she is generous, she will bring dishonor on her lord."[156] From this Philippe drew the conclusion: "A woman should not be generous."[157] Only the giving of alms should be permitted her. Philippe de Novare thought that women had an easier time of it than men. A man, after all, had to possess a number of virtues, he was supposed to be "courtly, generous, brave, and wise."[158] In contrast the perfection of a woman was essentially limited to a single issue: "If she preserves her body as a decent woman, all her other flaws will remain hidden, and she can walk with her head held high."[159]

Thomasin von Zirklaere held that in women moral qualities ranked above intellectual qualities. A woman needed only enough good sense "to be courteous and decent (*hüfisch unde gevuoc*). "If she has more intelligence, let her possess the propriety and wisdom not to show how much she has. She is not wanted as a ruler. A man should know many arts. The education of a noble lady prescribes that a lady who is decent and of good family should not possess too much intelligence. Simplemindedness suits the ladies well."[160] We encounter similar ideas, in connection with the notion (already documented in the Old Testament) that a woman's place was in the home, in a poem by Teichner (mid-fourteenth century): "It is unnecessary for a woman to talk much. To what end should she be able to talk? If she ensures the honor of the house, if she knows the Lord's Prayer, and if she reproaches the domestics and urges them on to proper conduct, she knows enough of speaking, and there is no need for the art of disputation from the seven higher arts."[161]

The moral instruction of noble girls was probably for the most part in the hands of clerics or those with clerical training. Not only in their youth, but later, as well, most noble women probably had more frequent and closer contact with clerics than their husbands had. We may assume, though this is difficult to prove historically, that the teachings of the Church were of greater importance for the self-perception of women, and that women moreso than men sought to live up to the ethical injunctions preached to them, if only because they were measured against them and because their standing within society was tied largely to their good name.

THE PARAMETERS OF WOMEN'S ACTIVITIES

The woman as ruler   To the end of the Salian period it was customary for the emperor to mention his wife as "co-ruler" (*consors regni*) in charters and official documents, and to describe his legal decrees as desired also by his wife or even initiated by her: "On the advice of our most beloved wife, august Theophano, co-ruler and consort in the emperorship and the kingship;"[162] "On the intercession of the most serene Empress Gertrude, partner in the royal highness and royal glory;"[163] "At the pious request of our most beloved consort Beatrice, Roman Empress and most noble ruler."[164] Such phrases were but seldom used by the Hohenstaufen emperors, and soon disappeared altogether. This change in language has not yet been sufficiently explained. It has been argued that it may attest to a factual decline of the political influence and public activity of female rulers. More likely the change in protocol mirrors a change in the concept of lordship. Whereas in Carolingian times the realm was seen virtually as the private possession of the ruling house, in the High Middle Ages the institutional character of lordship came more to the fore. The result may have been that in the language of protocol the familial motifs receded into the background. The wife of the ruler in the twelfth century was also called "Queen of the Romans" (*regina Romanorum*) or "Empress of the

Romans" (*imperatrix Romanorum*) if her husband had received the imperial crown. Circumstances permitting, the queen or empress was crowned together with her husband, though she received only the crown and not the other insignia of lordship. What happened at the royal coronation of Philip of Swabia in 1198 in Mainz was unusual: while the Byzantine Princess Irene was seated next to her husband on the throne, she was decorated only with a golden circlet and was not crowned herself. It is possible that in this case considerations of Byzantine protocol were decisive. When Philip had himself crowned again in Aachen in 1205, his wife received the crown along with him.

To what extent the queen would share in the rule of her husband depended for the most part on personal factors. The German empresses and queens of the twelfth and thirteenth centuries did not play as large a role in imperial politics as had their predecessors of the tenth and eleventh centuries. The primary reason for this is that the circumstances did not encourage a more assertive role. The majority of Hohenstaufen emperors were married to foreign princesses, some of whom, like Beatrice of Burgundy (d. 1184) and Constance of Sicily (d. 1198), held important positions of lordship in their own hereditary lands. Twelfth-century France had a number of prominent female rulers. Best known among them are Eleanor, the heiress of Aquitaine and Poitou (d. 1204), who as queen of England at times ruled her hereditary lands independently, and the Vicontesse Ermengarde of Narbonne (d. 1197). For decades two of the largest royal fiefs of France, Champagne and Flanders, were ruled by women. In the thirteenth century, Blanche of Castile (d. 1252), wife of Louis VIII (d. 1226), and Margaret of Provence (d. 1295), wife of Louis IX (d. 1270), had a decisive influence on the course of French history. In Germany, women exercised lordship largely in the context of regional history. Countess Matilda of Schwarzburg (d. 1191/92), the widow of Count Adolf II of Holstein (d. 1164), was a very energetic woman who during the minority of her son "wisely arranged the affairs of his house with full authority."[165] We are told that Duchess Elisabeth of Bohemia, the sister of King Bela III of Hungary (d. 1196) and wife of Duke Frederick of Bohemia (d. 1189), "ruled over Bohemia moreso than her husband."[166] After the death of Margrave Albrecht II (d. 1220), Emperor Frederick II appointed Archbishop Albrecht of Magdeburg (d. 1232) as guardian for his minor sons. Albrecht II's wife, Mechthild of Brandenburg (d. 1255), got rid of the archbishop by buying the feudal wardship from him for 1900 silver marks. And when the guardian for the dynastic possessions of the Ascanian heirs, Count

Henry I of Anhalt (d. 1252), renounced the exercise of his rights in 1225, Mechthild was able to rule the March all alone in the name of her sons. After the male line of the house of the Thuringian landgraves had died out, Landgravine Sophie (d. 1284), the daughter of Louis IV of Thuringia and St. Elisabeth, energetically and successfully defended, in years of struggle, her hereditary claim to Hessia against both the archbishop of Magdeburg and the margraves of Meißen. This historical evidence for the political activity of women in the German territories has not yet attracted the interest of scholars.

In France, women had the right of feudal succession to fiefs: in Germany they did not. Only to the Babenbergs did the emperor grant female succession as a special privilege when the duchy of Austria was established in 1156. In 1184 the same right was given to the counts of Hainaut and Namur, in 1204 to the dukes of Brabant, in 1235 to the dukes of Brunswick-Lüneburg. How strongly the princes were interested in this issue is revealed by the action of Landgrave Hermann I of Thuringia (d. 1217) when Emperor Henry VI offered the princes full hereditability of imperial fiefs in 1196. Hermann immediately decreed that his daughter Hedwig, still a minor, should succeed him since he had no sons at the time. No doubt this move was prompted more by dynastic considerations than by any desire to improve the legal position of daughters.

The history of the High Middle Ages offers much evidence that the right of feudal succession for women did not automatically give them a greater sphere of action. The greater the importance of the fief that fell into the hands of a woman, the greater the political interest directed at her. The French barons in the Kingdom of Jerusalem exercised their feudal right of wardship over the female heirs to the throne with exceptional ruthlessness. After the death of King Baldwin II (d. 1131), his three daughters ruled the kingdom in succession for over seventy years. The choice of their husbands was largely in the hands of the barons. When Sibylla died in 1190, her husband, King Guy of Lusignan (d. 1194), was deposed, since the right to the throne had passed on to Sibylla's sister Isabella. At that time Isabella (d. 1208) was married to Humphrey of Toron, whom the barons did not like. They forced the queen to divorce Humphrey and marry the man of their choice, Conrad of Montferrat (d. 1192), who only two years later was murdered by assassins. Her next husbands, Henry of Champagne (d. 1197) and Amalrich II (d. 1205), also died within a few years, so that at age thirty-one Isabella was divorced once and widowed three times.

When Sibylla of Palestine, after the death of King Baldwin V in 1186, asked the Patriarch of Jerusalem to place the crown on her head, he is said to have refused with the words, "I don't know why the crown should be yours, seeing that you are a woman."[167] The ecclesiastical prince was not the only one who held such an opinion. The annals of Prague tell the story of the origins of the house of the Premyslides and of Libussa, whom the Bohemian people had chosen as their ruler. But after a while the people began to speak disparagingly of her, saying "any woman is better suited for the embraces of men than for rendering justice over knights."[168] The *Rhetorica ecclesiastica* from the end of the twelfth century taught: "It is not the business of women to judge, to rule, to instruct, or to bear witness."[169] The German princes reportedly deprived Emperor Frederick II's widow, Agnes of Poitou (d. 1077), of the wardship over Henry IV, the heir to the throne, with the argument: "it is not right that a woman should rule the kingdom."[170] The author of the *Vita Heinrici IV* criticized the verdict of the princes by pointing out that "we hear of many queens who ruled kingdoms with the wisdom of men."[171] Such voices were rare. Courtly literature expressed the idea that women were unsuited for lordship in a variety of ways. Several stories recount how the hero reaches the land of a queen or princess who proves incapable of defending her realm against external foes. Our knight arrives in the nick of time to avert the decisive defeat and frees the lady from her distress. In most cases he then proceeds to marry her and takes over the governance of the land with manly vigor. The moral and social appreciation of woman could quite easily go hand in hand with a depreciation of her abilities as ruler. A woman should be beautiful and virtuous, but "she was not needed as a ruler."[172]

Among the few examples of positive depictions of female rule is Duchess Bene in *Wilhelm von Wenden*, who is offered the crown of an orphaned land after its nobility has exhausted itself in years of internal feuds. A perfectly realistic reason is given for entrusting the lordship to a woman: if she proves unsatisfactory she can be deposed again more easily than a strong man (U. v. Etzenbach, *Wilhelm v. Wenden* 4294 ff.). Bene's initial reaction to the offer is to declare her unfitness: "I am a weak woman. How could I be the ruler of the land?"[173] But after discovering that the princes' offer was quite serious, she accepts and proves to be an extraordinarily resolute and successful ruler. The poet describes in precise detail the various measures she takes to secure her lordship and pacify the land (4385 ff.). The first step is the promulgation of a general territorial peace and the restoration of her judicial sovereignty. There follows economic and financial decrees. To implement her decisions she reorganizes the court administration. Supervision of the administration of justice is placed into the hands of a judge suggested by the princes, who also functions as the chief advisor. Within a very short time, a land once shattered by internal wars is flourishing again, thanks to the superior exercise of lordship on the part of a woman. Since the figure of Duchess Bene was a tribute to Queen Guta of Bohemia (d. 1297), as the author made clear by equating the names *Bene = guote = Guta* (4667 ff.), it is not clear whether in this case nonliterary motivations determined the tone of the story. It is conspicuous, though, that the courtly poets used the image of the positive female ruler far less frequently than real life offered it to them.

This is even more noticeable in the case of military action. Our historical sources speak not infrequently of noble women who held their own even in war. In 1129, Marquise Sophie came to the aid of her brother, Duke Henry the Proud, "with eight hundred armored knights"[174] and took over the siege of castle Falkenstein for him. In 1159, Empress Beatrice led the knights she had levied across the Alps to reinforce the army of the emperor (Rahewin, *Gesta Frederici*, p. 602). In the year 1180, Countess Matilda of Holstein "tenaciously defended"[175] castle Segeberg against the assault of Henry the Lion. At Prague in 1184, Duchess Elizabeth of Bohemia and the burghers put up "effective resistance"[176] against the attacks of Wladislaw of Moravia. Yet the motif of the fighting lady is conspicuously rare in courtly poetry. It plays an important role only in Wolfram's *Willehalm*, where Marquise Gyburg and her ladies defend the city of Orange for weeks against the fury of a large pagan army. "Now lady Gyburg stood ready for battle with her sword raised high, as though eager to fight."[177] In other respects, as well, Gyburg transcended the narrow sphere of action usually drawn for women and proved herself in functions usually reserved for men.

From *Willehalm* we also learn that women sometimes had control of their own financial resources. Old Countess Irmenschart of Paveie, Willehalm's mother, hired a troop of mercenaries to support her son and didn't even have to clear this with her husband. Among her retinue was a merchant from Narbonne who functioned as her banker and who financed the entire equipping of the mercenaries (195.12 ff.). It was probably rare for princely ladies to have a regular income, unless they administered their hereditary lands independently. But it seems to have been customary that a certain percentage from tribute payments or other special revenues was expressly reserved for the wife of the ruler. When Siena did homage to Henry VI in 1186, the city paid four thousand marks to the king, six hundred marks to the queen, and four hundred marks to the court (MGH Const. 1, no. 313, p. 440). In the "Compact with the Count of Hainaut" (*Conventio cum comite Hainoensi*) from the year 1184, it was agreed that the count would pay a total of eight hundred marks in silver to Emperor Frederick I, his son Henry, and the court, and five marks in gold to Empress Beatrice (MGH Const. 1, no. 298, p. 423).

From literature we learn that queens also had their own court officials. A marshal of Queen Ginover is mentioned in *Parzival* (662.20), a seneschal of Queen Isolde in Gottfried's *Tristan* (8953), a chamberlain of Queen Beatrice in Rudolf von Ems's *Wilhelm von Orlens* (3856). We also hear that a queen occupied her own palace with her ladies (W. v. Grafenberg 222). In France the emergence of a court staff for the queen seems to have begun in the second half of the twelfth century. There is no comparable evidence for Germany.

One way in which women could have an effect on political events was through personal influence on their husbands. Historical sources rarely talk about this, while the poets used this theme more often. In both her marriages, Kriemhild brought up the most important decisions that required her husbands' consent in the conjugal bed: "One night, as the splendid lady lay beside the king and he caressed her in his arms as he was wont to do (for she was as dear to him as life), she was thinking of her enemies. She said to the king: 'My dear lord and husband, if you please I would like to ask you for something. . .'"[178] The poet did not comment on such bedroom politics, but his depiction probably strengthened the prejudices against women instead of dispelling them. It was exceptional for a woman's influence on her husband to be presented in a positive light. Such was the case with old Queen Isolde of Ireland in Gottfried's *Tristan*. She used the trust that her husband, King Gurmun, placed in her—he even allowed her to speak publicly in his name—in sovereign fashion by planning everything herself and carrying it out while constantly keeping in mind the interests of the entire realm.

What importance the Church attached to the influence of a ruler's wife is revealed by a number of papal letters to German queens. In 1208 Innocent III turned to the wife of King Philip of Swabia, asking her to prevail upon her husband to withdraw his support for Bishop Waldemar of Schleswig (Böhmer V.2, p. 1100). Surely the pope would not have taken such a step unless he thought there was a real chance of success. The notion that women were more receptive to exhortations from the Church was confirmed by experience. In the confessional of Thomas of Chobham from the year 1216, we read the following:

> The penance imposed on women must always be that they should be preachers to their husbands. For no priest can soften the heart of a man like a wife can. Therefore the sin of a man is frequently attributed to the woman, if through the negligence of his wife a man is not freed of faults. In bed and in the midst of his embraces she should address her husband lovingly; and if he is harsh and cruel and an oppressor of the poor, she shall move him to mercy. If he is a robber, she shall curse robbery. If he is avaricious, she shall arouse generosity in him, and she shall secretly give alms from their communal property. The alms that he neglects she shall give in full. For it is permitted a wife to give away much of her husband's possessions for his own good and for pious purposes, even if he doesn't know about it.[179]

Especially if the intent was to make a ruler lenient and conciliatory, it was believed that wives could exert considerable influence. There are many historical incidents where a vanquished enemy or someone who had fallen into disgrace asked the queen to intercede on his behalf, and apparently in many cases such intercession was in fact successful. This is why sometimes, if the ruler was determined to show no mercy, the supplicants were not even allowed to present their requests to the queen. Such was the case in 1162, when the Milanese surrendered to Emperor Frederick I and a festive procession of their envoys appeared in the imperial camp, each bearing a cross: "Hoping for mercy, however, they tossed the crosses they carried in their hands through the window grates into the chambers of the empress, since they had no access to her in person."[180]

In addition to the blamelessness of her personal conduct, a great lady's renown was measured by the extent of her charitable activities: "The magnitude of your intelligence, your noble character, your diligence, is revealed by your works, namely the various donations to monasteries and the support for clerics and the poor."[181] These words were addressed to Queen Judith of Bohemia, the wife of Wladyslaw II (d. 1175). The scale of pious donations by noble ladies in the twelfth century is best attested in the chronicle of Zwiefalten by the monk Berhold, who faithfully registered the monastery's property and its growth: "The chapel of St. Nicholas, an addition to the western end of the cathedral, was built by Countess Udelhilde of Zollern. For the chapel she also donated a chalice, a chasuble, a stole, and all necessary utensils. In addition she gave to the same church a homestead (*huba*) in

Stetten, one in Engstlatt, one in Hart, one in Streichen, and two in Thanheim."[182] "Sophie, the duchess of Moravia, sister of Richenza and wife of Duke Otto, donated a church banner, a white dalmatica, twelve curtains, six marks of silver, and much more, including also a reliquary box of ivory. Together with her sister Richenza she had the dining hall and dormitory of the lay brothers built from the ground up, and furnished it splendidly with her gifts."[183] "Setzibrana, a Slavic lady from Bohemia, sent to the heavenly Queen among other gifts a large tapestry of wool, onto which a depiction of the glory of the Lord and a portrait of Charlemagne had been embroidered."[184] "Gisela of Hiltensweiler, sprung from a free lineage, gave two homesteads in the village of Kohlberg along with the small adjoining wood called Bernbold."[185] "His [Bern of Dettingen's] wife Salome donated eight ounces of gold and a great amount of precious stones for the decoration of the cross brought to us from Jerusalem."[186] "The widow of Ulrich [of Gammertingen], Countess Adelheid, gifted to us two large linen cloths, in addition to other jewelry, which she gave away or made with her own hands . . . As long as she lived, she supplied us abundantly with grain and wine from the estates she had reserved for her usufruct, and the greater part of the convent for the nuns she erected at her own expense."[187] "Matilda of Spitzenberg, a sister of Count Werner of Frickingen, gave six homesteads in Burkhausen, that is to say, she gave the entire village."[188] "Matilda, the wife of Mangold of Sulmetingen, decorated a black chasuble most splendidly with broad gold embroidery, apart from other gifts she gave us."[189] "His [Duke Henry the Black of Bavaria's] wife Wulfhilde gave an ivory box, her red mantle for a hooded cloak, a blanket, also to be made into a hooded cloak, and a gold stole."[190] These examples from a very rich body of evidence also throw a light on the actual control noble women exercised over movable and immovable property. In courtly poetry the charitable activities of great ladies is mentioned for the most part only in passing. This is all the more remarkable, since we must assume that pious donations and charity towards the poor played an important role in the real life of noble women. Only their medical skills and knowledge were acknowledged by the poets.

The renunciation of the world   Many noble ladies unable or unwilling to marry entered a convent or joined communities of women living a religious life. This was frequently a question of providing for one's livelihood, but it appears that more and more women chose this path

out of an inner calling. From the end of the twelfth century there was a
steady rise in the number of women who demanded a religious life and
sought to realize the ideals of poverty, chastity, and the imitation of
Christ. Most of them found a refuge in the newly founded mendicant
orders. In the course of the thirteenth century about seventy Dominican
convents were established in the German region of the order alone;
some of them housed more than a hundred sisters. In addition there
were about twenty Franciscan convents. The new orders soon began to
resist this strong influx. Some women preferred to live a pious life in
Beguine communities, free groups without the protection of an order.
This thoroughly religious women's movement certainly had social
causes as well. It is hardly accidental that religious communities of
women were particularly numerous in regions with a richly developed
urban economy: Flanders, the Rhineland, and northeastern France. But
the argument that the movement grew from the social distress of urban
female workers is certainly not the whole truth. There is solid documentation that the women who desired to live in poverty included many
noble ladies, whose decision to renounce the world was not the result of
economic pressures, but sprang from a pious wish. How many of these
women were also motivated by a desire to escape a social order in
which they were in almost every respect disadvantaged and subject to
the arbitrary power of men, is difficult to determine. We can only note
that the religious life of women offered more room for self-
determination and self-realization than a normal life within noble
society.

An insight into the religiosity of women living in pious communities
without ecclesiastical organization can be gained from Jacques de Vitry,
who as an Augustinian canon at Oignies (near Namur), had close contact with the the Belgian Beguines. After 1213 he composed the life of
Marie of Oignies (d. 1213), who had been the spiritual leader of a
women's group in Nivelles. In the dedicatory letter to Bishop Fulques of
Toulouse at the beginning of the work, Jacques de Vitry depicts the
lifestyle of these "modern saints,"[191] who

> out of love for the heavenly kingdom despise the riches of this world, cling in
> poverty and humility to the heavenly groom, and gain their livelihood by the
> work of their own hands, even though their parents have an abundance of
> great wealth. These women, however, turned away from their families and
> their paternal homes, and preferred to bear privation and poverty rather
> than live in unlawfully acquired riches and remain in danger [to their souls]
> among the worldly people who love pomp.[192]

On a different occasion Jacques de Vitry says that the pious women "despise the riches of their parents, think little of proposed marriages to noble and powerful men, live in great and joyous poverty, own nothing except what they can acquire by spinning and the work of their own hands, and are content with simple clothes and modest food."[193]

Of great interest is Jacques de Vitry's description of different types of spiritual ecstasy in the prologue to the *vita* of Marie of Oignies. Some women lay in bed for years "sick with longing" and "had no other cause of illness except Him in desire of whom their souls pined away."[194] With others "the taste of honey from the honeycomb of spiritual sweetness in their hearts poured out so that they could actually taste it in their mouths."[195] And others, again, "were enraptured outside themselves in such great spiritual drunkenness"[196] that they lay like dead the entire day. These same forms of religious experience later shaped the religiosity of female monastic mysticism.

Some women encountered considerable difficulties from their families in trying to realize their desire for a religious life. One such case is recounted in the Life of Countess Jolande of Vianden (d. 1283), which Brother Hermann, who was well acquainted with the personal circumstances of the countess, composed in Middle High German verse probably soon after her death. Jolande was the daughter of Count Henry of Vianden (d. 1252) and his wife Margarete of Courtenay (d. 1270), who belonged to a family of the highest French nobility. Early in life Jolande took a liking to the religious life. At age twelve she decided to enter the Dominican monastery of Mariental (founded in 1232 near Luxembourg), just when the family council decided to marry her off to Count Walram of Montjoie, a relative of the counts of Luxembourg. Her mother got Jolande to participate once again in the entertainments of court life only by lying to her and promising that she would assist her in realizing her religious ambitions. "She sang, she walked, and she leapt in dance, but it was all against her will. No matter how joyous she was there, her heart was somewhere else. Her body could sing, dance, and leap, while her heart was troubled how she might carry out her good intentions."[197] The mother forbade all contact with the monastery and the Dominicans. Jolande faced additional problems from some female relatives of the Cistercian order who tried to win her to their own order. On a trip to Luxembourg in 1245, Jolande managed to escape her mother's supervision. In Mariental she cut her hair, took the vow, and was ceremoniously admitted into the convent. But with threats of violence against the convent, the count of Luxembourg forced

it to hand Jolande over to her family. Her mother took away the monastic garb and forced her to put on courtly dresses. Jolande now fell
seriously ill. Her brother Henry, the Cathedral provost at the episcopal
church in Cologne, came to Vianden and tried to talk her out of her
plans; but impressed by her determination, he came over to her side. At
great social events in Vianden Jolande was forced to participate and
perform in front of the guests. "She had to sing, and so it was: she sang,
she screamed, so that one could see flowing from her eyes the hot tears
which she could not restrain at any time. The good girl cried and sang,
and she walked like a nun. No matter how much one begged and asked
her, she did not dance the fireley. Her heart would not go along; her
walk disturbed the group dance, and she had to be excused."[198] The
family sought help in Cologne, from Albertus Magnus, who tried to
influence Jolande but eventually gave the advice not to force her against
her will. Meanwhile her fiancé, the count of Montjoie, was demanding
his bride or a substantial compensation. But he eventually found
another bride and abandoned the planned marriage to Jolande. All the
while there were repeated, unpleasant confrontations between Jolande
and her mother, who was carried away to uncontrolled outbursts of
anger. In 1247 a great family assembly gathered in Münstereifel, also
attended by the archbishop of Cologne, a relative of the counts of Vianden. Another attempt was made to persuade Jolande to change her
mind, but without success. Eventually the count decided to let Jolande
go to Mariental. But her mother remained opposed to the idea, and it
required further negotiations before she finally gave her consent as well.
In January of 1248—five years after she had decided to renounce a
worldly life—Jolande was taken to Mariental by her mother. She lived
there for another thirty-five years, after 1258 as the prioress of the
monastery, and was granted the joy of seeing her mother enter the convent. The fame of Jolande's holy life made the small convent known far
and wide. In 1283 she died there and was buried in the convent's
church.

Difficulties even greater than those experienced by Jolande of Vianden had confronted the English noblewoman Christina of Markyate (d.
after 1155), whose life in Latin prose was written around 1160 by an
unknown monk of the monastery of St. Albans. Christina came from a
well-known Anglo-Saxon family with large landholdings in the County
of Huntingdonshire. During a visit to the monastery of St. Albans as a
young girl, she made the vow to remain a virgin. Shortly thereafter
Bishop Ralph of Durham (d. 1128) visited the family. He took a liking to

Christina and had her brought to his chamber where he tried to violate her. "The lascivious bishop held the virgin shamelessly by one sleeve of her dress, and with his holy mouth, which normally said the mass, he tempted her to an abominable deed. What should the poor girl do caught in such distress? Alarm the parents? They had already gone to sleep. Under no circumstances did she want to give herself up. Neither did she dare to resist openly, for if she did she would undoubtedly suffer violence."[199] Through a ruse Christina managed to slip out of the room, but she had turned the bishop into her implacable enemy. In revenge he arranged for a young nobleman called Burthred to request her hand in marriage and made sure he obtained the consent of her parents. The family tried everything to talk Christina into accepting the marriage, and in a moment of weakness she agreed. She was immediately engaged to Burthred, but this did not change her attitude, and she remained determined "to let her neck under no circumstances be dishonored by the carnal embrace of a man."[200] Neither threats nor requests could change her mind. She was forbidden to have any contact with clerics and was even denied access to the chapel. Instead she was forced to attend public banquets and amusements, for it was hoped that she might thereby find enjoyment in the pleasures of the world. When this, too, proved fruitless, her parents—with whom Christina was still living—secretly admitted Burthred to her bedroom, "in order that he, finding the girl asleep, might suddenly overpower and violate her."[201] Christina, however, was dressed, and received her fiancé like a brother. She announced her willingness to follow him to his house as his wife, if he gave his consent that their marriage would remain chaste and that after a few years they would both enter a monastery. But the parents would have none of this, and they incited Burthred to try once more with force. This time Christina hid in her room: clinging with both hands to a hook and trembling with fear she hung between the curtain and the wall and was not discovered. At the third attack by Burthred she managed to escape from the room and scale a high fence. As the day of her wedding approached, she ran a high fever which could not be cured even by immersing her in cold water.

Eventually the matter was brought before Bishop Rober of Lincoln (d. 1123), who decided—incidentally without hearing Christina herself—that she should not be forced into marriage. A bribe by Christina's father made him reverse his decision and he declared that the marriage agreement was binding and that Christina belonged to her husband. But as Christina still refused to honor this verdict, she was treated at home like a prisoner. Her mother swore "that she didn't care who would violate her daughter if only she could be violated in some way."[202] Until the end of her life, Christina carried on her back the visible marks of the beatings she received from her mother. The author of her vita believed that two things could explain the behavior of the parents: one was their narrow-minded stubbornness, and the other was the fact that Christina was so remarkably intelligent, talented, and beautiful—"more lovely than all other women"[203]—that her parents were hoping to draw some material profit from her talents and wanted to see her exceptional abilities passed on to her children. By bribing the servants, Christina managed to contact the hermit Eadwin, who was to help in her escape from the parental home. Thanks to Christina's careful planning, the escape came off successfully. She first went to Flamstead to the female hermit Alfwin, where she had to hide for a long time in a small, dark room, because her parents were sending search parties all over, "who were to pursue her quickly and once they had apprehended her, return her with abuse, and kill anyone they found in her company."[204] Christina remained in Flamstead for two years. Then she moved to Markyate, to the famous hermit Roger, but there, too, she had to stay in hiding and live in extreme privation, since her parents and her fiancé had still not given up the search. After Roger's death she was hidden in different places but eventually returned to Markyate. Only after the bishop of Lincoln had died and Archbishop Thurstan of York had declared her marriage with Burthred invalid, was she able to continue her pious life as a hermit without any external threats. Apparently she never saw her parents again.

For most women, religious self-fulfillment could be attained only by rejecting the world and joining a religious community. But there were some women who tried to live their religious ideals as members of noble society. Duchess Hedwig (d. 1243), the wife of Duke Henry I of Silesia (d. 1238), and her niece, the Landgravine Elizabeth of Thuringia (d. 1231), aroused the amazement of their contemporaries by their saintly way of life. Both were canonized very shortly after their deaths. Everything we know about the pious lives of these noble women was written in connection with the canonization procedures and is therefore not without bias. But even a critical evaluation of the source documents that the religiosity of both women was characterized by a very personal engagement which also had to overcome opposition at the courts.

How courtly society looked upon the religious activities of noble women can be seen from Ulrich of Liechtenstein's *Frauenbuch*, where men and women hold each other responsible for the sorry state of their society. Women are told that courtly joy is gone because they no longer give men a friendly reception and want only to lead a pious life. Every woman is dressing and acting "as though she were a nun."[205] They pull the whimple down to their eyes and cover mouth and cheeks with the veil. And if a woman ever wore precious clothes, "the strip of sable hanging from her bosom had to be prayer beads."[206] One would think a woman like that "had entered the spiritual life out of pain."[207] Instead of dancing with the men, "you are seen in church day and night."[208] The women answer this criticism with the charge that men lack a courtly attitude. "You have given up the service of ladies and all you can do is brag."[209] Men are so rude and unfriendly "that we are afraid of you."[210] If a woman dresses up nicely and is attentive towards a man, she is instantly suspected of wanting to commit adultery. But if women try to embrace their husbands lovingly they are rebuffed by them. At the crack of dawn a man rides into the forest with his hunting dogs: "There he frolics the entire day and lets his virtuous wife lead a life without any joy."[211] When he finally returns home in the evening dead tired, "he stretches out over the table and his sole desire is that a board game be brought out. Then he plays half the night and drinks until his strength gives out. Then he goes to where his wife is still waiting for him, and she greets him with the words: 'welcome, my lord,' and rises courteously and courteously goes to meet him. But he does not respond and all he wants to do is lie down and sleep until morning."[212] Since her husband has no interest in her and since she is not allowed any contact with strangers, "there is nothing better for her than to devote herself completely with mind and soul to the service of God."[213]

If courtly poetry says little about the political influence of women as rulers, it says even less about their contribution to the religious poverty movements. It largely ignores precisely those spheres of real life in which noble ladies of the courtly age could achieve a certain measure of independence. The poetic ideal of women was not concerned with their possibility of self-realization. Instead, it was entirely in the service of a new concept of society that was focused on the perfection of the knight. A woman had her own place within this scheme only insofar as she fulfilled functions that furthered the perfection of a man: as the embodiment of courtly virtue, as a revered object of knightly minne service, and as the wife of a ruler striving for perfection.

3. COURTLY LOVE

Definitions   "Can anybody tell me what love is?"[1] The question as to
the nature of love became a central theme for the courtly poets. The
more they thought about it, the clearer it became that the human mind
alone could not fathom the mystery of love, which ruled over humankind with destructive power but was also the source of supreme happiness. "What can it be that all the world calls love? I do not believe that
anyone could find out."[2] Despite their diverse answers to the riddles of
love, the poets agreed on one thing: love was a matter of supreme importance in explaining the meaning of courtly character and courtly
perfection.

The phrase "courtly love" (*amour courtois*) was not coined until the
nineteenth century. Its creator was the French scholar Gaston Paris,
who in an 1883 essay on Chrétien de Troyes's "Lancelot" highlight-
ed four characteristics:

1. Courtly love is illegitimate, *illégitime*, and therefore necessarily
secretive. It includes total physical surrender.

2. Courtly love manifests itself in the submissiveness of the man,
who considers himself the servant of his lady and seeks to fulfill her
desires.

3. Courtly love demands that a man strive to become better and
more perfect in order to be more worthy of his lady.

4. Courtly love is "an art, a science, a virtue" with its own rules and
laws that the lovers must master.

This definition set off a great scholarly debate. It has been especially
vigorous in the last few decades, and an end is nowhere in sight. What
courtly love is seems less certain today than it was a hundred years ago.
Every detail and the very concept itself are disputed. It has even been
argued that courtly love is merely a figment of scholarly imagination.
Scholars are realizing more and more why an agreement on the concept
of courtly love has been so elusive: courtly literature has many different
depictions of love, and the variations have much to do with intrinsic
characteristics of the various literary genres in which they appear. Lyric,
epic, dawn song, minne canzone, crusading song, pastourelle, courtly
romance, rhymed story, and *Schwank*: each has its own kind of courtly

love. And within each genre the poets placed the accents very differently. Courtly love could be unrequited love or it could culminate in sensual fulfillment. Love could be directed at a lady of high nobility or at a woman of more humble descent. If the chosen lady was married, courtly love was adulterous in nature. On the other hand, love for one's own wife could also be courtly, as could the love between two unmarried people. Courtly love frequently demanded lengthy service by the man, yet sometimes it was quickly consummated without service. Most scholarly definitions of courtly love have to ignore some of these aspects for the sake of consistency. Unless we simply ignore these contradictions, it is clear that the phenomenon of courtly love cannot be satisfactorily grasped by concrete definitions, no matter how important they might be for a historical understanding of love. What remains as the one common characteristic of all manifestations of courtly love is still something very significant: the specifically courtly character of love, the fact that it is set within the framework of the poetic conception of courtly society.

Andreas Capellanus   At the center of the discussion about the nature of courtly life has always stood the Latin treatise *De amore* ("On love") by Andreas Capellanus, probably written between 1180 and 1190. Andreas tells us that he was "royal chaplain" (*aulae regiae capellanus*, p. 148), and this would place him at the court of King Philip II Augustus (1180–1223). The theory that he belonged to the court of the counts of Champagne, at that time a famous center of courtly and Latin literature, remains speculation. Capellanus divided his work into three books. Books I and II address the questions how to acquire and how to retain love; book III justifies why it is better to abstain from love altogether. The main argument against love was the alleged wickedness of women, which Capellanus proves with an elaborate catalog of vices. This change of attitude from books I and II to book III has been variously interpreted. Most scholars have been guided by the question in which part of the work the author expressed his personal opinion. Insufficient attention has been given to the fact that is was very common in the Middle Ages to examine an issue from two opposing viewpoints without presenting one as right and the other as wrong. Furthermore, Ovid himself, whose *Ars amatoria* ("Art of Love") influenced the basic approach of Capellanus's tract, appended a warning ("Remedies against Love" *Remedia amoris*) to his practical manual of love.

More difficult is the question what we are to make of the remarks on love in books I and II. In book I Capellanus defined and explained a variety of topics in the style of a scholarly treatise: "What love is" (*Quid sit amor*, chap. 1), "Between what persons love may exist" (*Inter quos possit esse amor*, chap. 2), "The origin of the word amor" (*Unde dicatur amor*, chap. 3), "What the effect of love is" (*Quis sit effectus amoris*, chap. 4), and so on. The learned character of the investigation could create the impression that the author was concerned with a systematic examination of love, and to this impression Capellanus's treatise owes its unique fame: it was, and to some extent still is today, regarded as evidence of a comprehensive theory of courtly love. If one wanted to know what courtly love was, all one had to do was familiarize oneself with the exposition of Capellanus. Almost all older scholarship took this approach. Only gradually has it become clear that the definitions and characteristics produced by this method apply to only a small portion of courtly literature. Modern Capellanus scholarship is dominated by the question whether the scholarly format reflects in any way a serious search for truth, or whether the work is instead ironic in character. More than half of the entire work consists of model dialogues between men and women of various social ranks, in which the man employs rhetorical devices in trying to seduce the woman into love and surrender. This fact alone is an indication that the author was less concerned with solving scientific problems than in presenting his theme in an interesting and humorous way to a court audience of clerics and educated laypeople. Some misunderstandings and mistakes in the interpretations of *De amore* have arisen because the pointed statements of the speakers have been read as the author's own beliefs.

In view of the existing scholarly disagreements all statements about the purpose of *De amore* can only be provisional. A new *opinio communis*, however, seems to be emerging in the view that the tract of Andreas Capellanus must not be read as a textbook of courtly love, and that the work is therefore of only limited usefulness in seeking to define the characteristics of courtly love. But this does not lessen its importance. No other literary work of that period gives us such precise information about the great role which discussions of love played in French courtly society of the twelfth century.

The idea of service   The great master of love, Ovid, had already taught that love was service: "Every lover serves . . ."[3] The troubadours and minnesingers elevated this idea to one of central importance. Certainly the most striking characteristic of courtly love is the peculiar setup of the minne relationship: man and woman do not interact as equals, instead the woman is a superior to whom the man looks up as a servant, and the deeds a man accomplishes to be worthy of love are seen as service. "From the moment I had understanding, my heart advised me to be in her service if ever I were to become a man. Now the time has come that I must serve her. So help me God that I might serve her well and suffer no sorrow from it. That splendid, noble woman, she is mistress over me and my heart. Is there anybody to whom I would rather belong?"[4] The duty of service to women held a prominent place within knightly ethics: "Serve them gladly, if you have any sense; you will live in higher honor for it. Blessed by God is he on whom their favor falls if he has served them honestly."[5]

The minnesingers served their ladies by composing songs in their praise. Service through martial deeds was the norm in epic poetry. Ulrich von Liechtenstein did both, at least according to his self-portrait in *Frauendienst*. Here he describes in great detail the life of a knight who has devoted himself to minne service. He travels from tournament to tournament to prove himself in service to his lady and in the hope of winning her favor with his knightly deeds. In addition he sends her every new song he writes in her praise. The humorous and ironical highlights in this autobiography of a minnesinger, coupled with the fact that it is composed entirely of literary motifs, would seem to indicate that the author was intent on bringing out the poetic and fictional character of the idea of service.

Ulrich von Liechtenstein never reveals the identity of the lady in service to whom he spent a large part of his life. But we can infer from his work that she outranked him in the aristocratic hierarchy (*Frauendienst* 18.5 ff.). Liechtenstein came from a ministerial family of Styria, and, according to his own account, at age twelve he was sent to a foreign court where he and other pages attended on the lady of the court (22.1 ff.). This lady he chose as his minne mistress and served her, as long as he was still not a knight, by picking flowers for her and drinking the water she had used to wash her hands (25. 5 ff.). Some scholars have maintained that this was the normal relationship, and that the concept of service can be explained by the fact that courtly love was always directed at a lady of higher standing. Some statements of the minnesingers would seem to support such an interpretation: "It is very painful when someone loves deeply in those lofty ranks where his service is completely despised."[6] "She rules and is mistress in my heart and is nobler than I am."[7] "I cannot resist her power: she is above and I am below."[8] But it is by no means certain whether "above" and "below" refer here to the social hierarchy. Where the poets describe the lofty standing of their lady in more detail, it becomes clear that they were thinking of courtly virtue and not of social rank.

Epic poetry confirms that the service idea was not linked to social rank. It is true that the lady was not infrequently of a higher social standing than the man. As lord of Parmenie and a vassal of the duke of Brittany, Tristan was not even a prince (though on his mother's side he was descended froom a royal family), while his lover was the queen of England and daughter of the king of Ireland. Gahmuret was the son of a king, but as the second-born he had no share in the kingship, and it was only through his marriage to the Queens Belakane and Herzeloyde that he became a king himself. Among the knights of the Round Table who attained kingship through marriage are Iwein (by marrying Laudine), Lancelot (by marrying Iblis), and Wigalois (by marrying Larie). But the opposite could also happen, that a man attached himself to a woman who did not hold a rank equal to his own. As the daughter of an impoverished count, Enite stood much lower than the crown-prince Erec. King Meljanz in *Parzival* even courted the daughter of one of his own vassals, Prince Lippaut. King Loys in *Willehalm* was married to the daughter of the count of Narbonne, one of his vassals. Notwithstanding such differences of rank, all these men and women were members of the exclusive circle of the highest nobility, and in this sense they were all peers. Marriages across class lines occur only in legendary stories (Hartmann von Aue, *Der arme Heinrich*) or in *Schwänke* (*Das Häslein*).

If minne service was unsuccessful, the minnesingers sometimes turned in anger from their lady, but only to offer their service straightaway to another lady, or—as Ulrich von Liechtenstein did for a while—to serve all ladies until they found one who would accept their services. Rarely was the renunciation of a minne relationship used as an occasion to question the idea of service as such. If it was, the poetic protest would criticize service for being one-sided and unrewarding, and it demanded instead a mutual relationship with the physical surrender of the woman. Here the social standing of the chosen lady played a role. In Hartmann von Aue's so-called "Song of displeasure" the poet responds to his friends' invitation: "Hartmann, let us go visit noble ladies,"[9] with the declaration: "I can have a better time with simple women,"[10] for they more readily obliged his desires: "What good is an unattainable goal?"[11] With the same question Walther von der Vogelweide justified his renunciation of service to ladies: "What good to me are those of the highest nobility?"[12] Following his new motto, "I will sing my songs of praise to those women who know how to show gratitude,"[13] Walther glorified in his *Mädchenlieder* young women who were not as "noble and rich"[14] as the courtly ladies of high minnesong. Instead of golden rings and gems they had only a "glass ring"[15] to decorate themselves, but they did bestow their favor on the poet. The interpretation of these critical voices, which incidentally had little appeal and could not damage the validity of the idea of service, is controversial. The emphasis was not on the differences of social rank between the poet and the *ritterlichen vrouwen* ("courtly ladies")—the poet, too, was a member of aristocratic society—but on the contrast between the cool ladies and the willing women of humble descent. This social typology also appears in the goliardic songs and the pastourelles. It was based on experiences in real life, insofar as it was difficult for women of humble social standing to resist the sexual advances of noble lords.

There were also minne relationships in which the idea of service played no role whatsoever. When Gawan arrived at Schampfanzun, the kiss of welcome from Antikonie initiated an immediate sexual relationship. The only reason it did not lead to physical consummation was the fact that they were interrupted by the entrance of a stranger. Wolfram von Eschenbach painted this scene with some ironic highlights, but he did not question the courtly character of this love affair. How the action unfolded when nobody interrupted is told in the first continuation of the *Conte du Graal*. Gawan was once again the hero, and his partner was in this case the sister of Bran de Lis. When she greeted Gawan, whom she had never seen before, she immediately offered him her love: "With a kiss he took possession of her. Then they conversed so much about love, about joyous conversation and courtliness, and laughed and joked sweetly until she lost the name of virgin."[16] Tristan did not serve Isolde before they became lovers, nor did Iwein serve Laudine, and in neither case did even the shadow of uncourtliness fall on their love. The clearest expression of quick love without service comes in Meinloh von Sevelingen, who is placed among the older minnesingers: "It cannot be called love if someone courts a woman for a long time. People will notice it and because of envy it will come to nothing. Indecisive friendship leads only to inconstancy. One must hurry to love; that is a good strategy against the guardians. To keep anyone from knowing before they have had their desire, one should keep it secret. Many who did it this way have succeeded."[17] These words, however, are fairly unique within minnesong, and this stanza can be properly understood only in relation to another stanza in which Meinloh has positive things to say about the idea of service: "Whoever wants to serve noble ladies must behave accordingly. If he knows how to behave properly towards them he must at times carry pangs of love in his heart; he may not tell it to anybody. Whoever serves ladies vigorously will receive from them a suitable reward."[18] Perhaps both viewpoints were discussed within noble society. Perhaps Meinloh's intention in contrasting these two approaches was to distinguish a correct and a wrong type of love. Be that as it may, in almost all cases where the nature of courtly love is explained, special importance is attached to the idea of service: "Who can have love without service? If I may tell you what I think, a man sins who carries off love without serving for it. He who strives for high minne must serve for it beforehand and afterwards."[19] In a Provençal *tenzone*, Guillem de la Tor and Imbert (Pillet-Carstens 236.8) debate the question whether a lady who leaves long service unrewarded is more lovable than one who grants her favor before she is even asked for it. Guillem de la Tor defends the proper attitude of service: "A true lover should not lose heart if his lady does not grant him her love right away, but he should serve, if he is generous and excellent, until the reward is given."[20] In *Tristrant*, Eilhart von Oberg recounts that Gymele, a court lady to Queen Isalde, rebuffed the advances of Prince Kehenis with these words: "Have you taken leave of your senses, that you ask me after so short a time for my love? It could not have escaped you that I am not a peasant wench. But I do think you are a peasant."[21]

Platonic and physical love   The idea that courtly love in its highest form was platonic was derived from the notion that the purifying and ennobling power of love could only take effect if a man's desires remained without final bodily fulfillment. The educative function of a woman and her unapproachableness were therefore closely related. Support for this attitude could be found in the troubadours and minnesingers, whose songs were filled with lamentations over the futility of their courtship. But above all one could invoke the words of Andreas Capellanus, who defined unfulfilled love as "pure love" (*amor purus*) and set it apart from the lower form of "fulfilled" or "mixed love" (*amor mixtus*). In his eighth dialogue, the lord of great nobility (*nobilior*) explains to his lady "that one kind of love is pure and one kind is called mixed. It is the pure love which binds the hearts of two lovers with perfect sentiments of joy. This kind consists in the contemplation of the mind and the affectation of the heart; it goes as far as the kiss and the embrace and the chaste touching of the naked lovers, but it omits the final pleasure, for that is not permitted to them who wish to love purely."[22] This love, our speaker continues, is of such great value "that from it arises all excellence of character."[23] Mixed love, on the other hand, is that "which gets its effect from every pleasure of the flesh and culminates in the final act of love."[24] Some scholars have tried to elevate this distinction of *amor purus* and *amor mixtus* to a kind of fundamental law of courtly love. They ignore the fact that the noble speaker in the dialogue uses these terms as part of his strategy of persuasion, the final aim of which is to seduce the lady into yielding to love. Characteristically enough the lady answered that to her these were "strange and unknown words" (*inaudita et incognita*), and that such pure love would be "considered unnatural by all people."[25] Furthermore, the fact that Andreas Capellanus in a different passage returned to these terms and declared that "properly looked at, however, *amor purus* in its essence is considered the same thing as *amor mixtus*,"[26] does not exactly indicate that he intended to establish rigid categories.

What Andreas Capellanus called "pure love"—a relationship allowing sexual contact but excluding complete surrender—is rare in courtly literature. A Provençale *tenzone* between Aimeric de Peguilhan and Elias d'Uisel (Pillet-Carstens 10.37) addressed the fact that Aimeric's lady had promised him a night with her if he were willing to be content with a kiss. The argument was over whether or not Aimeric should honor the agreement. A similar case was debated in a French "jeu-parti" between Guillaume le Vinier and Gilles le Vinier (Långfors, no. 129). A lady had promised her lover, as a reward for faithful service, to lie with him "totally naked" for one night,[27] but to go no further than kissing and embracing. The point of the debate was this: Who does more for the other person in the case of such chastity, the man or the woman? In German minnesong we find in Dietmar von Aist the idea of a "foolish sleeping together," which apparently referred to the same thing. As in Andreas Capellanus, it was the lady who rejected this kind of relationship: "What good was it that he lay with me like a fool? I never became his woman!"[28] In a different guise the idea also appears in Reinmar der Alte. In one song he says that he expects his love to remain unfulfilled, and he asks his lady if at least "once she could pretend as though it were real, and let me lie with her and for a while show me affection as though it were serious."[29] But such ideas always have something farcical and hypothetical about them.

In epic poetry the motif of chaste sleeping together is sometimes used

in a humorous tone. When Parzival and Condwiramus celebrate their
wedding, their inexperience keeps them from consummating their marriage: "He lay there with such restraint as would not suit many women
today."[30] The poet used his hero's behavior as an opportunity to vent
his spite on women who hid their desire for love behind social etiquette.
Wolfram contrasted this with the behavior of a faithful lover who finally receives his reward and who now, lying next to his beloved woman,
says to himself: "I have served this lady many years for her reward.
Now she has offered me solace, and here I lie. Once I would have been
content to be allowed to touch her gown with my bare hands. If I now
yield to my desire I would be disloyal to myself. Shall I exact it from her
and put us both to shame? Sweet words before bedtime best suit noble
ladies."[31] This attitude of the shy lover can be compared to what
Andreas Capellanus described as *amor purus*, but in the context of the
story of Parzival's wedding it was obviously meant to be funny.

In epic poetry courtly love almost always culminated in physical consummation. Unfulfilled love is the exception, as when the lady does not
requite the knight's love (Ulrich von Liechtenstein: *Frauendienst*), or
circumstances prevent the consummation (Konrad von Würzburg:
Herzmaere), or when death separates the lovers before they can yield to
their desire (Sigune und Schionatulander in *Parzival*). This motif was
more common in lyric. But few minnesingers professed such a self-
denying attitude as Reinmar der Alte, who persisted in loving adoration
of his lady even when there was no hope of obtaining his reward: "I
love her, and it seems to me that I mean absolutely nothing to her.
What's the point? I will put up with it and will remain sincerely devoted
to her."[32] Other minnesingers said bluntly what they hoped for from
the ladies: "The kiss of red lips, that is a joy to the heart, and along with
it the embrace of two lovely white arms."[33] Some poets dreamed of a
scale of love's pleasures: "Should it happen that you are successful and
a sweet woman grants your request, oh, what joys await you when she
stands defenseless before you: embracing, fondling, lying with her."[34]
The dawn songs and the *Frauenlieder* (women's songs) describe the full
enjoyment of sexual pleasure, and this dawn song love was no less
courtly than the complaints of the canzone poets about the futility of
their courtship.

High and low minne   If love became the object of reflection and one
wanted to fathom its inner nature, the approach was nearly always to
differentiate various kinds of love, usually good love and bad love. Fun-

damental to the medieval Christian philosophy of love was the distinction between "spiritual love" (*amor spiritualis*) and "carnal love" (*amor carnalis*), a distinction the Church Fathers had established. "That love which is false is called desire or lust: true love is called charity and love of God."[35] The difference between *caritas* ("religious love") and *cupiditas* ("sensual desire") remained fundamental for theological thinking during the High Middle Ages. "Love is a fire. There is good love, a good fire, this is the fire of *caritas*, and there is bad love, a bad fire, this is the fire of *cupiditas*."[36] "There are two kinds of love: one is good and pure and makes one cherish truth and virtue; the other is impure and bad, through it we are tempted to vice."[37] "A single spring of love arises inside and flows in two streams: one is love for the world, *cupiditas*; the other is love for God, *caritas*. *Cupiditas* is the root of all evil, *caritas* the root of all good."[38] When the poets for their part began to define true love, they referred to this kind of terminological differentiation. However, the theological duality "love of God"/"love of the world" played only a secondary role in courtly literature; it was used mostly by ecclesiastical didacticians. Lay poets employed it only in religious songs whose theme was the renunciation of the world and the abandonment of courtly minne service. The most powerful examples are Walther von der Vogelweide's songs of "Lady World" and Neidhart's songs of the "Sweetness of the World": "When I praise worldly love it pains my soul. My soul says it is merely a lie and foolishness. Only true love, it says, possesses perfect constancy; only it is good and everlasting. Walther, give up the love that condemns you, and cherish the love that lasts."[39] Crusading lyric also worked with this conflict of loves: the structure of many songs is such that the knight is caught between the demands of courtly minne service and the religious duty to fight for the faith. In Friedrich von Hausen, the first poet who used the crusading song, the decision already went against courtly love and in favor of the love for God: "I had lost my mind: love did that, it inflicts such distress on many. Now I will stick with God; he can deliver mankind from its woes."[40] Hartmann von Aue used the concept of religious love in his own crusading songs for a sharp attack on courtly minnesong as such: "You minnesingers, you will always be without reward. What harms you is empty fancy. I can boast that I can sing well of love, since love has taken possession of me and I of it. Why can you poor wretches not love such love as I do?"[41] But this was an extreme attitude that only a few poets advocated in this form. In many crusading songs the contrast between worldly and divine love was not set up as a sharp conflict, which enabled the idea to arise that it should be possible to combine both kinds of love harmoniously. The songs of Albrecht von Johansdorf are evidence of that. In *Willehalm*, Wolfram von Eschenbach gives, once again in the context of the crusading idea, an almost programmatic description of the harmonious fusion of courtly minne love and religious love of God. On the battlefield of Aliscans the Christians fight "for both types of love: for the reward of the ladies here on earth and for the song of the angels in heaven."[42]

If the poets tried to define courtly love, the contrast between worldly and spiritual love receded into the background. From the theologians the poets adopted the distinction between good love and bad love, though to them it meant not spiritual versus secular love but two kinds of worldly love. Good and bad love they defined as true and false love, as sensible and blind love, as high and low love. Particularly problematic was the question how to judge the obvious irrationality of sexual love. The courtly lyric poets described all the symptoms of the disease and the confusion of the senses that occurred in the service of love. Epic poetry knew many examples of a love that was blind with rage and destructive in effect: from the deadly madness of Queen Dido in Veldeke's *Eneit* to the foolishness of the great philosopher Aristotle, whose blind passion for the beautiful Phyllis made him trot around the garden as her riding animal, the laughingstock of the entire court (*Aristoteles und Phyllis*). Such blinding, confusing, and destructive love often became the target of bitter reproaches: "Love, you misfortune for all of us! The joy that you grant is so short, you are so very fickle. What is it that all the world loves in you? I see clearly that you repay her as a swindler would. Your final outcome is not as pleasant as you promise it to everyone when you entice them with brief joy to long sorrow. Your enchanting falseness, which surrounds itself with deceptive delight, deceives everything that lives."[43]

> Lady Love, your doing has always been deceit. You rob many women of their good name and prompt them to incestuous loves. Your power is such that many a lord has wronged his vassal, friends their companions, vassals their lords; your ways have become infamous. Mistress Love, you should be ashamed that you accustom the body to desires that harm the soul. Mistress Love, since you have the power to age the young when youth is already so brief, your works bear the mark of perfidy.[44]

To this blinding, lustful, deceitful love Wolfram von Eschenbach opposed "true love," love with *triuwe*: "True love is genuine *triuwe*,"[45] whereby *triuwe* means the absence of deceit and the sincerity of mutual commitment.

From the protest against blind and deceitful love arose the idea that proper love had to be controlled by reason. "To love wisely" (*sapienter amare*) became the aim, as the great noble lady (*nobilior*) in Andreas Capellanus expressed it: "There is nothing more praiseworthy in this life than to love wisely."[46] The rationalization of love, control of the emotions, and the sublimating of lust: these were indeed marks of courtly love. To attain these things it was good to approach love with scholarly methods, to investigate and organize this strange phenomenon, to find definitions and draw up rules. Courtly love was a science; one had to know its laws and follow its precepts. In the thirteenth-century French work "The art of love" (*L'art d'amour*), love was integrated into the system of the liberal arts. The author distinguished "liberal arts" (*ars liberaux*) and "nonliberal arts" (*ars non liberaux*), and he classed them according to whether the laws of the Church and the world permitted or prohibited them. Neither prohibited nor "prescribed" (*octroiees*) were, in the author's opinion, astronomy and the "art of love" (*l'art d'amours*): "She is not forbidden, for if she were, those wounded by love would not know where to look for healing and recovery, and would thus die or commit base sins against nature."[47]

In the end, however, there remained in love an inexplicable remnant which could not be unlocked with the tools of reason. One was forced to admit that there was always something irrational about love. As Wolfram von Eschenbach expressed it in the episode of the three drops of blood in the snow, "Lady Reason"[48] had to give way every time "Lady Minne" appeared and directed Parzival's entire thinking to love. In the French *Roman de la rose* the efforts of "Reason" (*Raison*) to influence the lover in his thoughts and actions were unsuccessful. The unresolved contradiction emerged very forcefully in the *Consaus d'amours* of Richard de Fournival. Here the love between man and woman was celebrated as "the root of all virtues and everything good,"[49] while at the same time it was said: "Love is a confusion of the spirit, an inextinguishable fire, an insatiable hunger, a sweet evil."[50] In the author's eyes the irrational nature of love was also revealed in the fact "that a king or a great lord will be seized by love for a low-born woman, that a poor man dares to love a queen and a common girl a king."[51]

The conflict between blind and sensible love, which so profoundly

influenced reflections on the nature of courtly love, was rarely formulated into a simple conceptual pair. If the poets wanted to describe the
positive and negative effects of love, they sometimes spoke of "high"
and "low" minne. Walther von der Vogelweide defined these terms in
his song to Lady *Mâze* ("Moderation") (46.31): "Low minne is the love
which so degrades that the body strives for worthless pleasure; this love
inflicts pain in a disgraceful manner. High minne encourage and makes
the spirit soar to high worth."[52] Scholarship has vigorously debated the
meaning of "high" and "low" in this context. If we stick to the reading
of the lines, it is clear that high and low do not refer in any way to the
social rank of the lovers. Nor is the conflict between sexual and platonic
love the main theme, even though the statement that low minne strives
"for worthless pleasure" (*nâch kranker liebe* 47.6) is undoubtedly a
reference to the sensual pleasures of love; we cannot infer from this,
however, that high minne had no physical consummation. The emphasis of Walther's words is apparently on the different worthiness of
love: high minne is aimed at "high worth" (*hôhe wirde* 47.9), low minne works "in disgraceful fashion" (*unlobelîche* 47.7). One type of love
elevates a person, the other degrades him. This is the most important
and most general statement regarding courtly love. Courtly love is a
value and a virtue, it dissociates itself from love without worth. "Where
the love of a woman increases the honor of the man, the woman and a
woman's love must be praised. But where a man loses honor and worth
through the love of a woman, there love is mixed with foolishness, even
if the man has everything else that I also possess."[53]

The courtly character of love (Love as a social value)   "Oh what a
wonderful thing love is, which lets people radiate with so many virtues
and teaches them such a wealth of noble morals."[54] On this point the
poets had no quarrel with Andreas Capellanus. The poets glorified love,
of whose dangers they had just warned, as the greatest worldly value
and the source of everything good. "Love is a treasure of all virtues."[55]
"From love everything good comes to us, love creates a virtuous
disposition."[56] Therefore love is the queen of virtues."[57] "A man becomes nobler than he is if he devotes himself to high minne."[58] "He
who wants to behave as love teaches, must refrain from everything that
is not good. This requires a constant effort and lasting attention to love.
Whoever wants to be among her retinue needs such an attitude that he
will do good with deeds more than with words. He may never break his
faith. Generosity and courage place themselves in the service of love."[59]

A love that made people better and more virtuous could not be a sin before God. "Love was never found among the sins. To a good man it can give true teachings. Many people say that un-love (*unminne*) is a sin. Love is free of all sins."[60] "He who loves as one should, entirely without deceit, stands before God without sin. This love ennobles and is good."[61] "Anyone who claims that love is a sin, he better think about it. Love possesses great renown, which one can rightly enjoy; and in her retinue are great constancy and bliss. She detests it if someone commits an injustice. I am not talking about false love, which is best called *unminne*; this love I will forever reject."[62] We don't know how such statements were received in their time. Their candor and confident tone indicate that the singers were counting on the audience's approval. But the clerics among the listeners no doubt crossed themselves when they heard that carnal love, condemned by a centuries-old theological tradition as *amor carnalis* and sinful lust, was elevated to something pleasing to God and the source of all virtues. More than anything else, this reevaluation of love reflects lay society's new demand that secular notions of the good things in life be accorded their own validity.

If courtly love was the "origin and cause of everything good,"[63] then the precepts of love were at the same time the precepts of ethics. "Love teaches great generosity, love teaches great virtue."[64] In *Jüngerer Titurel*, love was listed among the twelve "flowers of virtue"; courage (*belde*), purity (*küsche*), generosity (*milte*), honesty (*triwe*), moderation (*maz*), solicitude (*sorge*), chastity (*scham*), wisdom (*bescheiden*), constancy (*staete*), humility (*diemüte*), patience (*gedulde*), and love (*minne*; stanzas 1911 ff.). But courtly love was not only to guide the moral actions of people; it was also to impart the rules of social conduct. In the French *Roman de la rose* by Guillaume de Lorris, the god Amor himself announced the commandments of love, which everybody devoted to the service of love had to follow. First of all, the god demanded that all "boorishness" (*vilanie*) be kept from love. Let the lover follow the example of Gauvain, "who is praised for his courtliness."[65] He should be "pleasant and wise in speech,"[66] should not use ugly words and be the first to offer his greeting in the street. "Serve all ladies and honor them."[67] Their respect a lover must earn by deeds. "He who wishes to devote himself to love must cultivate a noble bearing;"[68] this included "beautiful clothes and beautiful ornaments."[69] A lover must find a good tailor who knows how to make sleeves "becoming and elegant."[70] He should frequently repair his boots and shoes, "and make sure they fit so snugly that the peasants will marvel how you get in and

out of them."[71] Gloves, belt, a flower hat, and a silk purse are also part
of courtly attire. Suitable attention must be paid to personal hygiene.
"Wash your hands, brush your teeth. And if a line of black appears
beneath your nails, do not let it remain. Lace up your sleeves tightly,
comb your hair, but do not apply makeup or paint yourself, for that is
suited for none but ladies and folk of ill repute, who through misfortune
have found a love contrary to nature."[72] In the service of love, "merri-
ment" (envoiseüre), "joy" (joie), and "delight" (deduit) shall hold
sway. Love "is a very courtly malady, in the midst of which one plays
and laughs and jokes."[73] It was a precept of love to be a good horseman, skilled at galloping and jousting; for "if you are beautifully
equipped with weapons you will be loved for it ten times more."[74]
Dancing, sweet singing, fiddling and flute playing all suited a lover well.
Great generosity, too, he had to show. "Whoever wishes to make Amor
his lord must be courtly and free of pride, gracious and merry, and
famous for his generosity."[75]

It may strike us as odd that this doctrine of courtly love addresses
none of the questions central to modern scholarship: whether the beloved lady is married or not, whether she is socially higher or lower in
rank, whether love cannot attain the final consummation: not a word
about any of this. Instead, what matters are tight boots and decorative
sleeves, clean fingernails, elegance and gaiety, and the art of elegant
speaking. The doctrine of courtly love has now become a social doctrine, and this seems the crucial point in trying to understand the nature
of courtly love. Courtly love was a thing of social value which manifested itself in the practice of courtly virtues and the adherence to
courtly etiquette. Courtly love was the love of a person who was striving
for courtly perfection. This idea appears also in Andreas Capellanus. In
the third dialogue a lady of higher nobility (nobilior) instructs a common man (plebeius) on what is demanded of him "who wants to be
considered worthy of serving in the army of love."[76] The first thing
she mentions is generosity. "It is considered a sign of great courtliness
and magnanimity"[77] if someone feeds the hungry poor. To his lord
he should offer due respect, and should honor God and the saints.
"He should show himself humble to all and stand ready to serve
everybody."[78] Let him disparage no man, "for evil tongues may not
remain within the house of curialitas."[79] Whoever seeks to love courteously should not mock anyone and not be quarrelsome. "In the presence of ladies he should moderate his laugh."[80] He should seek the
company of mighty lords "and should visit the great courts."[81] He

should pay little heed to the game of dice. "Let him study eagerly and take to heart the great deeds of the men of old."[82] He should be brave in battle, wise and cautious in dealing with his enemies. "He should not be a lover to several women at once, but should be a devoted servant to only one among all women."[83] He should devote only moderate attention to the adornment of his body and should "show himself wise and amiable to everybody."[84] A lover should not lie and should beware of excessive talking as well as excessive silence. He should not make hasty promises, should accept gifts with a friendly countenance, speak no ugly words, commit no misdeeds, be hospitable to all. He should say nothing nasty about the clergy or monks, but should render them due respect. He should go to church frequently and hear the Gospel of the Lord with a glad heart, "even though some people foolishly think that the women like it if they despise everything connected with the Church."[85]

Only the injunction that a man should not be a lover to several women at once was related in the narrower sense to how one should behave in love. Everything else was part of social teachings and courtly ethics. What the *plebeius* lacked for courtly love was *curialitas*, courtliness. That is why he was told to visit the great courts and learn refined etiquette. This bond that tied love to the court and to cultivated courtly manners explains why Andreas Capellanus pronounced peasants incapable of courtly love: "We declare that it is hardly possible for peasants to serve at the court of love; rather, they perform the works of love in a natural way, like horses and mules."[86] *Curialitas* ("courtliness"), *urbanitas* ("elegant deportment"), *probitas morum* ("refinement of manners"): these were to Andreas Capellanus the marks of courtly love. "The doctrine of love teaches us that no woman and no man in the world can be happy or attain *curialitas* or achieve anything good unless they are driven by the fire of love."[87] "For all *urbanitas* arises from the strength of the stream of love."[88] Through five qualities a man could win the love of a woman: physical beauty, refinement of manners, eloquence, wealth, and generosity. But only one of them, *probitas morum* (refinement of manners), made him loveable in the courtly sense: "A wise woman will therefore choose as a lover only a man who is distinguished by the refinement of his manners."[89]

Curialitas and *probitas morum* concerned not only the mastery of courtly etiquette, but everything that was demanded of a lover: constancy, honesty, devotedness, loyalty, chastity, selflessness, and patience. These terms are derived from traditional ethics. But in relation to love they took on a new meaning. Honesty among lovers did not exclude the possibility that they might deceive others in order to conceal their love. Constancy could mean adherence to a secrete relationship. Good sense in love might seem from the outside like total irrationality. Faithfulness sometimes entailed unfaithfulness towards the marriage partner. This re-evaluation of virtues was especially striking in the case of chastity. Chastity in love did not mean, as it did in Christian ethics, sexual abstention, but a monogamous relationship and the renunciation of polygyny. The world of love and *curialitas* had other rules than those of Christian morality. Courtly love had its own laws, and all those committed to the ideal of *curialitas* had to observe them. It was this claim to a separate law for courtly love that called forth the determined opposition of those who clung to the notion that Christian concepts of morality were binding on lay society. To the clerics, courtly love along with the entire ideal of courtly society, which placed itself under the sign of love, were symptoms of a dangerous moral decay and the corruption of the nobility. They said so very bluntly. But we would not be doing the phenomenon of courtly love justice if we were to see courtly love only from this perspective.

Courtly love was a social utopia. It was the codeword for a new and better society, a society that was unreal and could exist only in the poetic imagination. What differentiated the society of love from reality was the utopian idea that everything bad and boorish was excluded where love reigned. In the French *Roman de la rose*, the realm of love was an enclosed garden, on whose surrounding walls was depicted everything that was not allowed inside: hatred (*haine*), malice (*felonie*), villainy (*vilanie*), greed (*covoitise*), avarice (*avarice*), envy (*envie*), sorrow (*tristece*), old age (*vieillece*), hypocrisy (*papelardie*), and poverty (*povreté*). This meant that the reality of ordinary life was completely excluded. Only those were admitted who were willing and able to devote their life to courtliness (*cortoisie*), delight (*deduiz*), gaiety (*leece*), beauty (*biautez*), wealth (*richece*), generosity (*largece*), candor (*franchise*), carefreeness (*oiseuse*), and youth (*jonece*). Such an ideal mirrored the dreams of a thin aristocratic upper class which refused to be tied down to the demands of social responsibility. But we must not overlook that this garden of love was not merely a place of merry entertainment and pleasant idleness. Under the strict reign of Amor a lover had to learn the hard lessons of self-control and moral purification, until he had reached the goal of courtly perfection. The ethical demands made in the name of *curialitas* were hardly less severe than those of Christian moral doc-

trine. Whoever wished to enter into the service of love had to renounce
all deceit and violence. The iron gate locking the entrance to the minne
grotto in Gottfried's *Tristan* indicated that "falseness and violence were
locked out."[90] No doubt the utopia of courtly love remains unsatisfactory from the perspective of modern social theory. Nevertheless, we
must not fail to appreciate that twelfth and thirteenth-century aristocratic society, through its poets, pledged itself to an ideal that condemned
the brutality and ruthlessness with which this society pursed its interests
in real life, and called upon men and women to submit to the laws of
curialitas and love.

LOVE-MARRIAGE-ADULTERY

The incompatibility of love and marriage   Ever since scholars began
to examine the phenomenon of courtly love, the idea that this love
could find true fulfillment only outside of marriage was considered its
most striking and offensive characteristic. Some have spoken outright of
the adulterous nature of courtly love and have described the songs of
the troubadours and minnesingers as the poetry of adultery.

The thesis of the incompatibility of love and marriage is based primarily on Andreas Capellanus, specifically on the seventh dialogue, in
which a man of high nobility (*nobilior*) and a noble lady (*nobilis*) debate whether the love a married woman feels for her husband is a sufficient reason for her to reject a lover. The lady says it surely is, but the
man challenges that answer with the following argument: "I am greatly
surprised that you wish to misapply the name of love for the conjugal
affection which husband and wife are expected to feel for each other
after marriage, since it is quite clear that love can have no place between
a husband and a wife."[91] To justify his position the noble lord points to
the absence of secrecy in "marital affection" (*maritalis affectio*) and the
lack of jealousy between a husband and a wife. The lady raises the
moral objection that love "without sin"[92] is possible only in wedlock,
which the man counters by saying that even in a marriage, sexual pleasure "beyond the desire for offspring and the rendering of the marital
obligation. . . cannot be without sin."[93] The disputed point—"whether
true love could have a place between husband and wife"[94]—was finally
referred to the countess of Champagne, who announced her famous
verdict in a letter dated May 1, 1174: "We declare and firmly establish
that love cannot unfold its powers between married people."[95] The
countess justified her verdict with the argument that only lovers gave

themselves freely to each other, whereas husbands and wives were bound by the law of mutual obligation. Furthermore, through marital intercourse "neither person could increase in virtue."[96] There was also no jealousy among married couples.

According to Andreas Capellanus, much the same was said by the Vicontesse Ermengarde of Narbonne when confronted with the case of a lady who did not wish to continue an earlier affair after her marriage. "The improper conduct of this lady was condemned by Lady Ermengarde of Narbonne with these words: a marriage newly entered into does not abrogate an earlier love."[97] At the end of the second book of *De amore*, Andreas Capellanus compiled thirty-one "rules of love"[98] decreed by the god of Love. The first rule said: "Marriage is no real excuse for not loving."[99] As so much else in the "amour courtois" scholarship, the meaning of Capellanus's statements is hotly contested: do they reflect a prevailing attitude in courtly society at the time, or should they rather be understood as the product of a farcical wit? Whatever the answer, Andreas Capellanus's views are echoed elsewhere.

In his *Historia calamitatum* ("Story of my misfortunes"), Abelard reports that his lover Heloise refused to become his wife after giving birth to his child, saying "she would prefer it and it would be better for my reputation if she were called my lover and not my wife, so that I would be preserved for her solely by love and not bound by the fetters of marriage."[100] In her first letter to Abelard—I shall ignore the question concerning the authenticity of the correspondence—Heloise confirmed this attitude: "God is my witness, I never sought from you anything but yourself; only you I desired and not your possessions."[101] "The name of wife may seem loftier and more sacred, but sweeter to me was always the name of mistress or, if you do not consider it unworthy, that of concubine or whore."[102] Among the reasons "why I preferred love to marriage and freedom to chains,"[103] Heloise ranked highest that love is selfless and freely given.

According to Richard de Fournival, there were different kinds of worldly love: "There is worldly love that arises from the force of nature, and love that simply grows from the will of the heart."[104] Love compelled by nature was, to him, love between relatives and spouses: "It is the love among family members, how one loves one's father and mother, one's brothers, one's parents, one's relatives, and one's wife."[105] But the love rooted in the heart is the sexual love "between a man and a woman."[106] This was the love that bestowed all courtly virtues upon the lovers if their hearts were filled with noble-mindedness.

"Marital love is a love of obligation; the love of which I speak now is a love of favor. Though it is courtly to render what one owes, it is not a love for which one owes such gratitude as for the love that springs from favor and from the pure generosity of the heart."[107]

Similar arguments are found in some Provençale and French tenzones, which debate the question whether it was better to be the lover or the husband of one's beloved lady. In most cases the defenders of marriage brought up its practical advantages. What spoke in favor of love in the tenzone between Gui d'Uisel and Elias d'Uisel (Pillet-Carstens 194.2) was the claim that only love freely given elevated a man's worthiness: "That through which one is improved, Lord Elias, I consider better, and worse that through which one sinks lower. On account of a lady honor increases, and on account of a wife a man loses worthiness; one is praised for adoring a lady and mocked for adoring a wife."[108]

There are no comparable texts from Germany, undoubtedly because the kinds of writings best suited for discussing such questions—treatises on the theory of love and tenzones—did not make their way to that country. But the idea of a separation of love and marriage was not unknown in Germany, as we can see from the humorous use of this motif in Ulrich von Liechtenstein's *Frauendienst*. The singer who wore himself out in service to his lady was also a happily married man, even though the hardships of minne service rarely allowed him to be with his wife. One such opportunity came in 1227, as he was traveling through the land disguised as Venus and passed close to his ancestral estate: "I immediately sneaked away and rode joyously to where I found my dearly beloved wife; she could not be dearer to me."[109] For three days he enjoyed "the comfort and happiness"[110] of married life, until minne service called him back again. Elsewhere Liechtenstein said that his wife "was as dear to me as could be, even though I had another woman as mistress over myself."[111]

Liechtenstein's humorous self-portrait reveals that the idea of the incompatibility of love and marriage did not mean that one had to choose between the two. Liechtenstein was an exemplary servant of minne and at the same time a happy husband. It would seem that both roles could be combined very well. What the poets really meant to express was that love freely given had a different character and a different quality than marital love, and apparently this notion was widely agreed upon. This is also what the verdict of the countess of Champagne was all about: between husbands and wives there could not be the freely given love that exists among lovers. This was really no call to commit adultery and no justification for it, but rather the mere recognition of the fundamental difference in the quality of the relationship between a man and a woman within marriage and outside of it.

Marriage in theory and practice   It was observed long ago that the theoretical separation of love and marriage fit surprisingly well with the actual marriage practices within noble society and with the Church's doctrine of marriage at the time.

Feudal marriage   To the lay nobility, marriage was primarily a political institution, an instrument of dynastic politics. The most important function of a marriage was the continuation of one's family, in other words the begetting of legitimate heirs, especially legitimate sons. The dynastic principle demanded that only the husband be permitted to impregnate his wife. This was one of the reasons why adultery by a woman was a crime by secular law, whereas the extramarital affairs of a man were not a punishable offense. A wife's quality was measured first of all by her ability to bear children. Infertility of a woman was one of the most frequent causes of divorce. In addition to the continuation of the family line, feudal marriage also served to establish ties with other houses. In such cases marriage was almost always prompted by family politics: the securing or expansion of the family domain, the consolidation of political alliances, the reconciliation of old enmities, or marriage into families of higher nobility. Of central importance in such marriages, on the one hand, was the choice of the spouse and the contractual guarantees of the marriage bonds. If a great inheritance was at stake, the political intent of a dynastic marriage came to fruition in most cases only in the following generation, since it was the children of such a union that established the desired connections between the families involved. Hence feudal marriage pursued for dynastic reasons was also focused on offspring. On the other hand, it was in the interest of noble families that marriages could be dissolved. Family politics could not always be planned a full generation in advance. Sometimes an opportunity for a politically more favorable marriage arose, which could be taken advantage of only if an existing marriage was dissolved.

The prospects for marriage were not equal for all children. Central to the political considerations was the marriage of the eldest son, who was to continue the dynastic tradition. By comparison, the family's interest in getting the younger sons married was rather modest. If these sons established households of their own, they would have to be set up at the expense of the family property, unless they succeeded in marrying rich heiresses and setting up their own lordships. For the most part, therefore, the younger sons were destined for clerical careers: in high ecclesiastical offices they could later be of use to the family interests. This attitude, however, produced a distortion of the marriage market: a great many marriageable daughters were faced with few available sons. This lowered the value of women for the purpose of family politics. Only if a family was of high nobility was there no difficulty in marrying off all the daughters, since many considered it advantageous to be linked to such a family. Otherwise the expenses of dowries had no meaningful relationship to the expected benefits. Daughters were frequently married to men who stood a step lower in social rank. This could be very much in the dynastic interest of a family, since a husband was thereby more tightly linked to the house of his wife. For those daughters who could not be married off, the convent was usually the only option.

It is not to be expected that love played a significant role in marriages contracted under such circumstances. As a rule, the conditions and contracts of marriage were negotiated between the families, at best between the groom and the father of the bride. Sometimes children were betrothed as infants. It could also happen that the wedding was the first time the bride and groom saw each other face to face. Dynastic concerns could simply not permit the free choice of spouses. Women were particularly disadvantaged, since they very seldom had any say in the choice of their husbands. The verdict of St. Ambrose, "It is not suited to the decency of girls to choose the husband,"[112] quoted in the twelfth century in Gratian's *Decretum* (col. 1124), corresponded to actual conditions. If a girl from a great house violated the norm and refused to submit to her family's political plans, this attracted great attention and made it into the annals of history. In 1194, Agnes, the cousin of Emperor Henry VI and daughter of his uncle, the Count Palatine Conrad (d. 1195), secretly married Duke Henry, the eldest son of Henry the Lion. The emperor was supposedly planning to marry her to the French king, but Agnes "remained firm in her love to the duke, whom she had chosen."[113] The secret marriage succeeded only with the help of Agnes's mother, who approved of the union with the Welf duke. The emperor is said to have demanded from his uncle that the marriage be dissolved, but he did not get his way.

Family interests frequently were indifferent to whether or not spouses were suited for each other. Welf V (d. 1120) was seventeen when he married the rich, forty-year-old heiress Matilda of Tuscany (d. 1115). Greater still was the age difference when, in 1252, twenty-year-old King Ottokar II of Bohemia married the nearly fifty-year-old Margarete of Austria, sister of the last Babenberg duke of Austria. The marriage was childless, and Ottokar obtained a divorce after he had absorbed Austria, the patrimonial lands of his wife. But his rule there was of short duration. This case shows the limits of such ruthless marriage policy. Since the political purpose of marriage was only achieved with the birth of children, there had to be a minimum basis for a physical relationship between the spouses.

In those rare cases where personal motives were decisive in the choice of a partner, this often had negative political repercussions. Gislebert of Mons reports that young Count Baldwin II of Hainaut (d. 1098) was betrothed to the niece of Count Robert of Flanders (d. 1093). But the first time he saw her in person, "he scorned and despised her appearance disfigured by excessive ugliness."[114] Instead he married the daughter of Duke Henry II of Brabant (d. 1078/79). This change of mind cost him the castle of Douai: the count of Flanders had taken it into his power to guarantee the promised marriage and now refused to return it. A similar case occurred in Saxony in the twelfth century. Margrave Udo von der Nordmark planned to marry the daughter of the last Billunger, Duke Magnus (d. 1106), "but he lodged in the house of Count Helprich von Ploceke, and when he saw his very beautiful sister Ermengarda, he married her."[115] Once again, consideration for the looks of the bride had negative political repercussions, as "his vassals were greatly outraged, since they were of equal rank with Helprich, and some ranked even higher."[116]

In most cases the spouses resigned themselves to reality and lived together or separated. Uta of Calw, the wife of Duke Welf VI (d. 1191), spent most of her time on her estates beyond the Swabian Alps and had little contact with her husband, all the more "since he felt little for her and preferred the embraces of other women."[117] The situation was particularly unpleasant for a wife if her husband kept a concubine he loved. We hear this about Landgrave Albrecht ("the Degenerate") of Thuringia (d. 1314), who was married to a daughter of Emperor Frederick II: "In the year of our Lord 1265, this Albrecht treated Lady Margaret very unjustly on account of a court lady called Kunigunde of Isenberg, who was his concubine and whom he loved."[118] Incidentally, after the death of his wife, Albrecht married Kunigunde. Ottokar of Styria has left us a vivid description of the personality and political influence of the mistress of King Wenzel II of Bohemia (d. 1305). Agnes was "a beautiful woman, who could play music and sing and was courtly and skilled at it; she was shrewd enough in all those things with which women make themselves lovable and worthy to men."[119] The king was so fond of her that he even entrusted her with important diplomatic missions: "She delivered confidential messages from him to high princes and she was so skilled that he frequently sent her as an ambassador to other countries; through this she became so beloved and dear and trusted that the other noble lords all began to hate her for it."[120]

One result of concubinage was that at some courts a great number of bastards grew up. Gislebert of Mons reports that before his death, Count Baldwin V of Hainaut (d. 1195) "assigned estates to his children who were not born of his wife but of other noble ladies."[121] Emperor Frederick II was married four times and had ten children from his four wives. But there were also at least nine other children, the offspring of his liaisons with eight other women.

Typical of feudal marriage arrangements was the case of Margarete de Rivers, daughter of the chamberlain of the English king and widow of Earl Baldwin of Albermarle. Matthew of Paris reports that in 1215 King John I married her to the mercenary leader Fawkes de Bréauté, one of the most feared and detested men of his time. When the king exiled Fawkes in 1224, Margarete sought the anullment of her marriage from the king and the archbishop and "declared that she had never consented to being tied to him by the bond of marriage."[122] On the occasion of her death in 1252, Matthew of Paris wrote in reference to this marriage: "It was the marriage of a noble to an ignoble person, a pious to an impious person, a beautiful to a vile person, against her will and by force."[123] Matthew then cited a few (anonymous) verses that shed light on the nature of feudal marriage: "The law joined them, love and the harmony of the bed. But what kind of law? What love? What harmony? A lawless law, a hateful love, a discordant harmony."[124]

Of course there were also happy marriages. In 1208, King Andreas II of Hungary (d. 1235) betrothed his daughter Elisabeth, then just a year old, to the eldest son of Landgrave Hermann I of Thuringia. At age four she went to the court of Thuringia, at fourteen she celebrated her marriage to Ludwig IV (d. 1227). When Elisabeth was twenty her husband died; four year later she followed him to the grave. Our sources say that husband and wife "had loved each other with extraordinary affection."[125] In 1186, thirteen-year-old Count Baldwin VI of Hainaut

married twelve-year-old Marie, the daughter of Count Henry I of
Champagne (d. 1181). According to Gislebert of Mons, Marie had
already in her early youth displayed great piety. Likewise, "her husband
Baldwin, the young knight, led a chaste life, spurned all other women
and loved only Marie with ardent affection; it is something rare among
men that someone is so enamored of a single woman and is content
with her alone."[126]

One could list still other cases of marital love. But the fact that they
are reported in the chronicles, and in such an astonished and admiring
tone, is an indication that these were the exceptions. The circumstances
under which marriages were contracted in those days left little room for
love, which is why love is hardly the proper yardstick for measuring the
quality of a feudal marriage. The success of a marriage is better gauged
by observing whether husband and wife cooperated successfully in pursuing the dynastic interests that formed the basis of their union. The
twelfth and thirteenth centuries saw many noble women who, at their
husbands' sides or in their places, looked after the interests of their
families with great energy and skill. This aspect of historical reality—
the public and political sphere of action that a feudal marriage allowed
a woman—has not been sufficiently appreciated. No doubt in many
cases a successful cooperation between spouses established or deepened
a more intimate personal relationship between them; our historical
sources tell us virtually nothing about this. Nevertheless, such marital
affection was most likely of a very different quality than the passionate
feeling between lovers.

The Scholastic doctrine of marriage   The doctrine of the Church was
also aimed at a separation of love and marriage; at least it could be
interpreted that way. Everything the theologians had to say on the subject was marked by an extremely negative attitude towards sexual desire (*libido*). Sexual ethics of the old Church were dominated by the
ideal of immaculate virginity. It goes without saying that extramarital sex was always disapproved of, since its only purpose could be the
satisfaction of lust. Even within marriage, sexual intercourse was tar-
nished with the stigma of *libido*. Marriage was therefore regarded as the
second best option for all those who did not have the strength to remain
undefiled by anything sexual. But did not God himself command mankind to procreate with the words "Be fruitful and mulitply"?[127] Augustine resolved this contradiction with his theory of the dual establish-

ment of marriage, which the theologians of the twelfth century still accepted nearly in its entirety. This theory argued that one had to distinguish between marriage in paradise, which God had established with the words just cited, and marriage after the Fall. The purpose of marriage in paradise was procreation. This happened without sexual lust, since in paradise the sexual organs were still subject to and controlled by the will. *Libido* was born only with the fall of man, as something "evil" (*malum*), as a punishment for sinful humankind. The character of marriage was thereby fundamentally altered. While still serving the purpose of procreation, it now became primarily an institution to curb evil sexual desires, as St. Paul laid down in 1 Corinthians: "Because there is so much immorality, let each man have his own wife and each woman her own husband. A husband must give the wife her due, and the wife equally must give the husband his due."[128] As justification for marriage after the Fall, which was always afflicted with the *malum* of lust, theologians invoked the doctrine of the marital "goods." On this point, as well, twelfth-century theology adhered essentially to Augustine, who had identified the three goods of matrimony: offspring (*proles*), loyalty (*fides*), and sacrament (*sacramentum*). The procreation of children remained a supreme value after the Fall. "Loyalty" among spouses was usually regarded as a "remedy against lustfulness" (*remedium concupiscentiae*). The sacramental nature of marriage lay not in its ability to bestow grace, but in the fact that it reflected something higher: according to St. Paul (Ad Ephesios 5.23 ff.), the relationship of a husband to his wife mirrored in a mysterious way the relationship of Christ to his Church. The first two marital goods had their corresponding subjective motives for conjugal intercourse in the hope for children (*spes prolis*) and the mutual rendering of marital obligation (*debitum*). Opinions differed in the twelfth century on the question of *debitum*. If the willingness to engage in intercourse served to keep one's spouse from incontinence, it was generally regarded as free of sin, as was intercourse for the sake of procreation. If, however, marital intercourse was sought out of fear of one's own incontinence, most theologians already regarded this as a sin, though a venial one. Intercourse solely to satisfy lust was condemned as a sin even between spouses. Even the severe Augustinian position that marital intercourse was never without sin found many adherents in the twelfth and thirteenth centuries: "Sexual lust, without which no intercourse can take place, will truly always be a sin."[129]

The subjective purposes of marital intercourse could also be seen as reasons for marriage itself. In addition to the hope for children (*spes prolis*) and the avoidance of fornication (*vitatio fornicationis*), twelfth- and thirteenth-century marriage treatises not infrequently list secondary reasons for marriage; undoubtedly they did so not least because the discrepancy between Church doctrine on marriage and the actual conditions within lay society was too jarring. Walther of Mortagne, in his tract "On the Sacrament of Marriage" from the mid-twelfth century, separated the secondary motives into "honorable reasons" (*honestae causae*) and "less honorable reasons" (*minus honestae*). Honorable motives were in his view "the reconciliation of enemies" (*inimicorum reconciliatio*) and the "re-establishment of peace" (*pacis redintegratio*). Clearly, Walther has the feudal marriage in mind. Compared to these public motives, private and personal reasons for marriage were held in much lower regard. Among the less honorable reasons the author lists "the beauty of the man and of the woman, which frequently impels those inflamed with love to enter into marriage so that they might fulfill their desire,"[130] as well as "profit and love of wealth."[131] Peter Lombard (d. 1160) incorporated these regulations verbatim into his *Book of Sentences*, thereby assuring them a wide circulation. In keeping with his additional marriage reasons, Walther of Mortagne also expanded the list of marital goods: he included "the friendship that arises between a man and a woman from the marital union,"[132] and "the peace among people who were previously at enmity."[133]

The anonymous marriage tract *Sacramentum coniugii non ab homine*, also from the mid-twelfth century, lists among the usual motives for marriage special reasons for the choice of a husband and a wife: "In the choice of a husband, four points are usually considered: virtue, lineage, beauty, and wisdom. In the choice of wife, four things drive a man to love: beauty, lineage, wealth, and good conduct."[134] That a woman's wealth was listed as something that made her especially desirable as a wife can be regarded as a realistic motive. This same tract argued that all marriages were valid, even if the primary reasons had been ignored and a marriage had been contracted solely "because of peace or beauty or wealth."[135] The author adds by way of explanation: "Otherwise most of the marriages would have to be considered null and void, since people in our day are used to entering marriages for the above-named reasons, without thinking of the fundamental ones."[136]

The conflict between theory and practice   In some very important points the Christian doctrine of marriage was in agreement with the feudal practice of marriage: for both the main purpose of matrimony was procreation; in both there was hardly a word about love, about the personal bond between spouses. In other important points, however, the feudal and the Christian concepts of marriage stood in sharp conflict. Within aristocratic society, parents wanted to decide the marriages of their children, especially of their daughters, while the Church demanded the consent (*consensus*) of both spouses as the condition for a valid union. In noble society marriages within the extended kin were common, whereas the Church placed a strict prohibition upon marriages between relatives. Noble society took little offense if a man kept concubines and mistresses next to his wife, while the Church insisted on strict monogamy. In opposition to the practice of divorce and the repudiation of wives in noble society, the Church stood for the principle that marriages were indissoluble. From the Church's point of view, divorces were granted as nullifications on the basis of legal impediments discovered after the marriage. These opposing positions clashed head-on in the twelfth century. The results were spectacular confrontations in which, especially in France, even the ruling families were involved, and which caught the fancy of the public for a long time. On the whole, the trend was for an ever-increasing influence of the Church in all matters relating to marriage. From the end of eleventh century on, disputed matrimonial issues were adjudicated only in ecclesiastical courts. The codification of an ecclesiastical marriage law began with Gratian's *Decretum* (around 1140). Initially based on decisions and verdicts of individual popes, this law was systematically expanded in the course of the twelfth century, and reached its (temporarily) final form in the Decretals (*Liber decretalium*) of Pope Gregory IX (d. 1241). But the administration of justice was only one way in which the Church could exert influence on the matrimonial matters of the laity; other avenues were confessional and penitential practices. Furthermore, new forms of Church participation in marriage ceremonies developed. The ceremonial blessing of the marriage by a priest was an old demand of the Church which now gradually asserted itself. From the beginning of the thirteenth century, first in England and northern France, the proposed marriage was also publicly announced in church ahead of time; this was intended to counteract the practice of secret marriages.

The Church's claim to be the final arbiter in all matrimonial questions no longer met with any serious opposition in the thirteenth century. But the Church did not succeed in imposing its conception of marriage on aristocratic lay society without modifications. Quite often the conflict ended with a compromise. One example is the most famous matrimonial lawsuit of the age, one which kept all of Europe in suspense for two decades and in different ways even influenced international politics: the suit concerning the divorce of the French King Philip II Augustus, who had married the Danish Princess Ingeborg in 1193, only to repudiate her immediately following the marriage. Not until 1213 did he again acknowledge her as his legitimate wife. For the most part lay opposition to the Church's marriage regulations did not take the form of arguments—written objections—but expressed itself through the force of concrete action.

In most matrimonial lawsuits of the twelfth century, the question of the kinship of the spouses played a decisive role. Following a decision by Pope Alexander II (d. 1073) from the year 1059, Gratian's *Decretum* laid down that kinship to the seventh degree constituted a compelling impediment to marriage. This position, which threatened to render a great number of feudal marriages invalid, was untenable in the long run. At the Fourth Lateran Council in 1215, the canonical decision was revised to the effect that now only kinship to the fourth degree constituted a legal impediment. As it was, the prohibition of marriages between relatives turned out to be a double-edged sword. The fact that nearly all families of the high nobility were related in some way or another had two consequences: first of all, it meant that the canonical law was constantly violated while the Church was unable to do very much about it. Secondly, the canonical prohibition of incest turned out to be a convenient and approved way for the lay nobility to continue the old practice of divorce: one simply had to prove kinship to one's wife in order to obtain a canonical annulment of the marriage. Proof was furnished with the help of genealogical charts that had to be confirmed by the oaths of witnesses. We know for a fact that genealogies were manipulated for this purpose. A highly interesting document concerning such divorce arrangements is the "Table of Consanguinity" (*Tabula consanguinitatis*) preserved in the register of Abbot Wibald of Stablo (d. 1158). It established the kinship between Emperor Frederick I and his first wife Adele of Vohburg (d. after 1187), and apparently provided the basis for the dissolution of their marriage in 1153. The official version said that the emperor was divorced on account of illegal kinship. But rumors had it that very different reasons were behind the emperor's desire for a divorce: the infertility of the marriage or the prospects of a union with the Byzantine imperial house. Malicious gossip even suggested alleged adultery by the empress.

In other respects the Church hardened its position in the course of the twelfth century. Gratian's *Decretum* established as a principle "that no woman should be married to anyone against her will."[137] From that time on this so-called principle of consent formed the basis of canonical marriage law. But while Gratian still taught that the marriage was contracted by mutual consent and then consummated by intercourse, twenty years later Peter Lombard laid down in his *Book of Sentences* (*Libro* IV *sententiarum*) that mutual consent in itself established a valid marriage, regardless of whether the marriage was consummated. The later collections of decretals followed Peter Lombard's position. But in establishing the consent of bride and groom as the central act in contracting a marriage, the Church opposed prevailing custom, which in most cases paid no regard whatsoever to the wishes of the daughters to be married. At the same time, the Church was also emphasizing an aspect that had hitherto hardly entered into the discussion of marriage: the mutual affection of the future spouses. Gratian had already decreed that all those "who joined themselves in conjugal affection . . . are called spouses."[138] According to the tract *Sacramentum coniugii non ab homini*, three elements were involved in marital consent: "the union of wills, mutual love, the husband's protection of his wife."[139] Such statements indicate that the Church was slowly moving away from its conception of matrimony as a sexual union for the procreation of children and the prevention of immorality. The widest departure in the twelfth century was made by Hugh of St. Victor, who was one of the first to speak of "marital love,"[140] and to whom marriage "without the bond of love was worthless."[141] But such views placed Hugh of St. Victor on a lonely outpost in the twelfth century. Only in high Scholasticism, in Albertus Magnus, was the personal bond between spouses given greater weight.

Marriage and love in courtly literature   What the courtly didacticians had to say about the nature of marriage fit both the teachings of the Church and actual conditions.

> Before a manly man who values his reputation, a womanly woman shall rightly fold her hands. A manly man and a womanly woman should bear this in mind: he is to be master over her and her possessions; she is to obey his

will. He shall be a man and she shall be a woman: this is the proper way. He shall also honor her, and she shall do nothing without his advice: that is for her own good. Thus they can grow old joyfully.[142]

Traces of this attitude can also be found in epic poetry. Whenever we hear noble men boasting about their wives to one another and wagering on who had the best wife, the criteria for deciding the issue were always her humility and submissiveness. At the siege of Viterbo by the Romans as recounted in the *Kaiserchronik*, during breaks in the fighting the Roman leaders talked about heroes and good horses, hunting birds and beautiful women (4415 ff.). Some were happy to be away from their wives. Others praised the virtuousness of their women, most loudly Conlatinus, who was married to Lucretia: "I have the worthiest wife."[143] King Tarquinius wagered his soul's salvation that his own wife was even more virtuous, and they immediately rode back to Rome to make the test. When Conlatinus arrived at home in the middle of the night, "Lucretia jumped out of bed"[144] and ran to meet her husband and to greet him most kindly. She obeyed his gruff demand to prepare some food and personally served the two men at table. "When the noble lady served a drink, the host lifted the cup and poured the wine in her face. The liquid ran down her dress. She stood up and bowed courteously before him."[145] Without a word of complaint she changed her clothes, resumed serving at table, and looked after their guest until he had retired contentedly for the night. Very different was the reception they received the following night at the royal court. The queen refused to get up, and when the king asked her to prepare a meal for him, she answered: "At this court I am neither steward nor cupbearer, neither chamberlain nor cook. I don't know what you want from me. I don't care if you will still get something to eat."[146] Thereupon the king had to award the prize to Lucretia. Stories of this kind were apparently very popular with noble audiences.

Courtly epics portrayed the relationship between love and marriage in a variety of ways. In some stories love and marriage stood in conflict, in others the two were joined harmoniously. Most stories that revolved around a conflict of love and marriage confirmed the verdict of the countess of Champagne: true love was not found between spouses. Here we encounter the special case which has sometimes been seen as the norm of courtly love: love that found fulfillment in adultery. It is no coincidence that the concept of courtly love was drawn from an analysis of Chrétien de Troyes's Lancelot romance, which has the adultery motif. On the whole, however, adultery was the exception, though an important one that deserves separate treatment.

More numerous were the courtly romances and stories in which a conflict of love and marriage appeared not at all or only in subplots. Among them were the tales that told of love and marriage as an unproblematic progression: most frequently the love between two young people had to overcome a series of obstacles or tests before the couple, once again happily united, could marry. As a rule the wedding constituted the culmination, and the marriage itself ceased to be the subject of the story. Examples of this type are *Wilhelm von Orlens* by Rudolf von Ems and *Flore und Blanscheflur* by Konrad Fleck.

Much more interesting are those romances that tell of a quick wedding of the hero and of a marriage in which love still had to prove itself. Thanks to the outstanding artistic importance of Chrétien de Troyes's epics (*Erec et Enide, Yvain, Le conte du Graal*) and their German redactions by Hartmann von Aue and Wolfram von Eschenbach, this story line came to dominate the courtly romance in France and Germany. In these works the marriage theme was treated with a previously unknown degree of complexity. The special quality and variety of these motifs can only be brought out by a close textual analysis. As far as the development of the courtly ideal of society is concerned, the crucial point is that in these romances the verdict of the countess of Champagne proved invalid. In contrast to both Church doctrine and feudal reality, these romances assigned to love a central importance for an understanding of marriage. Through the plots themselves the poets made it clear that it took great effort on the part of the heroes to join love and marriage into a constructive relationship. In *Erec* and in *Iwein*, the quick marriage very soon reaches a crisis and virtually breaks up; only at the end, after a long trial period, is it renewed and reestablished. From the perspective of the final outcome, the point of the romances was the attainment of perfection through the harmony of love and marriage. This concept was given a unique accent through the incorporation of the theme of lordship. The marriages of Erec and Iwein were not threatened by a lack of love, but by the great difficulties the heroes had in doing justice to the political duties they had assumed through marriage. Both men had to learn first to combine love and marriage in such a way that their sense of responsibility as future rulers was enhanced. In the end the reconciled spouses were at the same time model ruling couples.

The poetic conception of such a harmonious union of love, marriage,

and lordship could be seen as a criticism of prevailing marriage practices, specifically of the impersonal nature of matrimonial ties. Perhaps
it was also a response to the Christian marriage doctrine, which had so
little to say about love between spouses. The marital love depicted in
the romances had essentially the same quality as the courtly love of the
minnesingers. Its courtly character is revealed by the fact that the lovers
are pledged to the same ideal of courtly perfection as the poets in the
minnesongs. But there were differences in regard to the position of the
woman. Her role as an exemplary wife manifested itself primarily in her
ability to subordinate herself, to serve, and to suffer. In this respect
Enite displayed the most amazing qualities. Condwiramurs, for her
part, had to bear the nearly five-year-long separation from Parzival without complaint, and even Laudine in the end was kneeling to her husband
(H. v. Aue, *Iwein* 8130). Only in exceptional cases did the epic poets
describe the relationship between the spouses in such a way that the
wife was an independent actor. Gyburg in Wolfram's *Willehalm* was
such an exception. In these motifs the depictions in the romances
proved to be more realistic than the purely imaginary world of love in
the minnesongs.

Adultery   To medieval legal thinking, adultery was an offense only
women could commit. On this point Germanic and Roman legal ideas
agreed. Only the Church tried to insist that men be treated no differently than women in this regard, but its demand did little to change the de
facto inequality. According to secular law, adultery was punishable by
death. Some legal codes granted the betrayed husband a special right to
kill the offenders, a right that seems, in fact, to have been invoked.

Adultery in society
    It is difficult to determine the frequency of adultery in noble society.
A few famous cases found their way into the annals of history, no doubt
primarily because of the draconian punishments exacted by husbands
who took the law into their own hands. In 1256, Duke Ludwig II of
Bavaria (d. 1294) had his wife, Maria of Brabant, decapitated on the
mere suspicion of adultery. This deed, which earned the duke the
epithet "the Severe," was recorded in many sources and in most instances drew a disapproving comment. Particularly harsh was the protest of
the *Spruch*-poet Stolle, who glorified the duchess as a "martyr" (16.9)
and placed her at the side of St. Catherine. In 1175, Count Philip of
Flanders (d. 1191) caught his wife, Elizabeth of Vermandois (d. 1182),

in flagrante delicto with the knight Gautier de Fontaines. Benedict of Peterborough recounts that Gautier was bound, tortured, and beaten with clubs and swords; finally "they suspended the healf-dead man by his feet head down over a disgusting sewage ditch"[147] until he died. The annals of Worcester report under the year 1230: "At Easter Llewellyn deceitfully invited William of Braose, whom he suspected of having commited adultery with his wife, then cut off his members and hung him from the gallows."[148] Castration seems to have been a popular punishment for adultery. Matthew of Paris recounts under the year 1248 that the knight Godfrey de Millers entered the house of another nobleman "with the intention of lying with his daughter."[149] With the help of the girl, "who was afraid of being turned into a concubine,"[150] he was caught, beaten, and castrated. The chronicler called the girl a "little whore"[151] and considered the punishment an "inhuman crime."[152] The king decreed that all who participated in this act—among them the girl's father—would forfeit their property and be banished. There are other cases we know of, and from this we can extrapolate a correspondingly greater incidence of undetected adultery. On the whole, however, one gets the impression that such scandals were rare enough to merit recording. We might be tempted to think that adultery was in the same category as instances of true marital love, which were also reported as remarkable exceptions. Noble society of that time had no tolerance for adultery. In fact, since the risks to a wife and her potential lover were enormous, we may suspect that few were willing to take a chance.

Finally, one could argue that adultery was frequent since it was discussed so often in contemporary penitential handbooks. The authors of these handbooks considered all kinds of scenarios: that both adulterers were married or only one of them, that the adultery was committed with a cleric or a nun, with a widower or a widow, with the sister of the wife, with a virgin, with a maid, with the wife or daughter of a neighbor, with a Jewess or a pagan woman, and so on. This list of questions alone shows that most cases dealt with the sexual liberties of men. Even though the penitentials took the position that fornication by a man should be judged no differently than fornication by a woman, we can see from many individual regulations that the theologians, too, took into account the actual differences in sexual morality. For example, the penitential code of manuscript Codex Vaticanus 4772 (eleventh century, of German provenance) asks about a prohibited position during intercourse: "Did you have intercourse with your wife or another woman from behind, as dogs do? If you have done that you shall do penance at bread and water for ten days."[153] The wording itself indicates that it was of secondary importance whether the man had been with his wife or some other woman. Nothing comparable is ever said in the penitentials regarding the sexual conduct of women.

Adultery in literature

Opinions differ as to the importance of adultery as a literary motif. The notion that the most typical form of courtly love was adulterous love could fall back on statements from the courtly age. A satirical poem of Der Stricker, entitled *Die Minnesänger*, opened with these words: "In former times, when the guardians were severely rebuked and when many a thoughtless host paid dearly for presenting his wife to his guests, if she then forgot her faithfulness and violated her duty and broke her marriage, this was called high minne."[154] The poet then proceeded to describe in detail what happened when a minnesinger was invited to the table of a hospitable lord: "While he [the host] made sure that the guest lacked nothing, the guest wooed the wife and estranged her from her husband."[155] To make the woman favorably disposed to his desires, the minnesinger praised the elevating power of secret love: "Secretive high minne possesses such great power that she promotes all virtues: she ennobles behavior, casts out depression, bestows greatness onto thinking, gives dignity to life, and is the precursor to bliss."[156] The author condemned such talk, which had the sole purpose of tempting the wife into adultery, as so much "apery and deceit."[157] If the woman did not offer stern resistance to such wooing, the poet recommended countermeasures to the husband: intimidate and strictly supervise your wife. The minnesingers, however, he should entertain in the manner they deserved: "If a guest thinks it is courtly that the host suffers an insult to his wife by a courtly man, a good response would be if the host treated the guest as he deserves, and let him know what his courtliness is worth. For when he sits down at the table eager to eat and drink, it would be very appropriate to serve him nice flowers, leaves, and grass, things which have always been the delight of courtiers, along with a bird that can sing sweetly and a fountain which springs from under a beautiful linden tree. Then he might understand how pleasant all that is of which he constantly sings."[158]

The same reproach was raised in a thirteenth-century strophe composed by the poetess or poet by name of Gedrut or Geltar. The verses warn the lords of Mergersdorf of the danger to their wives from the seductive arts of some poets mentioned by name:

> If I had a servant who sang of his lady, I would make him tell me clearly her name so that nobody would have to think it was my wife. Alram, Ruprecht, Frederick, who would have thought you capable of betraying the lords of Mergersdorf? If this went to court they'd be after your life. You are too fat for anyone to believe that you are suffering the lover's grief you complain about. If anyone seriously felt such great longing for minne, he'd be dead within a year.[159]

It is difficult to assess what such statements say about the real social background of minne lyric. If one took the minnesingers' declarations of love literally, one could easily turn the motif of secret minne into a suspicion of adulterous relationships. Adulterous affairs were imputed to many troubadours in the biographies (*vidas*) and song commentaries (*razos*) that were posthumously compiled with information drawn from their songs. In Konrad Bollstater's *Losbuch* from the fifteenth century, three well-known minnesingers of the courtly period—Heinrich von Morungen, Wolfram von Eschenbach, and Reinmar von Brennenberg—along with the otherwise unknown Fuß der Buhler, were depicted in miniatures under the title "The four paramours"[160]: all four are busy seducing women.

The minnesongs themselves offered little to nourish such suspicions. The troubadours occasionally mention "the husband" (*marit*) or "the jealous man" (*gilos*): in these cases the lady was apparently thought of as a married woman. Open professions of adultery occur only in the French "songs of the badly married" (chansons de mal-mariés): "My husband is too jealous, too conceited, deceitful, and arrogant. But soon he shall be a cuckold, when I meet my sweet friend, who is so courtly and affectionate."[161] In German minne lyric this theme was completely avoided. Characteristic of its depiction of love is the intentional vagueness of the social circumstances. Not even the dawn songs, a genre defined by the motif of the secretiveness and dangerousness of love, were an exception in this regard. The personal and familial circumstances of the noble lady who receives a knight into her chamber at night are never mentioned; neither is the strange familiarity between the lady and the watcher ever explained. If one wanted to interpret the situation in the dawn songs realistically—as Ulrich von Liechtenstein did in *Frauendienst* (1622.1 ff.)—one might ask whether the guard's complicity with the lovers did not prove his disloyalty to the lord of the castle. This is why Liechtenstein replaced the guard by a lady-in-waiting, who owed loyalty only to her mistress. But this isolated case merely shows that a realistic interpretation of the social context of love in lyric was not appropriate. The very fact that the poets are silent about the concrete social conditions reveals that love in the minnesongs had a poetic character uniquely its own.

In narrative literature, on the other hand, adultery was an established motif. We find it especially in those works that treat love in a light-hearted way, primarily in the *Schwänke* (bawdy tales), which by the thirteenth century were among the most popular literary forms. Adultery in a great many variations was virtually the main humorous theme of that genre. By contrast, serious literature shows a striking restraint towards the adultery motif, in Germany even moreso than in France. Rhymed tales not infrequently tell of the love of a noble knight for a married lady. Here the sympathy of the author is always with the lovers, and the moral dimensions of their actions are ignored. In these tales the emphasis is almost always on the purity and greatness of love, which must triumph over the suspicions and persecutions of the husband and society. In most cases the adultery itself was treated with noticeable timidity. Sometimes it never happened because the lover died before there was ever an opportunity for the physical union of the lovers: this was the case, for example, in *Frauentreue* and in Konrad von Würzburg's *Herzmaere*. In other stories the adulterous woman was married to a pagan—as was the case in *Heidin*—and went on to marry her Christian lover; under such circumstances the breakup of the marriage could be seen as an almost meritorious deed. The adultery could also occur—as it did in *Moriz von Craûn*—as a kind of rape, against the will of the woman; initially she had been willing to yield completely to her lover, but when she had second thoughts the disappointed lover punished her with forcible intercourse. Frequently these stories dealt with a specific case, a specific problem of how to act in a minne relationship. The plot in *Moriz von Craûn* raised the question of how a woman should act if she finds her lover asleep at the arranged rendezvous. *Heidin* posed the question of which part a knight should choose if his lover offers him the choice between the upper and the lower half of her body. Apparently such casuistry of love was very popular with the courtly audiences. In the context of such discussions, adultery became a hypothetical case which one could play through and debate and elaborate epically without having to address the moral implications of the situation.

In the courtly romances adultery is a rare motif, and when it occurs it is usually portrayed in a negative light. In Otte's *Eraclius*, for example, Empress Athanias herself condemned her adulterous love of Parides as a "crime" (*missetât*, 4054). Yet the theme of adultery was central in two famous epics from the stock of Celtic legends: the romances of Lancelot and Tristan. The fame of these two tales gave rise to the impression that adultery was a central theme in courtly epic. But in reality the poets approached this delicate topic very cautiously, especially in Germany. Chrétien de Troyes's *Lancelot*, which revolves around the hero's adulterous love for Queen Guinevere, was the only work of the great French poet that was not put into German; whether that had something to do with the prominent adultery motif is difficult to determine. In any case, as early as the end of the twelfth century, Ulrich von Zatzikhoven translated a different French Lancelot romance, one which lacked the adultery theme. Scholarly opinions today differ on the interpretation of Chrétien's *Lancelot*. Was it the poet's intention to glorify courtly love, which was stronger than all injunctions of morality? Or did he intend to take a stance of ironic aloofness from this kind of love? The fact that the work was never finished makes it that much harder to answer these questions.

The French *Tristan*, the other main work on the theme of adultery, was first translated into German by Eilhart von Oberg. Here the verdict on the adulterous relationship is unambiguous: the hermit Ugrim, whom the lovers in their distress approached for help, condemned the love of Tristan and Isolde as "a sin" (*sunde*, 4715) and "a wrong" (*unrecht*, 4719). All blame for the misfortune was placed on the magical powers of the love potion; when its effect subsided after four years, the lovers separated immediately and Isolde returned to her husband. Very different was the treatment of the theme a generation later at the hands of Gottfried von Straßburg. In his version, no hint of reproach touched the actions of the lovers, whose continued adultery did serious damage to the public reputation of the betrayed king. Since the love potion in Gottfried's story had no time limit, the adulterous relationship became a permanent affair which would end only with the death of the lovers. And Gottfried nowhere addresses the moral problem of this adultery. Instead, his depiction of this adulterous love is combined with a critique of the feudal marriage. Gottfried casts a negative light on the political motives behind marriages and on the greedy and lustful relationship of a husband to his wife. In Gottfried's view, these forms of marriage were well suited to a court society whose actions were guided by jealousy, envy, and intrigues. In opposition to a society of such questionable moral character, Gottfried made illicit love into a program for a better world: a world of *edelen herzen* ("noble hearts"), which knew neither falseness nor deceit, a world in which love became the sole criterion, and in which an action that expressed the highest loyalty seemed to outsiders like so much deception.

LOVE AND SOCIETY

The double standard of sexual morality   "It should be permitted to men, but not to women."[162] These words from a minnesong by Albrecht von Johansdorf could serve as the motto for a discussion of medieval sexual ethics. The following was said of the wedding night of Emperor Focas and Athanias: "He lay the beautiful woman into his bed, and then he played with her for the highest stake at a game that he knew well, but which she had never played before."[163] It seemed to go without saying that a man entered marriage with sexual experience, while a woman was expected to be a virgin. King Herwig of Seeland wanted to take his bride Kudrun home as his wife immediately after their engagement. Kudrun's mother, however, opposed that idea with the argument that she first wanted to prepare her daughter for her new role as queen. "Herwig was advised to leave his bride there, and for a year to while away the time with beautiful women elsewhere."[164]

Behind such attitudes stood the teachings of the moral theologians and the decretalists: because of the difference in pysical makeup, men and women displayed different forms of sexual behavior and were therefore subject to different rules of conduct. In men the sex drive was considered a "natural desire" (*appetitus naturalis*). The legal scholar Huguccio wrote at the end of the twelfth century: "For the man is driven by the natural desire of sensuality to unite physically with the woman."[165] In women, on the other hand, sexual desire was explained as arising from their weaker nature and was linked to their diminished resistance to the temptations of sin. The statement of the Church Father St. Jerome that "sexual desire arouses in virgins a greater desire because they think sweeter what they do not know,"[166] was quoted by the decretalists of the thirteenth century. Cardinal Hostiensis (d. 1271) spoke of "woman, whose vessel is always ready."[167] This was why a woman should be placed under strict supervision. To the question "why more was demanded of a woman than of a man,"[168] Pope Innocent IV (d. 1254) responded that a husband was allowed to have sexual contact with several women, whereas a wife was not allowed to have relationships with several men: "There is no harm if a man divides his flesh among many. But if a woman divides her flesh among many, the sacrament inside her is extinguished."[169] St. Augustine had already supplied a biblical justification for this unequal treatment: among the patriarchs a man had several wives, but not a single woman had several husbands. "And this does not violate the nature of marriage. For several women can be impregnated by one man, but one woman cannot be impregnated by several men."[170]

Andreas Capellanus applied this moral double standard to courtly love. He opposed "the old notion"[171] "that the same thing should hold in the case of a woman who committed a breach of faith, as did in the case of an unfaithful lover."[172] In courtly love, too, the inequality of the sexes was to be preserved.

> We shall never concede that forgiveness be extended to a woman who does not shy from uniting in carnal lust with two men. With men this is permitted because it happens more frequently and because the male sex has a privilege, which allows men to engage more freely in everything naturally sensual in this world. With women it is, on account of the modesty of their chaste sex, considered such an abomination that a woman who enters into multiple relationships is regarded as an unclean whore, and by common consent deemed unworthy of joining the company of other ladies.[173]

In the third book of *De amore*, Andreas Capellanus expressed this idea even more ironically: "Whereas with men, on account of the impudence of their sex, an excess of love and dissipation is tolerated, with women that is considered a detestable crime."[174]

This double standard was reflected in a person's social reputation. The didacticians knew "how very different the lives of women and men are: their disgrace is our honor. What degrades women we regard as the crowning achievement. If a man conquers many women, this does no harm to his renown. In contrast, women who care for their good name and avoid disgrace usually refrain from other men if they have a good lover."[175] The minnesingers put these words into the mouth of a woman: "If I yield to you, you would have the fame for it and I the mockery."[176]

The behavior of men   The historical sources tell us little about the sexual practices of the nobility. From the accounts of ecclesiastical writers we get the impression that excesses and violent behavior were commonplace. Pope Innocent III painted a bleak picture of the manners of his age in a letter (from 1209) to the bishop of Regensburg: "The

knights, who insist that for their sins they must not answer to an ecclesiastical court, commit adultery, fornication, and other sins with im-
punity and are not even rebuked for them."[177] Burchard von Ursberg's
portrayal of Duke Conrad of Swabia (d. 1196), a brother of Emperor
Henry VI, reveals that sexual excesses could go along quite well with
the more positive qualities of lordship: "He was a man thoroughly
given to adultery, fornication, defilement, and to every dissipation and
foulness; nevertheless he was vigorous and brave in battle and generous
to his friends."[178] Guibert de Nogent tells us that Enguerrand de Boves
(d. 1116), the count of Amiens, was "a very liberal, generous, and wealthy man,"[179] who honored the churches and bestowed rich gifts on
them; "he was, however, so addicted to carnal love that he surrounded
himself with all manner of women, decent ones and those who can be
bought, and he did almost nothing that was not prompted by their
wantonness."[180] Hermann von Reichenau (d. 1054) complained in his
poem "On the eight chief vices" that only the poor man, compelled by
his poverty, was content with a single woman, while the rich man had
many mistresses and did not shy from public intercourse with them:
"The poor man is constrained to have only a single legitimate wife, and
out of fear he enjoys sacred marriage only a little. The rich man, on the
other hand, debauches one, two, or more mistresses, being totally given
to his insatiable lasciviousness, and is not afraid to indulge publicly in
this whoring."[181] A strange case of polygamy is reported in the *Vita
Bertholdi Garstenis*, written in the second half of the twelfth century by
a monk of the monastery of Garsten. One day, the story goes, Abbot
Berthold met twelve women in the house of Ulrich von Berneke who
lived there in great luxury: "Since his wife had died, this lord always
had one of them in his bed according to his desire."[182] "Wherever
knights come together, there is a lot of talk about how many women
one or the other has debauched. They cannot keep quiet about their
misdeeds; their renown is measured solely by women. But whoever has
nothing to show in this respect feels pitiful among his companions."[183]

In assessing such statements, we must always bear in mind that most
of these authors were clerics. They were very distrustful of the worldly
doings of the nobility, and based their depictions of worldly life on
outdated interpretive schemes which they did not verify against reality.
Some clerical zealots even denounced excesses and immorality in cases
where their secular contemporaries saw a perfectly legitimate marriage.
Nevertheless, the impression that the noble lords often enough used the
prerogatives of their position to satisfy personal desires no doubt has a

certain degree of truth to it. Only against the background of such social conditions can we see clearly what high standards the idea of courtly love set for noble society.

In a didactic poem from the thirteenth century, King Tirol admonishes his son not to lay hands on the wives of his subjects: "Son, beware that in your heart you do not lust for the wives of your noble men and their beautiful daughters; you would impair the good name of your noble vassals."[184] Not all rulers seem to have listened to such advice. We are told that King John I of England (d. 1216) "raped the daughters and relatives of the noble men of his realm."[185] Among the reasons for the deposition of King Adolf of Nassau by the princes in 1298, Sigfrid of Balnhusen mentions this one: "Second, because he has violated virgins."[186] This case shows that such behavior was considered detestable and, in the right circumstances, could be used against the perpetrator. Occasionally we even hear of resistance to the sexual license of great lords. Mathias of Neuenburg reports the following about Count Heinrich of Freiburg under the year 1271: "When Henry had come to Neuenburg to receive the burghers' oath of loyalty on the following day, that evening he raped the wife of a burgher at the meat market. On account of this the Neuenburgers refused him the oath."[187]

Criticism of the sexual excesses of men came especially from the pens of the courtly poets: "A man who has a good wife and goes to another woman is like a pig. What is there that could be more wicked? He leaves the clear well and lies down in the muck. A lot of men act this way."[188] Polygyny was condemned along with adultery: "The man who treats women such that he likes to have many of them, that ill-intentioned man should be disgusting to noble women."[189] In *Parzival* we read that Urjans, a prince of Punturtoys, had raped a noble maid near Arthur's court and was condemned by the king to die at the gallows. On the intercession of the queen, Urjans's life was spared, but he was deprived of all his honors and for the deepest humiliation was locked into the dog pound: "Together with trackhounds and lead dogs he had to feed from a trough for four weeks. Thus the lady was revenged."[190] Not everyone had to fear such severe punishment. King Meljakanz was no better than Urjans: "Whether it was a married woman or a virgin, he always took love by force. He should be killed for it."[191] Meljakanz, however, remained a respected member of court society. Even the model knight Gawan was not blameless in this respect: "He did violence to a beautiful maid against her will, so that she cried and screamed."[192] Hartmann von Aue recounts that one day Iwein was traveling with a maid, and that they both found friendly lodging at a castle. At night they slept in one room, which drew this comment from the poet: "Now if anyone is amazed that a maid who was not his relative lay so close by him and he did not touch her, doesn't know that a decent man can refrain from everything he wishes to refrain from. But God knows, there are were few men like that."[193] The last sentence indicates just how far the courtly conduct of men in the poetic world was removed from real life.

The behavior of women   A very different set of rules applied to the sexual life of women. It was normal for a man to repudiate his wife and marry another woman. But if a woman left her husband to marry someone else, she exposed herself to the worst possible suspicions regarding her moral character. Countess Bertrade of Anjou (d. after 1115), the daughter of Count Simon I of Montfort, left her husband, Count Fulques IV of Anjou (d. 1109), in 1092 and married the French King Philip I (d. 1108). Both men involved were disreputable characters. Count Fulques had already repudiated two wives before; "inflammed with love,"[194] he took the beautiful Bertrade as his wife. The chronicle of the counts of Anjou calls him "a lecher."[195] King Philip I has gone down in history as a "lascivious king."[196] He repudiated his first wife, Bertha of Holland, to marry Bertrade. Nevertheless, most chroniclers blamed Bertrade for this scandal, which attracted great attention at the time; she was denounced as "that utterly evil woman,"[197] "a lustful woman,"[198] "adulteress"[199] and "shameless concubine."[200] The English historian William of Malmesbury held her social ambition responsible for everything: "Drawn by an itch for a loftier name,"[201] she gave up the count for the king.

A woman who left her husband had to expect even serious legal discrimination. The "Chronicle of Zwiefalten" by the monk Ortlieb tells the story of a woman from the family of the counts of Achalm. She married and went to live in Italy, but later left her husband and returned to Swabia where she demanded her share of the family inheritance: "But since she had lost her rightful claim through the disgraceful abandonment of her husband, on the opposing verdict of men learned in the law she received nothing. For a woman who loses her conjugal integrity also forfeits her right of inheritance."[202]

When it came to the fulfillment of personal happiness, a woman's sphere of action was tightly confined by society, and if she was not thoroughly passive in her behavior, she could easily fall under suspicion of wantonness. We can see this from the story of Countess Ida, the much-wooed heiress of the county of Boulogne. First she was married to Count Gerhard III of Gerldern, who died only two years after the wedding. Her second husband was the much older Duke Berthold IV of Zähringen (d. 1186), whom she also lost after a brief marriage. A widow for the second time, she returned to her county and, as Lambert of Ardres charges, "gave herself over to carnal desires and worldly pleasures."[203] Supposedly she began a love affair with the neighboring Count Arnald of Guines on her own initiative. But this love was not blessed with happiness. At the instigation of the French King Philip II Augustus, Count Renaud of Dammartin (d. 1227) kidnapped, imprisoned, and finally married Countess Ida.

Public accusations were also raised against the queen of France, Eleanor of Aquitaine, when her husband, King Louis VII (d. 1180), divorced her in 1152. The official reason was said to be a prohibited degree of kinship. The fact that Eleanor had born the king only daughters may also have had something to do with it. But rumors soon claimed that a love affair between the queen and Count Raymond of Antioch (d. 1149) was to blame for the breakup of the marriage. As Helinand of Froidmont put it, "she had behaved not like a queen but rather like a whore."[204] As evidence that her sensuality had found no satisfaction in her marriage to Louis VII, William of Newburgh cited her own statement that "she had married a monk, not a king."[205]

Under such conditions, women were compelled to make concern for their good name the guiding principle of their conduct. For a married woman it was best to be content with what her marriage could offer her. This was also expressed by the noble lady (*nobilis*) in Andreas Capellanus's tract: "All people should choose the kind of love that one can practice every day without reproach. This is why I must choose as the man who is to enjoy my embraces someone who can be both a husband and a lover to me."[206] An unmarried woman did well to follow the teachings of Winsbekin, who advised her daughter to avoid love altogether. But if minne compelled her to love a man, "you shall not yield to him: that is my wish."[207] Here are the social roots of the minne-song lady who persistently rejects the wooing of a man. It was the sexual double standard which compelled women to behave this way. This was clearly expressed in the so-called *Frauenstrophen*, verses which the minnesingers put into the mouths of ladies: "I refuse to give myself to the man I love dearly, not from a feeling of great hatred, but out of concern for my good name."[208] "Had I the courage to do it, I would

grant his desire, if I, a lady in love, did not have to fear for my reputation and for the life of the man who is everything to me."[209] "Love is
such a dangerous pleasure that I shall never dare to begin it."[210] "Now
he wants that for his sake I risk my good name and my life: this is my
misfortune!"[211] "What he desires, that is death and casts many into
ruin. Pale and red again it makes women. The men call it love, better it
were named un-love. Woe to him who has started with it."[212] The wish
to establish a friendship on the sole basis of conversations was usually
frustrated by the men, who were pushing for physical fulfillment. "Alas
that we women cannot make friends at conversations without them
wanting more; that depresses me. I do not want to make love."[213] It is
obvious that under such circumstances personal happiness was also sac-
rificed.

Now and then during the Middle Ages voices arose to protest the
moral double standard. "If a lady commits a misdeed, the kind a man
has committed a thousand times, her good name is supposed to be
ruined, while he is to derive fame from it. This is an unfair game. Such
law God does not want."[214] In the Latin *Ruodlieb* romance of the
eleventh century, the hero threatens his wife with death if she is not
faithful to him: "You must be faithful or be decapitated."[215] To which
the girl responds: "It is proper that both are subject to the same law.
Tell me, why shall I show a better faith to you than you to me? Tell me,
if you can defend that position, whether it would have been permitted
to Adam to keep a mistress next to Eve? If you were to keep company
with whores, would you want me to be a whore? Far be it from me to
bind myself to you with such a contract. Go, farewell, and whenever you
want to go whoring count me out."[216] St. Ambrose had taken the position that "to a man is not permitted what it not permitted to a
woman;"[217] in the twelfth century Gratian quoted this sentence in his
Decretum (Causa 32, Questio 4, chap. 4, col. 1128), but it proved impossible to make it fully accepted.

The conviviality of love   One can interpret courtly love as a counter-
program to the conditions of real life. In the world of courtly love everything was different: instead of violence and excesses, exquisite behavior
according to the rules of courtly etiquette; instead of a sexuality aimed
solely at physical satisfaction, an erotic culture in which musical talents,
eloquence, and literary education were of great importance; instead of
discrimination against and exploitation of women, a new distribution
of roles, where the lady is in a superior position and the man becomes a

servant who must strive for courtly perfection to earn the lady's favor. This conception of a new and better society with love as the central value was in essence a poetic idea, elaborated upon by the poets and no doubt largely a product of their imaginations.

But was there not also another side to real life? Was the courtly *Frauendienst* not also a social reality? The following example may illuminate how difficult it is to answer such questions. The French court chaplain Guillaume le Breton (d. 1224) wrote in his great Latin epic (*Philippis*) about the deeds of King Philip II Augustus. In recounting the Battle of Bouvines in 1214—where Emperor Otto IV and his Flemish allies suffered a humiliating defeat at the hands of the French—Guillaume relates that in the melée of battle, one knight called out "as though in jest"[218]: "Now let everyone think of his girl!"[219] Yet in his historical prose work on the same theme (*Gesta Philippi Augusti*) Guillaume omitted this detail. How can we explain this? Was the "jest" of the knight real but too unimportant to Guillaume the serious historian, or did Guillaume the poet merely embellish his battle account with a poetic-fictional motif? I know of only one piece of evidence from the courtly age which shows that a noble lord actually did perform knightly deeds in service to his lady and for the purpose of winning her favor. Salimbene of Parma reports under the year 1240 that Margrave Opizo of Este fought at a tournament and lost an eye in the action: "He did this, however, out of love for a woman who was present."[220] But anyone who thinks that this Italian margrave was a model courtly knight will be disappointed when he hears what Salimbene has to say next: "It was said that he had raped the daughters and wives of both the noble and the common people of Ferrara. He was even suspected of having had intercourse with his own sister and with the sister of his wife."[221] We can learn from this Opizo of Este that knightly service to ladies and violent sexual behavior could be combined without any apparent conflict.

It is impossible to determine how genuine the margrave's feelings were towards the lady for whom he fought the tournament. We do know, however, that talk of the ideals of knighthood and love were also used as a strategy of persuasion to make women willing instruments of one's desire. In the French *Lai du lecheor*, the ladies at court debated why the knights were so courtly and so brave: "Why are they good knights? Why do they love tournaments? Why do the young lords arm themselves? Why do they wear new clothes? Why do they hand out their jewelry, their ribbons and their rings? Why are they noble-minded and kind? Why do they beware of doing evil? Why do they love to woo, to caress, and to embrace?"[222] The answer was: "for a single thing only,"[223] and that was *con* (from Lat. *cunnus* "vagina") "All good deeds are performed for it."[224]

Older scholarship never doubted that the love songs of the troubadours and minnesingers were motivated by real life experiences. The chief witness for *Frauendienst* in action was Ulrich von Liechtenstein. His poetic self-portrait in *Frauendienst* offered everything one could expect of a minne-knight: years of self-denying courtship for the favor of a socially higher-ranking lady, in whose service the poet embarks on knightly journeys and for whose glory he peforms his songs. Today the unanimous view is that this work tells us little of historical value regarding the social reality of minnesong. Even if everything that Liechtenstein relates about his deeds in the service of minne were true, he still only imitated what courtly poetry had constructed. His autobiography of a minnesinger is composed almost entirely of literary motifs. The reality of courtly love is not to be found in the genuineness of the feelings of any one singer. In order to do justice to the character of love as a social function, we must seek out a different level of reality: that of courtly conviviality. Love had its place among the forms of entertainment in noble society.

The situation in France   It was not rare for troubadours to attach *tornadas* to their songs: these were accompanying stanzas, a few of which give the names of historically attested members of the southern French high nobility who were patrons and friends of the poets. In this way a link was established between the texts of the songs and the society for which the songs were intended. The same goes for the *senhals*—pseudonyms for the ladies who are addressed in these songs—which the troubadours mention in the tornadas as well as in the songs themselves. Although we have not been able to decipher a single one of these names, we must assume that they stood for actual people, since the game of concealment made sense only if there was something real behind it. What kind of relationship existed between the singers and the ladies they sang about so mysteriously is not clear. The theory that the pseudonyms served to hide real love affairs cannot be verified. Names such as "Beautiful Glance" (*Bel Esgar*), "Pure Joy" (*Fin Joy*), "Beautiful Hope" (*Bel Esper*), "Better than Good" (*Milhs de Be*), and so on, were probably social appelations, and the identity of the people they referred to would have been known within the circles of court society. In any case, the names themselves reveal that there was a direct relationship between the poets' songs and the social life at court.

What sort of relationship that was is revealed in a song by William IX of Aquitaine (d. 1126), the first known troubadour: "If you give me a love game, I am not so stupid that I wouldn't know how to pick out the better part among the bad ones."[225] Apparently the poet was referring here to a game which later came to be called "divided game" (Provençal *joc-partit*, French *jeu-parti*). Its basic premise was as follows: a variety of opinions regarding a love problem were offered for choice, and each player picked one opinion which he then had to defend in debate against others. It would seem that such games were the source from which sprang the partime, one of the main types of the Provençal debating songs, attested since the end of the twelfth century. In the partimes, two poets are confronted with a disputed issue in the form of an either-or dilemma ("is it this way or that?"); one poet chooses one position and the remaining position falls to the second poet. The two men then expound their opinion to each other in alternating stanzas, until finally they appeal for the verdict of the arbiter. The questions debated were nearly always concerned with courtly love. Sometimes the points discussed were of central importance. More often, though, the positions were extreme or overstated ("Who is easier to win over, the wife of an impotent man or the wife of a jealous man?" Pillet-Carstens 461.16); and not infrequently they were downright funny ("What do you prefer, warm clothing in winter or a courtly mistress in summer?" Pillet-Carstens 129.2; "If your lady will give herself to you on the condition of a night with a toothless old man, would you prefer to fulfill this condition before or afterwards?" Pillet-Carstens 144.1; "What is more likely to bring death, an Advent night with one's mistress or eight hours among infamous bandits?" Pillet-Carstens 129.3, etc.). We can see from this that the tenzones were not primarily concerned with intellectual solutions to specific questions, but with skillfull and witty argument. In other words, the entertainment value of this genre was at least as prominent as its didactic purpose.

The interest of French noble society in debating questions of love increased even further during the twelfth and thirteenth centuries. Two games which seem to have enjoyed special popularity were known as "The king who does not lie" (Le roi qui ne ment) and "The game of the king and queen" (Le jeu du roi et de la reine). One player was chosen as the king or queen, and proceeded to pose questions to the fellow players and vice versa. The questions concerned love; they could be drawn from literature or could refer to the personal situation of the person asked, and they had to be answered in as witty a way as possible. Such games were part of the entertainment program at the court feasts. In the poetic description of the tournament hosted by Count Louis of Laon in 1285 in Chauvency, we read the following: "Everywhere there was great pleasure in conversation and various games. Some dance in a circle, others in a line; those who truly love pose love questions; others settle among themselves on the game "Of the king and queen," and it is played according to the rules; a third group plays "The king who never lies"; another speaks intimately about love."[226] These quiz games were so popular that entire collections of questions and answers were compiled in the fourteenth century.

Among the minne entertainments in the Romance countries there were also love tournaments and performances of various kinds. Rolandinus of Padua reports in his chronicle that at a feast, hosted in 1214 in Treviso, a minne castle had been erected, which was defended by the ladies present and besieged by the men (see p. 221). We may assume that literary models were not infrequently used for such affairs. It was known from Ovid that the god of Love had "a castle of his own" (*sua castra*) (*Amores* I.9.1). The taking of a castle as an allegory for the conquest of a woman became a popular motif in the minne teachings of the thirteenth and fourteenth centuries.

Of all the forms of minne entertainment, the French love courts (*cours d'amour*) have attracted the most scholarly attention. A number of misconceptions used to exist about this institution, until it became clear that these courts were not real legal sessions but social events that were especially popular with women. The chief witness for the love courts is Andreas Capellanus, who included in his work a catalog of twenty-one "love verdicts" (*iudicia amoris*; p. 271 ff.), all of which were rendered by ladies. One such verdict was issued by a "court of ladies in Gascony"[227]; the other decisions Andreas Capellanus attributed to individual ladies of the high nobility, all of whom are mentioned by name, and most of whom were still alive when he wrote his work: Queen Eleanor of England (d. 1204), her daughter, Countess Marie of Champagne (d. 1198), Marie's cousin, Countess Elisabeth of Flanders (d. 1182), the Vicontess Ermengarde of Narbonne (d. 1192), and possibly also Queen Alice of France (d. 1206). In one passage Andreas described how the verdicts of these ladies came about or could come about: two members of noble society approached the countess of Champagne in writing, requesting a decision in a question of love; the countess re-

turned a letter with her verdict. Most cases in which a decision was
sought from the courts of ladies concerned violations of the rules of
courtly love, violations that were labeled and condemned as such. There
was, for example, the case of a man who had a love affair with a
woman. When he discovered that she was related to him, he wanted to
end the relationship, while the woman wanted to continue it. Queen
Eleanor decided—incidentally, in agreement with the rules of canonical
marriage law—that an "incestuous love"[228] violated all laws and therefore had to be given up. A smaller group of cases dealt with issues that
had to be settled by making a choice. For example, the question was put
to Queen Eleanor of who should be preferred as a lover, a young man
"distinguished by no virtue,"[229] or an older man "pleasing in every
virtue."[230] The queen decided against youth and in favor of virtue.
Questions of this sort call to mind the themes of the tenzones. Whether
or not the verdicts recorded by Andreas Capellanus are authentic, that
is to say, whether they were in fact rendered in this form by the ladies to
whom Andreas attributes them, cannot be determined. Occasionally it
is suggested that Andreas Capellanus invented the love decisions to ridicule the ladies associated with them, but such a view finds no support in
the texts. It also misjudges the importance attached to the discussion of
questions of courtly love within French aristocratic society. The *Council of Remiremont* (*Veris in temporibus*), a Latin debating poem from
the middle of the twelfth century, also mentions a number of historical
ladies (Elisabeth de Granges, Elisabeth de Faucogney, Eve de Danubrium, etc.), who acted as judges or experts in questions of love. If we
also add the names of the persons who are called upon to decide the
issues debated in the Provençal partimes, we get the impression that
discussions about courtly love were as popular as they were common
with the French nobility.

The situation in Germany   Only by looking at conditions in France
do we realize how very different the situation was in Germany. Virtually
all the elements that attest a lively minne entertainment in France during the courtly age are missing in Germany. The German minnesingers
did adopt the romance song types, but they omitted the *tornadas* at
the end of their songs, and with them the names of their patrons. The
German minnesingers adopted most of the descriptive techniques of the
troubadours, but the pseudonyms, the *senhals*, which pointed to the
social reality of the minne culture, remained unknown in Germany,
with a few exceptions. Also ignored were the debating songs, the par-

times, which in France were the main genre for discussing questions of love. No evidence exists to show that love games, such as "The king who never lies," were known to the German nobility. There is no documentation for love tournaments or love courts. Nothing indicates that members of the German high nobility were involved in decisions concerning love disputes. We are forced to conclude that the lively exchange which existed in France between minne poetry and minne entertainment was unknown in Germany. It would appear that courtly love reached Germany almost exclusively as a literary phenomenon; not as a form of aristocratic entertainment, but as a poetic ideal.

This does not mean, however, that court society in Germany did not also show an increasing interest in debates on questions of courtly love. But here the interest was focused mainly on poetry, where such questions were put up for discussion. This is attested by around the midtwelfth century in a scene from the *Kaiserchronik*: during a break in the fighting at the siege of Viterbo by the Romans, a noble lady from the besieged city addresses the Roman Totila with the following words: "Totila, you noble man, you may approach more closely to the ladies. You are so brave and a great hero in physical might. By God, answer me what I ask you: in all honesty, would you prefer that a beautiful lady made love to you all night, or that tomorrow you should meet in battle a man as brave as you. If you had the choice, what would you do, which of the two would you prefer?"[231] Such questions were also treated in the Provençal debating songs, for example in a partime between Sordel and Bertran d'Alamanon (Pillet-Carstens 437.10): here the issue was whether a man would rather lose favor with the ladies or his fame as a fighter. We must assume that the poet of the *Kaiserchronik* was aware of the custom of debating such questions, and that he either expected his audience to show an interest in this or intended to arouse such an interest. Incidentally, Totila did not really answer the question put to him. Instead he avoided making a choice by diplomatically praising both battle for *êre* as well as minne.

There are some dialogue songs by Albrecht von Johansdorf and Walther von der Vogelweide, in which a lord and a lady debate questions of courtly love in a humorous and pointed way. Although we certainly cannot take these songs as reflections of actual minne conversations, they do show clearly the court audience's interest in such discussions. These songs employed a minne casuistry similar to that discussed in France. Albrecht von Johansdorf, for example, addressed a question that was also treated by Andreas Capellanus: whether a knight may serve two ladies at the same time: "How he shall act, that is what I ask: whether it can be done with courtly decorum or whether it would not be unfaithful if he devoted himself to two women, to both in secret love. Tell me, milord, would that be unseemly?"[232] The lord responded: "It should be permitted to men but not to women."[233] Walther's dialogue song (70.22) also brings up the question whether a man devoted to his lady may in addition seek his pleasure with other women. The lady rejects this idea: "Whoever wants me as a lover should refrain from such inconstancy if he expects to win my favor."[234] Conversely, the minnesinger Rubin discussed what one should think of a lady who has taken three knights into her service (VII b, 4.1 ff.). The troubadours pondered the very same question. A partime between Savaric de Mauleon, Gaucelm Faidit and Uc de la Bacalaria (Pillet-Carstens 432.2) debates which of three lovers a lady loves more: the one she looks at lovingly; the one whose hand she holds; or the one whose foot she laughingly touches. What makes the German texts different from the French is the fact that all the dialogues from Germany are fictitious, whereas the Provençal tenzones were actual debates between various poets. The Middle High German *geteiltez spil* ("divided game") is the exact equivalent of the French *jeu-parti*, and was apparently created by way of imitation. In Germany, however, the word was not used to describe a separate genre. In minnesong it expresses a "dilemma," as, for example, when a lady weighs two equally bad options: "My friends have given me a 'divided game,' which in either case I must lose. I would rather refrain from choosing one or the other, since my choices are bad. My friends say that if I want to love, I must renounce it. But I would rather have both."[235] Reinmar der Alte put such an either-or question to himself in his famous *Preislied* (MF 165.10): "Two possibilities I have given myself to choose from, and they are battling each other with arguments inside my heart."[236] All this would be unthinkable without the model of the French and Provençal debating songs and minne disputations.

In German courtly epics based on French models we do find minne courts and minne verdicts. The first example occurs in Ulrich von Zatzikhoven's *Lanzelet*, where we hear that beautiful Elidida had been "judge in courtly matters"[237]: "Whenever there was a quarrel at court that led to a conflict of minne, she settled it with a final and exemplary decision."[238] Rudolf von Ems recounts in *Wilhelm von Orlens* how on the occasion of the great tournament of Puy, the most beautiful ladies of the land "come together six days before the beginning of the tournament and elect a queen who is to judge their complaints. For the entire week she renders minne justice, just as feudal law is administered before a lord."[239] Such tales are not proof that minne conversations with consultations and decisions by noble ladies were also practiced in Germany. But they do attest that such things were by no means unknown, and that court society took an interest in them.

A direct link to French minne casuistry is visible in the courtly poetic tale *Die Heidin*, which gives a central role to a problem already discussed by Andreas Capellanus: what a knight should do when his lady gives him the choice between her upper and her lower half: "I want to give you two options to choose from, both of which are courtly. Now listen, lord, and pick the best: if you want, you shall have what is above the belt; or take what extends from the belt down, if that is what you want. If you choose the best part, it will be to your happiness. You shall have the better half, leave the worse for me."[240]

It would seem that the interest in French forms of minne entertainment grew livelier in Germany towards the end of the thirteenth century. From this time comes the tale "The Two Unequal Lovers," which begins like an invitation to a *jeu-parti*: "My dear lady, I wish to present to your goodwill a dispute to be decided."[241] The question here was one that was also frequently discussed in France: who was preferable as a lover, a poor young man who knew how to love *hercenlich* (43), or a noble and rich man who lacked that quality. But unlike the Provençal partimes, in the German texts the two alternatives are not argued by two different people, nor was there a genuine choice, since the poet from the start sided with the poor but noble man.

Around the turn of the fourteenth century we also encounter in German lyric the first instance of a pseudonym for the beloved lady. Heinrich Hetzbolt von Weißensee (attested until 1345) addressed his lady as "The Beautiful Splendor,"[242] no doubt in imitation of the French examples. From the same period comes a group of texts from the middle Rhine ("The Minne Court" [*Der Minnehof*], "The Knightly Journey" [*Die Ritterfahrt*], "Minne and Society" [*Minne und Gesellschaft*]), in which historically attested ladies and lords from a circle of nobility around the courts of Katzenelnbogen and von Sayn appear as participants in minne games. "Minne Court" tells of a session of a minne court which has to consider the problem of how a lady could reward her knight without endangering her own honor and the knight's life. Here the Counts Gerhard of Jülich (d. 1327/28) and Johann of Sponheim (d. 1323/24), along with Lord Kraft of Greifenstein (attested until 1326) act as expert consultants (144 ff.). All three appear as witnesses in a charter of 1300 by Count William I (attested until 1331) and Diether IV (d. 1315) von Katzenelnbogen. The "Knightly Journey" recounts the campaign against the castle of the "beautiful lady of Limburg,"[243] who had transgressed the laws of courtly love by choosing a lover who "is neither knight nor servant."[244] Leader of the army was Countess Irmgard of Rheinfels (d. 1303), the wife of William I of Katzenelnbogen, and among the ladies and lords who joined the campaign were several well-known figures of the Rhenish nobility.

An even wider circle of people appears in "Minne and Society" (first half of the fourteenth century). These texts hold a special place in the German literature of this period, because such a direct involvement of the noble audience, for which the unknown authors wrote, is found nowhere else. Apparently the poets along the middle Rhine at the end of the thirteenth century were quite familiar with the French forms of minne entertainment.

To sum up the contrasting situations: until the end of the thirteenth century, courtly love in Germany was largely a literary phenomenon, whereas in France love was also a favorite theme of courtly entertainment. It is not clear what reasons account for the delayed adoption of French forms of minne entertainment. We must bear in mind that many details of French aristocratic culture were at that time transmitted by literature. The fact that the romance debating songs and minne disputations had such little appeal in Germany is no doubt related to differences in the level of lay education. The history of the Provençal partimes, as well as the enjoyment of the clever and witty debates of minne questions, must be seen in relation to the educational developments in France that gave rise to the Scholastic method. Dialectic and logic were the new sciences; they shaped a new style of thinking which in France also enriched the forms of entertainment of the educated laity. In Germany these sciences remained largely unknown (cf. p. 72), and since the German nobility of the thirteenth century was still for the most part illiterate, it lacked the intellectual preconditions for the adoption of such forms of entertainment.

CHAPTER VI

Criticism of Courtly Life

The material luxury at the great courts and the worldly attitudes of the nobility encountered frequent opposition and protest. The tone of the critique was set by the ecclesiastical authors, who regarded the openly displayed worldliness of courtly life as a symptom of an ominous moral decay, and condemned it as a violation of the basic principles of Christian ethics. A keen critic at the beginning of the twelfth century was the Norman monk Ordericus Vitalis, who was scandalized by the worldly doings of the young noblemen and noblewomen of northern France: "Now the laypeople in their wantonness seize upon fashions that suit their perverse lifestyle."[1] Particularly dubious in the eyes of this ecclesiastical writer was the fact that those noble men and women, who "live in their own pleasures without consideration for the law of God and the customs of their ancestors,"[2] met with such approval from their peers. The bearers of the new social activities were to Ordericus the "courtiers" (uiri curiales), who with their "fashionable innovations" (nouis adinuentionibus) aimed above all at pleasing the ladies: "The courtiers greatly flatter the women with every kind of wantonness."[3]

A few decades after Ordericus Vitalis, around the middle of the twelfth century, John of Salisbury composed the first thorough critique of the court culture then flourishing in France and England. He became the founder of a literature of court criticism, which in the following centuries became increasingly important. Central to John of Salisbury was the criticism of the uses, or rather abuses, of hunting, which he saw as a symbol of the unrestrained life of secular court society. John was apparently drawing on personal experiences at the English court. The extraordinary hunting passion of King Henry II (d. 1189) was criticized by various contemporary writers. It was said that nearly one third of England was turned into royal forests during the twelfth century. Violations against the hunting privileges of the court and the nobility were subject to severe punishments. John of Salisbury condemned the arbitrary and reckless conduct of the noble hunters and the injuries they inflicted upon the rural population: "Peasants are kept from their fields to allow the wild animals to pasture freely. To increase the pasturage for these animals even more, the peasants are deprived of their fields, the tenants of their land, the cowherds and shepherds of their pastures."[4] Excess and lack of restraint were for John of Salisbury the characteristics of hunting, through which human feeling and reason were ruined. Owing to "the immoderate impulse for pleasure,"[5] hunting belonged with other dissolute activites of court society, "feasts, drinking, eating, songs and games, overrefined luxury, excesses and every kind of dissipation,"[6] which endangered the soul and through which men were even more easily ruined than women. Also harmful was the nobility's interest in secular music, because it made men soft and effeminate: "Today noblemen are said to be educated if they know how to hunt, if they practice the damnable game of dice, if they subdue the natural vigor of their voices to a softer sound with clever tricks, if, unmindful of their manliness, they forget in songs and instrumental music the nature to which they were born."[7]

Under the influence of the *Policraticus*, a whole circle of Latin writers in the second half of the twelfth century, nearly all of whom had personal connections to the English court, continued the criticism of the modern social life of the secular nobility: Peter of Blois in his tract "Of the Flatterer and Yes-man" (*De palpone et assentatore*) and in his famous letter (no. 14) of 1175 to the court chaplains of King Henry II of England; John of Altavilla in *Architrenius* (around 1185); Nigellus Wireker in his "Tractate against the Courtiers and Court Clerics" (*Tractatus contra curiales et officiales clericos*) of 1193—these were the most prominent voices. In order to bring out the darker sides of court life, the courtier who concerned himself with trifles was compared to the philosopher, or life at court was contrasted with life in a monastery or at the schools. At the same time the main substantive critiques of the court were put into more concrete terms. Central to the criticism were charges of "flattery" (*adulatio*) and "ambition" (*ambitio*). Variations on the theme of *adulatio* were "hypocrisy" "mendacity," "slander," and "intrigue"; *ambitio* embraced "restlessness," "greed," and "venality." Most authors directed their criticism in particular at the noise, crowded conditions, and confusion at court, as well as at the worldly display of pomp, the luxurious clothes of the nobility, the wastefulness in the building of new houses, and the extravagance at courtly banquets. Critics were also fond of listing the unpleasant sides of court life: the poor quality of the food and lodging, the discomfort during travels, the daily hustle and bustle at the departure of the court, the moodiness of the lord of the court, and the exertions it required to get through to the lord. All these motifs would become firmly established elements in the literature of court ciriticism during the following centuries.

Twelfth-century court criticism in Latin was initially a discourse among learned men of letters. No doubt it was rare for those against whom the writings were directed to learn anything about their content. But by around the middle of the twelfth century, a religious and didactic literature written in the vernacular appeared in Germany. It addressed itself to an aristocratic audience and condemned its modern lifestyle with great severity. The "Discourse on Faith," composed probably between 1140 and 1160 by an author who called himself "poor Hartmann" (der arme Hartmann), lists everything that belonged to the furnishings of a great court: golden cups and silver bowls, gems and ivory, artfully woven gold braids, expensive jewelry, various silk cloths, scarlet, mantles, tapestries, rugs and curtains interlaced with gold filament, glittering armor, shining helmets, saddles and shields with gold decorations, riding horses and war chargers, long lances with silk pennants, rich tables with white bread, meat, and fish, a well-stocked cellar, a rich and comfortable bed, and at night a beautiful wife in one's arms. "Thus you are pleased, your heart rejoices in your breast over all this voluptuousness, with which you tempt the flesh and endanger your soul."[8] But, the poet continues, when death comes all worldly treasures are useless: they fall to the laughing heirs, while the body rots in the grave and all that matters are those things that were done for the salvation of the soul.

Somewhat later, the tract "Remembrance of Death" (*Von des tôdes gehugde*) took the same approach in depicting the worldly splendor of courtly-noble life. Its author—Heinrich von Melk—leads a noble lady to the bier of her deceased husband and shows her the decaying corpse as symbolic of the transitory nature of the world:

Now behold, where are his frivolous words with which he praised the pride of the ladies? See how the tongue lies in his mouth, the tongue with which he sang the love songs so agreeably; now he cannot utter a single word or tone. Look, where is the chin with the newfangled beard? Look at the unnatural position of the arms with which he caressed and embraced you in so many ways. Where are the feet on which he walked in courtly manner with the ladies? Many times you could admire how nicely his hose suited him: now they unfortunately no longer cling so tightly to his legs. He is now utterly foreign to you, he whose silk shirt you once pleated in such manifold ways. Look at him now: in the middle he is bloated like a sail.[9]

Court criticism was also the theme of the first rhymed treatise on ethics in the German language, written by Wernher von Elmendorf in Thuringia around 1170. The author warns of flatterers, scoffers, and babblers, of lies, deceit, and intrigue, of an overestimation of beauty, wealth, and nobility, of greed and a passion for fame, of gluttony and immoderation, and of wastefulness in the construction of new buildings. The subject was treated even more fully by the ecclesiastical didacticians of the thirteenth century, Thomas von Zirklaere and Hugo von Trimberg. "Sad to say, but today there are few courtiers who strive for heaven and think nothing of worldly fame."[10] Falseness and dissimulation are to Hugo of Trimberg the marks of the courtiers, "for they all talk sweetly, though their hearts are full of gall."[11] Upright and honest people were not to be found at court. "If someone deceives with sweet words,"[12] he is suitable for service at the court. Greed and flattery dominate the entire court society. "Courtiers, doctors, and lawyers have idols, the chests"[13] in which they hide their ill-gotten wealth. "Pride, greed, gluttony, and shamelessness teach the courtiers all manner of pretenses."[14] This criticism was directed not only at the courtiers but also at the lords themselves: "One thing I have observed: many a lord prefers a dishonest man who knows how to flatter over someone who looks after his [the lord's] wealth and good name."[15] This is why no honest and upright men are appointed to the princely council. In the old days "devious and evil councilors"[16] had no access to the courts of the great lords. "But now the life at the courts has changed completely for the worse, so that a man rarely attains any renown there unless he has seven tongues."[17] Hugo von Trimberg painted a picture of a thoroughly degenerate court society, in which traditional virtues had lost all value. "Uprightness, decency and truth, humility, modesty and guilelessness, purity, and moderation have been expelled from the court, and in their place exist lies, deceit, villainy, worthless and knavish character, falseness, dissipation, flattery, drinking, free-loading, sneering, gluttony, games, thievery, and mockery, and nobody thinks of God, of salvation and of death."[18]

Even the works that drew a positive picture of courtly life fell under the spell of this ecclesiastical criticism. We can see this from the didactic poem entitled *Der Winsbeke*, in which a noble father instructs his son on courtly virtue and knightly worthiness. In the thirteenth century a sequel to this text was composed: here the noble teacher himself was instructed, namely on the vanity of court life. At the end of this "Anti-Winsbeke," the father sells all his possessions and endows a poorhouse which he enters as a lay brother.

Ecclesiastical court criticism in Germany attained its widest impact at the end of the thirteenth century in the powerful sermons of the Franciscan friar Berthold of Regensburg. Castigating the extravagant life-style of court society as an expression of sinful pride, he painted the dangers that court life posed to the salvation of the soul in the harshest colors: "If someone can courteously pass on a message, or carry a key, or courteously offer a cup, and knows how to carry his hands politely or fold them in front of himself, some people will say: 'Ah, what a well-bred squire (or man or woman) that is! He is truly a virtuous person. Ah, how virtuously he behaves!' Behold, this virtue is a mockery before God and is nothing in the eyes of God."[19]

It is difficult to assess how great an impact this criticism had on the very people to whom it was addressed. On the whole, it would seem that the clerical objections had little effect. Neither the denunciations of courtly extravagance in dress nor the many ecclesiastical prohibitions had more than sporadic success. And the clerical admonitions could not prevent the social ethics of the nobility from becoming increasingly secularized and increasingly detached from the tutelage of the Church. With growing self-confidence, the laity demanded to set its own criteria for judging the life of this world, and to establish social practices on values that were thoroughly worldly in orientation. The court poets gave effective support in formulating and defending these demands with their depictions of an idealized society, in which the beautiful sides of courtly life were integrated harmoniously, and without any apparent conflict, with traditional Christian moral and ethical concepts.

But even the courtly poets had critical things to say, and we can assume that this kind of criticism stung much more than the reproaches of clerics, who were outsiders. In southern France as early as the first half of the twelfth century, Cercamon and especially Marcabru de-

nounced the dubious moral nature of the new culture of love. The
northern French epic poets, too, presented some of their courtly tales in
a way that raises doubts whether they really intended to glorify the
social practices of the nobility. A master of courtly irony was the unknown author of *Aucassin et Nicolette*, a *chantefable* (a tale composed
of alternating narrative and sung parts). Written around 1200, it tells
the story of the love of Aucassin, the young son of a count, for the
slave-girl Nicolette. The viconte who owned Nicolette tried to talk Aucassin out of his love for the girl: "Take the daughter of a king or a
count. Besides, what profit would you have had, had you made her your
lover and taken her to your bed? Very little you would have won, for
your soul would be in hell for eternity, and you would never enter
Paradise."[20] To which Aucassin replied:

> What am I to do in Paradise? I care not to enter, but only to have Nicolette,
> my sweetest friend, whom I love so dearly. For into Paradise enter only such
> people as I will tell you now: those aged priests and old cripples and the
> lame, who day and night sit before the altars and in the old crypts, those with
> worn mantles and old, tattered habits, who are naked and barefoot and with-
> out socks, those who die of hunger and thirst, of cold and wretchedness. It is
> they who enter Paradise, and I want nothing to do with them. I would much
> rather go to Hell, for to Hell go the fair clerks and handsome knights, who
> were slain in tournaments and in great wars, and the good squires and the
> loyal men. I shall go with them. And there go also the courtly ladies, who
> have two or three lovers besides their husbands. There go gold and silver,
> ermine and rich furs, harpers and minstrels, and the kings of this world. I
> shall go with these, if I can have with me Nicolette, my sweetest friend.[21]

It did not often happen that a courtly poet dared to regale his noble
audience with such words, which could easily be misunderstood as a
confirmation of the clerical denunciations of the sinfulness of court life.

In Germany, where literature on the whole had a less pronounced
character of entertainment and conviviality, the humorous and satirical
strains usually yielded to a positive depiction of the courtly ideal of
society. This left less room for critical views than in France. But in Germany, too, there existed a critical literature that deserves more attention
than it has received up to now.

In courtly lyric, the critical debate with the courtly concept of minne
began immediately with the first phase in the reception of romance
models. The rejection of worldly love in Friedrich von Hausen's crusading songs was, however, an exception, as was the criticism of the exalted
position of the lady and the futility of one-sided service in the songs of

Hartmann von Aue and Walther von der Vogelweide (cf. p. 364). Only in Neidhart did the satirical-critical approach assume a central importance. But a glance at recent Neidhart scholarship shows that there is still no agreement on the aim of his social critique. It has frequently been said that the highly overdrawn and satirical world of loutishness in Neidhart's songs should be seen as an appeal to the noble audience to return to courtly values, but this can scarcely be verified from the texts. In fact, these courtly values were probably the very target of his criticism. In the process of public reception, however, Neidhart's songs lost their sting: Neidhart was refashioned into an enemy of the peasants, and was thereby assimilated to the social self-image of the nobility.

Court criticism was more concrete in *Spruchdichtung*, especially in the *Sprüche* of Walter von der Vogelweide. "I don't know to whom I shall compare the court hounds (*hovebellen*)..."[22]: thus begins a strophe aimed at the conditions at the court of Carinthia under Duke Bernhard II (d. 1256). The use of the word *hovebellen* to describe the schemers and slanderers at the ducal court follows a Latin tradition that goes back to Boethius and was already used in court criticism in the eleventh century (*canes palatini*: "court dogs" = "courtiers"). Walther's epigram about the court of Thuringia, "if anyone suffers from an ear disease, I advise him to stay away from the Thuringian court,"[23] also uses motifs that were known in the Latin literature of court criticism in the wake of John of Salisbury's *Policraticus*: the loud noise and restlessness of court activities, the crowds around the lord, and the immoderation of the drinking bouts. "Even if a tun of wine cost a thousand pounds, the cups of the knights there would never be empty."[24]

The most interesting court criticism is found in the courtly epics. Among the oldest secular epics in Germany is *Reinhart Fuchs*, the first animal epic in German. It was written perhaps around 1180—the date is controversial—and the otherwise unknown Heinrich der Glichesere gives himself as the author. The poet used the well-known fable of "the court day of the lion" to draw a thoroughly negative picture of lion Frevel's royal court and its courtiers. The king's behavior was marked by ignorance, irresponsibility, cruelty, and selfishness, while the noble members of his court were conspicuous for their corruption, cowardice, and scheming. The conjecture that the contemporary allusions were aimed at the Hohenstaufen imperial court under Frederick I has much to recommend it, though it cannot be verified. We don't know who commissioned this satirical epic. It is among the most significant literary works of its time, but judging from the few scattered manuscripts in which it has survived, its influence was negligible.

In the Arthurian romances critical voices are rare. King Arthur and his court embodied courtly perfection, and admission to the Round Table was the highest honor a knight could hope for. Nevertheless, the king's actions did not always live up to the expectations of this idealized image. And the fact that such a shady character as Keie was, as steward, responsible for running the entire court, does not quite fit in with the court's function as role model. How these motifs should be interpreted is unclear. A political interpretation which tries to link the weakness of the king to the crisis of the German monarchy after 1198, and which tries to see in the figure of Keie a conflict with the ambitions of the ministerial class, goes beyond what the texts themselves reveal.

The heroic epics, which treated historical themes and were much closer to real life, offered wider scope for court criticism. The *Nibelungenlied* portrays the Burgundian royal court at Worms as a model of courtly order and courtly splendor. But behind the façade of courtly manners, there opened an abyss of hatred, deceit, lust for power, and treason. The king was too weak to secure by himself the continuation of his rule; the strongman at the court, Hagen, turned into a murderer because he saw in Siegfried a threat to the Burgundian kingship. The story culminates in the downfall of an entire society which had concealed its corruption behind a courtly mask.

The high point of poetic court criticism in Germany was the depiction of the English court in Gottfried von Straßburg's *Tristan*. King Mark's spring feast at the beginning of the poem presents the court initially in the full splendor of carefree, festive joy. Later, as young Tristan's brilliant court career arouses the jealousy of the barons, it is revealed that life at court is dominated by intrigues, as each courtier tries to destroy the others' influence with the king. Thanks to his superior intellect, Tristan initially succeeds in keeping the scheming barons at bay. But when the suspicion of adultery poisons personal relations, the king's character, too, grows increasingly gloomy. In contrast to the degenerate court life, Gottfried creates a realm of love free of intrigues and falseness. But Gottfried did make clear that in the long run, love stood no chance of realizing itself outside the existing social order. Moreover, the poet's cool irony makes it hard to know whether the critical depiction of the court was intended merely to denounce abuses, or whether

Gottfried wanted to show the flawed and brittle structure of the entire courtly social system.

The critical power inherent in the courtly epics of around 1200 seems to have had little appeal for noble audiences. In any case, in the thirteenth century the depiction of society rapidly lost depth and became much more one-dimensional. The *Nibelungenlied* was soon weakened by the poetic addition of the "Lament," and both Wolfram's *Willehalm* and Gottfreid's *Tristan* were reabsorbed into the norm of courtly idealization with the help of innocuous sequels that rendered the original messages harmless.

CHAPTER VII

The Literary Scene of the Courtly Age

Before the invention of the printing press, writers labored under conditions very different from those that have existed in more recent centuries. There was no publishing industry, no book trade, no copyright, and not much of a literate public. The costs of production were enormous. Every book had to be written by hand—longer works could take years—and for centuries the sole available writing material was expensive parchment, which had to be manufactured in a lengthy process from sheep, goat, or cow hides. Only the spread of paper manufacturing in the fourteenth century made it possible to lower costs significantly, which in turn led to a rise in the production of books. But even then, owning books remained a privilege of the wealthy. Writing was always done in the Latin alphabet, the use of which was acquired in the Latin school; this meant that only a very small group of people trained in Latin was directly involved in the production of literature.

Until the twelfth century, all literary activity lay in the hands of clerics or those with a clerical education. The literature of clerics and monks, whether Latin or vernacular, was for the most part practical religious literature: in part it served theology, liturgy, and exegesis; in part it had apologetic-missionary, scientific, and didactic purposes. Even the poetry composed in monasteries and at episcopal residences was intended for use in mass or for the glorification and strengthening of the Christian faith. Learned monks wrote poetry in the strophic forms of classical lyric, exchanged Latin rhymed letters and occasional poems, and celebrated in verse the quiet joys of the contemplative life.

But these poetic efforts were only pleasant diversions, and they were sometimes accused of lacking the proper spiritual seriousness. Secular poetry was the exception during these centuries, and it is found above all where literature was used to glorify worldly lordship (*Ludwigslied, Modus Ottinc*).

A completely new situation emerged in the twelfth century as the lay nobility began to influence the production of literature. At the great princely courts, which at this time developed into centers of literary activity, literary culture was determined by factors very different from those at the monasteries. The crucial element was the princely patrons who called the poets to their courts, supported them, and supervised their work. The poets' dependence on the goodwill of their patrons and the tastes of the court audience shaped their literary output. At the same time, the new interest which court society took in secular poetry accorded to literature a higher social rank than it had possessed before. Literature became the most significant artistic expression of lay society. The precondition for this was the establishment of organized writing at the secular courts.

1. ORAL CULTURE AND LITERACY IN COURTLY SOCIETY

LAY EDUCATION

Lay education in France   In France and Norman England we can observe that the creation of courtly literature in French went hand in hand with changes in the educational system. Modern court literature could develop only when and where the princely patrons themselves had a Latin education. The notion that an exemplary ruler should be literate was expressed at that time most bluntly in the saying: "An illiterate king is a crowned ass."[1] This sentence appears in the *Deeds of the English Kings*, written around 1120 by William of Malmesbury and dedicated to Earl Robert of Gloucester (d. 1147). William placed these words into the mouth of King Henry I (d. 1135), who supposedly uttered them in the presence of his uneducated father, King William I the Conqueror (d. 1087). A few decades later the sentence was quoted in John of Salisbury's *Policraticus* (circa 1160; vol. 1, p. 254), where the kings are admonished that "the pretext of knighthood"[2] could not be used to excuse ignorance of the Holy Scriptures. Rather, the holy books should be read every day: "This makes it quite clear how necessary a knowledge of Scriptures is for the princes, who in daily reading should ponder the laws of God."[3] In the second half of the twelfth century this was no longer an unrealistic demand. The French King Louis VII (d. 1180) and the English King Henry II (d. 1189) had both enjoyed a Latin education. The same was true for the great French crown vassals who at that time opened their courts to literary culture: Count Henry I of Champagne (d. 1181), his brother, Count Thibaut V of Blois (d. 1191), Count Philip of Flanders (d. 1191), and others.

The gradual spread of lay education in the French princely houses overlaps in many phases the rise of courtly culture. In southern France, the court of the counts of Poitou was already a center of higher studies and literary activities under William III (d. 1030). The count had books copied and corresponded with some of the most important scholars of his age, Fulbert of Chartres (d. 1028) and Leo of Vercelli (d. 1026). The historian Ademar of Chabannes (d. 1034) said about William III: "This duke was trained in the arts from childhood and had a good knowledge of literature. He kept a large number of books at his court, and if by chance he had time away from the bustle of the court, he devoted it to his personal reading and spent the better part of the night with books, until sleep overcame him."[4] His famous grandson, William IX (d.1126), the first troubadour, could profit from the tradition of education at the court of Poitiers.

In Anjou we find the first educated count as far back as the tenth century. He was Fulques II (d. 960), whose level of education is said to have inspired King Louis IV (d. 954) to proclaim: "Indeed, wisdom, eloquence, and education are particularly suited to kings and counts. The more elevated one's position, the more luminous should be one's manners and education."[5] Even if this statement hardly refers to historical fact, it does reveal what people at the great French courts thought about education in the twelfth century, when the comment was penned.

An exception among the secular princes of France was Count Fulques IV of Anjou (d. 1109), who personally composed a Latin history of his house, only fragments of which have survived (*Fragmentum historiae Andegavensis*). His grandson, Count Godfrey V (d. 1151) was, according to the *Gesta consulum Andegavorum*, "extraordinarily well educated and the most eloquent among clerics and laymen."[6] In his biography of Godfrey V (written around 1170–80), Jean de Marmoutier emphasized that the count combined knightly skill with a literary education: "he was devoted to the exercise of arms and to the liberal arts."[7] In 1127, the then fifteen-year-old Count Godfrey celebrated his engagement to Matilda, the emperor's widow and the daughter of King Henry I of England. Jean de Marmoutier's account of the festivities reveals how highly the French lay nobility valued education, elegance, and courtly manners, even by the first half of the twelfth century. Henry I, we are told, seated the young count next to himself and questioned him about many things in order to discover how intelligently he could answer. The young man "paid close attention to his choice of words, and decorated his speech with many rhetorical figures,"[8] to the great delight of the king, who was amazed at such sharpness of mind. From the marriage of Godfrey V of Anjou and Matilda was born King Henry II of England, who in his time was the greatest patron of literature and the liberal arts. No illiterate king would ever again occupy the English throne.

In the house of the Norman dukes, the beginnings of lay education also reach back into the tenth century. Even Richard I (d. 996) is said to have been educated in the arts. At his request Dudo von St. Quentin wrote the first family history of a French princely house: "On the Manners and Deeds of the First Dukes of Normandy" (*De moribus et actis primorum Normanniae ducum*). William the Conqueror (d. 1087) does not seem to have enjoyed a formal education, but his wife, Matilda of Flanders (d. 1083), was, as Ordericus Vitalis reports, distinguished by "beauty, high birth, a knowledge of letters, and the splendor of her manners and virtues."[9] Her son Henry I (d. 1135) was later given the epithet "Beauclerc" because of his education. His court became a meeting place of poets and scholars, in part because his two wives, Matilda of Scotland (d. 1118) and Adele (Aelis) of Brabant (d. after 1157), took an interest in literature. Adele was also the first to promote vernacular poetry at the English court. Henry I's sister, Countess Adele of Blois (d. 1137), was as well educated as her brother. She had close contact with the most famous Latin poets of her time, Baudri of Bourgueil and Hildebert of Lavardin, who glorified her in their songs. Her husband, Count Etienne-Henri of Blois-Chartres (d. 1102), was also literate in Latin. From this time on the tradition of education at the court of Blois continued without interruption.

In Flanders, a genealogy of the ducal house (*Genealogia Arnulfi comitis*) had already been compiled under Count Arnulf I (d. 965). Latin historiography, too, took on a decidedly dynastic cast much earlier here than anywhere else. Not much seems to be known about the level of education of the counts of the earlier period. The line of educated counts begins with Robert I (d. 1093), and during the second half of the twelfth century the court of Flanders became a flourishing center of French vernacular poetry. In a remarkable letter to Count Philip of Flanders (d. 1191), Philip of Harvengt, the abbot of Bonne-Espérance (near Mons), expressed the notion that knightly vigor and a learned education did not have to exclude each other; instead, a combination of the two suited a secular prince well, since "a prince who is not distinguished by any knowledge of letters is as unworthy as a peasant."[10] The clerics were not alone in propagating this idea, for it appears that it was well received by the lay nobility as well.

It would seem, however, that at the end of the twelfth century the custom of educating one's children still did not extend beyond the small circle of the great secular princes. But for southern France there is evidence from as early as the tenth and eleventh centuries that even members of smaller noble families were literate. This probably explains why in southern France courtly literature was cultivated even at the smaller courts, whereas in the north it was initially only the great princely courts that became literary meeting places. In his mirror of princes, Giraldius Cambrensis (d. 1233) mentioned approvingly that King Louis VIII of France (d. 1226) had devoted himself to the liberal arts in his youth, and he praised this as "a virtue, which, wherever it is found, is more precious and excellent to the same degree that it is rare among the princes of our time."[11] The same sentiment is expressed in a letter of Walther Map (d. after 1208) to Randulf of Glanville: "The nobles of our land either consider it beneath their dignity or they are too lazy to educate their children in letters."[12] Such words should caution us not to exaggerate the extent of lay education among the French nobility.

Lay education in Germany   The situation in Germany seems to have been very different. The evidence, however, is so poor that it is difficult to get a clear picture. This explains why opinions concerning lay education in Germany at times diverge quite drastically. A passage from the world chronicle of Ekkehard of Aura (d. after 1125) is often cited as evidence of a relatively high level of education among the German nobility by the beginning of the twelfth century. It reports, under the year 1110, that Emperor Henry V (d. 1125) instructed his chaplain, David, to write an account of the emperor's journey to Rome: "On the emperor's orders that man [David] wrote down in three books the course and events of this expedition, in a very easy style which hardly at all departed from colloquial speech; in this way he helped lay readers and other less educated folk, so that their intellect could grasp these things."[13] It is, however, entirely unclear who these "lay readers" were, for whom the historian showed such solicitous concern. Since the work was intended for the emperor, David—or Ekkehard, as the case may be—was possibly thinking of him and the lay society at the imperial court. While we know virtually nothing about the upbringing of Henry V, it would be surprising, given his father's excellent education, if he had not enjoyed at least some elementary instruction. In interpreting the Ekkehard passage, we must also keep in mind that the educated author's assurance that he tried to adjust his style to the humbler abilities of laymen sounds very much like a literary convention. Godfrey of Viterbo, in the dedication of his world history (*Memoria saeculorum*) to Emperor Henry VI, offered a similar justification why "in this work I have not made special efforts to bring out the elegance of words or to introduce artful expressions or decorative phrases."[14] He was adhering "to a middle level of style,"[15] in consideration of the lay mind to which the work was addressed: "This simple work I intended and adapted for you, a layman little trained in philosophy, and for other boys of your age."[16] We know that Henry VI was literate in Latin. If we may assume the same for Henry V, we can hardly draw from Ekkehard's passage the conclusion that at the beginning of the twelfth century the majority of the German nobility could read.

A more accurate picture of actual conditions is probably given by Wipo, chancellor to the Emperors Conrad II (d. 1039) and Henry III (d. 1056). In his *Tetralogus*, completed in 1041, he laments that in Germany a literary education of noble children was regarded as superfluous or even disgraceful. This prompted Wipo to call upon the emperor to make schooling compulsory by law:

> Pass now a decree throughout the German land, in order that the wealthy will teach their children letters and knowledge of the law, so they may be able to produce examples from their books when they have to negotiate with princes. Rome once lived honorably with this custom; with such learning it could bind mighty tyrants. The Italians adhere to this when they have grown past first childhood, and all youngsters there must sweat it out in school. Only in Germany it seems unimportant or disgraceful that someone should be educated unless he wants to become a cleric.[17]

In the twelfth century it was common in Germany to equate "lay" with "illiterate."[18] The attitude of the lay nobility to a learned education is revealed in the account of the upbringing of Abbot Dietrich of St. Hubert (d. 1086), written soon after his death. We are told that his mother had the young boy secretly instructed in the basics of the liberal arts. His father, however, "wanted to make him into what he himself was, namely a worldly fighter."[19] When he discovered what his wife was doing, "he had his son removed from his studies and ordered him placed under guard at home, and he threatened his wife with severe punishment if she dared to expose him again to these teachings."[20]

We can gather the most reliable information about the level of education among the German lay nobility by looking at the line of emperors and kings. From the tenth century on we always encounter the same situation: every time a new dynasty assumes the throne, the first emperor is illiterate. But in the second generation of the new houses, or at the latest in the third, we come upon educated rulers. Thus the princely families from whose midst the emperors were chosen were usually illiterate, but most rulers themselves thought it desirable to give their successors to the throne a formal education. This observation still holds true for the twelfth century. The successor to the last Salian emperor, Duke Lothair of Saxony (1125–1137) from the old princely house of Supplinburg, was uneducated. So was his successor, Conrad III (1138–1152), who begins the line of Hohenstaufen rulers. The Hohenstaufen were related by marriage to the Salian imperial house, and as dukes of Swabia they were among the most powerful imperial princes. Nevertheless, literacy and a literary education seem to have been as unknown among them as they were among the other great aristocratic families. Frederick I (1152–1190), Conrad III's successor, was also unlettered, but he gave his own children a thorough education: Henry VI (1190–1197) as well as his younger brother, Philip of Swabia (1198–1208), were both literate in Latin. Philip's case is a bit different, though, since he was originally intended for an ecclesiastical career and only afterwards returned to lay standing. His rival in the fight for the throne was Otto IV (1198–1218), the first emperor from the house of the Welfs. The Welf family had long laid claim to a rank equal to the king, but here, too, a literate education was unknown. Their family history, the *Historia Welforum* (composed around 1170), has not a single word about matters of education, even though Empress Judith (d. 843), to whom the Welfs traced back their genealogy, had held an important place in the literary life of the ninth century. We are not told that Otto IV could read and write, which in his case is surprising, since Otto spent the better part of his youth at the English and French courts.

All evidence indicates that the German princes in the second half of the twelfth century were usually uneducated. At the diet of Besançon in 1157, a Latin letter of Pope Hadrian IV (d. 1159) was read to the public assembly, and apparently none of the princes present understood the words. Only when the letter "had been carefully explained by Chancellor Rainald in a fairly accurate translation, were the assembled princes seized by great indignation."[21] Of importance in the discussion of education is the letter Landgrave Ludwig II of Thuringia (d. 1172) sent to the French King Louis VII in 1162 or 1163 (see p. 78) requesting the king's protection for his two sons who would travel to Paris to study. The landgrave explained his intentions as follows: "I plan for all my sons to learn to read and write, and the one who proves himself the brightest and most capable shall continue with his studies."[22] If the letter is authentic, it constitutes the most important testimony for this period about the educational ambitions of a German princely house.

A second report from the same period about the education of the son of a German prince concerns the Babenberg dynasty in Austria. We are told that the eldest son of Duke Leopold VI (d. 1230) "died during the lifetime of his father while he was attending the school at Klosterneuburg."[23] This occurred in the year 1216. We don't know, however, whether Duke Leopold VI was training his son for the succession or whether he was perhaps preparing him for an ecclesiastical career.

No studies exist on how lay education spread in Germany in the course of the thirteenth century. We do get the impression, however, that at the end of the thirteenth century the better part of the nobility still could not read or write. Berthold of Regensburg (d. 1272) addressed laypeople very matter-of-factly as illiterates: "Since you laypeople cannot read as we priests can..."[24] Also very informative is Ottokar of Styria's account of the diet of Augsburg in 1275. Bishop Wernhart of Seckau appeared there as the envoy of King Ottokar II of Bohemia. Before the king and the princes of the empire he delivered an artfully composed speech in Latin, in which he questioned the legitimacy of the election of King Rudolf of Hapsburg: "Had the laymen understood him he would have paid dearly for it. But they did not understand him."[25] Finally the king interrupted him and said he could speak Latin when he was negotiating with clerics: "But when you present a petition before me or the realm, I cannot follow your bookish words."[26] If he, the king, allowed imperial matters to be discussed in Latin, "the lay princes of the realm"[27] would all sit before him "like fools and mutes."[28]

After the interregnum, the election of Rudolph of Hapsburg (d. 1291) in 1273 once again brought to the throne a king from the German high nobility, and everything seems to indicate that once again the first representative of the new dynasty was illiterate, even though the counts of Hapsburg were among the greatest territorial lords in the southwestern lands. His successors, too, seem to have been uneducated, with the exception of Adolf of Nassau (d. 1298). Historians believe that an extant ordination ritual which makes special allowances for the new ruler's ignorance of Latin was intended for the coronation of Henry VII (d. 1313) in the cathedral of Aachen on January 6, 1309: "Since the king, as an illiterate and layman, does not understand the aforesaid questions and answers that are spoken in Latin, the archbishop of Cologne, either in person or through an appointed cleric, will recite to the lord king the aforesaid questions and answers in a more understandable form in our vernacular, that is to say, in German."[29] Ludwig the Bavarian (d. 1347), the first of the Wittelsbach dynasty to assume the throne, was also an illiterate.

But there always were some highly educated laymen. In the eleventh century, for example, there was Count Henry II of Stade (d. 1016), co-founder of the monastery of Harsefeld, who "was literate and very zealous in the divine services,"[30] or the Saxon Count Palatine Frederick II (d. 1088), who owned a collection of books which he bequeathed to the monastery of Goseck, and which included Gregory the Great's *Moralia*. But these were exceptional people; in nearly all cases it turns out that we are dealing with men who were destined for a clerical career but then returned to lay standing. Henry of Stade obtained no less than three dispensations from clerical vows, and Count Palatine Frederick II of Saxony, a third-born son, had been educated in the monastery of Fulda and was selected to become count palatine only after the death of his brother Dedo. The situation was very different with noble women within lay society, for they participated in educational life to a much greater extent than men.

Litteratus-illitteratus   The terms *litteratus* and *illitteratus*, which in the Latin sources of the period describe the educated and the uneducated, referred to elementary schooling. A "literate" (*litteratus*) person was someone who had learned to read and write Latin, that is to say someone who had been instructed in the basic subjects of the trivium— grammar and rhetoric—either in an ecclesiastical school or by a private tutor. An "uneducated" (*illitteratus*) person was someone who could neither read nor write, who was illiterate. This terminology was not without imprecision. The designation *litteratus* does not reveal whether a person had been instructed merely in the basics of Latin grammar or whether he had enjoyed a thorough training in the higher studies. *Litteratus* was only occasionally used in the classical sense of "learned," mostly by authors who were consciously following Roman-classical usage. John of Salisbury, for example, could say that "those who are without knowledge of the liberal arts are called *illitterati*, even if they can read and write."[31] Other authors had to rely on comparatives such as "very educated" (*nimio litteratus*) or "highly educated" (*litteratissimus*) in order to distinguish the scholar from the simple *litteratus*.

The terms *litteratus* and *illitteratus* were also unable to grasp the intermediate stages between literacy and illiteracy, which were of great importance especially in lay society. Some rulers who had grown up without the benefit of an education still managed to learn to read as adults. This is what we hear about Otto I (d. 973): "After the death of Queen Edith he learned the letters, of which he previously had been ignorant, so well that he was perfectly capable of reading and understanding books."[32] It would seem that it was not all that rare to find a lay prince who understood some Latin without having learned to read and write it. Emperor Frederick I was described by Bishop Sicardus of Cremona as an "illiterate"[33]; his biographer Rahewin says of Frederick (using the very same words with which Einhard had characterized Charlemagne's educational level): "In his native tongue he was very eloquent; Latin, however, he understood better than he could speak it."[34] We know of several princes of this period who sought access to Latin literature despite being illiterate. Henry the Lion (d. 1195) "ordered the ancient historical works to be collected, written down, and recited to him."[35] It is not clear, however, whether Henry knew enough Latin to follow the reading or whether he had a translation recited. Similar news reaches us about Landgrave Hermann I of Thuringia: "He never surrendered his tired limbs to sleep without having first listened to a piece from the Holy Scriptures or the deeds of famous princes of old; and he inclined his ever attentive ear to Latin as well as German works."[36] It appears that we are dealing with a conventional motif in the praise of princes, the truthfulness of which cannot be verified in individual cases. It is not clear whether Landgrave Hermann owned other Latin books besides the two richly decorated psalters that were written and painted on his commission. A manuscript of the *Bellum civile* by the Roman epic poet Lucan (first century A.D.)—now kept in Kassel (Landesbibliothek, 2° Mss. poet. et rom. 5)—bears the following marginal comment on the first folio: "H., by the grace of God Landgrave of Thuringia and Count Palatine of Saxony."[37] But it is entirely uncertain whether this entry was penned by Hermann I to indicate his ownership.

The most interesting case of an uneducated prince who took an interest in Latin books was Count Baldwin II of Guines (d. 1206). Lampert of Ardres recounts that Count Baldwin, "although only a layman and illiterate" (*licet omnino laicus esset et illiteratus*) and "entirely without any knowledge of the arts" (*omnino ignarus artium*), gathered theologians and scholars at his court, and by keeping company with them got so far that he could discuss the most difficult questions "like an educated person" (*quasi literatus*). But since he did not understand any Latin, he had a variety of works translated into French, among them the Psalms and a biography of St. Anthony, as well as a scientific treatise by the Roman geographer Solinus. "He also had the Holy Books, which were needed for services in church, copied and embellished and stored in his various chapels."[38] His librarian, Hasard of Aldehen, was also a layman, but through constant contact with the books of the count, he "had learned to write and had become literate."[39] Count Baldwin personally contributed to the composition of a French poetic work, which was given the title *Roman de Silence* (*Romanum de Silentio*) after its chief author, the master Walter Silens.

The figure of the count of Guines makes clear that the difference between *litteratus* and *illitteratus* could become completely blurred within lay society. An illiterate man as book collector and with the skill to engage in learned disputations: this no longer fits into the conventional categories. Count Baldwin was undoubtedly an exception. But the conditions at his court are well suited to shed some light on the literary situation in Germany. Common to both counts was the fact that noble lords who could not read or write acquired a knowledge of Latin literature by having it translated into their own language and recited out loud. This created a new kind of literature: here we find texts that were composed after written models and then in turn put down in writing; they could be read as books, but according to the intentions of the patrons, they were meant primarily for dissemination through oral presentation. A large portion of courtly literature in Germany falls into this category, which was created in response to the special educational environment of the lay nobility.

Unlike the count of Guines, the German princes were not so much interested in Latin literature as in modern French court poetry, about which they learned through translations and imitations. In this way the relationship between literature and writing underwent a profound change. Although the French texts received at the German courts usually also existed in written form—no different from the Latin texts only a literate person could use—one did not have to be able to read and write to understand French. Knowledge of the French language was transmitted orally, and an illiterate person could be exposed to French literature by having it read out loud. As a result, from the twelfth century on, there emerged a separate lay education alongside the Latin education, which continued to be tied to the study of grammar in school. This lay education was focused on French language and literature and was accessible even to the uneducated.

ORAL TRADITIONS

The laity had its own literature, one that was entirely unwritten. It is rather difficult to get a sense of the nature and significance of this oral literature: with the exception of a few traces preserved in writing, it has all but vanished. We have also lost the ability to think in categories of oral tradition. Only the observations on the nature of oral poetry that Milman Parry and Albert B. Lord derived from their study of twentieth-century Serbo-Croatian epic poetry have sharpened our understanding of the fact that orally composed works are subject to different creative constraints and laws than written literature:

— The oral poet performed as a singer. Unlike the poets who worked in written form, his intention was not to create a work, but to continue a narrative tradition. Anonymity was frequently a sign of oral transmission. The criterion by which the singer's achievement was measured was a correct rendition, and correctness meant adherence to tradition.

— The oral epic was not a text with fixed wording, but a plastic, variable entity that could be constantly retold in new and different ways, as is still the case today with jokes.

— An oral tale was composed of set formulae which the singer had learned in his exposure to tradition. The number of these preset formulae was limited.

— Oral works were not composed and afterwards recited: creation and performance coincided. The work was created in the process of recitation, whereby the circumstances of the performance became part of the work itself and were reflected, for example, in the varying length and varying emphases placed on certain themes.

The insights into the structural laws of oral poetry that were gained from the study of twentieth-century works can also be used to help us understand medieval traditions. But the many mistaken paths that the study of oral poetry has taken over the past decades warns us of drawing hasty conclusions. In most cases little is gained by merely calculating the percentage of formulaic elements in literary works based on oral traditions. Much more important is the fact that the study of Serbo-Croatian epics uncovered the mechanisms of an oral literary culture. In the process, Parry and Lord discovered basic laws of oral transmission, laws that may apply in similar ways to the oral literature of the illiterate lay society of the Middle Ages.

In the Middle Ages, oral tradition comprised the entire sphere of customs, manners, and law. Literary transmission must be seen within this broader context. Easiest to document is the oral transmisson of heroic epics. The historical allusions in texts written down much later reveal that the stories were passed on orally for centuries. It is rather unclear and controversial, especially in regard to the older period, who the bearers of this tradition were. In the eleventh-century Annals of Quedlinburg we read: "And this man was Theoderic of Bern, of whom the peasants used to sing."[40] This statement, long regarded as an important piece of evidence for the active role of the peasants in the transmission of oral heroic epics, is today regarded by scholars as a late addition from the fifteenth century. Moreover, whoever penned these words was probably thinking not of peasants but of *rustici* in the sense of *illitterati*, and was thus referring to the illiterate laity in general. The nobility's interest in orally transmitted heroic epics, on the other hand, is well documented. The popularity that heroic tales enjoyed in the eleventh century even at ecclesiastical courts is revealed by the figure of Bishop Gunther of Bamberg (d. 1065). In one of his letters, Meinhard, a teacher at the cathedral school in Bamberg, said about the bishop: "He never thinks of Augustine, never of Gregory; he is always pondering Attila, Amalung [= Theoderic of Bern] and other things of this kind."[41] In another letter Meinhard criticized the bishop for wasting his time "on soft pillows and with courtly tales."[42] If Meinhard here was once again referring to the bishop's fondness for the old heroic tales, we could interpret the phrase "courtly tales" (*fabulae curiales*) as an indication that the courts of the great lords were at that time seen as centers for the transmission of sagas and legends. A piece of evidence from the twelfth century seems to point to the same conclusion. In his "History of the Danes" (*Gesta Danorum*), Saxo Grammaticus reports that in 1131 the Danish King Magnus (d. 1134) treacherously invited his brother-in-law, Count Cnut of Jütland, to a meeting with the intent of murdering him. The invitation was delivered by a Saxon bard (*cantor*), who tried to warn the duke of the treachery by singing in front of him, "in the form of a very beautiful song, Kriemhild's well-known betrayal of her brothers."[43] Cnut did not understand the warning, went to the meeting, and was murdered. This episode is not only important evidence for the oral transmission of the *Nibelungenlied* long before it was put down in writing. It also reveals that the heroic songs were very popular with noble society. The Saxon bard knew, Saxo tells us, "that Duke Cnut was very fond of the delivery and sound of the Saxon language."[44] Furthermore, it is interesting that the bard himself belonged to noble society, or at least was so much trusted by his royal employer that he was dispatched on such an important diplomatic mission.

Allusions to the sagas of Theoderic and Gudrun in twelfth-century poetic works intended for a noble court audience are another indication that courtly society was more widely familiar with oral heroic tales. Heroic poetry played an important role for the historical consciousness of an illiterate aristocratic society. The cult of ancestors, the heroizing of one's own forefathers, and the extension of the family history back into the heroic age provided historical legitimation for the lay nobility. In the annals of the monastery of Pegau from the mid-twelfth century, the genealogy of the princely founder of the monastery, Margrave Wiprecht of Groitzsch (d. 1124), was traced back to the legendary Ostrogothic King Ermanaric—who appears here as the "German King Emelrich"[45]—and his brother, King Herlibo, the founding father of the legendary race of the Harlungen. The illiterate lay nobility must have taken a strong interest in historical traditions, especially in the history of their own families. Adam of Bremen tells us that the Danish King Sven Estridson (d. 1076) "had committed to memory the entire history of the barbarians, as though it were fixed in writing."[46] Count Hugh of Amboise (d. circa 1130), so we read, "retained in his mind, like a literate person, not only domestic but also foreign wars and events."[47] Oral traditions were probably also the source of most of the genealogical knowledge which members of the high nobility in the twelfth and thirteenth centuries presented and confirmed on oath at divorce proceedings.

Orally transmitted heroic epics were first put into written form towards the end of the twelfth century, when a regular literary life began at the courts of the worldly princes and the courtly poets there produced vernacular works on the basis of written models. The *Nibelungenlied* holds a unique position in that it straddles the realms of both oral and written literature. Oral transmission seems to be the source of its metric form (the long line stanzas), of some peculiarities of style, of the structure and the motivations, and of course of the material itself. But in compositional form and artistic ambition it was conceived as a written work, which reveals down to many details the poet's training in contemporary, written court poetry. It is difficult to define the place of the *Nibelungenlied* in the literary history of its time. One the one hand, it would seem that the poem, especially in the so-called C version, was a great literary success. On the other hand, several decades went by before it was imitated. Not until the second half of the thirteenth century do we find in *Kudrun* another heroic epic in written form; but this work also failed to achieve a breakthrough for this genre. Apparently the oral transmission of epic poetry was still so vigorous at this time that there was not much of a demand for written versions.

There are many indications that during the courtly age an intact oral literature existed side by side with written literature. It would therefore be one-sided and inadequate to approach the literary life of the lay nobility in this period only through an examination of the works extant in manuscripts. Much evidence attests that the oral transmission of heroic-epic traditions continued in the thirteenth century. Hugo von Trimberg speaks of traveling bards who earned their living by reciting heroic sagas: "Anyone who can tell of Lord Dietrich of Bern and of Lord Ecke and of the old warriors will have his wine paid for."[48] Oral poets were often pictured as blind bards: "This the blind sing to us, that Siegfried had a callus."[49] The most informative testimony is a strophe by der Marner, a *Spruch* poet of the mid-thirteenth century, who complained how varied the repertoire of a traveling bard had to be to fulfill all the wishes of the audience:

When I perform my songs for the listeners, the first one wants to hear how Dietrich von Bern left the land, the second where King Rother was at home; the third wants to hear of the war against the Riuzen; the fourth of Eckehard's distress; the fifth of Kriemhild's betrayal; the sixth takes more pleasure in hearing what became of the Wilzen; the seventh wants to hear of the battle against Heime or Lord Wittich, of the death of Siegfried or Lord Ecke; the eighth, on the other hand, wants only courtly minnesong; the ninth finds all this too boring; the tenth can't decide, he wants this and that, now here, now there. Moreover, some would like to hear of the treasure of the Nibelungen: it doesn't weigh much, believe me. Such a one thinks only of gold.[50]

This list of popular pieces raises many difficult questions. What is clear, though, is that der Marner was thinking of orally transmitted songs and tales, since most of the material he mentions had not yet been written down. Even the tales of Siegfried and King Rother probably did not refer to the twelfth-century Rother epos or to the *Nibelungenlied*, but to oral versions that continued to exist alongside the written versions of these sagas. The somewhat contemptuous tone in which der Marner speaks of the tastes and wishes of the audience indicates that he no longer saw himself as exclusively within the tradition of oral poetry. In fact, we know that, far from being illiterate, he was unusually well-educated. He was among the few courtly poets who also composed Latin verses. We can conclude from this that an overlapping and inter-mixing of oral and written traditions must have existed not only among the listeners but also among the poets.

There must have been other forms of oral poetry in addition to the heroic epics, but they are not as well documented. As far as sung lyric is concerned, there must have been above all dancing songs, which were very popular throughout the Middle Ages. The strange story of the dancers of Kölbigk, which attracted attention all over Europe in the eleventh century, can shed some light on the form of these songs. On Christmas Eve in 1018 (or 1021), so the story goes, a group of young people in the small town of Kölbigk (near Anhalt) disturbed the peace of the church with their riotous dancing. The priest cursed them for it, and as a punishment from God they were forced to dance for one year without interruption. One of the dancers, Theodericus by name, later testified: "We held our hands and lined up in the courtyard of the church for the dance of sin. The leader of your blind fury, Gerlef, struck up in jest the fateful song: 'Bobo rode through the green forest. He had the beautiful Merswind with him. Why do we stand? Why don't we go?'"[51] Whether this Latin text was in fact based on an eleventh-century Saxon dancing song must remain an open question. The ballad-like content, the simple stanzaic form of two long lines and a refrain, and the formulaic style are compatible with the pattern of oral trans-mission. The *Carmina Burana*, the famous collection of Latin goliardic songs from the monastery of Benediktbeuren, also contains a German dancing strophe of unknown provenance with a very old-fashioned sound to it: "All who dance in this round are maids. All summer long they want to go without men."[52] This strophe, which is very different from the artistic forms of the early minnesong, gives us a glimpse of what this popular dance lyric looked like. While these songs were probably widely known, another type of oral lyric, *Spruch* poetry, seems, once again, to have been intended largely for aristocratic society. Among its themes were the praise of rulers and patrons, riddles and aphorisms, religious instruction for the laity, wise sayings, and similar things. Evidence for the existence of this type of poetry comes from written literature. Among the oldest strata of courtly lyrics in Germany are the *Sprüche* that have come down to us under the name "Spervogel." Since there are neither Latin nor Romance models for this genre, we may assume that we are dealing with the continuation of a tradition of oral poetry.

THE DEVELOPMENT OF ORGANIZED WRITING AT THE SECULAR COURTS

The illiterate lay nobility did not live entirely without writing. Every court had chaplains and clerics who handled books; every noble family had close contact with the monasteries and convents in its territories, and if it wanted to fix a legal act in writing, it could avail itself of the monastic *scriptoria* (writing-rooms). Unable to read and write themselves, the great lords were accustomed to using the skills of the clerically educated in the exercise of lordship.

Family monastery and the lord's court: The beginnings of a dynastic historiography A particularly close connection existed between the lord's court and the family monastery. Family monasteries were monastic institutions that great noble houses established on their own property, and over which they exercised secular sovereignty as advocates. These monastic foundations served not only pious purposes. Alongside the construction of castles and the founding of cities, they were an important instrument for spreading and consolidating political authority in a territory. If the tomb of the founding family was located in the family monastery, which was frequently the case, the monastic community kept the memory of the dead alive for centuries and prayed for the salvation of their souls. Quite often the chaplains and court clerics, and sometimes also the doctors, teachers, and architects employed at the court, came from the family monasteries. The introduction of regular writing at the great courts profited from the fact that in some cases the family monasteries were integrated architecturally into the new palace structures built in the twelfth and thirteenth centuries; as a result a close physical connection was established between the court and the monastery or cathedral chapter. We can see an example of this in Brunswick, where even today the living quarters of Henry the Lion's palace of Dankwarderode and the massive monastic Church of St. Blasius—the modern-day cathedral—border the square in which the duke erected his famous lion statue in 1166.

In some cases the link between family monasteries and their founding dynasties was reflected in literary works as early as the eleventh century. In the course of compiling the first historical accounts, some monasteries recorded the history of their own foundation (*fundatio*), and in doing so they also remembered the secular founders and their families; sometimes the *fundatio* was expanded into what was almost a small chronicle of the founding family. These "founders' chronicles" are the beginnings of dynastic historiography in Germany.

Genealogical records were a second step in this development. The oldest princely genealogies come from Flanders, where by the tenth century the lineage of Count Arnulf I (d. 965) was already written down. In France these records begin in the eleventh century with the genealogies of the counts of Vendômes and of Anjou. The first example from Germany is the genealogy of the Welfs (*Genealogia Welforum*). It was compiled in Altdorf-Weingarten, the family monastery of the southern Welfs, possibly still during the lifetime of Henry the Black (d. 1126) or soon after his death. The genealogies of two other southern German princely houses also date to the twelfth century: that of the Babenberger, who were initially margraves of Styria and after 1156 dukes of Austria (*Genealogia marchionum Austriae*), and that of the Traungau margraves of Styria (*Genealogia marchionum de Stire*). The genealogy of the dukes of Zähringen (*Genealogia Zaringorum*) may also be of the twelfth century. The thirteenth century saw the compilation of the genealogies of the landgraves of Thuringia, of the Wettin dynasty in Meißen, of the Askanian dynasty in Anhalt and Brandenhurg, of the Wittelsbach family in Bavaria, of the dukes of Andechs-Meran, and of the Spanheim dukes of Carinthia. These are the same princely houses who were making a name for themselves as patrons and sponsors of

courtly literature. Genealogies of ducal families are still rare in the thirteenth century. Where we do find them, we are dealing either with
powerful families, such as the counts of Hapsburg, of Zollern, or of
Bogen, who were not far behind the great princes in consolidating their
territorial lordship, or with ducal families related to the ruling houses,
as for example the counts of Frombach. In nearly all cases the authors
of the genealogies are unknown. As far as we can tell, the majority of
these records were compiled in the family monasteries: the genealogy of
the dukes of Andechs-Meran in Dießen (at Lake Ammer), that of the
Spanheim dukes in St. Paul (in Carinthia), that of the Hapsburgs in
Muri (Switzerland). We can see from this that the link between family
monastery and princely court was still a stimulus to literary production
in the thirteenth century.

Another step towards the development of new forms of dynastic historiography were the independent family and regional histories which
had already attained an important literary rank in northern France and
Flanders in the twelfth century. There is only one twelfth-century work
from Germany that is on a level with this literature: the "History of the
Welfs" (*Historia Welforum*), written around 1170, probably at the request of Welf VI. The anonymous author explains in the prologue that
he unearthed "the generations of our princes"[53] from old chronicles
and charters. The account begins with Welf I, the father of Empress
Judith (d. 843), and it gets increasingly broader as it approaches the
present. The center of attention were Welf VI and his brother Henry the
Proud (d. 1139), whose battles to preserve and extend the reputation
and possessions of the family are described in detail. It has been
assumed that the author of the *Historia Welforum* was one of Welf VI's
court chaplains. If that is true, it would mean that the writing of dynastic history had in this case already shifted from the monastery to the
court. In all this, the question as to the readership of this Latin history
must remain open. As far as we know, Duke Welf VI was illiterate, and
apart from the chaplains, there were not many people at the court who
could be considered potential readers.

Far into the thirteenth century, Latin historiography, even when it
was strongly dynastic, had its home in the monasteries and not at the
courts. An important work of history, the *Historia Reinhardsbrunnensis*, was written around 1200 in Reinhardsbrunn, the family monastery
of the Thuringian landgraves. It recounts contemporary events from the
perspective of the Thuringian court. This work, however, has not survived in its original form; Oswald Holder-Egger reconstructed it from

the fourteenth-century *Chronica Reinhardsbrunnensis*. Works now lost
are also believed to have stood at the beginning of the territorial histories of the Welf dynasty in Brunswick and the Askanian dynasty in
the March of Brandenburg. All that survives from this period are a few
short accounts from Austria, Thuringia, and Meißen. Though most of
them are of little importance as historical sources, they are of interest as
documents of a historiography that was focused on the princely courts
and the princely houses. Among them is the "Brief Austrian Chronicle
from Melk" (probably written around 1177), whose author addressed
himself directly to Duke Leopold V of Austria (d. 1194) to instruct him
about his ancestors: "We want to bring to your memory, as you have
requested, the ancestral line of the princes of this land, your forefathers."[54] The account begins with Leopold I (d. 994), the first
Babenberg margrave of the Eastern March, and ends with the elevation
of Austria to the rank of a duchy in 1156. At about the same time, a
short work was compiled about Margrave Leopold III (d. 1136), the
founder of Klosterneuburg; it was probably written at Klosterneuburg
itself, the family monastery of the house of Babenberg. Around 1200 or
soon after, someone in Reinhardsbrunn put together, on the basis of
older accounts of the family history of the landgraves, the "Short History of the Princes of Thuringia" (*Historia brevis principum Thuring-
iae*); it had most to say about Ludwig der Springer (d. 1123), the founder
of Reinhardsbrunn and builder of the Wartburg. The genealogy of
the Wettin dynasty (*Genealogia Wettinorum*) was compiled in Lauterberg, the family monastery of the Wettin family, probably before 1215.
It deserves to be ranked with the early territorial histories, since it offers
much more than a mere list of names: it traces the family history of the
Wettin margraves of Meißen from the tenth century to the early thirteenth century. Finally, we could also mention in this context the vita of
Landgrave Ludwig IV of Thuringia (d. 1227) (*Gesta Ludowici*), which
the court chaplain Berthold penned after the death of the landgrave.
Unfortunately this first extensive princely biography has not survived.
We have to reconstruct it from a later rewriting, which in turn exists
only in a German translation of the fourteenth century (Friedrich Ködiz
von Salfeld, *Das Leben des heiligen Ludwig*).

   This early evidence for a new historiography seems altogether very
modest compared to the important works from Flanders (Walter of
Thérouanne, *Vita Karoli*, Galbert of Bruges, *Passio Karoli*), Anjou
(Jean de Marmoutier, *Historia Gaufredi ducis Normannorum et comitis Andegavorum*), Guines (Lambert of Ardres, *Historia comitum*

Ghisnensium), and Hainaut (Gislebert of Mons, *Chronicon Hano-niense*), where dynastic historiography was already flourishing in the period around 1200. In Germany the princely biographies and regional chronicles were very slow to develop, since the necessary educational preconditions for the reception of Latin literature did not exist at the courts.

The "Codex Falkensteinensis" Court literature also included fief books, land registers, and property records in Latin. These were drawn up at the request of the secular lords, and the princes, who could not read these documents themselves, used them in their political and administrative activities. The most impressive document is the "Codex Falkensteinensis" (now in the Bavarian Hauptstaatsarchiv in Munich), the oldest *Traditionsbuch* (register of land transfers) of a great German noble family, compiled between 1164 and 1170 at the request of the Bavarian Count Siboto IV of Neuburg-Falkenstein (d. around 1200). Count Siboto had the book written at the Canonic Foundation in Herrenchiemsee, whose advocate he had been since 1158; separate ducal chanceries did not exist anywhere in Germany at this time. The occasion for its compilation was apparently prompted by the count's concern for the continued existence of the family's property after his death. This is why the book begins with the appointment of a guardian: in the event of his own death, his father-in-law, Count Kuno IV of Mödling, was to look after the rights of his two minor sons. The actual body of the codex is made up of a register of fiefs and a land register, that is to say a record of the income and landholdings of the ducal lordship. These two sections are of great significance for both legal and economic history: along with the fief book of the imperial ministerial Werner of Bolanden (probably written after 1180), the register of fiefs from the "Codex Falkensteinensis" is the oldest record of its kind from Germany. The land register is absolutely unique for its time. It gives insights into the inner organization of a secular lordship, insights that are unequaled for the twelfth century. Of particular interest is the fact that the list of properties already evidences the early stages in the development of administrative entities. The land register is, in fact, arranged according to the four castles which the Counts of Falkenstein owned, and which acted as the political and administrative centers for the widely scattered landholdings of the comital family. The register is also a rich source for many details about the material culture and the social life at the court of the counts.

Fig. 35. Count Siboto of Falkenstein and his family. The count and his wife, seated side by side, instruct their two sons. From the *Codex Falkensteinensis* (Munich, Bayer. Haupstaatsarchiv, Kloster Weyarn 1). Twelfth century.

How much importance Count Siboto attached to these records is revealed not least by the costly decorations of the manuscript. The codex contains five large pictures and numerous marginalia. On the first folio we find a three-colored pen-and-ink drawing that takes up half the page and depicts the count and his wife, both in festive robes, together with their two sons (see fig. 35). This is the first true family portrait from Germany of which we know. The four figures hold a banner whose clearly legible right side reads: "We ask you, Beloved, to think of us when you read this. This goes for everyone, but especially for you, dearest son."[55] On the left side the writing is smaller and faded and barely decipherable. Here the text supposedly reads: "Say farewell to father! Speak well of your mother, oh sons!"[56] Apparently the inscription and the entire composition of the picture was directly related to the original purpose of the codex, the appointment of a guardian for Count Siboto IV's minor sons in the event of his death. If the reading of the left portion is correct, the count's departure on a lengthy trip may have prompted his precautionary arrangements. It has been speculated that Siboto's participation in Emperor Frederick I's fourth journey to Italy in 1166 was the concrete occasion. But the concern proved unjustified, for Count Siboto would live for another thirty years. During these three decades the codex continued to be used as a *Hausbuch* in the monastery of Herrenchiemsee. This portion of the manuscript is also unique, since we have no other *Hausbücher* of secular lordships from this period. As in the monastic *Hausbücher*, it primarily recorded transfers of property.

Scattered throughout the "Codex Falkensteinensis" are words and sentences in German, and two texts are written entirely in German. It has been inferred from entries and information supplied by users of the manuscript in the sixteenth and seventeenth centuries that a complete German translation was made soon after the completion of the records. If it were possible to prove the existence of this early German version, the codex would be even more significant for the development of writing at the secular courts, since we may assume that the translation of the entire collection into German was motivated by the count's ignorance of Latin. A new examination of the manuscript might yield more precise information.

The establishment of separate chanceries   The decisive step towards writing was taken with the establishment of separate chanceries at the courts of the secular princes. Henry the Lion was the first lay prince who had charters drawn up at his court in Brunswick. Until then the princes had ruled without their own scribes. Most sovereign acts did not require written confirmation. The verdicts of courts were as a rule pronounced orally. Enfeoffments, too, were usually performed in Germany by legally binding gestures, and were rarely verified by charters, unlike Italy, where the drafting of enfeoffment letters was customary. Before administration became established on a written basis, charters were drawn up primarily to record privileges and gifts. Naturally these written records were of special interest to the recipients, who were above all monasteries and churches. The oldest princely charters were therefore all written by the recipients or by third parties.

Yet separate secular chanceries did start developing after the middle of the twelfth century, and this phenomenon is certainly linked to the fact that the modern forms of territorial lordship everywhere necessitated a new administrative organization that made increasing use of writing. At the same time that the chanceries of secular princes were being created, there was also a considerable increase in the volume of written business transacted by the imperial chancery. Whereas less than three hundred charters were issued by the imperial chancery during the reign of King Conrad III (1138–1152), the number rises to fourteen hundred for his successor Frederick I (1152–1190). Even if we take into account that Frederick I occupied the throne longer, we are still looking at a doubling in volume. During the reign of Frederick II (1215–1250) we are already up to five thousand documents from his chancery. Compared to these figures, the early stages of the princely chanceries are very modest indeed. Only in the fourteenth century did their output reach four figures.

When the secular princes began issuing their own charters, the notaries took the royal charters as models. We can see this from the protocol, the structure of the text, and the external makeup. A good example is the charter issued by the Welf Duke Henry the Black of Bavaria (d. 1126) in 1125 for the cathedral chapter of Ranshofen. The document has a format of forty-four by thirty centimeters, and is written in a diplomatic minuscule similar to the one used by the imperial chancery. The decorative elements, too, are modeled after the imperial charters: a chrismon (a decorated C) preceding the text, *littera elongata* (ornamental writing with elongated shafts) in the first line, and at the end even a monogram of the duke. The charter was drafted "by the hand of the notary Wernhard."[57] It is unlikely that this Wernhard was a notary of the duke and that Henry the Black already had his own chancery. The duke may have enlisted the help of a neighboring ecclesiastical prince in drafting his charter. The oldest charters from the secular chanceries are characterized by their plain form and modest decoration. Frequently they were small, irregularly cut pieces of parchment, written to the very edges in plain bookhand, sometimes with awkward penmanship, and in many cases lacking the formulae and other emphatic devices common in the great charters. In some cases the oldest princely charters are in the simple form of undated notices of land transfers, in which the issuer did not speak in the first person but merely gave a plain account of the transaction. The first charter issued by Henry the Lion in 1144 in his own name was drafted as a letter from the duke to the archbishop of Mainz; it requested a confirmation of the duke's disposition in favor of the monastery of Bursfelde. The requested confirmation from Mainz is at the bottom of the page of parchment on which the seals of the duke and the archbishop have been imprinted. Uncertainties of protocol and a plain external makeup remained for a long time the marks of many princely charters. Only at the end of the thirteenth century do we see the beginnings of a change: the format of the charters was standardized and the wording became subject to fixed rules. This lengthy process documents how difficult it was to establish the regular practice of writing in lay society.

We must not picture the princely chanceries of the twelfth and thirteenth centuries as well-organized institutions. In most cases there was only a single notary (*notarius*), who not infrequently acted as his own scribe or who employed one or two scribes. Only the appearance of a protonotary (*protonotarius*) indicates that several people were regularly employed in the chancery and that the first steps towards a fixed organization were being taken. But it is very revealing that even in the thirteenth century the titles *notarius* and *protonotarius* changed frequently.

As a rule the notaries were clerics. The first layman is documented in 1296 in the chancery of Lower Bavaria. In selecting and appointing their notaries, the princes could frequently draw on their court chaplains. Like the chancellors at the imperial court, in whose hands lay the supervision of the imperial chancery, the notaries at the princely courts not only kept watch over all the correspondence, but were also enlisted for confidential services, especially diplomatic missions. In return they were rewarded with high ecclesiastical offices. Hartwig of Utlede (d. 1207), notary to Henry the Lion, became archbishop of Bremen; his notary Gerold (d. 1163) became bishop of Osnabrück; Gerold's notary Henry (d. after 1178) was made provost of the monastery of St. Stephen and Willehald in Bremen.

The Saxon chancery of Henry the Lion in Brunswick is attested from 1144 on. Six notaries are known by name; four of them worked simultaneously as court chaplains, and of these, three came from the monastery of St. Blasius. At times several notaries were employed at the chancery at the same time; in 1168, the notary Henry had the title *protonotarius*. The notaries examined and notarized charters. They dictated and sometimes personally wrote the documents drafted at the court. About half of the charters of Henry the Lion were drawn up in his chancery, while the others were issued by recipients. Occasionally the chancery produced large-format privileges with graphic decorations and solemn diction; next to them we find plain confirmation charters written on small parchment in simple bookhand. Even after his deposition (1180) and after his return from exile (1185), Henry the Lion continued to employ notaries. But his chancery did not last. Only after Brunswick-Lüneburg had been elevated to the rank of an imperial principality in 1235 did a new chancery begin to develop.

The early history of the chancery in Thuringia has never been thoroughly studied. The letter collections of the monastery of Reinhardsbrunn reveal that the landgraves used the scriptorium of their family monastery down to the mid-twelfth century. The history of the chancery at the court of the landgraves begins in 1168 with a charter of Ludwig II (d. 1172), which was drafted by the notary Gumbert. Gumbert was also court chaplain and *magister*, and he served as notary until 1189. In 1186 we already find two notaries at work in the Thuringian chancery. The notary Eckehard was the provost of Goslar and was probably in charge of the chancery until 1211. His successor was Henry von Weißensee, who supervised the activities of the chancery for several decades, until 1244. He appears in many charters as *notarius* and *scriptor*. Early German philologists suggested that this Henry was identical with the minnesinger called der Tugendhafte Schreiber, twelve of whose songs are contained in the Large Heidelberg Song Manuscript. This identification, however, remains very uncertain. Under Heinrich Raspe, who was elected to the German throne in 1246, the personnel of the Thuringian chancery was increased. Five notaries from this period are known by name.

Austria already showed a lively use of charters and seals from the first half of the twelfth century, though the existence of a margravian chancery cannot be proved. The first charter sealed by a member of the Babenberg family dates from 1115: Margrave Leopold III (d. 1136) issued it to the monastery of St. Florian. Close ties existed to the church in Passau and its chancery. Later, several Austrian notaries were simultaneously cathedral canons in Passau, and there is even one documented case of a Passau notary who entered into the service of the house of Babenberg. The monasteries also had a considerable influence on the use of charters in Austria. The archive in the monstery of Klosterneuburg had no parallels in other territories. Here, during the twelfth century, the most important charters of the Babenbergs were gathered and registered in chronological order: the great privileges of 1058 and 1156, imperial diplomas, treaties, foundations, and gifts. After the death of Duke Frederick II in 1246, the charters of Klosterneuburg took on great political importance. Duchess Margaret (d. 1267), the sister of Frederick II, took several important documents from the collection, and on the occasion of her marriage to King Ottokar II of Bohemia in 1252, she presented "the privileges of the land to her husband"[58] in a public ceremony and in the presence of the entire nobility from Austria and Styria. In addition to Klosterneuburg, the Schotten monastery in Vienna also influenced the court's use of charters in the twelfth century. We can see this from the charters that Duke Henry II (d. 1177) had drafted there: they contain classicistic and Byzantine names, which apparently served to glorify the princely house and were intended specifically as a laudatory allusion to the Byzantine descent of Duchess Theodora Comnena. A separate ducal chancery seems to have been established only under Leopold V (d. 1194). After about 1180, the form of the ducal charters becomes standardized to the point that we suspect centralized control over their production. The first ducal notary, however, is not documented until 1193: in a charter of Leopold V for the monastery of Seitenstetten, he introduces himself with the words: "I, Ulrich, have affixed the seal."[59] Ulrich was also head of the chancery under Dukes Frederick I (d. 1198) and Leopold VI (d. 1230), until he was made bishop of Passau in 1215. The chancery was already employing several people from 1203 onward, among them probably a certain Henry, who after Ulrich's departure took over and headed the chancery until 1227. Henry also served as the duke's personal doctor and was, like all Babenberg protonotaries, an influential and wealthy man. The most outstanding career was that of Ulrich of Kirchberg (d. 1268), who is attested as protonotary in 1241. In 1244 he became bishop of Seckau, and in 1256 archbishop of Salzburg.

In Bavaria the establishment of a separate chancery was delayed by the repeated change of rulers in the twelfth century. The older Welf dukes seem to have done largely without their own production of charters; the already mentioned charter of Duke Henry the Black (d. 1126) from the year 1125 (see p. 448) stands all alone. In contrast, the Babenbergs, who were dukes of Bavaria from 1139 to 1156, repeatedly issued charters in their capacity as dukes. Of particular interest is a charter of Leopold IV (d. 1141) for the monastery of Prüfening (dated 1140). Written in the chancery of King Conrad III, it was finished in Regensburg with the comment: "Given in Regensburg by the hand of the canon Rupert, the chaplain of Duke Leopold."[60] Whether this represents the first step towards the establishment of a Bavarian chancery of the Bebenbergs is unclear. Canon Rupert later seems to have been involved in the production of charters for the bishops of Regensburg. Henry the Lion, who ruled the duchy of Bavaria from 1156 to 1180, used his notaries from Brunswick to draft and issue charters in Regensburg, and did not establish a separate chancery for Bavaria. This explains why the Wittelsbachs, who became dukes of Bavaria in 1180, had to start from the beginning. The establishment of a Bavarian chancery occurred during the rule of Duke Ludwig I (d. 1231). The first secure evidence for a separate production of charters comes from 1209 (the notary Gerold) and 1213 (the notary Ulrich). Ulrich, from the Wittelsbach ministerial family of Losenaph, was provost of Illmünster, and in 1228 he appears as the ducal protonotary alongside his brother Conrad, who headed the palatine chancery as protonotary. After 1241 the Wittelsbach dynasty also held the county palatine of the Rhine, where they set up a separate chancery. Under Duke Otto II (d. 1253) the activities of the chancery gradually took on clearer and firmer lines. While the Ludowingen dynasty in Thuringia and the Babenberg dynasty in Austria became extinct around the middle of the thirteenth century, the extant charters from Bavaria reveal how a princely chancery was expanded in the course of the thirteenth century. After the division of Bavaria in 1255, two chanceries existed there. Under Ludwig II of Upper Bavaria (d. 1294), four notaries were already at work under the supervision of a protonotary. The charters now become increasingly uniform in style and structure. The old decorative elements disappear, the *arenga* atrophies, "*Nos*" ("We") before the name of the issuer establishes itself as the new introductory formula. Chancery and archival notes on the backsides of the charters are the beginnings of an orderly system of record-keeping. In Lower Bavaria the development initially proceeded somewhat slower under Duke Henry XIII (d. 1290). Only after the protonotary Henry began his service in 1270 did the activities of that chancery also experience a rapid increase.

These dates from the early history of the princely chanceries are also of great importance to literary history. They reveal the point in time when we may assume the existence of regular writing at the various courts, and they can be quite easily matched to the chronology of literary works. The first patron of vernacular literature was Henry the Lion. Literary activities began in Thuringia after 1170, in Austria shortly thereafter. The late establishment of writing at the Bavarian court was not without consequences for literary history. We would also have to trace the beginnings of the chanceries of the Wettin dynasty in Meißen, the Andechs-Meran dynasty in Bavaria, and the Zähringer dynasty in the southwest, in order to complete the chronological and geographic framework of courtly literature around 1200.

The drafting of charters was only one task of the newly established chanceries, and probably not the most important one. The system whereby the recipients themselves or third parties drew up charters had proved useful and continued in practice even after the establishment of princely chanceries. It was, above all, the new style of administering the territories that demanded the use of writing. Everywhere it proved necessary to compile precise registers of properties and revenues, on the basis of which an orderly administration of land and finances could be erected. The most detailed documents that issued from the princely chanceries were land registers, fief books, lists of offices, and business transactions, and later, account books and tax records as well. The first land register of a territorial prince seems to have been drawn up in Austria under Duke Leopold V (d. 1194). None of the extant Austrian land registers, however, is dated earlier than the second or third decade of the thirteenth century. Around that same time, probably between 1231 and 1237, the first land register was compiled in Bavaria, in this case in German. In the wake of the division of Bavaria in 1255, another record of land holdings was drawn up. Around 1280 there follows the great, two-volume, comprehensive land register from Upper Bavaria. The first extant Bavarian account book dates to 1291–1294. Extensive account books began to be kept in Tyrol in 1288 during the rule of Meinhard II (d. 1295). At the end of the thirteenth century, Tyrol possessed the most modern territorial administration in all of Germany.

To what extent the princes became personally involved in the activities of the chanceries at their courts is difficult to determine. After the Merovingian period we no longer find the signatures of rulers. A very peculiar, isolated case is the signature of Emperor Henry VI under the treaty he concluded on June 10, 1196 with the bishop of Worms and the monastery of St. Martin in the same city: *Henrichus Ro[manorum] imp[e]r[ator]* (Böhmer-Baaken no. 518, p. 210). It is likely, though beyond proof, that Henry wrote the signature with his own hand. Why the emperor—who was literate—took this step in this one instance is unknown. Not until Karl IV (d. 1378) do we find another emperor who signed his name in person. Under Frederick III (d. 1493) and Maximilian I (d. 1519) such signatures assumed a special legal significance.

The centuries-old tradition whereby the ruler validated a charter drafted in his name by drawing a signatory line through his monogram was also given up at the beginning of the twelfth century, most likely because by now the notion had come to be accepted that a charter was verified by the affixing of a seal. A sealed charter was considered a document personally confirmed by the ruler, even if the seal had been affixed only on his orders. At the end of the thirteenth century, Conrad of Mure declared in his treatise on diplomatics: "No charters, except for the very simple ones, must be confirmed with the seal of the lord without the express order of the prince."[61]

In some cases the wording of the charter was used to create the impression that the princely issuer had been personally involved in validating the document. For example, we read the following in a charter of Henry the Lion for the monastery of St. Moritz in Hildesheim from the year 1164: "We have confirmed the present page with our hand and have ordered it to be marked with the impression of our seal."[62] The formula "with our hand" (manu nostra) cannot be taken literally, however: the charter was drafted by the notary Hartwig, who used a similar wording in another document. Of the same formulaic character are references to the personal signature of the prince, for example in a charter of Duke Leopold VI of Austria from the year 1211: "I, Leopold, by the grace of God duke of Austria and Styria, sign."[63] In fact the validation and sealing of the charters was in the hands of his notary, who not infrequently signed the documents he issued with his own name. In charters drafted by recipients, space was sometimes left before the line containing the date to allow the notary to insert this formula datum per manum ("given through the hand of").

The use of seals was not a prerogative of princes. Some extant ducal seals are dated as early as the eleventh century (Count Dietrich of Holland 1083); in the twelfth century, the cities began to carry seals of their own; in the thirteenth century the nobility of the lowest rank used seals. There are also seals of artisans, scribes, and peasants. At the great courts the use of seals began long before the establishment of chanceries. Charters issued by recipients or third parties were confirmed by the princely seal. The Austrian sources document an extensive use of seals in the twelfth century: Margrave Leopold III (d. 1136) used no less than four seals; for his son Henry II (d. 1177), six seals are known from the period after 1156. We do not know who was in charge of the seals as long as no separate chanceries existed; later the protonotary kept the princely seal. The seals normally had a legend which gave the name and title of its owner in Latin. With the exception of liturgical books, these seal inscriptions are in fact the first writing that can be documented at the princely courts.

Charters witten in German   The penetration of writing into the administration of secular law was a process that stretched over several centuries. As long as the charters were drafted in Latin, the princes who commissioned them had no access to the documents written and sealed in their name. Only in the last decade of the thirteenth century did urban and princely chanceries switch over on a larger scale to writing charters in the German language; the imperial chancery took this step still later. A few scattered charters in German are found as early as the first half of the thirteenth century. Among the oldest extant pieces are the division agreement between the Counts Albrecht II and Rudolf III of Hapsburg from the year 1238/39 (*Corpus der altdeutschen Originalurkunden*, vol. 1, p. 20 f., no. 6), and the charter issued by King Conrad IV (d. 1254) on July 25, 1240, for a settlement between the imperial ministerial Volkmar of Kemenaten and the imperial city of Kaufbeuren (*Corpus*, vol. 1, p. 21 f., no. 7), the first and for a long time only royal charter in German.

A number of charters, especially from the early period, exist in both a German and a Latin version. The most famous one is the imperial peace of Mainz, promulgated by Emperor Frederick II in 1235. The conjecture that the German version is the original while the Latin text represents a later draft by the chancery, is today no longer accepted. Similarities in wording to the territorial peace of King Henry (VII) from the year 1234 establish the Latin version as the original. But the German version, too, was official in nature, as we can see from the fact that King Rudolf of Hapsburg (d. 1291) and his successors based their declarations of territorial peace on the German text of the peace of Mainz. Moreover, the *Königschronik* of Cologne reports that in 1235 in Mainz, "at the gathering of nearly all the princes of the German Empire, a peace was sworn, old laws were confirmed, new laws were issued and written in German on parchment, and publicly announced to everyone."[64] The chronicler apparently considered this procedure quite remarkable. Not a word is said about a Latin version.

The German charters would be unthinkable without the Latin charters as models. The structure and form of the German charters reveal their dependence on their Latin counterparts. In regard to the actual wording, however, the German documents are surprisingly independent. The very first German texts already show a developed and agile form, which was uniformly used in different areas where there is no evidence of cross-regional influence. There can be only one explanation for this: the German charters could follow in the footsteps of oral legal traditions. Syntactical studies of the language of German charters have shown its proximity to vernacular usage, whereas no connection could be established to the courtly language of the poets. This does not exclude the possibility, however, that the works of courtly literature and the legal texts in Germany were produced in the same scriptoria.

If we consider the total number of extant charters, the one thousand German pieces written before 1290 seem like a small batch. Of great interest is Conrad of Mure's comment on the use of the German language in charters, which appears in his treatise *Summa de arte prosandi* (1275). Conrad, a teacher and cantor at the Großmünster in Zurich, was aware of letters and charters in German, but he recommended them only for extrajudicial use "among friends" (*inter amicos*). Since he had personally experienced that even authentically sealed German documents were rejected in legal proceedings by the opposing party or the judge, Conrad gave the advice "to write letters and charters in Latin."[65]

What exactly caused the transition to the use of German is a much debated question with no clear answer. The hypothesis that the ministerial class played an important role in this development finds little support in the sources. Much more important were the urban scriptoria. The penetration of writing into the economy and the administration proceeded much more quickly in the cities than in the countryside, and from the beginning the vernacular carried more weight than Latin. But if we consider the chronology of the extant documents, major credit for the first efforts in the development of German charters belongs to the high nobility: to the counts of Hapsburg and of Freiburg in the southwest, to the counts of Jülich, of Berg, and of Sayn around Cologne. This dynastic nobility also played an important role in the development of new forms of aristocratic literature in the thirteenth century. By comparison, the great princely houses showed themselves rather cautious in the use of German for judicial matters. This may have something to do with the fact that resistance to linguistic innovation was strongest in places where chanceries had already been established with a regular use of Latin. It is quite unclear who drafted the German ducal charters and where, during the period when the dukes had no chanceries of their own. Sometimes professional scribes were already used in the thirteenth century. A comparison of language and writing has revealed, for example, that in the years 1260–1270, several noble families from Upper Swabia had their charters drafted by the same scribe, whose services were also employed by various monasteries, and in one instance even by the bishop of Constance, even though he had his own chancery.

In the use of German as a chancery language, a distinction was made between actual charters and other legal records. Among the oldest German-language documents collected in the *Corpus der altdeutschen*

Originalurkunden are the Jewish oath from Erfurt (around 1200), the city law of Brunswick (1227), the fief register of the county of Zweibrücken (around 1250), the privileges of Kulm (around 1252), and the *Geschworen brief* from the city of Lucerne (around 1252); in a formal sense, none of these are charters. If we add to them the oldest land registers in German and other texts of a legal nature which are preserved only in later copies, we get the picture of a fairly extensive use of German legal prose at a time when charters in German were a rarity. It is revealing that the Bavarian chancery of the Wittelsbach family already used the German language in compiling the first land register (1221–1237), whereas charters continued to be drafted exclusively in Latin for another half century.

It seems that the appearance of charters written in German was also related to changes in the use of legal evidence. In the older period, charters had the sole function of recording and confirming legal transactions that had been conducted orally and verifed by witnesses. During the thirteenth century, however, the notion gradually took hold that a transaction was made valid only with the drafting of a charter. As the *Schwabenspiegel* (around 1280) put it: "We declare that charters are better than witnesses. For witnesses die, while charters last forever."[66] It has been argued that this development is related to a change in the introductory formula used in charters. In Latin charters of the thirteenth century, and sporadically even in the twelfth century, the new formula offered that the text not only be read but also heard: "To all those who shall hear or read this page."[67] In the German-language charters this formula appears from the very beginning and with considerable regularity: "Whoever may see or hear this document"[68]; "to all those who shall read or hear this charter."[69] Of course we have no way of knowing whether these documents were actually read out loud in every case. But there is evidence for the public reading of charters. For example, in 1275, Henry of Hasenburg, the *Kirchherr* (proprietor of the church) of Wilhelmsau, confirmed "that this charter, sealed with the seal of the venerable abbot of St. Urban, was handed over to me by Ulrich, the son of H. the Tailor of blessed memory; I personally read out its words in the above-named church and translated it into the vernacular before a multitude of faithful."[70] If the charter was written in Latin, as was the case here, it had to be translated at the public reading. With charters in German this was obviously not necessary.

Finally, it is clear that the use of German was also linked to the state of education in lay society. Ingeborg Stolzenberg has noted that in the thirteenth century the decision whether a charter should be drafted in Latin or German did not rest solely with the issuer, but that consideration for the other party frequently was the deciding factor. The transactions of Count Conrad I of Freiburg (d. 1271) reveal that business with the Orders and the Church was almost always done with Latin charters, whereas charters to laymen were written in German, no doubt from a concern to make the document intelligible to the lay party involved. It is interesting that German was also the language of choice for legal transactions within the ducal family. Whether the members of the ducal house could already read the charters themselves remains an open question. At the end of the thirteenth century there were no doubt laymen who could read German texts without ever having learned Latin.

2. PATRONS AND SPONSORS

Many regard art on commission as an inferior kind of art, since they believe that an artist's dependence on his sponsor interferes with his creative freedom. But in the Middle Ages there was no choice between commitment to a patron or artistic self-realization. Instead, it was precisely a patron's commission which created the material and organizational framework in which works of art could be created and artistic individuality expressed. Although we cannot always prove patronage, and even though we may assume that not every work was done on commission, it would be misleading to make a distinction between works that sprang from an inner vision of the artist and works that were done on request.

Since the historical sources say very little about the activities of kings and princes as sponsors and almost never mention literary patronage, virtually everything we know is culled from the works themselves, primarily from the prologues and epilogues, where the authors talked about themselves, their work, and their patrons. In interpreting this information, it is important to bear in mind that the praise of one's sponsor and the dedicatory preface were literary devices shaped by a long rhetorical tradition stretching back into late antiquity. In some cases the dedicatory inscription seems to have had no connection whatsoever to real-life circumstances. In other cases the mention of patrons' names can be seen as just a polite phrase that tells us nothing about where to place a work historically. Some dedications were probably unsolicited. But none of this changes the fundamental fact that the production of literature was decisively shaped by patronage relationships and the commissioning of works. In each instance, however, these circumstances must be examined in detail.

For ecclesiastical authors, in whose hands lay all literary production up to the twelfth century, patronage played an insignificant role. Monks and canons were not dependent on the goodwill of patrons in pursuing their literary activities. The scriptoria and libraries in the monasteries and cathedral chapters supplied them with everything they needed. Finished works were often given a dedication and were sent off to writer friends or to ecclesiastical dignitaries, who could be considered the authors' patrons only in a very broad sense. It also happened that abbots and bishops commissioned specific literary works. But this did not establish a dependent patronage relationship; instead such a commission was seen as a great honor for the writer.

THE IMPERIAL COURT AS A LITERARY CENTER

Imperial patronage   Up to the twelfth century, the imperial court was the only place for literature outside the monasteries and cathedral chapters. The idea that the support of art and literature was among the emperor's duties was derived from Roman antiquity. Roman emperors had glorified their names through inscriptions and the erection of public buildings, through the promotion of education and the endowment of imperial appointments at the schools of rhetoric, and through literary patronage in the manner of Augustus. It is no coincidence that patronage at the imperial courts of the Middle Ages was always especially pronounced whenever a ruler modeled his style closely after Roman-classical traditions: under Emperor Charlemagne (d. 814), under Otto III (d. 1002), and under Frederick II (d. 1250). The artistic and literary activities initiated by the imperial court above all benefitted the Church. Next to the founding of monasteries and the building of churches, decorating existing churches and monasteries with costly furnishings was a very important activity. Panegyric court poetry and historical writings, to the extent that they were influenced by the imperial court, served to glorify the imperial name. In other cases the sending of a literary work to the emperor complete with an appropriate dedication was simply one way of making it public. If the work was received with interest at the court, its author could expect that it would soon be known in educated circles.

The personal involvement of emperors in the patronage of their courts differed from one ruler to the next. It was rare for all educational activities at the court to be as decisively shaped and guided by the emperor himself as was the case under Charlemagne and Frederick II. Most emperors simply lacked the educational background to become personally involved in literary life, since the literature at the imperial court was Latin up to the second half of the twelfth century. In many cases the initiative probably did not come from the emperor himself but from the clerics and clergy at the court, who were grouped together in the court chapel. A typical eleventh-century representative of a court clergy actively engaged in literary activities was the Burgundian Wipo, who was called to the court by Emperor Conrad II (d. 1039), and still served as chaplain under Henry III (d. 1056). In addition to religious poetry, his work comprised panegyrics to the two Salian emperors, didactic works in Latin verse (the *Proverbia centum* and the *Tetralogus*), which Wipo wrote in his function as tutor to the princes and dedicated to Henry III, as well as a historical work, the "Deeds of Conrad" (*Gesta Chuonradi*), which he presented to Emperor Henry with the words, "I dedicate this work to you, most exalted emperor."[1] The literary activities of the imperial chaplain Godfrey of Viterbo in the twelfth century revolved in a similar way around the emperor. Godfrey entered the imperial chapel under Conrad III (d. 1152), but most of his works were written during the reign of Frederick I. The "Mirror of Kings" (*Speculum regum*), a mirror of princes in the form of short royal biographies, was dedicated to young Henry IV, in whose education Godfrey was probably involved. Godfrey's chronicle of world history from the year 1185 was also dedicated to Henry.

In this last work, Godfrey of Viterbo described the adverse conditions under which literary activities at the imperial court took place. The court's mobility, the restlessness of daily business, and the varied tasks entrusted to the imperial chaplains did not create an atmosphere very conducive to continuous effort on a larger literary work:

> May my patient efforts and the excellence of the subjects treated, as well as the length of the work, find the more attention because I wrote this in the nooks of the imperial palace or on horseback on the road, under a tree or deep in the forest, whenever time permitted, during the sieges of castles, in the dangers of many a battle. I did not write this in the solitude of a monastery or in some other quiet place, but in the constant restlessness and confusion of events, in war and warlike conditions, in the noise of such a large court. As a chaplain I was occupied every day around the clock in the mass and all the hours, at table, in negotiations, in the drafting of letters, in the daily arrangement of new lodgings, in looking after the livelihood for myself and my people, in carrying out very important missions: twice to Sicily, three

times to the Provence, once to Spain, several times to France, forty times
from Germany to Rome and back. More was demanded of me in every exertion and restlessness than from anyone else my age at the court. The more
extensive and difficult all this is, the more miraculous it is that in such hustle
and bustle, amidst such great noise and disquiet, I was able to create this
work.[2]

Even if this description is somewhat exaggerated, it does convey a good
picture of the specific atmosphere of literary production at the great
courts.

The literature of the imperial court from Conrad III to Frederick II
Little is known about the literary activities at the imperial court
during the time of Conrad III (1139–1152), the first Hohenstaufen
king. The intellectual climate of the court was shaped by ecclesiastics
who held the leading offices: by Chancellor Arnold of Wied (d. 1156),
the builder of the church in Schwarzrheindorf (near Bonn), a structure
of great importance for the development of romance architecture in the
Rhineland; by Arnold of Selenhofen (d. 1160), the head of the court
chapel, who succeeded Arnold of Wied in the chancellorship in 1151
and eventually became archbishop of Mainz; by Bishop Anselm of
Havelberg (d. 1158), who was among the king's closest advisers and
became famous through his learned disputation with Byzantine theologians in 1146; and above all by Wibald (d. 1158), the abbot of the two
imperial monasteries of Stablo and Corvey, who was frequently at
the court—not a few of Conrad III's charters and letters were drafted
by him—and exerted the strongest influence on foreign policy and
especially relations with the papal curia. During Conrad III's crusade
(1147–1149), Wibald, as tutor of the then ten-year-old King Henry
(VI), acted practically as regent. The extent of his activities is revealed
by his large "letter book" (*Codex epistolaris Wibaldi*), a large portion
of which Wibald himself compiled, and which contains, in addition to
his own correspondence, many official documents (the extant section
contains the letters from the years 1147–1157). His letters also reflect
the breadth of his scholarly interests and the high esteem which he enjoyed among the educated men of his time. Of particular interest is his
correspondence with Rainald of Dassel (d. 1167), who was at that time
provost at the cathedral of Hildesheim. Wibald wrote to request that he
send the Cicero manuscripts kept at Hildesheim. In his reply, Rainald
asked as a surety for the loan of the manuscripts ("It is not customary
with us to hand over anything to anyone without a valuable deposit"[3])

a copy of Gellius's "Attic nights" (*Noctes Atticae*) as well as Origines's commentary on the Song of Songs. Since Wibald did not have Gellius's work available at that time, he sent instead the "Strategems" (*Stratege-mata*) of Frontin, then a very rare work. Wibald of Stablo's intimate acquaintance with the modern learning at the French schools is revealed by his letter to Manegold of Paderborn (Epistolae no. 167). Wibald describes a scene which occurred during a banquet at the royal court and which shows that King Conrad III took a personal interest in the scholarship of his courtiers:

> Our lord, King Conrad, is amazed at the clever things said by the scholars, and he declares that it cannot be proved that man is an ass. We were full of gaiety at the banquet, and most of those who were with us were not unedu-cated. I told him that this was not possible given the nature of things; how-ever, it could be drawn from a false conclusion if a truth is turned into a lie through an inadmissible premise. When he didn't understand this, I went at him with a facetious fallacy. I asked: 'Do you have an eye?' When he con-ceded that, I added: 'Do you have two eyes?' When he definitely affirmed this, I said: 'One and two make three. Thus you have three eyes.' Blinded by the play of words, he swore that he did not have more than two. But when he had learned through many similar examples to make distinctions, he said that the scholars lead a happy life.[4]

The reign of Conrad III saw the writing of the most important histor-ical work produced in twelfth-century Germany. Its author, Otto of Freising (d. 1158), was the half-brother of the king, born to their mother Agnes (d. 1143) in her second marriage to Margrave Leopold of Austria (d. 1136). As bishop of Freising, Otto had close personal and political contact to Conrad III, but it is doubtful whether the king ever saw his great work, "The History of the Two Cities" (*Historia de duabus civita-tibus*), also called *Chronica*, which Otto finished in 1146 and dedicated to Abbot Isingrim of Ottobeuren. Only eleven years later, in 1157, with Frederick I now on the throne, did Otto of Freising present a revised version of his chronicle to the court. He supposedly did this at the emperor's initiative, but there is no evidence whether Frederick I took a personal interest in it. The decisive impulse seems to have come from Rainald of Dassel, who, as imperial chancellor after 1156 and later also as archbishop of Cologne, exerted a crucial influence over Frederick I's Italian policy and over the intellectual life at the imperial court until his death in 1167. In 1157, Otto addressed a special letter to him with the request that his work be given a favorable reception at the court. It was probably also Rainald of Dassel who suggested that Otto of Freising be commissioned to write a new work about the deeds of Frederick I. Be that as it may, the imperial chancery published a summary account of the historical events from the first years of Frederick I's reign, which would serve Otto as the basis for his new work, and it could hardly have done so without the knowledge and the permission of its chancellor. At Otto's death his new history, "The Deeds of Frederick" (*Gesta Frederici*), was left unfinished, and his chaplain Rahewin continued and completed it in 1160. A new concept of historiography, different from what it had been in the *Chronica*, is apparent in its total focus on the glorification of the emperor. The imperial chancery developed or at least promoted this new concept, as we can see from the fact that during the height of Rainald of Dassel's influence at the court, numerous historical works with a similar tone were written in verse to glorify Emperor Frederick's military campaigns in Italy, specifically his victory over Milan. Among them are the long imperial poem "Hail, Lord of the World" (*Salve mundi domine*), composed by Archipoeta, who worked as Rainald of Dassel's court poet, and the historical epic "Poem of the Deeds of Frederick in Lombardy" (*Carmen de gestis Frederici I imperatoris in Lombardia*). The latter is the work of an unknown poet who wrote after 1160, and who must have had direct contact with the imperial court since he was familiar with the letters of Emperor Frederick to Otto of Freising and Wibald of Stablo.

After the death of Rainald of Dassel, Hohenstaufen historiography retained its fundamental courtly-dynastic outlook. We can see this from the "Deeds of Frederick" (*Gesta Frederici*) by Godfrey of Viterbo, and the *Ligurinus* of Gunther of Pairis. Both works were written in the second half of the 1180s, and both are primarily poetic accounts of Frederick I's wars in Italy. Godfrey of Viterbo was imperial chaplain and as such a member of court society. If we can believe what Gunther of Pairis himself tells us, he also served at the imperial court, at least temporarily, as tutor to the emperor's youngest son Conrad (d. 1196). Gunther had already dedicated his *Solymarius*, an epic on the First Crusade, to his "noble pupil,"[5] while his *Ligurinus* was inscribed to both the emperor and his five sons. His main source was the *Gesta Frederici* of Otto of Freising and Rahewin, though he also used the *Carmen de gestis Frederici*. In all likelihood, he had gained access to these texts at the imperial court itself or with the help of the imperial court.

It is not clear whether there also existed an epic in German about the deeds of Emperor Frederick I. In *Wilhelm von Orlens*, Rudolf von Ems mentions an otherwise unknown poet, Absolon (2209), who is said to have recounted the deeds and death of Frederick. Since the literary information in Rudolf von Ems is usually very realiable, we cannot simply dismiss the mention of Absolon. The German epic of Emperor Frederick, however, would belong to the early thirteenth and not to the twelfth century.

If Godfrey of Viterbo is to be believed, Frederick I owned an extensive library, which was housed in the imperial palace at Hagenau. In a laudatory poem about this palace (*De castro Haginowa*), Godfrey said the following: "The emperor's bookcases are full of the best [Roman] authors and the best Christian writers. If you want works of history, the court offers a market. Legal texts and scientific treatises are there along with all the poets. The great Aristotle, Hipocrates, and the medical science of Galen give out fitting advice and say what things to avoid."[6] If this description is true, the collection at Hagenau was among the most important court libraries of the High Middle Ages. The emperor himself, however, would not have been able to use it directly since he was not literate in Latin.

The works of goldsmithry commissioned by Frederick I also show the trend toward the glorification of the emperorship and the emperor himself. Among them are the huge circular chandelier in the cathedral of Aachen, which the dedicatory inscription identifies as a gift of the emperor and his wife Beatrice, as well as the precious arm reliquary of Charlemagne (today in Paris). Its side panels depict Frederick I together with his wife Beatrice, his father Frederick II of Swabia, and his uncle King Conrad III. There is also the famous Barbarossa head of Cappenberg (today kept in the church at Cappenberg), a silver portrait bust which the emperor gave to his godfather Count Otto of Cappenberg. It is not unlikely that the connections between the imperial court and the goldsmiths of the Maas and Rhine regions were established by Wibald of Stablo. From Wibald's letter to the imperial notary Henry von Wiesenbach we learn that after the royal coronation of Frederick I in Aachen on March 9, 1152, Wibald was charged with procuring the dies for the new royal seals. Only fourteen days later he was able to send to the royal court "the iron stamping device for the gold bulla"[7] along with a pewter seal and two finished gold bulla. Stylistic comparisons have shown that the gold bulla were crafted by the same anonymous master who also made the arm reliquary of Charlemagne, and who must be considered among the greatest artists of his time.

A look at the artistic endeavors of the imperial court must also include the splendid castles and palaces built by Emperor Frederick I (see p. 105). The high quality of the decorative elements that mark the extant remains in Gelnhausen and elsewhere, and their link to the architectural decorations used in churches, reveal that the emperor also enlisted the best artists for his architectural projects.

It is unclear what role the imperial court played in the development of courtly literature in the German language, which went from the first stirrings to a full flowering during the four decades of Frederick I's reign (1152–1190). The Hohenstaufen played an important part in the reception of French aristocratic culture, and we may assume that the emperor's marriage to Beatrice of Burgundy (d. 1184) stimulated the literary exchange. We know that Beatrice was active as a patroness of French poets even after her coronation as empress (see p. 76). Despite these favorable circumstances, remarkably little of the modern French literature can be linked to the imperial court. It is often believed that the court of Frederick I was a gathering place for the minnesingers. A sound piece of evidence is the fact that Friedrich von Hausen, one of the first to compose in the romance style, was among the emperor's closest advisers after 1186–87. In 1189 he accompanied Frederick on his crusade and died along the way, only a few weeks before the death of the emperor himself. The crusading theme figures prominently in Hausen's lyric, and this probably indicates that these songs were composed only during the last years of his life. It is true that the call for a new crusade never died down after the failed campaign of 1147–1149, but it was only Saladin's capture of Jerusalem in 1187 that rekindled the crusading fervor in the west. Hausen's songs had a strong influence on a whole group of poets, who are called the Hausen school. Among them are Ulrich von Gutenberg, Heinrich von Rugge, Bligger von Steinach, and Bernger von Horheim, all of whom were in some way or another connected to members of the Hohenstaufen family. It is possible that the court of Frederick I was the social focal point of this entire circle of poets. Almost all the documentary evidence, however, points to Italy. At that time Provençal lyric flourished at the courts of northern Italy, and there the German poets could become acquainted with their Provençal models.

Even more significant is the fact that no courtly epic can be linked directly to the Hohenstaufen court. During his lifetime, Frederick I's name was mentioned only once by a German epic poet: in the last part of his *Eneit*, Heinrich von Veldeke mentions the Mainz court feast of 1184 and goes on to celebrate the emperor's fame (see p. 206). It is believed that Veldeke was in Mainz in 1184, but we don't know in what capacity or in whose retinue. The landgrave of Thuringia, Ludwig II, came to Mainz with a large following of knights. In 1184, Veldeke was probably already attempting to finish his work on commission from the Thuringian princes. Under these circumstances it is unlikely that Veldeke had a literary relationship to the imperial court.

Under Emperor Henry VI (1190–1197) the style of Latin court literature hardly changed. Godfrey of Viterbo and Petrus de Ebulo dedicated their works to him. The "Book in Honor of the Emperor" (*Liber ad honorem augusti*) by the south Italian cleric Petrus de Ebulo, which for the most part glorifies Henry VI's battles for the Sicilian inheritance of his wife Constance, has survived in a richly decorated manuscript, probably the presentation copy (Bern, Burgerbibl. Cod. 120). The poem is divided into fifty-one sections, and each section is decorated with a full-page colored picture. The artistic merit of the pictures is not exceptional, but they do allow a very interesting glimpse at many details of court life. In this case, too, the court chapel had more to do with the production of this work than did the emperor himself. The commission for the writing of the poem came from Conrad of Querfurt (d. 1202), Henry VI's imperial chancellor. The dedicatory picture in the Bern manuscript (fol. 139^r) depicts the poet kneeling on the steps of the imperial throne; introduced to the emperor by Conrad of Querfurt, we see the poet in the act of presenting his work.

Petrus de Ebulo relates that Henry VI had his palace decorated with a great cycle of painted wall pictures. Five rooms depicted scenes from the Old Testament, from the Creation to the story of David. The sixth room was reserved for contemporary themes, the crusade and death of Emperor Frederick I:

> In the sixth chamber Frederick is shown in a pious robe, the aged emperor surrounded by the imperial offspring. Here Frederick has been painted as he departed joyously and with confidence in the midst of thousands, full of zeal to fight for Christ. Here an ancient grove has been painted, in which stood many oak trees, a forest through which only the sword could hew a path. Iron raged against the entire forest, reducing it to ashes and opening a way where previously there had been none. Here has been painted your hypocritical oaths, faithless Hungarian, and how Frederick continued the journey in spite of you.[8]

Several secenes were devoted to the siege and conquest of Constantinople. "But after they have satiated themselves with the treasures and the gold of Ikonium, they move on; they do not desire rest. Alas, at Tarsus

Fig. 36. The paintings in the imperial palace of Henry VI. Above: the paint-ings in rooms 1–5 (The Creation of the World, Noah's ark, Abraham, Moses, King David). Middle and below: the paintings in room 6 (Emperor Frederick and His Sons Henry and Philipp; Emperor Frederick with His Army on the Way to the Holy Land). From the Bern manuscript of the *Liber ad honorem Augusti* by Petrus de Ebulo (Burgerbibliothek, 120). End of the twelfth century.

they pitch their tents at a river, and there, as he swims, Frederick parts the roaring waves. He gets into dangerous waters, is carried away and loses his life. Now he serves before God and lives in eternity, Frederick, who never leveled a lance whose point did not find its mark."9 The Bern manuscript contains a matching illustrated page on which the paintings of the imperial hall are depicted according to the description of the text (see fig. 36). From the top, arranged by rooms: "First room: God creates everything. Second room: Noah's ark. Third room: Abraham. Fourth room: Moses, the Red Sea. Fifth room: King David."10 The middle and lower registers depict the paintings of the sixth room. In the center Emperor Frederick sits on his throne and blesses his two sons, Henry and Philip. The accompanying inscription reads: "Sixth imperial chamber: Emperor Frederick. Henry. Philip." The lower register shows the emperor on his way to the Holy Land: "Emperor Frederick gives the order to cut down the Hungarian forest."[11] We see the emperor at the head of his army, and in front of him two soldiers who are chopping down trees.

Unlike his father Frederick I, Henry VI was an educated man, "distinguished by the gifts of knowledge, wreathed by the flowers of eloquence and learned both in canon law as well as in the [Roman] laws of the imperial majesty."[12] In the dedicatory prologue to his *Königsspiegel*, Godfrey of Viterbo bestowed the greatest praise on the education of his pupil: "The learning with which I see your eminence, Henry, most blessed of all kings, educated, gives me much confidence in my work on the lineage of the emperors. I am delighted to have a philosophizing king, whose majesty does not need to beg from others his knowledge of affairs of state."[13] Henry VI had contact with the great prophet of his time, Abbot Joachim of Fiore (d. 1202), and he asked him to interpret the prophecies of Merlin and the Sibylline Books: "Your majesty orders you to interpret the British prophet Merlin and the Babylonian Sibyl."[14] The prophecies of the old Celtic bard Merlin, which were closely linked to the legendary material concerning King Arthur, had become known in the twelfth century through the work of Geoffrey of Monmouth.

Of particular importance for the history of German literature is the fact that Henry VI was active as a poet himself. Current scholarly opinion holds that he is the author of the songs listed under the name "Keiser Heinrich" in the Weingarten Song Manuscript and in the Large Heidelberg Song Manuscript. Although there is no actual proof of this, the arguments that used to be raised against his authorship are not convincing, either. If Henry VI was the author of these songs, it is easiest to place their composition in the years after 1186. After his marriage to Constance of Sicily (d. 1198) and his coronation as king of Italy, young Henry—he was twenty-one at the time—spent a good deal of time in Italy. In his circle were the minnesingers Friedrich von Hausen and Ulrich von Gutenberg, both of whom appear in Italian charters of 1186. At this time Henry VI had lively contact with the northern Italian princes and lords, at whose courts the Provençal minnesong had then found a home.

No German-language evidence of patronage exists from the period of Henry's emperorship. It is unclear what role his court played in the composition of the first German Lancelot epic by Ulrich von Zatzikhoven. The French model belonged to an English nobleman who had come to Germany in 1194 as a hostage for Richard the Lionheart. "Emperor Henry ordered them [the hostages] to come to him in Germany, for that is what he wanted. One of these hostages was called Hugh of Morville, in whose possession was the French book of Lancelot as we came to know it."[15] Apparently the Norman lord had brought along French reading to while away his time as a hostage in Germany. It is very likely that Ulrich von Zatzikhoven was given his model at the imperial court. But we don't know whether the emperor or his court were interested in a German adaptation of the French work; Ulrich does not mention a patron or sponsor.

Little is known about literary activities at the imperial court during the period of the civil war between Hohenstaufen and Welfs after the dual election of 1198. The Hohenstaufen prince Philip of Swabia (1198–1208), Henry VI's younger brother, had received a clerical education and had already assumed high ecclesiastical offices before he returned to lay standing at his brother's request. The Welf contender Otto IV (1198–1218), on the other hand, seems to have been uneducated. Both appear in the songs of Walther von der Vogelweide. Walther himself tells us that he was at Philip's court in 1198: "I found a good place at the fire: the empire and the king took me in."[16] It was probably here that he composed the three stanzas in the imperial melody (8.4, 8.28, 9.16) and the *Spruch* about the old crown and the young king. We are not sure how long Walther remained in the service of the Hohenstaufen king. *Spruch* 19.5 about the festive procession of the royal couple in Magdeburg on Christmas day of 1199 (see p. 219) already seems to reflect more the political interests of Landgrave Hermann of Thuringia than those of the imperial court.

The evidence for Walther's connection to the court of Otto IV is even more tenuous. The festive greeting of the emperor upon his return from Italy, "Lord emperor, welcome!"[17] may have been recited by Walther at the court day in Frankfurt in the spring of 1212. But allusions in this poem to the political situation in Germany seem to indicate that Walther von der Vogelweide was at this time in the employ of Margrave Dietrich of Meißen (d. 1221).

Emperor Frederick II (1215–1250) also appears in the verses of some *Spruch* poets, namely Walther von der Vogelweide, Reinmar von Zweter, and perhaps even Bruder Wernher. Under Frederick II the imperial court was a center of learning and the arts, and the emperor himself, as the author of a Latin hunting manual "On the Art of Hunting with Birds" (*De arte venandi cum avibus*) and of songs in the Italian vernacular, had a decisive influence on the literary and artistic activities of his court. But all this no longer belongs to a history of German literature, since the center of Frederick II's power lay in Italy, and he rarely visited Germany after his imperial coronation in 1220. But his sons Henry (VII) and Conrad IV, who were governing Germany in their father's name from 1220 and 1237 on, promoted courtly poetry. Between 1230 and 1250, their court was the center of an entire circle of lyric and epic poets. Here Rudolf von Ems and Ulrich von Türheim were commissioned to write various epics, and the minnesingers Gottfried von Neifen, Burkhart von Hohenfels, Ulrich von Winterstetten, Hiltbold von Schwangau, and perhaps even Schenk von Limburg were probably members of the noble society at the Hohenstaufen court. Yet the personal involvement of both kings in this kind of literature remains largely unknown. Henry (VII) was only nine years old when he was formally installed in 1220, and his half-brother was of the same age in 1237. We know the circle of advisers who determined the course of policy and who actually ran the government. They were also the ones who supported the literary efforts at the court. Outstanding among them was the imperial cupbearer Conrad of Winterstetten, who was mentioned as a patron by both Rudolf von Ems and Ulrich von Türheim. Later, probably after the death of Frederick II, Conrad IV (1250–1254) did become active as a patron himself. At his request Rudolf von Ems composed his world chronicle: "This is King Conrad, the son of the emperor, who has ordered me and graciously commissioned me to write this work."[18] But Conrad IV died four years after his father, and Rudolf's chronicle was left unfinished.

The kings from the period of the interregnum played no role in the history of German literature. Even Rudolf of Hapsburg (1273–1291) does not seem to have been a friend of the poets. The *Spruch* poets mocked his stinginess, and we have no epic poetry from his court. Only in the fourteenth century, under Ludwig the Bavarian (1314–1347) and Charles IV (1346–1378), did the imperial court once again become an important literary center.

THE PATRONAGE OF PRINCES

The literary interests of the princes   What gave the literary activities of the courtly age their decisive impulses was the emergence of the secular princes as patrons and sponsors from the second half of the twelfth century on. Their new role as supporters of literature must be seen in connection with the fact that the princes were developing during this period their own style of lordship in imitation of the representational forms of the royal court. As with the organization of their court administrations, the construction of their palaces, the minting of coins, and the style of their charters, the princes also followed the example of the kings in their patronage of learning and the arts.

But from the very beginning, the literary patronage of the princes had a character all its own. Two things reflect this: sponsorship was directed above all towards vernacular poetry, and the patrons displayed a much greater degree of personal involvement. The first point undoubtedly had something to do with the educational conditions. Whereas the literary activities at the imperial court remained largely Latin during the courtly age, courtly poetry in the vernacular flourished at the courts of the secular princes. Even after the establishment of separate chanceries, the number of people learned in Latin was apparently so small that authors writing in Latin did not have enough appeal at these courts. This distinguishes the German courts from those of the French princes, whose patronage embraced in equal degrees both Latin and vernacular literature.

While literary patronage at the imperial court was largely in the hands of the court chapel, it appears that the secular princes personally influenced the literary activities at their courts. A revealing piece of evidence is the epilogue to the *Eneit* with its information about how the work was created. We do not know on whose commission Heinrich von Veldeke began the translation of the French *Roman d'Eneas*. We do know that the countess of Cleves took an interest in the work before it was finished. In the epilogue we are told that Veldeke gave the unfinished manuscript to the countess "to read and to look at."[19] He did this at her marriage to Landgrave Ludwig III of Thuringia (d. 1190), which took place in 1175. On this occasion the manuscript, which Countess Margaret had given to a lady-in-waiting for safekeeping, was stolen by Count Henry: "For this the countess became enraged at Count Henry, who took the book away and sent it from there to his home in Thuringia."[20] It is usually assumed that the thief was Count Henry Raspe III (d. 1180), a younger brother of Landgrave Ludwig III. But several manuscripts have at this point the name Henry of Schwarzburgs (*heinrich von swartzburg* HE, *von swartzburg greve heynrich* G). The Schwarzburgs were an important comital family in Thuringia. The person in question could be Count Henry I (d. 1184), who is known for his feuds with the Ludowingian landgraves. In either case, it must have

been an unusual personal interest in modern courtly epic that drove
Count Henry to steal the manuscript. It was nine years before Veldeke's
work reappeared in Thuringia; and now it was the Count Palatine
Hermann (later Landgrave Hermann I, d. 1217) and Count Frederick
of Ziegenhain (d. after 1213), two brothers of Landgrave Ludwig III,
who prompted the poet to come to Thuringia, "where he met the count
palatine of Saxony, who handed the book over to him and requested
that he finish it."[21] Apparently it was thanks to the personal efforts of
the Thuringian princes that Veldeke's poetic work was brought to a
happy conclusion. The interest that the princes and lords took in the
new literature is also revealed by the fact that several of them not only
commissioned works but were active poets themselves. A not inconsiderable number of minnesingers of the twelfth and thirteenth centuries were members of the higher nobility. It is easy to imagine what made
courtly poetry so attractive to the great lords. The depictions of the
modern French social culture in epics modeled after French works
seems to have had great relevance for the noble audience in Germany;
and the new ideals of knighthood and love expressed an idea of noble
perfection which they tried to imitate on the festive occasions of courtly
conviviality.

When poets were called to a princely court, this was usually the first
step towards a relationship of literary patronage. Ulrich von Etzenbach
tells us at the end of his *Alexander* that the literary model for his work
was presented to him by two noble lords in the name of Archbishop
Frederick II of Salzburg (d. 1284). Along with it went an invitation to
the court at Salzburg: "Through them he offered me his support and
urgently invited me to join him."[22] The poet could afford to decline this
offer, since he held a permanent post at the court of King Wenzel II of
Bohemia (d. 1305) in Prague: "At that time I did not want to leave the
[Bohemian] lion, and still now I would be loathe to do it, whatever may
happen to me: I was born in his land, and next to God I have chosen
him as my lord."[23] We don't know how the material support of the
poets at court was organized. While the traveling *Spruch* poets depended on what each performance earned them, the livelihood of the
epic poets, who worked for years to finish a single project whose completion must also have been in the interest of the princely patron, was
no doubt guaranteed to a certain extent by regular donations and a
long-term supply of the necessary working materials.

In most cases the obligation of procuring the literary models would
have fallen to the patron, since the poets for financial reasons alone

would hardly have been in a position to acquire a manuscript containing the desired text. Wolfram von Eschenbach reveals in the prologue to *Willehalm* that the material had been obtained by his patron: "Landgrave Hermann of Thuringia introduced me to his [Willehalm's] story."[24] If the intended project was an adaptation of a French work, the first step was to procure the necessary text from France. We have several documented instances where this was organized by the princely patrons. Herbort von Fritzlar recounts that he composed his *Trojanerkrieg* on commission from Hermann of Thuringia: "Prince Hermann, the landgrave of Thuringia, ordered this. The model was sent to him by the count of Leiningen."[25] The counts of Leiningen were located in the palatine left of the Rhine (their family castle stood near Dürkheim), not far from the French language border. From here it was no doubt easier to obtain a copy of Benoît de Sainte-Maure's *Roman de Troie*, Herbort's model. The contact was probably Count Frederick I of Leiningen (d. 1220), whose close personal links to the Thuringian landgraves is also historically attested. He was possibly also the author of a minnesong listed in the Large Heidelberg Song Manuscript under the name "Graue Friderich von Liningen." In another case a noble lord brought the French manuscript back with him from a trip to France. Rudolf von Ems recounts in *Wilhelm von Orlens*: "This story was sent from France to Germany by a courtly and noble man, Johannes of Ravensburg. From French books he learned of the deeds of the hero. And so he brought them back to Germany as he found them written."[26] Sometimes it was a matter of pure chance. Ulrich von Zatzikhoven's *Lanzelet* could never have been composed if the English Lord Hugh of Morville had not brought with him "the French book of Lanzelot"[27] when he came to Germany in 1194 as a hostage for Richard Lionheart. In all likelihood the French models were only borrowed and returned again. Not a few French manuscripts must have circulated in Germany at that time, but not a trace has survived.

Through the procuring of sources the princely patrons also influenced the choice of material. The idea that Wolfram von Eschenbach could have been commissioned to work on *Tristan* or that Gottfried von Straßburg might have been told to compose a *Parzival* seems an almost unbearable thought to modern literary interpretation, which places such great emphasis on the affinity between an author and his material. Scholars believe that the choice of material corresponded to the author's inner disposition in the case of Hartmann von Aue. In the prologue to *Gregorius* the poet regrets that until now he has composed his verses "to please the world,"[28] an ambition he dismisses as a folly of youth. But now, mindful of his sinfulness, he wishes to turn to a religious theme. To this day these statements are interpreted autobiographically and are usually linked directly to the death of Hartmann's feudal lord, a death which left its mark in Hartmann's lyric (MF 206.14). It has not been sufficiently appreciated that the renunciation of secular literature is a frequent topos in religious poetry, and has biographical relevance in very few cases. For the most part the interests of the patron who commissioned a work are a sufficient explanation. Rudolf von Ems composed the legend of *Barlam und Josaphat* on commission from the abbot and the convent of the Cistercian monastery of Kappel (near Zurich), whereas he had secular sponsors for his worldly epics. But religious works were not composed exclusively for ecclesiastical patrons. Konrad von Würzburg wrote his legend of Pantaleon at the request of Johannes of Arguel (attested to 1311), a burgher of Basel, whereas his worldly tale *Heinrich von Kempten* was done on commission from Berthold of Tiersberg (d. 1277), provost at the cathedral of Straßburg. Decisive in each case was the patron's wish.

The extent to which the princely patron's personal interests shaped the choice of material is particularly clear in those instances where several works were created at the initiative of one sponsor. Landgrave Hermann of Thuringia made it possible for Heinrich von Veldeke to finish his *Eneit*; he asked Herbort von Fritzlar to produce an adaptation of the *Trojanerkrieg*, and he provided Wolfram von Eschenbach with the model for his *Willehalm*. In all three cases we are dealing with historical material from antiquity (*Trojanerkrieg, Eneit*) and the Carolingian period (*Willehalm*). It is striking that Hermann ignored the then-modern Arthurian epic. Hermann seems to have taken a greater pleasure in historical materials which, by contemporary opinion, contained more truth and wisdom than the fantastic Celtic tales of King Arthur and the knights of the Round Table. Similarly, the poetic kinship between Neidhart and Tannhäuser was not only the result of their personal relationship. Undoubtedly it also had something to do with their common patron, Duke Frederick II of Austria (d. 1246), who had a personal preference for the new forms and themes of courtly dancing lyric; both poets tell us that he personally participated in dancing lyric as a precantor.

The princely patrons sometimes also influenced the style of the composition itself. The rhymed prologue to *Lucidarius* recounts that Henry the Lion insisted the work be composed in prose, against the advice of

his chaplains who were charged with writing it: "[The duke] commanded them to write it without verses. It would not have been because of
the master: he would have versified it if he had been asked to."[29] But
when it came to the title, the master prevailed over the duke: "The duke
wanted the work to be entitled 'Aurea gemma'; the master, however,
thought it better to call it 'Lucidarius.'"[30] We may assume that such
interference on the part of the patrons happened far more often than the
direct evidence suggests. Reinbot von Durne composed his *Heiliger
Georg* on commission from the Bavarian Duke Otto II (d. 1253) and his
wife Agnes (d. 1267). In the prologue he apologizes for the plain poetic
style of his work by pointing out that the duchess forbade the use of
more elaborate rhetorical devices: "I don't possess so little artistic sense
that I couldn't have versified it much better and decorated it and
ornamented it through and through with lies. But the duchess of Bavaria, to whom I am humbly devoted, strictly forbade it."[31]

The great princely houses as patrons of literature   The chronology of
princely patronage must begin with the Welfs, with Henry the Lion
(d. 1195) and his uncle Welf VI (d. 1191), whose court in Altdorf-
Weingarten was a center of noble conviviality in the 1170s and 1180s.
The poets later sang of the duke's legendary generosity: "The generous
Welf"[32] was held up by Walther von der Vogelweide as an example to
the princes of the following generation, and still in the second half of
the thirteenth century Tannhäuser listed "Welf of Swabia"[33] among the
great patrons of the past. We reach solid ground in the history of patronage with the court of the Welfs at Regensburg, where around 1170
the German *Rolandslied* was written at the request of Henry the Lion.
We are now fairly certain that the Duke Henry mentioned in the epilogue of the *Rolandslied* ("Now we all together wish that God may
reward Duke Henry"[34]) refers to Henry the Lion and not to his father
Henry the Proud (d. 1139), as used to be believed. It can be no coincidence that the Welf dukes are the first attested patrons: until the sale of
their southern German dynastic estates to Emperor Frederick I (1179)
and the fall of Henry the Lion in 1180, they were the most powerful and
renowned family among the German princes. A decade or two before the *Rolandslied*, the *Kaiserchronik* had already been written in Regensburg, which, in the last section of the work where contemporary
events are discussed, recounts in detail the deeds of Henry the Proud.
This would indicate that the author of the *Kaiserchronik* was close to
the court of the Bavarian Welfs or was sponsored by it. But in view of

the eventful history of Regensburg in the middle of the twelfth century, and given the fact that no sponsor is mentioned, this attribution remains uncertain. This holds true even moreso for other epics from the period 1150 to 1180: Lamprecht's *Alexander, König Rother, Herzog Ernst*. They were all composed for a noble audience in Bavaria or at least were known early on in Bavaria, but not a single one contains a reference to a patron. The *Lucidarius* was written in Brunswick at the Saxon court of Henry the Lion, who charged his court chaplains with the task: "This book is called 'Lucidarius.' God implanted the idea into the duke, who commissioned it. He ordered his chaplains to search out the material in the books."[35]

If Eilhart von Oberg composed his *Tristrant* for the Saxon court—which must remain an uncertain conjecture since no sponsor is mentioned—the court in Brunswick would also have been of great importance for the early history of courtly epic. Firm clues are also missing for *Straßburger Alexander* and *Trierer Floyris*, which were probably written around 1170 in the middle and lower Rhine regions, respectively. We do not know which courts in the northwest sponsored such works at this time. There is evidence for an interest in modern courtly literature at the comital courts of Laon (in Brabant) and Cleves. Countess Agnes of Laon—either the wife of Duke Otto I of Bavaria (d. 1183) or her mother of the same name—sponsored Heinrich von Veldeke's work on his legend of Servatius: "Out of goodwill and affection the noble Countess Agnes of Laon commissioned him. She was very eager that he translate into German what he had learned from the vita of the saint."[36] Countess Margaret of Cleves was interested in Veldeke's *Eneit* (see p. 471). It is doubtful, however, whether the necessary conditions for the writing of large epic works existed at either of these comital courts. We know that work on *Servatius* was also supported by the sexton Hessel from the monastery of Servatius in Maastricht: "He was also commissioned by lord Hessel, whom we must call famous; he was in charge of the treasury at that place."[37]

The literary activities at the Thuringian court began under Landgrave Ludwig III (d. 1190). It is not known whether the landgrave shared the literary interests of his wife, Margaret of Cleves. His three brothers, however, hold a place in literary history: Henry Raspe (d. 1180) as the thief of Cleves, the other two, Hermann I and Frederick of Ziegenhain, as patrons of Veldeke. In *Krone*, Heinrich von dem Türlin mentions among the famous poets of old the minnesinger Hug von Salza (2445), not a single verse of whom has survived. A Hug von Salza appears as a witness in 1174 in a charter of Landgrave Ludwig III; if he is identical with the poet, there could have been courtly minnesong at the landgrave's court as early as the 1170s. Thuringian patronage emerges more clearly only after Veldeke was called to the court of Thuringia, and especially after Hermann I succeeded his brother Ludwig as landgrave in 1190. Under Hermann I (d. 1217) the Thuringian court became the most famous center of courtly poetry in Germany. Three great epics were composed on his request: Veldeke's *Eneit*, Herbort's *Trojanerkrieg*, and Wolfram's *Willehalm*. Several other works that contain no reference to patrons are believed to have a connection to Hermann of Thuringia: the adaptation of Ovid's *Metamorphoses* by Albrecht von Halberstadt, the anonymous epics *Graf Rudolf* and *Athis und Prophilias*, and a legend of Pilate. Perhaps Wernher von Elmendorf's tract on ethics was also intended for the Thuringian court. Lyric poetry, too, flourished in Thuringia: Walther von der Vogelweide belonged for a time to the princely household ("I belong to the retinue of the generous landgrave"[38]), and possibly Heinrich von Morungen as well. But the famous song contest at the Wartburg is probably no more than a legend. The work which recounts the event—the *Wartburgkrieg*, the oldest sections of which date to the second half of the thirteenth century—contains few historical motifs. The notion that the Wartburg was home to the Thuringian poets is probably also false. Landgrave Hermann seems to have spent little time there. Its splendid new palas, the so-called House of the Landgrave, was probably finished by his son Ludwig IV. Just how strongly the literary scene at the Thuringian court was shaped by the personality of Landgrave Hermann is revealed by the fact that his death in 1217 marked a clear break. During the rule of Ludwig IV (d. 1227) and his pious wife Elisabeth (d. 1231), a different literary taste seems to have taken over the court. We hear nothing about minnesong and courtly epic during this period. We do know that in 1227 Landgrave Ludwig put on a passion play in Eisenach, "as a sign of his great piety."[39]

The son-in-law of Landgrave Hermann I was Margrave Dietrich of Meißen (d. 1221), with whom the patronage of the Wettin family begins. In all likelihood, Heinrich von Morungen worked at his court, and Walther von der Vogelweide composed several verses about the "proud man from Meißen."[40] But the court of Meißen became an important center of literature only under Dietrich's son, Margrave Henry III (d. 1288), who also fell heir to the Ludowingians in Thuringia and thereby became one of the most powerful princes in Germany. Henry III appears in the songs of Reinmar von Zweter and Tannhäuser, and he composed minnesongs himself. Moreover, the oldest parts of *Wartburgkrieg* and the *Christherre-Chronik* may have been written at his request.

The patronage of the Babenberg family, who were dukes of Austria from 1156 on, goes back to the time of Duke Henry II (d. 1177). The last burgraves of Regensburg from the family of the counts of Riedenburg, Frederick (d. 1181) and Henry (d. 1184), were his nephews and are attested at this court. They and their half-brother Otto (d. 1183) are believed to be the minnesingers listed in the Large Heidelberg Song Manuscript under the names "Der Burggraue von Regensburg" and "Der Burggraue von Rietenburg," and who belong to the oldest group of courtly poets in Germany. If they practiced their art at their uncle's court, Vienna would have been the first center of German minnesong. This oldest circle of lyric poets in Vienna also included Dietmar von Aist, provided the poet is identical to the Baron Dietmar de Agist, who is historically attested in the entourage of Duke Henry II of Austria.

The heyday of the Viennese minnesong seems to have been the 1190s, when Reinmar der Alte and Walther von der Vogelweide worked there. The belief that both poets were active at the same court for a long period of time is inferred from the many allusions to each other in their songs. Walther left the Viennese court after the death of Duke Frederick I (d. 1198), possibly because he did not enjoy the favor of the new duke. How long Reinmar remained at the court we simply don't know. There is no reliable information about courtly poetry in Vienna during the rule of Leopold VI (1198–1230). Only under the last Babenger duke, Frederick II (d. 1246), did Vienna once again become a center of lyric poetry where Neidhart and later Tannhäuser set the tone.

The Bavarian counts of Wittelsbach and Scheyer became dukes of Bavaria in 1180. The first duke, Otto I (d. 1183), was married to Agnes of Laon. We know nothing about any literary activities at the court at this time. Duke Ludwig I (d. 1231) was mentioned once by Walther von der Vogelweide (18.17), but there is no evidence that he was the poet's patron. It is believed that Neidhart already worked in Bavaria under Ludwig I, but this is not firmly established. Clearly documented poetic work on commission begins in Bavaria only under Otto II (d. 1253) with Reinbot von Durne's *Heiliger Georg*. During the second half of the thirteenth century, Otto II's sons Duke Ludwig II of Upper Bavaria (d. 1294) and Duke Henry XIII of Lower Bavaria (d. 1290) welcomed many poets at their courts in Landshut and Munich. Ludwig II probably commissioned *Jüngerer Titurel*, and maybe even *Lohengrin*; both works stood in the tradition of Wolfram von Eschenbach. The Bavarian court in fact continued to be a center for the reception of Wolfram's work.

At the same time as the Wittelsbach family, the Bavarian counts of Andechs rose to the rank of imperial princes as margraves of Istria and dukes of Meran. Duke Berthold VI (d. 1204) may have already been a patron of courtly epic at his court: in *Wigalois*, Wirnt von Grafenberg laments the "death of the noble prince of Meran,"[41] and he may be referring to Berthold himself. Wirnt von Grafenberg could have finished his work under Berthold's son Otto I (d. 1234). Margrave Henry of Istria (d. 1228), the brother of Otto I, may have taught Ulrich von Liechtenstein the art of poetry. Liechtenstein commemorated him nobly in his *Frauendienst* (29.3 ff.), though the reading of Henry's name in the sole surviving manuscript is controversial. Another brother, Bishop Ekbert of Bamberg (d. 1237), the builder of the cathedral of Bamberg, was celebrated as a patron by Tannhäuser (VI. 122 ff.). The sister of Henry and Ekbert was Saint Hedwig (d. 1243), the wife of Duke Henry I of Breslau (d. 1238); with her began the literary history of Silesia.

The court of the dukes of Carinthia in St. Veit became receptive to courtly literature under Bernhard II (d. 1256). Walther von der Vogelweide was a guest there and dedicated two poems to the "noble Carinthian."[42] It is also said that Duke Bernhard commissioned Heinrich von dem Türlin's *Krone*, though this is no more than a conjecture. Equally uncertain is the assumption that his son Ulrich III (d. 1269), last of the Spanheim dukes, was a patron of Ulrich von dem Türlin.

In southwestern Germany the dukes of Zähringen built up their own dominion around Freiburg during the twelfth century. The last Zähringer duke, Berthold V (d. 1218), is known to have commissioned an epic of Alexander by Berthold von Herbolzheim. We know of this work only through Rudolf von Ems (*Alexander* 15772 ff.). The Zähringer owe the important place they hold in literary history even more to the belief that Hartmann von Aue, who mentions no patrons in any of his works, may have already worked at their court and on their commission under Berthold VI (d. 1186). There is, however, no concrete evidence to support this view.

Even if we make allowances for the fact that many epics fail to mention patrons—which means that we must accept the possibility that there were more literary centers than the information given by the poets would suggest—it is highly unlikely that a significant number of courts with an active literary life remained entirely unattested. All the evidence seems to indicate that in the period around 1200, courtly literature, and especially courtly epic, was found only at the few courts that already maintained their own chanceries. Their number seems to have risen only slightly during the thirteenth century. Many of the princely houses that were important in the early history of patronage died out in the thirteenth century: the Zähringer family, the house of Andechs-Meran, the Babenberg family, the Ludowingians in Thuringia, and the Spanheim family in Carinthia. Those remaining were the Wittelsbach family in Bavaria and the house of Wettin in Meißen, whose patronage really flourished only during the second half of the thirteenth century. Also remaining were the Welfs, who after 1235 returned to the rank of imperial princes as dukes of Brunswick-Lüneburg. Under Albrecht I (d. 1279) and his brother Johann I (d. 1277), the Brunswick court established itself once more as a center of poetry. It was here that the *Braunschweigische Reimchronik* was written, which is dedicated to the children of Duke Albrecht I; and it was here that Berthold von Holle composed his *Crane*—Duke Johann I had introduced him to the material (28 ff.)—and possibly also his other epics. This group of patrons was joined in the thirteenth century by those princely families that had risen to become great territorial lords in eastern Germany: the Askanians in the duchy of Saxony and in the march of Brandenburg, the Piast dynasty in Silesia, and above all the Premyslides as kings of Bohemia.

Among the Askanian princes, Count Henry I of Anhalt (d. 1252) is the most interesting figure for literary history, since he is considered the author of the minnesongs listed in the Large Heidelberg Song Manuscript under the name "Der Herzog von Anhalt" ("The Duke of Anhalt"). His brother, Duke Albrecht I of Saxony (d. 1261), was celebrated as a patron by Tannhäuser, though nothing is known of the literary activities at his court. The same goes for the Askanian relatives in the march of Brandenburg, who were also praised by Tannhäuser. It was only the next generation of the margraves of Brandenburg which stands out in the literary sphere: Otto IV (d. 1308), who wrote minnesongs himself and was sung about by Meißner, and his cousins Otto V (d. 1298) and Albrecht III (d. 1300), in whose honor Der Meißner and Der Goldener composed laudatory poems.

The patronage of the dukes of Silesia is attested by Tannhäuser (*Gedichte* VI.78 ff.). It is believed that Tannhäuser's laudation of his patron was addressed to Duke Henry III (d. 1266). But the minnesongs listed in the Large Heidelberg Song Manuscript under the name "Duke Henry of Pressla" are now generally attributed to his son Henry IV (d.

1290), who was also sung about by Frauenlob. The most important patron of courtly literature from the house of the Piasts seems to have been Duke Bolko I of Schweidnitz-Hauer (d. 1301), who commissioned the historical epic *Landgraf Ludwig's Kreuzfahrt* ("Landgrave Ludwig's Crusade"): "A blooming branch of the royal lineage, full of fame and princely deed, has engaged me for this work: the noble Duke Bolko."[43]

The most important center of courtly literature in the second half of the thirteenth century was the royal Bohemian court in Prague. King Wenzel I (d. 1253) kept a splendid court and also drew German poets to Prague: Meister Sigeher and Reinmar von Zweter. Under Ottokar II (d. 1278) the court at Prague displayed heights of splendor never seen before. Friedrich von Suonenburg, Sigeher and Der Meißner composed poems in praise of the king. Courtly epic began in Prague with Ulrich von dem Türlin, who dedicated his *Willehalm* to King Ottokar. Ottokar's son and successor, Wenzel II (d. 1305), composed minnesongs and employed Ulrich von Etzenbach at his court as an epic poet. Etzenbach's *Alexander* as well as his *Wilhelm von Wenden* were both written on commission from the king.

The patronage of the princely courts from northeast Germany is not as well documented. Duke Barnim I of Pomerania (d. 1278) was sung about by Rumslant, Duke Henry I of Mecklenburg (d. 1302) or his son of the same name (d. 1329) by Frauenlob, a duke of Silesia—possibly Waldemar IV (d. 1312)—by Hermann dem Damen, Prince Wizlav III of Rügen (d. 1325) by Goldener and Frauenlob. It would seem that the *Spruch* poets and their art of praise were welcome everywhere, but regular literary activity is not attested at any of these courts.

The patronage of princely ladies   The role that noble women played in the reception and spread of courtly literature in Germany is difficult to assess. Such influential personalities as the English Queen Eleanor of Aquitaine (d. 1204) and her daughters, Countesses Marie of Champagne and Alice of Blois, who were central to the development of courtly literature in France and England, did not exist in Germany. But there is evidence documenting the active participation of princely ladies in the patronage of courtly poetry, especially during the early period. The epilogue of the *Rolandslied* informs us that the work was adapted from the French at the request of Duke Henry: "The noble duchess desired this, the daughter of a mighty king."[44] In 1168 Henry the Lion had married Matilda, the daughter of King Henry II of England and his wife Eleanor of Aquitaine. It has been argued that Matilda was only twelve years of age when she got married, and that one can hardly attribute such literary influence to a mere child. Moreover, it made no sense that a daughter of Eleanor should have taken a special liking to the old *Chanson de Roland*, while her mother and her half-sisters Marie and Alice sponsored the modern courtly romances. The motifs of empire and crusade in the German *Rolandslied* undoubtedly appealed primarily to her husband's ideas and wishes. We must also consider that Matilda's name and her royal descent are mentioned with special emphasis in various foundations—in the dedicatory inscription of the altar of Saint Mary in Brunswick as well as in the dedicatory poem of the Gospel Book of Gmund—even though there is no evidence that the duchess was in any way personally involved in these works. Nevertheless, there is no reason to doubt the statement in the epilogue and to deny that Matilda had any part in the translation of the French *Chanson de Roland*. Moreover, if it is true that Eilhart von Oberg did in fact compose his *Tristrant* at the request of the court of Brunswick, Duchess Matilda would hold an even more important place in the development of literature in Germany.

At about the same time, Duchesses Agnes of Laon and Margaret of Cleves sponsored the poet who helped the courtly romance achieve its breakthrough in Germany: Heinrich von Veldeke. When Veldeke was called to the Thuringian court, nine years after the wedding in Cleves, Countess Margaret, as the wife of Ludwig III, was landgravine of Thuringia. There is no mention that she was in any way involved in bringing the poet to the Thuringian court, but the laudatory words that Veldeke dedicated to her in the epilogue indicate that the landgravine participated in the completion of the work: "This was the generous and noble countess of Cleves, full of a high disposition, who was splendid at giving. Her conduct was exemplary, as befits a lady."[45]

A favorite object of the patronage of noble ladies were legendary epics in the courtly style. That the ladies directed their literary interests to such works surely had something to do with the fact that the education of women had a much more pronounced religious slant than that of men. First in line was Countess Agnes of Laon, who commissioned Veldeke with the German adaptation of the Latin legend of Servatius. She was followed by Duchess Clementia of Zähringen, the wife of Duke Berthold V (d. 1218), at whose request the *Wallersteiner Margarete* was composed: "Since now the noble Duchess Clementia of Zähringen incites my meagre artistry to undertake it, I shall take heart for her sake and shall attempt the book of Saint Margarete..."[46] Reinbot von

Durne composed his *Heiliger Georg* ("Saint George") at the request of Duke Otto II of Bavaria (d. 1253) and his wife, Agnes of Brunswick: "He and his virtuous wife, the high-born princess, said to me: Reinbot, you are to compose a book . . ."[47] The execution of the work seems to have been supervised largely by the duchess, who also prescribed to the poet the style he was to employ (see p. 475).

The courtly epic poets repeatedly declared that their works were intended to win them the favor of noble ladies. Concrete relationships of patronage cannot be inferred from such statements. We may accept, however, that women comprised a not inconsiderable portion of the courtly audience, and that their reaction and judgment were decisive for the success or failure of a literary composition (see p. 509 f.).

Bishops and ecclesiastical dignitaries as patrons of courtly literature
The question to what extent ecclesiastical princes sponsored secular literature is of great importance, especially for the early history of courtly poetry. Around the middle of the twelfth century the Rhineland was the leading literary province of Germany. The religious poetry composed during that period at the episcopal sees of the Rhine and in the great monasteries is characterized by a sophisticated literary technique which the secular poets later could work from. If we could assume that the episcopal court in Cologne was also the site of secular poetry, such as the *Straßburger Alexander*, the literary history of the twelfth century would take on much clearer contours. Unfortunately there is no incontrovertible evidence that minnesong was performed or courtly epic commissioned at any of the ecclesiastical courts. How the educated ecclesiastical princes dealt with courtly literature is shown by the Latin epic of Duke Ernst (*Gesta Ernesti ducis*), written in hexameter by the Magdeburg cleric Odo at the request of the archbishop of Magdeburg, Albrecht of Käfernburg (d. 1232). Hartmann von Aue's *Gregorius* was also put into Latin verse (*Gesta Gregorii peccatoris*) by Abbot Arnold of Lübeck (d. 1211/14), who is also known as a historian. He composed the work at the request of Duke Henry of Brunswick-Lüneburg (d. 1213); it is not known whether the duke himself was educated in Latin.

An exception among the ecclesiastical princes was Wolfger of Erla (d. 1218), bishop of Passau from 1191 to 1204, and subsequently patriarch of Aquileia. To literary historians he is known as the patron of Walther von der Vogelweide. His travel account book, which documents that the bishop spent considerable sums to support and reward minstrels and wandering artists, contains this famous entry of November 12,

1203: "At Zei[selmauer] to the cantor Walther von der Vogelweide five large schillings for a fur coat."[48] We do not know what sort of achievements or services Bishop Wolfger was rewarding with such a princely gift, nor whether Walther at that time belonged to the bishop's retinue or whether he was merely visiting the court at Zeiselmauer (near Vienna). In Walther's laudatory poem on the three courts whose favor he had most sought, he lists "the renowned patriarch without faults"[49] along with the Viennese court of Leopold VI and the court of Leopold's cousin at Mödling. Since this poem is not securely dated, we cannot determine whether Walther was thinking of Wolfger or of his successor, Patriarch Berthold of Andechs (d. 1251). Wolfger von Erla's interests were not limited to courtly lyric. We now believe that during his episcopacy (and on his commission?) the *Nibelungenlied* was written in Passau, and that its author commemorated his ecclesiastical patron in the figure of Bishop Pilgrim. There is no clear proof for this assumption. However, the fact that the episcopal city at the Donau receives such striking attention in the poem, and that its location is described with such precision ("where the Inn with a strong current flows into the Danube"[50]), lends support to the view that the poet worked in Passau rather than somewhere else. If all this is indeed true, the court of Passau would hold a prominent place in the history of the patronage of courtly literature. As patriarch of Aquileia, Wolfger of Erla was the superior and possibly the sponsor of Thomasin von Zirklaere, who composed in 1215–1216 his large didactic work *Der Wälsche Gast*. Here we assume that the poet is identical to the "Thomasinus de Corclara canonicus" (von Kries, p. 6) who is mentioned in an undated entry in the death register of the cathedral chapter of Aquileia.

From the later thirteenth century there is a good deal of evidence for the sponsorship of courtly literature by ecclesiastical dignitaries. Archbishop Frederick of Salzburg (d. 1284) supplied Ulrich von Etzenbach with the model for his *Alexander*, and he tried to bring the poet to his court (see p. 472). In Zürich, high-ranking ecclesiastics participated in the minne entertainments of the noble upper class, as Johannes Hadloub reports in one of his songs (2.93 ff.): the prince-abbot of Einsiedeln, the prince-abbess at the Frauenmünster in Zürich, the abbot of the monastery of Petershausen, and the bishop of Constance, Henry von Klingenberg (d. 1306), to whom Hadloub dedicated a separate laudatory strophe (2.85 ff.). Henry von Klingenberg is thought to be the sponsor of one of the great song collections, the Song Manuscript of Weingarten, compiled in Constance probably around 1300. There are also laudatory poems to the bishops Hermann of Kammin (d. 1298), Conrad of Straßburg (d. 1299), and Giselbrecht of Bremen (d. 1306). The art of the *Spruch* poets was also appreciated at the ecclesiastical courts. Konrad von Würzburg found his patrons among the high clergy of Straßburg and Basel: the rhymed tale *Heinrich von Kempten* was composed on commission from Berthold of Tiersberg (d. 1277), the cathedral provost of Straßburg; his legend of Silvester at the request of the Basel archdeacon Liutolt of Roeteln (d. 1316); his *Trojanerkrieg* on commission from the Basel cathedral cantor Dietrich am Orte (documented to 1298). The latter instance is the only case in the thirteenth century where an ecclesiastical sponsor can be documented for a courtly epic. But we must judge the literary importance of Dietrich am Orte differently from that of the patronage of Wolfger of Erla: as far as we know, the social focal point in Basel was not the episcopal court, but a circle of ecclesiastical and secular lords of the town nobility who together or alternately sponsored Konrad von Würzburg.

THE SMALLER COURTS

It is often assumed that alongside the great princely courts, the small noble residences and castles were also centers of courtly poetry. The main witness is Wolfram von Eschenbach. In book five of *Parzival*, when Wolfram describes the great hall in the Grail castle of Munsalvaesche and its huge fireplaces, he comments that "here at Wildenberg"[51] no one has ever seen such great fireplaces. There is little doubt that this refers to castle Wildenberg in the Odenwald (near Amorbach), which was at that time being rebuilt. The lord of the castle was Baron Rupert von Durne, who belonged to the closest circle around Frederick I and Henry VI. But it remains uncertain whether this Rupert of Durne was in fact Wolfram's patron, and whether part of *Parzival* was actually composed in this isolated castle in the Odenwald.

Based on the information derived from references to patronage, we are well advised to make a distinction between *Spruch* poetry and great epic works. It would seem that *Spruch* poets received a friendly reception at the courts of the lesser nobility as early as the twelfth century. This is attested by Spervogel's lamentations on Wernhart of Steinsberg. Spervogel mentions the names of several patrons, at least two of whom can be historically documented: Baron Wernhart of Steinsberg, who appears in two imperial charters of Lothar III (1128 and 1129), and whose family seat still today towers over the Kraichgau; and Baron

Walther of Hausen, who appears in several charters of Emperor
Frederick I. This would indicate that the wandering *Spruch* poet Spervogel found his patrons at noble courts in southwestern Germany. This
finding is confirmed by the *Spruch* poetry of the thirteenth century.
Among the lords that the wandering poets sang about we find noblemen
of all ranks: princes, counts, barons, and ministerials. The barons included Lord Otte, about whom Bruder Wernher wrote a strophe; the
lord of Preuzzel, mentioned by Sigeher; Ulrich of Rifenberg, celebrated
by Freidrich von Suonenburg and Rumelant von Schwaben; as well as
Zabel of Redichsdorp and Zabel of Plawe, to whom Rumsland von
Sachsen dedicated a poem. Among the imperial ministerials were Volkmar of Kemenaten, praised by Kelin and Rumelant von Schwaben, and
Herdegen of Gründlach, the subject of a laudatory poem by Der Meißner. The *Spruch* poets did not depend on scribes and parchment. They
could practice their art even at the courts and residences where writing
was still unknown.

The situation was different with epic poets, who could only work
where writing materials were available. The first nonprincely sponsor of
courtly epic was the imperial ministerial Conrad of Winterstetten (d.
1243), to whom Rudolf von Ems (*Wilhelm von Orlens*) and Ulrich von
Türheim (*Tristan*) dedicated their works: "This is the noble cupbearer,
the high-minded Conrad of Winterstetten, who has commanded me to
strain my artistry for his sake and to compose for you in properly
rhymed verses."[52] But the social setting of these works was not one of
the castles belonging to the ministerial family of Tanne-Waldheim-
Winterstetten, but the Hohenstaufen court of King Henry (VII, d. 1242),
whose circle of advisers included the imperial cupbearer of Winterstetten. A connection to a great court also existed for Rudolf of Steinach, to
whom Rudolf von Ems dedicated his *Guter Gerhard*. The Steinach
family were ministerials of the bishops of Constance, and Rudolf of
Steinach held an honored position in that city. The familiar tone in
which the poet addresses his patron as "namesake"[53]—both were
called Rudolf and in rank both belonged to the class of ministerials—
raises doubts whether we are dealing with a conventional patronage
relationship at all. As late as the end of thirteenth century large-scale
epic works seem to have been written at smaller courts only under exceptional circumstances. From Bohemia we hear that Henry of Freiberg
composed his continuation of *Tristan* at the request of Raimund of
Lichtenburg (attested to 1329); and the so-called appendix to the *Alexander* of Ulrich von Etzenbach is dedicated to Borso II of Riesenburg

(attested to 1312). The Lichtenburgs and the Riesenburgs were among the most renowned and most powerful noble families of Bohemia and had close connections to the court at Prague. Whether their patronage, too, was focused on the royal court is not known.

THE BEGINNINGS OF LITERARY LIFE IN THE CITIES

The city had long been a setting for literature. The bishops had their seats in the cities, numerous monasteries and schools were located there, and from the second half of the twelfth century a growing number of secular princes also began to move their courts and residences into the urban centers. But we can speak of an urban literary life in the narrower sense of that phrase only where urban society itself, or at least part of it, participated in the literary scene. The earliest testimony comes from Straßburg, where from 1230 to 1240 the city scribe Hesse (*Hesso*) is attested as the head of the city's chancery (*notarius burgensium*, UB der Stadt Straßburg, vol. 1, no. 236, p. 186). This was a very influential post, since the city scribe was in charge of all the city's foreign correspondence. That Hesse also played an important role for contemporary literature is revealed by Rudolf von Ems in his *Wilhelm von Orlens*. In the prologue to book II, Rudolf answers Lady Aventiure's request to continue the story: "I would do it, if I knew that master Hesse, the scribe of Straßburg, would praise it if it so deserved. 'Yes, he will certainly do that! He is so knowledgeable! Whenever he examines a literary work that needs his correction, he makes the proper decisions, for he is very good at correcting."[54] According to these words, master Hesse was a widely respected connoisseur and critic of literature, who must also have dealt with courtly epic, since Rudolf von Ems submitted to his judgment. But we are completely in the dark concerning the social setting of Hesse's literary activities in Straßburg.

Urban patronage assumes clearer contours only towards the end of the thirteenth century in Basel and Zurich. Basel was where Konrad von Würzburg worked, and thanks to his detailed information about the sponsors of his various works, we can get a fairly good picture of the composition of the literary circle in that city. The members of this circle belonged to a thin upper social stratum, and most came from families eligible to sit on the city council. Characteristic was the cooperation of ecclesiastical and secular lords. Among Konrad's patrons were the cathedral cantor, Dietrich am Orte, the archdeacon and later cathedral provost, Liutolt of Roeteln (see p. 485), the mayor, Peter Schaler (attested to 1307), who commissioned the writing of *Partonopier und Meliur* after a French model, and Johannes of Arguel (attested to 1311), who requested the legend of Pantaleon. The two secular patrons were, incidentally, political opponents who headed the two great political factions in Basel, but they seem to have agreed in their literary tastes. It appears that Konrad von Würzburg was sponsored by a circle of lords with common literary interests who gave the poet financial support either in turns or jointly. It could happen that an ecclesiastical lord like Dietrich am Orte requested a secular epic, while a layman like Johannes of Arguel wanted a religious work. This urban upper class, of noble rank in its origins and way of life, disposed of sufficient means to finance large-scale literary projects such as *Partonopier und Meliur* and *Trojanerkrieg*, projects whose sponsorship had hitherto been in the hands of the great secular princely courts.

The literary interests of urban society were at this time directed at the traditional forms of courtly literature. While courtly epic in the French style experienced another flowering in Basel, Zurich became the gathering place of courtly lyric. Zurich, too, had one main poet, the minnesinger Johannes Hadloub, around whom was gathered a whole circle of patrons. This circle as well was made up of ecclesiastical and secular lords and ladies. The social center seems to have been the bishop of Constance, Heinrich von Klingenberg (d. 1306), who was frequently in Zurich. Among the secular members, town nobility and landed nobility were equally well represented: Count Frederick of Toggenburg (d. 1303–05), the barons of Regensburg and Eschenbach, the ministerials of Tellikon and Landenburg. Hadloub spoke especially highly of Rüdiger Manesse (d. 1304) and his son Johannes (d. 1297), members of the old Zurich town nobility, who compiled an extensive collection of courtly lyric (see p. 556). The literary interests of the Zurich circle seem to have been directed primarily at reviving the old noble ideals of knightly virtue and courtly minne. Forms unique to a specifically urban literature developed only much later.

3. AUTHOR AND AUDIENCE

THE SOCIAL STANDING OF THE POET

Until the beginning of the courtly age, vernacular literature was largely anonymous. This is true for all of the Old High German literature of the ninth century—the only name we know here is that of Otfrid von

Weißenburg—as well as for the early High Middle German religious poetry of the eleventh and twelfth centuries. The authors of the *Wiener Genesis* and of the *Annolied*, who were among the most important poets of their time, are unknown. The information that the *Ezzolied* is the work of the Bamberg canon and *scholasticus* Ezzo comes to us by pure chance. This situation changed abruptly around the middle of the twelfth century with the beginning of literary activities at the secular courts. The names of the oldest minnesingers were still known a century and a half later when the great manuscript collections were being assembled, and the epic poets usually introduced themselves, often with great emphasis, at the very beginning of their work. Pfaffe Lamprecht, with whom the history of the courtly epic begins in Germany, gave his name in the very first line: "Listen attentively to the epic we are creating. Its courtly character is excellent. Pfaffe Lamprecht composed it. He would like to tell us who Alexander was."[1] The development of the prologues and epilogues into sophisticated pieces of art has not a little to do with the fact that this is where the authors could introduce themselves to their audience. Only the *Spielmannsepik* and the heroic epics, which drew from oral traditions and for which anonymity was a fundamental characteristic, has been handed down without the authors' names. If, on the other hand, an epic that was based on a French or Latin source remained anonymous, the omission of the poet's name was almost always accidental. The mentioning of their names reflects a new self-confidence on the part of the authors, which was based not only on their own artistic talents, but even moreso on the high esteem in which courtly poetry was held by the noble society of the twelfth and thirteenth centuries.

What position the poets held in this society is in many cases unknown, owing to the lack of historical evidence. If a poet was called Spervogel ("Sparrow"), or Der Stricker ("The Knitter"), or Heinrich der Glichesere ("Henry the Dissembler"), any attempt at a historical identification is already thwarted by the names. Nor can we say any more about Walther von der Vogelweide, since a family von der Vogelweide cannot be attested for the period around 1200. In the case of Gottfried von Straßburg, it is unclear what exactly it signifies that he was named after this episcopal city on the upper Rhine. Even Wolfram von Eschenbach must be regarded as an unknown quantity as far as his social origin is concerned. A noble family von Eschenbach cannot be traced in the charters earlier than the second half of the thirteenth century in Wolframs-Eschenbach; whether the poet was their ancestor is no more than an unsubstantiated conjecture. Even when there is good contemporary evidence, it is still sometimes problematic to establish an identity. The chaplain Wernher von Elmendorf, who composed a German tract on ethics around 1170, was hardly a relative of Dietrich of Elmendorf, provost of Heiligenstadt, at whose request he wrote and whom Wernher mentioned with great reverence. Dependents frequently took the name of their lord. Rarely is there as much clarity as in the case of Friedrich von Hausen, who is almost certainly identical with the imperial ministerial of the same name.

Because poets such as Heinrich von Veldeke and Hartmann von Aue were both minnesingers and epic poets, the erroneous notion has taken hold that lyric and epic poetry of the courtly age both were the product of the same circle of poets. In fact there were very few poets who composed both lyric and epic poetry. The vast majority of the poets can be assigned to only one of the two genres, and when we do so we notice that the boundaries between the genres were often identical with the boundaries of social class.

The epic poets   The lengthy process of composition and the need for large quantities of working materials made the epic poets, in particular, acutely aware of their dependence on patrons and sponsors. We can assume that most of them were professional poets, which does not preclude the possibility that they also had other duties. In many cases the sheer length of the literary compositions indicates that the poets worked on them over extended periods of time. Pfaffe Lamprecht is the earliest poet with several surviving epic works: in addition to the *Alexander* he also composed a legend of Tobias. Large-scale epic from classical material and legendary poetry also exist side by side in Heinrich von Veldeke, who in addition composed many songs. Hartmann von Aue is represented with no less than four epics and one didactic work. Wolfram von Eschenbach composed nearly fifty thousand verses, and this number was soon surpassed by other poets. There are different ideas about the pace at which the epic poets worked. Undoubtedly a wide range existed from one poet to the next. Nevertheless, it is probably not wrong to assume that the production of an epic work comprising ten to twenty thousand verses usually took several years.

It would seem that the continuity of working conditions necessary for the successful completion of a large-scale epic was frequently disturbed: a great number of unfinished epics testifies to this. Scholars have almost always sought the reasons for a sudden breaking off with the poets themselves. There were no doubt instances were a poet died in the midst of his work. But in cases where several epics by the same author were left unfinished, this explanation fails. Wolfram von Eschenbach left two fragmentary epics (*Willehalm* and *Titurel*), as did Chrétien de Troyes (*Lancelot* and *Conte du Graal*), Rudolf von Ems (*Alexander* and *Weltchronik*), and others. And these were not the only cases where we can assume that outside interference prevented the continuation of the work. Since an epic poet could work only as long as his patron made it possible, the death of a patron or the loss of his favor—which had the same effect—must have had disastrous consequences for a work in progress, unless the poet succeeded in quickly finding a new sponsor. The poet of *Jüngerer Titurel*, of whom we know only his first name, Albrecht, after nearly six thousand verses of his long work complains, "My lance of support splintered against a prince."[2] A few hundred verses further on he abandoned his effort with the words: "Heavy poverty oppresses me."[3] Such declarations of failure are rare. In most cases silence is the sole indication of a sudden end. How precarious the position of a court poet was is revealed by the declaration of the unknown author of the *Wallersteiner Margaret* that he owed his very existence to Duchess Clementia of Zähringen: "I have so often bowed in thanks for her generosity that I would like to be sure that she, for whose sake I now attempt this small book, will not let me waste away in the street."[4] In several courtly epics we find indications that the poets temporarily interrupted their work. Philologists make these interruptions seem harmless by saying the poets simply took a break. But in all likelihood these passages testify to outside interference. A direct connection between an interruption and the change of patrons is attested for Veldeke's *Eneit*: the poet was prevented from continuing his work when a patron stole his manuscript (see p. 471), and he had to wait nine years before he found another patron who was influential enough to retrieve it. At the end of book six of *Parzival*, a discouraged Wolfram von Eschenbach passed the task of completing the work on to someone else: "Now let someone continue who knows how to write a romance and who is skilled in the art of versification."[5] In veiled statements Wolfram indicated that the word of an influential lady could allow work to go on or could stop it. Philological studies have confirmed that an interruption occurred at this point in the work, which seems to have been caused by the circumstances of patronage.

The information we get about the creation of Veldeke's works allows us to follow the courtly career of an epic poet as he went from one court to the next. Even though there is no final certainty about the chronological placement of Veldeke's *Servatius*, we are probably not wrong in assuming that Veldeke initially found his patrons in his more immediate homeland: at the court of the counts of Laon and at the imperial bishopric of Maastricht. His visit to the court of the counts of Cleves was then a step into the big world, for it was there that he met the princes of Thuringia, who determined the future course of his career. When Veldeke was called to the court of Thuringia nine years later, he joined the entourage of a great patron and became the esteemed center of the most important literary circle that existed in Germany at the time. The verses about the court feast of Mainz in 1184 in the last part of the *Eneit* (347.14 ff.) attest that Veldeke in the end even visited the imperial court; at that time he was probably a famous man.

The career of Rudolf von Ems seems to have followed a similar course. He, too, wrote his first works for sponsors from his immediate homeland, northern Switzerland: for the ministerial Rudolf of Steinach from Constance (*Der gute Gerhard*) and for the Cistercian monastery of Kappel in the canton of Zurich (*Barlaam und Josaphat*). Circumstances unknown to us later gave Rudolf von Ems access to the Swabian literary circle at the court of King Henry (VII) and Conrad IV. Henry (VII) is believed to have commissioned the *Alexander*, the *Weltchronik* is dedicated to Conrad IV.

Most authors of secular epics were educated. Contrary to the widespread notion that with the beginning of courtly literature clerics were replaced as authors by writers from the laity, we must emphasize that the epic poets usually had the kind of learned education that could only be acquired at the ecclesiastical schools. The discussion of this issue has often overlooked the fact that the Latin word *clericus* at this time did not describe primarily an ordained priest or the holder of an ecclesiastical office, but a man with a clerical education. In his commentary on St. John, the theologian Rupert of Deutz (d. 1130) complained in the dedicatory prologue to Abbot Kuno of Siegburg (d. 1132) that "it is common to apply the name *clericus* to a highly educated man of every rank and standing."[6] Philip of Harvengt (d. 1182) put it even more clearly: "When we ask someone if he is a *clericus*, we do not wish to know whether he is ordained to serve at the altar, but rather whether he is a *litteratus*. And so the person asked would respond properly by saying that he is a cleric if he is educated, and conversely, that he is a layman if he is uneducated."[7] The German word corresponding to *clericus* was *pfaffe*, and this word, too, was directed more at the level of education than at a particular office. In this sense even an educated layman could be a *pfaffe*: "A layman who is knowledgeable, even if he has no tonsure, is still called a *pfaffe* if he is literate."[8] Given this usage, it is understandable that the first writers of secular-courtly epics in Germany introduced themselves as *pfaffen*: "the *pfaffe* Lamprecht,"[9] the author of the *Alexander*, and "the *pfaffe* Konrad,"[10] who composed the Rolandslied. This is all we know about these two poets. It is known, however, that both understood not only French but also Latin. Because of their titles as *pfaffen* their works have been assigned to early Middle High German clerical poetry, even though there can be no doubt that these texts are courtly and not monastic literature.

Where the authors' names are completely missing it is usually impossible to discover anything about their social standing. It is assumed that the poets who wrote *Herzog Ernst* and *König Rother* were educated clerics, as may have also been the case with the poet of the *Nibelungenlied*. The author of the *Straßburger Alexander*, who worked from Latin sources was also of clerical standing. Heinrich der Glichesere, who composed *Reinhart Fuchs*, was in all likelihood a cleric. It is usually said that with Eilhart von Oberg and Heinrich von Veldeke the knightly laymen took the place of the clerical authors. They were the first epic poets with binomial names, the second part of which indicated their places of origin. The families von Oberg and von Veldeke are attested as ministerials of the bishops of Hildesheim and the counts of Laon, respectively, and it is not unlikely that the two poets were members of these families. But as concerns their level of education, they must be seen as clerics. We are absolutely certain of this in the case of Veldeke, since he composed his *Servatius* after a Latin source. In the case of Eilhart we are limited to conjecture. Clerical status is once again beyond doubt for Herbort von Fritzlar, author of the first German romance of Troy, who introduced himself as a "learned schoolmaster,"[11] and for Ulrich von Zatzikhoven, who composed the *Lanzelet*. Ulrich is identified with the Thurgau "chaplain Ulrich von Zatzikhoven, parish priest of Lommis,"[12] who appears in a charter (dated 1214) of the counts of Toggenburg for the monastery of Peterzell.

An exception is Hartmann von Aue, who said of himself: "There was a knight who was so learned that he could read books, everything that was written in them. His name was Hartmann and he was a ministerial at Aue."[13] As long as the notion prevailed that most courtly epic poets were knights, the special accent of Hartmann's statement could not be emphasized enough. The terms "knight" and "educated man," *miles*

and *clericus*, which in the minds of contemporaries represented oppo
sites, were joined in the case of Hartmann. A knight who could reac
books must have been regarded as a most unusual figure. What wa:
unusual, however, was not that this courtly epic poet could read—the)
nearly all could—but that Hartmann was a ministerial and a knight
How this paradox can be explained in Hartmann's case we just don'ı
know. Like the other educated laymen of this time, he had probably beer
destined for a clerical office, and then for some reason or another hac
returned to lay standing. Only one other epic poet of the thirteentb
century seems to have been in a situation similar to that of Hartmann:
Rudolf von Ems, who calls himself a *knappe* and *dienstman* of the
counts of Montfort (*Wilhelm von Orlens* 15627 ff.), but who was, as all
his works attest, highly educated. Most epic poets of the thirteenth century were literate in Latin, beginning with Gottfried von Straßburg, of
whom only one thing is certain: he was a learned man, a *clericus* par
excellence.

It probably never would have occurred to anyone that uneducated
laymen also played a role as authors of courtly epics, had not the most
famous of them, Wolfram von Eschenbach, confessed to his illiteracy:
"I cannot read a single letter."[14] There is a great diversity of opinion
about Wolfram's educational level. It is certain, though, that a fundamental difference existed between, on the one hand, the Latin-
educated epicists Veldeke, Hartmann, and Gottfried von Straßburg,
and, on the other hand, the uneducated layman versifier Wolfram von
Eschenbach. The awareness of this difference left an imprint both on
Wolfram's statements about his views on art and his colleagues, and on
Gottfried of Straßburg's verdict in the so-called "literary excursus" in
Tristan, which is marked by the educated man's sense of superiority and
the cleric's contempt for the uneducated layman. For while Gottfried
celebrates Hartmann as the greatest contemporary poet for the beautiful clarity of his "crystal words,"[15] Wolfram—who is not mentioned by
name, but to whom verses 4636 following certainly refer—is mocked as
"friend of the hare,"[16] who "high-skipping and far-browsing seeks out
poetry's field with dicing words."[17] Courtly epic was the preserve of the
educated literati, and it remained so even after Wolfram. That Wolfram
as a layman could measure himself against the educated was, even during his lifetime, considered his greatest claim to fame: "A lay mouth
never spoke more beautifully."[18] These words of praise from Wirnt von
Grafenberg were later often repeated. For all the influence that Wolfram's narrative style exerted on the epic poetry that came after him,

uneducated epicists remained a great rarity. His most ardent imitators, in particular, were highly educated.

The minnesingers   The Large Heidelberg Song Manuscript is a collection of the songs of 140 poets, and the authors are arranged by rank and social class: Emperor Henry heads the list, followed by Kings Conrad the Younger and Wenzel of Bohemia, and then dukes, margraves, counts, and a large number of lords. At the end of the collection are several singers who carry the title "master" (Meister Sigeher, Meister Rumslant), and others with typical minstrel names (Der alte Meißner, Der Gast, Spervogel, Boppe). This list may create the impression that all levels of society, from the highest nobility down to the lawless vagabonds, participated in the production of courtly lyric. Such an impression would be false. With few exceptions, the poets of the Heidelberg Manuscript represent only two social groups, both of which were internally fairly homogeneous: noble lords and wandering professional poets. Minnesong was the preserve of the nobility, *Spruch* poetry that of the minstrels.

Minnesong was aristocratic art: "He who begs for worn clothes is not worthy of the minnesong."[19] "Minnesongs are sung there, at the court and at feasts, whereas I am so desperately in need of used clothes that I don't sing of ladies."[20] Der Stricker expressed the same sentiment in the form of a fictitious protest from the audience: "Isn't it something that now Der Stricker, too, wants to praise the ladies. If he were wise he would not mention them in his pieces. His life and the praise of the ladies have nothing in common. A horse and used clothes would be more fitting objects of his praise."[21] A more positive expression of this same idea appears in *Armer Heinrich*, where Hartmann von Aue painted the ideal image of a noble knight, whose courtly virtues and qualities included the ability to sing of minne: "He was a pillar in counsel and sang beautifully of minne. Thus he could win fame and renown in the world. He was courtly and wise."[22]

Most minnesingers can be assigned to historically attested noble families. As for the oldest poets, those who still belong to the twelfth century, there are certain doubts and uncertainties about their social class. In particular Der von Kürenberg, the first German minnesinger known by name, cannot be identified. Nevertheless, the dominant role of the nobility in the older minnesong is clear enough. Of the high nobility were the burgraves of Regensburg and Rietenburg, descendants of the old Bavarian noble clan of the Papones, who were related by marriage to the Babenberg family. A link also existed between the Babenberg dynasty and Baron Dietmar von Aist (see p. 478). Count Rudolf von Fenis belonged to the powerful house of the counts of Neuenburg.

Minne scholarship has concerned itself strongly with the question of how great a share of courtly lyric can be attributed to the various levels of the nobility. Alois Schulte and Paul Kluckhohn sought to prove that most singers came from the class of ministerials. If we look at the index of the Large Heidelberg Manuscript, we notice how numerously the uppermost ranks of the nobility are represented: one emperor, two kings (the third king is the legendary King Tirol of Schotten), five princes, and eight counts head the collection. They are followed by members of well-known Swiss and southwest German baronial families: Warte, Klingen, Rotenburg, Sax, Rauenberg, and so on. The nobility below the rank of count in this manuscript bears only the title of "lord" (*her*). How many of these lords were barons and how many were ministerials has become something of a central problem of minnesong scholarship. According to Schulte, the group of barons extends to no. 34 (Heinrich von Morungen), and with no. 35 (Der Schenk von Limburg) the ministerials begin, who are said to occupy the entire middle section of the collection, up to no. 101 (Der Taler). But there are some who don't fit this pattern: Morungen is preceded by Veldeke (no. 16), who was certainly not a baron, and Schenk von Limburg is followed by the highly noble burgrave of Rietenburg (no. 42) and the Baron Bligger von Steinach (no. 58). This is enough to convince us that the sequence of poets in the Heidelberg Manuscript is not thoroughly consistent, even if the overall structure is arranged by social rank.

The number of ministerials among the noble minnesingers was apparently much smaller than used to be assumed. That the separation between barons and ministerials in fact has little meaning is revealed by the oldest securely attested ministerial among the minnesingers: Friedrich von Hausen. Friedrich belonged to the most important group of imperial ministerials around Emperor Frederick I, but his father, Walther von Hausen, is attested as a baron in several imperial charters. Legally speaking the entrance into the class of imperial ministerials did in fact constitute a step down in social rank, but practically speaking it entailed much greater proximity to the ruler and probably an actual rise in power and influence. The number of ministerials among the lyric poets seems to have increased to the same degree that the ministerial class became fused with the old nobility. In the course of the thirteenth century, many old noble families died out in Germany. It has been estimated that the nobility around 1300 was up to eighty percent ministerial. In view of these numbers the ministerial class is, if anything, underrepresented in the Heidelberg collection.

Where the noble poets practiced their art eludes us. We cannot exclude the possibility that the singers of the lower nobility sang at their own castles and residences; but this was certainly not the rule. Minnesong presupposes the kind of courtly festivity found at the great courts. Literary relationships among the singers, for example among the poets of the Hausen school, would suggest that their social life had a common focal point. For the Hausen circle this was probably the court of Henry VI; for the Swabian minnesingers in the thirteenth century it was most likely the Hohenstaufen royal court of Henry (VII) and Conrad IV. In such circumstances the noble poets were undoubtedly to a certain degree subject to the literary tastes of the lords of the courts, as we learn from the brief episode involving Baron Reinhart of Westerburg: Emperor Ludwig the Bavarian (d. 1347) rebuked him for his woman's song (see p. 330). But we must not confuse such forms of literary patronage with the constraints to which professional poets were subject.

It is rather unclear how the noble lords acquired the skill to manipulate complicated strophic schemes linguistically, metrically, and musically. In fact this phenomenon has not occasioned sufficient surprise. In the case of the Provençal and French poets, who served the Germans as models, we can frequently presuppose a literary education. But such is not the case with the noble minnesingers in Germany, who as a rule were undoubtedly illiterates. It would seem that the oldest poets around Kürenberg, who composed their verses primarily in long-line stanzas, based their poetic techniques on oral traditions. A more difficult task confronted those who worked from romance models. The problem could be solved most easily if one simply took over the complete strophic scheme of a romance song, the metric structure together with the melody. Such *contrafacta* were apparently of paramount importance for Hausen and his circle. Using the pattern of the adopted forms, it was then possible, through variation, to create similar works of lyric art. One could not expect great poetry to be created with this method. Nevertheless, an exceptional talent like Friedrich von Hausen did succeed in developing his own style and tone with borrowed tools.

On the whole, the artistic merit of the minnesongs composed by noble dilettantes was not very high. The poetic creations of the princely singers of the thirteenth century consistently lack power and expressiveness. That courtly lyric nevertheless did become great art in Germany is due largely to the minnesingers of lower social rank, especially the professional poets, most of whom had a literary education and thus approached their work from an entirely different educational background. In southern France, in addition to the princely poets such as William IX and Jaufré Rudel, professional singers had a hand in shaping the form of troubadour lyric as early as the first half of the twelfth century. Marcabru and Cercamon were the most prominent among them. Marcabru polemicised against the love practices of the nobility, and later, too, there were voices that accused the noble singers of corrupting courtly service to a lady.

The question of when professional minnesong began to be composed in Germany is one that has so far received little attention from minnesong scholarship. Since all poets were thought to be noblemen, including Walther von der Vogelweide and Neidhart, the question never arose in the first place. Today, however, we are certain that Walther was a professional singer of unknown background. The same goes for Neidhart and Tannhäuser. The fact that these poets are listed in the Large Heidelberg Song Manuscript with the title of lord, and that they are depicted with coats of arms and other noble attributes, says nothing about their actual social standing. Whether professional court singers existed before Walther's time is uncertain. Reinmar der Alte may have been in such a position, and possibly Heinrich von Morungen as well, whose noble birth was never questioned since he was identified with the "Henricus de Morungen" who is described in a charter (dated 1217) of the Margrave Dietrich of Meißen as a "retired knight" (*miles emeritus*). But the charter goes on to say that the margrave bestowed on him a yearly pension of ten talents "for the great services during his life,"[23] and this would seem to apply to a deserving retainer rather than a noble lord. Morungen also falls outside the normal pattern of noble poets in regard to his educational level: the many classical motifs in his songs indicate that he had enjoyed a scholarly education and knew Latin, as was probably also the case with Walther von der Vogelweide. If all this is true, it would mean that the greatest artists among the German minnesingers were professional poets. This would come as no surprise, since it was hardly possible to attain mastery of courtly lyric without literary training.

The professional court lyricists depended on the favor of princely patrons and were apparently in a situation similar to the epic poets working at the courts. Neidhart, for example, seems to have held a permanent position at the Viennese courts for years. But if we can believe his own words, even he was not spared the bitter experience of a change of patrons: "I have lost my lord's favor through no fault of mine. Therefore I have left everything I own in Bavaria: I'm on my way to Austria to place my hopes in the noble Austrian."[24] A poetic product of this situation was the patron minnesong, which combined the praise of the patron with the minne theme. We find it with Neidhart and Tannhäuser.

Scholars believe that the German minnesingers also included members of the clergy, but a thorough examination of this question remains to be done. The clearest evidence for clerical standing exists in the case of Rost von Sarnen, who is called "Rost. Kirchherr zu Sarne"[25] in the Heidelberg Manuscript. The family of Rost belonged to the town nobility of Zurich, and a Henry (d. 1330) is attested as *Kirchherr* (proprietary lord of the church) in Sarne and later as canon in Zurich. Hugo von Trimberg reported "that an abbot of St. Gall composed dawn songs."[26] Hadloub sheds light on the cultural-historical background: ecclesiastical dignitaries of both sexes participated in the minne entertainment of noble society in Zurich.

The traveling poets   Worst off were the traveling poets, who had no permanent home and were therefore outside the law. They had to make a living from their art, which they offered "at court and in the street."[27] Their domain was *Spruchdichtung*. Occasionally a *Spruch* poet, such as Der Marner or Der Kanzler, also composed a minnesong, but on the whole the two genres remained strictly separated as far as authorship is concerned. Only against this background does it become clear what a unique and exceptional place Walther von der Vogelweide occupies in the history of courtly lyric: he was the only poet who worked to equal degrees as *Spruch* poet and minnesinger. It is believed that the death of his patron, Duke Frederick I of Austria (d. 1198), led to the loss of his position as court singer in Vienna, forcing Walther to seek his livelihood as a wandering minstrel. Walther was also the one who brought the two genres, minnesong and *Spruchdichtung*, formally closer together by raising the *Spruche* to the artistic level of the songs. In doing so he became the founder of courtly *Spruchdichtung*.

Nothing certain is known about the social background of the wandering minstrels. In medieval society, those outside the law formed a separate group without any attributes of social rank. This needs to be stated very emphatically, since it has become quite common in literary history to bestow on the wandering poets social attributes that are borrowed from entirely different legal spheres. Most *Spruch* poets are said to come from a "burgher" background: this is a thoroughly misleading concept, since the word "burgher" in the legal sense at that time described only those city-dwellers who possessed the rights of burghers, which has not been attested for a single *Spruch* poet. It is also unlikely that a significant number of *Spruch* poets of the twelfth and thirteenth centuries came from the urban population. It is even less likely that there were noblemen among them. This idea used to be very popular with the older minnesong scholarship, and it became most relevant in reference to Walther von der Vogelweide: it was thought that he could have been the younger son of a ministerial, who had remained without an inheritance and was therefore forced to earn his living as a wandering minstrel. Other *Spruch* poets, too, were counted among the nobility: Friedrich von Suonenburg, Johannes von Ringgenberg, Pfeffel, von Wengen—primarily because their names are also documented as the names of noble families. But there is not a single case where a poet is securely attested as a member of such a family, nor is it very likely that any of them were. Certainly there were among the wandering minstrels some who were better off than others. The educated minstrels looked down with utter contempt on those who were practicing their art as illiterates. The sharp-tongued polemics that the poets aimed at one another reveals how tough the competition was.

The wandering *Spruch* poets are indistinguishable in social appearance from the jongleurs who performed in large numbers at festive occasions at court. In German philology, however, this fact has been vehemently denied, because no one wanted to admit that a poet like Walther von der Vogelweide was on a par with that "wretched musical riff-raff" (Hans Naumann) that was the jongleurs. But such judgments fail to do justice to the high esteem that instrumental musicians, in particular, enjoyed in lay society. It is well documented that the jongleurs had a broad palette of entertainment to offer, from acrobatic stunts and magic tricks to the recitation of sophisticated poetry. To Charlemagne's court feast in Landit

> there came more than four hundred minstrels, whom we call *speleman* and who also acted as *Wappensprecher*. Some of them knew how to sing of adventures and of things that happened in times gone by. There were also some there who told by heart of minne and love; some who let the fiddles sound out loud; some who blew the horn sweetly. Some performed as giants.

Some played artfully on the wood or bone flute. Some played musical pieces on the bagpipe. Some, whom one could listen to silently, played the harp and the violin. Some pleased sad hearts with the psaltery. Then there were some who had learned to play the zither in Paris. Some experienced masters did magic tricks under a hat. Some were good at turning the disk. Some struck the cymbals with drumsticks. Some made noise and leapt about; others were good at wrestling. Some had billy goats fight horses at will and let monkeys ride on their backs. Some could dance with dogs, and some could chew stones to little bits.[28]

The list did not end here: there followed a variety of magicians and especially the popular imitators of animal voices.

The size and varied composition of the class of minstrels and jongleurs is revealed most clearly by the travel accounts of the Passau bishop, Wolfger of Erla (d. 1218), which record the bishop's daily expenses on his travels through Austria and Italy in the years 1203 and 1204. Bishop Wolfger had a generous hand for all those who sought his support and crowded around him wherever he went. The "wandering folk" (*vagi, girovagi*) included the mass of the "poor" (*pauperes, pauperculi*), the "old" (*vetuli*), the "infirm" (*infirmi*), the "blind" (*caeci*), the "fat" (*pingues*), the many "pilgrims" (*peregrini, wallerii*) and "penitents" (*penitenciarii*), the "poor crusaders" (*pauperes cruciferi*), and the wandering "monks" (*monachi, moniales*). No less numerous were the scholars who, despite their education, had sunk to the same social level: the "poor clerics" (*pauperes clerici*), the "scholars" (*scolares*), the "wretched priests" (*lodderpfaffi*), and many an "old canon" (*vetulus canonicus*). Even larger was the group of wandering performers who came to meet the bishop on his travels. They were usually described with traditional ecclesiastical terminology as "jugglers" (*ioculatores*), "entertainers" (*histriones*), and "actors" (*mimi*). But we also find more precise names, which reveal that the musical offerings of "fiddlers" (*gigari*), "singers" (*cantores, discantores*), "female singers" (*cantatrices*), and a "girls' choir" (*puellae cantantes*) were especially appreciated. *Cantor* is also the designation given to Walther von der Vogelweide, and in this case the word is probably best translated as "wandering minstrel." The sums of money that are recorded in the account books shed some light on the different social status of the various groups. The bishop bestowed the richest rewards on the goliards and the scholars. But he spent almost as much on the jugglers and musical entertainers. Much more modest were the gifts to the great number of the poor and the pilgrims.

Even as a group, the *ioculatores* and entertainers were not homo-geneous, and the hierarchy was largely determined by what a person did. In a much-quoted passage from the *Summa confessorum* by Thomas of Chobham (d. after 1233), the entertainers are divided into three classes and judged from an ecclesiastical point of view:

> There are three kinds of entertainers. [First], those who twist and bend their bodies in disgraceful leaps and gestures, and who most disgracefully expose themselves or wear horrible armor or masks: they are all destined for damnation, unless they give up their profession. [Second], there are others, who do nothing else except stick their noses into the affairs of others; they have no permanent abode, but wander to the courts of the princes and spread scandal and ignominy about those who are absent. These, too, are destined for damnation; for the apostle forbids us to eat with such people. They are called *scurrae vegi* (wandering pranksters), because they are good for nothing besides stuffing themselves and speaking evil. There is a third category of entertainers who own musical instruments to delight the people, and of them there are two kinds. Some visit public banquets and frivolous feasts in order to sing lascivious songs to incite the people to wanton-ness. They are as worthy of damnation as the others. The second group, those who are called *ioculatores*, sing of the deeds of kings and of the lives of the saints, and they bring the people consolation in their sorrows and fears. These people can be saved.[29]

The Church's condemnation of the wandering folk of acrobats and entertainers had a long tradition stretching back to the time of the Church Fathers. Again and again, ecclesiastics as well as laymen were warned not to get involved with the entertainers, whose activities seemed to the strict preachers of morality the very embodiment of the sinful life of the world. But all these admonitions seem to have done very little. Like Bishop Wolfger of Erla, many other ecclesiastical princes were not embarassed to admit their fondness for the art of the jongleurs and minstrels. In the thirteenth and fourteenth centuries, the Church noted with special anxiety that more and more educated clerics, who apparently were unable to find an ecclesiastical position, took up the lifestyle of the wandering folk as *clerici vagi*, with some of them actually becoming all but *ioculatores*. A council in Salzburg in 1310 decreed that "clerics who deny their clerical status entirely and become entertainers or goliards or jesters"[30] shall forfeit all privileges of their clerical standing. The statutes of the Synod of Lüttich (1287) forbade clerics "to become jugglers, entertainers, bailiffs, secular foresters, or goliards."[31] Just how close clerics and jugglers were to each other in terms of their status is revealed by the Bavarian Territorial Peace of

1244. Under the heading "About vagrants and jugglers" (*De vagis et hystrionibus*), it decreed the following: "Clerics who wear a lay tonsure and who are vagrants are declared to be outside the peace, just like lay jugglers."[32]

The case of the entertainers shows how little success the Church's sermonizing had where noble society's desire for entertainment was concerned. The esteem in which the wandering entertainers were held by the secular nobility stood in marked contrast to the condemnation heaped upon them by the theologians. At all feasts and at all courts they were welcome and were loaded with rich presents. And if it happened that a lord behaved differently and turned the entertainers back, this was seen as unusual enough by contemporary chroniclers to merit recording (see p. 230). The favor that the wandering minstrels and jugglers enjoyed gave some of them the chance to improve their position. Disguised as an old entertainer, Tristran told this story in Ireland: "I was a court minstrel and was master of many courtly skills . . . Through this I acquired such riches until the wealth turned my head and I wanted more than was my due. And so I took up trading."[33] He joined up with another merchant and equipped a ship that sailed from Spain to England. This story was pure invention, but it was meant to sound believable, and apparently it did. At the English court, too, Tristan concealed his true identity, and he advanced solely on the basis of his courtly talents, first as hunter and then as an instrumental soloist. King Mark was so impressed by his musical offerings that he made Tristan a trusted companion who entertained him with "harping, fiddling, and singing"[34]; he also appointed him as the king's personal armorer. "And thus the homeless lad became a favorite at court."[35]

The Provençal work *Daurel et Beton* from the twelfth century, and the French work *Guillaume de Dole* by Jean Renart from the first half of the thirteenth century, also give a picture of the preferential positions a minstrel could attain if he had his lord's confidence. In *Guillaume de Dole*, Jouglet was the minstrel of the German Emperor Conrad, and no one at the court was closer to the emperor. Jouglet remained a servant always: he sang and made music for the emperor, he helped him dress, he went on diplomatic missions and looked after guests. At the same time he enjoyed the emperor's special affection: Conrad engaged him in intimate conversation and sang with him, and Jouglet was the only one at court to whom he entrusted matters of the heart. The musical skills of the professional singers and instrumentalists were always especially appreciated. In France it was customary by the twelfth century for art-loving princes to take individual minstrels into their service and give them a secure position at court. The evidence from Germany is sparser. In a charter issued in Speyer by King Henry VI on September 6, 1189, for the monastery of Steingaden, "Rupert, the king's minstrel"[36] appears among the witnesses. Bishop Wolfger of Erla also had his own *ioculator* who accompanied him on his travels.[37] King Manfred (d. 1266), the son of Emperor Frederick II, kept at his court a whole band of "violinists" (*gigaeren*) and "fiddlers" (*videlaeren*) to whom he granted great privileges.

Most wandering entertainers lived according to the motto "To take money for honor" (*guot umb êre nemen*). In the courtly period this phrase became almost a standard way of describing the profession of minstrels. Eneas "announced publicly that he was getting married, and that all those who wished to take money for honor should come with high hopes."[38] Even the legal texts used this phrase. In the *Schwabenspiegel*, we read in connection with the law of inheritance: "If a son becomes a minstrel by taking money for honor . . ."[39] The wording initially meant simply that the minstrels accepted material rewards (*guot*) for the praise (*êre*) they bestowed on the lords in their poems. But *guot umb êre nemen* could have another, degrading meaning: "To receive reward instead of respect." Here the word *êre* referred to the minstrels themselves, and the phrase expressed the notion that those who sang for material remuneration gave up their social standing by doing so. For Berthold of Regensburg, the entertainers belonged to the devil's own retinue: "They are the jokesters, the fiddlers and drummers, whatever they may be called, all those who take money for honor."[40]

The function of the wandering *Spruch* poets was to praise the great lords: "God has given them intelligence and understanding to make life easier for the great lords, to conceal their vices, and to make their good deeds known everywhere. Minstrels have been created to spread joy and entertainment everywhere."[41] The minstrels were often accused of unscrupulous behavior in following their calling: praising the wicked and denouncing the virtuous, or twisting praise into abuse behind the back of the one they had just eulogized. Once again the sharpest criticism came from Berthold of Regensburg: "For a man like that speaks the best of someone for as long as that person can hear it; and if he turns his back, he says the worst he can think of. And he reproaches many a person who is righteous before God and the world; and he praises someone who lives disgracefully before God and the world."[42] The poets themselves knew that their material dependence forced them to praise even someone who did not deserve it: "The old saying goes: If you want to eat a man's bread, you must sing his praise and dance to his tune."[43] In an argument between Gawein and Keie, from which these lines are taken, Gawein defended the position of the honorable *Spruch* poet who wanted to praise only the worthy: "One should gladly praise the lord if he deserves it. But I do not wish to be close to anyone I know to be disgraceful simply for the sake of his bread."[44] In his response, Keie made clear that this noble sentiment failed in the face of reality: "The great lords do not wish to be rebuked, and want you to praise everything they do. They can give great rewards for this. What use is, on the other hand, your honest song? Whereas an untrue 'yes' brings me rich rewards from them, your 'no', no matter how true, is useless."[45] Many *Spruch* poets had the worthy resolution to praise only those who deserved it: "Before I'd praise an evil rich man for a small gift, I'd rather live in poverty forever with the virtuous poor."[46] But many of them admitted that they "lied" to the wrong ones "with nice words."[47] "Because of my impoverishment I must now lie frequently."[48] "Many a time my mouth lied to them with words of praise."[49] "I must abandon truth and lie for the sake of mammon. Since I have neither possessions nor property despite great artistry, I will lie even worse than all my peers."[50]

What seemed to weigh even more heavily on the poets than false praise was the necessity to mock and rebuke others. Sometimes the entertainers were virtually classified according to whether they spoke praise or calumny: "There are so many minstrels; some are courteous, the others serve no other purpose but to speak evil and utter insult and great malice."[51] According to another view, the courtly *Spruch* poets also had to sing songs of insult: in Tristran's words, a "courtly minstrel"[52] should not only "play the lyre and the fiddle, the harp and the rebec," but should also know how to "jest and mock."[53] Of the German *Spruch* poets of the twelfth and thirteenth centuries, substantially more songs of praise have survived than songs of insult. Perhaps the negative lyric was not thought worth preserving to the same extent. What such songs of insult could sound like is revealed by the various verses about the stinginess of King Rudolf of Hapsburg (d. 1291). Few poets used mockery with such insulting sharpness as Walther von der Vogelweide in his *Spießbratenspruch* ("Spit-roast verse") (*Wir suln den kochen râten* 17.11) or in his verses about "Lord Otto" (26.23; 26.33). It was also Walther von der Vogelweide who expressed the connection between the poets' poverty and dependence and their obligation to compose insulting songs: "I was poor for too long now, against my will. I was so full of calumny that my breath stank."[54]

THE COURTLY AUDIENCE

Historical clues   If we try to picture the courtly audience, we depend largely on deduction and hypothesis, since there is no historical information. The only certain thing is that the poets found their audience at the courts. A slight exception may have to be made for the wandering *Spruch* poets, who may have offered part of their repertoire to a non-noble audience *an der strâzen* ("in the streets") (Walther von der Vogelweide 105.38). But for the minnesingers and the epic poets the court was the only conceivable setting for their art.

Chronicles and annals tell us little about the size and composition of a princely household (see p. 53). The princely account books that contain such information date only from the last years of the thirteenth century. The books of the counts of Tyrol, which begin in the year 1288, contain an inserted folio that was probably written around 1300 and bears the following heading: "This is the lord's *familia* in Tyrol."[55] Here we find listed about fifty people who, below the aristocratic courtiers, belonged to the administrative personnel or the domestic staff of the main ducal castle at Tyrol: a chaplain, a tutor, two jesters (Wolflinus Narro and Hartel Narre, p. 386), guards and gatekeepers, housekeepers, vintners, shepherds, foresters, millers, tailors, carpenters, a goldsmith, kitchen workers, and several servants. The only one on this list who carries the title of "lord" (*dominus*) is the notary Rudolf. Except for him, the chaplain, the tutor, and possibly the jesters, it is unlikely that anybody mentioned here participated in the literary activities of the court.

More informative is the Bavarian court rule from the year 1294. Promulgated by the brothers Otto III (d. 1310), Ludwig III (d. 1296), and Stephan I (d. 1310)—who ruled Lower Bavaria jointly from 1194 on—it lists the entire personnel of the Wittelsbach court. Each of the dukes had his own "chamberlain" (*chamrar*). The staff further included a joint "master chamberlain" (*chamermeister*) and a joint "chamber scribe" (*chamerschriber*), a "doorkeeper" (*tvrhvtt*), a "barber" (*scheraer*), a "tailor" (*snider*), a "kitchen master" (*chvchenmeister*), three "cooks" (*choch*), a "pantler" (*spiser*), a "chaplain" (*chapplan*), the "chief scribe" (*der oberist schriber*), the "court master" (*hofmeister*), the "marshal" (*marschalich*), several "archers" (*schvtzen*), a "falconer" (*valchner*), a "hunting master" (*jaegermeister*), eight "hunters" (*jaeger*), three "minstrels" (*spilman*), a "doctor" (*aerzt*), diverse servants, runners, and boys. The hierarchy of the court personnel can be read from the number of horses each person was entitled to. The highest rank was held by the chief scribe with six horses, followed by the court master with five horses. Next were the chamberlains and the chaplains with four horses. All others received fewer. Noble birth is likely only for those who confirmed the court rule on oath, namely "the officials, court master, master chamberlain, marshal, cellarer, food master, and kitchen master."[56] This group was probably also the one that was involved in the literary activities. At the Wittelsbach court it included further a noble lord from the class of *lantheren*, two members of the ministerial class (*dienstmannen*), two "court knights" (*hofritter*), and eight "young noblemen" (*junch herren*, p. 53), who were spending longer periods of time at the court. Altogether we reach a number of about twenty-five people of noble standing at the court, not counting the princely family itself, the court clergy, the ladies, or the guests. At the end of the thirteenth century the Wittelsbach court in lower Bavaria was among the most important courts in Germany. For the twelfth century we would probably be looking at smaller numbers.

Aristocratic court society is also reflected in the witness lists of charters. So far it has not yet been tested whether this source could yield reliable clues. As a first attempt I have evaluated the Thuringian charters from the time of Landgrave Hermann I (1190 to 1217). Dobenecker's collection for this period lists thirty-seven charters in which the witnesses are mentioned by name. The number of witnesses varies considerably from one charter to the next, between four and thirty-seven. In most cases somewhere between ten and twenty people are named. Thirteen of the thirty-seven charters indicate the place where they were issued. These thirteen documents come from ten different sites, evidence that Thuringia did not have a fixed center of lordship at this time. The Wartburg is not mentioned at all among these places. Only one charter was issued in Eisenach (1196). The Landgrave's castle of Eckartsberga appears most frequently with three charters (1195, 1197, 1199). Of the two other main castles of the Ludowingian family, Weißensee appears twice (both times 1201), and Neuenburg on the Unstrut once (1215).

Altogether more than 250 people are mentioned as witnesses in the charters of Landgrave Hermann. Among them are a few princes: the archbishop of Magdeburg and Margrave Dietrich of Meißen (d. 1221), about twenty Thuringian abbots and provosts, several canons, cantors, sextons, and priests, a large number of counts, barons, and ministerials—who formed the largest single group—as well as a few burghers from Eisenach and other cities. Most of these appear as witnesses only once. This shows that the court society was in a constant state of flux. But it also means that a great portion of the Thuringian nobility visited the Landgrave's court at least occasionally and had personal contact with the ruler of the land. Only a small group of about forty people is attested more than twice in the charters. Among them were the permanent members of the court administration, along with those counts and lords of the Thuringian nobility who were held in special confidence and who seem to have spent extended periods of time at the landgrave's court. The first group included the steward Günther of Schlotheim, who made no less than twenty appearances as a witness, the notary Eckehard, who headed the chancery until 1211, the marshal Heinrich of Eckartsberga, who was active at the court until 1200 and was frequently named as a witness during that time, as well as the burgrave Gotebold of Neuenburg and a few other ministerials. The old nobility was represented at court by Count Henry of Stolberg, Burchard of Mansfeld, Frederick of Beichlingen, and by Barons Manegold of Tannroda, Gozwin of Wengen, and a few others. We get the impression that it was a very small circle of confidants who were constantly with the landgrave, and that the continuity of the business of government was largely guaranteed by the holders of the court offices. On special occasions the court society probably increased considerably through the addition of guests: the great halls in the main Thuringian castles Weißensee and Wartburg offered room for one hundred to two hundred people.

In all likelihood, an examination of the charters of those princes who were active patrons during this time would produce similar findings. We can infer from this that only a small number of people could have participated continuously in the literary life at the courts: the princely patron himself and his family, the court clergy, the holders of the chief court offices with their wives, the closest advisers to the prince from the local nobility—altogether surely not more than twenty to twenty-five people. On festive occasions, when many guests visited the court, the audience was probably several times as large. But the literary program at these festive gatherings could not have offered more than short pieces or selections from longer works. If one wanted to hear a large epic of ten thousand to twenty thousand verses, one had to stay at the court much longer. We must assume that there were few people in

Thuringia who had heard Heinrich von Veldeke's *Eneit* from beginning to end, or all of *Willehalm*, to the extent that Wolfram had composed it. This observation is meant to sharpen our awareness that an understanding of literature in the Middle Ages involves categories different from the modern method of literary interpretation, which seeks to comprehend a work of art "in its entirety."

The role of women   The witness lists fail us once we ask about the role of women in the literary entertainment at court. But other clues reveal that women were active in court society not only as patrons, but also as readers and listeners, as lectors and copyists, as singers and dancers. Because they were better educated, women were more qualified than men to discuss literary matters. Furthermore, the themes and style of courtly poetry undoubtedly appealed particularly to the interests of women. In the case of minne lyric, we must assume that the songs were in many instances addressed to women, whether the poets, as Ulrich von Liechtenstein has decribed it, sent them their poetic works through messengers and letters, or whether the women were present at the public performance of the songs. A brief scene from the *Wartburgkrieg* reveals that women also played a role in the recitation of courtly epics. As Wolfram von Eschenbach was beginning to relate the story of Lohengrin, the landgrave of Thuringia interrupted him: "If you want to go on telling us the story, we must first send for the ladies."[57] And so it was done: "The landgravine also arrived there. On the palas of the Wartburg one could see her with forty or more ladies-in-waiting, eight of whom were noble countesses."[58] It would seem that a literary performance was hardly conceivable without the presence of women.

Not infrequently, the courtly epicists revealed through salutations to their listeners or readers that they had composed their works largely with an audience of women in mind: "You ladies . . . this work I wish to dedicate to you, for I have begun it for your sake."[59] "This book shall belong to noble women."[60] "The ladies should enjoy reading it."[61] 'Now I will have it copied in honor of all noble women."[62] "All ladies who read this book shall wish me God's blessing, and shall thank me for what I have done with it."[63] "You noble ladies, I mean you who live in virtue with unwavering faithfulness, now ask the Lord our God to give me the grace to finish this work."[64] Sometimes a poet dedicated his work to a single lady: "Thus I begin in God's name and also for a noble lady."[65] "A lovely lady asked me to compose it and put it into good verses. Now I have done it for her sake."[66] "O little book, wherever I may be, remain close to my lady; be my tongue and my mouth and speak to her of my honest love."[67] It also happened that a patron or sponsor commissioned a work specifically for a lady. Rudolf von Ems declares in *Wilhelm von Orlens* that he composed this work for Conrad of Winterstetten, so that his lady "would make him [Conrad] rich with joy, and through her excellence think well of his constancy."[68]

If women made up a significant portion of the audience at court, they undoubtedly also had considerable influence in shaping literary tastes. For many a poet the decisive question would have been how the women thought of him and his work. All of *Parzival* is permeated with traces of the poet's debate with an influential lady or a group of ladies, whose goodwill was necessary for bringing the work to a successful conclusion. It was apparently the objection of one or several ladies that interrupted the poem after book VI (see p. 491). At the end the poet declared: "If I have any well-wishers among noble ladies of discernment, I shall be valued all the more for having brought this tale to an end. I have done so to please one lady in particular; she must admit that I said some pleasant things."[69]

The audience as participant   For a courtly poet who was to such a high degree dependent on the favor of his patrons and the goodwill of his listeners, consideration of the intended audience must have played an important role even during the composing of the work, so that the creative process could almost be seen as a continuing dialogue between the author and his audience. In this way the listeners were drawn into the work itself—they became participants. In courtly lyric, court society was present in the role of the friends whose help and sympathy the singer was counting on and to whom he confided his minne lamentations. Epic poets used the prologue to strike up a conversation with the audience, to introduce the listeners to the story, and to win them over to their side. In many cases this conversation was carried on throughout the entire work, in the form of direct address, rhetorical questions, remarks and comments, jokes, or allusions to places and events with which the poet could expect his audience to be familiar. Now and then the listeners are given their own voices to demonstrate their participation in the story or raise questions and objections. A master of such fictitious interjections from the audience was Hartmann von Aue. When the narrator in *Erec* was about to describe the precious saddle of Enite's palfrey, he let a listener interrupt him:

"'Be quiet, dear Hartmann: do you think I can guess it?'—I'm quiet, speak quickly.—'I have to think about it first.'—Do it quickly then, I'm in a hurry.—'Do I seem a clever man to you?'—Of course. Speak, for God's sake.—'I will tell you.'—The rest you may keep to yourself.—'The saddle was of yoke elm.'—Yes, what else would it be?—'Beautifully gilded.'—Who told you that?—'With strong straps.'—You guessed it right.—'On top was scarlet.'—This makes me laugh.—'See, I could guess it right.'—Indeed, you are a true weather-prophet."[70]

Such dialogues seem naive to us. But this was a calculated naiveté, and it reveals the convivial nature of courtly story-telling. At the same time, the cleverness and curiosity of the fictitious listeners reflects the poet's desire for a real-life audience that participated in the stories and honored him as a great artist.

The formal expectations of the audience   The courtly poets acquainted their lay audience with complicated rhymes and strophic schemes, rhetorical and ornamental devices with which an oral culture could not have been familiar. This education in poetic aesthetics, which deserves a thorough study in itself, was so successful that the lay listeners soon placed high demands on the formal structure of the poet's art. We see this in the rapid development of poetic technique that took place in Germany from about 1170 on. In the course of only a few decades, the forms of literary expression and narration were brought to a previously unknown level of technical sophistication. To a certain extent this trend was initiated by the poets themselves, and should be seen as an expression of their growing power of poetic interpretation; perhaps it is also evidence for the competition at the courts. But the expectations of the audiences also played an important role, as we can see from the way in which the works were received and spread, a process which the poets did not directly influence. Literary works not completely up-to-date in their poetic technique apparently fell from favor quite rapidly, and were no longer copied and spread. In this way nearly all of early courtly literature composed before 1190 became obsolete very quickly and sank into oblivion, unless revised versions adapted them to the new demands of formal structure. The oldest German Alexander epic of Pfaffe Lamprecht has survived only in the Vorau anthology from the second half of the twelfth century. By around 1170, a courtly adaptation was written, which exists as the *Straßburger Alexander*. This version, too, was overtaken by the development of poetic technique and ceased to have any further influence. It was only Rudolf von Ems who composed a courtly *Alexander* that met all the formal requirements. The *Rolandslied* of Pfaffe Konrad was circulated widely soon after its appearance, but after 1200 it was hardly copied any more. Around 1200, Der Stricker produced a courtly adaptation (*Karl der Große*), and it was only in this form that the work lived on to the end of the Middle Ages. Several epics of the twelfth century—*Graf Rudolf, Trierer Floyris*, Heinrich's *Reinhart Fuchs*, the old epic of *Herzog Ernst*, Eilhart's *Tristan*—have survived only in fragments of manuscripts that were written before or around 1200. *Graf Rudolf* sank into complete oblivion. The story of Flore and Blanchefleur was translated from the French once again around 1220 by Konrad Fleck. *Reinhart Fuchs* went through a courtly rewriting in the thirteenth century. *Herzog Ernst*, as well, is known to us in its entirety only through a courtly version of the thirteenth century (*Herzog Ernst* B). The complete manuscripts of Eilhart von Oberg's *Tristrant* date only to the fifteenth century, but they undoubtedly go back to a thirteenth-century adaptation.

THE IMPACT OF LITERATURE

There is little evidence from the courtly period about how noble society at court reacted to the performance of literature. Much more numerous are statements by the poets themselves about the goal and purpose of their works, and about the effect they hoped to have. But we must remember that medieval poets who addressed such questions could select at will from a number of topoi. It was known from Horace's *Ars poetica* that "the poets wish to be useful or pleasing, or both at the same time."[71] This idea could be used in a variety of ways to clarify one's own intent:

> I will tell you the three-fold usefulness of stories and songs. One is that their lovely sound is very pleasing to the ear. The second is that their doctrine teaches the heart courtly breeding. The third is that these two make the tongue very eloquent. I believe that the art of song and story-telling conveys much elation and splendor to the people who follow their teachings: they instruct in courtly manners and virtuous behavior.[72]

A number of contemporary accounts reveal the great interest courtly society took in the epic material, especially in the tales of King Arthur and the knights of the Round Table. According to an anecdote from the *Dialogus miraculorum* of Caesarius of Heisterbach (d. after

1240), the knightly tales had an electrifying impact even on the monks in the monastery:

> When Abbot Bevard, the predecessor of the current abbot, would solemnly address to us words of admonition in the chapter hall, and when he saw that many, especially of the novices, were sleeping, some of them even snoring, he exclaimed: "Listen, brothers, listen, I have new and glorious things to report to you. Once upon a time there was a king, his name was Arthur." After these words he stopped and said: "Brothers, behold this great misery. When I speak of God, you sleep. But as soon as I throw in frivolous words, you wake up and begin to pay attention with ears cocked."[73]

Hugo von Trimberg (d. after 1313) also complained in *Renner* that mankind no longer wanted to hear anything about the miracles of God and the pious deeds of the saints: "Most people, both here and in other lands, are much more familiar with the books I have mentioned before: the books of Parzival and Tristan, Wigalois and Eneas, Erec and Iwein, and whoever else belonged to the Round Table at Caridol."[74] The ecclesiastical teachers saw it as an ominous sign that many people strove to imitate the knights of the Round Table rather than the models of Christian piety: "For many think they would be worthless unless they became heroes like the ones just mentioned."[75] In this context Hugo von Trimberg also described the moving effect that the theme of minne service had on noble ladies: "One hears many ladies lamenting and crying more often about how in former times the old heroes were beaten up for the sake of their ladies than about the holy wounds of our Lord Jesus Christ."[76]

Ecclesiastical chroniclers in the twelfth century noted with amazement how much concern and sympathy were evoked by the Celtic tales of King Arthur and the knights of the Round Table. A novice confessed: "I remember that the stories told in the vernacular of Arthur, about whom I know nothing else, sometimes moved me to tears."[77] Peter of Blois (d. after 1204) said:

> In the sad stories and other songs of the poets, and in the songs of the minstrels, a hero is often depicted who is wise, beautiful, brave, amiable, and exemplary in every respect. But the dreadful difficulties and insults that this hero suffers are also recounted. Thus the minstrels tell many a marvelous thing of Arthur and Gawain(?) and Tristan, whereby the hearts of the listeners, when they hear them, are shaken with pity and moved to tears.[78]

This account reveals that the listeners at that time became involved in the fortunes and dangers suffered by the knights of the Arthurian romances in a way that is difficult to conceive for a modern reader, who is used to very different literary devices of suspensefulness.

The frequency of certain names is also an indication that the members of noble society sought to establish a link between themselves and their families and the famous knights of the courtly romances. In 1269 we find a Thuringian noble called *Conradus dictus Parcseval*, in Bavaria in 1282 a *Parcefal* of Weineck, on the middle Rhine in 1324 a *Perceval* of Eltz. In 1287 there is a *Tristamus* of Aich, as early as 1210 a *Walewanus* of Hemmenrode, in 1293 an *Erekke* of Schwanberg, in 1360 a *Wigeleis* of Nordholz. Even more frequent are daughters named after literary characters: *Isalda* of Heinsberg (1217), *Enyta*, the daughter of Henry Zisel (1239), *Siguna* of Braunberg (1286), *Giburgis* of Krumbach (1331), *Herczeloyde* of Wickede (1354), and others. From the end of the thirteenth century on, such names are also found in the upper class of the urban population. These names need a critical examination on the basis of the cities' charter books.

In the literary excursus in *Tristan*, Gottfried von Straßburg described how courtly lyric affected listeners or was meant to affect them: "The voices of the nightingales [the minnesingers] are clear and beautiful, they elate our spirits and gladden our hearts deep inside. The world would be joyless and would live full of ill will, were it not for this sweet birdsong. . . . It arouses pleasant feelings that turn our thoughts inward, when the sweet birdsong begins to tell the world of its joy."[79] There are other contemporary statements that emphasized the effect of lyric poetry. In his lamentation on the death of Reinmar der Alte, Walther von der Vogelweide had these words for his colleague as the highest praise: "You knew how to increase the *vreude* of all courtly society."[80] Reinmar himself had sung: "I released a hundred thousand hearts from sorrow. . . . Truly, I was a consolation to all the world."[81]

According to Gottfried von Straßburg, the art of the "nightingales" exerted its power above all through the magic of music. In Walther von der Vogelweide he praised the beauty of his voice and the art of musical variation: "How it [the nightingale-Walter] carols over the heath in her clear voice! What wonders she performs! How artfully she sings in organon! How she varies her singing!"[82] The enchanting effect of courtly singing and of instrumental play was described by Gottfried von Straßburg in his depiction of Tristan's musical offerings at the English court: "He played so beautifully and plucked the harp so splendidly in the Breton style that many stood and sat there who forgot their own names. Hearts and ears turned deaf and numb and began to stray from their rightful paths."[83] On several occasions we are told that the beauty of the singing especially had an effect on women. In *Kudrun* it is recounted that Horant of Denmark sang so sweetly at the Irish court that the birds fell silent, the animals of the forest stopped grazing, and the fish in the water stood still. Even "the church bells no longer sounded quite as lovely as before."[84] When the old Queen Hilde heard his voice through the window of her palace, she asked Horant to sing for her every day. The princess Hilde, too, was so moved by his artistry that she had the singer secretly led into her chambers, which gave Horant a chance to present King Hetel's offer of marriage. In a woman's poem by Kürenberg, a courtly lady, who is described as the lady of the castle and the land, speaks of how the lovely singing of a knight aroused in her a desire for the singer: "I stood on the ramparts late at night. There I heard a knight from among the crowd sing very beautifully in Kürenberg's melody. I shall have him for myself or he will have to leave my land."[85] Heloise wrote in her first letter to Abelard: "You had besides, I admit, two special gifts with which you could at once capture the heart of any woman: the gift of composing verse and the gift of singing."[86] Ulrich von Liechtenstein talked in *Frauendienst* about the popularity of his own songs: "This song was often sung."[87] "Many liked the song."[88] But when Ulrich von Winterstetten has "an old hag" (*ein altes wîp*, 4.1.2) say about his songs: "They shout his songs day and night in the streets,"[89] we can't take this literally: in imitation of Neidhart, the courtly scene has been placed into a village setting for the purpose of satire.

The song of the *Spruch* poets aimed at a very different effect. They were not concerned primarily with the beauty of the melody but with the statement of the poem, with which they could either glorify or denigrate the great lords. An episode from the biography of Count Godfrey V of Anjou (d. 1151) reveals how highly the art of praising and insulting others was regarded by those who stood to profit from it. One day the count captured four knights from Poitou and handed them over to his seneschal, Josselin de Tours, for safekeeping. Josselin wanted to help the captives and gave them the following advice: "Now compose a song in verse about the virtue of the count, the kind of song which comes out easily and almost naturally among your people. If I get a chance, I will entertain the count here, and when he has come, I will show you from where you can sing for him what you have composed."[90] When the count came for a visit and was sitting in the great hall after a good meal, the seneschal hurried to the prisoners and said: "Come out and climb

up to the gallery of the tower, step up to the windows above and sing
the song you have composed about the count and do not be silent in
front of him. Overcome your sorrow, trust in the fulfillment of your
wishes and sing the song several times. Perhaps he will take pity on
you."[91] The count was so moved by the words that he ordered the
knights to his table, gave them gifts of new clothes, and sent them back
to their country.

The professional poets were best at flattering the great lords with
their songs of praise, which made their art much sought after everywhere: "Highly honored and much celebrated and greatly loved were
those who wrote down the deeds and composed the stories. Often the
barons and the noble ladies gave them lovely gifts so that they
would introduce their names into the story, which would preserve
their memory forever."[92] If a lord did not show the expected generosity,
the disappointed poet might withhold his praise. For example, it is said
that the poet of the French *Chanson d'Antioche* deliberately left out the
deeds that Count Arnald II of Guines accomplished on the first Crusade, thus to revenge himself for the fact that the count "had refused a
pair of scarlet shoes"[93] the poet had asked for. A great lord did not have
to fear such a slight if the singers were working at his request. We can
see this from the malicious account from 1191 by Bishop Hugh of
Coventry about William Longchamp, the bishop of Ely, who was chancellor of England under King Richard Lionheart (d. 1199): "In order to
increase the fame of his name, he had begging songs and flattering
poems composed, and through gifts he had procured singers and minstrels from France, who were to sing about him in public. And soon it
was said everywhere that there was no one like him in all the world."[94]

To the same degree that the praise of the poets was welcomed, their
rebuke and mockery was feared. Walther Map told of a man named
Galeran who enjoyed the special favor of King Louis II of France (d. 879)
because of his wit and sharp tongue. When Galeran noticed that the
chief court officials were cheating the king, "he composed a song in
French,"[95] in which he denounced the fraud of the officials. The latter
were so shaken by it that they defamed the poet to the king. And since
Galeran also made the mistake of directing his sharp tongue against
relatives of the king, he was exiled and his property was confiscated.
Not every ruler was as forgiving of poetic insults as the Danish King
Sven (d. 1157), of whom Saxo Grammaticus relates the following:

> Among other things a German singer had composed a song about the flight
> and exile of Sven and had introduced violent reproaches into the poem and

cast various insults into the king's face. While the poet's colleagues rebuked him sharply for it, Sven concealed his annoyance and bade him to sing freely about his misfortunes, declaring that he liked to remember the difficult times that were past.[96]

An episode from *Der Wartburgkrieg* reveals how dangerous it could be if a poet directed his praise or blame at the wrong person. We are told that the famous poets of the courtly period held a singing contest at the Thuringian court on the theme of who was the most generous of princes. Heinrich von Ofterdingen chose the duke of Austria, Walther von der Vogelweide the king of France, Der Tugendthafte Schreiber voted for Landgrave Hermann of Thuringia, and Biterolf for the counts of Hainaut. Reinmar von Zweter and Wolfram von Eschenbach, who initially served as judges, joined in the praise for Landgrave Hermann. In the end only Heinrich von Ofterdingen defended his own choice. It turned into a potentially deadly quarrel, for the executioner of Eisenach, a man by the name of Stempfel, was called in to enforce the verdict: "Stempfel of Eisenach shall stand by our heads with his broad sword and shall punish one of us like a robber."[97] Later chroniclers reported that the defeated Heinrich von Ofterdingen, "with his life in danger, crawled under the mantel of the landgrave's wife in the hope of finding refuge with her."[98]

Poetic mockery could deeply hurt or enrage the person at whom it was directed, as we learn from the account of Ordericus Vitalis about the English King Henry I (d. 1135), who in 1124 imprisoned and blinded the Norman noblemen who had risen against him: "He commanded that Luce de la Barre should also lose his sight on account of his mocking songs and his rash resistance."[99] When the count of Flanders pointed out to the king that it was unjust to maim captured knights, Henry I especially justified his cruel treatment of Luce: "This scoffer composed indecent songs about me and sang them in public to insult me. Thus he often provoked my enemies, who wish me evil, to laughter."[100]

For this period we possess only one piece of evidence from Germany about the effect of political *Spruch* poetry. It concerns the antipapal verses of Walter von der Vogelweide. In the malicious poem "Ah, how like a Christian the pope now laughs,"[101] Walther has the pope express his satisfaction over the fact that he has cast the empire into chaos and has enriched himself with the treasures of the Germans: "All their stuff is mine. Their German silver fills my Italian chest."[102] Only a few years later, Thomasin von Zirklaere, in his *Der Wälsche Gast*, referred to

these verses and complained about the injustice that had been done to
the pope: "How greatly he sinned against him, the good man, who in
his presumption once said the pope wishes to fill his Italian chest with
German goods."[103] According to Thomasin, Walther reached a wide
audience with his insulting verses: "For he misled a thousand people, so
that they ignored the commandments of God and of the pope."[104] We
must undoubtedly interpret these words to mean that Walther's antipapal invectives found a broad resonance in the noble society for which
his songs and sayings were intended.

4. THE PERFORMANCE AND SPREAD OF LITERATURE

The notion that literature is intended for readers and that a knowledge
of literature is transmitted through books, applies to the courtly society
of the High Middle Ages only with many qualifications. Most men and
women of the nobility were incapable of reading a book. But even those
who could read seem to have used this skill only infrequently, for courtly
literature was a social event, and its purpose lay in creating and confirming a sense of community. It is therefore impossible to understand
this literature historically unless one always keeps in mind its manner of
presentation. And so it is all the more unfortunate that the medieval
sources offer little evidence about the performance, forcing us to rely
largely on inferences and conjectures. Central to our discussion is the
relationship between the oral and written dimensions of literature.
Since courtly epic and courtly lyric differ considerably in this respect—
as they do in their manner of performance in general—it is best to
discuss these two genres separately.

COURTLY EPIC

Working conditions   The German poets worked from French or
Latin sources, which normally must have been available to them in the
form of books. If their own words can be believed, some poets engaged
in an extensive study of the sources before they decided on a specific
text. In the prologue of *Armer Heinrich*, we are told about the poet:
"He looked at many books, and searched in them for something that
might lighten his heavy hours."[1] Gottfried von Straßburg described in
even greater detail how he tracked down the romance of Tristan by
Thomas of Brittany: "What he had narrated of Tristan, the true and

authentic version, I began to search for in Romance and Latin books. I took pains to compose the story in the way he had told it. Thus I made many researches until I found in a book his entire tale."[2] We know nothing about the concrete circumstances of such work. What must have happened in many cases is that the poet received the written source along with a commission from a princely patron. The claim of having researched in books was a conventional motif of learned literature. Even epic poets who could not read themselves seem to have used written sources; passages in *Parzival* that echo the wording of the *Conte du Graal* are proof of this. Wolfram indicated that he became acquainted with his French sources through oral transmission. The French text could have been read aloud or paraphrased for him. A very similar method must have been employed by those poets who could read but did not understand any French, and who therefore depended on the help of translators (see p. 85).

Literate epicists probably wrote their works in their own hand or at least supervised the writing. Original manuscripts in a poet's own hand have not survived, but the consistent nature of the extant manuscripts presupposes that a written text stood at the beginning of the process of transmission. This also applies the works of Wolfram von Eschenbach, which were surely not written down by the poet himself. In all likelihood Wolfram dictated them to a scribe. In this way, a poet who could neither read nor write was able at that time to compose written works based on written models. Where the extant manuscripts of an epic work show significant textual deviations—which is really the case only with the *Nibelungenlied*—it is possible that no fixed text existed at the beginning. It is also possible that the deviant versions are the result of subsequent rewritings.

We are not able to discover whether the poets usually worked at court or at some location where they could escape the noise and restlessness of the itinerant court. But they must have stayed in contact with their patrons and their audience while composing their works, since the epics—at least those of the more famous poets—became known even before they were completed. We know that Heinrich von Veldeke loaned the unfinished manuscript of his *Eneit* to the countess of Cleves (352.35 ff.). Scholars have discovered that *Parzival* and *Tristan* contain allusions to each other, which can be explained most easily if we assume that the epics were "published" one section at a time. In the case of *Parzival*, there is other evidence that the final version of the work was preceded by earlier versions and piecemeal publication. The spread of manuscript copies of fragmentary works is further proof that the epics began to circulate before they were finished. Even unrelated pieces like the two *Titurel* fragments by Wolfram von Eschenbach were copied and spread in their unfinished state.

The circumstances of performance   In view of the educational situation within lay society, we can start from the assumption that a knowledge of courtly poetry was normally acquired by listening to it. The authors frequently referred to the performance, especially in shorter stories and *Schwänke*: "If you will now listen and be quiet, I will tell you a story."[3] "If it is agreeable to you, I will tell you the story in worthy fashion; you would like that. I ask all of you to be happy. All who want to hear how the story continues, be they man or woman, will not regret it. But I ask those who don't want to hear it to please sit in the back. Now the story begins."[4]

On what occasions and for what sort of audience courtly epics were recited must be inferred from a few hints. The scene that most people would tend to imagine is one in which the members of court society interested in literature gathered in the evening to listen to the poet's words. But strangely enough, this scenario is badly documented. "A short evening story" (*âbentmaerlîn*) is mentioned once, with a slight parodistic flavor, in the introduction to the *Schwank Das Häslein*: "For your entertainment and to spite the philistines, I will present a short evening story."[5] In *Huon de Bordeaux*, a chanson de geste from the thirteenth century, we read: "Honorable lords, I'm sure you see that evening is at hand, and I am very tired. Thus I ask all of you to return tomorrow after dinner."[6] The French Arthurian romance, "The Knight with the Two Swords," recounts the performance of an epic outdoors: the ladies and lords settled comfortably under shady trees in a meadow, and Queen Ginover "held a romance in her hand, from which she read to the knights and maids."[7]

Sometimes the lord of the court or a member of the lord's family arranged for a private reading: "The daughter of the king of Persia sat there in her tent in courtly joy, as usual. A beautiful maid read to her from a book the story of the destruction of Troy."[8] Readings were also held in the intimate family circle. When Iwein arrived at the Castle of the Dreadful Adventure, he met the lord of the castle with his wife in the garden, "and in front of them sat a girl who could read French very well, as I was told. She entertained them. She made them smile. What she read seemed delightful to them, for she was their daughter."[9] In *Mai*

und Beaflor, the king had his daughter read from French books to entertain the guests (230.30 f.). Noble women almost always did the reading
on such occasions.

The best evidence exists for the recitation of epic works at the great
court feasts. Accounts that describe in detail the varied entertainments
offered at these feasts usually also mention that songs were sung and
stories of adventure and love recited. At the court feast of King William
of England, one heard "different kinds of string instruments played with
lovely melodies, lovely singing of minne and artful tales of adventure
(which one ought to listen to decently), talk of minne and knighthood."[10] Arthur's court had "professional raconteurs,"[11] who on
festive occasions recited "stories and tales" (*fabel unde maere*). At
the court feast in Cluse, minnesongs were sung and French works recited: "A good deal was read there in French."[12] "They were told nice
stories of knights who fought each other."[13] For the most part it was
only a smaller section of the festive company that was interested in
literary performances, while others found greater pleasure in dancing,
athletic contests, or the acrobatics of the jugglers. The poets do not
mention which works were presented at the feasts. Only once, in *Helmbrecht*, is a title given: the passage recounts how the nobility in the old
days celebrated its feasts with dancing and all sorts of entertainment:
"When all this had come to an end, one of them came forward and read
out loud about someone called Ernst."[14] This is surely a reference to the
epic of *Herzog Ernst*, which was widely known in the thirteenth century. At six thousand verses it was among the shorter epic works. It is,
nevertheless, quite impossible that the entire poem was recited at a
feast. A presentation to the guests could have comprised only shorter
stories or selections from longer works.

Nothing is known about the technique of reciting epics. Were the
works memorized? Memorizing a longer poem would have posed no
great difficulty to a trained reciter. Nevertheless, we should assume that
the story was usually read from a manuscript. On a few occasions the
poets said so explicitly. Moreover, the terminology used to describe the
performance offers additional evidence: the Middle High German word
lesen meant not only "to read," but also "to read out to someone else";
the *leser* was accordingly also the "reciter" (Salman and Morolf 451 a,
4). A popular way of describing the recitation of an epic was the phrase
"to hear read."[15] Scholarly opinions differ about the manner of the
recitation. The widest support is now given to the notion that the
strophic epic—which was predominantly heroic epic—was sung,

whereas the epic in paired rhymes was spoken. In support of the "sing-ability" of the strophic epic one can point to the fact that the Nibe-lungen strophe is formally identical to the song-stanza of Kürenberg. There is also the melodic notation to one stanza of *Jüngerer Titurel* in a Viennese manuscript (Cod. Vindob. 2675) from the end of the thir-teenth century. Similar evidence does not exist for epic in paired rhymes. But the so-called "disyllabic cadences," (*klingende Kadenzen*), which must be read with two beats (e.g. *mínnè*), require a measured intonation. We probably come closer to the reality of performance if we don't distinguish between singing and speaking, but between *concentus* (melodic song) and *accentus* (recited song). Instrumen-tal accompaniment is unlikely for epics in paired rhymes. To what extent mimicry and gestures accompanied the recitation is completely unknown. All conjectures about this aspect have failed to yield any-thing concrete. It is also unclear whether the reciter had any room for improvisation.

The question as to the length and duration of an epic recitation has occupied scholarship since the early days of German philology. Today we must admit that we know nothing reliable. The discussion of this issue was profoundly influenced by Karl Lachmann's division of *Par-zival* into sixteen books in his critical edition of Wolfram in 1833. These books, whose average length is fifteen hundred verses—though individual books might deviate considerably from this figure—have often been regarded as units of performance. It was calculated that a reciter could get through about one thousand verses in an hour. An evening presentation of one book of *Parzival* would thus have taken about an hour and a half. The entire *Parzival* would have required twenty-four hours, *Iwein* eight, Gottfried's *Tristan* nineteen and a half. But it is questionable whether such calculations have any meaning beyond the theoretical. We cannot even guess the time frame in which an entire epic reached the listeners. It may have happened that a literary presentation was spread out over several days. But the idea that sixteen readings of an hour and a half each took place within a short period, so that the entire *Parzival* could be presented, is the product of modern expectations that the great epics must have become known to the public in their entirety. We must accept the idea that lengthy works were prob-ably known completely to only a few people.

Most epics show clearly visible beginnings of a rough overall struc-ture, which is marked either by particularly noticeable initials in the manuscripts, or by a division into "sections" (*distinctiones* in Herbort von Fritzlar), "aventiuren" (in the *Nibelungenlied*), or "books" (in *Alexander* by Rudolf von Ems). In a few cases we are certain that these divisions were made by the author himself. In other cases there is considerable uncertainty about how the author structured his work. The rough division apparently served the artistic arrangement of the material, in that units of action were separated from one another or sections that formed a coherent whole were made to stand out. Whether the authors were at the same time thinking of the publication of their works, that is, whether the sections were also intended as recitation units, is something we cannot determine. A structuring with an eye to performance cannot be securely documented for any German epic of the twelfth or thirteenth century. In all likelihood the authors did not provide a fixed format of presentation. The private forms of recitation, in the family circle, would not have adhered to such a format. And at the readings presented at the court feasts, the length of the presentation was probably determined less by any intentions the authors may have had, and more by the specific circumstances of the setting and the reception by the audience.

The private reading of epic works   The courtly epic poets, most of whom were educated in Latin, placed great emphasis on the fact that their works were fixed in writing, and that, unlike oral poetry, they could be read in addition to being heard. They made a point of informing the court audience, which was composed largely of illiterates, that they drew their material from "books," and they presented their own works to the listeners as "books." Ulrich von Türheim spoke in the epilogue of *Rennewart* of the "effort I have invested in this book."[16] Der Pleier asked the audience for its blessing on the poet, "because he has composed the book as entertainment."[17] Though Wirnt von Grafenberg was possibly among the uneducated epic poets, he had his poem speak of itself as a "book": "Which well-meaning person has opened me? If it is someone who can read and understand me, let him bestow his favor on me."[18] Even Ulrich von Liechtenstein, by his own admission illiterate, regarded his *Frauendienst* not without pride as a "book": "Everything that I ever sang in new melodies one will find entered here into this book."[19]

Some poets went even further by inserting decorative elements accessible only to a reader into their works intended for public recitation. The art of forming acrostics and anagrams had to be learned from Latin literature. Educated poets were fond of using such ornamental

devices for veiled references to their own names or these of their patrons. Gottfried von Straßburg seems to have been the first courtly epi-
cist in Germany to employ this technique. The first letters of every fifth
verse of the prologue in *Tristan* spell the name DIETRICH: this was
probably his patron's name. In *Krone*, the first letters of verses 182–
216, when read in succession, spell out the acrostic HEINRICH VON
DEM TVRLIN HAT MIKH GETIHTET (Heinrich von dem Türlin
composed me). His namesake Ulrich von dem Türlin mentioned both
his own name and that of his patron in the first letters of sections VII
and VIII of his *Willehalm*: MEISTER VLRICH VON DEM TVRLIN
HAT MIH GEMACHET DEM EDELN CVNICH VON BEHEIM
(Master Ulrich von dem Türlin made me for the noble king of Bohemia). The master of the acrostic among the thirteenth century epic poets
was Rudolf von Ems, who decorated his epic works richly with this
device. Some poets supplied instructions on how to discover and decipher the acrostic. Ebernand von Erfurt decorated his courtly legendary epic *Heinrich und Kunigunde*—which he personally wanted to
entitle *Emperor and Empress*—with a particularly elaborate acrostic.
It combined the first letters of all sixty or sixty-one sections into which
the work is divided into a text: EBERNANT SO HEIZIN ICH. DI
ERFVRTERE IRKENNINT MICH. KEISER VNDE KEISERINN
(Ebernand is my name. The people of Erfurt know me. "Emperor and
Empress."). At the end we read: "If the reader is bright and knowledgeable in artistic devices, let him read from beginning to end the main
letters with which the verses begin. If he is not a total child, he will
easily find the poet's name: the poem will tell him. The letters, read
from beginning to end, spell words. Thus he can find my name."[20]

Ebernand von Erfurt made clear that the acrosticon was not intended
for listeners but for readers; apparently he expected his work not only
to be recited but also to be read. For authors of religious poetry, it
seems to have gone without saying that their texts could and should be
read, even if they were addressing their works to a lay audience. The
author of the Middle German *Judith* (mid-thirteenth century) addressed
the individual reader at the end of the poem: "You and all those who
eagerly read this book in spiritual fashion..."[21] He anticipated that
his text would be copied, and he urged precision and care in doing so:
"I strongly urge that everyone who has this book copied take care to
have it occupied correctly."[22] In the prologue to his *Urstende* (first half of
the thirteenth century), Konrad von Heimesfurt protested "lest anyone
scrape off something with a knife or a pumice stone."[23] Otto von Freis-

ing said in *Laubacher Barlaam* in reference to his own work "that in order to make it known, it was written on parchment, so that anybody may understand it who can read."[24] A "Hail Mary" (*Mariengruß*) from the thirteenth century addressed the reader directly: "reader, it wants to tell you even more."[25] To what extent these texts were actually read by the lay public must remain unanswered. As long as most laypeople could not read, there remained a gap between the wishes of the ecclesiastical poets and reality.

Scholars today are debating whether the courtly poets, too, intended their works for readers, and whether by the thirteenth century we must reckon with a greater frequency of private reading of courtly epics in addition to the spread of literature by public recitation. Clarification of this issue is made more difficult by the fact that the Middle High German terminology of hearing and reading was decidedly imprecise. *Hoeren* meant not only "to hear," but also, in a broader sense, "to learn"; *lesen* meant not only "to read" or "to read out loud," but also "to tell"; *sagen* could also mean "to make known"; *schrîben* had the additional meaning of "to inform." This implies that the words *lesen* and *schrîben* do not by themselves prove a written transmission, just as *hoeren* and *sagen* cannot be seen as ready evidence for oral transmission. But notwithstanding this terminological vagueness, it is striking how frequently the epic poets mentioned that their works could also be read. In most cases they used the phrase "to hear or to read" (*hoeren oder lesen*), which expresses the notion that the poetic work could be heard in a public presentation or could be read privately. "I send this book as a messenger to those who will hear or read it;"[26] "those who read or hear it, and those to whom I will tell it or sing it in verses."[27] In a few cases the poet himself seems to have addressed the reader: "Whoever may read this book."[28] "My poem will be shown around and no doubt in some places it will also be read."[29] "Reader of this book, listen!"[30]

Given the level of education within lay society, potential readers of courtly epics would have been, apart from the court clerics, almost exclusively noble women. And in fact the poets revealed in a number of passages that the readers they were addressing were primarily women (see p. 509). Even Wolfram von Eschenbach, who refused to regard his own work as a "book" (Parzival 116.1), expected that many a lady "will see this story written down"[31] and will get to know it by reading it. To what extent women used their ability to read is difficult to determine. We should imagine a situation where listening and reading com-

plemented each other; it was not an either-or situation. But insofar as
the social effect is concerned, the oral presentation was surely the more
important medium of transmission.

Word and picture   In addition to public recitation and private reading, there was a third way for the noble audience to become acquainted
with the epic material: through pictures. Among the oldest manuscript
of epic works is the Heidelberg manuscript of the *Rolandslied* (Cpg
112) from the end of the twelfth century, which is decorated with
thirty-nine pen-and-ink drawings. The pictures were drawn with brown
ink and inserted into the text without borders. The fact that a second
manuscript of the *Rolandslied* (manuscript A, which was burned in
Straßburg) had similar pictures, and that a third manuscript (fragment S
from Schwerin) left room for them, supports the conjecture that the
original itself—or, better, the presentation copy—also contained pen-
and-ink drawings. This would mean that an illustrated presentation
manuscript stood at the very beginning of the history of patronage.
Based on their artistic characteristics, the drawings in the *Rolandslied*
can be attributed to the Bavarian painting school in Regensburg-
Prüfening or Freising. Since it is very likely that the *Rolandslied* was
composed in Regensburg, we can assume that there were contacts between the ducal court and the monastic painting schools.

The illustrated *Rolandslied* remained an exception. No other epic
from the older period was decorated in this way. And even in the
thirteenth century, when the illustration of secular texts gradually increased, courtly epics, and especially Arthurian epics, were largely excluded from this trend. Illustrations were provided for didactic poems
(Thomasin von Zirklaere), law books (*Sachsenspiegel*), historical works
(the world chronicle of Rudolf von Ems), and historical poems, among
which were counted both Heinrich von Veldeke's *Eneit* as well as Wolfram von Eschenbach's *Willehalm*. With few exceptions, the courtly
romances in the narrower sense of the term were not illustrated. In a
separate category are the three illustrated Munich manuscripts of *Parzival* (Cgm 19), *Tristan* (Cgm 51), and *Wilhelm von Orlens* by Rudolf
von Ems (Cgm 63), whose miniatures were painted separately on illustrated pages that were bound into the texts only later. This kind of
decoration was not much imitated. Not until the fifteenth century were
larger numbers of courtly epics illustrated.

But by the thirteenth century there was considerable interest in pictorial representations of themes from the courtly romances. This interest,

however, was not directed at the illustrations of books, but at more life-like media. We have fifteen *Iwein* manuscripts from the thirteenth century, and not a single one is illustrated. Yet from the same period come two large cycles of *Iwein* wall paintings: in castle Rodeneck in southern Tyrol (near Brixen), and in the so-called "Hessenhof" in Schmalkalden. We don't know the original purpose of the relatively small rooms, which are completely covered with paintings. Particularly precious are the life-size, beautifully colored figures in Rodeneck, which were only recently uncovered. They have been dated to soon after 1200, and if this is correct, they would be among the earliest and most important evidence for the reception of Hartmann's work. It is peculiar that in Rodeneck the paintings depict exclusively—and in Schmalkalden predominantly—scenes from the first part of *Iwein*, up to Iwein's wedding with Laudine. Perhaps this is an indication that the lengthier epics were hardly ever known or received in their entirety. The choice of the motifs is also very interesting. In Rodeneck we find a few specific scenes from the story about the magic well and the horrible wild man. But what dominates the rooms in both places are representative scenes of courtly life: the knightly duels between Iwein and Askalon in Rodeneck (see fig. 37), which fill an entire wall and are more detailed than the literary text; and the great banquet at the front wall in Schmalkalden, a scene which does not correspond directly to anything in Hartmann's work. This reveals that the painters were not primarily concerned to illustrate the text, but to emphasize those aspects that had special representative value for the image of courtly society.

The extant paintings are supplemented by literary evidence. The *Prosa-Lancelot* relates that Lancelot, while in captivity in the castle of Ragual, watched a fresco painter at work: "It happened one day that he stepped up to the window and saw a man painting an old story; and each painting had an inscription. It seemed to be the story of Aeneas, how he had fled from Troy. At this he seized upon the idea of painting the room in which he was kept with pictures of the woman he loved so much, and for whom he felt such great longing."[32] He asked for paint from the artists and bolted his door.

Thus he began to paint how the lady of Lac had brought him to King Arthur's court to become a knight, how he had ridden to Camelot, how he was startled by the beauty of his mistress, the queen, when he saw her for the first time, and how he took leave of her when he rode to the duchess of Noans to save her. All this he did on the first day; and the pictures were so beautifully and skillfully done as though he had been engaged in this handicraft all his life.[33]

Fig. 37. Duel between Iwein and Ascalon. The two charge each other with lowered lances. Wall frescoes in Castle Rodeneck, southern Tyrol. Thirteenth century.

On the following days he continued to work, scene by scene, on the story of his love for the queen. "And when Easter was over he had finished it all."[34]

For someone who lived in rooms painted with scenes from courtly epics, this literature was constantly before him in his daily life. Considering that the fresco cycles were preserved and rediscovered by sheer coincidence, it is not unlikely that such serial paintings existed in larger numbers. The great interest that people had in translating courtly literature into pictures of this sort is also attested by the many objects of daily use that are decorated with literary motifs. Scenes from the romance of Tristan were especially popular. The oldest piece, from the early thirteenth century, is a small ivory box (Forrer-box) from eastern France or the Rhineland, now kept in the British Museum. Carved into the lid and the sides are figurative scenes that probably refer to the story of Tristan and Isolde. Also from the thirteenth century are the painted tiles from Chertsey Abbey with many motifs from Tristan. Much more numerous are objects of this kind from the fourteenth and fifteenth centuries: rugs, wall hangings and quilts, boxes, combs, mirror cases, writing cases, tableware, and other things were decorated with figures from the Tristan legend. All these pieces were specifically courtly objects that existed only in noble households; more precisely, they were objects used by women. In this respect, as well, the pictorial evidence is a revealing clue to literary reception.

To supplement this evidence we must refer once again to literary testimony. In Hartmann's *Erec*, the precious saddle gear of Enite's horse was ornamented with images drawn from literature. On one side "the long song of Troy"[35] had been carved into the ivory saddle frame; on the other side one could see "how clever Eneas sailed across the sea."[36] In the back Dido's despair was shown, in the front Aeneas's subsequent adventures and his marriage to Lavinia. On the saddle cushion "was depicted how Thisbe and Pyramus, conquered by love, . . . came to a sad end."[37] Motifs from classical literature are especially frequent. Helmbrecht's courtly hood was embroidered on one side with the siege and capture of Troy and with the flight of Aeneas, and on the other with scenes from the *Rolandslied*, in the back with motifs from the legend of Dietrich, and in front with courtly dancing scenes (45 ff.). Even more abundant is the evidence from France. Scenes from the story of Troy and from the *Aeneid* appeared on sheets, tent walls, and clothes. Jean Renart's *Galeran de Bretagne* (first half of the thirteenth century) has a description of a cloth, into "one side of which the life of King Floire and of Blanchefleur had been interwoven with splendid artistry, the entire lives of the lovers."[38] Pictures of the Arthurian legends were also used. On the mantle which the queen of Garadigan wore at her wedding, one could see how Merlin took the form of Duke Gorlois; how Arthur was conceived in Tintagel; how Igerne accused her husband, and how it was decided that she should marry Uther Pendragon. Moroever, "portrayed on the mantle were the brave deeds that Arthur later accomplished."[39]

The circulation of manuscripts   From Germany we have just under twenty manuscripts of epic works which the paleographic evidence dates to the twelfth century or to the time around 1200. If we count the *Kaiserchronik* among the epics, the number increases by six. It is characteristic for the extant manuscripts of the older epics that only four are complete; all others are fragments. Since no comparative study of this oldest stratum of secular epics has yet been undertaken, the following statements are only provisional.

Based on their external appearance, the twelfth-century manuscripts can be divided into two groups: miscellanies and single-work manuscripts. The miscellanies include:

— The famous Vorau manuscript (Vorau, Stiftsbibl. 276) from the second half of the twelfth century, which contains Lamprecht's *Alexander* and the *Kaiserchronik*, along with numerous religious poems in German and the *Gesta Frederici* of Otto of Freising and Rahewin.

— The Straßburg-Molsheim manuscript (Straßburg, Universitätsbibl. C.V. 16.6.4), which was written after 1187. It was burned in 1871. The manuscript contained the *Straßburger Alexander* and a variety of religious poems.

The category includes two fragmentary miscellanies:

— The Stargard fragments (Berlin, Mgq 1418, currently Cracow, Bibl. Jagiellońska), written around 1200, which preserve a piece of Eilhart's *Tristan* and sections of Lamprecht's *Tobias* legend together with a *Tagzeitengedicht* (poem of the hours of the day).

— The Trier fragments (Trier, Stadtbibl., folder X, no. 13), probably from the beginning of the thirteenth century, which contain pieces of the *Trierer Floyris* along with pieces of *Trierer Agidius and Trierer Silvester*.

These collections belong to a larger group of miscellanies from the twelfth century, all of which contain religious poems in German and were probably written in monasteries or episcopal seats. The four manuscripts just mentioned differ from the others in that they all contain a secular epic amidst the religious poetry. What may have prompted the ecclesiastical compilers to put together such a mixture of texts is completely unclear. The least difficulty is posed by Lamprecht's *Alexander* in the Vorau manuscript: the story of Alexander the Great fits well into the world historical conception of this collection. In the other three manuscripts the secular text stands next to legendary poems, a combination also found in later manuscripts. It is not clear what interest caused the secular piece to be written down. That love romances like the *Trierer Floyris* and Eilhart's *Tristrant* were copied in the twelfth century for monastic use is surely out of the question. The possibility that the manuscripts were intended for episcopal courts must remain open. It has been suggested that the Vorau manuscript was written in Salzburg or Regensburg, since it is thought to be unlikely that such an extensive collection of texts could have been compiled in the small monastery of Vorau (in Styria), which was only established in 1163. Another possibility is that the manuscripts were produced for secular patrons. The question of who commissioned the manuscripts is of central importance for understanding the sociology of the spread of literature. But the fact that the identity of such a patron cannot be established beyond doubt for a single manuscript of the twelfth or thirteenth century that contains secular poetry in German, shows the limits to this path of inquiry. We cannot count on any solid results in this area.

A different picture confronts us with the single-work manuscripts of the twelfth century. We possess two complete manuscripts:

- The Heidelberg *Rolandslied* manuscript (Cpg 112).
- The Heidelberg manuscript of *König Rother* (Cpg 390).

The extant fragments don't reveal whether they come from anthologies or single-work manuscripts. But most fragments of the twelfth century show such a close similarity in lay-out to the single-work manuscripts that we can include them in this category. They are:

- The Schwerin fragments of the *Rolandslied*,
- The Arnstadt fragments of the *Rolandslied*,
- The Marburg fragments of *Herzog Ernst*,
- The Brunswick-Göttingen fragments of *Graf Rudolf*,
- The Regensburg fragments of Eilhart's *Tristrant*,
- The Magdeburg fragments of Eilhart's *Tristrant*,
- The Regensburg fragments of Veldeke's *Eneit*,
- The Klagenfurt fragments of the *Nibelungenlied*.

Somewhat later, perhaps, are the following:

- The Erfurt fragments of the *Rolandslied*,
- The Munich fragments of *König Rother*,
- The Kassel fragments of *Reinhart Fuchs*,
- The Munich fragments of Veldeke's *Servatius*,
- the Meran fragments of Veldeke's *Eneit*.

In most cases the paleographic evidence alone is not sufficient to date the writing of a manuscript to within a decade or two. That holds true for this list as well. Some of the manuscripts mentioned may not have been written until the thirteenth century; perhaps some others that are dated to the early thirteenth century really belong here.

The single-work manuscripts and the majority of the fragments differ from the miscellanies in their format and lay-out.

The format: The single manuscripts are consistently smaller and in many cases do not exceed the size of a small paperback book (7″ × 4″). The Heidelberg *Rolandslied* manuscript measures 8 3/4″ × 6″, the *König Rother* manuscript 6 3/4″ × 4 1/2″, and most of the old fragments fall within these dimensions. The smallest manuscript is that of the *Nibelungenlied* from Klagenfurt at 6″ × 4 3/4″. The only unusually large fragments are those of the Schwerin *Rolandslied* (10 1/4″ × 8 3/4″). But they don't even come close to the miscellanies from Vorau and Straßburg, which are twice the size. The Vorau manuscript measures 18 1/2″ × 13″. The one from Straßburg may have been even larger (exact measurements are missing): it had fifty-six lines in each column, the Vorau manuscript forty-six. The single manuscripts and fragments have only twenty to thirty lines per page. But smaller miscellanies also existed: the difference in format between the fragments from Trier and Stargarde and the single manuscripts is negligible.

The lay-out: In the great miscellanies, and also in the Trier fragments, the text is written in double columns. This arrangement had a long tradition in the transmission of religious literature. By comparison, the two single manuscripts and nearly all fragments of the twelfth century have continuous writing, a single column. Only the Kassel fragments of *Reinhart Fuchs* and the Meran fragments of *Eneit* are in double columns. The Meran *Eneit* manuscript is also the only older epic manuscript in which the verses are already individually set off, unlike the others, where the writing is continuous. The Meran manuscript may belong to the thirteenth century, and at the time it must have been the most modern epic manuscript.

We cannot discover anything certain about the provenance of the single manuscripts. The notion that the smaller, fairly plain manuscripts, whose only decoration were simple red initials, were pocketbook copies for professional storytellers, has no evidence at all to support it. The small format and the plain appearance must surely not be seen as signs that the person who commissioned them lacked the funds for more elaborate copies. More likely, it reflects the fact that secular literature at this time was not held in as high esteem as religious texts, which were often decorated at great expense. Really splendid and precious copies of secular epics, like the Vienna *Willehalm* manuscript for King Wenzel (d. 1419), did not exist before the fourteenth century.

Similarities in the external appearance of the old manuscripts of epic works suggest that we are dealing with a homogeneous circle of patrons. Given the historical background, these patrons could have existed only at the courts of the secular princes: the evidence shows that it was here that the texts contained in the manuscripts found their audience. Whether the manuscripts were also written at the courts is a different question, to which there is no clear answer. It would be worthwhile to compare the oldest pieces of writing from the princely chanceries with the manuscripts of the epic works. The charters that were drafted at the courts retained a very plain, undecorated form (see p. 448) far into the thirteenth century. Even more interesting would be a comparison with the oldest German texts from the princely chanceries: the ducal land register from Bavaria from the 1230s, or the fragment of the land register of the marshals of Pappenheim, which is dated back to the time of Henry of Kalden (d. 1214/15). Future studies must show whether such an approach could yield reliable insights.

We don't know how the epics were spread in written form. Could one request from a friendly court a copy of a work that had been written there? Or did one borrow the original manuscript in order to copy it? Were scribes sent to the court in question, or was the author invited to one's own court? Lively contacts must already have existed around 1200 between courts with an active literary scene. The extant manuscripts attest to the rapid spread of literature. Not counting the Heidelberg manuscript, five fragments of the *Rolandslied* are known which were probably also written in the twelfth century or at the beginning of the thirteenth. Eilhart's *Tristrant* is known to us from three fragmentary manuscripts from around 1200. Three old fragments also exist for Veldeke's *Eneit*. *König Rother* and *Herzog Ernst* were also copied repeatedly soon after their appearance. Measured against the small number of secular courts at which the literary life began before 1200, the number of extant manuscripts from this time is remarkably high.

In most cases clues to the geographic spread of the manuscripts come only from their language and occasionally from the place where they were found. But studies of the dialects used have often not produced the desired clarity, since many manuscripts show contradictory linguistic characteristics. Older studies started from the false assumption that each manuscript would necessarily reveal the dialect of its writer and could therefore be precisely located. Today we know that the language of a given text was influenced and shaped by a variety of factors, among which the dialect of the writer was only one. Of equal importance were the linguistic conventions of the scriptorium or chancery to which the scribe belonged, and the linguistic usage of the text that was being copied. If a scribe was working from a text that came from far away, contradictory forms of speech were almost unavoidable in the copy.

Some epics seem to have wandered pretty far. The Low German elements in the Schwerin fragments of the *Rolandslied* indicate that the Bavarian work had already made its way to northern Germany in the twelfth century. Conversely, traces of upper German dialect in the Regensburg fragments of Eilhart's *Tristrant* attest that this north-central German work was also known in southern Germany quite early. Most surprising of all is that all of the old versions of Heinrich von Veldeke's *Eneit*, which was finished in Thuringia, are of Bavarian or upper German dialect: the Regensburg fragments are classified as Bavarian-Swabian, the Meran fragments as upper German, the Pfeiffer fragments even as southern Bavarian. *König Rother*, which in the original seems to have had lower German idioms, was already transcribed in the twelfth century into Bavarian, as the Munich fragments attest. The Prague fragments of *Herzog Ernst* from the beginning of the thirteenth century show middle Frankish characteristics and were possibly intended for a Rhenish audience. The studies of Thomas Klein will shed more light on these relationships. The literary exchanges seem to have been especially intensive between the Rhineland and Bavaria, which must be seen against the background of the broad economic and cultural contacts between these two regions. We can also detect the literary connecting routes from the Rhineland to Thuringia, and from Saxony and Thuringia to Bavaria. The sponsors of this literary traffic must have been primarily the princely patrons.

Changes in manuscript appearance in the thirteenth century   In the first half of the thirteenth century, the appearance of the manuscripts of epic works underwent a noticeable change: they became larger and more elaborate. What had been an exception around 1200—the format and layout of the Meran *Eneit* fragments—soon became the norm. A quarto format about 9″ to 13″ high and 6 1/2″ to 8 3/4″ wide, writing in double columns, coordination of the beginning of a verse with the beginning of a new line: eighty to ninety percent of the manuscripts of epics from the thirteenth century look this way. The old form of the one-columned, mostly small-formatted manuscript was still used repeatedly in the early thirteenth century. The Prague fragments of *Herzog Ernst*, the Gießen *Iwein* manuscript, the Cologne *Wigalois* manuscript, the Vienna *Wigalois* fragments, the fragments of *Armer Heinrich* from St. Florian, and the St. Paul *Iwein* fragments all represent this older type, which disappeared almost completely during the second half of the thirteenth century. Among the few manuscripts that were still written this way at the end of the thirteenth century are the Munich fragments of Wolfram's *Titurel* and the Sagan fragments of *Herzog Ernst*. The latter, with a format of 4 1/4″ × 5″, is one of the smallest epic manuscripts of the thirteenth century. That this format was not a sign of cheapness is revealed by the tiny *Iwein* manuscript from Gießen (4″ × 3 1/4″), whose wide margins (the column of writing is only 3 1/2″ × 2 1/4″) and beautiful script with its artistic and colorfully decorated initials show that it was prepared with considerable care. It was rare for a larger epic manuscript in the thirteenth century to be written in a single column. The *Nibelungenlied* manuscript C from Donaueschingen, dated to before 1250, is such a rarity.

Altogether slightly more than twenty epic manuscripts with single-column writing from the thirteenth century have survived, most of them in fragmentary form. There are almost as many manuscripts with three columns of text on each page. This new type of layout, and the custom of beginning each verse with a new line, has been attributed to French influence. But this still needs to be documented. The oldest three-column manuscript in Germany is the Berlin *Eneit* manuscript (Mfg 282) from the first half of the thirteenth century, which is among the most interesting and most beautiful epic manuscripts of the courtly period. On the first pages the scribe wrote the text continuously in double columns, but then he switched to triple columns with separated verses, and he kept this format until the end. What makes this manuscript so precious is the unusually rich pictorial decoration. Each page of text is followed by a (subsequently inserted) page of illustration. There are a total of seventy-one pictorial pages, most of which are divided into an upper and a lower half by a horizontal line through the middle, so that the manuscript contains altogether 136 pictures (see fig. 38). The pictures are multicolored pen-and-ink drawings and are attributed to the circle of the Regensburg-Prüfening painting school. They are also of great importance for the study of material objects, for example the development of the shape of helmets and the emergence of heraldry. Some scholars have sought to discover in the heraldic de-

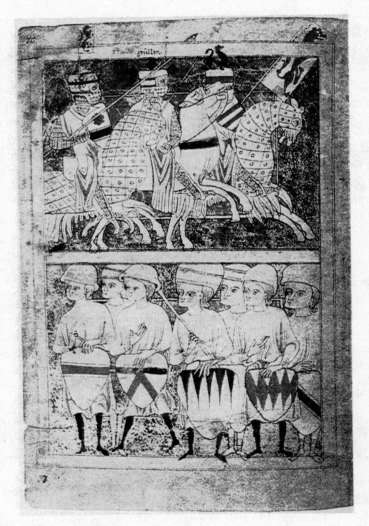

Fig. 38. The Berlin *Eneit* manuscript (Mgf 282). Illustration page and text page. Most of the illustrated folios are divided into two sections (above: the knights of Duke Turnus; below: the foot-soldiers of Duke Turnus). The text page has triple-column writing. Thirteenth century.

vices the identity of the person who commissioned the manuscript. But this approach cannot document any link to the house of the Thuringian landgraves. Judging from the shape of the letters, the manuscript is upper German, more precisely, east Frankish-Bavarian. It was probably intended for a court in southern Germany.

For a time epic manuscripts written in triple columns remained a rarity. The only other manuscript we can mention from the first half of the thirteenth century is the Wolfram manuscript in Munich (Cgm 19). The Salzburg fragments of *Wilhelm von Orlens* by Rudolf von Ems are dated to the middle of the century. All other manuscripts with triple columns were produced only at the end of the thirteenth or the beginning of the fourteenth century. Relatively few manuscripts with triple columns have a small format, such as the Berlin *Eneit* ($10'' \times 7''$); most are larger. The Berlin *Nibelungen* fragments O are one of the largest epic manuscripts of the thirteenth century, with dimensions of $17\,1/2'' \times 11''$ and seventy-eight lines per column. Almost as large is the Berlin *Willehalm* manuscript ($15\,1/4'' \times 11''$). But there are also double column manuscripts that reach such dimensions: the Nuremberg *Willehalm* fragments ($16\,3/4'' \times 12\,1/2''$), or the Ansbach-Wolfenbüttel-Berlin fragments ($16\,1/4'' \times 9\,1/2''$), which contain pieces of the *Eckenlied*, *Virginal*, *Ortnit*, and *Wolfdietrich*. For the most part the heroic or historical epics (*Willehalm*) have come down to us in these large-format manuscripts. The only courtly epic that was written several times in triple columns during the thirteenth century was *Parzival*: this is attested by the Weimar fragments (c), the Rein fragments (d), the Berlin fragments (f), the Gotha-Arnstadt fragments (h), and the Würzburg fragments (t), all of which, incidentally, belong to the manuscript category D.

Some manuscripts are rather plain, others are much more elaborate in the quality of the parchment used, the size of the margins, the careful script, and the precious decorations. But any kind of division into manuscripts intended for public reciting and manuscripts intended for reading is inappropriate for the thirteenth century. Even the precious codices show many signs of wear, which reveal that these manuscripts were heavily used. In the *Nibelungen* manuscript A from Munich, greasy fingermarks at the edges indicate that the manuscript was often held in the hand for reading or reciting. It was certainly not all that easy to read from a manuscript that was written without standard spelling and without punctuation. Friedrich Ranke discovered that the writer of the Innsbruck fragments of Gottfried's *Tristan*, which date from the first half of the thirteenth century, took into account in his writing the metric form of the text, accommodating in this way the needs of some-one who would read the work out loud. Whether this was an exception-al case still needs to be examined.

Apparently the manuscripts were not always immediately bound. The Heidelberg *Iwein* manuscript A from the mid-thirteenth century shows noticeably strong signs of wear on the front and back pages of each gathering, which can be most easily explained if we assume that the gatherings were initially stored separately. Were they also used individually for public reading? In the St. Gall miscellany (manu-script 857), signs of wear appear at the beginning of each poem; it would seem that the various parts were bound together only at a later date. The loss of entire gatherings—as in the Munich *Parzival* manu-script G^k—also indicates that a manuscript had already been used be-fore being bound. The Berlin *Nibelungen* manuscript J is damaged at the edges of the first and last folios; perhaps it was kept in a parchment folder before it was given a hard binding. It has been said that the small verse poems were probably circulated on unbound pages.

There are about 250 epic manuscripts from the thirteenth century, if we include those manuscripts dated "around 1300" or "thirteenth/ fourteenth century." Looking at the chronological spread, we notice that only a relatively small number of manuscripts are securely dated to the first half or the middle of the thirteenth century. The great majority come from the second half of the thirteenth century and from around 1300. Apparently the copying activities picked up only slowly after 1200, and not until the end of the thirteenth century was there a strong surge. Even if we take into account that many more of the older manu-scripts were lost than of the younger ones, we can still estimate that the production of manuscripts at the end of the thirteenth century had in-creased tenfold from what it had been at the beginning of the century. This indicates that profound changes occurred in literary life towards the end of the thirteenth century. Whether there is a link between the growing number of manuscripts and the appearance of charters in Ger-man in the last years of the thirteenth century, and whether the in-creased copying activity has a causal connection to the entrance of the landed nobility and the noble upper class of the cities into literary life, are questions which must for now remain open.

Where the many manuscripts were written and who commissioned them cannot be determined with certainty in a single case. In the Berlin anthology Mfg 1062—the so-called Riedegger Manuscript, written in Austria around 1300—the last page has this entry in a different hand:

"I, Otto of Hakenberg and Rabensburg, to his beloved relative Albero of Kuenring."[40] Scholars used to interpret this as a dedicatory note, and inferred from it that the manuscript was written at the request of the Austrian ministerial Otto of Hakenberg (attested 1276–1295), who then gave it to his brother-in-law Albero of Kuenring. But the words are merely a quote from the protocol of a letter or charter, and it must remain open whether the patron who commissioned the manuscript did in fact come from these families. Other notes on the last folio of the Riedegger Manuscript point to the Bavarian ducal family. In all likelihood most epic manuscripts of the thirteenth century were written at the request of secular princely courts. After the mid-thirteenth century, we must also reckon with patrons from the richer landed nobility, especially in the Austrian lands. To what extent the princely chanceries were involved in the production of manuscripts cannot be determined. The fact that most epic manuscripts of the thirteenth century were written by a single hand may perhaps be taken to indicate that they were produced in smaller scriptoria with a modest staff. Even some of the more extensive miscellanies, such as the Riedegger Manuscript, are the work of a single scribe. How the Riedegger collection was planned and carried out is revealed by the fact that at the end of the Neidhart collection, the back of folio 62 was left blank, and a new gathering started on folio 63[r] with the beginning of *Dietrichs Flucht*. Apparently the two parts of the manuscript were written separately. Decorated ascenders in the letters of the first lines are reminiscent of the script used in charters, and they suggest that the scribe worked in a chancery.

Very few epic manuscripts of the thirteenth century do not fit this pattern. The Munich Wolfram manuscript (Cgm 19) from the first half of the thirteenth century was written by six different scribes. The St. Gall miscellany (Stiftsbibl. 857) from the middle of the century—with 318 pages the largest epic manuscript of the thirteenth century—was the work of six or seven different hands. Five scribes were involved in producing the Vienna Stricker-manuscript (Nat.-Bibl. 2705) from the second half of the thirteenth century. The organization of the manuscripts and the distribution of the various hands reveal that several scribes worked on it simultaneously. In the production of the St. Gall manuscript, the work was divided such that each epic began with a new gathering. The main scribe first wrote the entire *Willehalm*, and then continued with *Parzival*, which had been begun by another scribe; eventually he was also involved in writing the *Nibelungenlied*. The scribes of the Munich Wolfram manuscript were assigned to various gatherings:

the first scribe began *Parzival* with section 1 (by modern counting), the second began with section 5, and the third with section 10. If the scribes worked simultaneously, the required space had to be calculated in advance. Minor inconsistencies were unavoidable with this method: thus in the ninth gathering of the Munich manuscript one page was left empty (fol 53^v), and the next page but one (fol 54^v) was only half written on. Apparently the beginning of the tenth gathering was already complete, and there was not enough text to fill up the ninth gathering completely. The first *Parzival* scribe later also wrote *Titurel*. This kind of division of labor shows that these manuscripts were produced in large, efficient scriptoria. We can fill in even a bit more about the Munich Wolfram manuscript, since it has been discovered that the Munich *Tristan* manuscript (Cgm 51) is the work of the same scribe who was the main writer of the Wolfram manuscript. The identical style of the illustration in both manuscripts is also an indication that they came from the same scriptorium. A third work from this scriptorium are the Salzburg fragments of Rudolf von Ems's *Wilhelm von Orlens*. This manuscript, like Cgm 19, is arranged in triple columns, and the manner of writing shows great similarities to scribe 1 of Cgm 19 and to the scribe of Cgm 51. The distribution of the initials in the Salzburg fragments also reminds us of the Munich Wolfram manuscript. The scriptorium in which these three manuscripts were written must have been among the leading producers of epic manuscripts around the mid-thirteenth century. The language of the three manuscripts points to Alemannic origin. Friedrich Ranke has advanced the thesis that the scriptorium was located in Straßburg, and that the head of the Straßburg chancery, Meister Hesse (see p. 487), organized the editing and writing of the texts. But a variety of reasons argue against this scenario. If we consider that two of the three manuscripts contain works dedicated to Conrad of Winterstetten—Rudolf von Ems's *Wilhelm von Orlens* and the *Tristan* continuation by Ulrich von Türheim (see p. 486)—we are rather led to believe that this group of manuscripts issued from the royal Hohenstaufen court of Henry (VII) and Conrad IV with its large, well-organized chancery, or at least that the mansucripts were commissioned from there.

There is no indication that the commercial production of epic manuscripts had already begun in the thirteenth century. The beginnings of a book market in Germany cannot be traced back beyond the fifteenth century, with the possible exception of Latin school books used at the universities. This means we must assume that each manuscript was written on request. This circumstance probably explains why some manuscripts were left unfinished, like some epic works themselves. One example is the Munich *Parzival* manuscript G^k from the end of the thirteenth century. It is an elaborately prepared codex, with a format of 12 1/2″ × 8 1/2″, and written in a careful script by a single hand. The original plan called for extensive illustrations, and room was left for them. But only the first miniature was finished. The initials planned by the scribe were also not carried out. The loss of complete gatherings indicates that the manuscript was left unbound for some time. In all likelihood the patron who commissioned it died or canceled his order. This dependence on patronage must have had a profound influence on manuscript production in the thirteenth century.

The number of manuscripts containing more than one epic increased gradually. It was particularly rare that the fragmentary works of the great masters—Gottfried's *Tristan* and Wolfram's *Willehalm*—were copied without continuations. Not a single manuscript of the thirteenth century has Gottfried's *Tristan* by itself: in the Munich manuscript M and in the Heidelberg manuscript H it is followed by Ulrich von Türheim's continuation; in the Florence manuscript F it is followed by the continuation of Heinrich von Freiberg. The situation is similar to that of *Willehalm*: in the Berlin manuscript B it appears between Ulrich von dem Türlin's prehistory (*Willehalm-Arabel*) and Ulrich von Türheim's continuation (*Rennewart*). The Berlin Türheim/Türlin fragments (Mgf 923.30 and 923.32) and the Berlin *Willehalm* fragments no. 16 attest that at the end of the thirteenth century Wolfram's work was regularly read and copied in this cyclical version. *Willehalm* survived only once without continuation in a thirteenth-century manuscript, the St. Gall miscellany. Even closer was the link between the *Nibelungenlied* and its early addition, the so-called *Klage* ("Lament"): in the thirteenth century these two works were never written separately.

A tendency to arrange cycles of works also appears in the transmission of the younger heroic epics. Not a single manuscript of the thirteenth century has one of these works by itself. A great collection from around 1300, which combined *Eckenlied*, *Virginal*, *Ortnit*, and *Wolfdietrich*, has survived only in fragments. In other manuscripts, *Dietrichs Flucht* and *Rabenschlacht* or *Sigenot* and *Eckenlied* were joined to works from other genres. This cyclical transmission of heroic epic was later continued in the *Heldenbücher* of the late Middle Ages.

Sometimes the last pages of a epic manuscript were filled up with shorter pieces of a different character. Thus the Vienna manuscript of the *Jüngerer Titurel* has the praise of the prince from the *Wartburgkrieg* on the final page. What accounts for this association, perhaps, is the fact that both the *Wartburgkrieg* and *Jüngerer Titurel* were composed in stanzas. Kleinepik (short epic) and *Spruch* poetry, along with religious and shorter didactic pieces, appear frequently on the unused pages. The Vienna manuscript of Rudolf von Ems's *Guter Gerhard* (A) has the short legend *Von Gottes Leichnam* by Nikolaus Schlegel at the end. At the end of the Berlin *Nibelungen* manuscript J, the *Klage* is followed by *Der Winsbeke* and *Die Winsbekin*. Whether in this case we are already looking at a consciously planned manuscript program cannot be determined.

The combination of several works into one manuscript often mirrors the taste and interests of the patron who commissioned it. Not infrequently the fact that epics were close in theme or dealt with similar material explains their association. This is quite clear when Veldeke's *Eneit* is once joined with Otte's *Eraclius* into one volume (M), and once with a poem of Alexander (Marburg, Hessisches Staatsarchiv, Index 147, folder A). The classical material determined the combination in these cases. In the fourteenth century, the *Eneit* was also combined with Herbort von Fritzlar's *Trojanerkrieg* (H). The *Willehalm* transmission was also influenced by such considerations. In the St. Gall miscellany (857), Wolfram's poem appears after Stricker's *Karl*, the courtly adaptation of the *Rolandslied* to which Wolfram referred several times in his *Willehalm*. The proximity of *Willehalm* and Heinrich von Hesler's *Evangelium Nicodemi*, which appear side by side in a fragmentary manuscript, is also revealed by their subsequent history. Both works were highly regarded in the Teutonic Order, and in the fourteenth century both were worked into Heinrich von München's rhymed world chronicle. Stricker's *Karl* was also used by Heinrich von München. The association of *Karl* with historical poetry is further attested by a St. Gall manuscript from the end of the thirteenth century, in which Stricker's work follows the *Weltchronik* by Rudolf von Ems. A bit strange is the joining of Stricker's *Karl* with Hartmann's *Gregorius* in a thirteenth-century Vatican manuscript. *Gregorius*, which appears here at the end of the manuscript, is also found in some other strange combinations. In a fragmentary manuscript (L) it shows up next to *Der Winsbeke*. Apparently there were a number of patrons who were interested in a combination of courtly epic and courtly didactic works. This is also attested by the Heidelberg *Tristan* manuscript H from the end of the thirteenth century, which contains Gottfried's work together with

Türheim's continuation. This manuscript also originally included the Freidank manuscript A, which was later removed. All three works were written by the same hand in direct succession.

As far as we can tell from the extant manuscripts of the thirteenth century, only once were the epic works of one poet compiled into a codex. The Munich manuscript Cgm 18, which combines *Parzival, Titurel,* and two dawn songs, was clearly planned as a Wolfram collection. The prose pieces that now appear on folio 75^r were added later by a different hand. Space had been left at the end of the *Titurel,* apparently in the hope that additional pieces of the fragmentary poem would be discovered. It is striking that *Willehalm* is missing from this anthology. When we consider what heights the veneration of the great poets from around 1200 reached during the thirteenth century, the absence of other anthologies of single authors is strange.

The most interesting insights into the literary tastes of the time come from the extensive anthologies that combined works of different character. Two collections have survived only in fragmentary form: the *Parzival* fragments h, which are part of a manuscript that also contained the Middle High German epic *Segremors*; and the Zurich fragments of a three-column manuscript from the second half of the thirteenth century (Staatsarchiv, C. VI/I, Mappe VI, no. 6), which transmitted pieces of *Parzival* and *Tristan.* Three great collections have survived intact:

— the St. Gall manuscript (Stiftsbibl. 857) from the middle of the thirteenth century, which contains Wolfram's *Parzival,* the *Nibelungenlied,* the *Nibelungenklage,* Stricker's *Karl,* Wolfram's *Willehalm,* and *Sprüche* by Friedrich von Suonenburg;

— the Berlin manuscript (Mgf 1062) or Riedegger Manuscript from around 1300, which combines Hartmann's *Iwein,* Stricker's *Pfaffen Amis,* Neidhart's songs, *Dietrichs Flucht,* and *Die Rabenschlacht*;

— the Donaueschingen manuscript (Fürstl. Fürstenbergische Hofbibl. 74), which was also written around 1300 or at the beginning of the fourteenth century. It contains Rudolf von Ems's *Wilhelm von Orlens,* Konrad von Fussesbrunnen's *Kindheit Jesu,* Konrad von Heimesfurt's *Himmelfahrt Mariä,* as well as *Sigenot* and the *Eckenlied.*

In all three collections, courtly epics were combined with heroic epics, and other genres are also represented: *Spruch* poetry in the St. Gall manuscript, *Schwank* poetry and songs in the Riedegger Manuscript, religious epics in the Donaueschingen manuscript. It would seem that in all three cases the patrons who commissioned the manuscripts wanted a sampling of courtly literature. What criteria determined the actual selection and combination of various pieces cannot be determined. The fact that one manuscript includes two legendary poems with New Testament themes might suggest that the personal tastes of the patron were responsible. Equally as unusual is the inclusion of a collection of lyric poetry in the Riedegger Manuscript. Most impressive of all is the arrangement in the St. Gall manuscript. The initiative for its production must have come from a great connoisseur of literature, who wanted to collect a number of the most important epics from around 1200. It is the only manuscript of the thirteenth century that combines *Parzival* with *Willehalm*, and the only one in which Wolfram's works appear with the *Nibelungenlied*. If we knew who commissioned this collection, our picture of the literary life of the thirteenth century would be enriched by an important detail.

COURTLY LYRIC

Lyric poetry for public performance, for dancing, and for reading   A lyric poem was always meant to be sung; text and music belonged together. While an epic was first created as a written work and was only then performed, the scenario was exactly the reverse for the song: it was primarily sung and may also have been written down. This different point of departure for lyric poetry has shaped the entire history of its transmission. With epics we are dealing with fixed written versions that were but little changed in the process of written transmission. With lyric, on the other hand, we must assume that there were phases of transmission during which the texts were changed in ways which modern scholarly methods of textual philology cannot correct or reconstruct. It is for this reason that the texts published in the critical editions of lyric works have a weaker claim to authenticity than the critical editions of epic poems.

How the songs of the minnesingers were performed and spread must largely be inferred from hints of the poets themselves; historical accounts about it do not exist. A glance at scholarship shows the great uncertainty that attaches to many points. As for the question of what role oral and written factors played in the spread of the songs, here the scholarly opinions diverge so drastically that it hardly seems possible at all to give a summary of the current consensus. This is why I shall limit myself here to the most important issues that are of significance for interpreting lyric poetry.

The usual form of presentation for courtly lyric was surely the performance of the songs in the festive circle of courtly society. The minnesingers often regarded it as their task to entertain the courtly audience with the beauty of their melodies and to arouse the elated feeling of courtly *vreude*. In all likelihood the poets themselves usually performed as singers and instrumentalists, accompanying their singing with a string instrument. In southern France it seems to have been customary for the noble troubadours to have singers who peformed their songs. Peire Cardinal "brought a jongleur with him who sang his sirventes."[41] Guiraut de Borneil "brought two singers with him who sang his songs."[42] Such a division of labor between poet and singer is also attested for Italy. In Germany, on the other hand, it seems to have been unknown in the twelfth and thirteenth centuries. A number of minnesingers mentioned that their songs were sung by others: "Whoever may sing these stanzas in her [the lady's] presence..."[43] "Quite often others lament to her in song my sorrows."[44] But undoubtedly the poets were not thinking of a performance organized by themselves, but of the use of their songs by members of court society or by other professional singers.

Epic texts can give us an idea of the lyric entertainment at court. The French *Roman de Horn* from the second half of the twelfth century describes how music was performed at the Irish royal court in the presence of foreign guests. The king's daughter, Lenburc, began to play the *Lai de Rigmel*, a song in praise of the Breton princess Rigmel; next her brother took up the harp, and the instrument then made the rounds, for "at that time everybody knew how to play the harp well. The more noble a person, the more skilled he was at it."[45] Gottfried von Straßburg depicted how Tristan, as a guest at the court of Arundel, entertained the society there with his songs. "Time and again when the entire court sat together—he, Isolde and Kaedin, the duke and the duchess, ladies and barons—he would compose songs, rondeaux, and little courtly melodies."[46] Every song that Tristan sang closed with a refrain mentioning Isolde's name. In the *Roman de Horn*, too, a song of praise for a lady was sung. We can see from this that the songs in praise of ladies were not only intended to be sung before those particular women. The *Nibelungenlied* tells of the performance of a noble singer before a lady of princely rank, when Volker of Alzey sings to Margravine Gotelind as the Burgundians seek lodging at Bechlarn: "Brave Volker stepped courteously before Gotelind with his fiddle and played lovely melodies and sang his songs for her."[47] The margravine rewarded his artistry with twelve golden bracelets. Surely we are not dealing with a minne relationship here.

It is probable—though undocumented—that occasionally at such entertainments in court circles minnesingers of low social rank who were employed as court singers also performed. Better attested, if only in poetic sources, is the appearance of professional minnesingers at the great court feasts. The literary entertainment offered to the guests on these occasions also included the performance of minnesong. At the coronation feast in Cluse, there were "twenty singers who sang minnesongs to dispel sorrow."[48] At the court feast of King William of England, one heard "different kinds of string music played in beautiful melodies, and sweet singing of minne."[49] We are not told whether these singers performed their own songs or whether they drew from a repertoire of songs composed by others. Among the troubadours, a poet might leave his songs to his jongleur, who then performed them for money. Raimon de Miraval, who composed around 1200, addressed the jongleur Bayona in one of his songs: "I know well, Bayona, that you have come to me for a sirvente. This is the third, two I have already written for you, with which you have earned gold and silver, many a used armor, and good and bad clothes."[50] In Germany such practices are not attested. But even here it seems to have been expected of professional singers that they could sing minnesongs. This probably explains why Der Marner, in listing the pieces that were especially popular among the courtly audience, mentions minnesong amidst themes from heroic epics: "The seventh wanted to hear something about the battle with Heime or with Wittiche, or Siegfried's death or Ecke's death. The eighth person, on the other hand, wants to hear nothing but courtly minnesong."[51]

The singing of songs in the convivial circle at court and the performance by professional singers at the court feasts seem to have been the most important ways in which courtly lyric reached its audience. That we must also reckon with other forms of transmission besides these is attested by Ulrich von Liechtenstein, whose statements about the performance and publishing of his songs are one of a kind. No other minnesinger reported in such detail about these aspects. In

Frauendienst we find neither the presentation in an intimate circle nor the public performance at feasts. Liechtenstein made his songs known in a variety of ways. They were

- sung by the poet to an all-male gathering;
- sung by noble knights as a traveling or tournament song;
- sung to a lady by a messenger;
- read to a lady by a messenger;
- read by the lady herself;
- danced and sung.

Minnesongs could thus be sung, danced to, or read. We would do well to consider these three possibilities as real factors of courtly literary practice.

Ulrich von Liechtenstein composed on his sick bed (*Frauendienst* 110.3 ff., 350.3 ff.), while on pilgrimage to Rome (416.7 ff.), and in prison (1726.1 ff.). Some of his songs were written in the winter (159.1 ff., 1356.1 ff.), but he also composed and sang during his summertime tournament circuits, where he met his peers from Austria and Styria (316.1 ff., 1424.6 ff.). The noble lords liked his songs so much that they learned and sang them themselves while traveling or at tournaments. "With this joyous traveling song many a good knight spent the summer on the road."[52] "The song was sung often. I am not lying: after the song many a knightly joust was ridden. The song was popular where the sparks flew from the helmet during jousting. Many knights liked it."[53] According to Liechtenstein's testimony, in the first half of the thirteenth century there already existed courtly lyric that was not meant for and did not reach the court, but was sung by members of the lay nobility during knightly games.

If Ulrich von Liechtenstein is to be believed, he sent most of his songs to ladies whose love he was courting. We hear that his first lady, whom he served for years without success, was the mistress of a great court. Liechtenstein could communicate with her only through a lady from among his own noble relatives, who gave his songs and letters to a messenger or presented them herself. To this end the songs were written down and were conveyed either orally or in writing. Sometimes the messenger sang the song to the lady: "Milady, through me he has sent you this song, be so kind and listen to it... He asked me, milady, to sing it to you."[54] Sometimes the song was read to the lady: "I read your new song to her."[55] Sometimes the lady read the song by herself: "The sweet and lovely woman read the letter which contained the song."[56] Whether Liechtenstein in fact dealt with his songs this way is beyond our knowing. Perhaps he borrowed the motif of the messenger from troubadour poetry, where it is often mentioned that the poets sent their songs—in written or oral form—to their ladies or patrons via messengers. "Without parchment I send this song, which we sing in plain Romance language, through Filhol to Uc le Brun."[57] The request that the lady sing the song, and the instructions to the messenger to sing it to her, also appear in Romance lyric: "Hugh, my courtly messenger, sing my song willingly before the queen of the Normans."[58] But it is remarkable that Liechtenstein could present his listeners with the notion that minnesongs were not only sung but also read. In reference to his lay, Liechtenstein even spoke in general terms of a reading audience of women: "The lay was well suited for singing. Many a beautiful lady read it with pleasure."[59]

Minnesongs were also danced to. Ulrich von Liechtenstein said about his song *Wol her alle, helfet singen* (no. 52): "This song was masterful, the rhymes were artfully fashioned. That is why many liked to sing it. The strophic melody was truly not too long: it was well suited for dancing. . . And it was often danced to."[60] He said similar things about other songs: "The song is truly good for dancing."[61] "The melody was often danced to."[62] One song he gave the title "Ladies' Dance": "This song is called 'Ladies' Dance.' It should be danced joyously."[63] Out of a total of fifty-eight songs, thirty-eight in *Frauendienst* have a title. Twenty-six of those are "dancing songs" (*tanzwîsen*). The manner of performance is probably also indicated by the title "singing melody" (*sincwîse*, four songs). The circumstances under which a song was used may be reflected in the title "traveling song" (*ûzreise*, two songs), while other designations refer to the structure of the songs: "lay" (*leich*, one song), "round" (*reien*, one song), "long melody" (*lange wîse*, two songs). To all this we must add one "dawn song" (*tagewîse*). The fact that most of these songs were declared "dancing songs" is remarkable above all because all were songs in canzona stanzas, which do not advertise themselves as dancing songs either in formal structure or in theme (no melodies for Liechtenstein's songs have come down to us). If these songs were dancing lyric, we have no formal characteristic to differentiate dancing lyric and sung lyric, unlike the situation in France, where dancing songs had their own structure.

The question from what time on songs in canzona form were intended for dancing can hardly be answered. It seems almost unthinkable that the songs of Morungen or Reinmar were already used for dancing, since their serious tone seems incompatible with dancing pleasure. But whether such arguments even get to the heart of the issue is an open question. Most scholars think dancing songs appear in the work of Walther von der Vogelweide. His song *Nemt, frowe disen kranz* (74.20) is also a canzona; but its allusion to dancing ("What if she is at this dance? Ladies, if you please, push back your hats!"[64]) could be an indication that the song was sung while dancing. Or was it only a reference to an imagined scenario? Dancing lyric in the grand style begins only with Neidhart. Both his summersongs with their nontripartite stanzas and his wintersongs composed in canzona form are considered dancing lyric. Scholars find confirmation in the melodies to Neidhart's songs: short musical units, frequent repetition, the absence of melismas, and a tonality similar to a major key are regarded as marks of dancing tunes. The great success of Neidhart's songs surely had something to do with their manner of performance.

The manuscripts and their precursors   The manuscript transmission of epic works reaches back to the lifetime of the poets who wrote them. Courtly lyric, on the other hand, has come down to us almost entirely in collections that were written only towards the end of the thirteenth and the beginning of the fourteenth centuries, more than a century after the older poems were composed. Even if we must reckon with many losses, the different distribution reveals that written versions apparently played a smaller role in the transmission of sung lyric.

The oldest written version of a poem by a minnesinger known by name dates back to the twelfth century. It is the lay of Heinrich von Rugge, which was subsequently written on the unused pages of a Latin manuscript (Munich, Clm 4570), following the collection of canons by Burchard of Worms. It was not uncommon that empty spaces in older manuscripts were used to record short single pieces, and lyric stanzas in their brevity were especially well suited. Some of the stanzas printed in the book *Minnesangs Frühling* under the title "Nameless Songs" also come from Latin manuscripts of the twelfth century. To what extent these anonymous verses are products of courtly lyric still needs to be examined; they do not bear comparison with the sophisticated artistic structure of Rugge's lay. Why this lay, among all the songs of the older minnesong, was deemed worthy of being recorded in writing so early we don't know. The fact the Rugge's lay is a religious poem probably had something to do with it. The poem's subtitle—"This is a lay of the Holy Sepulchre"[65]—called attention to the religious theme. An author's name is not mentioned; that the lay—which exists in no other manuscript—comes from the pen of the minnesinger Heinrich von Rugge is inferred from the name given at the end: "The foolish man von Rugge has given this wise advice."[66] It is remarkable that the text was written down without the melody. This reveals that courtly lyric in the twelfth century could already be regarded as text-lyric, as lyric to be read. However, the Latin manuscript from the monastery of Benediktbeuern was certainly not intended for a court audience.

Another strange and exceptional case is the second oldest text in the chronology of courtly lyric, once again found within the framework of a Latin manuscript. We are talking about the famous *Carmina Burana* (Munich, Clm 4660), the most extensive collection of goliardic songs. It is now believed that it was written during the first half of the thirteenth century in the region where the southern Bavarian dialect was spoken. Among the Latin texts are about fifty German strophes (we can ignore the religious poems at the end of the manuscript) that were individually added to Latin songs. Similarities in the formal structure seem to have determined the placement. It must have been a single editor who arranged the texts in this way. He probably selected or perhaps even composed the Latin songs in such a way that their stophic structure made them compatible with the German pieces. Occasionally the reverse must have occurred, and the German poem was composed after the model of the Latin song. A collection of such pairs then found its way into the manuscript of the *Carmina Burana*: here they are written together in a fairly compact sequence. From no. 135 to no. 183 almost every Latin song has a German addition; outside of this section German songs appear only sporadically. Names of authors are given neither for the Latin nor for the German pieces. But some of the German verses can be assigned to known minnesingers on the basis of other manuscripts: to Dietmar von Aist (CB 113a), Heinrich von Morungen (CB 150a), Reinmar der Alte (CB 143a, 147a, 166a), Walther von der Vogelweide (CB 151a, 169a, 211a), Otto von Botenlouben (CB 48a), and Neidhart (CB 168a). In most cases the German stanzas are the beginning stanzas of longer songs that were cited in this way. Among them are such famous pieces as Walther's "Song of Palestine": *Allerêrst lebe ich mir werde* (14.38 = CB 211a), and Neidhart's crusading song: *Ez gruonet wol diu heide* (11.8 = CB 168a). In a few instances the German stanzas were taken right from the middle of a song: the third stanza of Walther's

May-song: *Muget ir schouwen* (51.13) is cited once (CB 151a), as is the fourth stanza (CB 169a), while only the last stanza of the dawn song of Otto von Botenlouben is given: *Wie sol ich den ritter nû gescheiden* (no. 13) (CB 48a). We don't know how these selections were made. We are equally in the dark about where the other German stanzas come from; they are not transmitted anywhere else and can therefore not be linked to any poets. Some of them strike us as old-fashioned, while others adhere to the norms of high minnesong. Most German verses contain nature motifs; apparently the collector had a special preference for them. Other than that the themes represent a colorful mix: women's strophes, dancing tunes, parodies, classicizing verses, and pastourelle-like pieces. Some texts seem like imitations of well-known songs or allude to them in parody, which confirms the existence of a lively lyric scene. It is unclear whether the editor compiled the stanzas from oral traditions, or whether there already existed a written collection. The condition of the texts would suggest orally circulating song material. Apparently more minne lyric existed in the first half of the thirteenth century than the later miscellanies would indicate. Particularly valuable are the melodies in the Munich manuscript (see fig. 39). It is true that only a few pieces are accompanied by notes, and that the notation in neumes (some of them barely legible) written without lines above the text raises extraordinary difficulties of musical interpretation. But at least we have the melodies for a few German stanzas or pieces of stanzas, among them some for the songs of Morungen (150a), Reinmar (143a, 147a), and Walther (151a). The notes are clear proof that the poems were meant to be sung. We must not, however, imagine a secular audience for this Latin manuscript; scholars believe that it was produced at the request of and for an episcopal court.

All other written texts of thirteenth-century courtly lyric are of a later date. We can distinguish three types of lyric transmissions: 1. sporadic texts, 2. collections of a specific poet's work, and 3. the great song manuscripts.

1. Sporadic texts are entries of single stanzas or small groups of stanzas into manuscripts containing other texts. This practice already existed in the twelfth century, and it continued in the thirteenth. Almost everything that was recorded in this way is anonymous. Only where parallel transmissions exist do we know the identity of the poets. This is the case for the Spervogel verses in the Munich Ovid and Cicero manuscript (Clm 4612), for two stanzas of Konrad von Würzburg in a theological miscellany from Munich (Clm 27329), for two stanzas of

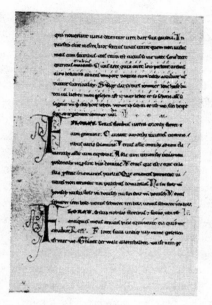

Fig. 39. Carmina Burana (Munich, Clm 4660). The oldest recorded melodies for German minnesongs. In the upper third of the page a strophe by Reinmar der Alte (Sage daz ih dirs iemmer lone). Thirteenth century.

Reinmar von Zweter in the Vienna *Seifried Helbling* manuscript (Nat.-Bibl. 324), and also for the five stanzas of Friedrich von Suonenburg on the last page of the St. Gall miscellany (manuscript 857). On the borderline between sporadic transmission and separate song book are the thirty-two anonymous *Spruch* verses—in the manner of the Spervogel *Sprüche*—in the appendix to the Heidelberg Freidank manuscript (Cpg 349). It is certainly no accident that *Spruch* verses almost always were transmitted this way. Among the sporadic texts we should perhaps also count the small collection of eight stanzas entered on the last page of the Zurich *Schwabenspiegel* manuscript (Zentralbibl. Z.XI.302), for once with the names of the poets ("von Zweter," "von Kolmas," "Walther").

2. Collections of a poet's work. When people began to collect and write down songs on a larger scale, they were usually guided by the names of the poets. In the thirteenth century, three poets overshadowed all others in fame: Walther von der Vogelweide, Neidhart, and Reinmar, whereby the name Reinmar sometimes stood for Reinmar der Alte and sometimes for Reinmar von Zweter. The first large collections of

poets' work from the thirteenth century have come down to us under
these three names:

The Neidhart collection R in the Riedegger Manuscript (Berlin, Mgf
1062), which was written around 1300 (see p. 544). The Neidhart
songs, just under four hundred stanzas, appear here between Stricker's
Pfaffe Amis and *Dietrichs Flucht*. The reason for this close association
with *Schwank* poetry may lie in the fact that Neidhart's songs contained
Schwank-like themes that by around 1300 gave the impetus for the
production of new *Schwank* songs.

The Reinmar von Zweter collection D in the Heidelberg Song Manuscript (Cpg 350), also written around 1300. On forty pages it contains
in careful thematic arrangement 193 *Spruch* stanzas of the younger
Reinmar, as well as some verses in Zweter's style, and in the appendix a
small Walther collection (stanzas 239–256). The *Sprüche* of Reinmar
von Zweter were gathered into a number of collections in the thirteenth
century. The fragments from Halle (V) transmit fifteen stanzas in the
same sequence as manuscript D. A third Reinmar collection of the thirteenth century is the newly discovered fragments from Los Angeles,
which contain fourteen stanzas in a different sequence. The unique feature of this new discovery is that the two parchment pieces (format
4 3/4" × 15 1/2") don't come from a codex but from a scroll.

An extensive collection of the songs and *Sprüche* of Walther von der
Vogelweide from the thirteenth century has not survived. But we do
know that Walther's poems were collected early on, and we possess
several fragments of manuscripts that contained such collections. The
oldest Walther collection is the fragments of Heiligenstadt (w^x, w^{xx}),
four pages with songs of old age and political *Sprüche* (eleven stanzas).
Next, from the end of the thirteenth century, are the Berlin fragments
(O) with forty-four stanzas, and the Wolfenbüttel fragments (U^x, U^{xx})
with forty-two stanzas. The Walther verses at the end of the Zweter
collection D could also be regarded as the remnants of a separate
Walther collection. There is a striking difference in external appearance: the three Walther manuscripts all have a small octavo format (w^x,
w^{xx}: 5 1/4" × 4 1/4"; O: 7" × 4 1/4"; U^x, U^{xx}: 6" × 4") and are written in
triple columns, whereas the manuscripts with the songs and *Sprüche*
of Reinmar von Zweter have a quarto format (D: 9 1/2" × 6";
V: 10 1/2" × 7 1/4") and double column writing. We must note that the
Wolfenbüttel fragments also contain songs of Reinmar der Alte: the
first extant page has the ending of a Reinmar stanza (no. 67, stanza 5),
and this is followed, without title, by the Walther collection. The other

such Walther-Reinmar double collection is known to us only from the fourteenth century, in the *Hausbuch* (E) of Michael de Leone (d. 1355). In E, the Reinmar collection ends with exactly the same stanza, and the Walther collections begin, as in U^x, U^xx, with *Mir tuot einer slahte wille* (113.31). The combining of two collections of poets' work was one step towards the great song manuscripts.

A unique author's collection is Ulrich von Liechtenstein's *Frauendienst*. In it the poet cited verbatim all his own songs. Perhaps the real purpose behind Liechtenstein's fictitious autobiography was to gather and comment on the songs. Liechtenstein tells us that the work was finished in 1255. We know of no other instance from the thirteenth century where a poet himself put together a collection of his own work. The next examples come only from around 1400.

3. "Song Manuscripts" is the name given to lyric collections in which a number of authors are represented with their poems. In France such collections were called *chansonniers*, and several of these were already compiled in the thirteenth century. Of the three great German song manuscripts—which compiled almost all the courtly lyric that existed in Germany—only one comes from the thirteenth century: The Small Heidelberg Song Manuscript (A). The other two, the Weingarten Song Manuscript (B) and the Large Heidelberg Song Manuscript (C), are dated to the first half of the fourteenth century. The Jena Song Manuscript (J) from the mid-fourteenth century belongs to the same category of manuscripts, even though it is actually not a song manuscript, since it contains almost exclusively *Spruchdichtung*. J is the only one among the great lyric collections that also has notation; A, B, and C are only collections of texts. A contains just under eight hundred stanzas of thirty-four named poets (and a few unnamed ones) on forty-five pages; B comprises 158 pages and about 750 stanzas (as well as a few pieces not meant for singing) under the names of twenty-five poets; C has 426 pages and over six thousand stanzas that are attributed to 140 different poets. In external appearance A and B resemble each other: they are relatively small (A: 7 1/2″ × 5 1/2″; B: 6″ × 4 1/2″) and are written in a single column. C and J, on the other hand, are large, double column manuscripts of great splendor (C: 14 1/4″ × 10″; J: 22 1/2″ × 16 1/2″), of the kind that was not found in the transmission of lyric in the thirteenth century. In arrangement and decoration, however, B and C are more closely related: in both the poets are organized according to their social rank, and in both every poet is represented by a full-page portrait. A seems simpler, but with its careful script, the names of

the poets written in different colors, and the beautiful decorative letters at the beginning of each new melody, it is a precious manuscript. A, B, and C all stem from the Alemannic language region. We don't know who commissioned any one of the manuscripts. A was probably written in the Alsace, possibly in Straßburg, in which case it may have been requested by its art-loving Bishop Conrad of Lichtenberg (d. 1299). B probably belongs to Constance and may have been produced there during the episcopacy of Bishop Henry of Klingenberg (d. 1306). C has been located in Zurich, where perhaps the entire circle of noble men and women who took an interest in literature—the circle which Hadloub mentions in his songs (see p. 488)—was involved in producing this large collection. Hadloub attests that Rüdiger Manesse (d. 1304) played the crucial role in this process:

> Where could one find so many songs all together? Nowhere in the entire kingdom could one find as many as are in the manuscripts in Zurich. This is why the people there are well versed in masterly singing. Manesse directed his efforts at this with success, and thus he now owns the song books. All singers should bow to his court and should spread its fame here and elsewhere. For there minnesong exists in all its fullness. If Manesse knew where else good lyric existed, he would quickly endeavor to obtain it.[67]

The Heidelberg manuscript could be a copy of the Manesse collection. With its exceptionally rich decoration, C is one of the most precious manuscripts of the Middle Ages. It also documents the work of an active collector: the later insertion of entire sections, the added stanzas in the margins, and the columns and pages left empty at the end of the collections of various authors—all this provides insights into how the collectors and editors worked. Apparently it was their aim to include everything they could get their hands on. The southwest German and Swiss poets are best represented in C. As for the lyric from other parts of Germany, we must assume that there are larger gaps. The Middle German Walther transmission in manuscripts E, O, U^x, U^{xx}, w^x w^{xx}, and Z attests that toward the end of the thirteenth century intensive collection was also going on in central Germany. A good deal of this does not seem to have reached Switzerland. Of the 212 Walther stanzas in manuscript E, forty-nine are missing in C and another twenty are listed there under different names.

The question what the sources and preliminary stages of the extant song manuscripts looked like has received much attention from scholars. The analysis and comparison of the surviving collections has yielded important insights into the transmission of lyric in the thirteenth century. The most significant result of these investigations was the demonstration that the collectors in the period around 1300 could draw on written sources, namely older song manuscripts no longer extant. The most important of these collections were AC, BC, and EC. (These inferred collections are designated by the abbreviations of the manuscripts for which they served as a source). In addition, a series of smaller collections can also be shown to have existed. For the chronology of transmission, this means that song collections already existed in Germany around the mid-thirteenth century. Incidentally, the oldest French chansonniers come from the same period. Brand new insights into the prehistory of the extant song manuscripts can be expected from an examination of the latest manuscript find: the Széchényi National Library in Budapest has acquired three pages of an illuminated song manuscript which is related to the Large Heidelberg Song Manuscript and which contains, among other verses, nine stanzas of von Kürenberg. (This information was provided to me by Dr. A. Vizkelety).

What the Small Heidelberg Song Manuscript reveals about its sources is particularly enlightening. Linguistic differences indicate that the collection was not cast in a single mold. The editor of A apparently used several written sources, which can be assigned to different types of lyric transmission:

One song collection of famous minnesingers. In the first part of A, which takes up almost half of the entire manuscript, we find four of the best-known poets with extensive collections of their songs: Reinmar der Alte (no. 1; he is followed, as nos. 2 and 3, by Reinmar der Fiedler and Reinmar der Junge, who were placed here probably because they have the same name), Walther von der Vogelweide (no. 4), Heinrich von Morungen (no. 5), and Der Truchseß von Singenberg (no. 6). The joining of the songs of Walther and Reinmar we have met before. All that A reveals is that there already existed in the second half of the thirteenth century a song book combining several collections of poets. The texts in this song book are of superior quality. The inclusion of Singenberg, who is represented with 118 stanzas, is unusual. Perhaps the Singenberg-corpus reflects the special interests of the patron who commissioned this collection.

Anonymous song books. These minne poets are followed in A by two anonymous song books under the names Niune (no. 8) and Gedrut (no. 9). A third book of this kind appears in no. 31 under the name Lutolt von Seven. We are apparently not dealing with collections of individual authors, since almost everything that appears in A under these three names is attributed to different names in other manuscripts. No less than fifty-five of the sixty stanzas listed under Niune can be distributed among thirteen different poets. Niune and Gedrut were probably not minnesingers, but the collectors or owners of song books. These song books combined the works of different authors, apparently without their names. The famous poets, such as Neidhart or Walther von der Vogelweide, are represented in the anonymous song books almost entirely with stanzas of doubtful authenticity. Other poets, such as Rubin von Rüdiger, Kunz von Rosenheim, or Geltar, to whom the songs listed in A under Gedrut are attributed in C, are entirely unknown quantities. We can deduce from this that the anonymous song books were filled largely with verses of unknown authorship, and that the poets who composed these verses were not infrequently imitating the style of well-known poets. It is unclear who had an interest in collecting and preserving such poetry. It has been suggested that Niune and Gedrut (a female name) were professional singers who traveled with this song repertoire.

Individual transmissions. The third part of A has twenty-two poets (nos. 13–34), all of whom—with the exception of Lutolt von Seven and his song book (no. 31)—are represented with just a few stanzas: Wolfram von Eschenbach with four stanzas, Albrecht von Johansdorf with six, Bruder Wernher with three, the burgrave von Regensburg with two, and so on. Even more striking is the fact that in this section of A, several names appear twice in similar forms: Heinrich der Riche (no. 14) and Heinrich von Rucche (no. 15), Rudolf von Rotenberc (no. 13) and Rudolf Offenburg (no.19), the Margraf von Hohenburc (no. 23) and the Margraf von Rotenburc (no. 29). Heinrich von Veldeke is also represented twice (nos. 22 and 24). In all likelihood these double names are derived from different sources. In the case of Heinrich von Veldeke this can be proved through a textual comparison. It would seem that the editor of A used two smaller collections in which several poets were represented with only a few stanzas each. The differences in the names are an indication that the older collections of lyric were beset by corruptions and uncertainties. What is remarkable, however, is that the collector of A did not attempt to reconcile the inconsistencies of his sources, but simply took what he found. This does have the advantage for the modern student that the various parts from which the A-collection was pieced together are still clearly visible, but as a document of lyric transmission, manuscript A, only the first part of which is well ordered, is a rather pitiful creation. It all fits in with the way in which additions were entered on the last sheets of the manuscript without the names of the authors.

Among the thirteenth-century song collections that can be inferred from extant manuscripts, one deserves special emphasis. Collection BC must have been not only one of the most extensive, but also one of the most careful and precious. It was characterized by its criterion of arrangement—according to the social rank of the poets—and by its rich pictorial decoration. In these respects manuscripts B and C followed their common source. In both, Kaiser Heinrich is listed at the beginning of the collection, followed by the counts and lords, while the poets without any noble title, like Gottfried von Straßburg and Frauenlob, can be found at the end. The idea of organizing the minnesingers by their social rank came to the editor of BC probably from France. Manuscript M, one of the most beautiful chansonniers of the thirteenth century (Paris, Bibl. Nationale, f. fr. 844), has the same arrangement. At the head are the prince of the Morea, the count of Anjou, the count of Bar, the duke of Brabant, and so on. They are followed by the lesser nobility, beginning with Gace Brulé and the Chastelain de Coucy. The rear is brought up by the poets of humble origin. It is unlikely that editors in France and Germany arrived at such an arrangement independently. The French manuscript is dated to between 1254 and 1270; the German collection BC could have been produced at about the same time or slightly later. Perhaps the hierarchic order was an expression of deference to the sponsor. The French manuscript may have been commissioned by Charles of Anjou (d. 1285), the brother of King Louis IX (d. 1270), or by some other member of the French royal house. We have no sure clues for BC. The fact that manuscripts B and C retained the hierarchic order of the poets indicates that it was not only royal patrons who considered such an arrangement appropriate. From this same French source the editor of BC may also have picked up the idea of decorating his song collection with portraits of the poets. In France we find several chansonniers with pictures of the authors, which were mostly integrated into the decoration of initials. But the German collector went beyond the French model in both format and pictorial program.

Oral and written aspects in the transmission of lyric   Central to our interest in the history of the spread of minnesong is the question of how the songs were passed on in the long period between their creation and the beginning of written transmission. In many instances the song texts, as they appear in the later collections, show corruptions. Sometimes different versions of a song have come down to us; quite often there are differences in the sequence or number of stanzas; not infrequently one

song is attributed to different poets; there are many songs that philological criticism does not consider the work of the poets to whom they are
attributed. No doubt a large part of this corruption is the product of
transmission. But it is also likely that there was not always a text that
was as clearly fixed in length and wording at the beginning of the lyric
transmission, as we must assume was the case for epic poems. A minnesinger may have recited the same song differently on different occasions.
In such a case we could no longer speak of a single original version, but
of several author's versions, which might have left their own mark on
the subsequent transmission of the song. For example, we have two
accompanying stanzas (tornadas) for the song *Ges de chantar no'm
pren talans* (no. 21) by the troubadour Bernart de Ventadorn, who
wrote in the second half of the twelfth century. The tornadas reveal that
the poet at one time dedicated his song to the English King Henry II,
and at another time sent it to his friends in Puy. Walther's song *Nemt,
frowe, disen kranz* (74.20) exists in three different versions, all of which
may have been intended by the poet himself; perhaps in this case several
original versions have survived. But it is unlikely that the majority of the
textual differences can be explained this way. We must reckon that
most changes occurred only after the fact. Apart from the typical mistakes that always appear when a text is repeatedly copied, we also find
among the changes traces of the kind of wear and tear common to oral
transmission.

The older scholarship worked with a model of minnesong transmission that is still today regarded as partly valid. According to this model,
the development went through three stages:

1. Loose pages. The songs were first written on loose pages of paper
or other writing material and were spread in this way.

2. Song booklets. At the second stage the pages with the songs of a
poet were collected and joined together to form a song booktlet.

3. Collections. Eventually the various songs booklets were combined into a large volume; such collections are extant in the surviving
song manuscripts.

This model was given a special accent in that the written versions of
stages one and two were attributed to the poets themselves, and that it
was further assumed that the poets arranged their songs into chronological order in the process of compiling the song booklets. These notions
have been most strongly challenged by the thesis that no written records

of any kind existed in the first phase of transmission, that the songs were at this stage spread exclusively in oral form, and that the writing down of individual songs and the compilation of collections of various kinds began at a later time, when people began to take a historical view of the achievement of the great poets of the period around 1200. Today the discussion moves between these two positions, whereby the willingness to assume the existence of early written records of lyric seems to be increasing once again.

First written records

Loose pages with single songs have not survived. But there is evidence, at least from France, that poets wrote down individual songs, or had them written down, and sent them in this form to their ladies or to friends and patrons. In Gontier de Soignies, who composed around 1200, we read in an accompanying stanza: "Gontier, who composed the words, was also the one who wrote them down. Thus this writing will be quickly brought to my lady. By God, I will have been born in a lucky hour if she reads my message."[68] In Bernart de Ventadorn: "She knows and understands writing, and I enjoy writing the words. If she so pleases, let her read them and make me happy by doing so."[69] Of the troubadour Peire Cardinal we are told in his *vida*: "He learned letters and could read and sing well."[70] Of Elias Cairel it was said: "He wrote words and melodies beautifully."[71] The writing down of single troubadour songs is also attested by an anonymous cobla with complicated rhymes, in which the author challenges a jongleur to compose a stanza with the same rhymes but different rhyming words: "I will give you a measure of rye if you can write on the paper I will line for you a cobla in which none of the rhyming words are repeated."[72]

In Germany, Ulrich von Liechtenstein is for this period the only witness for the written spread of minnesongs by a poet himself. Liechtenstein had most of his songs put into writing immediately and sent them to his lady (see p. 548). Both the text and the melody were written down: "In beautiful writing melody and words."[73] Whether Liechtenstein, in describing the written spread of his songs, was talking about a common practice cannot be verified. The idea that the poet sent a written version of his song to his lady through a messenger is apparently also reflected in the illustrations of the Large Heidelberg Song Manuscript. There we find several images depicting a minnesinger dispatching a messenger to his lady with a scroll for her. In the picture of Hartwig von Raute (see fig. 40), the messenger has taken hold of the scroll and is

Fig. 40.   Hartwig von Raute. The poet is dispatching a messenger who is holding an empty speech band. It is not clear why the messenger is being slapped.
From the Large Heidelberg Song Manuscript (Cpg 848). Fourteenth century.

already on his way. If the scroll contained the song of the poet, this
scenario would capture precisely the same situation that Ulrich von
Liechtenstein described.

We must not assume that the first written versions of minnesongs
were also put down on parchment. Expensive parchment was usually
used only when texts were meant to last and to be stored away. For
practical purposes there were other writing materials. Wax tablets, on
which the writing was done with a stylus, were very popular. They were
used for letters, accounts, and various kinds of notes. In noble lay society, wax tablets and styli were attributes primarily of women, who could
use them with greater skill than most men. When the royal princess
Lavinia refused to tell her mother the name of the man she secretly
loved, the queen ordered her to write the name: "She took her tablet
and golden stylus to write on it."[74] Lavinia probably carried these writing implements on her belt, in the manner often depicted in pictures. In
Hartmann's *Gregorius* (719 ff.) and in *Apollonius von Tyrland* (2079
ff.) it was also noble women who handled wax tablets and styli. In
Neidhart's songs even the peasant girls decorated themselves with them
(48.11). Excavations in Thuringian castles have unearthed large num-

bers of gaming dice and styli from the twelfth century. There is solid evidence that wax tablets were also used to record lyric poetry: "Stylus and tablets and Ovid's songs are the daily fare."[75] Before he broke the stylus he had used for ten years to write down his songs, Baudri de Bourgueil dedicated a lament to his writing instrument: "The great sorrow over the broken stylus"[76]; in another song he addressed his scribe Girardus, who transferred the poems from the wax tablets to parchment (no. 44). The use of wax tablets by German minnesingers is not attested. But the notion that courtly songs were written on tablets must have existed in the thirteenth century. Wax tablets also appear in the pictures of the Large Heidelberg Song Manuscript, as the attribute of the learned minnesinger (Der von Gliers) and as the instrument for recording the freshly composed text (Reinmar von Zweter). It is no surprise that not a trace has survived of this temporary form of writing.

Better attested than wax tablets for the recording of courtly lyric are scrolls. Compared to the codex, the scroll, made of strips of parchment sewn together, played a minor role in the Middle Ages. It was used primarily for texts of a documentary nature or in the form of registers: for account books, statutes and tariffs, necrologies, copies of charters, land registers, collections of legal decrees, and similar things. Literary texts were rarely written on scrolls, but if scrolls were used they were used especially for texts intended for stage performance rather than for reading. In addition to manuscripts in high format, the scroll is characteristic of the ecclesiastical plays that have been transmitted not as texts to be read but as stage books and performance manuals. Among the most interesting discoveries of recent years is that courtly lyric, too, was written on scrolls. Three fragments of scrolls, all of which may still belong to the thirteenth century, are now known:

— the Basel fragments (Universitätsbibl. F. IV. 12) with *Sprüche* by Konrad von Würzburg, Der Marner, and Der Kanzler;

— the Los Angeles fragments (University of California, Research Library, 170/575) with *Sprüche* by Reinmar von Zweter;

— the Berlin fragments (Geheimes Staatsarchiv, Stiftung Preußischer Kulturbesitz XX. HA. StA. Königsberg, MS. 33, 11) with *Spruch* verses from the *Wartburgkrieg*.

Franz H. Bäuml and Richard H. Rouse, the discoverers of the Los Angeles scroll, have argued that the entire transmission of lyric in Germany occurred through a first phase of writing in scrolls, but this thesis

Fig. 41. Reinmar von Zweter. The poet's eyes are closed; apparently he is dictating to the two young ladies. One is writing in a scroll, the other on wax tablets. From the Large Heidelberg Song Mansucript (Cpg 848). Fourteenth century.

will hardly stand the test. It is true, though, that scrolls were more important for the transmission of lyric than used to be believed. It is hardly coincidental that the three extant scrolls all preserve *Spruchdichtung*. If we can also extend to lyric the observation that texts written on scrolls were intended primarily for performance, we could infer from this type of transmission that the literary character of *Spruchdichtung*, which was still largely in the hands of wandering professional singers, was not yet very highly developed in the thirteenth century. In view of the new scroll discoveries, some of the portraits in the Large Heidelberg Song Manuscript also take on new meaning: Bligger von Steinach is dictating to a scribe who is writing on an open scroll; and Reinmar von Zweter is surrounded by two young ladies, one of whom is writing on a wax tablet and the other on a scroll (see fig. 41).

The use of wax tablets and scrolls shows that a model of transmission based on loose pages and song books as the first stages of written lyric does not do justice to the variety of written forms at this time. Precisely the temporary forms of writing, which were intended for use rather than preservation, must have played a large role in the first phase of putting lyric down in writing.

Song collections

The first minnesinger who is known to have collected his own songs and to have them written down is Ulrich von Liechtenstein. Inconsistencies in the numbering of the songs indicate that Liechtenstein, in composing his *Frauendienst*, could draw on an already extant collection of his songs. This source for *Frauendienst*, which was probably compiled before or around 1250, is the oldest known collection of an author's work in Germany. Liechtenstein tells us that he cited his songs in chronological order, but there are doubts concerning the validity of the chronological sequence. It is entirely possible that the poet introduced the chronological arrangement only later through the romance-like embellishment of his fictional autobiography. The arrangement of poems in the chronological order of their composition has probably at all times suggested itself more readily to philologists than to poets. The troubadour Peire Vidal is said to have collected sixteen of his songs in chronological sequence shortly after 1200. The first concretely attested song collection of a troubadour is much younger. In the Provençal song manuscript C (Paris, Bibliothéque Nationale, f. fr. 856) from the end of the thirteenth century, the songs of the troubadour Guiraut Riquier, who worked in the second half of the thirteenth century, are introduced with this comment: "Here begin the songs of Lord Guiraut Riquier of Narbonne, namely chansons, verses, pastourelles, retrouenges, descorts, albas, and various others, in the same sequence as he ordered them in his book; they are all transferred here from his book, which he wrote in his own hand."[77] Romance scholars assume that Guiraut Riquier, too, put his songs into a chronological order.

For Germany, a second chronologically arranged collection is believed to have existed around 1250. The Reinmar von Zweter collection in manuscript D from the end of the thirteenth century is very carefully organized according to thematic groups: God and Mary (stanzas 1–22), minne (23–55), teachings for lords (56–70), virtues and vices (71–124), political *Sprüche* (125–157). Gustav Roethe has discovered that in the last section all of Reinmar's datable poems from the years 1227–1240 are listed in chronological order. This has lead him to argue, first, that the collection was compiled by the poet himself, since only he could have known the sequence of the *Sprüche* so well; and second, that the collection was produced in 1240/41, since Reinmar's *Sprüche* dated after 1240 were not included. These theses have been widely accepted. We should consider, however, that the chronological sequence of Reinmar's political *Sprüche* is a good deal less certain than Roethe believed he could establish, and that the division into *Sprüche* before 1240 and after 1240 is very closely tied in with Roethe's reconstructed biography of the poet, for which we have very few concrete clues. But if the chronology of the *Sprüche* is problematic, then the argument that only the poet himself could have known the precise sequence no longer holds. In which case the entire collection could have been produced at a later time.

At the end of *Frauendienst*, Ulrich von Liechtenstein took stock of his songs: "Fifty-eight songs I have sung, they are listed here in their entirety."[78] A similar tallying is found in Neidhart's *weltsüeze*-song (Winterlied 28), which is probably among his later songs: "Eighty new songs that I have sung over a long period in the service of my lady and in her praise now accompany me free of their purpose [after Neidhart had withdrawn from service to his lady]. This is now the last song I want to sing."[79] Did Neidhart also count and collect his songs? The editions of Neidhart list seventy-seven "genuine" songs, a number that could be right. But the cited verses appear only in a manuscript of the fifteenth century and may not even be from the pen of Neidhart himself. The notion that every lyric poet normally collected his own songs is without basis as a general statement.

The songs of the poets could be compiled in a number of different ways. A chronological sequence may exist for the songs of Ulrich von Liechtenstein. A thematic arrangement is attested by the Zweter collection in manuscript D and by the Walther collection in the Heiligenstadt fragments. In other collections we can detect only hints at a division according to thematic criteria. Some collections were organized by genres. It appears that minnesong and *Spruch* poetry were transmitted separately. A mixing of these two genres, as in the Large Heidelberg Song Manuscript, is rare. Within minne lyric, Liechtenstein, in the titles of his songs in *Frauendienst*, attests a division according to genres and manner of performance (see p. 549). In addition there were also completely different possibilities for organizing the songs. Hermann Schneider has shown that the songs in the reconstructed collection BC were oftentimes arranged in such a way that the beginning of one song picked up where the previous song ended, be it through the assonance of a word or a rhyme, or through the continuation of a thought. Whether such an artistic interlinking was also used in other collections is controversial. We are still far from a full understanding of the arrangement of the songs in the great collections.

For most collectors the names of the poets were of great importance. The author's name appears either as the title in front of a poet's collected works or in front of every song, as in the Walther-Reinmar collection in manuscript E or in some of the Neidhart collections. As a rule the collectors must have taken the names from their written sources. But where did the names in those sources come from? Some have seen in the authors' names evidence that there existed a written tradition stretching from the poets to the later collections. In any case, the attribution could not have been made if there was a preceding phase of anonymous transmission. The many cases of erroneous attributions or multiple attributions show that the connection of a song to a name was subject to a variety of interruptions and corruptions. But it must be noted that even these interferences followed certain rules. For example, in the case of a song's attribution to two different poets, there are fixed pairs of Dietmar von Aist and Heinrich von Veldeke, Heinrich von Rugge and Reinmar der Alte, Reinmar der Alte and Walther von der Vogelweide. It would seem that in these cases the collected works of the poets came into contact early on and got somewhat mixed up. A different source of false attributions was the anonymous songbooks of the kind that appear in manuscript A under the names Niune and Gedrut.

That the names of the minnesingers were already known early on is attested by the catalogs of poets in the literature of the thirteenth century. These lists of poets have been interpreted as evidence for the existence of comprehensive song collections. But the oldest such list, in Heinrich von dem Türlin's *Krone*, does not square with such an interpretation. We read there after great praise of Hartmann von Aue and Reinmar der Alte: "I must also lament the noble Dietmar von Aist and the others, who were their foundation and support: Heinrich von Rugge and Freidrich von Hausen, Ulrich von Gutenburg and the noble Hug von Salza."[80] *Krone* cannot be dated precisely, but it is unlikely to have been written after 1230. It is very unlikely that at this time there already existed a song collection which would have had to be as large as the collection BC. Heinrich von dem Türlin could also have gotten the names from oral transmission.

The transmission of melodies

The transmission of German lyric in the thirteenth century is for the most part a pure transmission of texts. Apart from the melodies in the *Carmina Burana*, we know of only one other manuscript from this time which contains notation: a precious fragment, which has unfortunately disappeared, contained the melody for the fourth lay of Ulrich von Win-

terstetten, nicely written in neumes on a five-line system. We don't know
why the music was normally left out. We have to take into consideration that the copying of melodies required a good deal more work and
that changes in the notational system in the thirteenth century made it
more difficult to do so. Perhaps we must also reckon with the possibility
that the melodies were left out because it was assumed they were
known. In any case, the absence of melodies should not lead us to infer
in every case that the collectors were only interested in the texts. The
German transmission shows a striking difference in this respect to its
French counterpart. The French chansonniers of the thirteenth century
have an extraordinarily rich musical offering, containing more than a
thousand melodies. But there were also differences within France: the
southern French song collections of the thirteenth century, like the German ones, almost all lack notation. The troubadour melodies that we
know come either from northern French transmission or from two song
collections of the fourteenth century, the Milan manuscript G and the
Paris manuscript R. In Germany, too, we have more melodies from the
fourteenth century than from the thirteenth. This distribution shows
that it would be wrong to divide the history of lyric transmission into an
early performance tradition and a later text tradition. Surely Neidhart's
songs were still sung in the fourteenth and fifteenth centuries. But we
hardly dare ask about the authenticity of the later melodies.

In a few cases it is certain that the copyists who wrote down the
songs were no longer thinking of the recitation or performance of the
songs. In the Würzburg Walther-Reinmar collection (E), the rhyming
links have been broken up in such a way that the texts can no longer be
read out loud or sung. In France we even find collections that contained
only selections from troubadour songs: general aphorisms and weighty
maxims were detached from the song context. Here the didactic interest
in the texts must have been the major motivation.

Oral circulation

Naturally we know much less about the spread of the songs through
oral transmission. Whenever we hear that the ladies and lords of noble
society sang songs in a friendly gathering, or when professional singers
performed them at the court feasts, written versions are never mentioned. But singing from sheet music does not seem to have been entirely unknown, as we can see from statements by Ulrich von Liechtenstein
and the troubadours. In many cases one must have learned the songs by
heart while listening to them. Garin le Brun (second half of the twelfth

century) talks about this in his teachings for noble girls: "If you are with people who like to sing you should be joyful. If new verses and songs are performed in your presence, listen carefully, and it should give you pleasure to learn them by heart in sequence, if you can retain them in your memory. If you can't retain everything, remember only the most beautiful passages."[81]

How extensive this knowledge of lyric was and what use was made of it can be seen in the French epics with lyric interludes. Jean Renart was apparently the first to insert lyric pieces into an epic context. In the prologue to his *Roman de la rose ou de Guillaume de Dole*, which was probably written around 1227/28, the poet called attention to this innovation: "he has had beautiful songs copied down so that one might remember the poems."[82] In this way one could "sing or read from it, whatever one preferred."[83] Jean Renart's innovation was very popular. A few years later Gerbert de Montreuil adopted the technique of lyric interludes in his *Roman de la violette*; and in the course of the thirteenth century a whole series of other French texts were composed in this way: *Cléomades* by Adenet le Roi, the *Roman du châtelain de Coucy* by Jakemes, the anonymous *Châtelain de Saint Gille*, *Le tournou de Chauvency* by Jacques Bretel, the *Lai d'Aristote* by Henry d'Andeli, and others. These tales convey the impression that lyric and singing played a large role in the life of noble society. The ladies and lords apparently knew many songs by heart. The emperor himself joined in the singing, the princes and the high ladies sang, as did the pages and girls, the minstrels and the jongleurs. One sang alone or in pairs or in a choir; one sang after the meal at convivial gatherings, one sang to honor guests, one sang while out for a walk, while riding, and while dancing; noble ladies sang while doing their needlework; one sang when one was happy and when one was sad. Very popular in French society were the anonymous songs and refrains that have come down to us in large numbers: girls' songs (*cantigas de amigo*), pastourelles and romances, *chansons de toile*, *chansons d'histoire*, *chansons de femme*, *chansons de mal-mariée*, and the various kinds of dancing lyric. But people also sang the songs or individual stanzas from the songs of the well-known troubadours and trouvères. *Guillaume de Dole* has altogether forty-six lyric pieces, sixteen of which come from courtly songs. For the most part only the first stanza of a song was quoted, sometimes several stanzas, and it could also happen that a stanza was taken from the middle of a song. The selections attest that among the French trouvères the poets Gace Brulé and the Châtelain de Coucy were especially popular. Jean

Renart usually chose the lyric interludes in such a way that they fit very well into the narrative context of the story. For example, after Emperor Conrad received (false) word that his lover had gotten involved with another man, he sang a stanza from Gace Brulé, which declares it a thing "of great folly to make inquiries about a woman or friend, as long as one wants to love her."[84] In his grief the emperor also sang two stanzas from a lover's lament of Renaut de Sabloeil "in order to soothe his pain."[85] But once the suspicion against the beautiful Lienor was proved to be unfounded, and the court was once again full of joy, a knight sang the first stanzas of Bernart de Ventadour's famous lark song: "When I see the lark flying up towards the sun with joy . . ."[86] Sometimes the connection between the song text and the action in the epic is looser. One morning the emperor stood at the window and was thinking of his far-away lover, whom he had never seen in person, and he sang the first stanza of a crusading song by the Châtelain de Coucy. In it the poet expressed the desire "that I might hold her, to whom my heart and thoughts belong, naked in my arms before I set out for the Holy Land."[87] There is no proof that noble society in France did in fact know and sing so many songs. But the poets would hardly have recounted the singing of the songs of trouvères and troubadours on many different occasions if this had never actually happened. In this respect these texts have some value as evidence for lyric practice.

None of the French works with lyric interludes were translated into German. The reason for this is surely not to be sought in any reservations about this new style. Rather, it has to do with the changed literary situation in the thirteenth century: French works composed after 1220 did not extend their influence into Germany. But the German poets, too, recounted the occasions when noble society sang songs. When Erec rode into Brandigan, where a difficult adventure awaited him, "he was completely carefree. He rode towards the people and greeted them with a laugh. And he began to sing a happy song."[88] That people sang while walking and riding is attested by Ulrich von Liechtenstein: some of his songs were sung as traveling songs (see p. 548). When Liechtenstein arrived in Möllersdorf near Vienna during his Venus tour in 1227, his page handed over to him a message from his lady: "He rose before me courteously and presently sang a song. With it he informed me that he was bringing a message that made me happy. The song which the courtly and bright page sang penetrated into my heart and made me feel good inside, because it gave me joy. . . . Now hear the stanza; it went like this: 'You shall offer me a welcome, for it is I who brings

you news . . ."[89] What the page sang was the first stanza from the
"Preislied" of Walther von der Vogelweide (56.14). The song was
apparently so well known around the middle of the thirteenth century
that there was no need to mention the poet's name. Perhaps we may
infer from this that in Germany, too, the songs of the minnesingers were
sung more often than the written evidence would suggest.

Notes

INTRODUCTION: FICTION AND REALITY

1. . . . in Liguriam irruit, agros inflammat, vastat, vineas demolitur, ficus exterminat omnesque fructiferas arbores aut succidi aut decortari precepit totamque regionem depopulatur (*Gesta Frederici*, p. 594).

2. Vidimus enim otpima quaeque diripi, viculos nostros succendi, rapinis nos exponi, equos et iumenta nostra depopulari, et domos nostras absque habitatore relinqui (*Annales*, p. 214).

3. quendam lese maiestatis convictum pelle exutum decoriavit, quendam vero regno aspirantem coronari coronamque per timpora clavis ferreis transfigi precepit, quosdam stipiti alligatos piraque circumdatos exurens crudeliter extinxit, quosdam vecte perforatos ventretenus humo agglutinavit (*Chronica*, p. 61).

4. que quasi cottidie fiebant infra familiam sancti Petri (Weinrich, p. 100).

5. Sic mortuo imperatore mortua est simul iusticia et pax imperii (Gerlach von Mühlhausen, p. 709).

6. totus orbis in morte ipsius conturbatus fuit, qui multa mala et gwerre surrexerunt, quae postea longo tempore duraverunt (*Annales Marbacenses*, p. 70).

7. tamquam lupi rapaces (*Chronica regia Coloniensis*, p. 160).

8. per campos et vicos gregatim mortui fame inveniebantur (*Annales Marbacenses*, p. 71).

9. Pauperes per plateas iacebant et moriebantur (*Annales Reineri*, p. 652).

10. diversas calamitates et miserias superventuras universo Romano imperio denunciat (*Chronica regia Coloniensis*, p. 159).

11. VI ciphi cum copertoriis argentei et V craterę argentee sine copertoriis, tria peccaria argentea cum opertoriis et IIII sine opertorio . . . et coclearia duo argentea; . . . XV loricas, etiam octo ocreas ferreas . . . Sexaginta hastilia, id est spîzze, quatuor galeę, sex tubę, viginti federpete, tria wurfzâbel, tria scâhzâbel, elefantei lapides tam ad wurfzâbel quam scahzabel pertinentes (p. 67).

12. mitten in ir palas ein scône tier geworht was, daz was alliz golt rôt, alse siz selbe gebôt. daz tier was vil hêrlîch eineme hirze gelîch. an sîn houbit vorne hattiz dûsint horne. ûf allir horne gelîch stunt ein fugil hêrlîch. ûf dem tiere saz ein man scône unde wol getân, der fûrte zwêne hunde unde ein horn ze sînen munde. nidene an dem gewelbe lâgen viere und zwênzich blâsebelge. zaller belge gelîch gingen zwelif man crêftich. sô si di belge drungen, di fugele scône sungen an deme tiere vorn, sô blies ouh der man sîn horn, sô galpeden ouh di hunde. ouh lûtte an der stunden daz hêrlîche tier mit der stimmen als ein pantier (6001–26).

13. uz balgen gie dar in ein wint, daz ieglich vogel sanc in siner wise (392.4).

14. Aerea, sed deaurata quaedam arbor ante imperatoris sedile stabat, cuius ramos itidem aeraee diversi generis deaurataeque aves replebant, quae secundum species suas diversarum avium voces emittebant. Imperatoris vero solium huiusmodi erat arte compositum, ut in momento humile, exelsius modo, quam mox videretur sublime, quod inmensae magnitudinis, incertum utrum aerei an lignei, verum auro tecti leones quasi custodiebant, qui cauda terram percutientes aperto ore linguisque mobilibus rugitum emittebant (*Antapodosis*, p. 488).

15. diu tassel, dâ diu solten sîn, dâ was ein kleinez snuorlîn von wîzen berlîn în getragen. dâ hete diu schoene în geslagen ir dûmen vor ir linken hant. die rehten hete sî gewant hin nider baz, ir wizzet wol, dâ man den mantel sliezen sol, und slôz in höfschlîche inein mit ir vingeren zwein (10939–48).

16. der zadel fuogte in hungers nôt. sine heten kaese, vleisch noch prôt, si liezen zenstüren sîn, und smalzten ouch deheinen wîn mit ir munde, sô si trunken (*Parzival* 184. 7–11).

17. Ir sült die zende stüren niht mit mezzern (117–118).

18. E daz ir trinkt, so wischt den munt, daz ir besmalzet niht den tranc (93–94).

19. des wart der küene Iweret geslagen durch sîn barbel, daz der degen alsô snel bluoten begunde zer nasen und zem munde durch die vintâlen nider (4528–33).

20. mich jâmert waerlîchen, und hulfez iht, ich woldez clagen, daz nû bî unseren tagen selch vreude niemer werden mac der man ze den zîten pflac (*Iwein* 48–52).

21. diu werlt sich verkêret hât; ir vreude jaemerlîche stât; diu reht sint gevloehet; ir gewalt der is gehoehet; diu triuwe ist verschertet; untriuwe mit nîde hertet. diu zît hât sich verwandelt gar; ie lanc lenger boesent diu jâr (*Wigalois* 10259–66).

22. Dô man der rehten minne pflac, dô pflac man ouch der êren. nu mac man naht unde tac die boesen site lêren. Swer diz nu siht und jenez dô sach, owê, waz der nu klagen mac! tugende welnt sich nû verkêren (61.18–24).

23. Hie vor dô was diu welt sô schoene, nû ist si worden alsô hoene (23, 32–33).

24. Wâ von mac man niht vinden hiute alsô tugenthafte liute alsô man hie bevor vant? (6281–83).

25. dâ von daz wir haben niht Artûs inder imme lant (6328–29).

26. mais li prince sont si destroit, et dur, et vilain, et fellon (La bible 234–35).

27. as festes firent honor de biau despendre, et de doner, et de riche vie mener (252–54).

28. Bien sont perdu li biau repaire, li grant pallais dont je sospir, qui furent fait por cort tenir! (248–50).

29. Bî den alten zîten was daz ein ieglîch kint las: dô wâren gar diu edeln kint gelêrt, des si nu niht ensint. dô stuont ouch diu werit baz âne nît und âne haz (9197–9202).

CHAPTER 1: NOBLE SOCIETY OF THE HIGH MIDDLE AGES

1. BASIC CONCEPTS OF THE SOCIAL ORDER

1. Nieman ist so here so daz reht zware. wan got ist ze ware ein rehtir rihtaere (*Vom Rechte* 1–4).

2. Got ist selve recht, dar umme is em recht lef (p. 51 f.).

3. Dit recht hebbe ek selve nicht irdacht, it hebbet van aldere an unsik gebracht Unse guden vorevaren (151–53).

4. wan daz si habent einen sin: si dûhten sich ze nihte, si enschüefen starc gerihte. si kiesent künege unde reht, si setzent hêrren unde kneht (9.3–7).

5. Daz reht ist über al an allen dingen mâze, wâge, zal. ân reht mac niemen genesen (Thomasin v. Zirklaere 12375–77).

6. "Verfluocht si Chanaân Unde allez sîn geslehte Sol diener und eigen knehte Mîner zweier süne sin!" Nu merket, lieben friunde mîn: Alsus sint edel liute kumen Unde eigen (H. v. Trimberg 1376–82).

7. nicht in hat vns di natura bescheiden me denne den vihe an der weiden. si gab vns alle dinc gemeine. do begreif sumelich al eine, dez manic leben muchte (W. von Elmendorf 251–55).

8. Na rechter warheit so hevet egenscap begin van dwange unde van venknisse unde van unrechter gewalt, de men van aldere in unrechte gewonheit getogen hevet unde nu vor recht hebben wel (*Landrecht* III 42.6).

9. meliorum et maiorum terre consensus (MGH Const. 2, p. 420).

10. Got hât driu leben geschaffen: gebûre, ritter unde pfaffen (Freidank 27. 1–2).

11. Triplex ergo Dei domus est quae creditur una. Nunc orant, alii pugnant aliique laborant (Adalbero of Laon, *Carmen ad Robertum regem* 295–96).

12. Preterea tres janque status nostri statuerunt Philosophi veteres; nam clerum preposuerunt, Ut reliquos regeret, documentis. Inde locatur Armatus miles ut rem publicam tueatur; Istis agricole subsunt alii laicique, Quorum nanque labor victum largitur utrique (5071–76).

13. In driu geteilet waren von erste die liute, al ich las: buman, ritter und pfaffen. ieslich nach siner maze was gelich an adel und an art dem andern ie (VII, 22. 1–6).

14. unusquisque autem in suo ordine (I Corinthians 15.23).

15. die frigen . . . die ritere . . . die eigin lúte (p. 8, 14–15).

16. vürsten ritter knehte (R. von Ems, *Alexander* 19566).

17. grâven, vrîen, dienestman (R. v. Ems, *Guter Gerhard* 3415).

18. Die êrsten drîer leie liute daz sint die hoehsten unde die hêrsten, die der almehtige got selbe dar zuo erwelt unde geordent hât, daz in die andern siben alle undertaenic wesen suln und in dienen suln (vol. I, p. 142).

19. werltlîche rihter, herren und ritter, die dâ witwen unde weisen schirmen sullent (ibid.).

20. und alle werltlîche herre, die ritter unde herren sint, und alle die, den unser herre ûf ertrîche gerihte unde gewalt geben unde bevolhen hât (p. 144).

21. alle die gewant wirkent (p. 146).

22. alle die mit îsenînen wâfen arbeitent unde wirkent (p. 147).

23. alle die mit kouf umbe gênt (p. 148).

24. alle die dâ ezzen unde trinken veil habent (p. 150).

25. alle die daz ertrîche bûwent (p. 151).

26. alle die mit erzenîe umbe gênt (p. 153).

27. Daz sint die gumpelliute, gîger unde tambûrer, swie die geheizen sîn, alle die guot für êre nement (p. 155).

2. THE HIERARCHICAL STRUCTURE OF SOCIETY

1. Diu krône ist elter danne der künec Philippes sî (18.29).

2. Prima ministerialis, que etiam militaris directa dicitur (*Chronicon Ebersheimense*, p. 433).

3. adeo nobilis et bellicosa, ut nimirum libere condicioni comparetur (ibid.).

4. Secunda vero, censualis et obediens (ibid.).

5. que servilis et censualis dicitur (ibid.).

6. Nu net latet uch nicht wunderen, dat dit buk so luttel seget van denstlude rechte; went it is so manichvolt, dat is neman to ende komen ne kan. Under iewelkeme biscope unde abbede unde ebbedischen hebben de denstlude sunderlik recht (*Landrecht* III 42.2).

7. venator (Weinrich, p. 122).

8. se ipsos in proprietatem ip(sius) ecclesie ad ius ministerialium tradere... de infimo ordine videlicet de litis aut de censuariis facere ministeriales abbas potestatem habeat (MGH Dipl. K III, no. 181, p. 327 f.).

9. infimos homines et nullis maioribus ortos summis honoribus extulisset et eis noctes perinde ac dies in deliberationibus insumens, ultimum, si possit, nobilitati exterminium machinaretur (Lampert of Hersfeld, *Annales*, p. 384 f.).

10. Adeo sunt inter se sacramento coniuncti, quod nisi factam concederet coniurationem, denegarent universi introitum Cameraci reversuro pontifici (*Gesta episcoporum Cameracensium. Continuatio*, p. 498).

11. niemen wart sô tiuwer, sîn hôchvart waere kleine wan durch daz bû aleine (*Helmbrecht* 558–60).

3. THE ECONOMY

1. ad communes utilitates efficere (*Monumenta Boica*, vol. 28.2, no. 13, p. 221).

2. saluti totius (p)atri(e) utili(ter provide)tur (MGH Dipl. F I, vol. 2, no. 496, p. 422).

3. cum generalis utilitas... procuretur (*Lübeckisches UB*, vol. 1, no. 76, p. 83).

4. Post natale sancte Marie unusquisque comes septem boni testimonii viros sibi eligat et de qualibet provincia sagaciter disponat et, quanto pretio secundum qualitatem temporis annona sit vendenda, utiliter provideat (Weinrich, p. 220).

5. Regalia sunt hec:... vie publice, flumina navigabilia,... portus, ripatica, vectigalia, que vulgo dicuntur tholonea, monete, mulctarum penarumque compendia, bona vacantia... angariarum et parangariarum et plaustrorum et navium prestationes, et extraordinaria colllatio ad felicissimam regalis numinis expeditionem, potestas constituendorum magistratuum ad iustitiam expediendam, argentarie, et palatia in civitatibus consuetis, piscationum redditus et salinarum... (Weinrich, p. 246 f.).

6. XXX milia talentorum plus minusve redditibus publicis per singulos annos accessere (*Gesta Frederici*, p. 522).

7. pecunia infinita a rege Anglorum (*Continuatio Admuntensis*, p. 588).

8. novem milia marcarum (*Chronica regia Coloniensis*, p. 218).

9. her gaph im wol achte dhusent marc, daz her im svor hulde sicherliche zo helfene truweliche (*Braunschweigische Reimchronik* 5021–23).

10. Unus est dux Saxonie et hic habet duo milia marcarum in redditibus; unus palatinus, id est dux Bavarie, et hic habet viginti milia marcarum in redditibus, quinque milia de palatio et quindecim de ducatu; unus marchio Brandiburgensis, et hic habet quinquaginta milia marcarum; unus rex Boemie, et hic habet marcarum centum milia probatarum (*Descriptio Theutoniae*, p. 238).

4. THE KNIGHT AND KNIGHTHOOD

1. princeps exercitus (*Genesis* 39.1).
2. magister militum (*Genesis* 37.36).
3. si uerchöften in sâr einem riter putifar (77.7).
4. eineme herren hiez Putifâr (*Wiener Genesis* 3676).
5. einem fursten putifar (77.5).
6. Die trogin ritarlich gewant (*König Rother* 1824).
7. wol gewassen unde smal und rîterlîch ubir al, scône under den ougen (*Straßburger Alexander* 6047–49).
8. der allertiureste man, der rîters namen ie gewan (H. von Aue, *Iwein* 1455–56).
9. Karl ist selbe ein gût knecht (*Rolandslied* 2259).
10. de genere militari (1244), de militari stirpe (1252), de militari prosapia (1254) (Fleckenstein, p. 269).
11. ritter und chnappen von dem lande ze Osterrich (Schwind-Dopsch, no. 63, p. 125).

5. THE COURT

1. Mille porcos et oves, 10 carradas vini, 10 cervisie, frumenti maltra mille, boves 8 preter pullos et porcellos, pisces, ova, legumina aliaque quam plura

(*Annalista Saxo*, p. 622).

2. clericorumque atque militum multitudinem tantam, quod omnibus qui videbant ammirationem faciebat (*Gesta Alberonis*, p. 604).

3. cum 40 navibus cameratis, exceptis liburnis et honerariis atque coquinariis ratibus (ibid.).

4. quingentos adduxit milites, et triginta vini carratas et immensam copiam victualium secum advexit, carris fere opinione infinitis (p. 586).

5. Perpendit enim, plus conferre ad victoriam atque ad accendendos animos virorum vini copiam et aliorum victualium quam multa milia famelicorum (ibid.).

6. exceptis clericis et cuiuscumque conditionis hominibus (p. 156).

7. juxta veram estimationem (ibid.).

8. manic hovesc frowe (4351).

9. swer rehte wirt innen frumer wîbe minne, ist er siech, er wirt gesunt, ist er alt, er wirt junc. die frowen machent in genuoge hovesc unde kuone (4609–14).

10. Vnde ir warh mit sinir houisheit Daz die magit lossam. Ir uater inran (3776–78).

11. unkûsce er sich underwant er rait hovescen in diu lant, er hônde di edelen frouwen (16554–56).

12. Swer ze hove wil wol begârn, der sol sich deheime bewarn daz er nien tuo unhüfschlîchen, wan ir sult wizzen sicherlîchen daz beidiu zuht unt hüfscheit koment von der gewonheit (T. v. Zirklaere 653–58).

13. Vernemet scône hovescheit umbe ein pharît das si reit (H. v. Veldeke, *Eneit* 148.15–16).

14. er stach in zuo der erde tôt, als ez der hövesche got gebôt (*Erec* 5516–17).

CHAPTER II: THE ADOPTION OF FRENCH ARISTOCRATIC CULTURE IN GERMANY

1. SOCIETY

1. vicus Allemannorum (Bourquelot, p. 199).

2. Domus Allemannorum (ibid., p. 200 n. 1).

3. de domo sua Londonensi (*Hansisches UB* 1, no. 14, p. 8).

4. de regno Baldevvini (Laufner, p. 106).

5. pannos lineos vel laneos (*Hansisches UB* 3, no. 601, p. 386).

6. in Saxoniam (ibid., p. 387).

7. de Goslaria (*Hansisches UB* 1, no. 61, p. 32).

8. tanta erat copia piperis et aromatum, ut modiis ea et acervis maximis dividerent (Arnold of Lübeck, *Chronica*, p. 218).

9. magnam pacem Flandrensibus per terram imperatoris eundi ac redeundi (*Annales Blandinienses*, p. 29).

10. habebunt ascensum et descensum in Reno et in aliis aquis sive terris in imperio nostro (*Hansisches UB* 1, no. 23, p. 14 f.).

11. quatuor fora mercatoribus Flandriae (p. 14).

12. de Masthrihet et dexteris partibus (*Regensburger UB* 1, no. 43, p. 13).

13. dimidium fertonem argenti, libram piperis, duos calceos et cyrotecas (ibid.).

14. ad quantitatem pannorum, qui de Colonia ligati veniunt (*UB zur Geschichte der Babenberger* 1, no. 86, p. 118).

15. ad instantiam Ratisponensium (*Regensburger UB* 1, no. 43, p. 12).

16. es campanarum (*UB zur Geschichte der Babenberger* 1, no. 86, p. 118).

17. Ciues de Ache (Rauch, vol. 2, p. 106).

18. chaligas. almvcia uel alia chleinodia (p. 106).

19. pailles de Costentinoble v de Renesburgh (Bateson, p. 499).

20. Statutum est ut nullus scarlatas, aut barracanos, vel pretiosos burellos, qui Ratisboni, hoc est apud Rainesbors fiunt, sive picta quolibet modo stramina habeat (*Statuta congregationis Cluniacensis*, col. 1031).

21. commertia tuta (Rahewin, *Gesta Frederici*, p. 406).

22. ex petitione dilecti nostri Philippi comitis Flandriae (*Hansisches UB* 1, no. 23, p. 14).

23. ad instanciam nobilis viri A(lberti) ducis (de) Bruneswyk (*Hansisches UB* 1, no. 633, p. 219).

24. v pailles de Costentinoble v de Renesburgh v cheinsil v walebrun de Maence (Bateson, p. 499; the charter has survived only in a French translation).

25. accipitres (Laufner, p. 107).

26. Ze Vlander er hâte nâch rôtem scharlâte einen karrich gesant (*M. von. Craûn* 657–59).

27. zendal, siden und scharlat und aller hande riche wat (*Die Treueprobe* 260–61)

28. uf den jarmarkt ze Pruvis (256).

29. ane einer gemeiner straten van Engellant te Ungeren vore Colne ende vore Tungeren, ende also gelike van Sassen te Vrancrike, ende bit schepe, di des plegen, te Denemarken ende te Norwegen. die wege si samenen sich al da (972–79).

30. ANNO MILLENO CENTENO SEPTUAGENO / NEC NON UNDENO GWERNHERUS CORDE SERENO / SEXTUS PREPOSITUS TIBI VIRGO MARIA DICAVIT / QUOD NICOLAUS OPUS VIRDUNENSIS FABRICAVIT (Röhrig, p. 16).

31. qui quoniam domi, no iuxta Renum seu in Gallia doctus erat (*Anonymus Haserensis*, p. 261).

32. Ad quem audiendum cum multi nostratum confluant (p. 2).

33. etiam in nostris prouinciis (ibid.).

34. cum aliis quindecem qui secum venerant electissimis clericis (*Continuatio Claustroneoburgensis* I, p. 610 f.).

35. omnes in diversas dignitates promoti sunt (p. 611).

36. Teutonicus igitur in bella cohortibus itur (503).

37. Quo audito, factus est concursus clericorum Teutonichorum; et intrantes tabernam vulneraverunt hospitem domus (*Chronica*, vol. 4, p. 120).

38. fecit insultum in hospitium clericorum Teutonichorum (ibid.).

39. Accidit autem, cum in scolis esset Parisius, ut, contencione inter

burgenses et clericos orta, servientes ipsius ad auxilium clericorum ab eo missi homicidium committerent, pro qua de re sua promocione desperans, clericatum dicitur reiecisse (*Chronicon Montis sereni*, p. 204 f.).

40. Theutonicos furibundos, et in conuiuiis suis obscenos dicebant (Rashdall, vol. 3, p. 440).

41. In una autem et eadem domo schole erant superius, prostibula inferius. In parte superiori magistri legebant, in inferiori meretrices officia turpitudinis exercebant (ibid.).

42. Ecce quaerunt clerici Parisius artes liberales, Aurelianis auctores, Bononiae codices, Salerni pyxides, Toleti daemones, et nusquam mores. Nam de moribus non dico vltima, sed nulla fit quaestio. Vbique quaeritur scientia, et nusquam vita, sine qua non solum nihil prodest, sed et nihil est scientia (*Sermones*, p. 257).

43. Sunt enim Parisius omnia valde cara venalia, et tanta est ibi studiosorum copia, quod summa difficultate possunt reperiri hospitia (Pez, vol. 6, part 1, col. 427).

44. H. scolaris parysiensis (Rockinger, vol. 1, p. 372).

45. Hospitia in Gallia nunc me vocant studia (Werner, p. 134 f., numeration after Langosch, 1, 1–2).

46. Vale! dulcis patria! suavis Suevorum Suevia! Salve! dilecta Francia! philosophorum curia! (5.1–4).

47. Ad urbem sapientię denuo festino (8.1–2).

48. in Parisiensi civitate, in qua fons est totius scientiae (*Dialogus miraculorum*, vol. 1, p. 304).

49. quos rationum amplius delectat subtilitatis sublimitas (p. 120).

50. quos nunc adduximus de Francia (*Wibaldi epistolae*, p. 327).

51. qui ea, que a magistris audierunt, non segniter conscribere atque aliis transcribenda communicare consueverunt (Grabmann, vol. 2, p. 486 n. 1).

52. Cum igitur theologice discipline sectatores distinctiones magistri petri parisiensis ad partes teuthonicas detulissent (ibid.).

53. hic liber... Quem Otakarius archidiac. marchoni Otachario et ille nostre ecclesie contulit (Classen, p. 261).

54. Gallicanam subtilitatem et eloquentiam (*Chronica*, p. 318).

55. Cuius vocem cum audimus, non hominem sed quasi angelum de caelo loqui putamus; nam et dulcedo verborum eius et profunditas sententiarum quasi humanum modum transcendit (*Codex Udalrici*, p. 286).

56. Anselmum Laudunensem, Wilhelmum Parisiensem, Albricum Remensem, Hugonem Parisiensem et alios plurimos, quorum doctrina et scriptis mundus impletus est (*Wibaldi epistolae*, p. 278).

57. apud Parisius magistri insignes claruerunt (p. 13).

58. Deinde ex propria camera et ex redditibus ecclesiae cui preerat datis ei stipendiis, studii causa misit eum Parisius (*Continuatio Claustroneoburgensis* I, p. 610).

59. Procedunt pariter doctores discipulique, Omnes Romanum cupientes visere regem, Quorum te numerosa, Bononia, turba colebat, Artibus in variis noctuque dieque laborans (*Carmen de gestis Frederici* I, 463–66).

60. ut nemo studium exercere volentes Impediat stantes nec euntes nec redeuntes (496–97).

61. Inde rogat cives, ut honorent urbe scolares (500).

62. omnibus, qui causa studiorum peregrinantur scolaribus, et maxime divinarum atque sacrarum legum professoribus hoc nostre pietatis beneficium idulgemus, ut ad loca, in quibus litterarum exercentur studia, tam ipsi quam eorum nuntii veniant et habitent in eis securi (Weinrich, p. 258).

63. maioris causa scientiae scholas adire...ut maiore scientia imbutus ecclesiae tuae honestius militare et curiae nostrae, quando voluerimus, valeat servire (MGH Dipl. F I, vol. 2, p. 349).

64. Duo sane sunt, quae hominem ad legum scientiam vehementer impellunt, ambitio dignitatis, et inanis gloriae appetitus (*Epistolae*, col. 416).

65. pecunie vel laudis cupiditate (*Historia calamitatum*, p. 81).

66. cottidie sericis indumentis Grecorum arte laboratis...Ruthenis pellibus, que auri et argenti precio preferuntur, carnem perituram adornes (Roth, p. 316).

67. comitatus et expensae magnificentia omnes alios principes obscurabat (*Gesta Alberonis*, p. 604).

68. in equo residens, indutus thorace, et desuper tunica iacintina, habens in capite galeam deauratam, et in manibus clavam trinodem (Albert von Stade, p. 347).

69. quod asini sui exercitus maiores haberent expensas quam omnis familia imperatoris (ibid.).

70. swelh ritter ze Henegouwe, ze Brâbant und ze Haspengouwe ze orse ie aller beste gesaz (H. v. Aue, *Gregorius* 1575–77).

71. Hanegöwe Brâbant, Flandern Francrîch Picardîe hât sô schoenes niht (13.25–27).

72. facie pulcherrima, suavibus et blandis sermonibus...gracilis copore...litterata (*Historia*, p. 167 f.).

73. le quiens de Borgogne (322)

74. des gerte di edele herzoginne (9024)

75. diu edel herzoginne...von Zeringen Clêmende (20/22).

76. Filios enim meos omnes litteras discere proposui, ut qui majoris ingenii necnon majoris inter eos notaretur discretionis, in studio perseveraret (Denifle, vol. 1, p. 39).

77. Ex his vero duos ad presens nobilitati vestre mittere proposui, ut vestro juvamine necnon vestra defensione Parisius stabilius possent locari (ibid.).

78. clementer accepistis et clementius hactenus tenuistis (Jordan, p. 174).

79. etiam secularibus rebus instituendos Parisius mittunt (*Chronica*, p. 147).

80. usum Teutonicorum imitantes (p. 146).

81. Unum tamen est, quod nos plurimum angit et silentii omnino impatientes facit, videlicet quod honestas regni, quae temporibus priorum imperatorum veste et habitu nec non in armis et equitatione decentissime viguerat, nostris diebus postponitur, et ignominiosa Franciscarum ineptiarum consuetudo introducitur, scilicet in tonsione barbarum, in turpissima et pudi-

cis obtutibus execranda decurtatione ac deformitate vestium multisque aliis novitatibus, quas enumerare longum est (Giesebrecht, vol. 2, p. 718).

82. apud regem et quosdam alios principes familiariores habentur (ibid.).

83. Laicus namque cum sis et, juxta morem laicorum, barba minime rasa incedere deberes, tu encontra divinae legis contemptor quasi clericus barbam tuam rasisti (col. 243).

84. quod scilicet nemo laicorum radere barbam debeat (col. 244).

85. honestus patrum mos antiquorum (Historia ecclesiastica vol. 4, p. 188).

86. nouis adinuentionibus...longos crines ueluti mulieres nutriebant ...Crispant crines clamistro...nimiumque strictis camisiis...longis latisque manicis...Humum quoque puluerulentam interularum et palliorum superfluo sirmate uerrunt (ibid.).

87. leuibusque et nouitatum amatoribus...idque genus calciamenti pene cuncti diuites et egeni nimium expetunt (ibid., p. 186).

88. in dem snite von Franze (G. v. Straßburg 10905–06).

89. alse Franzoise wîp pflegent (U. v. Zatzikhoven 5804–05).

90. den frowentrit nâch Franzoysinne sit (U. v. d. Türlin 195.13–14).

91. Als mans ze Francrîche Pfliget (H. v. d. Türlin 2852–53).

92. nâch franzeiser sit dar ûf diu bet (K. v. Fussesbrunnen 2410).

93. nâch Franzoyser sit tischelachen wîze und manig twehel Parisîn (U. v. d. Türlin 169.16–17.).

94. der Franzoiser sit (R. v. Durne 2512).

95. in franzoiser wîse (G. v. Straßburg 8065).

96. tyrocinium, quod vulgo nunc turnoimentum dicitur, cum militibus eius extra exercendo usque ad muros ipsos progrediuntur (Gesta Frederici, p. 158).

97. in conflictibus Gallicis, qui hastiludia vel torneamenta vocantur (Historia Anglorum, vol. 1, p. 409).

2. LANGUAGE

1. Mark sach Tristanden an: "friunt", sprach er, "heizest dû Tristan?" "jâ, hêrre, Tristan. dê us sal!" "dê us sal, bêâs vassal!" "merzî", sprach er, "gentil rois, edeler künic Kurnewalois, ir und iuwer gesinde ir sît von gotes kinde iemer gebenedîet!" dô wart gemerzîet wunder von der hovediet. si triben niwan daz eine liet: "Tristan, Tristan li Parmenois, cum est bêâs et cum cûrtois!" (G. v. Straßburg 3349–62).

2. Hic etiam inter Francos Romanos et Teutonicos, qui quibusdam amaris et invidiosis iocis frequenter rixari solent, tamquam in termino utriusque gentis nutritus utriusque linguae scius medium se interposuit ac ad commanendum multis modis informavit (Otto of Freising, Chronica, p. 508).

3. idoneus illis videretur ad regendum abbatiam, quoniam Theutonica et Gualonica lingua expeditus (Gesta abbatum Trudonensium, p. 254).

4. nunc Latialiter, nunc Gallice Germaniceque fando (Saxo Grammaticus, vol. 1, p. 443).

5. er niht moht verstân deheinez irer wort (O. v. Steiermark 75424–25).

6. Tout droit a celui tans que je ci vous devis Avoit une coustume ens el tiois paÿs Que tout li grant seignor, li conte et li marchis Avoient entour aus gent françoise tous dis Pour aprendre françois lor filles et lor fis (148–52).

7. wälsch lâsen sie dâ vil (Stricker, *Daniel* 8173).

8. swer strîfelt sîne tiusche wol mit der welhsche sam er sol; wan dâ lernt ein tiusche man, der niht welhische kan, der spaehen worte harte vil (41–45).

9. Ich hort da wol tschantieren, die nachtegal toubieren. alda muost ich parlieren ze rehte, wie mir waere: ich was an alle swaere. Ein riviere ich da gesach: durch den fores gienc ein bach ze tal übr ein planiure. ich sleich ir nach, unz ich si vant, die schoenen creatiure: bi dem fontane saz diu klare, süeze von faitiure (Gedichte III, 24–33).

10. ad discendam linguam theutonicam et mores curie (Gislebert of Mons, p. 234).

11. et si quos habetis pueros, quos vel terram nostram vel linguam addiscere vultis, nobis transmittatis (Jordan, p. 174).

12. Herbergen ist loschiern genant. sô vil hân ich der sprâche erkant. ein ungefüeger Tschampâneys kunde vil baz franzeys dann ich, swiech franzoys spreche (237.3–7).

13. franzeis ich niht vernemen kan (212).

14. Ez mac wol curteis povel sîn. pittit mangier ist in gesunt (XI, 2.25–26).

15. mit sîner rede er vlaemet (82.2).

16. ein Sahs bürtic von Wienen (III, 332).

17. als ich von im vernomen hân, sô ist er ze Sahsen oder ze Brâbant gewahsen. er sprach "liebe soete kindekîn": er mac wol ein Sahse sîn (744–48).

18. Ey waz snacket ir gebûrekîn und jenez gunêrte wîf? mîn parit, mînen klâren lîf sol dehein gebûric man zewâre nimmer gegrîpen an (764–68).

3. LITERATURE

1. von Veldeken Heinrîch der sprach ûz vollen sinnen . . . er inpfete daz êrste rîs in tiutscher zungen (G. v. Straßburg 4724–25, 4736–37).

CHAPTER III: MATERIAL CULTURE AND SOCIAL STYLE

1. CASTLES AND TENTS

1. Man muoz vor iu knien unde gegen iu ûf stên unde muoz gein iu vorhte hân und habt vil wîte unde breit umb iuch unde rîtet schône unde gêt schône unde habt hôhe bürge und schoene frouwen (Vol. 1, p. 364 f.)

2. ubicumque voluerit in regno nostro castrum edificare in patrimonio suo aut in beneficio suo (MGH Dipl. K III, no. 138, p. 249).

3. Nobiles in villis turres parvulas habuerunt, quas sibi similibus vix defen-

dere potuerunt...Castra et castella in ea pauca fuerunt (*De rebus Alsaticis ineuntis saeculi* XIII, p. 236).

4. in desertis locis altos et natura munitos montes quaerere et in his huiusmodi castella fabricare, quae, si in locis competentibus starent, ingens regno firmamentum simul et ornamentum forent (Bruno, *Saxonicum bellum*, p. 212).

5. dum locos castellis quaereret (p. 228).

6. cui rei maturandae et diligenter exequendae dominum Bennonem praeesse constituit (Norbert, *Vita Bennonis*, p. 388 f.).

7. architectus praecipuus, cementarii operis solertissimus (p. 388).

8. Nam semper secundum alveum Rheni descendens, nunc castrum in aliquo apto loco edificans vicina queque coegit, nunc iterum procedens, relicto priore, aliud munivit (Otto of Freising, *Gesta Frederici*, p. 152).

9. Suscepit igitur eam cum patrimoniis et divitiis multis et trecentis quinquaginta castris (Arnold of Lübeck, p. 246).

10. ANNO MILENO POSTQUAM SALVS EST DATA SECLO / CENTENO JVNCTO QUINQUAGENO QUOQUE QUINTO / CAESAR IN ORBE SITVS FRIDERICVS PACIS AMICVS / LAPSUM CONFRACTVM / VETVS IN NIHIL ANTE REDACTVM / ARTE NITORE PARI REPARAVIT OPVS NOVIMAGI / IVLIVS IN PRIMO TAMEN EXTITIT EIVS ORIGO / IMPAR PACIFICO REPARATORI FRIDERICO (Hotz, p. 41).

11. ANNO AB INCARNATIONE / DOMINI NOSTRI IESV CHRISTI MCLXXXIIII / HOC DECVS IMPERIO CESAR FRIDERICVS ADAVXIT / IVSTICIAM STABILIRE VOLENS / ET VT VNDIQUE PAX SIT (Hotz, p. 102).

12. Palatia siquidem a Karolo Magno quondam pulcherrima fabricata et regias clarissimo opere decoratas aput Noviomagum et iuxta villam Inglinheim, opera quidem fortissima, sed iam tam neglectu quam vetustate fessa, decentissime reparavit et in eis maximam innatam sibi animi magnitudinem demonstravit (p. 712).

13. Domum insulariam Siutberti et Nuwemagen perfici facias et optime custodiri, quia perutile iudicamus (*Historia de expeditione Friderici*, p. 43).

14. Ein castel heizet daz. da ein tvrn stat. vnde mit einer mvre vmbefangin ist. vnde sich div zwei beschirmint. vnder einanderen (*Züricher Predigten*, p. 21).

15. ...graven alse dep, alse en man mit eneme spaden op sceten mach de erde...mit holte oder mit stene drier dele ho boven en ander, ene binnen der erden, de andere two boven, deste men ene dore hebbe in'me nederen gademe boven der erden knes ho (*Landrecht* III 66 § 3).

16. ...vesten enen hof mit tunen oder mit staken oder muren also ho, also en man gereken mach op eneme orse sittene; tinnen unde borstwere ne scal dar nicht an sin (ibid.).

17. ûz sô grôzen steinen daz man vil kûme ir einen mit drîn winden ûf gezôch (K. Fleck, *Flore* 4171–73).

18. due turres edificantur de lapidibus quadris tante quantitatis, ut lapis unus vix a duobus bubalis in curru trahatur (p. 327).

19. alsô was daz hûs zebreit mit den türnen. nâch ir zal sô was ir drîzec über al (7861–63).

20. den berc hete in gevangen ein burcmûre hôch und dic. ein ritterlîcher aneblic ziertez hûs innen. ez rageten vûr die zinnen türne von quâdern grôz (7845–50).

21. castrum fortissimum cum septuaginta septem turribus construxerat (*Chronica regia Coloniensis*, p. 243).

22. dâ lac ein burc, diu beste diu ie genant wart ertstift: unmâzen wît was ir begrift (Wolfram v. Eschenbach, *Parzival* 403. 18–20).

23. die türne gezieret obene mit goldes knophen rôt, der ieglîcher verre bôt in daz lant sînen glast (Hartmann v. Aue, *Erec* 7865–68).

24. dô nam er einer bürge war: âvoy diu gap vil werden glast (W. v. Eschenbach, *Parzival* 398.28–29).

25. ûzenân und innen schein siu betalle hêrlich, niden was der esterich von marmelsteine gemaht. diu mûre was der selben slaht, geschâzavelt genôte, wîz unde rôte, wârn die steine geviert (Ulrich v. Zatzikhoven 4102–09).

26. Ein palas hêt diu künigîn daz was märmelsteinîn, gezieret wol begarwe, von vier hande varwe: rôt, brûn, weitîn und gel; daz hûs daz was sinwel, beliewet umb und umbe wol (W. v. Grafenberg, 222–28).

27. Mit zwein siulen süezen Was ieglîch venster gezieret (H. v. d. Türlin, *Krone* 15776–77).

28. Gevenstert und gewelbet was Umb unde umb ein palas: Der was wol vünf hundert, Und wâren dâ gesundert Mit siulen maneger hande varwe (ibid., 20131–35).

29. von löubern und von tieren wâren si gehouwen, swer wunder wolte schouwen von meisterlichen dingen, der lie sîn ougen swingen an ir siule sinewel, dâ manic vremdez capitel stuont an gesniten unde ergraben (K. v. Würzburg, *Trojanerkrieg* 17514–21).

30. einhalp der kemenâten want vil venster hete, dâ vor glas (W. v. Eschenbach, *Parzival* 553.4–5).

31. dô kam ein juncfrouwe vîn reht als ein turteltiubelîn geslichen vür daz palastor und wolte gerne hân dâ vor des wazzers sich erlâzen (*Die halbe Birne* 227–31).

32. Der wirt mich dâ vil wol enpfie. sîn wîp, diu hûsvrouwe, gein mir gie mit vrouwen vil ein stiege zetal (*Frauendienst* 932.1–3).

33. diu venster sâzen vrouwen vol (*M. v. Craûn* 878).

34. in ein venster sî gestuont, als senendiu wîp dicke tuont, den leit von minne ist geschehen (ibid., 1705–07).

35. manig wurze unde krût (70).

36. Diu was gemachet umbe daz, daz der wirt dar inne saz, In dem sumer, wen er az: in dûht', in bekaem' diu spîse des baz (79–82).

37. Prima autem area fuit in superficie terre, ubi erant cellaria et granaria, ciste etiam magne, dolia et cupe et alia domus utensilia. In secunda autem area fuit habitatio et communis inhabitantium conversatio, in qua erant penora, hinc panetariorum, hinc pincernarum, hinc magna domini et uxoris sue, in qua accubabant, camera, cui contiguum erat latibulum, pedissequarum videlicet et puerorum camera vel dormitorium. Hinc in magne secretiori parte camere erat quoddam secretum diversorium, ubi summo diluculo vel in vespere vel in infirmitate vel ad sanguinis minutiones faciendas vel ad pedissequas vel ad pueros

ablactatos calefaciendos ignem componere solebant. In hac etiam are coquina domui continuata erat, in qua erant dure aree. In inferiori area hinc porci ad impinguescendum positi sunt, ad nutriendum hinc anseres, hinc capones et alia volatilia ad occidendum et ad vescendum semper parata. In altera autem coquine area conversabantur tantum coci et coquine provisores, et in ea preparabantur esce dominorum delicatissime et multimodo coquorum apparatu et labore confricate et ad vescendum parate. Ibi etiam familiariorum et domesticorum esce cotidiana provisione et laboris officio preparabantur. In superiori domus area fuerunt facta solariorum diversoria, in quibus his filii, cum volebant, illic filie, quia sic oportebat, domini domus accubabant; illic vigiles et ad custodiendam domum servientes positi et constituti et semper parati custodes quandocumque somnum capiebant; hic gradalia et meicula de area in aream, de domo in coquinam, de camera in cameram, item a domo in logium, quod bene et procedente ratione nomen accepit—ibi enim sedere in deliciis solebant ad colloquendum—a "logos," quod est sermo, derivatum; item de logio in oratorium sive capellam Salomoniaco tabernaculo in celatura et pictura assimilatam (p. 624).

38. Ich ne weiz war zo der uvrste sal. Her ne hatte ette wane schal. Mit vroweden in deme houe sin (*König Rother* 1543–45).

39. Mitten durch den palas manec marmelsûl gesetzet was under hôhe pfîlaere (*Willehalm* 270.1–3).

40. hundert krône (W. v. Eschenbach, *Parzival* 229.24).

41. kleine kerzen umbe an der want (229.27).

42. mit marmel was gemûret drî vierekke fiwerrame (ibid. 230.8–9).

43. sô grôziu fiwer sît noch ê sach niemen hie ze Wildenberc (230.12–13).

44. dâ hinc ein tûre umbehanc, der was breit unde lanc, von edelen golde durhslagen. mit sîdin wâren dar în getragen vogele unde tiere mit manicfalder ziere unde mit manigerslahte varwe. daz merketih alliz garwe. man mohte dar an scowen rîter unde frowen obene unde nidene mit wunderlîchen bilide. zô den enden und an den orten wâren tûre borten und elfenbeinîne crapfen, di hangeten an den ricken. alse man zouh den umbehanc, manic goltschelle dar an irclanc (*Straßburger Alexander* 5949–66).

45. Dâ was von golde geworht an, Wie von Kriechen entran Von Pârîs vrouwe Hêlenâ; Ouch was geworht anderswâ, Wie Troie zevüeret lac Unde der jaemerlîche slac, Der an Dîdôn ergienc, Dô sie Êneam enpfienc. Man sach ouch dâ schînen Von der schoenen Lavînen, Wie sie Êneas ervaht, Und der Rômaere slaht. Diu lache den sal umbe gie Und in mit staten bevie (H. v. d. Türlin, *Krone* 524–37).

46. Schoene gemêlde an palast wenden (H. v. Trimberg 17391).

47. an iegelîchem ende wâren dâ die wende wol gemâl sô vaste, daz ez alse ein münster glaste. daz himelze obene gemuoset waz, daz ez lûhte alse ein spiegelglas (*M. v. Crâun* 1101–06).

48. Astiterat dictans operantibus ipsa puellis, Signaratque suo quid facerent radio (103–04).

49. Cura sagax etenim comitissae praecipientis Hanc super effigiem composuit titulum (1330–31).

50. Aurea pictura thalami laquearia plura Omnia preterita recolunt mon-

strantque futura, Cunctorum regum signat ymago genus (Dinumeratio regnorum 145–147).

51. daz ich oben gemâlet hân daz hân ich gar von iu getân: ich hân gemâlet disen sal wie iuwer ritter über al mit iu dar in gênt unt bî iu schouwunde stênt (Stricker, *Pfaffe Amis* 669–74).

52. lectum culcitra et operimento precioso magnifice ornatum, sedemque eburneam cum cussino lecto prepositam (Arnold v. Lübeck, p. 171).

53. dâ stuont ein bette enmitten bî, vernemet, wie daz gemachet sî: dem wâren sîne stollen grôz unt gedrollen, unt von helfenbeine ergraben wâren tier ane erhaben, aller hande als siu diu erde treit, unt golt dar under geleit enmitten in das helfenbein, daz ir antlitze dar ûz schein. die rigel wâren alsus von holze, daz Vulcânus niht verbrennen enkan, unt wâren gestrecket dar an vier liebarten hiute (ditz hânt wan rîche liute), mit naeten zesamene gezogen. diu rede ist wâr unt niht gelogen, swie ich es niht beziugen mac. enmitten ûf den hiuten lac vil bette weich unde grôz, diu wâren decke niht blôz: ûf in wâren die ziechen, pfellelîn von Kriechen; dar obe lac ein golter dâ—ich waene vrou Cassandrâ nie bezzer werc volbraehte oder dehein ir geslähte—unde ûz sabene ein deckelachen. dâ hiezens under machen vedere, die man tiure galt (*M. v. Craûn* 1111–41).

54. hundert pette (W. v. Eschenbach, *Parzival* 229.28).

55. gât in die batstuben hin; dâ ist er inne (diu ist warm) (*Der nackte Bote* 16–17).

56. de loco cedente columna lignei caenaculi, in quo sederunt, cediderunt in locum balnei, quod aqua super montem ducta congruo tempore complevit (*Chronicon Eberspergense*, p. 14).

57. Unsere vorfaren haben ainest uf den hochen bergen in iren heusern und schlösern gewonet, do ist auch traw und glauben bei inen gewest, iezunder aber so lassen wir unsere bergheuser abgeen, bewonnen die nicht, sonder vilmehr befleißen wir uns in der ebne zu wonnen, damit wir nahe zum badt haben (Vol. 2, p. 481 f.).

58. Postquam vero praesidia in ipsis castellis collocata coeperunt in circuitu sui praedationes agere, non suos labores in suos usus comportare, liberos homines ad opus servile compellere, filias vel uxores alienas ludibrio habere: tunc primum, quid illa castella portenderent, intellexerunt (p. 212).

59. machet iwern gwalt wit. habt ritterlichen mannes mut, lat iu dienen liute und gut in der gegende swes ez si, des enlazet ir deheinen fri. ez chumt vil schiere an die frist daz daz ir beste vreude ist, daz si iwer hulde muezen han und sint iu gern undertan. so furhtent die richen iwer chraft, die armen sint iu diensthaft. wir chunnen mit gefugen dingen die liute wol dar zu bringen daz si iu dienent alle tage mit gutem willen ane chlage. swaz wir mit guten minnen noch hiute an in gewinnen, daz muezens ouch zejare geben. da geturrens nimmer wider streben, so muzzen siz ouch iemer tûn. swer iu hiute git ein hûn, der git iu ane geschrei zejare driu oder zwei. so waehset iemer mere iwer frum und iwer ere und wert werder danne ê. swelich geboure iu wider ste, den gewinnet zeinem ampt man: swaz er geleisten danne chan, daz ist iemer iwer eign. sus sult irs alle neigen mit listen unde mit gwalt, sus werdet ir mit eren alt (98–130).

60. dar umbe hât man bürge, daz man die armen würge (121.12–13).

61. Daz kristen liute sint worden wilde, Die bî wolfen und bî bern In rûhen welden wonent gern Und in wüestunge machent bürge, Daz man arme liute würge (22766–70).

62. Castrum hoc bonum habet portum, piscariis, salinis, lignis, pascuis et agris fertilibus habundat (p. 327).

63. uf ainer flû, da stossent vier lantstrasen zû, der och gewaltig ist der berg (6455–57).

64. gewelpten arken (6459).

65. vil manig kar und wagen dar úber wol geladen gat (6474–75).

66. alten rehten, lassen, zol (6491).

67. dú dez vil wol genússet daz da wasser flusset, schifrichs und michel (6507–09).

68. swas ain richer fúrst bedarf und des gesinde, daz man daz alles vinde da (6582–85).

69. von dem man hat diss gemach daz man da weschet, bachet, malt (6600–01).

70. daz man ob allen tischen (der wiger ist so visrich) hat ain geriht tǎglich (6616–18).

71. aychern, fúhse, kúngel, hasen, ve marder, swin (6628–29).

72. hirs, rech, tier, hinden (6631).

73. hebk, valken, sperwer (6636).

74. rebhúnrd und vasande (6642).

75. da wachset och der frowen werch, langer hanf und linder vlahs (6660–61).

76. da gat ain brunn da man saltz ús súdet (6666–67).

77. so si sich ald ire trut wellint hailen und baden (6730–31).

78. des oft sich verainent dar an der appenteger knaben, die krúter prechen, wurzen graben und sûchent spezzerie man siht durch erzenie (6744–48).

79. och siht man birsen, baitzen, jagen. wol von der burg hin ze tal (6776–77).

80. daz nummer hus da wirt bedaht wan von roten hafen ziegeln (6796–97).

81. aput Lutra domum regalem ex rubris lapidibus fabricatam non minori munificentia accuravit. Etenim ex una parte muro fortissimo eam amplexus est, aliam partem piscina ad instar lacus circumfluit, piscium et altilium in se continens omne delectamentum ad pascendum tam visum quam gustum. Ortum quoque habet contiguum cervorum et capreolorum copiam nutrientem. Quorum omnium regalis magnificentia et maior dictu copia opere pretium spectantibus exhibet (Gesta Frederici, p. 712).

82. ez was eht vil voll&#xNaN;clîche erziuget dirre wiltban und alsô daz dehein man der doch gerne wolde jagen nimmer dörfte geklagen daz er wildes niht envunde. ouch hete der wirt der hunde die smannes willen tâten diz jagehûs wol berâten (7149–57).

83. plura ceteris et pulchriora tentoria habuit (p. 155).

84. als ez ein turn wâre. zweinzich soumâre ne mohtenz dar niht getragen (247.11–13).

85. als ein palas (W. v. Eschenbach, Parzival 27.16).

86. Palas tvrne movr mit allen zinnen (*Jg. Titurel* 4408.3).

87. Zwölff camer wolgetan Warent auch darinne (2424–25).

88. diu winde was gevieret. (siu was hôch unde wît.) ein teil was ein samît, rehte grüene als ein gras. manic bilde drane was mit starken listen gemaht. ez was verre bezzer slaht dan ze Kriechen dehein phellel sî. daz ander teil was dâ bî ein rîcher triblât, brûn sô man uns gesaget hât: dar an rôtiu bilde, glîch vogelen und wilde, meisterlîche wol geworht. daz gezelt stuont unervorht vor aller slahte wetere. guldîn was daz etere, dâ mite zesamene was genât der samît und der triblât. ich sages iu niht nâch wâne, von rôtem barragâne was diu dritte sît. siu lûhte harte wîte in den grüenesten clê. im kunde nimer werden wê, dem daz in teile was getân, daz er drîn mohte gân, er hât an saelden grôzen prîs. ez was ein irdisch paradîs, des muoz man jehen zwâre. von wîzem visches hâre waz daz vierde ende . . . (U. v. Zatzikhoven 4808–39).

89. Inter que papilionem unum, quantitate maximum, qualitate bonissimum, perspeximus. Cuius si quantitatem requiris, nonnisi machinis et instrumentorum genere et adminiculo levari poterat; si qualitatem, nec materia nec opere ipsum putem aliquando ab aliquo huiuscemodi apparatu superatum iri (Rahewin, *Gesta Frederici*, p. 406).

90. miro spectanda decore Scena (*Ligurinus* VI, 172–73).

91. Materiam quaeris? peregrino stamine texta Creditur: artis opus? miras habuisse figuras (175–76).

92. tentorium optimum et domum desupter de scarlatto et tapete iuxta latitudinem et longitudinem ipsius domus (p. 171).

93. tentorium operosum, quod portare vix poterant tria plaustra (*Chronica regia Coloniensis*, p. 144).

94. tentoria innumera erecta, bissina, purpurea, cum capitibus aureis, et pro uniuscuiusque magnificentia vario decore ornata (Arnold v. Lübeck, p. 119).

95. tentorium aureum, quod totum incanduit gemmis et lapidibus preciosis (ibid.).

96. tentorium mirifica arte constructum, in quo ymagines solis et lune artificialiter mote cursum suum certis et debitis spaciis peragrant et horas diei et noctis infallibiliter indicant. Cuius tentorii valor viginti milium marcarum precium dicitur transcendisse (*Chronica regia Coloniensis*, p. 263).

97. ach, was hoher kost rich an die decke was gelait! diu aventůr hat gesait daz Luna, Mercurius, die planeten, und Venus, Sol, Mars, und Jupiter, Saturnus nach wunsches ger stůnden dran gemachet: so riche daz hertze lachet von der kost rich. zirkels wis gelich was ez dar gestellet, der stern kraiz gesellet was in daz firmament (J. v. Würzburg 15430–43).

98. inter thesauros regios (*Chronica regia Coloniensis*, p. 263).

2. CLOTHES AND CLOTH

1. dô riht er aver sâ umbe der bûliute gewaete. daz machte der bâbes dô staete. Nû wil ich iu sagen umbe den bûman, waz er nâch der pfaht solte an tragen: iz sî swarz oder grâ, niht anders reloubet er dâ; gêren dâ enneben, daz gezimet sînem leben; sînen rinderînen scuoch, dâ mit ist des genuoch; siben elne

se hemede unt ze bruoch, rupfîn tuoch. ist der gêre hinden oder vor, sô hât er sîn êwerch verlorn (14788–802).

2. rocke mit vir unde zwenzig oder drißig gêren (p. 36).

3. mit vier gêren und niht mê (O. v. Steiermark, 20028).

4. sîn lancreidez valwe hâr (102.14).

5. im und sînen tanzgesellen sol man hâr und kleider alsô stellen (nâch dem alten site gar), als manz bî künc Karel truoc (102.15–18).

6. dô man dem lant sîn reht maz, man urloubt im hûsloden grâ und des vîrtages blâ, von einem guoten stampfhart. dehein varwe mêr erloubt wart im noch sînem wîbe. diut treit nû an ir lîbe grüen, brûn, rôt von Jent (II, 70–77).

7. sie enmache ir gewant alsô lanc daz der gevalden nâchswanc den stoub erweche dâ si hin gê (*Erinnerung an den Tod* 323–25).

8. Nullus vario vel grisio vel sabellinis vel escarletis utatur (Cartellieri, vol. 2, p. 57).

9. Que ningun rric omme non faga mas de quatro pares de pannos al anno, nin otro cauallero nin otro omme ninguno. Et estos que non sean arminnados nin nutriados, nin con seda nin con orpel nin con argent pel, nin con cuerdas luengas nin bastonadas nin con orfres nin con çintas nin con perfil nin con otro adobo ninguno, sinon penna e panno; nin entallen vn panno sobre otro; e que ninguno non traya capa aguadera descarlata sinon el Rey, e que non fagan capas pielles sinon dos uezes en el anno, e la capa aguadera quela trayan dos annos, e que ninguno no uista çendal nin seda, sinon fuere Rey o nouel, sinon fuere enfforradura de pannos, e que ninguno non traya pennas ueras, sinon el Rey o nouel o nouio, si fuere rric omme o fi de rric omme, e que ningun rrico omme nin otro que non traya en capa nin en pellote plata nin christales nin botones nin cuerdas luengas nin arminnos nin nutria, sinon en perfil en capa piel, e que ningun rric omme non traya tabardo andando en corte (*Córtes de Valladolid de 1258*, p. 57).

10. Il est ordené que nus ne dux, ne cuens, ne prélaz, ne bers, ne autres, soit clers soit lais, ne puisse faire ne avoir en un anz plus de iiij paires de robes vaires (Duplès-Agier, p. 179).

11. Rex Francie precepit in omni regno . . . quod [nemo] rusticorum quantarum diviciarum vestibus militum uteretur (p. 206).

12. Item nobiliori quam griseo et viliori plabatico veste non utantur et calciis bovinis (Franz, p. 328).

13. welh ir roc waere? des vrâget ir kameraere: ich gesach in weizgot nie (H. v. Aue, *Erec* 8946–48).

14. gesniten al nâch der Franzoyser siten (W. v. Eschenbach, *Parzival* 313.8–9).

15. ein snit nâch der Franzoyser won (U. v. d. Türlin 171.11).

16. ein dem snite von Franze (G. v. Straßburg 10905–06).

17. gewant sîdîn, zendal und paltikîn, samît und siglât, phelle und pliât (O. v. Steiermark 69058–61).

18. Im wurde von Kriechen brâht Maneger varwe samît, Purper unde timît, Paile, rôsât, siglât, Dîasper und tribelât, Von golde geworhter blîalt, Von sîdîn lachen manecvalt, Diu man ze cleidern sneit, Dâ mit man die ritter cleit Und diu palas beleit (H. v. d. Türlin, *Krone* 510–19).

19. der aller besten purper ein, der ie ze Kriechen wart geweben (K. v. Würzburg, *Trojanerkrieg* 14930–31).

20. samittos plurimos, ita ut omnes milites suos vestiret samittis (Arnold v. Lübeck, p. 120).

21. mantellum et tunicam de optimo serico (ibid., p. 122).

22. cum multis pannis preciosis de serico (*Annales Marbacenses*, p. 65).

23. vestes et pallia et alia quaedam preciosa (p. 144).

24. auri et argenti, sericorum, preciosarum vestium atque gemmarum (ibid., p. 213).

25. aurum et argentum multum nimis, pannos sericos negotiatorum in habundantia, vestes preciosas et ornatum seculi cum varia suppellectili in superhabundantia (ibid., p. 250).

26. du si sach di cirheit, du verwan si die girecheit umbe einen pellen den si sach, de in der costerien lach, dure ende vele gut. dar tu stunt here der mut. van groten sunden dat et quam, dat si den pellen du nam. geswaslike si'ne danne druch. dat was misdat genuch dat si't i gedachte. du si'ne te hus brachte, di hertoginne rike, si dede'n cirlike scheppen ende gestellen, want het was ein dure pellen. des dede si di nade neien bit goltdrade. men ne durste's here nit verunnen, hadde si'ne wale gewunnen (5107–28).

27. tuoch von Gente (*Lohengrin* 3083); brûnez scharlach von Gint (W. v. Eschenbach, *Willehalm* 63.22); fritschal von Gent (*Gauriel* 2307); klaider- . . . von Iper (*Der Teufelspapst* 152–53); schürbrant von Arraze (W. v. Eschenbach, *Parzival* 588.19–20).

28. der ritter kleider muosten sîn und ouch der knappen von dem Rîn von Yper und von Gente (J. Enikel, *Fürstenbuch* 331–33).

29. Zechen tuoch von Jent ist ein soum. Ahte scharlachen ist ein soum. Zwelf tuoch von Eypper ist ein soum. Sehzehniu von Hoy ist ein soum. Zehen stampfart von Arra ist ein soum (Tomaschek, vol. 1, p. 7).

30. panni de Genta, panni de Ypra (Stolz, p. 58).

31. stotzen und stân von golde an allen enden (K. v. Würzburg, *Trojanerkrieg* 20060–61).

32. ich hân selbe sîden: nu schaffet daz man trage gesteine uns ûf den schilden, sô wurken wir diu kleit (*Nibelungenlied* 358.2–3).

33. Obir eynes ritters licham geborit sich wol eyn buntis cleid (1765–66).

34. Pannis rubeis aut viridibus, nec non mancicis aut calceis consutitiis non utantur (Schannat-Hartzheim, vol. 3, p. 659).

35. wîz, rôt, gel, grüene, swarz, grâ, blâ was ir wünneclicher schîn (K. v. Würzburg, *Partonopier* 12448–49).

36. als ein pfâwe (H. v. d. Türlin, *Krone* 8221).

37. pfâwen kleit (*Nibelungenlied* C 1320.1).

38. schâchzabelwîs gevieret (K. v. Würzburg, *Partonopier* 8710).

39. si truoc einen roc wîten, von zwein samîten gesniten vil gelîche, eben unde rîche; der eine was grüene alsam ein gras, der ander rôter varwe was, mit golde wol gezieret (W. v. Grafenberg, 746–52).

40. röcke geteilt (W. v. Eschenbach, *Parzival* 235.13).

41. daz was halbez plîalt, daz ander pfell vo Ninivê (235.10–11).

42. ex purpura et lino subtilissimo, aurifrigio etiam et laminis aureis, mar-

garitis et gemmis (*Vita Engelberti*, p. 248).

43. vestibus deauratis gemmisque decoratus (*Chronicon Colmariense*, p. 248).

44. Nobiles terrae, in amaritudine cordis flete regem vestrum, qui vestiebat vos coccino in deliciis, et praebebat ornamenta aurea cultui vestro, accincti velamine ornamentorum pretiosissimorum, quibus etiam fucatis ostro fimbriis radiantia fila pendebant (*Annales Otokariani*, p. 194).

45. von golt die besten wât (73094).

46. ouch kouften sie dâ bunt, hermîn unde grâ und luoden des manigen ballen (73105–07)

47. swaz man zuo der selben stunt in dem lande solher lîut erkande, ez waere wîp oder man, die sich die kunst naemen an, daz si ûf frouwen wât mit rîhen oder mit der nât, mit stricken oder mit sneisen von berlen und baleisen tier kunden wurken meisterlich, die wurden gemachet rîch (73112–22).

48. pro facienda slucha domine ducisse... pro 6 milibus berl. deauratis, 6 milibus corallis, tribus ligacionibus berlarum alterius coloris, berlarum albarum unc. 5 et serici 6 (Riedmann I, p. 542).

49. Sich hêt diu maget rîche vil harte hövischlîche in einen mantel gevangen, wîten unde langen, genagelt wol mit golde, bezogen als si wolde mit einer veder härmîn; dâ wâren gesnîten în von einer hiute vischîn—der hâr daz was weitîn, brâht von Îberne—mâne unde sterne (W. v. Grafenberg 801–12).

50. Swar man dinget bi koniges banne, dar ne scal noch scepen noch richtere kappen hebben an, noch hut noch hudeken noch huven noch hantscen. Mentele scolen se op den sculderen hebbben (*Landrecht* III 69, § 1).

51. Paligan uie sie unter sinin mantel, er troste die frouwin (7390–91).

52. ir mantels swanc se umb in ein teil (W. v. Eschenbach, *Willehalm* 291.5).

53. die schone kuniginnen intfienc mit vrolichem mûte den edelen greven gûten. sie tvanc in zu iren brusten, lipliche sie in cûste, sie nam in under iren mantel (*Graf Rudolf*, Ib 9–14).

54. daz mantelîn si ûfe tete unde enpfienc in drunder (K. v. Würzburg, *Engelhard* 3108–09).

55. al den werden er dô sant drîer hande rîch gewant: scharlachen rôt unversniten, diu zwei von phelle wol gebriten mit golde spaehe gar geworht (U. v. Etzenbach, *Wilhelm v. Wenden* 1777–81).

56. vestes preciosas (Rahewin, *Gesta Frederici*, p. 706).

57. cum diversorum colorum purpura, aromata multa nimis et in hac terra hactenus incognita (*Chronica s. Petri Erfordensis*, p. 172).

58. preciosissima pallia diversi generis et vestes operis mirabilis, auro et lapidibus presiosissimis ornatas (Vincent of Prague, p. 682).

59. al kleine wîz sîdîn ein hemde der künegîn, als ez ruorte ir blôzen lîp (W. v. Eschenbach, *Parzival* 101.9–11).

60. Nu nim von mir dis fúrspan, Geselle min, liebes trut! Das rûrte mine blossen hut (R. v. Ems, *Wilhelm von Orlens* 5446–48).

61. der het ir zeswen arm geruort (W. v. Eschenbach, *Parzival* 375.16).

62. dô wart der magede freude grôz. ir arm was blanc unde blôz: dar über hefte sin dô sân (390.27–29).

63. Ich hiez mir snîden vrowen cleit: zwelf röckel wurden mir bereit und drîzic vrowen ermel guot an kleiniu hemde, daz was mîn muot (*Frauendienst* 473.1–4.).

64. swar ich zer werlte kêre, dâ ist nieman frô: tanzen, singen zergât mit sorgen gar: nie kristenman gesach sô jaemerlîche schar. nû merkent wie den frouwen ir gebende stât: die stolzen ritter tragent dörpellîche wât (124.21–25; without the additions of Kraus).

65. prolixisque nimiumque strictis camisiis indui tunicisque gaudebant (*Historia ecclesiastica*, vol. 4, p. 188).

66. Humum quoque puluerulentam interularum et palliorum superfluo sirmate uerrunt. longis latisque manicis ad omnia facienda manus operiunt (ibid.).

67. Femineam mollitiem petulans iuuentus amplectitur (ibid.).

68. diu maget gap den ritter an ir mantel unde ir suckenîe (Pleier, *Tandareis* 13321–22).

69. einen pelz zôch si an der stet ab ir, der was lûter grâ; den sande si dem rîter dâ; hie mit kleite er sich sâ (W. v. Grafenberg 5937–40).

70. La reïne se fu vestue d'une chiere porpre vermeille, bendee d'or a grant merveille trestot le cors des i as hanches et ensement totes les manches. Un chier mantel ot afublé, menuëment a or goté, a un fil d'or ert galonee et sa teste ot d'orfreis bendee (1466–74).

71. Ir hemede daz was cleine, wîz unde wol genât. dar an was manich goltdrât. ez was gedwenget an ir lîb. si was ein wol geschaffen wîb, sô si baz endorfte sîn. ir belliz der was hermîn, wîz unde vile gût; die kelen rôt alse ein blût; die ermel wol ze mâzen wît, dar ûffe ein grûner samît nâch ir lîbe wol gesniten. daz hete si ungerne vermiten. der was wol gezieret und vil wol gezimieret mit berlen unde borden, die dar zû gehôrden. vile wol her ir gezam, dô sie in an sich genam, dâ si sich mite gorde daz was ein tûre borde geworht als si wolde mit silber und mit golde. Ir mantel der was ein samît grûne als ein gras; diu vedere wîz hermîn daz si niht bezer mohte sîn. der zobel brûn unde breit (59.28–60.15).

72. ir hemde daz was sîdîn: dar in was siu geprîset (U. v. Zatzikhoven 872–73).

73. daz vil minneclîche wîp het ze naehste an ir lîp ein hemede geprîset (Otte 3793–95).

74. mit golde zuo den sîten gebrîset was ir lîp dar în (K. von Würzburg, *Engelhard* 3042–43).

75. si nâte selbe mit ir hant in ein hemde daz magedîn (H. v. Aue, *Erec* 1541–42).

76. Ir rock waidenliche waz An jren zarten lib gesnitten (*Der Traum* 568–69).

77. der roc... tete sich nâhe zuo der lîch: ern truoc an keiner stat hin dan (G. v. Straßburg 10913–15).

78. ir roc was gezieret, wol gefischieret rîterlîche an ir lîp, alse Franzoise wîp pflegent, die wol geschaffen sint (U. v. Zatzikhoven 5801–04).

79. er leite sich nâh unde twanc an ir arme und an ir brust. dâ niden was er durch gelust geschrôten alsô rehte wît, daz manic valte bî der zît lac unden umbe ir füeze doch (K. v. Würzburg, *Partonopier* 12476–81).

80. dô truoc diu schoene ein hemde von sîden an ir lîbe, daz nie deheime wîbe ein kleit sô rehte wol gezam. ez was sô kleine, als ich vernam, daz man dar durch ir wîze hût (diu was alsam ein blüendez krût) sach liuhten bî den zîten. mit golde zuo den sîten gebrîset was ir lîp dar în. man sach ir senften brüstelîn an dem kleide reine strozen harte kleine, als ez zwên epfel waeren (K. v. Würzburg, *Engelhard* 3034–47).

81. daz hemde bî der erden nam vil manegen wünneclichen valt. der eine was alsô gestalt und was der ander sô getân. man sach si bî den füezen gân vil wildeclichen ümbe. si suochten fremde krümbe beidiu ze berge und hin ze tal. dirre der nam sînen val vil schône rehtehalp dar nider: sô vielt sich jener ûfe wider. der eine was geslitzet, reht als ein bilde gesnitzet, und was der ander vorne sleht. si wâren eben unde reht, her unde dar geschrenket (3062–77).

82. daz hemde stuont gelenket nâch einem fremden schrôte und suochte sô genôte an ir lîp vil ûz erkorn daz man des haete wol gesworn daz diu saeldenbaere einhalp des gürtels waere nacket unde enbloezet gar (3078–85).

83. dâ von enmohte niht der swanz die varwe sîn verliesen: er liez sich dâ wol kiesen von maneger hande valten (3092–95).

84. turbavit mulieres omnes cum quadam constitutione quam fecit; in qua continebatur quod mulieres haberent vestimenta curta usque ad terram et tantum plus, quanta est unius palme mensura. Trahebant enim prius caudas vestimentorum per terram longas per brachium et dimidium (*Chronica*, vol. 1, p. 246).

85. quod fuit mulieribus amarius omni morte. Nam quedam mulier familiariter dixit michi, quod plus erat ei kara illa cauda quam totum aliud vestimentum quo induebatur (ibid.).

86. ein haftel wol hande breit, daz was ein gelpher rubin (H. v. Aue, *Erec* 1561–62).

87. diu zwei, gedraet unde genaet, diu envollebrâhten nie baz ein lebende bilde danne daz (10958–60).

88. ze etlîchen zîten des mantels si ein teil ûf swanc: swes ouge denne drunder dranc, der sah den blic von pardîs (*Willehalm* 249.12–15).

89. Erat enim haec ipsa domina ad opera muliebria magno ingenio sollertissima, et feminas ad rerum textilium diversitatem doctas habuit, et in conficiendis vestibus preciosis mulieres multas superavit (Ebbo, *Vita Burchardi*, p. 837).

90. nigram casulam magno aurifrisio decentissime perornavit (Berthold, p. 226).

91. sî kunde liehte borten wol, edle waehe rîche würken meisterlîche (R. v. Ems, *Guter Gerhard* 2920–22).,

92. dô hiez ir juncfrouwen drîzec meide gân ûz ir kemenâten Kriemhilt diu künegin, die zuo solhem werke heten groezlîchen sin. Die arâbîschen sîden wîz alsô der snê unt von Zazamanc der guoten grüene alsam der klê, dar in si leiten steine; des wurden guotiu kleit. selbe sneit si Kriemhilt (*Nibelungenlied* 361.2–362.4).

93. ein juncvrouwe in naete in einen roc pfellîn (W. v. Grafenberg 699–700).

94. sô sint im die elenbogen in zwên gugelzipf gesmogen, die hangent verre hin zetal (*Seifried Helbling* I, 229–31).

95. an einem ermel haeten vier ze rehtem wâpenroc genuoc (ibid. I, 170–71).

96. Post haec pellicium mox induerat varicosum, Prae vel post fissum (*Ruodlieb* X. 123–24).

97. mit wunderlîcher rîcheit zesniten und zehouwen (G. v. Straßburg 672–73).

98. Zwô hosen durchsniten gar Vuorte er von rôtem scharlach, Dâ man diu bein durch sach (H. v. d. Türlin, *Krone* 3709–11).

99. ir beider hosen ûz gesniten, zerhouwen wol nâch hübeschen siten, dar über manic goltdrât. dâ durch schein diu lînwât wîzer danne kein snê (*Herzog Ernst* B 3005–09).

100. "seht", sprâchen sî, "der jungelinc der ist ein saeliger man. wie saeleclîche stât im an allez daz, daz er begât! wie gâr sîn lîp ze wunsche stât! wie gânt im sô gelîche inein diu sîniu keiserlîchen bein!" (G. v. Straßburg 702–08).

101. hosen streich er... an diu bein (W. v. Grafenberg 4088–89).

102. mit sô gelîmter beinwât (H. v. Aue, *Gregorius* 3399).

103. scharlachens hosen rôt man streich an in dem ellen nie gesweich. Avoy wie stuonden sîniu bein! (W. v. Eschenbach, *Parzival* 168.5–6).

104. in turpissima et pudicis obtutibus execranda decurtatione ac deformitate vestium (Giesebrecht, vol. 2, p. 718).

105. prolixis... camisiis... tunicisque (Vol. 4, p. 188).

106. zwên stival über blôziu bein (*Parzival*, 63.15).

107. quod cum morbi coactione faceret (*Gesta Alberonis*, p. 602).

108. ab aliis pro raritate facere videbatur (ibid.).

109. man siht im doch die stivaln von des rockes kürze; daz er in nider schürze, des hât er guoten rât, sô er zuo den liuten gât. ein ieslîch man selbe spür: vor gênt die hosenestel für, hinden sîner schanden gwant daz ist von mir ungenant (I.234–42).

110. Sincipite scalciati sunt, ut fures. occipitio autem prolixas nutriunt comas ut meretrices (*Historia ecclesiastica*, Vol. 4, p. 188).

111. Crispant crines calamistro (ibid.).

112. Ze strenen gewunden Und mit golde gebunden (H. v. d. Türlin, *Krone* 6884–85).

113. ouch was gebunden diu rein nâh der Franzoyser won (U. v. d. Türlin 298.14–15).

114. Irem kynn dem hat sie hoch gepunden. die gimpel gend Ir in den munndt. all nach dem hoffe sitt (Neidhart c, no. 37, II. 1–2).

115. Uf ruhte si ir gebende (*Nibelungenlied* 1351.1).

116. fuge lasciuiam puellarum, quae ornant capita, crines a fronte demittunt, cutem poliunt, utuntur lomentis, adstrictas habent manicas, uestimenta sine ruga soccosque crispantes (*Epistolae*, vol. 3, p. 199).

117. ... caeteris matronibus, quae apud modernos sunt... quarum magna pars menbratim iniuste circumcincta, quod venale habet in se, cunctis amatoribus ostendit aperte (*Chronicon*, 178).

118. quia videlicet multa superflua et luxoriosa mulierum ornamenta, quibus Graecia uti solet, sed eatenus in Germaniae Franciaeque provinciis erant incognita, huc primo detuli memeque eisdem plus quam humanae naturae con-

veniret, circumdans et in hujusmodi habitu novico incedens alias mulieres simi-
lia appetentes peccare feci (col. 373).

119. di guldinen copfe di silberinen nepfe daz edele gesteine daz ture gebeine
di manige goltborten wehe geworhten daz edele gesmide pellil unde side cindal
vnde samit di scarlachen da mit di mantele manicfalt in dine gewalt du heizis dir
machin di guten ruckelachen teppit vnde vorhanc vile breit vnde lanc gevollit
mit golde, alsiz din herze wolde, vnde andre zirde also vile, der ih reiten nit ne
wile (2410–29).

120. si hât vil guot gezowe, hemde unt röchel; ouch habent si die lochel alsô
chläine gedraet; die handschûch wol ginaet ziehent si an mit vlîzzen; die borten
sihet man glîzzen durch die gelwen rîsen; si beginnent sich vaste brîsen; die
hantschône! unt die spiegel! (*Priesterleben* 700–09).

121. mantella de Bruneta, nigra, sive mureta & pellicea de vario, & alias
exquisitas & sumptuosas pelles (Schannat-Hartzhaim, vol. 3, p. 535).

122. non habeant moniales manicas strictas vel consuricias, nec habeant
monilia, nec fibulas, nec annulos aureos vel argenteos, nec aurifrigia, nec cing-
ulos sericos, nec aliquem saecularem ornatum (ibid.).

123. des muoz mich nemen wunder grôz, daz sî mê denne halber blôz gânt
ob des gürtels lenge. ir kleit sint alsô enge daz ez mich lasters vil ermant, wan ir
in dem rocke spant der lîp mit lasterlîcher pfliht (15211–17).

124. her Adâm hête Lützel gêren an sîner wête: Prîsschuohe, hûben, gebildet
hemde Wâren im biz an sîn ende fremde (22753–56).

125. Ir herren einhalp mit versnitem gewande, und ir frouwen anderhalp
mit gilwen unde mit zwacken unde mit naewen (vol. 1, p. 527).

126. wie die ermel wol gestênt oder der sleiger oder daz gebende (vol. 1,
p. 415).

127. ir frouwen, ir machet ez gar ze noetlîche mit iuwern gewande, mit
iuwern röckelînen: diu naewet ir sô maniger leie unde sô tôrlîche, daz ir iuch
möhtet schamen in iuwerm herzen (vol. 1, p. 118).

128. ob ir ez eht alse hôhverteclîchen traget, daz ir iuwern lîp dâ mite brankieret unde gampenieret (ibid.).

129. kleider diu ze waehe gesniten sint oder zuogenaewet unde gemachet,
als ir frouwen pfleget ze tuon (vol. 1, p. 25).

130. Iuch genüeget niht, daz iu der almehtige got die wal hât verlân an den
kleidern, wellet ir brûn, wellet ir sie rôt, blâ, grüene, gel, swarz: dar an genüeget
iuch niht. Unde dar zuo twinget iuch iuwer grôziu hôhvart. Man muoz ez iu ze
flecken zersnîden, hie daz rôte in daz wîze, dâ daz gelwe in daz grüene; sô daz
gewunden, sô daz gestreichet; sô daz gickelvêch, sô daz witschenbrûn; sô hie
den lewen, dort den arn (vol. 1, p. 396).

131. Sô habent die frouwen met dem gelwen gebende groezer arbeit, denne
diu diemüteclîch ein wîzez treit, wan ir etelîche legent daz jâr wol halbez dar
an, niur an daz gebende, niur an sleir (vol. 2, p. 242 f.)

132. mit ir hôhvertigem gange unt mit vrömder varwe an dem wange unt
mit gelwem gibende (*Erinnerungen an den Tod* 327–29).

133. Ein magt mit einem gelwen swanze (12408).

134. Blôzer nac und gelwer kitel Lockent manigen valschen bitel, Snüere an
röcken, an kiteln bilde Machent meide and knappen wilde (ibid. 12577–80).

135. dc gelwe röckeli. uñ die gelwon stûchon (Grieshaber, vol. 2, p. 69).

136. owe rosenkrencz! owe myner swencz! owe gele gebende! owe myner wyßen hende! owe myner hoffart! (1996–2000).

3. WEAPONS AND HORSES

1. omne suum harnascha (Rahewin, *Gesta Frederici*, p. 456).

2. durch al der sarringe niet er sluoc den künec Malakîn (W. v. Eschenbach, *Willehalm* 442.26–27).

3. mit der finteilen niht bewart. Heimrîch was undern ougen blôz: diu barbier ez niht umbeslôz: sîn helm et hete ein nasebant (408.4–7).

4. Sin helm brûn lutir stâlin Mit lîstin wol gezierit Vnd uaste gebarbierit Uvor dŏgin vnd vûrz antlitz: Nach den aldin sitin spitz, Als sie phlâgin bi den tagin (E 102–07).

5. man sach da wunder gogelen von tieren und von vogelen ûf manegem helme veste, boum, zwî, unde ir este mit koste geflôrieret (W. v. Eschenbach, *Willehalm* 403.23–27).

6. sîn schilt was alt swaere lanc und breit, sîniu sper unbehende und grôz, halp er und daz ros blôz (H. v. Aue, *Erec* 747–49).

7. alsô wart der dritte var, von golde ûze und innen gar, dar ûf ein mouwe zobelîn, diu niht bezzer mohte sîn, dar über ein buckel geleit: von silber schône zebreit diu rîs, ze breit noch ze smal, si beviengen daz bret über al: daz bestuont diu mouwe. innerhalp ein vrouwe an dem vordern orte: der schiltrieme ein borte mit guotem gesteine: des enwas er niht eine. si wâren innen alle gelîch, die riemen alsamelîch (2304–19).

8. Der knoph und daz gehelze was golt unde gesmelze (H. v. Veldeke, *Eneit* 160.39–40).

9. sîn gehilze was guldîn, diu scheide ein porte rôt (*Nibelungenlied* 1784.2).

10. sô wârn im sîne velze mit buochstaben durchgraben guot (*Virginal* 37.10–11).

11. CHVNRAT VIL VERDER SHENKE VON VINTERSTETEN HOHGEMVT. HIE BI DV MIN GEDENKE. LA GANZ DEHAINE ISENHVT (Wegeli, p. 33).

12. des gehôrte er noch gesach sô wol ûz der îsenwaete als er blôzer taete (H. v. Aue, *Erec* 4157–59).

13. ich enmac mîn harnasch niht getragen ze vüezen, dêst ze swaere (Pleier, *Tandareis* 10233–34).

14. lûter als ein spiegelglas was der helm (W. v. Eschenbach, *Willehalm* 22.28–29).

15. dô sach man von in glesten harnasch wîz als ein zin (U. v. Zatzikhoven 786–87).

16. si sâhen in der vinster der liehten schilde schîn (*Nibelungenlied* 1602.2).

17. der ritter als ein engel stuont gewâpent ritterlîche (R. v. Braunschweig 8390–91).

18. er schein ein engel, niht ein man (U. v. Zatzikhoven 4430).

19. tunica iacintina . . . galeam deauratam (Albert v. Stade, p. 347).

20. diu decke reicht unz ûf den huof (U. v. Liechtenstein, *Frauendienst* 1404.4).

21. Si quis rusticus arma vel lanceam portaverit vel gladium, iudex, in cuius potestate repertus fuerit, vel arma tollat vel viginti solidos pro ipsis a rustico accipiat (Weinrich, p. 220).

22. an dem sunnentage sol er ze kirchen gân, den gart in der hant tragen. wirt daz swert dâ zim vunden, man sol in vuoren gebunden zuo dem kirhzûne: dâ habe man den gebûren unt slahe im hût und hâr abe (14805–11).

23. Thoraces vel ysenhut vel colliria vel juppas de pukramo vel cultrum latinum (Franz, p. 326).

24. hospites (p. 328).

25. langez swert alsam ein hanifswinge, daz treit er allez umbe (59.10–11).

26. cesari ad ecclesiam procedenti, circulo illius decoratus ensem imperatoris honorifice portavit (*Annales Magdeburgenses*, p. 184).

27. in coronamento illo principes potentissimi gestamentum gladii imperialis de jure reclamarent (p. 156).

28. nu kom ouch Heimrîch, der fürste krefte wol gelîch: ein barûn truoc vor im sîn swert, im volgete manec ritter wert (W. v. Eschenbach, *Willehalm* 143.13–16).

29. kein schiltaere entwürfe in baz denn alser ûfem orse saz (W. v. Eschenbach, *Parzival* 158.15–16).

30. mit fliegenden schenkelen, mit sporen und mit enkelen nam er daz ors zen sîten (G. v. Straßburg 6843–45).

31. ze nageln vieren ûf den schilt dâ sol dîn sper gewinnen haft, oder dâ der helm gestricket ist: diu zwei sint rehtiu ritters mâl und ûf der tjost der beste list (*Winsbeke* 21.6–10).

32. Dâ schilt und helme zesamen gât unt dâ den hals daz collir hât beslozen, dâ traf in mîn hant, sô daz daz collir wart entrant und daz der starke biderbe man ein teil sich neigen dâ began (U. v. Liechtenstein, *Frauendienst* 859.1–6).

33. dâ man die riemen heften siht bî den nageln ûf dem schilt, dar wart ze râme vil gezilt mit ritterlîchem sinne (R. v. Braunschweig 7340–43).

34. unz an die hant (H. v. Aue, *Erec* 9095).

35. ein waltswende (W. v. Eschenbach, *Parzival* 57.23).

36. daz tete er umbe daz daz ieman des möhte jehen daz im diu schande waere geschehen daz er in ligende hete erslagen (827–30).

37. palas unde türne von den slegen dôz, dô si mit swerten. hiuwen ûf die helme guot (*Nibelungenlied* 2359.2–3).

38. di fiures funchen uz den helmen sprungen (*Rolandslied* 4812–13).

39. der tet im fianze: daz spricht entiuschen sicherheit (W. v. Grafenberg 7817–18).

40. heten si dô gevohten ze orse mitten swerten, des sî niene gerten, daz waere der armen orse tôt von diu was in beiden nôt daz sî die dörperheit vermiten und daz sî ze vuoze striten. in heten diu ors niht getân (*Iwein* 7116–23).

41. daz ergienc zorse und niht ze fuoz (*Parzival* 263.23).

42. in sîner kintheit zEngellande, sam man seit, vil wol gelernet ringen (H. v. Aue, *Erec* 9282–84).

43. zwischen in und disen scharn wart ûf dem plân manic gegenrenn getân, als man noch durch hôhen muot zwischen den scharn tuot, daz mans hab dester tiur (O. v. Steiermark 11025–30).

44. quidam de exercitu, male affectate laudis avidi, prevenire alios... desiderabant...sperantes se aliquid memorabile facturos (Gesta Frederici, p. 470).

45. Certatur hastis primo, deinde strictis ensibus dimicatur (ibid.).

46. Fugiebant eum universi, neque vim hominis neque audaciam sustinentes (p. 470 f.).

47. et detracta galea atque thorace, capite cesus (p. 472).

48. ir wânt, ez waere hie gestalt als gegen den Franzoisen; ich weiz sô kurtoisen grâf Ybanen niht (25737–40).

49. ir herren dâ ûz Ôsterlant, nû sît ir alle wîgant. ir sult uns ritterlîch bestân und mit den swerten umbe gân und mit uns schône houwen durch willen aller vrouwen. ir werft in uns die zwecke durch die îsnîn decke, sô müez wir vallen ûf den plân, daz ist niht ritterlîch getân. der iu ie swert umb gebant, dem sî verfluochet sîn hant, und iu den schilt gesegnet hât, des sêl müez nimmer werden rât. er scholt einn kocher vollen pfîl iu gesegent haben in einer wîl, daz waer heidenischer sit, dâ waert ir wol geweret mit (J. Enikel, Fürstenbuch 3361–78).

50. arger schützen harte vil (W. v. Eschenbach, Parzival 183.9).

51. Artem autem illam mortiferam et Deo odibilem ballistariorum et sagittariorum adversus Christianos et catholicos exerceri de caetero sub anathemate prohibemus (Mansi, vol. 21, col. 533).

52. Hostes enim quodam genere armorum utebantur admirabili et hactenus inaudito; habebant enim cultellos longos, graciles, triacumines, quolibet acumine indifferenter secantes a cuspide usque ad manubrium quibus utebantur pro gladiis (Guillaume le Breton, vol. 1, p. 283).

53. mit zornes siten reit er ûf in unde trat in nider (Pleier, Tandareis 10881–82).

54. daz man im sîn ros bereite und ir pherit vrouwen Enîten (H. v. Aue, Erec 3059–60).

55. sedens in palefrido (Rahewin, Gesta Frederici, p. 456).

56. sedens in dextrario (ibid.).

57. qui habentur ad labores onerum vel tractus quadrigarum et redarum (p. 1378).

58. caballi fortissimi triginta...cum frenis argenteis et sellis optimis de pallio et ebore compositis (p. 122).

59. equos ferreis cooperturis ornatos (p. 197).

60. guldîn was sîn gügerel, ein boum mit löubern niht zu breit (U. v. Zatzikhoven 4438–39).

61. mit îserkovertiur verdact. ûf daz îsern was gestract ein phellel, des ir was ze vil. der orse muoter man niht wil sô hie ze lande zieren: wir kunnen de ors punieren (395.9–14).

62. Her Keiî li senetschas Der reit gein Hispanje Und brâhte gein Britanje Vil manec guot snellez marc, Hôhez, schoenez unde starc (H. v. d. Türlin 490–94).

63. nuncii regine Hyspanie affuerunt, qui pulcherrimos dextrarios et magnifica munera cesari attulerunt (*Chronica regia Coloniensis*, p. 268).

64. cum pretiosissima veste et equo, qui ad mille marcas estimabatur (*Annales Colmariensis*, p. 267).

4. FOOD AND DRINK

1. Rueben und kumpost Trug man nicht ze tisch; Wilprett und edel fisch Was mit gewurtz den heren wol perait. Mit speyse was da reychait Und dar zu der peste wein Der auff erden mag gesein Truncken di recken do (H. v. Neustadt, *Apollonius* 11407–14).

2. Manic gebûr wirt schimelgrâ, Der selten hât gezzen mensier blâ, Vîgen, hûsen, mandelkern: Rüeben kumpost âz er gern Und was im etwenne alsô sanfte Mit einem heberînen ranfte Als einem herren mit wilde und zam (H. v. Trimberg 9813–19).

3. boesen win, die boesten spise (25.6).

4. Sin kezzelkrut, sin spisebrot, sin boesen zuberwin, diu bringe er vür die hunde hin oder aber vür diu swin (25.9–10).

5. sûrez bier und roggîn was mîn almuosen für mîn tor, swenn ich den armen sach dâ vor (R. v. Ems, *Guter Gerhard* 946–48).

6. Et habebat ante se super mensam duas magnas concas argenteas, in quibus pro pauperibus ponebantur cibaria. Et portebat dapifer semper duo fercula de quolibet ciborum genere secundum diversitates ciborum et ponebat ante fratrem Rigaldum. Ille vero unum ferculum retinebat sibi, de quo comedebat, aliud vero pro pauperibus refundebat in concas. Et sic faciebat de qualibet appositione et diversitate ciborum (Salimbene of Parma, vol. 1, p. 628).

7. man schuof in zeiner lîpnar fleisch und krût, gerstbrîn, ân wiltpraet solden sie sîn, zem vasttag hanf, lins und bôn; visch und öl sie liezen schôn die herren ezzen, daz was sit (VIII.880–85).

8. nû ezzent sie den herren mit (886).

9. que ne dus, ne bers, ne cuens, ne prélaz, ne chevaliers, ne clers, ne autres dou réaume, en quel estat que il soit, ne puisse doner à mengier fors trois mès touz simples (Duplès-Agier, p. 177 f.)

10. se n'est à tarte ou en flaons (p. 178).

11. von edeler spîse vollen rât: vische, hüener, wiltbrât (*Mai u. Beaflor* 39.9–10).

12. den kranich noch den trappen, den reiger noch den kappen, daz rephůn noch den fasan (U. v. Türheim, *Rennewart* 16251–53).

13. der pfâwe vor im gebrâten stuont (W. v. Eschenbach, *Willehalm* 134.9).

14. allati sunt in pompatica gloria duo cigni vel olores ante regem, phalerati retibus aureis vel fistulis deauratis (*Flore historiarum*, vol. 3, p. 132).

15. hanboume stuonden blôz (W. v. Eschenbach, *Parzival* 194.7).

16. Fuerunt ibidem erecte due magne et spaciose domus intrinsecus, undique perticate, que a summo usque deorsum ita gallis sive gallinis replete fuerant, ut nullus eas suspectus penetrare potuerit, non sine ammiratione multorum, qui

tot gallinas in omnibus finibus illis vix esse credebant (Arnold of Lübeck, p. 152).

17. Hic piper atque crocus, hic gingiber atque galange Assunt et faciunt arte placere cibos. His condimentis odor et sapor et color addunt Delicias epulis sedulitate coci (Justinus, *Lippiflorium* 105–08).

18. in kleiniu goltvaz man nam, als ieslîcher spîse zam, salssen, pfeffer, agraz. dâ het der kiusche und der vrâz alle gelîche genuoc (W. v. Eschenbach, *Parzival* 238.25–29).

19. ein halp brot daz man da hiezet gastel—iz ist alumme sinuwel (*Graf Rudolf* H 30–32).

20. Swer machet eine hochzit, swie manege traht man git, da mac kein wirtschaft sin, da ensi guot brot unde wint (Tannhäuser, *Hofzucht* 213–16).

21. man sach da nieman trinken pier, man trank da win und claret, syropel gůt und sǔzen met (U. v. Türheim, *Rennewart* 32230–32).

22. Habuimus igitur illa die primo cerasas, postea panem albissimum; vinum quoque, ut magnificentia regia dignum erat, abundans et precipuum ponebatur... Postea habuimus fabas recentes cum lacte decoctas, pisces et cancros, pastillos anguillarum, risum cum lacte amigdalarum et pulvere cynamomi, anguillas assatas cum optimo salsamento, turtas et iuncatas et fructus necessarios habuimus abundanter atque decenter. Et omnia curialiter fuerunt apposita et sedule ministrata (*Chronica*, vol. 1, p. 322).

23. ine bin solch küchenmeister niht, daz ich die spîse künne sagn, diu dâ mit zuht wart für getragn (W. v. Eschenbach, *Parzival* 637.2–4).

24. das ich uch nu vil seit darab, was spise das man da gab, und auch die gericht: das mecht mir ein groß gebrecht und brecht doch keinen fromen, darumb will ich darvon komen (*Der Junker und der treue Heinrich* 1900–05).

25. ob mich nu ainer vragt wenne si iht aezzen, der ge zu andern vraezzen und la von spise im sagen (J. v. Würzburg 15176–79).

26. Von vil ezzens sage ain vraz (*Wilhelm v. Orlens* 14760).

27. iez vnd trinc daz dir di nature genuge (W. v. Elmendorf 894).

28. Trinkens und ezzens unmêzikeit Bringet manigen liuten ofte leit An lîbe, an sêle, an êren, an guote (H. v. Trimberg 9569–71).

29. deheines vrâzes er sich vleiz: abe einem huone er gebeiz drîstunt, des dûhte in genuoc (H. v. Aue, *Erec* 8648–50).

30. ferculorum multiplicitas...vinorum et poculorum diuersitas... omnium appositorum deliciositas (p. 266).

31. sed potius quędam specialia et leuia et deliciosa coenantibus apponuntur, maxime in curiis dominorum (ibid.).

32. temporis congruitas...loci opportunitas (p. 265).

33. In locis enim spatiosis, amoenis et securis, solent nobiles facere festa sua (ibid.).

34. vultus hilaritatem...Nihil enim valet coena vbi facies hospitis cernitur turbulenta (ibid.).

35. ministrorum vrbanitas seu honestas...cantorum et instrumentorum musicorum iucunditas...Sine enim cithara vel symphonia non solent coenae nobilium celebrari (p. 266).

36. luminarium et cereorum copiosa numerositas (ibid.).

37. . . . hiez schône und küniclîchen wol ummehengen sînen sal mit sper-
lachen über al, die glesten glanz von golde fin. mit tiuwern tepichen sîdîn wart
der estrich beleit und rôsen vil dar ûf gespreit (H. v. Freiberg, *Tristan* 2520–26).

38. dies sidelen wurden wol gedaht mit guoten gultern lieht gemâl. von sa-
mîte und von zendâl wârn plûmât und materaz. kein gesidel wart gezieret baz
(*Mai und Beaflor* 8.16–20).

39. Michel was diu hôchzît und daz gestûle vile wît (H. v. Veldeke, *Eneit*
345.5–6).

40. der truhsaeze vor dem tische stuont der dem herren die sedele gap. in
sîner hende was ein stap der die liute sitzen hiez (*Herzog Ernst* B 3160–63).

41. dô gienc aldâ mit sîme stabe des keisers truhsaeze und schihte daz man
aeze (K. v. Würzburg, *Heinrich v. Kempten* 74–76).

42. man sazte si alle hêrlîch, und doch alle niht gelîch (*Mai und Beaflor*
191.9–10).

43. Dar nach daz ir wirde was Er satzte sie vf die benke (H. v. Fritzlar
530–31).

44. Swer niden, mitten schône und oben Geste kan setzen, den sol man
loben (H. v. Trimberg 5473–74).

45. ieglichem fursten sunderlich was sîn gesidel ûz gemezzen, darinn er sold
ezzen (73398–400).

46. nû huop sich ein kriec hôch: der von Koln für zôch, ez waer alsô her
komen, swâ ein hof wurd genomen von dem rîch in tiutsche lant, dâ solde zuo
der zeswen hant ze naehst des kunigs gemezzen der von Kolne ezzen (73401–
08).

47. die tavel houbt noch ende hât nicht weder hie noch dort, nindert ecke
noch kein ort: die helde, die mit ritters tât ir manheit sô gewirdet hât und ritterlîch erworben hân daz sie gesitzen dar an, die sitzen alle hêrlîch, in einer hêrschaft alle glîch (H. v. Freiberg, *Tristan* 1340–48).

48. ze oberst an dem tische (K. Fleck 3003).

49. der tisch was nider unde lanc. der wirt mit niemen sich dâ dranc. er saz
al eine an den ort (W. v. Eschenbach, *Parzival* 176.13–15).

50. et là fu-je, et vous tesmoing que ce fu la miex arée que je veisse onques;
car à la table le roy manjoit, emprés li, li cuens de Poitiers, que il avoit fait
chevalier nouvel à une saint-Jehan; et après le conte de Poitiers, mangoit li cuens
Jehan de Dreues, que il avoit fait chevalier nouvel aussi; après le conte de
Dreues, mangoit li cuens de la Marche; après le conte de la Marche, li bons
cuens Pierres de Bretaigne. Et devant la table le roy, endroit le conte de Dreues,
mangoit messires li roys de Navarre, en cote et en mantel de samit, bien parez de
courroie, de fermail et de chapel d'or; et je tranchoie devant li (*Histoire de Saint
Louis*, p. 34).

51. Darière ces trois barons avoit bien trente de lour chevaliers, en cottes de
drap de soie, pour aus garder; et darières ces chevaliers avoit grant plentei de
sergans vestus des armes au conte de Poitiers, batues sur cendal (p. 34 f.).

52. ès hales de Saumur; et disoit l'on que li grans roys Henris d'Angleterre
les avoit faites pour ses grans festes tenir. Et les hales sont faites à la guise des

cloistres de ces moinnes blans; mais je croi que de trop loing il n'en soit nuls si grans (p. 35).

53. et uns Alemans de l'aage de dixhuit ans, que on disoit que il avoit estei fiz sainte Helizabeth de Thuringe; dont l'on disoit que la royne Blanche le besoit ou front par devocion, pour ce que elle entendoit que sa mère l'i avoit maintes foiz besié. Ou chief dou cloistre d'autre part estoient les cuisines, les bouteiller-ies, les paneteries et les despenses; de celi chief servoit l'on devant le roy et devant la royne, de char, de vin et de pain. Et en toutes les autres eles et eu prael d'en milieu mangoient de chevaliers si grans foisons, que je ne soy les nombrer; et distrent mout de gens que il n'avoient onques veu autant de seurcoz ne d'autres garnemens de drap d'or et de soie à une feste, comrne il ot là; et dist on que il y ot bien trois mille chevaliers (p. 35 f.).

54. Ruotlieb disposuit sedilia, ceu bene novit, In quo quisque loco sedeat sibi certificato, Dans geminis unam mensam dominis ad habendum (*Ruodlieb* XVI, 26–28).

55. Mit einander dâ âzen Ein ritter und ein vrouwe ie (H. v. d. Türlin, *Krone* 29301–02).

56. bî ieglîchem vürsten saz ein schoene vrowe, diu mit im az, süeze, reine unde guot; dâ von si wurden hôch gemuot (*Mai und Beaflor* 8.27–30).

57. zwênzic kameraere, Juncherren êrbaere, Mit michelen gevuogen (*Krone* 29275–77).

58. drîzic videlaere (29287).

59. Vil manege süeze wîse (29290).

60. zwêne knieten unde sniten: die andern zwêne niht vermiten, sine trüegen trinkn und ezzen dar, und nâmen ir mit dienst war (W. v. Eschenbach, *Parzival* 237.17–20).

61. si kniete nider (daz was im leit), mit ir selber hant si sneit dem rîter sîner spîse ein teil (ibid. 33.9–11).

62. swenn siz parel im gebôt, daz gerüeret het ir munt, sô wart im niwe freude kunt daz er dâ nâch solt trinken (ibid. 622.22–25).

63. vil hôhe kameraere, die hôchsten von dem lande, in rîchem gewande, die knieten unde buten dar die twehelen vil wîz gevar (*Herzog Ernst* B 3178–82).

64. Officium dapiferi sive pincerne, camerarii vel marscalci, non nisi reges vel duces aut marchiones amministrabant (Arnold of Lübeck, p. 152).

65. von golde ein kandel und einen koph von golde swaere fuort sîn hôhster kameraere. der schal wart ungefüeg und grôz von der pusûnen dôz; floiten und teubaere, schalmîen und pûkaere, mit grôzen hersumpern under einander pumpern—ez gap sô grôzen schal dâ über daz gevilde al, dâ diu gesidel wâren ûf, als ob ez allez ze hûf von dem dôze wolde gên. wîchen und ûf hôher stên muoste dâ meniclich, dô von Bêheim der kunic rîch mit sô hôchvertigen siten in diu gesidel kom geriten (O. v. Steiermark 73604–22).

66. den stap und diu trincvaz (73604–22).

67. den truhsaezen giengen mit busûner die in bliesen vor. man warf die tambûr enbor mit slegen daz der wîte sal dem gedoene engegen hal (W. v. Grafenberg 9484–52).

68. A chascun mes les trompes sonnent. Dames i avoit qui servoient; De

dras d'or parees estoient, Devant cascun mes vont cantant (Philippe de Remi, *Jehan et Blonde* 5998–6001).

69. sô stunden dâr an einen rinc tûsint jungelinge von irn ingesinde, die plâgen hubischeite vile mit allir slahte seitspile (6034–38).

70. alse di harfen clungen, di juncfrouwen sungen und tanzeten unde trâten (6055–57).

71. Sie ttunken unde âzen . . . unt sâhen maneger hande spil, des man vor in mahte vil (*Die Heidin* 708–10).

72. pastes de vis oiselés (2876).

73. köphe näphe goltrôt, die schüzzel von silber wol getân (*Herzog Ernst* B 2394–95).

74. scutellae etiam mensae eius ex auro puro et argento subtili opere fabricatae, ad omnia fercula licet mensae eius deferebantur (*Annales Otakariani*, p. 194.).

75. in mensa cottidiana vasa aurea et argentea, quibus cibi et pocula inferebantur, ad mille marcas sunt appreciata (Arnold of Lübeck, p. 204).

76. vasa ex argento et auro facta (*Gesta Frederici*, p. 706).

77. swaz er des mâles drinne vant von kostbaerlichen vazzen, daz warf er an die gazzen den gernden algemeine. guldîne köpfe reine und manec schüzzel silberîn wart von der milten hende sîn geworfen ûf die ritterschaft, diu noetic unde kumberhaft sîner helfe gerte (K. v. Würzburg, *Turnier von Nantes* 52–61).

78. vier karrâschen (*Parzival* 237.22).

79. ieslîchem gieng ein schrîber nâch, der sich dar zuo arbeite und si wider ûf bereite, Sô dâ gedienet waere (237.28–238.1).

80. Apud Neuuenpurch sunt VI ciphi cum copertoriis argentei et V craterȩ argentee sine copertoriis, tria argentea cum opertoriis et IIII sine opertorio . . . argenteus et coclearia duo argentea; hec sunt sedecim vasa argentea (p. 67).

81. unum lavachrum mirabile . . . , quod similitudinem pavonis in forma ostendebat (*Chronica majora*, vol. 5, p. 489).

82. summus . . . senescalcus totius comitatus Hainoie (p. 336).

83. summus . . . camerarius (ibid.).

84. summus . . . pincerna (ibid.).

85. emptor . . . escarum ad coquinam pertinentium et ipsarum custos escarum (p. 337).

86. Cujus precepto vinum ad curiam apportatur et in curia in mensis propinatur (ibid.).

87. propria manu debet vinum propinare coram domino comite vel coram domina comitissa (ibid.).

88. vinum ad curiam apportatum in vasis debet conservare et in cyffos vel in ollas ad propinandum infundere (p. 338).

89. Latores vini et cujuslibet poculi (ibid.).

90. ipsius precepto portatur panis ad curiam a domo pistoris hereditarii seu a venditoribus (bid.).

91. Pistor hereditarius (p. 339).

92. Custos panis aportati ad curiam et mensalium (ibid.).

93. Impositor mensarum et mensalium super mensas et portandi panem post panitarium ad serviendum et distribuendum in curia (ibid.).

94. habet de ministerio suo pallia seu capas omnium, qui hominagium faciunt domino comiti Hainoiensi (ibid.).

95. facere candelas precepto camerarii et per pondus camerario factas amministrare. Amministrare etiam aquam ipsi camerario, ut ipse camerarius eam porrigat comiti et comitisse, ipse autem minor camerarius clericis et militibus aquam debet porrigere (ibid.).

96. ministerium habet ministrandi ad curiam ollas figularias tam ad cameram quam ad coquinam et ad vinum propinandum necessarias (p. 340).

97. precepto panitarii Montensis debet condere lardarium comitis (ibid.).

98. ministerium habet custodiendi claves cellarii (ibid.).

99. ministerium habet quoddam colligendi redditus comitis in agnis et avena in villis circa Montes (ibid.).

100. Isci comencent les reules ke le bon eveske de Nichole Robert Grosseteste fist a la contesse de Nichole de garder e governer terres e hostel (*Rules*, p. 388).

101. La [disesetime] reule vus aprent coment vus devez asser genz al manger en vostre hostel. Fetes tote vostre fraunche maysnee e les hostes a plus ke lem poet ser a tables, de une part e de autre e ensemble, ne pas ci quatre et la treys . . . e vus memes tutes oures en miliu seez del haute table, ke voske presence a tuz uvertement (cum seignur ou dame aperge, e ke vous overtement) puissez de une part e de autre ver tuz e le servise e le defautes. A co seyez ententive ke iescun iur a vostre manger eyez overtement deus survues sur vostre hostel quaunt vus seez a manger (p. 402).

102. Comaundez ke vostre mareschal ententif soyt de estre present sur la mesnee, a numeement en sale, de garder la mesnee dehors e dedenz nette, e saunz tencun u noyse u vileyne parole; e a chescun mes apele les serviturs de aler a la quisine, e il memes auge tute voye devaunt vostre seneschal deske a vus e deske vostre mes seyt devaunt vus asis, e puis auge ester en miliu de la sale al chef, e veye ke ordeneement e saunz noyse augent les seriaunz ove les mes, de une part e de autre de la sale, a cels ki serrunt assingne de asser les, mes issi ke lem ne asete, ne serve desordeneement par especialte, dunt vus meymes eyez le oyl al service deske les mes seyent assis en hostel. Pus entendez a vostre manger e comaundez ke vostre esquele seyt issi replenie e tassee, e numeement des entremes, ke curteysement puissez partir de vostre esquele a destre e a senestre par tute vostre haute table, e la vus plarra, tut eyent eus de mesmes co ke vus avez devaunt vus (p. 404).

103. en quel vesture vos genz vus deyvent servir a vostre manger (p. 402).

104. le ostel al manger est servi de deus mes gros e pleners pur le aumone acrestre, e de deus entremes pleners par tote la fraunche meynee, e al soper de un mes de legere chose e ausi un entremes, e puis furmage, e si estraunges survenent al super lem lur sert sulunc co kil unt bosoyn de plus (p. 404).

105. nec comedas panem priusquam veniat aliud ferculum super mensam, ne dicaris impatiens; nec tantum ponas bolum in ore tuo, ut micae defluant hinc et inde, ne dicaris gluto; nec glutias bolum priusquam bene fuerit commastica-

tum in ore tuo, ne stranguleris; ne pocula sumas donec os sit vacuum, ne dicaris vinosus; nec loquaris dum aliquid in ore tuo tenueris (p. 37).

106. Wusch den mund mit diner hant! (p. 543).

107. ob ez aber also geschiht, so nemet hovelich daz gewant Und jucket da mit, daz zimt baz, denn iu diu hant unsuber wirt (111–14).

108. Sümliche bizent ab der sniten und stozents in die schüzzel wider nach geburischen siten; sülh unzuht legent die hübschen nider (Tannhäuser 45–48).

109. Ern ruochte wâ diu wirtin saz: einen guoten kropf er az, dar nâch er swaere trünke tranc (W. v. Eschenbach, *Parzival* 132.1–3).

110. Er verschoup alsô der wangen want mit spîse dier vor im dâ vant, dazz drîn niht dorfte snîen (W. v. Eschenbach, *Willehalm* 275.1–3).

111. dort haben wir manec geslende, dâ mite wir sulen den lîp gelabn (326.28–29).

112. sniten in öl gebrouwen (C 1497.3).

113. die êrsten traht (863).

114. ein krût vil kleine gesniten (867).

115. ein veizter kaese, der was mar (871).

116. ein huon gebrâten, einz versoten (881).

117. die gebûre nie bekande (888).

118. ich wil in loben immer für bûhurdieren und für tanz. crône, tschapel unde cranz, pfelle, samît und scharlât, swaz gezierede disiu werlt hât, die naeme ich niht für den wîn (*Weinschwelg* 44–49).

119. ichn hân niht jagehunde, noch winde, noch vederspil. ich hân ouch rosse niht sô vil, daz ich turnieren rîte noch ze ritterlîchem strîte. ich enweiz ouch niht der vrouwen, die mich iht gerne schouwen. ich hân ouch niht sô guot gewant, des ich ze vüeren in daz lant deheine vröude müge hân. sol ich ze tanze nacket gân? dâ bin ich ouch der liute spot (52–63).

120. ich . . . wil inz luoder treten (Steinmar 1.10).

121. Sît si mir niht lônen wil der ich hân gesungen vil, seht sô wil ich prîsen den der mir tuot sorgen rât, herbest der des meien wât vellet von den rîsen. ich weiz wol, ez ist ein altez maere daz ein armez minnerlîn ist rehte ein marteraere. seht, zuo den was ich geweten: wâfen! die wil ich lân und wil inz luoder treten (Steinmar 1.1–10).

122. wirt, du solt uns vische geben mê dan zehen hande, gense hüener vogel swîn, dermel pfâwen sunt dâ sîn, wîn von welschem lande. des gib uns vil und heiz uns schüzzel schochen: köpfe und schüzzel wirt von mir unz an den grunt erlochen (ibid. 22–28).

123. hovelîch und gemeit (921).

124. daz sind nû hovelîchiu dinc: "trinkâ, herre, trinkâ trinc! trinc daz ûz, sô trink ich daz!" . . . ein affe und ein narre waser, der ie gesente sînen lîp für guoten wîn umbe ein wîp. swer liegen kan der ist gemeit, triegen daz ist hövescheit (985–88; 1004–08).

125. her Frâz . . . her Slunt (10178).

126. unmaze des mundes (vol. 2, p. 204).

127. diu selbe sünde der ist niendert alsô vil, sô hie ze tiutschen landen und aller meiste herren ûf bürgen und burger in steten (p. 205).

128. Sun, beidiu, luoder unde spil sint lîbes und der sêle val (45.1–2).

CHAPTER IV: COURTLY FEASTS

1. COURT FEASTS

1. plures quam LXX (re)gn(i) . . . principes (*Annales Marbacenses*, p. 54).

2. incredibilisque multitudo hominum diversarum regionum vel linguarum ibi coadunata est (Otto of St. Blasien, p. 37).

3. Dat was de groteste hochtit en, de ie an Dudischeme lande ward. Dar worden geachtet de riddere uppe viertich dusent ân ander volk (p. 232).

4. exceptis clericis et cujuscumque conditionis hominibus (p. 156).

5. procerissime constructe sunt in circuitu (Otto of St. Blasien, p. 38).

6. de omnibus terris (p. 151).

7. que per descensum sive per ascensum Reni advecta fuerat (ibid.).

8. liberalissime (*Chronica regia Coloniensis*, p. 133).

9. singulis ad ostendendam sue dignitatis magnificenciam sumptus ambiciosissime conferentibus (Otto of St. Blasien, p. 38).

10. exquisitisque conviviis sumptuosissime exhibitis (ibid.).

11. in maxima gloria et honore (Albert of Stade, p. 350).

12. militibus captivis et cruce signatis (Gislebert of Mons, p. 156).

13. equi, vestes preciose, aurum et argentum (ibid.).

14. Principes enim et alii nobiles non solum pro dominorum suorum, scilicet imperatoris et ejus filiorum honore, sed eciam pro sui proprii nominis fama dilatanda, largius sua erogabant (ibid., p. 156 f.).

15. quamvis ceteris non esset corpore major vel decentior, tamen pre ceteris eum gerere scutum suum decebat (ibid., p 157).

16. sinistro casu (*Chronica s. Petri Erfordensis*, p. 192).

17. divino iudicio (*Chronica regia Coloniensis*, p. 133).

18. filiis huius seculi prudencia sua, que stulticia est apud Deum, in generatione sua abutentibus (Otto of St. Blasien, p. 38).

19. nominatum de consilio principum (Gislebert of Mons, p. 160).

20. tractatisque diversis imperii ab imperatore negociis (Otto of St. Blasien, p. 38).

21. sicut in convivio Assueri (p. 151).

22. ichn vernam von hôhzîte in allen wîlen mâre, diu alsô grôz wâre, alsam dô het Ênêas, wan diu ze Meginze dâ was, die wir selbe sâgen, desn dorfen wir niet frâgen, diu was betalle unmâzlîch, dâ der keiser Friderîch gab zwein sînen sunen swert, dâ manech tûsent marke wert verzeret wart und vergeben. ich wâne alle die nû leben deheine grôzer haben gesehen. ichn weiz waz noch sole geschehen, desn kan ich ûch niht bereiten. ichn vernam von swertleiten nie wârlîche mâre, dâ sô manech vorste wâre und aller slahte lûte. ir lebet genûch noch hûte, diez wizzen wârlîche. dem keiser Friderîche geschach sô manech êre, daz man iemer mêre wunder dâ von sagen mach unz an den jungisten tach, âne logene vor wâr. ez wirt noch uber hundert jâr von ime gesaget und gescriben (347.14–348.3).

23. In festo desponsationis imperatricis Ysabellae, sororis domini regis Angliae, erant tam apud Maguntiam quam Wermesiam quatuor reges, et un-

decim duces, et triginta comites et marchiones, praeter praelatos (Matthew of Paris, *Chronica majora*, vol. 3, p. 324).

24. Eodem etiam tempore, convocatis optimatibus tam Bawariae quam Sueviae, in plano Lici ultra Augustam, in loco qui dicitur Conciolegum, solempne penthechosten celebravit innumerabilemque multitudinem undecunque coadunatam laute pavit (*Historia Welforum*, p. 70).

25. Artûs der meienbaere man, swaz man ie von dem gesprach, zeinen pfinxten daz geschach odr in des meien bluomenzît. waz man im süezes luftes gît! (W. v. Eschenbach, *Parzival* 281.16–20).

26. ze ûz gândem aberellen (U. v. Zatzikhoven 8787).

27. ze îngênden meien (Otte 2817).

28. gekroenet als ein keiserîn (9354).

29. vrouwe Lârîe satzte im dô ûf sîn houbet schône die guldînen krône und bevalch in sîne hant ir lîp, ir liute und ir lant mit einem zepter guldîn (9433–38).

30. barûne und lanthêrren (H. v. Freiberg, *Tristan* 517).

31. grâven, vrîen, dienestman (*Mai und Beaflor* 69.14).

32. Min gewalt get so wide. Virsizzet iz daz geman. Der moz den liph virloren han (1554–56).

33. uns sol der koste niht beviln. wir suln uns rîch da erbieten, sie sô ze frôuden mieten und suln ir gemüete zenen daz sie sich nâch uns müezen senen (U. v. Etzenbach, *Wilhelm v. Wenden* 1384–88).

34. In quo novos milites creaverunt et honorabiliter vestierunt, munera distribuerunt, glorie sue divicias ostendentes, nobilibus terre se benivolos exhibentes, se in ipso ducatu arcius [read: acrius] imprimentes, ut adversarii, si qui essent, et emuli rubore perfunderentur et fideles ad ipsos fidelius firmarentur (vol. 1, p. 324).

35. ein künic sô rîchet der solte dicker (geste) sehen, als ir sît genennet und ich iu hoere jehen. er solte mit sînen helden ofte buhurdieren, dâ mite er sîniu erbe und sich selben solte . . . zieren (31.1–4).

36. Hei wie wol ez doch stuont! die vürsten des nû wênic tuont, daz si sô offenbaere sîn. ez ist ein swaerer pîn, swâ si sint bî liuten vil. ir deheiner ez nû lîden wil, daz a sich lâze dringen. si kunnent niewan twingen, den si solden vröude geben: die müezen von in in kumber leben. des ist vröude verdorben gar (87.29–39).

37. Qui porroit ce des princes croire, S'il ne v(o)it out oïst la voire, Qu'a maingier font fermer lor us? Se m'aïst deus, je ne m'an puis Taire, quant dïent cil usier: "Or fors! mes sires vuet maingier!" (*L'enseignement des princes* 73–78).

38. cum magno et honesto apparatu, tam vasis argenteis multis quam ceteris sibi necessariis, et cum servientibus honeste ornatis (Gislebert of Mons, p. 155).

39. Ad regales curias quando veniebat, spectaculum omnibus erat; solus admiratione dignus videbatur; comitatus et expensae magnificentia omnes alios principes obscurabat (Balderic, *Gesta Alberonis*, p. 604).

40. marschalke si vür sanden, die in solden enblanden umb herberge in der stat (*Mai u. Beaflor* 70.13–15).

41. hütten und gezelt (592).

42. guot vexillum ducis in eodem hospitio pro signo affixum in cloacam

deiceretur (Matthew of Paris, *Chronica majora*, vol. 2, p. 384).

43. ut bettegewaete unt ander hûsgeraete, kophe unt tischlachen von rîchlichen sachen, schüzzel unt becher swaere (4040–44).

44. tûsent kastelân (U. v. Zatzikhoven 56–7).

45. zwelf hundert râvîde (ibid. 5609).

46. tûsent tuoch wurden versniten von scharlach wîz unde rôt (*Weltchronik* 12930–31).

47. zweinzic hundert ballen von lî*nînen* tuochen (12952–53).

48. daz si gâben schuoch genuoc allen (den) die dar kâmen (12936–37).

49. zaeme und gereit (7689).

50. scharlach und brunât, paltikîn und siglât, grâ, hermîn unde bunt mêr dann umb zweinzic tûsent phunt muost man zder hôchzît koufen (7690–94).

51. daz darüber âne vorht zehen neben einander riten (7729–30).

52. daz ieglich hûfe groezer waere denn diu kirch ze Salhenouwe (7753–54).

53. unz daz des kunigs schrîbaere zuo der reitung sâzen: daz brôt, daz si dâ gâzen, und mit dem, daz über wart, der selben reitunge wart weizes tûsent mutte (7771–76).

54. Tanta fuit affluencia expensarum, ut modum excederet, et purpurarum variarum et scindati atque diversorum colorum vestium a Venetorum excredicione transvecta, ut usque ad hec tempora nondum sint soluta, et nobiles in agendis et cives ad duces Carinthie potentialiter indagati a Venetis in suis mercatibus tedia sint perpessi (Johann of Victring, vol. 1, p. 324).

55. der wirt engegen im gie verre vür daz bürgetor: dâ saluierte er in vor (H. v. Aue, *Erec* 8175–77).

56. innumera multitudo nobilium armatorum (Roger of Wendover, *Flores historiarum*, vol. 3, p. 111).

57. cereis accensis (Matthew of Paris, *Chronica majora*, vol. 3, p. 321).

58. cum processione solenni campanas pulsantes et cantica laetitiae modulantes (Roger of Wendover, vol. 3, p. 111).

59. magistri cujuscumque generis musicae artis cum suis instrumentis (ibid.).

60. qui in equis sedentes Hispanicis ad agilem eos cursum urgebant, dum hastas et arundines, quas ferebant in manibus, in alterutrum confregerunt (ibid.).

61. naves, quasi remigantes per aridam, equis absconditis et tectis sericis coopertoriis illas trahentibus; in quibus navibus clerici suaviter modulantes cum organis bene sonantibus audientibus inauditas cum stupore fecerunt melodias (Matthew of Paris, vol. 3, p. 322).

62. der busûnen lût erschal (482.7).

63. Dar nâch ein holreblâser sluoc einen sumber meisterlîch genuoc (485.1–2).

64. dar nâch zwêne fideler guot riten, die mich hôch gemuot machten: wan si fidelten hô ein reisenot (486.5–8).

65. nâch tugenden und nâch êren si al ir dinc rihten. ir schar si schône schihten (*Mai u. Beaflor* 70.20–22).

66. schône mit hovelîchen siten (70.36).

67. gar stolz was diu massenî. ie mit einer vrouwen reit ein edel ritter gemeit, der ir al die stunde die zît vertrîben kunde mit süezen maeren ûf der vart. sus riten si schône geschart (70.38–71.4).

68. man muose si neben den vrouwen buhurdieren schouwen (71.27–28).

69. ie zuo eim juncvröwelîn wart geschaft ein ritter dar der ir naem mit dienste war (Pleier, *Tandareis* 14941–43).

70. dô was guot kurzwîle des weges drî mîle. si vunden guote beize dâ: beide bach unde lâ lagen antvogele vol. swaz ein habech vâhen sol, des vunden si dâ vil (H. v. Aue, *Erec* 2034–40).

71. susceptus est ab archiepiscopo manuque deductus ad aecclesiam, accensis luminaribus cunctisque sonantibus campanis (p. 64).

72. ut tot sibi equos mitteret, quot duci campanas sonare vel quot coronas accendi preciperet (ibid., p. 66).

73. cum maximis sumptibus triumphali pompa preparata tota coronatur civitas, tapetibus sertisque diversi generis et precii competa illustrantibus, thure, myrra aliisque speciebus odoriferis intus et extra civitatem redolentibus plateis (p. 62).

74. omni faleramento equestri vestiumque varietate adornati, ordine stacionario (ibid.).

75. singulis quibusque pro suo modo vel arte cum omnibus musice discipline instrumentis plausum exhibentibus (ibid).

76. cunctis laudes affatim acclamantibus (p. 63).

77. mit hêrlîchem gedrange, mit phîfen und mit gesange, mit trumben unt mit seitspile (337.39–338.1).

78. mit phelle behangen (338.8).

79. in küniclîcher wirdekeit gecroenet unde rîch gecleit (1819–20).

80. hêrre, nû wese wir iur (1859).

81. die vrouwen sungen lîse (als sungen sie in süezer wîse got zuo êren) ein lobesanc dem hêren keiser Alexandrô (1891–95).

82. vor sanc der legum dominus, dem die andern alsus mit gesange alle des volgeten mit schalle (1913–16).

83. tambûren dôz, bûsinen snar was dâ manger leie dar. vil guoter vloitiere, hübischer videler viere an geleit nâch rîchen siten zenaehest vor dem hêrren riten, die ûf strichen guoter muoze die reisenote gar suoze (1939–46).

84. mit aller hande seitenspil (1957).

85. ir was vil, die nâch dem salter sungen und nâch der lîren sprungen, dise ruorten die zitôl, die andern suoze unde wol die rotten, harphen ruorten, die die jungen vuorten. der künste sie meister wâren (1958–65).

86. die hêrren hôher geburt die spil erlernten vor nieman, er muost daz adel zuo hân (1968–70).

87. diu schoene maget sprach: "sit willekomen, her Sîvrit, ein edel riter guot." dô wart im von dem gruoze vil wol gehoehet der muot. Er neic ir flîzeclîche; bi der hende si in vie. wie rehte minneclîche er bî der frouwen gie! (292.2–293.2).

88. Rex autem festum nativitatis Domini Magdeburch cum ingenti magnificentia celebravit, ipseque die sancto regalibus indumentis, imperiali dyademate insignitus, sollempniter incedebat sed et coniux sua Erina augusta regio

cultu excellentissime simul ornata, venerabili domna Agnete Quidelinghe-
burgensi abbatissa et domna Iuditta, Bernardi ducis Saxonie uxore, aliarumque
illustrium feminarum stipante caterva, regem fuit tam decentissime quam
venustissime prosecuta. Episcopi quoque qui aderant, pontificalibus indumentis
ornati, regem et reginam ex utroque latere tam reverenter quam honorabiliter
conduxerunt. Bernardus autem dux Saxonie, qui et ensem regium preferebat,
ceterique principes assistentes, viri quoque nobiles, comites et barones, omnisque generis plebs, colllecta in obsequio regis et tante sollempnitatis offitio,
sedulitate ferventes erant; omnesque qui aderant, quorum inconprehensibilis
exstitit numerus, corde gaudentes, animis exultantes, manibus applaudentes,
vocibus perstrepentes, opere vigilantes huic sollempnitati uniformiter
arriserunt, ipsam per omnia debite devotionis tripudio peragentes (*Gesta Hal-
berstadensis ecclesia pontificum*, p. 113 f.).

89. Ez gienc, eins tages als unser hêrre wart geborn von einer maget dier im
ze muoter hât erkorn, ze Megdeburc der künec Philippes schône. dâ gienc eins
keisers bruoder und eins kaisers kint in einer wât, swie doch die namen drîge
sint: er truoc des rîches zepter and die krône. er trat vil lîse, in was niht gâch:
im sleich ein hôhgeborniu küneginne nâch, rôs âne dorn, ein tûbe sunder gallen.
diu zuht was niener anderswâ (19.5–14).

90. Domnus autem Conradus, imperialis aule cancellarius, sagaciter cuncta
disposuit et prudenter et ut ordinate fierent omnia fideliter procuravit (p. 114).

91. mit gebaerden und mit grûze (U. v. Türheim, *Rennewart* 18940).

92. Got alrêst, dar nâch mir, west willekomen (W. v. Eschenbach, *Parzival*
305.27–28).

93. umbe wîbe gruoz (ibid. 456.21).

94. dâr bî men vorsten prîsen mûz daz sî di lûte grûzen wal (B. v. Holle,
Demantin 7204–05).

95. frouwe, iuch wil empfâhen hie der künec hêr. swen ich iuch heize
küssen, daz sol sîn getân: jane muget ir niht gelîche grüezen alle Etzelen man
(*Nibelungenlied* 1348.2–4).

96. mit grôzer zuht sî vor im stuont. Gâwân sprach "frouwe, iwer muont ist
sô küssenlîch getân, ich sol iweren kus mit gruoze hân." ir munt was heiz, dick
unde rôt, dar an Gâwân den sînen bôt. da ergienc ein kus ungastlich (405.15–
21).

97. si zwô si wâren under in süezer unmuoze mit zweier hande gruoze
grüezende unde nîgende, sprechende unde swîgende. ir reht was an in beiden
besetzet unde bescheiden: ir eine gruozte, diu ander neic, diu muoter sprach, diu
tohter sweic. diz triben di wol gezogen zwô (G. v. Straßburg 11014–23).

98. quedam curia solacii et leticie (*Chronica*, p. 45).

99. Factum est enim ludicrum quoddam castrum, in quo posite sunt dompne
ne cum virginibus sive domicellabus et servitricibus earundem, que sine alicuius
viri auxilio castrum prudentissime defenderunt. Fuit eciam castrum talibus
municionibus undique premunitum: scilicet variis et griseis et cendatis, purpur-
is, samitis et ricellis, scarletis et baldachinis et armerinis. Quid de coronis aureis,
cum grisolitis et iacintis, topaciis et smaragdis, piropis et margaritis, omnisque
generis ornamentis, quibus dompnarum capita tuta forent ab impetu pugnator-
um? Ipsum quoque castrum debuit expugnari et expugnatum fuit huiuscemodi

telis et instrumentis: pomis, datalis et muscatis, tortellis, piris et coctanis, rosis, liliis et violis, similiter ampullis balsami, amphii et aque rosee, ambra, camphora, cardamo, cinamo, gariofolis, melegetis, cunctis immo florum vel specierum generibus, quecunque redolent vel splendescunt (p. 46).

100. arbitrium et ordinacionem dompnarum et militum et totius curie sive ludi (ibid.).

101. Et jubente imperatore, plures vidit et cum delectatione inspexit ludorum ignotorum et instrumentorum musicorum, quae ad exhilarandam imperatricem parabantur, diversitates. Inter quas novitates obstupendas, unam magis laudavit at admirabatur. Duae enim puellae Saracenae, corporibus elegantes, super pavimenti planiciem quatuor globos sphericos pedibus ascendebant, plantis suis subponentes, una videlicet duos, et alia reliquos duos, et super eosdem globos huc et illuc plaudentes transmeabant; et quo eas spiritus ferebat, volventibus spheris ferebantur, brachia ludendo et canendo diversimode contorquentes, et corpora secundum modulos replicantes, cimbala tinnientia vel tabellas in manibus collidentes et jocose se gerentes et prodigialiter exagitantes. Et sic mirabile spectaculum intuentibus tam ipsae quam alii joculatores praebuerunt (*Chronica majora*, vol. 4, p. 147).

102. dâ was spil unde sank, buhurt unde gedrank, phîfen unde springen, videlen unde singen, orgeln unde seitspil, maneger slahte froude vil (H. v. Veldeke, *Eneit* 345.31–36).

103. swes der man gerte, dâ in sîn wille zuo truoc, des vant er alles dâ genuoc. buhurdieren, rîterschaft, schermen, schiezen den schaft, den stein werfen unde springen, videlen, herpfen, singen: man mohte dâ tanzen schouwen von magden und von frouwen (Otte 2830–82).

104. armbrust unde bogen die hulfen kurzewîlen mit pölzen und mit pfilen (Stricker, *Daniel* 8180–82).

105. dâ liefen knappen umb daz guot (ibid. 8171).

106. die liefen die barre (H. v. d. Türlin, *Mantel* 302).

107. sô schuzzen jene zuo dem zil (ibid. 304).

108. jene sprungen dise zuoloufes, jene von stete (ibid 295–96).

109. ringen (Pleier, *Garel* 20112).

110. Dise sluogen den bal (H. v. d. Türlin, *Krone* 692).

111. sô spilten die ûf dem brete mîle alde wurfzabels; dise phlâgen schâchzabels, jene teilten ir spil an den val (H. v. d. Türlin, *Mantel* 297–300).

112. duo scâhzâbel et II wrfzâbel (p. 68).

113. unum scahzâbel, unum wurfzabel (ibid.).

114. tria wurfzabel, tria scâhzâbel, elefantei lapides tam ad wurfzâbel quam ad scahzabel pertinentes (p. 67).

115. des sach man dâ genuoc, daz einer ûf der hant truoc eine burc unmâzen grôz. den des ze sehene bedrôz, der sach dâ liute die flogen (Stricker, *Daniel* 8175–79).

116. sumelîchiu ûf den kugelen gie, daz sî dem fuoze sich niht entseiten. sumelich sich sêr erbeiten mit sprüngen, an den lac flîz (U. v. d. Türlin 96.14–17).

117. Facto fine cibis vaga turba recurrit ad artes, Quisque suas repetens, inde placere volens. Hic canit, auditum dulcedine vocis amicans, Ille refert lyri-

co carmine gesta ducum, Hic tangit digitis distinctas ordine chordas, Hic facit arte sua dulce sonare lyram. Tibia dat varias per mille foramina voces, Dant quoque terribilem tympana pulsa sonum. Hic salit et vario motu sua membra fatigat, Se plicat et replicat, se replicando plicat, Pro pedibus docet ire manus, pes surgit in altum, Et caput ima petit: ecce Chymera patet! Hic profert varias magica velut arte figuras Ac oculos fallit mobilitate manus. Hic catulo vel equo populo spectacula praebet, Quos jubet humanos gesticulare modos. Hic forti gyro projectat in aera discum, Quem lapsum recipit huncque remittit item. Talibus ac aliis ludis festivus habetur Iste dies (Justinus 117–36).

118. di lewen also grimme mit den beren uechten (*Rolandslied* 646–47).

119. di adelaren daz zu gewenit waren, daz si scate baren (658–60).

120. helfande, löuwen unde bern zôch man durch kurzwîle für (K. v. Würzburg, *Partonopier* 17422–23).

121. contrefait les aventures de Bretaigne et de la Table ronde (p. 7).

122. ludus liberalis (*In Evangelium Lucae*, p. 493).

123. quia ipse ludus animum liberum et virtuosum reddit, et provocat ad virtutem et cordis lenitatem et mansuetudinem (ibid.).

124. ludus utilis, tamen mechanicus (ibid.).

125. ludus obscoenus et turpis (ibid.).

126. ludus scenicorum, qui nudi discurrunt, turpia tecta denudant, et ad turpia provocant (ibid.).

127. ludus taxillorum (ibid.).

128. Wälscher gîgaere, wizzic unde maere, der was dâ driu hundert (Stricker, *Daniel* 8141–43).

129. sehzic tiutscher spilman die hôrte man dâ strichen, den kunde niht gelîchen (8152–54).

130. man hôrte dâ hellen sumbere mit schellen. manger hande pfîfen (8155–57).

131. hundert harpfaere die machten dâ vil süezen dôn (8160–61).

132. zweinzic singaere (8163).

133. vrouwe Musica (*Krone* 22108).

134. Dort hoer ich die flöuten wegen, hie hoer ich den sumber regen. der uns helfe singen, disen reien springen, dem müeze wol gelingen zallen sînen dingen! (Tannhäuser, *Gedichte* 3.112–17).

135. Harpfen, rotten und gîgen Wil süeze andâht, zuht und swîgen: Urliuge wil toben und schrîen, Bûden, swegeln und schalmîen (H. v. Trimberg 5857–60).

136. immoderatum sonum faciant (*In politicorum continuatio*, p. 478).

137. nû seht! vür alle dise spil ich die videle loben wil, sie ist ze hoeren gesunt. welich herz mit riuwe ist verwunt, daz enphâht senfte gemüete vor ir süezer doene güete (U. v. Etzenbach, *Alexander* 14651–56).

138. weder mit tambur noch mit busine wolten sich die vrowen lan betôren. videlen, harpfen, rotten und ander sûze dône si wolden hôren (*Jg. Titurel* 1844.2–4).

139. kurzewîl man aldâ phlac: reien, springen, danzen, gar minniclîchen swanzen (U. v. Etzenbach, *Alexander* 26828–30).

140. hiure siht man megde reien (Kanzler IX.2.4).

141. in media curia imperatoris principes eius iuniores et alii milites more suo, eos ipso imperatore de imperiali suo palatio prospectante, choreas suas luderent (Vincent of Prague, p. 676).

142. ûf des küneges palas was vröude unt kurzwîle genuoc, unt manec juncvrouwe kluoc unt manec ritter wert erkant an dem man niht wan tugent vant die tanzten unde sprungen mit den vrowen unt sungen ze tanze manec hübschiu liet (Pleier, *Tandareis* 1090–97).

143. ie zwischen zwein frouwen stuont, als si noch bî tanze tuont, ein ritter an ir hende (*Helmbrecht* 97–99).

144. wir treten aber ein hovetänzel (Neidhart 40.23–24).

145. Springerwir den reigen (*Carmina Burana* 137 a. 1).

146. dâ wart ein wunneclicher tanz von in gemachet bî der zît, der nâch dem wunsche enwiderstrît wart dâ gesprungen und getreten (*Trojanerkrieg* 28192–95).

147. ein magt in süezer wîse, wol gebrîset, liehte varwe, sîten lanc; diu sanc vor, die andern sungen alle nâch (Stamheim 1, 10.5–7).

148. dâ gesach man schône ridewanzen. zwêne gigen; dô si swigen (daz was geiler getelinge wünne), seht, dô wart von zeche vor gesungen! (40.29–33).

149. sô die voretanzer danne swîgen, sô sult ir alle sîn gebeten, daz wir treten aber ein hovetänzel nâch der gîgen (40.21–24).

150. der unkiusche ingesinde, Bî den ich tanzen, reien vinde (H. v. Trimberg 12397–98).

151. Chorea enim circulus est, cujus centrum est diabolus (Lecoy de la Marche, p. 162, A.1).

152. nu sind sunderlich III stück, durch die der tûfel mit den frowen betrugt die manne: als sehen, reden vnd griffen; die III sint alle an dem tantz. da sint ansehung vnd winkung der augen, da sint vnkusche wort vnd geberd vnd gesanck, da sint angriffung der hende vnd des gantzen libes, da von das fuer der vnkuscheit entzundt vnd gemert wirt vnd manigs erbern kint verfellet (Böhme, p. 97).

153. mit vnzuchtigem vffspringen, sich entblôßen, dardurch man hermanet wird zu fleischlicher begirde (ibid., p. 100).

154. decenti motu corporis et membrorum (Albertus Magnus, *In evangelium Lucae*, p. 494).

155. Modernis enim temporibus tibie ac tube altitone fidulas morigeras a conviviis communiter fugant, et altisono strepitu certatim iuvencule saliunt ut cerve clunes illepide ac effeminaliter agitando (Konrad von Megenburg, *Ökonomik*, vol. 1, p. 256).

156. schouwen . . . vrouwen (H. v. Aue, *Lieder* 216.31–32).

157. man sach dâ, swaz man wolde sehen: dise fuoren sehen frouwen, jene ander tanzen schouwen; dise sâhen buhurdieren, jene ander justieren (G. v. Straßburg 614–18).

158. manech vorste rîche saz dâ frôliche und redeten mit den frouwen (H. v. Veldeke, *Eneit* 339.33–35).

159. dise sprâchen wider diu wîp, dise banecten den lîp, dise tanzten, dise sungen, dise liefen (H. v. Aue, *Iwein* 65–68).

160. sô schuzzen dise hie den schaft, sô wolten jene trinken wîn, sô wolten dis bî frouwen sîn werben nâ ir gruoze (R. v. Braunschweig 2914–17).

161. dise redten von seneder arbeit, dise von grôzer manheit (H. v. Aue, *Iwein* 71–72).

162. Dise retten von golde, Jene von der hôchzît; Dort was von den vrouwen strît, Wlhe dâ diu beste waere (H. v. d. Türlin, *Krone* 647–50).

163. Grôz was der ritter schouwen and den gemeiten frouwen. grôz was ir loben und ir prîsen . . . der eine frâgt, der underspricht, der sprach sîn liep, jener spehet, ein ander sprach dâ bî: "nu sehet dort lachende ougen unde grâ, hie brûne ougebrâ!" sô prîset der an frowen die site, der die ander, der die drite, der den hals, der die hende, nu den munt nu daz gebende nu die lîch süez unde klâr nur gelîch golde ein hâr nu der frouwen nu der meide, hie mit lobe von dirre beide nu die gebaerde nu den lîp. "ditz ist daz schoeneste wip!" ein ander sprach; sô stiez der den; "niht," sprach der, "sihstu jen? diu ist diu schoenest under in." "nein, dich triuget dîn sin. sihstu jene in dem samît?" hie verendet sich der strît und sie kômen dâ mit anz münster dâ intrôit der erzbischof gesanc (334–36, 343–66).

164. der künic Artûs wolte brechen sîne treskameren umbe daz, daz man in lobete dester baz, und wolte teilen sîn golt (U. v. Zatzikhoven 5596–99).

165. ûz voller hant al den herren besunder rîcher gâbe wunder, edel gesteine, silber, golt (U. v. Etzenbach, *Wilhelm v. Wenden* 1772–75).

166. drîer hande rîch gewant: scharlachen rôt unversniten, diu zwei von phelle wol gebriten mit golde spaehe gar geworht (1778–81).

167. ros unde phert (1785).

168. Ir gab deu chǔniginne wert erchant Ein gǔrtel und ein fǔrspang und ein vingerlein (Pleier, *Garel* 20234–35).

169. militibus et clericis curie et servientibus honesta distribuit dona, scilicet equos, palefridos, ronchinos, vestes preciosas, aurum et argentum (Gislebert of Mons, p. 237).

170. arma praeclara cum vestibus pretiosis curiae suae militibus et consociis idoneis temporibus ministrando (*Historia Welforum*, p. 72).

171. aurum et argentum, vasa ex argento et auro facta itemque vestes preciosas, beneficia feudorum aliaque donaria largiter et regaliter distribuebat (Rahewin, *Gesta Frederici*, p. 706).

172. ieslîchem man nâh mâze sîn (W. v. Eschenbach, *Parzival* 789.25).

173. den werden nâch ir wirde zil (W. v. Etzenbach, *Wilhelm v. Wenden* 340).

174. araebesch golt geteilet wart armen rîtern al gemeine, unt den küngen edel gesteine teilte Gahmuretes hant, und ouch swaz er dâ fürsten vant (W. v. Eschenbach, *Parzival* 100.28–101.2).

175. innumerabili multitudini ioculatorum et istrionum (*Kaiserchronik*, p. 262).

176. swer guot umb êre wolde, daz her frôlîch quâme und es sô vile nâme, daz ez im iemer mohte fromen und allen sînen nâchkomen (H. v. Veldeke, *Eneit* 336.4–8).

177. her bereite dô die spilman. der gâbe er selbe began, wander was der hêrste, von diu hûb herz alêrste, als ez kunege wol gezam. swer dâ sîne gâbe nam, dem ergiengez sâlichlîche, wander was des rîche sint unz an sîn ende und fromete sînem kinde die wîle daz ez mohte leben, wander konde wole geben unde hete ouch daz gût, dar zû den willigen mût. Dar nâch die vorsten rîche

gâben vollechlîche, ir ieslîch mit sîner hant, daz tûre phellîne gewant, golt unc
aller slahte schat, silber unde goltvat, mûle und ravîde, phelle und samîde ganz
und ungescrôten, manegen bouch rôten, dorchslagen goldîn, zobel unde harmîr
gâben die vorsten, wan siz tûn getorsten. herzogen unde grâven den spilmanner
sie gâven grôzlîchen unde sô, daz si dannen schieden frô und lob dem kunege
sungen ieslîch nâch sîner zungen (345.39–346.32).

178. rîcher kleinoete vil, den werden nâch ir wirde zil manic hundert mark
wert, den varnden kleider unde pfert (U. v. Etzenbach, *Wilhelm v. Wenden*
339–42).

179. ros unde wât (H. v. Aue, *Erec* 2183); ors und gewant (H. v. d. Türlin,
Krone 22534).

180. er hiez den spilliuten sagen, er wolt niu kleider tragen und wolt diu
alten hin geben. sie begunden all dar streben die der alten kleider wolden gern di
begund man all gewern (J. Enikel, *Weltchronik* 17689–94).

181. Imperator suadet principibus, ne hystrionibus dona solito more pro-
digaliter effundant, iudicans maximam dementiam, si quis sua bona mimis vel
ystrionibus fatue largiatur (*Chronica regia Coloniensis*, p. 266).

2. KNIGHTING CEREMONIES

1. armis virilibus, id est ense, cinxit (Astronomus, *Vita Hludovici*, p. 366).

2. sus wart her Gwîgâlois ze man (W. v. Grafenberg 1658).

3. er ist nû volleclîche ein man (K. Fleck 7774).

4. militem ordinare festinavit, ut terre dominium valeret obtinere (Gislebert
of Mons, p. 71).

5. militem fecit statimque eum, stupentibus cunctis et mirantibus, in regem
ungui praecepit et coronari (Gervaise of Canterbury, *Chronica*, vol. 1, p. 219).

6. armis cinctus nuptias magnifice celebravit (Otto of St. Blasien, p. 70).

7. Wart er ritter und nam wîp (H. v. d. Türlin, *Krone* 424).

8. wan er niht worden was ze man nâch ritterlîchem rehte. dô wart als
einem knehte sîn gemahel im versaget (R. v. Ems, *Guter Gerhard* 3546–49).

9. ez sol an eines knehtes arm mîn vrouwe nimmer werden warm (*Mai u.
Beaflor* 81.9–10).

10. sed ad eius (Elisabeth) amplexus nullatenus est admissus, nisi prius milicie cingulo cingeretur; quo cum maxima sollempnitate peracto eius thalamum
introivit (Johann of Victring, vol. 1, p. 194).

11. ad gradum milicie est provectus . . . indignum reputantes suum socerum
militem non esse (*Chronica regia Coloniensis*, p. 267 f.).

12. me fecit militem (p. 236).

13. armis militaribus adornare et honorare et ad militiam promovere et ordinare (Lambert of Arras, *Epistolae*, col. 664).

14. militem profiteri (p. 404).

15. arma sumere (*Continuatio Zwetlensis* II).

16. armis insigniri (Otto of St. Blasien).

17. gladio accingere, accingi (*Annales Pegaviensis*, *Annales s. Georgii*,
Continuatio Cremifamensis, *Continuatio Admuntensis*); gladio circumcingere
(*Annales Ratisponenses*); gladium accingere (Burchard of Ursberg).

18. ense succingere (*Continuatio Garstensis*).

19. gladio militari accingere (*Annales Marbacenses, Continuatio Claustroneoburgensis* III).

20. gladium militiae accingere (Arnold of Lübeck); ense militiae accingere (*Chronica regia Coloniensis*).

21. armis militae induere (*Continuatio Zwetlensis* II).

22. sacramentis militaribus implicari (*Chronica s. Petri Erfordensis*).

23. militare (*Annales Spirensis*).

24. militem facere (*Annales Aquenses, Chronicon Montis Sereni*).

25. militem declarare (Arnold of Lübeck).

26. novi milites ordinari (Gislebert of Mons).

27. (ze) ritter werden (*Eneit* 171.18 and elsewhere).

28. (ze) ritter machen (*Gregorius* 1646–47; *Nibelungenlied* 1755.3).

29. ritterschaft geben (W. v. Eschenbach, *Parzival* 123.6).

30. ze ritterschaft komen (W. v. Grafenberg 2328).

31. ze ritter segenen (H. v. Trimberg 19071).

32. ritters namen gewinnen (*Gregorius* 1665; *Nibelungenlied* 31.4).

33. ritters namen nemen (U. v. Türheim, *Rennewart* 11655).

34. ritters namen gern (R. v. Ems, *Wilhelm v. Orlens* 5260).

35. ritters namen enphâhen (R. v. Ems, *Guter Gerhard* 4934–35).

36. an ritters namen bringen (W. v. Eschenbach, *Parzival* 123.9).

37. ritters reht nemen (*Mai u Beaflor* 83.2–3).

38. ritters ambet enphâhen (O. of Steiermark 8114).

39. ine wil niht langer sîn ein kneht, ich sol schildes ambet hân (W. v. Eschenbach, *Parzival* 154.22–23).

40. uti tirocinii suscipiendi consuetudo expostulat (*Historia Gaufredi*, p. 179).

41. cyclade auro texto supervestitur (ibid.).

42. processit in publicum (ibid.).

43. miri decoris equus Hispaniensis (ibid.).

44. lorica . . . maculis duplicibus intexta (ibid.).

45. leunculos aureos ymaginarios habens (ibid.).

46. ad ultimum allatus est ei ensis de thesauro regio (ibid.).

47. mira agilitate (p. 180).

48. in ludi bellici exercitio (ibid.).

49. Et li prodon s'est abeissiez, Si li chauçca l'esperon destre: La costume soloit teus estre Que cil qui feisoit chevalier Li devoit l'esperon chaucier. D'autres vaslez assez i ot; Chascuns qui avenir i pot A lui armer a la main mise. Et li prodon l'espee a prise, Si li çainst et si le beisa Et dit que donee li a La plus haute ordre avuec l'espee Que Deus et feite et comandee: C'est l'ordre de chevalerie, Qui doit estre sanz vilenie (1624–38).

50. Li prodon maintenant le saingne, Si a la main levee an haut Et dist: "Biaus sire, Deus vos saut! Alez a Deu!" (1694–97).

51. Et la reîne fist estuves Et bainez chaufer an cinc çanz cuves, S'i fist toz les vaslez antrer Por beignier et por estuver, Et an lor ot robes tailliees, Qui lor furent apareilliees Quant il furent del baing issu. Li drap furent a or tissu, Et les panes furent d'ermines. Au mostier jusqu'aprés matines Li vaslet an estant veillierent, Qu'onques ne s'i agenoillierent. Au matin mes sire Gauvains Chauça a

chascun des ses mains L'esperon destre et çainst l'espee Et si li dona la colee. Lors ot il conpeignie viaus De cinc çanz chevaliers noviaus (*Conte du Graal* 9171–88).

52. In quibusdam etiam locis moris est, militem in crastinum consecrandum, totam noctem praecedentem pervigilem in orationibus ducere, et nec jacendi, nec sedendi habere licentiam (col. 744).

53. eidem comiti dudum in signum milicie gladium lateri et calcaria . . . sui militis pedibus adaptavit, et alapam collo eius infixit (p. 602).

54. sacramentis militaribus inplicantur (p. 192).

55. eine hôchzît (1625).

56. diu küniginne sande im sâ sehs rîter kleider; diu wâren der beider von scharlach und von pfelle (1613–34).

57. gap im ein ravît daz was guot (1636).

58. der künic im zwelf knappen liez; dar zuo er im geben swaz er haben solde, ieglîchez als er wolde (1638–41).

59. an dem heiligen pfingestage (1643).

60. die pfaffen gâben im den segen (1646).

61. dô gurte umbe sich der degen ein swert (1647–54).

62. der milte künic reichte im sâ den schilt selbe und einen schaft (1653–54).

63. sich huop dâ michel rîterschaft und schoene buhurdieren mit rîchen banieren (1655–57).

64. se rex arma bellica succinxit (p. 94).

65. sô gît man ime den ritters segen in einem tempel (2073–74).

66. vor ist im ein bat bereit, dar ûz er sich erwaschen muoz schôn von dem houbet ûf den fuoz (2077–79).

67. die naht er in dem tempel ligt (2082).

68. wie balde man ime daz swert umb bant! da enwas niergent kein wigant, er engebe ime mit kreften einen slac (2326–28).

69. leyt er yn in eyn kirchen, da er alle die nacht wachet biß and den tag und sprach sin gebete (vol. 1, p. 134).

70. So fúrte man dann zu dem mönster aller der wapen die des tags ritter wolten werden, und musten sich wapen in dem múnster, and da gab yn der konig den halßslag (p. 135).

71. Der graf von Tzil Herman genant Daz swert auz seiner schaide tzoch Und swencht ez in di luften hoch Und sprach tzu hertzog Albrecht: "Pezzer ritter wenne chnecht!" Und slug den erenreichen slag (IV.268–73).

72. des morgens dô der tac erschein ein bischof wart des enein, er sanc ein harte schoenez amt unt segent dô daz swert ze hant dem jungen künec von Tandarnas (Pleier, *Tandareis* 2043–47).

73. ze münster mit ein ander komen und heten messe vernomen und ouch enpfangen den segen, des man in dâ solte pflegen (5013–16).

74. Marke nam dô Tristanden, sînen neven, ze handen, swert unde sporn stricte er im an. "sich," sprach er, "neve Tristan, sît dir nû swert gesegnet ist und sît du ritter worden bist, nu bedenke ritterlîchen prîs." (5017–23).

75. Dô messe was gesungen, die hôchgemuoten jungen giengen nâch vil werder kür zuo mînem herren dort hin für. der segnet in diu swert aldâ. den

jungen niuwen helden sâ gurten stolze ritter wert umbe nâch ir rehte ir swert. nâch dem gotes segene drungen die swertdegene mit schalle für des münsters tür. ir ors verdaht mit rîcher kür funden sî bereit alhie (R. v. Ems, *Guter Gerhard* 3593–605).

76. swertes segen geben (*Lohengrin* 3809).

77. ze ritter segenen (H. v. Trimberg 19071).

78. Liupoldus dux Austriae et Stirie consecrationis ensis dignitate honorifice sublimatur (*Continuatio Mellicensis*, p. 506).

79. Heberhardo archiepiscopo Treverensi benedicente (*Annales Weissenburgenses*, p. 53).

80. Altera die rex in predicto campo ad quandam ligneam ecclesiam accedit, ibique ab episcopis—nam eo usque in puerilibus annis positus nondum militem induerat—accepta sacerdotali benedictione ad hoc instituta armis accingitur (*Gesta Frederici*, p. 196).

81. consuetudo solennis ut ea ipse die, qua quisque militari cingulo decoratur, ecclesiam solenniter adeat gladioque super altare posito et oblato quasi celebri professione facta seipsum obsequio altaris deuoueat (vol. 2, p. 25).

82. Sed et hodie tirones enses recipiunt de altari, ut profiteantur se filios Ecclesiae (*Epistolae*, col. 294).

83. Ordo ad armandum ecclesiae defensorum vel alium militem (Flori, p. 436).

84. Deinde cingat eum episcopus dicendo: Accipe hunc gladium cum Dei benedictione tibi collatum, in quo per virtutem spiritus sancti resistere et eicere valeas omnes inimicos tuos et cunctos sanctae Dei ecclesiae adversarios (p. 437).

85. Ordo ad regem benedicendum (Elze, p. 333).

86. toto ablutus corpore (ibid.).

87. Precingatur ense optimo aureo (ibid.).

88. ut hunc presentem militem ad dignitatem regalem sublevetis. (p. 334).

89. Wido, nobili stirpe progenitus ac militaribus armis precinctus (Winter, p. 63).

90. Liupoldus marchio Austrie accinctus est gladio (*Continuatio Claustroneoburgensis* I, p. 609).

91. factus iuvenis, arma succinxit (*Chronicon Gozecense*, p. 152).

92. arma accepit (*Annales Welfici Weingartenses*, p. 88).

93. accinctus est gladio (*Continuatio Claustroneoburgensis* I, p. 613).

94. militieque cingulum iam sumpserat (Otto of Freising, *Gesta Frederici*, p. 180).

95. quia a multis annis antea preteritis inauditum fuerat, ut aliquis comitum Hanoniensium filium militem. . .vidisset (p. 95).

96. copioso apparatu (*Continuatio Lambacensis*, p. 556).

97. iuvenis armis noviter praecinctus (p. 252).

98. eum accingi gladio. . .disposuit. . .Neque solus illa die balteo militari cinctus fuit, sed ob amorem et honorem filii multis pater coaetaneis arma dedit (p. 452).

99. Adelbertus filius marchionis Liupoldi cum aliis 120 accinctus est gladio (*Continuatio Claustroneoburgensis* I, p. 613).

100. multi quoque comites et nobiles quam plurimi accincti sunt ibi gladio (p. 519).

101. edelen kindelîn (28.2).

102. Vier hundert swertdegene (30.1).

103. Ex habundanti autem letitia, quam domnus inperator super tanta exercitus conceperat multitudine, militie ludum gaudens in propria persona ordinavit, et sexaginta iuvenes nobiles, qui armigeri nuncupantur, ad militarem habitum et cultum militie transtulit (Arnold of Lübeck, p. 172).

104. den künegen al zen êren (Nibelungenlied 646.2).

105. 144 iuvenes de terra sua nobiles apud Wiennam honorifice donavit gladio militari (Continuatio Garstensis, p. 597).

106. cum 118 militibus gladio militari se precinxit (Continuatio Sancruensis II, p. 644).

107. drîer slahte kleit ûz ir sunderkamern (W. v. Eschenbach, Willehalm 63.13–14).

108. quos omnes vestivit ad minus triplici vestimento, scilicet tunica preciosa, surgotum cum nobili vario, suchornam cum vario precioso (p. 224).

109. Die mit hoher richait Trûgent Wilhelmes clait, Die gabent wunneclichen schin; Samit, pfeller, paldegin Mit hârmine gefurrieret Und mit zobel wol gezieret Trûc der tugentriche man Und alle sin gesellen an (R. v. Ems, Wilhelm v. Orlens 5769–76).

110. Dar na worden de jungen heren van Sassen riddere und drogen so grote kost dat se to Magdeborch to inleger drungen worden umme schulde willen, der se nicht betalen konden (p. 160).

111. sublimare filium suum in militem (Grimm, vol. 3, p. 862).

112. inferioris conditionis iuvenes vel quoslibet contemptibilium etiam mechanicarum artium opifices... ad militie cingulum vel dignitatum gradus assumere (Gesta Frederici, p. 308).

113. ab honestioribus et liberioribus studiis tamquam pestem propellunt (ibid.).

114. swer vil kûme waere kneht, der wil nu rîter werden; des müezen die werden der boesen engelten. jâ geniuzet man vil selten der boesen gesellen. got müeze si vellen die dem immer swert gegeben der daz rîterlîche leben niht behalten künne, und der von sînem künne niht dar zuo sî geborn! daz alte reht hab wir verlorn (W. v. Grafenberg 2333–45).

115. Multi ignobiles facti milites in Argentina (p. 308).

116. achertrappen (O. of Steiermark 26195).

117. ein gebûr rîch und wert, sô man dem gesegent swert, des wirt unwert ein ritter (S. Helbling VIII.339–41).

3. TOURNAMENTS

1. qui torneamenta invenit (Chronicon Andagavense breve, p. 169).

2. ...lanceam levavit, et equo vehementer calcaribus impulso, adversus eum cucurrit, volensque eum militari ludo de equo suo deicere, lanceam ei in corde fixit, sine mora extinxit (Hermann v. Tournai, Liber de restauratione, p. 282).

3. pro honore terrae suae et pro exercitio militum suorum (*Passio Karoli comitis*, p. 564).

4. cum multis militibus quibus tunc temporis Hanonia florebat (p. 95).

5. Alrêst huop sich der turnei Als man in Vrankrîche pfliget (*Rittertreue* 570–71).

6. more Francorum (*Chronicon Anglicanum*, p. 179).

7. in conflictibus Gallicis (Matthew of Paris, *Historia Anglorum*, vol. 1, p. 409).

8. nec insultarent Galli Anglis militibus tanquam rudibus et minus gnaris (William of Newburgh, *Historia rerum Anglicarum*, vol. 2, p. 423).

9. Heinricus iuvenis de Habichisburc, plus quam decuit laetus, . . . in congressu infelicium ludorum, quibus periculose iocari saepius non destitit, infeliciter ictus occubuit (p. 240).

10. Adilbertus praefati Rudolfi filius, iuvenis armis noviter praecinctus, nimis hisdem incaute iocando in congressu eorundem ludorum innocenter occisus (p. 252).

11. Quae preludia militum cerneres pugnam simulantium in armis! Quam brevi spacio equum ferocem circumferri videres! Quales militum obviationes in equis, quali hastas fragore discindi perspiceres! Quales audires clamores horum insequentium, illorum terga vertentium! Qua arte simulatam attenderes fugam, quam subitas modo fugientium reflexiones, et precipiti cursu versam fortunam eorum qui iam sequebantur terga impellentium! Ibi notares milites modo condensatos, modo subito sese aperire, incursantemque hostem ingeniose quasi cedendo in sinum recipere, reflexisque cornibus eum concludere; mille ibi artes, mille fallendi modos discere dabatur (Balderic, *Gesta Alberonis*, p. 598 f.).

12. Πούτξη Ἀλαμανὲ (Johannes Cinnamus, col. 409 f.).

13. in exercicio militari, quod vulgo tornamentum vocatur (*Chronicon Montis Sereni*, p. 155).

14. Tantum autem idem pestifer ludus in partibus nostris tunc inoleverat, ut infra unam annum 16 in eo referantur milites periisse (ibid.).

15. Die Criechen vunden uns bereit Zu turneie und zu strîte Zu aller slachte zîte, Zu rosse unde zu vuze (Schieb-Frings 936–39).

16. swaz he togende îgewan zu tornei und zu strîte (1334–35).

17. der turnei wart gesprochen über drî wochen von dem naehsten mântage (2236–38).

18. baz turnierte ritter nie (2469).

19. drî maentage ich dâ vil gestreit (W. v. Eschenbach, *Parzival* 498.22).

20. Uber allú wålschú riche Der turnaý wart geworben (R. v. Ems, *Wilhelm v. Orlens* 5848–49).

21. Et ideo mandamus vobis et rogamus diligenter, quod ad torneamentum praedictum cum equis et armis ita provide veniatis, quod honorem inde habeatis (*Chronica majora*, vol. 2, p. 615).

22. Qui melius ibi faciet, habebit ursum, quem domina quaedam mittet ad torneamentum (ibid.).

23. Der sîn leben an ein swîn Wåget, an lewen oder an bern (H. v. Trimberg 11606–07).

24. wie Wir alhie turnieren (R. v. Ems, *Wilhelm v. Orlens* 6538–39).

25. Wie anders danne lant an lant? (6541).

26. alrêrst gedêch ûf einen strît der turnei, wan er toetlich wart (K. v. Würzburg, *Partonopier* 16170–71).

27. umbe al ritters habe (R. v. Ems, *Wilhem v. Orlens* 6563).

28. Umbe alles das er gewinnen kan (6566).

29. swie der man ze velde kam, daz solt ez allez gelten. bî der zît man selten
turnierte anders (R. v. Braunschweig 11216–19).

30. ez wart ein turney dâ her gesprochen: des enwart hie niht . . . den hât ein
vesperîe erlemt. die vrechen sint sô hie gezemt, daz der turney dervon verdarp
(W. v. Eschenbach, *Parzival* 95.14–19).

31. diu schar, diu den turney solde heben, si stapften bî ein ander eben und
habten sich zesamne wol, als man ze rehte gein vîenden sol (U. v. Liechtenstein,
Frauendienst 1586.5–8).

32. habt iuch zesamen: daz ist iu guot! (ibid. 262.3).

33. Nu drucket iuch zesamen gar! (ibid. 263.1).

34. Diu rotte waich. man sach sie jagen Ie naher mit gedrange, Das wichen
wert unlange E die flûhtigen kerten Und die jagenden lerten Wichen wider übers
velt (R. v. Ems, *Wilhelm v. Orlens* 6706–11).

35. fünf stiche mac turnieren hân, die sint mir mîner hant getân: einer ist
zem puneiz, ze triviers ich den andern weiz, der dritte ist zentmuoten, ze rehter
tjost den guoten hurteclîch ich hân geriten, und den zer volge ouch niht vermiten (812.9–16; punctuation according to Leitzmann).

36. rotte in rotte, schar in schar (R. v. Braunschweig 11268).

37. der turnei faste stuont enstet (U. v. Liechtenstein, *Frauendienst* 281.5).

38. dâ was der turnei als ein want stênde worden (U. v. Zatzikhoven 3288–
89).

39. Von kipperen ein michel rote Mit starken matziuwen, Die hinden nâch
bliuwen, Mohte man dâ schouwen (H. v. d. Türlin, *Krone* 776–79).

40. iegelîches harnasch was guot, ein panzier und ein îsenhuot und ein kiule
wol beslagen (H. v. Aue, *Erec* 2348–50).

41. den werden künic von Riuzen haet er gevangen in den zoum, und wolte
in under einen boum ziehen balde in sînen fride. sîn kneht der sluoc ûf sîniu lide
mit einem starken bengel. wand er alsam ein engel gezieret was mit golde, sô
wolte er hân ze solde daz ros und ouch den harnasch (2762–71).

42. der turnei was gebotten daz man keine kipper nam (R. v. Braunschweig
11214–15).

43. "Wie schaffet irz," sprach Rüedegêr "daz lât mich hoeren, künic hêr, sol
ez âne kipper sîn?" "jâ bî rehten triuwen mîn," sprach Gunthêr der rîche, "daz
lobe ich endelîche. swelhen ritter rüeret kippers hant, er sî knabe oder sarjant,
den des turneis niht bestê, daz ez im an die hant gê" (*Biterolf* 8579–88).

44. ad equestrem ludum, quod hastiludium vel torneamentum dicitur, cum
hastis et lineis armaturis . . . (Matthew of Paris, *Chronica majora*, vol. 2,
p. 650).

45. cujus mucro, prout deberet, non fuerat hebetatus (ibid., vol. 5, p. 318).

46. Swert, di doch niht scherfe sniten wan ze bûlen (2239.1).

47. iz waren krônlin, niht glevin gespitzet (ibid. 2005.3).

48. si îlten ûz an daz velt, vil michel wart ir gelpf, von bûhurt und von
springen, von tanzen und von singen (179–82).

49. Man vant da vrâuden vollen gelt. Swie der man wolte leben, Deu wal

waz im wol gegeben. Wolt er puhurdiren, Tanczen, tyostiren, Lauffen oder springen (Pleier, *Garel* 20106–11).

50. die rîter begunden alle vor ir buhurdieren mit rîchen banieren (W. v. Grafenberg 9011–13).

51. ez waere worden ein turnei, hêten si ir harnasch gehabet (ibid. 9021–22).

52. Gen dem gestůle unz an den schragen Wart ain groz gestôsse Mit mǎngem schilt gebôze (ibid. 5802–04).

53. der buhurt wart sô herte, daz maneger schiltgeverte mit rosse ensamet dar nider lac, dâ er sich ruowe gar bewac: wan im geschach von treten sô wê, daz in des tages gelust niht mê buhurdierens durch diu wîp. wan in swar et gar der lîp. daz schinbein manegem dürchel wart an der engen durchvart (*Mai u. Beaflor* 82.23–32).

54. Interim equites utrimque quasi ad spectaculum in campo mutuo coequitantes exercebantur (*Chronica regia Coloniensis*, p. 53).

55. Norici et maxime comites et nobiles, velut tyrocinium celebraturi, quod modo nundinas vocare solemus, in predicti comitis castro se recipiunt (Otto of Freising, *Gesta Frederici*, p. 180).

56. detestabiles illas nundinas vel ferias, quas vulgo torneamenta vocant (Hefele-Leclercq, vol. 5.2, p. 1102).

57. der site der ist noch rehte und offenlîche erkant über der Franzeise lant, daz man mit swerten und mit spern turnieret dâ; wil iemen gern jostierens mit den scheften, der mac sich dâ beheften mit starken stichen manicvalt. der turnei sam ein strît gestalt ist dâ ze lande, wizze Krist (K. v. Würzburg, *Partonopier* 15108–17).

58. ze samene sie geranden, als si beide luste. sie tâten eine juste harde ritterlîche zwein degenen gelîche, âne arge liste. ir neweder vermiste, beide sie wol stâchen, daz ir schafte brâchen, die sprundelen hôhe flogen (201.4–13).

59. ze rehter tjost (2510).

60. enzwischen den scharn (2586).

61. wir suln uns bêde des bewegen, mit rittern in ein fôreis legen; und al die wîle der tac dâ were, swer an uns ritterschefte gere, daz er der werd von uns gewert (*Frauendienst* 182.3–7).

62. Von Agley der patriarc sprach: "diu kost ist hie ze starc." von Babenperc der bischof sprach: "dêswâr ez ist mir ungemach, sül wir alsô umb sus hie sîn. mich bat her komen der bruoder mîn: ich meine den margrâven wert von Ysterrîch, der mîn her gert." (238.1–8).

63. dô hiez man künden in der stat, . . . der turney würd an dem mântage (243.4.8).

64. bouhordé, et contrefait les aventures de Bretaigne et de la Table ronde (Philippe de Novare, *Mémoires*, p. 7).

65. rotunda tabula (Rymer, vol. 1.1, p. 205).

66. tabula rotunda (Alberic of Troisfontaines, p. 937).

67. Anno quoque sub eodem, milites ut exercitio militari peritiam suam et strenuitatem experirentur, constituerunt non ut in hastiludio quod vulgariter torneamentum dicitur, sed potius in illo ludo militari qui mensa rotunda dicitur, vires suas attemptarent (*Chronica majora*, vol. 5, p. 318).

68. Ez was der tavelrunde gezelt (1514.1).

69. ein ritterlîch runttâfel (190).

70. Aynes turnays ward gedacht, Der ward auch schyr vollbracht: Fores und tavelrumen (18425–27).

71. hovesche breve (p. 168).

72. ein schone vruwen, de heit vrow Feie (ibid.).

73. dat se ores wilden levendes nicht mer ovede (p. 169).

74. ubi tanquam Aswerus cunctis regni Almanniae optimatibus convocatis divitias gloriae regni sui ostendit (*Annales Vetero-Cellenses*, p. 206).

75. et si quis comitum, baronum ibidem in magna multitudine congregatorum in hastiludio hastam suam super alium fregit, mox folium argenteum de arbore in signum virilitatis pro merito obtinebat. Si quis socium et comparem suum hasta de equo persistens dejecerat, mox folium aureum de dicta arbore promerebat (ibid.).

76. die stâchen hie durch hôhen muot, die andern dort wan umb daz guot: dâ tyostirt manges ritters lîp durch anders niht wan durch diu wîp: sô stâchen die durch lernen dâ, jen durch prîs dort anderswâ (U. v. Liechtenstein, *Frauendienst* 210.3–8).

77. turnieren wirdet mannes lîp: durch wirde lobent si diu wîp. turnieren daz ist ritterlîch (29.3–5).

78. mulieres in edituo murorum aspicientes (p. 458).

79. Aines tages gevuoctez sih sô, daz der kunic wart vil frô: Rômaere hêten grôze rîterscaft. daz maere kom ze Biterne in di stat. duo îlten alle die hovesken frowen oben an di zinnen scowen. duo Rômaere di frowen ersâhen, si îlten ie baz und baz dar zuo gâhen, daz die frowen jaehen, welhe guote rîter von Rôme waeren (4563–72).

80. Daz sî ir ritter hiezen Und daz niht enliezen Sine würden verhouwen Durch willen ir vrouwen (759–62).

81. daz die frouwen ab dem palas wol sâhn der helde arbeit (W. v. Eschenbach, *Parzival* 69.22–23)

82. Man seit, so vil der vrowen uber al uz allen richen den turnei solten schowen. durch daz wart er geordent werdiclichen. niht entwer mit knutteln ein ander klucken, mit tjosten hurticlichen woltens ander uz dem satel rucken (*Jg. Titurel* 1985 A, 1–4).

83. O simple voiz (3480).

84. un[s] chantereals (3485).

85. Mareschal, Kar me donez un boen cheval! (3489–90).

86. ir rosse er niene ruochte (H. v. Aue, *Erec* 2430).

87. vil wol wart er geprîset dâ (2452).

88. daz er ir deheinez nam, wan er dar niene kam ûf guotes gewin. dar an kêrte er sînen sin, ob er den prîs möhte bejagen (2618–22).

89. knaben von den wâpen (K. v. Würzburg, *Engelhard* 2755).

90. die grôjeraere, die sich nennent lantvaraere (O. v. Steiermark 74977–78).

91. vil varnder liute man dâ sach. maneger von den wâpen sprach, daz man krojieren nennet, an den man daz erkennet, daz sie die decke zerrent hin. wan dar an lît ir gewin (*Mai u. Beaflor* 88.25–30).

92. der gewin was ouch niht kleine, den sîne knappen nâmen, sô die ritter

nider kâmen, die ir herre von den rossen stach (U. v. Zatzikhoven 3058–61).

93. dâ wurden krôgierer gefröut, wand ûf den anger wart geströut samît, gesteine und edel golt (K. v. Würzburg, *Partonopier* 14533–35).

94. dô wurden einem zwô eln, dem dritten alse dem andern drî unde dem vierden dâ bî ze einem rocke genuoc (1046–49).

95. er warte, obe ieman quaeme, der ouch die hosen naeme: dannoch was dâ niemen (1071–73).

96. Den turnei selten er verlak. dâ er ofte suochen pflak Beide, tschost unde fôrest: und swâ er immer was gewest, Dâ jach an in der liute lop; wand sîn gabe was sô grop Spilliuten unde vrîen, daz sie muosten schrîen Mit offenlîchen worten sîn lob an allen orten (*Maria und die Hausfrau* 19–28).

97. swaz er mit sîner hant erstreit ross unde guoter dinge, daz gab er ûf dem ringe den cnappen algelîche, die von den schilten rîche und von den helmen sprâchen: dâvon si niht zebrâchen sîn lop noch sîne wirde. mit edels herzen girde croijiertens ûf in alle und riefen dô mit schalle gelîche und algemeine: "von Engellant der reine der ist ein fürst zeinem man! hurtâ hurt! wie wol er kan nâch hôhem prîse dringen" (K. v. Würzburg, *Turnier v. Nantes* 1102–17).

98. Car j'ai pris .v. cenz chevaliers Dont j'ai et armes et destriers E tot lor herneis retenu (18483–85).

99. man sach si werben dâ umb guot. si enruohten, wer vil sper verstach: umb guot man sî dâ werben sach noch mêr danne umb diu werden wîp (*Frauendienst* 303.4–7).

100. beidiu ir sin unde ir muot ranc nâch gewinne in turneis beginne. swâ siè daz vernâmen dâ liut ze samen kâmen durch turniern dâ vuorens hin durch anders niht wan durch gewin. sie wâren helde maere. sie vuorten soumaere unt ieclîcher zwelf knaben kluoc (*Tandareis* 12609–18).

101. Nû was der ritter maere ein rehter lantvaraere und haete ouch anders geldes niht wan daz er muoste, sô man giht, mit sînem schilde sich bejagen (K. v. Würzburg, *Engelhard* 2829–33).

102. manec ritter ûz erkorn dâ sêre nâch gewinne ranc den der kumber dar zuo twanc, die hôhen nâch prîse rungen (Pleier, *Tandareis* 16881–84).

103. Ze ritterschaft stuont al sîn muot, Biz daz er sînes vater guot Vertete wol diu zwei teil. Ze guote hete er kein heil. Er tet wol swaz er solde, Biz im sîn vater wolde Niht mêr geben sîns guotes . . . Daz quam von turneis schulden (*Rittertertreue* 37–43; 48).

104. want er truwerens (turnierens: v. d. Hagen) pflag, als er vor dett mangen tag. er verkaufft hute einen hoffe, das dett er alls durch lobe, biß zu letste das der biderbe verkaufft alles sin erbe (*Der Junker und der treue Heinrich* 85–90).

105. dô muosten dâ hin ze den juden varn si alle, di dâ gevangen wârn. man sach si setzen alzehant vil maniger hande kostlîchez pfant. die dâ gewunnen heten guot, die wâren vrô und hôch gemuot (311.3–8).

106. ses envoi au Liege batant a un borjois qui l'aime tant, qui li sieult fere ses creances; si li mande que .vi.xx. lances li face paindre de ses armes, et .iii. escuz, dont les enarmes soient de soië et d'orfrois, et si prie mout le borjois qu'en chascune ait un penoncel (1953–61).

107. nominatum de consilio principum (Gislebert of Mons, p. 160).

108. Dô sprach ir einer zorniclîch: "uns hât mîn herre ûz Oesterrîch enboten bî den triuwen mîn, daz wir hie turniren lâzen sîn: daz ist uns hertzenlîchen leit. juncherre, daz sî iu geseit: wir müezen im sîn undertân, durch in beidiu tuon und lân" (1598.1–8).

109. Detestabiles autem illas nundinas vel ferias, in quibus milites ex condicto convenire solent, et ad ostentationem virium suarum et audaciae temerariae congrediuntur (Hefele-Leclerq, vol. 5.1, p. 729).

110. . . . torneamentum quod futurum erat in sequenti epdomada penitus adnichillavit. Et in loco torneamenti sex predicatores constituit, qui verbum crucis efficatiter exposuerunt, plurimos signaverunt (Annales Reineri, p. 673).

111. Ad potentes et milites (Sermones vulgares, No. 52).

112. quum propter laudem hominum et gloriam maxime in circuitu illo impii ambulant et vani (p. 430).

113. quum unus alii invideat, quod magis strenuus in armis reputetur (p. 431).

114. quum unus alium percutit, et male tractat, et plerumque lethaliter vulnerat et occidit (ibid.).

115. quia non praevalent contra partem aliam, sed cum vituperio saepe fugiunt, valde contristantur (ibid.).

116. dum unus alium capit et redimit, et equum quem cupiebat, eum aufert illi contra quem pugnando praevaluit. Sed occasione torniamentorum graves et intolerabiles exactiones faciunt, et hominum suorum bona sine misericordia rapiunt, nec segetes in agris conculcare et (cod. formidare) foragiare (add: desistunt), et pauperes et agricolas valde damnificant et molestant (ibid.).

117. dum mutuo propter pompam mundi invitant ad prandia et invitantur, et non solum bona sua, sed et bona pauperum in superfluis comessationibus expendunt (ibid.).

118. quum placere volunt mulieribus impudicis, si probi habeantur in armis, etiam quaedam earum insignia portare consueverunt (ibid.).

119. grôzen hôhvart (vol. 1, p. 176).

120. Der ouch . . . tanzet oder tornei hât oder topelt oder unkiusche tuot oder roubet oder brennet oder stilt oder eide swert meines oder swelher leie sünde man dâ tuot, diu ist unserm herren gar herzeclîchen leit (vol. 1, p. 446).

121. Von stechen (11567 ff.).

122. Wenne ez hânt manige tumme leien Von justieren und von turneien Verlorn lîp, sêle und guot: Waz sol sôgetân übermuot? (11589–92).

123. Vil tiufel wont oben in den lüften: Die pflegent der die man siht güften Mit rossen, kleidern und mit koste Durch burdieren und joste Und durch liebes wîbes minne (11645–49).

124. Ûf einem starken rosse sitzet Und alle sîne gedanke spitzet Wie er der werlde wol gevalle (ibid. 11617–19).

125. Turnieren was ê ritterlîch, nû ist ez rinderlich, toblich, tôtreis, mundes rîch, mortmezzer unt mortkolbe, gesliffen aks gar ûf des mannes tôt. Sus ist der turnei nû gestalt: des werdent schoener vrouwen ir ougen rôt, ir herze kalt, swan si ir werden lieben man dâ weiz in mortlîcher nôt. Dô man turnierens phlac durch ritters lêre, durch hôhen muot, durch hübescheit unt durch êre, dô hete man umb eine decke ungern erwürget guoten man: swer daz nû tuot unt daz wol kan, der dunket sich ze velde gar ein recke (R. v. Zweter 106.1–12).

126. Die alten turnei sint verslagen und sint di niuwen für getragen. wîlen hôrt man kroyieren sô: "heyâ ritter, wis et frô!" nû kroyiert man durch den tac: "jagâ ritter, jagâ jac! stichâ stich! slahâ slach! stümble den der ê gesach! slach mir dem abe den fuoz! tuo mir disem hende buoz! dû solt mir disen hâhen und enen rîchen vâhen: der gît uns wol hundert phunt" (1023–35).

CHAPTER V: THE COURTLY IDEAL OF SOCIETY

1. THE CHIVALROUS KNIGHT

1. Iustitia vero regis est neminem iniuste per potentiam opprimere, sine acceptione personarum inter virum et proximum suum iudicare, advenis et pupillis et viduis defensorem esse, furta cohibere, adulteria punire, iniquos non exaltare, impudicos et striones non nutrire, impios de terra perdere, parricidias et periurantes vivere non sinere, ecclesias defendere, pauperes elemosynis alere, iustos super regni negotia constituere, senes et sapientes et sobrios consiliarios habere, magorum et hariolorum et pythonissarum superstitionibus non intendere, iracundiam differe, patriam fortiter et iuste contra adversarios defendere, per omnia in Deo confidere (p. 51 f.).

2. . . . Christum Dei virtutem, et Dei sapientiam (1.24).

3. sicut Salomonem fecisti regnum obtinere pacificum (Vogel-Elze, p. 250).

4. Nû suln alle werltkunige dâ bî nemen pilede, wi der edel kaiser Trajân dise genâde umbe got gewan, want er rehtes gerihtes phlegete (6083–87).

5. seht an Alexander, der gap unverspart: des vert sîn lop in allen rîchen wîten (Sigeher 7.12–13).

6. Karl was ain wârer gotes wîgant, die haiden er ze der cristenhaite getwanc. Karl was chuone, Karl was scône, Karl was genaedic, Karl was saelic, Karl was teumuote, Karl was staete, und hête iedoch die guote. Karl was lobelîch, Karl was vorhtlîch, Karl lobete man pillîche in Rômiscen rîchen vor allen werltkunigen: er habete di aller maisten tugende (*Kaiserchronik* 15073–87).

7. Igitur potiti terra et habitatione certa confortati, nostri vires suas ultra protendere et in diversis provinciis praedia et dignitates sibi accumulare coeperunt. Unde et in tantum ditati sunt, ut, divitiis et honoribus regibus praestantiores, ipsi quoque Romano imperatori hominium facere recusabant (*Historia Welforum*, p. 4).

8. Nune mugen wir in disem zîte dem chûninge Dauite niemen so wol gelichen so den herzogen Hainriche. got gap ime di craft daz er alle sine uiande eruacht. di cristen hat er wol geret, di haiden sint uon im bekeret: daz erbet in uon rehte an. zefluchte gewant er nie sin uan: got tet in ie sigehaft. in sinem houe newirdet niemir nacht. ich maine daz ewige licht: des nezerinnit im nicht. untruwe ist im lait, er minnit rechte warhait. io ŏbit der herre alle gotlike lere, vnt sin tuire ingesinde. in sime houe mac (man) uindin alla state unt alle zuht. da ist vrŏde unt gehucht, da ist kûske unt scham; willic sint ime sine man; da ist tugint unt ere. wa fraistet ir ie mere daz imen baz geschahe? sime schephere opherit er lip unt sele sam Dauid der herre (9039–68).

9. Labora sicut bonus miles Christi Jesu. Nemo militans Deo implicat se negotiis saecularibus (Ad Timotheum secunda 2.3–4).

10. mens humilis (*Vita sancti Geraldi*, col. 646).

11. sustentator indigentium . . . nutritor pupillorum . . . defensor viduarum . . . dolentium consolator (col. 692).

12. Erat enim fidelis defensor ęcclesiarum . . . , largitor elemosinarum, consolator miserorum, sublevator piissimus monachorum, clericorum, viduarum atque virginum in çenobiis Deo militantium (*Vita Burcardi*, p. 6).

13. prosapia vir progenitus generosa (I.1).

14. Tunc in consilio dando par est tibi nemo, Qui vel tam iuste ius dicat tam vel honeste Et qui sic viduas defendat sive pupillos, Propter avariciam cum damnabantur iniquam (V.238–41).

15. . . . fidem servantes dominis . . . ut Christianę non obvient religioni (*Liber de vita christiana*, p. 248).

16. His proprium est dominis deferre, predę non iniare, pro vita dominorum suorum tuenda suę vitę non parcere et pro statu rei publice usque ad mortem decertare, scismaticos et hereticos debellare, pauperes quoque et viduas et orphanos defensare, fidem promissam non violare nec omnino dominis suis periurare (p. 248 f.).

17. manus rei publicae armata (vol. 2, p. 2).

18. usus militiae ordinatae . . . Tueri Ecclesiam, perfidiam impugnare, sacerdotium uenerari, pauperum propulsare inurias, pacare prouinciam, pro fratribus (ut sacramenti docet conceptio) fundere sanguinem et, si opus est, animan ponere (vol. 2, p. 23).

19. Exaudi, quesumus, domine, preces nostras, et hunc ensem, quo hic famulus tuus N. se circumcingi desiderat, maiestatis tue dextera benedicere dignare, quatinus defensio atque protectio possit esse aecclesiarum, viduarum, orphanorum omniumque Deo servientium contra sevitiam paganorum, aliisque insidiantibus sit pavor, terror et formido (Vogel-Elze, p. 379).

20. ad faciendos novos milites (Flori, p. 273).

21. nunc fiant Christi milites, qui dudum exstiterunt raptores (Fulcher of Chartres, *Historia Hierosolymitana*, p. 136).

22. Indebita hactenus bella gessistis; in mutuas caedes vesana aliquotiens tela, solius cupiditatis ac superbiae causa, torsistis (Guibert of Nogent, *Historia*, p. 138).

23. Arma, quae caede mutua illicite cruentastis, in hostes fidei et nominis Christiani convertite (William of Tyre, *Historia*, p. 41).

24. Non vos protrahat ulla possessio, nulla rei familiaris sollicitudo, quoniam terra haec quam inhabitatis, clausura maris undique et jugis montium circumdata, numerositate vestra coangustatur, nec copia divitiarum exuberat et vix sola alimenta suis cultoribus administrat. Inde est quod vos in invicem mordetis et contenditis, bella movetis et plerumque mutuis vulneribus occiditis. Cessent igitur inter vos odia, conticescant jurgia, bella quiescant et totius controversiae dissensiones sopiantur. Viam sancti Sepulcri incipite, terram illam nefariae genti auferte, eamque vobis subjicite, terra illa filiis Israel a Deo in possessionem data fuit, sicut Scriptura dicit, "quae lacte et melle fluit" (*Historia Hierosolymitana*, p. 728).

25. Vos accincti cingulo militiae, magno superbitis supercilio; fratres vestros laniatis, atque inter vos dissecamini. Non est haec militia Christi, quae

discerpit ovile Redemptoris. Sancta Ecclesia ad suorum opitulationem sibi reservavit militiam, sed vos eam male depravatis in malitiam. Ut veritatem fateamur, cujus praecones esse debemus, vere non tenetis viam per quam eatis ad vitam: vos pupillorum oppressores, vos viduarum praedones, vos homicidae, vos sacrilegi, vos alieni juris direptores: vos pro effundendo sanguine Christiano expectatis latrocinantium stipendia; et sicut vultures odorantur cadavera, sic longinquarum partium auspicamini et sectamini bella. Certe via ista pessima est, quoniam omnino a Deo remota est. Porro si vultis animabus vestris consuli, aut istiusmodi militiae cingulum quantocius deponite, aut Christi milites audacter procedite, et ad defendendam Orientalem Ecclesiam velocius concurrite (*Historia*, p. 14).

26. Facultates etiam inimicorum vestrae erunt: quoniam et illorum thesauros expoliabitis (p. 15).

27. Non vos demulceant illecebrosa blandimenta mulierum nec rerum vestrarum, quin eatis (ibid.).

28. Cesset pristina illa non militia, sed plane malitia, qua soletis invicem sternere, invicem perdere, ut ab invicem consumamini... Habes nunc, fortis miles, habes, vir bellicose, ubi dimices absque periculo, ubi et vincere gloria, et mori lucrum (*Epistola* 363, p. 315).

29. Malitia fuit, non militia, quod hactenus Christianorum caedibus et rapinis et execrabilibus intenti ignem inexstinguibilem et immortalium cruciatus vermium meruerunt. Felix eis abest milita, in qua et vincere gloria, sed magis mori lucrum. Ad hanc invitat nos hodie, qui amat animas (*Epistola* 32, col. 250).

30. Deus..., cui servire regnare est (*Liber sacramentorum*, col. 206).

31. qui imperant serviunt eis, quibus uidentur imperare (*De civitate Dei*, vol. 2, p. 681).

32. Si quis ergo Deo vult servire, cui servire est regnare, et nomen habere milicie conspicuum et clarum, tollat crucem et sequatur Dominum et veniat ad tornamentum Domini, ad quod ab ipso Domino invitatur (p. 208).

33. Induitur cultu laicali, transit ad usum Armorum, servus portat herile jugum, Vult servire libens, non spernit ferre laborem, Promptus ad obsequium, non piger esse studet, Quem non compellit servire penuria rerum, Indita sed virtus, laus populique favor. Servit, abinde volens dominari; servit, ut inde Sit major (61–68).

34. daz er lûterlîchen got diende (14624–25).

35. durch frîgen muotgelust (14617).

36. ritterlîchen just (14618).

37. schouwen (14619).

38. sîner frouwen wolt dienen umb ir minne (14620–21).

39. lîden pîn (14626).

40. guot (14631).

41. durch kurzewîle (14633).

42. durch ruon (14635).

43. Ne attendant vultum mulieris. Periculosum esse credimus omni religio(so) vultum mulieris nimis attendere, et ideo nec viduam nec virginem nec matrem nec sororem nec amitam nec ullam feminam aliquis ex fratribus oscu-

lari presumat. Fugiat ergo feminea oscula Christi militia (*Regula commilitonum Christi*, p. 153).

44. Ut aliis diebus duo vel tria leguminis fercula sufficiant (p. 138).

45. Vestimenta quidem unius coloris (p. 140).

46. Ut pellibus agnorum utantur (p. 141).

47. ut aurum vel argentum, que sunt divitie peculiares, in frenis aut in pectoralibus vel calcaribus vel in strevis unquam appareat (p. 144).

48. Quod nullus cum ave accipiat aliam avem (p. 146).

49. Ut omnem occasionem venationis caveant (ibid.).

50. Scacos et aleas detestantur; abhorrent venationem, nec ludicra illa avium rapina, ut assolet, delectantur. Mimos et magos et fabulatores scurrilesque cantilenas, atque ludorum spectacula, tamquam vanitates et insanias falsas respuunt et abominantur (*Liber ad milites Templi*, p. 220).

51. pugnam quippe, non pompam, victoriam, sed non gloriam cogitantes (p. 221).

52. O res miranda, o milites egregii, quos animositas et probitas innata armorum exercicio famosos reddidit et pre ceteris gentibus insignivit. Miramur plurimum et miratione dignum est, quod in tanta necessitate erga deum sic modo turpiter alget et torpescit vestra devotio et obliti estis virtutis assuete velut degeneres et ignavi. Vestrum utique auditum mimus aliquis seu fabula theatralis demulcendo alliceret, et verba dei in vobis non capiunt que tam difficili et surdo percipitis intellectu (*Historia peregrinorum*, p. 123).

53. ne quis aut variis aut griseis seu etiam sericis utatur vestibus (*Epistola* 458, p. 436).

54. illi, qui Domino militant, . . . nequaquam in vestibus preciosis nec cultu forme nec canibus vel accipitribus vel aliis, que portendant lasciviam, debent intendere (Caspar, p. 304).

55. in vestibus variis aut grisiis, sive in armis aureis vel argenteis (ibid.).

56. Ut nullus enormiter juret. Et quod nullus ad aleas vel ad decios ludat. Et quod nullus vario vel grisio vel sabellinis vel escarletis utatur. Et quod omnes tam clerici quam laici duobus ferculis ex empto sint contenti. Et quod nullus aliquam mulierem secum in peregrinatione ducat, nisi lotricem peditem, de qua nulla suspicio habeatur. Et quod nullus habeat pannos decisos vel laceatos (Conrad, p. 123).

57. der vihtet niht nâch rîters reht der den armen man sleht, und der im nimt sîn guot, der treit unrîterlîchen muot. gedenket, rîtr, an iuwern orden: zwiu sît ir ze rîter worden? durch slâfen, weizgot ir ensît. dâ von daz ein man gerne lît, sol er dar umbe rîter wesen? ichn hânz gehoeret noch gelesen. waenet dar umbe ir rîter sîn, durch guote spîse und guoten wîn? dar an sît ir betrogen gar: jâ izzet daz vihe gern, deist wâr. durch kleider und durch schoene gesmît sît ir niht rîter (7765–80).

58. Swer wil rîters ambet phlegen, der muoz mêre arbeit legen an sîne vuor dan ezzen wol (7785–87).

59. Wil ein rîter phlegen wol des er von rehte phlegen sol, sô sol er tac unde naht arbeiten nâch sîner maht durch kirchen und durch arme liute. der rîter ist vil lützel hiute die daz tuon: wizzet daz, swerz niht entuot, ez waere baz daz er ein gebûre waere, er waere got niht sô unmaere. ir sult daz vür wâr wizzen, im

wirt sîn rîterschaft verwizzen, swer sîn rîterschaft sô hât daz er nien gît helfe unde rât (7801–14).

60. Dem kriuze zimet wol reiner muot und kiusche site, sô mac man saelde und allez guot erwerben dâ mite (H. v. Aue, *Lieder* 209.25–28).

61. beschirme die armen, daz ist ritterschaft, sprich ir wort, daz ist tugenthaft: so bist du vor Got wert: dar umbe segent man dir daz swert (*Der magezoge* 43–46).

62. Ritterschaft wart gemacht betalliclichen umb die heiligen kirchen zu beschutten und zu beschirmen (Vol. 1, p. 120).

63. alweg fechten umb den glauben zu stercken (p. 123).

64. ein ieslîch rîters êre gedenke, als in nu lêre, do er dez swert enphienc, ein segen, swer rîterschaft wil rehte pflegen, der sol witwen und weisen beschirmen von ir vreisen: daz wirt sîn endelôs gewin. er mac sîn herze ouch kêren hin ûf dienst nâch der wîbe lôn, dâ man lernet sölhen dôn, wie sper durch schilde krachen, wie diu wîp dar umbe lachen, wie vriundîn vriunts unsemftekeit semft. zwei lôn uns sint bereit, der himel und werder wîbe gruoz (W. v. Eschenbach, *Willehalm* 299.13–27).

65. Er was ain blůme ganzer tugent, Stǻter trúwe ain adamas, Milte und zúhte ain spiegelglas, Kúsch und demǔte Mit manlicher gǔte, Wis, beschaidenlichen gǔt, Ellenthaft und hohgemǔt (R. v. Ems, *Willhelm. v. Orlens* 12550–56).

66. minne in von allem mute (15); wene dich der tugent (17); vlis dich schoner gebere (21); sag niht schalkhaft mere (22); wis biberbe und wol gezogen (25); den geburen nit den vertrage (27); nige im der dir rehte sage (29); lerne tugent all tage (30); furht die helle (33); volge der Gotes lere (35); dinen vater und dine muter ere (36); hore gerne der wisen rat (37); beschirme die armen (43).

67. vlîzet iuch diemüete (W. v. Eschenbach, *Parzival* 170.28).

68. wis diemüete und wis unbetrogen (G. v. Straßburg 5027).

69. er tete sam die wîsen tuont, die des gote genâde sagent swaz si êren bejagent und ez von im wellent hân (H. v. Aue, *Erec* 10085–88).

70. vor allen dingen minne got (H. v. Aue, *Gregorius* 257).

71. lât derbärme bî der vrävel sîn (W. v. Eschenbach, *Parzival* 171.25).

72. im erbarmte diu ellende schar (H. v. Aue, *Erec* 9798).

73. sît got selve ein triuwe ist (W. v. Eschenbach, *Parzival* 462.19).

74. rehtiu scham und werdiu triwe gebent prîs alt unde niwe (ibid. 321.29–30).

75. staete und mâze swester sint, si sint einer tugende kint (T. v. Zirklaere 12339–40).

76. E daz ich mîn ritterlîche staete braeche an guoten wîben . . . (U. v. Liechtenstein, *Gedichte* XXV.67).

77. ich mac wol dîner güete jehn staete âne wenken (W. v. Eschenbach, *Parzival* 715.14–15).

78. die andern tugende sin enwiht, und ist dâ bî diu staete niht (T. v. Zirklaere 1819–20).

79. Mvter aller tvgende Gezimet wol der Jvgende Mazze ist so genant (*Die Maze* 1–3).

80. mâze diu hêre diu hêret lîp und êre. ezn ist al der dinge kein, der ie diu sunne beschein, sô rehte saelic sô daz wîp, diu ir leben under ir lîp an die mâze verlât (G. v. Straßburg 18017–23).

81. Firmissime itaque tene et nullatenus dubites ita omne honestum utile esse, quod nichil est utile nisi sit honestum (p. 69).

82. übel unde guot (5743).

83. beidiu man unde wîp hânt vümf dinc an ir lîp und vümfiu ûzem lîp; vür wâr, diu muoz diu sêle rihten gar, ode si bringent grôze untugent beidiu an alter und an jugent. diu vümf man imme lîbe treit: sterk, snelle, glust, schoene, behendekeit. ûzem lîbe hânt vümf kraft: adel, maht, rîchtuom, name, hêrschaft. swer diu zehen niht rihten kan mit sinne, der niht heizen man (9731–42).

84. an dem enwas vergezzen nie deheiner der tugent die ein ritter in sîner jugent ze vollem lobe haben sol. man sprach dô niemen alsô wol in allen den landen. er hete ze sînen handen geburt und rîcheit: ouch was sîn tugent vil breit. swie ganz sîn habe waere, sîn geburt unwandelbaere und wol den vürsten gelîch, doch was er unnâch alsô rîch der geburt und des guotes so der êren und des muotes (H. v. Aue, *Armer Heinrich* 32–46).

85. Man giht, daz nieman edel sî niwan der edellîchen tuot. und ist daz wâr, des mugen sich genuoge hêrren schamen, Die niht vor schanden sint behuot, jâ wont in valsch und erge bî: diu drî verderbent milte und êre und ouch den edelen namen. Ôwê daz er ie guot gewan, der sich die schande unde erge lât von manegen êren dringen! der solte sehen die armen hochgemuoten an, wie die mit höveischeit kunnen wol nâch ganzer wirde ringen. ein armer der ist wol geborn, der rehte vuore in tugenden hât; sô ist ein ungeslahte gar, swie rîche er sî, der schanden bî gestât (Bruder Wernher, no. 22).

86. niemen ist edel niwan der man der sîn herze und sîn gemüete hât gekêrt an rehte güete (3860–62).

87. Nieman ist edel denne den der muot Edel machet und niht daz guot (1417–18).

88. Swer tugent hât, derst wol geborn: ân tugent ist adel gar verlorn. Er sî eigen oder frî, der von geburt niht edel sî, der sol sich edel machen mit tugentlîchen sachen (54.6–11).

89. Aller manne schoen ein bluomen kranz (W. v. Eschenbach, *Parzival* 122.13).

90. "ir mugt wol sîn von ritters art." von den helden er geschouwet wart: Dô lac diu gotes kunst an im (123.11–13).

91. Est ergo pulchritudo realiter idem quod bonitas (Ulrich v. Straßburg, *De pulchro*, p. 76).

92. Quia enim in formis rerum visibilium pulchritudo earundem consistit, congrue ex formis visibilibus invisibilem pulchritudinem demonstrari dicit, quoniam visibilis pulchritudo invisibilis pulchritudinis imago est (Hugh of St. Victor, *Commentaria in hierarchiam coelestem*, col. 949).

93. Flôre hâte schoene hâr, minre brûn danne val, unde was daz über al allez ze mâzen reit: sîn tinne wîz unde breit, aller missewende frî: cleine brâwen dâ bî, als ez sich dar zuo gezôch, niht ze nidere noch ze hôch, nâch dem wunsche garwe, und wâren an der varwe sînes hâres genôz: diu ougen lieht unde grôz, mit süezem anblicke, als sie solten lachen dicke, daz im harte wol gezam. sîn nase was im alsam nâch wunsche eben unde sleht, wol geschaffen unde reht. dô

schuof der nâtûre flîz diu wangen rôt unde wîz alsô milch unde bluot. der munt was ouch behuot aller missewende gar, staeticlîche rôsenvar. gelîche zene cleine; von wîze lûhtens reine: und daz kinne sinwel: schoenen hals unde kel: sîn arme starc unde lanc, sîne hende sleht unde blanc, die vinger âne missewende, wol geschaffen an dem ende die nagele lûter als ein glas. sîn brust wol ûferhaben was, und iedoch enmitten smal. dar zuo was er über al wol geslihtet als ein zein. er hâte ritterlîchiu bein unde wolstânde waden, niht ze cranc noch überladen, and daz sie heizent holn fuoz. sît ich ez allez sagen muoz, der mâze zen zêhen, dorfte er niemen flêhen, daz ers im besnite baz; wan diu nâtûre vergaz an im deheiner zierde (6816–63).

94. er stahel, swa er ze strîte quam, sîn hant dâ sigelîchen nam vil manegen lobelîchen prîs (W. v. Eschenbach, *Parzival* 4.15–17).

95. er was schoene unde starc, er was getriuwe unde guot und hete geduldigen muot. er hete künste gnuoge, zuht unde vuoge (H. v. Aue, *Gregorius* 1238–42).

96. an fuoge unde an höfescheit hete er gewendet unde geleit sîne tage und sîne sinne (G. v. Straßburg 7709–11).

97. Cortesia es tals, se voleç saber cals: qui ben sap dir e far per c'om lo deia amar, e se garda d'enueis (427–31).

98. Cortesia es en guarnir e en gent acuillir; cortesia es d'onrar (damar, manuscript N) e es en gen parlar; cortesia es en solaz (457–461).

99. Vnde ir warh mit sinir houisheit Daz die magit lossam. Ir uater inran (3776–78).

100. (du)rch minen willen saltu phlegen wisen (zu der hov)ischeit unde leide ime die dorpericheit. (gevuge beh)urdieren daz saltu ime lieben, daz er sich (ouch d)ecke mit meschilde, dar zu wesen milde, zu (stete brin)gen sinen mut. daz ist ime an den eren gut. (zu den vr)ouwen sal er gerne gan, gezogentliche vor in (stan unde o)ouch bi in sizzen. zallen dingen sal er wizze (han na)ch sime rechte. sva er gute knechte horet reden (von m)anheit daz ne sal ime nicht wesen leit. daz sal (er horen) gerne. da bi mach er lerne daz ime zu den eren (wole stat) (γb 27–46).

101. tûsent jungelinge von irn ingesinde, di plâgen hubischeite vile mit allir slahte seitspile (*Straßburger Alexander* 6035–38).

102. Ob in vünf landen ûzerwünschet waere ein helt, des lîbes schoene in ganzen tugenden ûz erwelt, getriuwe, milte, staete in sînen worten; Er künde schrîben, lesen, tihten, seitenspil ouch birsen, jagen, schirmen, schiezen zuo dem zil, unt waere er guot in wâfen z'allen orten. Jâ künde er mit behendikeit diu swarzen buoch, ouch kunst der gramacîen, unt waere in sinnen wol bereit ze doenen, singen alle stempenien, unt wurfe er den blîden stein wol zwelf schuoh lanc vor allen sînen sellen, dâmit er kwaeme des in ein, daz er einn wilden beren künde vellen; unt alle vrouwen teilden im ir gruoz ze hôhem dinge, hete er der siben künste hort unt wîse unt wort-daz waer vil gar an im verlorn, unt hete er niht pfenninge (I.21).

103. Ez (daz guot) birt hochvart, hohen muot unt Gotes vil vergezzen (*Pseudo-Gottfried* III.6.5).

104. dâ was wünne und êre, vreude und michel rîterschaft und alles des diu überkraft des man zem lîbe gerte (H. v. Aue, *Iwein* 2442–45).

105. wis iemer höfsch, wis iemer frô! (G. v. Straßburg 5043).

106. den er fröude solte tragen, den was der hêrre in sînen tagen ein fröude berndiu sunne. er was der werlde ein wunne, der ritterschefte ein lêre, sîner mâge ein êre, sînes landes ein zuoversiht. an ime brast al der tugende niht, der hêrre haben solde (ibid. 251–59).

107. sîn hof wart aller vreuden bar unde stuont nâch schanden (H. v. Aue, *Erec* 2989–90).

108. Rum daz iz itel ere (W. v. Elmendorf 1183).

109. swes lebn sich sô verendet, daz got niht wirt gepfendet der sêle durch des lîbes schulde, und der doch der werlde hulde behalten kan mit werdekeit, daz ist ein nütziu arbeit (W. v. Eschenbach, *Parzival* 827.19–24).

110. behuoten ir sêle, behalten ouh werltlîch êre (5681–82).

111. Noch salich dich ein tugent lerin, di beide nutzze iz zu den erin vnd gibet dir gotis hulde (W. v. Elmendorf 647–49).

112. Ein man sol haben êre und sol iedoch der sêle under wîlen wesen guot, daz in dehein sîn übermuot Verleite niht ze verre (Spervogel 29.34–30.3).

113. Swer got und die werlt kan behalten, derst ein saelic man (Freidank 31.18–19).

114. morâliteit daz süeze lesen deist saelic unde reine. ir lêre hât gemeine mit der werlde und mit gote. si lêret uns in ir gebote got und der werlde gevallen; si ist edeln herzen allen ze einer ammen gegeben, daz sî îr lîpnar unde ir leben suochen in ir lêre, wan sîne hânt guot noch êre, ez enlêre sî morâliteit (8012–23).

115. wie man driu dinc erwurbe, der keines niht verdurbe. diu zwei sint êre und varnde guot, daz dicke ein ander schaden tuot: daz dritte ist gotes hulde, der zweier übergulde. die wolte ich gerne in einen schrîn (8.12–18).

116. jâ leider desn mac niht gesîn, daz guot und weltliche êre und gotes hulde mêre zesamene in ein herze komen (8.19–22).

117. Porro ordo militum nunc est, ordinem non tenere. Nam cujus os majore verborum spurcitia polluitur, qui destabilius jurat, qui minus Deum timet, qui ministros Dei vilificat, qui Ecclesiam non veretur, iste hodie in coetu militum fortior et nominatior reputatur (col. 294).

118. Olim se juramenti vinculo milites obligabant, quod starent pro reipublicae statu, quod in acie non fugerent, et quod vitae propriae utilitatem publicam praehaberent. Sed et hodie tirones enses suos recipiunt de altari, ut profiteantur se filios Ecclesiae, atque ad honorem sacerdotii, ad tuitionem pauperum, ad vindictam malefactorum et patriae liberationem gladium accepisse. Porro res in contrarium versa est; nam ex quo hodie militari cingulo decorantur, statim insurgunt in christos Domini, et desaeviunt in patrimonium Crucifixi. Spoliant et praedantur subjectos Christi pauperes, et miserabiliter atque immisericorditer affligunt miseros, ut in doloribus alienis illicitos appetitus et extraordinarias impleant voluptates (ibid.).

119. Qui contra inimicos crucis Christi vires suas exercere debuerant, potibus et ebrietatibus pugnant, vacant otio marcent crapula, vitamque degenerum in immunditiis transigentes nomen et officium militiae dehonestant (ibid.).

120. Quod si milites nostros ire in expeditionem quandoque oporteat, summarii eorum non ferro, sed vino, non lanceis, sed caseis, non ensibus, sed utribus, non hastis, sed verubus onerantur. Credas eos ire ad demum convivii, non

ad bellum. Clypeos deferunt optime deauratos, praedam potius hostium cupientes, quam certamen ab hostibus, et eos referunt, ut ita loquar, virgines et intactos. Bella tamen et conflictus equestres depingi faciunt in sellis et clypeis, ut se quadam imaginaria visione delectent in pugnis, quas actualiter ingredi, aut videre non audent (col. 296).

121. At pater, haeredem transitoriae possessionis desiderans, saecularis militiae insignia puero destinabat. Unde cum jam pupillares annos attigisset, eum cum coaevis urgebat equitare juvenibus, equum flectere in gyrum, vibrare hastam, facile clypeum circumferre, et, quod ille altius abhorrebat, spoliis instare et rapinis (Hildebert of Lavardin, *Vita Hugonis*, col. 860).

122. severe educaverat (Ekkehard IV, *Casus s. Galli*, p. 262).

123. Domum suam ordinatissime disposuit. Unde et nobilissimi quique utriusque provinciae filios suos eius magisterio educandos certatim commendaverunt (p. 22).

124. ad discendam linguam theutonicam et mores curie (Gislebert of Mons, p. 234).

125. viii junch heren (*Monumenta Wittelsbacensia*, section 2, no. 198, p. 53).

126. edelchinde von dem lande (p. 53 f.).

127. di vns ze tische dienent (p. 57).

128. moribus erudiendus et militaribus officiis diligenter imbuendus et introducendus (Lambert of Ardres, *Historia comitum Ghisnensium*, p. 603).

129. ir mugt wol volkes hêrre sîn (170.22).

130. erbarmen, milte, güete, diemüete (170.25 ff.).

131. gebt rehter mâze ir orden (171.13).

132. Reden und an bŭchen lesen (2765).

133. linguarum omnium quae sunt a mari Gallico usque ad Jordanem habens scientiam (Walther Map, *De nugis curialium*, p. 227).

134. multis linguis et variis loqui sciebat (Salimbene of Parma, *Cronica*, vol. 1, p. 508).

135. Preter facundiam enim Latinae et Teutonicae linguae Slavicae nichilominus linguae gnarus erat (Helmhold of Bosau, p. 190).

136. utens lingua Latina, Romana, Gallica, Graeca, Apulica, Lombardica, Brabantina, uti lingua materna (Albert of Stade, p. 347).

137. sciens Gallicum, Latinum et Germanicum (*Annales Colmarienses*, p. 257).

138. durch fremede sprâche in fremediu lant (G. v. Straßburg 2061).

139. In patria lingua admodum facundus (*Gesta Frederici*, p. 710).

140. more Italico longa continuatione peryodorumque circuitibus sermonem producturus . . . cum corporis modestia orisque venustate regalem servans animum ex inproviso non inprovise respondit (*Gesta Frederici*, p. 346).

141. vir magniloquus, forensis eloquentiae declamator facundissimus, coram regni principibus prudentia et consilio paene inter primos habitus (p. 244).

142. mit zühten sprechen (W. v. Grafenberg 1240).

143. kiuschiu wort (T. v. Zirklaere 389).

144. harpfen unde gîgen unde allerhande seiten spil, des kund er mê danne

vil, wand ez was dâ lantsite. die vrouwen lêrten in dâ mite baltlîche singen (U. v
Zatzikhoven 262–67).

145. Der ander meister, den er gewan, der lertîn wol mûsicam . . . unt vor
ime selben heven daz gesanc (Lamprecht, *Alexander* 177–78;82).

146. legere, scribere et cantare sciebat et cantilenas et cantiones invenir(
(Salimbene of Parma, vol. 1, p. 508).

147. Coniunx ducis Friderici, que civibus ad solatium a duce infra urben
relicta fuerat, fame et nuditate acriter afflicta, a rege Lothario regalibus doni:
liberaliter ditata, cum suis discessit (p. 766).

148. Adducitur autem uxor illius, quae et ipsa in castro obsessa fuerat.
quam dux benigne suscipiens et bene consolans patri suo palatino commisi1
(*Historia Welforum*, p. 40 f.).

149. Ibi recolligentes inconcinnos mores imperatoris, quos arbitrati sunt imperiali aule minime conducere, pro eo quod ecclesiasticis dignitatibus insultans.
archipresules simpliciter et vituperiose clericos, abbates monachos, reverandas
matronas mulieres appelans, universosque, quos Deus honorare precepit,
. . . inhonoravit (*Chronica s. Petri Erfordensis*, p. 209).

150. Vovit autem regis filius, quod nunquam duas noctes in uno loco
moraretur, quousque prosecuturus, quantum in ipso erat, votum paternum, in
Scotiam perveniret (Nicholas Trevet, *Annales*, p. 409).

151. Qu'il ne girra an un ostel Deus nuiz an trestot son aage . . . Tant que il
del graal savra Cui l'an an sert (Chrétien de Troyes, *Conte du Graal* 4728–29;
35–36).

152. Dedenz la chanbre a la roïne Avoit pendu une cortine; Tote ert pointe
de chevaliers (57–59).

153. Mais Blanchandins petit menja Quar aillors son penser torna Au chevaliers qu'il ot veüz Poinz en la chanbre fervestuz, Et jure Dieu que il querra
Tant aventure qu'il l'avra De joster et de tornoier (127–33).

154. von dem gemâlten bilde sint der gebûre und daz kint gevreuwet oft;
swer niht enkan verstên swaz ein biderb man an der schrift verstên sol, dem sî
mit den bilden wol. der pfaffe sehe die schrift an, sô sol der ungelêrte man diu
bilde sehen, sît im niht diu schrift zerkennen geschiht (1097–1106).

155. Idcirco enim pictura in Ecclesiis adhibetur, ut hi qui litteras nesciunt,
saltem in parietibus videndo legant quae legere in Codicibus non valent (*Epistolae*, col. 1027 f.).

156. swer guote rede minne und si gerne hoere sagen, der sol mit zühten
gedagen und merken si rehte: daz ist im guot. si getiuret (vil) manges mannes
muot, wand er vernimt vil lîhte dâ des er sich gebezzert sâ (82–88).

157. Swer ritterliche geverte sol ritterlichen triben in schimpf und ouch in
herte, der sol daz nimmer gern lan beliben, ern hôre da von lesen, sagen, singen.
daz git im kunst und ellen noch mere dann mit toren gampel ringen. Sprechen
und gebaren mit hovschen siten riche, des sol man gerne varen, daz man zu hove
kunne hoveliche werben gen den herren und den vrowen. erdaht durch tugende
schulde wart diutscher bûch mit triwen unverhowen. Tugende, manheit jehende
ist man den hohen werden, di wilent waren spehende niht wan daz si werdicheit
begerden. manheit, triwe, zuhte, maz und milte, der vrowen zuht mit kûsche, ir

beider wirde sich hie mit hohe zilte. Daz selbe, wene ich, hûte in al der werlde priset. alle werde lûte werdent des hie vil wol under wiset. swachiu dinc, di lert iz nieman werben. di diutsch nie lesen horten, der siht man tusent stunde mer verderben (2958.1–2961.4).

158. Juncherren suln von Gâwein hoeren, Clîes, Erec, Iwein, und suln rihten sîn jugent gar nâh Gâweins reiner tugent. volgt Artûs dem künege hêr, der treit iu vor vil guote lêr, und habt ouch in iuwerm muot künic Karln den helt guot (1041–48).

159. die âventiure sint gekleit dicke mit lüge harte schône (1118–19).

160. der tiefe sinne niht verstên kan, der sol die âventiure lesen (1108–09).

161. ich schilte die âventiure niht, swie uns ze liegen geschiht von der âventiure rât, wan si bezeichenunge hât der zuht unde der wârheit (1121–25).

162. sint die âventiur niht wâr, si bezeichent doch vil gar waz ein ieglîch man tuon sol der nâch vrümkeit wil leben wol (1131–34).

163. Doch sint diu buoch gar lügen vol (21644).

164. Swer gar sich flîzet an seltsên rîm, Der wil ouch, sinnes lîm Ûzen an schoenen worten klebe Und lützel nutzes dâr inne swebe. Alsô sint bekant durch tiutschiu lant Êrec, Îwan und Tristrant, Künic Ruother und her Parcifâl, Wigalois, der grôzen schal Hât bejaget und hôhen prîs: Swer des geloubt, der ist unwîs (1217–26).

165. Als ich mich versinnen kan, sô hât verlorn manigem man Sôgetâner tiutschen buoche lêre Lîp und sêle, guot und êre (21653–56).

166. Wenne maniger wênt er wêr enwiht, Würde er ein sôgetân degen niht Als die helde vor genant (21657–59).

167. swer noch behelte Der vor genanten singer doene Und ir getihte reine und schoene: Der vindet tugent, zuht und êre, Hübescheit der werlde und ouch die lêre, Von der sîn leben wirt genême Und selten ieman widerzême (1236–42).

168. regia stirpe genitus, regio obsequio morum elegantia idoneus (*Vita Meinwerci*, p. 7).

169. vir alti sanguinis valdeque curialis et honestus dulcique eloquio (Balderic, *Gesta Alberonis*, p. 596).

170. Ipse quoque ingenua liberalitate ac eximia largitate, morum quoque curialitate et tocius probitatis elegantia redimitus (*Gesta episcoporum Halberstadensium*, p. 114f.).

171. curialiter educatus et curialibus moribus instructus (Simon, *Gesta abbatum s. Bertini Sithiensium*, p. 661 f.).

172. curiales episcopi (*Contra clericos aulicos*, col. 472).

173. Ipse namque in omni actione sua, quod at paganis dignum laude videbatur, quandam a Spiritu sancto—hoc enim potissimum credo—cuiusdam singularis munditiae atque, ut ita dixerim, elegantis et urbanae disciplinae praerogativam habebat, ita ut nichil unquam indecens aut ineptum inhonestumve quid in cibo aut potu, sermone, gestu vel habitu admitteret, sed in omni officio exterioris hominis, quaenam esset compositio interioris, ostendebat, bonitate, disciplina et prudentiae cautela conspicuus (Herbord, *Dialogus de vita Ottonis*, p. 66 f.).

174. de magnis principibus unus et cui nihil in omni rerum humanarum

dignitate supra, natu scilicet, literarum etiam scientia, fortitudine atque divitiis satis prepollens, elegantia atque facundia bonis omnibus amabilis et affabilis (*Chronica*, p. 184).

175. curialibus disciplinis et splendida quadam claritudine mentem adeo informans, ut inter aulicos et viros mundana gloria prefulgidos nihil rusticanae simplicitatis admitteret omnibusque gloriosus appareret (p. 920).

176. quem scimus esse hominem curialem totumque urbanitati, ne dicamus vanitati, deditum (*Expositio Psalmorum*, p. 53).

177. Edissere mihi, pater karissime, veram nobilitatis definitionem (p. 9).

178. Accipe ait, talem qui septem liberalibus artibus sit instructus, industriis septem eruditus, septem etiam probitatibus edoctus, et ego hanc aestimo perfectam esse nobilitatem (p. 10).

179. Ne sit vorax, potator, luxoriosus, violentus, mendax, avarus et de mala conversatione (p. 11).

180. Equitare, natare, sagittare, cestibus certare, aucupare, scaccis ludere, versificari (p. 10).

181. wāde vns phase(t) saget eī bv̊h. von gv̊t mīnē gnŏc (15).

182. sver diz tv̊t alse ih ime rate. so ist sin er grv̊ne vn̄ state (33–34).

183. factus est per clericum miles Cythereus (*Carmina Burana* 92.41.3)

184. Quos scimus affabiles, gratos et amabiles; Inest curialitas clericis et probitas. Non noverunt fallere, neque maledicere, Amandi periciam habent, et industriam; Pulchra donant munera, bene servant federa (*Das Liebeskonzil zu Remiremont* 69–73).

185. a militibus quasi a quisbusdam portentis cauerae (Kühnel, p. 76).

186. Ipsi enim sunt per quos ut ita dicam reguntur iura curialitatis. ipsi sunt fons et origo totius honestatis (ibid.).

2. THE COURTLY LADY

1. sol ich der warheit iehen, so wart nie, nach der gotes kraft, nicht dinges so genadehaft so vrowen lip mit ir leben. die ere hat in got gegeben, daz man si uf der erde zu dem ho(e)hsten werde erkennen sol mit eren und ir lop immer meren (Stricker, *Frauenehre* 222–30).

2. seht an ir ougen und merkent ir kinne, seht an ir kele wîz und prüevent ir munt. Si ist âne lougen gestalt sam diu minne. mir wart von vrouwen so liebez nie kunt (H. v. Morungen 141.1–4)

3. alle ir tugende und ir schoene (H. v. Morungen 130.15).

4. ir schoene und ir güete (Rietenburg 19.29).

5. schoene ist ein niht wider güete (T. v. Zirklaere 956).

6. Ein toerscher man der siht ein wîp waz si gezierd hab an ir lîp. er siht niht waz si hab dar inne an guoter tugende und an sinne (ibid. 1304–07).

7. so ist ir uzer schoen entwiht, si ist schoene innerthalben niht (ibid. 951–52).

8. Nâch vrowen schoene nieman sol ze vil gevrâgen. sint si guot, er lâzes ime gevallen wol (H. v. Rugge 107.27–29).

9. wip sint voller urhap vollekomener dinge guot. wîp gebent tugentlîchen

muot, wîp hôhe fröude erweckent, wîp versêret herze erstreckent ze hôher stîge rihte mit froelîcher phlihte, wîp brechent vester sorgen bunt, wîp gebent süezes trôstes vunt, wîp tuont wesen ellenhaft, wîp sint an vînden sigehaft, wîp sint saelden voller teil werdiu wîp sint mannes heil (U. v. Etzenbach, *Wilhelm v. Wenden* 1418–30).

10. wer gît in heldes muot, wer gît in tugent? wer mûzet si ze vröuden, ezn tuo der vrouwen minniclich gewalt ? (R. v. Zweter 48.5–6).

11. daz Ritter Ritterlichen lebent, daz hant si von den vrowen (Stricker, *Frauenehre* 642–43).

12. Lange swîgen des hât ich gedâht (72.31).

13. mich enwil ein wîp niht an gesehen: die brâht ich in die werdekeit, daz ir muot sô hôhe stât. jon weiz si niht, swenn ich mîn singen lâze, daz ir lop zergât (73.1–4).

14. ir leben hât mînes lebennes êre: stirbe ab ich, sô ist si tôt (73.16–17).

15. Ir minnesinger, iu muoz ofte misselingen, daz iu den schaden tuot, daz ist der wân (*Lieder* 218.21–22).

16. ich waen, alle, die der sint, ein bezzer kint niht vunden, wan daz ir diu vüezel sint zerschrunden (49.1–2).

17. Brevis omnis malitia super malitiam mulieris . . . Ne respicias in mulieris speciem, et non cuncupiscas mulierem in specie. Mulieris ira, et irreverentia, et confusio magna . . . A muliere initium factum est peccati (Ecclesiastes 25.26–33).

18. inveni amariorem morte mulierem, quae laqueus venatorum est, et sagena cor ejus, vincula sunt manus illius (Ecclesiastes 7.27).

19. Tria sunt insaturabilia . . . Infernus, et os vulvae, et terra quae non satiatur aqua (*Liber proverbiorum* 30.15–16).

20. Omnia mala ex mulieribus (*Adversus Jovinianum*, col. 291).

21. Mulieres viris suis subditae sint, sicut Domino; quoniam vir caput est mulieris (Ad Ephesios 5.22–23).

22. Mulieres in ecclesiis taceant; non enim permittitur eis loqui, sed subditas esse, sicut et lex dicit (Ad Corinthios prima 14.34).

23. Mulier in silentio discat cum omni subjectione. Docere autem mulieri non permitto, neque dominari in virum (Ad Thimothaeum prima 2.11–12).

24. Est etiam ordo naturalis in hominibus, ut seruiant feminae viris (St. Augustine, *Quaestiones in Heptateuchum*, p. 59).

25. propter condicionem seruitutis, qua viro in omnibus debet subesse (col. 1254).

26. femina est mas occasionatus (*Summa theologiae*, part I, Quaestio 92, Articulus 1).

27. mulier naturaliter est minoris virtutis et dignitatis quam vir (ibid.).

28. in mulieribus non est sufficiens robur mentis ad hoc quod concupiscentiis resistant (ibid., part II, Quaestio 149, Articulus 4).

29. uxor regitur, et vir regit (ibid., part III, Supplementum, Quaestio 64, Articulus 5).

30. verbis, et verbere (ibid., Quaestio 62, Articulus 2).

31. varium et mutabile semper femina (*Aeneid* IV.569–70).

32. Qua potes in peius dotes deflecte puellae Iudiciumque brevi limite falle

tuum. Turgida, si plena est, si fusca, nigra vocetur; In gracili macies crimen habere potest (*Remedia amoris* 325–28).

33. Ille tamen gravior, quae cum discumbere coepit, laudat Virgilium, periturae ignoscit Elissae, committit vates et comparat, inde Maronem atque alia parte in trutina suspendit Homerum. cedunt grammatici, vincuntur rhetores, omnis turba tacet (*Saturae* VI.434–39),

34. mala stirps vitiosa propago (col. 1698).

35. Pulchior argento, fulvo pretiosior auro (col. 1700).

36. Quam nociva sint sacris hominibus femina, avaritia, ambitio.

37. esse debere causam et originem bonorum (p. 159).

38. Ob ich durch si den hals zubreche, wer reche mir den schaiden dan? (p. 29).

39. Da der vurgenant kaiser Ludewig daz lit gehorte, darumb so strafte he den herren von Westerburg unde saide, he wolde ez der frauwen gebeßert haben (ibid.).

40. In jamers noden in gar vurdreven bin durch ein wif so minnecliche (ibid.).

41. Que fame a plus de mil corages (*Yvain* 1436).

42. Et a bien pres totes le font, Que de lor folies s'escusent Et ce, qu'eles vuelent, refusent (1642–44).

43. doch tete sî sam diu wîp tuont: sî widerredent durch ir muot daz sî doch ofte dunket guot (*Iwein* 1866–68).

44. er missetuot, der daz seit, ez mache ir unstaetekheit: ich weiz baz wâ vonz geschiht daz man sî alsô dicke siht in wankelm gemüete: ez kumt von ir güete (1873–78).

45. er muoz mir diu lant rûmen, alder ich geniete mich sîn (8.7–8).

46. des gehazze got den dîn lîp! jô enwas ich niht ein eber wilde, sô sprach daz wîp (8.13–16).

47. Wîp unde vederspil diu werdent lîchte zam. swer sî ze rehte lucket, sô suochent sî den man (10.17–20).

48. Niemen darf mir wenden daz zunstaete, ob ich die hazze, die ich dâ minnet ê . . . ich waer ein gouch, ob ich ir tumpheit haete vür guot. ez engeschiht mir niemer mê (47.33–34; 48.1–2).

49. mit sumerlaten (73.22).

50. ich solte iu klagen die meisten nôt, niuwen daz ich von wîben niht übel reden kan (171.2–3).

51. wîp sint et immer wîp (W. v. Eschenbach, *Parzival* 450.5).

52. daz waegste selten wip getůt (U. v. Türheim, *Rennewart* 3386).

53. ich hân selten wîp gesehen, (ez waere maget ode wîp) den daz herze und der lîp ân allen wandel waere (Otte, *Eraclius* 2110–13).

54. Ez machet trûric mir den lîp, daz alsô mangiu heizet wîp. ir stimme sint gelîche hel: genuoge sint gein valsche snel, etslîche valsches laere (W. v. Eschenbach, *Parzival* 116.5–9).

55. Salomo der wise . . . sprichet der sie ein Vnd (Vnder) zehen kvme reine Die rechtliche stete si (H. v. Fritzlar 8519.25–27).

56. sît in daz von arte kumet, und ez diu natiure an in frumet (17971–72).

57. wan swelh wîp tugendet wider ir art, diu gerne wider ir art bewart ir lop,

ir êre unde ir lîp, diu ist niwan mit namen ein wîp umd ist ein man mit muote (ibid. 17975–79).

58. virilis ingenii femina (*Vita Henrici* IV, p. 414).

59. wâ nu, künec Gunther? wie verliesen wir den lîp! der ir dâ gert ze minnen, diu ist des tiuveles wîp (438.3–4).

60. Owê, gedâhte der recke, sol ich nu mînen lîp von einer magt verliesen, sô mugen elliu wîp her nâch immer mêre tragen gelpfen muot gegen ir manne (673.1–4).

61. dâ was vil manegiu under, diu der hôchzît wol hete enborn, wande sie hete verlorn den magetuom vor maneger zît, der maneger kurze freude gît. ir was ouch gnuoc unde vil, die von dem selben zabelspil mit worten heten vil vernomen und waern sîn gerne zende komen, mohten sies guot state hân (Otte, *Eraclius* 1914–23).

62. daz ist boese und heizet gîtecheit (2003).

63. ich gemache in wol zeinem affen, mînen herrn, swie wîse er ist (2066–67).

64. ze der swachesten waere wol bewant beide krône unde lant (2165–66).

65. Dô nam Keye scheneschlant froun Cunnewâren de Lâlant mit ir reiden hâre: ir lange zöpfe clâre die want er umbe sîne hant, er spancte se âne türbant. ir rüke wart kein eit gestabt: doch wart ein stap sô dran gehabt, unz daz sîn siusen gar verswanc, durch die wât unt durch ir vel ez dranc (W. v. Eschenbach, *Parzival* 151.21–30),

66. daz er si mit der hant sluoc alsô daz diu guote harte sêre bluote. er sprach: "ir ezzet, übel hût!" (H. v. Aue, *Erec* 6521–24).

67. ir strâfen was im ungemach. vil unsenfteclîche er sprach: "ir herren, ir sît wunderlich, daz ir dar umbe strâfet mich swaz ich mînem wîbe tuo. dâ bestât doch niemen zuo ze redenne übel noch guot, swaz ein mann sînem wîbe tuot. si ist mîn und bin ich ir: wie welt ir daz erwern mir, ich entuo ir swaz mir gevalle?" dâ mite gesweicte er si alle (6538–49).

68. swaz ouch mir mîn geselle tuot, daz dulde ich mit rehte. ze wîbe und ze knehte und ze swiu er mich wil hân, des bin ich im alles undertân (ibid. 3811–15).

69. ich hân unfuoge an ir getân (W. v. Eschenbach, *Parzival* 271.7).

70. Daz hât mich sît gerouwen, sprach daz edel wîp. ouch hât er sô zerblouwen dar umbe mînen lîp (*Nibelungenlied* 894. 1–2).

71. jâ gesprichet lîhte ein wîp des sî niht sprechen solde. swer daz rechen wolde daz wir wîp gesprechen, der müesse vil gerechen. wir wîp bedurfen alle tage daz man uns tumbe rede vertrage; wand sî under wîlent ist herte und doch ân argen list, gevaerlich und doch âne haz: wan wirne kunnen leider baz (H. v. Aue, *Iwein* 7674–84).

72. ouch wart in dâ ze hove gegeben in allen wîs ein wunschleben: in liebte hof und den lîp manec maget unde wîp, die schoensten von den rîchen (H. v. Aue, *Iwein* 43–47).

73. Swâ ein edeliu schoene frowe reine, wol gekleidet unde wol gebunden, dur kurzewîle zuo vile liuten gât, hovelîchen hôhgemuot, niht eine, umbe sehende in wênic under stunden, alsam der sunne gegen den sternen stât, -der meie bringe uns al sîn wunder, waz ist dâ sô wünnecliches under, als ir vil

minneclicher lîp? wir lâzen alle bluomen stân, und kapfen an daz werde wîp (46.10–20).

74. vil schiere sach ich komen, dô ich in die burc gienc, ein juncvrouwen diu mich enpfienc (H. v. Aue, *Iwein* 312–14).

75. hie vant ich wîsheit bî der jugent, grôze schoene und ganze tugent (339–40).

76. sî saz mir güetlichen bî: und swaz ich sprach, daz hôrte sî und antwurt es mit güete (341–43).

77. nu gevuogete ez sich dicke alsô, ir vater sô der was fröudehaft oder als fremediu ritterschft dâ ze hove vor dem künege was, daz Îsôt in den palas vür ir vater wart besant; und allez daz ir was bekant höfscher liste und schoener site, da kurztes im die stunde mite und mit im manegem an der stete (G. v. Straßburg 8040–49).

78. si sanc, si schreip und si las (8059).

79. ich lâze iu mîne tohter lesen swelch maere ir welt in franzois. mîn tohter ist sô kurtois, un welt ir zabelen mir ir, daz kan si wol: daz habet ûf mir. si tuot swaz ir wellet, ob si sich ziu gesellet (*Mai u. Beaflor* 230.30–36).

80. Gyburc mohte ir wâpenroc nu mit êren von ir legen: si unde ir juncfrouwen megn dez harnaschrâm tuon von dem vel. si sprach "gelüke ist sinewel. mir was nu lange trûren bî: dâ von bin ich ein teil nu vrî. Al mîne juncvrouwen ich man, leget iwer besten kleider an: ir sult iuch feitieren, vel und hâr so zieren, daz ir minneclîchen sît getân, ob ein minne gerender man iu dienst nâch minne biete, daz er sihs niht gâhs geniete, und daz im tuo daz scheiden wê von iu. daz sult ir schaffen ê: und vlîzt iuch einer hövescheit, gebâret als iu nie kein leit von vînden geschaehe. sît niht ze wortspaehe, ob si iuch kumbers vrâgen: sprechet 'welt irz wâgen, sone kêrt iuch niht an unser sage. wir sîn erwahsen ûzer klage: wan iwer künfteclîcher trôst hât uns vîntlîcher nôt erlôst. welt ir uns iwerr helfe wern, sô muge wir trûrens wol enbern.' nu gebâret gesellleclîche, nie fürste wart sô rîche, ern hoer wol einer meide wort. ir sitzet hie oder dort, parriert der rîter iuch benebn, dem sult ir die gebaerde gebn daz iwer kiusche im sî bekant. bî vriundîn vriunt ie ellen vant: diu wîplîche güete gît dem man hôhgemüete" (W. v. Eschenbach, *Willehalm* 246.24–248.2).

81. Precipue vero in IIII eas instruere conuenit et informare, sc. in pudicia siue castitate et in humilitate et in taciturnitate et in morum sive gestuum maturitate (p. 178).

82. Michi lauacra omnino displicent in adulta uirgine que se ipsam debet erubescere, nudamque videre non posse (p. 181).

83. animi est indicium (p. 181).

84. maturitas puellis seruanda sit in omni gestu, precipue tamen in aspectu, in quo precipue apparet pudicia et econtrario similiter impudicicia (p. 192).

85. honorare soceros, diligere maritum, regere familiam, gubernare domum et seipsam irreprehensibilem exhibere (p. 197).

86. ...et filiae meae, quoad psalterium discat, victum similiter praebeant (*Monumenta Understorfensia*, p. 146).

87. qui heit conoille, Ne teist, ne file, ne traoille... de sei faire belle et gente Et sei peindre blanche ou rovente (Etienne de Fougières 1053–58).

88. genuoge worhten under in swaz iemen würken solde von sîden und von

golde. genuoge worhten an der rame: der werc was aber âne schame. und die des niene kunden, die lâsen, diese wunden, disiu blou, disiu dahs, disiu hachelte vlahs, dise spunnen, dise nâten (6196–205).

89. litterarum et artium aliarum, distinguere auro gemmisque sacras vestes, peritissima fuit (*Vita s. Cunegundis*, p. 822).

90. . . . nichil umquam didicerit, nisi solum psalterium more nobilium puellarum (p. 330).

91. salter, unde alle buke, de to Goddes denste horet, de vrowen pleget to lesene (I.24 § 3).

92. alle naht unz ez taget liset sî an ir salter (K. Fleck, *Flore* 6222–23).

93. Si truoc ein salter in der hant (W. v. Eschenbach, *Parzival* 438.1).

94. an ir venje si den salter las (ibid. 644.24).

95. Herzentrût, mîn künigîn, . . . wilt du ein saltervrouwe wesen ? (Steinmar 11.34; 36).

96. litteris et Latino optime eruditam eloquio, . . . quod maxime domizellarum nobilium exornat decorem (Vincent of Prague, p. 664).

97. Pernez nule por sa beauté Ne nule ke soit en livre lettrié (A 151–52).

98. A fame ne doit on apanre letres ne escrire, se ce n'est especiaument por estre nonnain; car par lire et escrire de fame sont maint mal avenu. Car tieus li osera baillier ou anvoier letres, ou faire giter devant li, qui seront de folie ou de priere, en chançon ou en rime ou en conte, qu'il n'oseroit proier ne dire de bouche, ne par message mander (*Les quatre âges de l'homme*, p. 16).

99. la foiblece de la complexion de la fame (p. 17).

100. ouch sanc diu saeldenrîche suoze unde wol von munde (8000–01).

101. si kunde . . . brieve und schanzûne tihten, ir getihte schône slihten (8141–44).

102. si videlte ir stampenîe, leiche und sô fremdiu notelîn, diu niemer fremeder kunden sîn, in franzoiser wîse von Sanze und San Dinîse (8062–66).

103. si sang ir pasturêle, ir rotruwange und ir rundate, schanzûne, refloit und folate wol unde wol und alze wol (8076–79).

104. ein vrouwe sol niht vrevelîch schimphen (397–98).

105. ein vrouwe sol niht vast an sehen einn vrömeden man (400–01).

106. Ein juncvrouwe sol senfticlîche und niht lût sprechen (405–06).

107. zuht wert den vrouwen alln gemein sitzen mit bein über bein (411–12).

108. ein vrouwe sol ze deheiner zît treten weder vast noch wît (417–18).

109. ein vrouwe sol sich, daz geloubet, kêren gegen das pherstes houbet, swenn si rîtet; . . . si sol niht gar dwerhes sitzen (421–24).

110. ein vrowe sol recken niht ir hant, swenn si rît, vür ir gewant; si sol ir ougen und ir houbet stille haben (437–40).

111. Wil sich ein vrowe mit zuht bewarn, si sol niht âne hülle varn. si sol ir hül ze samen hân, ist si der garnatsch ân. lât si am lîbe iht sehen par, daz ist wider zuht gar (451–56).

112. si sol gên vür sich geriht und sol vil umbe sehen niht (461–62).

113. ein juncvrouwe sol selten iht sprechen, ob mans vrâget niht. ein vrowe sol ouch niht sprechen vil . . . und benamen swenn si izzet (465–69).

114. dehein biderbe wîp sol ane grîfen lân ir lip deheinn man der sîn niht reht hât (1392–94).

115. tot le beaul pas (73).

116. Saluez debonairemant (83).

117. Gardez que nus home sa main Ne laissiez matre en votre sain, Fors celui qui le droit i a (97–99).

118. Quant qu'il voudra, bien le sosfrez, Qu'obedience li davez (107–08).

119. Sovant regarder ne davez Nul home (145–146).

120. que ce soit par amor (154).

121. S'aucuns de votre amor vos prie, Gardez ne vos en vantez mie (169–70).

122. vilonie (171).

123. Aucune laisse desfermee Sa poit(e)rine, por ce c'on voi Confaitemant sa char blanchoie. Une autre laisse tot de gré Sa char aparoir ou costé; Une ses jambes trop descuevre (192–97).

124. Blanche gorge, blanc col, blanc vis, Blanche mains (203–04).

125. Que bele soit desoz ses dras (205).

126. li costent son honor (221).

127. Bele corroie ou bel coutel, Aumosniere, esfiche ou enel (241–42).

128. Sor totes choses de tancier Vos vuil je, dames, chestïer (255–56).

129. Ne remai(e)ent sans ne cortoisie (271).

130. En dame ne sai vilonie Nule plus grant que glotenie (305–06).

131. Cortoisie, beautez, savoir Ne puet dame yvre en soi avoir (311–12).

132. Dame, qui ai paule color Ou qui n'ai mie bone oudor (373–74).

133. D'ennis, de fenoil, de cumin, Vos desjuenez sovant matin (383–84).

134. Le tesmoing qu'a mostier avez, Bon ou mavais, toz jors l'avrez (401–02).

135. De molt rire, de mot parler Se doit on en mostier garder (407–08).

136. vos soigniez cortoisemant (417).

137. Se vos avez bon estrument De chanter, chantez baudemant. Beaux chanters en leu et en tans Est une chose molt plaisanz (453–56).

138. Beaux chanters ennue sovant (460).

139. Sovant les ongles recoupez (470).

140. Avenandise et natatez Vaut molt muez que ne fait beautez (475–76).

141. Totes les foiz, que vos bevez, Votre boiche bien essuez, Que li vins engraissiez ne soit (521–23).

142. Nuls ne doit amer ne servir Dame, qui par costume ment (542–43).

143. Mainte dame, quant on la prie D'amors, en est si esbaïe, Qu'ale ne set que doie dire (565–67).

144. dame, nuit et jor Me fait votre beautez languir (610–11).

145. Cului ainz je, que amer doi, A cui j'ai promise ma foi, M'amor, mon cors et mon servise Par loiauté de sainte yglise (698–701).

146. Trop parle (Robert de Blois, *Chastoiement des dames* 18).

147. Qui ne set les genz araisnier. Por ce ne set dame que faire (26–27).

148. wan schoene gebaerde und rede guot die kroenent daz ein vrouwe tuot (T. v. Zirklaere 203–04).

149. ir guote site, ir kiusche, it guot getaete, it triwe und ouch ir staete, ir prîs und ihr hüfscheit, ir guoten namen und edelkeit, it tugent (T. v. Zirklaere 1415–20).

150. ein vrouwe sich behüeten sol vor valsche harter dan ein man (970–71).

151. doch zimt diu milt den rîtern baz denn den vrouwen (975–76).

152. doch stêt diemüete den vrouwen baz (979–80).

153. ein vrowe sol vor unstaetekeit und vor untriuwen sîn behuot und vor hôhvart, daz ist guot. sint dise tugende an ir niht, so ist ir schoene gar enwiht (990–94).

154. car Nostre Sires comenda que fame fust touz jours en comendement et en subjecion (Les quatres âges de l'homme, p. 14).

155. en anfance doit ele obeïr a çaus qui la norrissent, et quant ele est mariée, outréemant doit obeïr a son mari, comme a son seignor (ibid.).

156. se ele est large, et li mariz larges, riens ne lor durra; et se li mariz est eschars, et ele est large, ele fait honte a son seignor (p. 15 f.).

157. Fame ne doit estre large (p. 15).

158. cortois et larges et hardiz et sages (p. 20).

159. se ele est prode fame de son cors, toutes ses autres taches sont covertes, et puet aler partot teste levée (p. 20).

160. sô have die zuht und die lêre, erzeig niht waz si sinnes hât: man engert ir niht ze potestât. ein man sol haben künste vil: der edelen vrouwen zuht wil daz ein vrouwe hab niht vil list, diu biderbe unde edel ist: einvalt stêt den vrouwen wol (842–49).

161. da leit nich an daz ain fraw vil reden chan. waz bedarf si reden mer? wann si schaft ir haus er und den pater noster chan und auch straft ir undertaân und die weist auff rechte fůg, dar an chan si rede gnůg, dazz nicht disputierns darf auss den siben chünsten scharf (470.149–58).

162. consilio dilectissimae coniugi nostrae Theophanu coimperatrici augustae nec non imperii regnorumque consortii (MGH Dipl. O II, no. 76, p. 92).

163. serenissimę, interventu Gerdrudis augustę consortis regię celsitudinis et glorię (MGH Dipl. K III, no. 32, p. 52).

164. pia petitione dilectissimę consortis nostrę Beatricis Romanorum augustę et illustrissimę imperatricis (MGH Dipl. F I, no. 279, p. 90).

165. . . . soluta a lege mariti, domum illius sapienter disponebat (Arnold of Lübeck, p. 130).

166. quae publicam rem Boemiae plus quam vir regebat (Gerlach of Mühlhausen, p. 691).

167. quomodo tibi corona debeatur, nescio, que femina es (Arnolf of Lübeck, p. 165).

168. quamlibet feminam magis virilibus amplexibus aptam, quam dictare militibus iura (Annales Pragenses III, p. 209).

169. Mulierum enim non est iudicare aut regnare aut docere aut testari (p. 2).

170. non decere regnum administrari a femina (Vita Heinrici IV, p. 416).

171. cum multae reginae legantur administrasse regna virili sapientia (ibid.).

172. man engert ir niht ze potestât (T. v. Zirklaere 844).

173. ein kranker wibes name ich bin. wie möhte ich landes frouwe sîn? (4363–64).

174. cum octingentis loricis (Historia Welforum, p. 30).

175. constanter (Arnold of Lübeck, p. 137).

176. firmiter resistebant (Gerlach of Mühlhausen, p. 705).

177. nu stuont vrou Gyburc ze wer mit ûf geworfeme swerte als op si strîtes gerte (227.12–14).

178. Dô si eines nahtes bî dem künege lac (mit armen umbevangen het er si, als er pflac die edeln frouwen triuten; si was im als sîn lîp), dô gedâhte ir vîende daz vil hêrlîche wîp. Si sprach zuo dem künege: "vil lieber herre mîn, ich wolde iuch bitten gerne . . ." (*Nibelungenlied* 1400.1–1401.2).

179. Mulieribus tamen semper in penitentia iniungendum est quod sint predicatrices virorum suorum. Nullus enim sacerdos ita potest cor viri emollire sicut potest uxor. Unde peccatum viri sepe mulieri imputatur si per eius negligentiam vir eius non emmendatur. Debet enim in cubiculo et inter medios amplexus virum suum blande alloqui, et si durus est et immisericors et oppressor pauperum, debet eum invitare ad misericordiam; si raptor est, debet detestari rapinam; si avarus est, suscitet in eo largitatem, et occulte faciat eleemosynas de rebus communibus, et eleemosynas quas ille omittit, illa suppleat. Licitum enim mulieri est de bonis viri sui in utiles usus ipsius et in pias causas ipso ignorante multa expendere (*Summa confessorum*, p. 375).

180. Illi autem spe misericordiae cruces, quas tenebant in manibus, per cancellos in caminatam imperatricis proiciebant, cum ante conspectum eius introitum non haberent (*Chronica regia Coloniensis*, p. 111).

181. quante sitis prudentie, nobilitatis et industrie, vestra indicant opera, monasteriorum videlicet diversi ornatus, clericorum et pauperum solatia (Vincent of Prague, p. 659).

182. Capella sancti Nicolai ad occasum in fine monasterii apposita ab Udilhilde comitissa de Zolro est constructa. Ad quam etiam calicem, casulam, stolam cum universis utensilibus necessariis contulit. Insuper unam hubam ad Stetin, unam ad Ingislatt, unam ad Harde, unam ad Striche, duas ad Danheim eidem ecclesiae dedit (p. 170 f.).

183. Sophia ductrix Morabiae, soror Richinzae, uxor Ottonis ducis, dedit unum vexillum, dalmaticam albam, XII pallia, VI marcas argenti aliaque perplura, capsam eburneam. Ipsa etiam cum sorore sua Richinza refectorium fratrum barbatorum cum dormitorio proprio sumptu a fundamentis extruit et omnibus bonis istum locum cum suis honoribus implevit (p. 174).

184. Setzibrana quaedam mulier slava ex Boemia inter alia dona dorsale magnum ex lana contextum, Maiestate et Caroli imagine insignitum, huc misit reginae coelorum (p. 178).

185. Gisela de Hiltiniswilare, libera propagine orta, dedit duos mansus in villa Colberc nuncupata cum adiacente silvula Berinbolt vocitata (p. 184).

186. Huius uxor Salome dedit VIII uncias auri et lapidum pretiosorum multitudinem copiosam ad sanctam crucem ornandam de Hierosolimis allatam (p. 186).

187. Huius vidua Adilhait comitissa . . . inter cetera ornamenta, quae dedit vel quae propriis manibus contexuit magna duo vela linea . . . Nam quamdiu vixit ex eis praediis, quae sibi usu fructuario retinuit, frumento et vino nos sufficientissime pavit et ecclesiam sanctimonialium cum claustro suo sumptu ex maxima parte construxit (p. 198).

188. Mahtilt de Spizzinberc, soror Werinheri comitis de Frikkingen . . .

dedit VI manus ad Burchusen, villam scilicet universam (p. 214).

189. Mathilt, uxor Manegoldi de Sunemotingen, inter alia dona, quae nobis contulit, nigram casulam magno aurifrisio decentissime perornavit (p. 226).

190. Huius uxor nomine Wolphilt dedit pixidem eburneam, mantellum suum rubeum ad cappam, unum pallium similiter ad cappam et unam stolam auream (p. 232).

191. sanctae modernae (*Vita s. Mariae Oigniacensis*, p. 638).

192. contemptis etiam amore regni caelestis hujus mundi divitiis, in pauper-tate et humilitate Sponso caelesti adhaerentes, labore manuum tenuem victum quaerebant, licet parentes earum multis divitiis abundarent. Ipsae tamen obli-viscentes populum suum et domum patris sui, malebant angustias et pauper-tatem sustinere, quam male acquisitis divitiis abundare, vel inter pomposos seculares cum periculo remanere (p. 636).

193. que divicias parentum contempnentes et maritos nobiles ac potentes sibi oblatos respuentes in magna et leta paupertate viventes nichil aliud habe-bant, nisi quod nendo et manibus propriis laborando acquirere valebant, vilibus indumentis et cibo modico contente (*Sermo ad virgines*, p. 47).

194. prae desiderio languerent...nullam aliam causam infirmitatis habentes nisi illum, cujus desiderio animae earum liquefactae (p. 637).

195. ex favo spiritualis dulcedinis in corde, redundabat mellis sapor sensi-biliter in ore (ibid.).

196. extra se tanta spiritus ebrietate rapiebantur (ibid.).

197. sy sanc, si danzet unde spranc. dat was doch sunder hiren danc: sô wat sy vrôiden plêge dâ, dat herze was doch anders wâ. der lîf wol mohte singen, jâ danzen unde springen, hir herze was in sorgen doch, wy sy vollbringen mohte noch den gůden willen den sy drůch (1301–09).

198. sy můste singen. dat geschach: sy sanc, sy schrê, dat man gesach dy heize trênen vlyzen und ůz den ôigen gyzen, des sy doch eine stunde sich nyt enthalden kunde. dy gůde weinede und sanc, vil klôsterlîche was ir ganc. den vyralley sy nyt entrat, wat man gevlêde, wat man bat. ir herze nyt enwolde dar, ir gân zebrach des danzes schar, dat man sy můste des erlân (3095–107).

199. impudicus episcopus virginem per alteram tunice manicam irreverenter arripuit et ore sancto quo misteria (divina solebat) conficere. de re nephanda (sollicitavit). Quid ergo faceret m(isera puell)a inter tales angustias appr(ehensa)? Clamaretne parentes? Iam (dor)mitum abierant. Consentire nullo modo voluit. aperte contradicere ausa non fuit. Qui si aperte contradiceret. proculdubio vim sustineret (*Vita Christinae*, p. 42).

200. collum suum nulla racione contaminandum fore carnali(bu)s viri amplexibus (p. 46).

201. quatinus si forte dormientem virginem reperiret: repente oppresse illuderet (p. 50).

202. quod non consideraret quis filiam suam corrumperet. (si) tantum aliquo casu corrumpi potuisset (p. 72).

203. super reliquas feminas esset amabilior (p. 66 f.).

204. qui velociter illam prosequerentur (et apprehen)sam reducerent cum contumelia interfecto quemcumque reperissent (in) eius comitatu (p. 94).

205. sam si ein swester sî (601.17).

206. der zobel underheftelîn muoz sâ ein pâter noster sîn, der an ir puosem hanget (601.27–29).

207. si hab sich begeben vor leide in ein geistlîch leben (601.31–32).

208. sô siht man iuch ze kirchen stân beidiu naht und ouch den tac (602.8–9).

209. ir habt iuch frowen dienst bewegen: ir künnet niht wan rüemens phlegen (600.15–16).

210. daz wir in vorhten gên iu sîn (599.27).

211. dâ rennet durch den tac sîn lîp und lât hie sîn vil reine wîp ân aller slahte freude leben (607.15–17).

212. ûf einen tisch legt er sich nider: ez ist sîn geschefte und ouch sîn pet, daz man im bringe dar ein pret: dâ spilt er unz an mitte naht, und trinket daz im gar sîn maht geswîchet und verswindet. sô gêt er dâ er vindet sîn wîp dannoch warten sîn. diu spricht "willkumen, herre min": mit zühten si gên im ûf stêt, durch ir zuht si gên im gêt. sô gît er ir antwurte niht, wan daz er vlîziclîche siht wâ er sich dâ sâ nider lege, slâfens unz an den morgen phlege (607.32–608.14).

213. so ist ir niht dinges alsô guot sô daz si herze unde muot wende an gotes dienst gar (609.13–15).

3. COURTLY LOVE

1. Saget mir ieman, waz ist minne? (W. v. Vogelweide 69.1).

2. Waz mac daz sîn, daz diu welt heizet minne? . . . ich wânde niht, daz ez iemen enpfunde (F. v. Hausen 53.15; 18).

3. Militat omnis amans . . . (*Amores* I.9.1).

4. Dô ich êrste sin gewan, dô riet mir daz herze mîn, obe ich immer wurde ein man, sô solte ich ir ze dienste sîn. nu ist mir komen diu zît daz ich ir dienen sol. nu helf mir got daz ich ir tuo den dienest schîn, dâ von ich leides mich erhol. Sî ist über mînen lîp frouwe und al des herzen mîn, sî vil wundern werdez wîp: nû wes solde ich gerner sîn (U. v. Liechtenstein, *Lieder* III.3.1–4.4).

5. sô diene in gerne, hâstû sin, dû lebest in êren deste baz. got sîn an saelden nie vergaz, dem ir genâde wirt beschert und er mit triuwen dienet daz (*Winsbeke* 16.3–7).

6. Ez tuot vil wê, swer herzeclîche minnet an sô hôher stat, dâ sîn dienst gar versmât (H. v. Morungen 134.14–16).

7. Sî gebiutet und ist in dem herzen mîn vrowe und hêrer, danne ich selbe sî (H. v. Morungen 126.16–17).

8. ich enmac ir kreften niht gestemen: sô ist si obe, sô bin ich unden (U. v. Gutenburg 72.39–40).

9. Hartman, gên wir schouwen ritterlîche vrouwen (216.31–32).

10. ich mac baz vertriben die zît mit armen wîben (216.39–217.1).

11. waz touc mir ein ze hôhez zil? (217.5).

12. waz hân ich von den überhêren (49.24).

13. ich wil mîn lop kêren an wîp die kunnen danken (49.22–23).

14. edel unde rîche (51.1).

15. glesîn vingerlîn (50.12).

16. Par un baisier l'en a saisie. D'amor, de jeu, de cortoisei Ont puis ensamble tant parlé Et bonement ris et jüé, Tant qu'a perdu non de pucele (2711–15; vol. 1, p. 74).

17. Ez mac niht heizen minne, der lange wirbet umbe ein wîp. diu liute werdent sîn inne und wirt zervüeret dur nît. unstaetiu vriuntschaft machet wankeln muot. wan sol ze liebe gâhen: daz ist vür die merkaere guot. Daz es iemen werde inne, ê ir wille sî ergân, sô sol man si triegen. dâ ist gnuogen ane gelungen, die daz selbe hânt getân (12.14–26).

18. Swer werden wîben dienen sol, der sol semelîchen varn. ob er sich wol ze rehte gegen in kunne bewarn, sô muoz er under wîlen senelîche swaere tragen verholne in dem herzen; er sol ez nieman sagen. Swer biderben dienet wîben, die gebent alsus getânen solt (12.1–11).

19. wer mac minne ungedienet hân? muoz ich iu daz künden, der treit si hin mit sünden. swem ist ze werder minne gâch, dâ hoeret dienst vor unde nâch (W. v. Eschenbach, *Parzival* 511.12–16).

20. E fins amams no is deu desconortar Si tot sidonz no il vol a comenssar Donar s'amor, mas s'el es larcs e pros Serva sidonz tro vegna guizerdos (Bertoni, p. 263).

21. wât tût ir hen ûwirn sin? jâ sêt ir wol daz ich nicht bin eine gebûrinne daz ir mich bittet umme minne in sô gar korzit zît: ich wêne ir ein gebûr sît (6679–84).

22. quod amor quidam est purus, et quidam dicitur esse mixtus. Et purus quidem amor est, qui omnimoda dilectionis affectione duorum amantium corda coniungit. Hic autem in mentis contemplatione cordisque consistit affectu; procedit autem usque ad oris osculum lacertique amplexum et verecundum amantis nudae contactum, extremo praetermisso solatio; nam illud pure amare volentibus exercere non licet (p. 182).

23. quod ex eo totius probitatis origo descendit (p. 183).

24. qui omni carnis delectationi suum praestat effectum et in extremo Veneris opere terminatur (p. 183).

25. Monstrosum namque iudicatur a cunctis (p. 184).

26. recte tamen intuentibus purus amor quo ad sui substantiam idem cum mixto iudicatur amore (p. 264).

27. Tout nu a nu (Långfors, no. 129, I.6; vol. 2, p. 113).

28. waz half, daz er toerschen bî mir lac? jô enwart ich nie sîn wîp! (41.6).

29. sô tuo gelîche deme, als ez doch wesen solde, Unde lege mich ir wol nâhen bî und biete ez eine wîle, als ez von herzen sî (167.7–9).

30. er lac mit sölhen fuogen, des nu niht wil genuogen mangiu wîp (W. v. Eschenbach, *Parzival* 201.21–23).

31. ich hân gedienet mîniu jâr nâch lône disem wîbe, diu hât mîme lîbe erboten trôst: nu lige ich hie. des hete mich genüeget it, oh ich mir mîner blôzen hant müese rüeren ir gewant. ob ich nur gîtes gerte, untriwe es für mich werte. solt ich si arbeiten, unser beider lasten breiten? vor slâfe süeziu maere sint frouwen site gebaere (202.6–18).

32. Si ist mir liep, und dunket mich, wie ich ir volleclîche gar unmaere sî. waz darumbe? daz lîde ich: ich was ir ie mit staeteclîchen triuwen bî (159.10–13).

33. ein kus von rôtem munde der fröit von herzen grunde, daz zuo ein umbevanc von zwein schoenen armen blanc (Kristan v. Hamle IV. 1.9–12).

34. Ist aber daz dir wol gelinget, sô daz ein guot wîp dîn genâde hât, hei waz dir danne fröiden bringet, sô si sunder wer vor dir gestât, halsen, triuten, bî gelegen (W. v. d. Vogelweide 91.35–92.1).

35. amor . . . qui cum prauus est, uocatur cupiditas aut libido; cum autem rectus, dilectio uel caritas (Augustine, *Enarrationes in Psalmos*, p. 66).

36. Amor est enim ignis: et est amor bonus, ignis bonus, ignis videlicet charitatis; et est amor malus, ignis malus ignis cupiditatis (Hugh of St. Victor, *Miscellanea*, col. 571).

37. Itidemque Amores duo; alter bonus et pudicus, quo sapientia et virtutes amantur; alter impudicus et malus, quo ad vitia inclinamur (*Mythographus Vaticanus* III, p. 239).

38. Unus fons dilectionis intus saliens duos rivos effundit. Alter est amor mundi, cupiditas; alter est amor Dei, charitas . . . Et omnium malorum radix cupiditas, et omnium bonorum radix charitas (Hugh of St. Victor, *Insitutiones in Decalogum*, col. 15).

39. lobe ich des lîbes minne, deis der sêle leit: si giht, ez sî ein lüge, ich tobe. der wâren minne giht si ganzer staetekeit, wie guot si sî, wies iemer wer. lîp, lâ die minne diu dich lât, und habe die staeten minne wert (W. v. d. Vogelweide 67.24–29).

40. von wîsheit kêrte ich mînen muot; daz was diu minne, diu noch manigem tuot die selben klage. nu wil ich mich an got gehaben, der kan den liuten helfen ûz der nôt (46.23–27).

41. Ir minnesinger, iu muoz ofte misselingen, daz iu den schaden tuot, daz ist der wân. ich wil mich rüemen, ich mac wol von minnen singen, sît mich diu minne hât und ich si hân . . . wan müget ir armen minnen solhe minne als ich? (218.21–24; 28).

42. durh der zweir slahte minne, Uf erde hie durh wîbe lôn und ze himel durh den engel dôn (16.30–17.2).

43. minne, al der werlde unsaelekeit! sô kurziu fröude als an dir ist, sô rehte unstaete sô du bist, waz minnet al diu werlt an dir? ich sihe doch wol, du lônest ir, als der vil valschafte tuot. dîn ende daz ist niht sô guot, als dû der werlde geheizest, so du sî von êrste reizest mit kurzem liebe ûf langez leit. dîn gespenstigiu trügeheit, diu in sô valscher süeze swebet, diu triuget allez, daz der lebet (G. v. Straßburg 1398–1410).

44. frou minne, ir pflegt untriuwen mit alten siten niuwen. ir zucket manegem wîbe ir prîs, unt rât in sippiu âmîs. und daz manec hêrre an sînem man von iwerr kraft hât missetân, unt der friunt an sîme gesellen (iwer site kan sich hellen), unt der man an sîme hêrren. frou minne, iu solte werren daz ir den lîp der gir verwent, dar umbe sich diu sêle sent. Frou minne, sît ir habt gewalt, daz ir die jugent sus machet alt, dar man doch zelt vil kurziu jâr, iwer werc sint hâlscharlîche vâr (W. v. Eschenbach, *Parzival* 291.19–292.4).

45. reht minne ist wâriu triuwe (ibid. 532.10).

46. in hac vita nil est laudabilius quam sapienter amare (p. 167).

47. si n'est mie deffendue du tout pur ce que aucuns qui avoient esté navrés d'amours ne savoient querre leur santé ne leur guarison, si en venoient a droite

mort et en villains pechiés contre nature (p. 67 f.).

48. frou witze (*Parzival* 288.14).

49. racine de toutes vertus et de tous biens (p. 9).

50. Amours est une foursenerie de pensée, fus sans estaindre, fains sans soeler, cous mals (ibid.).

51. que uns roys u uns grans sires est souspris de l'amour d'une femme de noient de pris . . . uns povres hom osera amer une royne et une garche osera amer un roy (ibid.).

52. Nideriu minne heizet diu sô swachet daz der lîp nâch kranker liebe ringet: diu minne tuot unlobelîche wê. hôhiu minne reizet unde machet daz der muot nâch hôher wirde ûf swinget (47.5–9).

53. Swâ wîbes minne mannes tugende mêret, dâ sî wîp unt wîbes minne gêret: swâ aber ein mann von wîbes minne an tugende, an wirden wehset abe, der habe im allez, daz ich habe, diu minne ensî gemischet mit unsinne! (R. v. Zweter 103.7–12).

54. O, quam mira res est amor, qui tantis facit hominem fulgere virtutibus tantisque docet quemlibet bonis moribus abundare! (Andreas Capellanus, p. 10).

55. minne ist aller tugende ein hort (W. v. Vogelweide 14.8).

56. Von minne kumet uns allez guot, diu minne machet reinen muot (H. v. Veldeke, *Lieder* 62.1–2).

57. da von ist die minne der tugende kuniginne (Stricker, *Frauenehre* 1259–60).

58. Ein man wirt werder, dan er sî, gelît er hôher minne bî (Freidank 100.18–19).

59. Swer ir lêre iht wil phlegen der muoz lâzen under wegen swaz anders heizet danne guot und minnen rehtes mannes muot. dâ hoeret arebeit zuo beide spâte unde vruo and daz man vil gedenke an sî. . . . Swer ir ingesinde wesen wil der bedarf sölhes muotes vil daz er gedenke dar zuo wie er mêre guotes getuo danne er dâ von gespreche: sîn triuwe durch nieman breche. milte unde manheit ist ir ze dienste niht leit (H. v. Aue, *Klage* 609–15, 21–28).

60. minne wart nie bî den sünden funden, sî kan guoten man wol rehte lêren. genuoge liute sprechent sô, daz unminne sünde sî. minne ist aller sünden frî (O. v. Brandenburg IV, 3.3–7).

61. Swer minne minneclîche treit gar âne valschen muot, der sünde wirt vor gote niht geseit. siu tiuret and ist guot (A. v. Johansdorf 88.33–36).

62. Swer giht daz minne sünde sî, der sol sich ê bedenken wol. ir wont vil manic êre bî, der man durch reht geniezen sol, und volget michel staete und dar zuo saelikeit: daz iemer ieman missetuot, daz ist ir leit. die valschen minne meine ich niht, diu möhte unminne heizen baz: der wil ich iemer sîn gehaz (W. v. d. Vogelweide 217.10–18).

63. Omnis . . . boni . . . origo et causa (Andreas Capellanus, p. 29).

64. diu minne lêret grôze milte, diu minne lêret grôze tugent (R. v. Zweter 31.9–10).

65. Par sa cortoisie ot de pris (2094).

66. De paroles douz e raisnables (2100).

67. Toutes fames serf e eneure (2115).

68. qui d'amors se viaut pener, Il se doit cointement mener (2133–34).

69. Bele robe e bel garnement (2148).

70. vestanz e cointes (2148).

71. E. gar qu'il soient si chauçant Que cil vilain aillent tençant En quel guise tu i entras E de quel part tu en istras (2151–54).

72. Lave tes mains, tes denz escure; S'en tes ongles pert point de noir, Ne l'i laisse pas remenoir. Cous tes manches, tes cheuves pigne, Mais ne te farde ne ne guigne: Ce n'apartient s'as dames non, Ou a ceus de mauvais renon, Qui amors par male aventure Ont trovees contre Nature (2166–74).

73. C'est maladie mout courtoise, Ou l'en jeue e rit e envoise (2179–80).

74. s'as armes es acesmez, Par ce seras dis tanz amez (2201–02).

75. Qui d'Amors viaut faire son maistre Cortois e senz orgueil doit estre; Cointes se teigne e envoisiez E de largece soit proisiez (2229–32).

76. Qui vult ergo dignus haberi in amoris exercitu militare (p. 64).

77. magna curialitas atque largitas reputatur (p. 65).

78. humilem se debet omnibus exhibere et cunctis servire paratus adesse (ibid.).

79. quia maledici intra curialitatis non possunt limina permanere (ibid.).

80. Modico risu in mulierum utatur aspectu (p. 66).

81. magnasque curias visitare (ibid.).

82. Magna debet antiquorum libenter gesta recolere atque asserere (ibid.).

83. Plurium non debet simul mulierum esse amator, sed pro una omnium debet feminarum servitor exsistere atque devotus (ibid.).

84. sapientem atque tractabilem et svavem se omnibus demonstrare (ibid.).

85. licet quidam fatuissime credant, se satis mulieribus placere, si ecclesiastica cuncta despiciant (p. 68).

86. Dicimus enim vix contingere posse, quod agricolae in amoris inveniantur curia militare, sed naturaliter sicut equus et mulus ad Veneris opera promoventur (p. 235).

87. amoris hoc nobis doctrina demonstrat, quod neque mulier neque masculus potest in saeculo beatus haberi nec curialitatem nec alique bona perficere, nisi sibi haec fomes praestet amoris (p. 118).

88. Quum enim omnis ex amoris rivuli plenitudine procedat urbanitas (p. 63).

89. Sapiens igitur mulier talem sibi comparare perquirat amandum, qui morum sit probitate laudandus (p. 15 f.).

90. valsch unde gewalte vor bespart (17034).

91. Vehementer tamen admiror, quod maritalem affectionem quidem, quam quilibet inter se coniugati adinvicem post matrimonii copulam tenentur habere, vos vultis amoris sibi vocabulum usurpare, quum liquide constet inter virum et uxorem amorem sibi locum vindicare non posse (p. 141).

92. sine crimine (p. 145).

93. ultra prolis affectionem vel debiti solutionem . . . crimine carere non potest (p. 147).

94. an scilicet inter coniugatos verus amor locum sibi valeat invenire (p. 151).

95. Dicimus enim et stabilito tenore firmamus, amorem non posse suas inter

duos iugales extendere vires (p. 153).

96. quum neutrius inde possit probitas augmentari (p. 154).

97. Sed huius mulieris improbitas Narbonensis Mengardae dominae taliter dictis arguitur: Nova superveniens foederatio maritalis non recte priorem excludit amorem (p. 280).

98. regulae amoris (p. 308).

99. Causa coniugii ab amore non est excusatio recta (p. 310).

100. et quam sibi carius existeret mihique honestius amicam dici quam uxorem ut me ei sola gratia conservaret, non vis aliqua vinculi nuptialis constringeret (p. 78).

101. Nichil umquam (Deus scit) in te nisi te requisivi: te pure, non tua concupiscens (ibid., p. 114).

102. Et si uxoris nomen sanctius ac validius videretur, dulcius mihi semper extitit amice vocabulum aut, si non indigneris, concubine vel scorti (ibid.).

103. quibus amorem conjugio, libertatem vinculo preferebam (ibid.).

104. Il est amours temporeus ki vient de force de nature et amours ki naist simplement de volenté de cuer (p. 8).

105. si est li amours ki est entre les amis carneus, si con d'amer son pere et sa mere, ses freres, ses parens, ses carneus amis et sa femme espousée (ibid.).

106. entre homme et femme (p. 9).

107. amours de mariage est amours de dete et l'amours dont je vous parole est amours de grace et ja soit ce que ce soit courtoise cose de bien paiier ce c'on doit, nepourquant ce n'est mie amours dont on doive savoir tant de gré con de celle amour ki vient de grace de pure franquise de cuer (p. 15).

108. La ren per c'om vai meilluran, N'Elias, tenc eu per meillor, E cella tenc per sordeior, Per c'om vai totz jorns sordeian. Per dompna vai bos pretz enan E per moiller pert hom valor, E per dompnei de dompna es hom grazitz E per dompnei de moiller escarnitz (Audiau XIV. 17–24).

109. von danne stal ich mich zehant und reit mit freuden, dâ ich vant die herzenlieben konen mîn: diu kunde mir lieber niht gesîn (707.5–8).

110. gemach und wunne (709.2–3).

111. diu künde mir lieber niht gesîn, swie ich doch het über mînen lîp ze vrowen dô ein ander wîp (1088.6–8).

112. non est enim virginalis pudoris eligere maritum (De Abraham, col. 476).

113. in ducis, quem elegerat, amore immobilis permanebat (Gerhard of Stederburg, p. 227).

114. quam visam nimia turpitudine indecentem sprevit et despexit (p. 35).

115. . . . declinavit in domum Helprici comitis de Ploceke, et videns valde pulchram sororem suam, Ermengardam, duxit eam (Albert of Stade, p. 326).

116. multum indignati sunt vasalli sui, qui pares erant Helprico, et quidam maiores (ibid.).

117. cum et illam minus diligeret et alienarum magis amplexibus delectaretur (Historia Welforum, p. 68).

118. Anno Domini 1265. hic Albertus multum persequebatur dominam Margaretham propter quandam pedissequam et concubinam ejus nomine Kunne von Ysenberg, quem dilexit (Chronicon terrae Misnensis, col. 326).

119. . . . einem wîbe wolgetân, diu kunde videln und singen und was ze solhen dingen hubsch unde kluoc und het ouch list genuoc zaller parat und zallen sachen, dâ sich diu wîp mit kunnen machen den man liep unde wert (86330–37).

120. si warp ouch heimlich botschaft von im ze hôhen fursten, si was ouch in den getursten, daz ers durch spehe sant dick in andriu lant, und darumb si im wart sô liep und sô zart unde sô gar heimlich, daz si die herren alle gelich darumbe hazzen begunden (86352–61).

121. Puerisque suis, quorum quosdam non de uxore sua, sed de mulieribus nobilibus genuerat, bona quedam assignavit (p. 311).

122. dixit se in eum nunquam consensisse ut illi matrimonio jungeretur (*Chronica majora*, vol. 3, p. 87).

123. Copulabatur tamen eidem ignobili nobilis, pia impio, turpi speciosa, invita et coacta (ibid., vol. 5, p. 323).

124. Lex connectit eos, amor et concordia lecti. Sed lex qualis? amor qualis? concordia qualis? Lex exlex, amor exosus, concordia discors (ibid.).

125. miro se affectu diligentes (*Libellus de dictis quatuor ancillarum*, p. 121).

126. quam vir ejus Balduinus, juvenis eciam miles, caste vivendo, spretis omnibus aliis mulieribus, ipsam solam cepit amare amore ferventi, quod in aliquo homine raro invenitur ut soli tantum intendat mulieri et ea sola contentus sit (p. 192).

127. Crescite, et multiplicamini (Genesis 1.28).

128. propter fornicationem autem unusquisque suam uxorem habeat, et unaquaeque suum virum habeat. Uxori vir debitum reddat, similiter autem et uxor viro (7.2–3).

129. Libido vero, sine qua coitus esse non potest, semper peccatum erit (Gandolf of Bologna, col. 536).

130. viri vel mulieris pulchritudo; quae animos amore inflammatos frequenter impellit ad ineundum conjugium ut suum valeant explere disiderium (*De sacramento conjugii*, col. 155).

131. Quaestus quoque et amor divitiarum (ibid.).

132. amicitia viri et mulieris ex societate procedens conjugali (col. 157).

133. pax inter homines sibi prius hostiliter adversantes (ibid.).

134. In eligendo autem marito iiii. spectari solent: Virtus, genus, pulchritudo, sapientia. Item in eligenda uxore iiii. res impellunt hominem ad amorem: Pulchritudo, genus, diutie, mores (Weigand, p. 45, A.14).

135. siue causa pacis siue pulcritudinis siue diuitiarum (ibid., A.13).

136. Alioquin ex maxima parte matrimonia irrita haberentur et uacua cum nostri temporis homines prefatis causis intercedentibus, immo sine constituentibus matrimonia contrahere consuescant (ibid.).

137. quod nisi libera uoluntate nulla est copulanda alicui (Causa 31, Questio 2, c. 4, col. 1114).

138. qui coniugali affectu sibi copulantur, . . . coniuges appelluntur (Causa 32, Questio 2, c. 5, col. 1121).

139. uoluntatis unio, mutua dilectio, uiri circa mulierem protectio (Weigand, p. 42, A.3).

140. amor conjugalis (*Epistola de virginitate beatae Mariae*, col. 876).

141. sine delectionis foedere cassa sit (ibid., col. 865).

142. Ein menlich man, der sich erlichen heldet, ein wiblich wib im billich ir hende veldet. ein menlich man, ein wiblich bib diz merken sol: Her sol sie meistem libes unde gůtes, sie si ein warterinne sines můtes. her si der man, sie si daz wib, daz vůget wol. Ouch sol er sie erlichen halten. sie ne sol ane sinen rat nicht tůn, daz ist ir gůt. So mügen sie an vreuden alten (Der Meißner II, 9.1–9).

143. ih hân daz aller frumigiste wîp (4444).

144. ûzer dem pette si spranc (4483).

145. alsô diu frowe ain trinken vur truoc, der wirt den kopf ûf huop, den wîn er ir under diu ougen gôz, daz trinken an ir gewaete flôz. si stuont, naic im gezogenlîche (4501–05).

146. ih enpin weder truhsaeze noh schenke, kamerâre noh koch uber allen disen hof. ih enwaiz waz dû mir wîzest: ih enruoch ob dû iemer ihtes enbîzest (4546–50).

147. semimortum suspenderunt illum per pedes, inclinato capite deorsum in quodam vilissimo cloacali foramine (*Gesta regis Henrici secundi*, vol. 1, p. 100 f.).

148. Lewelinus, vocato Willelmo de Breusa ad festum Paschale in dolo, suspicans eum adulteratum fuisse cum uxore sua, membris succisis fecit eum suspendi in patibulo (*Annales de Wigornia*, p. 421).

149. ut cum filia concumberet (*Chronica majora*, vol. 5, p. 34).

150. quae pellex fieri formidavit (ibid.).

151. meretricula (ibid.).

152. peccatum illud inhumanum (ibid.).

153. Concubuisti cum uxore tua vel cum alia aliqua retro, canino more? Si fecisti, decem dies in pane et aqua poeniteas (Schmitz, p. 421).

154. Hier vor do man die hu(o)te schalt und des sumlich wirt sere engalt, daz er lie sin husfrowen die geste gerne schowen, do si ir triwe uber sach und ir reht und ir ê zebrach, daz hiez hohgemutiu minne (1–7).

155. diewile er schuf umbe den gast, daz im da nihtes gebrast, die wile warp er umbe daz wip und leidet ir des wirtes lip (29–32).

156. ...diu hohe tougen minne. da ist so groze chraft inne, daz si...diu tugent alle richet. si edelt die gebaere, si vertribet alle swaere, si chan den gedanchen ere geben, si tiuret den lip und daz leben, si ist der selden vor louf (63–71).

157. daz aeffen und daz triegen (107).

158. swelch gast daz hat fur hofscheit, ob einem wirt ein herceleit von sinem hofschen libe geschaehe an sinem wibe, da wider waere ouch daz vil sleht, taete der wirt dem gaste sin reht und erzeiget im diu maere, wes sin hofscheit wert waere. swenne er dazetische saezze und gern trunch und aezze, so waere daz vil gefu(e)ge, daz man fur in tru(e)ge edel blu(o)men, loup und gras, daz ie der hofschaere vroude was, und einen vogel, der wol sunge, und einen brunnen, der da sprunge under einer schoenen linden; so mohte er wol bevinden, wie grozze froude ez allez git, da von er singet alle zit (223–42).

159. Hete ich einen kneht der sunge lîht von sîner frouwen, der müeste die bescheidenlîche nennen mir, daz des ieman wânde ez waer mîn wîp. Alram Ruoprecht Friderîch, wer sol iu des getrouwen, von Mergersdorf daz sô die

herren effet ir? waere gerihte, ez gienge iu an den lîp. ir sît ze veiz bî klagender nôt: waer ieman ernst der sich alsô nâch minnen senet, der laeg inners jâres friste tôt (I.1–9).

160. Die Vier Pûler (fol. 142).

161. Trop est mes maris jalos, Sorcuidiez, fel et estouz; Mes il sera par tens cous, Se je truis mon ami douz, Si gentil, li savoros (Etienne de Meaux 1.1–5; van der Werf, p. 142).

162. wan solz den man erlouben unde den vrouwen niht (89.20).

163. diu juncfrouwen wolgetân leite er an sîn bette. dô spilter ûf ir wette eines spiles, des er kunde, des sie ê nie begunde (Otte, *Eraclius* 2410–14).

164. Man riet Herwîgen, daz er si lieze dâ, daz er mit schoenen wîben ver-tribe anderswâ die zît und sîne stunde dar nâch in einem jâre (*Kudrun* 667.1–3).

165. Mouetur enim homo quodam naturali appetitu sensualitatis ut carnali-ter commisceatur femine (Brundage, p. 834, A.48).

166. Libido in virginibus maiorem patitur famen, dum dulcius esse putant quod nesciunt (ibid., p. 832, A.33).

167. . . . ex parte mulieribus, cuis vas semper paratum est (ibid., A.32).

168. quare magis exigitur in uxore quam in viro (ibid., p. 834, A.43).

169. ideo non nocet, si vir dividit carnem suam in plures; . . . unde si uxor in plures carnem suam dividat deficit in ea sacramentum (ibid.).

170. neque enim contra naturam nuptiarum est. Plures enim feminae ab uno viro fetari possunt; una vera a pluribus non potest (*De bono coniugali*, col. 387).

171. antiqua . . . sententia (p. 260).

172. ea penitus esse in muliere fallente servanda, quae sunt in fallaci ama-tore narrata (ibid.).

173. Absit enim, quod tali unquam profiteamur mulieri esse parcendum, quae duorum non erubuit libidini sociari. Quamvis enim istud in masculis toler-atur propter usum frequentem et sexus privilegium, quo cuncta in hoc saeculo etiam naturaliter verecunda conceduntur hominibus liberius peragenda, in muliere tamen propter verecundi sexus pudorem adeo iudicatur esse nefandum, quod, postquam mulier plurium se voluptati commiscuit, scortum quasi repu-tatur immundum et reliquis dominarum choris associari a cunctis iudicatur in-digna (p. 261).

174. Immo, quamvis in masculis propter sexus audaciam amoris vel lux-uriae toleratur excessus, in mulieribus creditur damnabile crimen (p. 324).

175. wie wibe und manne leben si gescheiden also sere: ir schande ist unser êre. des wip da sint gehoenet des welle wir sin gekroenet; swaz ein man wibe erwirbet, daz (er) doch niht verdirbet an sinen eren da von. dar under sin wir gewon an wiben die mit eren lebent und sich schanden begebent, diu einen guoten friunt hat, daz si der andern habe rat (*Zweites Büchlein* 698–710).

176. wert ich iuch, des hetel ir êre; sô waer mîn der spot (A. v. Johansdorf 93.35).

177. Praeterea milites quidem, qui se asserunt de suis excessibus non debere sacerdotum judicio subjacere, adulteria, incestus et alia peccata committunt im-pune, nec etiam corriguntur (*Epistolae*, vol. 3, col. 34 f.).

178. Erat enim vir totus inserviens adulteriis et fornicationibus et stupris,

quibuslibet luxuriis et immundiciis, strennuus tamen erat in bellis et ferox et largus amicis (p. 74).

179. vir fuit equidem admodum liberalis, largus et dapsilis (Guibert de Nogent, *De vita sua*, col. 910).

180. alias autem amori femineo adeo deditus ut quascunque circa se aut debitas aut usurarias mulieres haberet, nihil pene faceret, quod ei earumdem petulantia dictitaret (ibid.).

181. inops coactus publicam uxorem habet fors unicam et uel timore nuptiis parumper utetur piis. at diues unam vel duas aut concubinas plurimas constuprat haud explebili deseruiens libidini, et his stupris incumbere non pertimescit publice (*De octo vitiis principalibus* 1271–80).

182. quarum singulas, qui Conjux obierat, suo lecto ille vir pro libitu adesse semper praecipiebat (col. 116).

183. swâ sich diu rîterschaft gesamnet, dâ hebet sich ir wechselsage, wie manige der unt der behûret habe; ir laster mugen si nicht verswîgen, ir ruom ist niwan von den wîben. swer sich in den ruom nicht enmachet, der dunchet sich verswachet under andern sînen gelîchen (H. v. Melk, *Erinnerungen an den Tod* 354–61).

184. Sun, dîner werden manne wîp und ir schoenen tohter lîp: nû hüete, daz dir iht under brust in dîn herze kom der glust, dâ mit dû dînen werden man an êren mügest geswachen (*Tirol und Fridebrant* 32.1–6).

185. quod nobilium regni sui filias et consanguineas rapuit (Thomas Wykes, *Chronica*, p. 53).

186. secundus, quia virgines stuprasset (*Compendium historiarum*, p. 713).

187. Qui Heinricus cum Nuwenburg venisset animo recipiendi in crastino fidelitatem ab hominibus, in sero sub macellis cuiusdam burgensis uxorem stupravit, propter quod Nuwenburgenses illi fidelitatem facere renuerunt (*Chronica*, p. 17).

188. Swel man ein guot wîp hât unde zeiner ander gât, der bezeichnet daz swîn. wie möht ez iemer erger sîn? Ez lât den lûtern brunnen und leit sich in den trüeben pfuol. den site hât vil manic man gewunnen (Spervogel 29.27–33).

189. swelch man mit wîben sô umb gât daz er ir gerne manege hât, der selbe ungemuote man sol werden wîben widerstân (U. v. Liechtenstein, *Frauenbuch* 650.1–4).

190. ez waer vorlouft od leithunt, ûz eime troge az sîn munt mit in dâ vier wochen. sus wart diu frouwe gerochen (528.27–30).

191. ez waere wîb oder magt, swaz er dâ minne hât bejagt, die nam er gar in noeten: man solt in drumbe toeten (ibid., 343.27–30).

192. eine maget wol getân greif er über ir willen an, sô daz si weinde unde schrê (W. v. Grafenberg 1511–13).

193. swer daz nû vür ein wunder ime selbem saget daz im ein unsippiu maget nahtes alsô nâhen lac mit der er anders niht enpflac, dern weiz niht daz ein biderbe man sich alles des enthalten kan des er sich enthalten wil. weizgot dern ist aber niht vil (*Iwein* 6574–82).

194. amore... succensus (*Gesta Ambaziensium dominorum*, p. 103).

195. libidinosus (*Chronica de gestis consulum Andegavorum*, p. 65).

196. Rex libidinosus (ibid., p. 66).

197. Pessima illa (ibid., p. 67).

198. lasciua mulier (Ordericus Vitalis, vol. 4, p. 260).

199. adultera (ibid., p. 262).

200. peculans pelex (ibid., p. 260).

201. pruritu altioris nominis allecta (*Gesta regum Anglorum*, vol. 2, p. 293).

202. sed quia legalia iura propter turpem abiectionem mariti perdidit, contradicentibus legis peritis minime recepit, quippe quae maritalem castitatem amisit etiam iura hereditaria perdit (p. 24).

203. corporis voluptatibus et secularibus deliciis indulsit (*Historia comitum Ghisnensium*, p. 605).

204. quae non sicut regina, sed fere sicut meretrix habebat (*Chronicon*, col. 1058).

205. se monacho non regi nupsisse (William of Newburgh, *Historia rerum Anglicarum*, vol. 1, p. 93).

206. Ille enim amor ab omnibus est eligendus . . . qui sine crimine quotidianis potest actibus exerceri. Talis igitur est meis fruiturus amplexibus eligendus, qui mecum valeat mariti et amantis vice potiri (p. 144 f.).

207. der sol doch nâch dem willen mîn von dir belîben ungewert (27.9–10).

208. Der mir ist von herzen holt, den verspriche ich sêre, niht durch ungevüegen haz, wan durch mînes lîbes êre (Reinmar der Alte 186.25–28).

209. Getorste ich genenden, sô wolde ich im enden sîne klage, wan daz ich vil . . . sendez wîp ervürhten muoz der êren mîn und . . . des lebennes sîn, der ist mir alsam der lîp (F. v. Hausen 54.14–18).

210. minne ist ein sô swaerez spil, daz ichs niemer tar beginnen (Reinmar der Alte 187.19–20).

211. nu wil er-daz ist mir ein nôt-, daz ich durch in die êre wâge und ouch den lîp (ibid. 192.37–38).

212. Des er gert, daz ist der tôt und verderbet manigen lîp; bleich und eteswenne rôt, alse verwet ez diu wîp. Minne heizent ez die man unde mohte baz unminne sîn. wê ime, ders alrêst began (ibid. 178.29–35).

213. Daz wir wîp niht mugen gewinnen vriunt mit rede, si enwellen dannoch mê, daz müet mich. ich enwil niht minnen (ibid. 177.34–36).

214. tuot ein wîp ein missetât, der ein man wol tûsent hât, der tûsent wil er êre hân, und sol ir êre sîn vertân. daz ist ein ungeteilet spil: got solches rehtes niht enwil (Freidank 102.20–25).

215. Hanc (fidem) servare mihi debes aut decapitari (XIV.68).

216. Iudicium parile decet ut patiatur uterque. Cur servare fidem tibi debeo, dic, meliorem, Quam mihi tu debes? Dic, si defendere possis, Si licuisset Adae, maecham superaddat ut Evae? . . . Cum meretricares, essem scortum tibi velles? Absit, ut hoc pacto tibi iungar; vade, valeto Et quantumcunque scortare velis, sine sed me (XIV.70–73; 77–79).

217. nec viro licet quod mulieri non licet (*De Abraham*, col. 452).

218. quasi ludens (XI.142).

219. Nunc quisque sue memor esto puelle! (XI.143).

220. Faciebat enim talia amore cuiusdam muliercule, que presens aderat (vol. 1, p. 245).

221. Item dictum fuit de eo quod filias et uxores tam nobilium quam ignobilium de Feraria constupraret. Item diffamatus fuit quod proprias sorores cognoverit nec non et sororem uxoris (ibid.).

222. Par cui sont li bon chevalier? Por quoi aimment a tornoier? Por qui s'atornent li danzel? Por qui se vestent de novel? Por qui envoient lor joieaus, Lor treceors et lor aneaus? Por qui sont franc et debonere? Por qoi se gardent de mal fere? Por qoi aimment le donoier, Et l'acoler et l'embracier? (71–80).

223. Fors sol por une chose (82).

224. tuit li bien sont fet por lui (97).

225. E si·m partetz un juec d'amor No suy tan fatz No·n sapcha triar lo melhor D'entre·ls malvatz (6.11–14).

226. Partout demainent grant deduit En parler et en divers gieus: Cis qui plus set veut dire mieus, Desa karolent et cis dancent, Li vrai amant d'amors demandent, Et li autre en desterminent Li gieus del roi, de la roine, Qui est fait par commandement; Li tiers geue au roi qui ne ment, Et li autre d'amors consoile (Jacques Bretel, *Le tournoi de Chauvency* 2952–61).

227. Dominarum . . . curia in Guasconia (p. 291).

228. incestuosus amor (p. 279)

229. nulla probitate decorus (p. 278).

230. omni probitate iucundus (ibid.).

231. Tôtilâ, ain edel man, dû maht wol nâher zuo den frowen gân, dû bist kuone genuoc, des lîbes alzoges ain helt guot; wergot, sage mir des ih dih frâge, weder dir lieber waere an dîne triwe: ob dih ain scôniu frowe wolte minnen alle dise naht, ode dû morgen den tac in dînem gewaefen soltest gân, vehten mit ainem alsô kuonem man sô dû waenest daz dû sîst; waz dû tuon woltist, ob diu wal dîn waere, wederz dir baz gezaeme (4581–96).

232. Wie der einez taete, des vrâge ich, ob ez mit vuoge muge geschehen, waer ez niht unstaete, der zwein wîben wolte sich vür eigen geben, Beidiu tougenlîche? sprechent, herre, wurre ez iht? (89.15–19).

233. wan solz den man erlouben unde den vrouwen niht (89.20).

234. der mîn ze friunde ger, wil er mich ouch gewinnen, der lâze alselhe unstaetekeit (71.14–15).

235. Die vriunde habent mir ein spil geteilet vor, dêst beidenthalben verlorn: —doch ich ir einez nemen wil âne guot wal, sô waere ez baz verborn—Si jehent, welle ich minne pflegen, sô müeze ich mich ir bewegen. doch sô râtet mir der muot ze beiden wegen (H. v. Aue, *Lieder* 216.8–14).

236. Zwei dinc hân ich mir vür geleit, diu strîtent mit gedanken in dem herzen mîn (165.37–38).

237. rihtaere über die hübscheit (8035).

238. swer in der massenîe streit von ihte, daz an minne war, daz beschiet siu schône unde gar (8036–38).

239. Dar uf sinz sehs tag e Das der turnaý da erge, Und setzent aine kúnegin Ir clag ze rihter under in, Von der wirt in der wochen Minnen reht gesprochen, Als man rehte lehen reht Vor ainem herren machet sleht (7121–28).

240. Ich wil dir zwei geteiltiu geben, die doch beide hübesch sint . . . Sich, hêre; daz beste nim: oberhalp der gürtel mîn, wiltû, daz sol wesen dîn. Oder von der gürtel hin ze tal, wiltû, daz nim über al. Unt nimest dû daz beste teil, daz

wirt niht dîn unheil. Daz bezzer teil sol wesen dîn, daz erger lâz wesen mîn (1350–51; 58–66).

241. Liebiv frowe ich wil iv vf genade teilen ein spil (1–2).

242. der Schoene Glanz (II.2.4).

243. Von Limbůrg das vil scone wib (59).

244. He en ist ritter oder knecht (14).

CHAPTER VI: CRITICISM OF COURTLY LIFE

1. At modo seculares peruersis moribus competens scema superbe arripiunt (*Historia ecclesiastica*, vol. 4, p. 186).

2. extra legem Dei moremque patrum pro libitu suo ducebant (p. 188).

3. feminisque uiri curiales in omni lasciuia summopere adulantur (ibid.).

4. A noualibus suis arcentur agricolae, dum ferae habeant uagandi libertatem. Illis ut pascua augeantur, praedia subtrahuntur agricolis sationalia, insitiua colonis, compascua armentariis et gregariis (*Policraticus*, vol. 1, p. 31).

5. immoderato uoluptatis incursu (ibid.).

6. ... epulis, potationibus, conuiuiis, modulationibus et ludis, cultibus operosius exquisitis, stupris et uariis immunditiis (ibid., p. 33).

7. Nunc vero nobilium in eo sapientia declaratur, si uenaticam noverint, si in alea dampnabilius fuerint instituti, si naturae robur effeminatae uocis articulis fregerint, si modis et musicis instrumentis uirtutis immemores obliuiscantur quod nati sunt (ibid., p. 38).

8. so frowet sih din lib, din herze in diner bruste der manigen wol luste, da du daz flei(s)ch mite phezzis, dine sele da mite letzis (2485–89).

9. nû sich, wâ sint sîniu můzige wart dâ mit er der frowen hôhvart lobet unt säite; nû sich in wie getâner häite diu zunge lige in sînem munde dâ mit er diu troutliet chunde behagenlîchen singen—nûne mac si nicht fur bringen daz wort noch die stimme—; nû sich, wâ ist daz chinne mit dem niwen barthâre; nû sich, wie recht undâre ligen die arme mit den henden dâ mit er dich in allen enden trout unt umbevie! wâ sint die fûze dâ mit er gie höfslîchen mit den frowen? dem mûse dû diche nâch schowen wie die hosen stûnden an dem bäine, die brouchent sich nû läider chläine! er ist dir nû vil fremde dem dû ê die sîden in daz Hemde mûse in manigen enden witten. nû schowe in an: al enmitten dâ ist er geblaet als ein segel (607–31).

10. Man siht leider hiute Vil wênic hofeliute, Die gein himel trahten Und werltlicher êre niht ahten (H. v. Trimberg 661–64).

11. Wenne si gelobent alle wol, Swie doch ir herze sî gallen vol (665–66).

12. Swenne er mit süezen worten triuget (687).

13. Hofgesinde, erzte und juristen Habent abgöte, daz sint ir kisten (693–94).

14. Hôchfart, gîtigkeit, frâz, unkiusche Lêrent hofeliute vil manic getiusche (735–36).

15. Ein dinc ich ofte gemerket hân: Daz manigen herren ein falschaft man Vil lieber ist, der smeichen kan, Denne einer der guotes und êren in gan (743–46).

16. Schelke und boese râtgeben (1103).

17. nu ist daz leben In iren höfen gar verkêrt, Daz selten ieman dâ von wirt geêrt Der niht siben zungen hât (1104–07).

18. Triuwe, zuht und wârheit, Dêmuot, scham, einveltikeit, Kiusche und mâze sint vertriben Ze hofe und an ir stat sint beliben Liegen, triegen, ribaldîe, Loterfuor und buoberîe, Unkust, unzuht, leckerschimpfen, Trinken, slinden, nasen rimpfen, Luoder, spil, diube und spot, Lützel ahten ûf got, Ûf die sêle und ûf den tôt (1145–55).

19. Sô einer eine botschaft hovelîchen gewerben kan oder eine schüzzel tragen kan oder einer einen becher hövelîchen gebieten kan unde die hende gezogenlîche gehaben kan oder für sich gelegen kan, sô sprechent etelîche liute: "wech! welch ein wolgezogen kneht das ist (oder man oder frouwe)! daz ist gar ein tugentlîcher mensche: wê wie tugentlîche er kan gebâren!" Sich, diu tugent ist vor gote ein gespötte und engevellet gote ze nihte (vol. 1, p. 96).

20. prendés le fille a un roi u a un conte. Enseurquetot que cuideriés vous avoir gaegnié, se vous l'aviés asognentee ne mise a vo lit? Mout if ariés peu conquis, car tos les jors du siecle en seroit vo arme en infer, qu'en paradis n'enterriés vos ja (p. 5).

21. En paradis qu'ai je a faire? Je n'i quier entrer, mais que j'aie Nicolete, ma tresdoucé amie, que j'aim tant. C'en paradis ne vont fors tex géns con je vous dirai. Il i vont ći viel prestre et ćil viel clop et ćil manke, qui tote jor et tote nuit cropent devant ćes autex et en ćes viés creutes, et ćil a ćes viés capes ereses et a ćes viés tatereles vestues, qui sont nu et decaućet et estrumelé, qui moeurent de faim et de soi et de froit et de mesaisés. Ićil vont en paradis; aveuc ćiax n'ai jou que faire. Mais en infer voil jou aler; car en infer vont li bel clerc, et li bel cevalier qui sont mort as tornois et as rices gueres, et li boin serġant et li franc home. Aveuc ćiax voil jou aler. Et s'i vont les beles dames cortoises, que eles ont deus amis ou trois avoc leur barons, et s'i va li ors et li arġens et li vairs et li gris, et si i vont harpeor et jogleor et li roi del siecle. Avoc ćiax voil jou aler, mais que j'aie Nicolete, ma tresdouće amie, aveuc mi (p. 5 f.).

22. Ichn weiz wem ich gelîchen muoz die hovebellen (32.27).

23. Der in den ôren siech von ungesühte sî, daz ist mîn rât, der lâz den hof ze Dürengen frî (20.4–5).

24. und gulte ein fuoder guotes wînes tûsent pfund, dâ stüende ouch niemer ritters becher laere (20.14–15).

CHAPTER VII: THE LITERARY SCENE OF THE COURTLY AGE

1. ORAL CULTURE AND LITERACY IN COURTLY SOCIETY

1. rex illitteratus asinus coronatus (*Gesta regum Anglorum*, vol. 2, p. 467).

2. militiae praetextu (vol. 1, p. 250).

3. Ex quibus liquido constat, quam necessaria sit principibus peritia litterarum, qui legem Domini cotidie reuoluere lectione iubentur (ibid., p. 254).

4. Fuit dux iste a puericia doctus litteris, et satis noticiam scripturarum habuit. Librorum copiam in palatio suo servavit, et si forte a tumultu vacaret, lectioni per se ipsum operam dabat, longioribus noctibus elucubrans in libris, donec somno vinceretur (*Chronicon*, p. 176 f.).

5. Verum est quia sapientia et eloquentia et littere maxime regibus et consulibus conveniunt. Quanto enim quis prelatior, tanto moribus et litteris debet esse lucidior (*Gesta consulum Andegavorum*, Additamenta, p. 140).

6. optime litteratus, inter clericos et laicos facundissimus (p. 71).

7. civilibus armis et studiis liberalibus deditus (*Historia Gaufredi*, p. 176).

8. verborum compendio studens, eadem etiam verba rhetoricis exornans coleribus (ibid., p. 178).

9. forma, genus, litterarum scientia, cuncta morum et uirtutum pulchritudo (*Historia ecclesiastica*, vol. 2, p. 224).

10. princepts quem non nobilitat scientia litteralis, non parum degenerans sit quasi rusticanus (*Epistolae*, col. 149).

11. quae virtus quidem, quanto in principibus est hodie rarior, tanto, ubi affuerit, longe pretiosior et praeclarior (*De principibus instructio*, p. 7).

12. generosi partium nostrarum aut dedignantur aut pigri sunt applicare literis liberos suos (*De nugis curialium*, p. 8).

13. Hic itaque iussus a rege totam huius expeditionis seriem rerumque in illa gestarum stilo tam facili, qui pene nihil a communi loquela discrepet, tribus libris digessit, consulens in hoc etiam lectoribus laicis vel aliis minus doctis, quorum hęc intellectus capere possit (p. 254).

14. non multum studui in hoc opere verborum adhibere leporem, vel dictionis cameratas vel sermones faleratos inferre (p. 105).

15. mediocrem dictandi sequor urbanitatem (ibid.).

16. tibi layco moderate philosophanti et aliis quasi pueris tibi coetaneis ista simplicia dicta proposui et adaptavi (ibid.).

17. Tunc fac edictum per terram Teutonicorum, Quilibet ut dives sibi natos instruat omnes Litterulis legemque suam persuadeat illis, Ut, cum principibus placitandi venerit usus, Quisque suis libris exemplum proferat illis. Moribus his dudum vivebat Roma decenter, His studiis tantos potuit vincire tyrannos; Hoc servant Itali post prima crepundia cuncti, Et sudare scholis mandatur tota iuventus: Solis Teutonicis vacuum vel turpe videtur, Ut doceant aliquem, nisi clericus accipiatur (190–200).

18. ...laicorum scilicet illiteratorum (*Narratio de electione Lotharii*, p. 510).

19. qui eum, quod ipse erat, fieri terrenum militem...disponebat (*Vita Theoderici abbatis Andaginensis*, p. 39).

20. Qui filium suum a litteris abstractum domi servari iussit, interminatus uxori gravia, si posthac eum praesumeret tradere his disciplinis (ibid.).

21. litteris...per Reinaldum cancellarium fida satis interpretatione diligenter expositis, magna principes qui aderant indignatione commoti sunt (Rahewin, *Gesta Frederici*, p. 414).

22. Filios enim meos omnes litteras discere proposui, ut qui majoris ingenii necnon majoris inter eos notaretur discretionis, in studio perseveraret (Denifle, vol. 1, p. 39).

23. qui vivente patre cum frequentaret scolas Neunburch mortuus est (*Continuatio Claustroneoburgensis* I, p. 612).

24. Wan ir leien niht lesen kunnet als wir pfaffen (vol. 2, p. 233).

25. mohten sîn die leien hân vernomen, ez waer im harte übel komen; dô verstuonden si sîn niht (13085–87).

26. habt aber ir gegen mir oder gegen dem rîche iht ze suochen, des mac ich iu ûz den buochen mit worten niht gevolgen (13106–09).

27. des rîches leienfursten (13114).

28. als tôren unde stumben (13119).

29. Et quia rex tanquam illitteraturs et laicus premissas interrogationes et earum responsiones in latino dictas non intelligit, dominus Coloniensis per se vel per clericum unum cui faciendum mandaverit, premissas interrogationes et earum responsiones domino regi in vulgari nostro, id est in teutonico, manifestius declarabit (MGH Leges, vol. 2, p. 386 f.).

30. litteratus, et in divino servicio valde studiosus (*Annalista Saxo*, p. 661).

31. Qui enim istorum ignari sunt, illiterati dicuntur etsi litteras noverint (*Metalogicus*, p. 58).

32. post mortem Edidis reginae, cum antea nescierit, litteras in tantum didicit, ut pleniter libros legere et intelligere noverit (Widukind of Corvey, p. 118).

33. illiteratus (*Chronica*, p. 165).

34. In patria lingua admodum facundus, Latinam vero melius intelligere potest quam pronunciare (*Gesta Frederici*, p. 710).

35. antiqua scripta cronicorum colligi praecepit et conscribi et coram recitari (Gerhard of Stederburg, p. 230).

36. qui nec menbra lassa aliquando sopori dedit nisi preaudita collacione, modo de sacris apicibus, modo de magnanimitate principum antiquorum, quandoque latinizatis, aliquando theutonizatis aurem pervigilem adhibuit scriptis (*Chronica Reinhardsbrunnensis*, p. 564).

37. H. Dei gratia Thoringiae lantgravius et Saxonie comes palatinus (Struck, p. 12).

38. Sic sic divinos ei libros et in ecclesia ad cultum et venerationem Dei necessarios scribi fecit et parari et in capellis suis hic illic collocari (Lampert of Ardres, p. 598).

39. litteras didicisse et litteratum factum (ibid.).

40. Et iste fuit Thideric de Berne, de quo cantabant rustici olim (*Annales Quedlinburgenses*, p. 31).

41. Numquam ille Augustinum, numquam ille Gregorium recolit, semper ille Attalam, semper Amalungum et cetera id genus portare tractat (Erdmann-Fickermann, p. 121; portare is probably corrupt).

42. pulvillis fabulisque curialibus (ibid., p. 110).

43. speciosissimi carminis contextu notissimam Grimildae erga fratres perfidiam (vol. 1, p. 355).

44. quod Kanutum Saxonici et ritus et nominis amantissimum scisset (ibid.).

45. Emelricus, rex Theutoniae (*Annales Pegavienses*, p. 234).

46. omnes barbarorum gestas res in memoria tenuit, ac (si) scriptae essent (p. 278).

47. quasi litteratus non solum domestica, sed etiam extranea bella et facta omnia in memoria tenebat (*Gesta Ambaziensium dominorum*, p. 76).

48. Swer von hern Dietrîch von Berne Dâ sagen kan und von hern Ecken Und von alten sturm recken, Vür den giltet man den wîn (Renner 10348–51).

49. So singent uns die blinden, daz Sifrit hurnin were (*Jg. Titurel* 3364.1).

50. Sing ich dien liuten mîniu liet, sô wil der êrste daz wie Dietrîch von Berne schiet, der ander, wâ künc Ruother saz, der dritte wil der Riuzen sturm, sô wil der vierde Ekhartes nôt, Der fünfte wen Kriemhilt verriet, dem sehsten taete baz war komen sî der Wilzen diet. der sibende wolde eteswaz Heimen ald hern Witchen sturm, Sigfrides ald hern Eggen tôt. Sô wil der ahtode niht wan hübschen minnesanc. dem niunden ist diu wîle bi den allen lanc. der zehend enweiz wie, nû sust nû sô, nû dan nû dar, nû hin nû her, nû dort nû hie. dâ bî haete manger gerne der Nibelungen hort. der wigt mîn wort ringer danne ein ort: des muot ist in schatze verschort (XV. 14.261–78).

51. Conserimus manus et chorollam confusionis in atrio ordinamus. Ductor furoris nostri alludens fatale carmen orditur Gerlevus: Equitabat Bobo per silvam frondosam, Ducebat sibi Merswinden formosam. Quid stamus? cur non imus? (Schröder, p. 127).

52. Swaz hie gât umbe, daz sint alle megede, die wellent ân man allen disen sumer gân (MF 1.VI).

53. Generationes principum nostrorum (p. 2).

54. Avitam principum huius terre nostre, parentum scilicet vestrorum, prosapiam commemorare vobis, ut petitis, cupientes (*Breve chronicon Austriae Mellicense*, p. 70).

55. Qui legis hec, care, nostri petimus memorare. Hoc quidem cuncti; mage tu, carissime fili! (*Codex Falkensteinensis*, p. 29*, note 2).

56. Dic valeas patri? bene, fili, dicite matri! (ibid.).

57. per manum wernhardi notarii (*UB des Landes ob der Ems*, vol. 2, p. 162, no. 108).

58. privilegia terre marito suo exhibuit (*Annales Admuntenses, Continuatio Garstensis*, p. 600).

59. Ego Vlricus siggilavi (*UB zur Geschichte der Babenberger*, vol. 1, p. 120. no. 87).

60. Data Ratispone per manum Rouberti Canonici et Capellani ejusdem Ducis Liupaldi (*Monumenta Boica*, vol. 13, p. 171).

61. nulle littere, nisi valde simplices, debent domini sigillo conmuniri, nisi de scitu principis speciali (*Summa de arte prosandi*, p. 166).

62. presentem paginam manu nostra roboravimus et sigilli nostri impressione insigniri decrevimus (Jordan, p. 102, no. 68).

63. Ego Liupoldus dei gratia dux Austrie ac Stirię subscribo (*UB zur Geschichte der Babenberger*, vol. 1, p. 237, no. 177).

64. ...ubi fere omnibus principibus regni Teutonici convenientibus, pax iuratur, vetera iura stabiliuntur, nova statuuntur et Teutonico sermone in membrana scripta omnibus publicantur (p. 267).

65. ut littere et instrumenta...latino ydiomate conscribantur (p. 165).

66. Wir sprechen, daz brieve bezer sint danne geziuge. Wan geziuge die sterbent: sô belîbent die brieve immer staete (p. 34, § 34).

67. omnibus hanc (paginam) audientibus vel inspitientibus (*UB der Stadt u. Landschaft Zürich*, vol. 1, p. 281, no. 396, from the year 1219).

68. Swer dise schrift siht alde horet (*Corpus*, vol. 1, p. 20, no. 6).

69. Allen dien die disen brief werdent lesende oder hőrende (ibid., p. 25, no. 14).

70. quod quedam littera sigillata sigillo venerabilis Abbatis S. Urbani fuit michi ab Volrico filio H. bone memorie dicto Sartore presentata, cuius tenorem ego personaliter in ecclesia predicta legi et exposui vulgariter multis astantibus fide dignis (Schneller, no. 8, p. 161 f.).

2. PATRONS AND SPONSORS

1. Tibi, summe imperator, hoc opus devoveo (p. 522 f.).

2. Attendant magis humanos labores meos et rerum magnitudinem operisque prolixitatem, cum ego in angulis palatii imperialis, aut in via equitando sub aliqua arborum aut in silva aliqua absconsus ad horam ista scripserim in obsidionibus castrorum, in periculo preliorum multorum, non in heremo vel in claustro aut aliquo quietis loco positus hec dictaverim, set in omni motu et rerum turbatione assidue, et in guerra et in rebus bellicis, in strepitu tante curie, ubi me oportebat cotidie esse assiduum, upote capellanum, die ac nocte, in missa, in omnibus horis diei, in mensa, in causis agitandis, in epistolis conficiendis, in cotidiana cura novorum hospitiorum, in stipendiis conquirendis mihi meisque, in maximis legationibus peragendis, bis in Siciliam, ter in Provintiam, semel in Yspaniam, sepe in Franciam, 40 vicibus Romam de Alemania, et in omni labore et sollicitudine assidue magis, quam aliquis meus coetaneus in imperiali curia pertulisset. Que omnia quanto plura et graviora sunt, tanto mirabilius est, quod ego in tanto motu, in tanta crapula, tanto strepitu et sollicitudine esta potui operari (*Memoria saeculorum*, p. 105).

3. non est consuetudinis apud nos, ut sine bonis monimentis aliqui alicui concedantur (Wibald of Stablo, *Epistolae*, p. 327, no. 207).

4. Mirabatur dominus noster C(onradus) rex ea, quae á litteratis vafrę dicebantur; et, probari non posse, hominem esse asinum, aiebat. Iocundi eramus in convivio, et plerique nobiscum non illiterati. Dicebam ei, hoc in rerum natura non posse effici; set ex concessione indeterminata, nascens á vero mendatium, falsa conclusione astringi. Cum non intelligeret, ridiculo eum sophismate adorsus sum: "Unum" inquam "habetis oculum?" Quod cum dedisset, subieci: "Duos" inquam "oculos habetis." Quod cum absolute annuisset, "Unus" inquam "et duo tres sunt; tres igitur oculos habetis." Captus verbi cavillatione iurabat, se tantum duos habere. Multis tamen et his similibus determinare doctus, iocundam vitam dicebat habere litteratos (p. 283).

5. ingenuo... alumno (*Ligurinus* X.649).

6. Cesaris authorum sibi scrinia sunt meliorum, Plenaque sanctorum sibi scrinia sunt meliorum, Si petis hystorias, conferet aula forum. Leges aut artes ibi sunt, omnisque poeta, Magnus Aristotiles, Ypocras, Galiena dieta Dant ibi consilia digna, cavenda vetant (Delisle, p. 48).

7. ferramenta ad bullandum de auro (*Epistolae*, p. 506, no. 377).

8. Sexta Fredericum divo depingit amictu, Cesarea septum prole senile latus. Hic Fredericus ovans, in milibus undique fretus Fervidus in Christo miles iturus erat. Hic erat annosum multa nemus ylice septum, Non nisi per gladios silva datura vias. In nemus omne furit ferrum, nemus omne favillat, Fit via, quod dudum parte negabat iter. Hic erat, infide, tua fallax, Ungare, dextra, Qualiter invito te Fredericus abit (*Liber ad honorem augusti* 1581–90).

9. At postquam Conii spoliis saturantur et auro, Castra movent; nec eis cura quietis erat. Proh dolor, ad flumen ponunt temtoria Tharsis, Quo lacerat tumidas nans Fredericus aquas. Suspectas invenit aquas, qui raptus ab undis Exuit humanum, servit et ante deum, Vivit in eternum Fredericus, lancea cuius Nunquam fraudato cuspide versa fuit (1598–605).

10. Prima domus—Deus creans omnia. Secunda domus—Archa Noè. Tercia domus—Habraham. Quarta domus—Moyses—Mare rubrum. Quinta domus—David rex (fig. 49).

11. Sexta domus imperii—Fredericus Imperator—Henricus—Philippus. Fredericus Imperator iubet incidi nemus Ungarie (ibid.).

12. dotibus insignitus scientie litteralis et floribus eloquentie redimitus et eruditus apostolicis institutis et legibus imperatorie maiestatis (Alberic of Troisfontaines, *Chronica*, p. 858).

13. Scientia literarum, o Henrice omnium regum felicissime, qua tuam eminentiam video eruditam, scribenti michi de imperiali prosapia multam prebet audaciam . . . Gaudeo me regem habere philosophantem, cuius majestatem non oporteat in causis rei publice ab aliis mendicare (*Speculum regum*, p. 21).

14. Interpretari tua serenitas imperat Merlinum vatem Britannicum et Erytheam Babylonicam prophetissam (Waitz, p. 512).

15. die bevalch ab keiser Heinrich in tiutschiu lant umbe sich, als im riet sîn wille. Hûc von Morville hiez der selben gîsel ein, in des gewalt uns vor erschien daz welsche buoch von Lanzelete (U. v. Zatzikhoven 9335–41).

16. ich bin wol ze fiure komen, mich hât daz rîche und ouch diu krône an sich genomen (19.35–36).

17. Hêr kaiser, sît ir willekomen (11.30).

18. Das ist der kúnig Chûnrat, des keisirs kint, der mit hat geboten and das bete mich gerûchte biten des das ich durh in dú mere tihte (21663–67).

19. ze lesene und ze schouwen (352.36).

20. des wart diu grâvinne gram dem grâven Heinrîch, der ez nam unde ez dannen sande ze Doringen heim ze lande (353.7–10).

21. dâ her den phalinzgrâven vant von Sassen, der im daz bûch liez unde ez in volmachen hiez (353.18–20).

22. bî den bôt er mir sîn guot, vast er mich ze lande luot (27623–24).

23. dô woldich von dem lewen niht, und noch ungern, was mir geschiht: in des lande ich bin geborn, nâch gote ze hêrren habe ich in erkorn (27625–28).

24. lantgrâf von Dürngen Herman tet mir diz maer von im bekant (3.8–9).

25. Daz hiz der furste herman der Lantgraue von duringē lāt Diz buch hat im hergesant Der graue von Liningē (92–95).

26. Von Francriche in thiusche lant Wurden disiu mare gesant Bi ainem hoveschen werden man . . . Van Ravenspurg Johannes. Diu getat des werden

mannes Wart im an walschen bûchen kunt, Und brahte si do ze stunt Mit im her in thiusche lant, Alse er si geschriben vant (15601–03; 07–12).

27. das welsche buoch von Lanzelete (U. v. Zatzikhoven 9341).

28. nâch der werlde lône (4).

29. und bat sie daz sie ez dihten ane rimen wolden . . . ez enwere an dem meister niht beleben, er het ez gerimet ab er solde (*Lucidarius*-Prologue 14–15, 24–25).

30. Der herzoge wolde daz man ez hieze da "Aurea gemma," dô duhte ez dem meister bezzer sus daz ez hieze "Lucidarius" (26–30).

31. ich enbin der witze niht sô laz ich enkünne ez doch verre baz tihten unde zieren, mit lügenen florieren beider her unde dar: nû hât ez mir verboten gar von Beiern diu herzogin, der ich underhoeric bin (49–56).

32. der milte Welf (35.4).

33. Welf von Swaben (*Gedichte* VI.39).

34. Nu wnschen wir alle geliche dem herzogin Hainriche daz im got lone (9017–19).

35. Diz bûch heizet Lucidarius . . . got hat ime den sin gegeben, dem herzogen der ez schriben liez: sine capellane er hiez die rede sûchen an den schriften (*Lucidarius*-Prologue 1.10–13).

36. dore genade ende dore minne des heme ouch bat die gravinne van Lon, die edele Agnes. di bat luste heme des dat he't te dutschen kerde, alse heme di vite lerde (6177–82).

37. des bat heme her Hessel ouch, des man da wale ermanen mach, de du der costerien plach (6194–96).

38. Ich bin des milten lantgrâven ingesinde (35.7).

39. signum sue magne devotionis (Caesarius of Heisterbach, *Vita s. Elyzabeth*, p. 354).

40. der stolze Mîssenaere (18.16).

41. eines vil edeln vürsten tôt von Merân (8063–64).

42. edel Kerendaere (32.31).

43. des kuniclîchen stammes ein blûnder ast vol êren und furstlîcher tât mich zu dirre rede gebunden hât: der êrlîche herzoge Polke (5570–73).

44. des gerte di edele herzoginne, aines richen chûniges barn (9024–25).

45. daz was diu grâvinne von Cleve diu milde und diu gûte mit dem frîen mûte, diu konde hêrlîche geben. vil tugentlîch was ir leben, als ez frouwen wol gezam (352.38–353.3).

46. sît nu dar zuo gebeldet mîne kranke sinne diu edel herzoginne, daz ich duch sie genende, von Zeringen Clêmende, und ich mich versuoche an sant Margrêten buoche (18–24).

47. er und sîn reinez wîp, diu hôch edel fürstin, die . . . sprâchen zuo mir "Reinbot, du solt ein buoch tihten . . ." (6–8; 20–21).

48. apud Zei[zemurum] Walthero cantori de Vogelweide pro pellico. v. sol. longos (Heger, p. 86).

49. der biderbe patrîarke missewende frî (34.36).

50. dâ daz In mit fluzze in die Tuonouwe gât (1295.4).

51. hie ze Wildenberc (230.13).

52. Das ist der werde schenke, Der hoh gemûte Cûnrat Von Winterstetten der mich hat Gebetten durch den willen sin Das ich durch in die sinne mir Árbaite und úch tihte In rehter rime rihte (R. v. Ems, *Wilhelm v. Orlens* 2318-24).

53. genamen (6827).

54. Nu tâte ichz, ob ich wisse Ob mir maister Hesse Von Strasburg de sribaere Wolde disú mare Prisen ob si wårent gůt.—"Ja er, binamen ja, er tůt! Eı hat beschaidenhait so vil, Swa er tihte bessern wil, Das er ze rehte bessern sol. Da kumt sin úberhôren wol, Wan ez besserunge holt" (2279–89).

3. AUTHOR AND AUDIENCE

1. Diz lît, daz wir hî wurchen, daz sult ir rehte merchen. sîn gevûge ist vil reht. iz tihte der phaffe Lambret. er tâte uns gerne ze mâre, wer Alexander wâre (1–6).

2. mir zv brach der helfe lantze An einem fvrsten (5883.2–3).

3. mich drücket, aremuot diu swaere (Wolf I, p. 316).

4. ich hân sô dicke genigen ir vil milten hende, durch die ich nu genende an ditze selbe büechelîn, daz ich des wil vil sicher sîn daz sie mich niht lâze verderben ûf der strâze (62–68).

5. ze machen nem diz maere ein man, der âventiure prüeven kan unde rîme künne sprechen, beidiu samnen unde brechen (337.23–26).

6. quo nomine designari mos est cujuscumque ordinis vel habitus valenter litteratum (col. 203 f.).

7. interrogamus eum utrum clericus sit, non quaerentes scire utrum sit ad agendum altaris officium ordinatus, sed tantummodo, utrum sit litteratus. At ille ad interrogata consequenter respondens, dicit se clericum esse, si litteratus est; conversum vero laicum, si illiteratus est (*De institutione clericorum*, col. 816).

8. ain layg der sich verstatt Ob der nit ain platten hat Dannocht haist er ain pfaff dar von Das er die geschrift verstett vnd kan (*Ritter oder Knecht* 21–24).

9. der phaffe Lambret (4).

10. der phaffe Chunrat (9079).

11. Ein gelarter schulere (18451).

12. capellanus V̊lricus de Cecinchouin plebanus Lŏmeissae (*Turgauisches UB*, vol. 2, no. 99, p. 341).

13. Ein rittcr sô gelêret was daz er an dem buochen las swaz er dar an geschriben vant: der was Hartman genant, dienstman was er zOuwe (*Armer Heinrich* 1–5).

14. ine kan decheinen buochstap (*Parzival* 115.27).

15. sîne kristallînen wortelîn (4627).

16. des hasen geselle (4636).

17. ûf der wortheide hôchsprünge und wîtweide mit bickelworten welle sîn (4637–39).

18. leien munt nie baz gesprach (W. v. Grafenberg 6346).

19. swer getragener kleider gert, derst niht minnesanges wert (Buwenburc 6.47–48).

20. Man singet minnewîse dâ ze hove und inme schalle: so ist mir sô nôt nâch alder wât deich niht von frouwen singe (Gedrut-Geltar II, 1–2).

21. Ditz ist ein scho(e)ne mere, daz ouch nu der strickêre die vrowen wil bekennen. ern sole si niht nennen an sinen meren, wer er wis. sin leben und vrowen pris, die sint ein ander unbekant. ein pfert und alt gewant, die stunden baz in sinem lobe (*Frauenehre* 137–45).

22. er was des râtes brücke und sanc vil wol von minnen. alsus kunder er gewinnen der werlde lop unde pris. er was hövesch unde wîs (70–74).

23. propter alta vitae suae merita (*UB der Stadt Leipzig*, vol. 2, no. 8, p. 7).

24. Ich hân mînes herren hulde vloren âne schulde: . . . des hân ich ze Beiern lâzen allez, daz ich ei gewan, unde var dâ hin gein Ôsterrîche und wil mich dingen an den werden Ôsterman (74.31; 75.1–2).

25. Rôst. kilchherre ze Sarne. However, the preceding line reads: Her Heinrich der Rôst schriber (Pfaff, col. 947).

26. Daz ein abt von sant Gallen Tageliet machte (4192–93).

27. ze hove und an der strâzen (W. v. d. Vogelweide 105.28).

28. ouch quamen dare me dan viere hundert ministriere, die wir nennen speleman inde van wapen sprechen kan, sulche kunden singen van aventuren inde dingen die geschagen in alden jaren. sulche ouch da waren die van minnen inde lieve sprachen ane brieve. sulche die die vedelen zwaren daden luden offenbaren; sulich de wale dat horen blies, sulich geberde als ein ries; sulche floteden cleine mit holze inde mit beine, sulche bliesen mutet wale up deme muset; sulche harpen inde gigen, den man mochte swigen, sulche cum salterio druvige herzen machen vro, sulche die van zitole zů Paris hielden schole. sulche meistere gůde kouchelden under dem hůde. sulche kunden driven umbe wale die schiven; sulche wale die becken entfiengen mit den stecken; sulche tumelden inde sprungen, sulche die vil wale rungen; sulche als si is begerden, die bucke mit den perden daden si samen striden inde merkatzen riden. sulche die och kunden danzen mit den hunden; sulche die ouch steine kuweden harde cleine (*Morant u. Galie* 5145–84).

29. Sed notandum quod histrionum tria sunt genera. Quidam enim transformant et transfigurant corpora sua per turpes saltus vel per turpes gestus, vel denudando corpora turpiter, vel induendo horribiles loricas vel larvas, et omnes tales damnabiles sunt nisi relinquant officia sua. Sunt etiam alii histriones qui nihil operantur sed curiose agunt, non habentes certum domicilium, sed circueunt curias magnatum et loquuntur obprobia et ignominias de absentibus. Tales etiam damnabiles sunt, quia prohibet Apostolus cum talibus cibum sumere. Et dicuntur tales scurre vagi, quia ad nihil aliud utiles sunt nisi ad devorandum et maledicendum. Est etiam tertium genus histrionum qui habent instrumenta musica ad delectandum homines, sed talium duo sunt genera. Quidam enim frequentant publicas potationes et lascivas congregationes ut cantent ibi lascivas cantilenas, ut moveant homines ad lasciviam, et tales sunt damnabiles sicut et alii. Sunt autem alii qui dicuntur ioculatores qui cantant gesta principium et vitas sanctorum et faciunt solatia hominibus vel in egritudinibus

suis vel in angustiis suis . . . bene possunt sustineri tales (*Summa confessorum*, p. 291 f.).

30. Clerici qui clericali ordini non modicum detrahentes, se joculatores seu galiardos faciunt, aut buffones (Mansi, vol. 25, col. 227).

31. nec sint histriones, joculatores, ballivi, forestarii saeculares, goliardi (Mansi, vol. 24, col. 910).

32. Item clericos tonsuram laycalem deferentes, videlicet vagos, et etiam laicos istriones . . . ponimus extra pacem (MHG Const. 2, no. 427, p. 577).

33. ich was ein höfscher spilman und kunde genuoge höfischeit unde fuoge . . . dâ mite gewan ich sô genuoc biz mich daz guot übertruoc und mêre haben wolte, dan ich von rehte solte. sus liez ich mich an koufrât (G. v. Straßburg 7564–66; 73–77).

34. harphen, videln, singen (3728).

35. sus was der ellende dô da ze hove ein trût gesinde (3740–41).

36. Rubertus ioculator regis (Böhmer-Baaken, no. 90, p. 41).

37. Joc(u)latori episcopi (Heger, p. 90).

38. Enêas der mâre enbôt offenbâre, daz her brûten solde, swer gût umb êre wolde, daz her frôlîch quâme (H. v. Veldeke, *Eneit* 336.1–5).

39. ob ein sun ze einem spilmanne wirt, daz er guot vür êre nimt (§ 16, p. 20).

40. Daz sint die gumpelliute, gîgere unde tambûrer, swie die geheizen sîn, alle die guot fur êre nement (vol. 1, p. 155).

41. Car Diex sens leur donne et savoir Des gentilz homes soulacier, Pour les vices d'entr'eus chacier Et pour les bons noncier leur fais: Pour ce sont li menstrel fais, Que partout font joie et deduit (Watriquet de Couvins, *Li dis des trois vertus* 147–52).

42. Wan er ret eime daz beste daz er kan die wîle daz erz hoeret, und als er im den rücken kêret, sô ret er im daz boeste, daz er iemer mê kan oder mac, unde schiltet manigen, der gote ein gerehter man ist und ouch der werlte, unde lobet einen, der gote unde der werlte schedelîchen lebet (vol. 1, p. 155).

43. die alten sprüche sagent unz daz: swes brot man ezzen wil, des liet sol man ouch singen gerne, und spiln mit vlize, swes er spil (Der tugendhafte Schreiber XII.2.13–14).

44. man sol den herren gerne loben, da er ze lobene si: ja enwil ich nieman durch sin brot mit wizzende siner schanden wesen bi (XII.3.13–14).

45. Si wellent ane strafen leben, unt wellent, daz man alle ir vuore prise. dar ümbe kunnen si wol geben vil hohe miete: nu was touk danne iuwer slehtiu wise? so mir ein verlogenez Ja von in vil wol vergolten wirt, so weiz ich wol, daz iuwer Nein, swie war ez ist, iu lüzzel vrümen birt (XII.4.9–14).

46. E dan ich einen richen boesen prisete umb ein gebelin, e wolt' ich mit den milten armen immer arm sin (Der Litschower 5.9–10).

47. mit richen sprüchen angelogen (F. v. Suonenburg 47.2).

48. Nu muoz ich dikke liegen durch des libes not (Rumslant II.4.1).

49. Mîn munt der hât sie angelogen mit lobe an manigen stunden (Hermann der Damen IV.7.5–6).

50. ich muoz der warheit abe stan unde liegen umbe guot! Sit ich bi rehter

kunst bin gabe und guotes also bloz, so wil ich serer liegen denne müge einer min genoz (F. v. Suonenburg 18.3–6).

51. Mais il est tant de menestreus, Les uns cortois, les autres teus Qui ne siervient d'autre maistire Que de mesparler et de dire Ramposnes et grans felenies (Baudoin de Condé, *Li contes dou Wardecors* 77–81).

52. ein höfischer spilman (G. v. Straßburg 7564).

53. lîren unde gîgen, harphen unde rotten, schimpfen unde spotten (7568–70).

54. ich bin ze lange arm gewesen ân mînen danc. ich was sô voller scheltens daz mîn âten stanc (29.1–2).

55. Hec est familia domus in Tirol (Heuberger, p. 386).

56. die amptlevt, hofmaister, chamermeister, marschalch, chelner, spiser, chvchenmeister (*Monumenta Wittelsbacensia*, section 2, no. 198, p. 56).

57. wilt uns diu maere künden vürebaz, wir müezzen nâch den vrouwen allen senden (*Râtselspiel* 33.2–3).

58. Diu lantgrêvin quam ouch aldar: ze Wartberg ûf dem palas man wart dâ gewar bî ir wol vierzic vrouwen oder mêre. der ahte hôchgrêvinne sint (34.1–4).

59. Ir vrouwen . . . Dirre arebeit wil ich iu jehen, Wan ich ir durch iuch began (H. v. Türlin, *Krone* 29 990.95–96).

60. Ditz buoch sol guoter wîbe sîn (U. v. Liechtenstein, *Frauendienst* 1850.1).

61. die frowen süln ez gerne lesen (U. v. Liechtenstein, *Frauenbuch* 660.28).

62. nu wil ichz heizen schrîben ze êren guoten wîben (*Gute Frau* 3053–54).

63. swelhe vrouwen an disem buoche lesen, die suln mir wünschen heiles und danken mir mîns teiles, des ich dar an gesprochen hân (U. v. Türheim, *Tristan* 3658–61).

64. Nu wunschet, reine vrowen, ich mein, in tugent lebende mit triwen unverhowen, daz mir Altissimus di saelde gebende si, daz ich di aventûr geleite . . . (*Jg. Titurel* 66.1–3).

65. sus heb ich an in gotes namen und ouch durch ein gûtes wip (U. v. Türheim, *Rennewart* 140-41).

66. dô bat ein frouwe minniclîche mich, daz ich ez tihte und ez gerîmet rihte. nu hân ich ez durch sî getân (H. v. Wildonie, *Der nackte Kaiser* 8–11).

67. Kleinez büechel, swa ich si, so wone miner frowen bi: wis min zunge und min munt und tuo ir staete minne kunt (*Zweites Büchlein* 811–14).

68. Das si in frôden riche Und das si siner stâte Durch ir tugende raete Ze gûte an im gedenke (2314–17).

69. guotiu wîp, hânt die sin, deste werder ich in bin, op mir decheiniu guotes gan, sît ich diz maer volsprochen hân. ist daz durh ein wîp geschehn, diu muoz mir süezer worte jehn (827.25–30).

70. "nû swîc, lieber Hartmann: ob ich ez errâte?" ich tuon; nû sprechet drâte. "ich muoc gedenken ê dar nâch." nû vil drâte: mir ist gâch. "dunket ich dich danne ein wîser man?" jâ ir. durch got, nû saget an. "ich wil dir diz maere sagen." daz andere lâze ich iuch verdagen. "er waz guot hagenbüechîn." jâ. wâ von möhte er mêre sîn? "mit liehtem golde übertragen." wer mohte iuz doch rehte sagen? "vils starke gebunden." ir habet ez rehte ervunden. "dar ûf ein

scharlachen." des mac ich wol gelachen. "sehet daz ichz rehte errâten kan." jâ, ir sît ein weterwîser man (7491–511).

71. aut prodesse volunt aut delectare poetae aut simul (333–34).

72. ich zel iu drîer hande nutz, die rede bringet unde sanc. daz eine ist, daz ir süezer klanc daz ôre fröuwet mit genuht; daz ander ist, daz hovezuht ir lêre deme herzen birt; daz dritte ist, daz diu zunge wirt gespraeche sêre von in zwein. ich bin des komen über ein, daz beide fröude und êre sanc unde rede sêre den liuten bringent unde gebent, die nâch ir zweier râte lebent unde in beiden volgent mite. si lêrent hovelîche site und alle tugentlîche tât (K. v. Würzburg, *Partonopier* 8–23).

73. In sollemnitate quadam cum Abbas Gevardus praedecessor huius, qui nunc est, verbum exhortationis in Capitulo ad nos faceret, et plures, maxime de conversis, dormitare, nonnullos etiam stertere conspiceret, exclamavit: Audite, fratres, audite, rem vobis novam et magnam proponam. Rex quidam fuit, qui Artus vocabatur. Hoc dicto, non processit, sed ait: Videte, fratres, miseriam magnam. Quando locutus sum de Deo, dormitastis; mox ut verba livitatis inserui, evigilantes erectis auribus omnes auscultare coepistis (vol. 1, p. 205).

74. Vil manigem sint aber baz bekant Hie und über manic lant Diu buoch, diu ich vor hân genant: Parcifâl und Tristrant, Wigolais und Enêas, Êrec, Iwân und swer ouch was Ze der tafelrunne in Karîdol (21637–43).

75. Wenne maniger wênt er wêr enwiht, Würde er ein sôgetân degen niht Als die helde vor genant (21657–59).

76. wie hie vor die alten recken Durch frouwen minne sint verhouwen, Daz hoert man noch vil manige frouwen Mêre klagen und weinen ze manigen stunden Denne unsers herren heilige wunden (21692–96).

77. Nam et in fabulis, quae uulgo de nescio quo finguntur Arthuro, memini me nonnunquam usque ad effusionem lacrimarum fuisse permotum (Aelred of Rievaulx, *De speculo caritatis*, p. 90).

78. Saepe in tragoediis et aliis carminibus poetarum, in joculatorum cantilenis describitur aliquis vir prudens, decorus, fortis, amabilis et per omnia gratiosus. Recitantur etiam pressurae vel injuriae eidem crudeliter irrogatae, sicut de Arturo et Gangano et Tristanno, fabulosa quaedam referunt histriones, quorum auditu concutiuntur ad compassionem audientium corda, et usque ad lacrymas compunguntur (*Liber de confessione sacramentali*, col. 1088).

79. ir stimme ist lûter unde guot, si gebent der werlde hôhen muot und tuont reht in dem herzen wol. diu werlt diu waere unruoches vol und lebete rehte als âne ir danc, wan der vil liebe vogelsanc . . . ez wecket friuntlîchen muot. hie von kumt inneclîch gedanc, sô der vil liebe vogelsanc der werlde ir liep beginnet zalen (4757–62; 68–71).

80. dû kundest al der werlte fröide mêren (83.7).

81. Ich hân hundert tûsent herze erlôst von sorgen, . . . jâ was ich al der werlte trôst (184.31–33).

82. hei wie diu über heide mit hôher stimme schellet! waz wunders sî stellet! wie spaehe si organieret! wie si ir sanc wandelieret! (4800–04).

83. do begunde er suoze doenen und harphen sô ze prîse in britûnscher wîse, daz maneger dâ stuont unde saz, der sîn selbes namen vergaz. dâ begunden herze und ôren tumben unde tôren und ûz ir rehte wanken (3586–93).

84. die glocken niht (en)klungen sô wol alsam ê (390.3).

85. Ich stuont mir nehtint spâte an einer zinne, dô hôrt ich einen rîter vil wol singen in Kürenberges wîse al ûz der menigîn. er muoz mir diu lant rûmen, alder ich geniete mich sîn (8.1–8).

86. Duo autem, fateor, tibi specialiter inerant quibus feminarum quarumlibet animos statim allicere poteras, dictandi videlicet et cantandi gratia (*Historia calamitatum*, p. 115).

87. Gesungen wurden disiu liet vil (1621.1–2).

88. Diu liet gevielen manigem wol (1794.1).

89. si gelfent sînen sanc tac unde naht in dirre gazzen (4.1.9–10).

90. Nunc ergo, ait, de probitatibus consulis aliquem componite rimulum, quod genti vestre de facili et velut ex natura decurrit. Ego autem, cum opportunum fuerit, impsum hic hospitabor, quo cum pervenerit, dabo vobis locum ut in auribus ejus possitis cantare ea que dictata fuerint (Jean de Marmoutier, *Historia Gaufredi*, p. 195).

91. Exite, inquit, et, deambulatoria turris conscendentes, prominete ad fenestras superius et quod de comite composuistis canticum ne taceatis et ne detis silentium ei; vincite tristitiam, presumite quod optatis, frequentate canticum: forsitan miserebitur vestri (ibid.).

92. Mvlt soleient estre onure E mult preisie e mult ame Cil ki les gestes escriueient E ki les estoires faiseient. Suuent aueient des baruns E des nobles dames beaus duns, Pur mettre lur nuns en estoire, Que tuz tens mais fust de eus memoire (Wace, *Roman de Rou* III, 143–50).

93. duas caligas denegavit scarlatinas (Lambert of Ardres, p. 627).

94. Hic ad augmentum et famam sui nominis, emendicata carmina et rhythmos adulatorios comparabat, et de regno Francorum cantores et joculatores muneribus allexerat, ut de illo canerent in plateis: et jam dicebatur ubique, quod non erat talis in orbe (Roger of Hoveden, *Chronica*, vol. 3, p. 143).

95. carmen inde compsuit lingua Gallica (*De nugis curialium*, p. 213).

96. Inter cetera cantor Germanicus, fugam Suenonis exsiliumque cantilena complexus, varias ei contumelias, formatis in carmen conviciis, obiectabat. Quem ob hoc acrius a convivis increpitum Sueno, dissimulata molestia, fortunas suas liberius recinere iubet, perquam libenter se post aerumnas malorum meminisse confessus (vol. 1, p. 404 f.).

97. von Îsenache Stempfel muoz ob unser beider houbet stân mit sînem swerte breit, und richte über unser einen nâch roubes site (Fürstenlob 8.11–13).

98. Imminente itaque sibi mortis periculo, sub pallium conthoralis predicti lantgravii ob spem patrocinii confugit (*Annales Reinhardsbrunnenses*, p. 110).

99. Lucam quoque de Barra pro derisoriis cantionibus et temerariis nisibus orbari luminibus imperauit (*Historia ecclesiastica*, vol. 6, p. 352).

100. Quin etiam indecentes de me cantilenas facetus coraula composuit, ad iniuriam mei palam cantauit, maliuolosque michi hostes ad cachinnos ita sepe provocavit (ibid., p. 354).

101. Ahî wie kristenlîche nû der bâbest lachet (34.4).

102. ir guot ist allez mîn: ir tiuschez silber vert in mînen welschen schrîn (34.10–11).

103. Nu wie hât sich der guote kneht an im gehandelt âne reht, der dâ

sprach durch sînn hôhen muot daz der bâbest wolt mit tiuschen guot vüllen sîn welhischez schrîn! (11191–95).

104. wan er hât tûsent man betoeret, daz si habent überhoeret gotes und des bâbstes gebot (11223–25).

4. THE PERFORMANCE AND SPREAD OF LITERATURE

1. er nam im manige schouwe an mislîchen buochen: dar an begunde er suochen ob er iht des vunde dâ mite er swaere stunde möhte senfter machen (H. v. Aue, *Armer Heinrich* 6–11).

2. Als der von Tristrande seit, die rihte und die wârheit begunde ich sêre suochen in beider hande buochen walschen und latînen, und begunde mich des pînen, daz ich in sîner rihte dise tihte. sus treib ich manege suoche, unz ich an eime buoche alle sîne jehe gelas (155–65).

3. Welt ir nu hoeren unde dagen, sô wil ich iu ein maere sagen (H. v. Wildonie, *Der nackte Kaiser* 1–2).

4. Welt ir, ich tuon die rede iu kunt ze hoeren durch mîn selbes munt—ez laege iu wol—mit werdekeit. Ich bite iuch alle sîn gemeit, swer hoeren welle vürbaz, der sol ez lâzen âne haz, ez sî wîp oder man. Die ez wellen niht verstân, die bite ich sitzen hin dan; nû hebet sich diu âventiure an (*Die Heidin* 153–62).

5. Ich wil durch kurze wîle, den nîdaeren ze bîle Ein abent maerlîn welzen (5–7).

6. Segnor preudhomme, certes, bien le veés, Pres est de vespre, et je sui moult lassé. Or vous proi tous, . . . Vous revenés demain aprés disner (4976–78.80).

7. et si tenoit Vn romant dont ele lisoit As che ualiers et as pucieles (*Le chevalier aux deux epées* 8951–53).

8. Des küniges tohter von Persîâ diu saz in ir gezelte dâ mit vreuden, als ir sit was. ein schoeniu maget vor ir las an einem buoche ein maere wie Troje zevuort waere (W. v. Grafenberg 2710–15).

9. und vor in beiden saz ein maget, diu vil wol, ist mir gesaget, wälhisch lesen kunde: diu kurzte in die stunde. ouch mohte sî ein lachen vil lîhte an in gemachen: ez dûhte sî guot swaz sî las, wand sî ir beider tohter was (H. v. Aue, *Iwein* 6455–62).

10. maniger hande seitenspil in süezer wîse erklingen, von minnen schône singen, von âventiuren sprechen wol, daz man mit zuht vernemen sol, von minnen und von ritterschaft sprechen (R. v. Ems, *Guter Gerhard* 5982–88).

11. fabelieraere (H. v. d. Türlin, *Krone* 22112).

12. wälsch lâsen si dâ vil (Stricker, *Daniel* 8173).

13. man sagte in schoniu maere von rittern die sich sluogen (ibid. 8190–91).

14. als des danne nimmer was, sô gie dar einer unde las von einem, der hiez Ernest (955–57).

15. hoeren lesen (G. v. Straßburg 230; R. v. Ems, *Alexander* 20656).

16. die arbeit die ich han an ditz buch geleit (36493–94).

17. wan erz durch kurzwîle tet daz er daz buoch getihtet hât (*Tandareis* 4076–77).

18. Wer hât mich guoter ûf getân? sî ez iemen der mich kan beidiu lesen und verstên, der sol genâde an mir begên (*Wigalois* 1–4).

19. Swaz ich in niuwen doenen ie dar von gesanc, daz vindet man hie allez an dem buoche stân (1847.1–3).

20. ist der leser kluoc, hât er an kunste die gefuoc, er lese die houbtbuoch-stabe von êrst wan an daz ende herabe, darmite die verse erhaben sint. er ensî dan genzlîch ein kint, den namen vindet er lîhte, ez saget in daz getihte: diu buochstabe machent wort von êrst biz an des endes ort: sus mag er vinden mînen namen (4453–63).

21. du and alle die da mite, die in geistlichen site lesen vlizeclich diz buch (2725–27).

22. ich bit ouch vlizeclich hie na, swer diz buch im schriben la, daz er vlizic blibe, daz man ez rehte schribe (2753–56).

23. daz mir iemen iht dar abe. Mit pvmz oder mit mezzer. schabe (14–16).

24. daz man ez an die hiute geschriben hât ze diute, daz ez ein ieglîcher man wol vernimet der iht lesen kan (11–14).

25. Leser, ich wil dir sagen mê (821, cf. 791).

26. ditz buch zu boten ich sende an sie die ez horen oder lesen (U. v. Türheim, *Rennewart* 36510–11).

27. diez lesen oder hoeren, und der iz sag odr in dem dône singe (*Jg. Titurel*, Wolf II 6031.4).

28. swer daz buoch lese (Pleier, *Tandareis* 4074).

29. min getihte wirt gesehen Und vil lihte etteswa Gelesen da oder da (R. v. Ems, *Wilhelm v. Orlens* 5646–48).

30. leser dises buoches, vernim (H. v. Freiberg, *Tristan* 2644).

31. diz maere geschriben siht (337.3).

32. Und eins tages fugt es sich das er an ein fenster ging und sah von einem mann ein alt historien malen und off eim yglichen bild ein buchstaben stan. Es ducht yn die hystorye von Eneas syn wie er von Troya geflohen was; und gedacht, er wolt in der kamern maln, darinn er gefangen lag, von der die er so lieb hett und sere begeret zu sehen (vol. 2, p. 476).

33. Da hub er zum ersten an zu maln wie yn die fraw vom Lac in konig Artus hoff gebracht hatt ritter zu werden, und wie er geyn Camalot geritten were, und wie er erschrack von der schonheit syner frauwen der konigin als er sie von erst ane sah, auch wie der von ir urlaub nam als er reyt zur herczoginn von Noans sie zu entretten. Diß macht er alles des ersten tags; und die bild waren so wol und behentlich gemacht als hett er all syn leptag das hantwerck getriben (p. 477).

34. Und als die ostern vergangen waren, da hett er alles gedichtet (p. 478).

35. daz lange liet von Trojâ (7546).

36. wie der herre Ênêas, der vil listige man, über sê vuor (7553–55).

37. . . . was dar an entworfen sus wie Tispê und Pîramus, betwungen von der minne, . . . ein riuwic ende nâmen (7708–10; 12).

38. Du roy Floire et de Blancheflour Y ot la vie, d'une part, Tissue par merveilleux art, toute la vie des amans (516–19).

39. Et furent ou mantel portrait Et les proeces el li fait K'Artus fist dusqu'au ior de lores (*Le chevalier aux deux epées* 12195–97).

40. Ego Otto de Hakenberch et de Rabenspurch Dilecto Consanguineo suo. Alberonj de Chvnring (Pfeiffer, p. 54).

41. Menan ab si son joglar que cantava sos sirventes (Boutière-Schutz, p. 225 f.).

42. menava ab se dos cantadors que cantavon las soas chansons (ibid., p. 191).

43. Swer nu disiu liet singe vor ir (*Kaiser Heinrich* 5.20).

44. Doch klaget ir maniger mînen kumber vil dicke mit gesange (H. v. Morungen 127.18–20).

45. A cel tens sorent tuit harpe bien manïer; Cum plus fu gentilz hom e plus sout del mester (2824–25).

46. ofte unde dicke ergieng ouch daz, sô daz gesinde inein gesaz, er unde Îsôt und Kâedîn, der herzoge und diu herzogîn, frouwen und barûne, sô tihtete er schanzûne, rundate und höfschiu liedelîn (19209–15).

47. Volkêr der snelle mit sîner videlen dan gie gezogenlîche für Gotelinde stân. er videlte süeze doene und sanc ir sîniu liet (1705.1–3).

48. zweinzic singaere, die durch vertrîben swaere von minne lieder sungen (Stricker, *Daniel* 8163–65).

49. maniger hande seitenspil in süezer wîse erklingen, von minnen schônen singen (R. v. Ems, *Guter Gerhard* 5982–84).

50. Baiona, per sirventes Sai be qu'iest vengutz mest nos, Et ab aquest seran tres, Qu'ieu vo n avïa fatz dos, Dont mant aur et mant argent Avetz guazanhat, Baiona! E mant uzat garnimen E d'avol raub' e de bona (Witthoeft, p. 50).

51. der sibende wolde eteswaz Heimen ald hern Witchen sturm, Sigfrides ald hem Eggen tôt. Sô wil der ahtode niht wan hübschen minnesanc (XV 14.269–71).

52. Mit der ûzreise hôchgemuot fuor den sumer manic ritter guot (1352.1– 2).

53. Diu liet gesungen wurden vil. für wâr ich iu daz sagen wil: bî den lieden wart geriten manic tyost nâch ritters siten. diu liet man vil gerne sanc, dâ fiwer ûz tyost von helm spranc: si dûhten manigen ritter guot (1425.1–7).

54. Er hât, vrowe, liet bî mir ouch her gesant, diu gerne ir hoeren sült . . . er bat si, vrowe, mich singen iu (403.1–3.6).

55. ich las ir dîniu niuwen liet (74.2).

56. den brief diu süeze, wol getân las: dâ stuonden diu liet an (165.7–8).

57. Senes breu de parguamina Tramet lo vers, que chantam En plana lengua romana, A·n Hugo Bru per Filhol (Jaufré Rudel 2, V. 1–4).

58. Huguet, mos cortes messatgers, chantaz ma chanso volonters a la rëina dels Normans (Bernart de Ventadorn 33.43–45).

59. Der leich vil guot ze singen was: manic schoeniu vrouwe in gern las (*Frauendienst* 1374.1–2).

60. Diu liet diu wâren meisterlîch und ir rîm gar sinnerîch; dâ von sî gern maniger sanc. diu wîs was für wâr niht lanc: ze tanzen wâren si vil guot . . . si wurden oft getanzet vil (*Frauendienst* 1772.1–5.8).

61. diu liet . . . sint für wâr ze tanzen guot (1395.5.7).

62. Diu wîse wart getanzet vil (1359.1).

63. Disiu liet diu heizent frouwen tanz . . . blîdeclîchen man si tanzen sol (*Lied* 46.1.1.6).

64. waz obe si gêt and disem tanze? frowe, dur iur güte rucket ûf die hüete (75.5–7).

65. Diz ist ein leich von deme heiligen grabe (MF after 99.28).

66. Der tumbe man von Rugge hât gegeben disen wîsen rât (99.21–22).

67. Wâ vund man sament sô manic liet? man vunde ir niet im künicrîche, als in Zürich an buochen stât. des prüeft man dik dâ meistersanc. der Maness ranc dar nâch endlîche: des er diu liederbuoch nu hât. gein sîm hof mechten nigen die singaere, sîn lob hie prüevn und anderswâ: wan sanc hât boun und würzen dâ. und wisse er wâ guot sanc noch waere, er wurb vil endelîch dar nâ (8.1.1–11).

68. Ki k'ait les mos ajostés, Gontiers les mist en escrit, Si sera li briés portés A ma dame á cort respit. Dieus, de boine eure fuit nés, S'ele mon mesage lit (1.51–56).

69. ela sap letras et enten, et agrada·m qu'eu escria los motz, e s'a leis plazia, legis los al meu sauvamen (17.53–56).

70. et apres letras, e saup ben lezer e chantar (Boutière-Schutz, p. 225).

71. e ben escrivia motz e sons (ibid., p. 93).

72. Qu'eu darr' un moi de segle, S'en carta qu'eu te regle Poi scriver' una tal cobla S'un d'aquestz motz non s'i dobla (Witthoeft, p. 66).

73. mit guoter schrift wîse unde wort (Frauendienst 1100.4).

74. ir tavelen sie nam und einen griffel von golde, dar an si scrîben wolde (H. v. Veldeke, Eneit 282.10–12).

75. Stilus nam et tabule sunt feriales epule et Nasonis carmina (Carmina Burana 216.2.1–3).

76. De graphio fracto gravis dolor (no. 154).

77. Aissi comensan li can d'en Guiraut Riquier de Narbona enaissi cum es de cansos et de verse e de pastorellas et de retroenchas e de descortz e d'albas et d'autras diversas obras enaissi adordenadamens cum era adordenat en lo sieu libre, del qual libre escrig per la sua man fon aissi tot translatat (Guiraut Riquier, p. 19).

78. Zweier minner sehtzic doene ich hân gesungen: die stânt gar hier an (1846.1–2).

79. Ahzic niuwer wîse loufent mir nu ledic bî, diech ze hôhem prîse mîner vrouwen lange her ze dienste gesungen hân. ditze ist nû diu leste, die ich mêre singen wil (83.24–29).

80. Ouch muoz ich klagen den von Eist, Den guoten Dietmâren, Und die andern, die dâ wâren Ir sûl und ir brücke: Heinrîch von Rücke, Und von Hûsen Friderîch, Von Guotenburc Uolrîch, Und der reine Hûg von Salzâ (2438–45).

81. ab cels c'amont cantar, vos devez alegrar. Vers novels ni chançcons, qui las diz denan vos, escoltaz volonteira, e plaça vos, a teira voillas . . . saber, se podez retener; e si non podez toz, tenez los meillors moz (Enseignement 525–34).

82. il a fet noter biaus chans por ramenbrance des chançcons (2–3).

83. s'en vieult, l'en i chante et lit (19).

84. granz folie d'esprover ne sa moullier ne s'amie tant com l'en la veut amer (3626–28).

85. por sa dolor reconforter (3882).

86. Quant voi l'aloete moder . . . contre el rai (5212–13).

87. cele ou j'ai mist mon cuer et mon penser q'entre mes bras la tenisse nuete

ainz q'alasse outremer (928–30).

88. er was eht herzen sorgen vrî. nû reit er zuo und gruozte sî mit lachendem munde. nû huop er dâ ze stunde ein vil vroelîchez liet (8154–58).

89. er huob sich höfschlîch nâch mir sâ und sanc ein liet sân an der stunt. dâ mit sô tet er mir daz kunt, daz er mir braehte die botschaft, diu mir gaebe hôhes muotes kraft. Daz liet mir in daz herze klanc, daz dâ der höfsche, kluoge sanc: ez tet mir innerclîchen wol, wan ich dâ von wart freuden vol . . . nu hoert daz liet! daz sprach alsô: Ir sult sprechen willekomen: der iu maere bringet, daz bin ich (775.4–776.4; 776.8 f.).

Glossary

ABSCHNITTSBURG castle constructed as a succession of separate, fortified baileys.

BERGFRIED "keep," "great tower"; in German castles the main and generally highest tower. In peacetime it was usually uninhabited, unlike the Anglo-French *donjon*. In time of siege it would serve as the place of last retreat.

CANSO standard designation for the troubadour love song. By the early thirteenth century, the canso had become a rigidly defined genre. It was a lyric piece accompanied by a melody composed especially for it. Its stanzas, numbering five or six, were of identical structure.

CONTRAFACTUM term used in musicology to describe the substitution of one text for another while retaining the same, or nearly the same, music.

MINISTERIALS (*ministeriales* in Latin, *Dienstmannen* in German). The ministerialage was an institution unique to Germany. Predominantly of servile origin, the ministerials were employed in a number of capacities by their lords: as bailiffs, knights, castellans, and so on. They attained their greatest political importance in the twelfth century under the Hohenstaufen dynasty. Atter 1200 they merged with the surviving minor noble families.

PALAS the main building of a medieval German castle, housing the great hall and the lord's residential apartments.

SACHSENSPIEGEL Code of Saxon Law, written in Low German by Eike von Repgow between 1220 and 1230.

SCHILDMAUERBURG technical term to describe a castle located on the spur of a mountain with a strong curtain wall to protect the exposed slope side.

SCHWABENSPIEGEL name given in the seventeenth century to an anonymous German legal work dating from 1275/76 and originating in Augsburg. It draws on the *Deutschenspiegel*, a lawbook whose principal component is a thirteenth century High German adaptation of the *Sachsenspiegel*, and on additional material from Roman law, canon law, and other sources.

SCHWANK   in medieval literature a short humorous narrative, frequently bawdy in subject matter and tone.

SPIELMANNSEPIK   pre-courtly, anonymous romances whose plot revolves around the so-called *Brautwerbung*, the wooing of a bride. The older view that these works were composed by itinerant minstrels (*Spielmänner*, hence the name *Spielmannsepik*) is no longer accepted. This genre includes: *Herzog Ernst*, *König Rother*, *Ortnit*, *Salman und Morolf*, and *Orendel*.

SPRUCHDICHTUNG   "gnomic" or "didactic poetry." A *Spruch* was a didactic instructional poem of one or several strophes and, like love lyrics, was set to a melody. Dealing with matters of religion, moral conduct, politics, and polemics, its intent was social and instructional. *Spruchdichtung* was designed to teach people, mostly at the courts, how to make the right decisions.

STOLLEN   following the Romance *canso* form, the classical minnesong stanza had three parts: the *Aufgesang* (Latin *frons*) which was subdivided into two metrically identical sections called the *Stollen* (*pes*) and the *Gegenstollen* (*contra pes*), and the metrically different *Abgesang* (*cauda*).

TORNADA   at the end of an Old Provençal lyric there may be one or more tornadas, or half-strophes. The tornada serves as an epilogue, a poet's signature, a dedication to a day, patron, or friend, or as instructions to a jongleur.

WAPPENSPRECHER   professional poets specializing in the writing of descriptive heraldic poems.

Abbreviations

ABäG	Amsterdamer Beiträge zur älteren Germanistik
ABl.	Altdeutsche Blätter
AC	L'année canonique
ADAW	Abhandlungen der Deutschen Akademie der Wissenschaften zu Berlin. Klasse für Sprachen, Literatur und Kunst
AESC	Annales. Economies, sociétés, civilisations
AfD	Archiv für Diplomatik
AfdA	Anzeiger für deutsches Altertum
AGG	Archiv der Gesellschaft für ältere deutsche Geschichtskunde
AHR	The American Historical Review
AKG	Archiv für Kulturgeschichte
Al.	Alemannia
AM	Acta musicologica
AMw.	Archiv für Musikwissenschaft
AQ	Ausgewählte Quellen zur deutschen Geschichte des Mittelalters. Freiherr vom Stein-Gedächtnisausgabe
Arch.	Archiv für das Studium der neueren Sprachen und Literaturen
AUF	Archiv für Urkundenforschung
BDLG	Blätter für deutsche Landesgeschichte
BEC	Bibliothèque de l'Ecole des chartes
BMGN	Bijdragen en mededelingen betreffende de geschiedenis der Niederlanden
BON	Blätter für oberdeutsche Namenforschung
BPC	Bibliotheca patrum Cisterciensium
BPH	Bulletin philologique et historique

BRG	Bibliotheca rerum Germanicarum
BuS	Burgen und Schlösser
BzN	Beiträge zur Namenforschung
Ca.	Carinthia I
CC	Corpus Christianorum. Seria Latina
CC CM	Corpus Christianorum. Continuatio mediaevalis
CCM	Cahiers de civilisation médiévale
CIC	Corpus iuris canonici
CJ	The Classical Journal
CN	Cultura neolatina
Co.	Concilium. Internationale Zeitschrift für Theologie
CSEL	Corpus scriptorum ecclesiasticorum Latinorum
DA	Deutsches Archiv für Erforschung des Mittelalters
DALV	Deutsches Archiv für Landes- und Volksforschung
DU	Der Deutschunterricht
Eg.	Etudes germaniques
EHR	The English Historical Review
Eu.	Euphorion
FMLS	Forum for Modern Language Studies
FmS	Frühmittelalterliche Studien
Fr.	Francia
FS	French Studies
FuF	Forschungen und Fortschritte
GDV	Geschichtsschreiber der deutschen Vorzeit
Gf.	Der Geschichtsfreund. Mittheilungen des historischen Vereins der fünf Orte Lucern, Uri, Schwyz, Unterwalden und Zug
GGN	Nachrichten von der kgl. Gesellschaft der Wissenschaften zu Göttingen. Phil.-hist. Klasse
GLL	German Life and Letters
Gm.	Germania
GRM	Germanisch-Romanische Monatsschrift
HGb.	Hansische Geschichtsblätter
HJb.	Historisches Jahrbuch
HJL	Hessisches Jahrbuch für Landesgeschichte
HTb.	Historisches Taschenbuch
HZ	Historische Zeitschrift
IASL	Internationales Archiv für Sozialgeschichte der Literatur
JAMS	Journal of the American Musicological Society
JARG	Jahrbuch der Arbeitsgemeinschaft der Rheinischen Geschichtsvereine
JEGP	Journal of English and Germanic Philology
JfLF	Jahrbuch für fränkische Landesforschung
JGF	Jahrbuch für Geschichte des Feudalismus
JGoR	Jahrbuch für Geschichte der oberdeutschen Reichsstädte

JMH		Journal of Medieval History
JOWG		Jahrbuch der Oswald von Wolkenstein-Gesellschaft
Lili.		Zeitschrift für Literaturwissenschaft und Linguistik
LV		Landeskundliche Vierteljahrsblätter
Ly.		The Library
MA		Le moyen âge
MB		Monumenta Boica
MD		Musica disciplina
MDAI		Mitteilungen des Deutschen Archäologischen Instituts. Römische Abteilung
Me.		Merkur
MGES		Mitteilungen der deutschen Gesellschaft zur Erforschung Vaterländischer Sprache und Alterthümer
MGH		Monumenta Germaniae historica
	MGH Const.	Constitutiones et acta publica
	MGH Dipl.	Diplomata
	MGH Ep. BdK	Epistolae. Die Briefe der deutschen Kaiserzeit
	MGH SS	Scriptores
	MGH SS rer. Germ.	Scriptores rerum Germanicarum
MH		Mediaevalia et Humanistica, N. S.
MINF		Mémoires de l'Institut national de France. Académie des inscriptions et belles-lettres
MIÖG		Mitteilungen des Instituts für österreichische Geschichtskunde
MlJ		Mittellateinisches Jahrbuch
MLN		Modern Language Notes
Mo.		Monatshefte
MS		Monumenti storici
MSB		Sitzungsberichte der Bayerischen Akademie der Wissenschaften. Phil.-hist. Klasse
MSNH		Mémoires de la Sociéte néophilologique de Helsinki
MSt.		Medieval Studies
NA		Neues Archiv der Gesellschaft für ältere deutsche Geschichtskunde
NAV		Nuovo Archivo Veneto
Ne.		Neophilologus
NHJ		Neue Heidelberger Jahrbücher
NphM		Neuphilologische Mitteilungen
NZM		Neue Zeitschrift für Musik
ÖAW An.		Österreichische Akademie der Wissenschaften. Phil.-hist. Klasse. Anzeiger
OGS		Oxford German Studies
PBA		Proceedings of the British Academy
PBB		Beiträge zur Geschichte der deutschen Sprache und Literatur
PG		Patrologia Graeca
Ph.		Philobiblon

Pi.	Philologus
PJb.	Preußische Jahrbücher
PL	Patrologia Latina
PMLA	Publications of the Modern Language Association
PS	Der praktische Schulmann
QFIA	Quellen und Forschungen aus italienischen Archiven und Bibliotheken
RBM	Revue belge de musicologie
RBPH	Revue belge de philologie et d'histoire
RDC	Revue de droit canonique
RF	Romanische Forschungen
Rh.	Revue historique
RHC Occ.	Recueil des historiens des croisades. Historiens occidentaux
RHE	Revue d'histoire ecclésiastique
RHGF	Recueil des historiens des Gaules et de la France. Nouvelle édition
RIS	Rerum Italicarum scriptores
RJb.	Romanistisches Jahrbuch
RLR	Revue des langues romanes
RM	Revue de musicologie
Ro.	Romania
RR	Romanic Review
RS	Rolls Series. Rerum Britannicarum medii aevi scriptores
RSt.	Romanische Studien
RUB	Revue de l'Université de Bruxelles
RVjb.	Rheinische Vierteljahrsblätter
Sc.	Saeculum
SG	Studia Gratiana
SHF	Société de l'histoire de France
Si.	Signs. Journal of Women in Culture and Society
SiP	Studies in Philology
SM	Studi medievali
SMRH	Studies in Medieval and Renaissance History
Sp.	Speculum
SRA	Scriptores rerum Austriacarum
SRGS	Scriptores rerum Germanicarum praecipue Saxonicarum
TQ	Theologische Quartalschrift
Tr.	Traditio
TvR	Tijdschrift voor Rechtsgeschiedenis
UB	Urkundenbuch
Un.	Universitas
VfL	Vierteljahrsschrift für Literaturgeschichte
VHVO	Verhandlungen des Historischen Vereins für Oberpfalz und Regensburg

Vi.	Vivarium
Vr.	Viator. Medieval and Renaissance Studies
VSWG	Vierteljahrschrift für Sozial- und Wirtschaftsgeschichte
WS	Wolfram-Studien
WSB	Sitzungsberichte der kais. Akademie der Wissenschaften in Wien. Phil.-hist. Klasse
WZUG	Wissenschaftliche Zeitschrift der Ernst-Moritz-Arndt-Universität Greifswald. Gesellschafts- und sprachwissenschaftliche Reihe
WZUR	Wissenschaftliche Zeitschrift der Universität Rostock. Gesellschafts- und sprachwissenschaftliche Reihe
ZfbLG	Zeitschrift für bayerische Landesgeschichte
ZfdA	Zeitschrift für deutsches Altertum
ZfdB	Zeitschrift für deutsche Bildung
ZfdK	Zeitschrift für deutsche Kulturgeschichte
ZfdPh.	Zeitschrift für deutsche Philologie
ZfdSp.	Zeitschrift für deutsche Sprache
ZfdW	Zeitschrift für deutsche Wortforschung
ZffSL	Zeitschrift für französische Sprache und Literatur
ZfgSW	Zeitschrift für die gesamte Staatswissenschaft
ZfhF	Zeitschrift für historische Forschung
ZfhwF	Zeitschrift für handelswissenschaftliche Forschungen, N.F.
ZfhWK	Zeitschrift für historische Waffen- und Kostümkunde
ZfkT	Zeitschrift für katholische Theologie
ZfPG	Zeitschrift für preußische Geschichte und Landeskunde
ZfrPh.	Zeitschrift für romanische Philologie
ZfSG	Zeitschrift für Schweizerische Geschichte
ZfsT	Zeitschrift für systematische Theologie
ZFTV	Zeitschrift des Ferdinandeums für Tirol und Vorarlberg, Folge 3
ZGO	Zeitschrift für die Geschichte des Oberrheins
ZhVS	Zeitschrift des historischen Vereins für Steiermark
ZKG	Zeitschrift für Kirchengeschichte
ZRG GA	Zeitschrift der Savigny-Stiftung für Rechtsgeschichte. Germanistische Abteilung
ZRG KA	Zeitschrift der Savigny-Stiftung für Rechtsgeschichte. Kanonistische Abteilung
ZTZ	Zeitschrift für Tierzüchtung und Züchtungsbiologie

Bibliography

LATIN SOURCES

Abelard. *Historia calamitatum.* Edited by J. Monfrin. 4th edition, 1978.

Acerbus Morena. *Historia.* Edited by F. Güterbock. In: *Das Geschichtswerk des Otto Morena.* MGH SS rer. Germ N.S. 7: 130–76. 1930.

Adalbero of Laon. *Carmen ad Rotbertum regem.* Edited by C. Carozzi. 1979.

Adam of Bremen. *Gesta Hammaburgensis ecclesiae pontificum.* Edited and with German translation by B. Schmeidler and W. Trillmich. AQ 11: 135–499. 1961.

Ademar of Chabannes. *Chronicon.* Edited by J. Chavanon. 1897.

Aelred of Rievaulx. *De speculo charitatis.* Edited by C. H. Talbot. Opera Omnia, vol. 1, CC CM 1: 3–161. 1971.

Alberic of Troisfontaines. *Chronica.* Edited by P. Scheffer-Boichorst. MGH SS 23: 631–950. 1874.

Albert of Metz. *De diversitate temporum.* Edited by G. H. Pertz. MGH SS 4: 700–23. 1841.

Albert of Stade. *Chronica.* Edited by J. M. Lappenberg. MGH SS 16: 282–378. 1859.

Albertus Magnus. *De animalibus libri XXVI.* Edited by H. Stadler. 1920.

———. *Enarrationes in primam partem evangelii Lucae.* Edited by S. A. Borgnet. Opera Omnia, vol. 22, 1894.

Ambrose. *De abrahame libri duo.* Migne PL 14: cols. 437–524. 1882.

Andreas Capellanus. *De amore libri tres.* Edited by E. Trojel. Third edition, 1972.

Annales Admuntenses, Continuatio Garstensis, see Continuatio Garstensis.

Annales Aquenses. Edited by G. Waitz. MGH SS 24: 34–39. 1879.

Annales Blandinienses. Edited by L. Bethmann. MGH SS 5: 20–34. 1844.

Annales Colmarienses Maiores. Edited by P. Jaffé. MGH SS 17: 202–32. 1861.

Annales s. Georgii. Edited by G. H. Pertz. MGH SS 17: 295–97. 1861.

Annales Magdeburgenses. Edited by G. H. Pertz. MGH SS 16: 105–96. 1859.

Annales Marbacenses. Edited by H. Bloch. MGH SS rer. Germ 9. 1907.

Annales Otokariani. Edited by R. Köpke. MGH SS 9: 181–94. 1851.

Annales Pegavienses. Edited by G. H. Pertz. MGH SS 16: 234–70. 1859.

Annales Pragenses III. Edited by R. Köpke. MGH SS 9: 198–209. 1851.

Annales Quedlinburgenses. Edited by G. H. Pertz. MGH SS 3: 22–90. 1839.

Annales Ratisponenses. See Hugo of Lerchenfeld.

Annales Reineri. See Reiner of St. Jacob.

Annales Reinhards-Brunnenses. Edited by F. X. Wegele. 1854.

Annales Spirenses. Edited by G. H. Petz. MGH 17: 80–85. 1861.

Annales Stadenses. See Albert of Stade.

Annales Stederburgenses. See Gerhard of Stederburg.

Annales Vetero-Cellenses. Edited by J. O. Opel. 1874.

Annales Vincentii. See Vincent of Prague.

Annales Weissenburgenses. Edited by O. Holder-Egger. MGH SS rer. Germ. 38: 9–57. 1894.

Annales Welfici Weingartenses. Edited with German translation by E. König. In: *Historia Welforum* 86–95. 1938.

Annales de Wigornia. Edited by H. R. Luard. In: Annales Monastici, vol. 4. RS 36,4: 355–564. 1869.

Annalista Saxo. Edited by G. Waitz. MGH SS 6: 542–777. 1844.

Anonymous Haserensis. Edited by L. Bethmann. MGH SS 7: 253–67. 1846.

Ansbert. See *Historia de expeditione Friderici.*

Anselmus. *Vita Adalberti.* Edited by P. Jaffé. BRG 3: 568–603. 1866.

Arnold of Lübeck. *Chronica.* Edited by J. M. Lappenberg. MHG SS 21: 100–250. 1869.

Astronomus. *Vita Hludovici imperatoris.* Edited with German translation by R. Rau. AQ 5: 255–381. 1968.

Augustine. *De bono coniugali.* Migne PL 40: cols. 373–96. 1887.

———. *De civitate Dei.* Edited by B. Dombart and A. Kalb. Vols. 1–2, Opera 14. CC 47–48. 1955.

———. *Enarrationes in Psalmos I-L.* Edited by E. Dekkers and J. Fraipont. CC 38. 1956.

———. *Quaestiones in Heptateuchum.* Edited by J. Fraipont. CC 33,5: 1–377. 1958.

Balderic. *Gesta Alberonis archiepiscopi Treverensis.* Edited by G. Waitz, German translation by H. Kallfelz. AQ 22: 543–617. 1973.

Balderic of Dol. *Historia de peregrinatione Jerosolimitana.* RHC Occ. 4: 1–111. 1871.

Bartholomaeus Anglicus. *De proprietatibus rerum.* Edited by G. B. Pontanus. 1601.

Bateson, M. "A London Municipal Collection of the Reign of John." *EHR* 17: 480–511. 1902.

Baudri of Bourgeuil. *Les ouevres poétiques.* Edited by P. Abrahams. 1926.

Benedict of Peterborough. *Gesta regis Henrici secundi.* Edited by W. Stubbs. 2 vols. RS 49. 1867.

Bernhard of Clairvaux. *Epistolae*: 181–547. Edited by J. Leclercq and H. M. Rochais. Opera 8. 1977.

———. *Liber ad milites Templi de laude novae militae*. Edited by J. Leclercq and H. M. Rochais. Opera 3: 205–39. 1963.

Berthold of Zwiefalten. *Chronicon*. Edited with German translation by L. Wallach, E. König, and K. O. Müller. In: *Die Zwiefalter Chroniken Ortliebs und Bertholds*: 136–287. 2nd. ed. 1978.

Biblia Sacra Juxta Vulgatae. Edited by A. C. Fillion. 1887.

Böhmer, J. B. *Regestae imperii* IV,3: Die Regesten des Kaiserreiches unter Heinrich VI. Edited by G. Baaken. 1972; *Regesta imperii* V. Newly edited by J. Ficker and E. Winkelmann. Part 2. 1892–94.

Bonizo of Sutri. *Liber de vita Christiana*. Edited by E. Perels. 1930.

Bourquelot, F. *Etudes sur les foires de Champagne*. Vol. 1. 1865.

Breve Chronicon Austriae Mellicense. Edited by W. Wattenbach. MGH SS 24: 69–71. 1879.

Brundage, J. A. "Prostitution in Medieval Canon Law." *Si* 1: 825–45. 1976.

Bruno. *Saxonicum bellum*. Edited with German translation by E. Lohmann and F.-J. Schmale. AQ 12: 191–405. 1963.

Bullock-Davies, C. *Menestrellorum multitudo, Minstrels at a Royal Feast*. 1978.

Burchard of Ursberg. *Chronicon*. Edited by O. Holder-Egger and B. von Simson. MGH SS rer. Germ. 16. 1916.

Caesarius of Heisterbach. *Dialogus miraculorum*. Edited by J. Strange. 1851.

———. *Vita Engelberti*. Edited by F. Zschaeck. In: *Die Wundergeschichten des Caesarius von Heisterbach*. Edited by A. Hilka. Vol. 3: 223–328. 1937.

———. *Vita sanctae Elyzabeth lantgravie*. Edited by A. Huyskens. Ibid. 344–88.

Carmen de gestis Frederici imperatoris in Lombardia. Edited by I. Schmale-Ott. MGH SS rer. Germ. 62. 1965.

Carmina Burana. Edited by A. Hilka, O. Schumann, and B. Bischoff. Vols. 1–3. 1930–1970.

Cartellieri, A. *Philipp II. August*. Vol. 2. 1906.

Caspar, E. "Die Kreuzzugsbullen Eugens III." *NA* 45: 285–305. 1924.

Christina of Markyate. See *De s. Theodora virgine*.

Chronica de gestis consulum Andegavorum. Edited by L. Halphen and R. Poupardin. In: *Chroniques des comtes d'Anjou*: 25–73. 1913.

Chronica s. Petri Erfordensis Moderna. Edited by O. Holder-Egger. MGH SS rer. Germ. 42: 117–364. 1899.

Chronica Polonorum. Edited by G. Waitz. MGH SS rer. Germ. 18. 1880.

Chronica regia Coloniensis. Edited by G. Waitz. MGH SS rer. Germ. 18. 1880.

Chronica Reinhardsbrunnensis. Edited by O. Holder-Egger. MGH SS 30.1: 490–656. 1896.

Chronicon Andegavense Breve. RHGF 11: 169–70. 1876.

Chronicon Colmariense. Edited by P. Jaffé. MGH SS 17: 240–70. 1861.

Chronicon Ebersheimense. Edited by L. Weiland. MGH SS 23: 427–53. 1874.

Chronicon Eberspergense. Edited by W. Arndt. MGH SS 20: 9–16. 1868.

Chronicon Gozecense. Edited by R. Köpke. MGH SS 10: 140–57. 1852.

Chronicon Montis Sereni. Edited by E. Ehrenfeuchter. MGH SS 23: 130–226.
   1874.
Chronicon Terrae Misnensis. Edited by J. B. Mencken. SRGS 2: cols. 313–76.
   1728.
Cicero. *De officiis.* Edited by C. Atzert. Scripta 48. 4th ed. 1963.
Cipolla, C. "Discorso." *NAV* 10: 405–504. 1895.
Classen, P. "Zur Geschichte der Frühscholastik in Österreich und Bayern."
   MIÖG 67: 249–77. 1959.
Codex Epistolaris Wibaldi. See Wibald of Stablo.
Codex Falkensteinensis. Edited by E. Noichl. 1978.
Codex Udalrici. Edited by P. Jaffé. BRG 5: 1–469. 1869.
Conrad, H. "Gottesfrieden und Heeresverfassung in der Zeit der Kreuzzüge."
   ZRG GA 61: 71–126. 1941.
Conrad of Megenberg. *Ökonomik.* Edited by S. Krüger. Vols. 1–2. 1973–77.
Conrad of Mure. *Summa de arte prosandi.* Edited by W. Kronbichler. 1968.
Continuatio Admuntensis. Edited by W. Wattenbach. MGH SS 9: 579–93.
   1851.
Continuatio Claustroneoburgensis I. Ibid.: 607–13.
Continuatio Claustroneoburgensis III. Ibid.: 629–37.
Continuatio Cremifanensis. Ibid.: 544–49.
Continuatio Garstensis. Ibid.: 593–600.
Continuatio Lambacensis. Ibid.: 556–61.
Continuatio Mellicensis. Ibid.: 501–35.
Continuatio Sancrucensis I. Ibid.: 626–28.
Continuatio Sancrucensis II. Ibid.: 637–46.
Continuatio Scotorum. Ibid.; 624–26.
Continuatio Zwetlensis II. Ibid.: 541–44.
Corpus der altdeutschen Originalurkunden bis zum Jahr 1300. Vol 1. Edited by
   F. Wilhelm. 1932.
Cyprianus. See Pseudo-Cyprianus.
De rebus Alsaticis ineuntis saeculi XIII. Edited by P. Jaffé. MGH SS 17: 232–
   37. 1861.
De s. Theodora virgine quae et Christina dicitur. Edited by C. H. Talbot. 1959.
Delisle, L. *Littérature latine et histoire du moyen âge.* 1890.
Denifle, H. and E. Chatelain, eds. *Chartularium universitatis Parisiensis.* Vol. 1.
   1899.
Descriptio Theutoniae. Edited by P. Jaffé. MGH SS 17: 238–40.1861.
Dobenecker, O., ed. *Regesta diplomatica necnon epistolaria historiae Thuring-
   iae.* Vol. 2. 1900.
Ebbo. *Vita Burchardi episcopi Wormatiensis.* Edited by G. Waitz. MGH SS 4:
   829–46. 1841.
Ekbert of Schönach. See Roth.
Ekkehard IV. *Casus sancti Galli.* Edited with German translation by H. F.
   Haefele. AQ 10. 1980.
Ekkehard of Aura. *Chronica.* Edited with German translation by F.-J. Schmale
   and I. Schmale-Ott. AQ 15: 267–377. 1972.
Elze, R. "Königskrönung und Ritterweihe." In: *Institutionen, Kultur und
   Gesellschaft m Mittelalter. Festschrift für J. Fleckenstein*: 327–42. 1984.

Erdmann, C. and N. Fickermann, eds. *Briefsammlungen der Zeit Heinrichs IV*. MGH Ep. BdK 5. 1950.

Erfurter Chronik. See *Chronica s. Petri Erfordensis.*

Ermoldus Nigellus. *In honorem Hludowici christianissimi Caesaris Augusti.* Edited by E. Faral. 2nd ed. 1964.

Eudes of Saint-Maur. *Vita Burcardi.* Edited by C. Bourel de la Roncières. 1892.

Fleckenstein, J. "Zum Problem der Abschließung des Ritterstandes." In: *Historische Forschungen für W. Schlesinger:* 252–71. 1974.

Flores Historiarum. Edited by H. R. Luard. Vols. 1–3. RS 95. 1890.

Flori, J. "Chevalerie et liturgie." *MA* 84: 247–78, 409–42. 1978.

Franz, G., ed. *Quellen zur Geschichte des deutschen Bauernstandes im Mittelalter.* AQ 31. 1967.

Fryde, N. "Deutsche Englandkaufleute in frühhansischer Zeit." *HGB* 97: 1–14. 1979.

Fulcher of Chartres. *Historia Hierosolymitana.* Edited by H. Hagenmeyer. 1913.

Fulk IV of Anjou. *Fragmetnum historiae Andegavensium.* Edited by L. Halphen and R. Poupardin. In: *Chroniques des comtes d'Anjou:* 232–38. 1913

Galbert of Brugges. *Passio Karoli comitis.* Edited by R. Köpke. MGH SS 12: 561–619. 1856.

Gandolf of Bologna. *Sententiae.* Edited by J. de Walter. 1924.

Geoffrey of Monmouth. *Historia regum Britanniae.* Edited by A. Griscom. 1929.

Gerhard of Stederburg. *Annales.* MGH SS 16: 119–231. 1859.

Gerhoh of Reichersberg. *Expositio Psalmorum.* Edited by D. and O. van den Eynde and A. Rijmersdael. *Opera inedita,* vol. 21.1. 1956.

Gerlach of Mühlhausen. *Annales.* Edited by W. Wattenbach. MGH SS 17: 683–710. 1861.

Gervasius of Canterbury. *Chronica.* Edited by W. Stubbs. Vol. 1. RS 73,1. 1879.

Gesta abbatum s. Bertini Sithiensium. See Simon.

Gesta abbatum Trudonensium. Edited by R. Köpke. MGH SS 10: 213–448. 1852.

Gesta Alberonis. See Balderic.

Gesta Ambaziensium dominorum. Edited by L. Halphen and R. Poupardin. In: *Chroniques des comtes d'Anjou:* 74–132. 1913.

Gesta consulum Andegavorum, additamenta. Ibid.: 135–71.

Gesta episcoporum Cameracensium, continuatio. Edited by L. Bethmann. MGH SS 7: 489–500. 1846.

Gesta episcoporum Halberstadensium. Edited by L. Weiland. MGH SS 23: 73–123. 1874.

Giesebrecht, W. *Geschichte der deutschen Kaiserzeit.* Vol. 2, 5th ed. 1885.

Giraldus Cambrensis. *De principis instructione.* Edited by G. F. Warner. Opera 8. RS 21,8. 1891.

Gislebert of Mons. *Chronicon Hanoniense.* Edited by L. Vanderkindere. 1904.

Gottfried of Viterbo. *Dinumeratio regnorum imperio subjectorum.* Edited by L. Delisle (see under Delisle).

———. *Memoria saeculorum.* Edited by G. Waitz. MGH SS 22: 94–106. 1872.

————. *Speculum regum*. Ibid.: 21–93.

Grabmann, M. *Die Geschichte der scholastischen Methode*. Vol. 2. 1911.

Gratianus. *Decretum*. Edited by F. Freidberg. CIC 1. 1879.

Gregory the Great. *Epistolae*. Migne PL 77: cols. 431–1328. 1896.

————. *Liber sacramentorum*. Migne PL 78: 25–240. 1895.

Grimm, J., ed. *Weisthümer*. Vol. 3. 1842.

Guibert de Nogent. *De vita sua*. Migne PL 156: cols. 837–962. 1880.

————. *Historia quae dicitur Gesta Dei per Francos*. Edited by C. Thurot. RHC Occ. 4. 1879.

Guillaume le Breton. *Gesta Philippi Augusti*. Edited by H. F. Delaborde. In: *Oevres de Rogord et de Guillaume le Breton*. Vol. 1. SHF 69,1: 168–320. 1882.

————. *Philippis*. Ibid., vol. 2. SHF 69,2. 1885.

Gunther of Pairis. *Ligurinus*. Migne PL 212: cols. 255–476. 1855.

Hefele, C.-J. and H. Leclercq, eds. *Histoire des conciles d'après les documents originaux*. Vols. 1–8. 1907–21.

Heger, H. *Das Lebenszeugnis Walthers von der Vogelweide*. 1970.

Henry of Albano. *Epistolae*. Migne PL 204: cols. 215–52. 1855.

Heliand of Froidmont. *Chronicon*. Migne PL 212: cols. 717–1082. 1855.

————. *De bono regimine principis*. Ibid.: cols. 735–46.

————. *Sermones*. Edited by B. Tissier. BPC 7: 205–306. 1669.

Helmod of Bosau. *Chronica Slavorum*. Edited with German translation by B. Schmeidler and H. Stoob. AQ 19. 1973.

Heloise. See Abelard.

Herbord. *Dialogus de vita Ottonis episcopi Babenbergensis*. Edited by R. Köpke. MGH SS rer. Germ. 33. 1868.

Hermann of Reichenau. *De octo vitiis principalibus*. Edited by E. Dümmler. ZfdA 13: 385–434. 1867.

Hermann of Tournai. *Liber de restuaratione s. Martini Tornacensis*. Edited by G. Waitz. MGH SS 14: 274–327. 1883.

Heuberger, R. "Das Urkunden- und Kanzleiwesen der Grafen von Tirol." *MIÖG* suppl. vol. 9: 51–177. 265–394. 1915.

Hieronymus. *Adversus Jovinianum*. Migne PL 23: cols. 221–354. 1883.

————. *Epistolae*. Edited by I. Hilberg. Vol. 3. CSEL 56. 1918.

Hildebert of Lavardin. *Quam novica sint sacris hominibus femina, avaritia, ambitio*. Migne PL 171: cols. 1428–30. 1893.

————. *Vita s. Hugonis*. Migne PL 159: cols. 857–94. 1903.

Historia de expeditione Friderici imperatoris. Edited by A. Chroust. MGH SS rer. Germ. N.S. 5: 1–115. 1928.

Historia Peregrinorum. Ibid.: 116–72.

Historia Welforum. Edited with German translation by E. König. 1938.

Horace. *Ars poetica*. Edited by F. Klingner. Carmina: 229–41. 1940.

Hotz, W. *Pfalzen und Burgen der Stauferzeit*. 1981.

Hugo of Lerchenfeld. *Annales Ratisponenses, continuatio*. Edited by W. Wattenbach. MGH SS 17: 579–90. 1861.

Hugh of St. Victor. *Commentaria in hierarchiam coelestem s. Dionysii Aeropagitae*. Migne PL 175: cols. 929–1154. 1879.

————. *Epistolae de virginitate beatae Mariae.* Migne PL 176: cols. 857–76. 1880.

————. *Institutiones in Decalogum legis dominicae.* Ibid.: cols. 9–18.

————. *Miscellanea.* Migne PL 177: cols. 469–900. 1879.

Innocent III. *Epistolae.* Vol. 3. Migne PL 216. 1891.

Jacques de Vitry. *Historia occidentalis.* Edited by H. Rashdall (see Rashdall). Vol. 3: 439–40.

————. *Sermo ad virgines.* Edited by J. Greven: "Der Ursprung des Beginenwesens." *HJb.* 35: 43–49. 1914.

————. *Sermones vulgares.* Edited by J. B. Pitra. In: *Analecta novissima spicilegii solesmensis.* Vol. 2: 344–442. 1888.

————. *Vita b. Mariae Oigniacensis.* In: Acta Sanctorum Junii IV: 636–66. 1707.

Jean de Marmoutier. *Historia Gaufredii ducis Normannorum et comitis Andegavorum.* Edited by L. Halphen and R. Poupardin. In: *Chroniques des comtes d'Anjou*: 172–231, 1913.

Johannes Cinnamus. *Historiae.* Migne PG 133: 299–708. 1864.

John of Salisbury. *Metalogicus.* Edited by C. J. Webb. 1929.

————. *Policraticus.* Edited by C. J. Webb. Vols. 1–2. 1909.

Johannes of Victring. *Liber certarum historiarum.* Edited by F. Schneider. MGH SS rer. Germ. 36, vol. 1–2. 1909–10.

Jordan, K., ed. *Die Urkunden Heinrichs des Löwen.* MGH Dipl. Laienfürsten 1. 1949.

Justinus. *Lipiflorium.* Edited with German translation by H. Althof. 1900.

Juvenal. *Satirae.* Edited by U. Knoche. 1950.

Anonyme Kaiserchronik. Edited by J. Schmale and I. Schmale-Ott. AQ 15: 211–65. 1972.

Kries, F. W. von. *Textkritische Studien zum Welschen Gast Thomasins von Zerclaere.* 1967.

Kühnel, J., ed. *Dû bist mîn, ih bin dîn. Die lateinischen Liebes- (und Freundschafts-) Briefe des clm 19411.* 1977.

Lambert of Ardres. *Historia comitum Ghisnensium.* Edited by J. Heller. MGH SS 24: 550–642. 1879.

Lambert of Arras. *Epistolae et aliorum ad ipsum.* Migne PL 162: cols. 647–702. 1889.

Lampert of Hersfeld. *Annales.* Edited by O. Holder-Egger and W. D. Fritz, German translation by A. Schmidt. AQ 13. 1962.

Laufner, R. "Der älteste Koblenzer Zolltarif." *LV* 10: 101–7. 1964.

Lecoy de la Marche, A., ed. *Anecdotes historiques, légendes et aplogues tirés du recueil inédit d'Etienne de Bourbon.* 1877.

Libellus de dictis quatuor ancillarum. Edited by A. Huyskens. In: *Quellenstudien zur Geschichte der hl. Elisabeth*: 112–40. 1908.

Das Liebeskonzil zu Remiremont. Edited by C. Oulmont. In: *Les débats du clerc et du chevalier*: 93–100. 1911.

Liebhart of Prüfening. *Horreum formice.* Edited by M. Grabmann (see under Grabmann). Vol. 2: 486–87, note 1.

Lippiflorium. See Justinus.

Liutprand of Cremona. *Antapodosis.* Edited by J. Bekker, German translation by A. Bauer and R. Rau. AQ 8: 524–89. 1971.

Ludolf of Hildesheim. *Summa dictaminum.* Edited by L. Rockinger (see under Rockinger). Vol. 1: 439–534. 1861.

Magnus of Reichersberg. *Annales.* Edited by W. Wattenbach. MGH SS 17: 439–534. 1861.

Mansi, J. D., ed. *Sacrorum conciliorum nova, et amplissima collectio.* Vol. 21, 1776; vol. 24, 1780; vol. 25, 1782.

Marbod of Rennes. *Carmina varia.* Migne PL 171: cols. 1647–86. 1893.

———. *Liber decem capitulorum.* Ibid.: cols. 1693–1716.

Matheolus. *Liber lamentationeum.* Edited by A. G. van Hamel. Vols. 1–2. 1892–1905.

Mathias of Neuenburg. *Chronica.* Edited by A. Hofmeister. MGH SS rer. Germ. N.S. 4. 1924.

Matthew of Paris. *Chronica majora.* Edited by H. R. Luard. Vols. 1–7. RS 57. 1872–83.

———. *Historia Anglorum.* Edited by F. Madden. Vols. 1–3. RS 14. 1866–69.

Mayr-Adlwang, M. "Regesten zur tirolischen Kunstgeschichte." *ZFTV* Series 3, vol. 42: 117–203. 1898.

Ministeria curie Hanoniensis. Edited by L. Vanderkindere. In: *Gislebert of Mons*: 333–43.

Monumenta Boica. Vol. 13, 1777; vol. 28,1, 1829.

MGH Const.: *Constitutiones et acta publica imperatorum et regum.* 2 vols. Edited by L. Weiland. 1893–1896.

MGH Dipl. F I: Die Urkunden Friederichs I. Vol. 2. Edited by H. Appelt. 1979.

MGH Dipl. K III: Die Urkunden Konrads III. Edited by F Hausmann. 1969.

MGH Dipl. O II: Die Urkunden Ottos II. Vol. 1. Edited by T. Sickel. 1888.

MGH Leges. Vol. 2. Edited by G. H. Pertz. 1837.

Monumenta Understorfensia. MB 14: 111–70. 1784.

Moralium dogma philosophorum. Edited by J. Holmberg. 1929.

Mythographus Vaticanus III. Edited by G. H. Bode. In: Scriptores rerum mythicarum Latini tres Romae nuper reperti. Vol. 1: cols. 152–256. 1834.

Narratio de electione Lotharii regis. Edited by W. Wattenbach. MGH SS 12: 509–12. 1856.

Nicolas Treveth. *Annales.* Edited by T. Hog. 1845.

Nithard. *Historiae.* Edited by E. Müller, German translation by R. Rau. AQ 5: 385–461. 1968.

Norbert. *Vita Bennonis II episcopi Osnabrugensis.* Edited by H. Bresslau, German translation by H. Kallfelz. AQ 22: 372–441. 1973.

Odo of Cluny. *Vita s. Geraldi Auriliacensis comitis.* Migne PL 133: cols. 639–710. 1851.

Ordericus Vitalis. *Historia ecclesiastica.* Edited and transl. by M. Chibnall. Vols. 1–6. 1969–80.

Ortlieb of Zwiefalten. *Chronicon.* Edited with German translation by L. Wallach, E. König and K. O. Müller. In: *Die Zwiefalter Chroniken Ortliebs und Bertholds*: 2–135. 2nd. ed. 1978.

Otokar of Prague. See *Annales Otokariani.*

Otloh of St. Emmeram. *De cursu spiritali.* Migne PL 146: cols. 241–44. 1884.
———. *Liber visionum.* Ibid.: cols. 341–88.
Otto Morena. *Historia Frederici.* Edited by F. Güterbock. MGH SS rer. Germ. N.S. 7. 1930.
Otto of Freising. *Chronica sive Historia de duabus civitatibus.* Edited by A. Hofmeister and W. Lammers, German translation by A. Schmidt. AQ 16. 1961.
———. *Gesta Frederici.* Edited by G. Waitz, B. Simpson, and F.-J. Schmale German translation by A. Schmidt. AQ 17. 1965.
Otto of St. Blasien. *Chronica.* Edited by A. Hofmeister. MGH SS rer. Germn. 47. 1912.
Ovid. *Amores.* Edited with German translation by F. W. Lenz. 1965.
———. *Remedia amoris.* Edited with German translation by F. W. Lenz. 1960.
Petrus Alfonsi. *Desciplina clericalis.* Edited by A. Hilka and W. Söderhjelm. 1911.
Petrus Damiani. *Contra clericos aulicos.* Migne PL 145: cols. 467–72. 1867.
Petrus de Ebulo. *Liber ad honorem augusti.* Edited by E. Rota. RIS 31, 1. 1904.
Petrus Lombardus. *Libri VI sententiarum.* Edited PP. Collegii s. Bonaventurae. Vols. 1–2. 2nd ed. 1916.
Petrus Venerabilis. *Statuta congregationis Cluniacensis.* Migne PL 189: cols. 1023–48. 1890.
Petrus of Auvergne. *In politicorum continuatio.* In: Thomas Aquinas: *Opera omnia.* Edited by R. Busa. Vol. 7: 412–80. 1980.
Petrus of Blois. *Epistolae.* Migne PL 207: cols. 1–560. 1904.
———. *Liber de confessione sacramentali.* Ibid.: cols. 1077–92.
Pez, B. *Thesaurus novissimus anecdotorum.* Vol. 6, 1–2. 1721.
Pfeiffer, F. "Zwei ungedruckte Minnelieder." *Gm* 12: 49–55. 1867.
Philipp of Harvengt. *De institutione clericorum.* Migne PL 203: cols. 665–1206. 1855.
———. *Epistolae.* Ibid.: cols. 1–180.
Pseudo-Cyprianus. *De duodecim abusivis saeculi.* Edited by S. Hellmann. 1910.
Quintilianus. *Institutio oratoria.* Edited with German translation by H. Rahn. Vols. 1–2. 1972–75.
Radulf of Coggeshall. *Chronicon Anglicanum.* Edited by J. Stevenson. RS 66. 1875.
Rahewin. See Otto of Freising.
Rainald of Dassel. See *Codex epistolaris Wibaldi.*
Rashdall, H. *The Universities of Europe in the Middle Ages.* Vols. 1–3. 2nd ed. 1936.
Rauch, A., ed. *Rerum Austriacarum scriptores.* Vol. 2. 1793.
Regula commilitonum Christi. Edited by G. Schnürer. In: *Die ursprüngliche Templerregel.* 1903.
Reiner of St. Jacob. *Annales.* Edited by G. H. Pertz. MGH SS 16: 632–80. 1859.
Reinerus Alemannicus. *Phagifacetus.* Edited by H. Lemcke. 1880
Rhetorica Ecclesiastica. Edited by L. Wahrmund. 1906.
Riedmann, J. *Die Beziehungen der Grafen und Landesfürsten von Tirol zu Ita-*

lien bis zum Jahre 1335. 1977. (= Riedmann I).

———. "Adelige Sachkultur Tirols in der Zeit von 1290 bis 1330." In: *Adelige Sachkultur des Spätmittelalters* (cf. p. 708): 105–31. (= Riedmann II).

Robertus Monachus. *Historia Hierosolymitana.* RHC Occ. 3: 717–882. 1866.

Rockinger, L. *Briefsteller und Formelbücher des 11.-14. Jahrhunderts.* Vols. 1–2. 1863–64.

Roger of Hoveden. *Chronica.* Edited by W. Stubbs. 4 vols. RS 51. 1868–71.

Roger of Wendover. *Flores historiarum.* Edited by H. G. Hewlett. 3 vols. RS 84. 1884–89.

Röhrig, F. *Der Verduner Altar.* 1955.

Rolandinus of Padua. *Chronica.* Edited by P. Jaffé. MGH SS 19: 32–147. 1866.

Rösch, G. *Venedig und das Reich. Handels- und verkehrspolitische Beziehungen in der deutschen Kaiserzeit.* 1982.

Roth, E. W. E., ed. *Die Visionen der hl. Elisabeth und die Schriften der Äbte Ekbert und Emicho von Schönach.* 1844.

Ruodlieb. Edited by G. B. Ford, German translation by F. P. Knapp. 1977.

Rupert of Deutz. *Commentaria in Evangelium s. Joannis.* Migne PL 169: cols. 201–828. 1894.

Rhymer, T., ed. *Foedera, conventiones, litterae, et cujuscunque generis acta publica.* Vol. 1, 1. 4th ed. 1816.

Salimbene of Parma. *Chronica.* Edited by G. Scalia. 2 vols., 1966.

Saxo Grammaticus. *Gesta Danorum.* Edited by J. Olrick and H. Raeder. 2 vols. 1931–57 (vol. 2 edited by F. Blatt).

Schannat, J. F. and J. Hartzheim, eds. *Concilia Germaniae.* Vols. 3–4. 1760–61.

Schaube, A. *Handelsgeschichte der romanischen Völker des Mittelmeergebiets bis zum Ende der Kreuzzüge.* 1906.

Schmitz, H. J. *Die Bußbücher und das kanonistische Bußverfahren.* 1898.

Schneller et al., eds. "Vermischte Urkunden." *Gf* 7: 155–212. 1851.

Schröder, E. "Die Tänzer von Kölbigk." *ZKG* 17: 94–164. 1897.

Sicardus of Cremona. *Chronica.* Edited by O. Holder-Egger. MGH SS 31: 22–181. 1903.

Sigeboto. *Vita Paulinae.* Edited by J. R. Dietrich. MGH SS 30, 2: 909–38. 1934.

Sigfrid of Balnhusen. *Compendium' historiarum.* Edited by O. Holder-Egger. MGH SS 25: 679–718. 1880.

Simon. *Gesta abbatum s. Bertini Sithiensium.* Edited by O. Holder-Egger. MGH SS 13: 635–63. 1881.

Sprandel, R. "Die wirtschaftlichen Beziehungen zwischen Paris und dem deutschen Sprachraum im Mittelalter." *VSWG* 49: 289–319. 1962.

Stolz, O. *Der geschichtliche Inhalt der Rechnungsbücher der Tiroler Landesfürsten von 1288–1350.* 1957.

Stromer, W. von. "Bernardus Teotonicus und die Geschäftsbeziehungen zwischen den deutschen Ostalpen und Venedig vor Gründung des Fondaco dei Tedeschi." In: *Beiträge zur Handels- und Verkehrsgeschichte.* Edited by P. W. Roth: 1–15. 1978.

Struck, G. "Handschriftenschätze der Landesbibliothek Kassel." In: *Die Landes-*

bibliothek Kassel. Edited by W. Hopf. Part 2. 1930.

Sydow, J. "Beiträge zur Geschichte des deutschen Italienhandels im Früh- und Hochmittelalter." *VHO* 97: 405–13. 1956.

Thietmar of Merseburg. *Chronicon*. Edited by R. Holtzmann, German translation by W. Trillmich. AQ9. 1962.

Thomas Aquinas. *Summa theologiae*. Edited by R. Bus. *Opera omnia*, vol. 2: 184–926. 1980; part III *Supplementum*, cited after the edition of 1887.

Thomas of Chobham. *Summa confessorum*. Edited by F. Broomfield. 1968.

Thomas Wykes. *Chronica*. Edited by H. R. Luard. In: *Annales monastici*. Vol. 4. RS 36.4: 6–319. 1869.

Tomascheck, J. A., ed. *Die Rechte und Freiheiten der Stadt Wien*. Vol. 1. 1877.

Ulrich of Strassburg. *De pulchro*. Edited by M. Grabmann. MSB no. 5: 73–84. 1925.

Urkundenbuch zur Geschichte der Babenberger in Österreich. Vol. 1. Edited by H. Fichtenau and E. Zöllner. 1950.

Hansisches Urkundenbuch. 3 vols. Edited by K. Höhlbaum. 1876–86.

Urkundenbuch des Landes ob der Enns. Vol. 2. 1856.

Urkundenbuch der Stadt Leipzig. Vol. 2. Edited by K. Fr. von Poser-Klett. 1870.

Lübeckisches Urkundenbuch. Vol. 1. 1843.

Regensburger Urkundenbuch. Vol. 1. Edited by J. Widemann. MB 53. 1912.

Urkundenbuch der Stadt Strassburg. Vol. 1. Edited by W. Wiegand. 1879.

Thurgauisches Urkundenbuch. Vol. 2. Edited by J. Meyer and F. Schaltegger. 1917.

Urkundenbuch der Stadt und Landschaft Zürich. Vol. 1. Edited by J. Escher and P. Schweizer. 1888.

Vincent of Beauvais. *De eruditione filiorum nobilium*. Edited by A. Steiner. 1938.

Vincent of Prague. *Annales*. Edited by W. Wattenbach. MGH SS 17: 658–83. 1861.

Virgil. *Aeneis*. Edited by J. Götte. 1958.

Vita Adalberti. See Anselmus.

Vita Bennonis. See Norbert.

Vita Berholdi Garstensis. Edited by H. Pez. SRA 2: cols. 81–129. 1743.

Vita Burcardi. See Eudes of Saint-Maur.

Vita Burchardi. See Ebbo.

Vita Chirstinae. See *De s. Theodora virgine*.

Vita s. Cunegundis. Edited by G. Waitz. MGH SS 4: 821–28. 1841.

Vita s. Geraldi. See Odo of Cluny.

Vita Henrici IV imperatoris. Edited by W. Eberhard and F.-J. Schmale, German translation by I. Schmale-Ott. AQ 12: 407–67. 1963.

Vita Hludovici. See Astronomus.

Vita s. Hugonis. See Hildebert of Lavardin.

Vita Meinwerci episcopi Patherbrunnensis. Edited by F. Tenckhoff. MGH SS rer. Germ. 59. 1921.

Vita Paulinae. See Sigeboto.

Vita Ottonis. See Herbord.

Vita Theoderia abbatis Andaginensis. Edited by W. Wattenbach. MGH SS 12: 36–57. 1856.

Vogel, C. and R. Elze. *Le pontifical romano-germanique du dixième siècle.* 1963.

Waitz, G. "Beschreibung einiger Handschriften." *AGG* 11: 248–514. 1858.

Walter Map. *De nugis curialium.* Edited by T. Wright. 1850.

Walter of Mortagne. *De sacramento conjugii.* Migne PL 176: cols. 153–74. 1880.

Warnkönig, L. A. *Flandrische Staats- und Rechtsgeschichte bis zum Jahr 1305.* Vols. 1–2. 1835–36.

Weigand, R. "Liebe und Ehe bei den Dekretisten des 12. Jahrhunderts." In: *Love and Marriage in the Twelfth Century* (cf. p. 736 f.): 40–58.

Weinrich, L. ed. *Quellen zur deutschen Verfassungs-, Wirtschafts- und Sozialgeschichte bis 1250.* AQ 32. 1977.

Werner, J. *Beiträge zur Kunde der lateinischen Literatur des Mittelalters.* 1905.

Wibald of Stablo. *Epistolae.* Edited by P. Jaffé. BRG1:76–616. 1864.

Widukind of Corvey. *Res gestae Saxonicae.* Edited by H. E. Lohmann and P. Hirsch, German translation by A. Bauer and R. Rau. AQ 8: 1–183. 1971.

William of Malmesbury. *Gesta regum Anglorum.* Edited by W. Stubbs. 2 vols. RS 90. 1887–89.

William of Newburgh. *Historia rerum Anglicarum.* Edited by R. Howlett. In: *Chronicles of the Reigns of Stephen, Henry II., and Richard I.* 2 vols. RS 82,1–2. 1884–85.

William of Tyre. *Historia rerum in partibus transmarini gestarum.* RHC Occ 1, 1–2. 1844.

Winter, J. M. van. "Cingulum militae." *TvG* 44: 1–92. 1976.

Wipo. *Gesta Chuonradi II imperatoris.* Edited by H. Bresslau, German translation by W. Trillmich. AQ 11: 505–613. 1961.

———. *Tetralogus.* Edited by H. Bresslau. Opera. MGH SS rer. Germ. 51: 75–86. 3rd ed. 1915.

GERMAN SOURCES

Alber. *Tnugdalus.* Edited by A. Wagner. In: *Visio Tnugdali:* 119–86. 1882.

Albrecht. *Jüngerer Titurel.* Edited by W. Wolf. 2 vols. 1955–68 (to stanza 4394); edited by K. A. Hahn, 1842 (from stanza 4338). Edited by W. Wolf: "Wer war der Dichter des Jüngeren Titurel?" *ZfdA* 84: 309–46. 1952/53 (= Wolf I); edited by W. Wolf. *Altdeutsche Übungstexte* 14. 1952 (= Wolf II).

Albrecht von Johansdorf. *Lieder.* In: *Minnesangs Frühling.* no. 14, pp. 178–95; transl. by G. Schweikle, vol. 1: 326–51.

Strassburger Alexander. Edited by K. Kinzel. 1884.

Vorauer Alexander. See Lamprecht.

Meister Altswert. Edited by W. Holland and A. Keller. 1850.

Aristoteles und Phyllis. Edited by H. Niewöhner. In: *Neues Gesamtabenteuer.* Vol. 1, no. 34, pp. 234–43. 2nd ed. 1967.

Athis und Prophilias. Edited by C. von Kraus. In: *Mittelhochdeutsches Übungsbuch,* no. 3, pp. 63–82. 2nd ed. 1926.

Laubacher Barlaam. See Otto of Freising.

Berthold von Holle. *Demantin.* Edited by K. Bartsch. 1875.

Berthold von Regensburg. *Predigten.* Edited by F. Pfeiffer. 2 vols. 1862–80.

Die halbe Birne. Edited by G. A. Wolff. 1893.

Biterolf. Edited by O. Jänicke. In: *Biterolf und Dietleib:* 1–197. 1866.

Böhme, F. M. *Geschichte des Tanzes in Deutschland.* 2 vols. 1886.

Konrad Bollstatter. *Losbuch.* Facsimile edition. 1973.

Boppe. *Sprüche.* Edited by G. Tolle. 1894.

Der heimliche Bote. Edited by H. Meyer-Benfey. In: *Mittelhochdeutsche Übungsstücke,* no. 7, pp. 30–32. 2nd ed. 1920.

Die vrône Botschaft ze der Christenheit. Edited by R. Priebsch. 1895.

Sanct Brandan. Edited by C. Schröder. 1871.

Zweites Büchlein. Edited by H. Zutt. In: *Hartmann von Aue: Die Klage. Das (zweite) Büchlein:* 119–63. 1968.

Der von Buwenburg. *Lieder.* In: *Schweizer Minnesänger,* no. 23, pp. 256–64.

Deutsche Liederdichter des 13. Jahrhunderts. See Liederdichter.

Dietmar von Aist. *Lieder.* In: *Minnesangs Frühling,* no. 8, pp. 56–69; transl. by G. Schweikle, vol. 1: 136–59.

Dietrich von der Glezze. *Der Borte.* Edited by O. R. Meyer. 1915.

Ebernand von Erfurt. *Heinrich und Kunigunde.* Edited by R. Bechstein. 1860.

Eike von Repgow. *Sachsenspiegel, Landrecht.* Edited by K. A. Eckhardt. 1955.

Eilhart von Oberg. *Tristrant.* Edited by F. Lichtenstein. 1877; edited by H. Bußmann. 1969.

Tilemann Elhen von Wolfhagen. *Limburger Chronik.* Edited by A. Wyss. 1883.

Engelhart von Adelnburg. *Lieder.* In: *Minnesangs Frühling,* no. 20, pp. 283–84; transl. by G. Schweikle, vol. 1: 322–25.

Enikel. See Jans Enikel.

Die demütige Frau. Edited by H. Niewöhner. In: *Neues Gesamtabenteuer,* vol. 1, no. 36, pp. 251–54. 2nd ed. 1967.

Die gute Frau. Edited by E. Sommer. *ZfdA* 2 385–481. 1842.

Frauenlob. *Gedichte.* Edited by K. Stackmann and K. Bertau. 2 vols. 1981.

Freidank. *Bescheidenheit.* Edited by H. E. Bezzenberger. 1872.

Friedrich von Hausen. *Lieder.* In: *Minnesangs Frühling,* no. 10, pp. 73–96; transl. by G. Schweikle, vol. 1: 222–59.

Friedrich von Suonenburg. *Sprüche.* Edited by A. Masser. 1979.

Gauriel von Muntabel. Edited by F. Khull. 1885.

Gedrut-Geltar. *Gedichte.* In: *Deutsche Liederdichter des 13. Jahrhunderts,* vol. 1, no. 13, pp. 77–79.

Millstätter Genesis. Edited by J. Diemer. 2 vols. 1862.

Wiener Genesis. Edited by V. Dollmayr. 1932.

Der von Gliers. *Lieder.* In: *Schweizer Minnesänger,* no. 20, pp. 189–206.

Gottfried von Strassburg. *Tristan.* Edited by K. Marold. 3rd edition.

Graf Rudolf. Edited by P. F Ganz. 1964.

Grieshaber, F. K., ed. *Deutsche Predigten des XIII. Jahrhunderts.* Vol. 2. 1846.

Hadloub. *Lieder.* In: *Schweizer Minnesänger,* no. 27, pp. 283–361.

Der arme Hartmann. *Rede vom Glauben*. Edited by H. F. Maßmann. In: *Deutsche Gedichte des 12. Jahrhunderts*. Vol. 1: 1–42. 1837.

Hartmann von Aue. *Erec*. Edited by A. Leitzmann and L. Wolff. 5th ed. 1972.

———. *Gregorius*. Edited by H. Paul and B. Wachinger. 13th ed. 1984.

———. *Der arme Heinrich*. Edited by H. Paul and G. Bonath. 15th ed. 1984.

———. *Iwein*. Edited by G. F. Benecke, K. Lachmann, and L. Wolff. 2 vols. 7th ed. 1968.

———. *Klage*. Edited by A. Schirokauer and P. W. Tax. 1979.

———. *Lieder*. In: *Minnesangs Frühling*, no. 22, pp. 404–30.

Das Häslein. Edited by F. H. von der Hagen. In: *Gesamtabenteuer*. Vol. 2, no. 21, pp. 5–18. 1838.

Die Heiden. Edited by E. Henschel and U. Pretzel. In: *Deutsche Erzählungen des Mittelalters*: 135–63. 1971.

Kaiser Heinrich. *Lieder*. In: *Minnesangs Frühling*, no. 9, pp. 70–72; transl. by G. Schweikle, vol. 1, pp. 260–65.

Heinrich der Glichesere. *Reinhart Fuchs*. Edited by K. Düwel. 1984.

Heinrich von Beringen. *Schachbuch*. Edited by P. Zimmermann. 1883.

Heinrich von Freiberg. *Die Ritterfahrt des Johann von Michelsberg*. Edited by A. Bernt. In: *Heinrich von Freiberg*: 239–48. 1906.

———. *Tristan*. Ibid.: 1–211.

Heinrich von Melk. *Erinnerung an den Tod*. Edited by R. Kienast: 30–57. 1946.

———. *Priesterleben*. Ibid.: 9–29.

Heinrich von Morungen. *Lieder*. In: *Minnesangs Frühling*, no. 19, pp. 236–82; transl. by H. Tervooren. 1975.

Heinrich von Neustadt. *Apollonius von Tyrland*. Edited by S. Singer. 1906.

Heinrich von Rugge. *Lieder*. In: *Minnesangs Frühling*, no. 15, pp. 196–223.

Heinrich von dem Türlin. *Die Krone*. Edited by G. H. F. Scholl. 1852.

———. *Der Mantel*. Edited by O. Warnatsch. 1883.

Heinrich von Veldeke. *Eneit*. Edited by L. Ettmüller. 1852; edited by G. Schieb and T. Frings. 1964.

———. *Lieder*. In: *Minnesangs Frühling*, no. 11, pp. 97–149; transl. by G. Schweikle, vol. 1, pp. 166–205.

———. *Servatius*. Edited by T. Frings and G. Schieb. 1956.

Heinrich Hetzbolt von Weissensee. *Lieder*. In: *Deutsche Liederdichter des 13. Jahrhunderts*, vol. 1, no. 20, pp. 148–52.

Helmbrecht. See *Wernher der Gartenaere*.

Herbort von Fritzlar. *Liet von Troye*. Edited by G. K. Fommann. 1837.

Herger. See Spervogel.

Bruder Hermann. *Leben der Gräfin Jolande von Vianden*. Edited by J. Meier. 1889.

Hermann der Damen. *Sprüche*. In: *Minnesinger*, vol. 3, no. 28, pp. 160–70.

Herrand von Wildonie. *Der nackte Kaiser*. Edited by H. Fischer and P. Sappler. In: *Herrand von Wildonie*, no. 3, pp. 22–43. 3rd ed. 1984.

Herzog Ernst. Edited by K. Bartsch. 1869.

Ulmer Hofzucht. Edited by A. von Keller. In: *Erzählungen aus altdeutschen Handschriften*: 531–46. 1855.

Der saelden Hort. Edited by H. Adrian. 1927.

Hugo von Trimberg. *Der Renner.* Edited by G. Ehrismann. 4 vols. 1908–11.

Jans Enikel. *Fürstenbuch.* Edited by P. Strauch. 1900.

———. *Weltchronik.* Edited by P. Strauch. 1891.

Johann von Würzburg. *Wilhelm von Österreich.* Edited by E. Regel. 1906.

Mitteldeutsche Judith. Edited by R. Palgen and H.-G. Richert. 2nd ed. 1969.

Jüngerer Titurel. See Albrecht.

Der Junker und der treue Heinrich. Edited by K. Kinzel. 1880.

Kaiserchronik. Edited by E. Schröder. 1895.

Der Kanzler. *Gedichte.* In: *Deutsche Liederdichter des 13. Jahrhundters,* vol. 1, no. 28, pp. 185–217.

König Rother. Edited by T. Frings and J. Kuhnt. 1922.

König Tirol. See *Tirol und Fridebrant.*

Pfaffe Konrad. *Rolandslied.* Edited by C. Wesle and P. Wapnewski. 2nd ed. 1967.

Konrad Fleck. *Flore und Blanscheflur.* Edited by E. Sommer. 1846.

Konrad von Fussesbrunnen. *Die Kindheit Jesu.* Edited by H. Fromm and K. Grubmüller. 1973.

Konrad von Heimesfurt. *Urstende.* Edited by K. A. Hahn. In: *Gedichte des XII. und XIII. Jahrhunderts*: 103–28. 1840.

Konrad von Landeck. *Lieder.* In: *Schweizer Minnesänger,* no. 21, pp. 207–46.

Konrad von Würzburg. *Engelhard.* Edited by P. Gereke and I. Reiffenstein. 2nd ed. 1963.

———. *Heinrich von Kempten.* Edited by E. Schröder. In: *Konrad von Würzburg-Kleinere Dichtungen,* vol. 1, pp. 41–68. 3rd ed. 1959.

———. *Herzmaere.* Ibid.: 12–40.

———. *Partonopier und Meliur.* Edited by K. Bartsch. 1871.

———. *Trojanerkrieg.* Edited by A. von Keller. 1858.

———. *Turnier von Nantes.* Edited by E. Schröder. In: *Konrad von Würzburg-Kleinere Dichtungen,* vol. 2, pp. 42–75. 3rd ed. 1959.

Landgraf Ludwigs Kreuzfahrt. Edited by H. Naumann. 1923.

Kristan von Hamle. *Lieder.* In: *Deutsche Liederdichter des 13. Jahrhunderts,* vol. 1. no. 30, pp. 220–24.

Kudrun. Edited by K. Bartsch and K. Stackmann. 5th ed. 1965.

Der von Kürenberg. *Lieder.* In: *Minnesangs Frühling,* no. 2, pp. 24–27; transl. by G. Schweikle, vol. 1, pp. 118–23.

Pfaffe Lamprecht. *Alexander.* Edited by K. Kinzel. 1884.

Das Leben der hl. Elisabeth. Edited by M. Rieger. 1868.

Das Leben der Gräfin Jolande von Vianden. See Bruder Hermann.

Die beiden ungleichen Liebhaber. Edited by A. Mihm: "Aus der Frühzeit der weltlichen Rede." *PBB* 87: 416–18. 1965.

Deutsche Liederdichter des 13. Jahrhunderts. Edited by C. von Kraus. 2 vols. 2nd ed. 1978.

Limburger Chronik. See Elhen von Wolfhagen.

Der Litschower. *Sprüche.* In: *Minnesinger,* vol. 3, no. 15, pp. 46–47.

Lohengrin. Edited by T. Cramer. 1971.

Lucidarius. Edited by F. Heidlauf. 1915.

Lucidarius-Vorrede Edited by E. Schröder: "Die Reimvorreden des deutschen Lucidarius." *GGN* 1917: 153–72.

Der Magezoge. Edited by G. Rosenhagen. In: *Die Heidelberger Handschrift Cpg 341*, no. 36, pp. 21–29. 1909.

Mai und Beaflor. Edited by W. Vollmer. 1848.

Wallersteiner Margarethe. Edited by K. Bartsch. In: *Germanistische Studien* 1: 1–30. 1872.

Maria und die Hausfrau. Edited by F. H. von der Hagen. In: *Gesamtabenteuer*, vol. 3, no. 78, pp. 481–88. 1850.

Mariengrüsse. Edited by F. Pfeiffer. *ZfdA* 8: 274–98. 1851.

Der Marner. *Gedichte.* Edited by P. Strauch. 1876.

Die Maze. Edited by H. Meyer-Benfey. In: *Mittelhochdeutsche Übungsstücke*, no. 6, pp. 24–30. 2nd ed. 1920.

Meinloh von Sevelingen. *Lieder.* In: *Minnesangs Frühling*, no. 3, pp. 28–31; transl. by G. Schweikle, vol. 1, pp. 126–35.

Der Meissner. *Sprüche.* Edited by G. Objartel. 1977.

Minne und Gesellschaft. Edited by K. Mittaei. In: *Mittelhochdeutsche Minnereden*, vol. 1, no. 6, pp. 65–73. 1913.

Der Minnehof. Edited by A. Bach. In: *Die Werke des Verfassers der Schlacht bei Göllheim*: 220–26. 1930.

Die Schweizer Minnesänger (BSM). Edited by K. Bartsch. 1886.

Des Minnesangs Frühling (MF). Edited by H. Moser and H. Tervooren. 36th ed. 1977.

Minnesinger (HMS). Edited by F. H. von der Hagen. 4 vols. 1838.

Möncke, G., ed. and transl. *Quellen zur Wirtschafts- und Sozialgeschichte mittel- und oberdeutscher Städte im Spätmittelalter.* AQ 37. 1982.

Monumenta Wittelsbacensia. Edited by F. M. Wittmann. Part 2. 1861.

Morant und Galie. Edited by T. Frings and E. Linke. 1976.

Moriz von Craûn. Edited by U. Pretzel. 4th ed. 1975.

Die Nachtigall. Edited by F. H. von der Hagen. In: *Gesamtabenteuer*, vol. 2, no. 25, pp. 71–82. 1850.

Neidhart. *Lieder.* Edited by E. Wießner, H. Fischer, and P. Sappler. 4th ed. 1984.

Neidhart c. *Die Berliner Neidhart-Handschrift.* Edited by I. Bennewitz-Behr. 1981.

Nibelungenlied. Edited and transl. by H. Brackert. 2 vols. 1970–71.

Nibelungenlied C. *Das Nibelungenlied nach der Handschrift C.* Edited by U. Hennig. 1977.

Orendel. Edited by H. Steinger. 1935.

Ortnit. Edited by A. Amelung. In: *Ortnit und die Wolfdietriche*, vol. 1: 1–77. 1871.

Otte. *Eraclius.* Edited by H. Graef. 1883.

Otto von Botenlouben. *Lieder.* In: *Deutsche Liederdichter des 13. Jahrhunderts*, vol. 1, no. 41, pp. 307–16.

Otto von Brandenburg. *Lieder.* Ibid., no. 42, pp. 317–20.

Otto of Freising. *Laubacher Barlaam.* Edited by A. Perdisch. 1913 .

Ottokar von Steiermark. *Österreichische Reimchronik*. Edited by J. Seemüller. 2 vols. 1890–93.

Alsfelder Passionsspiel. Edited by R. Froning. In: *Das Drama des Mittelalters*. Vols. 2–3: 547–864. 1891–92.

Pfaff, F., ed. *Die große Heidelberger Liederhandschrift in getreuem Textabdruck*. 1909.

Der Pleier. *Garel vom blühenden Tal*. Edited by W. Herles. 1981.

————. *Meleranz*. Edited by K. Bartsch. 1861.

————. *Tandareis und Floribel*. Edited by F. Khull. 1885.

Züricher Predigten. Edited by W. Wackernagel. In: *Altdeutsche Predigten und Gebete*. 1876.

Prosa-Lancelot. Edited by R. Kluge. 3 vols. 1948–74.

Pseudo-Gottfried von Strassburg. *Gedichte*. In: *Minnesinger*, vol. 2, no. 124, pp. 266–78. 1838.

Vom Recht. Edited by W. Schröder. In: *Kleinere deutsche Gedichte des 11. und 12. Jahrhunderts*, vol. 2, no. 8, pp. 112–31. 1972.

Baunschweigische Reimchronik. Edited by L. Weiland. 1877.

Reinbot von Durne. *Der hl. Georg*. Edited by C. von Kraus. 1907.

Reinfried von Braunschweig. Edited by K. Bartsch. 1871.

Reinhart Fuchs. See Heinrich der Glichesere.

Reinmar der Alte. *Lieder*. In *Minnesangs Frühling*, no. 21, pp. 285–403.

Reinmar von Brennenberg. *Gedichte*. In: *Deutsche Liederdichter des 13. Jahrhunderts*, vol. 1, no. 44, pp. 325–33.

Reimnar von Zweter. *Sprüche*. Edited by G. Roethe. 1887.

Der Burggraf von Rietenburg. *Lieder*. In: *Minnesangs Frühling*, no. 5, pp. 34–37.

Ritter oder Knecht. Edited by J. Frh. von Laßberg. In: *Liedersaal*, vol. 2, no. 88, pp. 9–15. 1822.

Die Ritterfahrt. Edited by A. Bach. In: *Die Werke des Verfassers der Schlacht bei Göllheim*: 230–33. 1930.

Rittertreue. Edited by L. Pfannmüller. In: *Mittelhochdeutsche Novellen*, vol. 2: 5–26. 1912.

Robyn. *Sprüche*. In: *Minnesinger*, vol. 3, no. 6, p. 31.

Rolandslied. See Pfaffe Konrad.

Johannes Rothe. *Der Ritterspiegel*. Edited by H. Neumann. 1936.

Rubin. *Lieder*. In: *Deutsche Liederdichter des 13. Jahrhunderts*, vol. 1, no. 47, pp. 338–58.

Rudolf von Ems. *Alexander*. Edited by V. Junk. 2 vols. 1928–29.

————. *Der gute Gerhard*. Edited by J. Asher. 2nd ed. 1971.

————. *Weltchronik*. Edited by G. Ehrismann. 1915.

————. *Wilhelm von Orlens*. Edited by V. Junk. 1905.

Meisler Rumslant. *Sprüche*. In: *Minnesinger*, vol. 3, no. 20, pp. 52–68.

Ruprecht von Würzburg. *Die Treueprobe*. Edited by H. Niewöhner. In *Neues Gesamtabenteuer*, vol. 1, no. 37, pp. 255–68. 2nd ed. 1967.

Sachsenspiegel. See Eike von Repgow.

Der saelden hort. See Hort.

Salman und Morolf. Edited by F. Vogt. 1880.

Der Schlegel. Edited by L. Pfannmüller. In: *Mittelhochdeutsche Novellen,* vol. 2: 27–63. 1912.

Magdeburger Schöppenchronik. Edited by K. Janicke. 1869.

Der Tugendhafte Schreiber. *Gedichte.* In: *Minnesinger,* vol. 2, no. 102, pp. 148–53.

Schwabenspiegel, Landrecht. Edited by W. Wackernagel. 1840.

Schweikle, G. *Die mittelhochdeutsche Minnelyrik.* Vol. 1. 1977.

Schwind, E. Frh. von and A. Dopsch, eds. *Ausgewählte Urkunden zur Verfassungsgeschichte der detusch-österreichischen Erblande im Mittelalter.* 1895.

Seifried Helbling. Edited by J. Seemüller. 1886.

Sigeher. *Sprüche.* Edited by H. P. Brodt. 1913.

Trierer Silvester. Edited hy C. von Kraus. 1895.

Spervogel. *Sprüche.* In: *Minnesangs Frühling,* nos. 6–7, pp. 38–55.

Der von Stamhein. *Lieder.* In: *Deutsche Liederdichter des 13. Jahrhunderts,* vol. 1, no. 55, pp. 417–20.

Steinmar. *Lieder.* In: *Schweizer Minnesänger,* no. 19, pp. 170–88.

Stolle. *Sprüche.* In: *Minnesinger,* vol. 3, no. 1, pp. 3–10.

Der Stricker. *Der nackte Bote.* Edited by H. Fischer and J. Janota. In: *Der Stricker: Verserzählungen* I, no. 9, pp. 110–26. 4th ed. 1979.

———. *Daniel vom blühenden Tal.* Edited by M. Resler. 1983.

———. *Die Frauenehre.* Edited by W. W. Moelleken. In: *Die Kleindichtung des Strickers,* vol. 1, no. 3, pp. 15–91. 1973.

———. *Die Gäuhühner.* Edited by H. Mettke. In: *Fabeln und Mären von dem Stricker,* no. 24, pp. 78–87. 1959.

———. *Die Minnesänger.* Edited by W. W. Moelleken, G. Agler-Beck, and R. E. Lewis. In: *Die Kleindichtung des Strickers,* vol. 5, no. 146, pp. 83–97. 1978.

———. *Der Pfaffe Amis.* Edited by H. Lambel. In: *Erzählungen und Schwänke:* 1–102. 1883.

———. *Der Weinschlund.* Edited by H. Fischer and J. Janota. In: *Der Stricker: Verserzählungen* I, no. 13, pp. 155–60. 4th ed. 1979.

Peter Suchenwirt. *Werke.* Edited by A. Primisser. 1827.

Tannhäuser. *Gedichte.* Edited by J. Siebert: *Der Dichter Tannhäuser:* 81–126. 1934.

———. *Hofzucht.* Ibid.: 194–206.

Der Teichner. *Gedichte.* Edited by H. Niewöhner. 3 vols. 1953–56.

Der Teufelspapst. Edited by F. H. von der Hagen. In: *Gesamtabenteuer,* vol. 2, appendix no. 4, pp. 549–62. 1850.

Thomasin von Zirklaere. *Der Wälsche Gast.* Edited by H. Rückert. 1852.

Tirol und Fridebrant. Edited by A. Leitzmann and I. Reiffenstein. In: *Winsbeckische Gedichte:* 76–96. 3rd ed 1962.

Jüngerer Titurel. See Albrecht.

Tnugdalus. See Alber.

Der Traum. Edited by J. Frh. von Laßberg. In: *Lieder-Saal,* vol. 1, no. 25, pp. 125–49. 1820.

Ulrich von Etzenbach. *Alexander* (with addition). Edited by W. Toischer. 1888.

———. *Wilhelm von Wenden.* Edited by H.-F. Rosenfeld. 1957.

Ulrich von Gutenburg. *Lieder.* In: *Minnesangs Frühling,* no. 12, pp. 150–65; transl. by G. Schweikle, vol. 1: 284–315.

Ulrich von Liechtenstein. *Frauenbuch.* Edited by K. Lachmann. In: *Ulrich von Liechtenstein:* 549–660. 1841.

———. *Frauendienst.* Edited by R. Bechstein. 2 vols. 1888.

———. *Lieder.* In: *Deutsche Liederdichter des 13. Jahrhunderts,* vol. 1, no. 58, pp. 428–94.

Ulrich von Türheim. *Rennewart.* Edited by A. Hübner. 1938.

———. *Tristan.* Edited by T. Kerth. 1979.

Ulrich von dem Türlin. *Willehalm.* Edited by S. Singer. 1893.

Ulrich von Winterstetten. *Lieder.* In: *Deutsche Liederdichter des 13. Jahrhunderts,* vol. 1, no. 59, pp. 459–554.

Ulrich von Zatzikhoven. *Lanzelet.* Edited by K. A. Hahn. 1845.

Virginal. Edited by J. Zupitza. In: *Dietrichs Abenteuer:* 1–200. 1870.

Wackernagel, W., ed. *Lyrische Gedichte des XII., XIII. und XIV. Jahrhunderts.* Abl. 2: 121–33. 1840.

Walther von der Vogelweide. *Gedichte.* Edited by K. Lachmann, C. von Kraus, and H. Kuhn. 13th ed. 1965.

Der Wartburgkrieg. Edited by T. A. Rompelman. 1939.

Wegeli, R. *Inschriften auf mittelalterlichen Schwertklingen.* Dissertation. Leipzig. 1904.

Der Weinschwelg. Edited by H. Fischer and J. Janota. In: *Der Stricker: Verserzählungen* II, no. 18, pp. 42–58. 3rd ed. 1984.

Sächsiche Weltchronik. Edited by L. Weiland. 1877.

Bruder Wernher. *Sprüche.* Edited by A. E. Schönbach. 2 vols. 1904.

Pfaffe Wernher. *Maria.* Edited by C. Wesle, H. Fromm. 2nd ed. 1969.

Wernher der Gartenaere. *Helmbrecht.* Edited by F. Panzer and K. Ruhn. 9th ed. 1974.

Wernher von Elmendorf. *Moralium dogma philosophorum* (German). Edited by J. Bumke. 1974.

Wigamur. Edited by F. H. von der Hagen and J. G. Büsching. In: *Deutsche Gedichte des Mittelalters,* vol. 1, no. 3. 1808.

Williram von Ebersberg. *Paraphrase des Hohen Liedes.* Edited by J. Seemüller. 1878.

Der Winsbeke. Edited by A. Letizmann and I. Reiffenstein. In: *Winsbeckische Gedichte:* 1–45. 3rd ed. 1962.

Die Winsbekin. Ibid.: 46–66.

Wirnt von Grafenberg. *Wigalois.* Edited by J. M. N. Kapteyn. 1926.

Wisse, Claus and Philipp Colin. *Der Nüwe Parzifal.* Edited K. Schorbach. 1888.

Wolfdietrich A. Edited by H. Schneider. 1931; edited by A. Amelung, in: *Ortnit und die Wolfdietriche,* vol. I, pp. 79–163. 1873.

Wolfdietrich B. Edited by O. Jänicke. Ibid.: 165–301.

Wolfram von Eschenbach. *Parzival.* Edited by K. Lachmann. In: *Wolfram von Eschenbach:* 13–388. 6th ed. 1926.

———. *Titurel.* Ibid.: 389–420.
———. *Willehalm.* Ibid.: 423–640.
Froben C. von Zimmern. *Zimmerische Chronik.* Edited by P. Hermann. 4 vols. 1932.

ROMANCE SOURCES

Adenet le Roi. *Berte aus grans piés.* Edited by A. Henry. 1963.
L'art d'amour. Edited by B. Roy. 1974.
Aucassin et Nicolette. Edited by H. Suchier. 10th ed. 1932.
Audiau, J., ed. *Les poésies des quatres troubadours d'Ussel.* 1922.
Baudoin de Condé. *Li contes dou Wardecors.* Edited by A. Scheler. In: *Baudoin de Condé: Dits et contes,* vol. 1, pp. 17–29. 1866.
Bernart de Ventadorn. *Lieder.* Edited by C. Appel. 1915.
Bertoni, G., ed. *I trovatori d'Italia.* 1915.
Bertran de Born. *Lieder.* Edited by C. Appel. 1932.
Blancandin et l'orgueilleuse d'amour. Edited by F. P. Sweetser. 1964.
Boutière, J. and A.-H. Schutz, eds. *Biographes des troubadours.* 1950.
Le chevalier aux deux epées. Edited by W. Foerster. 1877.
Chrétien de Troyes. *Le conte du Graal (Perceval).* Edited by A. Hilka. 1932. Erste Fortsetzung. Edited by W. Roach, 3 vols. 1949–55.
———. *Yvain.* Edited and transl. by I. Nolting-Hauff. 1962.
Córtes de Valladolid de 1258. In: *Cortes de los antiguos reinos de Leon y de Castilla,* vol. 1, pp. 54–63. 1861.
Duplès-Agier, H., ed. *Ordonnances somptuaire inédite de Philippe le Hardi.* BEC 5: 1 76–81. 1854.
Etienne de Fougières. *Le livre des maniéres.* Edited by J. Kremer. 1887.
Etienne de Meaux. See H. van der Werf.
Floire et Blancheflor. Edited by M. Edélstand de Méril. 1856.
Garin le Brun. *Enseignement.* Edited by C. Appel. RLR 33: 404–32. 1889.
Gautier d'Arras. *IIIe et Galeron.* Edited by F. A. G. Cowper. 1956.
Gerbert de Montreuil. *Le roman de la violette.* Edited by D. L. Buffum. 1928.
Gontier de Soignies. *Lieder.* Edited by A. Scheler. In: *Trouvères belges,* vol. 2, no. 1, pp. 1–71. 1879.
Guillaume IX d'Aquitaine. *Lieder.* Edited by A. Jeanroy. 1927.
Guillaume de Lorris. *Le roman de la rose.* Edited with German translation by K. A. Ott. 3 vols. 1976–79.
Guiot de Provins. *La Bible.* Edited by J. Orr. 1915.
Guiraut Riquier. *Lieder.* Edited by U. Mölk. 1962.
Histoire de Guillaume le Maréchal. Edited by P. Meyer. 3 vols. 1891–1901.
Huon de Bordeaux. Edited by P. Ruelle. 1960.
Jacques Bretel. *Le tournoi de Chauvency.* Edited by M. Delbouille. 1932.
Jaufré Rudel. *Lieder.* Edited by A. Jeanroy. 1924.
Jean Renart. *Galeron de Bretagne.* Edited by L. Foulet. 1925.
———. *Le roman de la rose ou de Guillaume de Dole.* Edited by F. Lecoy. 1962.

Jean de Joinville. *Histoire de Saint Louis*. Edited by N. de Wailly. 1868.

Jungandreas, W. "Die Einwirkung des Französischen auf das Moselfränkische." *NphM* 70: 561–604. 1969.

Lai du Lecheor. Edited by G. Paris. In: "Lais inédits." *Ro* 8: 64–66. 1879.

Langfors, A., ed. *Recueil général des jeux-partis français*. 2 vols. 1926.

Philippe de Novare. *Mémoires*. Edited by C. Kohler. 1913.

———. *Les quatres âges de l'homme*. Edited by M. de Fréville. 1888.

Philippe de Remi. *Jehan et Blonde*. Edited by H. Suchier. 1885.

Pillet, A. and H. Carstens. *Bibliographie der Troubadours*. 1933.

Richard de Fournival. *Consaus d'amours*. Edited by W. M. McLeod. *SiP* 32: 1–21. 1935.

Robert Grosseteste. *Rules*. Edited by D. Oschinsky. In: *Walter of Henley and Other Treatises on Estate Management and Accounting*: 387–415. 1971.

Robert de Blois. *Le chastoiement des dames*. Edited by J. Ulrich. In: *Robert de Blois: Sämtliche Werke*, vol. 3, pp. 55–78. 1895.

———. *L'enseignement des princes*. Ibid.: 1–54.

Le roman d'Enéas. Edited by J. Salverda de Grave, transl. by M. Schöler-Beinhauer. 1972.

Le roman de Horn. See Thomas.

Sone de Nansay. Edited by M. Goldschmidt. 1899.

Thomas. *Le roman de Horn*. Edited by M. K. Pope. 1955.

Urbain le courteois A. Edited by H. R. Parsons. "Anglo-Norman Books of Courtesy and Nurture." *PMLA* 44: 398–408. 1929.

Wace. *Roman de Rou*. Edited by H. Andresen. 2 vols. 1877–79.

Watriquet de Couvins. *Dits*. Edited by A. Scheler. 1868.

H. van der Werf. *The Chansons of the Troubadours and Trouvères. A Study of the Melodies and Their Relation to the Poems*. 1972.

William IX of Aquitaine. See Guillaume IX.

Witthoeft, F. *Sirventes joglaresc*. 1891.

LITERATURE

This portion of the bibliography has been slightly altered and amended by the translator to reflect the needs of an English readership and to include some titles that have appeared since the publication of the original German edition.

INTRODUCTION

Basic for the material culture of the courtly age is A. Schultz, *Das höfische Leben zur Zeit der Minnesinger*. 2 vols. 2d ed. 1889. In addition: M. Heyne, *Fünf Bücher deutscher Hausaltertümer von den ältesten geschichtlichen Zeiten bis zum 16. Jahrhundert*. 3 vols. 1899–1903 (no more published).

I will not list the older works on cultural history, with the exception of the still valuable work of A. Luchaire, *La société française au temps de Philippe-Auguste*. 2d ed. 1909. Engl. transl. by E. Krehbiel, *Social France at the Time of*

Philip Augustus. 1967. Of the newer works, the following should be mentioned: H. Naumann, *Deutsche Kultur im Zeitalter des Rittertums.* 1938.—J. Hashagen. *Kultur des Mittelalters. Eine Einführung.* 1950—F. Heer. *The Medieval World: Europe 1100–1350.* 1962.—H. Kohlhaussen. *Ritterliche Kultur aus mittelalterlichem Hausrat gedeutet.* 1962.—M.W. Labarge. *A Baronial Household of the Thirteenth Century.* 1965.—F. H. Bäuml. *Medieval Civilization in Germany, 800–1273.* 1969.—J. Le Goff. *Time, Work, and Culture in the Middle Ages.* Transl. by Arthur Goldhammer. 1980.—W. H. Schwarz. *Sachgüter und Lebensformen. Einführung in die materielle Kulturgeschichte des Mittelalters und der Neuzeit.* 1970.—R. Delort. *Le moyen âge. Histoire illustrée de la vie quotidienne.* 1972.—A. Borst. *Lebensformen im Mittelalter.* 1973.—J. and F. Gies. *Life in a Medieval Castle.* 1975.—M. Pastoureau. *La vie quotidienne en France et en Angleterre au temps des chevaliers de la table ronde (XIIe–XIIIe siècles).* 1976.—O. Borst. *Alltagsleben im Mittelalter.* 1983.—H. Kühnel, ed. *Alltag im Spätmittelalter.* 1984.

Important sources for the modern study of material culture are the volumes published by the Institut für mittelalterliche Realienkunde Österreichs: *Die Funktion der schriftlichen Quelle in der Sachkulturforschung.* 1976.—*Das Leben in der Stadt des Spätmittelalters.* 2d ed. 1980.—*Klösterliche Sachkultur des Spätmittelalters.* 1980.—*Europäische Sachkultur.* 1980.—*Adelige Sachkultur des Spätmittelalters.* 1982.—*Die Erforschung von Alltag und Sachkultur des Mittelalters.* 1984.—*Bäuerliche Sachkultur des Spätmittelalters.* 1984.

For the material culture of the monasteries, see also G. Zimmermann, *Ordensleben und Lebensstandard. Die Cura Corporis in den Ordensvorschriften des abendländischen Hochmittelalters.* 1973.—L. Moulin. *La vie quotidienne des religieux au moyen âge, Xe–XVe siècle.* 1978.

The first summary of medieval archeology is offered by M. de Bouard, *Manuel d'archéologie médiévale. De la fouille à l'histoire.* 1975.

Exhibiton catalogs are very important sources of information and documentation: *Kunst und Kultur im Weserraum. 800–1600.* 2 vols. 3d, 4th eds. 1967.—*Rhein und Maas. Kunst und Kultur 800–1400.* 1972.—*1000 Jahre Babenberger in Österreich.* 1976.—*Die Zeit der Staufer. Geschichte—Kunst—Kultur.* 5 vols. 1977–79.—*Wittelsbach und Bayern.* Vol. 1: Die Zeit der frühen Herzöge. Parts 1 and 2. 1980.

On the question of the value of literary texts as sources, see the theoretical discussion by H. Schüppert, "Der Beitrag der Literaturwissenschaft für die mittelalterliche Realienkunde." In: *Die Erforschung von Alltag und Sachkultur des Mittelalters* (see above): 158–67.—The analysis of literary texts for their cultural historical content was a popular topic of older (and some more recent) dissertations. Very few of these studies have the high quality of the works by G. Siebel, *Harnisch und Helm in den epischen Dichtungen des 12. Jahrhunderts bis zu Hartmanns Erek.* Dissertation. Hamburg. 1968, and S. Zak, *Musik als "Ehr und Zier" im mittelalterlichen Reich. Studien zur Musik im höfischen Leben, Recht und Zeremoniell.* Dissertation. Frankfurt/Main. 1978. Still valuable in its own right is the extensive study of C.-V. Langlois, *La vie en France au moyen âge de la fin du XIIe au milieu du XIVe siècle.* 4 vols. 1924–28.

On the evidentiary value of pictures see E. Keyser, *Das Bild als Geschichts-*

quelle. 1935.—H. Pauer. "Bildkunde und Geschichtswissenschaft." *MIÖG* 71: 194–210. 1963.—H. Boockmann. "Über den Aussagewert von Bildquellen zur Geschichte des Mittelalters." In: *Wissenschaft, Wirtschaft und Technik. W. Treue zum 60. Geburtstag*: 29–37. 1969.

On the laudatio temporis acti see H. Delbrück, "Die gute alte Zeit." *PJb* 71: 1–28. 1893.—R. Koch. *Klagen mittelalterlicher Didaktiker über die Zeit*. Dissertation. Göttingen. 1931.—M. Behrendt. *Zeitklage und laudatio temporis acti in der mittelhochdeutschen Lyrik*. 1935.—H. Linke. "Der Dichter und die gute alte Zeit. Der Stricker über die Schwierigkeiten des Dichtens und des Dichters im 13. Jahrhundert." *Eu* 71: 98–105. 1977.

The topic literature and society in the Middle Ages has so far received only one comprehensive treatment, by the historian R. Sprandel, *Gesellschaft und Literatur im Mittelater*. 1982; with extensive bibliography.

CHAPTER I
NOBLE SOCIETY IN THE HIGH MIDDLE AGES

A good introduction into the problems of medieval social history is given by H. Boockmann, *Einführung in die Geschichte des Mittelalters*. 1978. On feudal society in the High Middle Ages see also M. Bloch, *La société féodale*. 2 vols. 1939–40. Engl. transl. by L. A. Manyon, *Feudal Society*. 2 vols. 1961.—K. Bosl. *Frühformen der Gesellschaft im mittelalterlichen Europa. Ausgewählte Beiträge zu einer Strukturanalyse der mittelalterlichen Welt*. 1964.—K. Bosl. *Die Grundlagen der modernen Gesellschaft im Mittelalter. Eine deutsche Gesellschaftsgeschichte des Mittelalters*. 2 vols. 1972.—G. Duby. *Hommes et structures du moyen âge. Recueil d'articles*. 1973.—G. Duby. *The Three Orders. Feudal Society Imagined*. Transl. by Arthur Goldhammer. 1978.—Of great value are the relvant articles in: *Geschichtliche Grundbegriffe. Historisches Lexikon zur politisch-sozialen Sprache in Deutschland*. Edited by O. Brunner, W. Conze, and R. Koselleck. To date: vols. 1–5 (A-Soz). 1972–84.

On the meaning and concept of law see F. Kern, "Recht und Verfassung im Mittelalter." *HZ* 120: 1–79. 1919. Critical: H. Krauss, "Dauer und Vergänglichkeit im mittelalterlichen Recht." *ZRG GA* 75: 206-51. 1958.—K. Kroeschell. "Recht und Rechtsbegriff im 12. Jahrhundert." In: *Probleme des 12. Jahrhunderts*: 309–35. 1968.—On the various legal spheres see K. Kroeschell, *Deutsche Rechtsgeschichte*. 2 vols. 1972–73. Also the relevant articles in *Handwörterbuch zur deutschen Rechtsgeschichte*. Edited by A. Erler and E. Kaufmann. To date: vols. 1–3. 1971–1984.

Some important essays on lordship as the basic concept of medieval constitutional history are collected in *Herrschaft und Staat im Mittelalter*. Edited by H. Kämpf. 1956. Some are accessible in English in *Lordship and Community in Medieval Europe*. Edited by Frederic L. Cheyette. 1968.—O. Brunner, *Land und Herrschaft. Grundfragen der territorialen Verfassungsgeschichte Österreichs im Mittelalter*. 4th ed. 1959. For a critique of this view see K. Kroeschell, *Haus und Herrschaft im frühen deutschen Recht*. 1968.—See also the volume *Ideologie und Herrschaft im Mittelalter*. Edited by M. Kerner. 1982.

On feudal law and the nature of feudalism see H. Mitteis, *Lehnrecht und Staatsgewalt. Untersuchungen zur mittelalterlichen Verfassungsgeschichte.* 1933.—*Studien zum Mittelalterlichen Lehenswesen.* 1960.—G. Droege. *Landrecht und Lehnrecht im hohen Mittelalter.* 1969.—F. L. Ganshof. *Feudalism.* Transl. by P. Grierson. 1961.—K.-F. Krieger. *Die Lehnshoheit der deutschen Könige im Spätmittelalter (ca. 1200–1437).* 1979.

On the medieval concept of estates see W. Schwer, *Stand und Ständeordnung im Weltbild des Mittelalters. Die geistes- und gesellschaftsgeschichtlichen Grundlagen der berufsständischen Idee.* 2d ed. 1952.—H. Stahleder. "Zum Ständebegriff im Mittelalter." *ZfbLG* 35: 523–70. 1972.—O. G. Oexle. "Die funktionelle Dreiteilung der 'Gesellschaft' bei Adalbero von Laon. Wirklichkeit i frühen Mittelalter." *FmS* 12: 1–54. 1978.—Georges Duby. *The Three Orders. Feudal Society Imagined.* Transl. by A. Goldhammer. 1980. T. Struve. "Pedes rei publicae. Die dienenden Stände im Verständinis des Mittelalters." *HZ* 236: 1–48. 1983.—O. G. Oexle. "Tria genera hominum. Zur Geschichte eines Deutungsschemas der sozialen Wirklichkeit in Antike und Mittelalter." In: *Institutionen Kultur und Gesellschaft im Mittelalter. Festschrift für J. Fleckenstein*: 483–500. 1984.

On medieval kingship see *Das Königtum. Seine geistigen und rechtlichen Grundlagen.* 1956.—T. Schieder, ed. *Beiträge zur Geschichte des mittelalterlichen deutschen Königtums.* 1973.—P. R. Mathé. *Studien zum früh- und hochmittelalterlichen Königtum, Adel und Herrscherethik.* 1976.—E. Schubert. *König und Reich. Studien zur spätmittelalterlichen deutschen Verfassungsgeschichte.* 1979.—On the terminology of lordship see E. Müller-Mertens, *Regnum Teutonicum. Aufkommen und Verbreitung der deutschen Reichs- und Königsauffassung im frühen Mittelalter.* 1970.—H. Beumann. "Die Bedeutung des Kaisertums für die Entstehung der deutschen Nation im Spiegel der Bezeichnungen von Reich und Herrscher." In: *Aspekte der Nationenbildung im Mittelalter*: 317–65. Edited by H. Beumann and W. Schröder. 1978.—Fundamental for the insignia of lordship is P. E. Schramm, *Herrschaftszeichen und Staatssymbolik. Beiträge zur ihrer Geschichte vom 3. bis zum 16. Jahrhundert.* 3 vols. 1954–56. Rich pictorial material is contained in the superbly documented volumes by P. E. Schramm and F. Mütherich, *Denkmale der deutschen Könige und Kaiser.* 2 vols. (vol. 2 by P. E. Schramm and H. Fillitz). 1962–1978. Specifically on the imperial jewels in Vienna see H. Fillitz, *Die Insignien und Kleinodien des Heiligen Römischen Reiches.* 1954.

On the position of the princes and the rise of territorial lordship see J. Ficker, *Vom Reichsfürstenstande. Forschungen zur Geschichte der Reichsverfassung, zunächst im XII. und XIII. Jahrhunderte.* Vol. 1, 1861; vol. 2, ed. by P. Puntschart. Parts 1–3. 1911–23.—W. Schlesinger. *Die Entstehung der Landesherrschaft. Untersuchungen vorwiegend nach mitteldeutschen Quellen.* 1941.—E. E. Stengel. "Land- und lehnrechtliche Grundlagen des Reichsfürstenstandes." *ZRG GA* 66: 294–342. 1948.—Th. Mayer. *Fürsten und Staat. Studien zur Verfassungsgeschichte des deutschen Mittelalters.* 1950.—H. Patze, ed. *Der deutsche Territorialstaat im 14. Jahrhundert.* 2 vols. 1970–71.

On the structural transformation of the medieval nobility see K. Schmid,

"Zur Problematik von Familie, Sippe und Geschichte, Haus und Dynastie beim mittelalterlichen Adel. Vorfragen zum Thema 'Adel und Herrschaft im Mittelalter'." *ZGO* 105: 1–62. 1957.—K. Schmid. "Über die Struktur des Adels im früheren Mittelalter." *JfLF* 19: 1–23. 1959.—W. Störmer. *Früher Adel. Studien zur politischen Führungschicht im fränkisch-deutschen Reich vom 8. bis zum 11. Jahrhundert.* 2 vols. 1973.—K. F. Werner. "Adel. A. Fränkisches Reich, Imperium, Frankreich." In: *Lexikon des Mittelalters.* Vol. 1, cols. 118–28. 1980.

On ministerials see K. Bosl, *Die Reichsministerialität der Salier und Staufer. Ein Beitrag zur Geschichte des hochmittelalterlichen deutschen Volkes, Staates und Reiches.* 2 vols. 1950–51.—K. Bosl. "Das ius ministerialium. Dienstrecht und Lehnsrecht im deutschen Mittelalter." In: *Studien zum mittelalterlichen Lehenswesen* (see p. 710): 51–94.—J. Fleckenstein, ed. *Herrschaft und Stand. Untersuchungen zur Sozialgeschchite im 13. Jahrhundert.* 1977.

On the history of the city in the Middle Ages see H. Planitz, *Die deutsche Stadt im Mittelalter. Von der Römerzeit bis zu den Zunftkämpfen.* 2d ed. 1965–*Untersuchungen zur Gesellschaftlichen Struktur der mittelalterlichen Städte in Europa* 1966.—C. Haase, ed. *Die Stadt des Mittelalters.* 3 vols. 1969–73.—B. Töpfer, ed. *Stadt und Stadtbürgertum in der deutschen Geschichte des 13. Jahrhunderts.* 1976.—H. Stoob, ed. *Alstständisches Bürgertum.* 2 vols. 1978.—E. Ennen. *The Medieval Town.* Translated by N. Fryde. 1979.—B. Diestelkamp, ed. *Beiträge zum hochmittelalterlichen Städtewesen.* 1982.

On the history of the peasantry see G. Franz, *Geschichte des Bauernstandes vom frühen Mittelalter bis zum 19. Jahrhundert.* 1970.—R. Wenskus et al., eds. *Wort und Begriff "Bauer".* 1974.—G. Franz, ed. *Deutsches Bauerntum im Mittelalter.* 1976.

On the economic history of the Middle Ages see *The Cambridge Economic History of Europe.* Edited by M. M. Postan et al. 3 vols. 1966 (vol. 1, 2d ed.), 1952, 1963.—H. Aubin and W. Zorn, eds. *Handbuch der deutschen Wirtschafts- und Sozialgeschichte.* Vol. 1, 1971.—H. Kellenbenz. *Deutsche Wirtschaftsgeschichte.* Vol. 1, 1977.—C. M. Cipolla and K. Borchardt, eds. *Europäische Wirtschaftsgeschichte.* Vol. 1, 1978.—H. Kellenbenz, ed. *Handbuch der Europäischen Wirtschafts- und Sozialgeschichte.* Vol. 2, 1980.—N. J. G. Pounds. *An Economic History of Medieval Europe.* 1974.—C. Cipolla. *Before the Industrial Revolution: European Society and Economy, 1000–1700.* 2d ed. 1980.—R.-H. Bautier. *The Economic Development of Medieval Europe.* 1971.

On the emergence of the money economy see Th. Mayer, "Geschichte der Finazwirtschaft vom Mittelalter bis zum Ende des 18. Jahrhunderts." In: *Handbuch der Finanzwissenschaft,* vol. 1, pp. 236–72. Edited by W. Gerloff and F. Neumark. 2d ed. 1952.—A. Suhle. *Deutsche Münz- und Geldgeschichte von den Anfängen bis zum 15. Jahrhundert.* 3d ed. 1964.—M. M. Postan. *Medieval Trade and Finance.* 1973.—R. Sprandel. *Das mittelalterliche Zahlungssystem nach hansich-nordischen Quellen des 13.–15.Jahrhunderts.* 1975.

On the development of technology see L. White, Jr., *Medieval Society and*

Social Change. 1962.—L. White, "Die Ausbreitung der Technik, 500–1000." In: *Europäische Wirtschaftsgeschichte* (see above), vol. 1, pp. 91–110.

On medieval long distance trade see the bibliographic references on pp. 714 ff.

On the economic foundations of kingship and territorial lordship see E. Bamberger, "Die Finanzverwaltung in den deutschen Territorien des Mittelalters (1200–1500)." *ZfgSW* 77: 168–255. 1922/23.—B. Heusinger. "Servitium regis in der deutschen Kaiserzeit. Untersuchungen über die wirtschaftlichen Verhältnisse des deutschen Königtums, 900–1250." *AUF* 8: 26–159. 1923.— H. Spangenberg. *Territorialwirtschaft und Stadtwirtschaft.* 1932.—H.-J. Riekenberg. "Königsstraße und Königsgut in liudolfingischer und frühsalischer Zeit (919–1056)." *AUF* 17: 32–254. 1941.—H. Oehler. *Das Itinerar des Königs, seine Ordnung und seine Beziehungen zur Regierungstätigkeit in der Zeit Kaiser Lothars III.* Dissertation. Freiburg i. Br. 1957.—J. Dikow. *Die politische Bedeutung der Geldwirtschaft in der frühen Stauferzeit.* Dissertation. Münster. 1958.—W. Metz. *Staufische Güterverzeichnisse. Untersuchungen zur Verfasungs- und Wirtschaftsgeschichte des 12. und 13. Jahrhunderts.* 1964.— U. Dirlmeier. *Mittelalterliche Hoheitsträger im wirtschaftlichen Wettbewerb.* 1966.—C. Brühl. *Fodrum, gistrum, servitium regis. Studien zur den wirtschaftlichen Grundlagen des Königtums im Frankenreich und in den fränkischen Nachfolgestaaten Deutschland, Frankreich und Italien vom 6. bis zur Mitte des 14. Jahrhunderts.* 2 vols. 1968.—A. Haverkamp. "Königsgastung und Reichssteuer." *ZfbLG* 31: 768–821. 1968.—G. Droege. "Die Ausbildung der mittelalterlichen territorialen Finanzverwaltung." In: *Der deutsche Territorialstaat im 14. Jahrhundert* (cf. p. 710), vol. 1, pp. 325–45.—C. Brühl. "Die Finanzpolitik Friedrich Barbarossas in Italien." *HZ* 213: 13–37. 1971.—W. Metz. *Das Servitium regis. Zur Erforschung der wirtschaftlichen Grundlagen des hochmittelalterlichen deutschen Königtums.* 1978.—H. Stehkämper. "Geld bei deutschen Königswahlen des 13. Jahrhunderts." In: *Wirtschaftskräfte und Wirtschaftswege,* vol. 1, pp. 83–135. Edited by J. Schneider. 1978.

On knighthood see the now obsolete surveys of K. H. Roth von Schreckenstein, *Die Ritterwürde und der Ritterstand.* 1886; and L. Gautier, *La chevalerie.* 1884.—From the newer scholarship on knighthood see S. Painter, *French Chivalry.* 1940.—A. Borst. "Das Rittertum im Hochmittelalter. Idee und Wirklichkeit." *Sc* 10: 213–31. 1959.—J. M. van Winter. *Rittertum. Ideal und Wirklichkeit.* 1969.—R. Barber. *The Knight and Chivalry.* 1970.—A. von Reitzenstein. *Rittertum und Ritterschaft.* 1971.—J. Fleckenstein. "Friedrich Barbarossa und das Rittertum. Zur Bedeutung der großen Mainzer Hoftage von 1184 und 1188." In: *Festschrift für H. Heimpel,* vol. 2, pp. 1023–41. 1972.— M. Foss. *Chivalry.* 1975.—A. Borst, ed. *Das Rittertum im Mittelalter.* 1976.— J. Fleckenstein. "Die Entstehung des niederen Adels und das Rittertum." In: *Herrschaft und Stand* (see p. 711): 17–39.—G. Duby. *The Chivalrous Society.* Transl. by Cynthia Postan. 1977.—R. Barber. *The Reign of Chivalry.* 1980.— J. Fleckenstein. "Über Ritter und Rittertum. Zur Erforschung einer mittelalterlichen Lebensform." In: *Mittelalterforschung. Forschung und Information:* 104–14. Edited by R. Kurzrock. 1981.—W. H. Jackson, ed. *Knighthood in*

Medieval Literature. 1981.—F. Cardini. *Alle radici della cavalleria medievale.* 1981.—J. Flori. *L'idéologie du glaive. Préhistoire de la chevalerie.* 1983.—K. Leyser. "Early Medieval Canon Law and the Beginnings of Knighthood." In: *Institutïonen, Kultur und Gesellschaft im Mittelalter* (see p. 710): 549–66.— W. Rösener. "Bauer und Ritter im Hochmittelalter. Aspekte ihrer Lebensform, Standesbildung und sozialen Differenzierung im 12. und 13. Jahrhundert." Ibid.: 665–92.—G. Duby. *William Marshal, The Flower of Chivalry.* Transl. by R. Howard. 1984.—F. Gies. *The Knight in History.* 1984.—M. Keen. *Chivalry.* 1984.—B. Arnold. *German Knighthood, 1050–1300.* 1985.—*Das Ritterbild in Mittelalter und Renaissance.* 1985.—Ch. Harper-Bill and R. Harvey, eds. *The Ideals and Practice of Medieval Knighthood.* 1987.—Popular accounts include the following: W. Hensen, *Die Ritter. Eine Reportage über das Mittelalter.* 1976.—M. Meyer and E. Lessing. *Deutsche Ritter—Deutsche Burgen.* 1976.—K. Brunner and F. Daim. *Ritter, Knappen, Edelfrauen. Ideologie und Realität des Rittertums im Mittelalter.* 1981.

On the emergence of the knightly class see E. F. Otto, "Von der Abschließung des Ritterstandes." *HZ* 162: 19–39. 1940.—J. Fleckenstein. "Zum Problem der Abschließung des Ritterstandes." In: *Historische Forschungen für W. Schlesinger:* 252–71. 1974.

On the history of the words "miles," "chevalier," and "ritter" and their meaning see P. Guilhiermoz, *Essai sur l'origine de la noblesse en France au moyen âge:* 331 ff. 1902.—G. Gougenheim. "De 'chevalier' à 'cavalier.'" In: *Mélanges de philologie romane et de littérature médiévale offerts à E. Hoepffner:* 117–26. 1949.—K.-J. Hollyman. *Le dévelopment du vocabulaire féodale en France pendant le haut moyen âge.* 1957.—P. van Luyn. "Les 'milites' dans la France du XIe siècle. Examen des sources narratives." *MA* 77: 5–51, 193– 238. 1971.—J. Johrendt. *'Milites' und 'Militia' im 11. Jahrhundert. Untersuchungen zur Frühgeschichte des Rittertums in Frankreich und Deutschland.* Dissertation. Erlangen-Nuremberg. 1971.—H. G. Reuter. *Die Lehre vom Ritterstand. Zum Ritterbegriff in Historiographie und Dichtung vom 11. bis zum 13. Jahrhundert.* 2d ed. 1975.—J. Flori. "La notion de chevalerie dans les chansons de geste du XIIe siècle. Etude historique de vocabulaire." *MA* 81: 211–44, 407–45. 1975.—K. O. Brogsitter. "'Miles,' 'chevalier,' und 'ritter.'" In: *Sprachliche Interferenz. Festschrift für W. Betz:* 421–35. 1977.—J. Bumke. *The Concept of Knighthood in the Middle Ages.* Transl. by W. T. H. and Erika Jackson. 1982.—J. Flori. "Chevalerie et liturgie. Remise des armes et vocabulaire 'chevaleresque' dans les sources liturgiques du XIe au XIVe siècle." *MA* 84: 247–78, 409–42. 1978.—H. Keller. "Militia. Vassalität und frühes Rittertum im Spiegel oberitalienischer miles-Belege des 10. und 11. Jahrhunderts." *QFIA* 62: 59–118. 1982.

On medieval itinerant kingship and the beginnings of the establishment of residences see A. Schulte, "Anläufe zu einer festen Residenz der deutschen Könige im Hochmittelalter." *HJb* 55: 131–42. 1935.—H. Sproemberg. "Residenz und Territorium im niederländischen Raum." *RVjb* 6: 113–39. 1936.— W. Berges. "Das Reich ohne Hauptstadt." In: *Das Hauptstadtproblem in der Geschichte. Festgabe zum 90. Geburtstag F. Meinekkes:* 1–29. 1952.—E.

Ewig. "Résidence et capitale pendant le haut moyen âge." *Rh* 230: 25–77.
1963.—H. C. Peyers. "Das Reisekönigtum des Mittelalters." *VSWG* 51: 1–21.
1964.—H. Koller. "Die Residenz im Mittelalter." *JGoR* 12/13: 9–39. 1966/
67.—H. Patze. "Die Bildung der landesherrlichen Residenzen im Reich
während des 14. Jahrhunderts." In: *Stadt und Stadtherr im 14. Jahrhundert*:
1–54. Edited by W. Rausch. 1972.

On the ceremony of traveling and especially on the arrival of the lord see E.
Peterson, "Die Einholung des Kyrios." *ZfsT* 7: 682–702. 1930.—H.-W. Kle-
witz. "Die Festkrönungen der deutschen Könige." *ZRG KA* 28: 48–96.
1939.—W. Bulst. "Susceptacula regum." In: *Corona quernea. Festgabe K.
Strecker zum 80. Geburtstag*: 97–135. 1941.—E. H. Kantorowicz. *Laudes re-
giae. A Study in Liturgical Acclamations and Medieval Ruler Worship*. 1946.—
A. M. Drabek. *Reisen und Reisezermoniell der römischen-deuschen Herrscher
im Spätmittelalter*. 1964.—W. Dotzauer. "Die Ankunft des Herrschers. Der
fürstliche 'Einzug' in die Stadt." *AKG* 55: 245–88. 1973.—H. M. Schaller.
"Der heilige Tag als Termin mittelalterliche Staatsakte." *DA* 30: 1–24. 1974.—
P. Willmes. *Der Herrscher-Adventus im Kloster des Frühmittelalters*. 1976.—
H. J. Berbig. "Zur rechtlichen Relevanz von Ritus und Zeremoniell im römisch-
deutschen Imperium." *ZKG* 92: 204–49. 1981.—S. Zak. "Das Tedeum als
Huldigungsgesang." *HJb* 102: 1–32. 1982.

On the history of the word *höfisch* see the unsatisfactory work of W. Schrad-
er, *Studien zum Wort 'höfisch' in der mittelhochdeutschen Dichtung*. 1935. For
a critique see P. Ganz, "Der Begriff des 'Höfischen' bei den Germanisten." *WS*
4: 16–32. 1977. On the history of the word *curialis* see R. Köhn, "Militia
curialis" (see chapter VI).—C. S. Jaeger. "The Courtier Bishop" (see p. 731).—
P. F. Ganz, "curialis/hövesch" (unpublished manuscript).

CHAPTER II
THE ADOPTION OF FRENCH ARISTOCRATIC
CULTURE IN GERMANY

On the historical relations between Germany and France in the High Middle
Ages see W. Kienast, *Deutschland und Frankreich in der Kaiserzeit (900–
1270). Weltkaiser und Einzelkönige*. 3 vols. 2nd ed. 1974–75. Kienast did not
discuss the social, cultural, and literary connections. Beyond this I refer the
reader to the works of the historian Karl F. Werner, who may be regarded as the
leading expert on German-French history.

The cultural ties between France and Germany in the Middle Ages used to be
seen almost entirely from nationalistic perspectives. The older literature no longer deserves to be mentioned. More recently the topic has been treated only by
the Romanist Fritz Neubert. See F. Neubert, "Ein Jahrtausend deutsch-
französischer geistiger Beziehungen." *Arch.* 188: 41–65. 1951; expanded in F.
Neubert, *Studien zur vergleichenden Literaturgeschichte*: 147–201. 1952.—F.
Neubert. "A propos des débuts des relations culturelles entre la France et l'Allemagne." In: *Homenaje à F. Krüger*, vol. 2, pp. 547–74. 1954.

On the international economic ties and trade links in the High Middle Ages, see in addition to the references for chapter I, W. Heyd, *Geschichte des Levanthandels im Mittelalter*. 2 vols. 1879—K Höhlbaum. "Kölns älteste Handelsprivilegien für England." *HGb*. 1882: 39–48.—A. Schulte. *Geschichte des mittelalterlichen Handels und Verkehrs zwischen Westdeutschland und Italien mit Ausschluß von Venedig*. 2 vols. 1900.—F. Keutgen. "Der Großhandel im Mittelalter." *HGb*. 1901: 65–138.—A. Schaube. *Handelsgeschichte der romanischen Völker des Mittelmeergebiets bis zum Ende der Kreuzzüge*. 1906.—R. Häppel. *Brügges Entwicklung zum mittelalterlichen Weltkmarkt*. 1908.—H. Bächtold. *Der norddeutsche Handel im 12. und beginnenden 13. Jahrhundert*. 1910.—F. Bastian. "Regensburgs Handelsbeziehungen zu Frankreich." In: *Festgabe H. Gauert*: 91–110. 1910.—W. Stein. "Der Streit zwischen Köln und Flandern um die Rheinschiffahrt im 12. Jahrhundert." *HGb*. 17: 187–213. 1911.—W. Stein. *Handels- und Verkehrsgeschichte der deutschen Kaiserzeit*. 1922.—G. Bens. *Der deutsche Warenfernhandel im Mittelalter*. 1926.—H. Laurent. *Un grand commerce d'exportation au moyen âge. La draperie des Pays-Bas en France et dans les pays méditerranées (XIIe—XVe siècle)*. 1935.— H. Ammann. "Deutschland und die Messen der Champagne." *JARG* 2: 61–75. 1936.—H. Ammann. "Die Anfänge der detusch-italienischen Wirtschaftsbeziehungen des Mittelalters." *RVjb*. 7: 179–94. 1937.—H. Ammann. "Untersuchungen zur Geschichte der Deutschen im mittelalterlichen Frankreich." *DALV* 3: 306–33, 1939; 5: 580–90, 1941.—H. Reincke. "Die Deutschlandfahrt der Flandrer während der hansischen Frühzeit." *HGb*. 67/68: 51–95. 1942/43.—H. Heimpel. "Seide aus Regensburg." *MIÖG* 62: 270–98. 1954.— H. Ammann. "Deutschland und die Tuchindustrie Nordwesteuropas im Mittelalter." *HGb*. 72: 1–63. 1954.—*Medieval Trade in the Mediterranean World*. Illustrative documents translated with introduction and notes by R. S. Lopez and I. W. Raymond. 1955.—J. Sydow. "Beiträge zur Geschichte des deutschen Italienhandels im Früh- und Hochmittelalter." Part 1. *VHVO* 97: 405–13. 1956.—H. Ammann. "Die Anfänge des Aktivhandels und der Tucheinfuhr aus Nordwesteuropa nach dem Mittelmeergebiet." In: *Studi in onore di A. Sapori*: 273–310. 1957.—H. Ammann. "Wirtschaftsbeziehungen zwischen Oberdeutschland und Polen im Mittelalter." *VSWG* 49: 289–319. 1962.—H. Kellenbenz. "Rheinische Verkehrswege der Hanse zwischen Ostsee und Mittelmeer." In: *Die Deutsche Hanse als Mittler zwischen Ost und West*: 103–18. 1963.—W. Rausch. *Handel an der Donau*. Vol. 1. 1969.—M. Mitterauer. *Zollfreiheit und Marktbereich. Studien zur mittelalterlichen Wirtschaftsverfassung am Beispiel einer niederösterreichischen Altsiedellandschaft*. 1969.—R. Schönfeld. "Regensburg im Fernhandel des Mittelalters." *VHVO* 113: 7–48. 1973.—M. Spallanzini, ed. *La Lana come materia prima. Atti della "Prima settimani di studio."* 1974.—H. Kellenbenz, ed. *Zwei Jahrtausende Kölner Wirtschaft*. Vol. 1. 1975.—T. H. Lloyd. *The English Wool Trade in the Middle Ages*. 1977.—W. von Stromer. "Bernardus Teotonicus und die Geschäftsbeziehungen zwischen den deutschen Ostalpen und Venedig vor Gründung des Fondaco dei Tedeschi." In: *Beiträge zur Handels-und Verkehrsgeschichte*: 1–15. Edited by P. W. Roth. 1978.—W. von Stromer. *Bernardus Teotonicus e i rapporti commerciali tra la Germania meridionale e Venezia prima della istituzione del Fondaco dei Tedes-*

chi. 1978.—N. Fryde. "Deutsche Englandkaufleute in frühhansischer Zeit." *HGb.* 97: 1–14. 1979.—T. H. Lloyd. *Alien Merchants in England in the High Middle Ages.* 1982.—G. Rösch. *Venedig und das Reich. Handels- und verkehrspolitische Beziehungen in der deutschen Kaiserzeit.* 1982.

On the rise of higher education in France and the so-called twelfth-century renaissance see the classic work by C. H. Haskins, *The Renaissance of the Twelfth Century.* 1927. Also: M. Clagett et al., eds. *Twelfth-century Europe and the foundations of modern society.* 1961.—M. de Gandillac and E. Jeauneau, eds. *Entretiens sur la renaissance du 12e siècle.* 1968.—P. Weimar, ed. *Die Renaissance der Wissenschaften im 12. Jahrhundert.* 1981.—R. L. Benson and G. Constable, eds. *Renaissance and Renewal in the Twelfth Century.* 1982.

On the beginnings of the universities see H. Rashdall, *The Universities of Europe in the Middle Ages.* 3 vols. 2d ed. 1936.—H. Grundmann. *Vom Ursprung der Universität im Mittelalter.* 2d ed. 1960.—J. Ehlers. "Die hohen Schulen." In: *Die Renaissance der Wissenschaften im 12. Jahrhundert* (see above): 57–85. On student life see C. H. Haskins, "The Life of Medieval Students as Illustrated by Their Letters." *AHR* 3: 203–29. 1898. On the German students in Paris see A. Budinsky, *Die Universität Paris und die Fremden an derselben im Mittelalter.* 1876.—A. Hofmeister. "Studien über Otto von Freising." Part 1. *NA* 37: 99–161, 633–768. 1912. On the connection between education and courtly culture see P. Classen, "Die Hohen Schulen und die Gesellschaft im 12. Jahrhundert." *AKG* 48: 155–80. 1966.

On the reception of early French scholasticism in Germany see H. Weisweiler, *Das Schrifttum der Schule Anselms von Laon und Wilhelms von Champeaux in deutschen Bibliotheken. Ein Beitrag zur Geschichte der Verbreitung der ältesten scholastischen Schule in deutschen Landen.* 1936.—P. Classen. "Zur Geschichte der Frühscholastik in Österreich und Bayern." *MIÖG* 67: 249–77. 1959.

A good survey of the linguistic influence of France is given by E. Öhmann, "Der romanische Einfluß auf das Deutsche bis zum Ausgang des Mittelalters." In: *Deutsche Wortgeschichte,* vol. 1, pp. 321–96. Edited by F. Maurer and H. Rupp. 3d ed. 1972. The entire material is collected in H. Palander, "Der französische Einfluß auf die deutsche Sprache im 12. Jahrhundert." *MSNH* 3: 75–204. 1902.—H. Suolathi. *Der französische Einfluß auf die deutsche Sprache im 13. Jahrhundert.* 2 vols. 1929–33. Also: E. Öhmann, *Studien über die französischen Worte im Deutschen im 12. und 13. Jahrhundert.* Dissertation. Helsinki, 1918.—E. Öhmann. *Die mittelhochdeutsche Lehnprägung nach altfranzösistchem Vorbild.* 1951.—T. Frings. *Germania Romana.* Vol. 1, 2d ed., 1966; vol. 2 (by G. Müller and T. Frings), 1968.—E. Öhmann. "Das französische Wortgut im Mittelniederdeutschen." *ZfdSP* 23: 35–47. 1967.

The literary connections between France and Germany in the Middle Ages have never been thoroughly studied. Brief overviews are given in the following works: V. Klemperer, "Romanische Literaturen (Einfluß auf die deutsche)." In: *Reallexikon der deutschen Literaturgeschichte,* vol. 3, pp. 73–107. Edited by P. Merker and W. Stammler. 1928–29.—H. Spanke. *Deutsche und französische Dichtung des Mittelaters.* 1943.—H. Schneider. "Deutsche und französische

Dichtung im Zeitalter der Hohenstaufen." *Un* 1: 953–66. 1946.—C. Minnis.
"Französisch-deutsche Literaturberührungen im Mittelalter." *RJb* 4: 55–123,
1951; 7: 66–95, 1955/56.—F. H. Oppenheim. "Der Einfluß der französischen
Literatur auf die deutsche." In: *Deutsche Philologie im Aufriß*, vol. 3, cols.
1–106. 2d ed. 1962.—J. Bumke. *Die romanisch-deutschen Literaturbeziehungen im Mittelalter*. 1967.—W. P. Gerritsen. "Les relations littéraires
entre la France et les Pays-Bas au moyen âge." In: *Moyen âge et littérature
comparée*: 28–46. 1967.—R. Schnell. *Zum Verhältnis von hoch- und spätmittelalterlicher Literatur*: 83 ff. 1978.

There are numerous specialized studies on the reception of the *roman
courtois*, but only a few works that are comprehensive in nature. See W.
Kellermann, "Altdeutsche und altfranzösische Literatur." *GRM* 11: 217–25,
278–88. 1923.—H. Hempel. "Französischer und deutscher Stil im höfischen
Epos." *GRM* 23: 1–24. 1935.—P. Tilvis. "Über die unmittelbaren Vorlagen
von Hartmanns Erec und Iwein, Ulrichs Lanzelet und Wolframs Parzival."
NphM 60: 29–65, 129–44. 1959.—C. Lofmark. "Der höfische Dichter als
Übersetzer." In: *Probleme mittelhochdeutscher Erzählformen*: 40–64. Edited
by P. F. Ganz and W. Schröder. 1972.—C. Lofmark. *The Authority of the
Source in Middle High German Narrative Poetry*. 1981.

On the theory of the *adaptation courtoise* see M. Huby, "L'adaptation courtoise: position des problèmes." In: *Moyen âge et littérature comparée*: 16–27.
1967.—M. Huby. *L'adaptation des romans courtois en Allemagne au XIIe et
au XIIe siècle*. 1968.—R. Pérennec. "Adaptation et société. L'adaptation par
Hartmann d'Aue du roman de Chrétien de Troyes, Erec et Enide." *Eg* 28: 289–
303. 1973.—D. Buschinger, ed. *Actes due colloque des 9 et 10 avril 1976 sur
"L'adaptation courtoise" en littérature médiévale allemande*. 1976.—J. Fourquet. "Les adaptations allemandes de romans chevaleresque français. Changement de fonction sociale et changement de vision." *Eg* 32: 97–107. 1977.—A.
Wolf. "Die 'adaptation courteoise.' Kritische Anmerkungen zu einem neuen
Dogma." *GRM* N.F. 27: 257–83. 1977.—J.-M. Pastré. "Raffinement du style
et raffinement des moeurs dans les oeuvres allemandes d'adaptation." In: *Littérature et société au moyen âge*: 71–87. Edited by D. Buschinger. 1978.—J.-M.
Pastré. *Rhétorique et adaptation dans les oeuvres allemandes du moyen âge*.
1979.—M. Huby. "Zur Definition der adaptation courtoise. Kritische Antwort
auf kritische Anmerkungen." *GRM* N.F. 33: 301–22. 1983.—R. Pérennec.
*Recherches sur le roman arthurien en vers en Allemagne aux XIIe et XIIIe
siècles*. 2 vols. 1984.

On the reception of Romance lyric see A. Lüderitz, *Die Liebestheorie der
Provençalen bei den Minnesingern der Stauferzeit*. 1904.—W. Nikkel. *Sirventes
und Spruchdichtung*. 1907.—O. Gottschalk. *Der deutsche Minneleich und sein
Verhältinis zu Lai und Descort*. Dissertation. Marburg. 1908.—F. Gennrich.
"Der deutsche Minnesang in seinem Verhältnis zur Troubadour- und
Trouvèrekunst." *ZfdB* 2: 536–66, 622–32. 1926.—H. Spanke. "Romanische
und mittellateinische Fromen in der Metrik von Minnesangs Frühling." *ZfrPh*
49: 191–235. 1929.—W. Bücheler. *Französiche Einflüsse auf den Strophenbau
und die Strophenbindung bei den deutschen Minnesängern*. Dissertation. Bonn.
1930.—T. Frings. *Minnesingers and Troubadours*. 1949.—T. Frings. "Erfors-

chung des Minnesangs." *FuF* 26: 9–13, 39–43. 1950.—I. Frank and W. Müller-Blattau, eds. *Trouvères et Minnesänger*. 2 vols. 1952–56.—H.H. S. Räkel. "Metrik und Rhythmus in der deutschen und französischen Lyrik am Ende des 12. Jahrhunderts." In: *Akten des V. Internationalen Germanisten-Kongresses Cambridge 1975*, vol. 2, pp. 340–49. Edited by L. Forster and H.-G. Roloff. 1976.—S. Ranawake. *Höfische Strophenkunst, Vergleichende Untersuchungen zur Formeltypologie von Minnesang und Trouvèrelied an der Wende zum Spätmittelalter*. 1976.

On the contrafacta see F. Gennrich, "Liedkontrafaktur in mittelhochdeutscher und althochdeutscher Zeit." *ZfdA* 82: 105–41. 1948/50.—U. Aarburg. "Melodien zur frühen deutschen Minnesang." *ZfdA* 87: 24–44. 1956/77; expanded version in: *Der deutsche Minnesang*: 378–423. Edited by H. Fromm. 1961.—E. Jammers. "Der Vers der Trobadors und Trouvères und die deutschen Kontrafakturen." In: *Medium Aevum Vivum. Festschrift für W. Bulst*: 147–60. 1969.—B. Kippenberg. *Der Rhythmus im Minnesang. Eine Kritik der literatur- und musikhistorischen Forschung mit einer Übersicht über die musikalischen Quellen*. 1962.

On the remaining genres see H. Schneider, "Deutsche und französische Heldenepik." *ZfdA* 51: 200–43. 1926.—E. Wechssler. "Deutsche und französische Mystik. Meister Ekkehart und Bernhard von Clairvaux." *Eu.* 30: 40–93. 1929.—H. Niedner. *Die deutschen und französischen Osterspiele bis zum 15. Jahrhundert*. 1932.—F. Panzer. "Die nationale Epik Deutschlands und Frankreichs in ihrem geschichtlichen Zusammenhang." *ZfdB* 14: 249–65. 1938.—H.P. Goodmann. *Original Elements in the French and German Passion Plays*. Ph.D. dissertation. Bryn Mawr College. 1951.—F. Frosch-Freiburg. *Schwankmären und Fabliaux. Ein Stoff- und Motivvergleich*. 1971.—A. Wolf. "Die Verschriftlichung der Nibelungensage und die französische-deutschen Literaturbeziehungen im Mittelalter." In: *Hohenemser Studien zum Nibelungenlied*: 53–71. Edited by A. Masser. 1981.

CHAPTER III
MATERIAL CULTURE AND SOCIAL STYLE

1. Castles and tents

On castle construction in the Middle Ages see O. Piper, *Burgenkunde*. 3d ed. 1912.—B. Ebhardt. *Der Wehrbau Europas im Mittelalter. Versuch einer Gesamtdarstellung der europäischen Burgen*. 2 vols. 1939–58.—E. Klebel. "Mittelalterliche Burgen und ihr Recht." *ÖAW* 89: 27–61. 1952.—P. Héliot. "Sur les résidence principières bâties en France du Xe au XIIe siècle." *MA* 61: 27–61. 1955.—W. Kiess. *Die Burgen in ihrer Funktion als Wohnbauten*. Dissertation. Stuttgart. 1961.—*Deutsche Königspfalzen. Beiträge zu ihrer historischen und archäologischen Erforschung*. 3 vols. 1963–79. This important work treats chiefly the older palace structures of the ninth through the eleventh centuries. For the courtly period see especially K. Bosl, "Pfalzen und Forsten" vol. 1: 1– 29, and K. Hauck, "Tiergärten im Pfalzbereich," vol. 1: 30–74.—H. Kunstmann. *Mensch und Burg. Burgenkundliche Betrachtungen an ostfränki-*

schen Wehranlagen. 1967.—H.-M. Maurer. "Die Entstehung der hochmittelalterlichen Adelsburg in Südwestdeutschland." *ZGO* 117: 295–332.—H. Ebner. "Entwicklung und Rechtsverhältnisse der mittelalterlichen Burg." *ZhVS* 61: 27–50. 1970.—W. Anderson. *Castles of Europe from Charlemagne to the Renaissance.* 1970.—P. Warner. *The Medieval Castle. Life in a Fortress in Peace and War.* 1971.—H. J. Mrusek. *Gestalt und Entwicklung der feudalen Eigenbefestigung im Mittelalter.* 1973.—H. Ebner. "Die Burgenpolitik und ihre Bedeutung für die Geschichte des Mittelalters." *Ca.* 164: 33–51. 1974.—J. and F. Gies. *Life in a Medieval Castle.* 1974.—C. Meckseper. "Ausstrahlungen des französischen Burgenbaus nach Mitteleuropa im 13. Jahrhundert." In: *Beiträge zur Kunst des Mittelalters. Festschrift für H. Wentzel:* 135–44. 1975.—L. Villena. *Glossaire. Burgenfachwörterbuch des mittelalterlichen Wehrbaus.* 1975.— H. Patze, ed. *Burgen im deutschen Sprachraum. Ihre rechts- und verfassungsgeschichtliche Bedeutung.* 2 vols. 1976. The following essays in this important collection should be mentioned: H. Ebner, "Die Burg als Forschungsproblem mittelalterlicher Verfassungsgeschichte," vol. 1: 11–84; F. Schwind, "Zur Verfassung und Bedeutung der Reichsburgen, vornehmlich im 12. und 13. Jahrhundert," vol. 1: 85–122; H.-M. Maurer, "Rechtsverhältnisse der hochmittelalterlichen Adelsburg vornehmlich in Südwestdeutschland," vol. 2: 77–190.—J. Gardelles. "Les palais dans l'Europe occidentale chrétienne du Xe au XIIe siècle." *CCM* 19: 117–34. 1976.—T. Martin. "Die Pfalzen im 13. Jahrhundert." In: *Herrschaft und Stand* (see p. 711): 277–301.—H. Ebner. "Die Burg in historiographischen Werken des Mittelalters." In: *Festschrift für F. Hausmann*: 119– 51. 1977.—R. Huber and R. Rieth, eds. *Burgen und feste Plätze. Der Wehrbau vor Einführung der Feuerwaffen.* 2d ed. 1977.—J. F. Burke. *Life in the Castle in Medieval England.* 1978.—W. Hortz. *Kleine Kunstgeschichte der deutschen Burg.* 4th ed. 1979.—F. Bottomley. *The Castle Explorer's Guide.* 1979.—G. Binding (et al.). "Burg." In: *Lexikon des Mittelalters,* vol. 2, cols. 957–1003. 1983. R. Allen Brown. *The Architecture of Castles: A Visual Guide.* 1984.—K. Reyerson and F. Rowe, eds. *The Medieval Castle: Romance and Reality.* 1984. This list of references does not include the rich castle scholarship on particular regions.

On the Hohenstaufen royal castles and palaces in particular see also G. Schlag, *Die deutschen Kaiserpfalzen.* 1940.—O. E. Wülfing. *Burgen der Hohenstaufen in Schwaben, Franken und Hessen.* 1960.—H.-M. Maurer. "Burgen." In: *Die Zeit der Staufer* (see p. 708), vol. 3, pp. 119–28.—F. Arens. "Die staufischen Königspfalzen." Ibid.: 129–42.—W. Hotz. *Pfalzen und Burgen der Stauferzeit. Geschichte und Gestalt.* 1981. There is also a whole series of important monographs on individual palaces and castles, which cannot be listed here.

On the evaluation of literary sources see H. Leo, "Über Burgenbau und Burgeneinrichtung in Detuschland vom 11. bis zum 14. Jahrhundert." *HTb* 8:165–245. 1837.—A. Schultz. *Über Bau und Einrichtung der Hofburgen des XII. und XIII. Jahrhunderts.* 1862.—H. Kupfer. *Die Burg in der deutschen Dichtung und Sage.* Part 1. Progr. Schneeberg. 1880.—A. Schultz. *Das höfische Leben zur Zeit der Minnesinger* (see p. 707), vol. 1, pp. 7 ff.—H. Schumacher. *Das Befestigungswesen in der alt-französischen Literatur.* Dissertation. Göttingen. 1906.—H. Lichtenberg. *Die Architekturdarstellungen in der mittelhochdeutschen Dichtung*: 66 ff. 1931.—M. Pfütze. "'Burg' und 'Stadt' in der deutschen Literatur des Mittelalters. Die Entwicklung im mittelfränkischen Sprachgebiet vom Annolied bis zu Gottfried Hagens Reimchronik (ca. 1100–1300)." *PBB* (Halle) 80: 271–320. 1958.—K.-B. Knappe. "Das Leben auf Burgen im Spiegel mittelalterlicher Literatur." *BuS* 15: 1–8, 123–31. 1974.—P. Riché. "Les répresentations du palais dans les textes littéraires du haut moyen âge." *Fr* 4: 161–71. 1976.—P. Wiesinger. "Die Burg in der mittelhochdeutschen Dichtung." *ÖAW An.* 113: 78–110. 1976.

On the history of furniture and furnishings see K. Seifart, "Das Bett im Mittelalter." *ZfdK* 2: 74–91. 1857.—A. Kerll. *Saal und Kemenate der altfranzösischen Ritterburg, zumeist nach dichterischen Quellen.* Dissertation. Göttingen. 1909.—H. Kohlhausen. *Geschichte des deutschen Kunsthandwerks.* 1955.—J. Hähnel. *Stube. Wort- und sachgeschichtliche Beiträge zur historischen Hausforschung.* 1975.—S. Hinz. *Innenraum und Möbel von der Antike bis zur Gegenwart.* 1976.—H. Appuhn. "Möbel des hohen und späten Mittelalters in den ehemaligen Frauenklöstern um Lüneburg." In: *Klösterliche Sachkultur des Spätmittelalters* (see p. 708): 343–52.—H. Stampfer. "Adelige Wohnkultur des Spätmittelalters in Südtirol." In: *Adelige Sachkultur des Spätmittelalters* (see p. 708); 365–76.—E. Penelope. *Medieval Furniture.* 1977.—Ph. B. Oates. *The Story of Western Furniture.* 1981.—E. Nellmann. "Ein zweiter Erec-Roman? Zu den neugefundenen Wolfenbütteler Fragmenten." *ZfdPh* 101: 28–78, esp. 65 ff. (on courtly pillow-terminology). 1982.

2. Clothes and cloth

The best overview of the history of costume in the Middle Ages is by E. Thiel, *Geschichte des Köstums. Die europäische Mode von den Anfängen bis zur Gegenwart.* 5th ed. 1980. Especially important among the older scholarship is G. Demay, *Le costume du moyen âge d'après les sceaux.* 1880. See also H. Weiss, *Kostümkunde. Geschichte der Tracht und des Geräthes im Mittelalter vom 4ten bis zum 14ten Jahrhundert.* 1864.—J. Quicherat. *Histoire du costume en France depuis les temps les plus reculés jusqu'à la fin du XVIIIe siècle.* 1875.—C. Pitton. *Le costume civil en France du XIIe au XIXe siècle.* 1913.—P. Post. "Das Kostüm." In: *Deutscher Kulturatlas*, vol. 2, folios 21–21e. Edited by G. Lüdtke and L. Mackensen. 1928–38.—E. Nienholdt. *Die deutsche Tracht im Wandel der Jahrhunderte.* 1938.—M. G. Houston. *Medieval Costume in England and France. The thirteenth, fourteenth and fifteenth Centuries.* 1950.—J. Evans. *Dress in Medieval France.* 1952.—O. Sronkova. *Gothic Woman's Fashion.* 1954.—M. Beaulieu. *Le costume antique et médiéval.* 3d ed. 1961.

On individual pieces of clothing see J. Wirsching, *Die Manteltracht im Mittelalter.* Dissertation. Würzburg. 1915.—P. Post. "Vom mittelalterlichen Schnurmantel." *ZfhWK* N.S. 4: 123–28. 1932/33.—K. Polheim. "Der Mantel." In: *Coronea quernea. Festgabe K. Strecker*: 41–64. 1942.—B. Schier. "Die mittelalterlichen Anfänge der weiblichen Kopftrachten im Spiegel des mittelhochdeutschen Schrifttums." In: *Beiträge zur sprachlichen Volksüberlieferung*: 141–55. 1953.—I. Fingerlin. *Gürtel des hohen und späten Mittelalters.* 1971.

On sumptuary laws see P. Kraemer, *Le luxe et les lois somptuaires au moyen âge*. Thèse. Paris. 1920.—L. C. Eisenbart. *Kleiderordnungen der deutschen Städte zwischen 1350 and 1700*. 1962.—G. Hampel-Kallbrunner. *Beiträge zur Geschichte der Kleiderordnungen mit besonderer Berücksichtigung Österreichs*. 1962.—V. Baur. *Kleiderordnungen in Bayern vom 14. bis zum 19. Jahrhundert*. 1975.

On the connection between clothes and the social order see R. Barthes, "Histoire et sociologie du vêtement. Quelques observations méthodiques." *AESC* 12: 430–41. 1957.—R. König and P. W. Schuppisser, eds. *Die Mode in der menschlichen Gesellschaft*. 1958.—M. E. Roach and J. B. Eicher, eds. *Dress, Adornment, and the Social Order*. 1965.—F. Piponnier. *Costume et vie sociale. La cour d'Anjou, XIVe–XVe siècle*. 1970.—A. Borst. *Lebensformen im Mittelalter* (see p. 708): 191 ff.—H. Platelle. "Le problème du scandale. Les nouvelles modes masculines aux XIe et XIIe siècles." *RBPH* 53: 1071–96. 1975.— M. Beaulieu. "Le costume, miroir des mentalités de la France médiévale (1350–1500)." In: *Mélanges offerts à J. Dauvillier*: 65–87. 1979.

On the descriptions of clothing by the courtly poets see M. Winter, *Kleidung und Putz der Frau nach den altfranzösischen Chansons de geste*. 1886.—A. Schultz. *Das höfische Leben zur Zeit der Minnesinger* (see p. 707), vol. 1: 222 ff.—M. Heyne. *Körperpflege und Kleidung bei den Deutschen*. 1903.—E. R. Goddard. *Women's Costume in French Texts of the eleventh and twelfth Centuries*. 1927.—E. Bertelt. *Gewandschilderungen in der erzählenden höfischen Dichtung des 12. und 13. Jahrhunderts*. Dissertation. Münster. 1936.—R. van Uytven. "Cloth in Medieval Literature of Western Europe." In: *Cloth and Clothing in Medieval Europe. Essays in Memory of E. M. Carus-Wilson*: 151– 83. 1983.—The following work appeared after I had completed this book: G. Raudszus, *Die Zeichensprache der Kleidung. Untersuchungen zur Symbolik des Gewandes in der deutschen Epik des Mittelalters*. 1985.—A new study of the German sources is being undertaken by E. Brüggen in her still unfinished dissertation at the University of Cologne. I was able to use her manuscript.

On the evaluation of pictorial art for the history of costume see M. Hauptmann, "Der Wandel der Bildvorstellung in der deutschen Dichtung und Kunst des romanischen Zeitalters." In: *Festschrift H. Wölfflin*: 63–81. 1924.—G. Barmeyer. *Die Gewandung der monumentalen Skulptur des 12. Jahrhunderts in Frankreich*. Dissertation. Frankfurt. 1933.—L. Ritgen. "Die höfische Tracht der Isle de France in der 1. Hälfte des 13. Jahrhunderts." *ZfhWK* Series 3, vol. 4, no. 1: 8–24. 1962.—L. Ritgen. "Kleidung der Isle de France in der 2. Hälfte des 13. Jahrhunderts." Ibid., no. 2: 87–111.—O. Rady. *Das weltliche Kostüm von 1250–1410 nach Ausweis der figürlichen Grabsteine im mittelrheinischen Gebiet*. 1976.—N. Rasmo. "Die Mode als Wegweiser für die Datierung von Kunstwerken des 14. Jahrhunderts." In: *Das Leben in der Stadt des Spätmittelalters* (see p. 708): 262–74.

On precious cloth see X. Francisque-Michel, *Recherches sur le commerce, la fabrication et l'usage des étoffes de soie, d'or et d'argent et autres tissus précieux en occident, principalement en France pendant le moyen âge*. Vol. 1. 1852.—J. H. Schmidt. *Alte Seidenstoffe. Ein Handbuch für Sammler und Liebhaber*. 1958.—R. Grönwoldt. "Kaisergewänder und Pergamente." In: *Die Zeit der Staufer* (see p. 708), vol. 1: 607–44—L. von Wilckens. "Seidengewebe in

Zusammenhang mit der heiligen Elisabeth." In: *Sankt Elisabeth. Fürstin, Dienerin, Heilige. Ausstellung zum 750. Todestag*: 285–302. 1981. On furs see R. Delort. *Le commerce des fourrures en occident à la fin du moyen âge (vers 1300–vers 1450)*. 2 vols. 1978. The terms for cloth and furs that appear in German and French texts from the courtly period have been collected by A. Schultz, *Das höfische Leben zur Zeit der Minnesinger* (see p. 707), vol. 1: 332 ff.

On ecclesiastical criticism of clothes see R. Harvey, "Gewez gebende. The Kulturmorphologie of a Topos." *GLL* 28: 263–85. 1975/76.—U. Ernst. "Der Antagonismus von vita carnalis und vita spiritualis im Gregorius Hartmanns von Aue." *Eu* 72: 160–226, 1978; 73: 1–105, 1979 ("Profane und sakrale Gewandung": no. 72: 212 ff.).—U. Lehmann-Langholz. *Kleiderkritik in mittelalterlicher Dichtung. Der Arme Hartmann, Heinrich "von Melk." Neidhart, Wernher der Gartenaere, nebst einem Ausblick auf die Stellungnahme spätmittelalterlicher Dichter*. Dissertation. Cologne. 1983. (The author did not permit me to use her study).

3. Weapons and horses
A good overview of the history of armaments in the Middle Ages is given by C. Gaier, *Les armes*. 1979. Useful aids are the drawings and explanations by O. Gamber, *Arma defensiva tabula*. 1972. Fundamental for the weapons of the courtly period is the work of G. Demay, *Le costume du moyen âge d'après les sceaux*. 1880. See also W. Boeheim, *Handbuch der Waffenkunde. Das Waffenwesen in seiner historischen Entwicklung vom Beginn des Mittelalters bis zum Ende des 18. Jahrhunderts*. 1890.—G. F. Laking. *A Record of European Armour and Arms Through Seven Centuries*. 5 vols. 1920–22.—B. Dean. *Handbook of Arms and Armor*. 1930.—H. Müller. *Historische Waffen. Kurze Entwicklungsgeschichte der Waffen bis zum 17. Jahrhundert*. 1957.—H. Nickel. *Der mittelalterliche Reiterschild des Abendlandes*. Dissertation. Freie Universität Berlin. 1958.—C. Blair. *European Armour. Circa 1066 to circa 1700*. 1958.—R. E. Oakeshott. *The Archeology of Weapons. Arms and Armour from Prehistory to the Age of Chivalry*. 1960.—A. Vesey and B. Norman. Arms and Armour. 1964.—B. Thomas, O. Gamber, and Hans Schedelmann. *Arms and Armour. Masterpieces by European Craftsmen from the Thirteenth to the Nineteenth Century*. Transl. by Ilse Bloom and William Reid. 1964.—H. L. Blackmore. *Arms and Armour*. 1965.—H. Seitz. *Blankwaffen*. 2 vols. 1965–68.—A. Vesey and B. Norman. *Warrior to Soldier, 449–1660*. 1966.—P. Martin. *Arms and Armour from the Ninth to the Seventeenth Century*. Transl. by Rene North. 1968.—H. Nickel. *Ullstein—Waffenbuch. Eine Kulturhistorie*. 1974.—K. Raddatz et al. "Bewaffnung." In: *Reallexikon der Germanischen Altertumskunde*, vol. 2: 361–482. 2d ed. 1976.—O. Gamber. "Die Bewaffnung der Stauferzeit," In: *Die Zeit der Staufer* (see p. 708), vol. 3: 113–18.—L. and F. Funcken. *Rüstungen und Kriegsgerät im Mittelalter. 8.–15. Jahrhundert*. 1979.—H. Nickel. "Arms and Armor." *Dictionary of the Middle Ages*, vol. 1: 521–536.

On the evaluation of the literary sources see San-Marte (i.e. A. Schulz), *Zur*

Waffenkunde des älteren deutschen Mittelalters. 1867.—A. Sternberg. *Die Angriffszahlen im altfranzösischen Epos.* 1886.—V. Schirling. *Die Verteidigungswaffen im altfranzöischen Epos.* 1887.—V. Bach. *Die Angriffswaffen in den altfranzösischen Artus- und Abenteuerromanen.* 1887.—A. Schultz. *Das höfische Leben zur Zeit der Minnesinger* (see p. 707), vol. 2: 1 ff.—J. Schwietering. *Zur Geschichte von Speer und Schwert im 12. Jahrhundert.* 1912.—F. Schmid. *De ritterlichen Schutz- und Angriffswaffen in der mittelhochdeutschen Literatur von 1170–1215.* Dissertation. Freiburg i. Br. 1922.—F. Doubel. "Studien zu den Waffennamen in der höfischen Epik." *ZfdPh* 59: 313–53. 1935.—G. Siebel. *Harnisch und Helm in den epischen Dichtungen des 12. Jahrhunderts bis zu Hartmanns Erek.* Dissertation. Hamburg. 1968.—D. Hüpper-Dröge. *Schild und Speer. Waffen und ihre Bezeichnungen im frühen Mittelalter.* 1983.—A. Masser. "Iwein-Fresken von Burg Rodenegg in Südtirol und der zeitgenössische Ritterhelm." *ZfdA* 112: 177–98. 1983.

On the knightly duel see F. Bode, *Die Kampfschilderungen in den mitelhochdeutschen Epen.* Dissertation. Greifswald. 1909.—K. Grundmann. *Studien zur Speerkampfschilderung im Mittelhochdeutschen.* 1939.—W. Harms. *Der Kampf mit dem Freund oder Verwandten in der deutschen Literatur bis um 1300.* 1963.—M. Désilles-Busch. *Doner un don—sicherheit nemen. Zwei typische Elemente der Erzählstruktur des höfischen Romans.* Dissertation. Freie Universität Berlin. 1970.—R. B. Schäfer-Maulbetsch. *Studien zur Entwicklung des mittelhochdeutschen Epos. Die Kampfschilderung in Kaiserchronik, Rolandslied, Alexanderlied, Eneide, Liet von Troye und Willehalm.* 1972.

On horses in the age of chivalry see F. Pfeiffer, *Das ross im altdeutschen.* 1855.–M. Jähns. *Roß und Reiter in Leben und Sprache, Glauben und Geschichte der Deutschen.* 2 vols. 1872.—A. Kitze. *Das Roß in den altfranzösischen Artus- und Abenteuer-Romanen.* 1888.—F. Rünger. "Herkunft, Rassezugehörigkeit, Züchtung und Haltung der Ritterpferde des Deutschen Ordens. Ein Beitrag zur Geschichte deer ostpreußischen Pferdezucht und der deutschen Pferdezucht im Mittelalter." *ZTZ* 2: 211–308. 1925.—H. Kolb. "Namen und Bezeichnungen der Pferde in der mittelalterlichen Literatur." *BzN* 9: 151–66.—A.-M. Bautier. "Contribution à l'histoire du cheval au moyen âge." *BPH* 1976: 209–49.

4. Food and drink

On the cultural history of eating and drinking see G. Schiedlausky, *Essen und Trinken. Tafelsitten bis zum Ausgang des Mittelalters.* 1956.—H. Wühr. *Altes Eßgerät. Löffel—Messer—Gabel.* 1961.—B. A. Henisch. *Fast and Feast. Food in Medieval Society.* 1976.—M. P. Cosman. *Fabulous Feasts. Medieval Cookery and Ceremony.* 1976.—P. Rachbauer. "Essen und Trinken um 1200." In: *Nibelungenlied. Ausstellung zur Erinnerung an die Auffindung der Handschrift A:* 135–46. 1979.—J. M. van Winter. "Kochkultur und Speisegewohnheiten der spätmittelalterlichen Oberschichten." In: *Adelige Sachkultur des Spätmittelalters* (see p. 708): 327–42. M. P. Cosman. "Cookery, European." *Dictionary of the Middle Ages*, vol. 2: 580–583.

On the evaluation of the literary evidence see A. Schultz, *Das höfische Leben zur Zeit der Minnesinger* (see p. 707), vol. 1: 360 ff.—F. Fuhse. *Sitten und Gebräuche der Deutschen beim Essen und Trinken von den ältesten Zeiten bis zum Schlusse des XI. Jahrhunderts.* Dissertation. Göttingen. 1891.—M. Heyne. *Das deutsche Nahrungswesen.* 1901.—O. Klauenberg. *Getränke und Trinken in altfranzösischer Zeit nach poetischen Quellen dargestellt.* Dissertation. Göttingen. 1904.—W. Pieth. *Essen und Trinken im mittelhochdeutschen Epos des 12. und 13. Jahrhunderts.* Dissertation. Greifswald. 1909.—G. F. Jones. "The Function of Food in Medieaeval German Literature." *Sp* 35: 78–86. 1960.—R. Roos. *Begrüßung, Abschied, Mahlzeit. Studien zur Darstellung höfischer Lebensweise in den Werken der Zeit von 1150–1320.* Dissertation. Bonn. 1975.

On books of table manners see P. Merker, "Die Tischzuchtliteratur des 12.–16. Jahrhunderts." *MGES* 11: 1–52. 1920.—S. Glixelli. "Les contenances de table." *Ro* 47: 1–40. 1921.—S. Gieben. "Robert Grosseteste and Medieval Courtesy-Books." *Vi* 5: 47–74. 1967. On the importance of the books of table manners for social history see N. Elias, *The History of Manners.* Transl. by E. Jephcott. 2 vols. 1978. The most important German texts have been collected in T. P. Thornton, ed., *Höfische Tischzuchten und Grobianische Tischzuchten.* 1957. A thorough study of the German texts and their relationship to the Latin tradition still needs to be done. The following work appeared after this book had gone to press: J. Nicholls, *The Matter of Courtesy. Medieval Courtesy Books and the Gawein-Poet.* 1985.

On the feasting and drinking literature see A. Hauffen, "Die Trinkliteratur in Deutschland bis zum Ausgang des 16. Jahrhunderts." *VfL* 2: 481–516. 1889 (unsatisfactory).—E. Simon. "Literary Affinities of Steinmar's Herbstlied and the Songs of Colin Muset." *MLN* 84: 375–85. 1969.—E. Grunewald. *Die Zeche- und Schlemmerliteratur des deutschen Spätmittelalters.* Dissertation. Cologne. 1976.

The oldest German cookbook is: *Daz Buch von guter Spise.* Edited by J. Hajek. 1958. This text was probably written at the beginning of the fourteenth century. Cf. H. Wiswe, *Kulturgeschichte der Kochkunst. Kochbücher und Rezepte aus zwei Jahrtausenden.* 1970.

CHAPTER IV
COURTLY FEASTS: PROTOCOL AND
ETIQUETTE

1. Court feasts

On the Mainz court feast of 1184 see J. Fleckenstein. "Friedrich Barbarossa und das Rittertum. Zur Bedeutung der großen Mainzer Hoftage von 1184 und 1188." In: *Festschrift für H. Heimpel*, vol. 2: 1023–41. 1972.—A. Borst. *Lebensformen im Mittelalter* (see p. 708): 85 ff.

The descriptions of feasts in literature of the courtly period have not yet been collected and evaluated. Some material can be found in A. Schultz, *Das höfische Leben zur Zeit der Minnesinger* (see p. 707), vol. 1: 486 ff. See also W. Mohr, "Mittelalterliche Feste und ihre Dichtung." In: *Festschrift für K. Ziegler:* 37–60.

1968.—Unsatisfactory is the work of H. Bodensohn, *Die Festschilderungen in der mittelhochdeutschen Dichtung.* 1936.—R. Marquardt. *Das höfische Fest im Spiegel der mittelhochdeutschen Dichtung (1140–1240).* 1985.

On the courtly forms of address and greeting see F. Schiller, *Das Grüßen im Altfranzösischen.* Dissertation. Halle. 1890.—G. Ehrismann. "Duzen und Ihrzen im Mittelalter." *ZfdW* 1: 117–49, 1901; 2: 118–59, 1902; 4: 210–48, 1903; 5: 127–220, 1903/04.—W. Bohlhöfer. *Gruß und Abschied in althochdeutscher und mittelhochdeutscher Zeit.* Dissertation. Göttingen. 1912.—P. Rettig. *Die Entwicklung der höfischen Anrede in der altdeutschen Dichtung.* Part 1. Dissertation. Gießen. 1922.—R. Roos. *Begrüßung, Abschied, Mahlzeit* (see p. 724).

On secular festive music and its instruments see the very informative work of S. Zak, *Musik als 'Ehr und Zier' im mittelalterlichen Reich* (see p. 708). See also C. Sachs, *Handbuch der Musikinstrumentenkunde.* 2d ed. 1930.—E. A. Bowles. "Haut and Bas. The Grouping of Musical Instruments in the Middle Ages." *MD* 8: 115–40. 1954.—E. A. Bowles. "Musical Instruments at the Medieval Banquet." *RBM* 12: 41–51. 1958.—E. A. Bowles. "La hiérarchie des instruments de musique dans l'Europe féodale." *RM* 42: 155–69. 1958.—W. Salmen. "Tischmusik im Mittelalter." *NZM* 10: 323–26. 1959.—E. A. Bowles. "Musical Instruments in Civic Processions during the Middle Ages." *AM* 33: 147–61. 1961.—R. Hammerstein. *Die Musik der Engel. Untersuchungen zur Musikanschauung des Mittelalters.* 1962.—H. Heyde. *Trompete und Trompetenblasen im europäischen Mittelalter.* Dissertation. Leipzig. 1965.—H. Steger. *Philologia musica. Sprachzeichen, Bild und Sache im literarisch-musikalischen Leben des Mittelalters: Lire, Harfe, Rotte und Fidel.* 1971.—R. Hammerstein. *Diabolus in musica. Studien zur Ikonographie der Musik im Mittelalter.* 1974.—D. Munrow. *Instruments of the Middle Ages and Renaissance.* 1976.—H. Giesel. *Studien zur Symbolik der Musikinstrumente im Schrifttum der alten und mittelalterlichen Kirche (von den Anfängen bis zum 13. Jh.).* 1978.—D. Buschinger, ed. *Musique, littérature et société au moyen âge. Actes du colloque 24–29 mars 1980.* 1980.—J. Montagu. *Geschichte der Musikinstrumente in Mittelalter und Renaissance.* 1981.

On the depiction of music and musical instruments in courtly literature see F. Brücker, *Die Blasinstrumente in der altfranzösichen Literatur.* 1926.—F. Dick. *Bezeichnungen für Saiten- und Schlaginstrumente in der altfranzösischen Literatur.* 1932.—D. Treder. *Die Musikinstrumente in den höfischen Epen der Blütezeit.* 1933.—H. Riedel. *Die Darstellung von Musik und Musikerlebnis in der erzählenden deutschen Dichtung.* 2d ed. 1961.—W. Relleke. *Ein Instrument spielen. Instrumentenbezeichnungen und Tonerzeugungsverben im Althochdeutschen, Mittelhochdeutschen und Neuhochdeutschen.* 1980.

On courtly dancing see F. M. Böhme, *Geschichte des Tanzes in Deutschland.* 2 vols. 1886.—J. Wolf. "Die Tänze des Mittelalters." *AMw* 1: 10–42. 1918/19.—C. Sachs. *Eine Weltgeschichte des Tanzes.* 1933.—W. Bahr. *Zur Entwicklungsgeschichte des höfischen Gesellschaftstanzes.* 1941.—D. Heartz. "Hoftanz und Basse Dance." *JAMS* 19: 13–36. 1966.—K. H. Taubert. *Höfische Tänze. Ihre Geschichte und Choreographie.* 1968.—A. Harding. *An Investigation into the Use and Meaning of Medieval German Dancing Terms.*

1973.—W. Salmen. "Ikonographie des Reigens im Mittelalter." *AM* 52: 14–26. 1980.—G. C. Busch. *Ikonographische Studien zum Solotanz im Mittelalter.* 1982.

On the minstrels see p. 742.

2. Knighting ceremonies

The history of the knighting ceremony has not yet been written. Fundamental are the following three, richly documented works: W. Erben. "Schwertleite und Ritterschlag. Beiträge zu einer Rechtsgeschichte der Waffen." *ZfhWK* 8: 105–67. 1918/20.—J. M. van Winter. "Cingulum militiae. Schwertliete en miles-terminologie als spiegel vanveranderend menselijk gedrag." *TvR* 44: 1–92. 1976.—J. Flori. "Les origines de l'adoubement chevaleresque. Etude des remises d'armes et du vocabulaire qui les exprime dans les sources historiques latines jusqu'au début du XIIIe siècle." *Tr* 35: 209–72. 1979.

On the historical evidence see also K. H. Roth von Schreckenstein, *Die Ritterwürde und der Ritterstand* (see p. 712): 203 ff.—P. Guilhiermoz. *Essai sur l'origine de la noblesse en France au moyen âge*: 393 ff. 1902.—C. Erdmann. *The Origin of the Idea of Crusade.* (see p. 729): 326 ff.—D. Sandberger. "Die Aufnahme in den Ritterstand in England." *AKG* 27: 74–93. 1937.—J. Flori. "Chevalerie et liturgie. Remise des armes et vocabulaire 'chevaleresque' dans les sources liturgiques du IXe au XIVe siècle." *MA* 84: 247–78, 409–42. 1978.—M. Keen. *Chivalry*: 64–82 ("The Ceremony of Dubbing to Knighthood"). 1984.

On the literary evidence for the ceremony of dubbing see K. Treis, *Die Formalitäten des Ritterschlags in der altfranzösischen Epik.* Dissertation. Berlin. 1887.—A. Schultz. *Das höfische Leben zur Zeit der Minnesinger* (see p. 707), vol. 1: 181 ff.—E. H. Massmann. *Schwertleite und Ritterschlag, dargestellt auf Grund der mittelhochdeutschen literarischen Quellen.* Dissertation. Hamburg. 1932.—F. Pietzner. *Schwertleite und Ritterschlag.* Dissertation. Heidelberg. 1934.—J. Flori. "Sémantique et société médiévale. Le verbe adouber et son évolution au XIIe siècle." *AESC* 31: 915–40. 1976.—J. Bumke. *The Concept of Knighthood in the Middle Ages* (see p. 713): 83 ff.—J. Flori. "Pour une histoire de la chevalerie. L'adoubement dans les romans de Chrétien de Troyes." *Ro* 100: 21–53. 1979.—R. Lénat. "L'adoubement dans quelques textes littéraires de la fin du XIIe siècle. Clergie et chevalerie." In: *Mélanges de la langue et littérature françaises du moyen âge et de la renaissance offerts à C. Foulon*, vol. 1: 195–203. 1980.

3. Tournaments

On the history of tournaments and their depiction in courtly poetry see F. Niedner, *Das deutsche Turnier im XII. und XIII. Jahrhundert.* 1881.—A. Schultz. *Das höfische Leben zur Zeit der Minnesinger* (see p. 707), vol. 2: 106 ff.—O. Müller. *Turnier und Kampf in den altfranzösischen Artusromanen.* Progr. Erfurt. 1907.—K. G. T. Webster. "The Twelfth-Century Turney." In: *Anniversary Papers by Colleagues and Pupils of G. L. Kittredge*: 227–34. 1913.—F. H. Cripps-Day. *The History of the Tournament in England and*

France. 1918.—R. C. Clephan. *The Tournament. Its Periods and Phases.* 1919.—N. Denholm-Young. "The Tournament in the Thirteenth Century." In: *Studies in Medieval History Presented to F. M. Powicke*: 240–68. 1948.—R. Harvey. *Moriz von Craûn and the Chivalric World* ("The Tournament", pp. 112–258). 1961.—G. Duby. *Le dimanche de Bouvines*: 111 ff. 1973.—P. Czerwinski. *Die Schlacht- und Turnierdarstellungen in den deutschen höfischen Romanen des 12. und 13. Jahrhunderts.* Dissertation. Freie Universität Berlin. 1975.—M.-L. Chênerie. "Ces curieux chevaliers tournoyers. Des fabliaux aux romans." *Ro* 97: 327–68. 1976.—R. Barber, J. Barker. *Tournaments.* 1985.

For the influence of courtly poetry on tournament practice see R. S. Loomis, "Chivalric and Dramatic Imitations of Arthurian Romance." In: *Medieval Studies in Memory of A. K. Porter*, vol. 1: 79–97. 1939.—E. Sandoz. "Tourneys in the Arthurian Tradition." *Sp* 19: 389–420. 1944.—R. H. Cline. "The Influence of Romances on Tournaments of the Middle Ages." *Sp* 20: 204–11. 1945.

On the *Histoire de Guillaume le Maréchal* see H. Winter, *Das Kriegswesen in der altfranzösischen Histoire de Guillaume le Maréchal.* Dissertation. Gießen. 1911.—S. Painter. *William Marshal. Knight-Errant, Baron, and Regent of England.* 1933.—A. Riedemann. *Lehnswesen und höfisches Leben in der altfranzösischen Histoire de Guillaume le Maréchal.* Dissertation. Münster. 1938.—L. D. Benson. "The Tournament in the Romances of Chrétien de Troyes and L'Histoire de Guillaume le Maréchal." In: *Chivlaric Literature*: 1–24, 147–52. Edited by L. D. Benson and J. Leyerle. 1980.—G. Duby. *William Marshal. The Flower of Chivalry.* Transl. by R. Howard. 1985.

On the depiction of tournaments in Ulrich von Liechtenstein's Frauendienst see R. Becker, *Ritterliche Waffenspiele nach Ulrich von Lichtenstein.* Progr. Düren. 1887.—O. Höfler. "Ulrichs von Liechtenstein Venusfahrt und Artusfahrt." In: *Studien zur deutschen Philologie des Mittelalters. F. Panzer zum 80. Geburtstag*: 131–52. 1950.—U. Peters. *Untersuchungen zu Ulrich von Liechtenstein und zum Wirklichkeitsgehalt der Minnedichtung* ("Ulrichs Artusfahrt und die literarisierte Turnierpraxis des europäischen Adels im 13. und 14. Jahrhundert," pp. 173–205). 1971.—H. Reichert. "Vorbilder für Ulrich von Lichtensteins Frisacher Turnier." In: *Die mittelalterliche Literatur in Kärnten*: 189–216. Edited by P. Krämer. 1981.

On Church criticism and prohibitions of tournaments see F. Merzbacher, "Das kirchliche Turnier- und Stierkampfverbot." In: *Im Dienste des Rechtes in Kirche und Staat. Festschrift zum 70. Geburtstag von F. Arnold*: 261–68. 1963.—On all aspects of tournament practice now see also the following important collection: *Das ritterliche Turnier im Mittelalter.* Edited by J. Fleckenstein. 1985.

CHAPTER V
THE COURTLY IDEAL OF SOCIETY

1. The chivalrous knight

The basic work for the mirrors of princes is W. Berges, *Die Fürstenspiegel des hohen und späten Mittelalters.* 1938. See also E. Booz, *Fürstenspiegel des Mittel-*

alters bis zur Scholastik. Dissertation. Freiburg i.Br. 1913.—L. K. Born. "The Perfect Prince. A Study in Thirteenth- and Fourteenth-Century Ideals." *Sp* 3 470–504. 1928.—J. Röder. *Das Fürstenbild in den mittelalterlichen Fürsten spiegeln auf französischem Boden.* Dissertation. Münster. 1933.—W. Kleineke *Englische Fürstenspiegel vom Policraticus Johanns von Salisbury bis zum Basili- kon Doron König Jakobs I.* 1937.—H. H. Anton. *Fürstenspiegel und Herr- scherethos in der Karolingerzeit.* 1968.—P. Hadot. "Fürstenspiegel." In: *Real- lexikon für Antike und Christentum,* vol. 8: cols. 555–632. 1972.—O Eberhardt. *Via regia. Der Fürstenspiegel Smaragds von St. Mihiel und seine literarische Gattung.* 1977.

On the traditional image of the ruler see J. Straub, *Vom Herrscherideal in der Spätantike.* 1939.—F. Taeger. *Charisma. Studien zur Geschichte des anti- ken Herrscherkults.* 2 vols. 1957–1960.—H. Wolfram. "Constantin als Vor- bild für den Herrscher des hochmittelalterlichen Reiches." *MIÖG* 68: 226–43. 1960.—H. Steger. *David rex et propheta. König David als vorbildliche Verkör- perung des Herrschers und Dichters im Mittelalter nach Bilddarstellungen des 8.–12. Jahrhunderts.* 1961.—H. Wolfram. *Splendor Imperii. Die Epiphanie von Tugend und Heil in Herrschaft und Reich.* 1963.—P. E. Schramm. "Das Alte und das Neue Testament in der Staatslehre und Staatssymbolik des Mitte- lalters." In: *La biblia nell'alto medioevo:* 229–55. 1963.—H. Kloft. *Liberalitas principis. Studien zur Prinzpatsideologie.* 1970.—F. Frh. von Müller. *Gloria Bona Fama Bonorum. Studien zur sittlichen Bedeutung des Ruhms in der früh- christlichen und mittelalterlichen Welt.* 1977.—M. McCormick. *Eternal Victory–Triumphal Rulership in Late Antiquity, Byzantium, and the Early Medieval West.* 1985.—A number of important essays are collected in the volumes *Ideologie und Herrschaft in der Antike,* ed. by H. Kloft, 1979, and *Das Byzantinische Herrscherbild,* ed. by H. Hunger. 1975.

On the ethic of nobility in the early and High Middle Ages and on the image of the ruler in medieval literature see A. Kühne, *Das Herrscherideal des Mittel- alters und Kaiser Friedrich I.* 1898.—F. Vogt. *Das Kaiser- und Königsideal in der deutschen Dichtung des Mittelalters.* 1908.—L. Sandrock. *Das Herrscher- ideal in der erzählenden Dichtung des deutschen Mittelalters.* Dissertation. Münster. 1931.—H. Schmitz. *Blustadel und Geistesadel in der hochhöfischen Dichtung.* 1941—H. Kallfelz. *Das Standesethos des Adels im 10. und 11. Jahr- hundert.* Dissertation. Würzburg. 1960.—F. Bittner. *Studien zum Herrscher- lob in der mittellateinischen Dichtung.* Dissertation. Würzburg. 1962.—J. Fechter. *Cluny, Adel und Volk. Studien über das Verhältnis des Klosters zu den Ständen (910–1156).* Dissertation. Tübingen. 1966.—A. Georgi. *Das latei- nische und deutsche Preisgedicht des Mittelalters in der Nachfolge des genus demonstrativum.* 1969.—M. F. Hellmann. *Fürst, Herrscher und Fürstengemein- schaft. Untersuchungen zur ihrer Bedeutung als politischer Elemente in mit- telhochdeutschen Epen.* Dissertation. Bonn. 1969.—D. Obermüller. *Die Tugendkataloge der Kaiserchronik. Studien zum Herrscherbild der frühmit- telhochdeutschen Dichtung.* Dissertation. Heidelberg. 1971.—G. Koch. *Auf dem Wege zum Sacrum Imperium. Studien zur ideologischen Herrschaftsbe- gründung der deutschen Zentralgewalt im 11. und 12. Jahrhundert.* 1972.—W. Störmer. *Früher Adel. Studien zur politischen Führungsschicht im fränkisch-*

deutschen Reich vom 8. bis 11. Jahrhundert. 2 vols. 1973.—K. Bosl. "Leitbilder und Wertvorstellungen des Adels von der Merowingerzeit bis zur Höhe der feudalen Gesellschaft." *MSB* no. 5, 1974.—E. Kleinschmidt. *Zur Disposition mittelalterlichen Aussageverhaltens, untersucht an Texten über Rudolf I. von Habsburg.* 1974.—K. R. Gürttler. *Künec Artûs ger guote. Das Artusbild der höfischen Epik des 12. und 13. Jahrhunderts.* 1976.—K. H. Borck. "Adel, Tugend und Geblüt. Thesen und Beobachtungen zur Vorstellung des Tugendadels in der deutschen Literatur des 12. und 13. Jahrhunderts." *PBB* 100: 423–57. 1978.—P. U. Hohendahl and P. M. Lützeler, eds. *Legetimationskrisen des deutschen Adels, 1200–1900.* 1979.—H. Wenzel, ed. *Adelsherrschaft und Literatur.* 1980.—D. Neuendorff. *Studien zur Entwicklung der Herrscherdarstellung in der deutschen Literatur des 9.–12. Jahrhunderts.* 1982.

The basic work on the pictorial representation of rulers is P. E. Schramm, *Die deutschen Kaiser und Könige in Bildern ihrer Zeit, 751–1190.* 2d ed. 1983. This work has not been continued. See also M. Kemmerich, "Die Porträts deutscher Kaiser und Könige bis auf Rudolf von Habsburg." *NA* 33: 461–513. 1908.—M. Kemmerich. *Die Deutschen Kaiser und Könige im Bilde.* 1910.— S. H. Steinberg and C. Steinberg-von Pappe. *Die Bildnisse geistlicher und weltlicher Fürsten und Herren.* Part 1: Von der Mitte des 10. bis zum Ende des 12. Jahrhunderts (800–1200). Text and Illustration. 1931.—K. F. A. Mann. *Das Herrscherbild der Hohenstaufenzeit.* Dissertation. Freie Universität Berlin. 1952.—H. Keller. *Das Nachleben des antiken Bildnisses von der Karolingerzeit bis zur Gegenwart.* 1970.—P. Bloch. "Bildnis im Mittelalter. Herrscherbild— Grabbild—Stifterbild." In: *Bilder vom Menschen in der Kunst des Abendlandes. Jubiläumsausstellung der Preußischen Museen Berlin*: 105–41. 1980.—J. Wollasch. "Kaiser und Könige als Brüder der Mönche. Zum Herrscherbild in liturgischen Handschriften des 9.–11. Jahrhunderts." *DA* 40: 1–20. 1984.

On the princely tomb sculptures see D. Schubert, *Von Halberstadt nach Meißen. Bildwerke des 13. Jahrhunderts in Thüringen, Sachsen und Anhalt.* 1974.—K. Bauch. *Das mittelalterliche Grabbild. Figürliche Grabmäler des 11.– 15. Jahrhunderts in Europa.* 1976. For the figures of the donors in Naumburg see W. Schlesinger, *Meißner Dom und Naumburger Westchor. Ihre Bildwerke in geschichtlicher Betrachtung.* 1952.—E. Schubert. "Der Westchor des Naumburger Domes. Ein Beitrag zur Datierung und zum Verständnis der Standbilder." *ADAW* 1964, no. 1.—W. Sauerländer. "Die Naumburger Stifterfiguren." In: *Die Zeit der Staufer* (see p. 708), vol. 5: 169–245.

On the idea of crusade and on the religious idea of knighthood see the seminal work of C. Erdmann, *The Origin of the Idea of Crusade.* Transl. by M. W. Baldwin and W. Goffart. 1977. Most recently J. Flori, *L'idéologie du glaive. Préhistoire de la chevalerie.* 1983. See also G. Wolfram, "Kreuzpredigt und Kreuzlied." *ZfdA* 30: 89–132. 1886.—U. Schwerin. *Die Aufrufe der Päpste zur Befreiung des heiligen Landes von den Anfängen bis zum Ausgang Innozenz' IV.* 1937.—V. Cramer. *Die Kreuzzugspredigt zur Befreiung des Heiligen Landes. 1095—1270.* 1939.—F.-W. Wentzlaff-Eggebert. *Kreuzzugsdichtung des Mittelalters. Studien zur ihrer geschichtlichen und dichterischen Wirklichkeit.* 1960.—W. Braun. *Studien zum Ruodlieb. Ritterideal, Erzählstruktur und Darstellungsstil.* 1962.—H. Hoffmann. *Gottesfriede und Treuga Dei.* 1964.—A.

Noth. *Heiliger Krieg und Heiliger Kampf in Islam und Christentum.* 1966.—F
Prinz. *Klerus und Krieg im früheren Mittelalter.* 1971.—R. R. Bolgar. "Hero or
Anti-Hero? The Genesis and Development of the Miles Christianus." In: *Con-
cepts of the Hero in the Middle Ages and the Renaissance*: 120–46. Edited by
N. T. Burns and C. J. Reagan. 1975.—P. Rousset. "L'idéal chevaleresque dans
deux Vitae clunisiennes." In: *Etudes de civilisation médiévale (XIe–XIIe siè-
cles). Mélanges offerts à E.-R Labande*: 623–33. 1975.—A. Wang. *Der Miles
Christianus im 16. und 17. Jahrhundert und seine mittelalterliche Tradition.
Ein Beitrag zum Verhältnis von sprachlicher und graphischer Bildlichkeit.*
1975.—R. C. Schwinges. *Kreuzzugsideologie und Toleranz. Studien zu
Wilhelm von Tyrus.* 1977.—J. Ashcroft. "Miles Dei—Gotes Ritter. Konrad's
Rolandslied and the Evolution of the Concept of Christian Chivalry." *FMLS*
17: 146–66. 1981.—G. Althoff. "Nunc fiant Christi milites, quid dudum ex-
titerunt raptores. Zur Entstehung von Rittertum und Ritterethos." *Sc* 32: 317–
33. 1981.—J. Flori. "La chevalerie selon Jean de Salisbury (nature, fonction,
idéologie)." *RHE* 77: 35–77. 1982.—S. Krüger. "Character militaris und character indelebilis. Ein Beitrag zum Verhältnis von miles und clericus im Mittelalter." In: *Institutionen, Kultur und Gesellschaft im Mittelalter* (see p. 710) 567–
80.—B. Z. Kedar. *Crusade and Mission. European Approaches toward the
Muslims.* 1984.

On the knightly military orders see J. Fleckenstein and M. Hellmann, eds.,
Die geistlichen Ritterorden Europas. 1980; especially the essay by J. Fleckenstein, "Die Rechtfertigung der geistlichen Ritterorden nach der Schrift De laude
novae militiae Bernhards von Clairvaux," pp. 9–22.

For a discussion of the knightly code of virtues see G. Eifler, ed., *Das ritterliche Tugendsystem.* 1970.

On the image of the knight in courtly poetry see S. Jauernick, *Das theore-
tische Bild des Rittertums in der altfranzösischen Literatur.* Dissertation. Göttingen. 1961.—G. Meissburger. "De vita christiana. Zum Bild des christlichen
Ritters im Hochmittelalter." *DU* 14, no. 6: 21–34. 1962.—D. Rocher. "'Chevalerie' et littérature 'chevaleresque'." *Eg* 21: 165–79, 1966; 23: 345–57,
1968.—C. Moorman. *A Knyght there Was. The Evolution of the Knight in
Literature.* 1967.—W. Schröder. "Zum ritter-Bild der frühmittelhochdeutschen
Dichter." *GRM* 53: 333–51. 1972.—W. P. Gerritsen. "Het beeld van feoda-
liteit en riderschap in middeleeuwse litteratuur." *BMGN* 89: 241–61. 1974.—
P. Ménard. "Le chevalier errant dans la littérature arthurienne." In: *Voyage,
quête, pèlerinage dans la littérature et la civilisation médiévale*: 289–311.
1976.—D. H. Green. "The King and the Knight in the Medieval Romance." In:
Festschrift for R. Farrell: 175–83. 1977.—L. D. Benson and J. Leyerle, eds.
*Chivalric Literature. Essays on Relations between Literature and Life in the
Later Middle Ages.* 1980.—Knighthood in Medieval Literature. FMLS 17, no.
2. 1981.—G. Kaiser. "Der Ritter in der deutschen Literatur des hohen Mittelalters." In: *Das Ritterbild in Mittelalter und Renaissance* (see p. 713): 37–49.

On the term "knight" and on the social dimensions of knighthood see
p. 710.

On the education of the nobility in the Middle Ages now see N. Orme, *From
Childhood to Chivalry. The Education of the English Kings and Aristocracy*

1066–1530. 1984. A criticial account does not yet exist for Germany. See the older work of E. Rust, *Die Erziehung des Ritters in der altfranzösischen Epik*. Dissertation. Berlin. 1888.—F. Tetzner. "Die Erziehung der junchherren in der Blütezeit des Rittertums." *PS* 38: 412–30, 481–500, 609–20, 671–86. 1889.—F. Meyer. *Jugenderziehung im Mittelalter, dargestellt nach den altfranzösischen Artus- und Abenteuerromanen*. Prog. Solingen. 1896.—N. Schneider. *Erziehergestalten im höfischen Epos*. 1935.—M. P. Cosman. *The Education of the Hero in the Arthurian Romance*. 1965.—A. Mundhenk. "Der Winsbecke oder Die Erziehung des Ritters." In: *Interpretationen mittelhochdeutscher Lyrik*: 269–86. Edited by G. Jungbluth. 1969.—S. Krüger. "Das Rittertums in den Schriften des Konrad von Megenberg." In: *Herrschaft und Stand* (see p. 711): 302–28.

On the exemplary quality of poetry and its influence on society see T. Hirsch, "Über den Ursprung der Preußischen Artushöfe." *ZfPG* 1: 3–32. 1864.—W. Störmer. "König Artus als aristokratisches Leitbild während des späten Mittelalters, gezeigt and Beispielen der Ministerialität und des Patriziats." *ZfbLG* 35: 946–71. 1972.—A. Ostmann. *Die Bedeutung der Arthurtradition für die englische Gesellschaft des 12. und 13. Jahrhunderts*. Dissertation. Freie Universität Berlin. 1975.—W. Störmer. "Adel und Ministerialität im Spiegel der bayerischen Namengebung (bis zum 13. Jahrhundert)." *DA* 33: 84–152. 1977.

On the importance of the court clerics in the formulation of the courtly ideal of society see H. Brinkmann, *Entstehungsgeschichte des Minnesangs*. 1926.—C. S. Jaeger. "The Courtier Bishop in Vitae from the Tenth to the Twelfth Century." *Sp* 58: 291–325. 1983.—C. S. Jaeger. "Beauty of Manners and Discipline (schoene site, zuht). An Imperial Tradition of Courtliness in the German Romance." In: *Barocker Lust-Spiegel. Festschrift für B. L. Spahr*: 27–45. 1984. After my book had already gone to press, an important work by C. S. Jaeger appeared: *The Origin of Courtliness. Civilizing Trends and the Formation of Courtly Ideals (939–1210)*. 1985.

On the debates about the virtues of the knight and the cleric see C. Oulmont, *Les débats de clerc et du chevalier dans la littérature poétique du moyen âge*. 1911.—E. Faral. "Les débats de clerc et du chevalier dans la littérature du XIIe et XIIIe siècles." *Ro* 41: 473–517. 1912.—H. Walther. *Das Streitgedicht in der lateinischen Literatur des Mittelalters*: 145 ff. 1920.—W. T. H. Jackson, "Der Streit zwischen miles und clericus." *ZfdA* 85: 293–303. 1954/55.—G. Tavani. "Il dibattito sul chierico e il cavaliere nella tradizione mediolatina e volgare." *RJb* 15: 51–84. 1964.

2. The courtly lady

Although a good deal of literature has appeared in recent years on the topic of women in the Middle Ages, there is still frequently a dearth of detailed and thorough studies. For France and England we should mention: A. Lehmann, *Le rôle de la femme dans l'histoire de la France au moyen âge*. 1952.—D. M. Stenton. *The English Woman in History*. 1957. For Germany there is only the richly documented but in its viewpoints completely outdated work of K. Weinhold, *Die deutschen Frauen in dem Mittelalter*. 2 vols. 3d ed. 1897. Supplemented by H. Finke, *Die Frau im Mittelalter*. 1913.

Of the more recent studies we should mention the following: P. Grimal, ed. *Histoire Mondiale de la femme*. 2 vols. 1965–66.—M. Bardèche. *Histoire des femmes*. 2 vols. 1968.—V. L. Bullough. *The Subordinate Sex. A History of Attitudes towards Women*. 1973.—S. Harksen. *Die Frau im Mittelalter*. 1974.—J. O'Faolian and L. Martines, eds. *Not in God's Image. A History of Women in Europe from the Greeks to the Nineteenth Century*. 1974.—R. T. Morewedge, ed. *The Role of Women in the Middle Ages*. 1975.—E. Power. *Medieval Women*. Ed. by M. M. Postan. 1975.—S. M. Stuard, ed. *Women in Medieval Society*. 1976.—G. Becker et al. "Zum kulturellen Bild un zur realen Situation der Frau im Mittelalter und in der frühen Neuzeit." In: *Aus der Zeit der Verzweiflung. Zur Genese und Aktualität des Hexenbildes*: 11–128. 1977.—F. and J. Gies. *Women in the Middle Ages*. 1978.—D. Baker, ed. *Medieval Women*. 1978.—G. Duby. *Medieval Marriage. Two Models from Twelfth-Century France*. Transl. by Elsborg Forster. 1978.—R. Pernoud. *La femme au temps des cathédrales*. 1980.—S. Shahar. *The Fourth Estate. A History of Women in the Middle Ages*. Translated by Chaya Galai. 1983.— P. Ketsch. *Frauen im Mittelalter*. 2 vols. 1981–84.—A. M. Lucas. *Women in the Middle Ages. Religion, Marriage and Letters*. 1983.—G. Duby. *The Knight, the Lady, and the Priest: The Making of Modern Marriage in Medieval France*. Transl. by B. Bray. 1983.—E. Ennen. *The medieval woman*. Transl. by E. Jephcott. 1989.—J. Kirshner and Suzanne F. Wemple, eds. *Women of the Medieval World. Essays in Honor of John H. Mundy*. 1985.—F. and Joseph Gies. *Marriage and Family in the Middle Ages*. 1987.

On the legal position of women see R. Bartsch, *Die Rechtsstellung der Frau als Gattin und Mutter. Geschichtliche Entwicklung ihrer persönlichen Stellung im Privatrecht bis in das 18. Jahrhundert*. 1903.—M. Weber. *Ehefrau und Mutter in der Rechtsentwicklung*. 1907.—H. Fehr. *Die Rechtsstellung der Frau und der Kinder in den Weistümern*. 1912.—J. Gilissen, ed. *La femme*. 2 vols. 1959– 62. On the conception of women in canon law and especially on the theme of woman as ruler, see W. Kowalski, *Die deutschen Königinnen und Kaiserinnen von Konrad III. bis zum Ende des Interregnums*. 1913.—T. Vogelsang. *Die Frau als Herrscherin im hohen Mittelalter. Studien zur consors regni—Formel*. 1954.—M. F. Facinger. "A Study of Medieval Queenship. Capetian France 987–1237." *SMRH* 5: 1–48. 1968.—D. Herlihy. *Women in Medieval Society*. 1971.—S. Konecny. *Die Frauen des karolingischen Königshauses. Die politische Bedeutung der Ehe und die Stellung der Frau in der fränkischen Herrscherfamilien vom 7. bis zum 10. Jahrhundert*. 1976.—R. Fossier. "La femme dans les sociétés occidentales." *CCM* 20: 93–102. 1977.—A. Kuhn et al. *Frauen in der Geschichte*. 4 vols. 1979–83.—P. Stafford. *Queens, Concubines, and Dowagers. The King's Wife in the Early Middle Ages*. 1983.

The position of women in economic life is the best-examined area. See K. Bücher, *Die Frauenfrage im Mittelalter*. 2d ed. 1910.—H. Wachendorf. *Die wirtschaftliche Stellung der Frau in den deutschen Städten des späteren Mittelalters*. Dissertation. Hamburg. 1934.—J. Barchewitz. *Von der Wirtschaftstätigkeit der Frau in der vorgeschichtlichen Zeit bis zur Entfaltung der Stadtwirtschaft*. 1937.—L. Hess. *die deutschen Frauenberufe des Mittelalters*. Dissertation. Königsberg. 1940.—B. Kuske. "Die Frau im mittelalterlichen deutschen

Wirtschaftsleben." *Zfhw* 11: 148–57.—E. Ennen. "Die Frau in der mittelalterlichen Stadtgesellschaft Mitteleuropas." *HGb* 98: 1–22.1980.—M. Wensky. *Die Stellung der Frau in der stadtkölnischen Wirtschaft im Spätmittelalter.* 1980.—K. Wesoly. "Der weibliche Bevölkerungsanteil in spätmittelalterlichen und frühneuzeitlichen Städten und die Betätigung von Frauen im zünftigen Handwerk (insbesondere am Mittel- und Oberrhein)." *ZGO* 128: 69–117. 1980.—B. Händler-Lachmann. "Die Berufstätigkeit der Frau in den deutschen Städten des Spätmittelalters und der beginnenden Neuzeit." *HJL* 30: 131–75. 1980.—E. Uitz. "Zu einigen Aspekten der gesellschaftlichen Stellung der Frau in der mittelalterlichen Stadt." *JGF* 5: 57–88. 1981.

On the upbringing and education of women see J. M. Ferrante, "The Education of Women in the Middle Ages in Theory, Fact, and Fantasy." In: *Beyond Their Sex. Learned Women of the European Past*: 9–42. Edited by P. H. Labalme. 1981. See also the work of A. M. Lucas mentioned above. Other than that there exist only some very old works: C. Jourdain, "L'education des femmes au moyen âge." *MINF* 28: 79–133. 1874.—F. Kösterus. *Frauenbildung im Mittelalter.* 1877.—A. A. Hentsch. *De la littérature didactique du moyen âge, s'adressant spécialement aux femmes.* Dissertation. Halle. 1903.—B. May. *Die Mädchenerziehung in der Geschichte der Pädagogik von Plato bis zum 18. Jahrhundert.* Dissertation. Erlangen. 1908.—H. Jacobius. *Die Erziehung des Edelfräuleins im alten Frankreich. Nach Dichtungen des XII., XIII. und XIV. Jahrhunderts.* 1908.

On the role of women in the literary and artistic life see H. Grundmann, "Die Frauen und die Literatur im Mittelalter. Ein Beitrag zur Frage nach der Entstehung des Schrifttums in der Volkssprache." *AKG* 26: 129–61. 1936.—R. Lejeune. "Rôle littéraire de la famille d'Aliénor d'Aquitaine." *CCM* 1: 319–37. 1958.—W. W. Kibbler, ed. *Eleanor of Aquitaine. Patron and Politician.* 1976.—T. Latzke. "Der Fürstinnenpreis." *MIJ* 14: 22–65. 1979.—S. G. Bell. "Medieval Women Book Owners." *Si* 7: 742–68. 1982.—E. Schraut and C. Opitz. *Frauen und Kunst im Mittelalter. Katalog zur Ausstellung.* 1983.

Only a few titles can be given here concerning the Christian attitude toward women: M. Bernards, *Speculum Virginum. Geistigkeit und Seelenleben der Frau im Hochmittelalter.* 1955.—M. Stoeckle. *Studien über Ideale in Frauenviten des VII.–X. Jahrhunderts.* Dissertation. München. 1957.—K. Thraede. "Frau." In: *Reallexikon für Antike und Christentum*, vol. 8, cols. 197–269. 1972.—M. M. McLaughlin. "Peter Abelard and the Dignity of Women. Twelfth-Century Feminism in Theory and Practice." In: *Pierre Abélard—Pierre le Vénérable*: 287–334. 1975.—A. Hufnagel. "Die Bewertung der Frau bei Thomas von Aquin." *TQ* 156: 133–47. 1976.—M.-T. d'Alverny. "Comment les théologiens et les philosophes voient la femme." *CCM* 20: 105–28. 1977.

On medieval biological and anthropological notions of women see A. Mitterer, "Mann und Weib nach dem biologischen Weltbild des hl. Thomas und dem der Gegenwart." *ZfkT* 57: 491–556. 1933.—V. L. Bullough. "Medieval Medical and Scientific Views of Women." *Vr* 4: 485–501. 1973.

On the religious women's movement see J. Grevin, *Die Anfänge der Beginen.* 1912.—E. W. McDonnel. *The Beguines and Beghards in Medieval Culture.* 1954.—H. Grundmann. *Religiöse Bewegungen im Mittelalter. Untersuchungen über die geschichtlichen Zusammenhänge zwischen der Ketzerei, den Bettelorden und der religiösen Frauenbewegung im 12. und 13. Jahrhundert und über die geschichtlichen Grundlagen der deutschen Mystik.* 2d ed. 1961.—G. Koch. *Frauenfrage und Ketzertum im Mittelalter. die Frauenbewegung im Rahmen des Katharismus und des Waldensertums und ihre sozialen Wurzeln (12.–14. Jahrhundert).* 1962.—G. Koch. "Die Frau im mittelalterlichen Katharismus und Waldensertum." *SM* Series 3a, vol. 5: 741–74. 1964.—E. McLaughlin. "Die Frau und die mittelalterliche Häresie." *Co* 12: 34–44. 1976.

On the tradition of misogynistic literature see A. Köhn, *Das weibliche Schönheitsideal in der ritterlichen Dichtung.* 1930.—W. Spiewok. "Minneidee und feudalhöfisches Frauenbild." *WZUG* 12: 481–90. 1963.—C. Soeteman. "Das schillernde Frauenbild mittelalterlicher Dichtung." *ABäG* 5: 77–94. 1973.—J. M. Ferrante. *Women as Image in Medieval Literature. From the Twelfth Century to Dante.* 1975.—R. Lejeune. "La femme dans les littératures françaises et occitanes du XIe au XIIIe siècle." *CCM* 20: 201–16. 1977.

On the image of woman in courtly lyric see C. Leube-Fey, *Bild und Funktion der domna in der Lyrik der Trobadors.* 1971.—W. D. Paden, Jr. "The Troubadour's Lady. Her Marital Status and Social Rank." *SiP* 72: 28–50. 1975.—L. Salem. *Die Frau in den Liedern des 'Hohen Minnesangs.'* 1980.—G. Schweikle. "Die frouwe der Minnesänger. Zu Realitätsgehalt und Ethos des Minnesangs im 12. Jahrhundert." *ZfdA* 109: 91–116. 1980.

On the image of woman in courtly epic see M. M. Mann, "Die Frauen und die Epik nach Gottfried von Straßburg." *JEGP* 12: 355–82. 1913.—H.-J. Böckenholt. *Untersuchungen zum Bild der Frau in den mittelhochdeutschen 'Spielmannsdichtungen.'* Dissertation. Münster. 1971.—A. K. Blumstein. *Misogyny and Idealization in the Courtly Romance.* 1977.—V. Mertens. *Laudine. Soziale Problematik im Iwein Hartmanns von Aue.* 1978.—G. J. Lewis. "das vil edel wîp. Die Haltung zeitgenössischer Kritiker zur Frauengestalt der mittelhochdeutschen Epik." In: *Die Frau als Heldin und Autorin*: 66–81. Edited by W. Paulsen. 1979.—E. Schäufele. *Normabweichendes Rollenverhalten. Die kämpfende Frau in der deutschen Literatur des 12. und 13. Jahrhunderts.* 1979.—I. Henderson. "Die Frauendarstellung im nachklassischen Roman des Mittelalters." *ABäG* 14: 137–48. 1979.—H. Göttner-Abendroth. "Die Herrin und ihr Held. Matriarchale Mythologie in der Epik des Mittelalters." In: H. Göttner-Abendroth, *Die matriarchalen Religionen in Mythos, Märchen und Dichtung*: 173–230. 1980.—N. C. Zak. *The Portrayal of the Heroine in Chrétien de Troyes' Erec et Enide, Gottfried von Straßburg's Tristan und Flamenca.* 1983.—P. Kellermann-Haaf. *Frau und Politik im Mittelalter. Untersuchungen zur politischen Rolle der Frau in den höfischen Romanen des 12., 13. und 14. Jahrhunderts.* Dissertation. Köln. 1983.

On the image of woman in the *Schwänke* see F. Brietzmann, *Die böse Frau in der deutschen Literatur des Mittelalters. 1912.*—M. Londner. *Eheauffasung und Darstellung der Frau in der spätmittelalterlichen Märendichtung.* Dissertation. Freie Universität Berlin. 1973.

On the portrayal of women in historical writing see M.-L. Portmann, *Die Darstellung der Frau in der Geschichtsschreibung des früheren Mittelalters.* 1958.

3. Courtly love

A very rich international bibliography exists on the concept of courtly love. I can mention here only some of the most important works. The most interesting viewpoints I have found in the studies of Rüdiger Schnell. A trusty guide to the sociological questions is the overview of current scholarship by Ursula Liebertz-Grün. The starting point for the scholarly debate about "amour courtois" was the essay by G. Paris, "Études sur les romans de la table ronde. Lancelot du Lac. 2. Le conte de la Charrette." *Ro* 12: 459–534. 1883. See also R. R. Bezzola, "Guillaume IX et les origines de l'amour courtois." *Ro* 66: 145–237. 1940.— A. J. Denomy. "Fin' Amors. The Pure Love of the Troubadours. Its Amorality and Possible Source." *MSt* 7: 139–207. 1945.—H. Kolb. *Der Begriff der Minne und das Entstehen der höfischen Lyrik.* 1958.—E. Lea. "Erziehen—im Wert erhöhen—Gemeinschaft in Liebe." *PBB* (Halle) 89: 255–89. 1967.—F. X. Newman, ed. *The Meaning of Courtly Love.* 1968.—H. Wenzel. *Frauendienst und Gottesdienst. Studien zur Minne—Ideologie.* 1974.—R. Schnell. "Ovids Ars amatoria und die höfische Minnetheorie." *Eu* 69: 132–59. 1975.—R. Boase. *The Origin and Meaning of Courtly Love. A Critical Study of European Scholarship.* 1977.—H. Kuhn. "Determinanten der Minne." *Lili.* 7, no. 26: 83–94. 1977.—R. Schnell. "Hohe und niedere Minne." *ZfdPh* 98: 19–52. 1979.

On the sociology of courtly love see E. Wechssler, "Frauendienst und Vasallität." *ZffSL* 24: 159–90. 1902.—W. Mohr. "Minnesang als Gesellschaftskunst." *DU* 6, no. 5: 83–107. 1954.—E. Köhler. "Die Rolle des niederen Rittertums bei der Entstehung der Trobadorlyrik." In: E. Köhler, *Esprit und arkadische Freiheit*: 9–27. 1966.—E. Köhler. "Vergleichende soziologische Betrachtungen zum romanischen und zum deutschen Minnesang." In: *Der Berliner Germanistentag 1968*: 61–76. Edited by K. H. Borck and R. Henß. 1970.—C. Wallbaum. *Studien zur Funktion des Minnesangs in der Gesellschaft des 12. und 13. Jahrhunderts.* Dissertation. Freie Universität Berlin. 1972.—U. Peters. "Niederes Rittertum oder hoher Adel? Zu Erich Köhlers historisch-soziologischer Deutung der altprovenzalischen und mittelhochdeutschen Minnelyrik." *Eu* 67: 244–60. 1973.—E. Kleinschmidt. "Minnesang als höfisches Zeremonialhandeln." *AKG* 58: 35–76. 1976.—U. Lieberts-Grün. *Zur Soziologie des amour courtois. Umrisse der Forschung.* 1977.—G. Kaiser. "Minnesang—Ritterideal—Ministerialität." In: *Adelsherrschaft und Literatur*: 181–208. Edited by H. Wenzel. 1980.

For Andreas Capellanus see W. T. H. Jackson, "The De Amore of Andreas Capellanus and the Practice of Love at Court." *RR* 49: 243–51. 1958.—F. Schlösser. *Andreas Capellanus. Seine Minnelehre und das christliche Weltbild des 12. Jahrhunderts.* 2d ed. 1962.—R. Schnell. "Andreas Capellanus, Heinrich von Morungen und Herbort von Fritzlar." *ZfdA* 104: 131–51. 1975.—F. Taiana. *Amor parus und die Minne.* 1977.—A. Karnein. "Auf der Suche nach einem Author. Andreas, Verfasser von De Amore." *GRM* N.S. 28: 1–20. 1978.—R. Schnell. *Andreas Capellanus. Zur Rezeption des römischen und kanonischen Rechts in De Amore.* 1982.—A. Karnen. *De Amore in volkssprachlicher Literatur. Untersuchungen zur Andreas Capellanus—Rezeption in Mittelalter und Renaissance.* 1985.

On the doctrine of marriage and the sexual ethics of Scholasticism and the canon law on marriage see P. Browe, *Beiträge zur Sexualethik des Mittelalters.* 1932.—J. Dauvillier. *Le mariage dans le droit classique de l'église depuis le décret de Gratien (1140) jusqu'à la mort de Clément V. (1314).* 1933.—H. Portmann. *Wesen und Unauflöslichkeit der Ehe in der kirchlichen Wissenschaft und Gesetzgebung des 11. und 12. Jahrhunderts.* 1938.—J. Fuchs. *Die Sexualethik des hl. Thomas von Aquin.* 1949.—M. Müller. *Die Lehre des hl. Augustinus von der Paradiesehe und ihre Auswirkung in der Sexualethik des 12. und 13. Jahrhunderts bis zu Thomas von Aquin.* 1954.—L. Brandl. *Die Sexualethik des hl. Albertus Magnus.* 1955.—J. G. Ziegler. *Die Ehelehre der Pönitentialsummen von 1200–1350.* 1956.—H. A. J. Allard. *Die eheliche Lebens- und Liebesgemeinschaft nach Hugo von St. Viktor.* 1963.—R. Weisgand. "Die Lehre der Kanonisten des 12. und 13. Jahrhunderts von den Ehezwecken." *SG* 12: 443–78. 1967.—J. A. Brundage. "The Crusader's Wife. A Canonistic Quandary." Ibid.: 425–41.—J. T. Noonan, Jr. "Marital Affection in the Canonists." Ibid.: 479–509.—R. Weigand. "Unauflösbarkeit der Ehe und Eheauflösungen durch Päpste im 12. Jahrhundert." *RDC* 20: 44–64. 1970.—R. Weigand. "Das Scheidungsproblem in der mittelalterlichen Kanonistik." *TQ* 151: 52–60. 1971.—R. Weigand. "Kanonistische Ehetraktate aus dem 12. Jahrhundert." In: *Proceedings of the Third International Congress of Medieval Canon Law:* 59–79. Edited by S. Kuttner. 1971.—J. T. Noonan, Jr. *Power to Dissolve. Lawyers and Marriages in the Courts of the Roman Curia.* 1972.—J. T. Noonan, Jr. "Power to Choose." *Vr* 4: 419–34. 1973.—H. Zeimentz. *Ehe nach der Lehre der Frühscholastik.* 1973.—J. A. Brundage. "Concubinage and Marriage in Medieval Canon Law." *JMH* 1: 1–17. 1975.— C. Donahue, Jr. "The Policy of Alexander the Third's Consent Theory of Marriage." In: *Proceedings of the Fourth International Congress of Medieval Canon Law:* 251–81. Edited by S. Kuttner. 1976.—V. Pfaff. "Das kirchliche Eherecht am Ende des 12. Jahrhunderts." *ZRG KA* 63: 73–117. 1977.—M. M. Sheehan. "Marriage Theory and Practice in the Conciliar Legislation and Diocesan Statutes of Medieval England." *MSt* 40: 408–60. 1978.—M. M. Sheehan. "Choice of Marriage Partner in the Middle Ages." *SMRH* 1: 1–33. 1978.—J. A. Brundage. "Rape and Marriage in Medieval Canon Law." *RDC* 28: 62–75. 1978.—C. N. L. Brooke. "Aspects of Marriage Law in the Eleventh and Twelfth Centuries." In: *Proceedings of the Fifth International Congress of Medieval Canon Law:* 333–44. Edited by S. Kuttner and K. Pennington. 1980.—J. A. Brundage. "Carnal Delight: Canonistic Theories of Sexuality." Ibid.: 361–85.—R. Weigand. "Zur mittelalterlichen kirchlichen Ehegerichtsbarkeit." *ZRG KA* 67: 213–47. 1981.

On marriage and sexuality among the medieval nobility see F. Frh. von Reitzenstein, *Liebe und Ehe im Mittelalter.* 1912.—P. Rassow. "Zum Kampf um das Eherecht im 12. Jahrhundert." *MIÖG* 58: 310–16. 1950.—J. F. Benton. "Clio and Venus. A Historical View of Medieval Love." In: *The Meaning of Courtly Love* (see p. 735): 19–48.—J.-F. Flandrin. "Contraception, mariage et relations amoreuses dans l'occident chrétien." *AESC* 24: 1370–90. 1969.—D. Herlihy. "The Medieval Marriage Market." In: *Medieval and Renaissance Studies:* 3–27. Edited by D. B. J. Randall. 1976.—*Il matrimonio nella società altomedievale.* 1977.—G. Duby. *Medieval Marriage. Two Models from the Twelfth Century.* Transl. by Elsborg Forster. 1978.—P. Dinzelbacher. "Über die Entdeckung der Liebe im Hochmittelalter." *Sc* 32: 185–208. 1981.-W. van Hoecke and A. Welkenhuysen, eds. *Love and Marriage in the Twelfth Century.* 1981.—J. Bumke. "Liebe und Ehebruch in der höfischen Gesellschaft." In: *Liebe als Literatur:* 25–45. Edited by R. Krohn. 1983.—J. Goody. *The Development of the Family and Marriage in Europe.* 1983.—D. Buschinger and A. Crépin, eds. *Amour, mariage et transgressions au moyen âge.* 1984.—G. Duby. *The Knight, the Lady, and the Priest: The Making of Modern Marriage in Medieval France.* Transl. by B. Bray. 1983.

On love and marriage in courtly literature see P. Schultz, *Die erotischen Motive in den deutschen Dichtungen des 12. und 13. Jahrhunderts.* Dissertation. Greifswald. 1907.—A. Drexel. *Über gesellschaftliche Anschauungen, wie sie in den mittelhochdeutschen höfischen und Volksepen hervortreten.* Dissertation. Kempten. 1909.—J. Coppin. *Amour et mariage dans la littérature française du nord au moyen âge.* 1961.—L. Pollmann. *Die Liebe in der hochmittelalterlichen Literatur Frankreichs.* 1966.—H. E. Wiegand. *Studien zur Minne und Ehe in Wolframs Parzival und Hartmanns Artusepik.* 1972.—H. Metz. *Die Entwicklung der Eheauffassung von der Früh- zur Hochscholastik in der mittelhochdeutschen Epik.* Dissertation. Cologne. 1972.—B. M. Faber. *Eheschließung in mittelalterlicher Dichtung vom Ende des 12. bis zum Ende des 15. Jahrhunderts.* Dissertation. Bonn. 1974.—W. Hofmann. *Die Minnefeinde in der deutschen Liebesdichtung des 12. und 13. Jahrhunderts.* Dissertation. Würzburg. 1974.—P. Wapnewski. *Waz is minne. Studien zur Mittelhochdeutschen Lyrik.* 1975.—J. M. Ferrante et al, eds. *In Pursuit of Perfection. Courtly Love in Medieval Literature.* 1975.—H. Eggers. "Die Entdeckung der Liebe im Spiegel der deutschen Dichtung der Stauferzeit." In: *Geist und Frömmigkeit der Stauferzeit:* 10–25. Edited by W. Böhme. 1978.—P. Wapnewski. "Das Glück der unglücklichen Liebe oder Schmerz laß nicht nach. Liebe als Dichtung: Minnesang." *Me* 34, no. 382: 238–47. 1980.—C. Muscatine. "Courtly Literature and Vulgar Language." In: *Court and Poet:* 1–19. Edited by G. S. Burgess. 1981.—R. Schnell. "Grenzen literarischer Freiheit im Mittelalter. Part I." *Arch* 218: 249–70. 1981.—L. P. Johnson. "Down with hohe minne." *OGS* 13: 36–48. 1982.—R. Schnell. "Von der kanonistischen zur höfischen Ehekausuistik." *ZfrPh* 98: 257–95. 1982.—R. Schnell. "Gottfrieds Tristan und die Institution der Ehe." *ZfdPh* 101: 334–69. 1982.—R. Schnell. "Praesumpta mors. Zum Widerstreit von deutschen, römischen und kanonischem Eherecht im Guten Gerhard Rudolfs von Ems." *ZRG GA* 100: 181–212. 1983.—X. von Ertzdorf. "Tristan und Lanzelot. Zur Problematik der Liebe in den höfischen Romanen des 12. und frühen 13. Jahrhunderts." *GRM* N.S. 33: 21–52. 1983.—G. Kaiser. "Liebe außerhalb der Gesellschaft. Zu einer Lebensform der höfischen Liebe." In: *Liebe als Literatur* (see above): 79–97.—H. Wenzel. "Fernliebe und Hohe Minne. Zur räumlichen und sozialen Distanz in der Minnethematik." Ibid.: 187–208.—R. Schnell. "Literatur als Korrektiv sozialer Realität. Zur Eheschließung in mittelalterlichen Dichtungen." In: *Non nova, sed nove. Mélanges de civilisation médiévale dédiés à W. Noomen:* 225–38. 1984.—X. von Ertzdorf and M. Wynn, ed. *Liebe- Ehe-Ehebruch in der Literatur des Mittel-*

alters. 1984.—R. Schnell. *Causa amoris. Liebeskonzeption und Liebesdarstellung in der mittelalterlichen Literatur*. 1985.

On minne conviviality, the debating songs and the love courts see P. Remy, "Les courts d'amour. Légende et réalité." *RUB* 7: 179–97. 1955.—E. Köhler. "Der Frauendienst der Trobadors, dargestellt an ihren Streitgedichten." *GRM* 41: 201–31. 1960.—S. Neumeister. *Das Spiel mit der höfischen Liebe. Das altprovenzalische Partimen*. 1969.—I. Glier. *Artes amandi. Untersuchungen zu Geschichte, Überlieferung und Typologie der deutschen Minnereden*. 1971.—U. Peters. "Cour d'amour—Minnehof. Ein Beitrag zum Verhältnis der französischen und deutschen Minnedichtung zu den Unterhaltungsformen ihres Publikums." *ZfdA* 101: 117–33. 1972.—C. Schlumbohn. *Jocus und Amor. Liebesdiskussion vom mittelalterlichen joc partit bis zu den preziösen questions d'amour*. 1974.—R. Schnell. "Facetus, Pseudo-Ars amatoria und die mittelhochdeutsche Minnedidaktik" *Zfd4* 104: 224–47. 1975.—I. Kasten. "geteiltez spil und Reinmars Dilemma." *MF* 165, 37. On the influence of the old Provençal sirvente on Middle High German literature, *Eu* 74: 16–54. 1980.—A. Karnein. "Europäische Minnedidaktik" In: *Europäisches Hochmittelalter*: 121–44. Edited by H. Krauss. 1981.—R. Schnell. "Zur Entstehung des altprovenzalischen dilemmatischen Streitgedichtes." *GRM* N.S. 33: 1–20. 1983.

CHAPTER VI
CRITICISM OF COURTLY LIFE

Latin court criticism of the twelfth century was ably treated by C. Uhlig, *Hofkritik im England des Mittelalters und der Renaissance. Studien zu einem Gemeinplatz der europäischen Moralistik*. 1973. Interesting new aspects have been developed by Rolf Köhn and C. Stephen Jaeger. See R. Köhn, "Militia curialis. Die Kritik am geistlichen Hofdienst bei Peter von Blois und in der lateinischen Literatur des 9.–12. Jahrhunderts." In: *Soziale Ordnung im Selbstverständnis des Mittelalters*, vol. I: 227–57. Edited by A. Zimmermann. 1979.—C. S. Jaeger. "The Court Criticism of MHG Didactic Poets. Social Structures and Literary Conventions." *MO* 74: 398–409. 1982.—C. S. Jaeger. "The Nibelungen Poet and the Clerical Rebellion against Courtesy." In: *Spectrum medii aevi. Essay in Early German Literature in Honor of G. F. Jones*: 177–205. 1983.—C. S. Jaeger. "The Barons' Intrigue in Gottfried's Tristan. Notes toward a Sociology of Fear in Court Society." *JEGP* 83: 46–66. 1984. A comprehensive analysis of the motifs of court criticism in Middle High German literature does not yet exist. See also I. von der Lühe and W. Röcke, "Ständekritische Predigt des Spätmittelalters am Beispiel Bertholds von Regensburg." In: *Literatur im Feudalismus*: 41–82. Edited by D. Richter. 1975.—D. Schmidtke. "Mittelalterliche Liebeslyrik in der Kritik mittelalterlicher Moraltheologen." *ZfdPh* 95: 321–45. 1976.—E. Türk. *Nugae curialium. Le règne d'Henri II Plantagenêt (1145–1189) et l'ethique politique*. 1977.—G. Scholz-Williams. "Against Court and School. Heinrich of Melk and Hélinand of Froidmont as Critics of Twelfth-century Society." *Ne* 62: 513–26. 1978.—H. Kiesel. *Bei*

Hof, bei Höll. Untersuchungen zur literarischen Hofkritik von Sebastian Brant bis Friedrich Schiller. 1979.

CHAPTER VII
THE LITERARY SCENE OF THE COURTLY AGE

1. Oral culture and literacy in courtly society

On oral tradition and writing in noble lay society see H. Fichtenau, *Mensch und Schrift im Mittelalter.* 1946.—P. Classen, ed. *Recht und Schrift im Mittelalter.* 1977.—H. Bekker-Nielsen et al., eds. *Oral Tradition, Literary Tradition.* 1977.—F. H. Bäuml. "Medieval Literacy and Illiteracy. An Essay toward the Construction of a Model." In: *Germanic Studies in Honor of O. Springer*: 41–54. 1978.—D. H. Green. "Oral Poetry and Written Composition. An Aspect of the Feud between Gottfried and Wolfram." In: *Approaches to Wolfram von Eschenbach*: 163–264. Edited by D. H. Green and L. P. Johnson. 1978.—M. T. Clanchy. *From Memory to Written Record. England 1066–1306.* 1979.—F. H. Bäuml. "Varieties and Consequences of Medieval Literacy and Illiteracy." *Sp* 55: 237–65. 1980.—J. Goody, ed. *Literacy in Traditional Societies.* 1968.—H. Vollrath. "Das Mittelalter in der Typik oraler Gesellschaften." *HZ* 233: 571–94. 1981.—A. and J. Assmann and C. Hardmeier, ed. *Schrift und Gedächtnis. Beiträge zur Archäologie der literarischen Kommunikation.* 1983.—B. Stock. *The Implications of Literacy. Written Language and Models of Interpretation in the Eleventh and Twelfth Centuries.* 1983.

On lay education in the High Middle Ages, the best information can be found in Thompson and Grundmann. J. W. Thompson, *The Literacy of the Laity in the Middle Ages.* 1939.—H. Grundmann. "Literatus—illiteratus. Der Wandel einer Bildungsnorm vom Altertum zum Mittelalter." *AKG* 40: 1–63. 1958.—See also the older and richly documented work of G. Zappert, "Über ein für den Jugendunterricht Kaiser Maximilian's I. abgefaßtes lateinisches Gesprächsbüchlein." *WSB* 28: 193–280. 1858.—Also: V. H. Galbraith, "The Literacy of the Medieval English Kings." *PBA* 21: 201–38.—P. Riché. "Recherches sur l'instruction des laïcs de IXe au XIIe siècle." *CCM* 5: 175–82. 1962.—K. Schreiner. "Laienbildung als Herausforderung für Kirche und Gesellschaft. Religiöse Vorbehalte und soziale Widerstände gegen die Verbreitung von Wissen im späten Mittelalter und in der Reformation." *ZfhF* 11: 257–354. 1984.—L. Grenzmann and K. Stackmann, eds. *Literatur und Laienbildung im Spätmittelalter und in der Reformationszeit.* 1984.

I can list here only a few titles from the extensive scholarship on oral poetry. The best description of oral composition was given by A. B. Lord, *The Singer of Tales.* 1960. A cross-section of the scholarship can be found in the volume *Oral Poetry. Das Problem der Mündlichkeit mittelalterlicher epischer Dichtung.* Edited by N. Voorwinden and M. de Haan. 1979. Additional bibliography can be found in E. R. Haymes, *Das mündliche Epos. Eine Einführung in die Oral Poetry-Forschung.* 1977. A critical view by M. Curschmann, "The Concept of Oral Formula as an Impediment to Our Understanding of Medieval Oral Poetry." *MH* 8: 63–79. 1977.

On the rise of dynastic historiography and the relationship of princely court and dynastic monastery see H. Patze, "Adel und Stifterchronik. Frühformen territorialer Geschichtsschreibung im hochmittelalterlichen Reich." *BDLG* 100: 8–81, 1964; 101: 67–128, 1965.

On the writing of charters and chanceries at the courts of the secular princes see O. Redlich, "Die Privaturkunden des Mittelalters." In: *Handbuch der Mittelalterlichen und Neueren Geschichte*, Section 4, vol. 1,3. 1911.—H. Bresslau. *Handbuch der Urkundenlehre für Deutschland und Italien.* 2 vols. 2d ed. 1912–31.—H. Patze. "Neue Typen des Geschäftsschriftgutes im 14. Jahrhundert." In: *Der deutsche Territorialstaat im 14. Jahrhundert* (see p. 710), vol. 1: 9–64.—J. Wild. *Die Fürstenkanzlei des Mittelalters. Anfänge weltlicher und geistlicher Zentralverwaltung in Bayern.* 1983.—*Landesherrliche Kanzleien im Spätmittelalter.* 2 vols. 1984.

On the chancery of Henry the Lion see F. Hasenritter, *Beiträge zum Urkunden- und Kanzleiwesen Heinrichs des Löwen.* MGH Dipl. Laienfürsten 1. 1949.—There is as yet no recent study of the chancery of the Thuringian landgraves. A brief discussion can be found in H. Patze, *Die Entstehung der Landesherrschft in Thüringen*, vol. 1: 527 ff. 1962. For the last years of the Ludowingians see D. Hägermann, "Studien zum Urkundenwesen König Heinrich Raspes (1246/47)." *DA* 36: 487–548. 1980.—For the chancery of the Babenbergs in Austria see O. Frh. von Mitis, *Studien zum älteren österreichischen Urkundenwesen.* 1912.—H. Fichtenau. *Das Urkundenwesen in Österreich vom 8. bis zum frühen 13. Jahrhundert.* 1971.—For the chancery of the Wittelsbach dynasty in Bavaria see S. Hoffmann, *Urkundenwesen, Kanzlei und Regierungssytem der Herzoge in Bayern und Pfalzgrafen bei Rhein von 1180 bzw. 1214 bis 1255 bzw. 1294.* 1967.—L. Schnurrer. *Urkundenwesen, Kanzlei und Regierungssystem der Herzöge von Niederbayern, 1255–1340.* 1972.

On the oldest land registers see W. Metz, *Staufische Güterverzeicchnisse. Untersuchungen zur Verfassungs- und Wirtschaftsgeschichte des 12. und 13. Jahrhunderts.* 1964.—W. Volkert. "Die älteren bayerischen Herzogsurbare." *BON* 7: 1–32. 1966.

On the emergence in the thirteenth century of charters written in German see M. Vancsa, *Das erste Auftreten der deutschen Sprache in Urkunden.* 1895.—F. Wilhelm, *Zur Geschichte des Schrifttums in Deutschland bis zum Ausgang des 13. Jahrhunderts. 1. Von der Ausbreitung der deutschen Sprache im Schriftverkehr und ihren Gründen.* 1920.—H. Hirsch. "Zur Frage des Auftretens der deutschen Sprache in den Urkunden und der Ausgabe deutscher Urkundentexte." *MIÖG* 52: 227–42. 1938.—R. Newald. "Das erste Auftreten der deutschen Urkunde in der Schweiz." *ZfSG* 22: 489–507. 1942.—H. G. Kirchhoff. "Zur deutschsprachigen Urkunde des 13. Jahrhunderts." *AfD* 3: 287–327.—I. Stolzenberg. "Urkundsparteien und Urkundensprache. Ein Beitrag zur Frage des Aufkommens der deutschsprachigen Urkunde am Oberrhein." *AfD* 7: 214–89, 1961; 8: 147–269, 1962.—B. Boesch. "Die deutsche Urkundensprache. Probleme ihrer Erforschung im deutschen Südwesten." *RVjb* 32: 1–28. 1968.—I. Reiffenstein. "Deutschsprachige Arengen des 13. Jahrhunderts." In: *Festschrift für M. Spindler*: 177–92. 1969.—H. de Boor. "Actum et Datum. Eine Untersuchung zur Formelsprache der deutschen Urkunden im 13. Jahrhundert." *MSB* no. 4. 1975.—U. Schulze. *Lateinischdeutsche Parallelurkunden des 13. Jahrhunderts. Ein Beitrag zur Syntax der mittelhochdeutschen Urkundensprache.* 1975.—F. Schubert. *Sprachstruktur und Rechtsfunktion. Untersuchung zur deutschsprachigen Urkunde des 13. Jahrhunderts.* 1979.

On the literary scene as a whole, see R. Krohn, "Literaturbetrieb im Mittelalter." In: *Propyläen Geschichte der Literatur*, vol. 2: 199–220. 1982.

2. Patrons and sponsors

On literary patronage in the Middle Ages see S. Moore, "General Aspects of Literary Patronage in the Middle Ages." *Ly. Ser. 3, vol. 4:* 369–92. 1913.—K. J. Holzknecht. *Literary Patronage in the Middle Ages.* Ph.D. dissertation. Univ. of Pennsylvania. 1923. Some more recent scholarly contributions to this topic have been collected in *Literarisches Mäzenatentum im Mittelalter.* Edited by J. Bumke. 1982.

On the imperial court as a literary center there is only the unsatisfactory account of W. C. McDonald, *German Medieval Literary Patronage from Charlemagne to Maximilian I. A Critical Commentary with Special Emphasis on Imperial Promotion of Literature.* 1973. See also J. Fleckenstein, *Die Hofkapelle der deutschen Könige.* 2 vols. 1959–66.—S. Haider. "Zum Verhältnis von Kapellanat und Geschichtsschreibung im Mittelalter." In: *Geschichtsschreibung und geistiges Leben im Mittelalter. Festschrift für H. Löwe:* 102–38. 1978.

On court historiography under Frederick I see R. Holtzmann, "Das Carmen de Frederico I imperatore aus Bergamo und die Anfänge einer staufischen Hofhistoriographie." *NA* 44: 252–313. 1922.—E. Ottmar. "Das Carmen de Friderico I. imperatore aus Bergamo und seine Beziehungen zu Otto-Rahewins Gesta Friderici, Gunthers Ligurinus und Burchard von Ursbergs Chronik." *NA* 46: 430–89. 1925.—I. Schmale-Ott. Introduction to *Carmen de gestis Frederici I Imperatoris in Lombardia:* XXIX ff. 1965.—W. Wattenbach and F.-J. Schmale. *Deutschlands Geschichtsquellen im Mittelalter. Vom Tode Kaiser Heinrichs V. bis zum Ende des Interregnum*, vol. 1: 46 ff. 1976.

Fundamental for patronage relationships in France is R. R. Bezzola, *Les origines et la formation de la littérature courtoise en occident (550–1200).* 3 vols. 1944–63. For England see W. F. Schirmer and U. Broich, *Studien zum literarischen Patronat im England des 12. Jahrhunderts.* 1962.—M. D. Legge. *Anglo—Norman Literature and Its Background.* 1963. On individual French courts see M. D. Stanger, "Literary Patronage at the Medieval Court of Flanders." *FS* 11: 214–29. 1957.—J. F. Benton, "The Court of Champagne as a Literary Center." *Sp* 36: 551–91. 1961. On the role of women in the literary and artistic life see p. 733.

On princely patronage in Germany see F. Wilhelm, *Zur Geschichte des Schrifttums in Deutschland bis zum Ausgang des 13. Jahrhunderts. 2. Der Urheber und sein Werk in der Öffentlichkeit.* 1921.—U. Müller. *Untersuchungen zur politischen Lyrik des deutschen Mittelalters.* 1974.—J. Bumke. *Mäzene im Mittelalter. Die Gönner und Auftraggeber der höfischen Literatur in Deutschland, 1150–1300.* 1979.

On the beginnings of the literary activities in the cities see U. Peters, *Literatur in der Stadt. Studien zu den sozialen Voraussetzungen und kulturellen Organisationsformen städtischer Literatur im 13. und 14. Jahrhundert*. 1983. For the situation in Basel see I. Leipold, *Die Auftraggeber und Gönner Konrads von Würzburg*. 1976. On the situation in Zurich see H.-E. Renk, *Der Manessekreis, seine Dichter und die Manessische Handschrift*. 1974.

3. Author and audience

On the courtly poets, their self-portrayal, and their place within society, see E. Köhler, "Die Selbstauffassung des höfischen Dichters." In: *Der Vergleich. Festgabe für H. Petriconi*: 65–79. 1955.—J. Gernentz. "Die gesellschaftliche Stellung des Künstlers in Deutschland um 1200." *WZUR* 9: 121–25. 1959/60.—F. Tschirch. "Das Selbstverständnis des mittelalterlichen deutschen Dichters." In: *Beiträge zum Berufsbewußtsein des mittelalterlichen Menschen*: 239–85. Edited by P. Wilpert. 1964.

On the social background of the minnesingers and the Spruch poets see F. Grimme, "Die Anordnung der großen Heidelberger Liederhandschrift." *NHJ* 4: 53– 90. 1894.—A. Schulte. "Die Standesverhältnisse der Minnesänger." *ZfdA* 39: 185–251. 1895.—F. Grimme. "Freiherren, Ministerialen und Stadtadlige im XIII. Jahrhundert. Mit besonderer Berücksichtigung der Minnesingér." *AI* 24: 97–141. 1897.—A. Wallner. "Herren und Spielleute im Heidelberger Liedercodex." *PBB* 33: 483–540. 1908.—P. Kluckhohn. "Ministerialität und Ritterdichtung." *ZfdA* 52: 135–68. 1910.—K. Franz. *Studien zur Soziologie des Spruchdichters in Deutschland im späten 13. Jahrhundert*. 1974.—J. Bumke. *Ministerialität und Ritterdichtung*. 1976.

On the minstrels and the wandering poets see E. Faral, *Les jongleurs en France au moyen âge*. 1910.—A. Mönckenberg. *Die Stellung der Spielleute im Mittelalter. 1. Spielleute und Kirche im Mittelalter*. Dissertation. Freiburg i.Br. 1910.—H. Naumann. "Versuch einer Einschränkung des romantischen Begriffs Spielmannsdichtung." *DVjs* 2: 777–94. 1924.—E. Frh. von Künssberg. "Swer einen spilman haben wil, der sol in auch beraten." In: *Deutschkundliches. F. Panzer zum 60. Geburtstag*: 61–69. 1930.—F. H. Wareman. *Spielmannsdichtung. Versuch einer Begriffsbestimmung*. 1951.—P. Bäuml. "Guot umb êre nemen and Minstrel Ethics." *JEGP* 59: 173–83. 1960.—A. Schreier-Hornung. *Spielleute, Fahrende, Außenseiter. Künstler der mittelalterlichen Welt*. 1981.— H. Kästner. *Harfe und Schwert. Der höfische Spielmann bei Gottfried von Straßburg* 1981—W. Hartung. *Die Spielleute. Eine Randgruppe in der Gesellschaft des Mittelalters*. 1982.—W. Salmen. *Der Spielmann im Mittelalter*. 1983.

There are few works on the audience of courtly literature See W. Fechter, *Das Publikum der mittelhochdeutschen Dichtung*. 1935.—F. P. Knapp. "Literatur und Publikum im österreichischen Hochmittelalter." In: *Babenberger Forschungen*: 160–92. Edited by M. Weltin. 1976.—M. S. Batts. "Author and Public in the Late Middle Ages." In: *Interpretation und Edition deutscher Texte des Mittelalters. Festschrift für J. Asher*: 178–86. 1981.

On noble given names drawn from courtly literature see I. V. Zingerle, "Die

Personennamen Tirols in Beziehung auf deutsche Sage und Literaturgeschichte." *Gm* 1: 290–95. 1856.—R. Müller. "Beiträge zur Geschichte der höfischen Epik in den österreichischen Landen, mit besonderer Rücksicht auf Kärnten." *Ca* 85: 33–51. 1895.—F. Panzer. "Personennamen aus dem höfischen Epos in Baiern." In: *Philologische Studien. Festgabe für E. Sievers*: 205–20. 1896.— E. Kegel. *Die Verbreitung der mittelhochdeutschen erzählenden Literatur in Mittel- und Niederdeutschland, nachgewiesen auf Grund von Personennamen.* 1905.

4. The performance and spread of literature

On the written and oral spread of literature see W. Wattenbach, *Das Schriftwesen im Mittelalter.* 3d ed. 1896.—G. H. Putnam. *Books and Their Makers during the Middle Ages.* 2 vols. 1896–97.—R. K. Root. "Publication before Printing." *PMLA* 28: 417–31. 1913.—R. Crosby. "Oral Delivery in the Middle Ages." *Sp* 11: 88–110. 1936.—H. J. Chaytor. *From Script to Print.* 1945.—S. Gutenbrunner. "Über Rollencharakteristik und Choreographie beim Vortrag mittelalterlicher Dichtung." *ZfdPh* 75: 34–47. 1956.—K. H. Bertau and R. Stephan. "Zum sanglichen Vortrag mittelhochdeutscher strophischer Epen." *ZfdA* 87: 253–70. 1956/57.—W. Mohr. "Vortragsform und Form als Symbol im mittelalterlichen Liede." In: *Festgabe für U. Pretzel*: 128–38. 1963.—G. Wolf. *Untersuchungen zur Literatursoziologie des deutschen Buches im Mittelalter. Mit besonderer Berücksichtigung der Schreibstuben des Meister Hesse in Straßburg und des Diebold Lauber in Hagenau.* Dissertation (typed). Innsbruck. 1963.—K. H. Bertau. "Epenrezitation im deutschen Mittelalter." *Eg* 20: 1–17. 1965.—G. Karhof. *Der Abschnitt als Vortragsform in Handschriften frühmittelhochdeutscher Dichtungen.* Dissertation. Münster. 1967.— A. C. Baugh. "The Middle English Romance. Some Questions of Creation, Presentation, and Preservation." *Sp* 42: 1–31. 1967.—R. M. Walker. "Oral Delivery of Private Reading? A Contribution to the Debate on the Dissemination of Medieval Literature." *FMLS* 7: 36–42. 1971.—F. O. Büttner. "Mens divina liber grandis est. Zu einigen Darstellungen des Lesens in spätmittelalterlichen Handschriften." *Ph* 16: 92–126. 1972.—F. Ohly. "Zum Dichtungsschluß Tu autem, domine, misere nobis." *DVjs* 47: 26–68. 1973.—A. Masser. "Wege der Darbietung und der zeitgenössischen Rezeption höfischer Literatur." In: *Deutsche Heldenepik in Tirol*: 382–406. Edited by E. Kühebacher. 1979.—M. G. Scholz. *Hören und Lesen. Studien zur primären Rezeption der Literatur im 12. und 13. Jahrhundert.* 1980; reviewed by D. Kartschoke in IASL 8: 253–66. 1983.—D. Kartschoke. "Ulrich von Liechtenstein und die Laienkultur des deutschen Südostens im Übergang zur Schriftlichkeit." In: *Die mittelalterliche Literatur in Kärnten*: 103–143. Edited by P. Krämer. 1981.—U. Mehler. *Dicere und cantare. Zur musikalischen Terminologie und Aufführungspraxis des mittelalterlichen geistlichen Dramas in Deutschland.* 1981.—M. Curschmann. "Hören—Lesen—Sehen. Buch und Schriftlichkeit im Selbstverständnis der volkssprachlichen literarischen Kultur Deutschlands um 1200." *PBB* 106: 218– 57. 1984.—C. Schmid-Cadalbert. "Mündliche Traditionen und Schrifttum im europäischen Mittelalter." *ABäG* 21/22: 85–114. 1984.—D. H. Green. "On the Primary Reception of Narrative Literature in Medieval Germany." *FMLS* 20: 289–308. 1984.—M. Wehrli. *Literatur im deutschen Mittelalter. Eine poetologische Einführung* ("Mündlichkeit und Schriftlichkeit", pp. 47–67). 1984.—D. H. Green. "Oral and Written Literature in Medieval Germany." In: *The Spirit of the Court*: 5–8. Edited by G. S. Burgess and R. A. Taylor. 1985.

On loud and silent reading in the Middle Ages see J. Balogh. "Voces paginorum. Beiträge zur Geschichte des lauten Lesens und Schreibens." *Pi* 82: 84–109. 1927.—G. L. Hendrickson. "Ancient Reading." *CJ* 25: 182–96. 1929/30.—P. Saenger. "Silent Reading. Its Impact on Late Medieval Script and Society." *Vr* 13: 367–414. 1982.

On the topic of text and picture see O. Söhring, "Werke bildender Kunst in altfranzösischen Epen." *RF* 12: 491–640. 1900.—R. S. Loomis. *Arthurian Legends in Medieval Art.* 1938.—W. Stammler. "Epenillustration." In: *Reallexikon der deutschen Kunstgeschichte*, vol. 5: cols. 810–57. 1967.—H. Frühmorgen-Voss. "Mittelhochdeutsche weltliche Literatur und ihre Illustration." *DVjs* 43: 23–75. 1969.—P. Kern. "Bildprogramm und Text. Zur Illustration des Rolandsliedes in der Heidelberger Handschrift." *ZfdA* 101: 244–70. 1972.—M. Lengelsen. *Bild und Wort. Die Federzeichnungen und ihr Verhältnis zum Text in der Handschrift P des deutschen Rolandsliedes.* Dissertation. Freiburg i.Br. 1972.—N. H. Ott and W. Walliczek. "Bildprogramm und Textstruktur. Anmerkungen zu den Iwein-Zyklen auf Rodeneck und in Schmalkalden." In: *Deutsche Literatur im Mittelalter*: 473–500. Edited by C. Cormeau. 1979.—W. Haug et al. *Runkelstein. Die Wandmalereien des Sommerhauses.* 1982.—N. H. Ott. "Geglückte Minneaventiure. Zur Szenenauswahl literarischer Bildzeugnisse im Mittelalter." *JOWG* 2: 1–32. 1982/83.—N. H. Ott. "Epische Stoffe in mittelalterlichen Bildzeugnissen." In: *Epische Stoffe des Mittelalters*: 449–74. Edited by V. Mertens and U. Müller. 1984.

To date there is only one unsatisfactory attempt at a history of the transmission of courtly literature: F. Neumann, "Überlieferungsgeschichte der altdeutschen Literatur." In: *Geschichte der Textüberlieferung der antiken und mittelalterlichen Literatur*, vol. 2: 641–702. 1964. See most recently K. Grubmüller, "Gegebenheiten deutschsprachiger Textüberlieferung bis zum Ausgang des Mittelalters." In: *Sprachgeschichte*, vol. 1: 214–23. Edited by W. Besch et al. 1984. It is not possible to list here the scholarly literature concerning the transmission of individual works, or the more recent works dealing with the methods and principles of textual criticism. On the geography of literature see the important study of T. Klein, *Untersuchungen zu den mitteldeutschen Literatursprachen des 12. und 13. Jahrhunderts.* Habilitation thesis (unpublished). Bonn, 1982. On the Munich manuscripts Cgm 19 and Cgm 51 and the question concerning their provenance, see F. Ranke, "Die Überlieferung von Gottfrieds Tristan." *ZfdA* 55: 157–278, 381–438. 1917.—G. Bonath. *Untersuchungen zur Überlieferung des Parzival Wolframs von Eschenbach.* 2 vols. 1970–71; reviewed by J. Heinzle in *AfdA* 84: 145–57. 1973. Both of the Munich manuscripts are available in facsimile editions.

On the transmission of lyric see W. Wilmanns, "Zu Walther von der Vogelweide." *ZfdA* 13: 217–88 ("Wie bildeten sich die größeren Liedersammlungen?", pp. 224–29). 1867.—W. Wisser. *Das Verhältnis der Minne-*

liederhandschriften B und C zu ihrer gemeinschaftlichen Quelle. 1889.—H. Schneider. "Eine mittelhochdeutsche Liedersammlung als Kunstwerk." *PBB* 47: 225–60. 1923.—E. H. Kohnle. *Studien zur den Ordnungsgrundsätzen mittelhochdeutscher Liederhandschriften.* 1934.—C. Bützler. "Die Strophenanordnung in mittelhochdeutschen Liederhandschriften." *ZfdA* 77: 143–74. 1940.—E. Jammers. *Das Königliche Liederbuch. Eine Einführung in die sogenante Manessische Handschrift.* 1965.—A. H. Touber. "Formale Ordnungsprinzipien in mittelhochdeutschen Liederhandschriften." *ZfdA* 95: 187–203. 1966.—G. Spahr. *Weingartner Liederhandschrift. Ihre Geschichte und ihre Miniaturen.* 1968.—H. Frühmorgen-Voss. "Bildtypen in der Manessischen Liederhandschrift." In: *Werk—Typ—Situation*: 184–216. 1969.—H. Kuhn. "Die Vorraussetzungen für die Entstehung der Manessischen Handschrift und ihre überlieferungsgeschichtliche Bedeutung." In: H. Kuhn, *Liebe und Gesellschaft*: 80–105, 188–92. Edited by W. Walliczek. 1980.—O. Sayce. *The Medieval German Lyric, 1150–1300.* 1982.—F. H. Bäuml and R. H. Rouse. "Roll and Codex. A New Manuscript Fragment of Reinmar von Zweter." *PBB* 105: 192–231, 317–30. 1983. All the Large Song Manuscripts are available in facsimile editions. On the German strophes of the *Carmina Burana* see B. Wachinger, "Deutsche und lateinische Liebeslieder. Zu den deutschen Strophen der Carmina Burana." In: *From Symbol to Mimesis*: 1–34. Edited by F. H. Bäuml. 1984. The sensational find of a new illustrated song manuscript was reported by A. Vizkelety and K.-A. Wirth after this book had already gone to press: "Funde zum Minnesang. Blätter einer bebilderten Liederhandschrift." *PBB* 107: 366–75. 1985.

On the French and Provençal chansonniers see G. Gröber, "Die Liedersammlungen der Troubadours." *RSt* 2: 337–670. 1875/77.—A. Jeanroy. *Bibliographie sommaire des chansonniers français du moyen âge.* 1918—G. Raynauds *Bibliographie des altfranzösischen Liedes.* Newly revised by H. Spanke. Part 1. 1955.—D'A. S. Avalle. *La letterature medievale in lingua d'oc nella sua tradizione manoscritta.* 1961—D'A. S. Avalle. "Überlieferungsgeschichte der altprovenzalischen Literatur." In: *Geschichte der Textüberlieferung der antiken und mittelalterlichen Literatur*, vol. 2: 261–318. 1964.

Index

Aachen, cathedral of, 464
Abelard, Peter, 74, 378
"About a Latin conversation booklet
    written for the education of young
    Emperor Maximilian I," 312
Absolon, 464
Accounting, 5–6
Acrostics, 523–525
Adalbert, 244
Adalbert of Anhalt, Count, 286
Adalbert I of Mainz, 69
Adalbert II, 69
Adam of Bremen, 438
"Adaptation courtoise," 100–101
Adele of Blois, Countess, 117, 118, 144,
    329, 428
Adele of Brabant, 428
Adele of Vohburg, 388
Adelheid, Countess, 353
Adelheid of Brunswick, 212
Ademar of Chabannes, 427
Adenet le Roi, 83, 569
Adolf of Altena, 3, 45
Adolf of Nassau, King, 315, 401, 433
Adolf I of Cologne, Archbishop, 63
Adolf II of Holstein, Count, 315, 347
Adolf III of Holstein, 287
Adultery, 390–391, 392–398; in litera-
    ture, 394–398; in society, 392–394
Aeneas, 229–230
Aeneid, 92
Agnes of Andechs, 77
Agnes of Brunswick, 483

Agnes of Laon, Countess, 78, 476, 478,
    482
Agnes of Poitou, Empress, 79, 153, 341,
    349
Agrant, King, 128
Agriculture, 39–40
Ahasuerus, banquet of, 184
Aist, Dietmar von, 367, 478, 496, 551,
    567
"Alba," 98
Alberich, 69
Alberic of Besançon, 88
Albero of Kuenring, 540
Albero of Montreuil, Archbishop, 74
Albero of Trier, Archbishop, 54, 148, 210
Albert of Lüttich, Bishop, 3
Albert of Metz, 144
Albert of Stade, 340
Albertus Magnus, 175, 224, 225, 356,
    389
Albrecht of Austria, Duke, 173
Albrecht of Käfernburg, 483
Albrecht of Magdeburg, Archbishop, 347
Albrecht of Thuringia, Landgrave, 382
Albrecht of Tyrol, 252
Albrecht I, Duke, 480
Albrecht I, King, 135–136, 178, 185,
    188–189, 277
Albrecht I of Braunschweig, Duke, 45
Albrecht I of Saxony, Duke, 245, 480
Albrecht II, Margrave, 347
Albrecht II of Hapsburg, Count, 455
Albrecht III of Austria, Duke, 239

Aldersbach Codex, 149
Aldersbach monastery, 141
Alexander, Emperor, 279–280
Alexander, 86, 91, 93, 217, 316, 472, 476, 481, 484, 490, 492, 512, 530
Alexander II, Pope, 388
Alfonse of Poitiers, Count, 185
Alfonse I of Aragon, King, 196
Alfonsi, Petrus, 196, 197, 323
Alfonso X of Castile, King, 129
Alice of Blois, 481
Alice of France, Queen, 408
Alsfelder Passion Play, 155
Amalrich II, 348
Ambrose, Saint, 381, 404
Anagrams, 523–525
Andreas Capellanus, 329, 361–362, 367, 368, 371, 374, 375, 377, 378, 399, 403, 408–409, 410–411, 412
Andreas II of Hungary, King, 383
Anfortas, King, *186*
Angliscu, Bartholomaeus, 182
Animals, as entertainment, 221, 222, 223–224
Annales Aquenses, 232
Annalist, 53
Annals of Colmar, 46, 104, 130, 245, 247
Annals of Prague, 349
Annals of Quedlinburg, 437
Annals of Worcester, 393
Anno II, Archbishop, 36
Annolied, 68, 489
Anselm, 68, 69
Anselm of Havelberg, Bishop, 461
"Anti-Winsbeke, " 419
Apollonius von Tyrland, 263, 562
Appollinart, Prince, 308
Aquinas, Thomas, 328
Archeology, 7
Archers, 173–174
Architecture, of Hohenstaufen castles, 16–17
Architrenius, 416
Aristocracy, rule of, 24
Aristocratic dress, 134–136
Aristocratic ethic, reform and, 290–293
Aristoteles und Phyllis, 370
Aristotelian logic, 71
Aristotle, 323, 370
Armament, history of, 155–157. *See also* Weapons
Arme Hartmann, der, 153
Armer Heinrich, 495, 518, 535
Armor, 158, 160, 164–167; for horses, 176–177. *See also Barbiere*; Chain mail; Hauberks; Helmets; Shields; Tabards; Weapons

Arnald of Guines, Count, 112–113, 313, 403
Arnald II of Guines, Count, 516
Arnold der Fuchs, 85
Arnold of Brienz, 161
Arnold of Lübeck, Abbot, 79, 127, 176, 483
Arnold of Mainz, Archbishop, 3
Arnold of Selenhofen, 461
Arnold of Wied, Chancellor, 461
Arnulf I, Count, 428, 442
Arofel, King, 174
Ars amatoria, 361
Ars poetica, 512
Art: artistic training of women, 340–342
Arthur, King, 15, 16, 92, 132, 177, 183, 214, 228, 231, 238, 270, 275, 281, 312, 318, 320–321, 333, 422, 512, 513; court of, 4; Round Table of, 9
"Arthurian courts," 318
"Arthurian journey," 270
Arthurian legends, 95–96
Arthurian romances, 95
Ascalon, *528*
Athanias, 398
Athis und Prophilias, 90, 94, 159, 477
"Attic nights, " 462
Aucassin et Nicolette, 420
Audience: courtly, 506–512; formal expectations of, 511–512; as participant, 510–511
Audita tremendi, 299
Aue, Hartmann von, 15, 49, 59, 85, 90, 92, 94, 95, 101, 110, 125, 126, 166, 171–172, 176, 238, 260, 315, 326, 330, 364, 369, 391, 401–402, 421, 473, 479, 483, 490, 493–494, 495, 510, *567*
Augsburg, guilds in, 37
Augustine, Saint, 295, 384–385, 399
Augustinian canons, 297
Augustus, 278, 279

Bacalaria, Uc de la, 411
Balderic, 74
Balderic of Dol, 294
Balduin of Trier, *184*
Baldwin of Albermarle, Earl, 383
Baldwin of Flanders, Count, 133
Baldwin II, King, 348
Baldwin II of Guines, Count, 237, 435
Baldwin II of Hainaut, Count, 382
Baldwin V, King, 349
Baldwin V of Hainaut, Count, 84, 205, 210, 231, 243, 248, 253, 287, 313, 383

Baldwin VI of Hainaut, Count, 229, 243, 383–384
Baligan, King, 136
Bamberg cathedral, 136
Bamberg ministerials, 34
Baniere, 164, 165. See also Pennants
"Banner-fiefs," 31
Banquets, *184, 186, 188, 198*; protocol of, 182–183; seating arrangements for, 183–187; splendor of, 187–191. *See also* Court feasts; Food and drink; Meals; Table service; Tableware
Barbarossa head of Cappenberg, 149, 283
Barbiere, 14, 156, 158–159, *160*
Barlam und Josaphat, 474
Barnim I of Pomerania, Duke, 481
Baths, 120–121
"Battle of Aliscans, The," 93
Baudri of Bourgueil, 428
Bauernspeise, 178
Bauernstand, 28
Bäuml, Franz H., 563
Bavarian court rule of 1294, 57, 313, 506
Bavarian Territorial Peace of 1244, 166, 502–503
Bawdy comedies, 333
Bayeux Tapestry, 116, *116*, 157, 161, 163
Beaflor, 335
Beard fashions, 149
Beatrice, Empress, 56, 76, 105, 350
Beatrice, Queen, 283, 351
Beatrice of Burgundy, 347, 465
Beaumont, Countess of, 117
Beauty: courtly knights and, 304–307; ideal of, 325–327; masculine, 146
Becket, Thomas, 237
Beds, 119–120
Behavior: rules of, for women, 342–344
Bela III of Hungary, King, 347
Bela IV of Hungary, King, 211
Belakane, Queen, 188, 364
Bellum civile, 434
Belrapeire, siege of, 12–13
Bene, Duchess, 349
Benedictio ensis noviter succincti, 293
Benedict of Peterborough, 393
Benno II of Osnabrück, Bishop, 104–105, 107
Bergfried, 109, 121–122
Beringen, Heinrich von, 238
Berlin manuscript, 544
Bernard of Clairvaux, 295, 297–298
Bernhard of Carinthia, Duke, 261
Bernhard of Saxony, Duke, 204
Bernhard II of Carinthia, Duke, 421
Bernhard II zur Lippe, Freiherr, 223, 296
Bern of Dettingen, 353

Bertha of Holland, 402
"Bertha with the Big Feet," 83
Berthold of Andechs, Patriarch, 484
Berthold of Regensburg, 103, 419, 432, 504
Berthold of Tiersberg, 474, 485
Berthold of Ziegenhain, Count, 286
Berthold of Zwiefalten, 243, 249
Berthold IV of Andechs-Merans, Duke, 77
Berthold IV of Zähringen, Duke, 77, 403
Berthold V of Zähringen, Duke, 77, 479
Berthold VI, 479
Bertrade of Anjou, Countess, 402
Bescheidenheit (Freidank), 123
Béthune, Conon de, 97, 98
Bezzola, Reto R., 59, 322
Bishops, as literary patrons, 483–485
Black Prince, 161
Blancandin et l'Orgueilleuse d'amour, 95, 319
Blanche of Castile, 186, 347
Blanschandin, 95
Blanscheflur, 335
Blessing ceremonies, 239–242
"Blessing of the newly-girt sword," 293
Blois, Robert de, 210, 342
Bohemian kings, 39
Bolanden, Werner von, 35
Bolko I of Schweidnitz-Hauer, Duke, 481
Bollstater, Konrad, 395
Bonizio of Sutri, 292
"Book in Honor of the Emperor," 466
Book of Lamentations, 26
"Book of Manners," 300
Book of Sentences, 386, 389
"Book of Ten Chapters," 329
"Book of the Christian ruler, The," 277
"Book of Visions," 152
"Book on the Christian Life," 292
"Book to the knights of the Temple in praise of the new knighthood," 297
Boppe, 308
Born, Betran de, 77
Borneil, Guiraut de, 546
Bornhöved, battle of, 45
Borso II of Riesenburg, 486
Botenlouben, Otto von, 321, 551, 552
Bourgueil, Baudri de, 117, 118, 144, 563
Bouvines, Battle of, 174, 405
Boves, Enguerrand de, 400
Brabant, Duke of, 295
Brandigan castle, 110
Braunschweig, cathedral of, 288
Braunschweigische Reimchronik, 480
Bréauté, Fawkes de, 383
Brechmunde, Queen, 136

Brennenberg, Reinmar von, 395
Bretel, Jacques, 569
Breton, Guillaume le, 405
"Brief Austrian Chronicle from Melk,"
    444
Brinkmann, Hennig, 322
Brulé, Gace, 97, 569, 570
Brun, Garin le, 308
Brunner, Otto, 21, 24
Buchs, Dietrich von, 268
Buchs, Otto von, 268
Buhler, Fuß der, 395
Bûhurt, 82, 259–260
Burchard of Mansfeld, 508
Burchard of Worms, Bishop, 3, 144, 550
Burgundian court, 191
Burkhardt of Endôme, Count, 291–292

Caballarii, 48
Caesarius of Heisterbach, 71, 135, 512
Cairel, Elias, 561
Cambrai, unrest in, 36
Candacis, Queen, 9, 48–49, 144, 189,
    308
Cantor, Peter, 72
Capital cities, emergence of, 55
Cardinal, Peire, 546, 561
Carmen de gestis Frederici, 463
Carmen in honorem Augusti, 162
Carmina Burana, 180, 440–441, 551,
    553, 567
Castles: architecture of, 108–112; as
    instruments of lordship, 121–126;
    twelfth and thirteenth century, 103–
    108
Cathedral schools, 68–69
Cercamon, 419–420, 498
Ceremonies: courtly ceremony of dress,
    136–138; dubbing, 50; of greeting
    and hospitality, 137; of knighting,
    137, 231–247; of knightly single com-
    bat, 168–175; of welcome, for court
    feasts, 219–220
Chain mail, 158
Champagne, Countess of, 377, 379, 390
Champagne, fairs at, 61
Chanceries, establishment of separate,
    447–454
Chanson d'Antioche, 516
Chanson de Roland, 85, 92, 482. See also
    Rolandslied
Chansonniers, 555, 557, 568
Chansons de geste, 48, 92, 93
Chantefable, 420
Charlemagne, Emperor, 128–129, 236,
    280, 459; court feast of, 500

Charlemagne cycle, 93
Charles of Anjou, 559
Charles of Flanders, Count, 248, 253
Charles the Bald, 231, 281
Charles IV, Emperor, 29, 189, 190
Charles V of France, King, 189
Charters, written in German, 454–458
Chartres cathedral, 139
Chastity, tests of, 333
Chastoiement des dames, 342
Château Gaillard, 121
Châtelain de Saint Gille, 569
Chertsey Abbey, 528
Chevalier, 47–49
Chivalrous knights, 276–325; courtly vir-
    tues and, 301–311; ideal versus reality
    of, 311–325; religious concept of
    knighthood, 290–301; traditional
    image of ruler and, 276–289
Choirs of mankind, 27–28
Christherre-Chronik, 478
Christian of Mainz, Archbishop, 74, 165,
    315
Christina, Countess, 152
Christina of Markyate, 356–358
Chronica, 462
Chronica Polonorum, 244
Chronica Reinhardsbrunnensis, 444
"Chronicle of Erfurt," 237
"Chronicle of Hainaut," 248
"Chronicle of Zwiefalten," 402
Church: criticism of dress by, 152–155;
    patronage of courtly literature and,
    483–485; role in knighting cere-
    monies, 239–242. See also Religion
Church of St. Jacob (Regensburg), 108
Cicero, 301, 304
Cities, 36–38; beginnings of literary life
    in, 487–488; economic activities of,
    41–43
Citizenship rights, 37
City of God, 295
Clementia of Zähringen, Duchess, 77–78,
    482, 491
Cléomades, 569
Clergy: clothing of, 134–135; of court,
    56; criticism of clothing by, 152–155
Clermont, Council of, 293–294
Cliges, 94
Clocks, invention of, 40
Clothing, 128–155; beginnings of courtly
    fashion, 138–140; church criticism of,
    152–155; courtly ceremony and,
    136–138; dress codes, 128–130; ex-
    travagance in, 134–136; history of
    costume, 130–132; men's, 145–149,

147, 148, 150; precious fabrics, 132–
134; terminology for, 131–132;
women's, 140–145, 141, 142, 145
Cluniac reform movement, 68
Cluniac Rule, 65
Cluse coronation feast, 547
Cnut of Jütland, 438
"Cobla," 99
Codex Balduini, 184
"Codex Falkensteinensis," 5, 192, 223,
445–447
Codex Vaticanus, 393
Coinage, 285–286; right of, 39
Colée, 236, 237, 238, 239
Colin, Philip, 85
Cologne: as commercial center, 41, 42; as
trade center, 63, 64; unrest in, 36
Cologne, Archbishop of, 29, 46, 62
Cologne Penny, 39
Comedies, bawdy, 333
Commena, Duchess Theodora, 451
Commentary on the Psalms, 72
Commerce, 41–43
"Common good," 43
"Compact with the Count of Hainaut,"
351
"Conditions in Alsace at the Beginning of
the thirteenth century," 104
Coniurationes, 36
Conrad. See also Konrad entries
Conrad, Count Palatine, 204
Conrad of Beichlingen, Count, 323
Conrad of Hessen, Landgrave, 285
Conrad of Lichtenberg, Bishop, 556
Conrad of Liechtenstein, Bishop, 245
Conrad of Luxembourg, Count, 81, 286
Conrad of Meißen, Margrave, 286
Conrad of Montferrat, 348
Conrad of Mure, 453–454, 456
Conrad of Querfurt, 466
Conrad of Swabia, Duke, 243, 249, 400
Conrad of Thuringia, Landgrave, 161
Conrad of Winterstetten, 163, 470, 486
Conrad of Zähringen, Duke, 36, 77
Conrad the Younger, King, 495
Conrad I of Freiburg, Count, 458
Conrad II, Emperor, 286, 430, 460
Conrad II, King, 104
Conrad III, Emperor, 431
Conrad III, King, 34, 81, 283, 447, 451,
464
Conrad IV, King, 455
Conrad VI, King, 232
Consaus d'amours, 371
Constance of Sicily, 347, 468
Constantine, Emperor, 280

Constantinople, conquest of, 466–468
Conte du Graal, 94, 235, 237, 238, 365,
519
Continuatio Sancruensis, 240
Continuatio Scotorum, 240
Contrafacta, 97, 497
Coradin of Babylon, 110
Coralus, Count, 4
Coronation ritual, knighting ceremony
and, 241–242
Corpus der altdeutschen Originalurkun-
den, 456–457
Corvey monastery, 34
Costume, sources for history of, 130–132
Coucy, Châtelain de, 569, 570
Council of Clermont, 68, 248, 293–294
Council of Remiremont, 409
Court, 52–60; development of organized
writing at secular courts, 441–458;
imperial court as literary center, 459–
470
Court cleric, role of, 321–325
Courtesy books, 196–199
Court feasts, 203–230; ceremony of wel-
come for, 219–220; entertainment
for, 220–228; festive entrance for,
213–219; gifts for, 228–230; lodging
and food for, 210–212; lordship and,
207–210; at Mainz, 46, 79, 168, 180,
188, 203–207, 237, 240, 270, 298.
See also Banquets
Courtliness, vocabulary of, 57–60
Courtly epics, 92–96, 518–545
Courtly fashion, 138–140
Courtly ideal of society, 275–413; chival-
rous knights, 276–325; courtly ladies,
325–359; courtly love, 360–413
Courtly ladies, 325–359
Courtly life, criticism of, 415–423
Courtly Life in the Age of the Minnesin-
gers (Schultz), 6
Courtly literature, marriage and love in,
389–392. See also Literature
Courtly love, 360–413; defined, 360–
361. See also Love
Courtly lyric, 96–99, 300–301, 545–571
Courtly poets, 301
Courtly society: modern scholarship and,
5–7; oral culture and literacy in, 426–
458
Courtoisie, 307–311
Court poets, vision of, 4–5
Court society, 55–57
Crafts, urban, 41
Crane, 480
Craûn, Moriz von, 267

Criminal justice, 2–3
Crop rotation, 40
Crossbows, 173–174
Crusade, Second, 250
Crusading literature, 293–297; vernacular translation of, 299–301
Crusading songs, 294, 420
Cunneware, 333
Curia regis Artus, 318
Curtius, Ernst Robert, 301–302

Dactyls, 96
Daily life: in castles, 111–112; in Middle Ages, 2
d'Alamanon, Bertran, 410
Damen, Hermann dem, 481
Damiani, Petrus, 322
Dancers of Kölbigk, 440
Dancing, 225–227; lyric poetry for, 545–550
d'Andeli, Henry, 569
Daniel vom bluhenden Tal, 95
Danubian minnesong, 96
d'Arras, Gautier, 76, 94
Daurel et Beton, 503
David, King, 279, 316
De amore, 329, 361, 362, 378, 399
Decretum, 278, 328, 381, 387, 388, 389, 404
Dedo of Wettin, Margrave, 288
"Deeds of Conrad, " 460
Deeds of the English Kings, 426
de Leone, Michael, 555
Delivery-of-arms ceremony, 232
Demay, Germain, 131
De officiis, 301
De proprietatibus rerum, 182
"Descorts," 98
"Description of Germany," 46
Deutsche Kultur im Zeitalter des Rittertums (Naumann), 7
Deutz, Rupert von, 68
Dialogue songs, 410
Dialogus miraculorum, 512
d'Ibelin, Jean, 224, 262
Didactic poetry, 23
Dienstmannen, 28
Dienstrecht (ministerial law), 22
Dietrich of Bern, 3
Dietrich of Elmendorf, 490
Dietrich of Meißen, Margrave, 469, 477, 498, 507
Dietrich of Naumburg, Bishop, 289
Dietrich of St. Hubert, Abbot, 430
Dietrich of Sommerschenburg and of Groitzsch, Count, 70
Dietrich V of Cleves, 287

Dietrichs Flucht, 540, 542, 544, 554
Dijon, Guiot de, 98
Disciplina clericalis, 196, 323
"Discourse on Faith," 417
Distinctiones, 72
"Disyllabic cadences," 522
Doctrine of the "nobility of virtue," 305
Dodone castle, 111
d'Oisy, Huon, 76
Domitian, Emperor, 310
Donaueschingen manuscript, 544
"Donjon," 109
d'Orange, Guillaume, 93
Dörper, 87
Dörperlich ("peasantish"), 14
Double standard of sexual morality, 398–399
Dress: the courtly ceremony of, 136–138; women's, 6
Dress codes, 128–130
Drinking cups, 191–192
Dubbing ceremonies, 50
d'Uisel, Elias, 367, 379
d'Uisel, Gui, 379
"Duke Henry of Pressla," 480
Duke of Brabant, 295
Durne, Reinbot von, 91, 475, 478, 482–483
Durne, Baron Rupert von, 107, 485
Dynastic connections, between France and Germany, 75–79
Dynastic historiography, beginnings of, 441–445

Eating habits, 6
Eberhard of Salzburg, 74
Eberhard of Trier, 240
Ebersberg, Richilde von, 121
Ebersheim Chronicle, 34
Ebulo, Petrus de, 118, 162, 214, 283, 466
Ecclesiastical courts, spread of aristocratic culture and, 75
Ecclesiastical dignitaries, as literary patrons, 483–485
Eckehard, 450
Eckenlied, 538, 542, 544
Economy, 39–46; importance of castles to, 124–125
Education: French influence on, 68–75; lay, 426–436; of nobility, 312–316; of women, 337–346
"Education of kings and princes, The," 277
Edward of Carnarvon, 245, 319
Edward I of England, King, 180, 246, 319
Eger castle, 114
Ehrismann, Gustav, 301, 302

Eichersberg, Magnus von, 244
Einschildritter, 28
Ekbert of Bamberg, Bishop, 479
Ekbert of Pütten und Formbach, Count, 173
Ekbert of Schönau, Abbot, 74
Ekkehard of Aura, 323, 429
Eleanor of Aquitaine, 77, 347, 403, 408–409, 481
Eleanor of England, Queen. *See* Eleanor of Aquitaine
Elephant, Frederick II's, 221, 222
Elisabeth of Bohemia, Duchess, 347, 350
Elisabeth of Flanders, Countess, 408
Elizabeth of Thuringia, Landgravine, 358
Elizabeth of Vermandois, 392
Elmendorf, Wernher von, 197, 418, 477, 490
Elsa of Brabant, 259
Emperors, itineraries of, 52–53
Empresses, habits of, 56
"Empress of the Romans," 346–347
Ems, Rudolf von, 67, 90, 163, 181, 233, 245, 254, 315, 351, 391, 411–412, 463–464, 470, 473, 474, 479, 486, 487, 491, 492, 494, 510, 512, 524, 526, 538, 541, 543, 544
Eneit, 60, 88–89, 90, 91, 126, 161, 165, 233, 251, 260, 465, 471, 474, 476, 477, 492, 509, 519, 526, 531, 532, 533, 534, *536–537*, 538, 543
Engelbert of Admont, Abbot, 277
Engelbert of Carinthia, Duke, 77
Engelbert of Cologne, Archbishop, 3, 135
Engelhardt, 257, 269
England, trade with, 62–63
Enikel, Jans, 211
Enite, 334
Ennius, 147, *147*, 149
Entertainment: for court feasts, 220–228; at courtly meals, 189–191; by women, 336
Entrances, 216–218
Epic poetry, 390
Epic poets, 490–495
Epics: courtly, 92–96, 518–545; French-style, 91
Epic works: circulation of manuscripts of, 529–534; illustrations in, 526–529; private reading of, 523–526
Epistles of St. Paul, 327
Eracle, 94
Eraclius, 332–333
Eraclius, 90, 94, 397, 543
Erben, Wilhelm, 237
Erec, 4, 49, 94, 110, 125, 127, 161, 171, 251, 391, 510, 529

Erec et Enide, 94
Erfurt, cathedral of, 288
Erfurt, Ebernand von, 524
Erfurt Chronicle, 318
Erla, Wolfger von, 484, 485, 501, 502, 504
Ermanaric, King, 438
Ermengarde of Narbonne, 347, 378, 408
Erzämter, 31–32
Eschenbach, Wolfram von, 12, 84, 85, 90, 91, 93, 94, 95, 98, 100, 101, 115, 132, 144, 148, 161, 172, 177, 192, 220, 234, 238, 365, 370, 371, 391, 395, 473, 474, 479, 485, 489, 490, 491, 494, 509, 517, 519, 520, 525, 526
"Estate of lords," 28
"Estate of peasants," 28
Estates, as basic concept of social order, 26–29
Estridson, King Sven, 438
Ethics, in women's education, 344–346
Etienne de Fougères, 300
Etienne-Henri of Blois-Chartres, Count, 428
Etiquette: rules of, 196–199; for women, 342–344
Etzel, King, 220
Etzenbach, Ulrich von, 217, 316, 472, 484, 486
Eudes of Saint-Maur, 291–292
Eugene III, Pope, 298–299
Eusebius of Caesarea, 280
Evangelium Nicodemi, 543
Evans, Joan, 150
Eve, courtly epics of, 332
Eve de Danubrium, 409
"Exposition of the Song of Songs," 69
Eyeglasses, invention of, 40
Ezzolied, 489

Fabrics, precious, 132–134
Facetus, 324
Fahnlehen, 31
Faidit, Gaucelm, 97, 411
Family monasteries, 33, 441–445
Fashion: changes in, 150–152; courtly, 138–140; women's, 6
Faucogney, Elisabeth de, 409
Feast days, everyday life and, 1–5
Feasting, literature of, 199–202. *See also* Court feasts; Food and drink
Felsberg castle, 112
Fenis, Rudolf von, 90, 496
Ferdinand of Portugal, 193
Festive entrances, for court feasts, 213–219
Feudal marriage, 380–384

Fighting, during tournaments, 255–256
Finances, tournaments and, 253–254
Fish, 179. *See also* Food and drink
Fitz Gilbert, Baron John, 248
Flaccus, *147*
Fleck, Konrad von, 90, 94, 238, 306–
    307, 391, 512
Floire et Blancheflor, 92, 94, 191
Florentin III of Holland, 287
Flore und Blanscheflur, 90, 391
Flori, Jean, 48
Florimont, 94–95
Fluchtburgen, 108
Focas, Emperor, 332, 398
Fondaco dei Tedeschi, 42, 65
Fontaines, Gautier de, 393
Food and drink, 178–202; courtesy
    books and, 196–199; for court feasts,
    210–212; food for nobility, 178–182;
    literature of feasting and carousing,
    199–202; organization of meal, 193–
    196; protocol of courtly banquet,
    182–183; seating arrangements for
    banquets, 183–187; service at table,
    187–191; tableware, 191–193
Forests, 125–126
Fournival, Richard de, 371, 378
Fourquet, Jean, 100
Fourth Lateran Council, 388
France: courtly love in, 406–409; lay
    education in, 426–429; social order
    in, 51
Frankfurt, diet of, 54
Frauenbuch, 359
Frauendienst, 15, 245, 251, 263, 270,
    313, 318, 363, 379, 395–396, 405,
    406, 479, 515, 523, 548, 549, 555,
    565, 566
Frauenlieder, 368
Frauenlob, 26, 481, 559
Frauenroth, monastic foundation of, 289
Frauenstrophen, 403
Frauentreue, 396
Frederick of Baumgartenburg, Abbot, 69
Frederick of Beichlingen, 508
Frederick of Bohemia, Duke, 53, 347
Frederick of Goseck, Count, 242
Frederick of Salzburg, Archbishop, 484
Frederick of Swabia, Duke, 53, 249, 283
Frederick of Toggenburg, Count, 488
Frederick of Ziegenhain, Count, 472
Frederick I, Emperor, 2, 30, 31, 43, 44,
    63, 65, 74, 76, 105, 106, 127, 137,
    157, 166, 168, 172, 175, 192, 205,
    206, 226, 243, 244, 282, 283, 298,
    315, 352, 388, 434, 446, 451, 463,
    465

Frederick I of Austria, Duke, 499
Frederick I of Cologne, Archbishop, 63
Frederick II, Count Palatine, 433
Frederick II, Emperor, 25, 30, 43, 44,
    163, 177–178, 206, 213, 221, 230,
    232, 315, 316, 347, 383, 455, 459,
    469; decrees of, 25; elephant of, 221,
    222
Frederick II of Austria, Duke, 55, 173,
    245, 450, 474
Frederick II of Salzburg, Archbishop, 472
Frederick II of Swabia, Duke, 81, 105,
    282, 317, 318, 323, 464
Frederick III, 30
Free peasants, 38
Freiburg, founding of, 36
Freiberg, Heinrich von, 319
Freidank, 123, 306
French aristocratic culture, 61–101;
    language and, 82–88; literature and,
    88–101; society and, 61–82
French court culture, language and, 82–
    88
French fashion, 131–132
French language, borrowed vocabulary
    from, 85–88
French literature: characteristics of
    adaptation of, 99–101; transmission
    of, 88–92
French love courts, 408
French social forms, adoption of, 79–82
French society, 13–14
Frescobaldi house, 65–66
Friedberg, Kuon von, 268
Friesach, tournament of, 252, 261, 270
Fritzlar, Herbort von, 90, 93, 156, 473,
    474, 493, 543
Frontin, 462
Fulbert of Chartres, 427
Fulques of Toulouse, Bishop, 354
Fulques II, 427
Fulques (Fulk) IV of Anjou, Count, 81,
    232, 402, 427
Furnishings, of castles, 112–121
Fussesbrunnen, Konrad von, 544

Gahmuret, 137, 148, 229, 364
Galbert of Bruges, 248
Galeran de Bretegne, 529
Game preserves, importance of, 125–
    126
Ganz, Peter F., 58
"Garden of Delight," 8
Gardolf of Halberstadt, Bishop, 322
Gaugi, Roger de, 268
Gäuhühner Die, 122–123
Gauriel von Muntabel, 211

Gawan (Gauvain, Gawain, Gawein), 4, 16, 138, 173, 235–236, 238, 365, 401
Gebhard of Passau, Bishop, 240
Gedrut, 394, 557, 558, 567
Gellius, 462
Gelnhausen castle, 106, 107, *107*, 112, 113, 114, *114*, 125, 465
Geltar, 394, *558*
Genealogia Welforum, 442
Genealogia Wettinorum, 444
Genealogical records, 442–443
Genealogy, of noble houses, 33
"Genre objectif," 99
Geoffrey of Monmouth, 265
Geoffrey of Namur, Count, 77
Geoffrey Plantagenet of Anjou, Count, 162, 234
Geoffrey II Martell of Anjou, Count, 286–287
Gepa, Countess, 340
Gerald of Aurillac, Count, 291
Geraldus of Cambrai (Giraldius Cambrensis), 277, 429
Gerburg, Countess, 340
Gerhard (merchant of Cologne), 178
Gerhard of Jülich, Count, 412
Gerhard of Stederburg, 2
Gerhard I of Mainz, Archbishop, 45
Gerhard III of Gerldern, Count, 403
Gerhoh of Reichersberg, 323
"German Alley," 61
German Culture in the Age of Chivalry, 7
German language, charters written in, 454–458
German states, development of, 32
Germany: courtly literature in, 3; courtly love in, 409–413; as elective monarchy, 29–30; itinerant kings in, 52–55; kingship in, 29–30; lay education in, 429–433; social order in, 51–52
Gertrude, Empress, 284, 346
Ges de chantar no'm pren talans, 560
Gesta consulum Andegavorum, 427
Gesta Ernesti ducis, 483
Gesta Frederici, 71, 82, 106, 232, 463, 530
Gesta Ludowici, 444
Gewere (lordship over things), 24
Geza II, King, 240
Gifts, for court feasts, 228–230
Gilbert, Baron John Fitz, 248
Gilbert of Tournai, 277
Ginover, Queen, 333, 351
"Girding with the sword," 232–233, 243, 244; ritual, 50
Gisela of Swabia, Empress, 341
Giselbrecht of Bremen, 485

Gislebert of Mons, 54, 126, 168, 176–177, 193, 204, 243, 248, 253, 382, 383, 384
Gislebrecht, Wilhelm von, 203
Gleichen, Count of, 288
Glichesere, Heinrich der, 421, 493
Glorjet castle, 115
Godfrey of Bouillon, 83
Godfrey of Viterbo, 430, 460, 463, 464, 466, 468
Godfrey V of Anjou, Count, 427–428, 515
"Golden Bull," 29
Goort, Gornemant de, 235
Gores (*gêren*), in clothing, 128–129
Goslar, 63
Gospel Book of Gmund, 284
Gotebold of Neuenburg, 508
Gottfried of Viterbo, 118, 314
Gouter kneht, 49
Gozwin of Wengen, 508
Gozzoli, Benozzo, 215
Grafenberg, Wirnt von, 15, 58, 91, 208, 238, 240, 320, 479, 494, 523
Graf Rudolf, 132, 151, 308, 477, 512, 531
Grail legends, 95–96
Grammatica, *142*
Grandes Chroniques, 189
Granges, Elisabeth de, 409
Gratian, 278, 328, 381, 387, 388, 389, 404
Great halls, 114–115
Gregorius, 75
Gregorius, 234, 473, 483, 543, 562
Gregory the Great, Pope, 295, 320, 433
Gregory VI I I, Pope, 296, 299
Gregory IX, Pope, 387
Grosseteste, Robert, 194–195
Guido of Crema, Cardinal, 322
Guido of Ponthieu, Count, 232
Guildhall, 42, 62
Guilds, 41–42
Guillaume de Dole, 269, 503, 569
Guinevere, Queen, 397
Gumbert, 450
Gunther of Bamberg, Bishop, 34, 437
Gunther of Paris, 127, 463
Günther of Schlotheim, 508
Gurmun, King, 351
Gurnemanz of Graharz, Prince, 302, 313
Güssing, Yban von, 173
Guta of Bohemia, Queen, 350
Gutenberg, Ulrich von, 90, 98, 465, 468. *See also* Gutenburg, Ulrich von
Gutenburg, Ulrich von, 567
Guter Gerhard, 67, 245, 254, 486, 543

Guy of Lusignan, King, 348
Gyburg, Marquise, 336–337, 350, 392

Hadamar of Kuenring, 252
Hadloub, Johannes, 200, 201, 331, 484,
    488, 499, 556
Hadrian IV, Pope, 431
Hagen, Kuno von, 107
Hagenau palace, 118, 125
"Hail, Lord of the World," 463
"Hail Mary," 525
Hainaut, counts of, 126, 176–177, 194,
    204, 243
Hairstyles, 149
Halberstadt, Albrecht von, 477
Halberstadt, diet of, 168
Halberstädter Bischofschronik, 218, 219
Handbuch der Kulturgeschichte (Kinder-
    mann), 7
Hardiz of Gascony, King, 253
Harrad of Landsberg, 340
Hartwig of Utlede, 449
Hasard of Aldehen, 435
Hastings, Battle of, 173
Hauberks, 158
Hausbuch, 555; "Codex Falkensteinen-
    sis" as, 446–447
Hausen, Friedrich von, 85, 90, 96, 97,
    331, 369, 420, 465, 468, 490, 496,
    497, 567
Hausen, Walther von, 496
Hausen school of poets, 465
Headdresses, 151–152
Hedwig, Duchess, 358
Heerschildordnung, 28
Heidelberg Freidank manuscript, 553
Heidelberg minnesinger manuscripts,
    151. *See also* Large Heidelberg Song
    Manuscript; Small Heidelberg Song
    Manuscript
Heidin, Die, 396, 412
Heiliger Georg, 91, 475, 478, 483
Heimesfurt, Konrad von, 524, 544
Heimliche Bote, Der, 324
Heinrich, Kaiser, 559
Heinrich of Eckartsberga, 508
Heinrich of Freiburg, Count, 401
Heinrich of Wolfratshausen, Count, 259
Heinrich und Kunigunde, 524
Heinrich von Kempten, 474, 485
Heldenbücher, 542
Helinand of Froidmont, 71, 236, 277,
    403
Helmarshausen, monastery at, 284
Helmbrecht, 15, 38, 88, 178, 200, 201,
    247, 273, 521
Helmets, 158–159, *160*

Heloise, 378
Henri of Saint Pol, Count, 295
Henry of Albano, 295
Henry of Brunswick-Luneburg, Duke,
    483
Henry of Carinthia, Duke, 212
Henry of Champagne, 348
Henry of Freiberg, 486
Henry of Hapsburg, 249
Henry of Hasenburg, 457
Henry of Istria, Margrave, 65, 479
Henry of Kalden, 533
Henry of Klingenberg, Bishop, 556
Henry of Lübeck, Bishop, 74
Henry of Stolberg, Count, 508
Henry of Straßburg, Bishop, 298
Henry of Vianden, Count, 355
Henry the Black of Bavaria, Duke, 286,
    442, 448, 451
Henry the Lion, 2, 55, 76–77, 78, 84, 91,
    127, 133, 205, 281, 283–284, 285,
    285, 288, 289, 434, 442, 447, 449,
    452, 454, 475, 481
Henry the Proud, Duke, 242, 281, 284,
    317, 318, 350, 443, 475
Henry the Wrangler, Duke, 283, *284*
Henry I, Margrave, 3
Henry I of Anhalt, Count, 347–348, 480
Henry I of Brabant, Duke, 45
Henry I of Breslau, Duke, 479
Henry I of Champagne, Count, 384, 427
Henry I of England, King, 196, 234, 247,
    426, 428, 517
Henry I of Mecklenburg, Duke, 481
Henry I of Schwarzburgs, Count, 471
Henry I of Silesia, Duke, 358
Henry II, Duke, 451, 478
Henry II, Emperor, 136, 283
Henry II of Austria, Duke, 161
Henry II of Brabant, Duke, 382
Henry II of England, King, 55, 62, 66, 77,
    115, 127, 129, 193, 231, 248, 284,
    299, 300, 311, 315, 416, 427, 428,
    560
Henry II of Stade, Count, 433
Henry III, Emperor, 79, 430
Henry III, Margrave, 477–478
Henry III of Carinthia, Duke, 286, *287*
Henry III of England, 221
Henry III of Meißen, Margrave, 264
Henry III of Silesia, Duke, 480
Henry III von Lowen, Count, 248
Henry IV, Emperor, 35, 36, 63, 104, 238,
    292, 322
Henry V, Emperor, 259, 429, 430
Henry VI, Emperor, 2, 3, 18, 23, 30, 45,
    84, 133, 192, 206, 216, 244, 310,

313, 348, 430, 453, 466–469; paintings belonging to, 467. *See also* Henry VI of Germany, King
Henry VI of Germany, King, 204–205, 282, 504. *See also* Henry VI, Emperor
Henry VII, King, 25, 455
Henry VII of Bavaria, Duke, 286, *286*
Henry XIII, Duke, 452
Heraldry, beginnings of, 33, 162
Herbolzheim, Berthold von, 479
Herdegen of Grundlach, 486
Hereford, Countess of, 300
Hereford, Earl of, 246
Heribert of Eichstatt, Bishop, 69
Herlibo, King, 438
Hermann Billung of Saxony, Duke, 216
Hermann dem Damen, 481
Hermann of Kammin, 485
Hermann of Kranberg, 252
Hermann of Meißen, Margrave, 12, *12*
Hermann of Ortenburg, 252
Hermann of Plothe, 288
Hermann I of Thuringia, Landgrave, 46, 90, 285, 348, 383, 434, 469, 472, 474, 507
Herrad of Landsberg, Abbess, 8, 141, 184
Herren, 51
Herrenspeise, 178
Herrenstand, 28
Hertnit of Orte, 252
Herwig of Seeland, King, 398
Herzeloyde, Queen, 4, 136, 229, 252, 364
Herzmaere, 396
Herzog Ernst, 476, 493, 512, 521, 531, 533, 534, 535
"Herzog von Anhelt, Der," 480
Hesdin Round Table tournament, 262
Hesler, Heinrich von, 543
Hesse, Meister, 541
Hesse (scribe of Straßburg), 487
"Hessenhof," 527
High Middle Ages, 18; material remains from, 8; weapons of, 155–157
High minne, 394
Hildebert of Lavardin, 329, 428
Hildeburg, 339
Hildegard of Bingen, 340
Himmelfahrt Maria, 544
Hincmar of Rheims, 277
Histoire de Guillaume le Maréchal, 250, 253, 254. *See also* "Life of William Marshal"
Historia calamitatum, 378
Historia Reinhardsbrunnensis, 443
"Historical Comparison of the Customs, Constitutions, and Laws, of Industry, Commerce, Religion, the Sciences, and the Schools of the Middle Ages with those of our own Century, considering the Advantages and Disadvantages of the Enlightenment, A" (Meiners), 1
Historiography, dynastic, 441–445
History: literature as a historical source, 7–14
"History of Anjou," 232
History of the Counts of Guines, 112–113, 237
"History of the Danes," 438
"History of the Saxons," 247
"History of the Two Cities, The," 462
"History of the Welfs" (*Historia Welforum*), 280, 282, 313, 431, 443
Höfisch (courtly), 14, 17, 57–60
Höfische Leben zur Zeit der Minnesinger, Das (Schultz), 6
Hofordnung, 57
Hofzucht, 197
Hohenberg monastery, 8
Hohenfels, Burkhart von, 470
Hohenstaufen castles, 16–17, 106–107, 110–111, 113–114, 122
Hohenstaufen dynasty, 15
Hohenstaufen period, 4
Hohenstaufen rulers, 431
Hoico, Count, 313
Holder-Egger, Oswald, 443–444
Holle, Berthold von, 95, 480
Holy Lance of Antioch, 167
"Holy law," 22
"Homogeneous order of knights," 50
Horace, 512
Horant of Denmark, 515
Horheim, Bernger von, 90, 465
Horse blanket, 165, 166–167
Horses, *167*; role in noble society, 175–178
Hortus deliciarum, 141, 158, 162, 184, 340
Hostiensis, Cardinal, 398
Houdenc, Raoul de, 95
Households: account books of, 5–6; composition of, 33–35
Hövescheit, 57, 307–311
Hugdieterich, 339
Hugh of Amboise, Count, 438
Hugh of Cluny, Abbot, 312–313
Hugh of Coventry, Bishop, 516
Hugh of Morville, 469
Hugh of Payens, 297
Hugh of St. Victor, 389
Hugh of Tufers, 252
Hugo of Morville, 79
Huguccio, 398
Humility, 302–303

Humphrey of Toron, 348
Hunfridingers, 32
Huon de Bordeaux, 520
Hygiene, 2

Ida of Boulogne, Countess, 77, 403
Ideal of beauty, 325–327
Ille et Galeron, 76, 94
Illiteratus (uneducated person), 433–436
Illustrations, in epic works, 526–529
Imbert, 366
Imperial court: as literary center, 459–
     470; literature of, 461–470
Imperial patronage, 459–461
Imperial peace of Mainz, 455
Imperial portraits, 281–289
Ingeborg of Denmark, Princess, 77, 388
Innocent II, Pope, 248, 271
Innocent III, Pope, 351, 399–400
Innocent IV, Pope, 398
Insignias, imperial, 30
Institutionelle Flächenstaat, 25
Invitations to tournaments, 252
Ipomédon, 94
Irene of Norway, Princess, 145, 218, 347
Irmenschart of Paveie, Countess, 350
Irmgard of Rheinfels, Countess, 413
Isabelle of England, 206, 213, 230
Isingrim of Ottobeuren, Abbot, 462
Isolde, 10, 220, 336, 341, 351
Italy, trade routes to, 65–66
Itinerant lordship, 52–55
Iwein, 364, *528*
Iwein, 4, 94, 95, 263, 339, 391, 522, 527,
     535, 539, 544

Jacob of Vitry, 227
Jaeger, C. Stephen, 322
Jakemes, 569
Jena Song Manuscript, 555
Jerome, Saint, 152, 327, 337, 398
Jeschute, 334–335
Joachim of Fiore, Abbot, 468
Jofrit of Brabant, Duke, 314
Johannes of Arguel, 474, 488
Johann of Michelsberg, 319
Johann of Sponheim, Count, 412
Johann of Victring, 209
Johansdorf, Albrecht von, 98, 370, 398,
     410, 558
John of Altavilla, 416
John of Bohemia, King, 262
John of Salisbury, 8, 241, 277, 292, 415–
     416, 421, 426, 434
John I of England, King, 248, 383, 401
John I of Trier, Archbishop, 46
Joinville, Jean de, 185

Jolande of Vianden, Countess, 355–356
Jonas of Orleans, 277
Jousting, 82, 170–173. *See also* Tourna-
     ments
Judith, 524
Judith, Empress, 431, 443
Judith of Bohemia, Queen, 341, 352
Jüngerer Titurel, 9, 91, 258, 320, 373,
     479, 491, 522, 543
Justice, 2
Juvenal, 328–329

Kaiserchronik, 57, 58, 60, 86, 128, 166,
     170, 233, 258, 265, 279, 281, 310,
     390, 410, 475, 529, 530
Kaiserslautern palace, 125
Kaiserwerth palace, 105, 106
Kalden, Heinrich von, 313
Kalogreant, 336
Kanvoleis, tournament of, 252, 255
Kanzler, der, 499
Karidol castle, 111
Karl, 543, 544
Karl IV, Emperor, 453
Karlmeinet, 93
Karl und Elegast, 93
Katzelsdorf, Round Table jousting at, 270
Katzenelnbogen, Diether IV von, 413
Kauffahrerhof, 62
Kaylet of Spain, King, 253
Kern Fritz, 22
Kindermann, Heinz, 7
Kindheit Jesu, 544
Kings: in hierarchy of society, 29–30;
     model, 279–280
Kippers, 256–257
Klage, 542, 543
Klein, Thomas, 534
Klingenberg, Heinrich von, 484, 488
Klosterneuburg: castle at 114; manuscript
     from, 293
Kluckhohn, Paul, 496
Knighthood, 46–52; religious concepts
     of, 290–301
Knighthood of Christ, 290
Knighting ceremonies, 137, 231–247;
     courtly ceremony of knighting, 234–
     239; customs of, 242–247; role of
     church in, 239–242
Knightly class, formation of, 50–52
Knightly code of virtues, 301–303
"Knightly Journey, The," 412, 413
Knightly single combat, 168–175
Knight of Riuwental, 4
Knights, 169; exemplary character of,
     302–303; weapons of, 157–164. *See
     also* Chivalrous knights

Knights' helmets, 14
Knights Templar, 298
Knight with the Two Swords, The, 520
Komarzi, tournament of, 253, 254
König Rother, 57, 58, 86, 132, 165, 183,
    209, 218, 233, 258, 308, 476, 493,
    531, 532, 533, 534
Königschronik, 110, 124, 127, 133, 295–
    296, 455
Königspiegel, 468
Konrad. *See also* Conrad *entries*
Konrad, Pfaffe, 75, 92, 493, 512
Konrad of Querfurt, 3, 314
Kraft of Greifenstein, Lord, 412
Kriemhild, Queen, 220, 335, 351
Kroeschell, Karl, 24
Kroijiraere, 267
Krone, 58, 67, 177, 333, 476, 479, 524,
    567
Kronechronik, 265
Kudrun, 209, 439, 515
Kunigunde, Empress, 283, 340
Kunigunde of Isenberg, 382
Kuno of Siegburg, Abbot, 492
Kuno IV of Mödling, Count, 445
Kürenberg, der von, 96, 331, 495, 515

Lachmann, Karl, 522
"Lady World" songs, 369
Lai d'Aristote, 569
Lai de Rigmel, 546
Lai du lecheor, 405
"Lais," 98
Lambert of Ardres, 112, 113, 237, 403,
    435
Lambert of Arras, Bishop, 232
"Lament of the Roasted Swan," 179
Lampert of Hersfeld, 238
Lamprecht, Pfaffe, 75, 86, 88, 89, 91, 93,
    476, 489, 490, 493, 511, 530
Lance charge, 169
Lancelot, 364; knighting ceremony of,
    239
Lancelot, 79, 397
Lancelot en prose, 95
Lances, *164*, 167–168; breaking and
    splintering of, 170; development of,
    163–164; fighting with, 171
Landeck, Konrad von, 76
Landenberg, Hermann von, 173
Landfriede (public peace), 22, 33
Landgraf Ludwig's Kreuzfahrt, 481
Landrecht, 340
Landsässiger Adel (landed gentry), 33, 35
Landsherren, 52
Landständische Verfassung, 52
Lanfranc, 68, 69

Lange swîgen des hât ich gedâht, 326
Language, French court culture and, 82–
    88
Lanzelet, 316
Lanzelet, 14, 79, 90, 94, 333, 411, 473,
    493
Laon, cathedral school of, 68
Large Heidelberg Song Manuscript, 223,
    225, 226, 228, 266, 450, 468, 473,
    478, 480, 495, 496, 498, 554, 555–
    557, 561, 563, 564, 566
Larie, Queen, 258, 364
Late Middle Ages, 18
Laubacher Barlaam, 525
Laudine, Queen, 330, 364
Lausitz, Dietrich von der, 250
Lauterberg Chronicle, 250
Law: as basic concept of social order, 22–
    23; legal position of burghers, 36–37;
    of ministerials, 34
Lay education, 426–436
Leicester, Countess of, 180
Leichtenstein, Ulrich von, 245, 479
Leonius, Abbot, 322
Leo of Vercelli, 427
Leopold III of Austria, Margrave, 242,
    286, 444, 450, 454
Leopold IV of Austria, Duke, 64, 451
Leopold V, Herzog, 90
Leopold V of Austria, Duke, 64, 79, 204,
    211, 444, 453
Leopold VI of Austria, Duke, 14, 65, 158,
    159, 179, 207, 240, 243, 245, 432,
    451, 454
Le tournou de Chauvency, 569
Liber ad honorem Augusti, 214, 283
Libussa, 349
Liechtenstein, Dietmar von, 261
Liechtenstein, Ulrich von, 112, 138, 159,
    170, 214, 251, 261, 263, 268, 269,
    270, 313, 318, 359, 363, 364, 379,
    395–396, 406, 509, 515, 523, 547–
    549, 555, 561–562, 565, 566, 568,
    570
Liet von Troie, 90
"Life of Archbishop Albero of Trier," 249
"Life of William Marshal," 248, 253,
    254, 266, 268, 316–317. *See also*
    Histoire de Guillaume le Maréchal
    Ligurinus, 463
Limburg, der Schenke von, 321, 470, 496
Limburg Chronicle, 330
Limburger Chronik, 128
Lincoln, Earl of, 246
Lippe family, 33
Lippiflorium, 223, 296
Literacy, 426–458

Literary scene of courtly age, 425–571;
authors and audiences, 488–518;
oral culture and literacy, 426–458;
patrons and sponsors, 458–488; performance and spread of literature,
518–571
Literature: adultery in, 394–398; beginnings of urban literary life, 487–488;
crusading, 293–297; of feasting and
carousing, 199–202; great princely
houses as patrons of, 475–481; as
historical source, 7–14; impact on
noble society, 512–518; of imperial
court, 461–470; imperial court as
literary center, 459–470; literary interests of princes, 470–475; literary
training of women, 340–342; misogynistic, 327–335; as model for the
nobility, 316–321; performance and
spread of, 518–571. See also Courtly
literature; Literary scene of the courtly
age
Litteratus (literate person), 433–436
Liutolt of Roeteln, 485, 487
Liutprand of Cremona, Bishop, 10
Locumer Artusepos, 91
Lodging, for court feasts, 210–212
Lohengrin, 259
Lohengrin, 479
Lombard, Peter, 386, 389
Lombard League, 53
London Psalter, 284
Longchamp, William, 516
Lord, Albert B., 436
"Lord Otto," 505
Lords' courts, connection to family
monasteries, 441–445
Lordship: as basic concept of social order,
23–25; court feasts and, 207–210;
economic foundation of, 43–46;
formation of permanent residences
for, 52–55
Lorris, Guillaume de, 373
Losbuch, 395
Lothair of Saxony, Duke, 431
Lothair of Sipplinburg, King, 81
Lothair (Lothar) III, Emperor, 137, 168,
284, 317
Louis of Laon, Count, 408
Louis the Bavarian, Emperor, 330
Louis the Pious, Emperor, 118, 231
Louis I of Laon, 78
Louis II of France, King, 516
Louis IV of France, King, 427
Louis IV of Thuringia, 348
Louis VII of France, King, 84, 78, 403,
427, 432
Louis VIII of France, King, 347, 429

Louis IX of France, King, 181, 185, 337,
347
Love: conviviality of, 404–406; courtly
character of, 372–377; in courtly
literature, 389–392; incompatibility
with marriage, 377–380; platonic and
physical, 366–368; service as, 363–
366; society and, 398–413. See also
Courtly love
Love courts, 408
Love games, 407–408, 410
Love tokens, clothing as, 137–138
Loys, King, 364
Lübeck, 41, 43, 45
Lübeck, Arnold von, 204, 206
Lucan, 434
Lucidarius, 27, 474, 476
Ludolf of Hildesheim, 71
Ludwig the Bavarian, Emperor, 433, 470,
497
Ludwig I of Bavaria, Duke, 3, 243, 244,
452, 478
Ludwig I of Thuringia, Landgrave, 341
Ludwig II of Bavaria, Duke, 392
Ludwig II of Thuringia, Landgrave, 78,
432, 466
Ludwig II of Upper Bavaria, 452
Ludwig III of Thuringia, Landgrave, 90,
92, 471, 476
Ludwig IV of Thuringia, Landgrave, 114,
383, 444
Lüttich, bishop of, 66
Luxury goods, 66–67
Lyric: courtly, 96–99, 300–301, 545–
571; transmission of, 559–571
Lyric poetry: manuscripts of, 550–557;
for performance, dancing, reading,
545–550

Maastricht, 67, 68
Mädchenlieder, 365
Magdalun castle, 124, 125
Magdeburg: cathedral of, 158; grail feast
of, 252
Magdeburger Schöppenchronik, 246, 263
Magezoge, Der, 302
Magnus of Denmark, King, 168, 438
Mahilda, 144
Mai, Prince, 232
Mainz, court feast of, 203–206, 298
Mai und Beaflor, 209, 520–521
Manegold of Paderborn, 462
Manegold of Tannroda, 508
Manesse, Rüdiger, 488, 556
Manfred, King, 504
Mantel, 228
Mantle of Charlemagne, 130
Manuscripts: changes in appearance of,

534–545; circulation of, 529–534; of
lyric poetry, 550–557
Map, Walther, 429, 516
Marbod of Rennes, Bishop, 329
Marcabru, 419–420, 498
Margaret, Duchess, 450
Margarete of Austria, 382
Margarete of Courtenay, 355
Margaret of Cleves, 92, 471, 476, 482,
519
Margaret of France, Queen, 193
Margaret of Lincoln, Countess, 194
Margaret of Provence, 347
Margot of Pozzident, King, 177
Marguerite of Blois, 76
Maria of Brabant, 392
Marienleben, 149
Mariental monastery, 355
Marie of Champagne, Countess, 408, 481
Marie of Oignies, 354, 355
Mark, King, 335; banquet of, 188
Marmoutier, Jean de, 234, 235, 237, 427,
428
Marner, der, 439, 499, 547
Marquart of Annweiler, 35
Marriage: in courtly literature, 389–392;
feudal marriage, 380–384; feudal ver-
sus Christian concepts of, 387–389;
incompatibility with love, 377–380;
marriage connections between France
and Germany, 76–78; scholastic
doctrine of, 384–386
Marseille, Folquet de, 97
Marshal, William (Guillaume le
Maréchal), 268
Martell, Geoffrey, 232
Martin of Parma, 178
Marveile, Schastel, 173
Material culture, 103–202; castles and
tents, 103–128; clothing, 128–155;
food and drink, 178–201; weapons
and horses, 155–178
Mathias of Neuenburg, 401
Mathilda of England, 329
Mathilda of Scotland, 329
Matilda, Duchess, 77, 288, 481–482
Matilda of Carinthia, 77
Matilda of Flanders, 428
Matilda of Holstein, Countess, 350
Matilda of Schwarzburg, Countess, 347
Matilda of Scotland, 428
Matilda of Spitzenberg, 353
Matilda of Tuscany, 382
Matthew of Paris, 81–82, 193, 221, 248–
249, 252, 257, 262, 383, 393
Maubuisson, Perrenelle de, 145
Mauleon, Savaric de, 411
Mayer, Theodor, 21, 25

Mâze, 303
Meals, organization of, 193–196. See also
Food and Drink
Meats, 180. See also Food and drink
Mechthild of Brandenburg, 288, 347
Medieval reality, 1–19
Meiners, Christoph, 1
Meinhard (teacher at Bamberg), 437
Meinhard II of Görz-Tyrol, Count, 209,
212, 232, 252, 453
Meinwerk of Paderborn, Bishop, 322
Meißner, der, 481
Melées, 251–258
Meljakanz, King, 401
Meljanz, King, 364
Melk, Heinrich von, 129, 153, 154, 233,
417–418
Melodies, transmission of, 567–568
Mémoires (Philippe de Novare), 224
Men: clothing for, 145–149; sexual be-
havior of, 399–402
Meraugis de Portlesguez, 95
Merchants, 61–68
Merschant, Heinrich, 85
Merseburg, cathedral of, 288
Merseburg, Thietmar von, 152, 216
Metamorphoses, 477
Mezze, Walther von, 167
Middle Ages, romantic picture of, 1
Middle High German, literary texts in, 7
Milan manuscript, 568
Miles, 46–47, 49
Miles-ritter, 50
Military religious orders, 297–299
Milites, 47
Milites Christi, 290
Milites Dei, 290, 293
Militia Christi, 290–301, 304
Militia diaboli, 290
Militia saecularis, 290, 297
Militia spiritualis, 297
Millers, Godfrey de, 393
Millstäter Genesis, 48
Mining, 125
Ministeriales, 45, 47
Ministerials, in the hierarchical structure
of society, 33–35
Minne, 15; high and low, 368–372
"Minne and Society," 412, 413
Minnelyric, 101
Minnesänger, Die, 394
Minnesangs Frühling, 550
Minnesinger manuscript, 112
Minnesingers, 89, 96, 495–499; song
collections of, 557
Minnesongs, 495, 548–549
Minstrels, gifts for, 229–230
Miraval, Raimon de, 547

"Mirror of Kings," 460
"Mirror of moral virtues, The," 277
Mirrors of princes, 276–279
Misogyny, 327–335. *See also* Women
Model kings, 279–280
Modern scholarship, courtly society and, 5–7
Money: circulation of, 39; role in politics, 45–46
Money economy, development of, 44–45
Mongol War of 1241, 299
Montreuil, Gerbert de, 569
Monumentum Ancyranum, 278
Moralia, 433
Morality: of food and drink consumption, 181–182; religious virtues of knight, 301–303; sexual, 398–399; among students, 70–71
Moralium dogma philosophorum, 304
Moral philosophy, Roman, 304
Morant und Galie, 93
Morena, Acerbus, 76
Moriz von Craûn, 265, 267, 396
Morungen, Heinrich von, 15, 97, 98, 321, 395, 477, 498, 551, 557
München (Munich), Heinrich von, 543
Munich Codex, 147
Munich manuscript, 552
Munich Tristan manuscript, 148–149, 187
Munich Wolfram manuscript, 540
Munsalvaesche banquet, *186*, 188, 192
Munsalvaesche castle, 115, 119, 187
Munt (lordship over people), 24
Münzenberg castle, 107
Murders, 2–3
Music, at courtly meals, 189–191

Nabuchodonosor, King, 230
Nachtigall, Die, 112
Narbonne, Heimrich von, 158–159
Naumann, Hans, 7
Naumburg, cathedral at, 11, *12*, 340
Needlework, women's education and, 339–340
Neidhart, 326–327, 369, 421, 478, 498, 499, 550, 551, 553, 554, 558, 562, 566
Neidharts Gefräß, 201
Neifen, Gottfried von, 321, 470
Nemt, frowe, disen kranz, 550, 560
Nesle, Blondel de, 97
Neuenburg on the Unstrut, castle at, 113–114
Neustadt, Heinrich von, 263
"New knighthood, the," 297–298
Nibelungenklage, 544

Nibelungenlied, 166, 199, 218, 234, 244, 332, 422, 423, 438, 439, 440, 484, 493, 519, 531, 532, 535, 540, 542, 544, 545, 546–547
Nibelungen manuscript, 538, 539, 543
Nicholas of Verdun, 68
Nideggen castle, 115
Nigellus, Ermoldus, 118
Nimwegen palace, 105, 106
Nithart, 247
Niune, 557, 558, 567
Niuwen site, 15
Nobiles, 47
Nobility, as knightly virtue, 304–307
Nobility, the: criticism of, 305–306; education of, 312–316; food of, 178–182; literature as model for, 316–321
Noble descent, 32–33
Noble knighthood, 49–50
Noble society: basic concepts of social order, 22–29; court and, 52–60; economy of, 39–46; hierarchical structure of, 29–39; historical background of, 21–60; impact of literature on, 512–518; knights and knighthood in, 46–52
Nogent, Guibert de, 400
Nonprincely nobility, in hierarchy of society, 32–33
Nordmark, Udo von der, 382
Notker of St. Gall, Abbot, 313
Nova militia, 297–298
Novare, Philippe de, 224, 341, 345
Nuremberg (Nürnberg), 41, 53; guilds in, 37
Nüwen Parzifal, 85

Oberg, Eilhart von, 82, 89, 90, 91, 244, 366, 397, 476, 482, 493, 512
Obilot, 138
Odo of Cluny, Abbot, 291
Oehler, 54
Offenburg, Rudolf, 558
"Offices of the Court of Hainaut," 57, 193
"Of kingship," 277
Ofterdingen, Heinrich von, 517
"Of the Flatterer and Yes-man," 416
"On Duties," 301
"On the Art of Hunting with Birds," 469
"On the education of children of the royal family," 277
"On the education of princes," 277
"On the education of royal children," 337
"On the Good Rule of a Prince," 236, 277
"On the governance of princes," 277
"On the Manners and Deeds of the First

Dukes of Normandy," 428
"On the Sacrament of Marriage," 386
"On the twelve evils of the world," 277
Opizo of Este, Margrave, 405
Oral culture, 426–458
Oral traditions, 436–441
Ordericus Vitalis, 80–81, 138–139, 147, 149, 415, 428, 517
Ordo ecclesiasticus, 51
Ordo equestris, 50
Ordo militaris, 50, 51
Ordo ministerialis, 51
Orendel, 232
Orendel, 239
Orff, Carl, 180
Organ-tree, 9
Origine, 462
Origins and Development of Courtly Literature in the West, The, 59–60
Orilus, Duke, 333, 334–335
Oringles, Count, 334
Ornamental role of women, 335–337
Orte, Dietrich am, 485, 487, 488
Ortlieb, 402
Ortnit, 538, 542
Otakar II of Styria, Margrave, 72
Otloh of St. Emmeram, 80, 152
Otte, Lord, 486
Otto of Bamberg, 107–108
Otto of Botenlouben-Henneberg, 289, 290
Otto of Burgundy, Count Palatine, 76
Otto of Cappenberg, Count, 283, 464
Otto of Carinthia, 5, 192
Otto of Freising, 69, 71–72, 73, 81, 240, 243, 246, 249, 251, 315, 462, 463, 524–525, 530
Otto of Kakenberg, 540
Otto of Lengenbach, 252
Otto of Maberg, Bishop, 322
Otto of St. Blasien, 2, 73
Otto of Scheyern, Count, 78
Otto of Streußlingen, 316
Otto I, Emperor, 29, 434
Otto I of Andechs-Meran, Duke, 65
Otto I of Bavaria, Duke, 476, 478
Otto II of Bavaria, Duke, 232, 452, 475, 483
Otto III, Emperor, 286, 313, 459
Otto III of Brandenburg, Margrave, 211
Otto IV, Emperor, 30, 45, 77, 105, 174, 405
Otto IV of Brandenburg, Margrave, 223
Otto V of Wittelsbach, Count Palatine, 318
Otto VI of Wolfratshausen, Count, 317, 318

Ottokar of Styria, 135–136, 382, 432
Ottokar I of Bohemia, King, 168
Ottokar II of Bohemia, King, 135, 172, 192, 211, 245, 382, 432, 450
Ottokar IV of Styria, Duke, 63
Ottonians, 32
Ovid, 328, 361, 362, 408, 477

Paintings, 116–119, 467
Palace-castles, 105
Palaces, architecture of, 108–112
Palas, 109
Paper, production of, 40
Paris, Gaston, 360
Paris manuscript, 568
Paris tax registers, 62
Parks, 125–126
Parry, Milman, 436
"Partimen," 99
Partimes, 407, 411
Partonopeus de Blois, 85, 89, 94
Partonopier, 260
Partonopier und Meliur, 85, 89, 233, 488
Parzival, 302, 306, 334; education of, 313, 314; knighting of, 235
Parzival, 13, 58, 86, 91, 94, 139, 151, 156, 186, 220, 238, 255, 313, 351, 364, 401, 485, 491, 510, 519, 522, 526, 538, 540, 541, 542, 544, 545
Pastourelle, 99
Patavinus, Rolandinus, 220
Patronage: imperial, 459–461; of princely ladies, 481–483; of princes, 470–485; in smaller courts, 485–487
Patrons, 458–488
Paul, Saint, 290, 385; epistles of, 327
Pavilions. *See* Tents
"Peace of Constance," 53
"Peace of God" movement, 50, 68, 291
Peasants: clothing of, 128, 130, 134; food of, 178, 179; free and unfree, 38; weapons and, 166–167
Pedites, 47
Peguilhan, Aimeric de, 367
Pembroke, Earl of, 248
Penefrec hunting lodge, 125
Pennants, 164, 167. *See also Baniere*
Performance: of epic works, 520–523; lyric poetry for, 545–550
Persenbeug castle, 121
Personenverbandsstaat, 25
Peter of Blois, 8, 74, 241, 311, 312, 416, 513
Peter the Venerable, 65
Peter III of Aragon, King, 174
Petershof, 42
Petrus of Auvergne, 225

Pfaffe Amis, 118–119, 544, 554
Pfalzburgen, 105
Pfert, 175, 176
Phagifacetus, 196, 199
Philip of Flanders, Count, 66, 254, 392, 427, 429
Philip of Harvengt, 429, 492
Philip of Swabia, King, 3, 30, 45, 168, 218, 219, 231, 243, 347, 431, 469
Philip I of France, King, 402
Philip Augustus. *See* Philip II of France, King
Philip II of France, King, 70, 77, 121, 129, 270, 299, 361, 388, 403, 405
Philip III of France, King, 83, 130, 179
Physical love, 366–368
Pine, Samson, 85
Pippin, 232; knighting of, 258
"Planh," 99
Plantagenet, Geoffrey. *See* Geoffrey Plantagenet of Anjou
Platonic love, 366–368
Pleier, der, 95, 523
Ploceke, Helprich von, 382
"Poem of the Deeds of Frederick in Lombardy," 463
Poetry, 3–5; castle descriptions in, 109–110; Provençal, 96; satirical, 88. *See also* Lyric poetry
Poets: courtly, 301; descriptions of material culture by, 8; epic, 490–495; image of society constructed by, 3–4; social standing of, 488–490; traveling, 499–506
Poitiers, great hall at, 115
Policraticus, 241, 277, 292, 416, 421, 426
Political murder, 2–3
Politics, role of money in, 45–46
Poppo of Stablo, Abbot, 79
Porrée, Gilbert de la, 72
Portraits, imperial and princely, 281–289
Post, Paul, 131
Potiphar, 48
Poultry, 179–180. *See also* Food and drink
Poverty, 2–3
"Praise of Times Gone By," 14–16
Preislied, 411, 571
Premyslides, house of, 349
Preuilly, Geoffroi de, 81, 247
Princely ladies, patronage of, 481–483
Princely seals, 285, 286–287
Princes: education of, 14; in hierarchical structure of society, 31–32; literary interests of, 470–475; patronage of, 470–485; princely portraits, 281–

289; transfer of royal attributes to, 280–281
Priscianus, *142*
Processions, 213–215, *215*
Prosa-Lancelot, 95, 96, 239, 301, 527
Protheselaus, 94
Provençal debating songs, 410
Provençal poetry, 96
Provençal renunciation songs, 331
Provençal song manuscript, 565
Proverbs of Solomon, 337
Provins, Guiot de, 16, 76, 79, 97
Prüfening, Liebhart von, 72

Quam divina patentia, 296
Quantam praedecessores, 298–299
"Queen of the Romans," 346
Querfurt, Conrad von, 219
Quintilian, 59

Rabenschlacht, Die, 542, 544
Radulf of Coggeshall, 248
Radulf of Diceto, 248
Ragual castle, 527
Rahewin, 2, 44, 106, 125, 127, 172, 192, 232, 434, 463, 530
Raimund of Lichtenburg, 486
Raimund of Provence, Count, 232
Rainald of Dassel, 72, 74, 83, 461–462, 462–463
Raitbücher, 57, 65
Ralph of Durham, Bishop, 356
Randulf of Glanville, 429
Ranke, Friedrich, 538, 541
Rappoltstein, Ulrich von, 85
Raspe, Count Henry III, 471
Raute, Hartwig von, 561, 562
Raymond of Antioch, Count, 403
Reading, lyric poetry for, 545–550
Receptions, 215–216
Reform, aristocratic ethic and, 290–293
Regalia, 44
Regensburg: as commercial center, 41; trade in, 64–65
Regensburg, Berthold von, 27, 154, 201, 272
Regensburg, der Burggraue von, 478
Regensburg-Prüfening painting school, 535
Reglindis, Margravine, 11, *12*
"Regulations for the Reception of the King," 216
Reichenau, Hermann von, 400
Reichsfürstenstand, 28
Reichsspruch, 310
Reinbrecht of Muoreck, 252
Reinerus Allemanicus, 196

Reinfried von Braunschweig, 153, 210, 263, 297
Reinhart Fuchs, 90, 421, 493, 512, 531, 532
Reinhart of Westerburg, Baron, 330, 497
Reinmar der Alte, 15, 98, 331, 367, 368, 411, 478, 498, 514, 551, 553, 554, 557, 567
Reinmar der Fiedler, 557
Reinmar der Junge, 557
Reitenburg, der Burggraue von, 478
Religion: military religious orders, 297–299; religiosity of women, 354–359; religious concept of knighthood, 290–301. *See also* Church
Religious orders, military, 297
"Remedies against Love," 328
"Remembrance of Death," 417
Renart, Jean, 269, 503, 529, 569, 570
Renaud of Dammartin, Count, 403
Renner, 123, 201, 225, 252, 513
Rennes, bishop of, 300
Rennewart, 523
Repgow, Eike von, 22, 24, 28, 29
Rhetorica, *148*
Rhetorica ecclesiastica, 349
Richard of Cornwall, Count, 221
Richard the Lionheart. *See* Richard I of England, King
Richard I of England, King, 45, 77, 79, 121, 161, 191, 192, 211, 249, 268, 428
Richardis of Holland, seal image of, *11*
Riche, Heinrich der, 558
Richenza, Empress, 284
Riedegger Manuscript, 539–540, 544, 545, 554
Ringgenberg, Johannes von, 500
Riquier, Guiraut, 565
Ritter, 47–49
Ritterlich (knightly), 17, 48
Ritterliches Tugendsystem, 301
Ritterspiegel, 134
Ritterstand, 28
Riuwental, 327
Rivers, Margarete de, 383
Robber knights, 123
Rober of Lincoln, Bishop, 357
Robert of Gloucester, Earl, 426
Robert the Monk, 294
Robert I, Count, 428
Rodeneck castle, 117, 527
Roethe, Gustav, 565–566
Roger of Hoveden, 70
Roger of Wendover, 257
Roger II, King, 133
Roland, knighting of, 236

Rolandinus of Padua (Rolandinus Patavinus), 220, 408
Rolandslied, 60, 77, 85, 88, 91, 92–93, 136, 156, 281, 300, 475, 481, 482, 512, 526, 529, 531, 532, 533, 534, 543. *See also Chanson de Roland*
"Romance of Lancelot," 94
Roman courtois, 99–100
Roman de Horn, 546
Roman de la rose, 371, 373, 376
Roman de la rose ou de Guillaume de Dole, 569
Roman de la violette, 569
Roman d'Eneas, 93, 140, 471
Roman de Silence, 435
Roman de Troie, 89, 93, 473
Roman du châtelain de Coucy, 569
Roman emperorship, German claim to, 29–30
Roman moral philosophy, 304
Romano-German Pontifical, 293
Romans antiques, 92, 93
Romans courtois, 92, 93, 94
"Roncaglian Decrees," 44
Rosenheim, Kunz von, 558
Rotelande, Hue de, 94
Rotenberc, Rudolf von, 558
Rotenburc, Margraf von, 558
Rothe, Johannes, 134
Round Table, 9, 15, 16, 92, 185, 238, 275, 281, 312, 364, 422, 512, 513
Round Table tournaments, 260–264, 318; in Walden, 257
Rouse, Richard H., 563
Royal insignia, 167–168
Royal power, basis of, 30
Royal tombs, 287–288
Rubin, 411
Rucche, Heinrich von, 558
Rudel, Jaufré, 498
Rüdiger, Rubin von, 558
Rudolf of Fenis-Neuenburg, Graf, 85, 97
Rudolf of Grüningen, 243
Rudolf of Hapsburg, King, 30, 135, 288, 432, 455, 470, 505
Rudolf of Steinach, 486, 492
Rudolf III of Austria, Duke, 83
Rudolf III of Hapsburg, Count, 455
Rudolph of Rheinfelden, 288
Rugge, Heinrich von, 15, 98, 465, 550–551, 567
"Rule of the aristocracy," 24
Rule of the Templars, 297–298
Rulers: portraits of, 281–289; traditional image of, 276–289; women as, 346–353. *See also* Kings
Rumslant, 481

Runkelstein castle, 117
Ruodlieb, 292, 316, 404
Rupert of Deutz, 492
Rural population, in the hierarchical
    structure of society, 38–39
Rürlein, Heinrich von dem, 67

Sabloeil, Renaut de, 570
Sachsen, Rumsland von, 486
Sachsenkrieg, 122
Sachsenspiegel, 22, 24, 28, 29, 31, 34,
    104, 108, 136, 340
Sachsische Weltchronik, 204
Sacramentum coniugii non ab homine,
    386, 389
Saelden Hort, Der, 124
Safety zone, in tournaments, 254
St. Blasien, monastery of: manuscript
    from, 9
St. Blasien, Otto von, 216
St. Blasius, church of, 289, 442
St. Elisabeth in Marburg, church of, 161
Sainte-Maure, Benoît de, 89, 93, 473
St. Gall manuscript, 544, 545
St. Gall miscellany, 539, 540, 543, 553
St. Jacob, church of (Regensburg), 108
St. Lorenz in Pegau, church of, 288
St. Quentin, Dudo von, 428
St. Truiden monastery, 83
St. Zeno, monastery at, 283
Salian emperors, 35, 39
Salimbene of Parma, 143, 181, 405
Salza, Hug von, 476–477, 567
Sarnen, Rost von, 499
Satirical poetry, 88
Saxo Grammaticus, 438, 516
Saxon Annalist, 53
"Sceptre-fiefs," 31
Schaler, Peter, 487
Schlegel, Nikolaus, 543
Schlesinger, Walter, 24
Schmalkalden castle, 117
Schöffenbarfreie, 28
Scholastic doctrine of marriage, 384–386
Schulte, Alois, 496
Schultz, Alwin, 6
Schwaben, Rumelant von, 486
Schwabenspiegel, 28, 457, 504, 553
Schwangau, Hiltbold von, 226, 470
Schwank Das Häslein, 520
Schwänke, 396
Schwank poetry, 544
Schwank songs, 554
Schwerin, Count of, 45
Scottus, Sedulius, 277
Seals: princely, 81, 285, 286–287; use of,
    454

Second Crusade, 295
Second Lateran Council, 174
Secular courts, development of organized
    writing at, 441–458
Seedorf shield, 161
Segremors, 95, 544
Seifried Helbling, 88, 129, 148, 179, 553
Seligenstadt palace, 126
Seneschal Keie, 333–334
Serfs, 33, 38
"Servants of Christ," 50
Servatius, 67, 133, 476, 492, 493, 531
Service, love as, 363–366
Serving role of women, 335–337
Sevelingen, Meinloh von, 365
Seven, Lutolt von, 557, 558
Seven sins, in criticism of tournaments,
    271–272
"Seven skills," 323
"Seven wise precepts," 323
Sexual behavior, 2
Sexual morality, double standard of,
    398–399
Shields, 160, 161–162
"Short History of the Princes of Thuring-
    ia," 444
Siboto IV of Neuburg-Falkenstein, Count,
    223, 445–446, 446
Sibylla of Palestine, 349
Sicardus of Cremona, Bishop, 434
Siegfried of Gorze, Abbot, 79, 147, 153
Sigeboto, 323
Sigeher, Meister, 481
Sigenot, 542, 544
Sigfrid of Balnhusen, 401
Silens, Walter, 435
Silk, 132–133, 134–135
Singenberg, der Truchseß von, 557
Single combat, 168–175
Single joust, 260–264
"Sirventes," 99
Small Heidelberg Song Manuscript, 555,
    557
Smaragdus of St. Mihiel, 277
Social order, basic concepts of, 22–29
Social prestige, courtly exemplariness
    and, 309
Social rank, dress and, 128
Social structure, estates and, 26–29
Society: economic ties in, 61–68; hierar-
    chical structure of, 29–39; love and,
    398–413. *See also* Courtly ideal of
    society; Court society
Soignies, Gontier de, 76, 561
Soldiers of Christ, 290
Soldiers of God, 50, 290
Solomon, King, 279

Solomon's bed, *120*
Solymarius, 463
Sone de Nansay, 262
Song: collections of, 565–567; first written records of, 561–565; oral circulation of, 568–571; transmission of, 559–571
Song books, anonymous, 557–559
Song manuscripts, 555
"Song of displeasure," 364
"Song of Palestine," 551
Sophie, Landgravine, 348
Sophie, Marquise, 350
Spanbette, 119
Spervogel, 486
Speyer cathedral, 108, 288
Spielmannsepik, 489
Spießbratenspruch, 505
"Spiritual Race, The," 80
Sponsors, 458–488
Sporadic texts, 552–553
Springer, Ludwig der, 444
Spruch, 99
Spruchdichtung, 7, 15, 30, 87, 99, 421, 499, 555, 564
Sprüche (Friedrich von Suonenburg), 544
Spruch poetry, 321, 441, 485–486, 495, 517, 543, 544, 553, 566
Spruch poets, 178, 308–309, 439, 472, 481, 485, 499, 500, 504–506, 515
Staete, 303
Stahleck, Count Palatine Hermann von, 249
Stapelrecht, 42
Statius, 92
Steiermark, Ottokar von, 173, 185, 211
Steinach, Bligger von, 90, 465, 496, 564
Steinmar, 200, 201, 331
Stephan of Auxonne, Count, 78
Stephan I, King, 249
Stolle, 392
Stolzenberg, Ingeborg, 457–458
"Storehouse of the Ant, The," 72
Straßburg: cathedral at, 151; city law of, 41–43; guilds in, 37
Straßburg, Gottfried von, 10, 58, 82–83, 85, 90, 95, 101, 144, 225, 233, 238, 240, 310, 315, 332, 341, 397–398, 422–423, 473, 489, 494, 514, 518, 524, 546, 559
Straßburger Alexander, 9, 93, 189, 476, 483, 493, 511, 530
Straßburg-Molsheim manuscript, 530
"Strategems" (Frontin), 462
Stretelingen, Heinrich von, 226
Stricker, der, 93, 95, 120, 122, 200, 394, 495, 512, 543

Suchenwirt, 239
Sumerlaten song, 331
Summa confessorum, 502
Summa de arte prosandi, 456
Summa dictaminum, 71
Suonenburg, Friedrich von, 178, 481, 486, 500, 544, 553
Superbia, *141*
Surety, 171
"Sweetness of the World" songs, 369
Sword fights, 171–172
Swords, 162–163, 167–168; blessing of, 239–242
Synod of Lüttich, 502
Széchényi National Library, 557

Tabards, 165, 166, *167*
Table manners, 12–13, 196–199, 323–324
"Table of Consanguinity," 388
Table ronde, 185
Table service, for banquets, 187–191
Tableware, 191–193
Tafelgüter, 44
Tagzeitengedicht, 530
Tancred of Sicily, King, 214, *215*
Tannhäuser, 197, 198–199, 478, 479, 480, 498, 499
Tannhäuser, 13
Tapestries, 115–117. *See also* Bayeux Tapestry
Taxes, 44
Teams, for tournaments, 252–253
Technology, progress in, 40
Tegernsee letter collection, 324
Teichner, 346
Telion, King, 335, 336
Templars, Rule of the, 297–298
Tents, 126–127
"Tenzone," 98
Teotonicus, Bernardus, 65
Terminology, of the knighting ceremony, 231–234
Terricus, 62
Territorial capitals, emergence of, 55
"Territorial lords," 25
Territorial Peace: of 1152, 166; of 1281, 52; of Bavaria, 130
Tetralogus, 430
Thebaid, 92, 93
Theodora, Princess, 207
Theodosius, Emperor, 280, 281
Theophano, Empress, 152, 346
"The teacher," 302
Thibaut IV of Blois, Count, 77
Thibaut V of Blois, Count, 76, 427
Thiel, Erika, 150

Thomas Aquinas, 328
Thomas of Brittany, 92, 94, 518
Thomas of Chobham, 352, 502
Three Wise Men, the, 150
Thurstan of York, Archbishop, 358
Tilting, 169–170
Tintagel, court feast at, 146
Tirol, King, 401
Tirol und Fridebrant, 264
Tobias, 530
Tombs, royal, 287–288
Topfhelm, 159, 160, 164
Tor, Guillem de la, 366
"To the English Queen," 329
"Tournament of the Ladies," 76
Tournaments, 82, 247–273; beginnings
    of, 247–251; bûhurt and, 258–260;
    mass tournaments (melées), 251–258;
    prohibitions and criticisms of, 271–
    273; significance of, 264–271; single
    joust and round table in, 260–264.
    See also Jousting; Wrestling matches
Tours, Josselin de, 515
"Tractate against the Courtiers and Court
    Clerics," 416
Trade, 41–43, 61–68; long-distance, 42
Trade routes, 62–63
Trades, rise of, 41
Trajan, Emperor, 279
Traveling poets, 499–506
Treuga Dei, 291
Trier, 1227 synod at, 153
Trierer Agidius, 530
Trierer Floyris, 89, 90, 94, 476, 512, 530
Trierer Silvester, 233, 530
Trimberg, Hugo von, 123, 154, 155, 201,
    272, 306, 321, 418, 439, 499, 513
Tristan, 302, 315, 316, 364, 365; knight-
    ing ceremony of, 309
Tristan, 10, 58, 351, 377, 397, 422, 423,
    473, 494, 512, 514, 519, 522, 524,
    526, 530, 538, 541, 542, 543, 544
Tristan tapestries, 116
Tristrant, 89, 90, 91, 94, 251, 366, 476,
    482, 512, 531, 533, 534
Trojanerkrieg, 9, 89, 93, 473, 474, 477,
    485, 488, 543
Troubadours, 96–99; Provençal, 97
Troyes, Chrétien de, 48, 49, 92, 94, 95,
    97, 101, 235, 237, 238, 330, 360,
    390, 391, 397, 491
Truce of God, 276, 291
Tugendhafte Schreiber, der, 450, 517
Tullius, 148
Türheim, Ulrich von, 93, 94, 470, 486,
    523, 541, 542
Türlin, Heinrich von dem, 58, 122, 187,
    211, 224, 228, 265, 333, 476, 479,
    567
Türlin, Ulrich von dem, 481, 524, 542
Turnus, Duke, 160, 536
Tusculanum, battle of, 165
Twelfth century: pictorial sources of, 8
"Two Unequal Lovers, The," 412
Tyrol: account books from, 5–6, 57, 136,
    212, 453; counts of, 5–6; trade in,
    65–66

Udalrich, 71
Udelhilde of Zollern, Countess, 352
Ugrim, 397
Ulmer Hofzucht, 198
Ulrich of Dachsberg, 339
Ulrich of Kirchberg, 451
Ulrich of Rifenberg, 486
Urbain le courtois, 341
Urban II, Pope, 68, 293–294
Urban population, in hierarchy of society,
    36–38
Urbanus, 324
Urjans, Prince, 401
Ursberg, Burchard von, 400
Urstende, 524
Uta of Calw, 382

Vagantes, 71
Varennes, Aimon de, 95
Vassalage, hierarchy of, 28
Veldeke, Heinrich von, 15, 60, 67, 78, 79,
    82, 85, 88–89, 89–90, 91, 93–94, 96,
    126, 133, 140, 161, 165, 166, 206,
    216, 233, 238, 251, 260, 370, 465,
    471, 474, 476, 477, 482, 490, 491–
    492, 493, 509, 519, 526, 534, 543,
    558, 567
Ventadorn, Bernart de, 97, 560, 561, 570
Verbruggen, Jans F., 264
"Verdun Altar," 68
Vesper, 254–255
Vesperie, 254
Vidal, Peire, 97, 565
Vienna Stricker-manuscript, 540
Viennese cart toll, 134
Viennese minnesongs, 478
Vincent of Beauvais, 152, 277, 337–339
Vincent of Prague, 341
Vinier, Gilles le, 367
Vinier, Guillaume le, 367
Virgil, 92, 328
Virginal, 538, 542
Virginity, protection of, 338
Virtue, knightly code of, 301–303
Vita Adalberti, 69–70
Vita Bertholdi Garstensis, 400

Vita Constantini, 280
Vita Heinrici IV, 349
Vita Paulinae, 323
Vitry, Jacques de, 70, 271–272, 354–355
Vivianz, knighting of, 245
Vogelweide, Walther von der, 5, 15, 23, 30, 56, 90, 97, 98, 99, 101, 138, 219, 310, 321, 326, 331, 335, 364–365, 369, 372, 410, 421, 469, 475, 477, 478, 479, 483, 484, 489, 498, 499, 500, 501, 505–506, 514, 517, 550, 551, 553, 554, 557, 558, 567, 571
Volkmar of Kemenaten, 486
Vom Glauben, 153
Von Gottes Leichnam, 543
Von hertzog Albrechts ritterschaft, 239
Vorau manuscript, 530, 532
Vreude, 138

Waldeck family, 33
Waldemar of Schleswig, Bishop, 351
Waldemar II, 45
Wallersteiner Margarete, 78, 482, 491
Wall paintings, 527–529
Walram of Montjoie, Count, 355
Wälsche Gast, Der, 197, 300, 324, 339, 484, 517–518
Walter of Châtillon, 304
Walther of Hausen, Baron, 486
Walther of Mortagne, 386
Walther-Reinmar collection, 567, 568
Wandering scholars, 71
War, use of mercenaries in, 45
Warfare, 2–3
Warriors, 50–51
Wartburgkrieg Der, 477, 478, 509, 517, 543
Was schaden tantzen bringt, 227
Water power, use of, 40
"Way of the king, The," 277
Weapons, 155–175; blessing of, 239–242; main weapons of knight, 157–164; new technology in, 40; social significance of, 164–168; terminology for, 156–157; for tournaments, 257–258. *See also* Armament; Armor
Wechselburg, castle-church of, 288
Weingarten minnesinger manuscripts, 151
Weingarten Song Manuscript, 468, 484, 555
Weinschlund, 200
Weinschwelg, 200
Weißenburg, Otfrid von, 488–489
Weißensee, Heinrich Hetzbolt von, 412
Weißensee, Henry von, 450
Welcome ceremony, for court feasts, 219–220

Welf I, 443
Welf IV, Duke, 45
Welf V, Duke, 313, 382
Welf VI, Duke, 207, 229, 382, 443, 475
Welfs, 32, 45–46, 76–77, 242, 475
Weltchronik, 72, 492, 543
Wenden, Wilhelm von, 137
Wenzel I of Bohemia, King, 173, 481, 495
Wenzel II of Bohemia, King, 132, 178, 189, 383, 472
Wergeld, 28
Werner of Bolanden, 445
Werner of Frickingen, Count, 353
Wernhart of Seckau, Bishop, 432
Wernhart of Steinsberg, Baron, 485–486
Wernher, Bruder, 149, 469, 558
Westminster castle, 115
Wibald of Stablo, Abbot, 72, 388, 461, 463, 464
Widukind of Corvey, 247
Wiener Genesis, 489
Wienhausen convent, 119
Wienhausen monastery, 116
Wigalois, 58, 91, 136, 320, 479, 535
Wigamur, 126
Wildenberg castle, 107, 485
Wilhelm of Champeaux, 68
Wilhelm of Orlens, 246, 258, 314, 315
Wilhelm of Wenden, Prince, 209, 230
Wilhelm von Orlens, 351, 391, 411–412, 463–464, 473, 487, 510, 526, 538, 541, 544
Wilhelm von Österreich, 128
Wilhelm von Wenden, 349, 481
Wilhelm IV of Jülich, Count, 169
Willehalm, Margrave, 245; address to troops, 301
Willehalm, 84, 90, 93, 127, 158, 168, 177, 199, 256, 337, 350, 364, 370, 392, 423, 473, 474, 477, 481, 509, 524, 526, 533, 538, 540, 542, 543, 544, 545
Willekin of Muntaburg, Count, 269
William. *See also* Wilhelm *entries*; Willehalm *entries*
William of Albineto, 252
William of Champeaux, 72
William of Conches, 304
William of Malmesbury, 402, 426
William of Newburgh, 403
William of Wenden, Duke, 218
William the Conqueror, 116, 117, 287, 426, 428, 521
William I, Count, 413
William I of England, King. *See* William the Conqueror
William I of Katzenelnbogen, 413

William II of Jülich, 287
William III of France, 427
William V of Aquitaine, Duke, 79
William IX of Aquitaine, Duke, 96, 407, 427
Williram of Ebersberg, Abbot, 69
Wines, 180–181. *See also* Food and drink
Winsbeke, Der, 202, 419, 543
Winsbekin, 403
Winsbekin Die, 543
Winter, Johanna Maria van, 237
Winterstetten, Ulrich von, 470, 515, 567–568
Wipo, 430, 460
Wiprecht of Groitzsch, Margrave, 288, 438
Wireker, Nigellus, 416
Wisse, Claus, 85
Wittelsbach court, 507
Wittelsbach dukes, 57
Wizlav III of Rügen, Prince, 481
Wladislav of Bohemia, Duke, 298
Wladislav I of Poland, King, 244
Wladislaw of Moravia, 350
Wladyslaw II, 352
Wolfdietrich, 538, 542
Wolfenbüttel fragments, 554
Wolfger of Erla, 5, 483
Wolfger of Gors, 252
Wolfger of Passau, Bishop, 56
Wolfhagen, Elhen von, 330
Wolfing of Stubenberg, 252
Wolfratshausen castle, 317
Wol her alle, helfet singen, 549
Women: beauty and, 306; behavior toward, 307–308; clothing for, 140–145; entertainment by, 336; etiquette for, 342–344; ideal of beauty and, 325–327; ornamental and serving role of, 335–337; parameters of activities for, 346–359; religiosity of, 354–359; renunciation of the world by, 353–359; role in literary entertainment at

court, 509–510; as rulers, 346–353; sexual lives of, 402–404; tests of chastity for, 333; tests of virtue for, 332; upbringing and education of, 337–346; worship of, 327–335. *See also* Courtly ladies; Misogyny
Wool, 134
Worms: church of, 3; guilds in, 41
Wormser Hofrecht, 3
Wrestling matches, 172
Writing: development of organized, 441–458; first written records of song, 561–565
Würzburg: guilds in, 41; tournament at, 82
Würzburg, Konrad von, 9, 85, 89, 90, 93, 94, 141–143, 226, 233, 257, 396, 474, 485, 487, 488, 552
Würzburg, Ruprecht von, 67

Yguerne, Queen, 235
Yvain, 94

Zabel of Plawe, 486
Zabel of Redichsdorp, 486
Zappert, Georg, 312
Zatzikhoven, Ulrich von, 14, 79, 90, 94, 333, 397, 411, 468–469, 473, 493
Zazamanc, 137, 145
Zechreden, 200
Zepterlehen, 31
Zimmern, Count Froben Christof von, 121
Zimmerschen Chronik, 121
Zirklaere, Thomasin von, 16, 84, 197, 199, 300, 304, 306, 319, 320–321, 324, 339, 342, 345, 418, 484, 517–518
Zweter, Reinmar von, 469, 478, 481, 517, 553, 554, 564, 565
Zwiefalten, Berthold von, 144
Zwiefaltener Chronik, 316

WITHDRAWN

GOSHEN COLLEGE - GOOD LIBRARY

3   01091453 7

WITHDRAWN

DATE DUE

OCT 2 8 1996			
JAN 8 8 1997			
MAR 2 5			
APR 0 3 2001			
APR 1 6 2001			
MAR 2 9 2004			
Oct. 31, 2007			
GAYLORD			PRINTED IN U.S.A.